Lecture Notes in Computer Science 966

Edited by G. Goos, J. Hartmanis and J. van Leeuwen

Advisory Board: W. Brauer   D. Gries   J. Stoer

Springer

Berlin
Heidelberg
New York
Barcelona
Budapest
Hong Kong
London
Milan
Paris
Tokyo

Seif Haridi Khayri Ali
Peter Magnusson (Eds.)

EURO-PAR '95
Parallel Processing

First International EURO-PAR Conference
Stockholm, Sweden, August 29–31, 1995
Proceedings

 Springer

Series Editors

Gerhard Goos, Karlsruhe University, Germany

Juris Hartmanis, Cornell University, NY, USA

Jan van Leeuwen, Utrecht University, The Netherlands

Volume Editors

Seif Haridi
Khayri Ali
Peter Magnusson
SICS (Swedish Institute of Computer Science)
Box 1263, S-164 28 Kista, Sweden

Cataloging-in-Publication data applied for

Die Deutsche Bibliothek - CIP-Einheitsaufnahme

Parallel processing : proceedings / EURO-PAR '95, First
International EURO-PAR Conference, Stockholm, Sweden,
August 1995. Seif Haridi ... (ed.). - Berlin ; Heidelberg ; New
York ; Barcelona ; Budapest ; Hong Kong ; London ; Milan ;
Paris ; Tokyo : Springer, 1995
  (Lecture notes in computer science ; 966)
  ISBN 3-540-60247-X
NE: Haridi, Seif [Hrsg.]; EURO-PAR <1, 1995, Stockholm>; GT

CR Subject Classification (1991): C.1-4, D.1-4,F.1-2, G.1-2

ISBN 3-540-60247-X Springer-Verlag Berlin Heidelberg New York

© Springer-Verlag Berlin Heidelberg 1995
Printed in Germany

Typesetting: Camera-ready by author
SPIN 10485367   06/3142 – 5 4 3 2 1 0   Printed on acid-free paper

Preface

The EURO-PAR'95 conference is organized in Stockholm by the Swedish Institute of Computer Science (SICS) and the Departmrnt of Teleinformatics at KTH. It is the first in a series of annual EURO-PAR conferences, formed by merging the PARLE and CONPAR-VAPP conference series on parallel processing, with the intent to create the main annual scientific event on parallel processing in Europe. The scope of the series covers the full spectrum of parallel processing, ranging from theory to design and applications. The objective is to provide a forum within which to promote the development of parallel computing, both as an industrial technique and as an academic discipline, extending the frontier of both the state of the art and the state of the practice.

The Call for Papers issued in August 1994 resulted in 180 submitted papers and 16 submitted posters by the February 1st deadline. All submissions were scanned by the Organizing Committee and dispatched to the most appropriate Programme Committee members. Most papers (152) were submitted in electronic form. Each paper was sent to at least four PC members and reviewed by at least three referees. All reviews (582) were submitted electronically by Programme Committee members. The Selection Meeting took place in Stockholm on March 30 and 31, 1995. Two days of intensive work resulted in 50 regular papers and 11 posters being accepted for presentation.

Another important but unpleasant result of the review process was the discovery of several cases of plagiarism. This led to an investigation of previous submissions of the authors involved, which revealed that some papers accepted at previous conferences were also cases of plagiarism. This matter is discussed further on page *vii*.

The rapidly improving information distribution mechanisms will undoubtedly affect the manner in which we assemble and publish research results, and we are excited to explore some of the possibilities. This proceedings is the first in the LNCS series to be published electronically. In cooperation with Springer-Verlag, EURO-PAR'95 will make the contents publicly available over the Internet, including a World Wide Web interface. Conference participants will have a chance to download papers of interest prior to travelling to the conference. The Programme Committee will have the ability to vote for best paper in good time before the conference.

In addition to the regular contributions, three invited talks will be given during the conference by Greg Papadopoulos (SUN Microsystems, USA), Björn Engquist (KTH, Sweden and UCLA, USA) and Gert Smolka (DFKI, Germany). The conference will end with a panel session on the topic Parallel Computing vs. Distributed Computing: Will They Merge in Future?

A specialized pre-conference workshop is organized by Anders Landin (SICS, Sweden) and Per Stenström (LTH, Sweden) on *Shared-Memory Multiprocessors*. Five basic and advanced pre-conference tutorials are organized by Chris Jesshope (Univ. of Surrey, UK) on *Scalable Parallel Computers*, Erland Fristedt and Per Öster (KTH, Sweden) on *Parallel Applications*, Per Stenström (Lund, Sweden) on *Multiprocessors and Multicomputers - Programming and Design*, Kam-Fai Wong (Chinese Univ., Hong

Kong) on *Parallel Database Systems Engineering*, and Richard Hofmann (Univ. Erlangen, Germany) on *ZM4/SIMPLE: a Universal Hardware Monitor and Trace Evaluation Package for Parallel and Distributed Systems*. EURO-PAR'95 also includes a vendor exhibition.

EURO-PAR'95 is endorsed by the European Commission, IEEE (TC on Computer Architecture and TC on Parallel Processing), Gesellschaft für Informatik/PARS, and European Research Consortium for Informatics and Mathematics (ERCIM). It is sponsored by the European Commission, the Swedish National Board for Technical and Industrial Development (NUTEK), TFR, Ericsson, Telia, and Wenner-Gren Scientific Foundation. This support is gratefully acknowledged.

We would also like to thank all members of the Organizing, Programme and Steering Committees, referees, invited speakers, panelists, tutorial presenters and workshop organizers for their efforts to make EURO-PAR'95 a successful event.

Finally, we would like to give our best wishes to the Organizing Committee of EURO-PAR'96, which will take place in France and be organized by ENS-Lyon (Ecole Normale Supérieure de Lyon).

Stockholm, June 1995

Seif Haridi   Khayri Ali   Peter Magnusson   Lars-Erik Thorelli

Important Note

The Program Committee of EURO-PAR'95 detected during its work that some submitted papers were not original contributions from the alleged authors but were in fact copied without permission from earlier work by other persons. Further investigations uncovered several related cases of plagiarism affecting several conferences and journals. The affected conferences included PARLE'94, one of the forerunners of EURO-PAR'95, which included the following two papers:

(1) Papadopoulos, C.V.: "A dynamic algorithm for online scheduling of parallel processes", Proc. PARLE'94, Springer-Verlag LNCS 817, 601-610, 1994.

Copied from:

A. Feldmann, M.-Y. Kao, J. Sgall, S.-H. Teng: "Optimal Online Scheduling of Parallel Jobs with Dependencies", Report CMU-CS-92-189, Carnegie-Mellon University 1992. - Also in STOC'93 ("25th Annual ACM Symposium on Theory of Computing").

(2) Papadopoulos, C.V.: "On the parallelism of data", Proc. PARLE'94, Springer-Verlag LNCS 817, 414-424, 1994.

Copied from:

V. Austel, R. Bagrodia, M. Chandy, M. Dhagat: "Relations + Reductions = Data-Parallelism", Report CSD-930009, UCLA 1993. (Also to appear in J. of Parallel and Distributed Computing.)

We ask you, the reader, to take notice of these facts, and to recognize the danger of similar plagiarism in the future.

The Program Committee wants to thank the referees of EURO-PAR'95 and all other persons who have helped to detect and investigate the above and other cases of plagiarism.

On behalf of the Program Committee for EURO-PAR'95

Lars-Erik Thorelli

Steering Committee

Chris Jesshope, Chairman (UK)
Kiril Boyanov (Bulgaria)
Agnes Bradier (EU)
Michel Cosnard (France)
Lucio Grandinetti (Italy)
Constantine Halatsis (Greece)
Seif Haridi (Sweden)

Ron Perrott (UK)
Ivan Plander (Slovakia/UK)
Dieter Reinartz (Germany)
Mateo Valero (Spain)
Richard Wait (UK)
Pierre Wolper (Belgium)

Organizing Committee

Conference Chair .... Lars-Erik Thorelli (Sweden)
Programme Chair .... Seif Haridi (Sweden)
Programme Co-Chair .... Khayri Ali (Sweden)
Japan & Asia Coordinator .... Makoto Amamiya (Japan)
North and South American Coordinator .... Doug DeGroot (USA)
Exhibition Chair .... Björn Lisper (Sweden)
Workshop Chair .... Peter Magnusson (Sweden)
European Union Liaison .... Michael Reeve (EU)
Central & East European Coordinator .... Valentin Voevodin (Russia)
Local Arrangements .... Abdel-Halim Smai (Sweden)
Treasurer .... Eva Skarbäck (Sweden)
Industrial Contacts .... Luis Barriga (Sweden)

Programme Committee

Emile H. L. Aarts (Neth.)
Gul Agha (USA)
Khayri Ali (Sweden)
Makoto Amamiya (Japan)
Francoise Andre (France)
B. Bergsten (France)
M. Boari (Italy)
Luc Bougé (France)
Kiril Boyanov (Bulgaria)
John Carter (USA)
Takashi Chikayama (Japan)
Andrzej Ciepielewski (Sw.)
Michel Cosnard (France)
Doug DeGroot (USA)
Michel Dubois (USA)
Paul Feautrier (France)
Robert Fowler (Denmark)
Guang R. Gao (Canada)
Geoffrey C. Fox (USA)
Wolfgang Gentzsch (Ger.)
Lucio Grandinetti (Italy)

Pascal Gribomont (Belgium)
Erik Hagersten (USA)
Constantine Halatsis (Greece)
Seif Haridi (Sweden)
M. Hatzopoulos (Greece)
M. Hermenegildo (Spain)
P.A.J. Hilbers (Netherlands)
Ladislav Hluchy (Slovakia)
Chris Jesshope (UK)
Peter Kacsuk (Hungary)
Yasunori Kimura (Japan)
Manolis Katevenis (Greece)
R. Kotagiri (Australia)
Björn Lisper (Sweden)
Peter Magnusson (Sweden)
Dimitris Maritsas (Greece)
Andrei Massalovitch (Russia)
Moray McLaren (UK)
Burkhard Monien (Germany)
Hiroshi Nakashima (Japan)
Rishiyur S. Nikhil (USA)

Ron Perrott (UK)
Ivan Plander (Slovakia)
Michael Reeve (Belgium)
Karl-Dieter Reinartz (Ger.)
Dirk Roose (Belgium)
Shuichi Sakai (Japan)
Joel Saltz (USA)
Paul Spirakis (Greece)
Per Stenström (Sweden)
Ondrej Sykora (Slovakia)
Peter Szeredi (Hungary)
Kazuo Taki (Japan)
Sergios Theodoridis (Greece)
Lars-Erik Thorelli (Sweden)
Evan Tick (USA)
Marian Vajtersic (Slovakia)
Mateo Valero (Spain)
Valentin Voevodin (Russia)
R. Wait (UK)
David H.D. Warren (UK)
Kam-Fai Wong (Hong Kong)

List of Referees

Emile H.L. Aarts
Clifford A. Addison
Vikram S. Adve
Gul Agha
Gagan Agrawal
Hallo Ahmed
Vassil N. Alexandrov
Khayri Ali
Jordi Garcia Alminyana
Makoto Amamiya
Hideharu Amano
D. Anagnostopoulos
Francoise Andre
Mark Astley
Philippe Audebaud
Eduard Ayguade
Godmar Back
Luiz Andre Barroso
Dmitry Barsky
Bernard Bauer
Martin Becka
Glenn S. Benson
Björn Bergsten
Bernard Berthomieu
Sergej Bezrukov
Maurelio Boari
Francois Bodin
Alex Bolychevsky
Luc Bouge
Kiril Boyanov
Thomas Brandes
Mats Brorsson
Francisco Bueno
George W. Byran
Daniel Cabeza-Gras
Montreal Canada
Manuel Carro
John Carter
Chialin Chang
Steve J. Chapin
Olivier Chéron
Takashi Chikayama
Anna Ciampolini
Andrzej Ciepielewski
Dominic Clark

R.A.W. Clout
Fabien Coelho
Jean-François Collard
Paul Connolly
Michel Cosnard
Yiannis Cotronis
Michel Couprie
Rita Cucchiara
Rune Dahl
Mads Dam
Alain Darte
Doug DeGroot
Ralf Diekmann
Miroslav Dobrucky
Patrick Dowd
Michel Dubois
Paul E. Dunne
Nahid Emad
Jocelyne Erhel
Luciano de Errico
K. Esselink
Karl-Filip Faxén
Zoltan Fazekas
Paul Feautrier
Rainer Feldmann
Agustin Fernandez
Bryan Ford
Stefano Foresti
Laurent Fournie
Robert J. Fowler
Geoffrey C. Fox
Joaquim Gabarro
Quim Gabarro
Guang R. Gao
Jorge Garcia
Alain Gefflaut
Joern Gehring
Marc Gengler
Wolfgang Gentzsch
Alessandro Giacalone
Bernard Girau
Antonio Gonzalez
R. Govindarajan
Håkan Grahn
Lucio Grandinetti

Pascal Gribomont
Ulf Gunneflo
Yike Guo
Erik Hagersten
Olof Hagsand
Costas Halatsis
Joacim Halén
Jonathan Cannon Hall
Per Hammarlund
Seif Haridi
Michalis Hatzopoulos
Steve Heller
Johan Håstad
Manuel Hermenegildo
P.A.J. Hilbers
Ladislav Hluchy
Juraj Hromkovic
Herbert H.J. Hum
Francois Irigoin
Jan Jansson
Claude Jard
Thierry Jeron
Chris Jesshope
Olof Johansson
Jan Jonsson
Pierre Jouvelot
Peter Kacsuk
Christos Kaklamanis
Linus Kamb
Sarantos Kapidakis
Roland Karlsson
Manolis Katevenis
Tetsuo Kawano
Hirota Kawasaki
Dilip Khandekar
Yasunori Kimura
Stephan Kindermann
Povl T. Koch
Martin Kochol
Jan Korst
Ramamohanarao Kotagiri
Andre Kramer
Chen-Chi Kuo
Ravindra Kuramkote
James S. Larson

Guy Leduc
Letizia Leonardi
Jay Lepreau
Hugues Leroy
Liang-Liang Li
Björn Lisper
Michel Loi
Pedro Lopez-Garcia
Reinhard Lueling
Johan Lukkien
Fredrik Lundevall
Ewing Lusk
Peter Magnusson
Olivier Maquelin
Dimitrios Maritsas
Evangelos Markatos
Andrei I. Massalovitch
Barton C. Massey
Hiroshi Matsuoka
Moray McLaren
Karl Meerbergen
Shamir Merali
D. Mery
Nikolaos M. Missirlis
Adrian Moga
Burkhard Monien
Shin-ichiro Mori
Henk Müller
Lenore R. Mullin
Peter Mysliwietz
Hiroshi Nakashima
Panagiotis Nastou
Juan J. Navarro
Ivailo Nedelchev
Brian Neilsen
M. Nicolaidou
Denis Nicole
Rishiyur S. Nikhil
Mara Nikolaidou
Haruko Nishimoto
M. Nocolaidou
Kazuaki Okamoto
Annika Olsson
K. van Overveld
Jean-Lin Pacherie
Rajendra Panwar
M.G. Peeters

Montse Peiron
Michael Pernice
G.-R. Perrin
Ron Perrott
Antoine Petit
Stephen Pink
Ivan Plander
Konstantin Popov
Steve Prestwich
German Puebla
Zsolt Puskas
Muhammad Abdul Qadar
Ramakrishnan Rajamony
Peter Rajcani
Lars Ramfelt
Xavier Redon
Michael Reeve
Karl Dieter Reinartz
Shangping Ren
Markus Roettger
Dirk Roose
Shuichi Sakai
Mariko Sakamoto
Joel Saltz
Vitor Santos Costa
Ulf-Peter Schroeder
Kees Schuerman
Juergen Schulze
Markus Schwehm
John Segers
Dimitrios Serpanos
Takeshi Shimizu
Osamu Shiraki
Jens Simon
Abdel-Halim Smai
Scott F. Smith
P. Spirakis
Ladislav Stacho
Paul W.A. Stallard
George D. Stamoulis
Luigi Di Stefano
H.P. Stehouwer
Per Stenström
Bruce Stephens
Daniel Sturman
Andy Sunderland
Ondrej Sykora

Andrzej Szepietowski
Peter Szeredi
Eiichi Takahashi
Kazuo Taki
Xinan Tang
Keith Taylor
Olivier Temam
Kevin Theobald
Sergios Theodoridis
Lars-Erik Thorelli
Claes Thornberg
Xinmin Tian
Evan Tick
Satoru Torii
Jordi Torres
Guy Tremblay
Staffan Truvé
Stefan Tschoeke
Hung-Yu Tseng
Sergi Girona Turell
Haruyasu Ueda
L.T. Uher
Tomas Uhlin
Walter Unger
Marian Vajtersic
Voevodin Valentin
Mateo Valero
Jesper Vasell
Jonas Vasell
Anjan K. Venkatramani
Tom Verhoeff
M. Verhoeven
Vladimir Vlasov
Vladimir V. Voevodin
Imrich Vrto
Richard Wait
Rolf Wanka
David Warren
Kam-Fai Wong
Handong Wu
Rong Yang
Derek F. Yates
Takashi Yokota

Table of Contents

Fault Tolerance and SIMD Arrays

Posters: Extended Abstracts

Keynote Speakers

Mainstream Parallelism:
Taking Sides on the SMP/MPP/Cluster Debate

Greg Papadopoulos

Greg Papadopoulos (Ph.D., MIT EECS) is the Chief Technology Officer for Sun Microsystems' Server Group. He has spent the last fifteen years developing scalable general and special purpose systems. Prior to joining Sun in the Fall 1994, he was Senior Architect at Thinking Machines Corporation and an Associate Professor at MIT. In addition, Greg is co-founder of three companies, including PictureTel Corp..

The Oz Programming Model

(Extended Abstract)

Gert Smolka[*]

Programming Systems Lab
German Research Center for Artificial Intelligence (DFKI)
Stuhlsatzenhausweg 3, 66123 Saarbrücken, Germany
email: smolka@dfki.uni-sb.de

Abstract. The Oz Programming Model (OPM) is a concurrent programming model that subsumes functional and object-oriented programming as facets of a general model. This is particularly interesting for concurrent object-oriented programming, for which no comprehensive and formal model existed until now. There is a conservative extension of OPM providing the problem-solving capabilities of constraint logic programming. OPM has been developed together with a concomitant programming language Oz designed for applications that require complex symbolic representations, organization into multiple agents, and soft real-time control. An efficient, robust, and interactive implementation of Oz is freely available.

Computer systems are undergoing a revolution. Twenty years ago, they were centralized, isolated, and expensive. Today, they are parallel, distributed, networked, and inexpensive. However, advances in software construction have failed to keep pace with advances in hardware. To a large extent, this is a consequence of the fact that current programming languages were conceived for sequential and centralized programming.

A basic problem with existing programming languages is that they delegate the creation and coordination of concurrent computational activities to the underlying operating system. This has the severe disadvantage that the data abstractions of the programming language cannot be shared between communicating computational agents. Thus the benefits of existing programming languages do not extend to the central concerns of concurrent and distributed software systems.

Given this state of affairs, the development of concurrent programming models is an important research issue in Computer Science. A concurrent programming model must support the creation and coordination of multiple computational activities. Since concurrency is the result of a generalized control structure, it must be accommodated at the heart of a programming model.

[*] Supported by the BMBF (contract ITW 9105), the Esprit Basic Research Project ACCLAIM (contract EP 7195), and the Esprit Working Group CCL (contract EP 6028).

The development of simple, practical, and well-founded concurrent programming models turned out to be difficult. The main problem was the lack of a methodology and formal machinery for designing and defining such models. In the 1980's, significant progress has been made on this issue. This includes the development of abstract syntax and structural operational semantics; the development of functional and logic programming, two declarative programming models building on the work of logicians (lambda calculus and predicate logic); the development of CCS [6] and the π-calculus [7], two abstract concurrent programming models developed by Milner and others; and the concurrent constraint model [4, 8], a concurrent programming model that developed from application-driven research in concurrent logic programming [11] and constraint logic programming [2].

The talk reports on the Oz Programming Model, OPM for short, which has been developed together with the high-level concurrent programming language Oz. OPM is an extension of the basic concurrent constraint model, adding first-class procedures and stateful data structures. OPM is a concurrent programming model that subsumes higher-order functional and object-oriented programming as facets of a general model. This is particularly interesting for concurrent object-oriented programming, for which no comprehensive and formal model existed until now. There is a conservative extension of OPM providing the problem-solving capabilities of constraint logic programming. The resulting problem solvers appear as concurrent agents encapsulating search and speculative computation with constraints.

Oz and OPM have been developed at the DFKI since 1991. Oz [16, 13] is designed as a concurrent high-level language that can replace sequential high-level languages such as Lisp, Prolog and Smalltalk. There is no other concurrent language combining a rich object system with advanced features for symbolic processing and problem solving. First applications of Oz include simulations, multi-agent systems, natural language processing, virtual reality, graphical user interfaces, scheduling, time tabling, placement problems, and configuration. The design and implementation of Oz took ideas from AKL [3], the first concurrent constraint language with encapsulated search.

Since January 1995, an efficient, robust, and interactive implementation of Oz, DFKI Oz, is freely available for many Unix-based platforms (see remark at the end of this extended abstract). DFKI Oz features a programming interface based on GNU Emacs, a concurrent browser, an object-oriented interface to Tcl/Tk for building graphical user interfaces, powerful interoperability features (sockets, C, C++), an incremental compiler, and a run-time system with an emulator and a garbage collector.

DFKI Oz proves that an inherently concurrent language can be implemented efficiently on sequential hardware. Research on a portable parallel implementation for shared memory machines has started. More ambitiously, we have also begun work towards a distributed version of Oz supporting the construction of open systems.

There is a full paper [15] corresponding to this extended abstract. The Oz

Primer [14] is an introduction to programming in Oz. There is a simple formal model underlying OPM [12]. The extension of OPM to constraint programming and encapsulated search is the subject of [10, 9]. More on modeling objects in OPM can be found in [1]. Basic implementation techniques for Oz are reported in [5].

References

1. M. Henz, G. Smolka, and J. Würtz. Object-oriented concurrent constraint programming in Oz. In V. Saraswat and P. V. Hentenryck, editors, *Principles and Practice of Constraint Programming*, chapter 2, pages 27–48. The MIT Press, Cambridge, MA, 1995. To appear.

2. J. Jaffar and M. J. Maher. Constraint logic programming: A survey. *The Journal of Logic Programming*, 19/20:503–582, May-July 1994.

3. S. Janson and S. Haridi. Programming paradigms of the Andorra kernel language. In V. Saraswat and K. Ueda, editors, *Logic Programming, Proceedings of the 1991 International Symposium*, pages 167–186, San Diego, USA, 1991. The MIT Press.

4. M. J. Maher. Logic semantics for a class of committed-choice programs. In J.-L. Lassez, editor, *Logic Programming, Proceedings of the Fourth International Conference*, pages 858–876, Cambridge, MA, 1987. The MIT Press.

5. M. Mehl, R. Scheidhauer, and C. Schulte. An abstract machine for Oz. In *Proceedings of PLILP'95*, Utrecht, The Netherlands, Sept. 1995. LNCS, Springer-Verlag. To appear.

6. R. Milner. *A Calculus of Communicating Systems*, volume 92 of *LNCS*. Springer-Verlag, Berlin, Germany, 1980.

7. R. Milner. Functions as processes. *Journal of Mathematical Structures in Computer Science*, 2(2):119–141, 1992.

8. V. A. Saraswat. *Concurrent Constraint Programming*. The MIT Press, Cambridge, MA, 1993.

9. C. Schulte and G. Smolka. Encapsulated search in higher-order concurrent constraint programming. In M. Bruynooghe, editor, *Logic Programming: Proceedings of the 1994 International Symposium*, pages 505–520, Ithaca, New York, USA, 13-17 Nov. 1994. The MIT Press.

10. C. Schulte, G. Smolka, and J. Würtz. Encapsulated search and constraint programming in Oz. In A. Borning, editor, *Second Workshop on Principles and Practice of Constraint Programming*, Lecture Notes in Computer Science, vol. 874, pages 134–150, Orcas Island, Washington, USA, 2-4 May 1994. Springer-Verlag.

11. E. Shapiro. The family of concurrent logic programming languages. *ACM Computing Surveys*, 21(3):413–511, Sept. 1989.

12. G. Smolka. A foundation for higher-order concurrent constraint programming. In J.-P. Jouannaud, editor, *1st International Conference on Constraints in Computational Logics*, Lecture Notes in Computer Science, vol. 845, pages 50–72, München, Germany, 7-9 Sept. 1994. Springer-Verlag.

13. G. Smolka. The definition of Kernel Oz. In A. Podelski, editor, *Constraints: Basics and Trends*, volume 910 of *Lecture Notes in Computer Science*, pages 251–292. Springer-Verlag, Berlin, Germany, 1995.

14. G. Smolka. An Oz primer. DFKI Oz documentation series, German Research Center for Artificial Intelligence (DFKI), Stuhlsatzenhausweg 3, D-66123 Saarbrücken, Germany, 1995.

15. G. Smolka. The Oz programming model. In J. van Leeuwen, editor, *Current Trends in Computer Science*, Lecture Notes in Computer Science, vol. 1000. Springer-Verlag, Berlin, Germany, 1995. To appear.

16. G. Smolka and R. Treinen, editors. *DFKI Oz Documentation Series*. German Research Center for Artificial Intelligence (DFKI), Stuhlsatzenhausweg 3, D-66123 Saarbrücken, Germany, 1995.

Remark. DFKI Oz and related papers are available through anonymous ftp from `ps-ftp.dfki.uni-sb.de` or through WWW from

`http://ps-www.dfki.uni-sb.de/oz/`.

Parallelism in Computational Algorithms and the Physical World

Björn Engquist

Department of Mathematics, UCLA Los Angeles and NADA, KTH Stockholm

1   Introduction

Most processes in the real world are local and contain a high degree of parallelism. A simple example is weather prediction. The weather at any location depends on the weather at earlier times in the neighborhood. Causality is, however, another important physical principle preventing parallelism. The weather at one instance must be known before the weather at later times can be computed. For problems of the size of weather prediction the required recursiveness in the algorithm does not, in practice, prohibit a high degree of parallelism. The parallel computation at each time instance saturates the computer.

The computational algorithms should capture the parallelism in these processes and map them efficiently onto the current architecture. Quite often the original physical process is approximated in such a way that the local dependence is lost. This happens, for example, when steady state is assumed. Furthermore, many modern computational methods are hierarchical and contain some global interconnection even if the underlying process is local. The overall efficiency depends on how well this connectivity is supported by the architecture. Different classes of modern methods in scientific computing and their parallel implementation will be discussed.

2   Explicit Time Dependent Algorithms

In this type of algorithm the unknown quantities are first given as initial values in a real array. Time is discretized and all these unknowns are updated at each discrete time level. In the update the new values in the array are computed as functions of a finite, and usually small, number of real values from the old array. This is the typical form of a finite difference or lumped finite element method approximating a partial differential equation, [4]. The partial differential equation is, by far, the most common mathematical model describing physical processes in many areas as, for example, weather prediction, electro-magnetic and elastic wave propagation, combustion and other chemical processes.

The update mentioned above is given by a fixed function of the old values in the array. These values are all physically close in the one, two or three dimensional space for the independent spatial variables of the simulation. This results directly from differentiation being a local operator.

A natural technique in modern coarse grain MIMD computers, as the IBM SP-1 and Cray T3D, is to decompose the the array following a decomposition

Language Implementation I

Execution of Distributed Reactive Systems *

Paul Caspi[†]   Alain Girault[‡]

Abstract

This paper addresses the problem of distributed reactive systems execution. We first show that a natural parallel description of such systems can be achieved with synchronous languages. Then, we explain how a centralized synchronous program can be executed in its environment, which is intrinsically asynchronous. For this purpose, we define a synchronous/asynchronous interface, which links the program logical time with the environment physical time. Finally, we motivate the need for distribution and show how a desired distribution can be easily achieved, thanks to the object code distribution algorithm implemented in the OC2REP tool. We then propose and discuss three solutions that allow distributed synchronous programs to be executed on an asynchronous network of processors.

Key words

parallel computing, program interface, reactive system, synchronous language.

1   Introduction

1.1   Reactive systems

Reactive systems are computer systems that react continuously to their environment, at a speed imposed by the latter [11]. This class of systems contrasts, on one hand with transformational systems (classical programs whose inputs are available at the beginning of their execution, and which deliver their outputs when terminating), and on the other hand with interactive systems (which react continuously to their environment, but at their own speed: for instance operating systems). Among reactive systems are most of the industrial *real-time* systems

---

*This work has been partially supported by GRECO Automatique Action C2A, Ministère de l'Enseignement Supérieur et de la Recherche and SCHNEIDER ELECTRIC.

[†]VERIMAG, Miniparc - ZIRST, rue Lavoisier, 38330 Montbonnot, FRANCE, tel: (33) 76.90.96.33, email: Paul.Caspi@imag.fr, VERIMAG is a joint laboratory of CNRS, Institut National Polytechnique de Grenoble, Université Joseph Fourier and VERILOG S.A. associated with IMAG

[‡]INRIA MEIJE project, Centre de Mathématiques Appliquées, BP 207, 06904 Sophia Antipolis cedex, FRANCE, tel: (33) 93.95.74.93, email: girault@cma.cma.fr

(control, supervision and signal-processing systems), as well as man-machine interfaces. These systems have the main following features:

- *Parallelism:* At least, the design must take into account the parallelism between the system and its environment. Moreover, these systems are often implemented on parallel architectures, whether for reasons of performance increase, fault tolerance or functionality (geographical distribution). Finally, it is convenient and natural to design such systems as sets of parallel components that cooperate to achieve the intended behavior.

- *Determinism:* These systems always react the same way to the same inputs. This property makes their design, analysis and debugging easier. Thus, it should be preserved by the implementation.

- *Temporal requirements:* These requirements concern both the input rate and the input/output response time. They are induced by the environment and must imperatively be satisfied. Hence, they must be expressed in the specifications, they must be taken into account during the design, and their satisfaction must be checked on the implementation.

- *Dependability:* This is perhaps their most important feature as these systems are often critical ones. For instance, the consequences of a software error in an aircraft automatic pilot or in a nuclear plant controller are disastrous. Therefore these systems require rigorous design methods as well as formal verification.

1.2 The synchronous approach

Synchronous languages [9] have been introduced in the 80's to make the programming of reactive systems easier. They are based on the simultaneity principle: all parallel activities share the same discrete time scale. This is the *synchrony hypothesis*. Each activity can then be dated on this scale; this has the following advantages [2]:

- Time reasonings are made easier.

- Interleaving-based non-determinism disappears, which makes program debugging and verification easier.

The main languages based upon the synchrony hypothesis are SML [4], the STATECHARTS [11], ESTEREL [3], LUSTRE [10], SIGNAL [12], SAGA [1] and ARGOS [13].

Finally, research on synchronous languages compilation has led to define an automaton encoding format: it is the OC format (OC standing for "object code" [14]). OC is the output format of the ESTEREL, LUSTRE and ARGOS compilers. It was recently extended to handle SIGNAL and SAGA programs as well [14]. The automaton transitions, whose execution time is statically computable, correspond to the system reactions to an input. Such an encoding allows to accurately checking the synchrony hypothesis validity, which is of paramount important for critical fields of applications.

1.3 Reactive systems execution

Synchronous languages can be compiled into finite state automata, with pieces of sequential code associated with each state. Yet, there remains the problem of their execution. Actually, the main constraint on the execution of synchronous programs is the *reactivity constraint*: a synchronous program implements a reactive system; it must thus remain reactive to its environment; in other words, it must react to any of the environment promptings.

It is convenient to view a synchronous program as a machine which transforms instantaneously input vectors into output vectors. This is the case of the OC programs, obtained when compiling synchronous programs. We thus add a *synchrony constraint*, enforcing a synchronous program to receive vectors of inputs. Now a synchronous program is embedded into its environment, which is asynchronous. This means that the input values are produced by the environment without any order. To ensure that the reactivity and the synchrony constraint are satisfied, there must be an *interface* whose job is to transform the input values produced by the asynchronous environment into input vectors for the synchronous program. Concerning the inputs, we distinguish continuous and impulse inputs:

- A *continuous input* can be seen as an electrical wire. It always has a value (in the same manner that an electrical wire always has a measurable potential). As a consequence, we can always read a continuous input value.

- An *impulse input*, on the contrary, is considered as an event. Such an input is present or not. The event "the input is present" can be seen as a Dirac impulse.

In this paper we present some *implemented solutions* for the execution of synchronous programs. We first present the general solution for centralized programs (i.e., executed as a single process). Then we motivate the need for distributed reactive systems, and present a distribution tool which implements an object code distribution method. We then introduce three execution methods for distributed synchronous programs, and discuss them.

2 Centralized execution

2.1 Synchronous/asynchronous interface

The interface is the link between logical time of the program and the physical time of the environment. It must satisfy both the reactivity and the synchrony constraints. We first present the general *sequential* execution mode, where the environment and the synchronous program behave in a sequential way (i.e., only one at a time is running). Then we present a particular *passive* execution mode, developed at SCHNEIDER ELECTRIC, where the synchronous program scans the inputs itself, which are updated by the environment in a passive way.

2.2 Sequential execution mode

The sequential execution mode [15] consists of two parts:

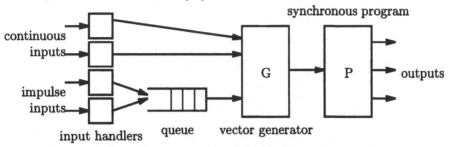

Fig. 1: A centralized sequential synchronous/asynchronous interface

The specialized input handlers which scan the inputs: impulse input values are serialized into a unique waiting queue, in their chronological order, and continuous input values are sampled when requested.

And the vector generator:

- does nothing while the queue is empty,

- extract from the queue the maximal word belonging to the program input language (to be defined later) and builds the corresponding input vector; any missing impulse input value is replaced by the absence value ε; as said in section 1.3, a continuous input always has a value.

- and finally invokes the synchronous program.

The synchronous program and the vector generator exchange control with each other. Only one at a time is running. The synchronous program computes an automaton transition each time it receives an input vector. It produces outputs, and then it gives the control back to the vector generator. In this execution mode, both the reactivity and the synchrony constraints are satisfied.

The vector generator must take into account the existing relations between inputs: exclusions, implications, clock constraints ... Such relations are environmental constraints that must be fulfilled by the interface. They are expressed in the *program input language*. When there are no relations, the generator has to build a new input vector each time the queue is not empty, by extracting from this queue the largest prefix including at most once each input.

For instance, consider four impulse inputs and the following values:

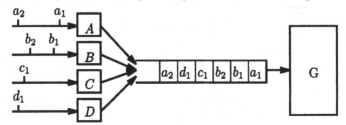

Fig. 2: An input value sequence with four impulse inputs

Then the vector generator successively builds the following vectors:

- $(a_1, b_1, \varepsilon, \varepsilon)$ because there are two consecutive values of B;

- (a_2, b_2, c_1, d_1) because it is the largest prefix that can be extracted from the queue.

Now the generator reading rate can be higher. It may for instance find its waiting queue empty, which we will represent by the value $\emptyset$. For instance, assume that it reads successively the following input values: a_1, b_1, b_2, c_1, $\emptyset$, d_1 and a_2. A $\emptyset$ means that two successive promptings are delayed. In such a case, the vector generator cannot wait for the missing input values necessary to build a full input vector: because of the reactivity constraint, it must build a new vector with the previously read values and as many ε as missing values.

In our example, the generator builds the following vectors:

- $(a_1, b_1, \varepsilon, \varepsilon)$ because there are two consecutive values of B;

- $(\varepsilon, b_2, c_1, \varepsilon)$ because there is a $\emptyset$ in the queue;

- $(a_2, \varepsilon, \varepsilon, d_1)$ because it is the largest prefix that can be extracted from the queue.

We conclude that, because of the generator reading rate, synchronous programming does not totally avoid *non-determinism*. It only rejects non-determinism at the interface level. This will have consequences on the distribution of interfaces, as we will see in section 3.

2.3 Passive execution mode

This solution, developed at SCHNEIDER ELECTRIC for SAGA programs, takes advantage of the fact that only continuous inputs are considered. This assumption is realistic since SAGA is used in the nuclear process control field, where inputs are physical values.

There is no waiting queue, and each input handler has to sample and give its last value when requested. Here the environment is considered as passive since the program itself scans these handlers each time it needs an input vector:

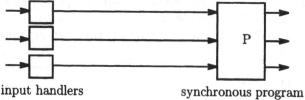

input handlers   synchronous program

Fig. 3: A centralized passive synchronous/asynchronous interface

The synchrony constraint is clearly satisfied since the program itself builds input vectors. Now, since the system only has continuous inputs, the notion of environment prompting depends on the variability of the inputs. Hence, the reactivity constraint is satisfied, provided that the synchronous program is quick enough. This can be easily checked thanks to the automaton structure of the object code [14] produced by the compiler.

3 Distributed execution

We now address the problem of distributed interfaces. We quickly motivate and introduce an implemented distribution tool, and then show how distributed interfaces can be implemented. Here again, the main concern is to ensure that the reactivity and the synchrony constraints are satisfied. We introduce three solutions, and show that only the third one is suitable.

3.1 Distribution method

Many reactive systems have to be *distributed* on several computing locations, for various reasons: performance increase, location of sensors and actuators, fault tolerance. This is the case of the CO3N4 control system, developed at SCHNEIDER ELECTRIC with SAGA for nuclear plants.

To achieve a distributed implementation of reactive systems, we propose to use the *object code distribution method*. This method consists in building the centralized transition system corresponding to the program behavior, debugging and verifying it, and then distributing it according to the system designer's specifications. This yields the following advantages: First, compiling the program into a single transition system may be useful, for debugging and verification purposes [16, 7]. Second, research on synchronous languages compilation has led to a common encoding format for automata: it is the OC format [14]. Hence the object code distribution method can be applied to any synchronous program.

The distribution algorithm, fully presented in [6], consists in:

1. assigning a unique computing location to each action, thanks to the designer's specifications;

2. replicating the program on each location;

3. eliminating on each location the actions not belonging to the considered location;

4. inserting sending actions in order to solve the data dependencies between two distinct locations;

5. inserting receiving actions in order to match the sending actions;

6. adding dummy communications in order to synchronize the distributed program.

It works because the program control structure is expressed in the automaton: we choose to replicate the control structure on each location, and to compute this algorithm only on the *sequential code* of the states (actually a directed acyclic graph of actions).

Then, some communication mechanism remains to be chosen. *Queues* allow to put back sendings and move forward receivings, therefore minimizing the waiting time induced by the communication network [8]. We choose to have two FIFO channels for each pair of locations, one in each direction. This is quite cheap in terms of execution environment, and has proved to work satisfactorily.

3.2 Distribution tool

This distribution method has been implemented and tested: it is the OC2REP tool. It acts as a post-processor for the various synchronous languages compilers. Starting from an OC program and a file of distribution specifications, it produces n OC programs, one for each computing location or process. The only requirement is that the network must preserve the integrity and the ordering of messages. Finally, an industrial version is being studied at SCHNEIDER ELECTRIC for SAGA applications. It is intended to be used for the future nuclear plant control system.

3.3 Centralized solution

First, we can adapt the centralized solution to the distributed case. It consists in using the vector generator, described in subsection 2.2, with the distributed program: the generated vectors have to be partitioned into as many sub-vectors as computing locations.

We assume that the program is distributed for n locations. The set of inputs is partitioned into n subsets, one for each component of the distributed program. This partition is directly deduced from the distribution specifications. Moreover, each sub-vector is obtained by projecting the input vector onto the corresponding subset of inputs.

For a program distributed on two locations, we have:

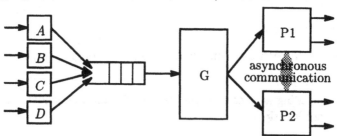

Fig. 4: A centralized interface linked with a distributed program

For instance, consider the case of four inputs A, B, C and D, such that A and B belong to location 1, and C and D to location 2. We keep the values of figure 2. The generated vectors are $(a_1, b_1, \varepsilon, \varepsilon)$ and then (a_2, b_2, c_1, d_1). Thus, the projected vectors are for program P1: (a_1, b_1) and then (a_2, b_2), and for program P2: $(\varepsilon, \varepsilon)$ and then (c_1, d_1).

The $(\varepsilon, \varepsilon)$ must not be considered as an empty input: indeed it forces P2 to react, thus allowing the communications with P1, and possibly the receipt of input values.

This execution mode satisfies both the reactivity and the synchrony constraint. However, it is not a distributed implementation. Here our goal is to distribute the interface as well as the synchronous program, so that each component of the distributed program is independent of the other components, and thus can be run separately.

3.4 Naïve distributed solution

The first distributed solution takes advantage of the existing *synchronization* of the distributed programs. Such a synchronization is intended to prevent the situation where one of the location programs behave as a value producer while others behave as value consumers. This could lead to queue overflow and loss of the temporal semantics of the centralized program. To ensure that the distributed programs remain synchronized, we can for instance add dummy communications between the distributed locations [6]. The result is that there cannot be more than one cycle overlap between any two location programs.

The naïve distributed solution consists in projecting the vector generator onto the input subset of each location. We thus obtain one vector generator for each location. For our program distributed on two locations, we have:

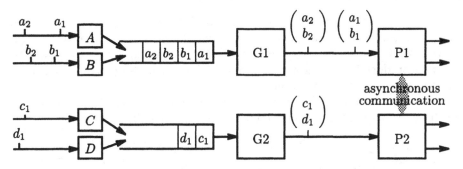

Fig. 5: A distributed interface with a distributed program

We keep the same input value sequence as in figure 2. The first vector generated by the couple G1/G2 is (a_1, b_1, c_1, d_1). The problem is that G1 and G2 should send synchronous input vectors to P1 and P2 respectively, which is not the case due to the delay between a_1/b_1 and c_1/d_1. In other words, the synchrony constraint is satisfied for each component of the distributed program, but not for the program as a whole. Moreover, this vector does not correspond to the first vector generated by the centralized interface (i.e., the $(a_1, b_1, \varepsilon, \varepsilon)$ vector).

In fact, G2 should be forced to build an input vector at the very moment when G1 sends its vector (a_1, b_1) to P1. In such a case, either the waiting queue of G2 is empty and it must build an empty vector (i.e., the $(\varepsilon, \varepsilon)$ vector), or it has already read some values and it must complete its new vector with as many ε as missing values.

Now consider a program with two inputs A and B, distributed such that A belongs to location 1 and B to location 2. Then assume that values for A are more frequent than for B. The reactivity constraint induces that each vector generator (G1 for location 1 and G2 for location 2) is able to take into account *each* input value. The synchronization between programs P1 and P2 ensures that they compute the same number of cycles. Two situations may arise:

- G1 and G2 run at the same rate, i.e., at the the fast input (A) rate: in that case, both programs P1 and P2 are activated the same number of times, even if P2 is sometimes activated with an empty input vector.

- G1 and G2 run at their own input rate: in that case, G1 runs at the fast input (A) and G2 at the slow input (B) rate. Then, since P1 and P2 are synchronized, they will run at the slow input rate and we will face an overflow in G1 waiting queue.

In order to avoid such an overflow, we must enforce G2 to build vectors at G1 rate. In other words, the distributed programs must run at the fast input rate. This is the solution presented in the next subsection.

3.5 Reactive distributed solution

The previous solution shows the need for some kind of synchronization between the vector generators, so that they produce input vectors equivalent to the centralized solution vectors, if possible. Several solutions can be considered. The one we introduce here is rather easy, and its implementation has proved to be efficient with respect to execution time.

We assume that a vector generator is able to know whether the corresponding synchronous program has received a value in any of its FIFO channels:

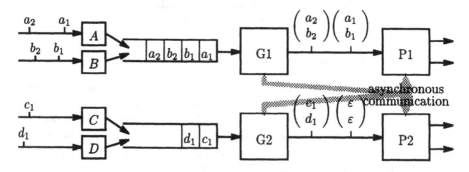

Fig. 6: A distributed interface with asynchronous link

If this assumption is valid, then a vector generator must activate its synchronous program each time that:

- the inputs read in the waiting queue allow to build a complete input vector, with respect to the subprogram input language: in such a case the program will be activated with this vector;

- the inputs read in the waiting queue do not allow to build a complete input vector but a data has been detected in one of the FIFO channels directed towards the program: this means that one of the other components of the distributed program is currently communicating with the considered component, and that this communicating component has already been activated by its own vector generator; the first vector generator must then activate its synchronous program with a vector including the currently read input values and as many ε as missing values.

This is a suitable solution. First, it satisfies the synchrony constraint, for the whole distributed program. Secondly, it ensures that the distributed program is reactive to its environment, since when one of its components react to a prompting, all other components are forced to do so, even if their respective inputs are absent.

Yet, non-determinism of the interface (see end of subsection 2.2) prevents us from proving the behavior equivalence (in terms of generated vectors) between the centralized and the distributed interface.

3.6 Implementation

We have developed a toy execution environment for synchronous programs, which works in conjunction with the OC2REP distribution tool. It is based on UNIX/INTERNET: FIFO channels are implemented as sockets. Sockets are well adapted since they preserve both the ordering and the integrity of messages. Moreover, they allow the vector generator to check for incoming messages. It has allowed to run an example of distributed program (the wristwatch with chronograph and alarm) between the University of Berkeley and the Centre de Mathématiques Appliquées of Sophia-Antipolis.

An industrial execution environment is currently being studied at SCHNEIDER ELECTRIC. It is based on the NERVIA [17] industrial network which uses a shared memory to implement communications between computation locations. This network, currently used in the control system of the 1450 MW nuclear plants, is also planned for the future control system. Here, the main difficulty is to implement communications so that the ordering of the messages is preserved. This was the case for the UNIX/INTERNET sockets, but is no longer valid for a shared memory. Once again, the reactivity and the synchrony constraints have to be carefully checked.

Finally, future work will include the execution of distributed programs with the PTOLEMY tool [5]. The PTOLEMY software is a system-level design framework that allows mixing models of computation. It is made of several *domains*, each of them being one computation model allowing to take into account communication and scheduling between processes. It is thus possible to execute the programs distributed by OC2REP within a PTOLEMY domain instead of UNIX sockets.

4 Conclusion

In this paper, we have studied the execution of reactive systems. Synchronous languages allow reactive systems to be programmed while preserving their natural parallelism and making time reasonings easier.

The synchrony hypothesis raises the problem of program execution. Indeed, the program logical time is assumed to be discrete: inputs must be synchronous. Yet, the environment is intrinsically asynchronous: no assumption can be made on the input occurring dates. In order to link the program logical time and the environment physical time, we need a synchronous/asynchronous interface. The main concern here is to ensure that the program remains reactive to its environment.

First, we have studied synchronous/asynchronous interfaces in the case of centralized programs (section 3). Then, we have motivated the need for distributed programs, particularly in the reactive systems field (for geographical, performance or fault tolerance reasons). Finally, we have presented and discussed three solutions for distributed synchronous/asynchronous interfaces (section 3). Only the third solution (subsection 3.5) is satisfactory because it allows a distributed implementation and it ensures that the program remains reactive to its environment. Unfortunately, the non-determinism due to the interface computing rate does not allow to prove formally that the distributed interface has the same behavior as the centralized one.

Finally, this execution method has been fully implemented on a UNIX/ INTERNET system. Thanks to the OC2REP distribution tool, it allows reactive systems to be easily programmed, compiled towards a parallel architecture, and efficiently executed.

References

[1] J.-L. Bergerand and E. Pilaud. SAGA : A software development environment for dependability in automatic control. In *SAFECOMP'88*. Pergamon Press, 1988.

[2] G. Berry, P. Couronné, and G. Gonthier. Programmation synchrone des systèmes réactifs, le langage ESTEREL. *Technique et Science Informatique*, 4:305–316, 1987.

[3] F. Boussinot and R. de Simone. The ESTEREL language. *Proceedings of the IEEE*, 79(9):1293–1304, September 1991.

[4] M.C. Browne and E.M. Clarke. Sml: a high-level language for the design and verification of finite state machines. In *International Working Conference*

from HDL Descriptions to Guaranteed Correct Circuit Designs, Grenoble, France, September 1986. IFIP.

[5] J. Buck, S. Ha, E.A. Lee, and D.G. Messerschmitt. PTOLEMY: a framework for simulating and prototyping heterogeneous systems. *International Journal of Computer SImulation*, April 1994.

[6] P. Caspi, A. Girault, and D. Pilaud. Distributing reactive systems. In *Seventh International Conference on Parallel and Distributed Computing Systems, PDCS'94*, Las Vegas, USA, October 1994. ISCA.

[7] E.M. Clarke, E.A. Emerson, and A.P. Sistla. Automatic verification of finite-state concurrent systems using temporal logic specifications. *TOPLAS*, 8(2):244–263, 1986.

[8] A. Dinning. A survey of synchronization methods for parallel computers. *Computer*, pages 66–76, July 1989.

[9] N. Halbwachs. *Synchronous programming of reactive systems*. Kluwer Academic Pub., 1993.

[10] N. Halbwachs, P. Caspi, P. Raymond, and D. Pilaud. The synchronous data flow programming language LUSTRE. *Proceedings of the IEEE*, 79(9):1305–1320, September 1991.

[11] D. Harel and A. Pnueli. On the development of reactive systems. In *Logic and Models of Concurrent Systems*, NATO. Springer Verlag, 1985.

[12] P. LeGuernic, T. Gautier, M. LeBorgne, and C. LeMaire. Programming real-time applications with SIGNAL. *Proceedings of the IEEE*, 79(9):1321–1336, September 1991.

[13] F. Maraninchi. Operational and compositional semantics of synchronous automaton compositions. In *CONCUR'92*. LNCS 630, Springer Verlag, August 1992.

[14] J.P. Paris and al. Les formats communs des langages synchrones. Technical Report 157, INRIA, June 1993.

[15] M.A. Péraldi. Conception et réalisation de systèmes temps-réel par une approche synchrone. Thesis, University of Nice-Sophia Antipolis, 1993.

[16] J.P. Queille and J. Sifakis. Specification and verification of concurrent systems in CESAR. In *International Symposium on Programming, LNCS 137*, pages 337–351. Springer Verlag, April 1982.

[17] SCHNEIDER ELECTRIC. *Manuel utilisateur NERVIA*. Document interne.

Relating Data–Parallelism and (And–) Parallelism in Logic Programs*

Manuel V. Hermenegildo and Manuel Carro

Universidad Politécnica de Madrid
Facultad de Informática
28660 Boadilla del Monte
Madrid — Spain
{herme,mcarro}@fi.upm.es

Abstract. Much work has been done in the areas of and–parallelism and data–parallelism in Logic Programs. Both types of parallelism offer advantages and disadvantages: traditional (and–) parallel models offer generality, whereas data–parallelism techniques offer increased performance for a restricted class of programs. The thesis of this paper is that these two forms of parallelism are not fundamentally different and that relating them opens the possibility of obtaining the advantages of both within the same system. Some relevant issues are discussed and solutions proposed. The discussion is illustrated through visualizations of actual parallel executions implementing the ideas proposed.

1 Introduction

The term *data–parallelism* is generally used to refer to a parallel semantics for (definite) iteration in a programming language such that all iterations are performed simultaneously, synchronizing before any event that directly or indirectly involves communication among iterations. It is often also allowed that the results of the iterations be combined by reduction with an associative operator. In this context a *definite iteration* is an iteration where the number of repetitions is known before the iteration is initiated.

Data–parallelism has been exploited in many languages, including C* [28], Data Parallel C [12], *LISP [27], etc. Recently, much progress has been reported in the application of concepts from data–parallelism to logic programming, both from the theoretical and practical points of view, including the design of programming constructs and the development of many implementation techniques [29, 3, 4].

On the other hand, much progress has also been made (and continues to be made) in the exploitation of parallelism in logic programs based on control-derived notions such as and–parallelism and or–parallelism [6, 10, 18, 19, 1, 17, 26]. It appears interesting to explore, even if only informally, the relation between these two at first sight different approaches to the exploitation of parallelism in logic programs. This informal exploration is one of the purposes of this paper, the other being to explore the intimately related issue of fast task startup.

---

* The authors have been partially supported by ESPRIT project 6707 *ParForce*

1.1 Data–Parallelism and And–Parallelism

It is generally accepted that data–parallelism is a restricted form of and–parallelism:[1] the threads being parallelized in data–parallelism are usually the iterations of a recursion, a type of parallelism which is obviously also supported in and–parallel systems. All and–parallel systems impose certain restrictions on the goals or threads which can be executed in parallel (such as independence and/or determinacy, applied at different granularity levels [15, 21, 7, 16]) which are generally the *minimal* ones needed in order to ensure vital desired properties such as correctness of results or "no–slowdown", i.e. that parallel execution be guaranteed to take no more time than sequential execution. Data–parallel programs have to meet the same restrictions from this point of view. This is generally referred to as the "safeness" conditions in the context of data–parallelism.

However, one central idea in data–parallelism is to impose *additional* restrictions to the parallelism allowed, in order to make possible further optimizations in some important cases. These restrictions limit the amount of parallelism which can be obtained with respect to a more general purpose and–parallel implementation. But, on the other hand, when the restrictions are met, many optimizations can be performed with respect to an unoptimized general purpose and–parallel model, in which the implementation perhaps has to deal with backtracking, synchronization, dynamic scheduling, locking, etc. A number of implementations have been built which are capable of exploiting such special cases in an efficient way (e.g. [4]). Often, a *a priori* knowledge of the sizes of the data structures being operated on is required (but this data is also obtained dynamically in other cases).

In a way, one would like to have the best of both worlds: an implementation capable of supporting general forms of and– (and also –or) parallelism, so that speedups can be obtained in as many programs as possible, and at the same time have the implementation be able to take advantage of the optimizations possible in data–parallel computations when the conditions are met.

1.2 Compile–time and Run–time Techniques

In order to achieve the above mentioned goal of a "best of both worlds" system, there are two classes of techniques which have to studied. The first class is related to detecting when the particular properties to be used to perform the optimizations hold; this problem is common to both control– and data–parallel systems, and equally difficult in both. The solution of allowing the programmer to explicitly declare such properties or use special constructs (such as "parallel map," "bounded quantifications" [2], etc.) which have built–in syntactic restrictions may help, but it is also true that this solution can be applied indistinctly in both of the approaches under consideration. Thus, we will not deal herein with how the special cases are detected.

The second class of techniques are those related to the actual optimizations realized in the runtime machinery to exploit the special cases. Admitting that data–parallelism constitutes a special case of and–parallelism, one would in principle expect the abstract machine used in data–parallelism to be a "pared down"

---

[1] Note, however, that data–parallelism can also be exploited as or parallelism [24].

version of the more general machine. We believe that this is in general the case, but it is also true that the data–parallel machines also bring some new and interesting techniques related to, for example, optimizations in memory management.

However, it should be noted that if the particular case is identified, the same optimizations can also be done in general–purpose abstract machines supporting and–parallelism (such as, for example, the RAP–WAM [14], the DAS–WAM [26] or the Andorra–I engine [25]), and without losing the capability of handling the general case, as shown in [23, 22].

On the other hand, a number of optimizations, generally related to the "Reform Compilation" done in Reform Prolog [20], are more fundamental. We find these optimizations particularly interesting because they bring attention upon a very important issue regarding the performance of and–parallel systems: that of the speed in the creation and joining of tasks. We will essentially devote the rest of the paper to this issue, because of the special interest of this subject, and given that, as pointed out before, the other intervening issues have already been addressed to some extent in the literature.[2]

2 The Task Startup and Synchronization Time Problems

The problem in hand can be illustrated with the following simple program:

```
vproc([],[]).
vproc([H|T],[HR|TR]):-
    process_element(H,HR),
    vproc(T,TR).
```

which relates all the elements of two lists. Throughout the discussion we will assume that the vproc/2 predicate is going to be used in the "forwards" way, i.e. a ground list of values and a free variable will be supplied as arguments (in that order), expecting as result a ground list. We use as process_element/2 a small–grained numerical operation, which serves to illustrate the issue:

```
process_element(H,HR):- HR is ((((H * 2) / 5)^2)+(((H * 6) / 2)^3))/2.
```

2.1 The Naive Approach

This program can be naively parallelized as follows using "control–parallelism" (we will use throughout &–Prolog [14] syntax, where the "&" operator represents a potentially parallel conjunction):

```
vproc([],[]).
vproc([H|T],[HR|TR]):-
    process_element(H,HR) & vproc(T,TR).
```

---

[2] Improving the performance of parallel systems in the presence of fine–grained computations can also be addressed by performing "granularity control" [9, 11, 31]. This issue can be treated orthogonally to the techniques discussed in this paper.

This will allow the parallel execution of all iterations. Note that the parallelization is safe, since all iterations are *independent*. The program can be parallelized using "data–parallelism" in a similar way.

However, it is interesting to study how the tasks are started due to the textual ordering of the goals. In a system like &–Prolog, using one of the the standard schedulers (which we will assume throughout the examples), the agent running the call to vproc/2 would create a process corresponding to the recursion, i.e. vproc(T,TR), make it available on its goal stack, and then take on the execution of process_element(H,HR). Another agent might pick the created process, creating in turn another process for the recursion and taking on a new iteration of process_element(H,HR), and so on. In the end, parallel processes are created for each iteration. However, the approach, or, at least, the naive program presented, also has some drawbacks.

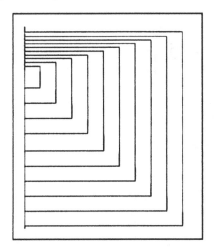

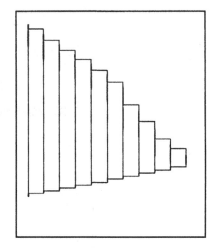

Fig. 1. List operation (10 el./1 proc.)

Fig. 2. List operation, giving away recursion (10 el./8 proc.)

In order to illustrate this, we perform the experiment of running the previous program with the goal "vproc(V, R)", where V has been instantiated to the list of integers from 1 to 10, and R is a free variable. This program (as well as the others) is run in &–Prolog on a Sequent Symmetry shared memory multiprocessor and instructed to generate trace files, which can be visualized using VisAndOr [5]. In VisAndOr graphs, time goes from top to bottom. Vertical solid lines denote actual execution, whereas vertical dashed lines represent waits due to scheduling or dependencies, and horizontal dashed lines represent forks and joins.

Figure 1 represents the execution of the benchmark in one processor, and serves as scale reference. The result of running the benchmark in 8 processors is depicted in Figure 2. As can be seen, the initial task forks into two. One is performed locally whereas the other one, corresponding to the recursion, is taken by another agent and split again into two. In the end, the process is inverted to perform the joins. A certain amount of speedup is obtained; this can be observed by comparing its length to Figure 1. However, the speedup obtained is quite small for a program such as this with obvious parallelism. This low speedup is in part due to the small granularity of the parallel tasks, and also to the slow generation of the tasks which results from giving out the recursion.

2.2 Keeping the Recursion Local

One simple transformation can greatly alleviate the problem mentioned above — reversing the order of the goals in the parallel conjunction, to keep the recursive goal local, and not even push it on to the goal stack:

```
vproc([],[]).
vproc([H|T],[HR|TR]):-
    vproc(T,TR) & process_element(H,HR).
```

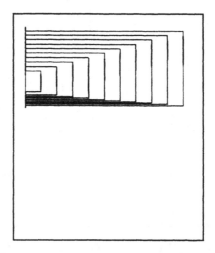

Fig. 3. List operation, keeping recursion (10 el./8 proc.)

The result of running this program is depicted in Figure 3, which uses the same scale as Figures 1 and 2. The first process keeps the recursion local and thus creates the tasks much faster, resulting in substantially more speedup. This transformation is normally done by the &–Prolog parallelizing compiler, unless the user explicitly annotates the goal for parallel execution by hand.

In applications which show much larger granularity than this example, task creation speed is not a problem. On the other hand, in numerical applications (such as those targeted in data–parallelism) the speed of the process creating the tasks will become a bottleneck, and speeding up tasks creation can greatly impact the performance of systems where the number of processes/threads cannot be statically determined and their creation is triggered at runtime.

2.3 The "Data–Parallel" Approach

At this point it is interesting to return to the data–parallel approach and, in particular, to Reform Prolog. Assuming that the recursion has already been identified as suitable for this technique, this system converts the list into a vector, noting the length on the way, and then creates the tasks associated with each element in a tight, low level loop. The following program allows us to both illustrate this process without resorting to low level instructions and measure inside &–Prolog the benefit that this type of task creation can bring:

```
vproc([H1,H2,H3,H4,H5,H6,H7,H8,H9,H10], [R1,R2,R3,R4,R5,R6,R7,R8,R9,R10]):-
    process_element(H1,R1) &
    process_element(H2,R2) &
    .
    .
    .
    process_element(H10,R10).
```

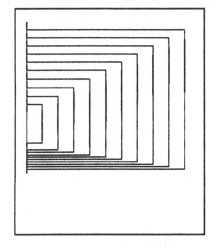
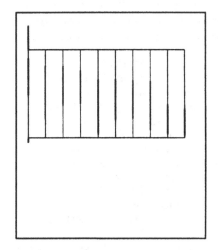

Fig. 4. List operation, keeping recursion (10 el./8 proc.)

Fig. 5. List operation, flattened for 10 elements (10 el./8 proc.)

Figure 4 represents the same execution as Figure 3, but at a slightly enlarged scale; this scale will be retained throughout the rest of the paper, to allow easy comparisons among different pictures.

The execution of the "data–parallel" program is depicted in Figure 5, which uses the same scale as Figure 4. The clear improvement is due to the much faster task creation and joining and also to having only one synchronization structure for all tasks. Note, however, that the creation of the first task is slightly delayed due to the need for unifying the whole list before creating any tasks and for setting up the tasks themselves. This small delay is compensated by the faster task creation, but can eventually be a bottleneck for very large vectors. Eventually, in a big computation with a large enough number of processors, the head unification will tend to dominate the whole computation (c.f. Amdahl's law). In this case, unification parallelism can be worthwhile [3].

In our quest for merging the techniques of the data–parallel and and–parallel approaches, one obvious solution would be to incorporate the techniques of the Reform Prolog engine into the PWAM abstract machine for the cases when it is applicable. On the other hand, it is also interesting to study how far one can go with no modifications (or minimal modifications) to the machinery.

The last program studied is an unfolding of the original recursion. Note that such unfoldings can always be performed at compile–time, provided that the depth of the recursion is known. In fact, knowing recursion bounds may actually be frequent in traditional data–parallel applications (and is often the case when parallelizing bounded quantifications [2]). On the other hand it is not really the case in general and thus some other solution must be explored.

2.4 A More Dynamic Unfolding

If the depth of the recursion is not known at compile time the previous scheme cannot be used. But instead of resorting directly to the naive approach, we can try to perform a more flexible task startup. The program below is an attempt at making the unfolding more dynamic, while still staying within the source–to–source program transformation approach:

```
vproc([H1,H2,H3,H4|T],             vproc([H1,H2|T],[R1,R2|TR]):- !,
      [R1,R2,R3,R4|TR]):- !,           vproc(T,TR)  &
   vproc(T,TR)  &                      process_element(H1,R1)  &
   process_element(H1,R1)  &           process_element(H2,R2).
   process_element(H2,R2)  &        vproc([H|T],[R|TR]):- !,
   process_element(H3,R3)  &           vproc(T,TR)  &
   process_element(H4,R4).             process_element(H,R).
vproc([H1,H2,H3|T],[R1,R2,R3|TR]):- !,  vproc([],[]).
   vproc(T,TR)  &
   process_element(H1,R1)  &
   process_element(H2,R2)  &
   process_element(H3,R3).
```

The results are shown in Figure 6, which has the same scale as Figures 4 and 5. A group of four tasks is created; one of these tasks creates, in turn, another group of four. The two remaining tasks are created inside the latter group. The speed is not quite as good as when the 10 tasks are created at the same time, but the results are close. This "flattening" approach has been studied formally by Millroth[3], which has given sufficient conditions for performing these transformations for particular cases such as linear recursion.

There are still two problems with this approach, however. The first one is how to chose the "reformant level", i.e. the maximum degree of unfolding used, which with this technique is fixed at compile–time. In the previous example the unfolding was stopped at level 4, but the ideal unfolding level depends both on the number of processors and the size of lists. The other problem, which was pointed out before, is the fact that the initial matching of the list (or the conversion to a vector) is a sequential step which can become a bottleneck for large data sets. A solution is to increase the task creation speed (for example, using low level instructions) but this has a limit, and it will also eventually become a bottleneck. Another solution is to use from the start, and instead of

---

[3] And has been used in &–Prolog compilation informally (see e.g. [30] and some of the standard &–Prolog benchmarks, in http://www.clip.dia.fi.upm.es).

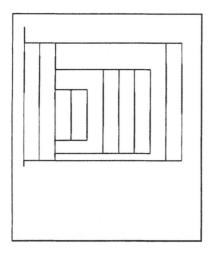

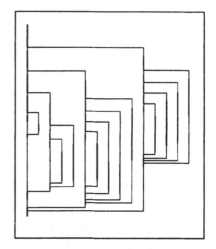

Fig. 6. List operation with fixed list flattening (10 el./8 proc.)

Fig. 7. List operation with flexible list flattening (10 el./8 proc.)

lists, more parallel data structures, such as vectors (we will return to this in Section 3).

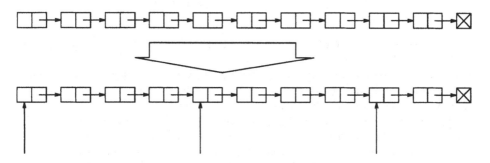

Fig. 8. "Skip" operation, 10 elements in 4

2.5 Dynamic Unfolding in Parallel

We now propose a different solution which tries to address at the same time the two problems above. The transformation has two objectives: speeding up the creation of tasks by performing it in parallel, and allowing a form of "flexible flattening". The basic idea, applied to lists, is depicted in Figure 8. Instead of performing a unification of a fixed length as encoded at compile–time, a builtin, skip/4, is used which will allow performing unifications of different lengths.

The predicate skip(L,N,LS,NS) relates a list L and an "unfolding increment" N with a suffix LS of L which is placed at most at N positions from the starting of L. NS contains the actual number of elements in LS, in case that N is less than the length of L (in which case LS = []). Several calls to skip(L,N,LS,NS) using the output list LS as input list L in each call will return pointers to equally–spaced suffixes of L, until no sufficient elements remain. Figure 8 depicts the pointers returned by `skip(L,N,LS,NS)` to a 10 elements list, with an "unfolding level" N = 4. This builtin can be defined in Prolog as follows (but can, of course, be implemented more efficiently at a low level):

```
skip(L,N,LS,NS):- skip(L,N,LS,NS,0).

skip(LS,0,LS,NS,NS):- !.
skip([],_,[],NS,NS).
skip([_|Ls],N,LRs,Ns0,Ns):-
    N1 is N-1,
    Ns1 is Ns+1,
    skip(Ls,N1,LRs,Ns0,Ns1).
```

We now return to our original program and make use of the proposed builtin (note that the "flattening parameter" N can be now chosen dynamically). The entry point is `vproc_opt/3`:

```
vproc_opt([],[],0).              vproc_opt_n(0,_,_).
vproc_opt(L,LR,N):-              vproc_opt_n(N,[L|Ls],[LR|LRs]):-
    N > 0,                           N > 0,
    skip(L,N,LS,NS),                 N1 is N-1,
    skip(LR,NS,LRS,NS),              vproc_opt_n(N1,Ls,LRs) &
    vproc_opt(LS,LRS,NS) &           process_element(L,LR).
    vproc_opt_n(NS,L,LR).
```

We have included the `skip/4` predicate as a C builtin in the &–Prolog system and run the above program. The result is shown in Figure 7. The relatively large delays are due to the traversal of the list made by `skip/4`. Note, however, how the tasks are created in groups of four corresponding to the dynamically selected increment, which can now be made arbitrarily large.

It is worth noting that, in this case, the predicate `skip/4` not only returns pointers to sublists of a given list, but is also able to construct a new list filled with free variables. This allows spawning parallel processes, each one of them working in separate segments of a list. This, in some sense, mimics the so–called *poslist* and *neglist* identified in the Reform Compilation at run–time.

If we want the splitting of the list to be used afterwards (for example, because it is needed in some further similar processing), we can construct a list containing pointers to suffixes of a given list, or, under a more logical point of view, a list describing sublists of the initial list by means of difference lists. Figure 9 depicts this situation, and Figure 10 shows the result of an execution where the input and output lists have been pre-processed using this technique. This list preprocessing does not appear in Figure 10, as an example of the reuse of a previously traversed list.

2.6 Performance Evaluation

In order to assess the relative performance of the various techniques discussed, we have run the examples on a larger (240 element) list. The execution times are presented in Table 1. The column *Relative Speedup* refers to the speedup with respect to the parallel execution on one processor, and the column *Absolute*

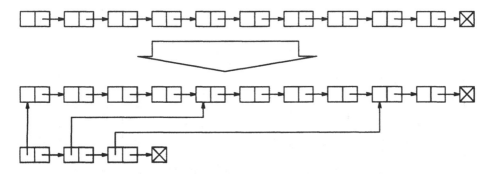

Fig. 9. "Skiplist" operation, 10 elements in 4

Method	Time (ms)	Relative Speedup	Absolute Speedup
Sequential	127	—	1
Parallel, 1 processor	153	1	0.83
Giving away recursion	134	1.14	0.94
Keeping recursion	41	3.73	3.09
Skipping (8)	30	5.1	4.23
Skipping (30)	28.5	5.36	4.45
Pre–built skipping list (8)	28	5.4	4.53
Pre–built skipping list (30)	26.5	5.77	4.79
Reform Compilation (8)	27	5.6	4.7
Data Parallel	26	5.88	4.88

Table 1. Times and speedups for different list access, 8 processors.

Speedup measures the execution speed with respect to the sequential execution. The numbers between parentheses to the right of some benchmark names represent the skipping factor chosen.

The speedups suggested by Figures 4 to 9 may not correspond with those in the table — the length of the benchmark and the skip/unfolding increment chosen in the two cases is different, and so is the distribution of the tasks. Processing larger lists can take more advantage from the proposed techniques, because the relative overhead from traversing the list is comparatively less, and tasks with larger granularity can be distributed among the processes.

Overheads associated with scheduling, preparing tasks for parallel execution, etc. make the parallel execution in one processor be slower than the sequential execution. This difference is more acute in very small grained benchmarks, as the one we are dealing with.

It can also be noted how a pre–built skipping list with a properly chosen increment beats the reformed program. Of course a reformed program with the same unfolding level would, in principle, at least equal the program with the pre–built list. But the point is that the reformed program was statically transformed, whereas the skiplist version can change dynamically, and be useful in cases where the same data is used several times in the same program.

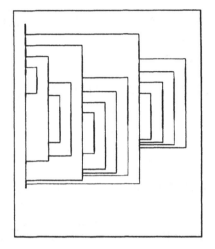 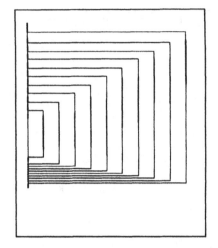

Fig. 10. List operation with prebuilt list (10 el./8 proc.)

Fig. 11. Vector operation, constant time access arrays (10 el./8 proc.)

3 Using Constant Time Access Arrays

Finally, and for the sake of argument, we propose a simple-minded approach to the original problem using standard Prolog terms, i.e., the real "arrays" in Prolog. The use of this technique is limited by the fact that term arity is limited in many Prolog implementations, but this could be easily cured. The "vector" version of vproc/3 receives a vector represented using a structure (which can have been either created directly or from a list) and its length. The access to each element is done in constant time using arg/3.

```
vproc(0,_,_).
vproc(_,V,VR):-
    I>0, I1 is I-1,
    vproc(I1,V,VR) & process_element_vec(I,V,VR).
```

The execution of this program is presented in Figure 11, where we are using a simple minded loop which creates tasks recursively. The same techniques illustrated in previous examples can be applied to this "real array" version: it is easy now to modify the above program in order to create the tasks in groups of N, but now without having to previously traverse the data structure, as was the case when using the skip builtin.

The result appears in Figure 12. It may seem that there is no performance improvement, but is due to the fact that the execution depicted is very small, and the added overhead of calculating the "splitting point" becomes a sizeable part of the whole execution. In Table 2 larger arrays and skipping factors were chosen, achieving better speedups than the simple parallel scheme. Since no real traversal is needed using this representation, the amount of items skipped can be dynamically adjusted with no extra cost.

A more even load distribution than that obtained with the simple recursion scheme can be achieved using a binary split. This is equivalent to dynamically

Method	Time (ms)	Relative Speedup	Absolute Speedup
Sequential	149	—	1
Parallel, 1 processor	174	1	0.85
Keeping recursion	45	3.8	3.31
Binary startup	38	4.5	3.92
Skipping (8)	31.2	5.57	4.77
Skipping (30)	29.5	5.89	5.05

Table 2. Times and speedups for vector accesses

choosing the splitting step to be half the length of the sub–vector assigned to the task. Figure 13 depicts an execution following this scheme. As in Figure 12, the comparatively large overhead associated with the determination of the splitting point makes this execution appear larger than that corresponding to the simple recursive case. But again, Table 2 reflects that for large enough executions, its performance can be placed between the simple recursion scheme and a carefully chosen skipping scheme.

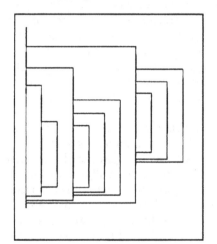 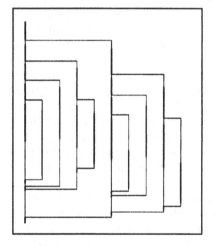

Fig. 12. Vector operation, constant time access arrays, skipping, 10 el./8 proc.

Fig. 13. Constant time access arrays, binary startup, 10 el./8 proc.

Some conclusions can be drawn from Tables 1 and 2. First, the structure–based programs are slightly slower than their list–based counterparts. This is understandable in that using structures as arrays involves an explicit index handling that is less efficient (or, rather, that has been less optimized) than in the case of lists. But the fact that accessing any element in a structure is, in principle, a constant–time operation, allows a comparatively efficient implementation of the dynamic *skip* strategy. This is apparent in that the speedups attained with the arrays version of the skipping technique are better than those corresponding to the list–based programs. The absolute speed is less, which can be attributed to the fact that the version of &–Prolog used has the **arg/3** builtin written in

C, with the associated overhead of calling and returning from a C function. This could be improved making **arg/3** (or a similar primitive) a faster, WAM–level instruction. Again, if we want (or have to) use lists, a low–level **vectorize/2** builtin could be fast enough to translate a list into a structure and still save time with respect to a list–based implementation processing the resulting structure in a divide–and–conquer fashion.

Finally, following on on this idea, we would like to point out that it is possible to build a quite general purpose "FORTRAN–like" constant access array library without ever departing from standard Prolog or, eliminating the use of "**setarg**", even from "clean" Prolog. The solution we propose in [13] is related to the standard "logarithmic access time" extensible array library written by D.H.D.Warren. In this case, we obtain constant (rather than logarithmic) access time, with the drawback that arrays are, at least in principle, fixed size.

4 Conclusions

We have argued that data–parallelism and and–parallelism are not fundamentally different and that by relating them in fact the advantages of both can be obtained within the same system. We have also argued that the difference lies in two main issues: memory management and fast task startup and management. Having pointed to recent progress in memory management techniques in and–parallelism we have concentrated on the issue of fast task startup, discussed the relevant issues and proposed a number of solutions, illustrating the point made through visualizations of actual parallel executions implementing the ideas proposed. In summary, we argue that both approaches can be easily reconciled, resulting in more powerful systems which can bring the performance benefits of data–parallelism with the generality of traditional and–parallel systems.

Our work has concentrated on speeding up task creation and distribution in a type of symbolic or numerical computations that are traditionally characterized by structural recursion over lists or arrays. We have shown some transformation techniques relying on a dynamic load distribution that can improve the speedups obtained in a parallel execution. However, the overhead associated with this dynamic distribution is large in the case of lists; better speedups can be obtained using data structures with constant access time, in which arbitrarily splitting the data does not impose any additional overhead.

There are other kinds of computations where the iteration is performed over a numerical parameter. While not directly characterizable as "data–parallelism" this type of iteration can also benefit from fast task startup techniques. This very interesting issue has been recently and independently discussed by Debray [8], and shown to also achieve significant speedups for that class of problems.

The techniques discussed in this paper probably cannot always match the performance of a native data–parallel system. But it is also true that, in principle, low level mechanisms can be designed which fit seamlessly within the machinery of a more general parallel system. In particular, entries in goal stacks *à la* &–Prolog can be modified to include pointers to the data the goals have to work with, thus tightly encoding both the thread to be executed and the relevant data. The resulting system should be able to achieve both maximum speedup for data–parallel cases while at the same time supports general and–parallelism.

Acknowledgments

We would like to thank Jonas Barklund, Johan Bevemyr, and Håkan Millroth for discussions regarding Reform Prolog and Bounded Quantifications, as well as Saumya Debray, Enrico Pontelli, and Gopal Gupta for interesting discussions regarding this work.

References

1. K.A.M. Ali and R. Karlsson. The Muse Or-Parallel Prolog Model and its Performance. In *1990 North American Conference on Logic Programming*, pages 757–776. MIT Press, October 1990.
2. Henrik Arro, Jonas Barklund, and Johan Bevemyr. Parallel bounded quantification—preliminary results. *ACM SIGPLAN Notices*, 28:117–124, 1993.
3. Jonas Barklund. *Parallel Unification*. PhD thesis, Comp. Sci. Dept., Uppsala Univ., Uppsala, 1990.
4. J. Bevemyr, T. Lindgren, and H. Millroth. Reform Prolog: the language and its implementation. In *Proc. 10th Intl. Conf. Logic Programming*, Cambridge, Mass., 1993. MIT Press.
5. M. Carro, L. Gómez, and M. Hermenegildo. Some Paradigms for Visualizing Parallel Execution of Logic Programs. In *1993 International Conference on Logic Programming*, pages 184–201. MIT Press, June 1993.
6. J. S. Conery. *The And/Or Process Model for Parallel Interpretation of Logic Programs*. PhD thesis, The University of California At Irvine, 1983. Technical Report 204.
7. M. García de la Banda, M. Hermenegildo, and K. Marriott. Independence in Constraint Logic Programs. In *1993 International Logic Programming Symposium*, pages 130–146. MIT Press, Cambridge, MA, October 1993.
8. S. Debray and M. Jain. A Simple Program Transformation for Parallelism. In *1994 International Symposium on Logic Programming*, pages 305–319. MIT Press, November 1994.
9. S. K. Debray, N.-W. Lin, and M. Hermenegildo. Task Granularity Analysis in Logic Programs. In *Proc. of the 1990 ACM Conf. on Programming Language Design and Implementation*, pages 174–188. ACM Press, June 1990.
10. D. DeGroot. Restricted AND-Parallelism and Side-Effects. In *International Symposium on Logic Programming*, pages 80–89. San Francisco, IEEE Computer Society, August 1987.
11. P. López García, M. Hermenegildo, and S.K. Debray. Towards Granularity Based Control of Parallelism in Logic Programs. In *Proc. of First International Symposium on Parallel Symbolic Computation, PASCO'94*, pages 133–144. World Scientific Publishing Company, September 1994.
12. Philip J. Hatcher and Michael J. Quinn. *Data-parallel Programming on MIMD Computers*. MIT Press, Cambridge, Mass., 1991.
13. M. Hermenegildo and M. Carro. A Note on Data–Parallelism and (And–Parallel) Prolog. Technical report CLIP 6/94.0, School of Computer Science, Technical University of Madrid (UPM), Facultad Informática UPM, 28660-Boadilla del Monte, Madrid-Spain, June 1995.
14. M. Hermenegildo and K. Greene. The &-prolog System: Exploiting Independent And-Parallelism. *New Generation Computing*, 9(3,4):233–257, 1991.
15. M. Hermenegildo and F. Rossi. Strict and Non-Strict Independent And-Parallelism in Logic Programs: Correctness, Efficiency, and Compile-Time Conditions. *Journal of Logic Programming*, 22(1):1–45, 1995.

16. M. Hermenegildo and the CLIP group. Some Methodological Issues in the Design of CIAO - A Generic, Parallel Concurrent Constraint System. In *Principles and Practice of Constraint Programming*, LNCS 874, pages 123–133. Springer-Verlag, May 1994.

17. L. Kale. Parallel Execution of Logic Programs: the REDUCE-OR Process Model. In *Fourth International Conference on Logic Programming*, pages 616–632. Melbourne, Australia, May 1987.

18. Y. J. Lin and V. Kumar. AND-Parallel Execution of Logic Programs on a Shared Memory Multiprocessor: A Summary of Results. In *Fifth International Conference and Symposium on Logic Programming*, pages 1123–1141. MIT Press, August 1988.

19. E. Lusk et. al. The Aurora Or-Parallel Prolog System. *New Generation Computing*, 7(2,3), 1990.

20. Håkan Millroth. Reforming compilation of logic programs. In Vijay Saraswat and Kazunori Ueda, editors, *Logic Programming, Proceedings of the 1991 International Symposium*, pages 485–502, San Diego, USA, 1991. The MIT Press.

21. L. Naish. Parallelizing NU-Prolog. In *Fifth International Conference and Symposium on Logic Programming*, pages 1546–1564. University of Washington, MIT Press, August 1988.

22. E. Pontelli, G. Gupta, and M. Hermenegildo. &ACE: A High-Performance Parallel Prolog System. In *International Parallel Processing Symposium*. IEEE Computer Society Technical Committee on Parallel Processing, IEEE Computer Society, April 1995.

23. E. Pontelli, G. Gupta, D. Tang, M. Hermenegildo, and M. Carro. Efficient Implementation of And–parallel Prolog Systems. Technical Report CLIP4/95.0, T.U. of Madrid (UPM), June 1995.

24. S. Prestwich. On parallelisation strategies for logic programs. In Springer-Verlag, editor, *Proceedings of the International Conference on Parallel Processing*, number 854 in Lecture Notes in Computer Science, pages 289–300, 1994.

25. V. Santos-Costa, D.H.D. Warren, and R. Yang. The Andorra-I Engine: A Parallel Implementation of the Basic Andorra Model. In *1991 International Conference on Logic Programming*, pages 825–839. MIT Press, June 1991.

26. K. Shen. Exploiting Dependent And-Parallelism in Prolog: The Dynamic, Dependent And-Parallel Scheme. In *Proc. Joint Int'l. Conf. and Symp. on Logic Prog.* MIT Press, 1992.

27. Thinking Machines Corp., Cambridge, Mass. *The Essential *LISP Manual*, 1986.

28. Thinking Machines Corp., Cambridge, Mass. *C* Programming Guide*, 1990.

29. Andrei Voronkov. Logic programming with bounded quantifiers. In Andrei Voronkov, editor, *Logic Programming—Proc. Second Russian Conf. on Logic Programming*, LNCS 592, Berlin, 1992. Springer-Verlag.

30. R. Warren and M. Hermenegildo. Experimenting with Prolog: An Overview. Technical Report 43, MCC, March 1987.

31. X. Zhong, E. Tick, S. Duvvuru, L. Hansen, A.V.S. Sastry, and R. Sundararajan. Towards an Efficient Compile-Time Granularity Analysis Algorithm. In *Proc. of the 1992 International Conference on Fifth Generation Computer Systems*, pages 809–816. Institute for New Generation Computer Technology (ICOT), June 1992.

On the Duality Between Or-parallelism and And-parallelism in Logic Programming

Enrico Pontelli & Gopal Gupta

Laboratory for Logic, Databases, and Advanced Programming
New Mexico State University
{epontell,gupta}@cs.nmsu.edu

Abstract. *Or-parallelism* and *And-parallelism* have often been considered as two distinct forms of parallelism with not much in common. The purpose of this paper is to highlight the inherently dual nature of the two forms of parallelism and the similarities that exist between them. The dualities and similarities observed are then exploited for gaining new insights into the design, implementation, and optimization of and- and or-parallel systems. The ideas developed in this paper are illustrated with the help of ACE system—a parallel Prolog system incorporating both and- and or-parallelism.
Keywords: Prolog, And-parallelism, Or-parallelism, Optimizations.

1   Introduction

Logic Programming is a declarative programming paradigm that is becoming increasingly popular. One of the distinguishing features of logic programming languages is that they allow considerable freedom in the way programs are executed. This latitude permits one to exploit parallelism implicitly (without the need for programmer intervention) during program execution. Indeed, three main types of parallelism—or-parallelism, independent and-parallelism, and dependent and-parallelism—have been identified and successfully exploited in logic programs. Parallel Execution of Logic Programs has been an active area of research since a decade [18, 8]. A great deal of effort has been spent in recent years in the design and development of parallel implementations of Logic Programming systems. However, parallel logic programming systems that can *efficiently exploit all* (profitable) forms of parallelism present in Logic Programs still elude us. This difficulty in combining the major forms of parallelism has been addressed in various ways—by introducing various forms of *restrictions* (e.g., allowing and-parallel execution of only deterministic subgoals as in the Andorra Model), by developing very complicated new mechanisms in which different forms of parallelism can co-exist to a certain extent, etc. The purpose of this work is to show that or- and and-parallelism are not two totally distinct forms, rather they *share* common traits. The utility of this observation is that mechanisms and methodologies that have been developed for one form of parallelism can be *re-used* for the other, suggesting new ways to implement/optimize individual implementations of or- and and-parallelism, and reducing the gap between the two forms of parallelism,thus simplifying the task of *efficiently* combining them in a single framework.

2 Parallelism in Logic Programming

Two forms of parallelism are typically identified in Logic Programming: or-parallelism and and-parallelism. Or-parallelism (ORP) arises when multiple rules define some relation and a call unifies with more than one rule head—the corresponding bodies can then be executed in *or-parallel* fashion. Or-parallelism is thus a way of efficiently searching for solution(s) to a goal. In principle, or-parallelism should be easy to implement, since the different branches of the parallel tree are actually computing different solutions *independently* of each other. This is only partially true, because multiple branches that are trying to compute different solutions to a goal share that goal's environment and may change it. The effect of one branch on the goal's environment must be shielded from the other branches. In a sequential implementation a single environment is sufficient for each clause, because the different bindings for a variable in a goal produced by different matching clauses are generated sequentially (through backtracking) and a single location for each variable is sufficient. In an or-parallel system this is not true anymore: different alternatives are concurrently explored and they may produce distinct bindings for the same variable (such variables are termed *conditional*). The problem of multiple environment management has to be solved by devising a mechanism where each parallel thread has a private area where it can store the locally produced bindings for the conditional variables. Typical solutions to this problem are: *(i)* creating distinct copies of the environment for each parallel thread (like in the Muse system); or *(ii)* maintaining private arrays/hash-tables in which the local bindings for conditional variables are stored (like in the Aurora system).

And-parallelism (ANDP) is generated by the parallel execution of a conjunction of subgoals. Two major classes of and-parallelism are typically identified, depending on whether and-parallel execution of subgoals accessing the same unbound variables is permitted or not: *(i) independent and-parallelism (IANDP)*: arises when conjunctive subgoals that do not share any unbound variables are executed in parallel. During IANDP no synchronization is required between parallel threads (as in &-Prolog [12] and ACE [9]); *(ii) dependent and-parallelism (DANDP)*: arises when conjunctive subgoals that share unbound variables are executed in parallel. DANDP can be further divided into two subclasses: *(a) restricted DANDP*: in which only subgoals satisfying certain conditions are allowed to execute in parallel (like in the Basic Andorra Model [2] and in non-strict IANDP [11]); *(b) general DANDP*: in which arbitrary subgoals can be executed in parallel (like the *Extended Andorra Model* [20], the *DDAS* [19], and in various committed-choice languages [18]). Whatever the model, and-parallel execution can be divided into 3 phases: **(i)** *ordering phase*: deals with the detection of dependencies among subgoals; **(ii)** *forward execution*: deals with the selection of subgoals and execution of the various resolution steps. The set of conjunctive subgoals that are executed in and-parallel is termed a *parallel call* (or a *parcall* for brevity); the corresponding descriptor that is placed in the stack when a parcall is made is called a *parcall frame*. Part of the forward execution phase is related to the scheduling of the subgoals among the active processors and, in the case of DANDP, the management of dependencies between subgoals; **(iii)** *backward execution*: deals with the sequence of steps taken on failure or when a new solution needs to be found. It requires extension of backtracking to the case of parallel execution.

3 Or-parallelism *vs* And-parallelism

In this section we draw a comparison between or-parallelism and and-parallelism. Table 1 compares and contrasts items of interest for the two forms of parallelism. The first two lines of the table relate and- and or-parallelism. Thus, while or-parallelism is obtained by parallel execution of *multiple alternatives in a choice point*, and-parallelism is obtained by executing *multiple subgoals in a parcall*. In both cases the parallel threads originate from a data structure containing a certain number of executions (choice points vs. parcall frames). Likewise, or-parallel execution produces multiple bindings for conditional variables, while and-parallel execution may do the same for shared variables. In both cases, during the execution of parallel threads, common variables can be concurrently accessed and/or bound. This creates possible *dependencies* that need to be resolved by adopting proper synchronization techniques (this issue is considered in section 4 and 5.3).

The duality between ORP and ANDP can be noted immediately in the way in which alternative executions are handled, since in ORP we are looking for *one* alternative to succeed (i.e., $\exists$), while in ANDP we are forced to verify that all the alternative executions are successful (i.e., $\forall \equiv \neg\exists$). The duality principle can also be seen in the way in which schedulers have been designed for the two kind of systems. In ORP a lot of effort has been spent in order to obtain *smart* schedulers, capable of selecting the alternative that is more likely to succeed as soon as possible; in ANDP the typical schedulers are quite simple (e.g., just push

Characteristic	ORP	ANDP
object of parall.	alternatives in a choice point	subgoals in a goal
dependency	on conditional variables	on shared variables
additional work	on failure	on success
speculativeness	on success	on failure
continuation	independent computations	join of computations

Table 1.: Comparison between ANDP and ORP

and pop and-parallel subgoals on goal stacks) due to the fact that ($\forall$) all the alternatives need to be tried. Nevertheless, as we will see in a later section, the duality noted above suggests ways to improve ANDP scheduling (section 5.2). This also suggests the possibility of managing ANDP work in an "ORP" way (section 5.1), leading to interesting improvements. Also, the dual nature of ORP and ANDP can be used to develop new approaches for dealing with dependent parallel executions (section 5.3).

The duality of or-parallelism and and-parallelism has been only indirectly investigated in the past. For example, it has been employed for *translating* or-parallelism to and-parallelism and vice-versa [3, 4]. The idea is to exploit both forms of parallelism, while implementing only one. This approach has its own pros and cons. On one hand the burden of developing complex mechanisms to integrate different forms of parallelism can be avoided and the other form of parallelism obtained effortlessly. On the other hand, such compile-time translations produce poor performance due to the extreme overhead introduced by the presence of an additional interpretation layer.

4 Applying And-parallel Concepts to Or-parallelism

In this section we discuss how the concepts developed for and-parallelism can be applied to or-parallelism. As we have seen, for each form of parallelism we can identify various "degrees" of implementation, depending on how strong the restrictions imposed are on the parallelism allowed. This suggests a possible classification of parallelism (independently from whether it is or- or and-), into three main classes: *(i)* **Independent Parallelism**: it is characterized by the fact that parallelism is allowed exclusively between threads which do not require any kind of synchronization during their execution, i.e. threads which are *independent*; *(ii)* **Restricted Dependent Parallelism**: this class consists of systems that allow parallel execution of threads which may have dependencies but will never produce any *solvable* conflict on them (i.e. an actual conflict corresponds to a failure of the computation). Interactions between threads are limited but require some care at the implementation level (e.g., use of locks); *(iii)* **Dependent Parallelism**: arbitrary dependent parallel computations are allowed. The first thing that we can notice is that these classes are in increasing order of complexity and **Independent ⊆ Restricted Dep. ⊆ Dependent**. This increasing order of complexity of control parallelism, though quite general, is inspired from the different types and restrictions of and-parallelism that have been considered in the literature (as mentioned in section 2). It is quite interesting to consider how this hierarchy of control parallelism applies to *or-parallelism*: **(1) Independent Parallelism**: this instantantion of or-parallelism is characterized by the independence of its parallel threads—which translates to allowing the parallel execution of alternatives in a choice point only if they do not access any unbound conditional variable. This may occur in various situations (e.g., predicates performing tests on the validity of their inputs, etc.). **(2) Restricted Dependent Parallelism**: this represents another type of or-parallelism in which parallel execution is only allowed between alternatives which may access conditional variable, but for which conflicting bindings will not be produced. This model of parallelism requires implementation mechanisms slightly more complicated, but still considerably simpler than those required for full ORP. **(3) Dependent Parallelism**: exploitation of full ORP. This is the model of ORP typically taken into consideration and requires complex mechanisms to deal with environment management. Although the independent and restricted forms of or-parallelism may appear to be too strict, it is worth taking them into account. First of all their implementation is extremely simple and could be realized with almost no overhead; independent or-parallelism requires only the ability of identifying the choice-points with work available—no other support for parallelism is required (e.g., no new environment representation schemes). In addition, the ability of identifying (e.g., through static analysis) these forms of or-parallelism may offer the chance of optimizing existing implementations (e.g., removal of binding array's entries in Aurora or removing the binding installation process in Muse for parts of the or-parallel computation that are determined to be independent or restricted).

Actually, independent and restricted and-parallelism have found applications in deductive databases where programs that submit to independent or-parallel execution are called *uniformly decomposable* [6]. Considerable research has been done in deductive database community for identifying uniformly decomposable programs [21, 6, 7].

5 Applying Or-parallel Concepts to And-parallelism

5.1 Choice Points vs. Parcall Frames

In ORP parallel work is represented by alternative subgoals that can be derived by using the different matching clauses associated with a certain choice point. In ANDP parallel work is represented by subgoals associated to a parcall frame (or a similar data structure). Given this similarity ($ChoicePoint \cong ParcallFrame$), the mechanisms needed to exploit ORP differ from those of ANDP exclusively because of the duality between ORP and ANDP, since

(1) scheduling in ORP is driven by "failure" ($ORP \equiv \vee$) (i.e., if a branch fails, search must continue with the next branch, else the search may stop since a solution has been found) while in ANDP it is driven by "success" ($ANDP \equiv \wedge$) (i.e., if a goal succeeds, search must continue with the next goal, else the execution may stop since the conjunction has failed.

(2) since $ORP \equiv \vee$, then $Success_{ORP} \equiv \bigvee_{Alternatives} Alternative$ while $ANDP \equiv \wedge$ and this means $Success_{ANDP} \equiv \bigwedge_{Alternatives} Alternative$ (where alternatives in the context of ANDP mean subgoals of a parallel conjunction). This translates to the fact that in ORP, whenever one of the alternatives succeed there is no need to verify the success of the others, while in ANDP a final "join" is required in order to determine the global consistency of the computation[1].

Nevertheless, the two differences mentioned above do not affect the actual phase of generation of the parallel threads— and this opens various possibilities in terms of importing ORP's implementation techniques to ANDP systems. In particular, management of

Goals	ACE Agents								
executed	1			3			5		
	Unopt.	Opt.	%	Unopt.	Opt.	%	Unopt.	Opt.	%
fibonacci	3692	3643	1%	1353	1313	3%	833	820	2%
takeuchi	1880	1821	3%	677	657	3%	428	408	5%
hanoi	2591	2514	3%	1000	979	2%	660	636	4%

Table 2.: Improvements avoiding pushing subgoals

choicepoints in ORP systems is typically quite efficient, while management of parcall frames in ANDP systems is extremely overhead prone. The following three subsections present ways that have been inspired by ORP to make management of parcall frames more efficient and reduce the overhead of exploiting and-parallelism.

(i) Elimination of Goal-stack: In ORP the or-parallel work is represented by a choice point, and such work is "made public" by notifying the existence of the choice point to the other processors working in the system. Each idle worker will access the *public* choice points and extract work from there. This approach has

---

[1] Although in ORP some synchronization points may be required to implement side-effects.

various advantages; one of the most important is that the cost of extracting the work from the choice point and initializing the proper information for parallel execution is spread between the different processors.

In the design of many ANDP systems (e.g. &-Prolog, DDAS), instead, the processor generating the parcall frame is also in charge of creating a *goal frame* for each and-parallel subgoal, initializing it with all the information required to allow its remote execution, and pushing it on a *goal stack*. The first level of optimization that we suggest is to avoid generation of a goal frame for each and-parallel subgoal. Instead, we adopt a mechanism in which the parcall frames containing unexplored alternatives (i.e. untried conjunctive subgoals) are "made public" and visible to all the processors (as happens for choice points in ORP), allow-

Goals	ACE Agents								
executed	1			3			5		
	Unopt.	Opt.	%	Unopt.	Opt.	%	Unopt.	Opt.	%
fibonacci	3643	3643	0%	1313	1284	2%	820	807	2%
takeuchi	1821	1821	0%	657	637	3%	408	386	5%

Table 3.: Distribution of descriptors creation

ing each idle processor to access one of these parcall frames and extract an unexecuted subgoal. This simple optimization, of treating parcall frames similarly to choicepoints, and not creating goal-stack entries has been implemented in the current version of the ACE system and the results are presented in table 2. The measured improvements vary on average from 1% to 5%, and are more pronounced when the computation generates a considerable number of and-parallel subgoals. This is the case of Takeuchi, which shows better results due to the larger number of parallel subgoals per parcall frame.

(ii) Distributed Allocation of Goal Slots: In a typical ANDP system each goal being executed in and-parallel has a *descriptor* associated with it. This descriptor is termed a *slot* in the &-Prolog and in the ACE systems. Descriptors are part of the parcall frame to which the corresponding subgoals belong, and they are generated together with the parcall frame. Borrowing ideas from or-parallel implementation we can improve this model: the task of creating the descriptors can be distributed between the different processors, i.e., each processor creates the descriptors for the goals it executes. This allows a better distribution of the overhead and an improvement in execution time. Some results of this optimization applied to ACE are reported in table 3. Again an average improvement of 3–5% is observed.

(iii) Parallelism on Demand: As we mentioned earlier, one of the characteristics of ORP is that each processor takes care of performing all the operations necessary to support the execution of the selected alternative. This implies that no parallel overhead (i.e., overhead spent to support exploitation of parallelism) will be incurred if no parallelism is exploited. This is hardly true for ANDP systems; in models like &-Prolog, ACE, DDAS, etc. overhead will be incurred even if the whole parallel call is actually executed by a single processor (since the creation of the parcall frame and other bookkeeping operations are still present). The desire is to allow ANDP to work with minimal overhead, especially when a parallel conjunction is executed sequentially due to lack of processors. This is in fact what happens in ORP, where sequential execution of alternatives in a *parallel* choice point is realized through ordinary backtracking, with

almost no overhead. We term the phenomenon in which overhead is incurred only

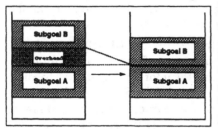

if parallelism is exploited, and no parallel overhead is incurred otherwise as *Parallelism on Demand*. For ANDP, part of this has been realized in the previous optimization, by distributing the task of creating a slot (i.e., and-parallel subgoal descriptor) to the processor which picks up the subgoal for execution. Nevertheless, this is far from being sufficient. In fact, even allowing distribution of this overhead, we still

Fig. 1.: Det. Proc. Optimization

have not solved the problem of removing the overhead during sequential execution of parallel subgoals (because the slots will still be needlessly allocated even though the execution is sequential). There has recently been some work in this direction [16, 13]. The proposal that come closest to the ideal "parallelism on demand" behaviour mentioned above is an optimization implemented in the current version of the ACE system. This optimization, termed *Processor Determinacy Optimization* (and described in more details in [16]) by us, is inspired by the following principle: *"two (potentially) parallel pieces of computation that are executed sequentially and in the proper sequential order should incur no parallel overhead"*. In the current implemented version of this optimization, whenever a subgoal is selected for execution a check is performed to verify whether the new subgoal is the "sequential" successor of the one previously executed; if the test is successful then most of the parallel overhead is avoided. Figure 1 shows schematically the behaviour of the system during this optimization. The performance figures for this optimization are quite impressive, especially considering this only approximates *Parallelism on Demand*.

Goals	ACE Execution	
executed	Unopt.	Opt.
Bt(0)	1461	1391 (5%)
pmatrix(30)	5598	5336 (5%)
listsum	2333	2054 (12%)
hanoi	2183	1790 (18%)
takeuchi	2366	1963 (17%)

Goals	ACE Execution	
executed	Unopt.	Opt.
Bt(0)	120	60
Deriv(0)	174	87
pmatrix(30)	1798	899
listsum	3000	1500
takeuchi	3558	2372
hanoi	4094	2047

Table 4.: Execution times (ms.) and memory usage (no. of structures)

The results obtained on some benchmarks in terms of improvement in sequential execution speed and in memory consumption (stack usage) are indicated in table 4. Work is in progress to obtain ideal implementation for parallelism on demand (avoiding allocation of parcall frames altogether in sequential executions).

5.2 Scheduling Related Issues

In most of the work on building and-parallel systems, the issue of scheduling is dealt with in a naive way. This is mainly due to the fact that ANDP systems are actually computing conjunctions of literals and, as such, they need in principle to execute *all* the subgoals associated to each parallel call. This is dual to the ORP case, where we are usually looking for *one* solution, and this requires success of at most one alternative out of each choice point built during the computation. This also relates to the duality between speculative computations in ORP and ANDP: in ORP success along one alternative of a choice point turns execution along other alternatives into speculative work[2], while in ANDP failure of a subgoal in a parallel call turns computation of subgoals to its right into speculative work. Nevertheless, the current approach taken in designing schedulers for ANDP systems seems to be too strictly oriented towards executions that are assumed to always succeed (e.g., CCL, &-Prolog, DDAS). The technique of trying failing subgoals first is never considered (e.g., in CCL the *right choices* are always assumed to be made). In ANDP systems, most of the time, the scheduling is based on simple goal-stacking, i.e., goals ready for parallel execution are pushed on a stack and from there picked up by idle processors. Only few variations have been suggested, like keeping track of the "best" sources of work [12] or using queuing instead of stacking [5].

Our claim, emerging from the duality between ORP and ANDP, is that even ANDP systems can take advantage of more sophisticated scheduling techniques, based on the same principles (or, better, their dual) that have been used for developing schedulers for ORP systems. In the case of ANDP, the ideal goal of a scheduler would be: *(i)* if the computation is going to succeed, we want to improve the speed-up and reduce the interactions between different processors; *(ii)* if the computation is going to fail (e.g., in an Independent ANDP computation one of the subgoals fails to find a solution), then the scheduler should ideally select first those subgoals that are more likely to fail, detecting the global failure as soon as possible (and reducing the amount of speculative work).

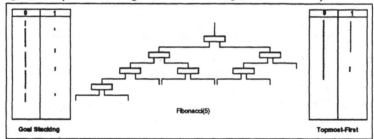

Fig. 2.: Comparison between Goal-stacking and Topmost-first

The issues that have to be considered in designing a scheduler for and ANDP system are essentially dual to those that are typically considered for ORP (e.g., see [1]). One possibility, in order to improve speed (cf. remark *(i)* above) during forward execution would be to get subgoals always from the parcall frames higher up in the computation tree, following the intuition that the granularity of these subgoals would be probably larger. This is essentially the same principle that has been used in the design of some of the schedulers adopted in ORP systems (like the *Manchester* scheduler for Aurora). A simplified version of this scheduler has been implemented in ACE and has resulted in improved performance.

Figure 2 shows the computation tree developed on the **fibonacci** benchmark. The distribution of ANDP work for the goal-stacking scheduler is shown

---

[2] This is not true if we want an *all-solutions* execution.

on the left, and for dispatching-on-topmost scheduler is shown on the right. Note that the one on the right is less fragmented, leading to higher granularity and better speedup. Table 5 contains the execution times on some benchmarks using the two schedulers; as we can see the behaviour is slightly worse for sequential execution (due to some additional costs incurred in the scheduler), but it improves when more processors are used, obtaining

Goals executed	ACE Agents								
	1			3			5		
	Unopt.	Opt.	%	Unopt.	Opt.	%	Unopt.	Opt.	%
fibonacci	3596	3701	-3%	1310	1296	1%	810	778	4%
matrixmult	5432	5545	-2%	1900	1877	1%	1166	1120	4%

Table 5.: Improvements using dispatching on topmost sched.

ing an average improvement of 4% using 5 processors. Similar techniques can be used to improve performance of the scheduler when dealing with failing computations (cf. remark 2 above). The ideal behaviour, the one in which failing computations are selected first, is clearly impossible to realize (since telling failing computations in advance is undecidable).

The typical solution in ORP systems for minimizing speculative work is to choose the parallel work that lies in the left part of the search tree so that parallel computation mimics sequential Prolog execution as much as possible. In ORP, if a processor is executing a branch that is potentially speculative, it will periodically check for the presence of "better" work (e.g., new alternatives in the leftmost part of the tree) and, if so, suspend the current computation and task-switch to one of the "better" alternatives [1]. The same technique is applicable to ANDP systems; focusing on the leftmost part of the computation tree seems to

Goal	Standard Scheduler	Lazy-Left Scheduler	Eager-Left Scheduler
failing matrix mult.	616	365	91

Table 6.: Execution Time (ms.) with Speculative work

be a reasonable assumption, considering that with respect to failure the subgoals on the right are more speculative that those on the left (named elsewhere *first-fail principle*). A scheduler capable of this is currently under development as part of the ACE project. Table 6 gives the results obtained by simulating the effect of this type of scheduler on a benchmark with speculative work (a failing matrix multiplication). In the table, the lazy-left scheduler always picks leftmost work but only after it finishes its current task, while the eager-left scheduler will voluntarily suspend its current task immediately if less speculative and-parallel work appears to the left.

5.3 DANDP

Another interesting application that can be developed from the dual nature of ORP/ANDP is related to the design of systems exploiting *Dependent And-parallelism (DANDP)*. As described earlier, a DANDP system allows and-parallel execution of two (or more) subgoals that share a common unbound variable (which may receive conflicting bindings from the two goals). The presence of these active dependencies requires the design of special mechanisms that ensure that the common variable is bound consistently, as in Prolog. To realize this, whenever a goal tries to bind a shared variable, it should perform a check in order to verify whether this binding may deviate the execution from the desired Prolog behaviour. This can be realized by introducing the notion of *producer* and *consumer* for each shared variable; at every point in the execution there should be only one producer for each shared variable (in Prolog semantics, the producer is the leftmost subgoal that has access to the variable). The producer subgoal is the only subgoal allowed to post a binding for the shared variable. All the other subgoals are designated as consumers and will suspend if they try to bind the shared variable. Suspended consumers will either wait for the variable to be bound by the producer or to become producers themselves (i.e., become leftmost in the computation tree). As discussed earlier, implementation of ORP has to deal with dependencies between parallel threads because different or-parallel threads may produce distinct bindings for the same (conditional) variable. The main difference is that in ORP the alternative threads are disjunct and consequently the bindings produced can be kept separate (since $\exists X(B_1(X) \vee B_2(X)) \equiv \exists X(B_1(X)) \vee \exists X(B_2(X)))$, while in the case of DANDP the bindings need to be kept consistent (since $\exists X(p(X) \wedge q(X)) \not\equiv \exists X(p(X)) \wedge \exists X(q(X)))$. Nevertheless we do not need to go to the extreme of keeping a unique location for these bindings, as done in most of the implementations (e.g., DDAS), since this requires complex synchronization mechanisms, locks, etc. An interesting alternative is exactly the one suggested by the duality principle above, by trying to split the existential quantification in two separate quantifications: $\exists X(p(X) \wedge q(X)) \equiv \exists X_1 X_2(p(X_1) \wedge q(X_2) \wedge X_1 = X_2)$ where the equality $X_1 = X_2$ is used to maintain consistency between the bindings produced by p and q. This gives rise to various degrees of possible implementations of DANDP, that differ from each other based upon the moment at which the equality $=$ is enforced. The simplest model is the one in which the parallel computations (e.g., $p(X_1)$ and $q(X_2)$) are carried on independently and '$=$' is applied only after they have both produced a binding for their variables. This essentially reduces DANDP to IANDP by delaying the dependencies after the end of the parallel execution (and has been adopted in some early works, e.g. [14]). Nevertheless, this is not too interesting and may lead to loss of Prolog semantics. Speculative work can appear (and, in extreme cases, it can be infinite—i.e., non-terminating computations). On the other hand, the most complex model is the one in which the $=$ is performed before starting the parallel execution, which leads to the various DANDP models implemented (like DDAS). We are interested in finding a solution between the two extremes.

Our solution is inspired from techniques for implementing or-parallelism. In or-parallelism different or-parallel threads may have dependencies between them, namely, through the conditional variables. The way this problem is solved there is that different or-parallel threads keep a different "view" of the variable with the help of the environment representation mechanism used. For example, in binding arrays [15], the common offset is stored in the stack location for that variable while the different bindings (that represent the different view of the variable for different or-parallel threads) are stored in the private binding arrays. In Muse, separate copies of the stack location for the variables are maintained by each thread. In DANDP, the problem is similar, the threads executing the producer and the consumer goals should have different "views" of the dependent variable.

That is, the thread executing the producer goal is allowed to bind the dependent variable, while the one executing the consumer goal is not (at least until the consumer goal becomes leftmost, in which case it becomes the producer). Thus, we can adapt a solution similar to the one used for or-parallelism. In particular, we use binding arrays.

Adapting BA to dependent and-parallelism requires some minor changes. Basically, a small BA is assigned to each subgoal, in which the "local view" of the shared variables associated to such subgoal will be stored. A *producer view* will be implemented as a direct pointer to the object. A *consumer view* will be realized as a pointer to the view of the immediately preceding subgoal. This is illustrated in figure 3. In this way the process of validating a variable access can be

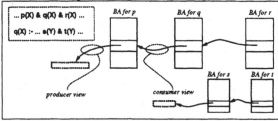

Fig. 3.: Use of BA for DAP

done concurrently while accessing its value—an indirection from one BA to another BA during dereferencing indicates that the subgoal has a consumer view of the shared entity. As in the BA model for or-parallelism, an *installation* phase is required upon scheduling of a computation to a computing agent. The installation step is executed by the agent to collect the BAs that represent the *shared environment* visible to the current computation. In figure 3, the shared environment for an agent executing t will be composed by the BA for t and the one for q.[3] Prolog semantics is respected by forcing any binding attempted through a consumer view to suspend. Furthermore, views may need to be modified upon completion of a subgoal (some consumer views may need to be transformed into producer views)—a simple bit associated to each BA and denoting the status of the corresponding subgoal (active or completed) is sufficient for this purpose. Our scheme is arguably superior to other implementation schemes for DANDP (like DDAS) [17]. Further details are not included here due to lack of space and can be found elsewhere [17].

6 Conclusions

In this paper we presented an analysis of the dual nature of the two major forms of parallelism—or- and and-parallelism—exploited in Logic Programming. The existence of this dual nature allows one to use techniques developed for realizing/optimizing one form of parallelism for realizing/optimizing the other. Our observations regarding duality of or-parallelism and and-parallelism, we hope, will also simplify the development of combined and-or parallel systems, while giving rise to a whole new set of optimizations and offering new ways to efficiently exploiting parallelism. Most of the techniques discussed in this paper

---

[3] A BA may be needed for each subgoal in the parallel call. Newly developed data-structures such as *Paged Binding Arrays* (PBA) [10] can be used for this purpose. Each subgoal can be allocated a page in the PBA, making the management of BAs simpler.

have been implemented in the ACE system, an and-or parallel implementation of Prolog, and the results have been reported.

The research presented has benefited from discussions with M. Carro, M. Hermenegildo, K. Shen, and V. Santos Costa, all of whom we would like to thank. Ongoing work is supported by NSF Grants 9415256, CCR 92-11732, and HRD 93-53271, and by NATO Grant CRG 921318, and by a fellowship from Phillips Petroleum to Enrico Pontelli.

References

1. K.A.M. Ali and R. Karlsson. Scheduling Speculative Work in MUSE and Performance Results. Technical report, SICS, 1993.
2. P. Brand, S. Haridi, and D.H.D. Warren. Andorra Prolog—The Language and Application in Distributed Simulation. In *Int'l Conf. on FGCS*. Tokyo, Nov. 1988.
3. M. Carlsson et al. A Simplified Approach to the Implementation of And-Parallelism in an Or-Parallel Environment. *ICLP*, 1988.
4. M. Codish, E. Shapiro. Compiling Or-Parallelism into And-Parallelism. *ICLP*, 1986.
5. J. Crammond. The Abstract Machine and Implementation of Parallel Prolog. Research report, Dept. of Computing, Imperial College, July 1990.
6. J. Du Pond and H.J. Hernandez. Parallelization of Right Uniform Datalog Programs and of Chain Sirups. *Journal of Computing and Information*, 1(1), 1994.
7. S. Tsur S. Ganguly, A. Silberschatz. A Framework for the Parallel Processing of Datalog Queries. In *Proc. of ACM SIGMOD Conf. on Manag. of Data*, 1990.
8. G. Gupta. *Multiprocessor Execution of Logic Programs*. Kluwer Press, 1994.
9. G. Gupta, M. Hermenegildo, E. Pontelli, and V. Santos Costa. ACE: And/Or-parallel Copying-based Execution of Logic Programs. In *ICLP*,MIT Press, 1994.
10. G. Gupta et al. Shared Paged Binding Arrays: Universal Data-structure for Parallel Logic Programming. NFS/ICOT workshop on Parallel Logic Progr., 1994.
11. M.Hermenegildo, F.Rossi. Non-Strict Independent And-Parallelism. In *ICLP*, 1990.
12. M.Hermenegildo. *Independent And-Parallel Prolog and its Architecture*. Kluwer, 1989.
13. M. Hermenegildo M. Carro. Backtracking families, unpublished manuscript, 1993.
14. L. Kale. Parallel Execution of Logic Programs: the REDUCE-OR Process Model. In *ICLP*, 1987.
15. E. Lusk and al. The Aurora Or-parallel Prolog System. *NGC*, 7(2,3), '90.
16. E. Pontelli, G. Gupta, and D. Tang. Determinacy Driven Optimizations of Parallel Prolog Implementations. Proc. of ICLP'95, MIT Press, 1995.
17. E.Pontelli, G.Gupta. Dependent And-Parallelism in Logic Programming. Internal Report, LLDAP, 1995.
18. E.Y. Shapiro, editor. *Concurrent Prolog: Collected Papers*. MIT Press, 1987.
19. K. Shen. *Studies in And/Or Rarallelism in Prolog*. PhD thesis, 1992.
20. D. H. D. Warren. The Extended Andorra Model with Implicit Control. In Sverker Jansson, editor, *Parallel Logic Programming Workshop*, June 1990. SICS.
21. O. Wolfson and A. Ozeri. A New Paradigm for Parallel and Distributed Rule Processing. In *SIGMOD Int'l Conf. on Manag. of Data*. ACM, 1990.

Functional Skeletons for Parallel Coordination

John Darlington   Yi-ke Guo   Hing Wing To   Jin Yang

Department of Computing
Imperial College
180 Queen's Gate, London SW7 2BZ, U.K.
E-mail: {jd, yg, hwt, jy}@doc.ic.ac.uk

Abstract. In this paper we propose a methodology for structured parallel programming using functional skeletons to compose and coordinate concurrent activities written in a standard imperative language. Skeletons are higher order functional forms with built-in parallel behaviour. We show how such forms can be used uniformly to abstract all aspects of a parallel program's behaviour including data partitioning, placement and re-arrangement (communication) as well as computation. Skeletons are naturally data parallel and are capable of expressing computation and co-ordination at a higher level of abstraction than other process oriented co-ordination notations. Examples of the application of this methodology are given and an implementation technique outlined.

1   Introduction

This paper proposes the use of skeletons as a coordination language for programming parallel architectures. The coordination language model, as proposed by Gelernter and Carriero, builds parallel programs out of two separate components, the *computation model* and the *coordination model* [4]. Applications written in this way have a two-tier structure. The coordination level abstracts all the relevant aspects of a program's parallel behaviour, whilst the computation level expresses sequential computation through procedures written in an imperative base language. Such a separation allows the task of parallel programming to focus on the parallel coordination of sequential components. This is in contrast to the low level parallel extensions to languages where both tasks must be programmed simultaneously in an unstructured way.

Although developing coordination languages has become a significant research topic for parallel programming, there is still no general purpose coordination language designed to meet the requirements of constructing verifiable, portable and structured parallel programs. In this paper, we propose an approach for parallel coordination using functional skeletons to abstract all essential aspects of parallelism including data distribution, communication and commonly used parallel computation structure. Applying skeletons to coordinate sequential components, we have developed a structured parallel programming framework, SPP(X), where parallel programs are constructed in a structured way. In the SPP framework, an application is constructed in two layers: a higher skeleton coordination level and a lower base language level. Parallel programs are constructed by using a skeleton based coordination language (SCL) to coordinate fragments of sequential code written in a base language (BL). The fundamental compositional property of functional skeletons naturally supports modularity of such programs. Using skeletons as the uniform means of coordination and composition removes the need to work with the lower level details of computation such as port connection. The uniform mechanism of high level abstraction of parallel behaviour means that all analysis and optimisation required can be confined to the coordination level which, being functional and constructed from pre-defined units, is much more amenable to such analysis and manipulation than the base language components or other coordination mechanisms.

This paper is organised into the following sections. In section 2, a skeleton coordination language, SCL, for is introduced and an example is presented to show its programming style and expressive power. In section 3, a concrete SPP programming language is proposed by taking Fortran as the base language for specifying sequential computation. Related work is overviewed in section 4. We finally summarise our work in section 5.

2 SCL: A Structured Coordination Language

We introduce a structured coordination language SCL as a general purpose coordination language by describing its three components: configuration and configuration skeletons, elementary skeletons and computational skeletons.

2.1 Configuration and Configuration Skeletons

The basic parallel computation model underlying SCL is the data parallel model. In SCL, data parallel computation is abstracted as a set of parallel operators over a distributed data structure. In this paper distributed arrays are used as our underlying parallel data structure, though this idea can be generalised to richer and higher level data structures. Each distributed array, called a parallel array, has the type ParArray index α where each element is of type α and each index is of type index. In this paper we use << ... >> to represent a ParArray. To take advantage of locality when manipulating such distributed data structures one of the most important issues is to coordinate the relative distribution of one data structure to that of another, i.e. data alignment. The importance of abstracting this *configuration* information in parallel programming has been recognised in other languages such as High Performance Fortran (HPF), where a set of compiler directives are proposed to specify parallel configurations [5]. In SCL, we abstract control over both distribution and alignment through a set of *configuration skeletons*.

A configuration models the logical division and distribution of data objects. Such a distribution has several components: the division of the original data structure into distributable components, the location of these components relative to each other and finally the allocation of these co-located components to processors. In SCL this process is specified by a partition function to divide the initial structure into nested components and an `align` function to form a collection of tuples representing co-located objects. This model, illustrated in Fig.1, clearly follows and generalises the data distribution directives of HPF. Applying

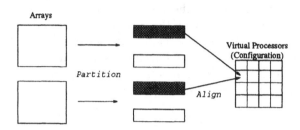

Fig. 1. Data Distribution Model.

this general idea to arrays, the following configuration skeleton `distribution` defines the configuration of two arrays `A` and `B`:

```
distribution (f,p) (g,q) A B =
      align (p o partition f A) (q o partition g B)
```

This skeleton takes two functions pairs, `f` and `g` specify the required partitioning (or distribution) strategies of `A` and `B` respectively and `p` and `q` are bulk data-movement functions specifying any initial data re-arrangement that may be required. The `distribution` skeleton is defined by composing the functions `align` and `partition`. `Partition` divides a sequential array into a parallel array of sequential subarrays:

```
partition :: Partition_pattern → SeqArray index α →
              ParArray index (SeqArray index α)
```

where `Partition_pattern` is a function of type ($index_s$ → $index_p$), where $index_s$ is associated with the `SeqArray` and $index_p$ addresses the `ParArray`. The type `SeqArray` is the ordinary sequential array type of our base language. Some commonly occurring partitioning functions are provided as built-in functions. For example, partitioning a $1 \times m$ two-dimensional array using `row_block` we will get:

```
partition (row_block p) A = << ii := B | ii ← [1..p] >>
   where B = SeqArray (1:1/p, 1:n)
          [(i,j) := A (i+(ii-1)*1/p,j) | i←[1..1/p], j←[1..n]]
```

Other similar functions for two-dimensional arrays are `col_block`, `row_col_block`, `row_cyclic` and `col_cyclic`. The `align` operator:

```
align::ParArray index α → ParArray index β → ParArray index (α,β)
```

pairs corresponding subarrays in two distributed arrays together to form a new configuration which is an `ParArray` of tuples. Objects in each tuple of the configuration are regarded as being allocated on the same processor. A more general configuration skeleton can be defined as:

```
distribution [(f,p)] [d] = p o partition f d
distribution (f,p):fl d:dl =
          align (p o partition f d) (distribution fl dl)
```

where `fl` is a list of distribution strategies for the corresponding data objects in the list `dl`.

Applying the **distribution** skeleton forms a configuration which is an array of tuples. Each element i of the configuration is a tuple of the form $(DA_1^i, \ldots, DA_n^i)$ where n is the number of arrays that have been distributed and DA_j^i represents the sub-array of the jth array allocated to the ith processor. As short hand rather than writing a configuration as an array of tuples we can also regard it as a tuple of (distributed) arrays and write it as $<DA_1, \ldots, DA_n>$ where the DA_j stands for the distribution of the array A_j. In particular we can pattern match to this notation to extract a particular distributed array from the configuration.

Configuration skeletons are capable of abstracting not only the initial distribution of data structures but also their dynamic redistribution. Data redistribution can be uniformly defined by applying bulk data movement operators to configurations. Given a configuration C: $<DA_1, \ldots, DA_n>$, a new configuration C': $<DA_1', \ldots, DA_n'>$ can be formed by applying f_j to the distributed structure DA_j where f_j is some bulk data movement operator defined specifying collective communication. This behaviour can be abstracted by the following skeleton **redistribution**:

```
redistribution [f₁ ,..., fₙ] <DA₁ ,..., DAₙ> = <f₁ DA₁ ,..., fₙ DAₙ>
```

SCL supports nested parallelism by allowing `ParArrays` as elements of a `ParArray` and by permitting a parallel operation to be applied to each of elements (`ParArrays`) in parallel. An element of a nested array corresponds to the concept of *group* in MPI [7]. The leaves of a nested array contain any valid sequential data structure of the base computing language. The following skeleton **gather** collects together a distributed array:

```
gather :: ParArray index (SeqArray index α) → SeqArray index α
```

Another pair of configuaration skeletons are **split** and **combine**:

```
split :: Partition_pattern → ParArray index α →
            ParArray index (ParArray index α)
```

```
combine :: ParArray index (ParArray index α) → ParArray index α
```

split divides a configuration into sub-configurations. **combine** is used to flatten a nested `ParArray`.

2.2 Elementary Skeletons: Parallel Arrays Operators

In the following we introduce functions, regarded as *elementary skeletons*, abstracting basic operations in the data parallel computation model.

The following familiar functions abstract essential data parallel computation patterns:

```
map :: (α → β) → ParArray index α → ParArray index β
map f << x₀,...,xₙ >> = << f x₀,...,f xₙ >>
```

$$\text{map} :: (\alpha \to \beta) \to \text{ParArray index } \alpha \to \text{ParArray index } \beta$$
$$\text{map } f \ll x_0,\ldots,x_n \gg \;=\; \ll f\,x_0,\ldots,f\,x_n \gg$$

$$\text{imap} :: (\text{index} \to \alpha \to \beta) \to \text{ParArray index } \alpha \to \text{ParArray index } \beta$$
$$\text{imap } f \ll x_0,\ldots,x_n \gg \;=\; \ll f\,0\,x_0,\ldots,f\,n\,x_n \gg$$

$$\text{fold} :: (\alpha \to \alpha \to \alpha) \to \text{ParArray index } \alpha \to \alpha$$
$$\text{fold } (\oplus) \ll x_0,\ldots,x_n \gg \;=\; x_0 \oplus \cdots \oplus x_n$$

The function **map** abstracts the behaviour of broadcasting a parallel task to all the elements of an array. A variant of **map** is the function **imap** which takes into account the index of an element when mapping a function across an array. The reduction operator **fold** abstracts tree-structured parallel reduction computation over arrays.

Data communications among parallel processors are expressed as the movement of elements in **ParArrays**. In SCL, a set of *bulk data-movement functions* are introduced as the data parallel counterpart of sequential loops and element assignments at the structure level. Communication skeletons can be generally divided into two classes: *regular* and *irregular*. The following **rotate** function is a typical example of regular data-movement.

$$\text{rotate} :: \text{Int} \to \text{ParArray Int } \alpha \to \text{ParArray Int } \alpha$$
$$\text{rotate } k\ A \;=\; \ll i := A((i+k) \bmod \text{SIZE(A)}) \mid i \leftarrow [1..\text{SIZE(A)}] \gg$$

For a $m \times n$ array, the following **rotate_row** operator express the data rotation of all rows:

$$\text{rotate\_row} :: (\text{Int} \to \text{Int}) \to \text{ParArray (Int,Int) } \alpha \to \text{ParArray (Int,Int) } \alpha$$
$$\text{rotate\_row } df\ A \;=$$
$$\ll(i,j) := A(i,(j+(df\ i)) \bmod n) \mid i \leftarrow [1..m],\ j \leftarrow [1..n]\gg$$

where **df** is a function and (**df** i) indicates the distance of rotation for the ith row. An operator **rotate_col** for rotating columns can defined in the same way.

Broadcasting can be thought as a regular data-movement in which a data item is broadcast to all sites and aligned together with the local data. This skeleton is defined as:

$$\text{brdcast} :: \alpha \to \text{ParArray index } \beta \to \text{ParArray index } (\alpha,\beta)$$
$$\text{brdcast } a\ A \;=\; \text{map (align\_pair } a)\ A$$

where **align_pair** groups a data item with the local data of a processor.

For irregular data-movement the destination is a function of the current index. This definition introduces various communication modes. Multiple array elements may arrive at one index (i.e. many to one communication). We model this by accumulating a sequential vector of elements at each index in the new array. Since the underlying implementation is non-deterministic no ordering of the elements in the vector may be assumed. The index calculating function can specify either the destination of an element or the source of an element. Two functions, **send** and **fetch**, are provided to reflect this. Obviously, the

fetch operation models only one to one communication. For the one dimensional definitions, two functions can be defined as:

```
send :: (Int → (SeqArray Int Int)) → ParArray Int α
          → ParArray Int (SeqArray Int α)
send f << x₀,...,xₙ >> = << [xₖ|0 in f k],...,[xₖ|n in f k] >>

fetch :: (Int → Int) → ParArray Int α → ParArray Int α
fetch f << x₀,...,xₙ >> = << x₍f 0₎,...,x₍f n₎ >>
```

The above functions can be used to define more complex and powerful communication skeletons required for realistic problems.

2.3   Computational Skeletons: Abstracting Control Flow

A key to achieving proper coordination is to provide the programmer with the flexibility to organise multi-threaded control flow in a parallel environment. In SCL this flexibility is provided by abstracting the commonly used parallel computational patterns as *computational skeletons*. The control structures of parallel processes can then be organised as the composition of computational skeletons. This structured approach of process coordination means that the behaviour of a parallel program is amenable to proper mathematical rigour and manipulation. Moreover, a fixed set of computational skeletons can be efficiently implemented across various architectures. In this subsection, we present a set of computational skeletons abstracting data parallel computation.

The **SPMD** skeleton, defined as follows, abstracts the features of SPMD (Single Program Multiple Data) computation:

```
SPMD []                  = id
SPMD (gf, lf) : fs  = (SPMD fs) ∘ (gf ∘ (imap lf ))
```

The skeleton takes a list of global-local operation pairs, which are applied over configurations of distributed data objects. The *local operations* are farmed to each processor and computed in parallel. Flat local operations, which contain no skeleton applications, can be regarded as *sequential*. The *global operations* over the whole configuration are parallel operations that require synchronization and communication. Thus, the composition of **gf** and **imap lf** abstracts a single stage of SPMD computation where the composition operator models the behaviour of *barrier synchronization*.

The **iterUntil** skeleton, defined as follows, captures a common form of iteration. The condition **con** is checked before each iteration. The function **iterSolve** is applied at each iteration, while the function **finalSolve** is applied when the condition is satisfied.

```
iterUntil iterSolve finalSolve con x
            = if con x
              then finalSolve x
              else iterUntil iterSolve finalSolve con (iterSolve x)
```

Variants of `iterUntil` can be used. For example, when an iteration counter is used, an iteration can be captured by the skeleton `iterFor` defined as follows:

```
iterFor terminator iterSolve x
      = fst (iterUntil iterSolve' id con (x, 1))
        where
              iterSolve' (x, i) = (iterSolve i x, i+1)
              con (x, j) = j > terminator
```

2.4 Parallel Matrix Multiplication: A Case Study

To investigate the expressive power of SCL, in this subsection we define the coordination structure of two parallel matrix multiplication algorithms using SCL. The two following matrix multiplication algorithms are adapted from [9].

Row-Column-Oriented Parallel Matrix Multiplication: Consider the problem of multiplying matrices $A_{l \times m}$ and $B_{m \times n}$ and placing the result in $C_{l \times n}$ on p processors. Initially, A is divided into p groups of contiguous rows and B is divided into p groups of contiguous columns. Each processor starts with one segment of A and one segment of B. The overall algorithm structure is an SPMD computation iterated p times. At each step the local phase of the SPMD computation multiplies the segments of the two arrays located locally using a sequential matrix multiplication and then the global phase rotates the distribution B so that each processor passes its portion of B to its predecessor in the ring of processors. When the algorithm is complete each processor has computed a portion of the result array C corresponding to the rows of A that it holds. The computation is shown in the Figure 2.

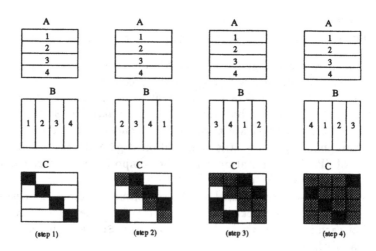

Fig. 2. Parallel matrix multiplication: row-column-oriented algorithm

The parallel structure of the algorithm is expressed in the following SCL program:

```
ParMM :: Int → SeqArray index Float →
         SeqArray index Float → SeqArray index Float
ParMM p A B = gather DC
    where
        C = SeqArray ((1,SIZE(A,1)), (1, SIZE(B,2))
            [ (i,j) := 0 | i ← [1..SIZE(A,1)], j ← [1..SIZE(B,2)] ]
        <DA, DB, DC> = iterFor p step dist
        fl = [(row_block p, id), (col_block p, id), (row_block p, id)]
        dl = [A, B, C]
        dist = distribution fl dl

step i <DA, DB, DC> =
    SPMD [(gf, SEQ_MM i)] <DA, DB, DC>
    where
        newDist = [id, (rotate 1), id]
        gf X = redistribution newDist <DA, DB, X>
```

where SEQ_MM is a sequential procedure for matrix multiplication. Data distribution is specified by the distribution skeleton with the partition strategies of [((row_block p), id), ((col_block p),id), ((row_block p),id)] for A, B and C respectively. The data redistribution of B is performed by using the rotate operator which is encapsulated in the redistribution skeleton. The example shows that, by applying SCL skeletons, parallel co-ordination structure of the algorithm is precisely specified at a higher level.

Block-Oriented Parallel Matrix Multiplication: This time we wish to multiply an $l \times m$ matrix A by an $m \times n$ matrix B on a $p \times p$ processor mesh with wraparound connections. Assume that l, m and n are integer multiples of p and p is an even power of 2. Initially both A and B are partitioned into mesh of blocks and each processor takes a $(l / p) \times (m / p)$ subsection of A and a $(m / p) \times (n / p)$ subsection of B (Fig.3(a)). The parallel algorithm staggers each block

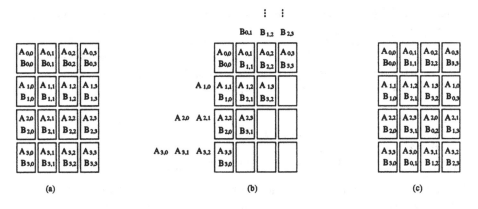

Fig. 3. Block-oriented algorithm: initial distribution

at row i of A to the left by i block column positions, and each block column i of

B upwards by *i* block row positions (Fig.3(b)) and the data is wrapped around (Fig.3(c)). The overall algorithm structure is also an SPMD computation iterated p times. At each step the local phase of the SPMD computation multiplies the pair of blocks located locally using a sequential matrix multiplication program and then the global phase moves the data: each processor passes its portion of A to its left neighbour and passes its portion of B to its north neighbour. The SCL code for this algorithm is shown below:

```
matrixMul :: Int → SeqArray index Float →
             SeqArray index Float → SeqArray index Float
matrixMul p A B = gather DC
    where
        C = SeqArray ((1,SIZE(A,1)), (1, SIZE(B,2))
            [ (i,j) := 0 | i ← [1..SIZE(A,1)], j ← [1..SIZE(B,2)] ]
        <DA, DB, DC> = iterFor p step dist
        fl = [((row_col_block p p), (rotate_row df1)),
             ((row_col_block p p), (rotate_col df1)),
             ((row_col_block p p), id)]
        dl = [A, B, C]
        dist = distribution fl dl
        df1 i = i (* to indicate the distance of rotation *)

step i <DA, DB, DC> =
    SPMD [(gf, SEQ_MM 0)] <DA, DB, DC>
    where
        newDist = [(rotate_row df2), (rotate_col df2), id]
        gf X = redistribution newDist <DA, DB, X>
        df2 i = 1 (* to indicate the distance of rotation *)
```

Abstraction. The above examples highlight an important feature of SCL. The parallel structure of a class of parallel algorithms for matrix multiplication can be abstracted and defined by the following SCL program:

```
Generic_matrixMul p distribustrategy redistribustrategy A B = gather DC
    where
        C = SeqArray ((1,SIZE(A,1)), (1, SIZE(B,2))
            [ (i,j) := 0 | i ← [1..SIZE(A,1)], j ← [1..SIZE(B,2)] ]
        dist = distribution distribustrategy [A, B, C]
        <DA, DB, DC> = iterFor p step dist

step i <DA, DB, DC> =
    SPMD [(gf, SEQ_MM i)] <DA, DB, DC>
    where
        gf X = redistribution redistribustrategy <DA, DB, X>
```

Thus, the row-column-oriented and the block-oriented parallel matrix multiplication program become instances of the generic parallel matrix multiplication code by instantiating the corresponding distribution and redistribution strategies. That is, the SCL code for generic parallel matrix multiplication defines an *algorithmic skeleton* for parallel matrix multiplication. This example shows how an application oriented parallel computation structure could be systematically defined.

3 Fortran-S: Coordinating Fortran Programs with SCL

As an exercise in developing a concrete SPP language we are designing a language, Fortran-S, to act as a powerful front end for Fortran based parallel programming. Conceptually, the language is designed by instantiating the base language in the SPP scheme with Fortran. Thus, to write a parallel program in Fortran-S, SCL is used as a coordination language to define the parallel structure of the program. Local sequential computation for each processor is then programmed in Fortran.

The matrix multiplication examples (section 2) can be coded in Fortran-S by instantiating the sequential local procedure SEQ_MM with the following Fortran subroutine for matrix multiplication (Fortran 90 syntax is adopted):

```
SUBROUTINE SEQ_MM (IT, IDX, X, Y, Z)
  INTEGER, INTENT (IN) :: IT, IDX
  REAL, DIMENSION (:,:), INTENT (IN) :: X
  REAL, DIMENSION (:,:), INTENT (IN) :: Y
  REAL, DIMENSION (:,:), INTENT (INOUT) :: Z
  INTEGER :: I, J

  START = ((IT + IDX) * SIZE(Y,2)) MOD SIZE(Z,2)

  DO I = 1, SIZE(X,1)
    DO J = 1, SIZE(Y,2)
      DO K = 1, SIZE(Y,1)
        Z (I,J+START) = Z (I,J+START) + X (I,K) * Y (K,J)
      END DO
    END DO
  END DO
END SUBROUTINE SEQ_MM
```

The *argument intent* of the parameters identifies the intended use of the variables. Variables specified with INTENT(IN) must not be redefined by the procedure, whilst INTENT(INOUT) variables are expected to be redefined by the procedure, and variables specified with INTENT(OUT) pass information out of the procedure.

In Fortran-S, the basic data type for SCL programming is the ParArray which is regarded as the parallel data structure whilst the basic data types, including arrays of Fortran are the sequential data structures. Thus, Fortran subroutines handle only Fortran data objects.

Fortran-S can be implemented by transforming Fortran-S programs into conventional parallel Fortran programs, that is sequential Fortran augmented with message passing libraries. Due to the functional nature of SCL source level transformation can be applied to optimise the parallel behaviour of the program, including granularity adjustment, nested parallelism flattening, optimised data distribution and interprocessor communication [2].

Currently, we are building a prototype system based on Fortran 77 plus MPI [7] targeted at a Fujitsu AP1000 machine [6]. The matrix multiplication example has been translated to Fortran77 plus MPI on an AP1000. Due to the richness of information provided by the Fortran-S code, the performance data is very encouraging, as shown in Fig. 4 for an array size of **400 × 400**.

nprocs	time(sec)	speedup
1	521.41	1.0
4	133.22	3.9
8	66.11	7.9
10	52.73	9.9
16	32.88	15.9
20	26.55	19.6
25	21.46	24.3
50	12.31	42.3
80	8.95	58.2
100	7.44	70.1

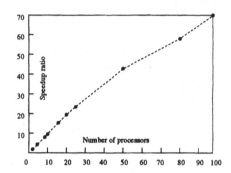

Fig. 4. Parallel matrix multiplication: speedup

4 Related work

Comparison with HPF. HPF supports data parallel programming by adding extensions to Fortran 90 including compiler directives for data distribution. Our work has been motivated by HPF. For example, there is a direct correspondence between the distribution specified by the HPF directives and the `distribution` skeleton. Configuration skeletons can be regarded as functional abstractions of HPF directives. Since SCL configuration skeletons are freely composable they are much more flexible than the fixed HPF directives. Moreover, the SCL operators are extendable and provide a more powerful means to express data distribution/re-distribution, alignment and movement.

Other coordination languages. One of the best known coordination languages is Linda, by Gelernter and Carriero [4]. As a coordination language, Linda abstracts MIMD parallel computation as an asynchronously executing group of processes that interact by means of an associative shared memory. Our work differs by extending the coordination language to describe all aspects of parallel coordination including partitioning and scheduling of parallel activities.

The coordination language PCN [3], promoted the concept of composing together modules by connecting together explicitly-declared communication ports. An interesting development of the PCN approach is the P^{3}L system [8]. Rather than using a set of primitive composition operators, a set of *parallel constructs* are used as program composition forms. Each parallel construct in P^{3}L abstracts a specific form of commonly used parallelism. This approach is based on the integration of the skeleton approach [1] and the PCN model. Such an integration, however, is not smooth since the high level abstraction of parallel computation structure is compromised by the lower level process model.

5 Conclusion

In this paper we have proposed functional skeletons as a new mechanism for developing general purpose parallel coordination systems. The work stems from our original work on functional skeletons to capture re-occurring patterns of parallel computation. This has been extended so that control of all aspects of parallel computation can be now expressed using skeletons. Therefore, it provides an ideal means for coordinating parallel computation. In this paper we have presented a coordination language, SCL, and a parallel programming scheme, SPP(X), obtained by applying SCL to coordinate computation programmed in a base language, X.

This work present a significant synthesis of some major developments of designing parallel programming systems including the coordination approach, data parallel programming, skeleton-based higher lever construction of parallel applications and declarative parallel programming. It provides a promising solution to the engineering problems of developing a practical structured programming paradigm for constructing verifiable, reusable and portable parallel programs.

Acknowledgements

The second author is supported by the ESPRC funded project GR/H77545 and the fourth author is supported by a British Council grant.

References

1. J. Darlington, A. J. Field, P. G. Harrison, P. H. J. Kelly, D. W. N. Sharp, Q. Wu, and R. L. While. Parallel programming using skeleton functions. In *Parallel Architectures And Languages, Europe: PARLE 93*. Springer-Verlag, 1993.
2. J. Darlington, Y. Guo, and H. W. To. Structured parallel programming: Theory meets practice. Technical report, Imperial College, 1995. unpublished.
3. Ian Foster, Robert Olson, and Steven Tuecke. Productive parallel programming: The PCN approach. *Scientific Programming*, 1(1), 1992.
4. David Gelernter and Nicholas Carriero. Coordination languages and their significance. *Communications of the ACM*, 35(2):97–107, February 1992.
5. High Performance Fortran Forum. *Draft High Performance Fortran Language Specification, version 1.0*. Available as technical report CRPC-TR92225, Rice University, January 1993.
6. Hiroaki Ishihata, Takeshi Horie, Satoshi Inano, Toshiyuki Shimizu, Sadayuki Kato, and Morio Ikesaka. Third generation message passing computer AP1000. In *International Symposium on Supercomputing*, pages 46–55, 1991.
7. Message Passing Interface Forum. *Draft Document for a Standard Message-Passing Interface*. Available from Oak Ridge National Laboratory, November 1993.
8. S. Pelagatti. *A Methodology for the Development and the Support of Massively Parallel Programs*. PhD thesis, Università Delgi Studi Di Pisa, 1993.
9. Michael J. Quinn. *Parallel Computing: Theory and Practice*. McGraw-Hill, second edition, 1994.

Architecture Design

On the Scalability of
Demand-Driven Parallel Systems

Ronald C. Unrau[1], Michael Stumm[2] and Orran Krieger[2]

[1] IBM Canada Ltd, North York, Canada, M3C 1V7
[2] Department of Electrical and Computer Engineering, University of Toronto,
Toronto, Canada, M5S 1A4

Abstract. Demand-driven systems follow the model where customers enter the system, request some service, and then depart. Examples are databases, transaction processing systems and operating systems, which form the system software layer between the applications and the hardware. Achieving scalability at the system software layer is critical for the scalability of the system as a whole, and yet this layer has largely been ignored.

In this paper, we characterize the scalability of the system software layer of demand-driven parallel systems based on fundamental metrics of quantitative system performance analysis. We develop a set of sufficient conditions so that if a system satisfies these conditions, then the system is scalable. We further argue that in practice these conditions are also necessary. In the remainder of the paper, we use the necessary and sufficient conditions to develop a set of practical design guidelines, to study the effect of application workloads, and to examine the scalability behavior of a system with only a limited number of processors.

1 Introduction

Demand-driven systems follow the model where customers enter the system, request some service, and then depart. Software-based demand-driven systems include databases, transaction processing systems, and operating systems. The design and implementation of scalable demand-driven parallel systems is difficult, yet important, if the performance potential of emerging large-scale parallel hardware bases is to be exploited.

Existing demand-driven parallel systems have typically been scaled to accommodate a large number of processors in an *ad hoc* manner, by repeatedly identifying and then removing the most contended bottlenecks. For example, on shared-memory multiprocessors, bottleneck contention is reduced either by splitting existing locks, or by replacing existing data structures with more elaborate, but concurrent ones. The process is long and tedious, and results in systems that 1) are fine-tuned for a specific architecture/workload and hence not easily portable to other environments with respect to scalability; 2) are not scalable in a generic sense, but only until the next bottleneck saturates; and 3) have a large number of locks that need to be held for common operations, with correspondingly large overhead.

Clearly, a more structured approach to designing scalable systems is needed. The key to finding an appropriate structuring is to first understand scalability itself. Although issues in scalability have been studied widely and many papers purporting scalable systems have been published [2, 4, 6, 9], little progress has been made towards a practical characterization of scalability. Most papers avoid defining scalability entirely, or simply state that their systems are targeted at some large number of processors [5].

An exception is Nussbaum and Agarwal's definition of scalability [8]: *The scalability of a machine for a given algorithm and problem size is the ratio of the asymptotic speedup on the real machine and the ideal realization of an EREW PRAM.* This definition is important because: 1) it recognizes that the applications and the architecture must work together if scalability is to be achieved; 2) it yields a quantitative measure of scalability, where a ratio of 1 indicates perfect scalability; and 3) it incorporates the notion of workload, in that the problem size is an explicit part of the definition.

However, the definition is not helpful for system designers for several reasons. First, the definition is based on speedup, while for demand-driven systems throughput is the more important performance metric[3]. Second, the definition of scalability is expressed in terms of inherent parallelism and asymptotic limits, and is therefore difficult to apply to real systems of fixed size and unknown inherent parallelism. Third, even if the definition could be used to evaluate the scalability of a real system, the quantitative number that is its result yields no insight into how to design or build a scalable demand-driven system.

In this paper, we develop an operational characterization of scalability that is applicable to demand-driven systems. Our development is based on an analysis of fundamental equations of quantitative performance evaluation, and is based on the definition that for a given workload, a system will scale if no resource saturates as the number of processors increases. From this definition, we argue that the following conditions are sufficient for a demand-driven system to scale:

1. The time at a particular resource devoted to servicing a particular request is bounded by a constant.
2. The number of resources available to service a particular class of request increases in proportion to p.
3. The system is balanced in its service capabilities.
4. The servicing of individual requests is localized and independent.

In addition, we believe that for practical systems, these conditions are necessary as well as sufficient for scalability.

The results we present are developed in a mathematical framework, which allows reasoning about asymptotic behavior, but the conditions are expressed in terms of physical quantities, so that they are of direct practical importance. In particular, Section 3 presents a set of design guidelines for building scalable

---

[3] It is interesting to note that Nussbaum and Agarwal specifically exclude the operating system from consideration in their definition and treat it as an extension of the hardware.

demand-driven systems that are derived from the scalability conditions. The mathematical derivation is based on broad assumptions of workload character-istics, and Section 4 refines these assumptions to see how real applications affect the scalability of a demand-driven system. Finally, Section 5 discusses issues in evaluating the scalability of existing systems, where only a limited number of processors are available.

While the following development is applicable to demand-driven systems in general, we are most familiar with parallel operating systems, and will therefore draw our examples from our experience in implementing an operating system for a scalable shared-memory multiprocessor [10].

2 Conditions for Scalability

In this section, we develop a set of conditions for the scalability of demand-driven systems. The development is based on an analysis of two fundamental perfor-mance metrics of computer systems: throughput and utilization. Section 2.1 re-views the definition of these metrics and discusses their properties in a scalable system. The assumptions upon which the scalability conditions are based and the conditions themselves are derived in Section 2.2.

2.1 Performance Metrics

The discussion examines throughput and utilization for servicing the requests of *customers* at *service centers*[4]. A particular class of customer is denoted as c, and a particular service center, or *resource*, as k. (In the following development, we use the terms resource and service center interchangeably.) Since a single service center can potentially support more than one class of customer, the subscripts ck are used to denote the customer class c at service center k.

In a demand-driven system, the notion of customers and service centers exists at multiple levels. At one level, applications are considered customers of the services provided by the system. For example, an operating system supports the services of creating a new process, or handling a page fault. The second level of customers and resources is within the system itself. At this internal level, the services are operations such as acquiring a lock, or allocating a descriptor for a physical page. The resources in these examples are the lock and the list of available page descriptors, respectively. The customers requesting service at the internal level are the servers and fault handlers of the operating system.

Throughput, X, is defined as the number of requests completed per unit time. An example of throughput is the number of page faults that are handled per second. Throughput can be measured at any service center in the system, where a service center is a resource as simple as a lock, or as complex as the system itself. The throughput for a customer class at resource k depends upon the arrival rate of requests, λ_c, and on the visit count at the service center, v_{ck}:

$$X_{ck} = v_{ck} \cdot \lambda_c \tag{1}$$

---

[4] The terminology and notation used is consistent with Lazowska *et al.* [7].

Formally, the visit count to resource k by customer class c is defined as the ratio of completions at resource k to the total number of system completions for class c. For a parallel demand-driven system, one intuitively expects the arrival rate of requests to the system to increase with the number of processors, either because there are more sequential applications, or because the parallel applications use more resources. However, we also expect the number of service centers to increase as more processors are added, so that the throughput of each resource need not necessarily be higher than for a sequential system. Hence, the visit count v_{ck} will typically decrease as the system size increases.

To illustrate this important point, consider a hash table with b bins that is used to access n elements; each bin and element in the table are locked separately. If b and n both increase with the size of the system, then the throughput required at each bin or element can remain relatively stable, assuming requests are distributed uniformly across the table resources.

Utilization, U, is defined as the percentage of time a resource spends serving requests. The utilization of a particular service center is related to throughput by the following equation:

$$U_{ck} = s_{ck} \cdot X_{ck} \tag{2}$$

where s_{ck} is the time required to service a request of type c at resource k. Over all customer classes, no resource can be busy more than 100% of the time, so that $1 \geq U_k = \sum_c U_{ck}$.

The resource with the highest utilization is designated the *primary bottleneck*; this is the resource that typically limits further increases in throughput, because of the queuing delay introduced by the resource. Performance can generally be improved by reducing the utilization of the primary bottleneck, either by reducing its service time or the number of requests it must service. These observations are the basis of the "lock-splitting" approach to scalability described earlier.

2.2 Development

Our development is based on the following two assumptions. First, we assume a workload with an arrival rate of requests for service, $\lambda_c(p)$, that increases in proportion to the number of processors in the system, p. Second, we assume that application service requests are spatially distributed across the system.

In a parallel environment, the utilization law of Equation 2 can be expressed as:

$$1 \geq U_k(p) = \sum_c U_{ck}(p) = \sum_c X_{ck}(p) \cdot s_{ck}(p) \tag{3}$$

where the components of the original equation are allowed to become general functions of the number of processors. If the system is to scale in p, then no resource k can saturate, or throughput will be limited. From these considerations, we define a scalable demand-driven system as one in which the utilization of any resource is bounded, such that saturation (ie. infinite queue lengths) never occurs.

From the definition and Equation 3 we conclude that the throughput and service times at resource k can only be functions of p if they are inversely proportional, so that their product is bounded for all p. In the remainder of the development, we use this observation to develop a set of properties sufficient for a demand-driven system to scale. We must consider the following three cases:

Case i. $s_{ck}(p)$ is independent of p,
Case ii. $s_{ck}(p)$ increases with p, and
Case iii. $s_{ck}(p)$ decreases with p.

We argue informally that case i, where service times are independent of p, is a reasonable base for structuring real systems, and derive the conditions sufficient to prevent saturation in this case. We further argue that case ii will make any system unscalable, and that case iii is unreasonable for real systems.

The discussion considers the class specific terms of Equation 3 ($s_{ck}(p)$ and $X_{ck}(p)$) because if any one of the class specific products is not bounded, it will dominate the sum and cause the resource to saturate. In addition, since all terms are functions of p, we will drop the explicit dependence in the notation for the remainder of the development.

Case i: Independent Service Time If service times are independent of the number of processors in the system, then operations such as creating a process or mapping a page, do not take longer to complete as the system grows. Keeping the service time bounded as the system grows seems an intuitive goal, albeit challenging to attain. Independent service time implies that the throughput for customer class c at resource k, X_{ck}, cannot increase as a function of p. From Equation 1, the throughput is proportional to both the system wide arrival rate, λ_c, and the visit count to the resource, v_{ck}. Since we expect λ_c to increase linearly in the number of processors, and since X_{ck} is to remain bounded, v_{ck} must decrease by at least $1/p$.

It is possible to have $v_{ck} \propto 1/p$ in practice if a) the number of instances of a resource grows proportional to the size of the system and b) requests are evenly distributed across the resource instances. This concept was illustrated by the hash table example of Section 2.1, where the number of hash bins grows with the size of the system, and is developed formally below. Define $\mathcal{R}_c$ as the set of identical resources available to service requests of class c, $K_c = | \mathcal{R}_c |$ as the number of resources in this set, and V_c as the total number of visits across the system that are needed to satisfy a request of class c:

$$V_c = \sum_{k \in \mathcal{R}_c} v_{ck} \tag{4}$$

If all v_{ck} within a set of identical resources are equal, (ie. $v_{ci} = v_{cj}, \forall i, j \in \mathcal{R}_c$) then the summation of Equation 4 can be replaced by a product:

$$V_c = K_c \cdot v_{ck} \quad \text{or} \quad v_{ck} = \frac{V_c}{K_c} \tag{5}$$

Since we need $v_{ck} \propto 1/p$, we must have $V_c/K_c \propto 1/p$. Below, we argue that in real systems, V_c should be independent of p, and K_c should increase proportional to p.

Equation 5 expresses v_{ck} as an *average*; it is likely not true at a given instant for a particular resource, but it must be true on average over time (and resources) if the system is to scale. In essence, Equation 5 requires a system to be balanced in its service capabilities to match the expected workload requirements. Note that to meet this requirement, the application load must be balanced across the system. Further, the servicing of individual requests must be independent of the servicing of other requests to different resources of the same class, otherwise concurrency will be compromised.

Case *ii*: Increasing Service Time We now consider the case where service times grow as an increasing function of p, $f(p)$, as processors are added to the system. This situation can occur, for example, if a list whose length increases with p must be searched linearly to service requests. However, we argue that systems with this property are unscalable.

If service time increases as $f(p)$, then the throughput at the resource must decrease as $1/f(p)$ if saturation is to be avoided. From the assumption of increasing λ_c and Equation 5, this requires $v_{ck} = V_c/K_c \propto 1/(pf(p))$. In real systems, it is not reasonable to expect V_c to decrease, because it implies that less work is required to satisfy requests of class c. Further, it is neither reasonable nor desirable to require K_c to grow faster than p. One reason this growth rate is unreasonable is that each resource has some space cost associated with it, so that if K_c grows faster than p, then the space costs will grow prohibitively as p becomes large. Note that the restriction that K_c grow no faster than p also restricts the growth of V_c, as given by Equation 5.

A second scenario that may appear to result in service times increasing with p are requests that require an identical operation simultaneously on many resources. We call this class of operations *compound* requests. Examples of compound requests include requests to destroy a parallel program containing many processes, or to invalidate data that has been replicated across several processors. From the point of view of the system, compound requests can be treated as multiple simultaneous but individual requests, each of which has service time independent of p.

Optimistically, one might hope to exploit concurrency in servicing compound requests, since multiple resources are involved. If the resources in the compound request are sufficiently independent, the service time for the n different resources of a compound request could even approach the service time for a single resource. However, in real systems the different resources are often coupled through shared resources such as locks. This coupling increases the demand on the shared resources, thus increasing the overall service time.

Case *iii*: Decreasing Service Time We now consider the case where service times decrease as a function of p, $1/f(p)$, and argue that this case is unrealistic.

In practical systems, service times can only decrease as $1/f(p)$ if the operation has speedup proportional to $f(p)$. To obtain this speedup, the service must be decomposed, or partitioned, into $f(p)$ independent operations that can be executed in parallel[5]. In practice, this partitioning is generally not possible. For example, operations such as creating a process or mapping a page act on a single process or page descriptor, so there is almost no potential for concurrency.

Having the service times decrease is also unrealistic because the assumption of increasing λ_c immediately precludes the possibility of applying multiple processors to the servicing of a particular request, because each processor must be available to service its share of the system-wide load. Even if all processors were involved in servicing each request, so that $s_{ck} \propto 1/p$, each processor would have to be involved in the handling of more requests, which requires the total visit count, V_c, to increase. This is only realistic under conditions of perfect speedup.

2.3 Conditions for Scalability

The previous discussion can be summarized as follows. We started with the definition that a demand-driven parallel system will scale if no resource saturates as the number of processors increases. We further assumed that the service request rate, λ_c, increases in proportion to the number of processors in the system, p, and that application requests are spatially distributed across the system. From the definition and these two assumptions, we have argued that the following conditions are sufficient for a demand-driven system to scale:

1. The time spent servicing request c at resource k, s_{ck}, is bounded by a constant independent of the number of processors in the system.
2. The number of resources available to service a request of class c, $K_c = |\mathcal{R}_c|$, increases in proportion to p.
3. The system is balanced in its service capabilities, so that $v_{ck} = V_c/K_c$ on average (Equation 5).
4. The servicing of individual requests is localized and independent, such that $V_c = \sum_{k \in \mathcal{R}_c} v_{ck}$ is independent of p.

As given, these properties form a set of sufficient conditions for a demand-driven system to scale. Further, we believe that: 1) any practical system must be based on the principle of bounded service times; 2) that the number of instances of a particular resource, K_c, can increase no faster than p; and 3) that the total system visit count for a particular class of operations, V_c is not a decreasing function of p. Given these assertions, the conditions above are both sufficient and necessary for scalability.

---

[5] It is important to note that parallelism in servicing a single request is different from the compound service requests discussed earlier, since compound requests are effectively identical operations performed on many similar resources.

3 Design Guidelines

The properties listed above identify conditions sufficient for a system to scale, but they do not directly specify how the requirements can be met. This section presents a set of design guidelines that are derived from the scalability criteria, and which can be used to design a scalable demand-driven system.

Preserving Parallelism *A demand-driven system must preserve the parallelism afforded by the applications.* Because we do not expect parallelism in servicing a single request, and because the system is primarily demand driven, parallelism within the system can only come from application demand. If several threads of a parallel application (or of simultaneously executing but independent applications) request independent services in parallel, then they must be serviced in parallel. This demand for parallel service can only be met if the number of service centers increases with the size of the system (scalability property 2), and if the concurrency available in accessing data structures also grows with the size of the system (scalability property 4).

Bounded Overhead *The overhead for each independent system service request must be bounded by a constant* [3]. This requirement follows directly from scalability property 1. If the overhead of each service call increases with the number of processors, the system will ultimately saturate, so the demand on any single resource cannot increase with the number of processors. For this reason, system-wide ordered queues cannot be used and objects must not be located by linear searches if the queue lengths or search lengths increase with the size of the system. Instead, structures that support search in order constant time, such as static positioning (for example, arrays), must be used.

The principle of bounded overhead is also applied to the space costs of the internal data structures. While the data structures are required (by scalability property 2) to grow at a rate proportional to the physical resources of the hardware, the principle of bounded space cost restricts growth to be no more than linear. For example, the size of memory management data structures should depend only on the amount of physical memory [1].

Preserving Locality *A demand-driven system must preserve the locality of the applications.* It is important to consider the memory access locality in large-scale systems, because, for example, many large-scale shared memory multiprocessors have non-uniform memory access (NUMA) times, where the cost of accessing memory is a function of the distance between accessing processor and the target memory, and because cache consistency incurs more overhead in large systems.

The mathematical model that we have developed is at the data structure level, and does not directly include effects due to memory placement or access latency. However, these effects are reflected through the service times, which will increase if remote accesses are made in a NUMA system. In particular, the latency to remote memory can be expected to increase as the system grows, and will increase even faster if the network is contended. Thus, the requirement that a demand-driven system preserves the locality of the applications is a direct consequence of scalability property 1.

Locality can be increased a) by properly choosing and placing data structures internal to the system, b) by directing requests from the application to nearby service points, and c) by enacting policies that increase locality in the applications' memory accesses and system requests. For example, policies should attempt to run the processes of a single application on processors close to each other, place memory pages in proximity to the processes accessing them, and direct file I/O to devices nearby. Within the operating system, descriptors of processes that interact frequently should lie close together, and memory mapping information should lie close to the processors that must access it to handle page faults.

4 Workload Effects

Previous sections have presented sufficient conditions for a demand-driven system to scale. However, a demand-driven system is only one part of the whole — the hardware, system, and applications must cooperate if scalability is to be achieved. Unfortunately, this means that no matter how well a system is designed, it is possible to construct an application that will saturate the system's resources. The mathematical model of Section 2.2 only considered independent, localized arrivals of requests for service. In practice, however, applications exhibit complex interactions and dependencies in their service requests. The application workload should therefore be considered in the design of a demand-driven system. This section examines how the workload affects the scalability of the system.

Consider a specific resource, k. As the number of processors is increased, we assume the arrival rate of requests for this resource will increase. To service the increasing number of requests, we require that the number of service centers, K_c, increase proportionally, so that the total demand placed on any service center is independent of the arrival rate, λ_c. However, an application program can undermine this strategy in two ways: (i) by creating an imbalance in its requests to the different instances of a particular resource, or (ii) by issuing requests that are not independent, and hence forcing resources to increase coordination as the arrival intensity increases. The effect of (i) is that some centers are idle while others saturate, which defeats the purpose of having multiple instances of a resource. Although the system can sometimes redistribute requests to idle centers, such load balancing does not come without cost, and is typically not effective for rapid, short-term changes in workload demand.

To illustrate (ii), consider a shared resource that is replicated across the processors of the system. Replicating objects is commonly used to improve access times by reducing contention and improving locality. Replicating the object increases the number of service centers because each replica is now available to service requests. However, performance will only improve if one can amortize both the cost of the replication and the cost of maintaining the consistency of the replicated object. The total demand[6] placed upon a service center, k, is thus the product of the percentage of requests which are directed to that replica (i.e., the visit count, v_{1k}), and the time required to access the data (i.e., the service requirement, s_{1k}) plus the product of the percentage of requests directed to center k due to maintaining consistency of the replicas (i.e., v_{2k}), and the amount of time required to perform the consistency operations (i.e., s_{2k}):

$$D_k = D_{1k} + D_{2k} = v_{1k} \cdot s_{1k} + v_{2k} \cdot s_{2k} \tag{6}$$

If the requests do not modify any of the replicas, then there is no cost in maintaining coherence, and D_{2k} of Equation 6 represents the one-time cost of replicating the object. If the requests modify the object, then the system must do work proportional to the p existing replicas to maintain coherence. Since this work is required for each modification, the system resources responsible for maintaining coherence will quickly saturate, and scalability is lost. Note also that if the object were not replicated it would saturate, since D_{1k} increases proportional to p.

For a workload with global writers then, the tradeoff between v and s (as well as their baseline costs) makes comparison between two systems with finite p possible. Balancing one against the other, even for small p, is reasonable. Notice that with a single instance of an object v grows linearly with p, and that when the object is replicated v can be made to grow logarithmically with p (if the auxiliary data structure is structured hierarchically). However, the baseline cost of replication (in this case s_{2k}), may be significantly higher than the other factors. Consequently, in mitigating the eventual saturation of the resource as p is increased the system designer may wish to facilitate a limited version of replication that balances time against frequency of access. This is the approach used in the design of the Hurricane operating system [10].

5 Evaluating Scalability

In principle, the properties that form our scalability criteria are observable quantities. However, their measurement in real systems can be non-trivial. For example, to prove a system is scalable, one must prove that s_{ck} and V_c are asymptotically bounded. For real systems, it is impossible to prove asymptotic independence through measurement alone, since there are only a finite number of processors. However, if a system is shown not to be scalable because of increasing service times, our set of conditions for scalability can yield more information than a simple yes or no answer to the question of scalability. This is because once one bases a system on bounded service times, a system that is found to be unscalable must violate one or more of the conditions for scalability.

Even if no resource saturates for a given workload and fixed p, the conditions for scalability can still be used to explore several interesting factors that affect

---

[6] Demand is related to utilization as $U_k = X \cdot D_k$.

the behavior of the system. For example, one can explore the rate of change of the system parameters as the size of the system is varied. Alternatively, one can vary the workload parameters for fixed p and examine the effects on the system. Finally, one can fix both the workload and system size, and tune the system for performance. The remainder of this section explores these options in detail.

Varying the Number of Processors For a fixed workload, it is possible to vary the number of processors and observe the effects on the system resources. In particular, if a resource saturates for some p, then the system has been proven unscalable for the given workload. If no resource saturates for a given range of processors, then the rate of increase in utilization, $\Delta U_k/\Delta p$, can be used as a first-order approximation to the range of processors for which the system resources do not saturate. An advantage of this approach is that $\Delta U_k/\Delta p$ can be determined empirically, typically by direct measurement of busy times or queue lengths. Ideally, if $\Delta U_k/\Delta p = 0$ then the utilization of resource k is independent of p. If this is true for all k, then the confidence that the system scales increases for the given workload. If $\Delta U/\Delta p > 0$, then the utilization of resource k is increasing as processors are added to the system and may eventually saturate. The rate of change of utilization, $\Delta U_k/\Delta p$, is not the only metric that can be used to estimate scalability. From the conditions for scalability, any of the metrics $\Delta s_{ck}/\Delta p$, $\Delta K_c/\Delta p$, or $\Delta V_c/\Delta p$ are useful. Ideally, $\Delta s_{ck}/\Delta p$ and $\Delta V_c/\Delta p$ should be 0, and $\Delta K_c/\Delta p$ should be p.

Varying the System The scalability criteria are also useful for comparisons between systems. From the perspective of scalability, the constants that bound service time and interaction need only be independent of the number of processors — no restriction is placed on the magnitude of the constants. However, if two systems are both proven to be scalable for a particular workload and number of processors, then the system with lower bounds will perform better, because its resources are less highly utilized.

To illustrate, consider a multiprocessor operating system targeted for a NUMA shared-memory architecture. At the level of abstraction used to develop the conditions for scalability, increased latency for accessing a remote memory is reflected in the service time, s_{ck}. Now consider two versions of an operating system data structure that are identical except for the way in which the K_c elements of the structure are distributed across the memories of the system. In one version, each element is placed local to the processor that has the highest probability of accessing it; in the other version the elements are distributed uniformly but randomly across the memories of the system. Since the data structures are identical at the programming level, we do not expect saturation for a given workload and system size (unless the interconnection network saturates because of the high number of remote accesses). However, we expect the highly localized version to perform better because the lower average access latencies result in lower average service times.

In practice, many systems will in fact trade scalability for performance. For example, a particular data structure may yield good performance for a small number of processors, but saturate quickly as the size of the system is increased. In a parallel operating system, this would be the case for, say, a single shared queue of processes that are ready to execute. This data structure provides good load-balancing and low overhead for a small number of processors, but will saturate as the number of processors increases if the queue of ready processes must be maintained in priority order. If the target system is small and load-balancing is deemed critical, some designers may trade-off the unscalability of the structure to obtain better performance.

Varying the Workload For a fixed number of processors and a given system configuration, one can vary the workload parameters and again observe the effect on system resources. This approach is useful for determining the range of workloads for which a system does not saturate.

To illustrate, consider a workload that shares a system resource among multiple processes. Clearly, this workload will eventually saturate the resource if the degree of sharing is allowed to increase arbitrarily. However, for a fixed number of processors, the resource may not saturate if the rate of requests for service (ie. the *granularity* of sharing) is low. As an example, a number of processes could share a single memory page of data in a NUMA multiprocessor environment. If the page is shared read-only, then it can be replicated as needed across the memories of the system to reduce access latency and network contention. If the page is subsequently modified, then the system must do work proportional to the degree of replication to maintain consistency (see Section 4). For a small degree of replication and/or a low rate of modifications to the page, the system resources can avoid saturation, but at some sharing granularity, the resources must saturate because the visit count, V_c, increases in proportion to the degree of replication. In effect, experiments that vary the workload are determining the granularity of sharing that can be tolerated by the system.

6 Conclusions

For a demand-driven parallel system to be scalable, all three layers of the system, the hardware, the system software, and the applications issuing requests, must be scalable. In this paper, we have focused on scalability issues at the system software layer. Our motivation for this study stems from the observation that this layer is critically important for scalability, but has typically been addressed only in a very *ad hoc* manner.

We presented an analytical model that characterizes the scalability of the system software layer, based on fundamental metrics of quantitative system performance analysis. In particular, a set of sufficient conditions was developed so that if a system satisfies these conditions then the system will be scalable. Further, it was argued that in practice these conditions are also necessary.

Analytical models typically have three limitations that prevent them from being practically useful. First, they yield no insight into how to build or design a scalable system. Second, they do not take into account the complex interactions exhibited by the workload of real applications. Finally, they are expressed in terms of asymptotic limits that make it difficult to evaluate the scalability of existing systems with only a limited number of processors.

We have addressed each of these limitations. First, the necessary and sufficient conditions we developed were translated into a specific set of practical design guidelines. Second, we explored how the application layer can impact the scalability of demand-driven systems. Finally, a number of techniques were presented that can be used to examine the scalability behavior of a system with only a limited number of processors.

References

1. Vadim Abrossimov, Marc Rozier, and Marc Shapiro. "Generic Virtual Memory Management for Operating System Kernels". In *Proc. 12th ACM Symposium on Operating System Principles*, pages 123–136, Litchfield Park, Arizona, Dec. 1989.
2. Ramesh Balan and Kurt Gollhardt. "A Scalable Implementation of Virtual Memory HAT Layer for Shared Memory Multiprocessor Machines". In *Summer '92 USENIX*, pages 107–115, San Antonio, TX, June 1992.
3. Amnon Barak and Yoram Kornatzky. Design principles of operating systems for large scale multicomputers. Computer Science RC 13220 (#59114), IBM Research Division, T.J. Watson Research Center, Yorktown Heights, NY 10598, Oct. 1987.
4. Amnon Barak and On G. Paradise. "MOS - Scaling up UNIX". In *Proc. USENIX Conference*, pages 414–418, December 1986.
5. John H. Howard, Michael L. Kazar, Sherri G. Menees, David A. Nichols, M. Satyanarayanan, Robert N. Sidebotham, and Michael J. West. "Scale and Performance in a Distributed File System". *ACM Transactions on Computer Systems*, 6(1):51–81, February 1988.
6. David V. James, Anthony T Laudrie, Stein Gjessing, and Gurindar S. Sohi. "Distributed-Directory Scheme: Scalable Coherent Interface". *Computer*, 23(6):74–77, June 1990.
7. Edward D. Lazowska, John Zahorjan, G. Scott Graham, and Kenneth C. Sevcik. *Quantitative System Performance*. Prentice-Hall Inc., Englewood Cliffs, NJ, 1984.
8. Daniel Nussbaum and Anant Agarwal. "Scalability of Parallel Machines". *Communications of the ACM*, 34(3):56–61, March 1991.
9. Mahadev Satyanarayanan. "Scalable, Secure, and Highly Available Distributed File Access". *Computer*, 23(5):9–21, May 1990.
10. Ron Unrau, Orran Krieger, Benjamin Gamsa, and Michael Stumm. "Hierarchical Clustering: A Structure for Scalable Multiprocessor Operating System Design". *Journal of Supercomputing*, To appear 1995.

Bounds on Memory Bandwidth in Streamed Computations

Sally A. McKee, Wm. A. Wulf, and Trevor C. Landon

University of Virginia, Charlottesville, VA 22903 USA

Abstract. The growing disparity between processor and memory speeds has caused memory bandwidth to become the performance bottleneck for many applications. In particular, this performance gap severely impacts stream-orientated computations such as (de)compression, encryption, text searching, and scientific (vector) processing. This paper looks at streaming computations and derives analytic upper bounds on the bandwidth attainable from a class of access reordering schemes. We compare these bounds to the simulated performance of a particular dynamic access ordering scheme, the Stream Memory Controller (SMC). We are building the SMC, and where possible we relate our analytic bounds and simulation data to the simulation performance of the hardware. The results suggest that the SMC can deliver nearly the full attainable bandwidth with relatively modest hardware costs.

1. Introduction

As has become painfully obvious, processor speeds are increasing much faster than memory speeds. To illustrate the current problem, a 300 MHz DEC Alpha can perform 24 instructions in the time to complete a single memory access to a 40ns DRAM.

Those programs that are limited more by bandwidth than by latency are particularly affected by this growing disparity — these include vector (scientific) computations, multi-media (de)compression, encryption, signal processing, text searching, etc. Caching provides adequate bandwidth for portions of such programs, but not for the inner loops that linearly traverse vector-like, "stream" data. Each stream element is visited only once during lengthy portions of the computation, and this lack of temporal locality makes caching less effective than for other parts of the program.

In this paper we develop analytic models that bound the performance of *any* uniprocessor or symmetric multiprocessor memory system on streams. We present highlights of these results, comparing them to the performance of a scheme we have proposed for accessing stream data — the *Stream Memory Controller* (SMC) [McK94a, McK94b]. There are two independent comparisons: a bus-level simulation, and a gate-level simulation of the SMC's VHDL description. Both forms predict the SMC consistently delivers nearly the maximum attainable bandwidth determined by the analytic bounds. While not reported here, preliminary tests of the actual hardware being conducted as this paper is written appear to confirm these results.

The performance of most memory systems is dependent upon the order of the requests presented to it. A multi-bank system, for example, performs better if the accesses permits concurrency among the banks. Order matters at an even lower level too: most memory devices provide special capabilities that make some access sequences faster than others [IEE92,Ram92,Qui91]. For illustration we focus on one such capability, fast-page mode. These devices behave as if implemented with a single on-chip cache line, or *page*. A memory access falling outside the address range of the current page is significantly slower than repeating accesses to the current page. Bandwidth can be increased by arranging requests to take advantage of such device capabilities.

Access ordering is any technique that changes the order of memory requests to increase bandwidth. Here we are specifically concerned with ordering vector-like *stream* accesses to exploit multi-bank systems using devices with special properties like page-mode. In this paper we buttress our previous results with both analytic models and (a few) gate-level simulations of the SMC being fabricated.

We first present the basic SMC architectures for uniprocessor and shared-memory multiprocessor systems. We then describe our multiprocessor task-scheduling strategy and how it affects memory performance. After explaining the assumptions underlying our analytic performance models and discussing the environment for our simulation experiments, we correlate the analytic performance curves with simulation results.

2. The SMC

There are many ways to approach the bandwidth problem, either in hardware or software. For instance, numerous designs of prefetching hardware have been proposed. These may prefetch into registers, cache, or special buffers [Bae91,Cal91,Chi94,Fu91, Gup91,Jou90,Kla91,Mow92,Skl92,Soh91]. Most of these schemes simply mask latency without increasing effective bandwidth. Such techniques are still useful, but they will be most effective when combined with complementary technology to take advantage of memory component capabilities.

Software access-ordering techniques range from Moyer's algorithms for non-caching register loads [Moy93] to schemes that stream vector data into the cache, explicitly managing it as a fast, local memory [Lee93,Los92,Mea92]. Moyer's scheme unrolls loops and groups accesses to each stream, so that the cost of each DRAM page-miss can be amortized over several references to the same page. Lee develops subroutines to mimic Cray instructions on the Intel i860XR [Lee93]. His routine for streaming vector elements reads data in blocks (using non-caching load instructions) and then writes the data to a pre-allocated portion of cache. Meadows describes a similar scheme for the PGI i860 compiler [Mea92], and Loshin and Budge give a general description of the technique [Los92].

Register-level schemes are restricted by the size of the register file, and cache-level schemes potentially suffer from cache conflicts. Moreover, optimal orderings cannot be generated without the address alignment information usually available only at run-time. Nonetheless, these techniques are useful to the extent to which they can be applied. McKee and Wulf examine access-ordering in depth, developing performance bounds for these and other access-ordering schemes [McK95]. The limitations inherent in compile-time techniques motivate us to consider an implementation that reorders accesses dynamically. Benitez and Davidson's algorithm can be used to detect streams at compile-time [Ben91], and the stream parameters can be transmitted to the reordering hardware at run-time.

Our analysis is based on the simplified architectures of Figure 1 and Figure 2. In these systems, memory is interfaced to the processor through a controller, or *Memory Scheduling Unit* (MSU). The MSU includes logic to issue memory requests and to determine the order of requests during streaming computations. For non-stream accesses, the MSU provides the same functionality and performance as a traditional memory controller.

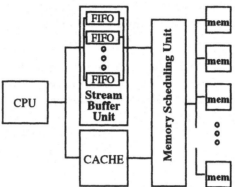

Figure 1 Uniprocessor SMC Organization

The MSU has full knowledge of all streams currently needed by the CPUs: using the base address, stride, and vector length, it can generate the addresses of all elements in a stream. The scheduling unit also knows the details of the memory architecture, such as interleaving and device characteristics. The access-ordering circuitry uses this information to issue requests for individual stream elements in an order that attempts to optimize memory system performance.

A separate *Stream Buffer Unit* (SBU) contains high-speed buffers for stream operands and provides memory-mapped control registers that the processor uses to specify stream parameters (base address, stride, length, and data size). Together, the MSU and SBU comprise a Stream Memory Controller (SMC) system.

The stream buffers are implemented logically as a set of FIFOs within the SBU, as illustrated in Figure 1. Each stream is assigned to one FIFO, which is asynchronously filled from (or drained to) memory by the access/issue logic of the MSU. The "head" of the FIFO is another memory-mapped register, and load instructions from (or store instructions to) a particular stream reference the FIFO head via this register, dequeueing or enqueueing data as is appropriate.

In the multiprocessor SMC system in Figure 2, all processors are interfaced to memory through a centralized MSU. The architecture is essentially that of the uniprocessor SMC, but with more than one CPU and a corresponding SBU for each. Note that since cache placement does not affect the SMC, the system could consist of a single cache for all processors or separate caches for each. Figure 2 depicts separate caches to emphasize the fact that the SBUs and cache reside at the same logical level of the memory hierarchy.

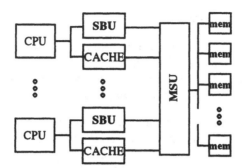

Figure 2 Symmetric Multiprocessor SMC Organization

3. Task Scheduling

The way in which a problem is partitioned for a multiprocessor system can have a marked effect on bandwidth. In particular, SMC performance is affected by whether the working sets of DRAM pages needed by different processors overlap during the course of the computation. If they overlap, the set of FIFOs using data from a page will be larger. With more buffer space devoted to operands from that page, more accesses can be issued to it in succession, resulting in greater bandwidth.

Here we focus on a scheduling model that distributes loop iterations among the CPUs, as in a FORTRAN DOALL. This parallelization scheme makes the *effective stride* at each of the M participating CPUs M times the original stride of the computation. If the number of memory banks is a multiple of the number of CPUs, this means that a different subset of banks will provide all the data for each CPU. Figure 3 illustrates the data distribution and code for this scheme. Since each of the M CPUs performs every Mth iteration, for stride-1 vectors all processors use the same DRAM pages throughout most of the computation (obviously, if the processors proceed at different rates, some may cross page boundaries slightly sooner than others).

vector x:

CPU_0's code:
```
for (i = 0; i < L; i += 2) {
    /* operations on x[i]*/
}
```

CPU_1's code:
```
for (i = 1; i < L; i += 2) {
    /* operations on x[i]*/
}
```

Figure 3 Data Distribution for a 2-CPU System

This model of scheduling maximizes the amount of DRAM page sharing, which in turn maximizes the SMC's ability to exploit memory bandwidth. We calculate the attainable bandwidth for an optimal data distribution, thus performance bounds derived for this scheduling model hold for other scheduling techniques. For details of SMC performance under other task-scheduling strategies, see our technical reports [McK94c, McK94d].

4. Modeling Assumptions

We have developed a number of reordering heuristics for the SMC, and we wish to evaluate their effectiveness. That was (and is) the motivation for the bounds derived here; however, even though our discussion is couched in terms of the SMC, our bounds apply to any scheme that performs batched ordering.

For the systems we consider, bandwidth is limited by how many page-misses a computation incurs. This means that we can derive a bound for *any* ordering algorithm by calculating the minimum number of page-misses, and we can use this bound to evaluate the performance of our heuristics. Similarly, we can calculate the minimum time for a processor to execute a loop by adding the minimum time the CPU must wait to receive all the operands for the first iteration to the time required to execute all remaining instructions.

This analysis provides us with two bounds on performance: the first gives asymptotic performance for very long vectors, and the second describes startup effects. The asymptotic model bounds bandwidth between the SMC and memory, whereas the startup-delay model bounds bandwidth between the CPUs and the SMC.

To make these bounds useful we want them to be upper bounds on what any real system can achieve; to that end we impose a number of constraints that real systems will not meet. We ignore bus turnaround delays and other external effects. We model the CPU as a generator of only non-cached loads and stores of vector elements; all other computation is assumed to be infinitely fast, putting as much stress as possible on the memory system. In calculating the number of page misses incurred by a multiple-stream computation, we assume that DRAM pages are infinitely large. In other words, we assume that misses resulting from crossing page boundaries are subsumed by the other misses calculated in our model. Finally, we derive our performance bounds by assuming that the SMC always amortizes page miss costs over as many accesses as possible: read FIFOs are completely empty and write FIFOs are completely full whenever the SMC begins servicing them.

As a practical consideration, we assume that the system is matched so that bandwidth between the CPUs and SMC equals the bandwidth between the SMC and memory; banks are assumed to be one word wide. The vectors we consider are of equal length and share no DRAM pages in common, and we assume a model of operation in which each CPU accesses its FIFOs in round-robin order, consuming one data item from each FIFO in each iteration. Each of these constraints tends to make the bound more conservative (larger) and hence harder to achieve in practice, but more useful as a yardstick for comparing access mechanisms.

We first look at how SMC startup costs impact overall performance, then we examine the limits of the SMC's ability to amortize page-miss costs as vector length increases asymptotically. We develop each of these models for uniprocessor SMC systems, then extend them to describe multiprocessor SMC performance.

5. Startup-Delay Models

Unlike the traditional performance concern over processor utilization, we focus on memory utilization for stream computations. Nonetheless, good overall performance requires that the processor(s) not be left unnecessarily idle.

Since we assume the bandwidth between the CPU and SMC equals that between the SMC and memory, optimal system performance allows each CPU to complete one memory access each bus cycle. Since the Memory Scheduling Unit attempts to issue as many accesses as possible to the current DRAM pages, most of our access-ordering heuristics tend to fill the currently selected FIFO(s) completely before moving on to service others. At the beginning of a computation on n streams, a CPU will stall waiting for the first element of the nth stream while the MSU fills the FIFOs for the first n-1 streams. By the time the MSU has provided all the operands for the first loop iteration, it will also have prefetched enough data for many future iterations, thus the computation can proceed without stalling the CPU again soon.

Deeper FIFOs cause the CPU to wait longer at startup, but if the vectors in the computation are sufficiently long, these delays are amortized over enough fast accesses to make them insignificant. Unfortunately, short vectors afford fewer accesses over which to amortize startup costs, thus the initial delays can represent a significant portion of the computation time.

To illustrate the problem, consider an SMC with FIFOs of depth f. If we disregard DRAM page misses, the total time for a computation is the time to fetch the first iteration's operands plus the time to finish processing all data. For a computation involving two read streams of length $l = f$, the CPU must wait f cycles (while the first FIFO is being filled) between reading the first operand of the first stream and the first operand of the second stream. According to our model (in which arithmetic and control are assumed to be infinitely fast), the actual processing of the data requires $2f$ cycles, one to read each element in each vector. For this particular system and computation, the time is at best $f + 2f = 3f$ cycles. This is only 66% of the optimal performance of $2f$ cycles (i.e., the minimum time to process all the stream elements). Figure 4 presents a time line of this example: the processor and memory both require the same number of cycles to do their work, but the extent to which their activities overlap determines the time to completion.

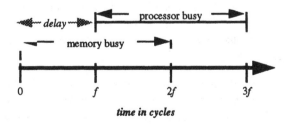

time in cycles

Figure 4 Startup Delay for 2 Read-Streams of Length f

In our analysis, a vector that is only read (or only written) consists of a single stream, whereas a vector that is read, modified, and rewritten constitutes two streams: a read-stream and a write-stream. Let s and s_{read} represent the total number of streams in a computation and the number of read-streams, respectively. The bandwidth limits caused by startup delays can then be described by:

$$\% \text{ peak bandwidth} = \frac{s \times l \times 100}{f(s_{read}-1) + (s \times l)} = \frac{s \times 100}{\left(\frac{f}{l}\right)(s_{read}-1) + s} \tag{1}$$

Figure 5 illustrates these limits as a function of the log of the ratio of FIFO depth to vector length for a uniprocessor SMC system reading two streams and writing one. When vector length equals the FIFO depth ($log(f/l) = 0$), this particular computation can exploit at most 75% of the system bandwidth. In contrast, when the vector length is at least 16 times the FIFO depth ($log(f/l) = -4$), startup delays become insignificant, and attainable bandwidth reaches at least 98% of peak.

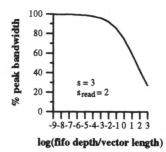

Figure 5 Performance Limits Due to Startup Delays

In a multiprocessor environment, we can bound the performance of the entire parallel computation by first calculating the minimum delay for the last processor to begin its share of the processing, and then adding the minimum time for that CPU to execute its remaining iterations. In developing these formulas, we assume all CPUs are performing the same operation, but are acting on different data. In our multiprocessor formulas, the length l reflects the portion of each vector being processed by a single CPU.

We can derive tighter bounds by tailoring our model to a particular SMC implementation. The way in which the MSU fills the FIFOs affects how long the CPUs must wait to receive the operands for their first iteration. If the MSU's ordering heuristic only services one FIFO at a time, then the last CPU must wait while the MSU fetches the read-streams for all other CPUs and all but one of its own read-streams. On the other hand, if the MSU can service more than one FIFO at a time, more than one CPU can start computing right away.

In the former case, when the MSU only services one FIFO at a time, the minimum number of cycles required to fill that FIFO is $1/N$ times the minimum for a uniprocessor system (because the bandwidth of the system is balanced, and there are now N CPUs that can each execute a memory reference per cycle). Let M represent the number of

CPUs participating in the computation. Then the CPUs are using M/N times the potential bandwidth, and the number of streams that must be fetched before the last CPU can start is $M \times s_{read} - 1$. The startup-delay formula under these circumstances is:

$$\%\text{peak bandwidth} = \frac{s \times 100}{\left(\dfrac{1}{N}\right)\left(\dfrac{f}{i}\right)(Ms_{read}-1) + s} \times \frac{M}{N} \tag{2}$$

For the latter case, let us assume that the MSU can perform accesses to M FIFOs at a time (one FIFO for each participating CPU). When $M = N$, the formula for startup delays is the same as for the uniprocessor SMC system (Equation 1). To see this, note that each CPU need only wait for all but one of its own read-streams to be fetched, and the average rate at which those FIFOs are filled will be one element per processor cycle. When $M < N$, the average time to fill a FIFO will be M/N times that for a uniprocessor, and the formula becomes:

$$\% \text{ peak bandwidth} = \frac{s \times 100}{\left(\dfrac{M}{N}\right)\left(\dfrac{f}{i}\right)(s_{read}-1) + s} \times \frac{M}{N}$$

$$= \frac{s \times 100}{\left(\dfrac{1}{N}\right)\left(\dfrac{f}{i}\right)(Ms_{read}-M) + s} \times \frac{M}{N} \tag{3}$$

The startup delays for the MSU servicing a single FIFO (Equation 2) and multiple FIFOs (Equation 3) differ only by a factor of $M - 1$ in the first term of the sum in the denominator. Thus Equation 3 also bounds bandwidth when the MSU fills one FIFO at a time; for simplicity, we use it as the basis for comparison with our simulation results.

6. Asymptotic Models

If a computation's vectors are long enough to make startup costs negligible, then the limiting factor becomes the number of fast accesses the SMC can make. The following models calculate the minimum number of DRAM page misses that a computation must incur — first for uniprocessors and then for multiprocessors.

6.1 Uniprocessor Models

The terms *stream* and *FIFO* will be used interchangeably, since each stream is assigned to one FIFO. For simplicity of presentation we refer to read-FIFOs unless otherwise stated; the analysis for write-FIFOs is analogous. We first present a model of small-stride, multiple-vector computations; we then extend this for single-vector or large-stride computations.

Multiple-Vector Computations

Let b be the number of interleaved memory banks, and let f be the depth of the FIFOs. Every time the MSU switches FIFOs, it incurs a page miss in each memory bank, thus the percentage of accesses that cause DRAM page misses is at least b/f for a stream whose stride is relatively prime to the number of banks. Strides not relatively prime to the number of banks prevent us from exploiting the full system bandwidth since they don't hit all banks. In calculating performance for vectors with these strides we must adjust our formulas to reflect the percentage of banks actually used. We calculate the number of banks used as the total number of banks in the system divided by the greatest common denominator of that total and the vector stride: $b/gcd(b, stride)$. The fraction of accesses that miss the page is thus at least $b/(gcd(b, stride) \times f)$.

Let v be the number of distinct vectors in the computation, and let s be the number of streams (s will be greater than v if some vectors are both read and written). If the CPU accesses the FIFOs (in round robin order) at the same rate as the memory system, then while the MSU is filling a FIFO of depth f, the CPU will consume f/s more data elements from that stream, freeing space in the FIFO. While the MSU supplies f/s more elements, the CPU can remove $f/(s \times s)$, and so on. Thus the equation for calculating the miss rate, r, for single-access vectors is:

$$r = \frac{b}{gcd(b, stride)} \times \frac{1}{f\left(1 + 1/s + 1/s^2 + 1/s^3 + ...\right)} \tag{4}$$

In the limit, the series in the denominator converges to $s/(s - 1)$, and our formula reduces to:

$$r = \frac{b(s-1)}{gcd(b, stride) \times fs}.$$

The number of page misses for each vector is the same, but a read-modify-write vector is accessed twice as many times as a read-vector and requires two FIFOs, one for the read-stream and one for the write-stream. Note that for such vectors, using a clever reordering scheme, the *percentage* of accesses that cause page misses is *half* that of a read-vector. To conservatively bound the average DRAM page-miss rate for the entire computation, we amortize the per-vector miss rate over all streams. If we assume that none of the banks is on the correct page when the MSU changes FIFOs, then this average is $R = r \times (v / s)$. But if:

1   the MSU takes turns servicing each FIFO, providing as much service as possible before moving on to service another FIFO;

2)   the MSU has filled all the FIFOs and must wait for the CPU to drain them before issuing more accesses; and

3)   the first FIFO to be serviced during the next "turn" was the last to be serviced during the previous one,

then the MSU need not pay the DRAM page-miss overhead again at the beginning of the next turn. Thus the MSU may avoid paying the per-bank page-miss overhead for one vector at each turn. When we exploit this phenomenon, our average page-miss rate, R, becomes:

$$R = \frac{v-1}{s} \times r = \frac{v-1}{s} \times \frac{b(s-1)}{gcd(b, stride) \times fs} = \frac{b(s-1)(v-1)}{gcd(b, stride) \times fs^2} \tag{5}$$

Let h be the cost of servicing an access that hits the current DRAM page, and let m be the cost of servicing an access that misses the current page. The maximum achievable bandwidth for a computation is equal to the percentage of banks used, thus we must scale our bandwidth formula accordingly, dividing by the greatest common denominator of the total number of banks and the vector stride. The asymptotic bound on percentage of peak bandwidth for the computation is thus:

$$\% \text{ peak bandwidth} = \frac{h \times 100}{(R \times m) + ((1 - R) \times h)} \times \frac{1}{gcd\,(b, stride)} \tag{6}$$

Single-Vector and Large-Stride Computations

For a computation involving a single vector, only the first access to each bank generates a page miss. If we maintain our assumption that pages are infinitely large, all remaining accesses will hit the current page. In this case, the model produces a page-miss rate of 0, and the predicted percentage of peak bandwidth is 100. We can more accurately bound performance by considering the actual number of data elements in a page and calculating the precise number of page-misses that the computation will incur.

Likewise, for computations involving vectors with large strides, the predominant factor affecting performance is no longer FIFO depth, but how many vector elements reside in a page. The number of elements is the page size divided by the stride of the vector data within the memory bank, and the distance between elements in a given bank is the vector stride divided by the number of banks the vector hits. We refer to this latter value as the *effective intrabank stride*, or *EIS*:

$$EIS = \frac{stride}{gcd\,(b, stride)} \tag{7}$$

For example, on a system with two interleaved banks, elements of a stride-two vector have an EIS of 1, and are contiguous within a single bank of memory.

Decreasing DRAM page size and increasing vector stride affect SMC performance in similar ways. Let d be the number of data elements in a DRAM page. Then for computations involving either a single vector or multiple vectors with large EIS values, the average page-miss rate per FIFO is:

$$R = EIS/d \tag{8}$$

For single-vector computations or computations in which *EIS/d* is less than the FIFO depth, we use Equation 7 instead of Equation 4 to calculate R. The percentage of peak bandwidth is then calculated from Equation 5, as before. Note that neither FIFO depth nor the CPU's pattern of interleaving accesses affects performance for large-stride computations.

6.2 Multiprocessor Extensions

Given the similarity of the memory subsystems for the SMC organizations described in Section 2, we might expect a multiprocessor SMC system to behave much like a uniprocessor SMC with a large number of FIFOs. For multiprocessor systems, though, some of the assumptions made in the uniprocessor models no longer hold. For instance, we can no longer assume that each read-vector occupies only one FIFO. The distribution of vectors among the FIFOs depends on how the workload is parallelized, since this affects the CPUs' pattern of DRAM page-sharing, which in turn affects performance. We bound multiprocessor SMC performance for all scheduling methods by calculating the minimum number of page misses for the extreme case when *all* CPUs share the same DRAM pages.

Recall that the system is balanced so that if each of N CPUs can consume a data item each cycle, the memory system provides enough bandwidth to perform N fast accesses in each processor cycle. Each CPU can only consume data from its set of FIFOs, while the MSU may arrange for all accesses to be for a single FIFO at a time: this means that the memory system can now fill a FIFO N times faster. Let M be the number of CPUs participating in the computation. When all CPUs use the same DRAM pages, we have essentially distributed each of our s streams over M FIFOs, which is analogous to using a single FIFO of depth $F = M \times f$ for each stream.

As before, we assume a model of computation in which each CPU accesses its FIFOs in round-robin order, consuming one data item from a FIFO at each access. It takes the MSU F/N cycles to supply F items for a stream. During this time, each CPU will consume F/Ns more data elements from this stream, for a total of MF/Ns freed FIFO positions. While the MSU is filling those FIFO positions (in MF/N^2s cycles), the CPU can remove M^2F/N^2s^2 more, and so on. Thus the page-miss rate of a vector is:

$$ r = \frac{b}{gcd\,(b,\, stride)} \times \frac{1}{F\left(1 + \frac{M}{Ns} + \left(\frac{M}{Ns}\right)^2 + \left(\frac{M}{Ns}\right)^3 + \ldots\right)} \tag{9} $$

The equation for the average page-miss rate is:

$$ R = \frac{r\,(v-1)}{s} = \frac{v-1}{s} \times \frac{b\,(Ns-M)}{gcd\,(b,\, stride) \times FNs} = \frac{b\,(Ns-M)\,(v-1)}{gcd\,(b,\, stride) \times FNs^2} \tag{10} $$

And the percentage of peak bandwidth is computed as in Equation 5:

$$ \%\,\text{peak bandwidth} = \left(\frac{h \times 100}{(R \times m) + ((1-R) \times h)} \times \frac{1}{gcd\,(b,\, stride)}\right) $$

7. Simulation Environment

In order to validate the SMC concept, we have simulated a wide range of SMC configurations and benchmarks, varying FIFO depth; dynamic order/issue policy; number of CPUs; number of memory banks; DRAM speed and page size; benchmark kernel; and vector length, stride, and alignment with respect to memory banks. Complete uniprocessor results, including a detailed description of each access-ordering heuristic, can be found in [McK93a]; highlights of these results are presented in

[McK94a,McK94b]. Complete shared-memory multiprocessor results can be found in [McK94c]. Since our concern here is to correlate the performance bounds of our analytic model with our functional simulation results, we present only the maximum percentage of peak bandwidth attained by any order/issue policy simulated for a given memory system and benchmark. All simulation results here were generated using DRAM pages of 4K bytes.

Recall that in order to put as much stress as possible on the memory system, we model the processor as a generator of non-cached loads and stores of vector elements. Instruction and scalar data references are assumed to hit in the cache, and all stream references use non-caching loads and stores.

The simulations we discuss here focus on two kernels, the results for which define the ends of the performance spectrum with respect to our set of benchmarks: *scale*, which involves one vector (two streams); and *vaxpy*, which involves three vectors (four streams). *Vaxpy* denotes a "vector axpy" operation: a vector *a* times a vector *x* plus a vector *y*. Our technical reports explore a larger space, simulating the performance of a suite of kernels found in real scientific codes. All our experiments indicate that the SMC's ability to optimize bandwidth is relatively insensitive to vector access patterns, hence the shape of the performance curves is similar for all benchmarks — asymptotic behavior approaches 100% of peak bandwidth [McK93a,McK94c]. Kernels are chosen, of course, because they are the portion of the applications that perform streamed accesses, which is the focus of this work; total system performance improvements obviously depend upon the fraction of time they spend in these kernels.

8. Comparative Results

All results are given as a percentage of the system's peak bandwidth, the bandwidth necessary to allow each processor to perform a memory operation each cycle. The vectors used for these experiments are 100, and 10,000 doublewords in length. Given the overwhelming similarity of the performance trends for most benchmarks and system configurations, we only discuss highlights of our results here. Although it is unlikely that system designers would build an SMC system with a FIFO depth less than the number of memory banks, we include results for such systems for completeness and for purposes of comparison.

Figure 6 represents the performance of a uniprocessor SMC system with two memory banks, depicting bandwidth as a function of FIFO depth. The graphs on the left show performance for *scale*, and those on the right are for *vaxpy*. The top graphs use 100-element, unit-stride vectors. The bottom graphs use stride-1 vectors of 10,000 elements.

Short vectors hinder the SMC's ability to amortize startup and initial page-miss costs. Even though *scale*'s simulation performance approaches 100% for both vector lengths, the percentage of peak bandwidth delivered for the vectors in Figure 6(a) is slightly lower than for those in Figure 6(c). Performance differences due to vector length are even more pronounced for multiple-vector computations. For the 100-element *vaxpy* computation in Figure 6(b), the startup-delay bound is the limiting performance factor.

Note that performance is constant for FIFO depths greater than the vector length. For longer vectors, as in Figure 6(d), startup-delays cease to impose significant limits to achievable bandwidth, and simulation performance approaches the asymptotic bound of over 97% of peak.

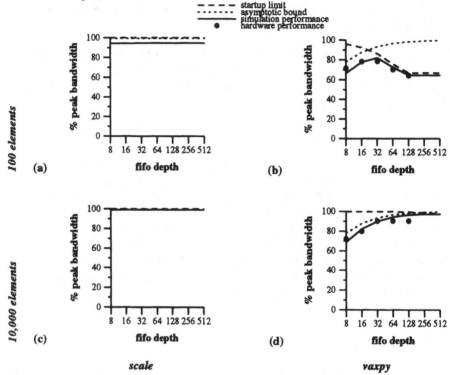

Figure 6 Uniprocessor SMC performance

The hardware data points in Figure 6 were generated via gate-level simulation of our initial implementation. The system parameters of the prototype differ slightly from the systems simulated; in particular, the hardware incurs extra delays (e.g. bus-turnaround) that have been abstracted out of our models, thus performance is limited to about 90% of the system peak. Nonetheless, this data gives us some indication of how actual SMC behavior relates to our models. It is still too early to make definitive claims, but the trends suggested in Figure 6 appear to agree with our other analysis and simulations.[1]

For deep FIFOs, if we increase the number of memory banks, we decrease the number of vector elements in each bank: doubling the number of banks affects performance much like halving the vector length. Alternatively, if the FIFO depth is small relative to the number of banks, increasing the number of banks further behaves like reducing the FIFO depth further since each FIFO holds items from more banks and this reduces the

---

1. These hardware simulations results are preliminary; we expect to have more data by the time of publication.

number of items from each DRAM page. Figure 7 demonstrates this phenomenon for stride-one *vaxpy* on 10,000-element vectors on a uniprocessor systems with two and eight banks. Decreasing the number of elements per bank limits the SMC's ability to amortize overhead costs, thus performance for systems with more banks is farther from the asymptotic limits. Note that systems with more banks deliver a smaller portion of a much *greater* bandwidth, as shown in Figure 7(c).

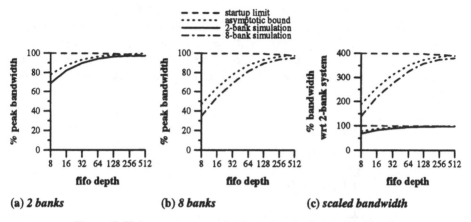

(a) *2 banks* (b) *8 banks* (c) *scaled bandwidth*

Figure 7 Uniprocessor *vaxpy* Performance for Increasing Banks

Figure 8 compares theoretical performance bounds to simulation results for our long-vector *vaxpy* computation on multiprocessor systems with two to eight CPUs. As the number of CPUs grows and the amount of data processed by each CPU decreases, performance becomes more limited by the startup-delay bound. For instance, this bound only begins to dominate performance at FIFO depths 128 and 256 for the 2-CPU system in Figure 8(a), but the crossover point between the startup-delay and the asymptotic bounds is between 64 and 128 for the 8-CPU system in Figure 8(c). All three systems deliver over 94% of peak for an appropriate choice of FIFO depth (in these cases 128).

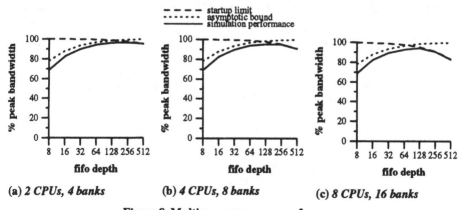

(a) *2 CPUs, 4 banks* (b) *4 CPUs, 8 banks* (c) *8 CPUs, 16 banks*

Figure 8 Multiprocessor *vaxpy* performance

The graphs in Figure 8 emphasize the importance of adjusting the FIFO depth to the computation. Deeper FIFOs do not always result in a higher percentage of peak bandwidth: for good performance, FIFO depth must be adjustable at run-time. Compilers can use the models presented here to calculate the optimal depth.

All examples thus far have used unit-stride vectors, but the same performance limits apply for vectors of any small stride. Figure 9 illustrates simulation results and performance limits for increasing strides on a uniprocessor SMC system with one bank, a FIFO depth of 256, and DRAM pages of 4Kb. We use the large-stride model from Section 6 to compute the asymptotic limits, since for these system parameters and strides, the number of elements in a page is never larger than the FIFO depth. Performance is constant for strides greater than 128, for at these strides only one element resides in any page.

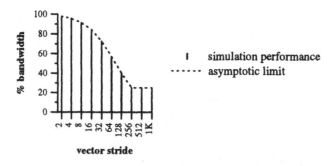

Figure 9 Asymptotic Limits for Increasing Strides

Figure 10 illustrates what happens when not all CPUs participate in a computation. If the MSU's ordering circuitry only services a single FIFO at a time, using fewer CPUs may optimize performance. For instance, by using one fewer CPUs for the task-scheduling scheme described here (in which each of M CPUs performs every Mth loop iteration), the effective stride of the computation becomes relatively prime to the number of memory banks. In such cases, the percentage of peak system bandwidth delivered becomes limited by the percentage of CPUs used, which lowers the startup-delay bound. The graph in Figure 10 shows SMC performance when only three CPUs of a four-CPU system are used to compute *vaxpy* on 10,000 element-vectors.

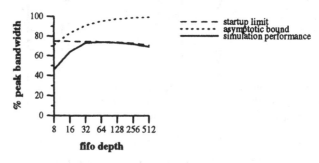

Figure 10 Using Only 3 CPUs of a 4-CPU System with 8 Banks

9. Conclusions

As processors become faster, memory bandwidth is rapidly becoming the performance bottleneck in the application of high performance microprocessors to important stream-oriented algorithms. These computations lack the temporal locality required for caching alone. Dynamic access ordering, however, can optimize such accesses. Previous papers have shown that by combining compile-time detection of streams with execution-time selection of the access order, we achieve high bandwidth relatively inexpensively.

Although our previous studies suggested good performance, we did not know how close our heuristic SMC algorithms were to optimal. Here we have described analytic models to bound the performance of both uniprocessor and symmetric multiprocessor SMC systems with memories comprised of multiple banks of page-mode DRAMs. Two different limits govern the percentage of peak bandwidth delivered:

- startup-delay bounds, or the amount of time a processor must wait to receive data for the first iteration of an inner loop; and
- asymptotic bounds, or the number of fast accesses over which the SMC can amortize DRAM page-miss costs.

Our analysis and simulation indicate that for sufficiently long vectors, appropriately deep FIFOs, and any of several selection heuristics, SMC systems can deliver nearly the full attainable memory system bandwidth.

In addition, our results emphasize an important consideration in the design of an efficient SMC system that was initially a surprise to us — FIFO depth must be run-time selectable so that the amount of stream buffer space to use can be adapted to individual computations. Using the equations presented here, compilers can either compute optimal depth (if the vector lengths are known), or they can generate code to perform the calculation at run-time.

Acknowledgments

This work was supported in part by a grant from Intel Supercomputer Division and by NSF grants MIP-9114110 and MIP-9307626. Other members of the SMC team, past and present, are Assaji Aluwihare, Jim Aylor, Alan Batson, Charlie Hitchcock, Bob Klenke, Sean McGee, Steve Moyer, Chris Oliver, Bob Ross, Max Salinas, Andy Schwab, Chenxi Wang, Dee Weikle, and Kenneth Wright.

References

[Bae91]   Baer, J. L., Chen, T. F., "An Effective On-Chip Preloading Scheme To Reduce Data Access Penalty", Proc. Supercomputing'91, Nov. 1991.

[Ben91]   Benitez, M.E., and Davidson, J.W., "Code Generation for Streaming: An Access/ Execute Mechanism", Proc. ASPLOS-IV, April 1991.

[Cal91]   Callahan, D., Kennedy, K., and Porterfield, A., "Software Prefetching", Proc. ASPLOS-IV, April 1991.

[Chi94]   Chiueh, T., "Sunder: A Programmable Hardware Prefetch Architecture for Numerical Loops", Proc. Supercomputing '94, Nov. 1994.

[Fu91]   Fu, J.W.C., and Patel, J.H., "Data Prefetching in Multiprocessor Vector Cache Memories", Proc. 18th ISCA, May 1991.

[Gup91]   Gupta, A., et. al., "Comparative Evaluation of Latency Reducing and Tolerating Techniques", Proc. 18th ISCA, May 1991.

[IEE92]   "High-speed DRAMs", Special Report, *IEEE Spectrum*, 29(10), Oct. 1992.

[Jou90]   Jouppi, N., "Improving Direct-Mapped Cache Performance by the Addition of a Small Fully Associative Cache and Prefetch Buffers", Proc. 17th ISCA, May 1990.

[Kla91]   Klaiber, A.C., and Levy, H.M., "An Architecture for Software-Controlled Data Prefetching", Proc. 18th ISCA, May 1991.

[Lee93]   Lee, K. "The NAS860 Library User's Manual", NAS TR RND-93-003, NASA Ames Research Center, Moffett Field, CA, March 1993.

[Los92]   Loshin, D., and Budge, D., "Breaking the Memory Bottleneck, Parts 1 & 2", Supercomputing Review, Jan./Feb. 1992.

[McK93a]   McKee, S.A, "Hardware Support for Access Ordering: Performance of Some Design Options", Univ. of Virginia, Department of Computer Science, Technical Report CS-93-08, August 1993.

[McK94a]   McKee, S.A., et. al., "Experimental Implementation of Dynamic Access Ordering", Proc. 27th Hawaii International Conference on Systems Sciences, Jan. 1994.

[McK94b]   McKee, S.A., Moyer, S.A., Wulf, Wm.A., and Hitchcock, C., "Increasing Memory Bandwidth for Vector Computations", Proc. Programming Languages and System Architectures, Zurich, Switzerland, March 1994.

[McK94c]   McKee, S.A., "Dynamic Access Ordering for Symmetric Shared-Memory Multiprocessors", Univ. of Virginia, Technical Report CS-94-14, April 1994.

[McK94d]   McKee, S.A., "Dynamic Access Ordering: Bounds on Memory Bandwidth," Univ. of Virginia, Technical Report CS-94-38, Oct. 1994.

[McK95]   McKee, S.A., and Wulf, Wm.A., "Access Ordering and Memory-Conscious Cache Utilization", Proc. High Performance Computer Architecture, Jan. 1995.

[Mea92]   Meadows, L., et.al., "A Vectorizing Software Pipelining Compiler for LIW and Superscalar Architectures", Proc. RISC'92.

[Mow92]   Mowry, T.C., Lam, M., and Gupta, A., "Design and Evaluation of a Compiler Algorithm for Prefetching", Proc. ASPLOS-V, Sept. 1992.

[Moy93]   Moyer, S.A., "Access Ordering and Effective Memory Bandwidth", Ph.D. Thesis, Department of Computer Science, Univ. of Virginia, Technical Report CS-93-18, April 1993.

[Qui91]   Quinnell, R., "High-speed DRAMs", EDN, May 23 1991.

[Ram92]   "Architectural Overview", Rambus Inc., Mountain View, CA 1992.

[Skl92]   Sklenar, Ivan, "Prefetch Unit for Vector Operation on Scalar Computers", Computer Architecture News, 20(4), Sept. 1992.

[Soh91]   Sohi, G. and Franklin, M., "High Bandwidth Memory Systems for Superscalar Processors", Proc. ASPLOS-IV, April 1991.

StarT-ng: Delivering Seamless Parallel Computing

Derek Chiou[1], Boon S. Ang[1], Robert Greiner[2], Arvind[1], James C. Hoe[1],
Michael J. Beckerle[2], James E. Hicks[2], and Andy Boughton[1]

[1] MIT
[2] Motorola

Abstract. StarT-ng is a joint MIT-Motorola project to build a high-performance message passing machine from commercial systems. Each *site* of the machine consists of a PowerPC 620-based Motorola symmetric multiprocessor (SMP) running the AIX 4.1 operating system. Every processor is connected to a low-latency, high-bandwidth network that is directly accessible from user-level code. In addition to fast message passing capabilities, the machine has experimental support for cache-coherent shared memory across sites. When the machine requires memory to be kept globally coherent, one processor on each site is devoted to supporting shared memory. When globally coherent shared memory is not required, that processor can be used for normal computation tasks. StarT-ng will be delivered at about the time the base SMP is introduced into the marketplace. The ability to be both a collection of standard SMP and an aggressive message passing machine with coherent shared memory makes StarT-ng a good building block for incrementally expandable parallel machines.

1 Introduction

The past few years have seen the demise of many companies dedicated to making high performance parallel computers. Some members of the computing community have gone as far as saying that parallel processing, in a classic sense, is dead. Although we strongly disagree with this assessment, we do agree that parallel computing is still at an adolescent stage in its development. We believe the problem is two-fold; it is too hard to program parallel computers, and the hardware, especially for *massively* parallel machines, costs too much for the node performance they deliver and supports too little off-the-shelf software. We are trying to solve the first problem by using implicitly parallel functional languages like Id[16, 5] and pH, and multithreaded languages such as Cid[17] and Cilk[6]. This paper, however, concentrates on StarT-ng, our solution to the second issue.

With personal computers (PC's) selling in the millions, mainstream computers have become commodities, resulting in lower computer prices, sped up product time tables, and rapid performance improvements. Parallel computers, on the other hand, have traditionally employed a lot of custom hardware and software. By the time the machine is ready, its processing node is generally a generation or two out-of-date, and a factor of two or more slower than the then current commercial microprocessors. The small customer bases and, therefore, small development teams cannot find and solve problems very quickly, making these custom machines and their software unreliable.

Coupling unreliability with the high cost of custom development, the general lack of shrink-wrapped software and the difficulty in writing custom applications, buying a parallel computer is difficult to justify. One would buy such a system only if one's application was critical enough to warrant a dedicated, *expensive* machine and the associated custom software development and maintenance cost. Massively parallel computers have fallen into the class of traditional supercomputers, rather than being affordable, widely-available high-performance computers as originally envisioned.

START-NG[3], a joint project between MIT and Motorola, tries to address these problems. START-NG is based on a commercial symmetric multiprocessor (SMP) *system* that uses PowerPC 620 processors. The goal of the project is to deliver very aggressive parallel performance by making small, manageable changes to the base SMP. We have added support for low overhead, high-bandwidth, user-level messaging, and support for globally coherent shared memory. Starting from a commercial system allows us to leverage infrastructure such as the processor, operating system, memory subsystem, and I/O subsystem. By borrowing most of the system technology, we dramatically reduce development time and cost, allowing us to deliver START-NG at approximately the same time the base SMP is introduced. START-NG, though a research machine, is *commercially* competitive in parallel performance as a message passing machine, and also runs stock sequential and SMP applications efficiently. START-NG extends the sharing of processor, memory and I/O resources made possible on a small scale by bus based SMP beyond the scaling constraints of buses.

While there are many advantages to using an entire system as the building block of a parallel machine, there are many technical challenges as well. Not only is our design constrained to using the stock PowerPC 620 microprocessor, which is optimized for sequential execution, but it cannot even change the system implementation in any significant way. Our design reuses all of the stock system implementation except for the boards carrying the processors. Observing these tight constraints while providing competitive performance is the topic of this paper.

Organization: In Section 2, we present an overview of the START-NG hardware. This is followed in Section 3 with a discussion of message passing support on START-NG. Section 4 discusses how shared memory is implemented on START-NG. Finally, we compare START-NG with some related work in Section 5 before concluding with the current status of the machine.

---

[3] START-NG is the latest incarnation of the *T or START project. For a history of the different versions of *T, see [4].

2 Overview of STARt-NG

A *site* in STARt-NG is a commercial PowerPC 620 SMP augmented with special hardware for message-passing and shared memory. The PowerPC 620 is a 64-bit, 4-way superscalar processor with a dedicated 128-bit wide L2 cache interface and a 128-bit wide L3 path to memory. It employs some of the most sophisticated techniques for pipelining instructions and memory management. It also has a novel feature that allows the processor to communicate with coprocessors over its L2 cache interface.

The STARt-NG SMP has 4 processor card slots that are connected to the main memory by a data crossbar. The crossbar has substantially better through-put than a traditional bus. In the commercial version, each processor card con-tains 2 processors and their L2 caches. STARt-NG replaces one to four of these processor cards with network-endpoint-subsystem (NES) cards, each containing a single 620 processor, 4 MBytes of L2 cache and a network interface unit (NIU). The NIU allows the 620 to communicate with an MIT-developed Arctic network router chip[7]. The STARt-NG system delivered to MIT will have 4 NES boards per site and will have a total of 8 sites.

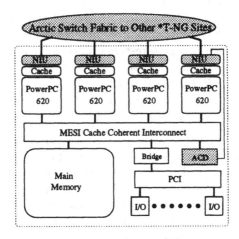

Fig. 1. A STARt-NG site: the white areas comprise the base SMP. The grey areas are our additions.

One of the NES boards at each site has an address capture device (ACD) which allows a designated processor at the site to monitor and respond to bus transactions. When used in this role, a processor is called a service processor(sP); when used to run application code, it is called an application processor (AP). The ACD and sP, collectively called the Shared Memory Unit (SMU), will be used to implement globally shared coherent memory, with coherence controlled at cache-line granularity. The ACD can be disabled when global shared memory is not needed making it completely invisible to the system, allowing all four processors at a site to serve as APs. Since all NES boards will actually have ACD's, it may be possible (depending on motherboard specifics) to use more than one as an SMU, dividing up the global space between them.

3 Messaging Support

START-NG's user-mode message-passing capabilities are provided by a fat-tree network built from Arctic[7] routers, and accessed through a tightly-coupled hardware network interface unit (NIU) attached to each 620 processor's L2 *coprocessor interface*. The NIU's packet buffers can be memory-mapped into an application's address space, allowing user programs to send and receive messages without kernel intervention by directly manipulating the buffers. Standard communication protocols, such as TCP/IP, PVM, MPI and Active Messages can be easily and efficiently implemented over START-NG's networking facilities.

The Arctic routing chip designed at MIT is a 4-by-4 packet-switched router capable of implementing a variety of staged networks. Implemented in .6 micron CMOS gate-array, Arctic is expected to run at 50 MHz, delivering 400 MByte/sec/full-duplex-link at a latency of 6 Arctic cycles per hop. A full fat-tree with 32 end-points delivers close to 6.4 GB/s of bisection bandwidth, and has a maximum of 8 hops between two end-points, resulting in a network latency of less than 1 μs. Based on the approximate PowerPC 620 timings available to us at this time, each 620 processor can achieve a maximum bandwidth of 180MB/s for message receiving or 278 MB/s for message sending.

Arctic supports variable-sized messages of up to 96 bytes of which 8 bytes are routing, control and CRC overhead. It provides two virtual prioritized networks, allowing the implementation of two-priority deadlock-free protocols (often known as separate request-reply) on a single physical network. Arctic also enforces secure space partitioning and employs sophisticated buffer management that allows it to sustain close to its peak bandwidth. Link-level flow control is implemented in hardware. Extensive error checking is designed into Arctic, including Manchester encoding of link-level flow control signals, and 16-bit CRC for every packet. Error rates are, however, low enough so that error recovery is unnecessary under normal operating conditions. Arctic is designed with a set of commercial-quality test, control and error detection and recording features. It was necessary to design our own router because no commercial equivalent, in functionality or performance, was available to us. Further details about Arctic can be found in [7].

3.1 620 Coprocessor Interface

START-NG's fast messaging capabilities are built on the L2 coprocessor interface found in the PowerPC 620 processor, which provides a low-latency, high-bandwidth connection to memory-mapped slave devices. Coprocessor device interfaces are required to look exactly like L2 cache sRAM, including having the same read/write timing characteristics. Since the coprocessor is accessed using normal load/store operations, individual pages in the coprocessor region can be accessed either in an uncached, cached with write-through, or cached with write-back fashion, where caching refers to caching in L1.

There are tradeoffs between using uncached, write-back cached, and write-through cached accesses to the coprocessor interface. Accesses to the L2 interface, though partially pipelined, have latencies significantly longer than accesses to the L1 cache. Caching the coprocessor interface allows the L2 access latency to be amortized across an entire cache-line and allows burst transfers. But because the coprocessor devices are slave devices, the L2 interface is not automatically kept coherent. In order to read new data, the 620 must first explicitly flush the previously read cache-line. Write-back cached writes also require flushes to force data to the coprocessor and take advantage of burst transfers to the L2 interface. Write-through cached writes and uncached writes do not require flushes but may not use the L2 interface as efficiently. We intend to experiment with the actual machine to determine the most efficient approach.

A common way to transfer a message consisting of multiple words is to first transfer the data, then indicate commitment of the transaction. If commit is indicated by writing to a coprocessor register, the ordering of writes, as seen by the coprocessor, becomes crucial. The implementation must guarantee that the commit write is not visible to the coprocessor before the data transfer has completed. Though simple in older microprocessors, such a guarantee is complicated in the 620 due to its weak memory ordering, which only ensures that memory operations to the same location occur in program order. No ordering guarantee, however, is provided for operations to different memory locations. Modern microprocessors provide synchronization instructions, which block the execution of subsequent instructions until all the prior memory operations have completed, to solve this problem. Such instructions, however, can be expensive. There are some possible 620-specific techniques which will be tried that may allow us to eliminate many of the otherwise necessary synchronization.

3.2 Network Interface Unit (NIU) Architecture

The START-NG NIU interfaces to the 620 coprocessor interface through a dual-ported SRAM. The 620 interacts with the NIU by reading and writing to specific regions in the buffer. Generally, the 620 will poll the NIU by reading specific memory locations to see if messages have arrived. The user process, however, has the option of configuring the NIU to interrupt the 620 processor when certain conditions, such as the arrival of a certain class of message, occur. This feature allows the user program to avoid the overhead of polling the network if it is known that messages arrive very infrequently. If the high priority network is devoted to the kernel, enabling the high-priority message arrival interrupt is an easy way to signal a kernel message arrival.

As shown in Figure 2, the dual-ported buffer space is logically partitioned into four data regions and one status/control region. The status/control region, located on a separate page accessible only to kernel, contains a 32-bit control

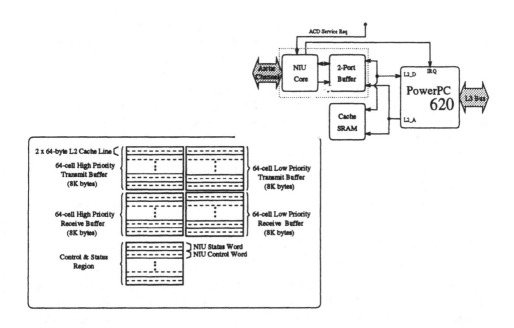

Fig. 2. NIU/620 Configuration, with organization of interface buffers shown in box.

word and a 32-bit status word through which all relevant NIU internal states can be read and written. This is used by the kernel to initialize the NIU, and perform context switching. The status word also contains the ACD service request signal. Normal user-level message sends and receives do not require access to this region, thus enabling ordinary page access control to protect the NIU, without performance penalty, from user corruption.

The four data regions of the NIU interface allow receiving and transmitting messages at both high and low priorities. Each data region occupies two memory pages (8 KBytes), allowing independent specification of protection and caching. Each transmit and receive data region, subdivided into 64 packet cells of 128 bytes, is jointly managed by the 620 processor and the NIU as a circular queue. For the transmit buffers, the 620 processor acts as the producer of the queue while the NIU serves as the consumer. For the receive buffers, their roles are reversed.

A v-bit in each packet cell indicates whether it contains a valid message. The consumer polls the v-bit at the head of the circular queue. When the v-bit is *valid*, the consumer càn proceed to retrieve the message from the cell, after which it frees the cell by resetting the v-bit to *invalid*. Prior to storing a new message into the queue, the producer first checks the v-bit of the cell it wishes to fill to ensure that the cell is free (v-bit invalid). After storing the message, the producer marks the v-bit *valid* to indicate to the consumer that the cell now holds valid data.

To handle timing asynchrony due to crossing of clock domains between the processors and the Arctic network, the NIU must first write the entire message, except the v-bit, into the receive buffer. The entire message actually includes the quad-word containing the v-bit; however, the v-bit is written as invalid. After a sufficient settling time, the v-bit alone is written, to the valid state. When reading messages from the sRAM, the NIU must first read the v-bit and, after it is valid, give sufficient settling time before reading the rest of the quad-word containing the v-bit.

With the use of the v-bit, there is no explicit exchange of queue indices between the 620 processor and the NIU to manage the circular queues. The dual-ported sRAM and the v-bit scheme provide a bridge across the processor and network clock domains, handling all the meta-stability and race concerns.

3.3 Transmit and Receive Cell Formats

The v-bit handshake between the NIU and the 620 requires that the v-bit be written last by the producer, and read first by the consumer relative to the data that it guards. When the 620 accesses the NIU through a cached interface, data transfer between the 620 and the dual-ported sRAM occurs in multiple cycles in an order dictated by the 620. In order to make sure that the v-bit is written last to the sRAM, the transmit cells take on the awkward format shown on the left side of Figure 3, where the v-bit is in the last quad-word (128 bits) of the first cache line.

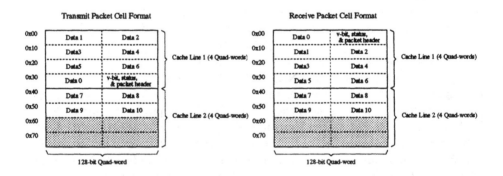

Fig. 3. Transmit cell and receive cell packet formats.

To further optimize the performance for uncached and write-through interfaces, the v-bit is placed in the last double-word of the last quad-word. This takes advantage of 620's *store-gather* capability, where two 64 bits stores to contiguous, ascending memory locations that occur one after another are packed into a single 128 bit transfer over the L2 interface. The v-bit and header are placed into the first cache-line of the transmit cell since smaller messages will only use one cache-line of the cell. For the receive cell, the v-bit is in the *first* quad-word of a receive packet cell (see right side of Figure 3), because the transfer of a cache line to the 620 starts by reading the first quad-word.

The START-NG NIU is optimized to support short, frequent messages, common in fine-grain parallel computation. The processor overhead of transmitting a 96-byte message (including an eight-byte header) by a user-level process using data already in its 620's registers is estimated at 42 cycles, assuming uncached access to the transmit buffers and buffer pointer already in register. Reading a 96-byte message takes 65 cycles under the same assumptions.

4   Shared Memory Support on STARt-NG

In addition to being a message passing machine, STARt-NG includes experimental support for building cache coherent shared memory. The main goals of this work are to explore: (i) the OS and virtual memory management (VMM) issues of a cache coherent distributed shared memory (CCDSM) system, (ii) hardware organization necessary to prevent deadlocks, and (iii) suitable memory models for programming. The emphasis in this research is on the necessary mechanisms to implement CCDSM correctly, rather than on the efficiency of the whole system.

4.1   Shared Memory Implementation

STARt-NG's cache-line coherent shared memory is implemented completely in software, allowing flexibility in the choice of coherence protocols. We plan to start with a simple directory-based, fixed home-site approach.

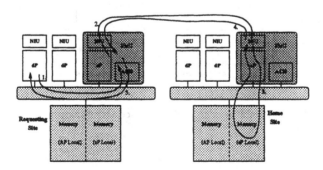

Fig. 4. Servicing a global memory cache miss, assuming a clean copy is available at the home site and no remote coherence action is needed.

Figure 4 shows how a cache miss of a global location is serviced. The cache miss results in a bus operation that is claimed by the local SMU (step 1) acting like memory. A high order bit of the physical address space is used to distinguish between global and local address spaces (more on address spaces later), allowing the SMU to detect operations to a global location by examining the address. The physical address of a global location is further divided into two parts: a field indicating the address's home, and the remainder indicating the actual cache-line address. The home site field enables the SMU to forward the request to the home-site SMU (step 2) which maintains directory information and initiates the appropriate coherence actions. In our example, no further coherence action is needed. Thus, after updating the directory information and reading the cache-line from the local dRAM (step 3), the SMU returns the requested data (step 4) to the requesting site, where the SMU returns the data to the requesting processor (step 5). This example is, of course, a specific case. In general, coherence action request messages may have to be sent out to invalidate remote caches or flush a dirty cache-line to reclaim ownership. It is important to note that the details of the directory-based protocol are flexible since they are implemented in software/firmware by the SMU.

In START-NG, the SMU uses a 620 at each site as a service processor (sP) to provide the processing power. Using a 620 provides flexible and inexpensive implementation, since it is fully programmable and can share system resources. An ACD is provided to allow the sP to observe, initiate and respond to bus transactions. In our current design, the sP reads and writes the ACD over the L3 snoopy bus itself. Faster designs, which allow the sP to communicate to the ACD through the coprocessor interface, were examined but not chosen for the initial implementation to reduce design complexity.

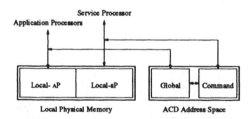

Fig. 5. Physical Address Space Organization

The user applications on the AP's see two regions of virtual memory which translate to two distinct regions of physical memory: (i) AP local memory which is accessed through the local memory controller without the SMU's involvement; and (ii) global memory, which is mapped to the SMU. This distinction is made because global memory accesses that go through the ACD are slow, while many objects in parallel programs, such as program text and stack frames, are local.

The sP also sees two regions of memory: (i) sP local memory and (ii) the ACD command interface. All global address space handled through the ACD is eventually mapped to some sP's local address space. Although both the AP and sP local memory reside in dRAM accessed through the local memory controller, they must either be completely disjoint or shared in a non-cached fashion in order to avoid deadlocks.

Deadlocks were a serious concern in the design of START-NG's shared memory. Deadlock-free implementation requires that the ACD be able to *selectively* flow-control requests due to lack of buffers, including software-based buffers in the sP. In particular, new cache-line read requests must be separated from write-back requests to avoid the possibility of reads consuming all buffering resources and causing deadlocks. Coherence-initiated cache-line flushes must be issued by the ACD and not the sP in order to avoid deadlocks. Deadlock issues are discussed in other papers[3, 2].

4.2 Access to Local-Global Memory

A *local-global* access is an access to a global location that has its home on the same site as the requesting processor. Our current design requires all global accesses, including local-global accesses, to be processed by the SMU in order to do the correct directory checks and maintenance. The SMU path overhead, however, is undesirable for local-global accesses, since the desired memory is local and often does not require remote coherence action. An all-software improvement, which we will try, would be to integrate network shared memory[15] and the cache-line level shared memory supported by the SMU (see Section 4.3). In the next paragraph, we discuss other local-global optimizations to START-NG which could not be implemented due to resource limitations.

One improvement has the SMU instruct the memory controller to deliver the desired data directly to the requesting processor once the directory check passes, bypassing the SMU during the return path. Yet another optimization modifies the memory controller to allow it to initiate dRAM access for local-global access but returns the cache-line only after the SMU determines and signals the memory controller that it is safe to do so. When data should come from a remote, dirty site, the SMU squashes the data read by the memory controller, and takes over the responsibility for returning the data. This scheme can be implemented without changing the memory controller by moving the filtering mechanism to the NES cards. Overall, however, it is probably more efficient to implement the SMU in the memory controller itself, which results in a FLASH-like design.

4.3 Operating System and Virtual Memory Management on START-NG

A major difference between START-NG and other CCDSM machines is in the OS and VMM. Some current CCDSM machines, such as Alewife, do not support virtual memory while others, like Dash, implement VMM with an SMP-like OS that has a single OS image and a single set of page tables for the entire machine. Each site of START-NG runs its own copy of an enhanced commercial SMP

OS with its own site-local page tables. A message-passing-based paging layer is added to achieve inter-site global virtual memory.

The VMM implementation has two layers: local and global. The first layer is the standard SMP VMM, handling local memory, but is augmented to also cache information about global memory. Initially, all global pages are protected against any access. When an access to such a page is first made on a site, the access is trapped and processed by the second layer which can either bring the page into local dRAM (sP local space), or provide a physical address translation if the page is already in another site's memory. In either case, the translation has to be set correctly so that the generated address falls into the AP global address space, and the home-site ID is in the appropriate field. The first layer VMM caches this until it is changed by the second layer.

This VMM approach will enable techniques similar to NVM[15, 9] that support coarse grain sharing and replication of pages by mapping global virtual pages into the AP's local physical memory, allowing accesses to those pages to bypass the SMU. STARt-NG therefore offers the flexibility of keeping coherence for global data at either page, or cache-line levels. At any time, each page has to be using only one scheme, but the selection can be changed dynamically, and independently for each page.

From the OS perspective START-NG looks like a high-speed network interconnection of multiple autonomous systems. This multiple OS image approach has significant advantages in fault tolerance; an OS crash at one site will not necessarily crash the other sites, killing only applications which depend on the crashed site. Another advantage is the fact that the SMP OS requires very minimal, if any, modifications. A third advantage is that TLB and other VMM-specific bus operations do not need to be broadcast across the entire machine whenever they occur. Finally, the use of site-local page tables offers software a choice of the granularity at which coherence is maintained. If desirable, it is easy to maintain page-level coherence, rather than the usual cache-line-level coherence, for selected pages.

4.4 Expected Performance of STARt-NG's Shared Memory System

This section presents estimated service times for global cache misses in START-NG. As noted earlier, the primary goal of shared memory support is *not* performance. The previous sections noted areas which could be improved but were not done for the START-NG implementation because of resource limitations. Not surprisingly, START-NG's shared memory performance is not particularly strong. Due to START-NG's very large caches (4 MB) and the improved locality due to its SMP nature, we hope cache miss rates will be low enough to make the coherent shared memory performance acceptable.

The penalties of cache-misses are shown in Figure 6. The times are given in processor cycles, and are approximate and conservative for START-NG. The penalties do not include network latencies, which is an orthogonal implementation issue. The corresponding penalties for the Stanford FLASH, as reported

Type of Miss	StarT-NG (proc cycles)	FLASH (proc cycles)
L3 Hit	157	54
Local Clean	199	54
Local Dirty Remote	575	198
Remote Clean	520	202
Remote Dirty at Home	575	202
Remote Dirty Remote	955	250

Fig. 6. Expected miss penalties excluding network latency in processor cycles. StarT-NG has a 133 MHz clock cycle while FLASH has a 200 MHz clock. The numbers for FLASH are taken from [10].

in [10] are given for comparison. To the first order, the miss penalties for StarT-NG are between 3 and 4 times longer than FLASH.

The actual impact of these numbers on performance depends on the miss rates and the percentage of memory operations in a program. When all other parameters are the same, a factor x increase in miss penalty requires a factor x decrease in miss rate to maintain the same overall run-time. Thus, if all parameters are the same, we would require a miss rate of between 3 and 4 lower than FLASH's to get to the same level of performance. The parameters are, however, not all the same. StarT-NG is based on SMP's which reduces the number of sites so that a larger fraction of references should be local-global. We also plan to make aggressive use of network virtual memory (mapping global pages to local pages) to further increase locality and reduce SMU utilization.

Large objects can be prefetched or steamed into a large software cache (L3 cache) maintained by the sP, further improving locality. Because the system continues to provide coherence maintenance, the user code can safely provide hints for prefetching based only on approximate information.

Another way to circumvent miss penalties is to switch threads when a cache-miss occurs. When the cache-line is returned, the thread is restarted where it left off. The penalty of a cache-miss is simply the time to swap out the thread and swap it in later, plus the cost of checking for cache-misses. Such a scheme is required to cache memory locations with synchronizing semantics such as I-structures[5].

Without special hardware support to detect and handle cache-misses, StarT-NG must implement this scheme in software. We plan to use a *miss pattern* as the returned data to indicate a cache miss. The application code tests all global loads to determine if a cache miss has occurred. The SMU returns the miss pattern after an access fails to hit in the L3 cache. If the miss pattern is encountered, the application thread sends a message to obtain the cache-line, then swaps itself out and schedules the next thread. The cache-line request includes information on how to restart the thread. The requested data is returned directly to the suspended thread and the cache-line to the sP for insertion into the L3 cache, ensuring that the scheme will work even if real data is equivalent to the miss pattern. An upper bound on the overhead of access to global memory would be around 300 cycles. Speculation and superscalar execution should remove most, if not all of the miss-checking overhead.

5 Related Work

START-NG is heavily influenced by dataflow architectures. Its message passing architecture emphasizes low-latency delivery of *small* messages rather than high-bandwidth transfer of large messages, although its bandwidth is very competitive. Achieving low overhead sending of small messages is a more difficult objective to achieve but allows finer granularity parallel execution. Machines that have influenced us in this area are the original *T project[19], MIT's Monsoon[18], ETL's EM-4[22], the J-Machine[8] and the M-Machine[11].

START-NG's software approach to cache-coherency is shared by other projects as well. The Wisconsin Wind Tunnel[20] (WWT) uses minimal hardware support[4] to implement shared memory. Network Virtual Memory[15, 14] (NVM) takes advantage of virtual-memory management hardware to maintain coherency at page-granularity.

START-NG is remarkably similar in some ways to Typhoon[21], an architecture developed at the University of Wisconsin. Typhoon, however, is not SMP based and proposes a much larger degree of custom hardware for its message passing and shared memory support than START-NG.

Alewife[1] and FLASH[10] use varying degrees of software in their coherency processing. Alewife has hardware support for maintaining coherence, but traps to software for exceptional cases not supported in hardware. Each Alewife site consists of a modified SPARC 2 processor and a fully custom memory controller, the CMMU. Unlike START-NG, Alewife cannot use standard commercial software such as operating systems.

Cache-coherency on FLASH, like on START-NG, is maintained completely in software. That software, however, runs on a special piece of hardware, the Magic chip, which replaces the standard memory controller. The Magic chip is much more aggressive than the SMU, and achieves better global cache-miss performance, but requires much more design effort both in the special hardware and in the system software to use it. FLASH's shared memory design is conceptually cleaner since it avoids unnecessarily recrossing the L3 and thus eliminates some potential deadlock situations.

The Stanford DASH[13, 12] is similar to START-NG in that it uses SMPs as building blocks for parallel machines. It adds custom shared memory boards to provide cache-coherent shared memory across multiple SMP sites. Unlike START-NG, all the protocol processing is performed by hardware on the shared memory board. All the directory memory also resides on this board. DASH's

---

[4] They hijack the ECC bits and handlers rather than adding any additional hardware. Unfortunately, this strategy cannot be supported on more aggressive processor architectures which do not provide precise ECC exceptions.

shared memory implementation, unlike START-NG's, allows access to local-global memory to proceed like a purely local access, unless coherency action has to be carried out on remote sites. However, the protocol is fixed in hardware.

START-NG's approach to shared memory uses much simpler hardware than any of the hardware supported shared memory schemes that we have encountered, allows finer-grained coherency control than NVM, and works with much more aggressive processors than the Wisconsin Wind Tunnel. We believe that this system will be an extremely competitive message passing machine which will also enable research into global shared memory issues.

6   Current Status and Conclusions

START-NG's delivery schedule is partitioned into 3 phases. Phase 1, to be delivered to MIT at the beginning of 1996, will consist of a machine with 8 sites, each containing 4 NES boards. The Phase 1 NES boards will communicate with their NIU's at either a third or a half of the processor clock rate. The ACD will run at a fourth of the processor clock rate, forcing the memory bus to run at that speed when the ACD is enabled and at L2 speeds otherwise. The ACD and NIU will be built from off-the-shelf parts, such as FPGA's and dual-ported sRAM's. The 620 clock rate may have to be reduced slightly to accommodate the ACD and NIU.

Phase 2 will raise the 620 processor to its maximum rated speed and the NIU clock to one half of the 620 clock. The ACD clock-speed remain a factor of 4 slower than the 620 necessitating the 620 L3 bus to run at that speed when the ACD is turned on. Phase 2 is due in the middle of 1996.

Phase 3 will boost ACD clock rate to one half of the 620 clock rate, making the SMP sites of the machine run at full commercial speeds even when the ACD is turned on. Phase 3 is currently planned for delivery perhaps in September of 1996, but will be influenced by results from experiments conducted on the phase 1 machine.

START-NG is an improvement over networks of workstations, capturing most of their advantages while significantly out-performing them. START-NG will deliver very aggressive message passing performance and will provide mechanisms to experiment with cache-coherent shared memory. Intensive effort to develop simulators, compilers, operating system support and coherency protocols are underway. START-NG should be a cost-effective, realistic platform for research as well as commercial parallel computing.

References

1. A. Agarwal et al. The MIT Alewife Machine: A Large-Scale Distributed-Memory Multiprocessor. In *Proceedings of Workshop on Scalable Shared Memory Multiprocesors*. Kluwer Academic Publishers, 1991.

2. B. S. Ang and D. Chiou. Finding Deadlocks in Cache-Coherent Distributed Shared Memory Machines. In *Proceedings of the 1995 MIT Student Workshop on Scalable Computing, Wellesley, MA*, August 1995. (To appear).

3. B. S. Ang et al. Issues in Building a Cache-Coherent Distributed Shared Memory Machines using Commercial SMPs. CSG Memo 365, Laboratory for Computer Science, MIT, Cambridge MA, December 1994.

4. B. S. Ang et al. StarT the Next Generation: Integrating Global Caches and Dataflow Architecture. In *Advanced Topics in Dataflow Computing and Multithreading, IEEE Press*, 1995.

5. Arvind et al. Executing a Program on the MIT Tagged-Token Dataflow Architecture. *IEEE Transactions on Computers*, 39(3):300–318, March 1990.

6. R. D. Blumofe et al. Cilk: An Efficient Multithreaded Runtime System. Submitted for publication, December 1994. Available via anonymous FTP from theory.lcs.mit.edu in /pub/cilk/cilkpaper.ps.Z.

7. G. A. Boughton. Arctic Routing Chip. In *Parallel Computer Routing and Communication: Proceedings of the First International Workshop, PCRCW '94*, volume 853 of *Lecture Notes in Computer Science*, pages 310–317. Springer-Verlag, May 1994.

8. W. J. Dally et al. Architecture of a Message-Driven Processor. *IEEE Micro*, 12(2):23–39, 1992.

9. S. Dwarkadas et al. Evaluation of Release Consistent Software Distributed Shared Memory on Emerging Network Technology. In *4th. ACM Symposium on Principles and Practice of Parallel Programming (PPoPP)*. ACM, 1993.

10. M. Heinrich et al. The Performance Impact of Flexibility in the Stanford FLASH Multiprocessor. In *Proceedings of the Sixth International Conference on Architecture Support for Programming Languages and Operating Systems, San Jose, CA*, pages 274 – 285, October 1994.

11. S. W. Keckler et al. Processor Coupling: Integrating Compile Time and Runtime Scheduling. In *Proceedings of The 19th Annual International Symposium on Computer Architecture, Gold Coast, Australia*, pages 202–213, 1992.

12. D. Lenoski et al. The Directory-Based Cache Coherence Protocol for the DASH Multiprocesor. In *Proceedings of The 17th Annual International Symposium on Computer Architecture, Seattle, WA*, pages 148–159, 1990.

13. D. Lenoski et al. The DASH Prototype: Implementation and Performance. In *Proceedings of The 19th Annual International Symposium on Computer Architecture, Gold Coast, Australia*, pages 92–103, May 1992.

14. K. Li. *Shared Virtual Memory on Loosely Coupled Multiprocessors*. PhD thesis, Yale University, September 1986. (Also as YALE/DCS/RR-492).

15. K. Li et al. Shared Virtual Memory Accommodating Hetergeneity. CS-TR 210-89, Princeton University, Department of Computer Science, February 1989.

16. R. S. Nikhil. Id Reference Manual, Version 90.1. CSG Memo 284-2, Laboratory for Computer Science, MIT, Cambridge MA, September 1990.

17. R. S. Nikhil. Cid: A Parallel "Shared-memory" C for Distributed-memory Machines. In *Proceedings of the 7th Annual Workshop on Languages and Compilers*

for Parallel Computing, Ithaca, NY, Lecture Notes in Computer Science. Springer-Verlag, August 1994.

18. G. M. Papadopoulos. *Implementation of a General-Purpose Dataflow Multiprocessor*. The MIT Press, 1991. Research Monograph in Parallel and Distributed Computing.

19. G. M. Papadopoulos et al. *T: Integrated Building Blocks for Parallel Computing. In *Proceedings of Supercomputing '93, Portland, Oregon*, pages 624–635, November 1993.

20. S. K. Reinhardt et al. The Wisconson Wind Tunnel: Virtual Prototyping of Parallel Computers. In *ACM SIGMETRICS*, May 1993.

21. S. K. Reinhardt et al. Tempest and Typhoon: User-Level Shared Memory. In *Proceedings of the 21st Annual International Symposium on Computer Architecture, Chicago, Il*, pages 325–336, April 1994.

22. S. Sakai et al. An Architecture of a Dataflow Single Chip Processor. *Proceedings of the 16th Annual International Symposium on Computer Architecture, Jerusalem, Israel*, pages 46–53, 1989.

Costs and Benefits of Multithreading with Off-the-Shelf RISC Processors

Olivier C. Maquelin[1], Herbert H.J. Hum[2], Guang R. Gao[1]

[1] McGill University, School of Computer Science
3480 University St., Montréal, Canada, H3A 2A7
[2] Concordia University, Dept. of Electrical and Computer Engineering
1455 de Maisonneuve W., Montréal, Canada, H3G 1M8

Abstract. Multithreaded architectures have been proposed for future multiprocessor systems due to their ability to cope with network and synchronization latencies. Some of these architectures depart significantly from current RISC processor designs, while others retain most of the RISC core unchanged. However, in light of the very low cost and excellent performance of off-the-shelf microprocessors it seems important to determine whether it is possible to build efficient multithreaded machines based on unmodified RISC processors, or if such an approach faces inherent limitations. This paper describes the costs and benefits of running multithreaded programs on the EARTH-MANNA system, which uses two Intel i860 XP microprocessors per node.

1 Introduction

Multithreaded architectures [1, 2, 12] have been promoted as potential processing nodes for future parallel systems due to their inherent ability to tolerate network and synchronization latencies. These delays are hidden by letting the processing unit switch to a different thread of execution instead of idling until the operation has completed. Due to the additional synchronization overhead when taking advantage of parallelism at a finer level, many architects question whether multithreading support can be made transparent to sequentially executing code and still be useful. However, preliminary results gained with the EARTH-MANNA system show that multithreading can indeed be useful, even on machines built with conventional RISC microprocessors. Even though the Intel i860 XP processor used in EARTH-MANNA was not designed for multithreading, benchmark results show that good speedups can be achieved, even compared with an efficient sequential implementation. Moreover, a detailed analysis of the multithreading overheads shows that they could be reduced significantly without having to switch to a custom processor design.

1.1 The EARTH-MANNA system

The results discussed in this paper were gained with our implementation of the EARTH *(Efficient Architecture for Running THreads)* model [4, 6, 5] on top of the *MANNA* (Massively parallel Architecture for Non-numerical and Numerical Applications) multiprocessor [3] developed at GMD-FIRST in Berlin, Germany. Each node of a MANNA machine consists of two Intel i860 XP RISC CPUs, clocked at 50 MHz, 32 MB of dynamic RAM and a bidirectional network interface capable of transferring 50 MB/s in each direction. This dual-processor design is similar to the EARTH model (see Fig. 1), which separates the processing node into an *Execution Unit* (EU) and a *Synchronization Unit* (SU).

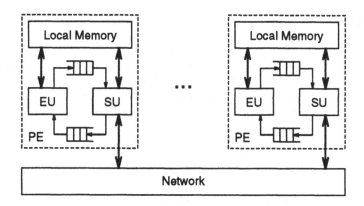

Fig. 1. The EARTH architecture

As demonstrated in [5], it is possible to implement multithreading support for such a machine without a major impact on performance. Performance of the parallelized code on a single node can be close to that of the sequential code because substantial portions of the code can often be executed in the normal sequential way. As shown in Sect. 3.3, performance gains can also be achieved by taking advantage of the SU to off-load data transfers from the main CPU. It is also interesting to note that for the EARTH-MANNA system the cost of saving and restoring registers is only a relatively small fraction of the total context switch costs (see Sect. 2.4). This means that better hardware support for multithreading should focus primarily on reducing the remaining costs, which are mostly due to communication between the EU and SU.

1.2 Synopsis

The next section discusses the overall performance of the EARTH-MANNA system and the costs associated with the multithreading support, such as the overhead to issue a split-phase transaction and the context switching costs. Then, Sect. 3 gives some insights into the relative performance of single-processor vs. dual-processor node designs. The costs for all internal operations involved in a remote memory access are shown for both cases, and finally some experimental results showing the benefit of a second processor are discussed.

2 Performance of the Multithreading Support

This section discusses the performance of the EARTH-MANNA multithreading support. It first shows the performance of some typical operations, then goes into more details to describe the EU overhead. The cost of communication between EU and SU is shown to be significant, mainly due to the necessary DRAM accesses. In contrast, the costs due to function invocation and to saving or restoring registers are shown to be relatively modest.

2.1 Performance of Typical EARTH Operations

In order to exploit parallelism at a finer level of granularity, it is important to reduce the costs of small messages, such as remote function calls or single-word remote memory accesses. While more conventional architectures focus primarily on high network bandwidth, the EARTH-MANNA system also tries to achieve very low latencies for the most important operations (see Table 1).

EARTH Operation	Sequential Local	Sequential Remote	Pipelined Local	Pipelined Remote
Spawn thread	2354 ns	4286 ns	2003 ns	1570 ns
Load word	2648 ns	7109 ns	1137 ns	1908 ns
Store word	2560 ns	6458 ns	1060 ns	1749 ns
Function call	5296 ns	9216 ns	3188 ns	2792 ns

Table 1. Execution time of some EARTH operations

These are overall costs, which include the network delays and the synchronization overhead. A substantial part of these costs can be hidden through multithreading. The actual costs to the EU will be described in more detail in Sect. 2.2. Because the EARTH model implements split-phase transactions, two or more EARTH operations are necessary to implement the operations in Table 1. See Sect. 3.1 for an example showing the detailed costs for a remote load.

Four numbers are shown in Table 1, each corresponding to a different usage of the operation. The typical latency depends on the location of the data that is referenced or the thread that is started. Remote references necessitate network accesses, which slows down execution. *Sequential* and *Pipelined* are two extremes of the typical usage. The sequential value indicates how long it takes to perform the complete operation, including context switching. In the pipelined case, on the other hand, operations are issued as fast as possible, without the need to synchronize before issuing the next operation. Obviously, the pipelined numbers are lower, as the EU, SU and network can all work in parallel.

These numbers compare well with other architectures, even those with hardware support for remote memory accesses. For example, in the Stanford DASH multiprocessor [8] a remote load takes $3\,\mu s$. In the Stanford FLASH architecture [7], a remote load will be performed in about $1\,\mu s$. However, the processor and network speed of the FLASH architecture are about $4 - 6$ times faster than the corresponding numbers in the MANNA architecture. The relative speed of communication vs. computation will therefore not be very different.

Performance of bulk data transfers is also excellent, with a maximum bandwidth of 41 MB/s in one direction and 61 MB/s when data is transferred in both directions simultaneously. The limiting factor in the first case is the packetization overhead, which reduces the usable link bandwidth by nearly 20%. In the second case the i860 XP's memory interface becomes the bottleneck. These values are especially good considering that our fastest local memory to local memory copy routine achieves 77 MB/s.

2.2 EU Overhead for the EARTH Operations

The execution times shown in Table 1 consider the total execution time. However, because the EU and SU can work in parallel, the EU can switch to a different thread while the SU performs the actual work. Table 2 shows the remaining EU overhead for some typical EARTH operation, as well as the time needed by the local SU and the remote SU to do the actual work. The EU overhead is the only part of the execution costs that can not be masked by multithreading. A more complete table can be found in [5].

EARTH Operation	Local EU Overhead (ns)	Local SU Costs (ns)	Remote SU Costs (ns)
SYNC (local)	700	200	0
SYNC (remote)	700	500	700
GET_SYNC (local)	780	300	0
GET_SYNC (remote)	780	500	800
DATA_SYNC (local)	780	300	0
DATA_SYNC (remote)	780	500	800
INVOKE (local)	800–1500	300–1000	0
INVOKE (remote)	800–1500	500–2000	500–2000
END_FUNCTION	750	0	0
END_THREAD	720	0	0

Table 2. Costs of some EARTH operations

As an example, a GET_SYNC (read word) operation where the data happens to be local costs the EU 780 ns on the average, while it takes the local SU only about 300 ns to perform the actual operation. These numbers are only averages, as the actual cost depends on many factors, such as cache hit rate and bus contention. Also, the EU overhead includes the EU $\leftrightarrow$ SU communication costs, but these costs are not included in the SU numbers.

Again, these numbers compare well with similar architectures. For example, with Active Messages on the CM-5 [13] the overhead to send a message is $1.6\,\mu s$. However, because communication is not off-loaded to a second processor, the overhead of receiving that message $(1.7\,\mu s)$ and executing the corresponding handler also has to be taken into account. The costs for the complete operation are therefore significantly larger than the typical 700 – 800 ns EU overhead of the EARTH-MANNA system. The J-Machine [10] achieves better performance, due to its hardware support for communication and synchronization. However, it still takes $0.9\,\mu s$ to send and receive an Active Message handler on that machine. Moreover, handlers are executed on the same processor, thus further slowing down the computation.

Considering that on MANNA each off-chip access takes about 200 – 300 ns, the run-time system is quite efficient. For such low-level code the number of instructions alone is not sufficient to get a good approximation of the execution time. Because communication between the EU and SU goes through software queues in the local memory, and because this information is shared between both processors, a certain number of cache misses and invalidations can not be avoided. For example, Fig. 2 shows the code for an END_THREAD operation (which switches to the next ready thread).

```
1:      ld.l 16(r14), r1      // load instruction pointer
        ld.l 20(r14), fp      // load frame pointer
        bte 0, r1, 1b         // branch back if queue empty
        st.l r0, 16(r14)      // mark element empty
        bri r1                // branch to specified address
        ld.l 0(r14), r14      // fetch address of next element
```

Fig. 2. Implementation of END_THREAD

The processor first loads the new instruction and frame pointers, branching back if the queue element turned out to be empty. After successfully loading the new pointers it marks the element empty, branches to the thread address and moves the queue pointer to the next element. This instruction sequence is quite short and little can be done to make it more efficient without additional hardware support. However, it takes on the average 720 ns to execute, which is significantly more than the 140 ns it would ideally take to execute these 6 instructions (*bri* needs two cycles to execute, for a total of 7 cycles).

The reason for the difference is that this code always involves at least one cache miss and one off-chip write, as shared data has to be transferred from the cache of the first processor to the cache of the second processor and consumed elements have to be freed. Bus conflicts also slow down communication, as the EU has to wait for the SU to release the bus. With today's RISC processors, maximum performance can only be achieved with good cache hit rates, or in other words when no off-chip accesses are performed. However, communication with another processor necessarily causes off-chip accesses. This turns out to be a crucial factor when using two CPUs per node.

With only the conventional, bus-based communication mechanisms, little can be done to improve performance. However, it is quite possible to improve hardware support for EU ↔ SU communication while still using an off-the-shelf processor as execution unit. This could be done e.g. with hardware queues that bypass the memory hierarchy (see Sect. 3.2). With adequate support it should be possible to lower the EU overhead for sending a request to around 100 – 200 ns, which would be less than the typical cost of a cache miss.

2.3 Function Invocation

The EARTH-MANNA system distinguishes between 4 different types of function invocations: normal sequential call, sequential call of a threaded function, invocation on a specific remote node, and invocation on an arbitrary node through dynamic load balancing. The frame of a *threaded* function, i.e. a function that contains threads or that calls other threaded functions, is allocated dynamically from the heap. Such functions can then invoke other threaded functions, or they can call sequential functions with the normal stack-based mechanism.

Frame allocation from the heap is necessary for threaded functions, as they can run in parallel with each other and therefore terminate in an arbitrary order. By keeping free lists for the most common frame sizes (i.e. the smallest frame sizes), the typical overhead for dynamic frame allocation can be kept down to around 200 ns. Because normal function calls use the sequential, stack-based calling mechanism, such functions run at the same speed as in a sequential implementation, which is crucial for good overall performance. This also allows the standard system libraries to be used unchanged.

2.4 Context Switching

Typical context switching implementations on conventional machines have to save and restore a large number of processor registers. However, the set of registers that are really active at context switch points, i.e. that really must be saved or restored, is often much smaller. This fact also motivated other architects to develop new mechanisms to speed up context switches, such as e.g. the Named-State Register File [11].

In the EARTH-MANNA system, context switches among threads are explicit and known to the compiler. The EARTH Threaded-C compiler can therefore analyze register usage at thread boundaries and minimize the number of registers saved and restored. The resulting save set is in general a conservative estimate of the registers that are really active, due to the presence of conditional branches and due to other simplifying assumptions made by the compiler. However, even with these limitations it turns out that on the average only a few registers need to be saved or restored. Table 3 shows context switching information that was gathered from five widely different benchmarks. See [5] for a detailed performance evaluation of these benchmarks.

Benchmarks	Context Switches	Total Saved	Total Restored	Average Saved	Average Restored
Ray Tracing	258	518	516	2.01	2.00
Protein Folding	65493	150327	177128	2.30	2.70
Paraffins	294	287	2	0.98	0.01
Tomcatv	77776	27131	154123	0.35	1.98
N-Queens	3780338	9868155	9868155	2.61	2.61

Table 3. Registers saved and restored

The average number of registers saved and restored is quite low for all five programs. This seems to be more or less independent of the average thread run-length, which ranges from $14\,\mu s$ for N-Queens to about $1\,s$ for Ray Tracing. These numbers are specific to the code generator we are using (the EARTH Threaded-C compiler is based on a commercial C compiler from The Portland Group Inc.), as different compilers will keep different variables in registers. However, a closer look at the generated object code did not reveal any serious shortcomings in register usage, but rather reinforced our conviction that the number of active registers at context switch points is often quite low.

Moreover, our experiences showed that in most cases good cache hit rates can be achieved for the loading and saving of registers. This means that the cost per load or store is only about 20 ns. On EARTH-MANNA the save/restore overhead is therefore only a small fraction of the total thread switching costs. It seems therefore much more important to support the EU $\leftrightarrow$ SU communication in hardware than to add support for multiple register sets.

3 Single Processor vs. Dual Processors: a Case Study

This section discusses the benefits of using a dual-processor node design in more detail. A detailed breakdown of costs for the remote load operation gives some insights into what could be expected from a single-processor implementation and what could be gained from better hardware support. Nevertheless, we then show that even without such hardware support some remote memory accesses can be masked by taking advantage of multithreading and a second processor.

3.1 Detailed Execution Costs

To better understand the advantage of having a second processing unit, it is first necessary to understand how much time is spent in each part of a typical operation. Table 4 shows a detailed breakdown of costs for a remote load.

Operation	Delay
EU send request to SU	780 ns
SU fetch request from EU	500 ns
SU generate and send message	500 ns
Transmission and polling delay	1000 ns
Remote SU read message from link	500 ns
Remote SU perform GET operation	300 ns
Remote SU generate and send response	500 ns
Transmission and polling delay	1000 ns
SU read response from link	500 ns
SU store result and sync	300 ns
SU insert into ready queue	500 ns
EU fetch next thread information	720 ns
Total	7100 ns

Table 4. Breakdown of costs for the remote load operation

In order to offer the same functionality in a single-processor node, some sort of interrupt (or other periodic polling) mechanism has to be implemented. Table 5 shows the estimated breakdown of costs for an interrupt-driven implementation.

Operation	Delay
EU generate and send message	800 ns
Transmission delay	500 ns
Remote EU interrupt latency	1000 ns
Remote EU read message from link	500 ns
Remote EU perform GET operation	300 ns
Remote EU generate and send response	800 ns
Transmission delay	500 ns
EU interrupt latency	1000 ns
EU read response from link	500 ns
EU store result and sync	200 ns
EU fetch next thread information	200 ns
Total	6300 ns

Table 5. Costs for an interrupt-driven implementation of remote loads

These numbers are estimates, as no interrupt-driven version of the run-time system has been implemented yet. For example, it is difficult to exactly predict the costs of interrupt latencies. A rather optimistic value was chosen for that delay to make sure that our comparison is not unfair to the interrupt-driven version.

In the single-processor, i.e. the interrupt-driven implementation, it is not necessary to send messages through the second processor; thus the total elapsed time for a remote load operation is smaller (6300 ns instead of 7100 ns). However, with a dual-processor node the amount of work done by the EU is much smaller, as most of the work can be off-loaded to the SU. Therefore the total EU overhead adds up to only 1500 ns, while in the single-processor case it is 5300 ns. This means that the dual-processor version can achieve a higher throughput.

A dual-processor node design is therefore expected to achieve better overall execution time if the remote access latencies can be masked by multithreading, but could perform worse if this is not the case. In any case, however, the EU costs for a single operation are still quite high compared with the typical costs for loads and stores to the local memory. It is therefore necessary to further reduce this overhead if parallelism is to be exploited efficiently at the level of individual reads and writes.

3.2 Gains through better Hardware Support

On MANNA it turns out that the EU $\leftrightarrow$ SU communication costs dominate the EU overhead. This is in part due to the lack of support for direct cache-to-cache updates, which forces all such communication to go through DRAM. More efficient cache strategies would help, but without additional hardware support it will not be possible to drastically lower the EU overhead.

In order to achieve significant improvements it would be necessary to significantly simplify the communication protocol, e.g. by supporting EU $\leftrightarrow$ SU queues in hardware. Hardware flow control would eliminate the need for test and branch instructions and eliminate some off-chip accesses. Also, bypassing the system bus would reduce the amount of bus collisions. With such hardware support it should be possible to reduce the cost for issuing a request or switching to the next thread to around 100 – 200 ns, less than the typical cost of a cache miss. This is only an estimate, as the exact numbers depends on the amount of hardware spent for supporting communication.

However, some costs are still likely to remain in a dual-processor node configuration. For example, the value returned by a remote load would still have to go through the system bus, as the EU expects the SU to store it in the local memory. Single-processor node designs will not suffer in the same way from inefficiencies due to the memory hierarchy, as no data needs to be transferred from one processor to the other. However, there are also efficiency limits due to the interrupt latency and to the fact that in a single-processor design all the work has to be performed by the main processor. Therefore, the dual-processor approach still seems the most promising for high-performance multiprocessors.

3.3 Benefits of Dual Processors

Even without extensive hardware support, significant gains can sometimes be achieved with a second processor. As an example, we discuss the multithreaded execution of Livermore Loop 7 [9]. The body of this parallel loop is a moderately complex expression, which reads from several arrays and writes to a different one. For the purposes of our experiment we forced one array to be remote and the others to be local. We also forced the whole loop to execute on a single node, even though it could run in parallel. The only use of parallelism in this case is to mask latencies. In order to experiment with other communication to computation ratios we also artificially increased the amount of communication by fetching the data two, four or more times.

The purpose of this experiment was to measure how well the system is able to hide the communication latencies. In order to compare with the multithreaded code, a version was developed where all the communication is performed at the beginning, before the loop starts. The execution time of that version therefore corresponds to no overlap between communication and computation and no multithreading overhead (because the normal sequential code can be executed after the data has been fetched). In order to get meaningful results we also increased the loop count from 990 to 9900, as with 990 iterations it takes only $190\,\mu s$ to perform all communication.

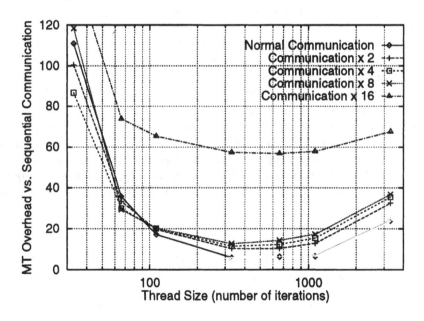

Fig. 3. Percent of communication time masked

Figure 3 compares the total communication overhead for both implementations. A value of 100% means that the total overhead for the multithreaded code was the same as if the data had been fetched all at once at the beginning. A value of 0% would mean that the execution time for the multithreaded code was the same as for the sequential code (i.e. communication perfectly hidden). This comparison was made for different thread sizes and for different amounts of communication.

With small thread sizes the costs are high, as the communication and multi-threading overheads increase. At the other hand of the spectrum, the amount of parallelism becomes too small to efficiently hide the communication. In between, there is a wide range of thread sizes for which a substantial percentage of the communication time could be hidden. The optimum size in this example is 330 iterations, in which case the total communication and multithreading overhead was just 5.8% of the sequential data transfer time. With increased communication the machine behavior remains roughly unchanged until the communication time becomes larger than the computation time (with 16 times the normal amount of data transferred). At that point, of course, it becomes impossible to hide all the communication.

4   Conclusion

We have implemented a multithreading layer on top of the MANNA architecture, a machine based on off-the-shelf RISC processors. Our experiences with the EARTH-MANNA system indicate that it does not introduce substantial overheads. Moreover, the possibility to overlap computation with communication can provide additional performance improvements, significantly reducing the overall costs of remote memory accesses.

The costs associated with multithreading support turned out to be dominated by the EU ↔ SU communication overhead. In order to efficiently hide latencies at the level of individual loads and stores this overhead has to be drastically reduced. This seems to be possible with appropriate hardware support. On the other hand, the cost of saving and restoring registers during context switches proved to be lower than expected. Multithreading seems to be a promising approach for future multiprocessor systems based on off-the-shelf RISC processors.

5   Acknowledgment

We would like to thank the Natural Sciences and Engineering Research Council (NSERC) for their support of this research. Also, the second author received funding from the Concordia FRDP and the third author received support from FCAR. Special thanks go to the MANNA developers at GMD-FIRST for the MANNA machines and for their technical support. Without them there would be no EARTH-MANNA system. Thanks go also to all the other members of the EARTH group for their contributions to the project.

References

1. Gail Alverson, Bob Alverson, David Callahan, Brian Koblenz, Allan Porterfield, and Burton Smith. Integrated support for heterogeneous parallelism. In *Multi-*

threaded Computer Architecture: A Summary of the State of the Art, chapter 11, pages 253–283. Kluwer Academic Pub., Norwell, Mass., 1994.

2. Boon Seong Ang, Arvind, and Derek Chiou. StarT the Next Generation: Integrating global caches and dataflow architecture. CSG Memo 354, Computation Structures Group, MIT Lab. for Comp. Sci., Aug. 1994.

3. Gesellschaft für Mathematik und Datenverarbeitung mbH. *MANNA Hardware Reference Manual*. Berlin, Germany, 1993.

4. Herbert H. J. Hum and Guang R. Gao. Supporting a dynamic SPMD model in a multi-threaded architecture. In *Digest of Papers, 38th IEEE Comp. Soc. Intl. Conf., COMPCON Spring '93*, pages 165–174, San Francisco, Calif., Feb. 1993.

5. Herbert H. J. Hum, Olivier Maquelin, Kevin B. Theobald, Xinmin Tian, Xinan Tang, Guang R. Gao, Phil Cupryk, Nasser Elmasri, Laurie J. Hendren, Alberto Jimenez, Shoba Krishnan, Andres Marquez, Shamir Merali, Shashank S. Nemawarkar, Prakash Panangaden, Xun Xue, and Yingchun Zhu. A design study of the EARTH multiprocessor. In *Proc. of the Intl. Conf. on Parallel Architectures and Compilation Techniques, PACT '95*, Limassol, Cyprus, Jun. 1995. IFIP WG 10.3, ACM SIGARCH, and IEEE-TCCA. To appear.

6. Herbert H. J. Hum, Kevin B. Theobald, and Guang R. Gao. Building multithreaded architectures with off-the-shelf microprocessors. In *Proc. of the 8th Intl. Parallel Processing Symp.*, pages 288–294, Cancún, Mexico, Apr. 1994. IEEE Comp. Soc.

7. Jeffrey Kuskin, David Ofelt, Mark Heinrich, John Heinlein, Richard Simoni, Kourosh Gharachorloo, John Chapin, David Nakahira, Joel Baxter, Mark Horowitz, Anoop Gupta, Mendel Rosenblum, and John Hennessy. The Stanford FLASH multiprocessor. In *Proc. of the 21st Ann. Intl. Symp. on Computer Architecture*, pages 302–313, Chicago, Ill., Apr. 1994.

8. Daniel Lenoski, James Laudon, Truman Joe, David Nakahira, Luis Stevens, Anoop Gupta, and John Hennessy. The DASH prototype: Implementation and performance. In *Proc. of the 19th Ann. Intl. Symp. on Computer Architecture*, pages 92–103, Gold Coast, Australia, May 1992.

9. Frank H. McMahon. The Livermore FORTRAN Kernels: A computer test of numerical performance ranges. Tech. Rep. UCRL-537415, Lawrence Livermore Nat. Lab., Livermore, Calif., Dec. 1986.

10. Michael D. Noakes, Deborah A. Wallah, and William J. Dally. The J-Machine multicomputer: An architectural evaluation. In *Proc. of the 20th Ann. Intl. Symp. on Computer Architecture*, pages 224–235, San Diego, Calif., May 1993.

11. Peter R. Nuth and William J. Dally. Named state and efficient context switching. In *Multithreaded Computer Architecture: A Summary of the State of the Art*, chapter 9, pages 201–212. Kluwer Academic Pub., Norwell, Mass., 1994.

12. Shuichi Sakai, Kazuaki Okamoto, Hiroshi Matsuoka, Hideo Hirono, Yuetsu Kodama, and Mitsuhisa Sato. Super-threading: Architectural and software mechanisms for optimizing parallel computation. In *Conf. Proc., 1993 Intl. Conf. on Supercomputing*, pages 251–260, Tokyo, Japan, Jul. 1993.

13. Thorsten von Eicken, David E. Culler, Sech Copen Goldstein, and Klaus Eric Schauser. Active messages: a mechanism for integrated communication and computation. In *Proc. of the 19th Ann. Intl. Symp. on Computer Architecture*, pages 256–266, Gold Coast, Australia, May 1992.

Semantics and Tools

Transformation Techniques in PEI

S. Genaud, E. Violard and G.-R. Perrin

ICPS, Université Louis Pasteur, Strasbourg
Boulevard S. Brant, F-67400 Illkirch
e-mail: genaud,violard,perrin@icps.u-strasbg.fr

Abstract. This article presents a few examples of program transformation strategies in the language PEI [Vio94]. Three strategies are developed : a simplification of the communications, the introduction of broadcasts by removing recursion from data field definitions, and the introduction of a reduction operator. These transformations emphasize the relationships between several programs solving a given problem, especially in the data parallelism area.

Keywords. Abstraction, Broadcast, Communication, Data-parallelism, Reduction, Refinement.

1 Introduction

Among the various parallel programming models that have recently emerged, the *data-parallel* paradigm is of particular interest and a few customized languages have been defined in this area, extending classical expressions such as C or Fortran. Hence, manipulation of regular data and control structures in the framework of a synchronous programming model only requires a small amount of effort to adapt from sequential programming to data-parallelism.

Nevertheless, studies have still to be carried out about this parallel programming model, especially in semantics, proof, program design methodologies or program transformations. This requires the definition of a theoretical foundation for data-parallel programming. Besides a few proposals (see for example [BL92]), PEI was defined [Vio94, VP94] in order to address the crucial question of program refinement through a straightforward generalization of equational notations ([Mau89, CCL91]), which were previously designed to implement nested loop parallelization methods in the so-called *Polytope model* [Len93].

PEI provides a formal framework to describe problem specifications and a means to reason on programs. Its semantics lies on a small but powerful set of mathematical issues since PEI statements describe operations on multisets of values. In order to access to these values, they are mapped onto discrete domains and form *data fields*, that are the basic objects of the language. From an operational point of view, such domains can abstract the mapping of calculations onto a mesh of virtual processors, whereas from a specification point of view, they can express the natural geometry of data structures such as arrays, for example. The set of data fields is supplied with three external operations which either compute values of data fields, or express data dependencies, or redraw the discrete domains underlying data fields. These operations are bricks for a refinement calculus allowing program derivation or transformation. Programs themselves are sets of equations between data fields. Moreover, reduction in PEI is defined as the *inverse* of some operations and the refinements it involves can lead to different reduction or scan functions.

This article aims to emphasize the way transformations can apply to refine, or conversely abstract parallel programs. Some fundamental rules are presented and lead to the definition of transformation strategies. Starting from an initial statement, several programs can be deduced : they can be considered as different implementations of an original function, according to different execution models and to the control and communication primitives they involve. Section 2 recalls the main features of PEI. Section 3 presents the concept of program refinement which is the foundation to transform the programs. Three transformation strategies are then developed in section 4 : a simplification of the communications, the introduction of broadcasts and then of a reduction operator by removing recursion from data field definitions.

2 Definition of Pei

2.1 Specifications and programs

PEI specifies a problem as a relation between *multisets of values*, called its *inputs* and *outputs*. Values of a multiset are supposed to be mapped onto discrete domains and form a *data field*. A specification is expressed as a system of unoriented equations on data fields [1]. It is called a *program* if these equations define a function, i.e. the system has at most one solution.

Example 1. Summation of two matrices

```
MATSUM:(A,B) ↦ C
⎧ A = matrix :: A
⎨ B = matrix :: B
⎩ C = add ▷ (A /&/ B)
matrix=λ(i,j) |(0<=i,j<n)
add    =λ(a·b).(a+b)
```

- the two first equations define the input data fields A and B. They express that A and B are invariant by applying a so-called *change of basis* operation (notation ::). This change of basis is the identity on the square domain $(0<=i,j<n)^2$,

---

[1] PEI means Parallel Equations Interpretor and pays homage to the architect of the Pyramide du Louvre.

[2] Without loss of generality, we assume that any vectorial data structure (vector, matrix, etc.) is expressed by a data field defined on the same geometry. So, the value A[i,j] is mapped on the index (i,j) of the data field A in $\mathbb{Z}^2$.

– the third equation defines the output data field C. The right hand side defines the *superimposition* of A and B (notation /&/), i.e. the set of couples (a·b), with a in A and b in B. The *function* add is applied on every element of the resulting data field (notation ▷).

2.2 Objects and expressions

Basic objects in PEI are data fields and functions. We only need here an intuitive idea about what is a data field : as we said before, it is a set of values mapped onto some discrete domain. In the following A, B, X, etc. denote data fields, whereas f, g, etc. denote functions. The PEI notation for functions is derived from the lambda-calculus : any function f of domain $dom(f) = \{x \,|P(x)\}$ is denoted as $\lambda x \,|(P(x)).f(x)$. Moreover, we denote $\lambda x.f(x)$ for $\lambda x \,|(\text{true}).f(x)$, and $\lambda x \,|(P(x))$ for $\lambda x \,|(P(x)).x$. Last, a function f defined on disjunctive subdomains is denoted as f1 # f2, and the domain of a composed function f ∘ g is $\{x \in dom(g) \,|\, g(x) \in dom(f) \}$.

Expressions are defined by applying operations on data fields. PEI defines one internal operation on the data field set, called *superimposition* : it is denoted as /&/ and builds the sequences of values of its arguments. Three external operations are defined too, and associate a data field with a function :

– *the functional operation*, denoted as ▷ , applies a function f (which may be a partial function) on values of a data field X (notation f ▷ X),
– *the change of basis* (denoted as ::). Let h be a bijection, h :: X defines a data field that maps the values of X onto an other discrete domain,
– *the routing operation*, denoted as ◁ , moves the values of a data field on its domain : the data field X ◁ g is such that its value mapped on some index z, $z \in dom(g)$, "comes from" X at index $g(z)$.

Example 2. A vector rotation

```
SHIFT:A ↦ B
{ A = vector :: A
{ B = A ◁ rotate
vector=λi |(0<=i<n)
rotate=λi.((i-1) mod n)
```

The routing operation has an inverse in PEI. It defines the so-called *geometrical reduction*, denoted as $g \cdot \triangleright X$, which "routes" at index z the sequence (in an arbitrary order) of all the values mapped in X at indices y, such that $y \in dom(g)$ and $g(y) = z$.

Example 3. A global summation
```
GSUM:X ⊢→ S
⎧ X = vector :: X
⎩ S = sum ▷ (reduce · ▷ X)
vector=λi |(0<=i<n)
reduce=λi.(n-1)
```

An equation in PEI expresses that both left and right hand side expressions define the same data field. A program is a set of equations within function definitions. The next section presents the semantical aspects for these constructions.

2.3 Semantics

The semantics of PEI is founded on the notion of discrete domain associated with a multiset. We call *drawing v* of a multiset M of values in V, a partial function from Z^n in V whose image is M. Since several drawings of a given multiset can be deduced one from another by applying a bijection, we define a data field X as the abstraction of any drawing :

Definition 1. A *data field* X is a pair $(v : \sigma)$, composed of a drawing v of a multiset M_X and of a bijection σ such that $dom(v) \subset dom(\sigma)^3$.

This formal definition means that a data field $X = (v : \sigma)$ can be interpreted as the function $[\![X]\!] = v \circ \sigma^{-1}$. External operations in PEI are defined as following :

Definition 2. Let f be a partial function from V to W and $X = (v : \sigma)$ a data field of values in V. The *functional operation* defines the data field $f \triangleright X$ of values in W as the data field $(f \circ v : \sigma)$.

Proposition 3. $[\![f \triangleright X]\!] = f \circ [\![X]\!]$.

Definition 4. Let h be a bijection from $dom(v)$ onto Z^p and $X = (v : \sigma)$ a data field drawn in Z^n. The *change of basis* defines the data field $h::X$ as $(v \circ h^{-1} : \sigma \circ h^{-1})$.

Proposition 5. $[\![h::X]\!] = [\![X]\!]$.

Definition 6. Let g be a partial function from Z^n to $dom(v)$ and $X = (v : \sigma)$ a data field drawn in Z^n. The *routing operation* defines the data field $X \triangleleft g$ as $(v \circ g : \sigma)$.

Proposition 7. $[\![X \triangleleft g]\!] = [\![X]\!] \circ \sigma \circ g \circ \sigma^{-1}$.

To complete this semantical presentation, let us consider the *geometrical reduction*. Let g be a partial function from $dom(v)$ to Z^n and $X = (v : \sigma)$ a data field drawn in Z^n. The geometrical reduction defines $g \cdot \triangleright X$ as some data field $(w : \sigma)$ such that $dom(w) = g(dom(v))$ and $w(z)$ is a sequence of the values $v(y)$, y such that $g(y) = z$.

---

[3] the function $v \circ \sigma^{-1}$ then defines another drawing of M_X.

3 Refinement

Refinement process [Mor90] is a powerful programming concept, that applies to parallelism in Unity [CM88] for example. In PEI, any equation whose arguments are only inputs defines *preconditions* on these input data fields. Any other one, whose arguments may be intermediates or outputs defines *postconditions* on these data fields. Intuitively, we will say that a statement S is refined by a statement S' if any solution of S' is equivalent to a solution of S for some *equivalent* parameters.

Definition 8. Two data fields $X = (v : \sigma)$ and $Y = (v' : \sigma')$ are said to be equivalent (denoted as $X \equiv Y$) if v and v' represent the same multiset of values and $Card(dom(\sigma)) = Card(dom(\sigma'))$.

Definition 9. Let S and S' be two statements. S is said refined by S', denoted as $S \sqsubseteq S'$ (or S abstracts S', denoted S' $\sqsupseteq$ S)[4]

- either if $Pre \Rightarrow Pre' \wedge Post' \Rightarrow Post$, where Pre, Pre' and $Post$, $Post'$ are the predicates associated with pre- and postconditions of S and S',
- or if S is identical to S' by substituting $h :: X$ for all occurrences of X.

These two kinds of refinement, respectively called the *denotational refinement* and the *operational* one, may apply whatever the step in the design of a solution. Since it is monotonic, this refinement definition induces a *refinement calculus* which is founded on the following rules :

$$
\begin{array}{llll}
Y = (f1 \circ f2) \triangleright X & \equiv & Y = f1 \triangleright (f2 \triangleright X) & (1) \\
Y = X \triangleleft (g1 \# g2) & \equiv & Y = (X \triangleleft g1) \;/\&/\; (X \triangleleft g2) & (2) \\
Y = X \triangleleft (g1 \circ g2) & \sqsubseteq & Y = (X \triangleleft g1) \triangleleft g2 & (3) \\
Y = (f \triangleright X) \triangleleft g & \sqsubseteq & Y = f \triangleright (X \triangleleft g) & (4) \\
Y = h :: (X \triangleleft h^{-1} \circ g \circ h) & \sqsubseteq & Y = (h :: X) \triangleleft g & (5) \\
Y = h :: (f \triangleright X) & \sqsubseteq & Y = f \triangleright (h :: X) & (6) \\
Y = (X1 \;/\&/\; X2) \triangleleft g & \equiv & Y = (X1 \triangleleft g) \;/\&/\; (X2 \triangleleft g) & (7) \\
Y = h :: (X1 \;/\&/\; X2) & \equiv & Y = (h :: X1) \;/\&/\; (h :: X2) & (8) \\
Y = (g1 \# g2) \cdot \triangleright X & \sqsubseteq & Y = (g1 \cdot \triangleright X) \;/\&/\; (g2 \cdot \triangleright X) & (9) \\
Y = (g1 \circ g2) \cdot \triangleright X & \sqsubseteq & Y = g1 \cdot \triangleright (g2 \cdot \triangleright X) & (10)
\end{array}
$$

Notice that rule (2) holds provided functions $g1$ and $g2$ are defined on disjunctive sub-domains and rule (5) is an equivalence provided h is bijective on $dom(X)$ which denotes the drawing domain of X. The two last rules associated with the following proposition define transformations of a reduction in some composition of routing operations.

Proposition 10. $g \cdot \triangleright X$ *is equal to* $X \triangleleft g^{-1}$ *if and only if* g *is bijective.*

---

[4] If S and S' refine one each other then $S \equiv S'$.

4 Transformation strategies

The refinement calculus is used to refine the initial specification accordingly to particular issues we want to achieve in the new solution. Conversely, the initial specification can be seen as an *abstract* version of the refined specification. In the following, we present strategic transformations, in one way or the other to reach particular goals such as minimization of data movements, introduction of broadcasts or reduction functions for instance.

These transformations are illustrated by the matrix-vector multiplication problem. First of all we consider a kind of systolic solution (cf. program MATVECT1) in which regular neighbour-to-neighbour communications "schedule" the execution. Assuming the same execution model, the equivalent program MATVECT2 is deduced by simplifying the communications. This last solution allows to abstract a data-parallel solution (cf. program MATVECT3) by discovering a non-recursive definition of the data fields : this new definition yields broadcasts of the original matrix and vector. Assuming such a broadcast primitive is available in the execution model, the schedule of the solution can then be changed and leads to an elegant data-parallel expression (cf. program MATVECT4). This program can then be completed by introducing a step by step summation (cf. program MATVECT5) and then generalized in a global summation through a reduction operator (cf. program MATVECT6).

4.1 Communications simplification

The first transformation technique we describe aims at simplifying routing functions by finding a suitable change of basis which, when applied to equations results in new definitions with simpler communication schemes. The simplification is possible provided that all routing functions are of the general form : $f(p, z) = ((p+az+b) \bmod n, z-1)$ where n is a structure parameter of the problem, the dependency in z is uniform (the argument z could represent the time direction for instance) and the other dependencies are piecewise *quasi-uniform* refering to z. Although these conditions may appear to be strong, this refinement technique addresses a broad class of algorithms.

Definition 11. Let z be an argument of f. Any other argument p of f is said to be *quasi-uniform* refering to z if its dependency is an affine expression of z.

Example Let us consider a first program, which is a systolic version of $p = A \times b$, where b is a vector of length n, initially lying on the diagonal of matrix A. In the first part of the example we will only consider the products computations and we leave to the second part the products summations. At each step k, n computations $p_{i,i} = A_{i,i} \times b_i$ occur on the diagonal. All elements of A are then shifted one position left, the elements of b being moved up-left along the diagonal (all communications are processed toroïdally) before the next computation takes place (see figure 1). In the end we get all the desired products on the diagonal plane $(i = j)$ of the cube.

The algorithm described above is transcribed by the following PEI program : P is defined as being the superimposition of data fields A and B, both recursively defined using routing functions `left` and `upleft` and initial values A0 and B0 defined from data M and V.

```
MATVECT1:(M,V) ↦ P
⎧ M = aligna :: A0
⎪ V = alignb :: B0
⎨ A = A0 /&/ (A ◁ left)
⎪ B = B0 /&/ (B ◁ upleft)
⎩ P = prod ▷ (A ◁ diag /&/ B)
doma=λ(i,j,k) |(0<=i,j<n & k=0)
domb=λ(i,j,k) |(0<=i,j<n & i=j & k=0)
aligna o doma=λ(i,j,k) |(0<=i,j<n & k=0).(i,j)
alignb o domb=λ(i,j,k) |(0<=i,j<n & i=j & k=0).(i)
left   =λ(i,j,k) |(0<k<n & 0<=i,j<n).(i,(j+1) mod n,k-1)
upleft=λ(i,j,k) |(0<k<n & 0<=i,j<n).((i+1) mod n,(j+1) mod n,k-1)
prod  =λ(a·b).(a*b)
diag  =λ(i,j,k) |(0<=i,j<=n & i=j)
```

Routing decomposition Both `left` and `upleft` can be decomposed so that a common routing (bijective) function α appears in the expressions :

```
left   =λ(i,j,k) |(0<=j<n).(i,(j+1) mod n,k) o
        λ(i,j,k) |(0<k<n & 0<=i,j<n).(i,j,k-1)   =α o prev
upleft=λ(i,j,k) |(0<=j<n).(i,(j+1) mod n,k) o
        λ(i,j,k) |(0<=i,j<n).((i+1) mod n,j,k) o
        λ(i,j,k) |(0<k<n & 0<=i,j<n).(i,j,k-1)   =α o up o prev
```

The names given to the new functions we obtain in this decomposition reflect the fact that moving points along the diagonal is equivalent to moving them left and then up. The idea is thus to demonstrate that a program that keeps the matrix A steady while the B vector is moved up is equivalent to the previous program, or in other words that we can simplify the routing functions by removing the α parts from both routing functions. Such a result comes from a general strategy presented hereunder.

Simplification strategy Let us consider the equation A = A0/&/ (A ◁ f) and some change of basis h whose domain contains $dom(A)$. Then, from the rules of the refinement calculus

$$(E1) \qquad \text{A = A0/\&/ (A ◁ f)}$$
$$\equiv \quad \text{h :: A = h::(A0/\&/ (A ◁ f))}$$
$$\equiv \quad \text{h :: A = (h :: A0)/\&/ (h::(A ◁ f))} \qquad (8)$$
$$\equiv \quad \text{h :: A = (h :: A0)/\&/ ((h :: A) ◁ f')} \quad (5 \text{ as } dom(A) \subseteq dom(h))$$
$$(E2) \quad \equiv \quad \text{A' = (h :: A0)/\&/ (A' ◁ f')}$$

where $f' = h \circ f \circ h^{-1}$ and $A' = h::A$

Therefore any bijection satisfying the previous conditions allows to transform $(E1)$ in $(E2)$; we now show a sufficient condition for it exists a particular bijection h such that $f = \alpha \circ f'$.

Theorem 12. *Assume a definition of the form $(E1)$ where $f = \lambda(p,z).((p + az + b) \bmod n, z - 1)$, and let $\alpha = \lambda(p,z)|(0 \le p < n).((p + b') \bmod n, z)$, it then exists a bijection h built from α, such that $(E1)$ can be transformed into an equivalent definition $(E2)$ with f' such that $f = \alpha \circ f'$.*

Proof. Let us consider a set of bijections h_i defined on disjunctive domains varying with z (the uniform argument) and h_i is obtained by recursive compositions of the bijective function $\alpha = \lambda(p,z)|(0 \le p < n).((p + b') \bmod n, z)$ with itself such that $h_i = \lambda(p,z)|(z = i).\alpha^i(p,z)$. We thus have

$$h_1 = \lambda(p,z)|(z = 1 \wedge 0 \le p < n).((p + b') \bmod n, z)$$
$$= \lambda(p,z)|(z = 1 \wedge 0 \le p < n).((p + zb') \bmod n, z)$$
$$h_2 = \lambda(p,z)|(z = 2 \wedge 0 \le p < n).((p + 2b') \bmod n, z)$$
$$= \lambda(p,z)|(z = 2 \wedge 0 \le p < n).((p + zb') \bmod n, z)$$
$$\vdots$$
$$h_r = \lambda(p,z)|(z = r \wedge 0 \le p < n).((p + rb') \bmod n, z)$$
$$= \lambda(p,z)|(z = r \wedge 0 \le p < n).((p + zb') \bmod n, z)$$

Let $h = h_1 \# h_2 \# \ldots \# h_r$. As $z \in [1 \ldots r]$, we find that $h = \lambda(p,z)|(0 \le p < n).((p + zb') \bmod n, z)$ which is a bijection. Given

$$f = \lambda(p,z).((p + az + b) \bmod n, z - 1)$$
$$\alpha = \lambda(p,z)|(0 \le p < n).((p + b') \bmod n, z)$$
$$f' = \lambda(p,z).((p + az + b - b') \bmod n, z - 1)$$

we have $f = \alpha \circ f'$, and h is a change of basis such that

$$h \circ f \circ h^{-1}$$
$$= h \circ \lambda(p,z).((p + az + b) \bmod n, z - 1) \circ \lambda(p,z).((p - zb') \bmod n, z)$$
$$= h \circ \lambda(p,z).((p - zb' + az + b) \bmod n, z - 1)$$
$$= \lambda(p,z).((p + zb') \bmod n, z) \circ \lambda(p,z).((p - zb' + az + b) \bmod n, z - 1)$$
$$= \lambda(p,z).((p + az + b - b') \bmod n, z - 1)$$
$$= f'$$

□

Example (continued) In order to apply the previous strategy and find a new program with simplified routing functions we search h as shown previously. Since in our example $\alpha = \lambda(i,j,k)|(0 \le j < n).(i, (j + 1) \bmod n, k)$ then we deduce $h = \lambda(i,j,k)|(0 \le j < n).(i, (j + k) \bmod n, k)$. Note that theorem 12 fully applies on MATVECT1 since $dom(A)$, $dom(B)$ and $dom(P) \subseteq dom(h)$, and h :: A0 reduces to A0 and h :: B0 reduces to B0. We thus get the following MATVECT2 program:

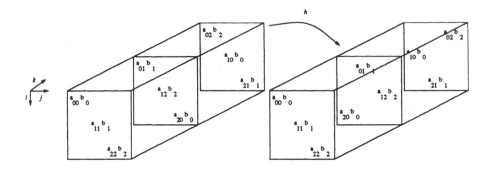

Fig. 1. Transformation of `MATVECT1` in `MATVECT2` for $n = 3$

```
MATVECT2:(M,V) ↦ P'
  M = aligna :: A0
  V = alignb :: B0
  A' = A0 /&/ (A' ⊲ prev)
  B' = B0 /&/ (B' ⊲ up o prev)
  P' = prod ▷ (A' ⊲ diag' /&/ B')
prev  = λ(i,j,k) |(0<k<n & 0<=i,j<n).(i,j,k-1)
up    = λ(i,j,k) |(0<=i,j<n).((i+1) mod n,j,k)
diag' = λ(i,j,k) |(i=(j+k) mod n)
```

4.2   Removing recursion from data fields definition

The previous program is a typical systolic program since all its routing functions
are point-to-point communications. If we assume a broadcasting communication
operator is available the communications can be rewritten in a data-parallel style.
The relationship between recursive definitions of data fields and broadcasting can
be stated as follows :

Theorem 13. *Let g be a function defined by the recursion* $g = i \# g \circ s$, *where
i is the identity and s a function. The* PEI *equation* Y = X ⊲ g *is refined by the
following recursive definition of* Y : $\quad$ Y = X ⊲ i /&/ Y ⊲ s

Proof. From rules of the refinement calculus :
$$
\begin{aligned}
&\text{Y} = \text{X} \lhd g \\
\equiv\ &\text{Y} = \text{X} \lhd (i \# g \circ s) \\
\sqsubseteq\ &\text{Y} = \text{X} \lhd i \text{ /\&/ } \text{X} \lhd (g \circ s) &&(rule\ 2) \\
\sqsubseteq\ &\text{Y} = \text{X} \lhd i \text{ /\&/ } (\text{X} \lhd g) \lhd s &&(rule\ 3) \\
\equiv\ &\text{Y} = \text{X} \lhd i \text{ /\&/ } \text{Y} \lhd s
\end{aligned}
$$
□

This is the only clue we need to write another program `MATVECT3` refined by
the `MATVECT2` program. Note that the new program uses broadcasting of data,
which is a main feature of the data-parallel paradigm.

```
MATVECT3:(M,V) ↦ P'
⎧ M = aligna :: A0
⎪ V = alignb :: B0
⎨ A' = A0 ◁ spreada
⎪ B' = B0 ◁ spreadb
⎩ P' = prod ▷ (A' ◁ diag' /&/ B')
spreada = λ(i,j,k) |(0<=k<n).(i,j,0)
spreadb = λ(i,j,k) |(0<=k<n & 0<=i<n).((i+k) mod n,j,0)
```

Proof. From theorem 13, the last statement is obtained by writing functions
spreada and **spreadb** in the following way :

```
spreada = λ(i,j,k) |(0<=k<n).(i,j,0)
        = λ(i,j,k) |(k=0) # λ(i,j,k) |(0<k<n).(i,j,0)
        = λ(i,j,k) |(k=0) # λ(i,j,k) |(0<=k<n).(i,j,0)
        o λ(i,j,k) |(0<k<n).(i,j,k-1)
        = i # spreada o prev
spreadb = λ(i,j,k) |(0<=k<n & 0<=i<n).((i+k) mod n,j,0)
        = λ(i,j,k) |(k=0 & 0<=i<n).((i+k) mod n,j,0) #
          λ(i,j,k) |(0<k<n & 0<=i<n).((i+k) mod n,j,0)
        = λ(i,j,k) |(k=0 & 0<=i<n) #
          λ(i,j,k) |(0<=k<n & 0<=i<n).((i+k) mod n,j,0)
        o λ(i,j,k) |(0<=i<n).((i+1) mod n,j,k-1)
        = i # spreadb o up o prev
```

□

From definition of data field **P'**, we come to the conclusion that products
are only defined on the diagonal plane of the cube and that these results could
be packed in a two-dimensional data field. The transformation is formally described by applying an appropriate change of basis h such that h o **diag'** =
λ(i,j,k) |(i=(j+k) mod n).(i,j). Definition of **P'** becomes :

```
h :: P' = prod ▷ (h :: (A' ◁ diag') /&/ h :: B')
```

If we let A''= h :: (A' ◁ diag'), B''= h::B'
then   A'' = h :: ((A0 ◁ spreada) ◁ diag')
        ⊒ A'' = h :: (A0 ◁ spreada o diag')   (3)
        ≡ A'' = (h :: A0) ◁ h o spreada o diag' o h⁻¹ (5)
        ≡ A'' = M ◁ λ(i,j) |(0<=i,j <n) = M
and   B'' = h :: B'
        ≡ B'' = h :: (B0 ◁ spreadb)
        ≡ B'' = (h :: B0) ◁ h o spreadb o h⁻¹   (5)
        ≡ B'' = (h :: B0) ◁ λ(i,j) |(0<=i,j<n).(j,j)

If we rename V' = h :: B0 and P'' = h :: P' then we get the abstract version :

MATVECT4 : $(M,V') \mapsto P''$
$$\begin{cases} A'' = M \\ B'' = V' \lhd \text{spreab'} \\ P'' = \text{prod} \rhd (A'' / \& / B'') \end{cases}$$
spreadb' $= \lambda(i,j) \,|\, (0{<}{=}i,j{<}n) . (j,j)$

4.3 Introduction of a reduction operator

We have only focused so far on the first phase of the algorithm, and we shall now complete the previous program with the summation of products. Once again it is a "systolic" version where we explicitly describe the communication path for the points to be added, to eventually reach a "data-parallel" version in which a reduction operator is used.

MATVECT5 : $(M,V) \mapsto R$
$$\begin{cases} A = M \\ B = V \lhd \text{spreadb'} \\ P = \text{prod} \rhd (A / \& / B) \\ S = P / \& / S \lhd \text{pre} \\ R = \text{sum} \rhd (S \lhd \text{last}) \end{cases}$$
pre $= \lambda(i,j) \,|\, (0{<}{=}i{<}n \ \& \ 0{<}j{<}n) . (i,j{-}1)$
last $= \lambda(i,j) \,|\, (0{<}{=}i{<}n \ \& \ j{=}n{-}1)$
sum $= \text{id} \ \# \ \lambda(a{\cdot}b) . (a{+}\text{sum}(b))$

Note that the field S is the result of an operator called *scan* in the data-parallel style. As previously, the recursive definition of S in the last statement can be abstracted to a non-recursive one (from theorem 14).

Theorem 14. *Let f be a function defined by the recursion $f = i \# f \circ s^{-1}$, where i is the identity and s is bijective. The PEI equation $Y = f \cdot \rhd X$ is refined by the following statement, which involves the recursive definition of an intermediate data field T :* $\quad T = X \ / \& / \ T \lhd s$
$\qquad\qquad\qquad\qquad\qquad\qquad Y = T \lhd i$

Proof. From rules of the refinement calculus:
$Y = f \cdot \rhd X$
$\equiv Y = (i \# f \circ s^{-1}) \cdot \rhd X$
$\sqsubseteq Y = i \cdot \rhd X / \& / (f \circ s^{-1}) \cdot \rhd X$ $\qquad\qquad$ (*rule* 9)
$\sqsubseteq Y = i \cdot \rhd X / \& / f \cdot \rhd (s^{-1} \cdot \rhd X)$ $\qquad\qquad$ (*rule* 10)
$\equiv Y = X \lhd i / \& / f \cdot \rhd (X \lhd s)$ $\qquad\qquad$ (*proposition* 10)
$\sqsubseteq Y = X \lhd i / \& / (X \lhd s) \lhd i / \& / f \cdot \rhd ((X \lhd s) \lhd s)$
$\equiv Y = T \lhd i$

□

It leads to the following statement expressing a reduction in the data-parallel programming model:

$$\text{MATVECT6}:(\text{M},\text{V}) \mapsto \text{R}$$

$$\begin{cases} \text{A} = \text{M} \\ \text{B} = \text{V} \lhd \text{spreadb'} \\ \text{P} = \text{prod} \rhd (\text{A} /\&/ \text{B}) \\ \text{R} = \text{sum} \rhd (\text{red} \cdot \rhd \text{P}) \end{cases}$$

$$\text{red} = \lambda(\text{i},\text{j}) \mid (0<=\text{i},\text{j}<n).(\text{i},\text{n}-1)$$

Proof. From theorem 14, function **red** can be rewritten as :

$$\text{red} = \lambda(\text{i},\text{j}) \mid (0<=\text{i},\text{j}<n).(\text{i},\text{n}-1)$$
$$= \lambda(\text{i},\text{j}) \mid (0<=\text{i}<n \ \& \ \text{j}=n-1).(\text{i},\text{n}-1) \ \#$$
$$\lambda(\text{i},\text{j}) \mid (0<=\text{i},\text{j}<n \ \& \ \text{j}<n-1).(\text{i},\text{n}-1)$$
$$= \text{last} \ \# \ \text{red} \ o \ \lambda(\text{i},\text{j}) \mid (0<=\text{i},\text{j}<n \ \& \ \text{j}<n-1).(\text{i},\text{j}+1)$$
$$= \text{last} \ \# \ \text{red} \ o \ \lambda(\text{i},\text{j}) \mid (0<=\text{i},\text{j}<n).(\text{i},\text{j}-1)^{-1}$$
$$= \text{last} \ \# \ \text{red} \ o \ \text{pre}^{-1}$$

□

5 Conclusion

This article was an attempt to use a refinement calculus and its reverse abstraction to transform programs within some target constraints of the execution model. Examples of such transformations were developed in this article, all founded on routing operations rewriting. Note that abstraction might be seen as a *reverse engineering* method to prove the correctness of refined programs since the most abstract version is the closest from the specification. PEI offers a convenient foundation for all these concepts because it enables these formal transformations. Further work could consist in the implementation of these strategies and would benefit from recent work like reduction detection([Red95]).

References

[BL92] L. Bougé and J.-L. Levaire. Control structures for data-parallel SIMD languages: semantics and implementation. *FGCS*, 8:363–378, 1992.

[CCL91] M. Chen, Y. Choo, and J. Li. *Parallel Functional Languages and Compilers*. Frontier Series. ACM Press, 1991. Chapter 7.

[CM88] K.M. Chandy and J. Misra. *Parallel Program Design :* A foundation. Addison Wesley, 1988.

[Len93] Christian Lengauer. Loop parallelization in the polytope model. June 1993.

[Mau89] C. Mauras. ALPHA : *un langage équationnel pour la conception et la programmation d'architectures parallèles synchrones*. PhD thesis, U. Rennes, 1989.

[Mor90] C. Morgan. *Programming from specifications*. C.A.R. Hoare. Prentice Hall Ed., Endlewood Cliffs, N.J., 1990.

[Red95] Xavier Redon. *Détection et exploitation des récurrences dans les programmes scientifiques en vue de leur parallélisation*. PhD thesis, U. Paris 6, Jan 1995.

[Vio94] E. Violard. A mathematical theory and its environment for parallel programming. *Parallel Processing Letters*, 4(3):313–328, 1994.

[VP94] E. Violard and G.-R. Perrin. Reduction in PEI. *CONPAR'94, LNCS*, 1994.

On the completeness of a proof system for a simple data-parallel programming language (extended abstract)*

Luc Bougé **, David Cachera

LIP, ENS Lyon, 46 Allée d'Italie, F–69364 Lyon Cédex 07, France

Abstract. We prove the completeness of an assertional proof system for a simple loop-free data-parallel language. This proof system is based on two-part assertions, where the predicate on the current value of variables is separated from the specification of the current extent of parallelism. The proof is based on a Weakest Precondition (WP) calculus. In contrast with the case of usual scalar languages, not all WP can be defined by an assertion. Yet, partial definability suffices to prove the completeness thanks to the introduction of hidden variables in assertions. The case of data-parallel programs with loops is briefly discussed in the conclusion.

Keywords: Concurrent Programming; Specifying and Verifying and Reasoning about Programs; Semantics of Programming Languages; Data-Parallel Languages; Proof System; Hoare Logic; Weakest Preconditions.

1 Introduction

The development of massively parallel computing in the last two decades has called for the elaboration of a parallel programming model. The data-parallel programming model has proven to be a good framework, since it allows the easy development of applications portable across a wide variety of parallel architectures. The increasing role of this model requires appropriate theoretical foundations. These foundations are crucial to design safe and optimized compilers, and programming environments including parallelizing, data-distributing and debugging tools. They are also the way to safe programming techniques, so as to avoid the common waste of time and money spent in debugging.

Existing data-parallel languages, such as HPF, C*, HYPERC or MPL, include a similar core of data-parallel control structures. In previous papers, we have shown that it is possible to define a simple but representative data-parallel kernel language (the $\mathcal{L}$ language), to give it a formal operational [5] and denotational semantics [4], and to define a proof system for this language, in the style of the usual Hoare's logic approach [10, 4]. The originality of our approach lies in the treatment of the *extent of parallelism*, that is, the subset of currently active

---

* The full version of this paper can be found in [2].

** Authors contact: Luc Bougé (Luc.Bouge@lip.ens-lyon.fr). This work has been partly supported by the French CNRS Research Program on Parallelism, Networks and Systems(PRS).

indices at which a vector instruction is to be applied. Previous approaches led to manipulate lists of indices explicitly [6, 11], or to consider context expressions as assertions modifiers [8]. In contrast, our proof system for $\mathcal{L}$ describes the activity context by a vector boolean expression distinct from the usual predicates on program variables.

We have shown that our proof system for $\mathcal{L}$ is *sound*, that is, any provable property of a program is actually valid. In this paper, we address the converse *completeness* problem: *Can any valid property of a program be proved in our system?* In some sense, completeness guarantees that the rules of a proof system actually catch all the semantic expressiveness of the language under study.

The completeness of proof systems for scalar Pascal-like languages has been extensively studied [1]. In attacking such a problem, the main tool is the *weakest preconditions calculus*. This notion has been introduced by Dijkstra [7]. It plays a central role in the formal validation of scalar programs, as shown in [9] for instance. The case of data-parallel programs is much more complex than the case of scalar programs, as one has to cope *both* with the variable values and with the manipulations of the activity context. Yet, we have shown in [3] that it is possible to define a weakest preconditions calculus for $\mathcal{L}$, at least for loop-free (so-called straight-line or *linear*) programs.

The contribution of this paper is to apply these results to prove the completeness of our proof system for *all linear* programs. We proceed as follows. We first present the $\mathcal{L}$ language, and give its denotational semantics. We describe a sound assertional proof system for this language, as defined in [4], and its weakest preconditions calculus as described in [3]. Then, we prove the completeness of the proof system in a restricted case: *plain* specifications formulae and *regular* programs. To handle non-regular programs, we extend the proof system with an additional rule. It enables to introduce and eliminate auxiliary *hidden* variables in assertions. We prove that this extended proof system is complete for linear programs without any restriction.

2 The $\mathcal{L}$ Language

An extensive presentation of the $\mathcal{L}$ language can be found in [5]. For the sake of completeness (if we dare say so!), we briefly recall its denotational semantics as described in [3].

2.1 Informal Description

In the data-parallel programming model, the basic objects are arrays with parallel access. Two kinds of actions can be applied to these objects: *component-wise* operations, or global *rearrangements*. A program is a sequential composition of such actions. Each action is associated with the set of array indices at which it is applied. An index at which an action is applied is said to be *active*. Other indices are said to be *idle*. The set of active indices is called the *activity context*. It can be seen as a boolean array where *true* denotes activity and *false* idleness.

The $\mathcal{L}$ language is designed as a common kernel of data-parallel languages like C*, HYPERC or MPL. We do not consider the scalar part of these languages, mainly imported from the C language. For the sake of simplicity, we consider a unique geometry of arrays: arrays of dimension one, also called *vectors*. Then, all the variables of $\mathcal{L}$ are parallel, and all the objects are vectors of scalars, with one component at each index. As a convention, the parallel objects are denoted with uppercase letters. The component of parallel object X located at index u is denoted by $X|_u$. The legal expressions are usual *pure* expressions: the value of a pure expression at index u only depends on the values of the variables components at index u. The expressions are evaluated by applying operators *component-wise* to parallel values. We do not specify the syntax and semantics of such expressions any further. A particular vector expression is called *This*. The value of its component at each index u is the value u itself: $\forall u : This|_u = u$. Note that *This* is a pure expression and that all constructs defined here are *deterministic*. The set of $\mathcal{L}$-instructions is the following.

Assignment: $X:=E$. At each active index u, component $X|_u$ is updated with the local value of *pure* expression E.

Communication: get X from A into Y. At each active index u, *pure* expression A is evaluated to an index v, then component $Y|_u$ is updated with the value of component $X|_v$. We always assume that v is a valid index.

Sequencing: $S;T$. On the termination of the last action of S, the execution of the actions of T starts.

Iteration: loop B **do** S. The actions of S are repeatedly executed with the current extent of parallelism, until *pure* boolean expression B evaluates to false at each currently active index. The current activity context is not modified.

Conditioning: where B **do** S. The active indices where *pure* boolean expression B evaluates to false become idle during the execution of S. The other ones remain active. The initial activity context is restored on the termination of S.

2.2 Denotational Semantics of $\mathcal{L}$

We recall the semantics of $\mathcal{L}$ defined in [3] in the style of denotational semantics, by induction on the syntax of $\mathcal{L}$.

An *environment* σ is a function from identifiers to vector values. The set of environments is denoted by Env. For convenience, we extend the environment functions to the parallel expressions: $\sigma(E)$ denotes the value obtained by evaluating parallel expression E in environment σ. We do not detail the internals of expressions any further. Note that $\sigma(This)|_u = u$ by definition.

Definition 1 (Pure expression). A parallel expression E is *pure* if for any index u, and any environments σ and σ',

$$(\forall X : \sigma(X)|_u = \sigma'(X)|_u) \Rightarrow (\sigma(E)|_u = \sigma'(E)|_u).$$

Let σ be an environment, X a vector variable and V a vector value. We denote by $\sigma[X \leftarrow V]$ the new environment σ' where $\sigma'(X) = V$ and $\sigma'(Y) = \sigma(Y)$ for all $Y \neq X$.

A *context* c is a boolean vector. It specifies the activity at each index. The set of contexts is denoted by Ctx. We distinguish a particular context denoted by *True* where all components have value *true*. The context *False* is defined the same way. For convenience, we define the activity predicate $Active_c$: $Active_c(u) \equiv c|_u$.

A *state* is a pair made of an environment and a context. The set of states is denoted by *State*: $State = (Env \times Ctx) \cup \{\perp\}$ where $\perp$ denotes the undefined state. The semantics $[S]$ of a program S is a *strict* function from *State* to *State*. $[S](\perp) = \perp$, and $[S]$ is extended to sets of states as usual.

Assignment: At each active index, the component of the parallel variable is updated with the new value.

$$[X{:=}E](\sigma, c) = (\sigma', c),$$

with $\sigma' = \sigma[X \leftarrow V]$ where $V|_u = \sigma(E)|_u$ if $Active_c(u)$, and $V|_u = \sigma(X)|_u$ otherwise. The activity context is preserved.

Communication: It acts very much as an assignment, except that the assigned value is the value of another component.

$$[\text{get } X \text{ from } A \text{ into } Y](\sigma, c) = (\sigma', c)$$

with $\sigma' = \sigma[Y \leftarrow V]$ where $V|_u = \sigma(X)|_{\sigma(A)|_u}$ if $Active_c(u)$, and $V|_u = \sigma(Y)|_u$ otherwise.

Sequencing: Sequential composition is functional composition.

$$[S;T](\sigma, c) = [T]([S](\sigma, c)).$$

Iteration: Iteration is expressed by classical loop unfolding. It terminates when the *pure* boolean expression B evaluates to false at each active index.

$$[\text{loop } B \text{ do } S](\sigma, c) = \begin{cases} [\text{loop } B \text{ do } S]([S](\sigma, c)) \\ \qquad \text{if } \exists u : (Active_c(u) \wedge \sigma(B)|_u) \\ (\sigma, c) \quad \text{otherwise} \end{cases}$$

If the unfolding does not terminate, then we take the usual convention: $[\text{loop } B \text{ do } S](\sigma, c) = \perp$.

Conditioning: The denotation of a **where** construct is the denotation of its body with a new context. The new context is the conjunction of the previous one with the value of the pure conditioning expression B.

$$[\text{where } B \text{ do } S](\sigma, c) = (\sigma', c)$$

with $[S](\sigma, c \wedge \sigma(B)) = (\sigma', c')$.

If $[S](\sigma, c \wedge \sigma(B)) = \perp$, then we put $[\text{where } B \text{ do } S](\sigma, c) = \perp$. Observe that the value of c' is ignored here.

3 A Sound Assertional Proof System for the $\mathcal{L}$ Language

3.1 Assertion Language

We define an *assertion language* for the correctness of $\mathcal{L}$ programs in the lines of [1]. Such a specification is denoted by a formula $\{P\} \; S \; \{Q\}$ where S is the program text, and P and Q are two logical assertions on the variables of S. This formula means that, if precondition P is satisfied in the initial state of program S, and if S terminates, then postcondition Q is satisfied in the final state. A proof system gives a formal method to derive such specification formulae by syntax-directed induction on programs.

We recall below the proof system described in [3]. As in the usual sequential case, the assertion language must be powerful enough to express properties on variable values. Moreover, it has to handle the evolution of the activity context along the execution. An assertion shall thus be broken up into two parts: $\{P, C\}$, where P is a predicate on program variables, and C a pure boolean vector expression. The intuition is that the current activity context is exactly the value of C in the current state, as expressed in the definition below.

Definition 2 (Satisfiability). Let (σ, c) be a state, and $\{P, C\}$ an assertion. We say that (σ, c) *satisfies* the assertion $\{P, C\}$, denoted by $(\sigma, c) \models \{P, C\}$, if $\sigma \models P$ and $\sigma(C) = c$. By convention, $\perp$ satisfies any assertion. The set of states satisfying $\{P, C\}$ is denoted by $[\![\{P, C\}]\!]$. When no confusion may arise, we identify $\{P, C\}$ and $[\![\{P, C\}]\!]$.

Observe that there are many sets of states which cannot be described by any assertion. This is in strong contrast with the case of scalar Pascal-like languages.

Lemma 3 (Restricted power of assertions). Let $\{P, C\}$ an assertion. For any environment σ, there exists at most one activity context c such that $(\sigma, c) \in [\![\{P, C\}]\!]$, namely $c = \sigma(C)$.

So, if a set of states contains two states (σ, c) and (σ, c') with $c \neq c'$, then it cannot be described by any assertion.

Definition 4 (Assertion implication). Let $\{P, C\}$ and $\{Q, D\}$ be two assertions. We say that $\{P, C\}$ implies $\{Q, D\}$, and write $\{P, C\} \Rightarrow \{Q, D\}$, iff
$$(P \Rightarrow Q) \qquad \text{and} \qquad (P \Rightarrow \forall u : (C|_u = D|_u))$$

Proposition 5. Let $\{P, C\}$ and $\{Q, D\}$ be two assertions. Then
$$\{P, C\} \Rightarrow \{Q, D\} \quad \text{iff} \quad [\![\{P, C\}]\!] \subseteq [\![\{Q, D\}]\!]$$

Our assertion language manipulates two kinds of variables, *scalar* variables and *vector* variables. As a convention, scalar variables are denoted with a lowercase initial letter, and vector ones with an uppercase one. We have a similar distinction on arithmetic and logical expressions. As usual, scalar (resp. vector) expressions are recursively defined with usual arithmetic and logical connectives. Basic scalar (resp. vector) expressions are scalar (resp. vector) variables and constants. Vector expression can be subscripted. If the subscript expression is a scalar expression, then we have a scalar expression. Otherwise, if the subscript expression is a vector expression, then we have another vector expression. The meaning of a vector expression is obtained by component-wise evaluation. We introduce a scalar conditional expression with a C-like notation $c?e : f$. Its value is the value of expression e if c is true, and f otherwise. Similarly, the value of a conditional vector expression, denoted by $C?E : F$, is a vector whose component at index u is $E|_u$ if $C|_u$ is true, and $F|_u$ otherwise.

Predicates are usual first order formulae. They are recursively defined on boolean scalar expressions with logical connectives and existential and universal quantifiers on scalar variables. Note that we do not consider quantification on vector variables.

We introduce a substitution mechanism for vector variables. Let P be a predicate or any vector expression, X a vector variable, and E a vector expression. $P[E/X]$ denotes the predicate, or expression, obtained by substituting all the occurrences of X in P with E. Note that all vector variables are free by definition of our assertion language. The usual Substitution Lemma [1] extends to this new setting.

Lemma 6 (Substitution Lemma). *For every predicate on vector variables* P, *vector expression* E *and environment* σ,

$$\sigma \models P[E/X] \quad \text{iff} \quad \sigma[X \leftarrow \sigma(E)] \models P$$

We can define the validity of a specification of a $\mathcal{L}$ program with respect to its denotational semantics.

Definition 7 (Specification validity). Let S be a $\mathcal{L}$ program, $\{P,C\}$ and $\{Q,D\}$ two assertions. We say that specification $\{P,C\}$ S $\{Q,D\}$ is valid, denoted by $\models \{P,C\}$ S $\{Q,D\}$, if for all states (σ,c)

$$((\sigma,c) \models \{P,C\}) \Rightarrow (\llbracket S \rrbracket(\sigma,c) \models \{Q,D\}).$$

Since $\bot$ satisfies any assertion, validity is relative to partial correctness.

3.2 Proof System

We recall on Fig. 1 the proof system defined in [3]. This system is a restricted proof system, in the sense that it only manipulates a certain kind of specification formulae, precisely these formulae $\{P,C\}$ S $\{Q,D\}$ such that the boolean vector expression D describing the final activity context may not be modified by the program S. More formally, using the notations of [1], we define the following sets of variables.

Definition 8. Let E be an expression. $Var(E)$ is the set of all variables appearing in E. Expression E may only depend on the values of these variables. We extend this definition to a $\mathcal{L}$-program S: $Var(S)$ is the set of all variables appearing in S.

Let S be a $\mathcal{L}$-program. $Change(S)$ is the set of program variables which appear on the left-hand side of an assignment statement or as the target of a communication statement. Only these variables may be modified by executing S.

A sufficient condition to guarantee the absence of interference between S and D is thus $Change(S) \cap Var(D) = \emptyset$. If a specification formula $\{P,C\}$ S $\{Q,D\}$ is derivable in the proof system, then we write $\vdash \{P,C\}$ S $\{Q,D\}$.

Theorem 9 (Soundness of $\vdash$ [4]). *The $\vdash$ proof system is sound: If $\vdash \{P,C\}$ S $\{Q,D\}$, then $\models \{P,C\}$ S $\{Q,D\}$.*

The contribution of this paper is to address the converse problem:

Is any valid specification provable? Does $\models \{P,C\}$ S $\{Q,D\}$ imply $\vdash \{P,C\}$ S $\{Q,D\}$?

In the case of scalar programs, the completeness of the proof systems for loop-free (so-called *linear*) programs is a not-so-difficult consequence of the existence of a weakest preconditions calculus. In contrast, studying the completeness with respect to programs including loops requires sophisticated methods. Indeed, this is tightly connected to the expressivity of the underlying logic.

In the case of data-parallel programs, even the simplest case of loop-free programs is already non-trivial. In this paper, we therefore restrict ourselves to this case. The case of loops is discussed in the conclusion.

Definition 10 (Linear $\mathcal{L}$-programs). A data-parallel $\mathcal{L}$-program S is *linear* if it is made of assignments, communications, sequencing and conditioning only.

Assignment Rule	$$\dfrac{X \notin Var(D)}{\{Q[(D?E:X)/X],D\}\ X{:=}E\ \{Q,D\}}$$
Communication Rule	$$\dfrac{Y \notin Var(D)}{\{Q[(D?X|_A : Y)/Y],D\}\ \text{get } X \text{ from } A \text{ into } Y\ \{Q,D\}}$$
Sequencing Rule	$$\dfrac{\{P,C\}\ S\ \{R,E\},\ \{R,E\}\ T\ \{Q,D\}}{\{P,C\}\ S;T\ \{Q,D\}}$$
Conditioning Rule	$$\dfrac{\{P,C \wedge B\}\ S\ \{Q,D\},\ Change(S) \cap Var(C) = \emptyset}{\{P,C\}\ \text{where } B \text{ do } S\ \{Q,C\}}$$
Consequence Rule	$$\dfrac{\{P,C\} \Rightarrow \{P',C'\},\ \{P',C'\}\ S\ \{Q',D'\},\ \{Q',D'\} \Rightarrow \{Q,D\}}{\{P,C\}\ S\ \{Q,D\}}$$
Iteration Rule	$$\dfrac{\{I \wedge \exists u : (C|_u \wedge B|_u),C\}\ S\ \{I,C\}}{\{I,C\}\ \text{loop } B \text{ do } S\ \{I \wedge \forall u : (C|_u \Rightarrow \neg B|_u),C\}}$$

Fig. 1. The $\vdash$ proof system for $\mathcal{L}$

4 Completeness of the Proof System for Plain Specifications and Regular, Linear Programs

4.1 Weakest Preconditions Calculus

Our main tool to prove the completeness of our system is a weakest preconditions calculus. This calculus has been presented in [3], and we briefly recall the main results below. Let us first motivate its use. We want to demonstrate that

$$\models \{P,C\}\ S\ \{Q,D\} \quad \Rightarrow \quad \vdash \{P,C\}\ S\ \{Q,D\}.$$

Let $\{P,C\}\ S\ \{Q,D\}$ be a valid specification formula. Assume for a while that we can find an assertion $\{P',C'\}$ such that $\vdash \{P',C'\}\ S\ \{Q,D\}$ holds, and moreover $\{P,C\} \Rightarrow \{P',C'\}$. Then, using the Consequence Rule, we have demonstrated

$$\vdash \{P,C\}\ S\ \{Q,D\}.$$

Definition 11 (Weakest preconditions). Let S be a linear $\mathcal{L}$-program and $\{Q,D\}$ an assertion. We define the *weakest preconditions* as

$$wp(S,\{Q,D\}) = \{s \in State \mid [\![S]\!](s) \models \{Q,D\}\}$$

Observe that

$$\models \{P,C\}\ S\ \{Q,D\} \quad \Leftrightarrow \quad [\![\{P,C\}]\!] \subseteq wp(S,\{Q,D\}).$$

As we have restricted ourselves to linear programs, observe that we do not need to take into account problems of divergence.

We have shown in a previous paper [3] that the set of states $wp(S,\{Q,D\})$ cannot generally be described by some assertion $\{P,C\}$ and thus be manipulated in the proof system. It is only the case when certain syntactic non-interference conditions on S and D are satisfied. These conditions are summed up in the following definitions.

Definition 12 (Plain specification). A specification formula $\{P, C\}\, S\, \{Q, D\}$ is said to be *plain* if we have $Var(D) \cap Change(S) = \emptyset$.

Definition 13 (Regular program). A program P is *regular* if, for any subprogram of P of the form **where** B **do** S, we have $Var(B) \cap Change(S) = \emptyset$.

Observe that any subprogram of a regular program is regular, too. The detailed definability results are listed up on Fig. 2. In spite of the restrictions, they are sufficient to guarantee the following property.

Proposition 14 (Restricted definability of wp for regular programs [3]). Let S be a regular, linear $\mathcal{L}$-program, and let $\{\ldots\}\, S\, \{Q, D\}$ be a plain specification for S. Then there exists an assertion $\{P, D\}$ such that $[\{P, D\}] = wp(S, \{Q, D\})$ In particular, $\models \{P, D\}\, S\, \{Q, D\}$.

Construct	Conditions	Weakest Precondition
Assignment	$X \notin Var(D)$	$wp(X := E, \{Q, D\})$ $= \{Q[(D?E : X)/X], D\}$
Communication	$Y \notin Var(D)$	$wp(\text{get } X \text{ from } A \text{ into } Y, \{Q, D\})$ $= \{Q[(D?X|_A : Y)/Y], D\}$
Sequencing	—	$wp(S_1; S_2, \{Q, D\})$ $= wp(S_1, wp(S_2, \{Q, D\}))$
Conditioning	$(Var(D) \cup Var(B)) \cap Change(S)$ $= \emptyset$ $wp(S, \{Q, D \wedge B\}) = \{P, C\}$	$wp(\text{where } B \text{ do } S \text{ end}, \{Q, D\})$ $= \{P, D\}$

Fig. 2. Definability properties of weakest preconditions for regular, linear $\mathcal{L}$-programs

4.2 Proving the Restricted Completeness

We now want to establish the completeness for the proof system described on Fig. 1. As it concerns plain specifications and regular programs, we call it *restricted* completeness. More formally, we aim at proving the following theorem.

Theorem 15 (Restr. compl., plain specif., regular, linear progr.). Let $\{P, C\}\, S\, \{Q, D\}$ be a plain specification, with S a regular, linear program.
$$\text{If } \models \{P, C\}\, S\, \{Q, D\}, \quad \text{then } \vdash \{P, C\}\, S\, \{Q, D\}.$$

Proof. The proof of this theorem follows the lines of [1]. It uses the weakest preconditions calculus. For any regular, linear program S and any plain specification $\{P, C\}\, S\, \{Q, D\}$, there exists some assertion $\{P', C'\}$ such that

$[\{P', C'\}] = wp(S, \{Q, D\})$. Using the Consequence Rule, it suffices to demonstrate that

$$\vdash wp(S, \{Q, D\})\ S\ \{Q, D\}.$$

The proof is by induction on the structure of the regular, linear program S, using the definability properties of Fig. 2.

The cases of the assignment, communication, and sequencing constructs are straightforward. Let us consider the case of the conditioning construct, with $S \equiv$ where B do T. As S is regular by hypothesis, we have $Change(T) \cap Var(B) = \emptyset$. As the specification is plain, we have $Change(S) \cap Var(D) = \emptyset$. As $Change(T) = Change(S)$, we also have $Change(T) \cap Var(D) = \emptyset$. The Definability Property 14 yields an assertion $\{P, D \wedge B\}$ such that $\{P, D \wedge B\} = wp(T, \{Q, D \wedge B\})$.

Program T is regular and linear as S is so. Specification $\{P, D \wedge B\}\ T\ \{Q, D \wedge B\}$ is plain.

Thus, the induction hypothesis yields $\vdash \{P, D \wedge B\}\ T\ \{Q, D \wedge B\}$. As $(Var(B) \cup Var(D)) \cap Change(T) = \emptyset$, the where Rule of the proof system applies, and we get $\vdash \{P, D\}$ where B do $T\ \{Q, D\}$.

Furthermore, the Definability Property gives $wp(\text{where } B \text{ do } T, \{Q, D\}) = \{P, D\}$. Hence the desired result:

$$\vdash wp(\text{where } B \text{ do } T, \{Q, D\})\ \text{where } B \text{ do } T\ \{Q, D\}.$$

$\square$

5 Extending the Proof of Completeness to Non-regular, Linear Programs

We have demonstrated the completeness of the proof system for plain specifications and regular, linear programs. In the presence of non-regular programs, we are no longer able to find any assertion that expresses the weakest preconditions. Thus, we first have to transform a non-regular program into a regular one. This can be done by introducing an *auxiliary variable*, which stores the value of the vector boolean expression: program where B do S is transformed into $Tmp := B$; where Tmp do S

Using such a variable can be interpreted as keeping track of the nested activity context in a stack. Each new variable Tmp is a cell of the stack.

But, instead of transforming programs in order to be able to prove them, we claim that it is possible *to encapsulate* this transformation into the proof system itself. The notion corresponding to syntactic *auxiliary* variables in programs is that of semantic *hidden* variables in assertions.

Rule 1 (Elimination of hidden variables) *Let E be any vector expression.*

$$\frac{\{P, C\}\ S\ \{Q, D\}, \quad Tmp \notin Var(S) \cup Var(Q) \cup Var(D)}{\{P[E/Tmp], C[E/Tmp]\}\ S\ \{Q, D\}}$$

We denote by $\vdash^* \{P, C\}\ S\ \{Q, D\}$ that a specification formula is derivable in the $\vdash$ proof system augmented with this new rule.

Theorem 16 (Soundness of $\vdash^*$). *The $\vdash^*$ proof system is sound:*

$$\text{If } \vdash^* \{P\}\ S\ \{Q\}, \quad \text{then } \models \{P\}\ S\ \{Q\}$$

Proof. Easy, using the Substitution Lemma — see [2]. □

Theorem 17 (Restr. completeness, plain specif., linear program). *Let* $\{P, C\}$ S $\{Q, D\}$ *be a plain specification, with* S *a linear program.*

$$\text{If} \models \{P, C\}\ S\ \{Q, D\}, \quad \text{then} \vdash^* \{P, C\}\ S\ \{Q, D\}$$

We first state that, thanks to the introduction of hidden variables, we retain the properties of definability of the weakest preconditions. The following proposition guarantees the existence of some assertion describing the weakest preconditions of any conditioning construct.

Proposition 18 (Non-regular conditioning [3]). *Let* $Tmp \notin Var(S) \cup Var(Q) \cup Var(D)$. *If*

$$wp(S, \{Q, D \wedge Tmp\}) = \{P, C\},$$

then

$$wp(\text{where } B \text{ do } S, \{Q, D\}) = \{P[B/Tmp], D\}$$

Theorem 19 (Restricted definability of WP). *Let* S *be a linear program. Let* $\{\ldots\}$ S $\{Q, D\}$ *be a plain specification for* S. *Then there exists an assertion* $\{P, D\}$ *such that* $[\![\{P, D\}]\!] = wp(S, \{Q, D\})$. *In particular,* $\models \{P, D\}$ S $\{Q, D\}$.

We can now prove Completeness Theorem 17 for non-regular programs.

Proof. The proof is similar to that of the Completeness Theorem 15 for regular programs. It uses a structural induction on S. The only new case to consider is $S \equiv$ where B do T, with $Var(B) \cap Change(T) \neq \emptyset$. Pick up a "new" variable Tmp such that $Tmp \notin Var(S) \cup Var(Q) \cup Var(D)$. Such a variable exists because the expressions from the program and from the assertion language are finite terms. By Theorem 19, we know there exists some assertion $\{P, D \wedge Tmp\} = wp(T, \{Q, D \wedge Tmp\})$.

By the induction hypothesis, we have $\vdash^* \{P, D \wedge Tmp\}$ T $\{Q, D \wedge Tmp\}$. We also have $\{P \wedge B = Tmp, D \wedge B\} \Rightarrow \{P, D \wedge Tmp\}$.

We can thus apply the Consequence Rule. This yields $\vdash^* \{P \wedge B = Tmp, D \wedge B\}$ T $\{Q, D \wedge Tmp\}$. Then, we apply the where Rule, and we get $\vdash^* \{P \wedge B = Tmp, D\}$ where B do T $\{Q, D\}$. Thanks to the Consequence Rule, this rewrites into $\vdash^* \{P[B/Tmp] \wedge B = Tmp, D\}$ where B do T $\{Q, D\}$.

Finally, applying the Elimination Rule with $E \equiv B$ yields $\vdash^* \{P[B/Tmp], D\}$ where B do T $\{Q, D\}$. According to Proposition 18, $wp(S, \{Q, D\}) = \{P[B/Tmp], D\}$. Thus $\vdash^* wp(S, \{Q, D\})$ S $\{Q, D\}$. As before, we conclude the proof with the Consequence Rule and the Definability Property 19. □

6 Extending the Proof of Completeness to Non-plain Specifications

We now focus on general specifications, where $Var(D) \cap Change(S)$ may be not empty. Surprisingly enough, the Elimination Rule is sufficient to prove the completeness in this case, and there is no need of any other additional rule.

Theorem 20 (Completeness, linear programs). Let S be a linear program.

$$\text{If } \models \{P, C\} \ S \ \{Q, D\}, \quad \text{then} \vdash^* \{P, C\} \ S \ \{Q, D\}.$$

Proof. Assume $\models \{P, C\} \ S \ \{Q, D\}$. As the expressions of the assertion language are finite terms, there exists a "new" hidden variable Tmp such that $Tmp \notin Var(S) \cup Var(Q) \cup Var(D)$. Let us show that

$$\models \{P \wedge Tmp = C, C\} \ S \ \{Q \wedge Tmp = D, Tmp\}$$

Let (σ, c) be in $[\![\{P \wedge Tmp = C, C\}]\!]$. We have in particular $(\sigma, c) \models \{P, C\}$. By hypothesis, we get $[\![S]\!](\sigma, c) = (\sigma', c) \models \{Q, D\}$.

Furthermore, we have $\sigma(Tmp) = \sigma(C) = c$. As $Tmp \notin Var(S)$, we have $\sigma'(Tmp) = \sigma(Tmp) = c$, and $(\sigma', c) \models \{Q, D\}$ gives $\sigma'(D) = c$. We conclude that $(\sigma', c) \models \{Q \wedge Tmp = D, Tmp\}$.

As $Tmp \notin Var(S)$, we are in the case of a plain specification, so the Completeness Theorem 17 applies and yields $\vdash^* \{P \wedge Tmp = C, C\} \ S \ \{Q \wedge Tmp = D, Tmp\}$.

As $\{Q \wedge Tmp = D, Tmp\} \Rightarrow \{Q, D\}$, we can apply the Consequence Rule. It yields $\vdash^* \{P \wedge Tmp = C, C\} \ S \ \{Q, D\}$. Applying then the Elimination Rule with $E \equiv C$ yields $\vdash^* \{P \wedge C = C, C\} \ S \ \{Q, D\}$.

Finally, as $\{P, C\} \Rightarrow \{P \wedge C = C, C\}$, we deduce by another application of the Consequence Rule that

$$\vdash^* \{P, C\} \ S \ \{Q, D\}$$

□

7 Conclusion

We have proved the completeness of a proof system associated with a simple data-parallel programming language. This proof system is based on a two-part assertion language, which enables a convenient treatment of activity context specifications.

We restricted ourselves to loop-free (so-called *linear*) programs. The proof of completeness given here relies on a weakest preconditions calculus, as in similar proofs for usual scalar (sequential) languages. The main technical difficulty is to cope with context manipulations. We first established restricted results of completeness, assuming syntactic restrictions on the conditioning constructs and on postconditions in the specification formulae. In a second step, we introduced a notion of *hidden* variables, together with an additional proof rule to manipulate them. We could then establish that this augmented proof system is complete for unrestricted programs and specifications formulae.

This completeness result can be extended to programs with loops using techniques similar to the usual scalar cases. Observe that handling loops in the $\mathcal{L}$ language is a subtle task, as the loop construct of the $\mathcal{L}$ language introduces a global logical OR on *infinite* boolean vectors. To illustrate the expressive power of this construct, consider the following example. Let I be an integer vector variable, and let $Halt$ be a boolean vector expression defined as follows: $\sigma(Halt)|_u = false$ if Turing Machine number $\sigma(I)|_u$ stops within $|u|$ steps. Let n be a positive integer. Consider the following program

$$I:=n;\ B:=Halt;\ Div:=true;$$
$$\text{loop } \neg B \text{ do } (Div:=false;\ B:=true)$$

This program always terminates, and $Div|_0$ is true iff Turing Machine number n diverges. Observe that this somewhat surprising fact does not prohibit the existence of some complete proof system, as the Consequence Rule considers all valid formula of the underlying logic as axioms, even though no complete proof system may exist for it.

More conceptually, programs of $\mathcal{L}$ encapsulate two kinds of divergences. The first kind comes from the *virtualisation loops* implicitely specified by each data-parallel assignment to infinite vectors. It may be called *spatial divergence*, and it is not visible at the level of semantics of $\mathcal{L}$. The second kind is due to explicit iterations loops. It may be called *temporal divergence*. It is denoted by $\perp$ in the semantics. Studying the semantics of $\mathcal{L}$ and the completeness of the associated proof systems leads thus to stratify the diverging behaviors of usual scalar programs into these two classes. As such, it definitely deserves further studies.

References

1. K.R. Apt and E.-R. Olderog. *Verification of Sequential and Concurrent Programs.* Text and Monographs in Computer Science. Springer Verlag, 1990.
2. L. Bougé and D. Cachera. On the completeness of a proof system for a simple data-parallel programming language. Research Report 94–42, LIP ENS Lyon, France, December 1994. Available at URL ftp://ftp.lip.ens-lyon.fr/pub/Rapports/RR/RR94/RR94-42.ps.Z.
3. L. Bougé, Y. Le Guyadec, G. Utard, and B. Virot. On the expressivity of a weakest preconditions calculus for a simple data-parallel programming language. In *ConPar'94–VAPP VI*, Linz, Austria, September 1994.
4. L. Bougé, Y. Le Guyadec, G. Utard, and B. Virot. A proof system for a simple data-parallel programming language. In C. Girault, editor, *Proc. of Applications in Parallel and Distributed Computing*, Caracas, Venezuela, April 1994. IFIP WG 10.3, North-Holland.
5. L. Bougé and J.-L. Levaire. Control structures for data-parallel SIMD languages : semantics and implementation. *Future Generation Computer Systems*, 8:363–378, 1992.
6. M. Clint and K.T. Narayana. On the completeness of a proof system for a synchronous parallel programming langage. In *Third Conf. Found. Softw. Techn. and Theor. Comp. Science*, Bangalore, India, December 1983.
7. E.W. Dijkstra. *A Discipline of Programming.* Prentice-Hall, 1976.
8. J. Gabarró and R. Gavaldà. An approach to correctness of data parallel algorithms. *Journal of Parallel and Distributed Computing*, 22(2):185–201, August 1994.
9. M.J.C. Gordon. *Programming Language Theory and its Implementation.* Prentice Hall International, 1988.
10. C.A.R. Hoare. An axiomatic basis for computer programming. *Comm of the ACM*, 12:576–580, 1969.
11. A. Stewart. An axiomatic treatment of SIMD assignment. *BIT*, 30:70–82, 1990.

An Implementation of Race Detection and Deterministic Replay with MPI

C. Clémençon[1], J. Fritscher[1], M.J. Meehan[2] and R. Rühl[1]

[1] CSCS–ETH, Centro Svizzero di Calcolo Scientifico,
6928 Manno, Switzerland
[2] Dept. of Computer Science, Univ. of North Carolina,
Chapel Hill, NC 27599-3175, U.S.A

Abstract. The *Parallel Debugging Tool* (PDT) of the *Annai* programming environment is developed within the *Joint CSCS-ETH/NEC Collaboration in Parallel Processing* [1]. Like the other components of the integrated environment, PDT aims to provide support for application developers to debug portable large-scale data-parallel programs based on HPF and message-passing programs based on the MPI standard. PDT supports MPI event tracing for race detection and deterministic replay for manually parallelized MPI programs as well as for code generated with the advanced techniques of a data-parallel compiler. This paper describes the tracing and replaying mechanisms included in PDT as well as their efficiency by presenting execution time overheads for several benchmark programs running on the NEC Cenju-2/3 distributed-memory parallel computers.

1 Introduction

The lowest-level programming paradigm employed often on Distributed-Memory Parallel Processors (DMPPs) is pure message passing. Until recently, proprietary message-passing libraries have been used a majority of the time, which has made porting of applications from a given DMPP to a system of another vendor difficult. In addition, message passing has been recognized to be tedious and error prone. To provide a higher-level programming interface, several data-parallel languages have been proposed. To allow for portability, the low-level Message-Passing Interface (MPI) and the high-level High Performance Fortran (HPF) have been defined and both have been accepted as standard by most DMPP vendors. HPF allows for the integration of MPI primitives into high-level source code through extrinsic procedures.

Many problems still remain regarding the usability of DMPPs. Debugging of DMPP programs for correctness is difficult because of possible deadlocks and non-determinism. Non-determinism may be either unintended or intended. Unintended non-determinism is a programming error and should be detectable by a DMPP debugger. The intended non-determinism used in some programming models (such as the *master/worker* model described in Section 2) can cause problems for the debugger because it might not be possible to re-produce an error condition if it is dependent on the execution order of a non-deterministic section of a program.

We are currently developing a fully interactive, source-level debugger for large-scale DMPP programs. The debugger is called Parallel Debugging Tool (PDT) [2], and is integrated into the programming environment *Annai* [3]. Annai also includes a Parallelization Support Tool (PST) [4], a Performance Monitor and Analyzer (PMA) [5] and an OSF/Motif-based graphical User Interface (UI). PMA supports performance debugging, while PDT supports debugging for correctness. Among the major design objectives for all tools are application-oriented design, portability, scalability, and support of both MPI at the low level and extended HPF at the high level. A group of application developers is continuously evaluating tool prototypes and providing feedback for functionality enhancements.

This paper reports results about the race detection and deterministic replay facilities built into PDT. Although first DMPP debuggers have been built which include deterministic replay features, they are either research systems targeting at a single communication interface and lacking the portability of MPI, or they emphasize other features than replay efficiency and scalable interactive debugging. In contrast to these systems (see also Section 3.1), PDT provides portable scalable interactive debugging support for both low and high-level programming paradigms. This includes a complete MPI instrumentation for the detection of non-determinism and for deterministic replay.

The next section gives an example of the two main types of non-determinism which can occur in MPI programs. Then we summarize related work and describe the integration of the various Annai components in more detail. After a summary of the algorithms used for race detection and deterministic replay, we present measurements of tracing and replay overhead on NEC Cenju-2/3 DMPPs.

2   An MPI Example

In Fig. 1 we show a simple code segment with calls to MPI which cause races. These races are due to blocking receives which use the `MPI_ANY_SOURCE` wildcard for matching the source processors of incoming concurrent messages. Although the code segment has no application and was constructed solely for benchmarking purposes (see also Section 5.2), it illustrates one kind of race possible in MPI programs: $p - 1$ processors send messages "concurrently" to the same processor which accepts messages using a wild-card for increased parallelism and efficiency. In the benchmark this is repeated $n \times (p - 1)$ times (loops at lines 5 and 6) and each processor plays the role of a receiver n times.

The situation is again depicted in Fig. 2 in a space-time diagram for four processors. Throughout the paper we denote a message as $\text{MSG}(a, b)$, where a defines the id of the source processor of a message, and b a serial event counter on that source. Analogously, the respective receive events are denoted as $\text{RECV}(a, b)$, where the serial number b is computed on the receiver.

Fig. 2 shows a triple race between $\text{MSG}(0, 1)$, $\text{MSG}(2, 1)$ and $\text{MSG}(3, 1)$. If replay information about $\text{MSG}(0, 1)$ and $\text{MSG}(3, 1)$ (the first two messages to be received) is stored in a first execution of the code segment and during re-execution the order of these two messages is guaranteed, then $\text{MSG}(2, 1)$ goes to $\text{RECV}(1, 3)$ as desired and the first execution is deterministically replayed.

A second type of non-determinism can occur in MPI due to the use of the nonblocking probe operation `MPI_Iprobe` (further on called *iprobe*). With iprobes,

Void RECEIVEBENCHMARK(Int n, MPI_Comm c)

```
1:    MPI_Status s;
2:    Int i, j, k, x, p, myid;
3:    MPI_COMM_SIZE(c, &p);
4:    MPI_COMM_RANK(c, &myid);
5:    for i := 1 to n
6:        for j := 0 to p − 1
7:            if j = myid
8:                for k := 1 to p − 1
9:                    MPI_RECV(&x, 1, MPI_INT, MPI_ANY_SOURCE, TAG, c, &s);
10:               end for
11:           else
12:               MPI_SEND(&myid, 1, MPI_INT, j, TAG, c);
13:           end if
14:       end for
15:   end for
```

Fig. 1. RECEIVEBENCHMARK is a typical example MPI code segment with races due to receives with wild-card source specification.

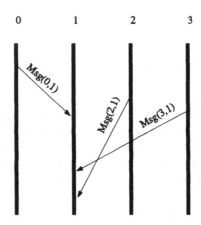

Fig. 2. Simple three message race.

non-determinism can occur on as few as two processors, because when replaying, depending on communication delays, the same sequence of iprobes may result in a non-deterministic sequence of booleans indicating the success of the operations. The example in Fig. 3 shows how a user can emulate a blocking receive using iprobes. For repeated executions of a program using EMULATEDRECV, with the same input, the loop at line 3 of Fig. 3 may be executed a different number of times. Note that in our implementation of MPI, MPI_Recv is actually based on non-blocking probes similar to what is shown in the figure.

Void EMULATEDRECV(Void ∗a, Int n, Int src, Int tag, MPI_Comm c, MPI_Status ∗s)

```
1:    Int true_src;
2:    Boolean f;
3:    repeat
4:       MPI_IPROBE(src, tag, c, &f, s);
5:    until f;
6:    MPI_GET_SOURCE(s, &true_src);
7:    MPI_RECV(a, n, MPI_INT, true_src, tag, c, s);
```

Fig. 3. EMULATEDRECV emulates a blocking receive using non-blocking probe operations.

3 Background

3.1 Related Work

The first step towards correct tracing and replay of communication events of a DMPP program, is the definition of the order of the events. Lamport [6] has first defined the *happens before* (or *causality*) relation "→", an irreflexive, partial order on a set of events E. For two events $e_1, e_2 \in E$, $e_1 \rightarrow e_2$ is the smallest transitive relation satisfying the following conditions: either e_1, e_2 are happening on the same processor and e_1 precedes e_2, or e_1 is a send event and e_2 is the respective receive event on the destination of e_1. If two events do not causally affect each other, they are called *concurrent*. A time stamp added to each message can be used to compute on each processor for the events e_1, e_2 logical clocks $C(e_1), C(e_2)$ which satisfy the *clock condition*:

$$e_1 \rightarrow e_2 \Rightarrow C(e_1) < C(e_2)$$

Fidge [7] has first used *vector clocks* to define the exact causal order of events in DMPPs. On a DMPP with p processors, vector clocks have p elements, and their computation in general requires appending of a vector time stamp of length p to each message. For the many DMPP programs which feature communication locality, however, such overhead can be drastically reduced by only communicating incremental vector clock changes [8] which typically adds constant overhead independent of the number of processors.

Netzer and Miller [9] have first described how to use vector clocks to trace and replay *frontier races*. A *frontier* is drawn across a space-time diagram of a DMPP program, which divides communication send and receive events into two sets such that (1) two (or more) sends are just after the frontier, (2) a receive that could have received either of the respective messages is just after the frontier, and (3) all receive events before the frontier also have their senders before the frontier. For simple message patterns, frontier races are traced and replayed with minimum overhead. An evaluation of six programs on a 32 node iPSC/2 is carried out which shows that only 1-2% of all message receives need tracing, and that tracing execution time overhead is less than 14%.

Damodaran-Kamal and Francioni [10] present the mdb debugger which allows the user to detect races using *controlled execution*: at certain points, the running program is suspended and the user is allowed to permute messages in send or receive queues. A set of commands is presented which can be applied to a suspended program; among others a sequential debugger can be used to inspect processor states. mdb does not support fully interactive low-level debugging in a scalable fashion. However, it supports the debugging of portable PVM programs.

Leu and Schiper [11] have built a system which integrates replay of non-determinism with ParaGraph-like visualization of message-passing programs. On the one hand, because the same trace format is used for visualization, race debugging and deterministic replay, both global and local behavior can be observed simultaneously. On the other hand, complete event tracing is necessary which introduces large trace overhead.

May and Berman [12] describe Panorama, a portable extensible system for both performance and correctness debugging of DMPP programs. A graphical interface runs on a user workstation and drives a vendor base debugger on the actual parallel platform. Deterministic replay is provided using complete message tracing. Measurements are shown on both an iPSC/860 and on an nCUBE, and for small messages, tracing accounts for an execution-time overhead of 7-55% on the iPSC and of 40-90% on the nCUBE, respectively, independent of the machine size.

3.2 Annai and its Parallel Debugging Tool (PDT)

Annai accepts high-level extended HPF programs and low-level message-passing source code. PST acts as a compiler for both paradigms. We are separately developing two other tools, one for correctness debugging (PDT) and one for performance analysis and tuning (PMA). For the reduction of trace overhead, each tool uses independent trace information, i.e. our basic communication platform MPI includes two orthogonal instrumentations.

The overall debugging support of Annai is split into two components, the Tool Services Agent (TSA) and PDT. TSA constitutes the machine interface of Annai, and provides a collection of basic debugging functions, for loading, executing, halting and inspecting a parallel program. TSA can be viewed as the back-end, low-level debugger of Annai and parts of it run on the target platform. PDT runs on the user workstation and its role is to provide more elaborate, higher-level debugging functions built from sequences of TSA commands. The high level debugging functions supported by PDT include global displays of distributed data structures and various breakpointing mechanisms. PMA uses TSA for interactive instrumentation of the target program. TSA is currently based on the GNU gdb debugger from the Free Software Foundation and plays a role similar to the basic vendor debugger underlying Panorama: while at the application level, portability is supported through the use of MPI and HPF, at the system level, TSA eases porting of the whole tool environment. Currently, we support the NEC Cenju-2, Cenju-3, and a DMPP emulator running on a Solaris workstation.

4 MPI Race Detection and Deterministic Replay

MPI provides three different kinds of tags as a basis for receiving a message: the source, the communicator (thus defining a context or group), and a conventional tag. Except for the communicator, there are wild-cards available for these tags. The communicator allows grouping of processes. Intra-group and inter-group communication is only possible through different communicators.

In a correct implementation of MPI, the order of messages with matching tags, sources and communicators is preserved (FIFO). Messages with different tags are allowed to overtake, however, even if they come from the same sender.

As already pointed out in Section 2 two classes of races can occur in MPI programs: races due to blocking receives and probes with equal tags, communicators and message-source wild-cards (for instance with MPI_Recv, MPI_Probe and MPI_Wait), and races due to asynchronous probe operations which non-deterministically test for message arrival in the system's message buffer (for instance with MPI_Iprobe and MPI_Test).

4.1 Blocking Probes and Receives

Race Detection and Tracing We use the same technique as Netzer and Miller to determine causality between messages and to trace racing receive primitives. Each processor maintains a vector time stamp and appends it to each message sent. On each processor, an internal scalar logical clock is incremented by one upon each send event. On processor i, the i-th element of the vector time stamp is equivalent to the processor's scalar clock. The remainder of the vector is determined by doing a component-wise maximum on the current time stamp and any time stamp received at the end of an incoming message.

Given two incoming messages a and b, the first arriving from processor p_a the second from p_b and their vector time stamps V_a and V_b, one can determine if they race by comparing the p_a-th value of the vector time stamps. If the p_a-th value of V_a is larger than the p_a-th value of V_b, then the two messages are concurrent and race. For message a to happen before b, the p_a-th value (p_a's internal clock) would have to be incorporated into message b's time stamp, because the p_a-th value would be passed along through the chain of messages linking the two.

Fig. 4 (a) demonstrates this. MSG(2, 1) ($p_a = 2$) arrives before MSG(0, 1) ($p_b = 0$) so the third (p_a-th) value of their time stamps must be compared. The third value of MSG(2, 1)'s time stamp is 1 and the third value of MSG(0, 1)'s time stamp is 0, therefore the two messages race. Considering MSG(2, 2) and MSG(0, 1), we see that the first value of the MSG(0, 1)'s time stamp is 1 and the first value of MSG(2, 2)'s time stamp is also 1, so the first message *happens before* the second message.

A *block race* is a collection of special frontier races which denotes races between a message and a set of messages. If the same message is concurrent to more than one message from the same processor, then it races with all of them. Fig. 4 (b) shows a block race. MSG(2, 1) is concurrent to both MSG(0, 1) or MSG(0, 2), therefore it races with both of them. Since MSG(2, 1) races with these messages, trace information about RECV(1, 1) and RECV(1, 2) must be stored. There also exists a block race between MSG(0, 3) and the pair MSG(2, 2) and MSG(2, 3) which results in storing information about RECV(1, 3) and

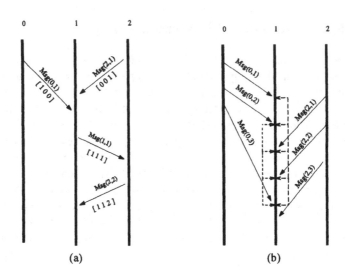

Fig. 4. On the left we show how vector time stamps are used to identify message races. On the right a block race is depicted.

RECV(1, 4). Due to the FIFO nature of the MPI communication channels, it is possible to store block races as single trace file entries. In our MPI implementation, block races can occur when long messages are chopped into pieces to fit into communication buffers of limited size.

To detect block races, a buffer of time stamps stemming from recently received messages must be stored for each tag. The buffer does not have to store all past time stamps. A time stamp can be taken out if a message of its tag has been received from every processor (excluding the time stamp's source and receiving processor). If a message of the same tag is received from another processor, then the message either races with the current message or it doesn't. If the new message races with the old, then the old message's trace information is stored in the trace file and the old time stamp is removed from the buffer. If the new message does not race with the old, then the new one's time stamp is added to the buffer and the old one remains.

In MPI, blocking and non-blocking probes can affect a program's execution when polling for racing messages. If any of the information from the probe is used in the program (for instance, existence of the message, the message's source or length), then the race affects the program.

Blocking probes can be traced in the same manner as receives. To trace them correctly, all of the operations for tracing a receive must be performed during the probe except for the removal of the message from the system buffer. The incoming time stamps are compared to those of the receives and other blocking probes, stored and removed from the buffer upon the same conditions and stored identically in the trace file if they race.

When a blocking probe is traced, the same actions performed for an equivalent receive are performed, including incrementing the same internal clock for each occurrence. If on a processor p there have been two blocking receives and three blocking probes, then the internal clock is incremented by five.

Deterministic Replay To replay a race condition, one needs to know which messages should arrive at all critical receives and should be able to hold off reception until the correct message arrives. To determine which messages race, given that the original execution has been traced correctly, one needs to read in the trace file which will indicate all critical receives and the correct messages for each.

Because FIFO message passing is assumed, the order of arrival of messages from a given processor is guaranteed. Therefore, the only piece of information necessary to determine the correct message for a critical receive is the sending processor's number. Assuming that all messages up to a certain critical receive arrive in the correct order, then the next message to come from the critical receive's desired source will be the correct one.

For a processor to replay deterministically, it needs to know which receives are critical and which messages should be received at each. To know which receives are critical, the trace file must—for each processor—supply the number corresponding to the internal clock of the original receive. Since the internal clock is incremented in the same manner as in the original execution, the algorithm can compare its current internal clock and the numbers of the critical receives to determine which receives must be controlled.

To implement re-execution, the program reads in the trace file and determines what the next critical receive is. The program executes without any interference until the first critical receive (since all of the preceding receives are already deterministic). Upon the first critical receive, the program blocks until the correct message arrives. This process is repeated again for the next and all proceeding critical receives.

One should note that this does not guarantee the order of *arrival* of messages. It simply guarantees the order of reception of the messages. The messages can still arrive in any order and must be buffered until their correct reception time. Netzer and Miller have proposed a handshake protocol for the correct replay of message arrivals. However, the MPI user is only affected by different message arrivals if message buffer overflows occur. In our MPI implementation, buffers are fairly large, and we refrained from implementing the above handshakes because of efficiency considerations.

4.2 Non-blocking Probes

Non-blocking probes (*iprobes* as defined above) can also cause non-deterministic behavior. As with blocking probes, if any of the information from an iprobe is used in a program (for instance existence, source or message length), it can cause non-determinism. Iprobes cannot be traced in the same manner as blocking probes and receives, since they are simply checks for existence of messages. Instead, the outcome of every non-blocking probe must be recreatable from a trace file.

Keeping the trace information for every iprobe would be expensive. One would have to store each iprobe's outcome (true or false) and the probed message's source if the iprobe was successful and was of a class that can detect messages from more than one source. For instance, in the Traveling Salesman Problem considered in Section 5.3, less than one percent of the iprobes executed return successfully. In such an application, tracing only successful iprobes can significantly reduce tracing overhead.

For deterministic replay of the iprobes, the traces are read into a buffer. Every time an iprobe is called, a respective counter is incremented. This iprobe event counter and trace files are separate and distinct from those used for the blocking receives and probes. Regardless of the existence of messages in the buffer, the replay mechanism forces the iprobe to return value FALSE until the iprobe counter matches the value for the next true iprobe. When the counter does match, value TRUE must be returned. To re-execute properly, the iprobe blocks until it has received the correct message before it returns a true value. Once again, only the source number of the message needs to be known for the critical iprobes.

5 Performance Measurements

5.1 The NEC Cenju-2 and Cenju-3

The NEC Cenju-3 installed at CSCS is configured with 128 processing nodes, each comprising a 75 MHz VR4400SC RISC processor, 32 Kbytes primary on-chip cache, 1 Mbyte of secondary cache and 64 Mbytes main dynamic memory. Processors communicate via a packet-switched multi-stage interconnection network composed of 4×4 crossbar switches. At CSCS, a 16 processor Cenju-2 (a predecessor of the Cenju-3) is also installed. The Cenju-2 features a similar network but is based on the slower 25 MHz MIPS R3000 processor. Some of the measurements shown in this paper were collected on the smaller Cenju-2, because it features a less intrusive timing function. The back-end C compiler used on both systems is the GNU gcc compiler, version 2.5.7.

5.2 Single Communication Primitives

To measure the impact of tracing and deterministic replay on the execution time of single MPI primitives we run the code segment of Fig. 1 ("Receive Benchmark") with $n = 500$ on our Cenju-2. The system timer on that machine features low intrusiveness and therefore average execution times of single MPI primitives can be measured reliably. To measure tracing and replaying overhead for iprobes, the benchmark was modified by replacing the MPI_Recv (Fig. 1, line 9) with the emulated receive of Fig. 3 ("Iprobe Benchmark"). Fig. 5 shows results of our performance measurements by breaking down the execution time spent in the three MPI primitives. Only the access time to trace buffers in memory is included in the measurements, but not the I/O necessary for writing and reading these buffers to and from disk.

The measurements show that with no instrumentation approximately half the time for a receive is spent waiting for the message arrival inside a loop of non-blocking probes. The other half is spent in receiving the message, which consists of bookkeeping and copying from system to user space. When tracing races, the overhead introduced in MPI_Recv is more expensive than for iprobes, because of the respective complexities of either tracing algorithm. When racing messages are traced in the receive benchmark,

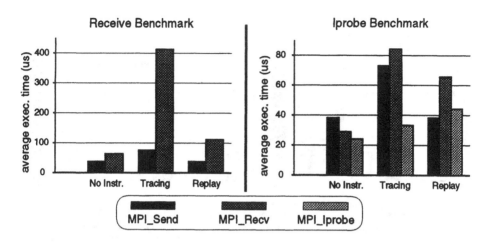

Fig. 5. Race detection and deterministic replay of single communication primitives on a 16 processor Cenju-2 in the benchmark of Fig. 1.

sends and receives are slowed down by approximately a factor of 2 and 6, respectively. Racing receives are replayed with less than a factor of 2 overhead with no noticeable performance difference for the respective sends. The relative execution-time overhead during replay is similar for both benchmarks.

5.3 Applications

We benchmarked two example programs:

TSP solves a traveling salesman problem on 18 randomly distributed cities using a parallel branch-and-bound algorithm. TSP is implemented in C with explicit MPI calls using a master-worker execution model (see also Section 2): the master processor constructs a queue of tasks which then are dynamically distributed to worker processes. The most important communication routine used for master-worker communications is `MPI_Iprobe`.

The **BiCGSTAB** solver from SPARSKIT [13] is applied to a simple sparse matrix, namely a banded random matrix of 16384 rows and a total bandwidth of 201. Our results refer to the performance of the iterative solver in steady state. BiCGSTAB is implemented in HPF with PST extensions, and compiled by PST, which intentionally introduces races for increased efficiency.

Fig. 6 shows the results of our measurements regarding the overhead of race detection and replay for TSP and BiCGSTAB, respectively. Both benchmarks were run on different Cenju-3 configurations without instrumentation, with race detection and with deterministic replay instrumentation. For TSP we show parallel execution times compared to an equivalent sequential program run; for BiCGSTAB MFLOPs are given. In TSP, the main source of non-determinism is the use of MPI non-blocking probe primitives. As the results show, replay is significantly slower than tracing: in the worst case performance is reduced by a factor of two compared to the non-instrumented code. In BiCGSTAB, few races are introduced by PST in blocking receive primitives. Our

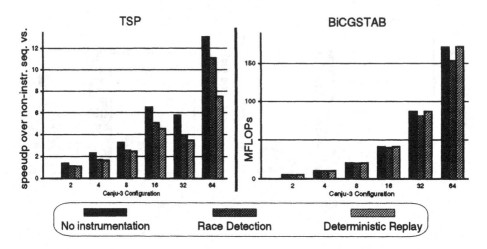

Fig. 6. The performance of TSP (left) and BiCGSTAB (right) without instrumentation, with race detection and with deterministic replay instrumentation is measured on several Cenju-3 configurations.

measurements show that only the performance of race detection is affected for large machine configurations, because the instrumentation requires longer messages to be communicated. The performance difference between non-instrumented and deterministically replayed program runs is negligible.

6 Conclusions

We have summarized the functionality of the Annai tool environment which integrates a compiler for extended HPF, a performance monitor and a parallel debugger. Since the whole tool environment aims at portable support of both extended HPF and MPI, one of the main features of the parallel debugger is race detection and deterministic replay. We have implemented such replay functionality in MPI with support for both frontier races of message receives with source-id wild-cards and for non-blocking probes (which are another type of race and require separate treatment).

We have measured the overhead introduced by both tracing and replay in a worst-case artificial benchmark where all messages race, as well as in two application programs, one parallelized using a master/worker model and non-blocking probes, and another data-parallel program where races are introduced for increased efficiency by the high-level compiler. We believe that the measurements show that the overhead introduced is acceptable, even for the debugging of large scale programs on many processors.

While the individual components of the debugger are not new to the research community, we believe we are the first to have integrated efficient race detection and deterministic replay into MPI and a tool environment which is portable and supports application portability.

Acknowledgments

The development of Annai has been a joint effort with A. Endo, A. Müller, and B. Wylie. Other project members, V. Deshpande, N. Masuda, W. Sawyer, and F. Zimmermann have generously been patient while evaluating our prototypes. We are grateful for many useful comments and careful proofreading of K. M. Decker and the EURO-PAR'95 reviewers.

References

1. C. Clémençon, K. M. Decker, A. Endo, J. Fritscher, G. Jost, N. Masuda, A. Müller, R. Rühl, W. Sawyer, E. de Sturler, B. J. N. Wylie, and F. Zimmermann. Application-Driven Development of an Integrated Tool Environment for Distributed Memory Parallel Processors. In R. Rao and C. P. Ravikumar, editors, *Proceedings of the First International Workshop on Parallel Processing (Bangalore, India, December 27–30)*, 1994.
2. C. Clémençon, J. Fritscher, and R. Rühl. Execution control, visualization and replay of massively parallel programs within Annai's debugging tool. In *Proc. High Performance Computing Symposium, HPCS'95, Montréal, CA*, July 1995.
3. C. Clémençon, A. Endo, J. Fritscher, A. Müller, R. Rühl, and B. J. N. Wylie. The "Annai" Environment for Portable Distributed Parallel Programming. In Hesham El-Rewini and Bruce D. Shriver, editors, *Proc. of the 28th Hawaii International Conference on System Sciences, Volume II (Maui, Hawaii, USA, 3–6 January, 1995)*, pages 242–251. IEEE Computer Society Press, January 1995.
4. A. Müller and R. Rühl. Extending HPF for the Support of Unstructured Computations. In *Proc. ACM International Conference on Supercomputing, ICS'95, Barcelona, Spain*, July 1995.
5. B. J. N. Wylie and A. Endo. Design and realization of the Annai integrated parallel programming environment performance monitor and analyser. Technical Report CSCS-TR-94-07, CSCS, CH-6928 Manno, Switzerland, November 1994.
6. L. Lamport. Time, clocks, and the ordering of events in a distributed system. *Communications of the ACM*, 21(7):558–565, July 1978.
7. C. J. Fidge. Partial orders for parallel debugging. *Proceedings of the ACM SIGPLAN/SIGOPS Workshop on Parallel and Distributed Debugging*, 24(1):183–194, January 1989. Published in ACM SIGPLAN Notices.
8. M. Singhal and A. Kshemkalyani. An efficient implementation of vector clocks. *Information Processing Letters*, 43(10):47–52, August 1992.
9. R. H. B. Netzer and B. P. Miller. Optimal tracing and replay for debugging message-passing parallel programs. In *Proceedings of Supercomputing '92*, pages 502–511, Minneapolis, MN, November 1992.
10. S. K. Damodaran-Kamal and J. M. Francioni. *mdb*: A semantic race detection tool for PVM. In *Proceedings of the Scalable High-Performance Computing Conference*, pages 702–709, May 1994.
11. E. Leu and A. Schiper. Execution replay: A mechanism for integrating a visualization tool with a symbolic debugger. In *Proceedings of CONPAR '92*, pages 55–66, September 1992.
12. J. May and F. Berman. Panorama: A portable, extensible parallel debugger. In *Proceedings of ACM/ONR Workshop on Parallel and Distributed Debugging*, pages 96–106, San Diego, California, May 1993.
13. Y. Saad. SPARSKIT: A basic tool kit for sparse matrix computation. CSRD Technical Report 1029, University of Illinois, IL, August 1990.

Formal and experimental validation of a low overhead execution replay mechanism*

Alain Fagot and Jacques Chassin de Kergommeaux

IMAG, APACHE project
46 avenue Félix Viallet,
F-38031 Grenoble Cedex 1, France.
{Alain.Fagot,Jacques.Chassin-de-Kergommeaux}@imag.fr

Abstract. This paper presents a mechanism for record-replay of parallel programs written in a remote procedure call (RPC) based parallel programming model. This mechanism, which will serve as a basis for implementing a user-level debugger, exploits some properties of the programming model to limit drastically the number of records that need to be done. A formal proof of the equivalence between recorded and replayed executions is given. Systematic measurements of the time overhead of the recording indicate that it is sufficiently low for the recording mode to be considered as normal execution mode. Similar techniques can be applied to other programming models.

Keywords: Instant Replay, parallel debugging, deterministic reexecutions, Remote Procedure Call.

1 Introduction

This paper presents a mechanism allowing programmers to cope with the inherent non-determinism of parallel executions, when debugging programs written in a remote procedure call (RPC) based programming model, designed for parallel multiprocessors. Many parallel programs present a non-deterministic behavior, even if they produce deterministic computation results. Non-deterministic execution behaviors originate mainly in execution environments of programs. Such an environment depends on a large number of factors that cannot be controlled by the programmer, such as the initial contents of cache memories, the behavior of the operating system, etc. Programs adapting to the execution environment for efficiency reasons, using dynamic load balancing techniques, for example, are very prone to exhibit non-deterministic execution behaviors. Non-deterministic execution behavior of erroneous parallel programs may result in transient errors which appear very unfrequently or vanish when debugging tools are used, because of changes introduced by these tools in the causal relationship between parallel processes.

---

* This work was partially supported by the French Ministry of Research under the inter-PRC project **Trace**.

The most classical technique used to catch transient errors appearing during executions of parallel programs is to *record* an initial execution and to *force* subsequent executions to be deterministic with respect to the initial execution, using the recorded information. Debugging an erroneous program then amounts to record an erroneous execution and to apply cyclic debugging techniques during subsequent replayed executions. In order for this technique to be effective, the perturbation resulting from the recording operation ought to be kept sufficiently low so that errors appearing in un-recorded executions do not vanish in recorded ones and vice-versa. If this overhead is low enough, recording can be left active during each execution of a parallel program, so that an error occurring unfrequently can be captured and subsequently reproduced.

Efficient record-replay techniques are mostly based upon the "Instant Replay" mechanism of LeBlanc and Mellor-Crummey [5]. The efficiency of the instant replay comes from the observation that it is sufficient to record the order of accesses to shared objects to be able to reproduce "indistinguishable" executions. The instant replay mechanism was adapted to message passing programming models [6], where each process records on a tape the identifiers of received messages. The replay system forces re-executing processes to treat incoming messages in the same order as during the initial recording. This mechanism was used as a basis for the implementation of parallel debuggers [8, 6, 3].

This paper describes an optimized record-replay mechanism for ATHAPASCAN[2], the programming model of the APACHE research project. APACHE aims at designing and implementing a parallel programming environment for parallel computers, providing both static and dynamic load balancing facilities [9]. The mechanism described in the sequel of this paper, exploits the characteristics of remote procedure calls to reduce drastically the volume of traces that need to be recorded in order to be able to replay programs deterministically with respect to the original recorded computation. This mechanism can be applied to any RPC-based programming model. A formal proof of the equivalence of executions controlled by the described mechanism is also given. In addition the time overhead of recording is measured systematically, for the most classical parallel numerical algorithms, showing that it always remains very low.

2 The Athapascan programming model

In ATHAPASCAN, the execution of parallel programs is performed by a set of identical *virtual processors* operating asynchronously [2]. Expression of parallelism is achieved by blocking and non-blocking remote procedure calls (requests), thereby hiding the underlying communication protocols under the parameters and results transmission mechanisms. Thus the ATHAPASCAN model is well suited for expressing control parallelism. Each virtual processor includes several *Entry Points*, which are the targets of remote procedure calls (see figure 1). No other communications are available in ATHAPASCAN.

---

[2] ATHAPASCAN is the language of the Apaches.

A remote procedure call results in the execution of a light-weight process (thread) within the virtual processor holding the target entry point. This thread may in turn create new threads by issuing remote procedure calls. Upon completion, each thread returns a result to its caller thread. Several light-weight processes execute concurrently within each virtual processor to hide the latency of communications in parallel systems. ATHAPASCAN offers two types of remote procedure calls:

- blocking (*Call*): control is returned to the caller after receiving the result of the called procedure,
- non blocking (*Spawn*): control is returned to the caller after the creation of the remote thread. Two operators are provided to test (*TestSpawn*) or wait (*WaitSpawn*) for the completion of non-blocking remote procedure calls.

3   Minimal trace recording

The non-deterministic behavior of an ATHAPASCAN program execution is due to the variable order in which requests are handled by entry points and to the results of non-deterministic primitives which are related to the current state of the system. The two causes can be tracked down separately.

3.1   Basic mechanism

The principle of the control driven replay is to record the order of accesses to shared resources. Classical implementations of Instant Replay record the order of system-level primitives for passing messages [6] or accessing shared variables [5]. In the ATHAPASCAN model, shared resources are entry points, accessed by requests. Our record-replay mechanism uses an intermediate level of abstraction where several system-level events can be abstracted in one, thereby reducing the number of records while being independent of the underlying communication system.

Each call to an entry point results in a typical sequence of such "abstract" events. Figure 1 represents a complete sequence of events generated by a call to an entry point, from the request emission (event **a**) to the result receipt (event **d**) passing through the request receipt (event **b**) and the result emission (event **c**). A replay can be driven by forcing the execution order of request receipts (event **b**). Since an entry point controls racing requests, it can be responsible for recording the order in which it serves incoming requests.

The order of request emissions (event **a**) is not recorded since an emitting thread will reproduce this order if all its non-deterministic operations produce the same values. However, this order may not be significant since the ATHAPASCAN model does not impose this order to be followed by the request receipts.

The order of request receipts (event **b**) is the order in which incoming requests are processed by an entry point. This fundamental order represents the order in which access is granted to shared resources and is recorded by each entry point.

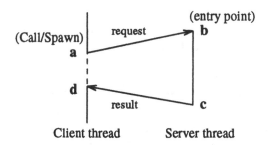

Fig. 1. Sequence of events for a call to an entry point.

The order of result emissions (event c) is not significant since a single result is emitted by a thread and this occurs at the end of its execution.

The order of result receipts (event d) is not visible from the point of view of the client thread. A client thread is informed of the presence of the result only through primitives *TestSpawn* and *WaitSpawn* in the case of a non blocking call or implicitly in the case of a blocking call.

Each entry point is responsible for recording its request receipt history (event b). This history contains the order of request unique identifiers. A request identifier is constructed independently by the client thread emitting the request in a deterministic way: in particular, it is independent of the other threads sharing the same virtual processor. For the ATHAPASCAN model, it has the following form: ⟨VirtualProcessorID, EntryPointID, ThreadID, RequestID⟩.

3.2   Non-deterministic primitives

Non-deterministic primitives may be considered as predefined non-deterministic entry points of the ATHAPASCAN kernel. For this type of entry points, results cannot be computed during replayed executions as during a recorded execution. Therefore, the instant replay mechanism must record the results computed for each non-deterministic request along with the request identifier in order to provide the same result to the same request during the replay. This technique mixes data driven replay with the general control driven strategy. It is used to record-replay the ATHAPASCAN *TestSpawn* primitive whose result is dependent on communication delays.

3.3   Interest of the proposed mechanism

The simplifications brought to the classical model result from the communication simplicity of the ATHAPASCAN-0 model. Processes obey a Client-Server protocol which is a sub-class of the model of communicating processes. Each request corresponds to a result and a result is emitted only if a request was received. The ATHAPASCAN request and result transmissions can be implemented in several different ways without consequences on the design of the record-replay mechanism. This independence leads to a reduction of the number of trace-points for some implementations, up to a factor of six relative to the classical solution of implementing the record-replay at the system level. This reduction factor is obtained at low cost since no additional information is appended to the messages.

4 Execution equivalence demonstration

In this section, we prove formally that using the record mechanism defined in section 3 results in deterministic replayed executions of ATHAPASCAN programs with respect to an original recording. An execution model is given for ATHAPASCAN, in the framework of which it is possible to define the equivalence between two executions of the same program. The notion of equivalence is such that equivalent executions of a program exhibit the same behavior from the programmer point of view.

The demonstration is similar to the demonstration of equivalence given by Mellor-Crummey in [8]. A parallel program execution is composed of a set of (light-weight) processes, each of which executes a function to compute the response (result) to a request. A mapping relation M defines the bijection between emitted requests and computing processes. The demonstration shows that it is sufficient to enforce the same mapping relation M in both executions to make them equivalent. The modified ATHAPASCAN run-time kernel implements the record-replay mechanism by recording the mapping relation of the initial execution and forcing the replayed execution to follow this mapping relation.

4.1 Execution model

Assumptions. In the following, we will assume that:

1. *Recorded* and *replayed* executions of a parallel ATHAPASCAN program are done using a fixed and ordered set of virtual processors VP. Each execution is started with the same initial parameters. Each virtual processor offers a fixed and ordered set of entry points EP_{vp}. All replayed executions can use at least the same amount of resources as the initially recorded one: processors, memory and disk space, etc.

2. The global variables of any *Entry Point* can only be accessed through a call to this *Entry Point*. Such an *Entry Point* declaration defines the limit of concurrent accesses allowed for these global variables. Therefore the state of each *Entry Point* during the computation of an ATHAPASCAN program is only determined by the order according to which the requests are received and processed by the *Entry Point*.

3. ATHAPASCAN programs do not use system non-deterministic primitives. The equivalence result obtained for such programs can be simply extended for programs using non-deterministic primitives, provided the results of these primitives are recorded in the recording phase and read in subsequent replayed phases.

4. The use of inputs/outputs in ATHAPASCAN programs is restricted. The programmer must ensure that the inputs of replayed executions are the same as the inputs of the recorded one. Access to shared output devices need to be encapsulated in ATHAPASCAN *Entry Points*.

5. Transmission times of requests and results are finite.

Definition 1. A *history of request receipts* $hr_{vp,ep}$ is associated with each entry point of each virtual processor. It defines the order according to which incoming requests are handled. The denotation of the history of request receipts of entry point ep of virtual processor vp is the following:

$$hr_{vp,ep} = c_0^{vp,ep}, c_1^{vp,ep}, c_2^{vp,ep}, \ldots$$

The execution model refers to the histories of request receipts $hr_{vp,ep}$ which are defined as the sequence of processes executed on the entry point. Each computation $c_{th}^{vp,ep}$ is performed by the process identified with the unique triple $\langle vp, ep, th \rangle$ expressing the thread th running the entry point ep on the virtual processor vp.

Definition 2. A *history of request emissions* he_p is associated with each process $p = \langle vp, ep, th \rangle$. It defines the sequence of requests emitted by this process during execution. The denotation for the history of request emissions of process p is the following:

$$he_p = e_0^p, e_1^p, e_2^p, \ldots$$

Each request emission $e_i^p = \langle vp, ep \rangle$ is directed towards entry point ep on virtual processor vp. For each process p, the history of request emissions he_p reflects the interactions of this process with the rest of the program.

Definition 3. The *mapping relation* M is a set of triples in the form $\langle p_1, i, p_2 \rangle$ indicating that the request emission $e_i^{p_1} = \langle vp, ep \rangle$ is computed by process $p_2 = \langle vp, ep, th \rangle$.

The relation M realizes a bijection between the set of emitted requests and the set of computations. This bijection guarantees that each emitted request is computed and each process computation corresponds to a request.

Following these definitions, the execution X is characterized by the triple $\langle H, E, M \rangle$, where H is the set of histories of request receipts, E is the set of histories of request emissions and M is the mapping relation.

In the following we assume that for all the computations of the same programs, the same mappings are enforced.

4.2 Execution equivalence

Definition 4. Two executions X and X' are said to be equivalent if for each process $p = \langle vp, ep, th \rangle$ both executions assign the same history of request emissions to process p. The equivalence of two executions X and X' is denoted as $X \approx X'$.

This definition of execution equivalence is suitable for debugging a program since the behavior of each individual process is identical in all equivalent executions. These identical behaviors enable a programmer to refine his understanding of the execution of a program through repeated executions. A cyclic debugging technique can then be applied.

Lemma 5. *Sequential* ATHAPASCAN *processes having no external interaction are deterministic.*

This lemma expresses the basic hypothesis of all instant replay mechanisms.

Consequences:

1. For any execution of a parallel ATHAPASCAN program, a process started with the same initial conditions will emit the same first request or the same result, if it does not emit any request.
2. For any execution of a parallel ATHAPASCAN program, a process started with the same initial conditions and whose previously emitted requests were identical and returned the same results, will emit the same following request or result, if it does not emit any more request. Here the difference is that the process interacts with its environment. However its interactions remain the same through all its computations.

For the purpose of the equivalence demonstration, let us define a vector clock [7] for ATHAPASCAN.

Definition 6. A *vector clock* for ATHAPASCAN is defined as a vector whose dimension is the number of Entry Points used by an ATHAPASCAN program execution and updated for each Entry Point in the following way:

1. The ith component of the vector clock of an Entry Point is incremented each time an incoming request $c_{th}^{vp,i}$ is handled on the Entry Point, that is a new process is created and started:

$$VC_i[i] := VC_i[i] + 1 = th$$

2. The vector clock VC_i of EP_i is piggy-backed to each message sent by a process of EP_i, be it a request or a result message.
3. The vector clock VC_i of EP_i is updated on receipt of each message by the Entry Point: if the message is a request, it is when starting a new process, just before incrementing the ith component of the vector clock (see above); otherwise, if the message is a response, the incrementation takes place when the message is passed to the requesting process. Updating performs the following operation:

$$VC_i := sup(VC_i, VC_{mes})$$

sup being a component-wise maximum operation.

We now use this vector clock to define a partial order on the messages emitted during a computation. Let n be the number of Entry Points during both computations. Let m_i and m_j be two messages emitted from Entry Points EP_i and EP_j during the computation of an ATHAPASCAN program and VC_i and VC_j the values of the vector clocks piggy-backed to m_i and m_j.

Definition 7. The partial order between messages induced by the ATHAPASCAN vector clock will be denoted $\prec_{VC}$:

$$m_i \prec_{VC} m_j \Leftrightarrow VC_i \prec VC_j$$

with

$$VC_i \prec VC_j \Leftrightarrow VC_i[k] \leq VC_j[k], \forall k \in [1, n]$$

$\prec_{VC}$ is a partial order since non causally linked messages cannot be ordered. Several requests emitted by the same process p may hold the same vector clock. However they can be ordered by using the indice o of the request emission e_o^p to extend the order $\prec_{VC}$.

Theorem 8. *Let $X = \langle H, E, M \rangle$ be an ATHAPASCAN program execution. Let X' be an execution of the same program under the assumptions defined above (see beginning of section 4.1).*

For X' to be equivalent to X, it is sufficient to map all requests of X' using M.

Proof: The proof is done by contradiction. Let us assume there exists at least one message of X' without corresponding identical message in X. If there exist several messages of this kind, there exists a set of smallest messages, under the $\prec_{VC}$ relation. Let $r_i'^j$ be one of the messages of this set, the jth message emitted by process i. Two possible cases may arise:

1. Either $j = 1$, which means that $r_i'^j$ is the first request emitted by process i, or the answer emitted by process i if it does not emit any request. Again two possible cases:

   (a) Either $i = 1$, $r_1'^1$ is the first request emitted during the ATHAPASCAN program execution. The program was started with the same input parameters in X and X' and therefore the sequential computations before the first request emissions should be identical in X and X' (consequence of lemma 5). Therefore requests r_1^1 and $r_1'^1$ are identical.

   (b) Or $r_i'^1$ is the first request emitted during the computation of process i or the answer of process i, if it does not emit any request. Since process i:
   - was created as a consequence of the same request in both executions X and X', this request being lower than $r_i'^1$ in the order $\prec_{VC}$,
   - was started under the same initial conditions because the mapping M defined by execution X is used during execution X'.
   - did not receive any other external input before emitting $r_i'^1$,

it will perform the same sequential computation between its initialization and the emission of $r_i'^1$ (consequence of lemma 5). Therefore $r_i'^1$, emitted during X' is identical to r_i^1 emitted during X.

2. Or $j > 1$. But prior to the emission of $r_i'^j$, process i:
   - was started under the same initial conditions because the mapping M defined by execution X is used during execution X'.
   - received the same inputs, in the same order as in execution X, since otherwise there would be some message m_i' of X' with $m_i' \prec_{VC} r_i'^j$ without corresponding identical message m_i in X, which contradicts the assumption above.

Because of lemma 5, it is not possible for $r_i'^j$ to be different from the jth request of process i in X and the assumption of the proof is contradictory.

The assumption done is proven false under any circumstances which demonstrates by contradiction that every request from X' has a corresponding request in X. A similar reasoning proves that it is impossible for a request of X not to have its counterpart in X'. □

5 Time-overhead measurement of trace recording

A prototype ATHAPASCAN kernel was instrumented with the mechanism described in this paper. The kernel is built on top of PVM and several thread libraries available for different hardware architectures. The determinacy of reexecutions was tested with a highly non-deterministic process-farm implementation of the N-queens problem, by observing the order of solutions in the result list.

5.1 Time-overhead measurement method

Performance measurements were done using the ANDES (Algorithms aNd DE-Scription) modeling language and synthetic programs generator (see figure 2) [4] which was adapted to model and generate ATHAPASCAN programs. A synthetic parallel program is a real program whose resource consumption, processor, memory and communication, can be easily controlled. The main advantages of synthetic programs are the possibility to generate them automatically and the ease of changing parameters regulating the consumption of resources. Synthetic programs can be used to measure the overhead of trace recording since this overhead is the same for real or synthetic programs. Another advantage of this method was the availability of a set of existing ANDES models. This is the approach of the ALPES project (ALgorithms, Parallelism, and Evaluation of Systems), combining synthetic program generation tools with software monitoring of parallel programs [11].

From a model of algorithm written in ANDES, it is possible to generate a wide range of different synthetic programs with different structures. For example with the *Prolog-like search tree* algorithm, it is possible to change the branching factor of the nodes or the depth of the tree. In the experiments, only one structure was

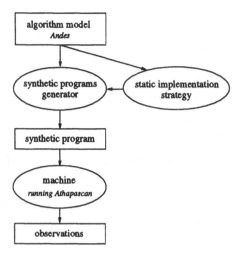

Fig. 2. Evaluation chain.

retained for each model of algorithm. The computation/communication ratio of synthetic programs was adjusted by tuning the values of the parameters of the program models. Experiments were performed by generating, for each model of algorithm, a synthetic program for each of the selected ratios. Execution threads defined in the models were mapped on the virtual processors executing the synthetic programs using one of the greedy algorithms of the mapping toolbox of the APACHE project [1]. From these mappings and the ANDES models of algorithms, synthetic ATHAPASCAN programs were generated. Then the execution times of all synthetic programs were measured, for all the selected ratios.

We restricted ourselves to program models having a deterministic behavior. The behavior of a non-deterministic program can indeed be so different for each of its executions that comparisons become impossible, as it was experienced with the N-queens program where some executions recording traces executed faster than unmonitored executions. For programs whose behavior is non-deterministic, it is not possible to apply a statistical measurement method, based on the hypothesis that observed executions have similar behaviors. The selected models include the following structures of algorithms *Divide and Parallelize* (balanced tree), *Prolog-like Search Tree* (unbalanced tree), *Regular Iteration* (same number of forks in each step), *Master-Slaves* (variable number of forks in each step) and *Strassen's Matrix Product* [10] (recursive numerical algorithm).

To measure the time overhead of the recording, the execution times of synthetic programs were measured "with" and "without" the recording mode set. For each benchmark, the desired precision was to make sure that, with a probability of 95%, the real mean execution time was enclosed within an interval of 3% of the mean execution time centered around the estimated mean execution time. The whole experiment represented 2400 different executions of ATHAPASCAN programs. Each overhead was computed as the ratio of the difference of mean execution time "with" recording mode set and mean execution time "without" recording mode set, divided by the mean execution time "without" recording mode set. The division between two results known with a precision of 95% each reduced the precision of the overheads to a certitude of 90%. Synthetic programs were executed by a prototype of the ATHAPASCAN kernel running on a 32 nodes IBM SP1 entirely dedicated to the measurements.

5.2 Time–overhead measurement results

Measurement results are summarized in figure 3 which displays the measured recording overheads with their confidence ranges. The main outcome from these measures is that recording overheads are lower than 5%, even for the improbable cases where communication costs represent 10 times computation costs. No algorithm seems pathological with respect to the time overhead of recording.

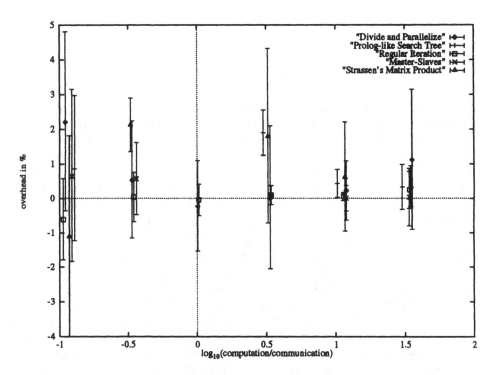

Fig. 3. Preliminary results.

6 Conclusion

Cyclic debugging of inherently non deterministic parallel programs can be done using the Instant Replay technique. This paper describes an adaptation of the

Instant Replay mechanism to a hierarchical, RPC-based programming model, where parallel programs are executed by a potentially high number of light-weight processes, grouped in virtual processors. This adaptation was optimized by exploiting the characteristics of the programming model, resulting in an important reduction of the number of records necessary to replay programs deterministically. The techniques described in the paper can be used for any RPC-based parallel programming model such as applications structured according to a Client-Server architecture. Similar techniques could be adapted to some object-oriented parallel programming models.

A prototype implementation of the RPC-based ATHAPASCAN programming model including record-replay techniques was done and tested. Systematic measurements indicated that the costs of the recording –time overhead and volume of recorded traces– remain very limited and that the recording mode can be used as the normal ATHAPASCAN execution mode, enabling to capture unfrequent errors as soon as they occur and debug them using a cyclic method. The implementation of the instant replay mechanism will serve as a basis for the development of an ATHAPASCAN debugger which is currently being designed.

References

1. P. Bouvry, J. Chassin, and D. Trystram. Efficient solutions for mapping parallel programs. In *Proceedings of EuroPar'95*. Springer-Verlag, August 1995.
2. M. Christaller. ATHAPASCAN-0A control parallelism approach on top of PVM. In *Proc PVM User's group meeting*. University of Tennessee, Oak Ridge, 1994.
3. H. Jamrozik. *Aide à la Mise au Point des Applications Parallèles et Réparties à base d'Objets Persistants*. PhD thesis, Université Joseph Fourier, Grenoble, 1993.
4. J. P. Kitajima and B. Plateau. Modelling parallel program behaviour in *ALPES*. *Information and Software Technology*, 36(7):457–464, July 1994.
5. T.J. LeBlanc and J.M. Mellor-Crummey. Debugging Parallel Programs with Instant Replay. *IEEE Transactions on Computers*, C-36(4):471–481, 1987.
6. E. Leu and A. Schiper. Execution replay: a mechanism for integrating a visualization tool with a symbolic debugger. In *CONPAR 92 - VAPP V*, volume 634 of *LNCS*, September 1992.
7. F. Mattern. Virtual time and global states of distributed systems. In *Proceedings of the Workshop on Parallel and Distributed Algorithms*, Bonas, France, September 1988. North Holland.
8. J.M. Mellor-Crummey. Debugging and Analysis of Large-Scale Parallel Programs. Technical Report 312, University of Rochester, September 1989.
9. B. Plateau. Présentation d'APACHE. Rapport APACHE 1, IMAG, Grenoble, December 1994. Available at `ftp.imag.fr:imag/APACHE/RAPPORTS`.
10. V. Strassen. Gaussian Elimination is not Optimal. *Numerische Mathematik*, Band 13(Heft 4):354–356, 1969.
11. C. Tron et al. Performance Evaluation of Parallel Systems: the ALPES environment. In *Proceedings of ParCo93*. Elsevier Science Publishers, 1993.

Interconnection Networks I

On Efficient Embeddings of Grids into Grids in PARIX*

Thomas Römke[1], Markus Röttger[2], Ulf-Peter Schroeder[2], Jens Simon[1]

[1] Paderborn Center for Parallel Computing (PC²)
[2] Department of Mathematics and Computer Science, University of Paderborn
D-33095 Paderborn, Germany
e-mail: [tomtom, roettger, ups, jens]@uni-paderborn.de
phone: +49 +5251 60 3302,   fax: +49 +5251 60 3515

Abstract. A hardware independent method of programming a massively parallel machine (MPP) can best be supported by a well-designed run-time environment. An important problem in this design is the ability of efficiently simulating networks different from the hardware topology. We will describe the mapping kernel of the virtual processors library for the commercial run-time system PARIX[3]. This kernel contains description classes for several topologies (so-called *virtual topologies*) and implementations of respective embeddings which map given instances of virtual topologies onto others or onto the hardware. Using these functions, PARIX is able to establish concrete virtual topologies with corresponding communication channels. The implemented functions were selected with respect to the well-known criteria for graph embeddings: *equal load* and *small dilation*. Additionally, we focus on *fast distributed computation* and *universal applicability*. As an example, we will show new methods for efficiently embedding an arbitrary 2-dimensional grid as a guest graph into any 2-dimensional grid as a host graph.

Key words: parallel run-time system, PARIX, virtual processors, embedding, grids

1   Introduction

To achieve optimal system performance of a parallel computer, high performance processors as well as high performance communication facilities are needed. Essentially the architecture of the system determines the overall communication throughput. The limited communication performance of a parallel computer requires a careful placement of the communicating processes of a parallel program.

---

* This work was partly supported by the EU ESPRIT Basic Research Action No. 7141 (ALCOM II) and the EU Human Capital and Mobility project: "Efficient Use of Parallel Computers: Architecture, Mapping and Communication".
[3] PARIX (**PAR**allel extensions to Un**IX**) is a trademark of the Parsytec GmbH, Germany.

The mapping of processes onto processors is in graph theoretic terms an embedding of a guest graph into a host graph. There exist several well-known cost measures to rate the quality of an embedding (e.g. *load, dilation, congestion*). The *load* of a host node is the number of guest nodes assigned to it. This is the most important measure, because an equal load – i.e. the loads of the processors differ at most 1 – ensures a good exploitation of the parallel system. Many parallel computer systems still do not have special routing chips (i.e. direct communication is only possible between neighboring processors) and therefore the routing software consumes processor performance. Thus, a minimum *dilation* value (i.e. the maximum distance in the host graph between the images of adjacent guest nodes) is also important. For more details on embeddings see [14].

Most parallel applications are developed w.r.t. the interconnection structures of the process graph. This knowledge can be used to calculate an optimal embedding of the process graph into the hardware, where, in this context, optimization relates to the run-time of a parallel program. Each embedding induces an individual communication load. This load has to be worked off by the network and influences the execution time.

In PARIX 1.x (see [16]) the concept of *virtual topologies* was integrated. A virtual topology consists of a set of processes and a set of fixed connections (virtual links) between them, which build a specific structure. The virtual topology library is aimed at efficient support for simulating the most important classes of these interconnection structures on the underlying hardware. We used some results from the areas "graph embedding" and "simulation among networks" with respect to special optimization criteria and achieved a speed-up for communication-intensive parallel applications. Similar approaches were introduced by [2, 12, 15]. In [2] a collection of mapping functions is presented which efficiently embed some networks with regular structures into a hypercube of the same size. In [12] a functional embedding kernel is designed which supports mappings of higher dimensional grid or torus process graphs onto the 2-dimensional grid network of the IBM Victor Multiprocessor. Moreover, in [15] the concept of virtual topologies as programming abstraction is described and it is shown that this concept offers significant performance improvements because of improved communication locality.

The newest version of PARIX will include a Virtual Processors layer and many-to-one mappings as well as mappings w.r.t. sub-topologies. We will explain these aspects, the user-interface, and the selection criteria in Sec. 2. Because of space limitations we cannot describe all the implemented mapping functions in detail. As an example we will describe an improvement of the *chaining* technique [18] which efficiently maps the nodes of an arbitrary 2-dimensional grid onto the nodes of any 2-dimensional grid as a host graph. The embeddings can be computed in constant time and ensure equal loads and small dilations. Considering 2-dimensional grids is very important, since the interconnection networks of many existing parallel systems are based on them. Furthermore, many algorithms are designed to run on a grid communication structure (e.g. numerical algorithms like the FEM or conjugate gradient methods).

2 The PARIX Structure

PARIX is a run-time environment for MPP systems. It is developed and distributed by Parsytec and contains support for the system administration as well as for the development and execution of applications. From the PARIX point of view, such an MPP system consists of homogeneous or heterogeneous computing nodes and special service nodes, e.g. front-end systems or file servers. PARIX is therefore divided into two parts, a small kernel running on the computing nodes and a complex server running on top of the operating system of the front-end.

The PARIX kernel contains the basic message passing routines, process management, a communication library (based on the message passing routines), Remote Procedure Calls, and numerical libraries. This small kernel is loaded onto all processors prior to the application code and has a direct link to the other part running on the front-end. The latter provides access to unix and network services as well as to peripherals. Furthermore, environments and tools are supplied for the cross-development of applications including compilers, debuggers, and monitoring tools.

Fig. 1. The new PARIX structure

PARIX has recently been extended to fulfill the needs of the next generation of MPP systems where one has a handful of high-performance processors instead of a large number of slow ones. It aims at easy-to-use and efficient object oriented user-interfaces and will provide extensive libraries. See Fig. 1 for its four level structure.

The bottom level of PARIX, called the *nanoKernel*, consists of routines for simulating an abstract sequential processor including, for example, process and memory management, interprocess communication, and I/O. The provision of such a virtual processor hides the real architecture and makes programming and porting much easier.

The Task Library (TaskLib) provides high-level routines for typed and untyped communication, task handling, topologies, and corresponding data structures. It is implemented in C++ and based on the Kernel functions. On the other hand compatibility to previous PARIX versions is supplied in this level. Since the TaskLib is more extensive, PARIX 1.x functions run in a TaskLib emulation box.

The next layer (VP PARIX) is also implemented in C++. It mainly consists of facilities to provide topologies of virtual processors, i.e. to simulate more processors than are available and to group them to structures. Let us consider the request of a 2^{10} node hypercube on an 8 processor machine configured as a 2×2 mesh of 2-processor nodes. VP PARIX ensures that this hypercube and all the other topologies provided in this level are mapped as optimal as possible (optimality is explained in the end of this section). Thus, an algorithm designed for such a topology can be expected to run with a small or even without any loss of efficiency. The VP PARIX concept consequently follows the idea of Virtual Topologies [16]. However, the Virtual Topologies Library was restricted to one-to-one mappings, whereas VP PARIX includes many-to-one mappings and mapping w.r.t. sub-topologies (topologies with some nodes missing).

The user interface level is open and is able to use the complete functionality of the other levels. It will at least contain a C++ and an MPI conform interface (C, Fortran).

Our Work within the PARIX Layers

The work on the virtual processors layer is twofold. On the one hand, we implemented descriptor classes for a number of topologies, i.e. **grids** and **tori**[4], **pipes** and **rings** as special cases of these, **star**[5], **hypercubes, deBruijn, Clique,** and **trees**. A description of a topology contains general information about the requested topology, e.g. member functions or fields to identify the dimension, number of nodes, diameter, the node id of a given coordinate w.r.t. the topology, membership of a given coordinate, the number and coordinates of neighbors, the structure of the topology coordinates, etc.

The more sophisticated work, however, was on the mapping functions from each of the mentioned topologies onto the others. We have implemented several well-known embedding methods as well as a lot of new techniques which we have explicitly developed within this project. All these routines are member functions of the respective topology classes and are called by the Task Systems when needed. If no mapping function is defined for the topology in mind, a more or less efficient default mapper is chosen. For now a simple mapper is integrated, but we have immediate plans to implement a high-level default mapper based on heuristics. We have a long term experience in these techniques (e.g. Distributed Simulated Annealing[7] and diffusion approach[4] algorithms) and they have proven to be very useful for solving hard combinatorial optimization problems.

---

[4] Even incomplete, i.e. some of the wrap-around edges are missing

[5] A star has a dedicated center node and the only connections are from this node to all the others.

How to Use the Functionality

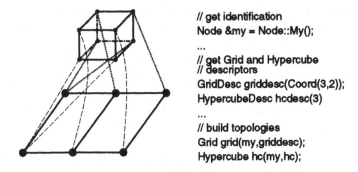

```
// get identification
Node &my = Node::My();

...
// get Grid and Hypercube
// descriptors
GridDesc griddesc(Coord(3,2));
HypercubeDesc hcdesc(3)

...
// build topologies
Grid grid(my,griddesc);
Hypercube hc(my,hc);
```

Fig. 2. Mapping example

As mentioned earlier, we focus on easy-to-learn and easy-to-use interfaces for the virtual processors facilities. Figure 2 shows how to run an algorithm for a 2^3 node hypercube. For reasons of simplicity, let us assume that the actual hardware is unknown and that we also need a 3×2 grid.

The first step is the unique identification of the actual node. This identification is provided by the TaskLib and needed for communication and as a parameter to some of the topology constructors.

Secondly, descriptors are generated for both the grid and the hypercube. The HypercubeDesc is quite a simple construction: A hypercube of dimension 3 is generated. The constructor for the grid, however, accepts a *Coord* argument, which is a vector of numbers. The length of this vector is the dimension of the grid and the numbers represent the size of each dimension.

Until now, no new topology has been built, but all necessary information is readily available. When the *Grid* constructor takes place, a 3×2 grid is established and mapped onto the actual topology or onto the hardware[6]. Furthermore, the *Hypercube* constructor establishes a 2^3 node hypercube, maps it onto the grid and sets up links between the hypercube nodes and the nodes they are mapped onto. All this is done automatically by the TaskLib, hidden from the user, and it is the only point at which the mapping functions are called.

Selection Criteria for Embedding Functions

The implementation of a Mapping Library was motivated by the intention that PARIX should support the hardware independent implementation of parallel applications, which leads to a portable programming concept. To conceal hardware details from a PARIX user and to prevent the problems of graph embedding, the

---

[6] This mapping is not shown here because it depends on whether or not other topologies have been created so far.

frequently used topologies and the mapping functions from each of the topologies onto the others are implemented in the VP library.

Besides an *equal load* and a *small dilation* the used embeddings have to satisfy the following criteria: *Fast distributed computation* and *universal applicability*. A distributed computation of the embedding is desirable because in a central computation of the embedding we have to broadcast the information where each process is allocated to the involved processors which slows down the run-time. Furthermore, we have focused our work to achieve a constant parallel run-time of the computation of the embedding. In case we have to embed hypercubes, deBruijn networks or complete k-ary trees the parallel run-time is logarithmic in the number of nodes of the network. Otherwise we will always get run-time $\mathcal{O}(1)$. Besides that, many algorithms on graph embedding are only applicable to special instances of a topology. These algorithms could be a part of the library as long as there are additional algorithms to handle the remaining instances of the topology.

3 Embedding Grids into Grids

In this section we take a closer look on an embedding technique called *chaining*. This technique can be applied to map nodes of an arbitrary $a \times b$ grid as a guest onto the nodes of any $x \times y$ grid as the host graph. An embedding can be described in graph-theoretic terms as follows:

Let $G = (V_G, E_G)$ and $H = (V_H, E_H)$ be finite undirected graphs. An *embedding* f of G into H is a mapping $f : V_G \longrightarrow V_H$. G is called the *guest* graph and H is called the *host* graph of the embedding f. If f is an injective function we get a *one-to-one* mapping, otherwise we get a *many-to-one* mapping.

The basic idea of the chaining technique was introduced in [5, 6] to embed 2-dimensional grids into hypercubes. In [18] the chaining technique was generalized to embed 2-dimensional grids into smaller grids, i.e. $a \geq x, b \geq y$ must hold, with dilation 3 and without equal load. We have improved the chaining technique, which implies a more widely applicable embedding technique and a decrease of the dilation w.r.t. the method mentioned above. Additionally, we will show that it is possible to compute the corresponding embedding in constant time.

Let us explain our technique by using an example: the 7×2 grid as the guest and the 5×3 grid as the host. We align the guest in the host grid compressing 2 rows of length 7 to length 5. This compression is shown in Fig. 3. Note that each row of the guest – called *chain* – can be described by a vector of length 5 which determines how many nodes of each chain are in the same column of the host grid. The vector $(2, 1, 2, 1, 1)$, for example, corresponds to the first chain, the vector $(1, 2, 1, 2, 1)$ to the second. Thus an embedding of a guest into a host grid via chaining results in an *embedding matrix* and a description of how the elements of each chain are connected. In the following we will show the set-up of the embedding matrix and we will prove that it is not necessary to compute the matrix explicitly to achieve the embedding.

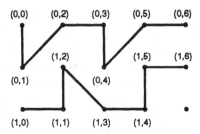

Fig. 3. Embedding of the 7×2 grid into the 5×3 grid via chaining.

Let us arrange the dimension sizes a, b, x and y in such a way that $b \geq y$. Note that this is not possible iff $\max\{a, b\} < \min\{x, y\}$, but, obviously, in this case the guest grid is a subgraph of the host grid. Let z be the smallest integer such that $zy \geq ab$, i.e. $z = \lceil \frac{ab}{y} \rceil$. We call $z \times y$ an *ideal grid* of $a \times b$.

Using the chaining technique we embed the guest grid into the ideal grid. If $ab > xy$ we group some of the nodes of the ideal grid in order to compress it into the host grid. Otherwise the ideal grid is a subgraph of the host grid. Let f_{ideal} denote the embedding of the guest graph into the ideal grid. To compute f_{ideal} we define an *embedding matrix* $W = (w_{ij}), 0 \leq i < a, 0 \leq j < y$ as follows:

– The first row of W is the vector

$$\left(\left\lceil \frac{b}{y} \right\rceil, \left\lceil \frac{2b}{y} \right\rceil - \left\lceil \frac{b}{y} \right\rceil, \ldots, \left\lceil \frac{(j+1)b}{y} \right\rceil - \left\lceil \frac{jb}{y} \right\rceil, \ldots, \left\lceil \frac{yb}{y} \right\rceil - \left\lceil \frac{(y-1)b}{y} \right\rceil \right),$$

– We get the ith row by a cyclic right shift of row $i - 1, 1 \leq i < a$.

Hence, for $a = 9$, $b = 7$, and $y = 5$ the embedding matrix W is:

$$W = \begin{pmatrix} 2\,1\,2\,1\,1 \\ 1\,2\,1\,2\,1 \\ 1\,1\,2\,1\,2 \\ 2\,1\,1\,2\,1 \\ 1\,2\,1\,1\,2 \\ 2\,1\,2\,1\,1 \\ 1\,2\,1\,2\,1 \\ 1\,1\,2\,1\,2 \\ 2\,1\,1\,2\,1 \end{pmatrix}$$

Note that $w_{ij} = \left\lceil b \frac{j-i+1}{y} \right\rceil - \left\lceil b \frac{j-i}{y} \right\rceil$ with $i \in \{0, .., a-1\}$, $j \in \{0, .., y-1\}$.

Theorem 1. The embedding matrix W has the following properties:

(I) $w_{ij} \in \{\lfloor \frac{b}{y} \rfloor, \lceil \frac{b}{y} \rceil\}$ for $0 \leq i < a$ and $0 \leq j < y$,

(II) $\sum_{j=0}^{y-1} w_{ij} = b$ for $0 \leq i < a$,

(III) $\sum_{i=0}^{a-1} w_{ij} \in \{\lfloor \frac{ab}{y} \rfloor, \lceil \frac{ab}{y} \rceil\}$ for $0 \leq j < y$.

Proof: Let $i \in \{0, .., a-1\}$ and $j \in \{0, .., y-1\}$. Using $w_{ij} = \left\lceil b\, \frac{i-i+1}{y} \right\rceil - \left\lceil b\, \frac{i-i}{y} \right\rceil$ and $\left\lceil \frac{k+l}{m} \right\rceil - \left\lceil \frac{l}{m} \right\rceil \in \{\lfloor \frac{k}{m} \rfloor, \lceil \frac{k}{m} \rceil\}$ for any integers k, l and m, property (I) follows. Note that one can compute a partial sum in any row $r \in \{0, .., a-1\}$ of the matrix W in constant time as follows:

$$\sum_{j=k}^{l} w_{rj} = \left\lceil b\, \frac{l-r+1}{y} \right\rceil - \left\lceil b\, \frac{k-r}{y} \right\rceil, \quad 0 \le k \le l < y. \tag{1}$$

Therefore $\sum_{j=0}^{y-1} w_{rj} = \left\lceil b\, \frac{y-r}{y} \right\rceil - \left\lceil b\, \frac{-r}{y} \right\rceil = b + \left\lceil -\frac{br}{y} \right\rceil - \left\lceil -\frac{br}{y} \right\rceil = b$.

In the same way one can compute a partial sum in any column $c \in \{0, .., y-1\}$:

$$\sum_{i=k}^{l} w_{ic} = \left\lceil b\, \frac{c-k+1}{y} \right\rceil - \left\lceil b\, \frac{c-l}{y} \right\rceil, \quad 0 \le k \le l < a. \tag{2}$$

Thus: $\sum_{i=0}^{a-1} w_{ic} = \left\lceil \frac{b(c+1)}{y} \right\rceil - \left\lceil \frac{b(c-a+1))}{y} \right\rceil = \left\lceil \frac{ab+(bc+b-ab)}{y} \right\rceil - \left\lceil \frac{bc+b-ab}{y} \right\rceil \in \{\lfloor \frac{ab}{y} \rfloor, \lceil \frac{ab}{y} \rceil\}$ $\square$

Now we are able to define the embedding f_{ideal} of the $a \times b$ grid into its ideal grid, the $z \times y$ grid, i.e. $f_{ideal} : \{0, .., a-1\} \times \{0, .., b-1\} \longrightarrow \{0, .., z-1\} \times \{0, .., y-1\}$ without the necessity of explicitly computing the embedding matrix. Let (a', b') be an arbitrary node of the $a \times b$ grid. For its (unique) image node (z', y') must hold:

$$\sum_{j=0}^{y'-1} w_{a'j} < b'+1 \le \sum_{j=0}^{y'} w_{a'j}, \tag{3}$$

$$\text{and} \quad z' = \sum_{i=0}^{a'-1} w_{iy'} + \begin{cases} b' - \sum_{j=0}^{y'-1} w_{a'j} & \text{if } y' \text{ is even,} \\ \left(\sum_{j=0}^{y'} w_{a'j}\right) - b' - 1 & \text{if } y' \text{ is odd.} \end{cases} \tag{4}$$

Figure 4(a) shows the embedding of a 9×7 grid into its ideal grid, the 13×5 grid, using the chaining technique with dilation 3. There are 9 chains of length 7 which are aligned in the 13×5 grid. Chain i corresponds to row i of the matrix W, i.e. this row determines how many nodes of chain i are in the same column of the host grid.

In the following we show that it is possible to compute the embedding f_{ideal} in constant time. At first we have to compute $y' \in \{0, .., y-1\}$ with $\sum_{j=0}^{y'-1} w_{a'j} < b'+1 \le \sum_{j=0}^{y'} w_{a'j}$. Note that $\sum_{j=0}^{-1} w_{a'j} = \left\lceil b\, \frac{-1-a'+1}{y} \right\rceil - \left\lceil b\, \frac{-a'}{y} \right\rceil = 0$, i.e. we can apply (1) for all desired partial sums. Thus, we have:

$$\left\lceil b\, \frac{y'-a'}{y} \right\rceil - \left\lceil b\, \frac{-a'}{y} \right\rceil < b'+1 \le \left\lceil b\, \frac{y'-a'+1}{y} \right\rceil - \left\lceil b\, \frac{-a'}{y} \right\rceil.$$

Let us set $c := \left\lceil b\, \frac{-a'}{y} \right\rceil$. It follows:

$$\left\lceil b\, \frac{y'-a'}{y} \right\rceil - c < b'+1 \le \left\lceil b\, \frac{y'-a'+1}{y} \right\rceil - c.$$

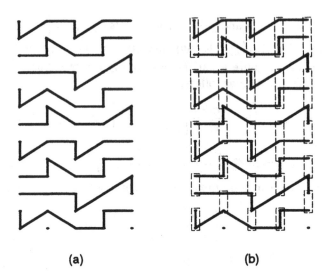

Fig. 4. Embedding of the 9×7 into the 13×5 (a) and 5×5 grid (b), via chaining.

Since b' must be an integer, it holds:

$$b \frac{y' - a'}{y} - c < b' + 1 \leq b \frac{y' - a' + 1}{y} - c + 1$$

and thus:

$$y \frac{b' + c}{b} + a' - 1 \leq y' < y \frac{b' + 1 + c}{b} + a'.$$

Since y' must be an integer, it holds:

$$\left\lceil y \frac{b' + c}{b} \right\rceil + a' - 1 \leq y' < \left\lceil y \frac{b' + 1 + c}{b} \right\rceil + a'.$$

With $y \frac{b' + c + 1}{b} - y \frac{b' + c}{b} = \frac{y}{b} \leq 1$ it follows that

$$y' = \left\lceil y \frac{b' + c}{b} \right\rceil + a' - 1 \quad \text{or} \quad y' = \left\lceil y \frac{b' + c}{b} \right\rceil + a'.$$

Note that only one of the two values for y' fulfill (3). Therefore, we initialize y' with $\left\lceil y \frac{b' + c}{b} \right\rceil + a'$ and decrease y' by one if $\left\lceil b \frac{y' - a'}{y} \right\rceil - c \geq b' + 1$ holds.

Now we are able to compute $z' \in \{0, .., z - 1\}$. If y' is even then $z' = \sum_{i=0}^{a'-1} w_{iy'} + b' - \sum_{j=0}^{y'-1} w_{a'j}$. Note that $\sum_{i=0}^{-1} w_{iy'} = \left\lceil b \frac{y' + 1}{y} \right\rceil - \left\lceil b \frac{y' - (-1)}{y} \right\rceil = 0$, i.e. we can apply (2) for all desired partial sums. Thus, we have:

$$z' = \left\lceil b \frac{y' + 1}{y} \right\rceil - \left\lceil b \frac{y' - a' + 1}{y} \right\rceil + b' - \left\lceil b \frac{y' - a'}{y} \right\rceil + \left\lceil b \frac{-a'}{y} \right\rceil.$$

If y' is odd then $z' = \sum_{i=0}^{a'-1} w_{iy'} + (\sum_{j=0}^{y'} w_{a'j}) - b' - 1$ and therefore

$$z' = \left\lceil b \frac{y'+1}{y} \right\rceil - \left\lceil b \frac{y'-a'+1}{y} \right\rceil + \left\lceil b \frac{y'-a'+1}{y} \right\rceil - \left\lceil b \frac{-a'}{y} \right\rceil - b' - 1.$$

Theorem 2. The function f_{ideal} defines a one-to-one embedding of the $a \times b$ grid into its ideal grid, the $z \times y$ grid, with dilation at most $\lceil \frac{b}{y} \rceil + 1$.

To the proof: Using Theorem 1, it is not difficult to see that f_{ideal} is an injective mapping of the nodes of the $a \times b$ grid onto the nodes of the $z \times y$ grid. Furthermore, it is obvious that the following holds: $|\sum_{i=0}^{l} w_{ic} - \sum_{i=0}^{l} w_{ic+1}| \le 1$ for $c \in \{0, .., y-2\}$ and $l \in \{0, .., a-1\}$ and $|\sum_{j=0}^{l} w_{rj} - \sum_{j=0}^{l} w_{r+1j}| \le 1$ for $r \in \{0, .., a-2\}$ and $l \in \{0, .., y-1\}$. Additionally, if a chain changes the column within the ideal grid it changes its direction from the bottom to the top or vice versa (see Fig. 4). Considering all these facts, we can conclude that adjacent nodes of the guest grid being in the same chain are in distance of at most 2 in this grid (one vertical and one horizontal edge). Furthermore, adjacent nodes of the guest grid belonging to different chains are at most $\lceil \frac{b}{y} \rceil$ vertical edges and one horizontal edge or at most $\lceil \frac{b}{y} \rceil + 1$ vertical edges apart. The full proof is obvious but too technical and was omitted because of space limitation. □

In comparison with the lower bounds given in [11], the dilation achieved with the chaining technique is asymptotically optimal. For completeness' sake we have to mention the work done in [10] that was independently developed. It is quite similar to the above construction except that its embedding cannot be computed in constant time. The authors use an embedding matrix just as we do but their more careful arrangement of the elements of the matrix provides dilation of at most $\lceil \frac{b}{y} \rceil$.

If the ideal grid is a subgraph of the considered $x \times y$ host grid, f_{ideal} already defines an embedding of the guest into the host grid. Otherwise we have to group some of the nodes of the ideal grid in order to compress it into the host grid. Since we require an equal load, we group $\lfloor \frac{ab}{xy} \rfloor$ or $\lceil \frac{ab}{xy} \rceil$ nodes in the ideal grid. In other words, we distribute $s = \sum_{i=0}^{a-1} w_{iy'} \in \{\lfloor \frac{ab}{y} \rfloor, \lceil \frac{ab}{y} \rceil\}$ nodes in column y' of the ideal grid on x nodes of the host grid in such a way that each node of the host grid is provided with at least $\lfloor \frac{s}{x} \rfloor$ nodes and at most $\lceil \frac{s}{x} \rceil$ nodes. Let f_{host} denote the embedding of the $a \times b$ grid into the $x \times y$ host grid, (a', b') an arbitrary node of the guest and $f_{host}(a', b') = (x', y')$ the image of (a', b'). To compute f_{host} as described above, we define y' as in (3) and with $s = \sum_{i=0}^{a-1} w_{iy'}$ we define:

$$x' = \begin{cases} \lfloor z'/\lceil \frac{s}{x} \rceil \rfloor & \text{if } z' < \lceil \frac{s}{x} \rceil (s \bmod x), \\[2mm] \lfloor (z' - s \bmod x)/\lfloor \frac{s}{x} \rfloor \rfloor & \text{otherwise.} \end{cases}$$

Figure 4(b) shows the embedding of a 9×7 grid into the 5×5 grid with dilation 2 using the technique described above. We group 2 or 3 nodes of the 13×5 grid to one node of the 5×5 grid.

Theorem 3. If $ab \geq xy$ and still $b \geq y$, the function f_{host} embeds the $a \times b$ grid into the $x \times y$ grid with an equal load and dilation of at most $\lceil \lceil \frac{b}{y} \rceil / \lfloor \frac{ab}{xy} \rfloor \rceil + 1$.

To the proof: Note that, as mentioned before, adjacent nodes of the guest grid are at most $\lceil \frac{b}{y} \rceil$ vertical edges and one horizontal edge or at most $\lceil \frac{b}{y} \rceil + 1$ vertical edges apart. Since we group nodes which are in the same column of the ideal grid, the vertical distance within the host grid of adjacent nodes of the guest grid decreases at least by the factor $\lfloor \frac{ab}{xy} \rfloor$.   □

Considering Theorem 3 with $ab \geq x(y + b)$, dilation 2 follows. If only $a \geq x$, we can guarantee dilation 3. If additionally $y \mid b$, then adjacent nodes are only one horizontal edge apart, since all elements in the matrix W are identical. Table 1 gives an overview of the used embeddings and upper bounds for the achieved dilations. Additionally, we have implemented the *folding* technique introduced in [1] that provides dilation 2 under certain conditions (see Table 1).

Table 1. Embeddings of the $a \times b$ grid into the $x \times y$ grid.

	condition	maximum dilation	method
one-to-one	$a \leq x \wedge b \leq y$	1	subgraph
one-to-one	$a \lceil b/y \rceil \leq x \wedge y \geq a$	2	folding
one-to-one	—	$\left\lceil \frac{\max\{a,b\}}{\min\{x,y\}} \right\rceil + 1$	chaining
many-to-one	$y \mid b \wedge a \geq x$	1	chaining
many-to-one	$ab \geq x(y + b) \wedge b \geq y$	2	chaining
many-to-one	$a \geq x \wedge b \geq y$	3	chaining
many-to-one	—	$\left\lceil \lceil \frac{\max\{a,b\}}{\min\{x,y\}} \rceil / \lfloor \frac{ab}{xy} \rfloor \right\rceil + 1$	chaining

4   Conclusion

We have presented the facilities of PARIX with respect to the Virtual Processors layer and given a detailed description of a modified chaining technique. This, however, was only a small part of our work within the VP PARIX layer. We also implemented well-known embedding methods for grids into hypercubes [5, 6, 9, 13, 17], trees into pipes and grids [8], and deBruijn into hypercubes [3]. The other embedding functions, e.g. hypercube into grid or torus into hypercube, though implemented, are not described here because of space limitations. Our work will continue to complete the VP library. A high-level default mapper based on heuristics will be implemented for those mappings which are not covered by our implementations or for arbitrary topologies defined by users.

References

1. R. Aleliunas, A. Rosenberg: *On Embedding Rectangular Grids in Square Grids*, IEEE Transactions on Computers, Vol. C-31, No. 9, September 1982.
2. F.S. Annexstein: *Parallel Implementations of Graph Embeddings*, Parallel Architectures and their efficient use, Lecture Notes in Computer Science, Vol. 678, 1992.
3. M. Baumslag, M.C. Heydemann, J. Opatrny, D. Sotteau: *Embeddings of shuffle-like graphs in hypercubes*, Parallel Architectures and Languages Europe (PARLE'91), Springer LNCS 505, pp. 179–190, 1991.
4. J.E. Boillat, P.G. Kropf: *A fast distributed Mapping Algorithm*, Proc. of CONPAR '90, Springer LNCS 457, 1990.
5. M.Y. Chan: *Embedding of Grids into Optimal Hypercubes*, SIAM J. Computing, Vol. 20, No. 5, pp. 834–864, 1991.
6. M.Y. Chan, F.Y.L. Chin: *Parallelized simulation of grids by hypercubes*, Technical Report, University of Hong Kong, October 1990.
7. R. Diekmann, R. Lüling, J. Simon: *Problem Independent Distributed Simulated Annealing and its Applications*, Applied Simulated Annealing, Lecture Notes in Economics and Mathematical Systems, Springer LNEMS 396, 1993.
8. R. Heckmann, R. Klasing, B. Monien, W. Unger: *Optimal Embedding of Complete Binary Trees into Lines and Grids*, Proc. 17th Int. Workshop on Graph-Theoretic Concepts in Computer Science (WG91), Springer LNCS 570, pp. 25–35, 1991.
9. C.T. Ho, S.L. Johnsson: *Embedding Meshes in Boolean Cubes by Graph Decomposition*, Journal of Parallel an Distributed Computing, 8, pp. 325–339, 1990.
10. S.-H. Huang, H.L. Liu, R. Verma: *A New Combinatorial Approach to Optimal Embeddings of Rectangles*, Intern. Parallel Processing Symposium, 1994.
11. S.R. Kosaraj, M.J. Atallah: *Optimal Simulations Between Mesh-Connected Arrays of Processors*, ACM Symposium on Theory of Computing, pp. 264–272, 1986.
12. E. Ma, D.G. Shea: *The Embedding Kernel on the IBM Victor Multiprocessor for Program Mapping and Network Reconfiguration*, Proceedings of the Second IEEE Symposium on Parallel and Distributed Processing, 1990.
13. Z. Miller, I.H. Sudborough: *Compressing Grids into Small Hypercubes*, Networks, Vol. 24, pp. 327–358, 1994.
14. B. Monien, I.H. Sudborough: *Embedding one Interconnection Network in Another*, Computing Suppl. 7, pp. 257–282, 1990.
15. J. Philbin: *Virtual Topologies: A New Concurrency Abstraction for High-Level Parallel Languages*, DIMACS Workshop on Interconnection Networks, 1994.
16. M. Röttger, U.-P. Schroeder, J. Simon: *Implementation of a Parallel and Distributed Mapping Kernel for PARIX*, Intern. Conference and Exhibition on High-performance Computing and Networking, (HPCN Europe'95), pp. 781–786, 1995.
17. M. Röttger, U.-P. Schroeder, W. Unger: *Embedding 3-dimensional Grids into optimal Hypercubes*, Proc. of the 1st Canada-France Conference on Parallel Computing (CFCP '94), Springer LNCS 805, pp. 81–94, 1994.
18. F.C. Sang, I.H. Sudborough: *Embedding Large Meshes into Small Ones*, Proc. of the IEEE Symposium on Circuits and Systems, Vol. 1, pp. 323–326, 1990.

Optimal Emulation of Meshes
on Meshes of Trees

Alf-Christian Achilles[*]

Department of Computer Science
University of Karlsruhe
Germany
achilles@ira.uka.de

Abstract. Many problems can be solved more efficiently on a mesh of trees network than on a mesh. Until now it has been an open problem whether the mesh of trees is always at least as fast as the mesh. In this paper, we present an emulation of N-node meshes on $O(N)$-node meshes of trees with constant slowdown, even though any embedding of a mesh into a mesh of trees requires dilation $\Omega(\log N)$. This demonstrates that the mesh of trees is strictly more powerful than the mesh. As an application, we show how to construct an optimal $O(\sqrt{N})$ sorting algorithm for the mesh of trees that improves on the best previously known algorithm by a logarithmic factor.

1 Introduction

Fixed interconnection networks for parallel computers determine to a large degree the algorithms used. They define the available locality any algorithm must try to exploit to be efficient. One of the important questions regarding interconnection networks is their relative computational power which can be determined by emulating one network on the other. An emulation describes how any algorithm for one network can be transformed to run on another network with a defined slowdown. Efficient emulations thus contribute to the portability of algorithms across interconnection networks, sometimes even to the discovery of new, faster algorithms for certain problems, as is the case in this work regarding the problem of sorting.

In this work we show that the mesh of trees is strictly more powerful than the mesh by emulating the mesh on the mesh of trees with constant slowdown (open problem 2.5 in [6]), and use that result to show the existence of an optimal $\Theta(\sqrt{N})$ algorithm for the sorting problem on the mesh of trees.

In this paper we investigate the emulation of meshes by mesh of trees networks that are at most a constant factor larger than the emulated mesh. First we discuss the properties of the mesh of trees and present previous work on the emulation of meshes by meshes of trees. The following sections describe the

---
[*] This work was supported by the Graduiertenkolleg "Controllability of Complex Systems" (DFG Vo 287/5-2)

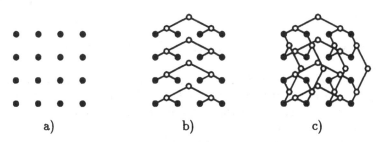

Fig. 1. A 4×4 mesh of trees: **a)** Mesh-like layout of the leaves. **b)** Addition of row trees. **c)** Addition of column trees.

emulation model used in this work and the application of neighborhood covers for the construction of the emulation. Finally we show how to parameterize the emulation such that both the expansion and the slowdown of the emulation are constant.

1.1 The Mesh of Trees

An $m \times m$ mesh of trees, $m = 2^i$ for $i \in \mathbb{N}$, is basically a 2-dimensional square mesh whose edges have been removed and have been replaced by complete binary trees on each column and row, thus additionally introducing new nodes in the internal nodes of the trees. Figure 1 shows a 4×4 mesh of trees.

An $M = m \times m$ mesh of trees contains $3m^2 - 2m = O(M)$ nodes and has a diameter of $4 \log m$. The mesh of trees is a recurrent network: By removing the root nodes and their incident edges in all trees the mesh of trees is partitioned into four disconnected $\frac{m}{2} \times \frac{m}{2}$ meshes of trees. Vice versa, a $2^i \times 2^i$ mesh of trees can be composed of 2^{2p}, $p \in \mathbb{N}$, $2^q \times 2^q$ submeshes of trees, $p + q = i$, by arranging the submeshes of trees in a grid pattern and adding the necessary tree nodes in each row and column.

The mesh of trees is an area-universal network, thus it can emulate any network of equal VSLI layout area with a polylogarithmic slowdown. Due to its small diameter, the mesh of trees can solve a number of problems more quickly than the 2-dimensional mesh. In particular, certain graph-theoretic problems such as the computation of the transitive hull or the minimum spanning tree can be solved on the N-node mesh of trees in time $O(\log^2 N)$, compared to $O(\sqrt{N})$ steps on the mesh. The capabilities of the mesh of trees are extensively discussed in [6].

However, there are problems whose best known solutions require asymptotically more steps on the mesh of trees than on the mesh. An important example is sorting N elements. The best previously known sorting algorithm for the mesh of trees needs $O(\sqrt{N} \log N)$ steps whereas on the mesh only $\Theta(\sqrt{N})$ steps are needed (see e.g. [12, 10, 5]).

1.2   Previous Work

Most of the work on interconnection networks has focused on finding efficient embeddings.

An embedding of a network $G = (V_G, E_G)$ into a network $H = (V_H, E_H)$ is a mapping of the nodes of G onto the nodes of H and a mapping of the edges of G onto paths in H such that the endpoints of an edge e are mapped to the endpoints of the image of e.

An embedding is generally characterized by three parameters: The *load* l of the embedding is the maximal number of nodes in G that are mapped to the same node in H. The *dilation* d is the maximal length of a path in H that is an image of an edge in G. The *congestion* c is the maximal number of paths in H that are images of an edge in G and share a common edge in H.

The emulation of G by H as described by an embedding consists of sending a packet along all the image paths in H for each step of G to be simulated and computing the next state for all the nodes of G. Both the dilation d and the congestion c are lower bounds for the transport of packets so that the transport takes $\Omega(d+c)$ steps. Since $\Omega(l)$ steps are needed for the computation of the next state of the nodes in G, at least $\Omega(d + c + l)$ steps are needed to emulate one step of the computation of G in H.

Previous work on the emulation of meshes by meshes of trees has relied on embeddings of the mesh into the mesh of trees. The intuitive embedding of an N-node mesh into an $O(N)$-node mesh of trees consists of a one-to-one mapping of the nodes of the mesh onto the leaf nodes of the mesh of trees and connecting the images of neighboring mesh nodes by paths in the trees. That embedding has load 1, congestion 2 and dilation $\Theta(\log N)$, which yields an emulation with a slowdown of $\Theta(\log N)$. In fact, this is also an asymptotically optimal embedding, since — as a consequence of the much more general result in [1] — any embedding of a mesh into a mesh of trees has dilation $\Omega(\log N)$. Therefore any emulation of meshes on meshes of trees that is based on embeddings must have slowdown $\Omega(\log N)$.

Probably due to the fact that the intuitive embedding already matches the dilation lower bound for embeddings, not much work has been done on this topic. A different model for emulations was needed that allows to overcome that dilation lower bound.

2   Emulations

There exists a more general but still realistic model for emulation of interconnction networks that has been proven to lead to stronger results.

A network is described by a directed graph $G = (V, E)$ with anti-parallel edges, where each vertex $v \in V$ in the graph designates a processor and each edge $e \in E$ a communication link between two processors. A computation on the network G is performed in disrete time steps as follows: at time step t each processor $v \in V$ has a state (v, t). To compute $(v, t + 1)$ it obtains a packet

(e, t) of constant length from one incoming communication link e incident to v, computes the next state $(v, t + 1)$ as a function of this packet and (v, t) and generates a packet $(e', t + 1)$ for one outgoing communication link e'.

An emulation of a network G on a network H begins with an initial distribution of all $(v, 0)$, $v \in V_G$, to vertices in H. The emulation then proceeds by computing the states of the vertices in V_G for the next time steps according to the computation rules for G. At each emulation step, each processor u in H can receive an edge packet (e, t) from one of its incident incoming edges, compute the state of a node in G, if all the necessary data is present on u, and send a packet along one incident outgoing edge.

G has been emulated for T_G time steps if for every $v \in G$ there exists at least one (v, T_G) in one of the vertices of H. Let the number of steps in H needed for the emulation be T_H.

Definition 1. The *slowdown* S of an emulation of T_G steps of G in T_H steps on H is defined as $S = T_H / T_G$. The *expansion* $|V_H| / |V_G|$ indicates the relative size of G and H.

Only slightly different models have already been employed to construct universal parallel computers [8, 9], to emulate meshes on butterflies with constant slowdown [4], to show the equivalence of bounded-degree networks derived from the hypercube [11], to tolerate faults in some interconnection networks [7] and to emulate planar graphs on various classes of networks [2, 3].

Please note that the model makes no assumption about the size of the state of a processor (as in [4] and [2]), except that the computation of the next processor state takes constant time.

This emulation model allows to hide latency by pipelining the routing of information which has been computed locally with the aid of multiple copies of processor states to distant processors such that the amortized time necessary for the emulation decreases compared to emulations based on embeddings where the dilation is a lower bound for the slowdown.

3 Our approach

We use a more general emulation model than embeddings that allows processors of the host network to be emulated in more than one processors in the guest network, as described above. We will describe the use of neighborhood covers and show how to generate neighborhood covers for the mesh.

3.1 Emulation through neighborhood covers

The concept of t-neighborhood covers, formalized in [2], is very useful to construct emulations:

Definition 2. Let $G = (V, E)$ be a graph. The *t-neighborhood* of a vertex $v \in V$ consists of all the nodes in V whose distance to v is at most t. The t-neighborhood of a subset $V' \subset V$ is the union of the t-neighborhoods of all the nodes in V'.

A node $v \in V$ can be emulated for t steps by emulating its t-neighborhood, if the states of the nodes in the t-neighborhood at step $t = 0$ are known.

Definition 3. A *t-neighborhood-cover* of an undirected graph G is a set of subgraphs $\{S_1, S_2, \ldots, S_h\}$ of G such that for every v in G there is an S_i that contains the t-neighborhood of v in G.

Obviously, the graph G can be emulated for t steps by emulating t steps of the subgraphs in a t-neighborhood cover, since the t-neighborhood of each node in G is contained in some subgraph in the t-neighborhood. To proceed with the emulation beyond the first t steps information has to be exchanged between the subgraphs: Each node $v \in S_i$ with $(u, v) \in E$, $u \notin S_i$, obtains the edge packets $((u, v), 1), ((u, v), 2), \ldots, ((u, v), t)$ from the node $v \in S_j$ where S_j is a subgraph that contains the t-neighborhood of v and therefore has been emulated for the full t steps. $v \in S_i$ is called an *importer* and $v \in S_j$ the corresponding *exporter*.

The emulation of the subgraphs in a t-neighborhood cover can be performed recursively with the aid of neighborhood covers for the sugraphs. Finally, the subgraphs in the last level of the recursion are embedded into the emulating network. A node in the final subgraphs can be an exporter on each of the levels of the recursion and its emulating node in H must send edge packets to each of the nodes emulating a corresponding importer.

3.2 Generating neighborhood covers for the mesh

In the following we show how the neighborhood covers are recursively generated for the $n \times n$ mesh to be emulated. The levels of the recursion are denoted by k, $0 \leq k \leq \kappa(N)$, where $k = 0$ be the first and $\kappa(N)$ the last level.

Global neighborhood covers First we create global t_k-neighborhood covers for the complete $n \times n$-mesh by dividing the mesh into equally sized submeshes of decreasing size $n'_k \times n'_k$, which we call the *cores* of the neighborhood cover, such that they are aligned with the lower left corner (node $(0, 0)$) of the mesh (Figure 2a). The submeshes are then augmented by their $2t_k$-neighborhood (Figure 2b) to form a t_k-neighborhood cover consisting of $n_k \times n_k$ submeshes, where $n_k = n'_k + 4t_k$.

Actually, enlarging the submeshes by their t_k-neighborhood would have been sufficient to create a t_k-neighborhood cover, but the neighborhood cover we created has the convenient property that a corresponding exporter for each importer on the edge of an enlarged submesh is in the same column (row) in adjacent submeshes, such that any communication between submeshes needs to take place only vertically (horizontally). Figure 3 shows four overlapping submeshes and the position of the corresponding exporters and importers. A node that is an importer (exporter) along the horizontal direction or the vertical direction in a t_k-neighborhood cover will be called a *level k horiontal importer (exporter)* or a *level k vertical importer (exporter)*.

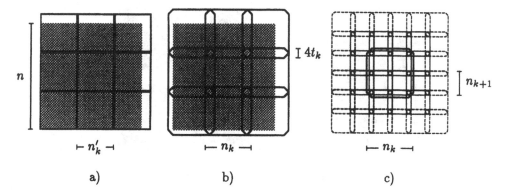

Fig. 2. Generation of a t_k-neighborhood cover in the mesh: **a)** Partitioning the mesh (grey area) into submeshes where some submeshes may extend beyond the borders of the mesh. **b)** Augmenting the submeshes by their $2t_k$-neighborhood. The border lines of the extended submeshes describe the set of exporters and importers. **c)** Recursive decomposition using those submeshes (solid lines) of the global t_{k+1}-neighborhood cover that have common nodes with a submesh in the t_k-neighborhood cover.

Bounding the number of importers and exporters in a row We will now take a close look at the set of nodes marked as exporters or importer by the global neighborhood covers up to level k. Each global t_k-neighborhood cover marks certain nodes of the mesh as exporters or importers. We will show that the nodes marked by all the neighborhood covers can be spread relatively evenly throughout the mesh. We require the following relationships between the t_k's and n_k''s, where $x \mid y$ denotes the fact that y is an integral multiple of x:

$$t_k \mid n_k' \tag{1}$$
$$t_{k+1} \mid t_k \tag{2}$$
$$t_k \geq n_{k+1} \tag{3}$$

Let P_k be a set of nodes in the mesh along equidistant parallel vertical, horizontal and diagonal lines of nodes in the $n \times n$ mesh:

$$P_k = \{(i, j) : (i \mid t_k) \vee (j \mid t_k) \vee ((i + j) \mid t_k) \vee ((i - j) \mid t_k)\}$$

It can easily be seen that with Equation 1 the exporters and importers in the t_k-neighborhood cover of the full mesh are contained in p_k (see Figure 2). Horizontal lines of nodes can contain vertical exporters and vertical lines can contain horizontal exporters, whereas diagonal can contain both types.

Furthermore, with the additional requirement of Equation 2 it follows that $P_{k+1} \subseteq P_k$ holds. Therefore all the nodes marked as exporters up to level k are contained in P_k.

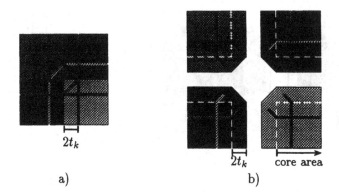

Fig. 3. Position of importers and exporters in adjacent submeshes in a t_k-neighborhood cover: **a)** Extension of the cores by their $2t_k$-neighborhood. The extension areas are delineated by lines of the same color as the core areas. These lines indicate the set of exporters of the neigborhood cover. **b)** Disentangled submeshes in the neighborhood cover showing the position of exporters (same color as the mesh they export to) corresponding to the importers (on the edge of adjacent submeshes). All exporters are at a distance of at least t_k from the borders of their respective submeshes.

Lemma 4. *At most 3 nodes per row (column) in any $n_k \times n_k$ submesh in the recursive neighborhood covers have been marked as horizontal (vertical) exporters or importers in levels $< k$.*

Proof. Since the parallel lines in P_k are t_k nodes apart we can infer that at most $\lceil n_{k+1}/t_k \rceil$ lines of each type traverse any $n_{k+1} \times n_{k+1}$ submesh. Both types of diagonal lines and the vertical (horizontal) lines can contain horizontal (vertical) exporters or importers and each line contributes one exporter or importer. With Equation 3 it follows that $3\lceil n_k/t_{k-1} \rceil \leq 3$. $\qquad\square$

Generating recursive neighborhood covers Using the global t_k-neighborhood covers we recursively decompose the mesh into t_k-neighborhood covers: We start with the complete mesh which is decomposed using the global t_1-neighborhood cover. The decomposition proceeds recursively by decomposing each resulting $n_k \times n_k$ submesh into those $n_{k+1} \times n_{k+1}$ submeshes in the global t_{k+1}-neighborhood cover whose core areas share nodes with the submesh (Figure 2c). Conceptually, each submesh in a neighborhood cover will be emulated by repeatedly emulating the submeshes in the next stage.

4 Emulation of meshes on meshes of trees

To emulate an $N = n^2$-node mesh on an $m \times m$ mesh of trees with $O(m^2)$ nodes we recursively create t_k-neighborhood covers as described above until the

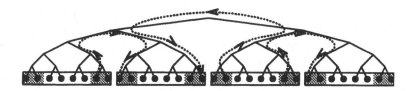

Fig. 4. Layout of paths connecting the exporters to the corresponding importers in one level of the emulation on the mesh of trees (*only some paths are shown*).

resulting submeshes are of a constant size $n_{\kappa(N)}$. These submeshes are embedded into the leaves of the smallest $m_{\kappa(N)} \times m_{\kappa(N)}$ mesh of trees that can contain them and these meshes of trees are recursively combined to $m_k \times m_k$ meshes of trees according to the recursive neighborhood covers to form the mesh of trees that emulates the complete mesh. Each $n_k \times n_k$ mesh will thus be emulated by an $m_k \times m_k$ mesh of trees.

4.1   Connecting importer and exporters

We need to route paths between the exporters and the importers on each level of the recursion within the submesh of trees that contains the neighborhood cover.

Note that for each level k horizontal (vertical) importer in the mesh of trees there is a level k horizontal (vertical) exporter on the same row (column) within the submesh of trees at level k that contains the importer. It follows that any communication paths between exporters and importers in the mesh of trees are contained either within only a column or within a row of the mesh of trees. For the rest of this paper we will therefore only investigate the communication between horizontal exporters and importers, since any observations can be applied to the communication between vertical row exporters and importers in an analogous and independent fashion. Hence, we will restrict ourselves to a description of the paths along the horizontal dimension of the mesh of trees as the other dimension is treated identically.

At each level k of the recursion we will assume that paths with constant congestion have already been laid out from each level $\leq k + 1$ importer and exporter to the row roots of their respective $m_{k+1} \times m_{k+1}$ submeshes of trees.

We then need to connect the level $k+1$ importers and exporters by connecting the roots of adjacent meshes of trees as shown in Figure 4, generating a constant congestion.

Additionally we must provide paths from level $\leq k$ importers and exporters to the roots of the $m_k \times m_k$ mesh of trees from the roots of the respective submeshes of trees containing those exporters or importers. With Lemma 4 there are at most 3 exporters (importers) for the levels $< k$ and an additional 2 level k exporters and importers in in each row these paths only add a constant to the congestion.

Since the paths routed for each level of the emulation are on different levels of the mesh of tree the congestion is constant and the latency for any packet travelling along a path depends only on the length of the path which is bounded by twice the height of the tree ($2 \log m_{k-1}$).

4.2 Parameters for the recursive neighborhood covers

We now choose the parameters that determine how the t_k-neighborhood covers are generated at each level k of the recursion. All logarithms are to the base of two.

$$t_k = 2^{\lceil 2 \log \log n_{k-1} \rceil}$$

Since all t_k's are integral powers of two, Equation 2 holds. n'_k is the width of the cores generated at level k and n_k is the width of the extended submeshes at level k.

The number of submeshes of width n'_k in one row of a recursive neighborhood cover is at most n_{k-1}/n'_k. We set

$$\nu_k = 2^{\left\lfloor \log \frac{n_{k-1}}{\log^4 n_{k-1}} \right\rfloor} \qquad \text{and} \qquad n'_k = \left\lceil \frac{n_{k-1}}{\nu_k - 1} \right\rceil_{t_k}$$

where $\lceil x \rceil_p$ is defined as the smallest integral multiple of p that is less than or equal to x. It follows that ν_k is an upper bound on the number of submeshes in one row at level k. Furthermore ν_k is an integral power of two, allowing the combination of the submeshes of trees to form a complete, larger mesh of trees at each level of the recusion.

$$n_k = n'_k + 4t_k = \left\lceil \frac{n_{k-1}}{2^{\left\lfloor \log \frac{n_{k-1}}{\log^4 n_{k-1}} \right\rfloor} - 1} \right\rceil_{t_k} + 4 \cdot 2^{\lceil 2 \log \log n_{k-1} \rceil}$$

Note that the constraint required earlier in Equation 1 is satisfied. The recursion stops at level $\kappa(N)$ where $\kappa(N)$ is the first level such that that $n_{\kappa(N)}$ is smaller than some chosen constant or $t_{\kappa(N)-1} < n_{\kappa(N)}$ (thus complying with Equation 3).

It is easy to show that

$$\frac{\log^4 n_{k-1}}{2} \le n_k = O(\log^4 n_{k-1}) \tag{4}$$

4.3 The size of the meshes of trees

In the following we show that the size of a mesh of tree at each level of the recursion is only by a constant factor larger than the mesh it is emulating. This information is needed to determine the lengths of the paths used to route packets between the exporters and the importers as well as to show that the complete emulation has a constant expansion. The width m_k of a mesh of trees at level k is the number of submesh of trees multiplied by the width m_{k+1} of the submesh of trees:

$$m_k = \nu_{k+1} m_{k+1} \le \frac{n_k}{n_{k+1}} \frac{n_{k+1}}{n_k} \nu_{k+1} m_{k+1}$$

$$\le \frac{n_k}{n_{k+1}} \left(1 + \frac{1}{\frac{n_k}{\log^4 n_k} - 1} + \frac{20}{\log^2 n_k} \right) m_{k+1}$$

Therefore

$$m_k \le \frac{n_k}{n_{\kappa(N)}} \prod_{i=k}^{\kappa(N)} \left(1 + \frac{1}{\frac{n_k}{\log^4 n_k} - 1} + \frac{20}{\log^2 n_k} \right)$$

With Equation 4, both $\sum_{i=0}^{\kappa(N)} \frac{1}{\frac{n_k}{\log^4 n_k} - 1}$ and $20 \sum_{i=0}^{\kappa(N)} \frac{1}{\log^2 n_k}$ are bounded by a constant for all N and the above product converges. Since $n_{\kappa(N)}$ is a constant we obtain

$$m_k = O(n_k)$$

Therefore the paths between exporters and importers at level k are $O(\log n_k)$ hops long and the overall emulation has constant expansion since $M = O(m_0^2) = O(n_k^2) = O(N)$.

4.4 Slowdown of the emulation

In this section we show that the emulation has constant slowdown. Let T_k be the number of steps needed to emulate a mesh of width n_k for t_k steps on an $m_k \times m_k$-MOT.

In each stage k of the recursive emulation, we emulate a mesh of width n_k for t_k steps by emulating the submeshes of width n_{k+1} for t_{k+1} steps and sending t_{k+1} packets from each exporter to its importer. This must be repeated $\left\lceil \frac{t_k}{t_{k+1}} \right\rceil$ times. The emulation of the submeshes takes T_{k+1} steps and, since the paths are of length $2 \log m_k = 2 \log O(n_k) = O(\log n_k)$, the last packet will arrive $O(\log n_k)$ steps later. Thus the time for the emulation of t_k steps on the $n_k \times n_k$ mesh is

$$T_k = \left\lceil \frac{t_k}{t_{k+1}} \right\rceil (T_{k+1} + O(\log n_k))$$

$$T_{\kappa(N)} = O(m_{\kappa(N)}) = O(n_{\kappa(N)}) = O(1)$$

Note, that $\left\lceil \frac{t_k}{t_{k+1}} \right\rceil = \frac{t_k}{t_{k+1}}$ since $t_{k+1} \mid t_k$. The recurrence can be unfolded as

$$T_0 = \sum_{k=0}^{\kappa(N)-2} \left(\prod_{i=0}^{k} \frac{t_i}{t_{i+1}} \right) O(\log n_k) + T_{\kappa(N)-1} \prod_{k=0}^{\kappa(N)} \frac{t_k}{t_{k+1}}$$

$$= \sum_{k=0}^{\kappa(N)-2} \frac{t_0}{t_{k+1}} O(\log n_k) + O(1) \frac{t_0}{t_{\kappa(N)}} = t_0 \sum_{k=0}^{\kappa(N)-2} \frac{O(\log n_k)}{t_{k+1}} + O(t_0)$$

$$= t_0 \sum_{k=0}^{\kappa(N)-2} \frac{O(\log n_k)}{2^{\lceil 2\log\log n_k\rceil}} + O(t_0) \leq t_0 O\left(\sum_{k=0}^{\kappa(N)-2} \frac{1}{\log n_k}\right) + O(t_0)$$

With Equation 4 we can infer that $\log n_{k+1}/\log n_k < 0.9$ for $n_k \geq 4$ and therefore the sume converges. Therefore we obtain $T_0 = O(t_0)$ and thus a constant slowdown:

$$S = \frac{T_0}{t_0} = O(1)$$

The result for the expansion and the slowdown of the emulation described above allows us to state the following.

Theorem 5. *Any N-node mesh can be emulated on an $O(N)$-node mesh of trees with constant slowdown.*

5 Sorting on the mesh of trees in optimal time

By emulating a sorting algorithm for the mesh we can also sort on the mesh of trees in the same asymptotic number of steps as on the mesh.

Lemma 6. *Any one-to-many offline routing problem on the leaves of an N-node mesh of trees can be solved in $O(\sqrt{N})$ steps.*

Proof. Omitted. □

Theorem 7. *N elements can be sorted on an $\sqrt{N} \times \sqrt{N}$ mesh of trees in time $O(\sqrt{N})$.*

Proof. Let the elements to be sorted reside in the leaves of an $\sqrt{N} \times \sqrt{N}$ mesh of trees. The leaves form a mesh which is emulated by an $O(\sqrt{N}) \times O(\sqrt{N})$ mesh of trees which is itself embedded into the $\sqrt{N} \times \sqrt{N}$ mesh of trees. To initialize the emulation we need to distribute the elements to be sorted to multiple leave nodes. This initialization of the emulation can be accomplished with a constant number of one-to-many offline routing phases, each taking $O(\sqrt{N})$ steps. We then use any of the well-known $O(\sqrt{N})$ sorting algorithm for the mesh and finally perform an inverse initialization to route the sorted elements to the correct leave node in the mesh of trees. □

6 Conclusion

We have shown that by recursively generating suitable neighborhood covers we can emulate a mesh on a mesh of trees of about the same size with constant slowdown, which is optimal except for a constant factor. This improves the slowdown of the previously best known emulation by a logarithmic factor.

This emulation is one of the rare cases where a general emulation actually also serves to discover a new, faster algorithm for an important problem: The emulation described above implicitly prescribes how to construct an algorithm for sorting on the mesh of trees in asymptotically optimal $O(\sqrt{N})$ steps.

The results presented here can easily be extended for higher dimensional meshes and meshes of trees.

References

1. S. N. Bhatt, F. R. K. Chung, J.-W. Hong, F. T. Leighton, and A. L Rosenberg. Optimal simulations by butterfly networks. In *Proceedings of the 20th Annual ACM Symposium on Theory of Computing*, pages 192–204, May 1988.

2. Christos Kaklamanis, Danny Krizanc, and Satish Rao. New graph decompositions and fast emulations in hypercubes and butterflies. In *5th Annual ACM Symposium on Parallel Algorithms and Architectures (SPAA 93)*, pages 325–334. ACM SIGACT, ACM SIGARCH, ACM Press, June 1993.

3. Christos Kaklamanis, Danny Krizanc, and Satish Rao. Universal emulations with sublogarithmic slowdown. In *Proceedings of the 34th IEEE Symposium Foundations of Computer Science (FOCS)*, pages 341–350, 1993.

4. Richard R. Koch, F. T. Leighton, Bruce Maggs, Satish B. Rao, and Arnold L. Rosenberg. Work-preserving emulations of fixed-connection networks. In *Proceedings of the 21st Symposium on Theory of Computation*, pages 227–240, May 1989. Extended abstract.

5. M. Kunde. Routing and sorting on mesh-connected arrays. In J. Reif, editor, *Proceedings of the 3rd Aegean Workshop on Computing: VLSI Algorithms and Architectures*, volume 319 of *Lecture Notes in Computer Science*, pages 423–433. Springer-Verlag, July 1988.

6. F. Thomson Leighton. *Introduction to Parallel Algorithms and Architectures: Arrays • Trees • Hypercubes*, volume I. Morgan Kaufmann, San Mateo, CA 94403, 1992.

7. Tom Leighton, Bruce Maggs, and Ramesh Sitamaran. On the fault tolerance of some popular bounded-degree networks. In *Proceedings of the 33rd Annual Symposium on Foundations of Computer Science*, pages 542–552, October 1992.

8. Friedhelm Meyer auf der Heide. Efficient simulations among several models of parallel computers. *SIAM Journal on Computing*, 15(1):106–119, February 1986.

9. Friedhelm Meyer auf der Heide and Rolf Wanka. Time-optimal simulations of networks by universal parallel computers. In *Proceedings of the 6th STACS*, pages 120–131, 1989.

10. C. Schnorr and A. Shamir. An optimal sorting algorithm for mesh connected computers. In *Proceedings of the Eighteenth Annual ACM Symposium on Theory of Computing*, pages 255–263, May 1986.

11. Eric J. Schwabe. On the computational equivalence of hypercube-derived networks. In *2nd Annual ACM Symposium on Parallel Algorithms and Arichitectures*, pages 388–397. ACM, ACM Press, July 1990.

12. C. Thompson and H. Kung. Sorting on a mesh-connected parallel computer. *Communications of the ACM*, 20(4):263–271, 1977.

Optimal Embeddings in the Hamming Cube Networks *

Sajal K. Das and Aisheng Mao

Department of Computer Science
University of North Texas
P. O. Box 13886
Denton, TX 76203, USA
{das, masheng}@cs.unt.edu

Abstract. This paper studies network embeddings in the Hamming cubes, a recently designed interconnection topology for multicomputers. The Hamming cube networks are supergraphs of incomplete hypercubes such that the additional edges form an extra binomial spanning tree. The recursively constructible and unit incremental Hamming cubes have better properties than hypercubes, including half of logarithmic diameter and higher fault-tolerance. They also support simple routing and efficient broadcasting schemes. In this paper, we show that Hamiltonian paths and cycles of all lengths, complete binary trees and their several variants are subgraphs of Hamming cubes. Our embeddings have both dilation and expansion equal to one. Furthermore, taking advantage of the enhanced edges in the Hamming cubes, tree machines can be embedded with dilation of one and expansion of $\frac{7}{6}$. Thus, Hamming cubes provide embeddings at a lower cost than (incomplete) hypercubes of the same size.

Keywords: Network embedding, dilation, interconnection network, Hamming cube, incomplete hypercube, binary tree, hypertree, tree machine.

1   Introduction

The demand for high-performance, reliable computing motivates the study of massively parallel, distributed-memory machines. Many static interconnection network topologies have been proposed for multicomputers [Lei92]. Such a network is usually modeled as an undirected graph $G = (V, E)$, where the node-set V represents the processor-memory modules and the edge-set E represents the communication links among these modules.

Among the existing networks, the binary hypercubes have received significant attention because of such attractive characteristics as node and edge symmetries, logarithmic diameter, high fault-tolerance, scalability, simple communication mechanisms, and embeddability of other networks. An n-dimensional binary hypercube is defined as $Q_n = (V, E)$, where $V = \{v_i = BR(i) \mid 0 \le i \le 2^n - 1\}$ consists of labeled nodes and $BR(i)$ is the binary representation of integer i. An edge $(v_i, v_j) \in E$ exists if and only if the *Hamming distance*, $\rho(v_i, v_j)$, between nodes v_i and v_j is one.

---

* This research is supported by Texas Advanced Technology Program TATP-003594031.

The hypercube topology grows its order by a power of two. There exist two variants, namely *incomplete* hypercubes [Kat88], IQ_k^n, of $2^n + 2^k$ nodes, where $0 \leq k < n$, and *generalized incomplete hypercubes* [TY91], $IQ(N)$, for $N \geq 1$, with incrementabilities of 2^k and 1, respectively. The network IQ_k^n consists of two "complete" hypercubes, Q_n (the *front* cube) and Q_k (the *back* cube), while $IQ(N)$ is composed of several complete hypercubes of different orders. These three networks can be classified as the *hypercube-family*.

Recent efforts have been made to improve the performance of the hypercube-family of networks with additional links, leading respectively to *folded* hypercubes [EAL91], *enhanced incomplete* hypercubes [CT92], and *enhanced generalized incomplete* hypercubes [DM94]. For example, an n-dimensional folded hypercube, FQ_n, has the *complementary* edges $(v_i, v_{\overline{i}})$ for every node v_i in the hypercube Q_n, where $\overline{i}$ is the address with all bits of i complemented. These networks can be categorized into the *enhanced* hypercube-family. Another example of this family is the *incrementally extensible hypercubes* [SS92].

There exist networks which modify the hypercube topology in order to derive new networks according to various design options. For example, a *twisted n-cube* [ENS87] twists a pair of edges in the shortest cycle (consisting of four nodes) of the hypercube Q_n. A *crossed cube* [Efe92], on the other hand, recursively twists pairs of edges. These networks can be regarded as the *hypercube-like* family.

We have recently derived *Hamming cubes* as another member of the enhanced hypercube-family [DM94a]. Our design is based on a theoretical network model, called the *incremental Hamming group*. These networks are supergraphs of incomplete and folded hypercubes. As shown in [DM94a, DM94b], the Hamming cubes have better topological and performance properties than the hypercubes (complete or incomplete) of the same size, without incurring much additional cost. These properties include recursive scalability, unit incrementability, half of logarithmic diameter, high fault-tolerance, simple routing and broadcasting schemes.

The embedding or mapping of one network architecture into another is an important problem because this way parallel algorithms developed for one architecture can be easily ported to another architecture. The (incomplete) hypercubes can efficiently simulate many other networks with a small factor of slowdown [Lei92, TCC90, OD95]. For example, binary hypercubes have only Hamiltonian cycles of even lengths [SS88, SSB93]. The $(2^n - 1)$-node complete binary tree is a subgraph of Q_{n+1}, and also can be embedded into Q_n with dilation two [BI85].

In this paper, we study the embeddability of the Hamming cubes, showing that several standard topologies including Hamiltonian paths and cycles, complete binary trees and their variants, and tree machines can be optimally embedded. These embeddings are better than those into (incomplete) hypercubes. For example, Hamming cubes are *pancyclic*, i.e. cycles of all lengths can be embedded as subgraphs. The complete binary tree is a subgraph of the same-sized Hamming cube, and also tree machines can be embedded at a lower cost than into hypercubes.

The rest of this paper is organized as follows. Section 2 introduces the Hamming cubes and summarizes their properties. Section 3 deals with embeddings of guest topologies into the Hamming cubes, while Section 4 concludes the paper.

Let us define a few notations to be used throughout this paper. Let $BR(i) = (b_k b_{k-1} \ldots b_1)$ be the binary representation of a non-negative integer i, where b_1 is the least significant bit. If there is no confusion, for brevity, $BR(i)$ and i will be used interchangeably. For convenience, the following notations are also defined: $i^{[j]} = (b_k b_{k-1} \ldots \overline{b_j} \ldots b_1)$ in which the jth bit of i is complemented; $\overline{i} = (\overline{b_k b_{k-1} \ldots b_1})$, i.e. all bits of i are complemented; and $i^{\{m\}} = (b_k b_{k-1} \ldots \overline{b_m} \ldots b_1)$ such that the rightmost m bits of i are complemented.

2 Hamming Cubes

This section formally introduces the Hamming cube networks originally due to Das and Mao [DM94a]. It also summarizes some of their properties relevant for the subsequent sections.

2.1 Network Definition

A *Hamming cube* of order $N \geq 2$, denoted as $HC(N) = (V, E)$, is an undirected, connected graph in which $V = \{v_i = BR(i) \mid 0 \leq i \leq N - 1\}$ is the set of labeled nodes. (For simplicity, node v_i will also be donted as i.) Let v_i and v_j, for $i < j$, be two nodes in $HC(N)$, each being represented by $\lceil \log(j + 1) \rceil$ bits. Then an edge $(v_i, v_j) \in E$ exists iff any one of the following two conditions is satisfied [DM94a]:

(E1): The Hamming distance $\rho(v_i, v_j) = 1$; or
(E2): $\rho(v_i, v_j) = h = \lceil \log(j + 1) \rceil$ for $j \geq 1$.

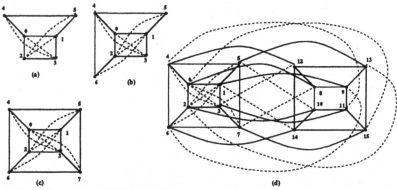

Fig. 1. Hamming cubes $HC(N)$ for $N = 6$, 7, 8 and 16.

The edges defined by Conditions (E1) and (E2) are designated as *E1-edges* and *E2-edges*, respectively. Clearly, the E1-edges define the underlying incomplete hypercube topology of $HC(N)$. An E2-edge v_i and v_j is said to be n_h-*dimensional* (or in dimension n_h), if $\rho(v_i, v_j) = h = \lceil \log(j + 1) \rceil$ and $j \geq 1$. Note that $(0, 1)$ is an E1-edge as well as an E2-edge. Figures 1(a)-(d) depict Hamming cubes $HC(N)$ for $N = 6$, 7, 8 and 16, where the E2-edges are distinguished by the broken lines. For example, since $\rho(v_3, v_{12}) = 4 = \lceil \log(12 + 1) \rceil$, there exists an n_4-dimensional E2-edge between the nodes v_3 and v_{12} in $HC(16)$. Similarly, $\rho(v_1, v_6) = 3$ implies that v_6 is linked to v_1 through an n_3-dimensional E2-edge. For conformity, $HC(2^n)$ will be called the n-*dimensional Hamming cube*, denoted as HC_n.

A *binomial spanning tree* is a binomial tree which spans all nodes in a network. Such a tree of height n has the characteristic that the number of nodes at

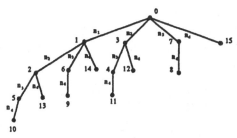

Fig. 2. A binommial spanning tree of HC_4, rooted at node v_0, using the $E2$-edges.

level i is $\binom{n}{i}$, for $0 \le i \le n$. A binomial spanning tree rooted at node v_0 can be constructed in HC_n with the help of the $E2$-edges (see Figure 2 for an example), which precisely gives a physical interpretation of these extra edges. By definition, there exists n_n-dimensional $E2$-edges in HC_n between all node-pairs v_i and v_j such that $\rho(v_i, v_j) = n$. Such edges correspond to the *complementary* edges in the folded hypercube [EAL91], which is thus a spanning subgraph of HC_n.

2.2 Topological Properties

Several important topological properties of the Hamming cube networks, including the edge complexity, node degree, and diameter are derived in [DM94a]. The Hamming cube $HC(N)$, where $N = 2^n$ and $n \ge 1$, has $E(N) = \frac{N}{2}\log N + N - 2$ edges, and its diameter is at most $\lceil \frac{\log N}{2} \rceil$. Thus, using only $2^n - 2$ extra edges compared to Q_n, the diameter of the n-dimensional Hamming cube (HC_n) reduces to $\lceil \frac{n}{2} \rceil$.

For an arbitrary order $N \ge 2$, the diameter of $HC(N)$ is given by $\lceil \frac{\lfloor \log N \rfloor}{2} \rceil + 1$. Also the Hamming cubes have been shown to be optimally fault-tolerant since the node-connectivity is equal to the minimum degree [DM94a]. We have shown that the minimum and maximum node-degrees of HC_n are $n + 1$ and $2n - 1$, respectively.

Table 1 compares the topological properties of several hypercube-like networks. Note that $Q(N)$, $TQ(N)$, $FQ(N)$, and $CC(N)$ have incrementability of $N = 2^n$ and $EIQ(N)$ has incrmentability of 2^k for $0 \le k \le n$. Whereas the rest of the networks in Table 1 have unit incrementability.

Clearly, the diameter of the Hamming cube $HC(N)$ of an arbitrary order N is the smallest among all the unit-incremental networks mentioned here. The fact that Hamming cubes are recursive in nature (that is, a smaller order HC is an induced subgraph of a larger order HC) implies that they do not require reconfiguration while expanding, as opposed to the incrementally extensible hypercubes. Also, the diameter of HC_n is almost the same as the n-dimensional crossed cube and folded hypercube at the cost of $2^n - 2$ and $2^{n-1} - 2$ extra edges, respectively. However, folded hypercubes are not recursive in nature.

2.3 Recursive Decomposition

Due to the definition of the Hamming cubes, HC_n can be recursively decomposed into $(n-1)$ induced and disjoint subgraphs, denoted as $HC_n = \{HC_2, Q_2, \ldots, Q_{n-1}\}$. Note that HC_2 consisting of the node-set $V^1 = \{v_0, v_1, v_2, v_3\}$ forms a complete graph of four nodes. The node-sets of other subgraphs Q_i are given by $V^i = \{v_\alpha \mid 2^i \le \alpha < 2^{i+1}\}$, for $2 \le i \le n - 1$. The nodes in each induced subgraph of this decomposition have the same degree and satisfy the node-symmetry [DM94a].

Table 1. Topological comparison of several hypercube-like networks.

Networks of N nodes	# Edges $E(N)$ for $N = 2^n$	Degree (ϕ) for $N > 2$	Regular?	Diameter for $N > 2$	Reconfiguration required?
Binary Hypercube $Q(N)$	$\frac{N}{2} \log N$	$\log N$	yes	$\log N$	no
Twisted hypercube $TQ(N)$	$\frac{N}{2} \log N$	$\log N$	yes	$\log N - 1$	yes
Folded hypercube $FQ(N)$	$\frac{N}{2}(\log N + 1)$	$\log N + 1$	yes	$\lceil \frac{\log N}{2} \rceil$	yes
Crossed cube $CC(N)$	$\frac{N}{2} \log N$	$\log N$	yes	$\lceil \frac{\log N+1}{2} \rceil$	no
Enhanced Incomplete Hypercube $EIQ(N)$ $N = 2^n + 2^k$ for $0 \le k < n$	$\frac{N}{2}(\log N + 1)$	$2 \le \phi \le \log N + 1$	no	$\lfloor \frac{\log N}{2} + 1 \rfloor$	yes
Incomplete hypercube $IQ(N)$	$\frac{N}{2} \log N$	$1 \le \phi \le \log N$	no	$\log N$	no
Enhanced Generalized Incomplete hypercube $EGIQ(N)$	$\frac{N}{2}(\log N + 1)$	$2 \le \phi \le \log N + 1$	no	$\lceil \frac{\log N}{2} \rceil$	no
Incrementally Extensible Hypercubes $IEQ(N)$	$\frac{N}{2} \log N$	$\log N \le \phi \le \log N + 1$	no	$\lfloor \log N \rfloor + 1$	yes
Hamming cube $HC(N)$	$\frac{N}{2} \log N + N - 2$	$2 \le \phi \le 2 \log N - 1$	no	$\lceil \frac{\log N}{2} \rceil + 1$	no

In $HC(N)$, where $2^{k-1} < N < 2^k$ and $k > 1$, we can partition the node-set into several subsets. Let $N = \sum_{i=1}^{l} 2^{p_i}$, where $1 \le l \le k$ and $p_{i+1} > p_i$. The l number of node-subsets are $V^{p_l} = \{v_\alpha \mid 0 \le \alpha < 2^{p_l}\}$ and $V^{p_{(l-i)}} = \{v_\alpha \mid \sum_{j=l-i+1}^{l} 2^{p_j} \le \alpha < \sum_{j=l-i}^{l} 2^{p_j}\}$ for $1 \le i \le l - 1$. The subgraph induced by the node-subset V^{p_l} forms a p_l-dimensional Hamming cube, HC_{p_l}, and the other subgraphs induced by $V^{p_{(l-i)}}$ form the binary hypercubes $Q_{p_{(l-i)}}$. Such a decomposition will be denoted as $HC(N) = \{HC_{p_l}, IQ(N - 2^{p_l})\} = \{HC_{p_l}, Q_{p_{l-1}}, \ldots, Q_{p_1}\}$. For example, $HC(15) = \{HC_3, Q_2, Q_1, Q_0\}$, where HC_3 consists of the nodes $\{v_0, v_1, \ldots, v_7\}$, Q_2 of $\{v_8, \ldots, v_{11}\}$, Q_1 consists of $\{v_{12}, v_{13}\}$, and Q_0 is v_{14}.

3 Embeddings in Hamming Cubes

The *embedding* of a *guest* graph $G = (V_G, E_G)$ into a *host* graph $H = (V_H, E_H)$ is to find two functions, Φ and Ψ, such that $\Phi : V_G \longrightarrow V_H$ is a mapping of their vertices while $\Psi : E_G \longrightarrow \{ \text{paths in } H \}$ is a mapping from edges in E_G to paths in H.

There are four metrics to measure the cost of an embedding. The *dilation* of an edge e in G is the length of the path $\Psi(e)$ in H. The dilation of G in an embedding is the maximum dilation over all edges. The *expansion* of an embedding is the ratio $\frac{|V_H|}{|V_G|}$. The *edge-congestion* is the maximum number of edges in G which are mapped by function Ψ to a single edge in H. The *load* is the maximum number of nodes in G mapped by Φ to a single node in H. In our study, the node-mapping function Φ is considered as one-to-one, thereby the maximum load is 1.

If each of dilation and edge-congestion is equal to 1, the guest network is a subgraph of the host. Since there is a trade-off between the dilation and expansion, by *optimal embedding* we mean one with unit dilation and minimum expansion.

In this section, we present subgraph and/or optimal embeddings of various networks into the Hamming cubes.

3.1 Hamiltonian Cycles

Binary hypercubes are Hamiltonian and, in fact, all cycles of even lengths can be embedded in Q_n. It is easy to see that the sequence of nodes traversed along the *binary reflected Gray Codes* [SS88] forms an embedded Hamiltonian cycle. Since there are $n!$ different Gray code sequences of length n, each of which corresponds to a permutation of the set $D = \{0, 1, \ldots, n-1\}$ of dimensions of edges in Q_n, hence Q_n can have $n!$ different Hamiltonian cycles. (Two embedded Hamiltonian cycles are said to be *different* if they differ in at least one edge.) However, it can be shown that Q_n has $2^{n-3}n!$ different Hamiltonian cycles [SSB93]. For the sake of completeness, let us sketch this scheme. A pair of nodes in the hypercube is connected by an i-dimensional edge if and only if their binary labels differ at the $(i+1)$th bit, where the least significant bit corresponds to $i = 0$. A sequence of dimensions, S, determining the traversal of edges in an embedded Hamiltonian cycle is obtained from D as follows [SSB93].

Algorithm Sequencing /* Construct the sequence S of dimensions */
begin
1.   Arbitrarily choose a dimension $d_1 \in D$ and let $D = D - \{d_1\}$.
2.   Let $S_1 = d_1$.
3.   For each i, $2 \le i \le n$, choose a dimension $d_i \in D$ and let $D = D - \{d_i\}$.
        Let $S_i = S_{i-1} \bullet d_i \bullet S_{i-1}$, where $\bullet$ indicates the concatenation operation.
4.   Let $S = S_n \bullet d_n$.
end

Given a node v_i and a sequence S_π of dimensions, where $\pi = d_1 d_2 \ldots d_n$, a Hamiltonian cycle $C(v_i, S_\pi)$ is traversed which starts at v_i and follows the cycle-edges determined by S_π. Since there are 2^n possible choices of the node v_i and $n!$ possible choices of permutation π, there are at most $2^n n!$ embedded Hamiltonian cycles in Q_n. However, only $2^{n-3}n!$ of them are different, as constructed by Algorithm Sequencing.

In the following, we show that the Hamming cubes are *pancyclic* networks, i.e. cycles of all lengths are embeddable, which is an advantage over binary hypercubes.

Hamiltonian Cycles in HC_n. By definition, the Hamming cube HC_n has two kinds of edges: the $E1$-edges (hypercube edges) and $E2$-edges (enhanced edges). There exist an n_n-dimensional $E2$-edge $(v_i, v_{\bar{i}})$ for every node v_i. Therefore, the size of the dimension-set $D = \{0, 1, \ldots, n-1, n_n\}$ in HC_n is $n + 1$, which implies that we have $(n + 1)!$ potential choices for the permutation π. Therefore, Algorithm Sequencing applied to HC_n leads to the following theorem.

Theorem 1. *The network HC_n has $2^{n-3}(n + 1)!$ different Hamiltonian cycles.*

Example 1: Consider an embedding of a Hamiltonian cycle $C(v_0, S_\pi)$ in HC_4, where the permutation of dimensions is $\pi = 20n_41$. The sequence of dimensions is $S_{20n_41} = 202n_42021202n_42021$ and $C(v_0, S_{20n_41}) = (0,4,5,1,14,10,11,15,13,9,8,12,3,7,6,2,0)$. Note that $(1, 14)$ and $(12, 3)$ are n_4-dimensional edges in this cycle.

Hamiltonian Cycles in $HC(N)$, where $2^{k-1} < N < 2^k$. We consider two cases depending on the value of N.

Case 1: For $2^{k-1} < N \le 2^{k-1} + 2^{k-2}$ and $k \ge 3$.

Let $N = 2^{k-1}+m$, where $1 \leq m \leq 2^{k-2}$. By Section 2.3, the decomposition yields $HC(N) = \{HC_{k-1}, IQ(m)\}$ in which the subgraphs HC_{k-1} and the incomplete hypercube $IQ(m)$ are induced by the node-sets $V(HC_{k-1}) = \{v_\alpha \mid 0 \leq \alpha < 2^{k-1}\}$ and $V(IQ) = \{v_\alpha \mid 2^{k-1} \leq \alpha < 2^{k-1} + m\}$, respectively. By the definition of Hamming cubes, each node v_i in $IQ(m)$ is linked to two different nodes $v_{i[k]}$ and $v_{i\{k\}}$ in HC_{k-1} through the k-dimensional $E1$-edge and n_k-dimensional $E2$-edge, respectively. Recall here that $i^{[k]}$ is obtained by complementing the kth bit of i, and $i^{\{k\}}$ is obtained by complementing the rightmost k bits of i. Since the Hamming distance $\rho(v_{i[k]}, v_{i\{k\}}) = k - 1$, there exists an (n_{k-1})-dimensional $E2$-edge between the nodes $v_{i[k]}$ and $v_{i\{k\}}$. Thus, we have:

Property 1. *Let v_α and v_β be two nodes in HC_{k-1} for $k \geq 3$, such that v_α is linked to v_β through an (n_{k-1})-dimensional $E2$-edge, i.e. $\alpha = \beta^{\{k-1\}}$. Then in HC_k, there exists a path $P = (v_\alpha, v_\gamma, v_\beta)$ of length 2, which goes through node v_γ such that $\alpha = \gamma^{[k-1]}$ and $\beta = \gamma^{\{k\}}$.*

By Theorem 1 and Property 1, Hamiltonian cycles can be embedded into the Hamming cubes of orders satisfying Case 1. We first apply Algorithm Sequencing to construct the Hamiltonian cycle $C(v_i, S_\pi)$ in the subgraph HC_{k-1}. Then in the permutation $\pi = (p_1, p_2, \ldots, p_{k-1})$, we choose the element $p_1 = n_{k-1}$ while the other elements are arbitrarily chosen from the set $D = \{0, 1, \ldots, k - 2\}$. Note that the starting node v_i can be any node in HC_{k-1}. The resulting sequence of dimensions corresponding to π has the form $S_{n_{k-1}p_2 \cdots p_{k-1}} = n_{k-1}p_2 n_{k-1}p_3 n_{k-1}p_2 n_{k-1} \cdots$. Let the required Hamiltonian cycle be $C(v_i, S_{n_{k-1}p_2 \cdots p_{k-1}}) = i a_2 a_3 \ldots, a_{2^{k-1}-1} i$, in which we search those pairs of nodes that are linked via the (n_{k-1})-dimensional $E2$-edges. Then, between those node-pairs. we appropriately insert the nodes of the subgraph $IQ(m)$ following Property 1.

Since there are 2^{k-1} possible choices of the starting node v_i and $(k-1)!$ possible choices of π, the subgraph HC_{k-1} has $2^{k-4}(k-1)!$ different Hamiltonian cycles, for $k \geq 4$. For each of these cycles, the edges that are (n_{k-1})-dimensional $E2$-edges, are expanded as paths of length two to include the nodes of the subgraph $IQ(m)$. Furthermore, by Property 1, the edges used in the expanded paths are different from those used in the Hamiltonian cycle in HC_{k-1}. Therefore, we have the following lemma.

Lemma 1. *The Hamming cube $HC(N)$, where $2^{k-1} < N < 2^{k-1}+2^{k-2}$ and $k \geq 4$, has $2^{k-4}(k-1)!$ different Hamiltonian cycles.*

Example 2: Consider $HC(11) = \{HC_3, IQ(3)\}$, where $V(HC_3) = \{v_\alpha \mid 0 \leq \alpha \leq 7\}$ and $V(IQ) = \{v_8, v_9, v_{10}\}$. Let $\pi = n_3 20$ and v_6 be the starting node. Then $S_{n_3 20} = n_3 2 n_3 0 n_3 2 n_3 0$. The Hamiltonian cycle in HC_3 is $C(v_6, S_{n_3 20}) = (6, 1, 5, 2, 3, 4, 0, 7, 6)$. Now inserting v_8, v_9, and v_{10} into the node-pairs $(0, 7)$, $(6, 1)$, and $(5, 2)$, respectively, the Hamiltonian cycle in $HC(11)$ is obtained as $(6, 9, 1, 5, 10, 2, 3, 4, 0, 8, 7, 6)$.

Case 2: For $2^{k-1} + 2^{k-2} < N < 2^k$ and $k \geq 3$.

Let $N = 2^{k-1} + m$, where $2^{k-2} < m < 2^{k-1}$, and $HC(N) = \{HC_{k-1}, IQ(m)\}$. This case has been proved rigorously by dividing it into two subcases depending on whether m is even or odd. The basic idea involves how to combine the embedded

Hamiltonian cycles in HC_{k-1} and $IQ(m)$ in order to construct the required cycle in $HC(N)$. We summarize the results here. For details, refer to [DM95].

Lemma 2. *The Hamming cube* $HC(N)$*, where* $2^{k-1} + 2^{k-2} < N < 2^k$ *for* $k \geq 3$*, has* Δ *(*$\lceil \log(N - 2^{k-1}) \rceil - 2)!$ *different Hamiltonian cycles, where* $\Delta = (k-1)!$ *for* N *even and* $\Delta = (k-2)!$ *for* N *odd.*

From Lemmas 1 and 2 we obtain

Theorem 2. *The Hamming cube of order* N*, where* $2^{k-1} < N < 2^k$ *for* $k \geq 3$*, has* $(k-2)!(\lceil \log(N - 2^{k-1}) \rceil - 2)!$ *different Hamiltonian cycles.*

The above results also prove that $HC(N)$ is a *pancyclic* network, for $N \geq 3$.

3.2 Complete Binary Trees and Related Variants

Both the complete binary tree and binary hypercube are bipartite graphs. A node of the hypercube Q_n is said to have *even parity* if its binary representation has an even number of one bits; otherwise, it has an *odd* parity. Also, Q_n has 2^{n-1} even parity nodes and 2^{n-1} odd parity nodes. In the bipartite partition of the binary tree, the nodes at the even (or odd) levels are put together. Therefore, it can be shown that the complete binary tree $CBT(n-1)$ of height $n-1$ and consisting of $2^n - 1$ nodes is not a subgraph of Q_n. However, the 2^n-node *two-rooted* complete binary tree is a subgraph of Q_n [BI85, Lei92]. Thus $CBT(n-1)$ can be embedded into Q_n with dilation two, while it is a subgraph of Q_{n+1}.

In this section, we will show that $CBT(n-1)$ is a subgraph of the n-dimensional Hamming cube, HC_n, consisting of 2^n nodes. This result clearly shows that Hamming cubes have better performance (in terms of tree embeddings) than binary hypercubes of the same size.

The decomposition yields $HC_n = \{HC_{n-1}, Q_{n-1}\}$, induced by the vertex-subsets $V' = \{v_\alpha \mid 0 \leq \alpha < 2^{n-1}\}$ and $V'' = \{v_\alpha \mid 2^{n-1} \leq \alpha < 2^n\}$, respectively. Due to the recursive structure, $HC_{n-1} = \{HC_{n-2}, Q_{n-2}\}$ and $Q_{n-1} = \{Q_{n-2}^1, Q_{n-2}^2\}$. Therefore, $HC_n = \{HC_{n-2}, Q_{n-2}, Q_{n-2}^1, Q_{n-2}^2\}$ such that the nodes in these four subgraphs have the labels (00*), (01*), (10*), and (11*), respectively, where $* \in \{0,1\}^{n-2}$. The following property can be stated for a node $v_i \in HC_{n-2}$.

Property 2. *Let* $HC_n = \{HC_{n-2}, Q_{n-2}, Q_{n-2}^1, Q_{n-2}^2\}$ *for* $n \geq 2$*, in which the subgraphs are induced by the vertex-subsets* $V^1 = \{v_\alpha \mid 0 \leq \alpha < 2^{n-2}\}$*,* $V^2 = \{v_\alpha \mid 2^{n-2} \leq \alpha < 2^{n-1}\}$*,* $V^3 = \{v_\alpha \mid 2^{n-1} \leq \alpha < 2^{n-1} + 2^{n-2}\}$*, and* $V^4 = \{v_\alpha \mid 2^{n-1} + 2^{n-2} \leq \alpha < 2^n\}$*. A node* $v_i \in HC_{n-2}$ *is linked to* $v_{i|[n]} \in Q_{n-2}^1$ *and* $v_{i(*)} \in Q_{n-2}^2$*, through the* $(n-1)$*-dimensional* $E1$*-edge and the* n_n*-dimensional* $E2$*-edge, respectively.*

Let us now construct, by induction, the embedded $CBT(n-1)$ in HC_n. Let v_0 be the root of the single node tree. Let $CBT(n-2)$ be the embedded complete binary tree in HC_{n-1}, having the leaves in the set V^2. The embedded $CBT(n-1)$ in HC_n grows from $CBT(n-2)$ by making the nodes in the set $V'' = V^3 \cup V^4$ as the children of the leaves of $CBT(n-2)$ through the $(n-1)$-dimensional $E1$-edges and n_n-dimensional $E2$-edges.

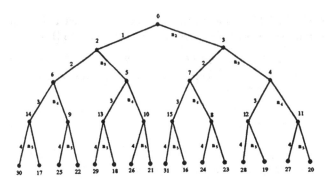

Fig. 3. The embedding of the complete binary tree $CBT(4)$ of height four in HC_5.

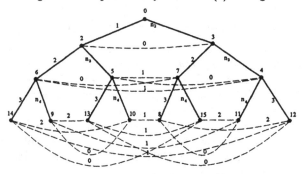

Fig. 4. The embedding of tree-cube $TC(3)$ rooted at node v_0 in HC_4.

Theorem 3. *The $(2^n - 1)$-node complete binary tree $CBT(n - 1)$ is a subgraph of the n-dimensional Hamming cube HC_n, having 2^n nodes.*

Figure 3 is an embedding of $CBT(4)$ in HC_5. An edge label indicates its dimension. Since the subgraph of HC_n induced by the set $V'' = V^3 \cup V^4$ forms the hypercube Q_{n-1}, the nodes at each level j, for $0 \le j < n$, of the embedded $CBT(n - 1)$ in HC_n are connected as a j-dimensional binary hypercube, Q_j, consisting of the nodes $V(Q_j) = \{v_i \mid 2^j \le i < 2^{j+1}\}$. Let us call such a network architecture a *tree-cube*, $TC(n - 1)$, of height $n - 1$. Figure 4 shows the embedding of the tree-cube $TC(3)$ in the Hamming cube HC_4. The hypercube edges are shown as broken lines. Due to this structure, several variants of complete binary trees with additional links between the nodes at the same level can be embedded in the n-dimensional Hamming cube.

For example, a *hypertree* structure $HT(n - 1)$ of height $n - 1$ is a complete binary tree such that the additional links at each level are chosen to be a subset of a hypercube [GS81]. So $HT(n - 1)$ is a subgraph of the tree-cube $TC(n - 1)$, and hence a subgraph of HC_n. With the help of the embedded tree-cubes and using the fact that the binary hypercubes are Hamiltonian, the full-ringed (hence half-ringed) binary tree of height $n - 1$ can also be embedded into HC_n.

3.3 Tree Machines

A *tree machine*, $TM(n)$, of dimension n consists of two $CBT(n)$'s – called the *upper* and *lower* trees – which are connected back to back along the common leaves. Thus, $TM(n)$ has $(3 \cdot 2^n - 2)$ nodes and $(2^{n+2} - 4)$ edges. It can be embedded in the hypercube Q_{n+2} with expansion approximately equal to $\frac{4}{3}$ and dilation one [Efe91].

It is also shown [OD95] that $TM(n)$ can be embedded in the incomplete hypercube $IQ(3 \cdot 2^n)$ with both dilation and edge congestion equal to 2.

We will show that the $TM(n)$ is a subgraph of the Hamming cube $HC(3 \cdot 2^n + 2^{n-1})$, implying that dilation is 1 and expansion is approximately $\frac{7}{6}$. Note that with the same expansion of $\frac{7}{6}$, the tree machine $TM(n)$ cannot be embedded as a subgraph into the incomplete hypercube $IQ(3 \cdot 2^n + 2^{n-1})$. Again, this provides an advantage of the Hamming cubes over the same-sized hypercubes.

Let us view the structure of the tree machine as follows. In $TM(n)$, the 2^n common leaves and their 2^n parents (half of them in the upper tree and the other half in the lower tree) form 2^{n-1} *building blocks*, each being a hypercube Q_2. These building blocks are then connected by the upper and lower complete binary trees of height $n-1$, one less height than the original trees in $TM(n)$. Note that the leaves of these two new trees are now the parents of the cornerwise nodes in the building blocks. When the dimension of the tree machine increases, say from n to $n+1$, the number of building blocks is doubled, from 2^{n-1} to 2^n. Thus, we need 2^n new leaves for each upper and lower tree to connect the new set of 2^n building blocks.

In the Hamming cube $HC(3 \cdot 2^n + 2^{n-1})$ for $n \geq 3$, each node label has length $n+2$. According to the first and second lowest bits of these labels, we can decompose $HC(3 \cdot 2^n + 2^{n-1})$ into $3 \cdot 2^{n-2} + 2^{n-3}$ building blocks, Q_2^i, for $0 \leq i \leq 3 \cdot 2^{n-2} + 2^{n-3} - 1$. Since the upper and lower trees in $TM(n)$ are symmetric along their common leaves, without loss of generality, we can concentrate on only one tree.

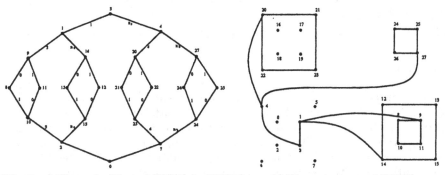

Fig. 5. a) The embedding of $TM(3)$ in $HC(28)$.   b) The upper tree of $TM(3)$.

Let nodes v_3 and v_0 in Q_2^0 be respectively the roots of the upper and lower trees in $TM(n)$. The root v_3 has the children v_1 and v_4 through the 1-dimensional $E1$-edge and the n_3-dimensional $E2$-edge. SImilarly, v_0 has the children v_2 and v_7,

In the embedded $TM(n)$ for $n \geq 3$, an internal node v_i at level j, for $1 \leq j \leq n-3$, of the upper tree has the left child $v_{i[2j+2]}$ and the right child $v_{i(2j+2)}$ linked through a $(2j+1)$-dimensional $E1$-edge and (n_{2j+2})-dimensional $E2$-edge, respectively. By this way, we can construct the top $n-1$ levels of the upper tree. The remaining step is to construct the leaves of the upper tree which are those parents of the cornerwise nodes in the building blocks.

We divide the nodes at level $n-2$ into two subsets, V' and V'' such that V' consists of the first 2^{n-3} nodes from the left, while V'' consists of the remaining 2^{n-3} nodes on that level. A node $v_i \in V'$ has two leaves $v_{i[n+1]}$ and $v_{i(n+1)}$ linked through the n-dimensional $E1$-edge and (n_{n+1})-dimensional $E2$-edge, respectively, in the Hamming cube. While a node $v_i \in V''$ has two leaves $v_{i[n+2]}$ and $v_{i(n+2)}$. Thus, the entire upper tree is constructed.

By the same method, the lower tree rooted at node v_0 can also be constructed. The common leaves for both the trees are then determined by the parent nodes of the building blocks, which are the leaves of upper and lower trees, through the $E1$-edges of dimensions 0 and 1.

Theorem 4. *The tree machine $TM(n-1)$ can be embedded as a subgraph into the Hamming cube $HC(3 \cdot 2^{n-1} + 2^{n-2})$ with an asymptotic expansion of $\frac{7}{6}$.*

Example 3: Figure 5a) shows the embedding of the tree machine $TM(3)$ in $HC(28)$ and Figure 5b) shows the upper tree. This figure includes all nodes of $HC(28)$, but omits the edges which are not used in the tree. There are four building blocks (i.e., Q_2's) formed by the 0- and 1-dimensional $E1$-edges, and one can clearly see the geometric relation of these building blocks in $HC(28)$.

Table 2. Comparison of embedding results.

Guest Networks	Binary Hypercube Q_n (# of nodes $N = 2^n$)	Incomplete Hypercube $IQ(N), N > 2$	Hamming cube $HC(N)$
Ring $R(m)$	For $0 \le m \le 2^n$, • Subgraph, when m is even; • $D = 2$, $EC = 1$, when m is odd.	For $0 \le m \le N$, • Subgraph, when m is even; • $D = EC = 2$, when m is odd.	pancyclic
Complete Binary Tree $CBT(m)$	• Subgraph $CBT(n-2)$ • $CBT(n-1)$ with $D = EC = 2$	• $CBT(n-1)$ in $IQ(2^n - 1)$ with $D = EC = 2$	• Subgraph $CBT(n-1)$
X-tree $X(m)$	• $X(n-1)$ with $D = EC = 2$	• $X(n-1)$ in $IQ(2^n - 1)$ with $D = EC = 2$	• Subgraph $X(n-1)$
Hypertree $HT(m)$	• $HT(n-1)$ with $D = 2$	• $HT(n-1)$ in $IQ(2^n)$ with $D = 2$	• Subgraph $HT(n-1)$
Tree Machine $TM(m)$	• Subgraph $TM(n-2)$	• $TM(n-1)$ in $IQ(3 \cdot 2^{n-1})$ with $D = EC = 2$	• Subgraph $TM(n-1)$ in $HC(3 \cdot 2^{n-1} + 2^{n-2})$

4 Conclusions

We have studied the embeddability of the recently proposed Hamming cube networks [DM94a]. Several topologies including Hamiltonian paths and cycles, complete binary trees and their variants, and tree machines are optimally embedded into the Hamming cubes with unit dilation ($\mathcal{D}$) and edge-congestion ($\mathcal{E}$), and minimum expansion. Table 2 compares our embedding results with (incomplete) hypercubes.

Due to the bipartiteness of incomplete hypercubes, a Hamiltonian cycle of odd length cannot be embedded with dilation of one. Using the additional enhanced edges in the Hamming cubes, Hamiltonian cycles of all lengths can be embedded as subgraphs, implying that Hamming cubes are *pancyclic* networks.

Although a complete binary tree is not a subgraph of the same-sized binary hypercube, it is a subgraph of the same-sized Hamming cube. Additionally, X-trees, hypertrees, full-ringed and half-ringed binary trees are all subgraphs of Hamming cubes with unit expansion.

Tree machines can also be embedded into the Hamming cubes with dilation of one and expansion of $\frac{7}{6}$. Whereas, tree machines can be embedded into the incomplete hypercubes with expansion approximately equal to one, and both dilation and edge congestion being equal to two. With the same expansion of $\frac{7}{6}$, the embedding of tree machines into the incomplete hypercubes still have dilation and edge congestion of two. This provides another advantage of the Hamming cubes.

Our future research will aim at the fault-tolerant embedding of guest networks into the Hamming cubes.

References

[BI85]   S. N. Bhatt and I. Ipsen. How to embed trees in hypercubes. Tech. rep. rr-443, Department of Computer Science, Yale University, New Heaven, CT, 1985.

[CT92]   H. L. Chen and N. F. Tzeng. An effective approach to the enhancement of incomplete hypercube computers. *J. Parallel Distri. Comput.*, 14:163–174, 1992.

[DM94]   S. K. Das and A. Mao. On enhanced generalized incomplete hypercubes. Tech. Rep. CRPDC-94-3, Dept Comput Sci, Univ North Texas, Denton, Jan 1994.

[DM95]   S. K. Das and A. Mao. Embeddings of Cycles and Tree-Related Networks in the Hamming Cubes. Tech. Rep. CRPDC-95-2, Dept Comput Sci, Univ North Texas, Denton, Jan 1995.

[DM94a]   S. K. Das and A. Mao. An interconnection network model and the Hamming cube networks. In *Proceedings of the 8th International Parallel Processing Symposium*, pages 18–22, Cancun, Mexico, Apr 1994.

[DM94b]   S. K. Das and A. Mao. Broadcasting trees in Hamming cubes. *Proc. Int. Conf. Parallel and Distri. Comput. Syst.*, pp 587–592, Las Vegas, Nevada, Oct 1994.

[EAL91]   A. El-Amawy and S. Latifi. Properties and performance of folded hypercubes. *IEEE Transactions on Parallel and Distributed Systems*, 2(1):31–42, Jan 1991.

[Efe91]   K. Efe. Embedding mesh of trees in the hypercube. *Journal of Parallel and Distributed Computing*, 11:222–230, 1991.

[Efe92]   K. Efe. The crossed cube architecture for parallel computation. *IEEE Transactions on Parallel and Distributed Systems*, 3(5):513–524, Sep 1992.

[ENS87]   A-H. Esfahanian, L. M. Ni, and B. E. Sagan. The twisted n-cube with application to multiprocessing. Tech. Rep., Michigan State Univ, Dec 1987.

[GS81]   J. R. Goodman and C. H. Sequin. Hypertree: A multiprocessor interconnection topology. *IEEE Trans. on Comput.*, C-30(12):923–933, Dec 1981.

[Kat88]   H. P. Katseff. Incomplete hypercubes. *IEEE Transactions on Computers*, 37(5):604–608, May 1988.

[Lei92]   F. T. Leighton. *Introduction to Parallel Algorithms and Architectures: Arrays, Trees, Hypercubes*. Morgan Kaufmann Publishers, San Mateo, CA, 1992.

[OD95]   S. Oehring and S. K. Das. Embeddings of tree-related networks in incomplete hypercubes. *J. Parallel and Distributed Computing*, 26(1):36-47, Apr 1995.

[SS88]   Y. Saad and M. H. Schultz. Topological properties of hypercubes. *IEEE Transactions on Computers*, 37(7):867–872, 1988.

[SS92]   S. Sur and P. K. Srimani. Incrementally extensible hypercube (IEH) graphs. *Proc. Int. Conf. Computers and Communication*, pp. 1–7, Phoenix, Apr 1992.

[SSB93]   A. Sen, A. Sengupta, and S. Bandyopadhyay. On some topological properties of Hypercubes, Incomplete Hypercube and Supercube. *Proc. 7th Int. Parallel Processing Symposium*, Newport Beach, California, Apr 1993.

[TCC90]   N. F. Tzeng, H. L. Chen, and P. J. Chuang. Embeddings in incomplete hypercubes. *Proc. Int. Conf. Parallel Processing*, vol III, pp. 335–339, 1990.

[TY91]   J-Y Tien and W-P Yang. Hierarchical spanning trees and distributing on incomplete hypercubes. *Parallel Computing*, 17:1343–1360, 1991.

Hierarchical Adaptive Routing Under Hybrid Traffic Load

Ziqiang Liu[*]

Department of Teleinformatics, Royal Institute of Technology
Electrum 204, 164 40 Kista, Sweden

Abstract. In actual multicomputer networks, communications consist of *hybrid traffic*, a mix of short and long messages.Typically, the short messages are used to support synchronization, global combining, and multicasting where the latencies are critical to the execution time of whole parallel program. However, in normal wormhole routed networks without packetization, the presence of long messages degrades network performance of short messages dramatically, qualitatively changing network behaviour. In this paper, we extend one existing adaptive routing framework, Hierarchical Adaptive Routing (HAR) to a hybrid traffic model, to form a new simple and efficient adaptive routing framework called Hybrid-HAR. Hybrid-HAR has four important advantages. Firstly, without packetization, the impact of long messages on short messages is very small. Secondly, it supports fully adaptive routing to both short and long messages for high communication performance. Third, the implementation complexity of Hybrid-HAR is compatible to standard routing algorithms such as Dimension Order Routing. Fourth, Hybrid-HAR is applicable to a wide variety of network topologies. High level implementation and simulation studies of a Hybrid-HAR for 2D mesh networks are presented.

1 Introduction

In highly parallel machines, a collection of computing nodes works in concert to solve large application problems. The nodes communicate data and coordinate their efforts by sending and receiving messages through a routing network. Consequently, the achieved performance of such machines depends critically on the performance of their routing networks. Network performance depends on a variety of factors, not only network architecture (topology, routing and flow control), but also the characteristics of communication that is actually carried on the network such as message sizes and traffic patterns.

Many recent multicomputer networks use cut-through or *wormhole routing* [9, 3], a technique which reduces message latency by pipelining transmission over the channels along a message's route. In these networks, a message spans multiple channels which couples the channels tightly together, so blockage on one channel can have immediate impact on another. Tight coupling between channels means that one long message can block the progress of many other messages, and as a result, even a small fraction of long messages can affect overall network performance significantly. In these networks, channel coupling effects make performance quite sensitive to message size.

There are a number of factors which give rise to non-uniform message sizes. First, applications may generate a range of message sizes directly [2, 7]. Second, many

---

[*] Ziqiang Liu died in December 1994, leaving his work to the members of his research group.

synchronous message passing implementations implement a three-phase protocol to allocate buffer storage. This translates a large application message into two short control messages, followed by a long (application size) message. Third, typical message passing libraries implement some form of packetization, breaking long messages into some maximum physical transfer size (256, 512, or 1024 bytes, typically). In addition, message-passing library functions such as global synchronization, reduction and multicast operations give rise to short messages. Finally, system software needs to move large blocks of data to provide services such as parallel input/output and distributed virtual memory.

Typically, in multicomputer applications, the short messages are used to support synchronization, global combining, and multicasting where their latency is critical to the execution time of whole parallel program. However up to today, little work has been done to reduce the short message latency under a hybrid traffic model in wormhole routed networks. In this paper we propose *Hybrid-HAR* as a promising technique to reduce the impact of long messages on short messages. In the interconnection network, a certain amount of virtual channel resource is exclusively allocated to short messages, which almost eliminates the possibility that a short message will be blocked by a long message. In the network interface, separate injection and sink channels, and incoming and outgoing buffers are provided for short and long messages, which guarantee that the send and receive of short messages at the source and destination nodes will not be affected by long messages. Thus Hybrid-HAR dramatically decreases both the variance and the average of short messages without packetization. By providing fully adaptive routing, Hybrid-HAR also gives good overall network performance. The implementation complexity of Hybrid-HAR is compatible to standard routing algorithms such as DOR, provided the same number of virtual channels is used. Also Hybrid-HAR is applicable to a variety of network topologies.

The next section gives the relevant background and related work. After that, Section 3 describes the general Hybrid-HAR framework for a variety of network topologies with hybrid traffic model. Section 4 shows an application of Hybrid-HAR to a 2D mesh network. This produces a simple fully adaptive routing algorithm for hybrid traffic load yielding high performance. Section 5 examines the performance of Hybrid-HAR router in 2D mesh networks. Finally, Section 6 concludes the paper, summarizing the results.

2 Background

All networks examined in this paper are wormhole-routed, k-ary n-cube, direct networks. With *wormhole* routing, the packet is not completely buffered at each node. As soon as the header of a packet comes into a node, it is forwarded to the requested outgoing channel if free. If not, the packet is stopped in place. This achieves the pipelined packet transmission with only modest buffering requirements for each router. Typically in wormhole-routed network, each physical link is split into multiple virtual channels. Each virtual channel has its own buffer queue and control signals, sharing the bandwidth of the corresponding physical link [3]. Virtual channels can be used to avoid deadlock and support adaptive routing for high network performance.

In wormhole-routed networks, channel coupling can cause achieved network throughput to be much less than the network capacity. Several studies have shown that the channel coupling increases with message length, reducing the performance [1, 6]. There are three techniques to reduce the impact of long messages on short messages: *packetization*, *multipath routing* and *virtual channel allocation*.

Packetization reduces the impact of long messages on other messages because long messages are split into a number of small packets, reducing the maximum blocking time. However, packetization has two significant drawbacks. First, it requires a mechanism for conversion between messages and packets. Second, packetization increases the network load; each packet must contain routing and sequencing information in its header.

Multipath routing, virtual channels and adaptive routing can reduce the interference of long messages on short messages [11]. Virtual channels [3] virtualize the physical channels, multiplexing them among several messages. The multiplexing allows a short message to pass a blocked long message. Adaptive routing allows a message to use any one of several paths from source to destination [8, 5, 14, 10, 13]. This can allow a short message to circumvent a blocked long message. With multipath routing, the possibility that a short message will be blocked by a long message is reduced, but not totally eliminated, especially when the long messages dominate the traffic [11]. The combination of multipath routing and packetization can further eliminate the blocking and minimize the effect of the remaining blocking [11].

In the virtual channel allocation scheme, a certain amount of virtual channels are exclusively assigned to short messages. The remaining virtual channels are shared by both short and long messages [16]. This totally eliminates the possibility that a short message will be blocked by a long message. However, previous research works in this field have been limited to non-adaptive routing, and the design of router could be complicated when the number of virtual channels is large [15].

In this paper, Hybrid-HAR is introduced as a combination of multipath routing and virtual channel allocation. Hybrid-HAR has four important advantages. Firstly, one set of virtual channels is exclusively allocated to short messages, which almost eliminate the possibility that a short message will be blocked by a long message Secondly, fully adaptive routing is provided to both short and long messages to give good overall network performance; Third, the hierarchical design makes the implementation of Hybrid-HAR simple, which is compatible to the standard static routing such as DOR provided the same amount of virtual channels is used. Fourth, it is applicability to a wide variety of network topologies.

3 Hybrid Hierarchical Adaptive Routing (Hybrid-HAR)

In this section, Hierarchical Adaptive Routing (HAR) is extended with virtual channel allocation for hybrid traffic load. A new adaptive routing framework called Hybrid-HAR is introduced to increase the performance of short messages.

3.1 Hybrid-HAR Framework

Hybrid-HAR is a combination of hierarchical adaptive routing, as described in [13], and virtual channel allocation scheme, which provides a simple and efficient framework to networks with bimodal traffic load. As shown in Figure 1, Hybrid-HAR divides a physical network into several virtual networks. There are two *connection* channels between two adjacent virtual networks, one for short messages and another for long messages. The connection channel allows blocked messages in the higher level to move to the lower level. Two separate injection and sink channels are provided, both for short and long messages. Different routing algorithms can be used in different virtual networks for different purposes. Initially, when a message is generated, it is injected into the first level virtual network and routed towards the destination. However, if at some point there are no free output channels in the first level virtual network (due to congestion), the message can be moved to the second level virtual network through the connection channel. If this happens again at another node, message can then be moved into the third level virtual network and so on.

Notation:
FAR: Fully Adaptive Routing (minimal); DOR: Dimension Order Routing
CCS: Connection Channel for Short Message; LVN: Lowest Level Virtual Network
CCL: Connection Channel for Long Message; OVC: Output Virtual Channel
SVN: Successive Virtual Network; DFR: Deadlock-Free Routing
C_1 : First Set of Virtual Channels in LVN; C_2 : Second Set of Virtual Channels in LVN

Hybrid-HAR Routing Algorithm

Upper Level Virtual Networks:
1   If one OVC is free by FAR, forward the message along that channel
2   else,
3.1   If the message is short and CCS is free, move it into SVN;
3.2   If the message is long and CCL is free, move it into SVN;
4   otherwise, block the message.

Lowest Level Virtual Network:
5.1   If the message is short and one OVC in C_2 is free by DFR, forward it;
5.2   If the message is short and one OVC in C_1 is free by DFR, forward it;
5.3   If message is long and one OVC in C_1 is free by DFR, forward it;
6   otherwise, block the message.

In any actual router design, there is only a finite number of virtual networks. When a packet enters into the lowest virtual network (LVN), it must be routed to the destination node entirely within that virtual network. The LVN must be deadlock-free for both short and long messages. However, the routing algorithms at the upper level virtual networks can be fully adaptive for higher performance. Also at LVN, one set of virtual channels is exclusively allocated to short messages to avoid that a short message will be directly blocked by a long message. As indicated in Figure 1, the virtual channels from the set C_2 are only used by short messages.

For any network topology, if there is a known deadlock-free routing algorithm, Hybrid-HAR can be used to produce a fully adaptive routing algorithm for hybrid traffic load. A virtual network with fully adaptive routing for both short and long messages needs to be added on the top of deadlock-free virtual network. One extra virtual channel needs to be added in the deadlock-free virtual network, which is used only by short messages. The routing algorithm on the extra virtual channel for short messages can be adaptive, as long as the whole routing algorithm is deadlock-free.

4 Hybrid-HAR in 2D Mesh

In this section, Hybrid-HAR is applied in a 2D mesh network to develop a simple and efficient fully adaptive routing algorithm for hybrid traffic load. A restricted Duato Adaptive Routing (DAR) algorithm is applied in the lowest virtual network to guarantee freedom from deadlock for both short and long messages, and to reduce the impact of long messages on short messages. We show that the possibility that a long message will be blocked by a long message is rare.

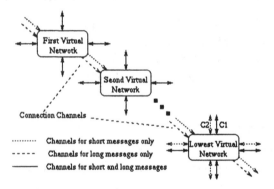

Fig. 1. Hybrid Hierarchical Adaptive Routing Framework

Hybrid-HAR in 2D mesh networks requires that each physical channel split into four virtual channels. The physical network is then divided into two equal virtual networks, which are connected through two internal connection channels, one for short and another for long messages. Separate injection and sink channels are used for short and long messages from and to the network interface. In the upper virtual network, fully adaptive minimum path routing is used on two sets of virtual channels (called FAR virtual network). At the lower level, the restricted Duato Adaptive Routing is used (called DAR virtual network) [5]. When a message, short or long, is injected into the network, it enters the FAR virtual network and uses the virtual channels there to move toward the destination. However, when there is congestion in the network, it is possible that all valid output virtual channels are busy. In such a case, if the corresponding connection channel to the DAR virtual network is free, the message is moved into the DAR virtual network.

In the lower level virtual network, the restricted DAR algorithm is applied. Both short and long messages can route over the first set of virtual channels $\langle C_1 \rangle$ with dimension order routing; However, only short messages can route over the second set of virtual channels $\langle C_2 \rangle$ with fully adaptive minimum path routing. In the original DAR algorithm, there is no distinction between short and long messages. Dimension order routing and fully adaptive routing can be chosen by any message at any step according to the status of output channels.

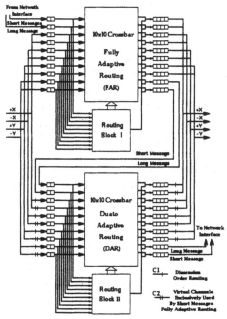

Fig. 2. Hybrid Hierarchical Adaptive Routing in 2D Mesh Network

In Hybrid-HAR, the probability that a short message will be blocked by a long message is very small. Firstly, a short message will never be blocked by a long message in the higher virtual network, since the connection channel will allow the blocked short message in the higher virtual network to move into the lower virtual network. Secondly, the chance that a short message will be blocked by a long message in the lower virtual channel is small. Two conditions must be satisfied. Firstly, a cycle dependency must exist in C_2 formed by several short messages due to the fully adaptive routing, which itself has no restriction on routing to avoid deadlock. Each message would occupy one virtual channel from C_2, requested by another short message. Secondly, all the corresponding virtual channels in C_1 must be occupied by long messages. In such a case, all those short messages in the dependency cycle are directly blocked by a long message. The simulation results in [10] have shown that the probability that a dependency cycle will occur with fully adaptive routing is actually very small. In Hybrid-HAR, it is even smaller with hierarchical adaptive routing and a larger number of virtual channels. Further more, the probability that the second condition will be true is small too. In one word, the probability that a short message will be blocked by a long message is very small in Hybrid-HAR. A proof that the restricted DAR algorithm is deadlock-free can be established using the theory described by Duato in [5].

5 Performance

In this section, we evaluate the performance of Hybrid Hierarchical Adaptive Routing compared to Dimension Order Routing (DOR) using a register-transfer level simulation. Firstly, the simulation modelling is presented. Then the simulation experiment results with uniform and non-uniform traffic patterns are given.

5.1 Simulation Modelling

The simulator is a 2000 line C program based on the HSMPL sequential discrete-event simulation environment [12]. It simulates 16x16 mesh networks at the flit-level. A flit transfer between two nodes and through the crossbar is assumed to take place in one clock cycle. The routing information fits in a single flit (the header flit), and a routing decision requires two clock cycles. In all cases, each physical channel has been split into four virtual channels. Routers are connected by dual unidirectional channels.

The models of DOR and Hybrid-HAR are similar to each other. The detailed modelling of Hybrid-HAR router has been presented in Section 3 and shown in Figure 2. Similar to Hybrid-HAR, the DOR router has two levels of virtual networks and each has almost identical 10x10 crossbars. Message has to finish routing in the X dimension before starts routing in the Y dimension. The Hybrid-HAR router has almost the same complexity as the DOR router, except routing decision is slightly complicated due to the fully adaptive routing and virtual channel allocation. Due to the same complexity, Hybrid-HAR and DOR routers will have same latency for data-through or cycle time. It is assumed that Hybrid-HAR router and DOR router has the same cycle in the simulation.

At each node, messages are generated by a Poisson process, whose mean value is determined by applied network load rate. Applied network loads are all normalized with respect to the network's maximum wire capacity, defined as all of the network channels transmitting simultaneously. Generated short or long messages which are not accepted by the network are source queued in a short or long messages queue which is allowed to grow without bound. Thus, the message latency numbers include the waiting time in the source queue. Three traffic patterns are considered: *uniform* and non-uniform *transpose* and *center-reflection*.

The traffic model is a bimodal distribution of message sizes, short and long. The length of short messages is fixed at 32 flits. If flits are eight bits, this short message size is comparable to a cache line or a procedure invocation record. The length of long messages is fixed to 256 flits. The traffic mixes contain 0%(short messages only), 25%, 50%, 75% and 100%(long messages only) long messages, respectively. The proportions are percentages by traffic volume.

5.2 Uniform Traffic

In the uniform traffic pattern, each node sends messages to all other nodes with equal probability and there is no congestion in the network. DOR has slightly better performance than adaptive routing. The reason is that with uniform traffic, non-adaptive routing preserves the traffic's uniformity, while adaptive routing disturbs it.

Figure 3 shows average short message latency (S-latency). DOR has slightly lower S-latency than Hybrid-HAR when the percentage of long messages (P) is less than 75%. As P is increased from 0% to 50%, S-latency increases in both DOR and Hybrid-HAR due to the increasing impact of long messages on short messages. However, further increasing P to 75%, S-latency is decreased in both DOR and Hybrid-HAR. Especially in Hybrid-HAR, S-latency is very low when P is 75% due to less congestion on those virtual channels exclusively allocated to short messages.

Figure 4 shows the average long message latency (L-latency). DOR has slightly lower L-latency than Hybrid-HAR. L-latency increases with the increased P in both DOR and Hybrid-HAR. Figure 5(a) shows that DOR has higher throughput than Hybrid-HAR with all traffic mixes. Throughput decreases with increased P, since channel coupling increases with message length, reducing the performance.

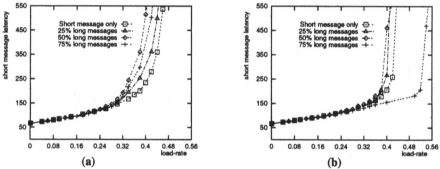

Fig. 3. The average short message latency under uniform traffic pattern when the routing algorithm is (a) DOR and (b) Hybrid-HAR.

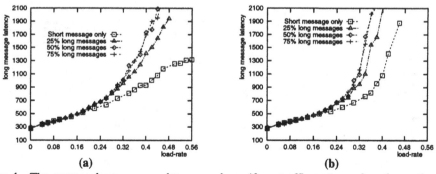

Fig. 4. The average long message latency under uniform traffic pattern when the routing algorithm is (a) DOR and (b) Hybrid-HAR.

The short message latency distribution is shown in Figure 6. All short messages in Hybrid-HAR are delivered with lower latency than in DOR. When there is no long messages in the network, all short messages are delivered in less than 900 cycles in Hybrid-HAR, versus 1250 in DOR. Fully adaptive routing in Hybrid-HAR reduces the possibility that short messages will block each other. With long messages present, a substantial fraction of short messages are delivered with extremely high latencies in

DOR. For example when P is 50%, the largest delay in DOR reaches 3400 clock cycles, where only 1300 in Hybrid-HAR.

5.3 Non-Uniform Traffic

Two non-uniform traffic patterns, transpose and center-reflection, have been examined to compare the performance of Hybrid-HAR with DOR. In the transpose traffic pattern, node (x,y) sends messages to node (y,x). For DOR, there are congestions in the lower left and upper right corners. In the center-reflection traffic pattern, node (x,y) sends messages to node (16-x,16-y). There is traffic jam in DOR at the left and right edges of the network. Due to the fully adaptive routing, Hybrid-HAR reduces the traffic jams significantly and has much better performance than DOR. The performance under transpose traffic pattern is similar to the one under center-reflection. All simulation results with center-reflection except the throughput have been omitted in the paper.

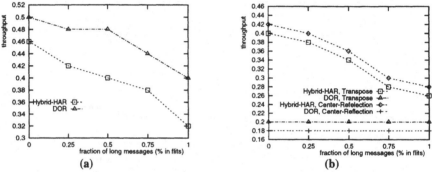

Fig. 5. The overall throughput under traffic with a range of traffic mixes. The traffic pattern are (a) Uniform and (b) Transpose and center-reflection

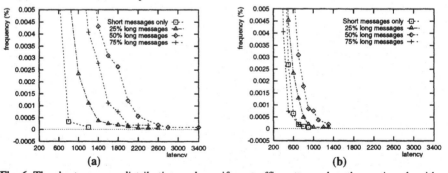

Fig. 6. The short message distribution under uniform traffic pattern when the routing algorithm is (a) DOR and (b) Hybrid-HAR. The applied load-rate is 0.36.

Figure 5(b) describes the throughput of DOR and Hybrid-HAR under two non-uniform traffic patterns. Hybrid-HAR out-performs DOR significantly, especially when P is low. The throughput of DOR in non-uniform traffic patterns is very low, only 0.20 and 0.18 respectively. It tends to be constant with all traffic mixes. The reason is that the congestion remains almost the same in the DOR network, regardless of the traffic mix. In Hybrid-HAR, throughput decreases with increased P, since channel coupling increases with message length, reducing the performance.

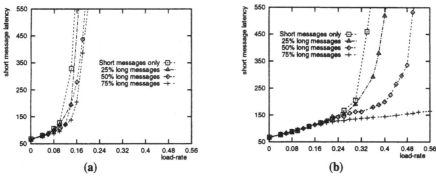

Fig. 7. The average short message latency under transpose traffic pattern when the routing algorithm is (a) DOR and (b) Hybrid-HAR.

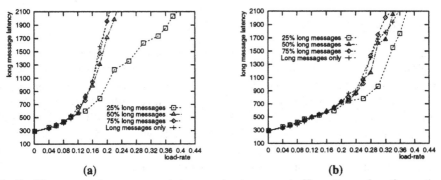

Fig. 8. The average long message latency under transpose traffic pattern when the routing algorithm is (a) DOR and (b) Hybrid-HAR.

Figure 7 shows that Hybrid-HAR has much lower S-latency than DOR with all traffic mixes. In DOR, S-latency decreases slightly with the increased P due to lower short messages traffic load. In Hybrid-HAR, however, S-latency decreases much quickly with the increased P. As P is increased, the short message traffic load decreases dramatically. There is much less congestion on those virtual channels exclusively allocated to short messages. Figure 8 shows that Hybrid-HAR has slightly lower L-latency than DOR with all traffic mixes.

Under transpose traffic pattern, all short messages in Hybrid-HAR are delivered with much lower latency than in DOR, as shown in Figure 9. All short messages in Hybrid-HAR are delivered in less than 600 clock cycles with all range of traffic mixes, versus at least 1600 in DOR. The distributions of short message latency differ dramatically as traffic mix changes in DOR. The largest delay in DOR is 9000, 1600, 7600 and 1600 clock cycles when P is 0, 0.25, 0.50 and 0.75 respectively. However, the longest delay in Hybrid-HAR is less than 600 clock cycles with all traffic mixes. Fully adaptive routing and virtual channels allocation scheme in Hybrid-HAR dramatically reduces the impact of long messages on short messages under non-uniform traffic pattern.

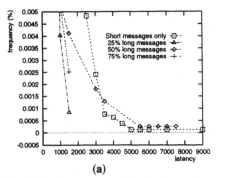 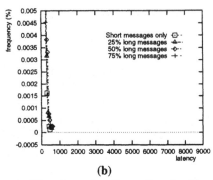

(a)   (b)

Fig. 9. The short message distribution under transpose traffic pattern when the routing algorithm is (a) DOR and (b) Hybrid-HAR. The applied load-rate is 0.20.

6 Conclusion

In this paper, we have extended the hierarchical adaptive routing to a hybrid-traffic model and produced a framework for fully adaptive deadlock-free wormhole routing (Hybrid-HAR). Hybrid-HAR divides the physical network into two levels of virtual networks. Fully adaptive routing is used in the higher level virtual network for higher performance. Another fully adaptive routing (by Duato) is used in the lower level virtual network to avoid deadlock. One set of virtual channels with fully adaptive routing are exclusively allocated to short messages in the lower level virtual network, which gives very good performance for short messages with all traffic mixes.

A draft implementation outline of Hybrid-HAR router for 2D mesh network has shown that it has almost the same complexity as the DOR router, when the same amount of virtual channels is used. All simulation results have confirmed the high performance of Hybrid-HAR. Under non-uniform traffic pattern, with fully adaptive routing, Hybrid-HAR out-performs DOR substantially. Under uniform traffic pattern, Hybrid-HAR gives compatible performance. Under both uniform and non-uniform traffic patterns, Hybrid-HAR can guarantee that short messages are delivered with much lower latency than DOR, with all traffic mixes. The conclusion is that Hybrid-HAR is a new fully adaptive routing scheme worth to be introduced for actual multicomputer application, where the traffic model is hybrid.

References

1. A. Agarwal. Limits on interconnection network performance. IEEE Transactions on Parallel and Distributed Systems 2(4):398--412, 1991.

2. R. Cypher, A. Ho, S. Konstantinidou, and P. Messina. Architectural requirements of parallel scientific applications with explicit communication. In Proceedings of the International Symposium on Computer Architecture, pages 2--13, 1993.

3. W. Dally and C. Seitz. Deadlock-free message routing in multiprocessor interconnection networks. IEEE Transactions on Computers, C-36(5):547--53, 1987.

4. W. J. Dally, et. al. Design and implementation of the message-driven processor. In Proceedings of the 1992 Brown/MIT Conference on Advanced Research in VLSI and Parallel Systems, T. Knight and J. Savage, eds., pages 5--25. MIT Press, 1992.

5. J. Duato. On the design of deadlock-free adaptive routing algorithms for multicomputers: design methodologies. In Proceedings of Parallel Architectures and Languages Europe, pages 390--405, 1991.

6. F. Hady. A Performance Study of Wormhole Routed Networks Through Analytical Modelling and Experimentation. PhD thesis, University of Maryland, 1993.

7. J. M. Hsu and P. Banerjee. Performance measurement and trace driven simulation of parallel cad and numeric applications on a hypercube multicomputer. IEEE Transactions on Parallel and Distributed Systems, 3(4):451--464, 1992.

8. C. R. Jesshope, P. R. Miller, and J. T. Yantchev. High performance communications in processor networks. In Proceedings of the International Symposium on Computer Architecture, pages 150--7, 1989.

9. P. Kermani and L. Kleinrock. Virtual cut-through: A new computer communications switching technique. Computer Networks, 3(4):267--86, 1979.

10. Jae Kim, Ziqiang Liu, and Andrew A. Chien. Compressionless routing: A framework for adaptive and fault-tolerant routing. In Proceedings of the International Symposium on Computer Architecture, pages 289--300, 1994.

11. Jae H. Kim and Andrew A. Chien. Network performance under bimodal traffic loads.To appear in the Journal of Parallel and Distributed Computing.

12. Z. Liu, L-E Thorelli, and H. Wu. Hsim: A hybrid sequential and parallel simulation. In Proceedings of the Information Processing, pages 372--378, 1992.

13. Ziqiang Liu and Andrew A. Chien. Hierarchical adaptive routing: A framework for fully adaptive and deadlock-free wormhole routing. In Sixth IEEE Symposium on Parallel and Distributed Processing, 1994.

14. L. Ni and C. Glass. The turn model for adaptive routing. In Proceedings of the International Symposium on Computer Architecture, pages 278--87, 1992.

15. Abdel-Halim Smai and Lars-Erik Thorelli. Dynamic allocation of communication bandwidth in multicomputers. In Parallel Architectures and Languages Europe, pages 677--687, 1994.

16. Abdel-Halim Smai and Handong Wu. Evaluation of a priority flow control scheme for multicomputer networks. In Euromicro Workshop on Parallel and Distributed Processing, pages 111-116, 1994.

Parallel Algorithms I

Tight Bounds on Parallel List Marking

Sandeep N. Bhatt[1], Gianfranco Bilardi[2], Kieran T. Herley[3],
Geppino Pucci[2], Abhiram G. Ranade[4]

[1] Bell Communications Research, Morristown NJ 07960, USA
[2] Dip. di Elettronica e Informatica, Univ. di Padova, Padova 35131, Italy
[3] Dept. of Computer Science, Univ. College Cork, Cork, Ireland
[4] Computer Science Div., Univ. of California at Berkeley, Berkeley CA 94720, USA

Abstract. The list marking problem involves marking the nodes of an ℓ-node linked list stored in the memory of a (p, n)-PRAM, when only the location of the head of the list is initially known. Under the assumption that memory cells containing list nodes bear no distinctive tags distinguishing them from other cells, we establish an $\Omega\left(\min\{\ell, n/p\}\right)$ randomized lower bound for ℓ-node lists and present a deterministic algorithm whose running time is within a logarithmic additive term of this bound. In the case where list cells are tagged in a way that differentiates them from other cells, we establish a tight $\Theta\left(\min\left\{\ell, \ell/p + \sqrt{(n/p)\log n}\right\}\right)$ bound for randomized algorithms.

1 Introduction

Linked structures are widely used in non numerical as well as sparse numerical computations. Therefore, it is important to ascertain whether parallelism can be exploited to process such structures effectively.

In this paper, we focus on lists, possibly the simplest type of linked structures, and on a very basic operation, which we call *marking*, consisting of writing a given value in each node of a given list. The essence of marking is that each node in the list has to be affected and no other. This feature is common to several basic list operations such as searching an element or ranking all nodes (determining their distance from the head). Marking itself is used in important practical applications, such as garbage collection, for identifying active structures in a large memory heap.

The complexity of parallel list operations crucially depends on the list representation, and is often affected by features that are irrelevant to sequential complexity. When managing lists in parallel, a favourable case arises if the the growth process affords keeping all list nodes in a compact region of memory. Specifically, the list could be represented as an array of ℓ records, each record corresponding to a list node, with a field storing the array index of its successor. Indeed, most list-based parallel algorithms in the literature (e.g., searching and ranking [2]) do assume such compact representation.

In other scenarios, unfortunately, list nodes become naturally scattered throughout a portion of memory whose size is much larger than the length of the list.

This case arises when a sequence of concatenations and splittings is performed on a set of lists.

We also distinguish between tagged and untagged lists, a tagged list being one where each node contains a *tag* that uniquely identifies the list. Tags can be maintained with small overhead if lists are modified only by insertion and deletion of nodes. However, the overhead is not negligible if other operations, such as concatenation and splitting, are allowed.

We investigate the extent to which parallelism, randomization, and tagging can be profitably exploited to improve upon sequential performance when lists are scattered throughout the memory. Specifically, we develop deterministic and randomized upper and lower bounds for marking a (tagged or untagged) list of ℓ nodes stored in the memory of a p-processor PRAM with n memory cells, when only the location of the head of the list is initially known.

1.1 Related Work and New Results

A restricted version of the list marking problem was introduced and analyzed by Luccio and Pagli in [7]. Under the assumption that list elements are distinguishable from non-list elements by inspection, the authors prove a deterministic $\Omega(\min\{\ell, n/p\})$ lower bound and provide a tight upper bound when $p = O(\ell/\log \ell)$ and $n = O(\ell \log \ell)$. In this paper we improve and generalize these results in the following directions:

1. In the case where list elements are indistinguishable from non-list elements, we prove that an $\Omega(\min\{\ell, n/p\})$ lower bound also holds for randomized algorithms. Moreover, we give a deterministic algorithm optimal to within a logarithmic additive term, therefore showing that randomization can not be exploited in any significant way in this setting.
2. In the case where list elements are tagged in a way that makes them recognizable by inspection, we establish a tight $\Theta\left(\min\left\{\ell, \ell/p + \sqrt{(n/p)\log n}\right\}\right)$ bound for randomized algorithms, showing that, for a wide range of list lengths, considerable speedups can be attained by means of randomization.

1.2 Preliminaries

We will assume that each memory cell has the same format and contains a memory address which will be interpreted as a pointer (called the *successor pointer*) to another cell, a *tag field*, capable of holding a distinctive symbol, a *data field*, and a small constant amount of additional space, called *scratch space*. The head of the list, denoted by h, occupies cell 0 and its data field contains some arbitrary symbol which we will refer to as the *signature* of the list. Finally, each node points to the next node in the list, and the pointer field of the last node r contains the address of cell 0, which we will interpret as a *nil* pointer.

We identify two variants of the problem. The list is *untagged* if list nodes bear no distinctive mark or symbol that renders them instantly identifiable as such. The list is *tagged* if each list node bears a distinctive symbol in its tag field which no non-list node bears, thus allowing list nodes to be identified by inspection. In both cases, the goal of the list marking problem is to copy the signature into the data field of every node in the list; the data fields of all other nodes should remain unchanged. A node is said to be *marked* once its data field bears the appropriate signature.

Since each memory cell contains a successor pointer, the entire memory can be interpreted as a directed graph G of n nodes. Each node must have outdegree zero or one, but a node (including list nodes) may have indegree zero (*leaves*), one (*unary nodes*), or higher. Such a graph is known as a *pseudoforest*. (Such structures feature in some connected component algorithms, for example [5].) Within the pseudoforest, the chain of list nodes forms a directed path in a structure T that we may interpret as a tree, the edges of which are oriented from child to parent. The node h is a leaf of T and the list nodes are the ancestors of h in T located along the directed path from h to r, the root of T. In fact, G consists of T plus a collection of node-disjoint components each of which is either a tree or one or more trees joined by a cycle connecting their roots. In this setting, the objective is to mark all those nodes in G that are ancestors of h in T.

The algorithms presented here all assume the ARBITRARY CRCW variant of the PRAM model of shared-memory computation [5]. Thus concurrent reads and writes are permitted. Whenever a number of processors attempt to write simultaneously to a cell, one of them, chosen arbitrarily, succeeds, while the others fail. For convenience, we will refer to a PRAM with p-processors and n-cells of memory as a (p, n)-PRAM and will assume throughout that $p \leq n$. We will also assume that each processor has a private area of $O(1)$ storage for workspace.

In Section 2 we investigate the problem of marking untagged lists and present a randomized lower bound and an almost matching deterministic upper bound. Section 3 deals with the tagged case. Section 4 offers some concluding remarks.

2   Marking Untagged Lists

In this section we determine the complexity of the untagged variant of the list marking problem. In Subsection 2.1, we prove that any randomized *Las Vegas* algorithm for the problem requires $\Omega\left(\min\{\ell, n/p\}\right)$ time with high probability. In Subsection 2.2, we give a deterministic algorithm whose running time is within an additive logarithmic term of the lower bound, thereby proving that randomization can not be conveniently exploited in this case.

2.1   A Randomized Lower Bound

The intuition behind the lower bound is that a list element becomes distinguishable from a non-list element only when every element along the directed path from the head of the list to that element has been marked. Therefore random probes of the memory cells will not speed-up the computation in any significant way. This argument is formalized in the following theorem.

Theorem 1. *Suppose that with probability $1 - o(1)$ a randomized parallel algorithm on a (p, n)-PRAM marks every element of a list of length ℓ within t time steps. Then $t = \Omega\left(\min\{\ell, n/p\}\right)$.*

Proof. Observe that a randomized algorithm can be seen as one chosen uniformly at random from a set $\mathcal{D}$ of deterministic algorithms (each deterministic algorithm being characterized by the outcome of a sequence of random choices). In order to prove our lower bound for the untagged case, we construct a set of inputs with the property that *every* algorithm in $\mathcal{D}$ fails to mark the list in less than the time prescribed by the lower bound for a constant fraction of the inputs. From this, it immediately follows that, for some input in the set, a constant fraction among all the deterministic algorithms fail to mark the list in the prescribed time. Therefore, the failure probability of a randomly chosen algorithm, on that particular input, is bounded below by a positive constant.

We will assume that ℓ is fixed and will restrict our attention to the following set of inputs. The contents of the memory are organized as a circular list of length n. The target list of length ℓ is stored as a contiguous sublist, and the address of the head and tail of the target list is given as input to the algorithm. There are $n!$ different inputs, corresponding to the $(n - 1)!$ different circular lists of length n and the choice for the address of the head of the target list. This formulation of the problem is essentially equivalent to that presented in the introduction, but more convenient in the current context.

Without loss of generality, suppose that $t \leq \frac{n}{2p}$. At any time step, the algorithm probes a set of at most p memory cells. At step $i \leq t$, we can think of the nodes on the circular list to be grouped into *sublists*. A sublist consists of a maximal set of adjacent probed nodes terminated by an unprobed node. According to this definition, we initially have n sublists, each consisting of a single distinct unprobed node. When a node v is probed, its pointer to the next element v' in the list becomes known, and their corresponding sublists merge. We will refer to the sublist containing the head of the target list as the *principal* sublist. This sublist will contain a prefix of the target list that grows in length as the algorithm executes. Notice that each step of the algorithm causes up to p merges and hence at least $n - pi$ sublists remain after i steps.

At the beginning of the ith step, suppose that the nodes are partitioned into a total of k_i sublists of various lengths (including the principal sublist), and let n_i^j denote the number of nonprincipal sublists of length j. Note that $\sum_{j=1}^n n_i^j = k_i - 1$. For convenience, we assume that each step consists of a first substep during which $p - 1$ arbitrary cells are probed, followed by a second substep when the tail of the principal sublist is probed, which has the effect of grafting a single sublist onto the end of the principal sublist. Clearly, conforming to this discipline will not alter the running time of an algorithm by more than a constant factor. The merges provoked by the $p - 1$ probes of the first substep yield k_{i+1} nonprincipal sublists. With the possible exception of the single sublist that will be grafted onto the principal sublist during the second substep, there are at most n_j^{i+1} sublists of length j. One of these sublists is grafted onto the principal sublist during this step, and because all input lists are equally likely, each of these sublists is equally likely to be chosen. Thus, the expected value of δ_i, the increase in the length of the principal sublist during step i, is bounded as follows

$$E[\delta_i] \leq \sum_{j=1}^{n} \frac{jn_j^{i+1}}{k_{i+1}} + \frac{n}{k_{i+1}} \leq \frac{2n}{n - pi} \leq 4 ,$$

since $k_{i+1} \geq n - pi \geq n/2$. (Note the sum accounts for all but one of the nonprincipal sublists; the term n/k_{i+1} accounts for the contribution of the remaining one.)

Therefore, only constant progress is made, on average, at each step on the prefix of the list, and the proof follows.

Note that the above bound is obtained under the optimistic assumption that a node belonging to the target list is marked as soon as all the other nodes between the head of the target list and that node are probed, even though the algorithm, by the time it touches the corresponding memory cells, may not have sufficient information to determine that these cells actually contain list elements.

2.2 A Deterministic Upper Bound

We begin by outlining a relatively simple but slightly inefficient deterministic algorithm for the untagged list marking problem. We then provide a fast technique to transform the input instance into an equivalent, smaller one so that the running time of the algorithm on the new instance is within the desired bound. The "shrinking" process is accomplished by deleting nodes and rearranging edges of the pseudoforest underlying the original input instance.

Consider an untagged list of ℓ nodes stored in the memory of a (p, n)-PRAM, and let h be the (given) distinguished pointer to the head of the list. As we observed in Section 1.2, the nodes to be marked are the ancestors of h in a tree T whose root is r, the tail of the list. Suppose that we are given the preorder and postorder number of every node in T. Then, a particular node x is an ancestor of h if and only if $preorder(x) \leq preorder(h)$ and $postorder(x) \geq postorder(h)$. Although the Euler-tour techniques of Tarjan and Vishkin[8] can be used to efficiently compute the preorder and postorder numberings in trees, these may not be applied immediately in the present context. Firstly, the presence of other components in the pseudoforest may complicate matters, and secondly the techniques rely on an adjacency list representation for trees.

We circumvent the first difficulty as follows. Using a straightforward pointer-jumping technique, each node in T can identify the root r in $O(\log n)$ time per node or $O((n/p) \log n)$ time overall. Nodes not in T executing the same algorithm will "converge" on some node other than r and will hence be clearly identifiable as not belonging to T. All such nodes will remain dormant for the remainder of the algorithm.

Having eliminated all nodes not in T, we may now construct an adjacency list representation for T. Label the ith cell C_i with the pair $< s, i >$ where s is the address of its parent in T. By sorting the cells lexicographically using Cole's algorithm [1], the children of each node occupy adjacent positions, and so they may be easily linked together in an adjacency list for that node. (These linking pointers are distinct from the successor pointers for the nodes and are stored in the scratch storage associated with the nodes in question.) The cells are then resorted with respect to their original addresses in order to reconstruct the original structure of T and to attach adjacency lists to the appropriate tree nodes. The implementation details are straightforward. The sorting steps dominate the running time and so the adjacency list representation for T can be constructed in $O((n/p) \log n)$ time.

Given the adjacency list representation for T, the preorder and postorder numberings can be computed in $O((n/p) \log n)$ time. The identification and marking of the ancestors of h can be completed within the same time bounds. Interleaving this $O((n/p) \log n)$ algorithm with the obvious $O(\ell)$ sequential algorithm, we obtain the following result.

Proposition 2. *An untagged list of length ℓ in the memory of an (p, n)-PRAM can be marked deterministically in $O(\min\{\ell, (n/p) \log n\})$ time.*

We now proceed to extend Proposition 2 to provide a more work-efficient algorithm. Our algorithm will consist of a sequence of *pruning* steps applied to the pseudoforest G. Each pruning step will be applied to the result of the previous one and each will reduce the size of the problem (the number of nodes in the pseudoforest) by a constant factor by deleting some nodes and rearranging pointers among the active (undeleted) nodes. After a certain number of stages, the original pseudoforest G will have been reduced to one G' of significantly smaller size. Because of its smaller size, it is faster to identify and mark the ancestors of h in G' than in G using the techniques of Proposition 2. Moreover, the ancestors of h in G' are among the ancestors of h in G and so the marking of G' can be extended to mark all the ancestors of h in G.

The following lemma provides the basis for pruning steps.

Lemma 3. *There is a constant $\mu < 1$ such that for any pseudoforest $H = (V, E)$ containing h, there is a subset $W \subseteq V$ consisting entirely of leaves and unary nodes, but not containing h, such that :*

(i) $|W| \geq \mu |V| - 1$;
(ii) *No pair of nodes in W are neighbours in H.*

Moreover, set W can be computed in $O(|V|/p + \log n / \log \log n)$ time.

Proof. Let $H = (V, E)$ be a pseudoforest. We show that there exists an independent subset W of V consisting entirely of leaves and unary nodes that has size at least $\mu |V| - 1$.

The nodes eligible for inclusion in W are the nodes in H of indegree at most one apart from h. This set induces a set of maximal node-disjoint linear chains of eligible nodes. Apply the following operation to each such chain. If the chain is of length one or two, select the first node; if the chain length has length three or more select a subset of the nodes such that (i) no two adjacent nodes are selected, and (ii) the maximum number of consecutive unselected nodes on the chain is two. The union of the selected nodes for the various chains forms the desired set W.

The identification of nodes in H of indegree at most one is straightforward and requires only constant work per node. The selection of nodes belonging to chains of length three or greater is instead accomplished by applying the 2-ruling algorithm of Cole and Vishkin [2] and selecting the nodes in the ruling. (The latter algorithm is formulated in terms of circular lists, but this is not an essential restriction.) This latter step can be completed in $O(|V|/p + \log n/\log\log n)$ time.

Consider a chain of length k. If $k \le 2$ then, clearly at least $k/2$ of the nodes on the chain are selected. If $k \ge 3$, then each pair of selected nodes is separated by at most two unselected nodes. Allowing for the possibility that the first two nodes on a chain might be unselected, we see that the number of selected nodes is at least $\lceil (k-2)/3 \rceil \ge (1/9)k$.

If we let s denote the number of nodes in H of indegree at most one (including h), it is clear that $s \ge (|V|+1)/2$. However the $s-1$ eligible nodes are arranged into chains of length one, two, or greater, and so we are guaranteed that at least $(1/9)(s-1) \ge (1/18)|V| - 1$ nodes are selected.

Notice that it is easy to delete a node w in W from H by redirecting the edge incident on w (if any) to point to w's parent. (Recall that w has at most one child.) By the above lemma, the graph H' thus obtained contains significantly fewer nodes than H (at most $(1-\mu)|V|+1$). It is also easy to verify that for every pair of nodes x and y in H', x is an ancestor of y in H' if and only if x is an ancestor of y in H. Thus, while smaller in size, the graph H' retains some of the ancestor-descendent information of the original graph H.

Before we describe the implementation of the pruning step in greater detail, we must introduce some auxiliary data structures employed by the algorithm, the role of which will become clear in due course.

Each processor maintains a private stack that is empty before the first pruning. When a processor deletes a node during a pruning step, it pushes that node onto its stack. This facilitates the reconstruction of the graph at a later stage in the algorithm. Each processor also has a private list called its work list. Collectively the p work lists hold all the active nodes in the graph. Between pruning steps, nodes are redistributed among work lists to ensure that each processor's work list contains an equal number of items. A processor is responsible for performing whatever operations are required for the nodes on its work list during a pruning step.

It should be emphasized that the only space overhead for these stacks and work lists is $O(1)$ per processor for a header pointer: the objects in these structures are nodes linked by pointers. These linking pointers are distinct from the successor pointers of the nodes in question and are represented within the scratch space of the nodes.

The pruning step applied to $H = (V, E)$ may be described as follows.

1. Identify the set W.
2. Perform the following step for each active node x in W: mark x deleted, label the node with the current time and the name of its lone child, and push the node onto the local stack. For each active node c whose parent x is in W do the following: redirect c's successor pointer to point to x's parent, or to *nil* if x has no parent. (Each processor is responsible for the nodes on its own work list.)
3. Update the work lists.

From Lemma 3 it follows that Step 1 is completed in $O(|V|/p+\log n/\log\log n)$ time. Assuming for the moment that every processor list holds $O(|V|/p)$ items at the start of the pruning step, it is easy to see that Step 2 requires $O(|V|/p)$ time. To update the work lists in Step 3, each processor scans through its own list removing the deleted nodes and counting the active nodes. Let a denote the total number of active nodes. Using a straightforward combination of parallel prefix [3] and routine pointer manipulations, it is possible to redistribute the active nodes among the work lists so that each processor's list receives at most $\lceil a/p \rceil$ in $O(a/p + \log n/\log\log n)$ time. Thus, each stage can be completed in $O(|V|/p + \log n/\log\log n)$ time.

The following recurrence provides an upper bound governing the number of active nodes remaining active after the ith pruning step:

$$a_i = \begin{cases} (1-\mu)a_{i-1} + 1, & \text{for } i > 0 , \\ n, & \text{for } i = 0 . \end{cases}$$

Thus, $a_i \leq (1-\mu)^i n + \sum_{j=0}^{i-1}(1-\mu)^j$, which is bounded above by $\mu^{-1}n/\log n$ for $i \geq \lceil \log\log n/\log(1-\mu)^{-1} \rceil$. Selecting k to be this latter quantity, we see that the number of active nodes can be reduced to at most $\mu^{-1}n/\log n$ in

$$O\left(\sum_{i=0}^{k-1} \frac{(1-\mu)^i n + \mu^{-1}}{p} + k\log n/\log\log n \right) = O\left(n/p + \log n \right)$$

time.

In conclusion, the overall algorithm is as follows.

1. Apply k stages to G to produce G' of size at most $\mu^{-1}n/\log n$.
2. Apply the algorithm of Proposition 2 to mark all nodes in G' that are ancestors of h.
3. Reincorporate the nodes deleted during Step 1 in the reverse order to which they were deleted. In other words, first undo the deletions of the kth pruning, then those of the $(k-1)^{st}$ pruning, and so on. For each reinserted node, mark it if its child is marked.

We have already noted that Step 1 runs in $O(n/p + \log n)$ time, and since Step 3 is similar, it too has the same time bound. By Proposition 2, Step 2 requires $O(((\mu^{-1}n/\log n)/p)\log n) = O(n/p + \log n)$ time.

By using the facts that an ancestor of a node x in G' is also an ancestor of x in G, and that only leaves and unary nodes are deleted, it is not difficult to see that all of the nodes marked by this algorithm are ancestors of h in G. On the other hand, suppose that some node along the directed path from h to r is not marked by the algorithm, and let x be the first such node. This node must have been deleted during one of the pruning operations in Step 1, otherwise it would have been marked during Step 2. Suppose that c was the lone child of x at the time that x was deleted. By assumption, the node c is marked by the algorithm, and so when x is reinserted during Step 3, it too would be marked.

The main result of this section is summarized in the following theorem:

Theorem 4. *An untagged list of length ℓ stored in the memory of a (p, n)-PRAM may be marked deterministically in $O\left(\min\{\ell, n/p + \log n\}\right)$ time.*

3 Marking Tagged Lists

Recall that in a tagged list each node carries a special symbol in its tag field so that it can be distinguished from non-list elements by inspection. Although deterministic list-marking algorithms cannot exploit this property to improve upon the worst-case performance of Theorem 4 [7], we sketch a simple but optimal randomized strategy which takes advantage of these tags.

The randomized algorithm is quite simple and proceeds in two stages. In the first stage, each processor randomly accesses q memory locations and retains the addresses of those locations that contain list elements. Successful probes partition the original list into chains of nodes whose heads are marked and randomly distributed among the processors. Our intuition is that the qp random probes in the first stage will select list elements so that g, the length of longest chain, is sufficiently small. Once the list has been "chopped" this way, in second stage we invoke a standard randomized search algorithm [6] that marks all the list nodes while balancing the load among the processors in time $O(\ell/p + g)$, with high probability. Note that this idea is not new: Greene and Knuth [4] have analyzed it in the context of graph traversal, and Ullman and Yannakakis [9] have used it for searching graphs.

By interleaving the above strategy with the straightforward $O(\ell)$ sequential algorithm we can see that the list can be marked in $O(\min\{\ell, \ell/p + q + g\})$ time, with high probability. The following lemma illustrates the tradeoff between the parameters q and g, the two quantities that determine the running time of the algorithm.

Proposition 5. *Suppose that a tagged list of length ℓ is stored in the memory of a (p, n)-PRAM, into which t probes are made at random. Let random variable X denote the length of a longest contiguous subsequence of unprobed list elements. Then $Pr(X > g) < \ell e^{-tg/n}$.*

Proof. The probability that no probes are made within a fixed subsequence of length $g \leq \ell$ equals $(1 - g/n)^t < e^{-tg/n}$, and there are at most $\ell - g + 1$ such subsequences.

With p processors making a total of pq probes, we have $Pr(X > g) < \ell e^{-pqg/n}$. Setting $q = g = \sqrt{k(n/p)\log n}$ where k is an arbitrary positive integer, we can see that

$$Pr(X > \sqrt{k(n/p)\log n}) < \ell n^{-k} \leq n^{-(k-1)} \ .$$

Thus our algorithm runs in $O(\min\{\ell, \ell/p + \sqrt{(n/p)\log n}\})$ time, with high probability.

Next, we establish a lower bound that is within a constant factor of this upper bound.

Theorem 6. *For any randomized list marking algorithm, if the probability that it terminates in time t is at least $1 - n^{-k}, k > 0$, then*

$$t = \Omega(\ell/p + \min\{\ell, \sqrt{k(n/p)\log n}\}) \ ,$$

where ℓ is the length of the input list stored in a memory of size n.

Proof. First note that ℓ/p is a trivial work-based lower bound for the problem. Next, assume that in i steps the first i list elements are marked, for all $1 \leq i \leq \ell$. This assumption does not weaken the argument for the lower bound.

Let W_j be the event that each of the first $j + 1$ list elements is marked within the first j steps. Also, let C_t be the event that every list element has been marked within t or fewer steps. Assuming for the moment that $t < \ell$, we can see $C_t \subseteq W_t$, which means that $Pr(C_t) \leq Pr(W_t)$ and, therefore $Pr(\overline{C_t}) \geq Pr(\overline{W_t})$.

Now, the probability that the $(i+1)st$ list element was touched by a random probe within the first i steps does not exceed pi/n. Hence, $Pr(W_i|\overline{W_{i-1}}) \leq pi/n$, and consequently, $Pr(\overline{W_i}|\overline{W_{i-1}}) \geq 1 - pi/n$. Combining this with the observation that $Pr(\overline{W_1}) = 1 - \frac{p}{n}$, we can see that

$$\begin{aligned}
Pr(\overline{W_t}) &\geq \prod_{i=1}^{t}(1 - pi/n) \\
&\geq (1 - pt/n)^t \\
&= e^{\Omega(-pt^2/n)},
\end{aligned}$$

for $t > 1$.

Thus, if $Pr(\overline{C_t}) \leq n^{-k}$, it must be the case that $n^{-k} = e^{\Omega(-pt^2/n)}$, hence

$$t = \Omega(\sqrt{k(n/p)\log n}) \ ,$$

and the theorem follows.

4 Conclusions

The results of this paper are summarized in the following table.

Deterministic and Rand. Untagged	$O\left(\min\{\ell, n/p + \log n\}\right)$ $\Omega\left(\min\{\ell, n/p\}\right)$
Rand. Tagged	$\Theta\left(\min\left\{\ell, \ell/p + \sqrt{(n/p)\log n}\right\}\right)$

The table shows that in all cases, speed-ups over sequential performance can be obtained only for a number of processors larger than a certain threshold p_0. Namely, $p_0 = \Theta(n/\ell)$ and $\log n = o(\ell)$ in the deterministic untagged case, and $p_0 = \Theta(n \log n/\ell^2)$ for the randomized tagged case. Moreover, in the untagged case, the deterministic upper bound and the randomized lower bound match except for $p = \Omega(n/\log n)$, therefore randomization can not be exploited in any significant way. In the case of tagged lists, however, for ℓ in the range $\sqrt{(n/p)\log n} \leq \ell \leq n/p + \log n$ the speedup attainable by exploiting randomization can be considerable.

Finally, preliminary investigations indicate that aspects of the above behaviour remain when extending the algorithms for marking to other basic operations and/or to broader classes of linked structures.

Acknowledgments

This research was supported, in part, by the Istituto Trentino di Cultura through the Leonardo Fibonacci Institute, in Trento, Italy. Further research support for G. Bilardi and G. Pucci by MURST and CNR of Italy, and by the ESPRIT III Basic Research Programme of the EC under contract No. 9072 (project GEPPCOM); for K.T. Herley by the ESPRIT III Basic Research Programme of the EC under contract No. 9072 (project GEPPCOM).

The authors wish to thank the referees for their thoughtful reading of the paper and their many suggestions, which resulted in improvements of the manuscript.

References

1. R. Cole. Parallel merge sort. *SIAM Journal on Computing*, 17(4):770–785, 1988.
2. R. Cole and U. Vishkin. Deterministic coin tossing with applications to optimal parallel list ranking. *Information and Control*, 70:32–53, 1986.
3. R. Cole and U. Vishkin. Faster optimal prefix sums and list ranking. *Information and Computation*, 81(3):344–352, 1989.
4. D. H. Greene and D. E. Knuth. *Mathematics for the Analysis of Algorithms*. Birkauser, Boston MA, 1982.
5. J. JaJa. *An Introduction to Parallel Algorithms*. Addison-Wesley, Reading MA, 1992.
6. R. M. Karp and Y. Zhang. A randomized parallel branch and bound procedure. In *Proceedings of the 20th Annual ACM Symposium on Theory of Computing*, pages 290–300, May 1988.

7. F. Luccio and L. Pagli. A model of sequential computation with pipelined access to memory. *Mathematical Systems Theory*, 26:343–356, 1993.

8. R. E. Tarjan and U. Vishkin. Finding biconnected components and computing tree functions in logarithmic time. *SIAM Journal on Computing*, 14(4):862–874, 1985.

9. J. D. Ullman and M. Yannakakis. High-probability parallel transitive closure algorithms. In *Proceedings of the 2nd Annual ACM Symposium on Parallel Algorithms and Architectures*, pages 200–209, July 1990.

Optimization of PRAM-Programs with Input-Dependent Memory Access*

Welf Löwe

Institut für Programmstrukturen und Datenorganisation, Universität Karlsruhe, 76128 Karlsruhe, Germany.

Abstract. There exist transformations of PRAM programs with predictable communication behavior to existing architectures. We extend the class of tractable programs to those with communication depending on the input. First, we define this class of programs. Second, we give source code transformations to simplify the programs and to eliminate indirect addresses and conditionals. Third, we show how to derive the communication behavior statically. Fourth, we show how to compute the mapping at compile time. Finally, we give upper time bounds for execution on existing architectures.

1 Introduction

In sequential computing the step from programming in machine code to programming in machine independent high level languages has been done for decades. Although high level programming languages are available for parallel machines todays parallel programs highly depend on the architectures they are planed to run on. Designing efficient parallel programs is a difficult task that can be performed by specialists only. Porting those program to other parallel architectures is nearly unpossible without a considerable losts of performance. Abstract machine models for parallel computing like the PRAM model are accepted by theoreticians but have no practical relevance since these models don't take into account properties of existing architectures.

The PRAM model consists of a shared memory and a number of processors with local memory. Processors only communicate via their shared memory. The computation steps are performed in a synchronous lock-step manner. Memory access to different memory locations can be performed at the same time. Several types of PRAMs are distinguished by their ability to access in parallel the same memory location. For an overview, see [KR90]. In this paper we exclude concurrent writes. Most parallel algorithms are designed for flavors of the PRAM models. The model has been successfully applied, because it allows to focus on the potential parallelism of the problem at hand. In particular, there is no need to consider a network topology and a memory distribution. For these reasons the model is often chosen to design parallel algorithms and programs.

---

* An extended version of the paper can be obtained via "World Wide Web": http://i44www.info.uni-karlsruhe.de/~loewe

On the other hand, almost all parallel computers and local area networks are distributed memory architectures. As shown in [ZK93] implementations of the PRAM model on real parallel machines are practically expensive, although theoretically optimal results exist [Val90]. The reason is the expensive synchronization, communication latency, communication overhead, and network bandwidth. In the LogP machine [CKP+93], these communication costs are taken into account. However, the number of processors are constant w.r.t. the problem size, and the synchronization must be programmed explicitly. The architecture dependent parameters of the LogP machine are the following. The *communication latency* L is the time a (small) message requires from its source to its destination. Observe that L is an upper bound on all source-destination pairs. The *communication overhead* o is the time required by a processor to send or receive a message. It is assumed that a processor cannot perform operations while sending or receiving a message. The *gap* g is the reciprocal of the communication bandwidth per processor. It means that when a processor has sent (or received) a message, the next message can only be sent or received after time g. The *number of processors* P is the last parameter. These parameters have been determined for the CM-5 in [CKP+93] and for the IBM SP1 machine in [DMI94]. Both works found the prediction on expected running times of programs on these machines confirmed by practice.

However, designing programs directly for distributed, asynchronous machines is a difficult task. Usually, it can be performed by specialists only. The programs are often very complicated, not understandable, and not portable without a dramatic lost of performance. It is therefore beneficial to develop a method transforming programs for the PRAM into distributed programs in a systematic way to ensure correctness. For this task, two main steps are necessary, to transform the synchronous program into an equivalent asynchronous program, and to distribute the shared memory to particular processes.

We define the class of *non-oblivious* programs. These programs have no predictable communication behavior. Many massively parallel algorithms[2] belong to this class, e.g. almost all parallel algorithms on graphs are non-oblivious. We show that non-oblivious algorithms can be transformed into a LogP program such that the execution time is optimal within the LogP model. However, the transformation itself may require much time. Therefore, we give some efficient, but non-optimal transformations. Furthermore, we prove bounds for the expected running time of the resulting programs.

2 Classification of Parallel Programs

For classifying parallel programs some assumptions have to be made. First, we assume that the programs are executed at the statement level, and that the running time is measured in the number of assignments executed. Second, the only

---

[2] A program is *massively parallel* iff the number of required processors increases with the size of the input.

composite data structures we use are arrays. This is no restriction as the shared memory may be considered as an array of integers. We allow the introduction of several arrays. Third, inputs are usually measured by their size. We use the overall number of single array elements. Finally, $P_A(n)$ denotes the maximum number of processors used by an algorithm A on inputs of size n and $T_A(n)$ denotes the worst-case running time of algorithm A on inputs of size n. We say that processor i *communicates at time t with processor j* iff there is a memory cell m which was either written by processor j at time t' or $t' = 0$, no processor writes into m between time t' and time t, and processor i reads at time t from m. We denote this by the predicate $comm(i, t, j, t')$. Conditions in conditional statements and loops are treated as assignments but without writing into the shared memory.

Definition 1. A *communication structure* of a PRAM algorithm A for an input x of size n is a directed acyclic graph $G_{A,x} = (V_{A,x}, E_{A,x})$, where

$$V_{A,x} = \{\langle i, t \rangle : 0 \leq i < P_A(n) - 1, 0 \leq t \leq T_A(n)\},$$

$$E_{A,x} = \{(\langle j, t' \rangle, \langle i, t \rangle) : t' < t \wedge comm(i, t, j, t')\}.$$

A *communication scheme* of a PRAM algorithm A for inputs of size n is a directed acyclic graph $G^*_{A,n}$, that is the union of all communication structures of A with a valid input of size n.

Definition 2. A parallel algorithm is called *oblivious* iff its communication structure and its communication scheme are the same for all inputs the same size. Otherwise, it is called *non-oblivious*.

Important problems where non-oblivious implementations may be desired are e.g. operations on sparse matrices, adaptive multi-grid-methods for the numerical solution of partial differential equations, graph algorithms. Observe that none of these algorithms is implemented to work in parallel. In fact, engineers prefer to implement these problems mainly sequentially as the sequential execution time is currently better than the execution time of a parallel implementation. Even Valiants PRAM simulation [Val90] that yields theoretically optimal results requires approximately $10 - 20ms$ for one PRAM step on a MASPAR [ZK93].

3 Deriving Communication Schemes

In this section we show how the communication scheme can be derived statically. From definition 1 it follows immediately that the communication structure of an oblivious program only depends on the size of the input and its communication scheme is equal to this communication structure. If we knew the size of the input and the fact that the program is oblivious, we could derive the communication structure just by a (synchronous) sample execution of the program.

If the program is non-oblivious there are some communications depending on the input of the program. In this case we assume that all possible communication occurs. All further transformations are based on the following assumptions: First, the input size n is known at compile time[3], and second, the program representation is a control flow graph. We assume that the control flow graph is a directed graph $CFG = (V, E)$ whose vertices are program points and $(v_1, v_2) \in E$ iff there is a direct control flow from v_1 to v_2. There are two types of vertices: AND-vertices arise from a **pardo**, i.e. the control flows to all successors, and OR-vertices arising from loops or conditional statements, i.e. the control flows to one successor.

First, we show how to decide whether a parallel program is oblivious or not. While deciding this we simplify the program. Second, we include a transformation making some non-oblivious programs oblivious. Finally, we derive the communication scheme from the simplified, transformed program. The basic techniques applied on oblivious programs can be found in [ZL94].

3.1 Simplifying PRAM Programs

Our goal is to transform the CFG into an acyclic directed graph whose vertices are AND-vertices by loop unrolling, procedure inlining, and recursion elimination[4], see algorithm 1. The size of the resulting code is limited by the work done by the PRAM algorithm. Therefore, the size of the code is at most $O(T(n) \times P(n))$. Hence, if the original algorithm is polynomial in the required time and processors, the size of the resulting code is also polynomial.

Lemma 3. *Let P be a parallel program. If constant folding, loop unwinding, recursion elimination, and procedure inlining is successfully applied to P, then the control flow graph of the transformed program is acyclic.*

Proof. As there is no loop and no recursion in the transformed program, the corresponding CFG must be acyclic.

---

[3] For many applications this is no restriction (assume e.g. the data is generated by sensors). For others there exist design methods for reducing the required number of processors to a constant (as e.g. for all divide & conquer algorithms). As a side effect, this constant equals to the input size of the resulting program. Finally, if the input size is bound by an upper and a lower limit it is possible to perform the following optimizations for all sizes in between these limits. If $G^*_{A,n} \subset G^*_{A,m}, m > n$ the optimizations can be implemented efficiently, i.e. schemes needn't be optimized redundantly.

[4] For non-recursive procedures and functions, procedure inlining is no problem. When all recursions can be eliminated, then procedure inlining is no problem. Sometimes it is not possible to check statically the number of recursions or iterations, even if it is constant or a function of the input size that is constant, as well. However, we believe that this case doesn't happen too often in practice. In Fortran-programs most of the loops are for-loops. For non-for loops and recursion techniques like [FSZ91, Zim91] of automatic complexity analysis can be used to derive the number of iterations of a loop and recursive calls of a recursive procedure, respectively.

Algorithm 1. *Simplify a PRAM Program and Check Obliviousness.*

(1) apply constant folding to P;
(2) eliminate recursion from P;
(3) unwind loops in P;
(4) inline all procedures of P;
(5) **repeat**
(6)   apply constant folding to P;
(7)   eliminate dead code from P;
(8) **until** P does not change;
(9) compute control flow graph (*CFG*) for P;
(10) mark each vertex v if v is not **pardo**;
(11) compute for each marked v:
(12)   number m_v of marked vertices;
(13)   on the longest path to v in *CFG*;
(14) label each marked v with t_v where:
(15)   PRAM completion time $t_v = m_v + 1$;
(16) **if** *CFG* has an OR-vertex $\lor$ *CFG* contains indirect addressing
(17) **then** output *CFG* and *P is not oblivious*;
(18) **else** output *CFG* and *P is oblivious*;
(19) **fi**;

3.2   Reducing the Non-obliviousness

After the above transformations a parallel program may contain indirect addresses on the left side of assignments, as e.g. in Tree Contraction. Suppose processor i executes an assignment $a[f(a, i)] := expr$ where $expr$ is an expression and $f(a, i)$ is an index function without side-effects (especially it doesn't raise exceptions like a division by 0). We transform the above assignment into:

distributed

    forall $j := 0$ **to** $|a| - 1$ **do in parallel**
        if $j = f(a, i)$ **then**
            $a[j] := expr$;
        end; $-$**if**
    end; $-$**forall**

where j doesn't occur neither in $f(a, i)$ nor in $expr$ and $|a|$ is the size of the shared address space. We add this transformation after line (4) of algorithm 1[5].

Lemma 4. *Let P be a simplified PRAM program. The above transformation of P doesn't change its semantics.*

---

[5] This transformation doesn't make the program more oblivious since the conditional statement cannot be eliminated by constant folding because $f(a, i)$ is not a constant. With a similar transformation we could eliminate the indirect addresses on the right side of assignments, as well. We don't do so. As we will see, these indirect addresses do not cause an all to all communication in the resulting distributed asynchronous program. Hence, it doesn't make sense to waste processors or time.

Proof. Because $f(a, i)$ is a function without side-effects we can call it arbitrarily often. This function $f(a, i)$ returns an index of a. There are only $|a|$ many possible return values of $f(a, i)$. Hence, we can check all indices if they are equal to the return value of $f(a, i)$ and execute the assignment for the index equal to this value. There are no dependencies between all these checks, hence, we can execute them in parallel.

Note, that a program running on p processors before this transformation requires at most $p \times |a|$ processor afterwards. Of course, instead of the **pardo** statement we could use a **for** loop. In this case our algorithm doesn't require more processors but time $t + |a|$ if t is the running time of the original program. However, we save an all to all communication in the resulting asynchronous program.

A parallel program may contain a conditional checking some predicate on the state of the shared memory. E.g. the Game of Life checks how many of the neighbor cells are dead. These conditionals can be removed by pessimistic assumption that each branch has to be computed for computing the conditional statement [ZL94].

3.3 Deriving Communication Schemes

After the transformations given in the last sections the control flow graph of PRAM programs only contain **pardo** and assignment vertices. The only remaining source of non-obliviousness in these programs is indirect addressing on the left hand side of assignments.

Algorithm 2. Compute a Communication Scheme.

$\mathbf{t = 0} :$ $G_0 = (V_0, E_0)$ where $V_0 = \{(a[i], 0) : 0 \leq i < p\}$ and $E_0 = \emptyset$
$\mathbf{t > 0} :$ $G_t = (V_t, E_t)$ where $V_t = V_{t-1} \cup V_t'$ and $E_t = E_{t-1} \cup E_t' \cup E_t''$
$\qquad V_t' = \{(x, t) : \exists v \in CFG : t_v = t \wedge v \text{ contains } x := c\}$
$\qquad E_t' = \{((y, t'), (x, t)) : \exists v \in CFG : t_v = t \wedge v \text{ contains } x := c \wedge$
$\qquad\qquad y \text{ is operand in } c \ \wedge t' = \max\{\bar{t} : (y, \bar{t}) \in V_{t-1}\}$
$\qquad E_t'' = \{((a[i], t'), (x, t)) : 0 \leq i < p \ \wedge \ exists v \in CFG :$
$\qquad\qquad t_v = t \ \wedge v \text{ contains } x := c \ \wedge a[f(a)] \text{ is operand in } c \ \wedge$
$\qquad\qquad t' = \max\{\bar{t} : (a[i], \bar{t}) \in V_{t-1}\}\}$
Let $G^* = G_m$ if m is the highest label of all vertices in CFG.

Theorem 5. Let P be a simplified PRAM program without indirect addressing on the left hand side of assignments and without conditionals. Algorithm 2 computes a graph containing all vertices and edges of the communication scheme G^* of P.

Proof. The proof is by induction on the steps of the PRAM program: G_0 is computed correctly since it contains a vertex for each memory cell. There is no communication at PRAM step 0. Therefore, E_0^* is empty. We assume that G_{t-1} is computed correctly. Vertices in the CFG labeled with t correspond to the PRAM assignment executed at time t. This labeling is well-defined since the CFG is acyclic by lemma 3. Hence, for each PRAM processor that executes an assignment at time t a vertex v is added to G_t. If a memory cell is read in the left hand side of the assignment an edge from the vertex u corresponding to the last assignment that wrote this cell to v is added to the set of edges of G_t. Hence, all oblivious communication to vertices v corresponding assignments executed at time t have a corresponding edge in G_t. If the left side of an assignment executed at time t contains an indirect address, edges from all vertices corresponding to the last write accesses to each memory cell is added. Hence, for all non-oblivious communications that possibly occur at time t there exist an edge in G_t. Therefore, G_t is a communication scheme of the PRAM program executing the first t steps of P. Let m be the highest label in CFG. There is no assignment executed at time $t > m$. Therefore, the construction of G terminates after m steps. That completes the proof.

4 Compiling Non-oblivious Programs

For transforming PRAM programs to LogP programs two tasks must be performed: first consideration of the asynchronous execution model and second, the distribution of the shared memory. We construct the communication scheme where every node corresponds to an assignment:

$$a[f(i, a)] := \Phi(a[f_1(i, a)], \ldots, a[f_m(i, a)]).$$

4.1 Program Transformation

First, we discuss the index functions in more detail. Therefore, we number the nested indirections in addressing. Observe, that all nestings of indirect addresses end up in a direct address, i.e. with a index function independing of the memory's state. We extend the above assignment by the number of nested indirect addresses:

$$a[f_0^0(i, a)] := \Phi(a[f_1^0(i, a)], \ldots, a[f_m^0(i, a)])$$

where $f_k^j(i, a)$ is defined as:

$$\Psi_k^j(i, a[f_{k,1}^{j+1}(i, a)], \ldots, a[f_{k,n}^{j+1}(i, a)])$$

if index expression Ψ_k^j contains further indirect addresses. Otherwise it simplifies to $f_k^j(i)$. Since for all nested indirect addresses there exist direct addresses, the communication structure can be computed partially. For oblivious communications of a non-oblivious program sender and receiver can be computed at compile time. For non-oblivious communications they have to be computed at run time. After having received all data the expression Φ can be computed. If the left hand side of the assignment doesn't contain indirect addressing the result can be sent via a channel to the next process as in oblivious programs. If it does, the next process has to be computed at run time and a message has to be sent to this process. We assume that there is no indirect addressing on the left side of the assignments. Hence, an assignment A has the form:

$$a[f_0^0(i)] := \Phi(a[f_1^0(i,a)], \ldots, a[f_m^0(i,a)]).$$

The necessary transformations of an assignment A executed at PRAM-time t is shown below.

Algorithm 3. *Remove Indirect Addresses.*

(1) **repeat**
(2)   substitute $a[f_k^j(i,a)]$ with $process[f_k^j(i,a)].get\_arg(f_0^0(i),t)$;
(3)   substitute $f_k^j(i,a)$ with $\Psi_k^j(i, a[f_{k,1}^{j+1}(i,a)], \ldots, a[f_{k,n}^{j+1}(i,a)])$;
(4) **until** A does not change;
(5) **repeat**
(6)   substitute $a[f_k^j(i)]$ with $a_{f_k^j(i)}$;
(7) **until** A does not change;

Process $a[f_0^0(i)] := \Phi(a[f_1^0(i,a)], \ldots, a[f_m^0(i,a)]).$

(1) **process** $(f_0^0(i), t)$ – *simulates A executed by processor $f_0^0(i)$ at time t*
(2)   **entry** *start* **is**
(3) $[a_{f_1(i)} \cdots a_{f_m(i)}] := [\mathbf{recv}(f_1(i), t_1) \ldots \mathbf{recv}(f_m(i), t_m)]$
                 $-- comm(f_0^0(i), t, f_{1 \cdots m}(i), t_{1 \cdots m})$
(4) A transformed by algorithm 3;
(5) $[\mathbf{send}(a_{f_0^0(i)}, (\iota_1, \tau_1)) \cdots \mathbf{send}(a_{f_0^0(i)}, (\iota_n, \tau_n))]; --comm(\iota, \tau, f_0^0(i), t)$
(6)   **end** *start*;
(7)
(8)   **entry** *get_arg*(i, τ) **is**
(9) $\mathbf{send}(a_{f_0^0(i)}, (i, \tau))$;
(10)   **end** *get_arg*;
(11) **end** $--$ **process** $(f_0^0(i), t)$

Each of the transformed assignments A is associated to a single process $(f_0^0(i), t)$. Additionally, the initial state of each memory cell must be provided by separate processes. For oblivious communications we use a channel-oriented model. We assume that each edge in the communication structure is a channel through which communication has to go. The semantics of $recv(f_x(i), t_x)$ is that the process receives the data sent by process $(f_x(i), t_x)$. The receiving of data and the assignment to the local variables $a_{f_1(i)} \cdots a_{f_m(i)}$ is executed in arbitrary order. The $send(data, (\iota, \tau))$ operation is dual to the receive operation, i.e. process (i, t) sends $data$ to process (ι, τ). A $recv$ operation is terminated if it received the data. Furthermore, we assume that processes can send without any synchronization with the receiving processes, and that the channels are safe.

Lemma 6. *Let P be a simplified PRAM program. After having applied algorithm 3 to P it doesn't contain any indirect access to the shared memory.*

Proof. The array *process* will contain the addresses of all processes that possibly contain an argument for computing A. In contrast to array a, array *process* can be computed statically, since we know all processes at compile time. The length of *process* is at most equal to the length of a. The message $get\_arg(f_0^0(i), t)$ sent to a process returns the argument stored in this process to the sender, i.e. to process $(f_0^0(i), t)$ (line 4). The index functions f can be computed at compile time since they depend only on i and not on the array a (line 12).

Theorem 7. *Let P be a simplified PRAM program. The processes $(f_0^0(i), t)$ can be executed asynchronously and with memory. They compute the same function as the original PRAM program did.*

Proof. Assuming that constant folding, loop unrolling and recursion elimination have been applied complete and correctly to P. Then P has a finite number of statements, because of lemma 3. Therefore, all indirect addresses on the left hand side of assignments and all conditionals can be eliminated. Because of lemma 4 these transformations are correct also. Therefore, the transformed PRAM program is semantical equivalent to the original one. By lemma 6 all accesses to the shared memory can be eliminated. Hence, each process must only contain the array cell that it writes. Therefore, the shared memory can be distributed. The correctness of the asynchronous execution is proven by induction on a topological ordering of the vertices in the communication scheme G^* of P. By theorem 5 G^* can be computed statically and contains all possible data dependencies of P. A vertex $(i, 0)$ in G^* corresponds to a process providing $a[i]$ at time 0. A vertex $(i, t), t > 0$ in G^* corresponds to a process $(f_0^0(i), t)$. We label each vertex that has been computed as finished. We assume that processes $(i, 0)$ contain the correct initial value of the array cell $a[i]$, i.e. all vertices with depth 0 in G^* can be labeled initially. A vertex v in G^* can be computed if all data needed in v is available. By induction hypothesis all predecessors of v are labeled (oblivious communication) and have sent the correct values to v (oblivious communication). Hence, the processors containing further values needed in v can be computed. Also by induction hypothesis all potential predecessors of v are labeled (non-oblivious communication). Therefore, v can order these values and computes correctly. After computation it sends the correct value to its (oblivious) successors and provides this value for further (non-oblivious) requests. v can be labeled as finished, as well.

Lemma 8. *Let d be the maximal depth of indirect addresses in a program P and dg the maximal degree of vertices in $G^*(P)$. The over all time L_{max} for communication from a vertex to its direct successor (in G^*) is at most:*

$$L_{max} \leq ((1 + 2d) \times (L + 2o + (dg - 2) \times max[o, g]).$$

Proof. Assume that a message is the last to be sent from a vertex. Then there are $out - degree - 1$ messages sent before. Hence, $out - degree - 1$ gaps have to be guaranteed. Then, sending the message takes time o and the communication delay is L. The same holds for receiving the message where in-degree -1 gaps have to be guaranteed. After one necessary oblivious communication for each nested indirect addressing two messages have to be sent in sequence.

Theorem 9. *Let P be a parallel program whose communication scheme G^* has diameter T. Let C be the maximal computation time for the vertices in G^*. Its execution time is at most: $T_{max} \leq (T-1) \times L_{max} + T \times C$.*

Proof. On the longest path T tasks have to be computed, $T-1$ communications occur sequentially. Each computation requires at most time C, each communication requires at most time L_{max}. There is no waiting necessary because we chose the longest path.

4.2 Program Optimization

Merging some of the processes into one processor saves time required for communication. On the other hand, the degree of parallelism is decreased. In fact we *cluster* the computations done in the vertices of a communication scheme onto the processors of the LogP machine such that the execution time is minimal. We can implement any oblivious PRAM program as an optimal LogP program w.r.t. its computation time. However, the transformations themselves are exponential. In [PY90] Papadimitriou and Yannakakis showed that finding an optimal clustering is NP-hard, even if $o = g = 0$ and $P = \infty$. We can therefore not expect to find an efficient and optimal transformation. It is also known that approximative solutions which are better than $2 \times T_{optimal}(G)$ cannot be found in polynomial time when $o = g = 0$, unless $P = NP$. However, in [LZ95] it is proven that the optimal solution can be found in polynomial time if G is coarse grained. Furthermore, Gerasoulis and Yang demonstrated in [GY93] that a solution guaranteeing $2 \times TIME_{opt}(G)$ without vertex duplications can be found for coarse grained communication structures assuming that $o = g = 0$. All these works assumed oblivious algorithms. However, we can extend the results to non-oblivious algorithms. Therefore, we define the notion of granularity of communication schemes. Informly speaking, the granularity of a communication scheme G^* is the ratio of computation and communication costs in G^* on a distinct parallel machine.

Definition 10. Let $PRED_v$ be the set of all direct predecessors u of a vertex v in a communication scheme G^*. Let $L_{max}(u, v)$ be the maximal overall communication cost for sending a message from vertex u to vertex v (including overheads and gaps). Let C_u be the time for computing u. The *granularity of a vertex* is defined as

$$g(v) = \frac{\min\limits_{u \in PRED_v} \{C_u\}}{\max\limits_{u \in PRED_v} \{L_{max}(u, v)\}}.$$

and the granularity of a communication scheme is defined as $g(G^*) = \min\limits_{v \in G^*} \{g(v)\}$. G^* is *coarse grained* if $g(G^*) \geq 1$, otherwise it is called *fine grained*.

Note, that the granularity of a communication schemes can be computed at compile time even if the program is non-oblivious. In contrast to other more qualitative definitions of granularity we can give upper bounds for the execution time of a program on a parallel machine in terms of the granularity of the corresponding communication schemes.

Theorem 11. *Any clustering of a communication scheme G^* computing only vertices of the same path in G^* on one processor leads to a program running in at most:* $T_{cluster} \leq (1 + \frac{1}{g(G^*)}) \times T_{optimal}(G^*)$.

Proof. Let $\mathcal{P}$ be the path from a vertex v_i with $idg_{v_i} = 0$ to a vertex v_o with $odg_{v_o} = 0$ with the maximal sum of computation times of its vertices and communication delay between these vertices. For the optimal clustering of G^* it holds: $T_{optimal}(G^*) \geq \sum_{v \in \mathcal{P}} C_v$. Let $L_{max}(v) = L_{max}(u,v)$ where u is the immediate predecessor of v in path $\mathcal{P}$. Set $L_{max}(v_i) = 0$. For the naive implementation of G^* it holds:

$$T_{naive}(G^*) \leq C_{v_o} + \sum_{v \in \mathcal{P}} C_u + L_{max}(v) \leq C_{v_o} + \sum_{v \in \mathcal{P}} C_u(1 + \frac{L_{max}(v)}{C_u})$$

$$\leq C_{v_o} + \sum_{v \in \mathcal{P}} C_u(1 + \frac{1}{g(v)}) \leq C_{v_o} + (1 + \frac{1}{g(G^*)}) \sum_{v \in \mathcal{P}} C_u$$

$$\leq (1 + \frac{1}{g(G^*)})(C_{v_o} + \sum_{v \in \mathcal{P}} C_u) \leq (1 + \frac{1}{g(G^*)}) \sum_{v \in \mathcal{P}} C_v$$

$$\leq (1 + \frac{1}{g(G^*)}) \times T_{optimal}(G^*)$$

Because a clustering along the paths in G^* cannot increase the running time compared to the naive implementation, the proof is complete.

Note, that for coarse grained communication schemes G^* the time bound reduces to $2 \times T_{optimal}(G^*)$ even if $o \neq 0, g \neq 0$, and the program is non-oblivious. Heuristic solutions for clustering communication structures where $g \neq 0$ and $o \neq 0$ can be found in [ZL94]. The techniques for clustering communication structures can be applied to communication schemes without any modifications.

5 Conclusions

We showed for another subclass of parallel programs for PRAMs that the gap between theory and practice can be bridged by mapping this class onto an asynchronous machine with distributed memory - the LogP machine. This class of *non-oblivious* parallel program is characterized by their communication behavior which varies for inputs of size n. From a practical point of view this class is large. It contains for example basic techniques as for instance pointer jumping, pebble game and tree contraction. Almost all parallel algorithms on graphs are non-oblivious. If the the input size of a program is limited before compiling, its communication scheme can be derived statically. With this information, we are able to include the transformation from non-oblivious PRAM programs to distributed programs running existing parallel machines into compilers. Therefore, the clustering and scheduling algorithms for mapping oblivious PRAM programs onto the LogP machine can be applied for non-oblivious PRAM programs, as well. Hence, for correct execution of non-oblivious PRAM programs, it is not necessary to perform expensive the PRAM-simulation. Additionally, we can give upper time bounds for execution for the resulting programs on existing architectures. Future work will consider the behavior of clustering and scheduling heuristics applied to the communication schemes of several graph algorithms. Beside the upper time bounds it would be interesting to determine average running times of the resulting programs. Therefore, we want to label the non-oblivious communications with the possibility of their occurrence.

References

[CKP+93] D. Culler, R. Karp, D. Patterson, A. Sahay, K. E. Schauser, E. Santos, R. Subramonian, and T. von Eicken. LogP: Towards a realistic model of parallel computation. In *4th ACM SIGPLAN Symposium on Principles and Practice of Parallel Programming (PPOPP 93)*, pages 1–12, 1993. published in: SIGPLAN Notices (28) 7.

[DMI94] B. Di Martino and G. Ianello. Parallelization of non-simultaneous iterative methods for systems of linear equations. In *LNCS 854, Parallel Processing: CONPAR'94-VAPP VI*, pages 254–264. Springer, 1994.

[FSZ91] P. Flajolet, B. Salvy, and P. Zimmermann. Average case analysis of algorithms. *Theoretical Computer Science*, 1991.

[GY93] A. Gerasoulis and T. Yang. On the granularity and clustering of directed acyclic task graphs. *IEEE Transactions on Parallel and Distributed Systems*, 4:686–701, june 1993.

[KR90] R. M. Karp and V. Ramachandran. Parallel algorithms for shared memory machines. In *Handbook of Theoretical Computer Science Vol. A*, pages 871–941. MIT-Press, 1990.

[LZ95] W. Löwe and W. Zimmermann. On finding optimal clusterings of task graphs. In *Aizu International Symposium on Parallel Algorithm/Architecture Synthesis*. IEEE Computer Society Press, 1995.

[PY90] C.H. Papadimitrou and M. Yannakakis. Towards an architecture-independent analysis of parallel algorithms. *SIAM Journal on Computing*, 19(2):322 – 328, 1990.

[Val90] L. G. Valiant. General purpose parallel architectures. In J. van Leeuwen, editor, *Handbook of Theoretical Computer Science Vol. A*, pages 945–971. MIT-Press, 1990.

[Zim91] Wolf Zimmermann. The automatic worst case analysis of parallel programs: Simple parallel sorting and algorithms on graphs. Technical Report TR-91-045, International Computer Science Institute, August 1991.

[ZK93] Wolf Zimmermann and Holger Kumm. On the implementation of virtual shared memory. In *Programming Models for Massively Parallel Computers*, pages 172–178, 1993.

[ZL94] W. Zimmermann and W. Löwe. An approach to machine-independent parallel programming. In *LNCS 854, Parallel Processing: CONPAR'94-VAPP VI*, pages 277–288. Springer, 1994.

Optimal Circular Arc Representations

Lin Chen

FRL, P. O. Box 18345, Los Angeles, CA 90018

Abstract. We investigate some properties of minimal interval and circular arc representations and give several optimal parallel recognition and construction algorithms. We show that, among other things, given an $s \times t$ interval or circular arc representation matrix,
- deciding if the representation is minimal can be done in $O(\log s)$ time with $O(st/\log s)$ EREW PRAM processors, or in $O(1)$ time with $O(st)$ Common CRCW PRAM processors;
- constructing a minimum interval representation can be done in $O(\log(st))$ time with $O(st/\log(st))$ EREW PRAM processors, or in $O(\log t/\log\log t)$ time with $O(st \log\log t/\log t)$ Common CRCW PRAM processors, or in $O(1)$ time with $O(st)$ BSR processors.

1 Preliminaries

Circular arc graphs are well-known intersection graphs and properly contain interval graphs. Benzer [4] showed overlap data involving fragments of a certain gene could be modeled by intervals. This finding confirmed the hypothesis that DNA has a linear structure within genes and helped him win a Nobel Prize. Circular arc graphs also find applications in some other areas such as register allocation. The best way to allocate registers corresponds to an optimal coloring of an interference graph which is often a circular arc graph or even an interval graph (see, e.g., [16]). Many algorithms on circular arc graphs work on circular arc representations (see, e.g., [15]), which can be constructed from circular arc graphs (see, e.g., [9]). In this paper, we study the properties of minimal interval and circular arc representations and present some efficient recognition and construction algorithms.

Given a family S of nonempty sets, the intersection graph G has vertices corresponding to the sets in S and two distinct vertices of G are adjacent iff the corresponding sets in S intersect. S is called an *intersection representation* (IR) for G. If S is a family of arcs on a circle, G is called a *circular arc graph*. If, in addition, the family of arcs satisfies the Helly property (*i.e.*, if several arcs mutually intersect, then the intersection of these arcs is nonempty), G is called a *Helly circular arc graph* (a.k.a. Θ circular arc graph). G is called an *interval graph* if S is a family of intervals on a real line.

In this paper, we often use a pair of the two endpoints of an arc to denote a closed arc. If we move along an arc in the clockwise direction, the last point on the arc is *clockwise endpoint*. The other endpoint is *counterclockwise endpoint*. If we use $[l_0, l_1]$ to denote an arc, l_1 and l_0 represent clockwise and counterclockwise endpoints, respectively.

The aforementioned classes of graphs can also be defined as intersection graphs on some discrete objects. Take the circular arc graphs for example. Let D be a circularly ordered set (such as points on a circle). A circular arc of D is defined as any set of contiguous elements in D. Let S be a set of circular arcs on D. The intersection graph G of S is a circular arc graph and the pair (D, S) is a circular arc representation. Two IRs (D_1, S_1) and (D_2, S_2) are said to be *equivalent* if there exists a one-to-one onto function $f: S_1 \to S_2$ such that x and y in S_1 intersect iff $f(x)$ and $f(y)$ in S_2 intersect. An IR (D, S) is said to be *minimal* if there does not exist an equivalent IR (D', S'), where $D' \subset D$. An IR (D, S) is said to be *minimum* if, for any other equivalent IR (D', S'), $|D'| \geq |D|$. We call $|D|$ the *size* of the IR (D, S). An element, say d, in D is called an *intersection point* (IP) if there exist two elements (not necessarily distinct), say s_1 and s_2, in S such that $s_1 \cap s_2 = \{d\}$. An IR, say (D, S), is often denoted by a $|S| \times |D|$ $(0, 1)$-matrix. A row, say R, of the matrix corresponds to an element in S. $R(i) = 1$ iff the ith element of D is contained in the element of S. We simply refer to the matrix as an IR if no confusion arises.

Suppose $D_1 = \{\clubsuit, \diamond, \heartsuit, \spadesuit\}$, and $S_1 = \{\{\clubsuit, \diamond\}, \{\diamond, \heartsuit\}, \{\heartsuit, \spadesuit\}, \{\spadesuit\}\}$. The corresponding matrix is M_1. Let $D_2 = \{\text{J, Q, K, A}\}$, and $S_2 = \{\{\text{J}\}, \{\text{J, Q, K}\}, \{\text{Q, K, A}\}, \{\text{A}\}\}$. Then the corresponding matrix is M_2. It is easy to verify these two interval representations are equivalent. The minimal interval representation is M_3, which can be obtained by deleting a column from M_1 or M_2.

$$M_1 = \begin{bmatrix} 1 & 1 & 0 & 0 \\ 0 & 1 & 1 & 0 \\ 0 & 0 & 1 & 1 \\ 0 & 0 & 0 & 1 \end{bmatrix}, M_2 = \begin{bmatrix} 1 & 0 & 0 & 0 \\ 1 & 1 & 1 & 0 \\ 0 & 1 & 1 & 1 \\ 0 & 0 & 0 & 1 \end{bmatrix}, M_3 = \begin{bmatrix} 1 & 0 & 0 \\ 1 & 1 & 0 \\ 0 & 1 & 1 \\ 0 & 0 & 1 \end{bmatrix}$$

The computation models employed in this paper are more or less standard. One model used is the well known PRAM. Some of our algorithms are implemented on EREW PRAM. Some other algorithms are designed for the Common CRCW PRAM. Also mentioned is a stronger submodel called Priority CRCW PRAM. A more powerful model known as Broadcasting with Selective Reduction (BSR) introduced in Akl and Guenther [2] is also used here.

A PRAM algorithm is said to be *work-optimal* if the processor-time product matches the time lower bound of the sequential algorithm. We say an algorithm is *time-optimal* if its time bound matches the lower bound on the corresponding model.

In designing PRAM algorithms, we often use the following result, usually attributed to Brent [5], to obtain the best tradeoff between the time and processor bounds.

Theorem 1. *If a problem can be solved in $O(T)$ time with $O(P)$ PRAM processors, the problem can also be solved in $O(TP/P')$ time with $O(P')$ PRAM processors, for $P' < P$.*

Cook, Dwork and Reischuk [12] established the following lower bound.

Theorem 2. *Computing the OR of n bits requires at least $\Omega(\log n)$ time on exclusive-write machines.*

A lower bound on CRCW PRAM is given in Beame and Hastad [3].

Theorem 3. *Checking parity for n bits requires at least $\Omega(\log n / \log \log n)$ time on a Priority CRCW PRAM if a polynomially bounded number of processors are used.*

We say a problem is in NC if there is an algorithm for it that runs in polylog time with a polynomial number of processors. Such an algorithm is called NC algorithm. Any parallel algorithm mentioned in the paper is meant to be an NC algorithm.

One very useful procedure in parallel computing is the prefix computation. It is not hard to see the above PRAM lower bounds apply to the prefix computation. It is known that all prefix sums for an array of n elements can be obtained in $O(\log n)$ time using $O(n / \log n)$ EREW PRAM processors [17], or in $O(\log n / \log \log n)$ time using $O(n \log \log n / \log n)$ Common CRCW PRAM processors [11], or in $O(1)$ time using $O(n)$ BSR processors [18].

One problem discussed in Chen [8] is the subarray computation. Given an array, say $a[1:n]$, composed of two types of elements, the problem is to obtain a subarray $b[1:k]$ of $a[1:n]$ such that $b[j]$ is the jth element in a of type 1, for $0 < j \leq k$, where k is the number of elements in a of type 1. The problem can be solved using the procedure for computing the prefix sums. It is now easy to conclude the following.

Theorem 4. *The subarray computation can be done in $O(\log n)$ time with $O(n / \log n)$ EREW PRAM processors, or in $O(\log n / \log \log n)$ time with $O(n \log \log n / \log n)$ Common CRCW PRAM processors. Both procedures are work-optimal. On the BSR model, the problem can be solved in $O(1)$ time with $O(n)$ processors. The algorithms are all time-optimal.*

These results are used frequently in designing other parallel algorithms. We may not make explicit reference to these results every time we use them later in this paper. In this paper, the minimal IR matrices are obtained thru column deletion. So the lower bound for subarray computation also applies to computing minimal representations.

2 Properties

In this section, we present some properties of minimal interval and circular arc representations. The proofs, if not given here, can be found in our earlier works [6] [10].

Lemma 5. *Suppose (D, I) is an interval representation. An element $d \in D$ is an IP iff there exist intervals I_i and $I_j \in I$ (I_i and I_j may be the same interval) such that d is the left endpoint of I_i and the right endpoint of I_j.*

Lemma 6. *Suppose (D, I) is an interval representation, and M is the corresponding matrix. An element of D is an IP iff the corresponding column of M is not contained in any other column.*

Theorem 7. *Suppose* (D, I) *is an interval representation and* M *is the corresponding matrix. The following four assertions are equivalent:*

1. (D, I) *is a minimum interval representation.*
2. (D, I) *is a minimal interval representation.*
3. *Every element of* D *is an IP.*
4. *No column of* M *contains another.*

Note the analogous statements of Theorem 7, Lemma 5 and Lemma 6 for circular arc representations are not true,. We will instead give the following results for the circular arc representation.

Lemma 8. *Suppose* (D, A) *is a circular arc representation, and* M *is the corresponding matrix. A column of* M *is not contained in any other column if the corresponding element of* D *is an IP.*

Theorem 9. *Suppose* (D, A) *is a circular arc representation and* M *is the corresponding matrix. For the following four assertions, one implies the next:*

1. (D, A) *is a minimum circular arc representation.*
2. (D, A) *is a minimal circular arc representation.*
3. *Every element of* D *is an IP.*
4. *No column of* M *contains another.*

Proof. $(1 \Longrightarrow 2)$ By definition.
$(2 \Longrightarrow 3)$ Analogous to the corresponding part of the proof of Theorem 7.
$(3 \Longrightarrow 4)$ Immediate from Lemma 8. $\qquad\qquad\square$

Theorem 10. *Suppose* (D, A) *is a circular arc representation. The representation is minimal iff every element of* D *is an IP.*

However, for circular arc representation satisfying the Helly property, the analogous statement of Theorem 7 is true. The proof is also analogous. We only list the result below.

Theorem 11. *Suppose* (D, A) *is a* Θ *circular arc representation and* M *is the corresponding matrix. The following four assertions are equivalent:*

1. (D, A) *is a minimum* Θ *circular arc representation.*
2. (D, A) *is a minimal* Θ *circular arc representation.*
3. *Every element of* D *is an IP.*
4. *No column of* M *contains another.*

The following theorem tells us something about the relation between minimal Θ circular arc representations and minimal circular arc representations.

Theorem 12. *If* (D, A) *is a minimal* Θ *circular arc representation for* G, (D, A) *is also a minimal circular arc representation for* G.

Proof. If (D, A) is a minimal Θ circular arc representation for G, then every element of D is an IP, by Theorem 11. Now the result follows from Theorem 10.
$\qquad\qquad\square$

3 Algorithms

In this section we give concrete computational procedures for the recognition and construction of minimum interval and circular arc representations. We begin with the problem of testing for minimum interval representations. We note that if an $s \times t$ matrix is a minimum interval representation matrix, then $s \geq t$. The reason is, if the matrix is a minimum interval representation, then all columns of the matrix correspond to IPs by Theorem 7. Thus, the number of left endpoints and therefore the number of rows is at least t. Consequently, if $s < t$, we can conclude immediately the representation is not minimum. Suppose we have an interval representation matrix with size $s \times t$ ($s \geq t$). We first check which columns correspond to the IPs. Obtaining the IPs is easy. By Lemma 5, a column corresponds to an IP iff it corresponds to a left endpoint and a right endpoint. For each row, we can decide its two endpoints in $O(1)$ time with t EREW PRAM processors. It then follows easily that all the IPs can be identified in $O(1)$ time with $O(st)$ Common CRCW PRAM processors. On the EREW PRAM model, the problem cannot be solved in $O(1)$ time. In fact, we have established a lower bound stated in the following theorem.

Theorem 13. *Deciding if an $s \times t$ interval representation matrix is minimum requires at least $\Omega(\log s)$ time on a CREW PRAM, for $s \geq t$.*

Proof. We prove the theorem by a reduction from computing the OR. Let $b[1]$, $b[2]$, ..., $b[n]$ be n bits. We construct an $n \times n$ matrix M as follows.

$$M[i, j] = \begin{cases} 1 \text{ if } b[i] = 1 \wedge 0 < j \leq n \\ 0 \text{ if } b[i] = 0 \wedge i \neq j \wedge 0 < j \leq n \\ 1 \text{ if } i = j \end{cases}$$

Obviously, M can be constructed in constant time with $O(n^2)$ processors. According to the construction, all columns correspond to IPs iff all bits of b are 0, or equivalently, iff the OR of the n bits is 0. By Theorem 7, all columns of M correspond to IPs iff M is a minimum interval representation. Now the bound follows easily from Theorem 2. $\square$

The $\Omega(\log s)$ lower bound also applies to the problem of deciding if an $s \times t$ (Θ) circular arc representation is minimal.

Below we show deciding if an interval representation is minimum can be done in $O(\log s)$ time by an optimal EREW PRAM procedure. The following is a procedure that computes the left endpoints.

```
0    for i := 1 to t codo l[i] := 0 odoc; {initialize l}
1    for i := 1 to s codo {initialize ml}
2      for j := 1 to t codo
3        ml[i, j] := 0;
4      odoc;
5    odoc;
6    for i := 1 to s codo ml[i, b[i]] := 1 odoc;
7    for i := 1 to t codo l[i] := ∨ₛⱼ₌₁ ml[j, i] odoc;
```

260

After executing the above code, $l[i] = 1$ iff Column i corresponds to a left endpoint. The only step that requires more than constant time is Line 7, which can be done in $O(\log s)$ time on an EREW PRAM. All steps can be done optimally. In an analogous way, we can also decide which columns correspond to right endpoints. So we can now conclude the following.

Theorem 14. *Given an $s \times t$ interval representation matrix, deciding if the representation is minimum can be done in $O(\log s)$ time with $O(st/\log s)$ EREW PRAM processors, or in $O(1)$ time with $O(st)$ Common CRCW PRAM processors. Both algorithms are time-and-work-optimal.*

If an interval representation matrix is not minimum, we can obtain a minimum one by deleting some columns. However, we cannot obtain such a matrix by simply deleting all columns that do not correspond to IPs initially, since one column may become to correspond to an IP as a result of deleting a neighboring column. Below we describe a sequential procedure for obtaining a minimum interval representation.

First compute $l[i]$ and $r[i]$ for $0 < i \le t$. Then perform the following task.

```
0    for i := 1 to t do m[i] := l[i] ∧ r[i] od;
1    i := 1;
2    while i <= t do
3       if l[i] = 1 ∧ r[i] = 0 then
4          while r[i] = 0 do i := i + 1 od;
5          m[i] := 1;
6       fi;
7       i := i + 1;
8    od;
```

Line 0 sets $m[i]$ to 1 iff Column i corresponds to an IP. Then we scan the columns from left to right (Lines 2–8). If a column corresponds to a left endpoint but not a right endpoint, we will repeatedly remove columns (keep $m[i]$ as 0) until we have reached a column that corresponds to a right endpoint (Line 4). Then the column corresponds to an IP and will remain (set $m[i]$ to 1 at Line 5). When the above procedure terminates, the columns that correspond to IPs ($m[i] = 1$) form a minimum interval representation.

The parallel procedure can work as follows. First, set $m[i]$'s as Line 0. Then, for each left endpoint that does not correspond to an IP, find the closest right endpoint, say k, to its right, and set $m[k]$ to 1. This can be easily done within the resource bounds for parallel prefix computation. Once we have identified all the columns corresponding to maximal cliques, we simply apply subarray computation on all the rows. It is now easy to conclude the following.

Theorem 15. *Given an $s \times t$ interval representation matrix, a minimum interval representation can be obtained in $O(\log(st))$ time with $O(st/\log(st))$ processors by a time-and-work-optimal EREW PRAM algorithm, or in $O(\log t/\log\log t)$ time with $O(st \log\log t/\log t)$ processors by a time-and-work-optimal Common CRCW*

PRAM algorithm, or in $O(1)$ time with $O(st)$ processors by a time-optimal BSR algorithm.

Next we consider the problem of deciding if a circular arc representation is minimal. If follows from Theorem 10 that the problem can be solved by checking if each column of the representation matrix corresponds to an IP. For the same reason as above, if the input matrix is of size $s \times t$ and $s < t$, we can conclude immediately the representation is not minimal. So we only need to consider the case $s \geq t$.

The procedure works as follows. We first locate all the clockwise and counterclockwise endpoints. Then for each column, say i, perform the following task. If the column corresponds to both clockwise and counterclockwise endpoints, then find the shortest arcs, say a and b, whose clockwise and counterclockwise endpoints are i, respectively. Then i is an IP iff the size of intersection of a and b is 1. Both a and b can be found using a variation of the procedure for finding the first 1 in a $(0, 1)$-array, which takes $O(1)$ time and $O(t)$ Common CRCW PRAM processors [13], or $O(\log t)$ time and $O(t/\log t)$ EREW PRAM processors. It is now easy to conclude the following.

Theorem 16. *Given an $s \times t$ circular arc representation matrix, deciding if the representation is minimal can be done in $O(\log s)$ time with $O(st/\log s)$ EREW PRAM processors, or in $O(1)$ time with $O(st)$ Common CRCW PRAM processors. Both algorithms are time-and-work-optimal.*

Below we consider how to construct a minimal circular arc representation. The method is sketched as follows. First we obtain all the clockwise endpoints $e[i]$'s and counterclockwise endpoints $b[i]$'s. Then starting from the first column, we perform the following task for each column: Check, based on the values of $b[i]$'s and $e[i]$'s, if the current column, say c, corresponds to an IP. If so, set $m[c]$ to 1. Otherwise, delete the column (keep $m[c]$ as 0) and update $b[i]$'s and $e[i]$'s if applicable. At the end of the iteration, each remaining column corresponds to an IP, and all the remaining columns form a minimal circular arc representation, by Theorem 10.

We are now going to present an efficient implementation of the algorithm. For the convenience of the description, we assume, in the following, that the indices of the first row and the first column are both 0. We also assume, without loss of generality, that the input matrix does not contain an all-1 row.

```
0    for i := 0 to s − 1 do {compute b and e}
1        for j := 0 to t − 1 do
2            if M[i, j] = 1 ∧ M[i, (j + 1) mod t] = 0 then e[i] := j fi;
3            if M[i, j] = 1 ∧ M[i, (j + t − 1) mod t] = 0 then b[i] := j fi;
4        od;
5    od;
6    for i := 0 to t − 1 do m[i] := 0 od; {initialize m}
7    for i := 0 to t − 1
8        find shortest arc, say j, whose clockwise endpoint is i;
9        find shortest arc, say k, whose counterclockwise endpoint is i;
```

```
10      if both j and k exist and size of their intersection is 1 then m[i] := 1 fi;
11      if m[i] = 0 then {delete Column i}
12        for j := 0 to s − 1 do {update b and e, if applicable}
13          if b[j] = i then b[j] := (i + 1) mod s fi;
14          if e[j] = i then e[j] := (i − 1 + s) mod s fi;
15        od;
16      fi;
17    od;
```

Computing the $b[i]$'s and $e[i]$'s (Lines 0–5) is straightforward and takes $O(st)$ time. Lines 8–9 can be easily done in $O(t)$ time. If both j and k exist, we have two arcs $[b[j], i]$ and $[i, e[k]]$. The size of their intersection can be decided in constant time. So we can now conclude the following.

Theorem 17. *Given an $s \times t$ circular arc representation matrix, a minimal circular arc representation can be obtained in $O(st)$ time.*

Suppose M_4 is the input circular arc representation. None of the columns correspond to any IP. When Columns 0 and 1 have been deleted, Column 2 becomes to correspond to an IP. So Column 2 is not removed, according to the above procedure. Then the rest of the columns are all deleted. So the minimal circular arc representation matrix is a column that consists of six 1's only.

$$M_4 = \begin{bmatrix} 1 & 1 & 1 & 0 & 0 & 1 \\ 0 & 1 & 1 & 1 & 0 & 0 \\ 0 & 0 & 1 & 1 & 1 & 1 \\ 0 & 1 & 1 & 1 & 1 & 0 \\ 1 & 1 & 1 & 1 & 0 & 0 \\ 1 & 1 & 1 & 1 & 1 & 0 \end{bmatrix}, \quad M_5 = \begin{bmatrix} 1 & 1 & 0 \\ 0 & 1 & 0 \\ 0 & 1 & 1 \\ 0 & 1 & 1 \\ 1 & 1 & 0 \\ 1 & 1 & 1 \end{bmatrix}$$

To obtain an efficient parallel algorithm, we make some observations. It is easy to see that deleting a column that does not correspond to an IP yields an equivalent circular arc representation. Moreover, being an IP is not affected by deleting some columns. Nevertheless, a column can change status and become to correspond to an IP as a result of deleting another column, even though the two columns are not next to each other. Suppose we have two arcs $[i, j]$ and $[j, i]$. If Column i is deleted, Column j becomes to correspond to an IP and cannot be deleted. We say two arcs *embrace* if they intersect at both endpoints but neither is contained in the other. If we delete a column, the two neighboring columns and any embracing columns may change status. It should be obvious that several columns can be deleted simultaneously if the deletion of one column does not affect the status of another column. So, if we can identify those columns efficiently, we can also obtain a more compact circular arc representation efficiently.

```
0     compute b and e in parallel;
1     for i := 0 to t − 1 codo m[i] := 0 odoc; {initialize m}
2     min := 0; n := t;
3     while min = 0 do {consider odd columns}
```

```
4     set lend[i, j] and rend[i, j] to 0, for 0 ≤ i, j < n;
5     for i := 1 step 2 to n − 1 codo {compute lend and rend}
6         for j := 0 to s − 1 codo
7             if e[j] = i then lend[b[j], i] := 1 fi; {lend[i, j] = 1 means [i, j] is an arc}
8             if b[j] = i then rend[e[j], i] := 1 fi; {rend[i, j] = 1 means [j, i] is an arc}
9         odoc;
10        if i is an IP then m[i] := 1 fi;
11    odoc;
12    construct G = (V, E), where V = {v_i | i mod 2 = 1 ∧ m[i] = 0 ∧ 0 < i < n}
13        and E = {(v_i, v_j) | lend[i, j] = rend[i, j] = 1};
14    find a maximal independent set V′ of G;
15    m[i] := 1 for all v_i ∈ V − V′;
16    delete Column i of M and m[i] if i mod 2 = 1 and m[i] = 0, for 0 < i < n.
17    let n′ be the number of columns in the resulting matrix.
18    if n′ = n then min := 1 else update b and e fi;
19    n := n′;
20 od; {next consider even columns}
21    set lend[i, j] and rend[i, j] to 0, for 0 ≤ i, j < n;
22    for i := 0 step 2 to n − 1 codo {compute lend and rend}
23        for j := 0 to s − 1 codo
24            if e[j] = i then lend[b[j], i] := 1 fi;
25            if b[j] = i then rend[e[j], i] := 1 fi;
26        odoc;
27        if i is an IP then m[i] := 1 fi;
28    odoc;
29    construct G = (V, E), where V = {v_i | i mod 2 = 0 ∧ m[i] = 0 ∧ 0 ≤ i < n − 1}
30        and E = {(v_i, v_j) | lend[i, j] = rend[i, j] = 1};
31    find a maximal independent set V′ of G;
32    m[i] := 1 for all v_i ∈ V − V′;
33    delete Column i of M and m[i] if i mod 2 = 0 and m[i] = 0, for 0 ≤ i < n − 1.
34    if the last column does not correspond to an IP then remove it fi;
```

In order to achieve a polylog time bound, we must identify columns that can be deleted simultaneously. We first consider odd columns (columns whose indices are odd numbers) that do not correspond to IPs. Obviously, none of them are neighbors. However, we may not remove all those columns since there may be some embracing arcs. To resolve this problem, we construct a graph (Lines 12–13) as follows. Associate each such column (endpoint) with a vertex. If two arcs embrace and the size of their intersection is 2, then link the two vertices corresponding to the two endpoints. So, if two vertices are adjacent in the resulting graph, only one of the two columns can be deleted. If several vertices are mutually independent , then all of the columns can be deleted simultaneously. Therefore, we compute a maximal independent set of the graph (Line 14). Because of the maximality, any vertex not in the independent set is adjacent to a vertex in the independent set. Consequently, the columns associated with the vertices outside the independent set become to correspond to IPs when the columns associated with the vertices inside the independent set have been deleted. After the deletion of some columns, some even columns may become odd columns. So we repeat this process and consider the odd columns again until all odd columns correspond to IPs (Lines 3–20).

Then, in an analogous way, we consider even columns among Columns from 0 to $(n-2)$ (we do not consider Column $(n-1)$ for the time being since Columns 0 and $(n-1)$ are neighbors) that do not correspond to IPs. However, in this case, after some columns are deleted, we do not need to repeat the process since all columns except possibly the last one now correspond to IPs. Finally, we check if the last column corresponds to an IP. If not, simply delete it. It is now easy to conclude the procedure correctly constructs a minimal circular arc representation, by Theorem 10.

If the procedure runs on M_4, Lines 12–13 construct a graph with three vertices corresponding to Columns 1, 3, and 5, respectively. The graph does not contain any edge. So all three columns are removed at Line 16 and the intermediate matrix is M_5. Then Column 1 corresponds to an IP and the **while** loop cannot remove any more column, so the control goes on to Line 21 and we consider even columns. The first column of M_5 is removed at the end of Line 33. And finally Line 34 deletes the last column.

Before deriving efficient resource bounds for the above procedure, we make some additional assumptions. The first one is $s = O(t^2)$. If this is not true, the input matrix contains some identical rows. In this case, we can simply remove and make row duplicates at the beginning and at the end, respectively. We claim this can be done within $O(\log(st))$ time and $O(st)$ work. Obviously, any row, say i, can be represented by a pair, $(b[i], e[i])$, where $0 \le i < s$ and $0 \le b[i], e[i] < t$. First we sort the rows using radix sort. Then we can identify row duplication in constant time with $O(s)$ EREW PRAM processors. We sort $e[i]$'s by actually sorting $e'[i]$'s, where $e'[i] = se[i] + i$. So each $e'[i]$ is distinct and is in the range $[0, st - 1]$. Such numbers can be sorted in $O(\log(st))$ time with $O(st/\log(st))$ EREW PRAM processors [7]. Then $b[i]$'s can be sorted using the same method. Now, the validity of the claim follows immediately.

The next assumption is $t = O(s)$. If this is not true, some columns do not correspond to any endpoint. In this case, we simply delete those columns. This can obviously be done in $O(\log(st))$ time and $O(st)$ work on an EREW PRAM.

With the above assumptions, let's now consider the resource requirements of the procedure. It is easy to see the most expensive part is the **while** loop (Lines 3–20). Lines 5–11 can be done in $O(\log s)$ time with $O(st)$ work on EREW PRAM. One challenging step is to find a maximal independent set (Line 14). Currently, the most efficient algorithm solves the problem in $O(\log^3 v)$ time with $O((v+e)\log^2 v)$ work on an EREW PRAM [14], where v and e denote, respectively, the number of the vertices and the edges in a graph. In our case, $v \le t/2 = O(t)$. Since each edge corresponds to two embracing arcs (rows), we have $e \le s/2 = O(s)$. Therefore, Line 14 takes $O(\log^3 t)$ time with $O((s+t)\log^2 t)$ work on an EREW PRAM. The total work of the loop body (Lines 4–19) is $O(st + (s + t)\log^2 t) = O(st)$ since $t = O(s)$. The total time of the loop body is $O(\log s + \log^3 t)$. By Assumption 1, $\log s = O(\log t)$. So the loop body takes $O(\log^3 t)$ time. Since the loop iterates $O(\log t)$ times, the loop takes $O(\log^4 t)$ time and $O(st \log t)$ work. Now the total resource bounds follow easily.

Theorem 18. *Given an $s \times t$ circular arc representation matrix, a minimal circular arc representation can be obtained in $O(\log s + \log^4 t)$ time with $O(st \log t/(\log s + \log^4 t))$ processors on an EREW PRAM.*

The time lower bound on the EREW PRAM is $\Omega(\log(st))$ and does not match the above upper bound. We conjecture the algorithm is not time-optimal. The algorithm is work-optimal within a factor of $O(\log t)$. If the input is a Θ circular arc representation matrix, then the above algorithm is definitely not time-optimal. Below we describe a time-optimal procedure.

First, we eliminate all column duplication. Then, we check, for each column, if it is contained in another column. If so, delete it. It follows that, in the resulting matrix, no column contains another. So the resulting matrix gives a minimum Θ circular arc representation by Theorem 11, and also a minimal circular arc representation by Theorem 12. Deciding whether Column i contains Column j takes constant time with $O(s)$ Common CRCW PRAM processors. There are $O(t^2)$ pairs of columns. So all the IPs can be identified in constant time with $O(st^2)$ Common CRCW PRAM processors. On the EREW PRAM, this can be done in $O(\log(st))$ time with $O(st^2)$ work. Once all the IPs are identified, we can obtain a minimum Θ circular arc representation by applying subarray computation on all the rows. Now, it is easy to conclude the following.

Theorem 19. *Given an $s \times t$ Θ circular arc representation matrix, a minimum Θ circular arc representation (also a minimal circular arc representation) can be obtained in $O(\log(st))$ time with $O(st^2/\log(st))$ EREW PRAM processors, or in $O(\log t/\log \log t)$ time with $O(st^2 \log \log t/\log t)$ Common CRCW PRAM processors, or in $O(1)$ time with $O(st^2)$ BSR processors. All algorithms are time-optimal.*

Although the above procedure for computing Θ circular arc representations is time-optimal, the total work involved moves away from optimality.

4 Discussion

In this paper, we have studied the properties of minimal interval and circular arc representations and have given some efficient algorithms for the recognition and construction of such representations. The models of parallel computation used in this paper include EREW PRAM, CRCW PRAM, and BSR. We have presented algorithms for each of these models and they are of independent interest. One might ask the following questions: Which model is the best? Is it sufficient to design algorithms on only one of the models? It is often debatable whether one model is better than another. There is no universal agreement on the answer. It seems premature to tell at this point. There is an interesting project on building PRAM-type computers (see, *e.g.*, [1]). BSR is a relatively new model; the analogous project is not known currently but it is technically feasible (see, *e.g.*, [18]). As in the way of deciding Gordon Bell Prize winners, probably a good way to compare the performance between PRAM and BSR computers is to run sample programs

on both types of machines, in which case efficient algorithms on both PRAM and
BSR are needed. Perhaps someday, the algorithms in this paper will also be used
for this purpose.

References

1. F. Abolhassan, R. Drefenstedt, J. Keller, W. J. Paul, and D. Scheerer. On the physical design of PRAMs. *Computer Journal*, 36(8):756–762, December 1993.
2. S. G. Akl and G. R. Guenther. Broadcasting with selective reduction. In G. X.
   Ritter, editor, *Proceedings, 11th IFIP World Computer Congress*, pages 515–520,
   1989. North-Holland.
3. P. W. Beame and J. Hastad. Optimal bounds for decision problems on the CRCW
   PRAM. *Journal of the ACM*, 36(3):643–670, July 1989.
4. S. Benzer. On the topology of the genetic fine structure. *Proceedings, Nat. Acad.
   Sci.*, 45:1607–1620, 1959.
5. R. P. Brent. The parallel evaluation of general arithmetic expressions. *Journal of
   the ACM*, 21:201–208, 1974.
6. L. Chen. Efficient parallel algorithms for several intersection graphs. In *Proceedings,
   22nd Int'l Symp. on Circuits and Systems*, pages 973–976. IEEE, 1989.
7. L. Chen. Efficient deterministic parallel algorithms for integer sorting. In S. G.
   Akl, F. Fiala, and W. W. Koczkodaj, editors, *Proc. International Conference on
   Computing and Information, Lecture Notes in Computer Science, Vol. 468*, pages
   433–442. Springer-Verlag, 1990.
8. L. Chen. Optimal parallel time bounds for the maximum clique problem on intervals.
   Information Processing Letters, 42(4):197–201, June 1992.
9. L. Chen. Efficient parallel recognition of some circular arc graphs, I. *Algorithmica*,
   9(3):217–238, March 1993.
10. L. Chen. Revisiting circular arc graphs. In D.-Z. Du and X.-S. Zhang, editors,
    *Proceedings, 5th Annual International Symposium on Algorithms and Computation,
    Lecture Notes in Computer Science, Vol. 834*, pages 559–566. Springer-Verlag, 1994.
11. R. Cole and U. Vishkin. Faster optimal parallel prefix sums and list ranking. *Infor-
    mation and Computation*, 81(3):334–352, June 1989.
12. S. A. Cook, C. Dwork, and R. Reischuk. Upper and lower time bounds for parallel
    random access machines without simultaneous writes. *SIAM Journal on Computing*,
    15(1):87–97, 1986.
13. F. E. Fich, P. L. Ragde, and A. Wigderson. Relations between concurrent-write
    models of parallel computation. In *Proc. 3rd ACM Symp. on Principles of Distributed
    Computing*, pages 179–189. Association for Computing Machinery, 1984.
14. M. Goldberg and T. Spencer. Constructing a maximal independent set in parallel.
    SIAM J. on Discr. Math., 2(3):322–328, August 1989.
15. U. I. Gupta, D. T. Lee, and J. Y.-T. Leung. Efficient algorithms for interval graphs
    and circular-arc graphs. *Networks*, 12:459–467, 1982.
16. J. L. Hennessy and D. A. Patterson. *Computer Architecture: A Quantitative Ap-
    proach*. Morgan Kaufmann, 1990.
17. R. E. Ladner and M. J. Fischer. Parallel prefix computation. *Journal of the ACM*,
    27(4):831–838, October 1980.
18. L. F. Lindon and S. G. Akl. An optimal implementation of broadcasting with selec-
    tive reduction. *IEEE Transactions on Parallel and Distributed Systems*, 4(3):256–
    269, March 1993.

Cache Systems

Exploiting Parallelism in
Cache Coherency Protocol Engines

Andreas Nowatzyk, Gunes Aybay, Michael Browne,Edmund Kelly,
Michael Parkin, Bill Radke, Sanjay Vishin

Sun Microsystems Computer Corporation
Technology Development Group
Mountain View, CA 94043

Abstract: Shared memory multiprocessors are based on memory models, which are precise contracts between hard- and software that spell out the semantics of memory operations. Scalable systems implementing such memory models rely on cache coherency protocols that use dedicated hardware. This paper discusses the design space for high performance cache coherency controllers and describes the architecture of the programmable protocol engines that were developed for the S3.mp shared memory multiprocessor. S3.mp uses two independent protocol engines, each of which can maintain multiple, concurrent contexts so that maintaining memory consistency does not limit the system performance. Programmability of these engines allows support of multiple memory organizations, including CC-NUMA and S-COMA.

1 Introduction

Shared memory multiprocessors are gaining popularity due to their programming model, which tends to ease software development. In fact, most current multiprocessor systems use the shared memory paradigm, which leads to a growing body of software that is based on the assumption that all threads of a parallel application may access all memory. However, most of these machines use buses, which limits the number of supported processors to about 10. There are numerous proposals for scalable shared memory multiprocessors [1,2,3,4,5] that either have been built or are being implemented. Common to all of these machines is the use of a scalable switching fabric that passes messages between the processing nodes, which consist of one or more processors, I/O and memory. Generally, such switching fabrics do not support broadcasting, which means that the relatively simple memory consistency methods (snooping) from bus based MPs cannot be used. Instead, memory consistency is typically maintained by means of a directory and a cache coherency protocol that defines how memory transactions are translated into message exchange sequences between nodes that share data.

Cache coherency protocols for scalable, non-broadcast systems are more complex than those for bus-based multiprocessors. While it is possible to implement a scalable CC-protocol completely in random logic [3], it is preferable to use a more structured approach that uses a combination of hardware and software, where the hardware is accelerating the common operations and the software is handling infrequent, but complicated, corner cases [1,2].

This paper addresses the problem of designing efficient protocol engines to maintain cache coherency for scalable, shared memory multiprocessors. Following this introduction is a brief overview of several existing implementations. Subsequently, a discussion of the design space for high performance protocol engines addresses the specific needs to support memory consistency. In the remainder of this paper, the architecture of the S3.mp protocol engines is described and evaluated.

1.1 Background

Remote memory references in the Stanford DASH [3] are processed by two units, the *reply controller* (RC) and the *directory controller* (DC), each of which are a collection of hardwired functional units (data paths controlled by finite state machines). Both the RC and DC use field programmable logic devices (FPGAs, Xilinx) and programmable read only memories (PROMs) that offer a very limited amount of programmability, which is mainly used to accommodate late design changes. The RC and DC use different, specific hardware structures and support only a limited degree of concurrency (local bus operations may proceed while a remote access is being processed).

The MIT Alewife [2] machine integrates the protocol processing onto one chip, the A-1000 CMMU [10]. This controller is tightly coupled to one processor chip and serves as its cache controller as well as the memory controller. This central position allows lower latencies. It also simplifies the logic because there is no need to support a local snoopy bus protocol in addition to the global CC-protocol, hence the hardwired coherency engine in the CMMU is smaller than the controllers in DASH. Alewife uses a hybrid approach to protocol processing where exceptional cases are handled by the local processor. This is made possible through the use of a special CPU chip that supports fast context switching. Because of the intimate relationship between the CMMU and a fast context switching CPU, multiple outstanding transactions are supported.

The PLUS [5] multiprocessor uses dedicated hardware (FPGAs) to tie one processor to local memory and an interconnection network. The memory consistency protocol is simpler and requires modifications to the application software.

The main contribution of the Data Diffusion Machine [4] is the concept of a cache only architecture where data is no longer bound to a physical memory location. Instead, all of memory is structured as one multilevel cache hierarchy were data migrates to where it is used. This memory architecture complicates the cache coherency protocol. The first implementations of cache only memory architectures (COMA) systems, such as the KSR-1, used hardwired logic.

Fig. 1. Basic Node Architectures

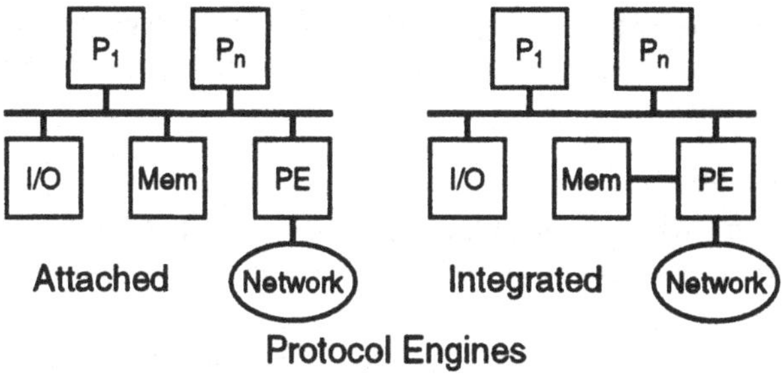

Protocol Engines

2 Protocol Engine Design Space

The architecture of a cc-protocol engine (PE) is strongly influenced by the way it is connected to the rest of the processing node. In general, it is only part of the multiprocessor hardware and is embedded in functional blocks that deal with the network, processor and memory interfaces. However for the purpose of providing a high level overview, the discussion of this support logic is deferred to the next section.

In the case of an attached protocol engine (Figure 1) the processing node was not specifically designed to be part of a shared memory multiprocessor, rather it is a conventional computing system (workstation, PC, etc.) that uses a bus to connect one ore more processors to memory and I/O devices. The advantage of the attached design is that the starting point is a fully functional computing environment and that the shared memory interface may be added to existing machines. However, the attached PE needs to deal with a design that did not anticipate its needs. This leads to extra complexity and overhead. For example, a snoopy bus generally assumes that all attached caches can perform the tag-lookup in a relatively short and fixed amount of time. However, the PE is representing a large, remote memory with interconnect latencies that tend to be much higher that local bus transactions. In order to be able to participate in a snoopy bus without slowing it down, the attached PE needs to have the ability to conservatively predict the need to interfere with a bus transaction in a timely manner, which may require significant amount of fast, static memory dedicated to a fast directory lookup table.

In the case of integrated PE, the designer exerts more influence over the memory design. In particular, it becomes possible to increase the memory bandwidth such that remote memory requests can be served without using up bandwidth on the local system bus. Furthermore, since most bus structures allow for variable memory response time, the snooping timing constraints are easy to meet. Continuing this line of architecture evolution is the merging of the PE with the CPU chip, so that the first/second level caches become accessible to the PE without cumbersome and time consuming bus protocols.

PE designs can also be classified by their implementation technologies. Early PE designs were almost exclusively hardwired. However the trend is to more programmable designs because it becomes clear that cc-protocols have not matured yet. In fact this is an active area with considerable innovation potential. For example, automatic detection of migratory data objects has been shown to be effective while requiring only modest changes to a cc-protocol [11, 18]. At the far end of this implementation spectrum is the use of standard RISC processor cores, which are provided by many ASIC vendors as compact, fully tested megacells [12]. While shortening the design cycle, the use of a standard RISC core does however increase the number of cycles necessary to process the cc-protocol.

2.1 System Interfaces

The primary interfaces for the PE are the interconnect network and the connection to the processor. In the case of an integrated PE, it must also interface to the main memory.

For attached PEs, the processor interface is essentially the system bus, which also serves to access main memory. The challenge is to design the PE so that it can deal with a given system bus, which generally did not anticipate the needs of a PE. As mentioned above, participating as a third party in snoopy bus transactions faces stiff timing constraints, which generally requires the use of expensive, fast and power hungry static memory devices (SRAM) to hold tables of memory locations that have been cached by remote nodes. Dealing with a system bus also complicates matters because it generally supports a multitude of transaction types, word sizes and alignments. A particular troublesome issue is the support of bus-locking, which tends to cause deadlocks in a scalable system without broadcasting.

The interconnect network is generally tailored towards the need of the PE. Critical issues are bandwidth, message insertion rates and latency. It is desirable to have the ability to insert multiple messages concurrently. Furthermore, the use of either independent networks for requests and replies or the support for multiple priorities can eliminate the need for deadlock recovery methods.

While the memory interface requirements don't differ much from that of an ordinary processing node, it is advantageous to support multiple banks and to have the ability to process several concurrent requests. Advanced DRAM devices, such as RamBus and S-DRAM, offer improved interfaces that allow multi-banked systems with modest effort.

2.2 Sources of Parallelism

The most obvious source of parallelism within a PE stems from the fact that the PE plays two roles, that of a client which initiates transactions and that of a server that has to respond to remote requests. The demand on both units in terms of number of transactions and the complexity of each transaction is roughly equal.

Higher performance systems generally need ways to hide the latency of remote memory references, most of which result in a demand for more bandwidth and more concurrent transactions. Prefetching and lockup free caches will both supply the PE with multiple transactions before one has completed. Given that it is much easier to design interconnect networks with higher bandwidth than with lower latency, this parallelism can be readily used. However the PE design becomes more complicated due to the need to coordinate multiple transactions, allocate resources in a non-blocking fashion and keep transactions separate. Furthermore, maintaining the proper memory semantics becomes more difficult.

Finally, there is a certain amount of parallelism within each transaction itself, which is best matched with a pipelined design that schedules data movement and control transfers separately.

2.3 Protocol Families

The two main classes of cache coherency protocols are labeled nonuniform memory access (NUMA) and cache-only memory architecture (COMA). The non-uniformity in NUMA refers to the fact that the memory latency becomes a function of the location of the memory block. The PE support for NUMA requires a mechanism to keep track of the cached copies of a particular memory block. Typically, this is done by maintaining a directory. Directories can either be stored at the location of the main memory [1,2,3] or a the location of the (processor-) caches [7,8]. While the latter approach requires less dedicated storage for the directory, it does require a more intimate connection to the processor, which is typically not possible in the attached PE configuration due to the characteristics of the system bus.

In addition to the directory, NUMA systems benefit from a cache that stores the data from remote memory references. It turns out that in PE designs that use the client/ server approach, the directory is only updated by the server while the cache for remote data is maintained exclusively by the client.

In addition to the facilities of a NUMA system, a COMA supporting PE needs to have a mechanism to locate the data for a given address. This involves the support for table with semi-associative lookup capability, much like the tag-store of conventional caches.

3 The S3.mp Protocol Engines

The S3.mp scalable, shared memory multiprocessor is an experimental research project that is being implemented by SMCC's Technology Development group. The S3.mp architecture is similar to systems mentioned in section 1.1, however unlike these conventional CC-NUMA MP's, S3.mp is optimized for a large collection of independent and cooperating parallel applications that share common computing resources which may be spatially distributed. Consequently, support for concurrent I/O operations, as in a video server, is important besides the traditional parallel applications. S3.mp nodes may be spatially separated by up to 200m, which means that a S3.mp system could be distributed over an entire building.

Fig. 2. S3.mp System Overview

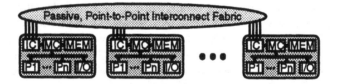

Figure 2 shows the generic S3.mp components: each node is essentially equivalent to a workstation with one or more processors, memory and I/O. The two S3.mp specific components are the interconnect controller (IC) and the memory controller (MC). The IC is a topology independent router that allows the construction of switching fabrics without centralized switches that have a bisection bandwidth that is comparable to that of a Cray T3D, but at much lower costs [13]. The interconnect fabric is composed of either fiber optic links or electrical connections that can carry bit serial data at rates exceeding 1.3 Gbits/sec. For the purpose of the subsequent discussion, the IC network should be regarded as a black box that can transport messages reliably between any two nodes in the system. This interconnect systems offers 4 levels of priorities. Because of the adaptive routing algorithm used by the IC, the message delivery order is not maintained.

The memory controller includes the protocol engines that are responsible for translating between local bus transactions and the messages that are transmitted over the interconnect system. There are two identical protocol engines, each with its own writable microcode memory.

3.1 The S3.mp processing element

Each S3.mp node consists of 2 gate arrays with about 200K gates combined that are part of one multi chip module (Figure 3). The MC interfaces directly to the memory chips, the local processor bus (Mbus) and the interconnect controller (IC). Normally, the MC serves memory operations from the local bus to the local memory, just like a conventional memory controller. However, it maintains a global 64 bit address space and allows the local processor to issue memory operations for remote data. The MC can also initiate transactions on the Mbus as a result of messages received from remote nodes. In the base configuration, two processors are connected to each MC through the Mbus.

Fig. 3. A S3.mp Node

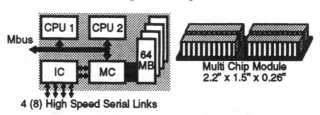

The MC is designed to directly drive a 64 to 256 Mbyte memory array that uses 16 or 64 Mbit synchronous DRAM devices. Coherency is maintained on memory blocks of 32 bytes, which is the size of one cache line on Mbus based systems. The architecture is not tied to a particular cache line size because remote data is cached in the MC and the MC could maintain subblocks or multi-line objects.

The MC uses 18 bits of ECC overhead and 14 bits of directory overhead for every 32-bytes of memory. 14 bits provide sufficient storage to keep a 12-bit node pointer and 2-bit state for each cache line.

The Mbus of each S3.mp node can be connected to other devices, which is the primary facility to attach I/O devices to the system. In particular, it is possible to plug a S3.mp module into any Mbus slot (for example into a Sparc Station 10 or 20 Workstation).

3.2 The Memory Controller

The MC is responsible for handling accesses to local and remote memory and for implementing directory based cache coherence protocols. In addition to operating as a normal memory controller, the MC performs the following functions:

1. Maintaining the directory information for the local memory under its control

2. Constructing and sending messages to remote nodes on the network initiated by local MBUS transactions that require remote access or in response to messages received from other nodes on the network

3. Performing memory operations and MBUS cycles on the local node in response to messages received from remote nodes

4. Maintaining an Inter-Node Cache (INC) which is used to store a copy of every cache line retrieved from a remote node

5. Sending and receiving diagnostic messages to or from other nodes to program configuration parameters, handle errors, etc.

Fig. 4. Datapaths Through The Mc

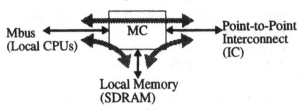

Mbus
(Local CPUs)

MC

Point-to-Point
Interconnect
(IC)

Local Memory
(SDRAM)

From the CPU's point of view, the MC operates as a virtual bus extender. CPUs connected to the MC on the local Mbus can assume that they are talking to a cache coherent bus. Except for the extra latency in accessing remote locations, details of getting data from remote nodes and distributed cache coherence protocols are completely hidden from these processors. Parallel application software targeted for a shared-bus cache-coherent multiprocessor system, written in accordance with the SPARC memory models [7], should execute correctly on a S3.mp system without any modification. However, performance tuning may be necessary to achieve good performance for some applications. The MC, acting as a virtual bus extender, allows single-threaded programs to utilize the collective physical memory in a cluster of workstations for memory intensive applications and allow uniform access to all I/O devices for high performance server applications.

The MC is structurally divided into the following set of modules (Figure 5):

1. A bus controller to interface to the Mbus

2. A memory sequencer to interface to SDRAMs

3. the protocol engines to implement distributed cache coherency protocols (RAS and RMH)

4. A configuration controller unit to take care of configuration management, errors, diagnostics, etc.

5. Input and output queues for interfacing to IC (or to a general purpose point-to-point interconnect)

Fig. 5. The MC Structure

MBUS

MBUS
controller

configuration
controller

output
queue

TIC

addr&data

Remote
Memory
Handler

packets

Remote
Access
Server

input
queue

TIC

memory
controller

scheduler

SDRAM

3.3 The MC Environment

The MC is designed like a system on a chip. Modules are designed to be as functionally self-sufficient as possible. Each module can generate and receive a small number of transactions. The number of signals going between modules are kept to an absolute minimum. Functional units communicate with each other through an address bus, a data bus and a packet bus. Access to these buses are managed by a central controller, the *scheduler*. The scheduler receives dedicated request lines from each master module and ready lines from each slave module (Figure 6) and sends dedicated grant lines to each master and dedicated request lines to each slave. Requests requiring data or acknowledgments to be returned are handled as split transactions. In addition, most slaves are required to be able to function as a master and initiate transactions to return data and/or acknowledgments.

Fig. 6. Centralized Communication Control

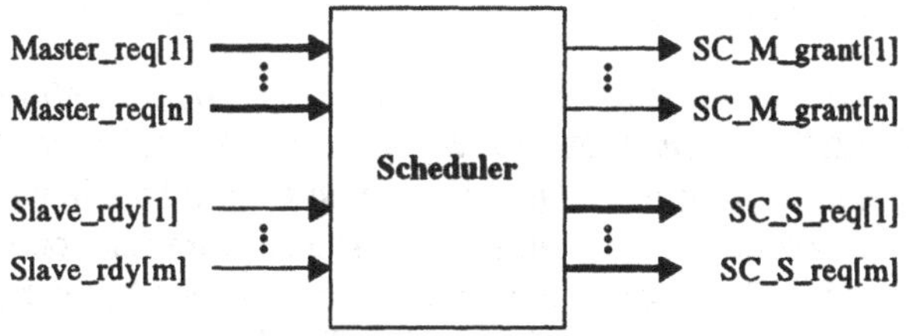

A typical transaction proceeds as shown in Figure 7:

1. The initiator asserts its dedicated request line (R_req) to the scheduler. R_req is a multi-bit signal including information about the resources to be used (i.e. A-bus, D-bus, P-bus), the number of cycles required for the transaction, module ID of the target unit and the type of the transaction. Each unit has its own dedicated R_req line going to the scheduler.

2. Slave modules assert a dedicated ready line (T_rdy) to the scheduler whenever they are ready to accept transactions.

3. Every cycle, the scheduler examines request inputs from master modules and ready lines from slave units. When the scheduler determines that all resources required for a request are available, it schedules a transaction for that request. Necessary communication resources are reserved for the duration of the transaction. A grant signal (SC_R_grant) is sent to the requestor and the request type and requestor ID is relayed to the target module (with SC_T_req signal).

4. Requestors are responsible for driving data on the bus as soon as they receive the grant signal from the scheduler. Typically, requestors latch the data into their output registers in the cycle they assert their request. The grant signal from the scheduler is used as an enable to drive data from these registers to the buses in the same cycle the transaction is scheduled.

Fig. 7. Internal Bus Protocol of MC

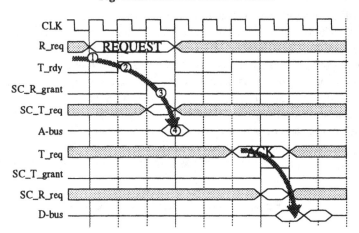

The main transaction initiators within the MC, *the MBUS Controller, the Remote Memory Handler* and *the Remote Access Server,* compete for access to the memory controller. The memory controller is designed to be able to handle two simultaneous transactions to a 4-banked memory subsystem. The split transaction communication protocol used in the MC reduces the contention on internal buses by reserving the buses only when data transfer is taking place. The data bus has a bandwidth of 1 Gbyte/sec, that connects the Mbus (320 MB/sec peak), the memory (640 MB/sec peak) and the two protocol engines (sharing the I/O queues with 440 MB/sec). Using split transactions such that data is always pushed by the sending unit which initiates arbitration also introduces a level of parallelism *and* pipelining. It is possible to send the address for a transaction on the address bus while an independent data transfer is taking place on the data bus. Moreover, since acknowledges are generated by the target module as new transactions, communication is clock-delay independent. Changes in the cycle timings of transactions (i.e. time taken to respond to a certain request) does not affect the overall functionality.

This design methodology does not necessarily result in the fastest possible implementation, however, it makes design management and verification simpler. The concept is similar to object oriented programming. Each module has a small set of externally visible data structures and a set of transactions (methods) that operate on these structures. Modules can be tested independently of the whole system by constructing simple test modules. Multiple implementations of modules can be maintained and cost-performance trade-offs can be postponed until late in the design process. Also, it is easy to reuse parts of the design targeted at different platforms and/or technologies. For example, the memory controller module has a very simple functional definition: it either reads or writes a 32-byte block of memory (a cache line) of memory. This requires that some of the logic to handle byte insertion, etc. is moved into other modules, but it makes the memory controller extremely modular. A Rambus or DRAM based version of the memory controller could be used in a future version of the MC design with minimal interface redesign effort.

This modular design methodology also decreases the complexity of the verification. Part of the development effort is to verify the correctness of the inter-module communication protocol using formal verification tools. Simple module interfaces and the small set of transactions supported by each module makes it possible to deal with the communication protocol at a high level of abstraction where formal verification tools like *Murφ* [14] and SMV [15] are applicable. At the module level, a simple interface and a small set of transactions enable designers to test their modules almost exhaustively before integration of the full-chip model. With the simple interface approach, integration of modules at different levels of abstraction is also possible.

3.4 Protocol Engines - RAS and RMH

The S3.mp cache coherency protocols are implemented by two protocol engines on the MC chip, the *Remote Memory Handler* (RMH) and the *Remote Access Server* (RAS). The RMH is responsible for locally initiated memory operations that refer to remote memory. It retrieves data from remote nodes, services invalidation and data forwarding requests, and maintains the INC. The RAS serves requests by remote nodes to the local memory. It services data request messages from remote nodes, maintains the directory and generates invalidation and data forwarding messages.

Fig. 8. Protocol Engine Datapath

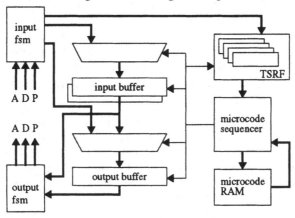

The RMH and RAS each use an instance of the microcode controlled datapath shown in Figure 8. This is a special purpose protocol controller with a simple instruction set that is tailored specifically towards the execution of cache coherency protocols. Each engine consists of 3 independently operating components: the input FSM, the actual micro controller and an output FSM. The input FSM receives requests from the system interface, which can be either a new packet from the input queue or a request from the bus interface unit. In either case, the input FSM receives the request and places it in the input buffer. It also interprets the request and decides if it belongs to one of the currently executing threads or if a new thread needs to be created. In the later case, the input FSM initializes all registers in the transaction state register file (TSRF) that collectively forms the state of a thread (addresses, program counter, auxiliary data, timer, retry counter, state variables, etc.). A TSRF entry has a total of 121 bits. The micro sequencer may be executing on a different, active thread while the input FSM operates.

The micro sequencer schedules a thread for execution once the input FSM has completed the initialization or when a thread is suspended or terminated while there is at least one other active thread in the TSRF. Context switches essentially require no extra time: the micro sequencer can be executing an instruction from TSRF entry #1 and #2 in adjacent clock cycles (15 nsec or 66 Mhz). The instruction set of the micro-sequencer includes a number of data move, test and set instructions that aid in the assembly and interpretation of messages. It also includes several more complicated instructions, such a performing a 3 way set-associative table lookup or a receive instruction that suspends the current thread until either a matching reply is received or a time-out occurs. Most instructions include a multi-way branch (2-16 ways). Instruction fetch, decode and branch take place within one clock cycle without branch delay slots.

The output FSM is invoked by the micro-sequencer to send replies or requests to other units (memory, output queue and bus interface). It off-loads the need to arbitrate for resources and control the data transfer from the micro-sequencer, which can proceed to work on another thread.

The key point of this design is that it implements a logical pipeline with three stages that receive transactions, process them and distribute the replies via dedicated agents that share resources.

The cache coherency protocols are separated into two parts, the server (RAS microcode) and the client (RMH microcode). Microcode is stored in two on-chip RAMs, so that it is possible to program different protocols.

The typical operation of the protocol engines is shown in Figure 9. In the most common case, there are two kinds of transactions performed by the protocol engines:

1. Transactions that require an acknowledge. This kind of transaction typically has a short burst of local activity (i.e. local cycles, memory cycles) which is terminated by sending a request packet. From this point on, the microcode waits for a reply from a remote node. This wait period is in the order of microseconds in the current implementation of the S3.mp system. When the reply is received, the transaction is terminated with another short burst of local activity.

2. Transactions that do not require an acknowledge. These are typically initiated by receiving a request packet and can be served using only the local resources of the receiving node. They are terminated by sending an acknowledge packet to the requestor.

Due to the long latency associated with waiting for a reply, it would have been inefficient to run the protocol engines in a mode where the microcode sequencer was kept busy for the entire duration of the transaction. This is the rational that led to the design with multiple contexts. The TSRF has several sets of registers to keep track of multiple concurrent transactions. The lowest 7 bits of the cache block address (bits [11:5] of the local address for 32-byte cache lines) are used as a tag for transactions. These 7 bits are preserved during address translation, thus, they effectively divide the global address space into 128 sets. Any protocol engine can be working on N of these sets concurrently where N is the number of register windows in the TSRF of that protocol engine. The current implementation of the MC chip uses 4 TSRF windows. The optimal number of contexts is a function of the available concurrency, which is limited by the current set of CPUs that issue only one memory reference at a time. 4 contexts roughly match the remote traffic that can be expected from 2 CPUs, provided that there is some support for prefetching and block copy operations that can proceed in the background and may be used for I/O or page migration. Once processors with lockup free caches, speculative execution and the ability to issue multiple outstanding memory references become available, the number of TSRF entries will need to be increased.

Fig. 9. S3.mp Protocol Engine Activity

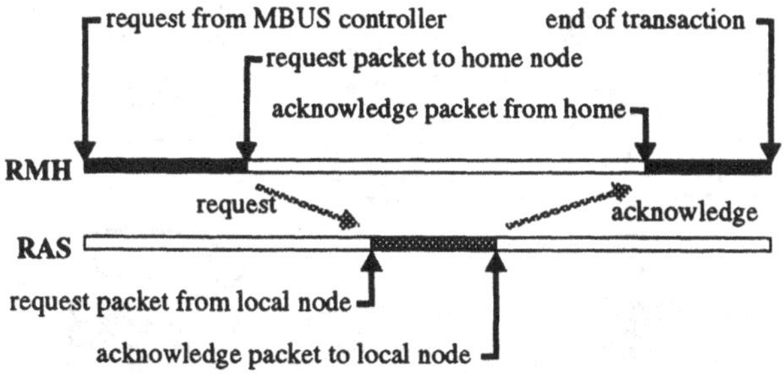

Transactions received by the protocol engines can be of two types: request or acknowledge. Request transactions require a new microcode thread to be generated. For transactions received from the local bus controller, the transaction type relayed by the scheduler is used as an entry point into the microcode. For packets received from the input queue, type information from the packet is used as the entry point. The next available TSRF window is assigned to this transaction and a new thread is generated and marked as ready to execute. When the microcode sequencer detects that this thread is ready to run, it starts executing this thread. The TSRF entry corresponding to this thread becomes part of the state space of the microcode sequencer for the duration of this execution. Until this thread is completed, all other subsequent transactions having the same ID will be suspended by the input FSM. Once the microcode sequencer completes the initial set of local operations and sends a request packet to a remote node, the current thread goes to sleep and any other thread which is marked as ready to execute can start running on the microcode sequencer.

When an acknowledge packet is received by the RAS or the RMH, ID field of this packet is compared to the ID fields of threads that are currently sleeping in that module. A sleeping thread waiting for the particular acknowledge packet is found. This thread is woken up, i.e., marked as ready to run. The microcode sequencer picks up the thread whenever it is available and continues executing after the point where the thread had gone to sleep previously. Basically, a thread goes to sleep whenever it needs to communicate with a remote node and is woken up whenever the acknowledge message is received. Between these two events, microcode sequencer is free to service other transactions.

A set of watchdog timers, one for each TSRF thread, are used to deal with the case where an acknowledge is expected but never received from a remote node. Whenever a thread waits for a reply, its timer is programmed to generate an error acknowledge if an acknowledge is not received within a preset amount of time.

In addition to providing a way of matching waiting threads and acknowledge messages from remote nodes, the ID field provides a convenient way to lock the directory and/or the INC while these data structures are in a transient state. The RAS can potentially lock N out of 128 slices of the directory independently, where N is the number of register windows in the TSRF. The RMH can also lock accesses to the INC with the same mechanism. By convention, the RAS does not touch the INC while the RMH does not access the directory. ID-locking is utilized exclusively by S3.mp directory protocols to implement delay independent operation. The example in Figure 10 illustrates the ID-locking feature.

Fig. 10. INC Locking Mechanism

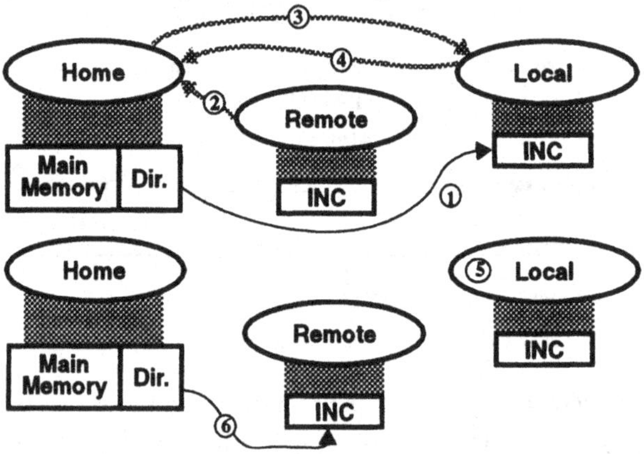

1. Initially, the directory is in the *Shared_Remote* state and the local node has a valid copy of the cache line.
2. A remote node issues a write to the same line and sends an exclusive ownership request to the home node.
3. The home node sends an invalidation request to the local node.
4. Before receiving the invalidation request from the home node, the local node decides to discard the line and sends an uncache request to the home node. This request and the invalidation request from the home pass each other in the interconnect network.
5. The local node receives an invalidation request while it was expecting an acknowledgment for its uncache request. Since the ID's match[1], the waiting RMH thread resumes execution. The invalidation request is treated as an acknowledgment and the thread is terminated.
6. The home node receives an uncache request message while it was expecting an invalidation acknowledge. The home node can safely treat this request as an acknowledgment to its invalidation request since the processors on the local node cannot access the INC for the same address until the invalidation request is received by the local node. The transaction is completed and ownership of the cache line is transferred to the remote node by changing the directory to *Exclusive_Remote* state.

---

1. Once the input FSM has matched the ID of the received message against all active TSRF entries, a subsequent address match is performed if there was an ID hit. Because of the uniqueness of the ID, only one such match is possible, hence only one address comparator is needed.

3.5 Flowcontrol and Deadlocks

Given that there is only a finite number of TRSF entries, flow control is needed to avoid acceptance of a request without the required resources. The input and output queues provide flow control and the scheduler will not grant a request unless the destination unit is ready. However, simply refusing to accept new messages can result in deadlocks because transactions may require acknowledge messages to complete. To avoid such deadlocks, the message exchange subsystem (I/O queues and IC network), support multiple levels of priority. The protocol engines have two virtual ports with independent flow control such that secondary messages can be sent at an elevated priority while blocking new requests that have lower priority.

3.6 MC Directory Operation

As mentioned above, the directory is actually part of main memory, hence it is read on every normal memory read operation. The local bus controller checks the directory on every memory access without increasing latency. On local references that need to recall or invalidate remotely cached data, the RAS is called to perform these operations. Only the RAS may change the directory state.

The MC reserves a programmable fraction of the main memory and uses this storage for the INC, which is required to include all locally cached blocks of remote memory and which is used for an address compression scheme that minimizes bandwidth demand for control messages. Since remote references have at least 3x higher latency than local memory references, even a relatively slow INC is beneficial. The INC is programmable in size and may occupy up to 50% of the total memory. It is implemented as a 3-way set associative cache with LRU replacement policy. Although S3.mp in this configuration is still fundamentally a CC-NUMA architecture, it does have many of the properties of a cache only memory architecture (COMA). Hence S3.mp offers a variable degree of COMA behavior that can be used to fine tune the system for specific applications.

Fig. 11. Reading Data from a Remote Node

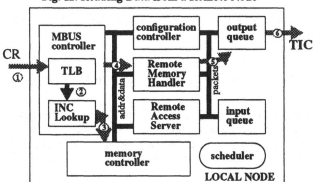

3.7 Putting it all together

This section contains a brief description on how one remote memory transaction progresses through the MC. The first agent is the local bus controller, which receives the transaction (1) in Figure 11 and identifies it as a reference to a remote part of the address space (2). The bus controller has read-only access to both the directory state and the INC state. It is capable of performing all operations that do not require assistance from a remote node, for example processing an INC hit (3).

In the case of an INC miss, the bus controller aborts the bus transaction, freeing it for other transactions[2], and forwards a copy of the INC state to the RMH (4). In this transaction, all state pertaining to a transaction is handed over to the RMH. This saves time because the RMH does not need to read the INC state. However, it also introduces a problem: the INC state may be become stale before the RMH processes the request. A mechanism similar to the Load-Linked/Store-Conditional instruction pair for synchronizing multiprocessors is used to track the validity of the INC state.

Once the new thread begins executing in the RMH, it will queue a request message (5) according to the CC-protocol and wait for a reply.

Fig. 12. Servicing Remote Read Request

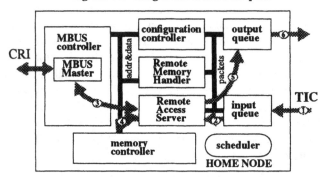

When the request packet is received by the home node (Figure 12), the following sequence of events happen:

1. The request packet is removed from the interconnect by the input queue

2. The input queue decodes the type of the packet to determine the destination unit and sends the packet to the RAS

3. The RAS requests a snoop cycle on the home Mbus. If one of the home caches have an exclusive copy of this cache line, data is read from this cache. This snoop action is necessary since the current S3.mp protocols do not distinguish between the resident directory state and states where a cache line is shared or owned by one of the CPUs at the home node.

4. If the snoop cycle has failed, the RAS reads the cache line and the associated directory information from the main memory.

---

2. The Mbus is a tenured bus, but allows a relinquish&retry reply, which is an approximation to a split transaction protocol, which would have superior performance.

5. If the directory is valid (i.e. the directory is not in *Exclusive_Remote* state), an acknowledge packet including the data is constructed and sent to the output queue. The RAS updates the directory information in the main memory if necessary. Assuming that no other node had a copy of the cache line involved in this transaction, directory state will be changed from *Resident* to *Shared_Remote* and the directory pointer will be updated to point to the local node.

6. The acknowledge packet including the data is sent back to the local node through the interconnect.

Fig. 13. Completion of a Remote Read

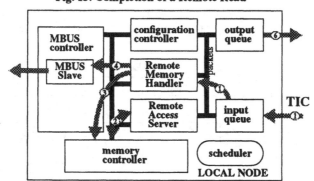

After the acknowledge packet is received by the remote node (Figure 13):

1. The acknowledge packet is removed from the interconnect by the input queue and sent to the RMH. This packet wakes up the sleeping RMH process which had initiated the request for this transaction.

2. The RMH reads the INC tags corresponding to the address of the cache line from the memory and allocates an INC entry. If there are no free INC entries available, RMH victimizes an existing INC entry in LRU fashion.

3. Data from the packet is written to the INC and INC tags are updated.

4. The MBUS controller is acknowledged to complete the transaction.

3.8 Cache Coherency Protocols

S3.mp was initially designed exclusively to support a CC-NUMA protocol and a large internode cache that resides in main memory and that could be changed in size when the system is initially turned on (static configurability). Advances in the ASIC technology during the design of the MC made it possible to replace the mask-programmed ROMS in the RAS and RMH with writable microcode SRAMS.

Discussions with Ashley Saulsbury from the Swedish Institute of Computer Science (SICS) showed that his ideas on how to implement a Simple-COMA [16] system are applicable to the S3.mp nodes with only minor extensions to the protocol engines. The most significant modification concerns the INC access logic, which was modified to support a data-less mode that only stores the tag and state information. This turns the INC into a reverse translation table.

3.9 Evaluation and Comparison

Alewife and S3.mp use roughly comparable technology (LSI Logic ASICs) for the PE, both of which can be expected to perform better than the implementation with standard components that was used in DASH. Unlike Alewife and DASH, S3.mp uses microcoded engines that offer programmability without slowing the design. A dual RISC core implementation was considered for S3.mp, which would have reduced the design time and increased versatility. This option requires roughly the same amount of chip area (RISC core + SRAM), but would need about 10x more cycles to process the cc-protocol. For a comparable design, the RISC core needs to be augmented by a larger register files to support rapid context switching and by a packet handler to assemble and decode messages efficiently and that could utilize the co-processor interface of the RISC core.

TABLE 1 : Protocol Engine Performance

	S3.mp	Alewife	DASH
Client #of gates	28 K	13 K	45 K
Server #of gates	28 K	16 K	23.5 K
Clock frequency	66 Mhz	30 Mhz	33 Mhz
Client #of concurrent operations	4	>= 3 (SW assisted)	1
Server #of concurrent operations	4	>= 3 (SW assisted)	1
Client #cycles for simple read	6+3	~8	10+11
Server #of cycles for simple read	8	~8	11

The S3.mp protocol engines achieve very good performance in terms of low flow through latency and high throughput with a relatively modest amount of logic. This opens the possibility that these PEs can be integrated onto the processor, which is one of the project goals. At the same time, programmability allows to adopt advances in cache coherency protocol designs.

4 Summary

Hardware accelerators to process cache coherency protocols are critical component of scalable shared memory multiprocessors. While there is a wide range of implementation choices for such protocol engines, it was shown that adding programmability by either microcoding or the use of embedded RISC cores are viable design options. It is advantageous to provide multiple context so that latency hiding techniques may use sever concurrent memory transaction to deal with high network latencies.

The S3.mp project opted to use microcoding to build a relatively small PE that is balanced with the other components of the memory controller chip.

5 References

[1] Nowatzyk, A., Aybay, G., Browne, M., Kelly, E., Parkin, M., Radke, W., Vishin, S., *"S3.mp: Current Status and Future Directions"*, Workshop on Shared Memory Multiprocessors, ISCA'94, Chicago (to be released as a Technical Report of the University of Southern California, Los Angeles)

[2] Agarwal, A.,Kubiatowicz J., Kranz, D., Lim, B., Yeung, D., D'Souza, G., Parkin, M. *"Sparcle: An Evolutionary Processor Design for Large-Scale Multiprocessors"*. IEEE Micro, June 1993, pages 48-61.

[3] Lenoski, D. *"The Design and Analysis of DASH: A Scalable Directory-Based Multiprocessor"*. PhD Dissertation, Stanford University, December 1991.

[4] Hagersten, E., Landin, A., and Haridi, S. *"DDM - A Cache-Only Memory Architecture"*. IEEE Computer 25,9 (September 1992), 44-54.

[5] Bisiani, R., and Ravishankar, M. K. *"Design and Implementation of The Plus Prototype"*. Technical Report, Carnegie Mellon University, August 1990.

[6] Li, K., *"Shared Virtual Memory on Loosely Coupled Multiprocessors"*. PhD Dissertation, Yale University, September 1986.

[7] IEEE Std 1596-1992, *"Scalable Coherent Interface"*. Institute of Electrical and Electronics Engineers, Inc., Service Center, 445 Hoes Lane, PO Box 1331, Piscataway, NJ 08855-1331

[8] Thapar, M., Delagi, B., and Flynn, M., *"Linked List Cache Coherence for Scalable Shared Memory Multiprocessors"*, Proceedings of the 1993 International Conference on Parallel Processing, pages 34-43.

[9] Nowatzyk, A., *"Communications Architecture for Multiprocessor Networks"*. PhD Dissertation, Carnegie Mellon University, December 1989.

[10] Kubiatowicz, J., *"The Alewife-1000 CMMU: Addressing the Multiprocessor Communications Gap"*, HotChip Symposium 1994, Stanford California

[11] Dubois, M., Skeppstedt, J., Ricciulli, L., Ramamurthy, K., Stenstrom, P., *"The Detection and Elimination of Useless Misses in Multiprocessors"*, ISCA'93, San Diego, California

[12] LSI Logic Product Information on R4000 embedded controller RISC core, LSI Logic, 1551 McCarthy Blvd., Milpitas California 95035.

[13] Nowatzyk, A., Parkin, M., *"The S3.mp Interconnect System and TIC Chip"*, HotInterconnects'93, Stanford CA, Aug. 1993

[14] Dill, D., Drexler, D., Hu, A., Yang, C. *"Protocol Verification as a Hardware Design Aid"*. 1992 IEEE International Conference on Computer Design: VLSI in Computers and Processors, (October 1992), 522-52

[15] McMillan, K., *"Symbolic Model Checking"*, 1992, Carnegie Mellon University PhD Thesis, Pittsburgh, PA 15213

[16] Hagersten, E., Saulsbury, A., Landin, A., *"Simple COMA Node Implementations"*, 27th Hawaii International Conference on System Sciences, 1994

[17] Kendall Square Research, *Technical Summary*. 1992. 170 Tracer Lane, Waltham, MA 02154-1379

[18] Cox, A., Fowler, R., *"Adaptive Cache Coherency for Detecting Migratory Shared Data"*, ISCA'93, San Diego

Verifying Distributed Directory-based Cache Coherence Protocols: S3.mp, a Case Study

Fong Pong, Andreas Nowatzyk*, Gunes Aybay* and Michel Dubois

Department of EE-Systems
University of Southern California
Los Angeles, CA 90089-2562

*Sun Microsystems Computer Corporation
Technology Development Group
Mountain View, CA 94043

Abstract. This paper presents the results for the verification of the S3.mp cache coherence protocol. The S3.mp protocol uses a distributed directory with limited number of pointers and hardware supported overflow handling that keeps processing nodes sharing a data block in a singly linked list. The complexity of the protocol is high and its validation is challenging because of the distributed algorithm used to maintain the linked lists and the non-FIFO network. We found several design errors, including an error which only appears in verification models of more than three processing nodes, which is very unlikely to be detected by intensive simulations. We believe that methods described in this paper are applicable to the verification of other linked list based protocols such as the IEEE Scalable Coherent Interface.

1 Introduction

S3.mp (*Sun's Scalable Shared memory MultiProcessor*) is a research project which implements a distributed cache-coherent shared-memory system [12]. In S3.mp, cache coherence is supported by a distributed directory-based protocol with a small, fixed number of pointers and a hardware supported overflow mechanism which keeps processing nodes sharing a data block in singly linked lists. Cache coherence protocols that use linked lists have been proposed by Thapar [18] and are also used in the Scalable Coherent Interface (SCI) protocol [7].

To verify the S3.mp protocol is very difficult because the linked lists are maintained by a distributed algorithm. The addition and deletion of nodes from the linked list reorganize the list. In addition to the complexity of maintaining linked lists, the S3.mp protocol behavior is unpredictable because the non-FIFO (First-In-First-Out) interconnect network does not preserve the order in which messages are delivered between nodes.

We have applied the Stanford Murφ [4] tool and a specialized method based on a Symbolic State Model (SSM) [13] to establish the correctness of the S3.mp cache coherence protocol. During the verification, several design errors were discovered. We will describe two subtle errors which were found in the validation of S3.mp cache protocols. The first error violates *Store Atomicity* [3], which is a property of all SPARC memory models [17] prohibiting several processors from observing an inconsistent order of store operations. The loss of consistency occurs when the protocol allows more than one dirty cache line or the coexistence of shared and dirty copies. This condition, however, is too narrow to cover all possible protocol errors. The values of all data copies must also be tracked. The second error was detected in cases with more than three processors but was not detected in intensive simulation runs. The result indicates that there is a need for methods which can deal with protocol models with a large number of processors. Verification and simulation runs on small models are not always sufficient to establish the correctness of complex protocols.

2 Overview of the S3.mp System and Cache Coherence Protocol

The S3.mp implements a *CC-NUMA (Cache-Coherent Non-uniform Memory Access)* multiprocessor system (Fig. 1). A specialized interconnect controller is added to the memory subsystem of a standard workstation [11]. The S3.mp is then built by interconnecting clusters of workstations to form multiprocessor workgroups which efficiently share memory, processors and I/O devices [12].

Each node may have several processors with private caches which are kept coherent via a snooping protocol supported on the *Mbus*. This is the system bus in the Sparcstation-10 and Sparcstation-20 series. Each processing node maintains a fraction of a globally shared address space. When a processor accesses a remote memory location, the memory controller translates the bus transaction into a message that is sent across the network to the remote memory controller.

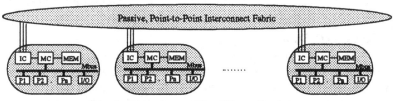

Fig. 1. Overview of the S3.mp System.

2.1 Distributed Directory-based Protocol

In the S3.mp, data consistency is maintained using distributed directories with a limited number of pointers. Pointer overflows are handled by a protocol with a directory organized as singly linked lists. Every memory block is associated with a *home* node which is the node where the physical memory page containing the memory block resides [9]. The home node serializes concurrent requests to the block and maintains a pointer to the head node of the linked list.

Part of the physical memory at each node is allocated as a large *InterNode Cache (INC)*. A copy of every cache block retrieved from remote nodes is loaded into the INC. This copy is maintained in the INC for as long as there is a copy in one of the processor caches at that node. This *inclusion* property is exploited by the directory protocol. In addition to providing support for the protocol, the INC cuts the network traffic. The size of the INC is programmable up to half of the main memory at a node to provide support for data migration. As a result, capacity misses to shared remote data due to the small size of processor caches are served from the much larger INC (up to 32 Mbytes).

We will not model the processor caches. This simplification is justified by two facts. First, the Mbus snooping protocol supporting the first-level coherent caches and the mechanisms for maintaining the inclusion property are well-understood -- whenever the INC receives a write-invalidation from the network, an invalidation is broadcast on the local Mbus to remove all potential copies in the first-level caches. Second, verifying the coherence protocol between the second-level INCs is our primary goal.

2.1.1 Directory and InterNode Cache States

We refer to the "state of the block in the INC" as the "cache state" and the "state of the block in the memory directory" as the "directory state". For every memory block, the home directory can be in one of four stable states: *Resident* (RES; the block only resides in the home node. The first-level processor caches are looked up and/or invalidated by incoming requests from remote nodes), *Shared_Remote* (SR; the memory copy is up to date and consistent with remotely cached read-only copies. The directory contains a pointer to the head node of the linked list formed by nodes sharing the block), and *Exclusive_Remote* (ER; the memory copy is stale and the block is *owned* and modified by one remote node. The home directory contains a pointer to the remote owner of the block).

Every cache block in the INC can be in one of three stable states: *Invalid* (Inv; the cache does not have a valid copy), *Read-Only* (RO; the cache has a clean copy which is potentially shared with other caches), and *Read-Write* (RW; the cache *owns* an exclusive copy of the block). INC tags also provide additional storage space for protocol information; they are used specifically to store '*pointers*' for the linked lists used by the protocol.

2.1.2 Cache Algorithm

The S3.mp protocol is an ownership-based, write-invalidate protocol. A read hit or a write hit to an owner copy do not cause coherence transactions. A cache miss is always serviced by the home node if there is no owner copy in the system. When an owner copy is present, the owner node is requested to provide the data. In the S3.mp, the requesting node always becomes the new head of the linked list.

When a write miss occurs, the linked list is cleared by an *ordinary* invalidation process. Invalidation is initiated by the home node which sends an invalidation to the head node of the linked list. The invalidation then propagates through the list and the last node acknowledges the home node to complete the invalidation process.

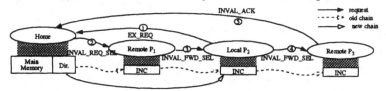

Fig. 2. Procure Ownership.

In the case of requesting for ownership, the home node initiates a *selective* invalidation cycle to remove all other cached copies but the requesting node copy. The transaction is shown in Fig. 2. The local node P_2 sends a request for ownership (EX_REQ) of the block to the home node. When the home node receives the request, it issues a selective invalidation request (INVAL_REQ_SEL) to the head node P_1 of the linked list. This invalidation message carries a null ID, which is not associated with any node. When P_1 receives the invalidation, it invalidates its copy and forwards the invalidation request (INVAL_FWD_SEL) to P_2. When P_2 receives the invalidation, it checks the node ID carried in the message. If it finds a null ID, it replaces the null ID with its own ID before propagating the message. In this case, P_2 will become the new exclusive owner of the block. If the message carries any other ID, P_2 will invalidate its copy and forward the invalidation to the next node in the list. Therefore, if more than one processor tries to write, the first one in the list will be granted ownership. This mechanism deals with the possibility that multiple processors in the list may issue EX_REQ messages concurrently, hence the number of outstanding EX_REQ messages are not known to the home node. After processing the first EX_REQ message, subsequent EX_REQ messages are obsolete and cause only harmless invalidations once they are processed by the home node. In the example, when P_3 receives the invalidation, it invalidates itself and acknowledges the home node.

Replacing a block in the state RW causes a write-back to the home node. If the victimized block is in state RO, a *conditional* invalidation message is used to remove the node containing this block from the sharing list. As shown in Fig. 3, the local node P_2 first sends an *uncache* request (UNC_REQ) to the home node, which subsequently sends a conditional invalidation (INVAL_REQ_COND) to the head node P_1. This invalidation message contains a *null* ID. When P_1 receives the invalidation, it updates its next pointer with the received ID. P_1 then forwards P_2 an invalidation message (INVAL_FWD_COND) which includes its own ID. When P_2 receives the invalidation, it invalidates itself and propagates to P_3 the same message received from P_1. When P_3 receives the invalidation message, it changes its pointer to the ID of P_1. P_3 acknowledges the home, which promotes P_3 to the new head node of the linked list. The conditional invalidation is similar to the selective invalidation, except that it removes only the cache blocks which are waiting to be discarded in one pass through the sharing list and reverses the linked list. Linked list reversal solves the problem of unnecessarily invalidating part of the sharing list while invalidating a single node, which has been considered a disadvantage for protocols utilizing single linked lists [18]. The home node can tell from the acknowledgment when the last outstanding copy is discarded.

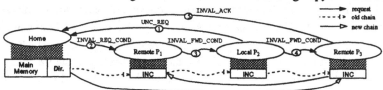

Fig. 3. Replace a Block in Shared State.

A *Recall* operation occurs when a processor at the home node has an access miss and there exists a remote owner. The current owner is asked to relinquish its copy and to return the new data to the home memory. The S3.mp supports a special operation called *Write-All* which allows a node to update an entire 32-byte memory block and forces *all* cached blocks to be invalidated using ordinary write-invalidation process. This operation accelerates bulk data moves or I/O operations.

3 Verification of the Protocol

3.1 Protocol Model

In the formal verification model several abstractions are made in order to construct a model with manageable complexity. Only one block is modeled and no information is kept on transactions to other memory locations [10,13]. We assume that replacements can take place at any time and we model them as processor accesses.

With respect to a single memory block, we abstract the architecture by the model of Fig. 4. The model consists of a home node and multiple processor-cache pairs. The first-level cache is explicitly modeled for the home processor in order to test the *Recall* operation. For remote processors, the first-level caches are not modeled as explained in section 2.1. Each processing node has only one processor which is associated with one *message sending channel (CH!)* and one *message receiving channel (CH?)* to model the message flow between caches and main memory. All message channels are characterized as non-FIFO buffers to simulate the network. Furthermore, we assume that messages are never lost.

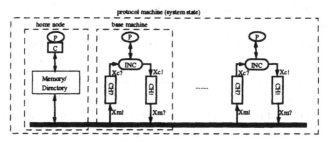

Fig. 4. Verification Model.

Another important abstraction made in the model is to allow only one *ghost* or *unresolved* message (per message type) in any message channel [2,14]. Ghost requests are caused by messages whose meaning is lost between their transmission and their reception because some other message has changed the state of the block. In the cases of uncache and ownership requests, there is a slight possibility in the S3.mp protocol to leave ghost requests in the network. For example, consider the case where processors P_1 and P_2 initially share the block and issue requests for ownership of the block concurrently. Suppose that P_1's request wins the race so that P_2's copy is invalidated. P_2 is therefore forced to re-initiate a request for an '*exclusive copy*' of the block, leaving an out-of-date ghost request for ownership of the block floating in the system. The other source of ghost messages occurs when processors P_1 and P_2 send requests to discard their copies at the same time. If P_1's request arrives at the home node first, both P_1's and P_2's copies are discarded (a conditional invalidation removes *all* entries scheduled to be discarded), while P_2's request remains pending.

Ghost requests for ownership and for block replacement are designed to be harmless to the correctness of the S3.mp protocol. In a correct design, unresolved requests for ownership merely purge the linked list and unresolved uncache requests only reverse the linked lists. However, obsolete requests waste network bandwidth and slow down the system, as well as exacerbating the complexity of the verification. On the other hand, protocols that are free of ghost-messages require more message exchanges and limit the concurrency, which results in lower performance for the common case. Due to the non-FIFO interconnect network, the number of ghost messages is not bounded, which prevents convergence of the verification process. Limiting ghost messages in any given message channel to one per message type does not compromise the validity, but greatly simplify the verification. Because the network is non-FIFO and a ghost message can be indefinitely delayed in the model, processors may receive ghost messages in arbitrary states. An alternative approach to model ghost messages consists in using *pseudo processors* which only act only as *event generators* injecting ghost messages into the verification model unconditionally. In section 4.4, we will explain how the SSM method automatically supports this alternative.

3.2 Modeling of Data Consistency

The S3.mp supports three memory consistency models: *Total Store Order, Partial Store Order,* and *Relaxed Memory Order* [15]. The strict *Sequential Consistency* model [8] is not supported. Rigorously speaking, the S3.mp cache protocol only guarantees the property of consistency: the value of a load access *La* to memory location *a* is the value written by the most recent store *Sa* that was globally performed or by the most recently initiated store by the same processor. The "globally performed order" among stores is defined by the program order and the execution order of synchronization accesses [1]. The programmer can specify the order constraints of memory accesses either implicitly by the choice of memory model or explicitly by using *memory-barrier* (MEMBAR) instructions [17].

To verify the property of consistency, we need to keep track of values of all data copies. Extending the abstraction in [13], the value of any cached copy can be in one of five states: NoData (the cache has no valid copy), GlobalFresh (the cache has an up-to-date copy; value is defined by the latest globally performed write), GlobalFresh_Hold (the cache writes a new value which is not yet visible to other processors), LocalFresh (a valid copy for read; a new value defined by another processor is not yet visible to the cache), and Obsolete (the cache has an out-of-date copy). The memory copy can also be one of the above states.

Consider the case of a write miss handled by the S3.mp protocol in Fig. 5. Initially, processors P_1, P_2, and P_3 share the block. Their copies are globally fresh as well as the memory copy. When processor P_0 experiences a write miss, it sends a request to the home node which provides a data copy to P_0 and initiates an invalidation cycle to purge the linked list. As soon as P_0 receives the data, it performs the pending write and immediately defines a new value, whereas P_2 and P_3 have not yet received the invalidation. As a result, inconsistency may exist among data copies cached by P_0, P_2, and P_3, nevertheless, the system still operates correctly in conformance with the SPARC consistency models by "hiding" the value stored by P_0 from other nodes until the invalidation cycle is complete. In our abstraction, when P_0 performs the write, it defines a new value (GlobalFresh_Hold), but this value is not yet visible to other processors. Processors P_2 and P_3 are still allowed to read their locally fresh (Local-Fresh) copies. Thus, the read accesses by P_2 and P_3 appear ahead of the write access by P_0 in a legal order of execution. As shown in Fig. 5, the MEMBAR instruction orders the store access and memory accesses after the MEMBAR instruction. The MEMBAR instruction stalls processor P_0 until the completions of preceding accesses. When finally receiving an acknowledgment from home, P_0 holds the most recent value, and all other copies in the system (including the home memory copy) become obsolete.

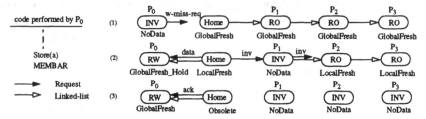

Fig. 5. Trace Values of Data Copies.

From this abstraction, we verify that the S3.mp protocol never allows a processor to read a memory location with an obsolete value.

3.3 Verification Methodologies

3.3.1 State Enumeration

First, we use the Stanford Murφ system [4] to verify the protocol. The Murφ implements a state enumeration method which explores all possible system states. We start the expansion process with an initial state in which all processors are in the Invalid (INV) state, and the home node is in the Reside (RES) state. All possible transitions are exercised, leading to a number of new states. The same process is applied repeatedly for every new state until no new states are generated. (Some transitions may lead back to states which have already been generated.)

To deal with the large state space, the Murφ exploits the symmetry of the system by grouping together states whose representations are permutations of each other [6]. According to the symmetry as shown in Fig. 4, the contexts of processors (represented as base machines) can be swapped without affecting the behavior of the system. Given a protocol model with n processors, the maximum reduction is $n!$. The Murφ also incorporates state encoding to reduce memory usage and hash tables to speed up the search and comparison operations.

We have successfully applied the Murφ to verify completely a system model including one home node and two remote nodes. Many design errors were found quickly in this small model. The trace generation facility provided in the Murφ has proven to be very useful. However, this model is fairly small and a moderately larger model is needed to obtain more reliable verification results.

3.3.2 Symbolic State Model (SSM)

Based on the *symmetry* and *homogeneity* of cache protocols (e.g., all bases machines in Fig. 4 are symmetrically and functionally identical), the SSM method differs from other state enumeration methods in the ways of representing and pruning global states. Since, in all existing protocols, data consistency is enforced by either broadcasting writes to all copies or by invalidating the copies in all other caches, the exact number of data copies in a shared state is irrelevant to protocol correctness. What is critical is whether there exists 0, 1, or multiple copies in a particular state (such as more than one RW copy). As a result, the SSM maps system states to more abstract states which do not keep track of the exact number of copies. The following repetition constructors are used to represent global states (for a detailed justification, see [13-14]).

Definition 1. (Repetition Constructors)

1. **Null** *(0) indicates zero instance.*
2. **Singleton** *(1) indicates one and only one instance.*
3. **Plus** *(+) indicates one or multiple instances.*
4. **Star** *(*) indicates zero, one or multiple instances.*

In a system with an unspecified number of caches, we group base machines (Fig. 4) in the same state into a *state classes* and specify the number of caches in the class by one of the repetition constructors. For example, we can represent all the global states such that "one or multiple caches are in the Invalid state, and zero, one or multiple caches are in the Read-Only state" by $(\text{Inv}^+, \text{RO}^*)$. This representation includes a large set of states, which would otherwise be listed explicitly in a state enumeration method.

Unfortunately, this abstract representation is not sufficient to represent linked lists. Therefore, we use a *hybrid* model in which processors in the linked lists are explicitly maintained and other processors are represented by the abstraction. The formal definition of a global state (called composite state) is defined as follows.

Definition 2. (Composite State) *With respect to a given block, a composite state represents the state of the protocol machine for a system with an arbitrary number of caches. It is constructed over an explicit linked list which contains the states of processors sharing the block. Processors that are not kept in the linked list are grouped and represented by the abstraction of the symbolic state model. Specifically, a composite state has the form*

$$\left(q_{\mathcal{MM}} \to {}_{R_1} C_1{}_{S_1} \to {}_{R_2} C_2{}_{S_2} \to \cdots \to {}_{R_k} C_k{}_{S_k}, \left({}_{R_{k+1}} C_{k+1} {}_{S_{k+1}}^{r_{k+1}}, \ldots, {}_{R_n} C_n{}_{S_n}^{r_n} \right) \right),$$

where C_i is the cache state, R_i and S_i represent the states of the message receiving and sending channel respectively, $r_{i:k+1..n} \in [0, 1, +, *]$ and $q_{\mathcal{MM}}$ is the state of the home memory. The arrows represent the pointers in the linked list.

Repetition constructors are ordered by the possible states they specify. The resulting order is $1 < + < *$; the null instance is ordered with respect to $*$, i.e., $0 < *$. These two orders lead to the definition of *state containment*.

Definition 3. (Containment) *Composite state S_2 contains composite state S_1, or $S_1 \subseteq S_2$, if*

1. *S_1 and S_2 have exactly identical linked list,*

2. *$\forall {}_R C_S^{r_1} \in S_1 \ \exists {}_R C_S^{r_2} \in S_2$ such that ${}_R C_S^{r_1} \leq {}_R C_S^{r_2}$ i.e. $r_1 \leq r_2$ and*

3. *$q_{\mathcal{MM}1} = q_{\mathcal{MM}2}$*

where $r_1, r_2 \in [0, 1, +, *]$.

This definition is an extension of our previous work which deals with snooping and central directory-based protocols [13,14]. We have added the requirement that two global states must have exactly identical linked lists in order to model the distributed directory structure of the S3.mp. As shown before, the SSM abstraction leads to a *monotonous containment relation* such that, if $S_1 \subseteq S_2$, then the family of states represented by S_2 is a superset of the family of states represented by S_1. Augmenting the abstraction with the explicit linked list does not affect this property of monotonicity. Because S_1 and S_2 must have the same linked lists, states evolving from activities of processors in the linked lists of S_1 and S_2 are identical.

Theorem 1. (Monotonicity) *If $S_1 \subseteq S_2$, then for every $\overline{S}_1$ reachable from S_1 there exists $\overline{S}_2$ reachable from S_2 such that $\overline{S}_1 \subseteq \overline{S}_2$.*

As the expansion process progresses, the SSM only keeps composite states which are not contained by any other state. At the end of the expansion process, the state space is partitioned into several families of states (which may be overlapping) represented by *essential* states.

Definition 4. (Essential State) *Composite state S is essential if and only if there does not exist a composite state $\overline{S}$ such that $S \subseteq \overline{S}$.*

Based on the monotonicity property of the SSM abstraction, we run the verification incrementally. The verification is started by limiting the maximum number of processors allowed to actively share the block to two (the length of the linked list). This number is then increased by one in each consecutive run. The set of essential states reported at the end of the current run is used as the set of initial states for the next run in order to quickly accumulate the state information. As the model size grows, the state space expands. We therefore run the verification until we run out of memory to store the state information.

4 Verification Results

Because of the high complexity of the S3.mp protocol, we have used a technique called *case-splitting* to avoid dealing with the entire protocol at one time. We have identified and isolated events that can be verified separately. For instance, the reason for modeling the first-level cache of the home processor is to test the *Recall* operation. The *Recall* operation occurs when an access misses in the cache of the home node while an exclusive copy exists in a remote node. To test *Recall* operation, we first run a small model of three processors with the full set of operations; then the home processor cache and the accesses from the home processor are removed in larger models. This simplification is justified because the small model covers the case in which a remote owner exists; regardless of the model size, only one owner is allowed in the system, and concurrent transactions are serialized by the home directory. When the home processor initiates a *Recall* transaction, there must exist only one owner copy and this transaction is guaranteed to complete before the next coherence transaction is executed by the home directory. This makes it possible for coherence transactions initiated by home processors to be checked in small models and eliminated from larger model so that the doubling of the size of the state space is avoided.

The *Write-All* access can be dropped in larger models for the same reason, i.e. a *Write-All* access essentially results in an ordinary write-invalidation which clears the sharing list. Since the home directory is locked during the propagation of invalidations, the invalidation caused by a *Write-All* request is equivalent to a normal write-invalidation operation. Therefore, in larger models, we do not need to repetitively model the *Write-All* operation.

4.1 Efficiency of the SSM Method

All the verifications were ran on a Sun4/690 system with 500Mb of physical memory. The performance of the verifications for all model sizes from 2 to 5 processing nodes is listed in Table 1. As shown in the table, the verification process is memory-intensive, partly because the SSM state information is not encoded in the SSM and, since the state classes are dynamically created and discarded, a large amount of memory is needed to maintain the complete representation of a global state in the SSM. The verification time increases rapidly with the number of nodes in the sharing list. Because we use the results generated in a current run as the set of starting states for the next run, the verification time accumulates. Most of the time is wasted for generating, searching and comparing states which have been produced. In fact, the efficiency of the SSM method depends on how fast the final set of essential states are generated. Unfortunately we do not have a very good heuristic to this end. The results listed in Table 1 are obtained by using a a *depth-first* expansion scheme. Namely, the next expansion path is explored only when the current expansion path is exhausted.

TABLE 1 : The Verification Results by Using the SSM Method.

Sharing Degree	Verification Time	Memory (Mb)
2	11.33	0.03
3	7,419.57	28.32
4	326,413.80	352.46
5	402,638.63[a]	500

a. This run is not fully completed.

As expected, the hybrid SSM method does not generally avoid the state explosion problem because processors sharing a memory block are explicitly tracked.

4.2 Data Inconsistency Caused by Stale Write-Backs

Although requests in the S3.mp protocol are always acknowledged, messages are *context sensitive*. Two nodes may concurrently send two independent request messages for the same memory location, such that each request is regarded as the acknowledgment by the recipient. For example, the home node may issue a *Recall* request while at the same time the remote owner sends a *write-back* request to the home node. No additional messages are generated to complete this exchange. The advantage of context sensitive semantics is lower latency and less traffic in some cases, but the design and verification of the protocol are more complex.

An error of data inconsistency caused by a stale *write-back* is shown in Fig. 6. Initially cache P_0 has a dirty copy of the block, and performs a write-back (WB_REQ) to the home node. In order to guarantee that the memory receives the block safely, cache P_0 keeps a valid copy of the block until it receives an acknowledgment. Meanwhile, cache P_1 sends a request (CRE_REQ) for an exclusive copy to the home node. Cache P_0 then processes the *data-forward-request* (D_FWD_E_REQ) from home, sends the data to P_1, and continues, ignoring the acknowledgment from the home node. P_1 then performs its write and victimizes the block after some unrelated misses. As shown in Fig. 6, a race condition exists between the two write-back requests. If the write-back from P_1 wins the race, the stale write-back from P_0 overwrites the values updated by P_1. Note that, in this example, all state transitions are permissible.

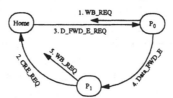

Fig. 6. Data Inconsistency Caused by Stale Write-Back.

If we do not keep track of the values of the data copies, this error goes undetected because the system correctly allows only one exclusive owner copy at any time. In our abstraction, when P_1 performs its write, it defines a globally fresh copy as compared to the obsolete copy carried by P_0's write-back message. This error is easily detected.

4.3 Data Inconsistency Found in a Larger Model

A fairly complex error which only appears when the verification model includes more than three processors was found and the sequence of events leading to this error shown in Fig. 7 is as follows:

1. Initially processor P_0 writes back its exclusive copy (WB_REQ) to the home node. Also, processor P_1 and P_2 request shared copies (CR_REQ). P_0 keeps a valid copy of the block until it receives an acknowledgment from the home node.
2. The home node receives the request for a shared copy from P_1. The home node establishes a new link pointing to P_1 and issues a data-forward request (D_FWD_REQ) to the current owner P_0. Processor P_1 is considered to be the new head of the list.
3. The data-forward-request from the home node, is interpreted by P_0 as an acknowledgment. P_0 forwards its copy to P_1 (by DATA_FWD_E) and invalidates its copy. When the home node receives the write-back from P_0, it updates the memory copy and releases the directory entry locked by the transaction from P_1. The directory changes to the stable state SR.
4. Home receives the request for shared copy from P_2. The home memory copy is supplied to P_2, which becomes the new head of the list. P_1 is now the second node in the list. P_1, meanwhile, is still waiting for the copy forwarded by P_0.
5. Home receives a harmless ghost request for replacement of a read-only copy (UNC_REQ, section 3.1). This request merely reverses the linked list in a correct protocol. When P_1 receives the conditional invalidation passed by P_2, P_1 needs to keep its pointer to P_2 to set up the list correctly.

6. When P_1 receives the forwarded exclusive data from P_0, P_1 nullifies its pointer since it thinks that it has the only copy. This causes the chain to be broken and P_2 is left off the list. When other processors write to the block, P_2's copy is not properly invalidated.

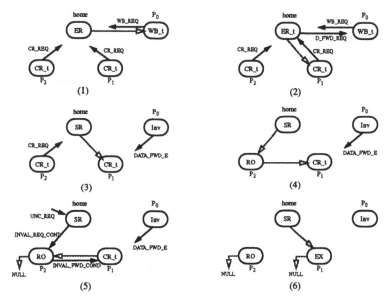

Fig. 7. Data Inconsistency due to a Broken Chain.

This error only occurs when at least four processors are involved. It was not detected in the model with two or three processors.

4.4 Generation of Events in the SSM

It should be noted that the state enumeration method and the hybrid SSM abstraction do not deal with the extreme case that the sharing list is infinitely long. To some extent, the SSM method loses some of its advantages over other approaches of verifying cache coherence protocols for arbitrary number of processors [13]. Nevertheless, we still exploit the other advantages provided by the symbolic state model in spite of this constraint.

Given a limited amount of memory and computation time, the advantage of using the SSM model versus a state enumeration method is that more test sequences are generated than in the state enumeration method which has a fixed number of processors. The state enumeration method only explores the interactions between the set of processors included in the model. The hybrid SSM model generates additional sequences of memory accesses initiated by processors out of the linked lists. When a processor is retired from the linked list, it moves to the part of the state representation abstracted by repetition constructors and interacts with the rest of the system for the rest of the expansion process.

Consider the scenario shown in Fig. 8. In S_0, processors P_0, P_1 and P_2 initially share the block and issue requests (EX_REQ) for ownership of the block at the same time. Other processors have no copies and are grouped in the abstracted part of the representation. In the example, some processors are in the INV state and some processors are in the CRE_t transient state with issued requests for the owner copy of the block in their sending channels. In accordance to the protocol, when P_2's request wins the race, it obtains an exclusive copy. P_0 and P_1 are retired from the sharing list and are forced to regenerate requests (CRE_REQ) for owner copies. The states of P_0 and P_1 are combined into a new class in the abstraction, this new class evolves with the state expansion and never vanishes as shown in the transition from S_2 to S_3. As a result, processors grouped in the abstracted part of the representation act as *event generators* which constantly inject new memory transactions into the system. The original requests (EX_REQ) issued by P_0 and P_1 are ghost messages in S_2 and S_3.

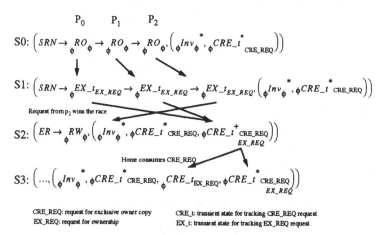

Fig. 8. State Expansion and Event Generation in the Hybrid SSM Method.

The SSM method can be simplified even more by dropping the plus (+) constructor. The plus constructor was introduced to track the existence of a data copy. For the S3.mp protocol, we do not have to be concerned about the exact number of processors in a particular state class since deterministic information such as the processors sharing the same memory block is maintained in the linked lists. The plus constructor can therefore be dropped without affecting the validity of the SSM method.

5 Conclusion

We have presented the results of verifying the S3.mp cache coherence protocol. The difficulty in verifying a distributed directory protocol is to abstract the linked lists efficiently, while correctly preserving properties that need to be checked. Since correct maintenance of the linked lists is orthogonal to maintaining data consistency, a possible solution is to isolate the problem of verifying the integrities of the linked lists from the problem of verifying data coherence. We think that the techniques applied to the S3.mp cache coherence protocols are applicable to other linked-list based cache coherence protocols, for example the SCI [7].

We have also demonstrated how to formulate the condition of data consistency in the context of relaxed memory consistency models. The approach in this paper only verifies the property of consistency, for which the state of a single memory block must be tracked. A more difficult problem is the verification of correct memory ordering of all memory accesses according to the memory consistency model. No formal method has been conceived as of today to tackle this problem. Even if a formal framework is found, the states and the values of multiple memory locations would have to be tracked, and this requirement would no doubt exacerbate the state space explosion problem.

References

[1]   Adve, S.V. and Hill, M.D., "Weak Ordering--A New Definition", *Proc. of the 17th Int'l Symposium on Computer Architecture*, May 1990, pp.2-14.

[2]   Archibald, J., "The Cache Coherence Problem in Shared-Memory Multiprocessors", Ph.D Dissertation, University of Washington, Feb. 1987.

[3]   Collier, W.W., Reasoning About Parallel Architectures, Prentice Hall, Englewood Cliffs, New Jersey.

[4]   Dill, D.L., Drexler, A.J., Hu, A.J. and Yang, C.H., "Protocol Verification as a Hardware Design Aid", *Int'l Conf. on Computer Design: VLSI in Computers and Processors*, pp. 522-525, Oct. 1992.

[5]   Holzmann, G.J., "Algorithms for Automated Protocol Verification", *AT\&T Technical Journal*, Jan./Feb. 1990.

[6]   Ip, C.N. and Dill, D.L., "Better Verification Through Symmetry", *Proc. 11th Int'l Symp. on Computer Hardwae Description Languages and Their Applications*, pp. 87-100, Apr. 1993.

[7]   James et al., "Scalable Coherent Interface", *IEEE Computer*, June 90, Vol 23, No. 6, pp 71-82.

[8]   Lamport, L., "How to Make a Multiprocessor Computer that Correctly Executes Multiprocess Programs", *IEEE Trans. on Computers*, Vol. C-28, No.9, Sept. 1979, pp.690-691.

[9]   Lenosky, D., *et al.*, "The Directory-Based Cache Coherence Protocol for the DASH Multiprocessor", *Proc. of the 17th Int'l Symposium on Computer Architecture*, June 1990, pp. 148-159.

[10]   McMillan, K.L. and Schwalbe, J., "Formal Verification of the Gigamax Cache Consistency Protocol", *Proc. of the ISSM Int'l Conf. on Parallel and Distributed Computing*, Oct. 1991.

[11]   Nowaztyk, A. and Parkin, M., "The S3.mp Interconnection System and TIC Chip", Hot *Interconnects* 1993.

[12]   Nowatzyk, A., Aybay, G., Browne, M., Kelly, E., Parkin, M., Radke, B. and Vishin, S., "The S3.mp Scalable Shared Memory Multiprocessor", *HICCS*, 1994.

[13]   Pong, F. and Dubois, M., "The Verification of Cache Coherence Protocols", *Proc. of the 5th Annual Symp. on Parallel Algorithm and Architecture*, pp.11-20, June 1993.

[14]   Pong, F. and Dubois, M., "Formal Verification of Complex Coherence Protocols Using Symbolic State Models", *Technical Report CENG-94-01, University of Southern California.*

[15]   Sindhu, P.S., Frailong, J-M. and Cekleov, M., "Formal Specification of Memory Models", In Dubois M. and Thakkar, S., Editors. *Scalable Shared Memory Multiprocessors.* Kluwer, Norwell, MA, 1992.

[16]   Stenström, P., "A Survey of Cache Coherence Schemes for Multiprocessors", *IEEE Computer*, Vol. 23, No. 6, pp. 12-24, June 1990.

[17]   The SPARC Architecture Manual, Version 9, Prentice Hall.

[18]   Thapar, M. and Delagi, B., "Stanford Distributed-Directory Protocol", *IEEE Computer*, June 1990, pp. 78-80.

Efficient Software Data Prefetching for a Loop with Large Arrays *

Se-Jin Hwang and Myong-Soon Park

Department of Computer Science
Korea University
Seoul, Korea, 136-701
{hsj,myongsp}@cslab1.korea.ac.kr

Abstract. In this paper, we propose a software data prefetching mechanism to cope with following two unfavorable phenomenons from large arrays. One is the failure of the reuse, and the other is the effect of the presence of unnecessary prefetching instructions. Also, we realized the proposed mechanism into a preprocessor,*LOOP*.

1   Introduction

The memory latency problem by cache miss is very serious in superscalar microprocessor that allows the simultaneous issuing of multiple instructions[2]. Therefore, techniques to reduce or tolerate large memory latency become essential for achieving high processor utilization. As one of the techniques to mitigate the large memory latency, the researches on data prefetching have been done for a few years[1, 2, 3, 4].

Prefetching transaction can be triggered either by a dedicated instruction[1, 4] or by a hardware auto-detection[3]. We call the former as software data prefetching, and the latter hardware data prefetching. The major drawback of software data prefetching is extra processor cycles to execute prefetching instructions inserted by a compiler[4]. Henceforth, the effectiveness of a software scheme is sensitive to how well the compiler inserts these instructions.

Mowry *et al* proposed a selective prefetching mechanism[4] which inserts prefetching instructions for array elements likely to show cache miss. The reuse analysis by the compiler makes it possible that we should insert only necessary prefetching instructions. In this mechanism, it is very crucial that the compiler should insert *necessary prefetching instructions* and transform a loop to exploit *data reuse*. However, these two items can be threatend by large arrays.

Unless a cache could hold one row of array accessed non-sequentially, some elements might be displaced from a cache[5]. Such fact urges us to load again data that used to be in the cache.

In addition, larger the size of an array becomes, more the number of prefetch instructions must be executed. When the array has LCD^2, same elements of the

---

* This paper was supported (in part) by NON DIRECTED RESEARCH FUND, Korea Research Foundation

^{2} We abbreviate loop carried dependency to 'LCD' in the rest of this paper.

array may be used at different loop iterations. Such fact may turn out many prefetching instructions to be unnecessary, if they were inserted uncarefully. To make matters worse, provided that the array were large, the amount of wasted cycles to execute the unnecessary prefetching instructions could be non-negligible.

In this paper, we propose software data prefetching mechanism which considers LCD, and the size of a cache along with the number of data that will be referenced. The proposed mechanism has two philosophies to cope with the failure of the data reuse: One is to reuse it desparately, and the other to give it up. Also, in order to eliminate unnecessary prefetching instructions for an array with LCD, it apropriately transforms a loop based on an accurate analysis.

The organization of the rest of this paper is as follows. First, section 2 discribes the motivation of this work. Section 3 proposes software data prefetching mechanism to mitigate the problem indicated in section 2. Section 4 describes the simulation method to measure the execution cycles of loops transformed by LOOP[6]. LOOP is a preprocessor that transforms a loop in order to insert prefetching instructions by using proposed scheme. We finally conclude in section 5.

2 Motivation

In this section, we address the types of performance degradation by large arrays in a loop.

2.1 The failure of data reuse by large arrays

When the non-sequentially accessed array is so large that a cache cannot hold one row of the array, some element could be displaced before reuse[5]. Therefore, it is necessary that we should reload data that used to be in the cache.

To estimate how successfully array elements can be reused as the array size increases, we transformed VPENTA[3] using the selective prefetching mechanism[4]. VPENTA is a nested loop with depth 2, and has eight array variables within a body. Furthermore, since all arrays in VPENTA are accessed non-sequentially, it is heavily sensitive to the size of the arrays. When we applied such selective mechanism into VPENTA, we assumed that the size of cache line is twice as much as that of one array element. Two innermost loops are generated after transforming VPENTA with the selective mechanism. The first one includes prefetching instructions, but the second does not, in order to use elements that have been brought into a cache during the execution of the first innermost loop.

We estimated the hit ratio of accessing array Y in the second innermost loop in VPENTA varying the size of the array. Graphs in Figure 1 present how well the array Y can be reused with increasing the size of it. In general, the graph for the size of 64×64 shows higher hit ratio than that for the size of 256×256.

It indicates that the larger the size of array is, the fewer the possiblity of reusing data accessed non-sequentially is. This phenomenon means that more

---

[3] VPENTA is a benchmark loop included in NAS kernels

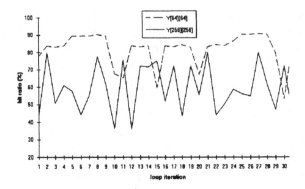

Fig. 1. Degree of reusability of array Y in VPENTA

reloading costs must be paid as the number of accessed array elements is increased.

To remove such overhead, our proposed mechanism examines whether array elements will be held in a cache or not. Unless we can reuse them in the cache, it applies indiscriminate prefetching mechanism[1] proposed by Porterfield. Otherwise, we applies the selective mechanism.

2.2 The negative effect of large arrays with LCD

Unnecessary prefetching instructions for an array with LCD might be easily inserted into a loop. Unfortunately, when the array is large, the total waste cycles to execute such instructions comes to be considerable. Therefore, it is essential that we consider prudently LCD to achieve efficient software data prefetching.

To illustrate how many prefetching instructions are turned out to be unnecessary by LCD, we present Figure 2. When we insert the prefetching instruction, we assume that the size of cache block is twice as much as that of an element of the array A.

```
for(i=0;i < 100;i++){
    prefetch(&(A[i]));
    A[i + 1] = A[i] + ...;
}
```
(a) a prefetching instruction for A[i] is inserted

```
for(i=0;i<100;i++){
    prefetch(&(A[i + 1]));
    A[i + 1] = A[i] + ...;
}
```
(b) a prefetching instruction for A[i + 1] is inserted

Fig. 2. Two cases of a loop which includes a prefetching instruction for an array A with LCD

Under this assumption, we can presume that the percentage of executed unnecessary prefetching instructions will be 99% at the execution of the loop in

Figure 2(a). All executed prefetching instructions, except for the first, will be unnecessary, since the object of the prefetching has been already cached before one iteration.

In case the argument of the prefetching instruction is substituted with '&($A[i+1]$)' as in Figure 2(b), the percentage of unnecessary prefetching instructions comes to be about 50% with the same presumption described above. At every two iterations, the inserted prefetching instruction tries to access array element which has been already cached in.

From Figure 2, we can know that LCD is should be taken into account on inserting prefetchinging instructions. Our proposed mechanism transforms properly a loop with consideration of LCD of an array. To avoid inserting unnecessary prefetching instructions, it peels as well as unrolls the loop.

3 Proposed Software Data Prefetching

In this section, we propose a software data prefetching mechanism to cope with the problems indicated in section 2. First, in subsection 3.1, we describes memory reference pattern of an array within a loop. From subsection 3.2 to 3.4, we propose loop transformation algorithms to insert efficiently prefetching instructions into the loop, according to the memory reference pattern. We put these algorithms all together to be applicable to general nested loop in subsection 3.5.

3.1 Memory reference pattern

We denote the k-th loop nest in nested loop by L_k ($1 \leq k \leq n$, n : the depth of nested loop). As the level of a loop is proceeded one by one from the innermost to the outermost, we assume that the value of k increases by one. I_k also refers to the loop control variable of the L_k. We use $Loc(I_k)$ as a notation to express the corresponding position of loop control variable I_k into subscripts of an array. P^a_k stands for the memory reference pattern that comes out at running an iteration of L_k. Since memory reference pattern is intrinsically the sequence of repeated cache hit and miss, we can describe P_k as ($M^a H^b$), here, M and H mean cache miss and hit respectively. a and b refers to the number of repetition of cache miss and hit respectively. F_k also represents the upper bound of L_k.

Memory reference pattern can be classified by comparing $Loc(I_k)$ with $Loc(I_{k-1})$ of all array variables into a loop body : sequential, non-sequential, fixed-positional reference patterns. As the corresponding position of I_k into array subscripts is moving from the right to the left, we assume that $Loc(I_k)$ is increasing by one. In case that I_k corresponds to no position of the array subscripts, $Loc(I_k)$ is 0. We describe the features of memory reference patterns, and the corresponding result of comparing $Loc(I_k)$ with $Loc(I_{k-1})$ as follows.

- Sequential memory reference pattern
  The adjacent array elements can be reused only a few iterations later.

$$Loc(I_1) = 1 \, , \, (k = 1) \tag{1}$$

$$Loc(I_k) \, > \, Loc(I_{k-1}) \, , \, (k > 1) \tag{2}$$

– Non-sequential memory reference pattern
  The adjacent array elements can be reused after one row of the array was entirely accessed.

$$Loc(I_1) \neq 1 \ , \ (k = 1) \tag{3}$$

$$Loc(I_k) < Loc(I_{k-1}) \ , \ (k > 1) \tag{4}$$

– Fixed-positional memory reference pattern
  This array element comes to be reused, after the first compulsory miss.

$$Loc(I_k) = 0 \tag{5}$$

From subsection 3.2 to 3.4, three loop transformation algorithms are introduced. They insert efficiently prefetching instructions into a loop, according to the correspoding memory reference pattern.

3.2 Loop transformation algorithm for sequential reference pattern

When we access an array sequentially in a loop, we come to reference the adjacent elements in a memory. Therefore, more than one cache hit will occur, after one cache miss. It is the sequential reference pattern. This sequence will be repeated during our references to this array. $P^a{}_k$, sequential access pattern of an array a can be represented at k-th loop nest as follows.

$$P^a{}_1 = (\ M \ H^v \ )^{F_1/(v+1)} \ , \ (k = 1) \tag{6}$$

$$P^a{}_k = (P^a{}_{k-1})^{F_k/(v+1)} \ , \ (k > 1) \tag{7}$$

Above, v can be calculated by

$$v = \frac{array\ element\ size}{cache\ line\ size} - 1. \tag{8}$$

Since the memory reference pattern of the lower level is preserved as shown in the above expression (7), transformation algorithm only have to work at the innermost loop level.

When an array has LCD, many references to the array exist within a loop body. Therefore, we can express the memory reference pattern of this array at k-th loop nest as $P^{a_n}{}_k, (n > 0)$. Here, n means the number of memory references which access the array a within a loop body. Sequential reference pattern of the array a with LCD can be expressed like the following.

$$P^{a_n}{}_k = (\ P^a{}_k \ H^x \ ) \ , \ (x \geq 0) \tag{9}$$

We can interpret the expression (9) that a reference to an array with LCD tends to access an array without LCD for a while, but, it always comes to show cache hit after the particular loop iteration. From such particular loop iteration, this reference uses array elements which have been already in the cache by other references with larger subscript. The reference with largest subscript accesses the array as if it had no LCD. Therefore, the value of x in expression (9) of such reference is 0.

Based on expression (6),(7) and (9), we present an algorithm for an array with sequential reference pattern in Figure 3.

```
if( LCD appears ){
    unrolling = the smallest x in expression (9).
    /* unrolling indicates how many iterations will be peeled. */
    peel iterations as much unrolling.
}
if( k = 1 ){
    /* k indicates the level of a nested loop */

    unroll the k-th loop v + 1 times.
    insert prefetching instructions in the body of unrolled loop.
    split unrolled loop.
    /* we split the loop into prologue, body
    and epilogue loops, to secure enough prefetch distance. */
}
```

Fig. 3. Loop transformation algorithm for an array with sequential reference pattern

3.3 Loop transformation algorithm for non-sequential reference pattern

Non-sequential reference pattern can be represented as follows.

$$P^a{}_1 = (M^{F_1} \ H^{F_1 \times v}) \ , \ (k = 1) \tag{10}$$

$$P^a{}_k = ((P^a{}_{k-1}\{M\})^{F_k} \ (P^a{}_{k-1}\{H\})^{F_k \times v}) \ , \ (k > 1) \tag{11}$$

Here, $P^a{}_{k-1}\{M\}$ and $P^a{}_{k-1}\{H\}$ represent a sequence of cache hit and a sequence of cache miss of memory reference pattern at L_{k-1} respectively. v can be calculated using expression (8). As we can see from the expression (11), the sequences of cache hit and miss shown at the execution of the $(k-1)$th loop are preserved at k-th loop nest. Therefore, we only have to unroll the k-th loop v times. After unrolling, our algorithm for this pattern inserts prefetching instructions only into the first $(k-1)$th loop. If the number of array elements that are referenced during the excution of k-th loop is so large that the cache cannot hold all referenced elements, some of these will conflict with old cached ones. Such conflicts among array elements prevent us from analyzing which elements can be reused. By examining the expression (12), we can determine whether such conflicts will occur or not.

$$F_k \times na \geq CS \times 2. \tag{12}$$

Here, na means the number of array elements that will be referenced, and CS the cache size. If the expression (12) is satisfied, memory reference pattern will be the followings.

$$P^a{}_1 = (M^{F_1}) \ , \ (k = 1) \tag{13}$$

$$P^a{}_k = P^a{}_{k-1}{}^{F_k} \ , \ (k > 1) \tag{14}$$

We present the loop transformation algorithm for non-sequential reference pattern in Figure 4. It considers the number of array elements that will be referenced, and meet with the case that we can hardly exploit the reuse property of the cache. The algorithm in Figure 4 has two opposite philosophies: one is to ignore the reuse property, and the other to exploit it.

```
if( we can hardly reuse array elements in a cache ){
    /* the condition can be examined using expression (12) */
    inserts prefetching instructions for all arrays accessed at the k-th loop nest.
    /* Here, we ignore the reuse property in the cache,
    and, prefetch array elements indiscriminately */
}else{
    unrolls the body of k-th loop nest.
    inserts prefetching instructions only the first (k − 1)-th loop.
    /* Here, we unroll the loop based on the pattern
    of expressions (10),(11) to exploit reuse property */
}
```

Fig. 4. Loop transformation algorithm for an array with non-sequential reference pattern

3.4 Loop transformation algorithm for fixed-positional reference pattern

If an array does not include I_k as a subscript, this will be referenced like a single variable at the execution of k-th loop. This array is not affected by the decrement or increment of the value of the I_k. So, all accesses to this element will show cache hit continuously after one cache miss at the first time. We refer to such reference pattern as fixed-positional reference pattern. It can be represented as follows.

$$P^a{}_1 = (M \ H^{F_1-1}) , (k = 1) \tag{15}$$
$$P^a{}_k = (P^a{}_{k-1} \ H^{F_k-1}) , (k > 1) \tag{16}$$

Since only one cache miss is shown in expression (15), peeling one iteration is enough measure to optimize the number of prefetching instructions. We express it as an algorithm in Figure 5.

3.5 Generalized Algorithm

Algorithms from Figure 3 to Figure 5 can be applicable to only one loop level, and to only one memory reference pattern. It is practically essential that we should

peel the body of the k-th loop.
if($k = 1$) inserts prefetching instructions above the loop.

Fig. 5. Loop transformation algorithm for an array with fixed-positional reference pattern

$k \leftarrow 1$. /* the innermost loop level */
while($k \leq$ the outermost loop level)
    $P_s \leftarrow$ memory reference patterns shown at level k.
    /* P_s : temporary buffer holding reference patterns. */
    if(P_s includes sequential memory reference pattern)
        apply the algorithm in Figure 3.
    if(P_s includes non-sequential memory reference pattern)
        apply the algorithm in Figure 4.
    if(P_s includes fixed-positional memory reference pattern)
        apply the algorithm in Figure 5.
    $k \leftarrow k + 1$. /* navigates to the upper loop nest */
}

Fig. 6. Generalized loop transformation algorithm

make these algortihms cooperate one another to transform a general nested loop and to insert prefetching instructions into it.

Therefore, we generalize three algorithms to insert prefetching instructions efficiently into a nested loop. Figure 6 shows a generalized loop transformation algorithm. It navigates every loop nests from the innermost to the outermost. It identifies memory reference patterns of all arrays at each loop nest, and then transforms a loop using a corresponding algorithm.

4 Simulation

In this section, we describe a simualtion method in order to measure the execution cycles of loops transformed by $LOOP$[6]. We also present our simulation results.

4.1 Environments

We defined our own $mutated - C$ language[6]. Our $mutated - C$ includes only for, if and $assignment$ statements.

The preprocessor, $LOOP$, can understand only such restricted specifications of $mutated - C$. $LOOP$ transforms 'for' statements in $mutated - C$, and transforms it with prefetching instructions. The prefetching instructions inserted into the loop like an external function call, for example, '$prefetch(\&(A[i][j]));$'. The argument of this function is the address of one array element. The loop produced from the preprocessor takes a form of the program written in an original C language.

We obtain machine codes of the transformed loop using *dlxcc*, the compiler in DLX simulator. After compilation with *dlxcc*, the prefetching instructions inserted by *LOOP* are changed into DLX machine code, *jal*. However, since DLX simulator cannot support our requests, such as a prefetching request buffer, we made our own simulator using C.

To execute the DLX machine codes in our simulator, it is necessary that we should change every DLX machine codes into functions defined in our simulator. However, it was so laborious and monotonous work that we made a converter called *DLX2C*[6] that performs the dirty work only in a few seconds.

DLX2C produces a C program that describes the DLX machine instructions. After linking it with our simulator, we can obtain an executable file. This executable file keeps track of the machine codes of the loop transformed by *LOOP*, and calculates execution cycle, processor idle cycle etc. To quantify the execution cycle, we assume that the cycle time spent at the execution stage of individual instructions of DLX as Table 1.

Table 1. Assumed instruction cycle

DLX instructions	cycles
add addi addui sub subi movfp2i movi2fp lhi sll jal j	*1*
sleu slt sle sgtu sge sgt bnez beqz	*2*
multf divf	*3*

Benchmarks evaluated in this paper are a part of Lawrence Livermore Loop and VPENTA. LLLs of number 1, 7, 9, 11, 18 and 21 are used. LLL 1, 7, 11, 18 loop have arrays with sequential reference pattern. LLL 9 has only one array variable with non-sequential reference pattern. We set the size of arrays in these loops to be 1000.

All arrays accessed in VPENTA have only the non-sequential reference pattern, whereas, all arrays in LLL 21 have three kinds of reference pattern. On simulating VPENTA, we vary the size of array variables in it to 64×64, 128×128, 256×256 and 512×512. We also vary the total iteration number of LLL 21 to the followings: $20 \times 20 \times 100$, $20 \times 20 \times 500$, $20 \times 20 \times 1000$, and $20 \times 20 \times 2000$. Since cache pollution phenomenon breaks out seriously in VPENTA, we increase the size of array variables by adding prime number to avoid it intentionally[4].

A secondary cache miss is assumed to be delayed by as much as 30 cycles, when it tries to access memory, and a primary cache miss is assumed to spend 13 cycles. To handle prefetching, the hardware has a prefetch issue buffer, which can hold up to 16 prefetching requests.

Processor is assumed to have an on-chip primary data cache of 2K bytes, and a secondary cache of 64K bytes. Both caches are direct-mapped and use 8 bytes blocks. The size of array elements that is mentioned in this paper is assumed to be 4 bytes. The primary cache is operated by write-through manner, and the secondary cache by write-back manner.

4.2 Evaluation

In each bar of all graphs from Figure 7 to 10, the bottom section is the amount of time spent executing instructions, and the upper section is the processor idle time due to memory access. We use the following characters to denote the prefetching method applied to experimented loops: I, S, P. Each of these represents indiscriminate prefetching method, selective prefetching method and proposed one repectively. Character N denote a loop which is not reorganized.

Figure 7 presents the performances of LLL1, LLL 7, LLL 9, LLL 11 and LLL 18. Since LLL 18 is a nested loop with depth 2, we can see rather good performance by avoiding the insertion of unnecessary prefetching instructions for arrays with LCD.

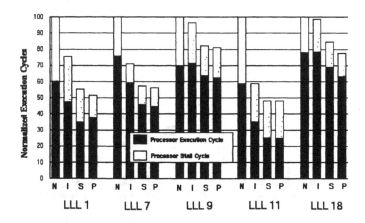

Fig. 7. Normalized execution cycles of simulated loops

Figure 8 shows the simulation results of LLL 21, the loop of matrix multiplication. Only three arrays are accessed within the body of LLL 21. We applied four prefetching methods to LLL 21 with different number of iterations. From the rightmost to the leftmost of each title, each number represents a loop bounds of the each loop nest from the innermost to the outermost. Cache can hold all arrays accessed within a loop body when the loop bounds of the innermost loop is 100. Meanwhile, as the iterations of the innermost loop is larger and larger, proposed method shows somewhat better performance than the selective method.

Figure 9 shows the simulation results of VPENTA. Since VPENTA is composed of only eight arrays with non-sequential memory reference pattern, heavy conflict comes to appear at run time. Henceforth, in Figure 9, we can find it that only a few cycles are saved with increasing of the iteration of innermost loop. Leftmost four graphs in Figure 9 is the results of simulations in case that array variables in VPENTA has 64 × 64 elements. Since such small number of array elements can be loaded in cache without conflict,

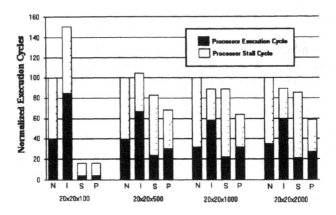

Fig. 8. Normalized execution cycles of LLL 21

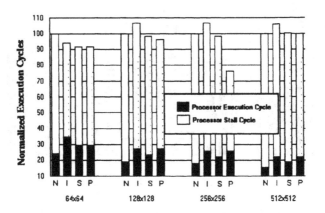

Fig. 9. Normalized execution cycles of VPENTA

Figure 10 shows a percentage of unnecessary prefetching instructions. Our proposed algorithm is more wasteful than the selective one. However, as the iteration of loop is larger and larger, the percentage of unnecessary prefetching instructions are getting smaller and smaller.

5 Conclusion

In this paper, we propose a software data prefetching mechanism to mitigate the problem which can occur by large array. To attack the problem of the failure of reusng data which is accessed non-sequentially, proposed algorithm has two opposite tactics: downright ignorance of it[1] and exhaustive consideration[4]. Additionally, our mechanism can successfully avoid inserting unnecessary prefetching instructions.

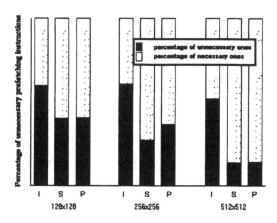

Fig. 10. Percentage of unnecessary prefetching instructions (VPENTA)

We realize our proposed algorithm into a preprocessor, *LOOP*[6]. After simulation using it, we can see that our method shows better performance than previous prefetching methods.

In the future, we will consider the type of the reference to an array, *load* or *store*. Relying on these types, the prefetched elements will be appropriately kept within a hardware which we plan to design and add. This extra hardware holds some prefetched array elements, and manages it in cooperation with a secondary cache. The preprocessor, *LOOP*, should transform a loop in the consideration of this hardware.

References

1. D. Callahan, K. Kennedy and A. Porterfield: Software prefetching. Proc. 5th ASPLOS. (1991) 40-52
2. Chen, T. F.: Data Prefetching for High-Performance Processors. TR 93-07-01, Dept. of Computer Science and Engineering, University of Washington, (1993)
3. Fu, J. W. C. and Patel, J. H.: Data Prefetching in Multiprocessor Vector Memories, Proc. 18th ISCA, (1991) 54-63
4. Mowry, T., Lam, M. S. and Gupta, A.: Design and evaluation of a compiler algorithm for prefetching. Proc. 5th ASPLOS. (1992) 62-73
5. M. E. Wolf and M. S. Lam: A Data Locality Optimizing Algorithm. Proc. SIGPLAN '91 PLDI (1991) 30-44
6. Se-Jin Hwang and Myong-Soon Park: Loop Reorganizing Algorithm for Data Prefetching. TR KUCS-CS-94-004, Korea University, (1994) (in Korean)

Loop Parallelization

Generation of Synchronous Code for Automatic Parallelization of while Loops

Martin Griebl[1] and Jean-François Collard[2]

[1] Universität Passau, FMI, Innstraße 33, D-94032 Passau, Germany.
`Martin.Griebl@fmi.uni-passau.de`
[2] ENS Lyon, LIP, 46 Allée d'Italie, F-69364 Lyon Cedex 07, France.
`Jean-Francois.Collard@lip.ens-lyon.fr`

Abstract. Automatic parallelization of imperative programs has focused on nests of do loops with affine bounds and affine dependences, because in this case execution domains and dependences can be precisely known at compile-time. When dynamic control structures, such as while loops, are used, existing methods for conversion to single-assignment form and domain scanning are inapplicable. This paper gives an algorithm to automatically generate parallel code, together with an algorithm to possibly convert the program to single-assignment form.

1 Introduction

Automatic parallelization of imperative programs has focused on nests of do loops with affine bounds and affine dependences [10], mainly because dependences can then precisely be known at compile-time. Data or "memory-based" dependences are due to reuse of memory cells, and thus are language- and program-dependent, whereas dataflows or "value-based dependences" denote transmissions of values and thus are algorithm-dependent. Memory-based dependences can be eliminated if a memory cell is associated with each program operation (the program is then in *single-assignment form*). Intuitively, cancelling memory-based dependences allows to extract more parallelism, hence the interest in automatic parallelization for algorithms to convert programs automatically to equivalent single-assignment form. Then, parallelization through space-time mapping boils down to finding a new coordinate system where some dimensions correspond to time and the others to (virtual) processor coordinates. Code generation then consists of producing a program which scans the execution domain in the new coordinate system.

However, using while loops and/or ifs introduces two main problems:

1. The flow of data is not precisely known at compile-time and must generally be approximated, the ambiguity being resolved at run time. Thus, existing algorithms for automatic conversion to single-assignment form fail.
2. The lack of regularity in execution domains of dynamic control programs forbids scanning schemes to be entirely static. One needs a way of scanning a conservative superset of the execution domain, and of checking on the fly whether a given point corresponds to an actual execution.

This paper proposes solutions to both problems. Our assumed target machine is some abstract shared-memory machine. Section 2 first gives some necessary definitions. Section 3 gives the algorithms for code generation, which are the topic of this paper.

2 Definitions

Mathematical Definitions. The k-th element of a given vector x is denoted by $x[k]$. Furthermore, $\ll$ ($\leqslant$) denotes the (strict) lexicographical order on such vectors. "max" denotes the maximum operator according to order $\ll$. The modulo operation is denoted by %, and the true and false boolean values by tt and ff, respectively. A Z-*polyhedron* is the intersection of an integer lattice and a convex real polyhedron [1].

Program Model. We shall restrict ourselves to the following program model:

- The only data structures are arrays of basic types, where array subscripts are affine functions of the counters of surrounding loops and parameters.
- Basic statements are assignments to scalars or array elements.
- The only control structures for a *static control program (SCP)* are the sequence and the do loop; *dynamic control programs (DCP)* include, in addition, while or repeat loop, and conditional if..then..else constructs, without restriction on predicates of while loops and ifs.

Statements and Their Instances. An *operation* is a *dynamic instance* of a (syntactic) statement. The instance of a statement in a do loop nest is identified by the statement's name and the corresponding loop counter's values. The vector of these values is called *iteration vector*.

While Loops. Since we also want to identify the operations specified by while loops, we simply add an artificial counter to every while loop. (Note that some variables may be used implicitly as counters, and that there exist algorithms to detect such variables.) The initial value of every such artificial counter is some arbitrary value lb (often 0), its step is 1, and its upper bound is not known. Hereafter, we shall write while loops as: do $w := lb$ while (*cond*) S.

A nest of while loops that fits our program model is declared in program WW:

```
        program WW
G₁ :   do w₁ := 0 while ( P₁(w₁) )
G₂ :       do w₂ := 0 while ( P₂(w₁, w₂) )
S :            a[w₁+w₂] := a[w₁+w₂−1]
```

The iteration vector is (w_1, w_2), thus an operation is identified by $\langle S, w_1, w_2 \rangle$. The *execution domain* is the set of values that the iteration vector takes in the course of the execution. If the surrounding loops are only do loops, then the execution domain is a finite $\mathbb{Z}$-polyhedron. Since we cannot predict statically the flow of control of programs containing while loops, their execution domains have to be approximated. The smallest possible *approximate execution domain* of S in program WW is the $\mathbb{Z}$-polyhedron $\mathbf{D}(S) = \{(w_1, w_2)|\,(w_1, w_2) \in \mathbb{N}^2, w_1 \geq 0, w_2 \geq 0\}$. Dimensions of the approximate execution domain that correspond to while loops are infinite, but only a finite subset of the infinite polyhedron is executed at run time.

If there is at least one while loop not at the outermost level, the execution domain is not convex. Together with its control dependences, it looks more like a (possibly, multi-dimensional) comb (Figure 5a). The sequence of points along a line of arrows in the execution comb—we call it a *tooth*—corresponds to the execution of one entire while loop.

The maximal value that a while loop counter takes during program execution will be stored in a variable called a *placeholder*; its value is calculated dynamically. For instance, let δ_1 and δ_2 be the placeholders for w_1 and w_2 in program WW. Then, we can approximate the execution domain by $\{(w_1, w_2)|\,0 \leq w_1 \leq \delta_1, 0 \leq w_2 \leq \delta_2\}$ after the execution terminates.

Finally, note that unpredictable execution domains imply that data dependences have to be approximated as well.

For now, we suppose that predicates P_1 and P_2 in program WW do not depend on array a, but only on w_1, and w_1 and w_2, respectively. This simplification allows us to concentrate on code generation (the focus of this paper) without having to deal with parallelization methods such as speculative execution [3].

Parallelization in the Polyhedron Model. A parallelization is a relaxation of the execution order of the instances of S while preserving the dependences together with the termination properties of the input program. Actually, the execution order of while loop nests, such as program WW, is over-constrained. To show this, we proceed in several steps.

First, we apply a preprocessing step to the source program, in which we (1) explicitly guard the loop body with a predicate *executed* and (2) add a boolean variable *terminated* that stores the current global state of the execution. Then, data dependence analysis and, optionally, conversion to single-assignment form are applied. Based on these results, we derive a *space-time mapping*, i.e., we calculate for every iteration when and where it shall be executed. Finally we *scan* the space-time mapped index domains to generate the (parallel) target loop nest. In the following subsections, we describe each of these steps in more detail and demonstrate the problems that occur.

3 Parallelization Process

3.1 Control Flow in while Loops

The flow of control in nests of while loops is less constrained than it may appear. For instance, if $P_1(0)$ evaluates to tt, then the program's semantics is not changed if the operation $P_1(1)$ immediately follows $P_1(0)$—provided the input program is correct, i.e. all **while** loops terminate and no fatal exception occurs.

More formally, program **WW** is equivalent to the program in Figure 1.

$(\forall\,(w_1, w_2) : w_1 \geq 0, w_2 \geq 0 : \textbf{do begin}$
$E:$ if $executed(w_1, w_2)$
$S:$ then $a[w_1 + w_2] := a[w_1 + w_2 - 1]$ **endif** ;
         if $terminated$ then STOP **endif**
    end)

Fig. 1. Program equivalent to program **WW**

In this recurrent form, the execution order is not over-specified anymore. STOP should be understood as a global immediate program stop. $executed(w_1, w_2)$ tests on the fly whether the current instance (operation) should execute or not; $executed(w_1, w_2)$ depends on some "previous" instances of this predicate, thus implicitly giving some constraints on the execution order. As mentioned earlier, $terminated$ is a global, shared boolean scalar variable that stores the current global execution status.

Predicate executed. The body of a nest of **while** loops (e.g., S in **WW**) is executed at point x with level r, iff, for all points x' at level $r' \leq r$ whose coordinates $x'_1, \cdots, x'_{r'}$ are identical to $x_1, \cdots, x_{r'}$, respectively, all predicates of **while** loops surrounding x' evaluate to tt. Formally, $executed$ is defined recursively, where $executed$ at some level r means that the body of the loop at level r must be executed—no matter whether it is a statement or another loop:

$executed(x_1, \cdots, x_d) = executed_d(x_1, \cdots, x_d)$ where $(\forall\,r : 1 \leq r \leq d :$
$executed_r(x_1, \cdots, x_r, lb_{r+1}, \cdots, lb_d) =$

if $x_r > lb_r$ $\rightarrow executed_r(x_1, \cdots, x_r - 1, lb_{r+1}, \cdots, lb_d) \wedge cond_r(x_1, \cdots, x_r)$
[] $x_r = lb_r \wedge r > 1 \rightarrow executed_{r-1}(x_1, \cdots, x_{r-1}, lb_r, \cdots, lb_d) \wedge cond_r(x_1, \cdots, x_r)$
[] $x_r = lb_r \wedge r = 1 \rightarrow cond_1(x_1)$
[] $x_r < lb_r$ $\rightarrow ff$
endif)

A more detailed explanation is given in [8]. Note that the recursive definition of predicate $executed_r$ follows the **while** dependences. If the space-time mapping respects these dependences we can be sure that, during scanning, predicate $executed$ never is evaluated at any point x before it was evaluated at x's predecessor.

Termination Problem. A subtle communication scheme for detecting termination in a distributed-memory model where only local communications exist was proposed in [8]. In this paper, shared memory is assumed and detecting termination is simpler.

The execution of a **while** loop nest terminates when the outermost **while** loop has terminated and all instances of inner **while** loops have terminated, too. To implement this, we use a shared global counter that is incremented by every tooth in any dimension that started its execution, and that is decremented by every terminating tooth in any dimension. Thus, the whole program terminates iff there are no active teeth at all, i.e., the counter has been reset to 0.

A formalization of this idea can be added to an imperative specification of *executed* such that the calculation of *terminated* is hidden as a side effect of the masking function *executed* in the target program ($exec_r$ is an r-dimensional persistent array that stores the value of $executed_r(x_1, \cdots, x_r, lb_{r+1}, \cdots, lb_d)$). Function *executed* is called for each scanned point in the approximate execution domain.

$$executed(x_1, \cdots, x_d) \equiv$$
$$r := level(x_1, \cdots, x_d) ;$$
$$\text{if } exec_r[x_1, \cdots, x_{r-1}, x_r - 1] \wedge \neg cond_r(x_1, \cdots, x_r) \text{ then } decr(count) \text{ endif} ;$$
$$exec_r[x_1, \cdots, x_r] := exec_r[x_1, \cdots, x_r] \wedge cond_r(x_1, \cdots, x_r) ;$$
$$\text{do } k := 1 + level(x_1, \cdots, x_d) \text{ to } d$$
$$\quad exec_k[x_1, \cdots, x_k] := exec_{k-1}[x_1, \cdots, x_{k-1}] \wedge cond_k(x_1, \cdots, x_k) ;$$
$$\quad \text{if } exec_k[x_1, \cdots, x_k] \text{ then } incr(count) \text{ endif}$$
$$\text{enddo} ;$$
$$barrier ;$$
$$terminated := (count = 0) ;$$
$$\textbf{return } (exec_d[x_1, \cdots, x_d])$$

where functions $incr(count)$ and $decr(count)$ increment and decrement *count* by 1, respectively. $cond_0()$ and $executed_0()$ must be initialized to *tt*. The *level* of a point is defined as d minus the number of trailing *lb* coordinates.

Case distinction by calculating the *level* above yields the code generation scheme for *executed* in Fig. 2. The generated code for *executed* in the case of program WW is as follows:

```
function executed(w₁, w₂)  : boolean
if w₂ > 0 then
    if exec₂[w₁, w₂−1] and not P₂(w₁, w₂) then decr(count) endif ;
    exec₂[w₁, w₂] := exec₂[w₁, w₂−1] and P₂(w₁, w₂) ;
else if w₁ > 0 then
    if exec₁[w₁−1] and not P₁(w₁) then decr(count) endif ;
    exec₁[w₁] := exec₁[w₁−1] and P₁(w₁) ;
    exec₂[w₁, w₂] := exec₁[w₁] and P₂(w₁, w₂) ;
    if exec₂[w₁, w₂] then incr(count) endif
else /* w₁ = w₂ = 0 */
    exec₁[w₁] := P₁(w₁) ;
    if exec₁[w₁] then incr(count) endif ;
    exec₂[w₁, w₂] := exec₁[w₁] and P₂(w₁, w₂) ;
    if exec₂[w₁, w₂] then incr(count) endif
endif ;
barrier ;
terminated := (count = 0) ;
return ( exec₂[w₁, w₂] )
```

Algorithm *executed_generator*
Input:
- The d **while** loop conditions.
- The d loop counters $(x_1, \cdots, x_d)$ (become the arguments to *executed*).

Output: Code implementing function *executed*

```
generate( function executed(x₁, ⋯ , x_d)  : boolean )
for r:=d downto 0
    if r ≥ 1 then
        generate( if x_r > 0 then )
        generate( if exec_r[x₁, ⋯ , x_{r-1}, x_r −1] and not cond_r(x₁, ⋯ , x_r)
                then decr(count) endif )
        generate( exec_r[x₁, ⋯ , x_r] := exec_r[x₁, ⋯ , x_{r-1}, x_r −1] and
                cond_r(x₁, ⋯ , x_r) )
    end if
    for k := r+1 to d
        generate( exec_k[x₁, ⋯ , x_k] := exec_{k-1}[x₁, ⋯ , x_{k-1}] and
                cond_k(x₁, ⋯ , x_k) )
        generate( if exec_k[x₁, ⋯ , x_k] then incr(count) endif )
    end for
    if r ≥ 1 then generate ( else ) else generate ( endif )
end for
generate( barrier )
generate( terminated := (count = 0) )
generate( return ( exec_d[x₁, ⋯ , x_d] ) )
```

Fig. 2. Algorithm *executed_generator* for automatic generation of the code for *executed*.

Lemma 1. *The implementation of terminated via the counters is correct.*

Sketch of the Proof. The following properties ensure that, at a given time step t, *terminated* is not set to tt if some **while** loop iteration has not terminated in the execution domain:

- For every tooth in every dimension *count* is incremented once (at its root) and decremented once (at its tip)—in this order. During execution every tooth contributes 1 to the global value of *count*, whereas before the start and after termination there is no contribution to *count*.
- If there is at least one processor evaluating some $executed_r(x_1, \cdots, x_d)$ $(1 \leq r \leq d)$ to tt at time t then the tooth τ at level r through $(x_1, \cdots, x_r, lb_{r+1}, \cdots, lb_d)$ has started but not yet finished. Thus, at this point in time, τ is contributing 1 to *count*.
- The barrier synchronisation ensures that all updates to *count* occurred before the processors read the value of *count*. Since the order in which increments and decrements take place is not relevant to the final value, all processors see the same value.
- Since every tooth with some executing point on it contributes 1 to *count* and since there could not have been more decrements than increments *count* must at least have the value 1, thus preventing termination.

Remark. In data-parallel languages with the construct *whilesomewhere*, termination detection by the counter scheme can be replaced by formulating the outermost loop on time as $whilesomewhere(executed_{level}(x_1, \cdots, x_d))$.

3.2 Dependence Analysis

Let E be the statement calling *executed* in Fig 1. Dependences due to access to arrays $exec_1$ and $exec_2$ are one-to-one, corresponding to edges e_1 and e_2 in Figure 3. In contrast, dependences on S have to be approximated by sets because we cannot predict at compile-time which operations execute and which do not. Hence, in the case of dynamic control programs, elaborate dependence analyses have to be applied [5]. For instance, an analysis of program WW tells that the source of the datum read by $\langle S, w_1, w_2 \rangle$ is

$$
\left|
\begin{array}{l}
\textbf{if } w_2 \geq 1 \\
\textbf{then } \{\langle S, w_1, w_2-1 \rangle\} \\
\qquad \left|
\begin{array}{l}
\textbf{if } w_1 \geq 1 \\
\textbf{then } \{\langle S, \alpha, \beta \rangle \mid \alpha + \beta = w_1 - 1, \alpha \geq 0, \beta \geq 0, \alpha < w_1\} \\
\textbf{else } \{\bot\}
\end{array}
\right.
\end{array}
\right. \tag{1}
$$

The first leaf of (1) is a singleton, meaning that if $w_2 \geq 1$, only one operation can be the source of the flow of $a[w_1, w_2-1]$ to $\langle S, w_1 w_2 \rangle$. In contrast, the second leaf is a non-singleton set of possible sources. The last leaf only contains $\bot$, the "undefined" value, meaning that the read has no source in the given program. The two non-bottom leaves yield edges e_3 and e_4 in Figure 3. Similarly, edges e_5 and e_6 correspond to memory-based, output and anti dependences respectively.

To eliminate memory-based dependences, the input program may be converted into single-assignment form by applying the following rules:

- Replace lhs expressions by an array subscripted by iteration vectors.
- Replace rhs expressions by the result of the dataflow analysis (such as (1)):
  - replace singleton leaves by references to the array cells written by the corresponding operation, or by initial references if the leaf is $\{\bot\}$,
  - replace non-singleton leaves by a call to a function *last* (defined later).

Example 1. A single-assignment version of program WW is:

$$
(\forall (w_1, w_2) : w_1 \geq 0 \wedge w_2 \geq 0 : \textbf{do}
$$

```
        begin
                if executed(w₁, w₂)
S :          then A[w₁, w₂] :=if w₂ ≥ 1 then A[w₁, w₂−1]
                              else if w₁ ≥ 1 then last_{A,a}(w₁, w₂)
                                   else a[w₁+w₂−1]
             if terminated then STOP
        end)
```

Edges	Description	Conditions
e_1	$\langle E, w_1, w_2-1 \rangle \rightarrow \langle E, w_1, w_2 \rangle$	$w_2 \geq 1$
e_2	$\langle E, w_1-1, 0 \rangle \rightarrow \langle E, w_1, 0 \rangle$	$w_1 \geq 1$
e_3	$\langle S, w_1, w_2-1 \rangle \rightarrow \langle S, w_1, w_2 \rangle$	$w_2 \geq 1$
e_4	$\{\langle S, \alpha, \beta \rangle \mid \alpha+\beta = w_1+w_2-1, \alpha \geq 0, \beta \geq 0, \alpha < w_1\} \rightarrow \langle S, w_1, 0 \rangle$	$w_1 \geq 1, w_2 = 0$
e_5	$\{\langle S, \alpha, \beta \rangle \mid \alpha+\beta = w_1+w_2, \alpha \geq 0, \beta \geq 0, \alpha < w_1\} \rightarrow \langle S, w_1, w_2 \rangle$	$w_1 \geq 1$
e_6	$\{\langle S, \alpha, \beta \rangle \mid \alpha+\beta-1 = w_1+w_2, \alpha \geq 0, \beta \geq 0, \alpha < w_1\} \rightarrow \langle S, w_1, w_2 \rangle$	$w_1 \geq 1$

Fig. 3. Dependences in program WW.

Predicate *executed* restores the flow of control [8, 9], and function *last* dynamically restores the flow of data. In other words, predicate *executed* checks whether the current loop iteration corresponds to an actual execution of statement S. Function *last* returns the value produced by the operation executed last (according to order $\ll$), which wrote into memory cell $a(w_1+w_2-1)$. Function *last* is similar to the ϕ-function proposed by Cytron et al. [6], and implements the result of an array dataflow analysis since the returned value is the one produced by the last possible source that was executed, or by the initial element of array a if no possible source was executed. An implementation for *last* is:

```
function last_{A,a}(w_1, w_2)  : datum
do α := w_1 - 1 to 0 step -1
    β := w_1 + w_2 - 1 - α
    if exec_2[α, β] then return ( A[α, β] )
enddo
return ( a[w_1+w_2-1] )
```

Automatic Generation of Function last. In Figure 4, we propose an algorithm *last_generator* to generate automatically the code for function *last*. This algorithm scans a given $\mathbb{Z}$-polyhedron $\mathcal{D}$ in opposite lexicographical order. u_k (l_k) stores the upper (lower) bound on the kth coordinate of scanned operations and is equal to the floor (ceiling) of the first component of the projection of $\mathcal{D}$ on the $n-k+1$ first dimensions. u_k and l_k can be computed by thanks to software such as PIP [7]. If the upper bound is undefined, then u_k is set equal to the corresponding placeholder (Section 2).

When the current point corresponds to an actual execution, then *last* returns the corresponding cell in array A (passed as a second argument to *last_generator*). If no scanned point corresponds to an executed operation, then a read from the original cell of array a is returned.

Example 2. For program WW, the first argument to *last_generator* is the non-bottom part of the second leaf of (1), i.e. $\{\alpha, \beta \mid \alpha+\beta = w_1-1, \alpha \geq 0, \beta \geq 0, \alpha < w_1\}$; so, $n = 2$. The remaining arguments are array A, the initial array expression

Algorithm *last_generator*
Input:
- A $\mathbb{Z}$-polyhedron $\mathcal{D}$ given by a system of affine constraints.
- An array A.
- An array expression e.
- The loop counters w (become the arguments to *last*).

Output: Code implementing Function *last*.

```
generate( function lastA,a ( w ) : datum )
let n be the dimension of D
for k := 1 to n
        compute lk := ⌈min≪ {αk,...,αn| α ∈ D}[1]⌉
        compute uk := ⌊max≪ {αk,...,αn| α ∈ D}[1]⌋
        if uk = ∞ then uk := δk
        if lk = uk then
                generate( αk := lk )
        else
                generate( do αk := uk to lk step -1 )
        if k = n−1 then
                generate( if execn[α] then return ( A [ α ]) )
        if lk ≠ uk then
                generate( enddo )
end for
generate( return ( e ) )
```

Fig. 4. Algorithm *last_generator* for automatic generation of the code for *last*.

$e = a[w_1 + w_2 - 1]$, and the counters of the loops surrounding the call to *last*, i.e. $w = (w_1, w_2)$. For $k = 0$, $\min_{\ll} \{(\alpha, \beta)| (\alpha, \beta) \in \mathcal{D}\} = (0, w_1 + w_2 - 1)$, hence $l_0 = 0$. Symmetrically, $\max_{\ll} \{(\alpha, \beta)| (\alpha, \beta) \in \mathcal{D}\} = (w_1 - 1, w_2)$, thus $u_0 = w_1 - 1$. Hence the bounds of the outermost do loop. For $k = 1$,

$$l_1 = \min_{\ll} \{(\beta)| (\alpha, \beta) \in \mathcal{D}\} = (w_1 + w_2 - \alpha - 1)$$

$$u_1 = \max_{\ll} \{(\beta)| (\alpha, \beta) \in \mathcal{D}\} = (w_1 + w_2 - \alpha - 1)$$

Since $u_1 = l_1$, a simple assignment to β is generated instead of an inner loop.

3.3 Finding Space–Time Mappings

Finding space–time mappings, i.e. schedules and processor mappings, is beyond the scope of this paper. For more details on the subject, the reader is referred to [10].

If program WW is not converted to single-assignment form, then a possible schedule for both S and *executed*, is: $\theta(\langle S, w_1, w_2 \rangle) = 3w_1 + w_2 + C$. ($C$ is some arbitrary additive constant.) A possible processor mapping is w_1, yielding a unimodular space–time mapping.

In the case of single-assignment form, getting rid of dependences e_5 and e_6 allows a faster schedule. The method proposed in [4] derives the following scheduling function (for both S and *executed*, as before): $\theta(\langle S, w_1, w_2 \rangle) = w_1 + w_2$. A possible processor mapping is also w_1.

In both cases, the target code will have to scan all operations that are really executed and avoid "holes". Figure 5 shows, on the left, a possible execution of program WW; black dots represent real executions and grey dots denote approximated operations. When mapping $t = w_1 + w_2, p = w_1$ is applied (right), only three operations should be spawned at time step 3 and one (operation $(3,2)$) should be skipped. Code generation is responsible for ensuring this [8].

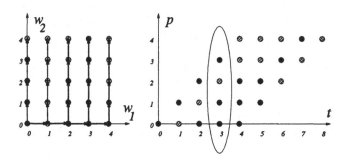

Fig. 5. A given execution of Program WW (left) and the target execution domain (right) with mapping $t = w_1 + w_2, p = w_1$.

3.4   Code Generation

After applying the space-time mapping we must re-construct a target loop nest. For that purpose, we shall first present the target loops themselves according to standard techniques [10], then show how the body and the auxiliary functions *executed* and possibly *last* are reindexed according to [2], and finally solve implementational problems for the arrays *exec*.

Without Single-Assignment. With the space-time mapping shown above, the scanning of the target domain yields:

```
do t := 0 while ( not terminated )
    doall p := 0 to ⌊t/3⌋
        if executed(w₁, w₂) then  a[w₁+w₂] := a[w₁+w₂−1]
```

Reindexing. Let T be the space-time transformation. It is defined by: $t = 3w_1 + w_2$, $p = w_1$, so its inverse T^{-1} is: $w_1 = p$, $w_2 = t - 3p$. Let L be the subscripting function; subcript $L(w_1, w_2)$ is replaced by $T(L(T^{-1}(t, p)))$. For instance, when $L(w_1, w_2) = (w_1, w_2 - 1)$, then $L(T^{-1}(t, p)) = (p, t - 3p - 1)$ and eventually the new subscript is $(3p + (t - 3p - 1), p) = (t - 1, p)$.

Thus, $executed(t, p)$ is derived from $executed(w_1, w_2)$ in Section 3.1 by replacing the array subscripts for $exec_r$ by the result of $T(L(T^{-1}(t, p)))$, and by replacing all other occurrences of w_1, w_2 by $p, t-3p$, respectively.

Memory Allocation. Since the size of the arrays $exec_r$ (for $1 \leq r \leq d$) can grow dynamically, we must use dynamic data structures instead of arrays. In general, for reducing memory requirements, we fold the time dimension of the arrays for $exec_r$ according to the delay of accesses on them [2], and we bound the space dimensions by expressions w.r.t. time.

In our concrete example, the longest delay of accesses on array $exec_2$ is from time t to time $t-1$, i.e., 1. Thus, we may fold the first dimension of array $exec_2$ by modulo 2. The second dimension is bounded by $p = w_1 = (t-w_2)/3 \leq \lceil t/3 \rceil$. Therefore, we have to insert the memory allocation statements $exec_2[t \% 2]$:=malloc ($\lceil t/3 \rceil$) and free $((t-1) \% 2)$ as the first and the penultimate statement of the body of $executed$, respectively.

With Single-Assigment. The mapping presented in Section 3.3 is invertible $(w_1 = p, w_2 = t-p)$, so program WW becomes:

```
program WW
do t := 1 while ( not  terminated )
   doall p := 0 to t−1
      if exec₂[t, p] then
         A( t,p ):= if t−p−1 ≥ 1   then A( t−1,p )
                    else if p ≥ 1  then last(p,t−p) else a(t−2)
```

Functions *executed* and *last* have to be reindexed according to the space-time transformation:

```
function last(w₁, w₂)
do α := w₁−1 to 0 step −1
   β := w₁+w₂−1−α
   if exec₂[α, β] then return ( A( α + β,β ) )
return ( a[w₁+w₂−1] )
```

executed also has to be reindexed as explained in 3.4. Similarly, dynamic allocation is used as described in Paragraph 3.4.

4 Conclusions

Automatic parallelization of dynamic control programs, e.g. including while loops, requires not only appropriate dependence analysis and scheduler, but an appropriate code generator, too. This paper proposed algorithms for this purpose.

To eliminate memory-based dependences while coping with unpredictable data flows, a new mechanism (function *last*) has been introduced and an algorithm to generate the code implementing *last* has been proposed. Several other implementation schemes for *last* can be imagined, and thorough experiments are necessary to select the most effective one; the scheme presented in this paper is the simplest, most abstract one.

Scanning irregular non-dense execution domains requires some run-time tests, and thus incurs an execution overhead; it may also yield unbalanced workloads on processors. Both properties mainly depend on the application, and we expect that parallelizing nests of while loops will prove to be efficient only for some types of algorithms.

On the other hand, we believe that one of the main drawbacks of current automatic parallelizers is their severe syntactical restrictions on input programs. The methods proposed in this paper allow code generators in automatic parallelizers to accept a much wider range of programs than current implementations do.

Acknowledgments

Thanks for the support by the German-French research exchange program PRO-COPE, the DFG project RecuR, the CNRS program PRS, PRC/MRE contract ParaDigme, and the DRET contract 91/1180.

Many thanks to Nils Ellmenreich for a careful reading and to Chris Lengauer and Gil Utard for the perusal and fruitful comments on this paper.

References

1. C. Ancourt. *Génération automatique de codes de transfert pour multiprocesseurs à mémoires locales.* PhD thesis, Univ. of Paris 6, Paris. March 1990.
2. J.-F. Collard. Code generation in automatic parallelizers. In C. Girault, editor, *Proc. of the Int. Conf. on Applications in Parallel and Distributed Comp., IFIP W.G 10.3*, pages 185–194, Caracas, Venezuela. North Holland, April 1994.
3. J.-F. Collard. Automatic parallelization of while-loops using speculative execution. *Int. J. Parallel Programming*, 1995. To appear. Earlier version: *Proc. 1994 Scalable High Performance Comp. Conf.*, pages 429–436. IEEE, May 1994.
4. J.-F. Collard and P. Feautrier. A method for static scheduling of dynamic control programs. Tech. Report 94-34, LIP, Ecole N. S. de Lyon. December 1994.
5. J.-F. Collard, D. Barthou and P. Feautrier. Fuzzy array dataflow analysis. In *Proc. of 5th ACM SIGPLAN Symp. on Principles and Practice of Parallel Prog..* Santa Barbara, CA. July 1995.
6. R. Cytron et al. An Efficient Method of Computing Static Single Assignment Form. In *Proc. of 16th ACM Symp. on Principles of Programming Languages*, pages 25–35. January 1989.
7. P. Feautrier. Parametric integer programming. *RAIRO Recherche Opérationnelle*, 22:243–268, September 1988.
8. M. Griebl and C. Lengauer. On scanning space-time mapped while loops. In B. Buchberger and J. Volkert, editors, *Parallel Processing: CONPAR 94 – VAPP VI*, LNCS 854, pages 677–688. Springer-Verlag, 1994.
9. M. Griebl and C. Lengauer. On the parallelization of loop nests containing while loops. In N. Mirenkov, editor, *Proc. Aizu Int. Symp. on Parallel Algorithm/Architecture Synthesis (pAs'95)*, pages 10–18, Aizu-Wakamatsu, Japan. IEEE, March 1995.
10. C. Lengauer. Loop parallelization in the polytope model. In E. Best, editor, *CONCUR'93*, LNCS 715, pages 398–416. Springer-Verlag, 1993.

Implementing Flexible Computation Rules with Subexpression-level Loop Transformations

Dattatraya Kulkarni*, Michael Stumm*, and Ronald C. Unrau**

*Department of Computer Science and
Department of Electrical & Computer Engineering
University of Toronto, Toronto, Canada, M5S 1A4
Email: kulki@cs.toronto.edu

**Parallel Compiler Development
IBM Toronto Laboratory
Toronto, Canada, M3C 1V7

Abstract. Computation Decomposition and Alignment (CDA) is a new loop transformation framework that extends the linear loop transformation framework and the more recently proposed Computation Alignment frameworks by linearly transforming computations at the granularity of subexpressions. It can be applied to achieve a number of optimization objectives, including the removal of data alignment constraints, the elimination of ownership tests, the reduction of cache conflicts, and improvements in data access locality.

In this paper we show how CDA can be used to effectively implement flexible computation rules with the objective of minimizing communication and, whenever possible, eliminating intrinsics that test whether computations need to be executed or not. We describe CDA, show how it can be used to implement flexible computation rules, and present an algorithm for deriving appropriate CDA transformations.

1 Introduction

In a SPMD framework such as HPF [7], data alignments and distributions are usually specified by the user or suggested by some automatic tool such as PARADIGM [8]. Given the data alignments and distributions, the compiler then maps computations to processors using a computation rule. The choice of computation rule can have a significant impact on performance, since it affects the amount of communication generated and the number of intrinsics needed in the code.

Traditionally, computation rules have been *fixed* in that they do not take alignments and distributions of all references into account. For example, the owner-computes rule is a fixed rule and is used almost exclusively. It maps a statement instance to the processor which owns the *lhs* (left hand side) data element of the statement [7], even if it would be more efficient to compute the statement on another processor, and it always maps a statement instance in its entirety. Fixed computation rules provide a general schema for computation mapping and hence simplify code generation, especially the insertion of communication code.

In contrast, *flexible* computation rules take into account the location of all the data needed for the computation and the cost of communication when deciding where a computation is to be executed [5]. The granularity of the computation being mapped is usually at the subexpression level. It is therefore possible to achieve optimal or near optimal computation mappings. However, the code generation is much more complex. Flexible computation rules are also important on shared memory multiprocessors. For example, it is important to minimize remote memory accesses on shared memory multiprocessors with non-uniform access times. Moreover, the location of computations can significantly affect cache locality and interference patterns.

In this paper, we show how the recently proposed CDA loop transformation framework [13, 14] can be used to efficiently implement a flexible computation rule called *P-Computes*. Section 2 briefly reviews the most important related work. Section 3 introduces the P-Computes rule. We show by example how P-Computes can be implemented with CDA in Section 4 and present the formal algorithms in Section 5.

2 Related Work

There has been much work in developing techniques that improve the performance of SPMD code. Linear loop transformation is a general technique developed in 1990 that changes the execution order of the iterations [4, 15, 17, 23] and can be used, for example, to reduce communication overhead by moving communications to the outer loop levels [17, 23]. However, linear loop transformations are limited in their optimization capabilities, since they leave iterations unchanged as they map the original iteration space onto a new one.

Over the last three years, Computation Alignment (CA) frameworks have been proposed that extend the capabilities of linear transformations [9, 12, 21] by transforming loops at the granularity of statements.[1] By applying a separate transformation to each statement in the loop body they change the execution order of each statement, thus effectively changing the constitution of the iterations. CA transformations have been applied to improve SPMD code in a variety of ways [12, 22]. For example, CA may be used to align the statements in the loop body so that all lhs data elements accessed in an iteration are located on the same processor in the hope of eliminating the need for ownership tests.

Computation Decomposition and Alignment (CDA) [13] is a generalization of CA and goes a step further in that it can transform computations of granularity smaller than a statement. Instead of transforming the statements as written by the programmer, CDA first partitions the original statements into finer statements and then aligns the statements at this finer granularity. This creates

---

[1] The origins of CA can be traced to loop alignment [1, 19], which is a special case of CA.

additional opportunities for optimization. In later sections we show how CDA can be used to implement flexible computation rules.

A number of optimization techniques have been proposed that reduce communication by transforming data. Bala and Ferrante [3] proposed the insertion of XDP directives that explicitly move data to transfer ownerships. XDP can thus be used to implement variations of owner-computes rule. In this context, dynamic data alignment [11] can be considered as a structured form of implicit data movement. Earlier approaches resorted to static solutions by deriving best data alignments [16] and distributions [2, 8] considering global constraints.

Chatterjee et al. [5] developed algorithms that derive communication optimal flexible computation rules for a class of expressions. They take the machine topology into account to find optimal mappings of subexpressions onto processors in polynomial time.

3 P-Computes Rules

The P-Computes operator, $\otimes$, can be used to specify flexible computation rules. A P-Computes rule, $\otimes_p (expr)$, specifies that the expression $expr$ is to be executed on processor p. Generally, p and $expr$ will be functions of the enclosing loop iterators. If $expr$ does not assign value to a lhs, then the result of executing $\otimes_p(expr)$ is to be sent to the processor designated by the enclosing P-Computes operator.

The specification of p in $\otimes_p(expr)$ can be either *direct* or *indirect*. If the processor is specified as a direct function of the iterators, then the P-Computes rule is direct. Otherwise, if the processor is specified in terms of the location of array elements, then the rule is indirect. The indirect specification can be achieved through an intrinsic similar to iown(e) used by owner-computes that evaluates to *true* on the processor that owns data element e. Here we use a variant, owner(e), that returns the processor that has data element e. Hence, iown(e) is equivalent to the conditional (myid = owner(e)).

The $\otimes$ operator is very general and can be used to express a variety of computation rules. For example:

$$\otimes_{\mathbf{owner}(e_1)}(e_1 = e_2 + e_3)$$
$$\otimes_{\mathbf{f}(I)}(e_1 = \otimes_{\mathbf{g}(I)}(e_2 + \otimes_{\mathbf{h}(I)}(e_3 + e_4)))$$
$$\otimes_{\mathbf{owner}(A(I))}(e_1 = \otimes_{\mathbf{owner}(B(I))}(e_2 + e_3) + \otimes_{\mathbf{owner}(C(I))}(e_4 + e_5))$$

are all valid P-Computes rules, where the e's are subexpressions. The first example above is equivalent to the application of the owner-computes rule. The second example specifies the processors directly as a function of the loop iterators, whereas the mapping is indirect in the last example.

To compare the difference between a P-Computes rule and the owner-computes, consider the following loop:

```
for i = 1,n
   for j = 1,n
      S₁ :  ⊗owner(A(i,j)) (A(i, j) =
                  ⊗owner(A(i-1,j)) (A(i - 1, j) + A(i - 1, j - 1) + B(i - 1, j))
            +B(i, j + 1) + A(i, j - 1))
      S₂ :  ⊗owner(B(i,j-1)) (B(i, j - 1) = A(i, j - 1) + B(i, j))
   end for
end for
```

Assume that each iteration is mapped onto a different processor and that $B(i,j)$ is aligned to $A(i,j)$, perhaps due to constraints from a previous loop. If the owner-computes rule were applied directly, then six non-local accesses would be necessary. In contrast, the specified P-Computes rule requires five non-local accesses, one of which is due to sending the result from $\otimes_{owner(A(i-1,j))}$ in statement S_1. Thus, the P-Computes rule can reduce communication by taking the location of data into account. As we will see in Section 4, CDA transformations can be applied to further reduce the number of communications to three.

4 CDA Implementation of P-Computes Rules

To implement a flexible computation rule specified with P-Computes operators, we transform the loop in a three stage process. The first two stages correspond to CDA, as described in [13]. In the first stage, the statements in the loop are decomposed so that statements can be assigned to processors in their entirety. This may require the introduction of new temporary arrays. Second, the (possibly new) set of statements are linearly transformed so as to eliminate (or reduce) the need for intrinsics. Finally, in a third stage, the newly introduced temporary arrays are data aligned to the existing arrays so that the given computation rule can be specified relative to the ownership of the lhs temporaries. In this section we give an overview of how these techniques can be applied, using the example of Section 3.

4.1 Computation Decomposition

Computation Decomposition is the first stage of our method. It decomposes the loop body into statements so that each statement can be mapped in its entirety to a processor. The P-Computes rules specify how the loop is to be decomposed. In a first step, each P-Computes rule that contains more than one statement is split, so that an equivalent P-Computes rule is applied to each statement separately. In a second step, those statements containing more than one P-Computes rule are split into multiple statements so that each new statement has a single $\otimes$ operator. If a statement must be split, then the expression of the embedded P-Computes rule will be elevated to the status of a statement and a temporary array is introduced to accumulate the results of the expression and to pass the result to the statement corresponding to the enclosing $\otimes$ operators. The temporary variables are typically chosen as arrays in order to reduce the number of dependences introduced by the decomposition, allowing for more freedom in the subsequent search for alignments.

Considering the example of Section 3, statement S_1 is decomposed into statements $S_{1.1}$ and $S_{1.2}$. $S_{1.1}$ corresponds to the expression of the P-Computes rule embedded in statement S_1. The result of evaluating that expression is assigned to the temporary t so that it can be passed to the remainder of S_1, namely $S_{1.2}$. The loop body after computation decomposition becomes:

```
for i = 1,n
    for j = 1,n
        S1.1 : ⊗owner(A(i-1,j)) (t(i,j) = A(i-1,j) + A(i-1,j-1) + B(i-1,j))
        S1.2 : ⊗owner(A(i,j)) (A(i,j) = t(i,j) + B(i,j+1) + A(i,j-1))
          S2 : ⊗owner(B(i,j-1)) (B(i,j-1) = A(i,j-1) + B(i,j))
    end for
end for
```

There are three things worth noting in this loop. First, each new statement has a single P-Computes rule. Second, each statement is mapped to a different processor, so it is necessary to evaluate intrinsics, resulting in considerable overhead. Stage 2 will attempt to eliminate the need for the intrinsics. Finally, note that $S_{1.1}$ as is does not use owner-computes. Stage 3 of our process will translate the existing P-Computes rule to an owner-computes rule.

If the programmer does not explicitly specify the P-Computes rule (as in the above example), then the compiler will have to derive it automatically. A part of that process is to decide which subexpressions are to be elevated to the status of statements. The other part is deciding which processors those subexpressions should be mapped onto.

4.2 Computation Alignment

The computation decomposition of Section 4.1 produces a new loop body that can have more statements than the original. We can now employ CA to separately transform each statement of the new loop body in attempting to eliminate the need for intrinsics [12, 22]. Intuitively, the mapping causes a relative movement of the statement instances across iterations. The idea is to move the computations so that those that are mapped to the same processor belong to the same iteration.

Just as there is an iteration space for the loop body, there is a computation space for a statement S, $CS(S)$, which is an integer space representing all execution instances of S in the loop. CA applies a separate linear transformation to each computation space. That is, if the decomposition produces a loop body with statements $S_1, \ldots, S_K$, which have computation spaces $CS(S_1), \ldots, CS(S_K)$, then we can separately transform these computation spaces with linear transformations $T_1, \ldots, T_K$, respectively. Before the alignment, an iteration $(i_1, \ldots, i_n)$

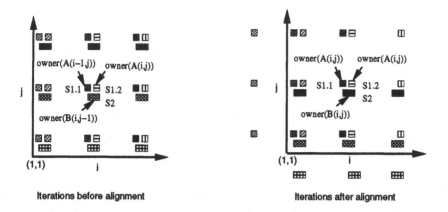

Fig. 1. Movement of computations in the computation space.

consists of computations $\{(i_1,\ldots,i_n;S_1),\ldots,(i_1,\ldots,i_n;S_K)\}$, where $(i_1,\ldots,i_n;S_j)$ is the execution instance of statement S_j in iteration $(i_1,\ldots,i_n)$. After the alignment, iteration $(i_1,\ldots,i_n)$ consists of computations $\{(T_1^{-1}\cdot(i_1,\ldots,i_n);S_1),\ldots,(T_K^{-1}\cdot(i_1,\ldots,i_n);S_K)\}$.

This type of computation movement at the statement level can be used to redefine the iterations so that all (most) computations in an iteration belong to the same processor. The basic idea in choosing an alignment can be illustrated with a simple example. Suppose we want to align statement S_1 below to statement S_K, where S_K assigns to the original lhs array, say $A(i,j)$.

$$S_1 : \otimes_{\text{owner}(B(i-c1,j-c2))}(t_1(i,j) = \ldots)$$
$$S_K : \otimes_{\text{owner}(A(i,j))}(A(i,j) = t_1(i,j) + \ldots)$$

Also assume that $A(i,j)$ and $B(i-a1,j-a2)$ are collocated due to a prior data alignment. We can align S_1 to S_K by applying a transformation that shifts the S_1 computations by $(c1-a1,c2-a2)$ relative to the computations of S_K. Doing so modifies the statements to become:

$$S_1 : \otimes_{\text{owner}(B(i-a1,j-a2))}(t_1(i+c1-a1,j+c2-a2) = \ldots)$$
$$S_K : \otimes_{\text{owner}(A(i,j))}(A(i,j) = t_1(i,j) + \ldots)$$

and both statements are now to be executed by the same processor.[2] We can align the statements of the decomposed loop of Section 4.1 in a similar way to eliminate the need for intrinsics. The $S_{1.1}$ computations are moved along the i direction to bring $(i+1,j;S_{1.1})$ to iteration (i,j). Similarly, the S_2 computations are moved along the j direction so that $(i,j+1;S_2)$ is now executed in iteration (i,j). Figure 1 shows these alignments. The resulting CDA transformed loop is:

---

[2] The alignment is legal when all dependences between S_1 and S_2 remain positive.

```
for  i = 0, n
   for  j = 0, n
      S_{1.2} :  (i > 0 ∧ j > 0)
               ⊗_owner(A(i,j))  (A(i, j) = t(i, j) + B(i, j + 1) + A(i, j − 1))
      S_2 :   (i > 0 ∧ j < n)
               ⊗_owner(B(i,j))  (B(i, j) = A(i, j) + B(i, j + 1))
      S_{1.1} :  (i < n ∧ j > 0)
               ⊗_owner(A(i,j))  (t(i + 1, j) = A(i, j) + A(i, j − 1) + B(i, j))
   end for
end for
```

and all statement instances in an iteration are now mapped to the same processor so that the intrinsics can be eliminated altogether.

Such a computation alignment changes the references and the dependences in the loop, as well as the loop bounds. If computation space $CS(S)$ is transformed by T, then reference matrix R of each reference r in S is changed to RT^{-1}. We represent data flow constraints in the loop with *dependence relations* [20], and we keep the exact dependence information between each pair of read and write [6, 18]. Consider a read reference r in statement S_r flow dependent on a write reference w of statement S_w. The dependence relation $w[d_{wr} \cdot I] \rightarrow r[I]$ between the references is changed to $w[d_{wr} \cdot T_w \cdot T_r^{-1} \cdot I] \rightarrow r[I]$, when T_w is applied to $CS(S_w)$ and T_r is applied to $CS(S_r)$. The alignment is legal if all new dependence relations are positive.

The new loop bounds are obtained by projecting all computation spaces onto an integer space that becomes the iteration space of the aligned loop. Because each statement can potentially be transformed by a different linear transformation, the new iteration space can be non-convex. There are two basic strategies that can be pursued to generate code. First, it is possible to take the convex hull of the new iteration space and then generate a *perfect* nest that traverses this hull. This is the strategy chosen to generate the above loop, but requires the insertion of *guards* that disable the execution of statements where necessary. A second, alternative strategy is to generate an *imperfect* nest that has no guards. Guard-free code is usually desirable for better performance, but a perfect loop may be desirable in some cases, for instance to avoid non-vector communications or to avoid loop overheads. Algorithms to generate code employing both strategies can be found in the literature [9, 10, 12, 21, 22].

4.3 Aligning the Temporary Arrays

In the third stage, each temporary array is data aligned to the array used by the ⊗ operator to specify the processor onto which the computations are to be mapped. The idea is to collocate the lhs reference of a statement (assuming it is to a temporary) and the array reference in the ⊗ operator. This allows the P-Computes rule to be interpreted as the owner-computes rule. In our running example, $t(i + 1, j)$ is data aligned to $A(i, j)$, so that owner($A(i, j)$) is equivalent to $\text{owner}(t(i + 1, j))$. Hence, we implement a flexible computation rule, but can retain the simplicity of owner-computes for code generation.

4.4 Properties of CDA Transformed Loops

Notice that the transformed loop implements the specified P-Computes rule. For instance, subexpression $A(i - 1, j) + A(i - 1, j - 1) + B(i - 1, j)$ is computed on the owner of $A(i - 1, j)$. The transformation has separated out the complex computation rule into its constituent simpler rules, which happen to be owner-computes here. Moreover, the computation alignment has made the loop efficient by moving the computations relative to each other so that all computations in an iteration are to be computed by the same processor, namely $\text{owner}(A(i, j))$. The intrinsics can now be eliminated altogether by changing the loop strides. The end result is a loop that requires only three non-local accesses, compared to six in the original (assuming again that each iteration is mapped to a different processor).

One drawback of our approach is that the computation alignment may change the loop independent dependences on the temporaries to become loop carried dependences. This can reduce the degree of available parallelism in the loop.

5 Algorithms

In this section we outline specific algorithms that implement a given P-Computes rule under the assumption that there is one statement in the original loop body. The algorithms correspond to the three stages discussed in Section 4. They can be easily extended to handle the case where the original loop body has multiple statements. We assume that the references are affine functions of iteration vector I and are represented by a reference matrix. The affine function f in a reference $A(f(I))$ is used to denote the reference matrix as well. Data alignments also have a matrix representation, and data alignment of d_j on an array changes each reference r to the array to be $d_j r$.

Algorithm *comp-decomp* decomposes the statement so that each P-Computes operator maps a separate statement. In each iteration of the algorithm, each innermost $\otimes$-subexpression is rewritten as a full statement with a new temporary array element as its lhs, and the $\otimes$-subexpression is replaced by the corresponding reference to the temporary.

Algorithm : *comp-decomp*
Decompose statement S : $\otimes_{\text{owner }(A(f(I)))}$ ($\text{lhs} = \text{rhs}$)
begin
    $i \leftarrow 1$
    while rhs of S has a P-Computes operator
        Choose an innermost $\otimes_{\text{owner }(B(g(I)))}$ (expr) in S
        $t_i \Leftarrow$ new temporary array
        generate statement S_i : $\otimes_{\text{owner }(B(g(I)))}$ ($t_i(I) = \text{expr}$)

   replace $\otimes_{\text{owner } (B(g(I)))}$ (**expr**) in rhs by $t_i(I)$
   $i \leftarrow i + 1$
  end while
  $K \leftarrow i$
  generate S_K : $\otimes_{\text{owner } (A(f(I)))}$ (**lhs = rhs**)
end

The second stage uses algorithm *comp-align* in attempting to find a computation alignment that aligns the K statements generated by the decomposition stage so that all statement instances in an iteration are mapped to the same processor. The search space of all legal computation alignments is large, and therefore it is not possible to exhaustively search this space in reasonable time. For this reason, we apply a heuristic.

We know that a statement S_j with P-Computes operator $\otimes_{\text{owner } (A_j(f_j(I)))}$ can be aligned to statement S_i with operator $\otimes_{\text{owner } (A_i(f_i(I)))}$ by applying a transformation $T_j = f_i^{-1}d_jf_j$ to S_j, where array A_j is data aligned to array A_i by transformation d_j. Since there are K statements in the loop, we can construct K computation alignments, $\alpha = \{\alpha_1, \ldots, \alpha_K\}$, with computation alignment α_i aligning each statement of the loop to statement S_i. Some of these computation alignments may be illegal. If there are legal alignments, then the algorithm will choose the one that results in a loop with the minimal communication overhead. If there are no legal alignments, then the algorithm attempts to make an illegal computation alignment legal by discarding individual statement alignments that violate dependences. The algorithm then selects the computation alignment with the fewest discarded statement alignments.

Algorithm : *comp-align*
Given: statements $S_1; \ldots; S_K$,
where S_i has the P-Computes operator $\otimes_{\text{owner } (A(f_i(I)))}$. Statements $S_1; \ldots; S_{K-1}$ have temporary variables on the lhs. S_K has the same lhs as the original statement.

begin

  Step 1: Construct a set of K computation alignments, α. Each alignment $\alpha_i \in \alpha$ contains K statement alignments, $\alpha_i = \{T_1, \ldots, T_K\}$, such that T_j aligns S_j to S_i. Hence, $T_j = f_i^{-1}d_jf_j$, where array A_j is data aligned to A_i by d_j.

  Step 2: If α contains no legal computation alignments, then go to Step 3. Otherwise, choose alignment $\alpha_i \in \alpha$ that (1) is legal and (2) results in a transformed loop with lowest communication overhead. Return α_i.

  Step 3: If none of the K computation alignments in α are legal, then modify each $\alpha_k \in \alpha$ to make it legal:
   (i) **While** the alignment α_k is illegal due to a violated flow dependence on a temporary

Choose such a dependence
Assume it is from S_i to S_j
   (that is the lhs of S_i is accessed in S_j and $T_i \not\leq T_j$)[3]
Set $T_i \leftarrow T_j$

(ii) **While** the alignment α_k is illegal due to a violated dependence on the lhs
   of S_K
   Choose such a dependence
   If it is a flow dependence from S_K to S_i
      then set $T_i \leftarrow T_j$ where T_j is chosen such that $T_i < T_j$
         and there is no other T_r with $T_i < T_r < T_j$
   else (it is an anti-dependence from S_i to S_K)
      then set $T_i \leftarrow T_j$ where T_j is chosen such that $T_i > T_j$
         and there is no other T_r with $T_i > T_r > T_j$

Return the computation alignment with the fewest discarded statement alignments.

end

Finally, algorithm *data-align-temp* aligns the temporaries to existing arrays so that P-Computes rules can be replaced by simple owner-computes rules.

Algorithm : *data-align-temp*
Data Align the temporary arrays introduced in Stage 1.
The alignment chosen in stage two is $\alpha_k = \{T_1, \ldots, T_K\}$.
begin
   for each statement $S_i : \otimes_{A_i(f_i(I)T_i - 1)} (t_i(T_i^{-1}I) = \ldots)$
      data align t_i to A_i by f_i
   end for
end
As discussed before, this data alignment makes it possible to convert the P-Computes rule for the loop into the familiar owner-computes rule, assuming the P-Computes rule for statement S_K is $\otimes_{owner} (A_K(f_K(I)))$.

6   Concluding Remarks

We have shown how P-Computes, a representative flexible computation rule, can be effectively implemented by using CDA loop transformations. The implementation eliminates intrinsics whenever possible. Since the P-Computes rule is finally translated into the familiar owner-computes rule, the code generation for a given P-Computes is simpler than if the rule were implemented directly.

We have assumed that the P-Computes rule was specified by the programmer so as to minimize communication. Ideally, a compiler should be able to automatically derive the most appropriate P-Computes rules. However, the derivation of

---

[3] $T_i \leq T_j$ denotes that for all iterations I, $T_i I$ is lexicographically less than or equal to $T_j I$.

an optimal P-Computes is still an open problem. We believe that it is possible to produce near optimal computation rules by first deriving CDA transformations that minimize the number of distinct references, and then employing existing algorithms that derive flexible computation rules [5]. For example, previous work by Chatterjee et al. shows that subexpressions can be optimally mapped to processors in polynomial time [5]. However, their results have to be extended if CDA transformations are taken into account. If each data element in the statement

$$A(i,j) = A(i-1,j) + A(i-1,j-1) + A(i,j-1) + A(i,j)$$

is mapped to a different processor, then Chatterjee's algorithm would map the execution of this statement to the processor that owns $A(i,j)$, resulting in three remote accesses. However, the statement can be CDA transformed to:

$$t(i+1,j) = A(i,j) + A(i,j-1)$$
$$A(i,j) = t(i,j) + A(i,j-1) + A(i,j)$$

With the temporary appropriately data aligned, the original statement is now effectively executed on two different processors, namely those that own $A(i-1,j)$ and $A(i,j)$. The execution of the transformed statements require only two remote accesses.

CDA is a general subexpression-level transformation framework which we applied here only for SPMD code optimization. CDA can be used in several other optimization contexts, for example to remove data alignment constraints, improve locality, eliminate cache conflicts, or reduce register pressure [13, 14].

Our current work includes the development of efficient algorithms that derive P-Computes rules and an analysis of their complexity. We are also working on more efficient algorithms to eliminate intrinsics that take intermediate alignments into account while constructing partial alignments.

References

1. R. Allen, D. Callahan, and K. Kennedy. Automatic decomposition of scientific programs for parallel execution. In *Conference Record of the 14th Annual ACM Symposium on Principles of Programming Languages*, pages 63–76, Munich, West Germany, January 1987.
2. J. Anderson and M. Lam. Global optimizations for parallelism and locality on scalable parallel machines. In *Proceedings of the ACM SIGPLAN '93 Conference on Programming Language Design and Implementation*, volume 28, June 1993.
3. V. Bala, J. Ferrante, and L. Carter. Explicit data placement (xdp): A methodology for explicit compile-time representation and optimization of data movement. In *Proceedings of the 4th ACM SIGPLAN Symposium on Principles and Practice of Parallel Programming*, volume 28, pages 139–149, San Diego, CA, July 1993.
4. Utpal Banerjee. Unimodular transformations of double loops. In *Proceedings of Third Workshop on Programming Languages and Compilers for Parallel Computing*, Irvine, CA, August 1990.
5. S. Chatterjee, J.R. Gilbert, , R. Schreiber, and S. Teng. Optimal evaluation of array expressions on massively parallel machines. *ACM Transactions on Programming Languages and Systems*, 17(1):123–156, January 1995.
6. P. Feautrier. Dataflow analysis of array and scalar references. *International Journal of Parallel Programming*, 20, 1991.

7. HPF Forum. HPF: High performance fortran language specification. Technical report, HPF Forum, 1993.

8. M. Gupta. Automatic data partitioning on distributed memory multicomputers. Technical report, Dept of computer Science, University of Illinois at Urbana Champaign, 1992.

9. W. Kelly and W. Pugh. A framework for unifying reordering transformations. Technical Report UMIACS-TR-92-126, University of Maryland, 1992.

10. W. Kelly, W. Pugh, and E. Rosser. Code generation for multiple mappings. Technical Report UMIACS-TR-94-87, University of Maryland, 1994.

11. K. Knobe, J.D. Lucas, and W.J. Dally. Dynamic alignment on distributed memory systems. In *Proceedings of the Third Workshop on Compilers for Parallel Computers, Vienna*, pages 394–404, 1992.

12. D. Kulkarni and M. Stumm. Computational alignment: A new, unified program transformation for local and global optimization. Technical Report CSRI-292, Computer Systems Research Institute, University of Toronto, January 1994.

13. D. Kulkarni and M. Stumm. CDA loop transformations. In *Proceedings of Third workshop on languages, compilers and run-time systems for scalable computers*, Troy, NY, May 1995.

14. D. Kulkarni, M. Stumm, R. Unrau, and W. Li. A generalized theory of linear loop transformations. Technical Report CSRI-317, Computer Systems Research Institute, University of Toronto, December 1994.

15. K.G. Kumar, D. Kulkarni, and A. Basu. Deriving good transformations for mapping nested loops on hierarchical parallel machines in polynomial time. In *Proceedings of the 1992 ACM International Conference on Supercomputing*, Washington, July 1992.

16. J. Li and M. Chen. The data alignment phase in compiling programs for distributed memory machines. *Journal of parallel and distributed computing*, 13:213–221, 1991.

17. W. Li and K. Pingali. A singular loop transformation framework based on nonsingular matrices. In *Proceedings of the Fifth Workshop on Programming Languages and Compilers for Parallel Computing*, August 1992.

18. D.E. Maydan, J.L. Hennessy, and M.S. Lam. Efficient and exact data dependence analysis. *SIGPLAN Notices*, 26(6):1–14, 1991.

19. D. Padua. Multiprocessors: Discussion of some theoretical and practical problems. PhD thesis, University of Illinois, Urbana-Champaign, 1979.

20. W. Pugh. Uniform techniques for loop optimization. In *International Conference on Supercomputing*, pages 341–352, Cologne, Germany, 1991.

21. J. Torres and E. Ayguade. Partitioning the statement per iteration space using non-singular matrices. In *Proceedings of 1993 International Conference on Supercomputing*, Tokyo, Japan, July 1993.

22. J. Torres, E. Ayguade, J. Labarta, and M. Valero. Align and distribute-based linear loop transformations. In *Proceedings of Sixth Workshop on Programming Languages and Compilers for Parallel Computing*, 1993.

23. M.E. Wolf and M.S. Lam. An algorithmic approach to compound loop transformation. In *Proceedings of Third Workshop on Programming Languages and Compilers for Parallel Computing*, Irvine, CA, August 1990.

Synchronization Migration for Performance Enhancement in a DOACROSS Loop

Rong-Yuh Hwang

Dept. of Electronic Engineering, National Taipei Institute of
Technology, Taipei, Taiwan, R. O. C.
ryh@en.tit.edu.tw

Abstract. An efficient technique for migrating the synchronization operations is proposed. This technique rewrites the original statements, *Send_Signal(S)* to be moved up and *Wait_Signal(S, i − d)* to be moved down, or rearranges the sequence of statements or the position of array element in a synchronization region by data dependence analysis to migrate the synchronization operations. Theorems show that the migration of synchronization operation can reduce the parallel execution time of loop significantly. Perfect benchmarks are employed to measure the system performance after migration. Experimental result shows that the enhancement is very significant.

Keywords. *Code migration, Data dependence, LBD, LFD, Synchronization, Synchronization region*

1   Introduction

Data dependences between different loop iterations are called loop-carried dependence, DOACROSS loop [4]. According to the statistics [2], the DOACROSS loops are significant parallelism sources, but not yet fully exploited. If a DOACROSS loop is executed sequentially, the system performance degrades seriously. To enforce the loop-carried dependences, synchronization instructions to coordinate data accesses from different processors are needed. There have been some works on multiprocessor data synchronization for DOACROSS loop. These include three kinds of data synchronization instructions [3]: 1) statement-oriented instructions such as P/V operations on semaphores, *Lock/Unlock* in the Cray XMP, *Advance/Wait* in [5], *Set/Wait* and *Send/Wait* in [10], *Post/Wait* in [11], 2) process-oriented instructions proposed in [3], and 3) data-oriented instruction such as *Full/Empty* tag scheme in HEP, integer-key scheme in the Cedar machine [1], *synch_read* and *synch_write* in [8]. For the data-oriented schemes, the synchronization operations are maintained during the memory accesses. These schemes incur a heavy memory space and initialization overhead. For the statement-level synchronization scheme, there exists a performance enhancement which is not yet exploited by all current synchronization schemes.

The basic approach for synchronization operation insertion is as follows:
1) generate a send statement immediately following dependence source S in the program text: *Send_Signal(S)*, and

2) generate a wait statement immediately before dependence sink S': *Wait_Signal(S, i − d)*, where *d* is dependence distance and *i − d* is iteration number.

For example, there exists three dependences, A[I] and B[I], inside the iteration in Fig. 1(a). Synchronization operation insertion is not needed in this case but the executing sequence can not be changed. On the other hand, there are two loop-carried dependences in Fig. 1(a). Array elements A[I] in statement S and A[I−1] in statement S_i exist a flow dependence with distance 1. Similarly, array elements B[I] in statement S and B[I−2] in statement S_k exist an anti-dependence with distance 2.

In order to maintain the correct execution, synchronization operations *Send_Signal(S)*, *Wait_Signal(S, I − 1)*, and *Wait_Signal(S, I − 2)* are inserted immediately after statement S, before statement S_i, and before statement S_k respectively. The synchronization operation insertion is shown in Fig. 1(b). It is possible to migrate *Wait_Signal* down and *Send_Signal* up. For example, an array element can be converted into several three address codes. The corresponding three address codes of the statements in Fig. 1(b) are shown in Fig. 2. Observing Fig. 1(b), *Wait_Signal(S, I − 1)* is inserted for the dependence sink A[I−1]; however, *Wait_Signal(S, I − 1)* has nothing to do with array elements E[I] and A[I] in statement S_i. And array elements A[I−1], E[I], and A[I] are 'read' operation.

Therefore, we can interchange the sequence of these elements. If the three address codes of array element A[I−1] is migrated after array elements E[I] and A[I], then *Wait_Signal(S, I − 1)* can be moved down. Evidence shows that the system performance is improved if *Send_Signal* can be migrated up or *Wait_Signal* can be migrated down. We had proposed an migration technique at instruction level to migrate *Send_Signal* up or *Wait_Signal* down [8, 9]. In this paper, we propose alternate techniques by moving synchronization operations at statement level to enhance the system performance.

DO I = 1, 100
  S_i: B[I] = A[I−1] − E[I] * A[I]
  S_j: D[I] = E[I] + A[I]
  S_k: B[I−21 = C[I] + E[I−2]
  S: A[I] = B[I] + G[I−3] * H[I]
END DO

(a) an example of Do loop

DOACROSS I = 1, 100
  Wait_Signal(S, 1 − 1)
  S_i: B[I] = A[I−1] − E[I] * A[I]
  S_j: D[I] = E[I] + A[I]
  Wait_Signal(S, I − 2)
  S_k: B[I−21 = C[I] + E[I−2]
  S: A[I] = B[I] + G[I−3] * H[I]
  Send-Signal(S)
ENDDO

(b) synchronization operation insertion in (a)

Fig. 1 *Synchronization operation insertion in a loop*

2   Related Work

The performance enhancement by migrating the synchronization operation is not discussed in any paper except [8]. In [8], we had proposed an efficient and intelligent migration technique. In this paper, an alternate efficient migration technique will be proposed.

The related theorems of code migration had made in [8]. Here, we only list the results with LFD and LBD cases.

Theorem 1: For a LFD loop, assume that the *Send_Signal* is at position i, and the *Wait_Signal* is at position j. (1) The parallel execution time of LFD loop is equal to the number of instructions in an instruction. (2) If *Wait_Signal* is moved down from j to j', the parallel execution time will be reduced by 0 time units. ($j < j'$)

Theorem 2: For a LBD loop, assume the *Send_Signal* is at position i, *Wait_Signal* is at position j, and the average distance is d. (1) the parallel execution time before migration is $\lfloor \frac{n}{d} \rfloor * (i-j+1)$, where $n > d$ (2) If *Send_Signal* is moved up to the position i', the parallel execution time of loop will be reduced by $\lfloor \frac{n}{d} \rfloor * (i - i')$ time units, where $i > i' > j$ (3) If *Wait_Signal* is moved down to the position j', the parallel execution time of loop will be reduced by $\lfloor \frac{n}{d} \rfloor * (j - j')$ time units, where $i > j' > j$.

Theorem 3: For any n dependence distances $d_1, d_2, ..., d_n$ with N iterations in a loop, where $N = i * LCM(d_1, d_2, ..., d_n)$, and i is a positive integer, the critical path which leads to the maximal parallel execution time in a loop only consists of a dependence distance.

Theorem 1 shows that the migration of synchronization operation in a LFD loop does not affect its parallel execution time. From the discussion above, the parallel execution time of LFD loop is always smaller than the parallel execution time of LBD loop. Therefore, the performance enhancement is achieved if LBD can be converted into LFD. From theorem 2, the more *Send_Signal* is moved up or *Wait_Signal* is moved down, the less the parallel execution time. Theorem 3 is very important, it tells that the parallel execution time is only formed by a dependence distance d_i, and this means that we need not migrate all LBDs. When the synchronization operation in the critical path is reduced by means of code migration, the parallel execution time can be improved.

3   Code Migration Technique

Now, we propose techniques to move *Send_Signal* up and *Wait_Signal* down. We discuss them in several aspects. First, we propose an algorithm to deal with the migration between statements. The parallel execution time is minimum if a LBD can be converted into a LFD. However, if LBD still exists after migration between statements, then migration in a statement is executed. For the migration in a statement, we describe how to rewrite statement to improve the system performance.

Finally, an advanced performance improvement is done by moving some array elements, which have not any dependence relation, out of the range between *Send_Signal* and its corresponding *Wait_Signal*.

3.1 Migration between Statements

The executing sequence of two statements S_1 and S_2 can be exchanged if there do not exist any dependence among their elements in the same iteration. For example, statements S and its corresponding *Send_Signal(S)* in Fig. 1 (b) can precede statements S_k and its corresponding *Wait_Signal(S, I − 2)* because all array elements in statements S and S_k do not depend on each other in the same iteration. Though array elements B[I] and B[I−2] have a loop-carried dependence, they do not depend on each other in the same iteration. After exchanging statements S and S_k, the dependence relation for array elements B[I] and B[I-2] is converted from LBD into LFD. According to theorem 2, the parallel execution time for LFD is minimum. Similarly, we try to exchange statements S and S_j; however, the exchanging fails because there exists an anti-dependence, A[I], in the same iteration. On the other hand, statements S_i and S_j have not any dependence in the same iteration. Therefore, statements S_i and its corresponding *Wait_Signal(S, I − 1)* can be interchanged with statement S_j. This leads to *Wait_Signal(S, I − 1)* to be moved down, and the performance enhancement is finished. The result of code migration is shown in Fig. 2. Now, we propose a technique to do migration between statements. Assuming the corresponding number of instructions for each statement is known.

Definition: For a backward data dependence $S_i\delta_\beta S_j$, the contiguous instructions from a *Send_Signal(S_i)* to its corresponding *Wait_Signal(S_j, I − d)* is called a backward synchronization region $SR(S_i\delta_\beta S_j)$, the notation for the corresponding parallel execution time of $SR(S_i\delta_\beta S_j)$ is $T(S_i\delta_\beta S_j)$, and the number of instruction in $SR(S_i\delta_\beta S_j)$ is $N(S_i\delta_\beta S_j)$.

Definition: For a backward data dependence $S_i\delta_\beta S_j$, an instruction $I \in SR(S_i\delta_\beta S_j)$ iff it belongs to the synchronization region $SR(S_i\delta_\beta S_j)$.

By (1) of theorem 2, the parallel execution time of $T(S_i\delta_\beta S_j)$ is

$$T(S_i\delta_\beta S_j) = \lfloor \frac{n}{d} \rfloor * N(S_i\delta_\beta S_j) + l \quad (1)$$

Observing (1), $T(S_i\delta_\beta S_j)$ will increase if $N(S_i\delta_\beta S_j)$ becomes large. Therefore, if S_i, dependence source, is moved to $S_{i'}$ which is in a backward synchronization region $SR(S_k\delta_\beta S_l)$, then $T(S_k\delta_\beta S_l)$ will increase, and the migration of S_i is useless if $T(S_{i'}\delta_\beta S_j) > T(S_i\delta_\beta S_j)$. Conversely, if $S_{i'}$ does not belong to any synchronization region, then the migration succeeds because it never increase the parallel execution time of any synchronization operation. After S_i is moved up to $S_{i'}$, its corresponding *Send_Signal(S_i)* is moved immediately following $S_{i'}$. Similarly, dependence sink S_j and its corresponding *Wait_Signal(S, I − d)* are to be moved down.

The algorithm for migrating statements is shown in algorithm 1. In this algorithm, all backward synchronization regions are found firstly. According to theorem 3, the synchronization region which has the largest parallel execution time is selected to be migrated. For a migration of *Send_Signal*, the migration succeeds if it is not moved into any backward synchronization region and there is not any dependence relation; however, if it is moved into one or more backward synchronization regions $SR(S_k \delta_\beta S_l)$, the parallel execution time for all $SR(S_k \delta_\beta S_l)$ need be recalculated. If any $SR(S_k \delta_\beta S_l)$ is larger than $SR(S_i \delta_\beta S_j)$, the migration fails. Conversely, the migration for *Wait_Signal* is similar to *Send_Signal*. Code migration is continued until each parallel execution time of synchronization region is smaller than the current maximal parallel execution time. Assuming array elements A[I], B[I], C[I], D[I], and H[I] in Fig. 1 (b) each is two instructions, array elements A[I-1], B[I-2], E[I-2], and G[I-3] each is translated into 3 instructions, and each operation needs 1 instruction. For simplicity, assuming each synchronization operation is corresponding to one instruction. In Fig. 1 (b), there are two LBDs whose dependence distances are 1 and 2. According to (1) of theorem 2, the parallel execution time for distance of 2 is 50×(1+3+2+3+2+2+2+3+2+3+1) = 1200 time units, and the parallel execution time for distance of 1 is 100× (1+2+3+2+2+3+2+2+2+2+1+3+2+3+2+2+2+3+2+3+1) = 4500 time units. Therefore, the parallel execution time in Fig. 1 (b) is 4500 time units. On the other hand, there exist one LBD and one LFD in Fig. 2. From (1) of theorem 1, the parallel execution time for LFD is 42 time units; however, the parallel execution time for LBD in Fig. 2 is (2+2+2+2)+100× (1+2+3+2+2+3+2+2+2+2+2+3+2+3+1)+1+(3+2+3+2)=2619 time units. Therefore, the parallel execution time in Fig. 2 is 2619 time units. There are 1881 time units improvement. As shown in the example, the performance enhancement after code migration is significant.

3. 2   Migration in a Statement

In this section we discuss how to migrate synchronization operations in a statement. Let $f_n(\alpha)$ be an expression with n operands, *op* is an operator and there are n dimension in a loop.

1) Migration of Send_Signal

Send_Signal can not precede its corresponding dependence source; otherwise, the processor waiting for the corresponding *Send_Signal* might access a stale data. Let array element A_{src} be a dependence source.

Case 1: A_{src} is on the right-hand side of ':='.

$B[] := A_{src}[]\ op\ f_n(\alpha)$

Send_Signal

In order to move *Send_Signal* up, these two statements can be rewritten as

$Temp[i_1, ..., i_n] := A_{src}[]$

Send_Signal

$B[] := Temp[i_1, ..., i_n]\ op\ f_n(\alpha)$

DOACROSS I = 1,100
S_j: D[I] = E[I] + A[I]

    Wait_Signal(S, I − 1)

S_i: B[I] = A[I−1] −E[I] * A[I]

S: A[I] = B[I] + G[I−3] * H[I]

    Send_Signal(S)

    Wait_Signal(S, I − 2)

S_k: B[I−2] = C[I] + E[I−2]

END DO

Fig. 2 *After migration between statements for Fig. 1 (b)*

DOACROSS I = 1,100
S_j: D[I] = E[I] + A[I]

    Temp[I] = A[I−1] −E[I] * A[I]

    Wait_Signal(S, I − 1)

S_i: B[I] = A[I−1] −Temp[I]

S: A[I] = B[I] + G[I−3] * H[I]

    Send_Signal(S)

    Wait_Signal(S, I − 2)

S_k: B[I−2] = C[I] + E[I−2]

END DO

Fig. 3 *After migration in a statement for Fig. 2*

Algorithm 1: Migration_between_statements

1. Calculate the parallel execution time of all backward synchronization regions in the program;

2. For the backward synchronization region $SR(S_i\delta_\beta S_j)$ whose $T(S_i\delta_\beta S_j)$ is maximal do

   2.1 moving S_i up to $S_{i'}$ by dependence analysis

     if $S_{i'} \in SR(S_k\delta_\beta S_l)$, $k \neq i$ and $l \neq j$ **then**

       {recalculated the parallel execution time, $T'(S_k\delta_\beta S_l)$, of $SR(S_k\delta_\beta S_l)$

        if $T'(S_k\delta_\beta S_l) \geq T(S_i\delta_\beta S_j)$ then migration fails; quit;}

      moving *Send_Signal(S_i)* immediately following S_i;

  2. 2 moving S_j down to $S_{j'}$ by dependence analysis

     if $S_{j'} \in SR(S_k\delta_\beta S_l)$, $k \neq i$ and $l \neq j$ **then**

       {recalculated the parallel execution time, $T'(S_k\delta_\beta S_l)$, of $SR(S_k\delta_\beta S_l)$

        if $T'(S_k\delta_\beta S_l) \geq T(S_i\delta_\beta S_j)$ then migration fails; quit;}

      moving *Wait_Signal(S_i, I − d)* immediately preceding S_j

3. Recalculated the parallel execution time, $T_{new}( )$, of $SR(S_i\delta_\beta S_j)$;

4. If there exists synchronization region whose parallel execution time is larger than $T_{new}( )$ and is not migrated then goto step 2;

After rewriting, *Send_Signal* is moved across $f_n(\alpha)$. According to (2) of theorem 2, the performance is enhanced. This technique creates an extra true dependence for $Temp[i_1, ..., i_n]$; however, this dependence is not a loop-carried dependence and can be resolved with hardware such as pipeline technique.

Case 2: A_{src} is on the left-hand side of ':='. For such case, *Send_Signal* can not be moved up because array element $A_{src}[]$ is placed at the last position of three address code.

2) Migration of Wait_Signal

In order to maintain order dependence, *Wait_Signal* can not be behind its corresponding dependence sink; otherwise, the processor waiting for the corresponding *Send_Signal* always accesses the dependence sink without suspending. Let A_{snk} be a dependence sink.

Case 1: A_{snk} is on the right-hand side of ':='.

    Wait_Signal
    $B[] := A_{snk}[] \; op \; f_n(\alpha)$

In order to move *Wait_Signal* down, these two statements can be rewritten as

    $Temp[i_1, ..., i_n] := f_n(\alpha)$
    Wait_Signal
    $B[] := Temp[i_1, ..., i_n] \; op \; A_{snk}[]$

For such arrangement, *Wait_Signal* can be moved after $f_n(\alpha)$. According to (3) of theorem 2, the parallel execution time of loop will be reduced.

Case 2: A_{snk} is on the left-hand side of ':='.

    Wait_Signal
    $A_{snk}[] := f_m(\alpha)$

In order to move *Wait_Signal* down, these two statements can be rewritten as

    $Temp[i_1, ..., i_n] := f_m(\alpha)$
    Wait_Signal
    $A_{snk}[] := Temp[i_1, ..., i_n]$

For such case, *Wait_Signal* can be moved after $f_m(\alpha)$. According to (3) of theorem 2, the performance is enhanced.

3) Migration of multiple dependence source/sink

An array element is called multiple dependence source/sink if it is both a dependence source and a dependence sink. Let $A_{src/snk}$ be a multiple dependence source/sink.

Case 1: $A_{src/snk}$ is on the right-hand side of ':='.

    Wait_Signal
    $D[] := A_{src/snk}[] \; op \; f_n(\alpha)$
    Send_Signal

For such case, either *Send_Signal* or *Wait_Signal* can be migrated. This is similar to case 1 of migration of *Send_Signal* or *Wait_Signal* respectively. If we move *Send_Signal* up, these three statements can be rewritten as

> *Wait_Signal*
> Temp[] := $A_{src/snk}$[]
> *Send_Signal*
> D[] := Temp[] *op* $f_n(\alpha)$

If we move *Wait_Signal* down, these three statements can be rewritten as

> Temp[] := $f_n(\alpha)$
> *Wait_Signal*
> D[] := $A_{src/snk}$[] *op* Temp[]
> *Send_Signal*

According to theorem 2, the performance is also enhanced.

Case 2: $A_{src/snk}$ is on the left-hand side of ':=' .

For such case, *Send_Signal* can not be moved up. Therefore, *Wait_Signal* is to be moved down and this is similar to case 2 of migration of *Wait_Signal*.

For example, the loop in Fig. 2 can be migrated as shown in Fig. 3 by applying case 2 of *Wait_Signal* migration. From theorem 2, the parallel execution time in Fig. 3 is 8 + 12 + 100×(1+2+3+2+2+2+2+3+2+3+1)+ 1 + 10=2331 time units.

> DOACROSS I = 1,100
> S_j: D[I] = E[I] + A[I]
>   Temp[I] = A[I−1] −E[I] * A[I]
>   Temp1[I] = G[I−3] * H[I]
>   *Wait_Signal(S, I − 1)*
> S_i: B[I] = A[I−1] −Temp[I]
> S: A[I] = B[I] + Temp1[I]
>   *Send_Signal(S)*
>   *Wait_Signal(S, I − 2)*
> S_k: B[I−2] = C[I] + E[I−2]
> END DO

Fig. 4 *After moving independent out of the synchronization region for Fig. 3*

3.3 Advanced Migration Techniques: Redundant Element Elimination

From the discussion in Section 2, the performance is improved if *Send_Signal* is moved up or *Wait_Signal* is moved down. In other word, the performance will be improved if the number of array element in the synchronization becomes small. Therefore, we try to reduce the number of array element in the synchronization region. Basically, an array element can be migrated to a new position if there is not any dependence in the same iteration between the old and new position. An array element in the synchronization region is redundant if this element can be moved out of that region. A statement that has a dependence sink will not have any redundant array elements after performing *migration in a statement*. For the other statements in the synchronization region, we need to check redundant element statement by statement. For example, statement S_j in Fig. 3 is the statement which exists a dependence sink A[I−1]. Therefore, there is not any redundant element in this statement. However, statement S in Fig. 3 has two redundant array elements G[I−3] and H[I]. We can migrate them out of the synchronization region shown in Fig. 4. G[I−3] * H[I] is replaced by a new temporary array element Templ[I]. After such arrangement, the parallel execution time is reduced as 1940 time units.

4 Experimental Results

4.1 Benchmark and Statistical Model

The Perfect Benchmarks (**PERF**ormance Evaluation for Cost-effective Transformations) is a suite of 13 FORTRAN 77 programs [7]. In this section, we use nine of the Perfect Benchmarks to make a statistics of dependence position. In these statistics, we apply Parafrase compiler to detect the loops which cannot be executed in parallel. The statistic model is constructed as follows. First, we use Parafrase compiler to convert a benchmark (*.f) into parallel source code (*.gen). Then, we extract DO loops which cannot be parallelized by Parafrase from the parallel source code. Chen and Yew [2] measured the contributions of individual restructuring techniques. The transformations examined are recurrence replacement, synchronized DOACROSS loops, induction variable substitution, scalar expansion, forward substitution, reduction statements, loop interchanging, and strip-mining. Surprisingly enough, the restructuring techniques have little effect on the speed of the codes. There are a few exceptions, however. Of all the restructuring techniques examined, scalar expansion had the greatest effect on performance of the codes. Reduction replacement is another transformation that significantly improves the performance of several codes.

According to their measurement, we use scalar expansion, reduction replacement, and induction variable substitution to convert a do loop into DOACROSS loop. And then we insert synchronization operations to execute DOACROSS loop in parallel. Similarly, synchronization operations are also inserted into the original DOACROSS loop. Then, an evaluator is constructed to collect some information about the position of each dependence event.

4.2 Statistical Results

According to the statistics in [7], there are 6 types of DOACROSS loop. These types are control dependence, anti-output dependence, induction variable, reduction operation, simple subscript expression and others that are not included in the above categories. Now, we explain some statistics gathered by using types 3 (induction variable), 4 (reduction operation), 5 (simple subscript expression), and part of type 6. First, we want to see the percentage of flow, anti-, and output dependences. These are listed in table 1. From this table, flow dependence is the major dependence type (90%) because reduction replacement is always converted as a flow dependence. Then we want to know the percentage of LBD and LFD. This measurement is listed in table 2. In this table, we find that benchmarks FLQ52, BDNA, TRFD, QCD, and TRACK are all LBD. The percentage of LBD is about to 95%. From the discussion above, we find that almost all dependences are *flow* LBD type of dependence. The flow dependence cannot be eliminated by any current compiler technique such as scalar renaming. On the other hand, LBD is the major factor for increasing the parallel execution time. These statistics display that code migration is necessary for the DOACROSS loop on the multiprocessor system.

Now, we investigate the migrating potential of code migration. Basically, a dependence source and its corresponding sink can be in the same statement or in different statements. If a dependence source and its corresponding sink are in the same statement, then the statement can not be converted from LBD into LFD. But, it is possible to reduce the parallel execution time by migrating *Send_Signal* up or *Wait_Signal* down. The number of array element between two array elements is named *distance*. For a dependence with LBD and flow dependence, migration at statement level can migrate *Wait_Signal* near the dependence source with distance 2. The statistics about dependence in a statement are listed in table 3. In this table, we find that benchmark ARC2D has the largest number of dependences in a statement. The average distance of a *dependence source* and its corresponding *dependence sink* in a statement is 3.2. Assuming each loop has 100 iterations, and each array element has 3 corresponding instructions whose numbers are minimum, the improved percentage for migration in a statement at statement level is as listed in Fig. 5. Benchmark MDG has significant improvement because reduction replacement is the major source of loop in MDG. The average improvement at statement level in a statement is 37.4%.

Now, we investigate the improved percentage in migration between statements. According to tables 4 and 5, we know the percentage for the dependence between statements is 30.5%. Benchmarks ARC2D, MDG, ADM, and SPEC77 contain this kind of dependence. Finally, we investigate the improved percentage for migration between statements with redundant element elimination. The total distance between statements of each benchmark is listed in table 4. Among these benchmarks, SPEC77 has the largest distance between statements, which means that SPEC77 will have a significantly improved percentage. After migration, the distance between statements is as listed in table 4. We find that benchmark SPEC77 has a significant improvement (98.4%), while the others get about 50% ~ 80% improvement. The position of a *Src* in benchmark SPEC77 is far away from its corresponding *Snk*; therefore, a significant performance enhancement is carried out. The improved percentage for migration between statements at instruction level is listed in Fig. 5. This figure displays that there is 80.4% improvement for the migration between statements with redundant element elimination. In summary, the improvement for migration at statement level is as shown in Fig. 5. The average improvement is about to 62.9%.

Table 1 *Total number of various dependence types*

Items Benchmark	Total number of flow dependence	Total number of anti dependence	Total number of output dependence
FLQ52	7	0	0
BDNA	34	0	0
ARC2D	159	3	0
TRFD	5	0	0
QCD	2	0	0
MDG	38	0	0
TRACK	4	0	0
ADM	11	6	3
SPEC77	12	1	17
Total	272	10	20

Table 2 *Total number of LFD and LBD*

Items Benchmark	Total number of LFD	Total number of LBD
FLQ52	0	7
BDNA	0	34
ARC2D	3	159
TRFD	0	5
QCD	0	2
MDG	6	32
TRACK	0	4
ADM	6	14
SPEC77	0	30
Total	15	287

Table 3 *Statistics in a statement*

Items Benchmark	Total number of dependence in a statement	Total distance in a statement
FLQ52	7	18
BDNA	34	97
ARC2D	114	297
TRFD	5	14
QCD	2	6
MDG	19	149
TRACK	4	14
ADM	13	30
SPEC77	12	46
Total	210	671

Table 4 *Statistics between statements*

Items Benchmark	Total number of dependence between statements	Total max. distance between statements	Total max. distance after migration
FLQ52	0	0	0
BDNA	0	0	0
ARC2D	48	342	160
TRFD	0	0	0
QCD	0	0	0
MDG	19	45	19
TRACK	0	0	0
ADM	7	17	3
SPEC77	18	571	9
Total	92	975	191

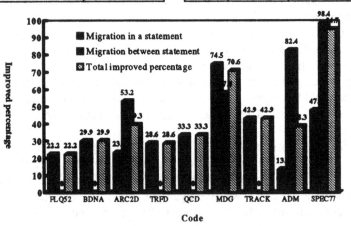

Fig. 5 *Percentage of improvement for migration*

5 Conclusion

We have proposed an efficient technique to enhance the system performance. The enhancement can be easily implemented by rewriting the original statement or migrating the statement sequence by dependence analysis. All cases for migration in a statement are considered and a better rewriting form is proposed. An algorithm is developed for the migration between statements. Finally, the redundant array elements are moved out of the synchronization region. The major feature of migration at statement levels is that it never increases the parallel execution time during statement migration. Experimental result shows that these techniques can reduce the overhead of synchronization operation significantly.

References

1. C. Q. Zhu and P. C. Yew, 'A scheme to enforce data dependence on large multiprocessor systems', *IEEE trans. Software Eng.* June 1987, 726-739.
2. D. K. Chen and P. C. Yew, 'An empirical study on DOACROSS loops', *Proc. of supercomputing.* November 1991, 18-22.
3. H. M. Su, and P. C. Yew, 'On data synchronization for multiprocessors', *Proceeding l 6th Annual International Symposium on Computer Architecture,* May 1989, 416-423 .
4. J. R. Allen and K. Kennedy, 'Automatic translation of FORTRAN programs to vector form', *ACM trans. Programming Language and Syst,* October 1987, 491-542.
5. M. Wolfe, 'Multiprocessor synchronization for concurrent loops', *IEEE Software,* January 1988, 34-42.
6. P. Tang, P. C. Yew and C. Q. Zhu, 'Compiler techniques for data synchronization in nested parallel loops', *Proc. 1990 International Conference on Supercomputing, Amsterdam,* Holland, May 1990, 177-186
7. R. Eigenmann, J. Hoeflinger, Z. Li, and D. Padua, 'Experiences in the automatic parallelization of four perfect-benchmark programs', *Proceeding of the Fourth Workshop on Languages and Compilers for Parallel Computing.* August 1991, pp. 87-95.
8. Rong-Yuh Hwang and Feipei Lai, 'An Intelligent Code Migration Technique for Synchronization Operations on a Multiprocessor', *IEE Proceedings-E Computers and Digital Techniques,* March 1995, pp107-116.
9. Rong-Yuh Hwang and Feipei Lai, 'Intelligent Code Migration Technique for Synchronization Operations on a Multiprocessor', International Symposium on a Parallel Architectures, Algorithms, and Networks, December 1994, pp121-127.
10. S. P. Midkiff and D. A. Padua, 'Compiler algorithm for synchronization', *IEEE trans. Comput,* C-36, 12, December 1987, pp1485-1495.
11. Z. Li, 'Compiler algorithms for event variable synchronization', *Proc. 1991 ACM International Conference on Supercomputing,* July 1991, pp85-95.

An Array Partitioning Analysis for Parallel Loop Distribution

Marc Le Fur, Jean-Louis Pazat and Françoise André *

IRISA, Campus de Beaulieu, F-35042 Rennes Cedex, FRANCE

Abstract. This paper presents the compilation techniques implemented in a compiler for a HPF-like language. The stress is especially put on the description of an optimized scheme which is dedicated to the compilation of parallel nested loops. The generation of the SPMD code is based on the polyhedral model and allows for the partitioning of the arrays involved in the loop in order to achieve symbolic restriction of iteration domains and message aggregation. Experimental results for some well-known kernels are shown.

1 Introduction and Motivation

The data parallel model is often shown as a promising way to easily write programs for distributed memory computers or clusters of workstations.

Among data parallel languages, High Performance Fortran [12] and its precursors embed data partitioning features in a sequential language as a means to drive the parallelization and the distribution of programs. With this paradigm, the programmer is still provided with a familiar uniform logical address space and a sequential flow of control. The compiler generates code according to the SPMD model and the links between the code execution and the data distribution are enforced by the *owner-computes rule*: each processor executes only the statements that modify the data assigned to it by the user-specified distribution.

This approach constitutes the basis of several compilers [17, 6] and is also applied in the PANDORE environment [4].

A simple scheme called *runtime resolution* [5] permits the translation of any sequential program into communicating processes. The first experiments have shown that aggressive optimization techniques are needed to generate efficient code.

The paper presents an optimized translation scheme, implemented in the PANDORE compiler, dedicated to the compilation of parallel loop nests with one statement. The importance of parallel loop nests in scientific applications is manifest. On the one hand, these loops form most computation-intensive parts of scientific programs. On the other hand, these loops can be produced thanks to automatic parallelization techniques such as affine-by-statement scheduling [10, 9] or automatic vectorization [1].

---

* mlefur@irisa.fr, pazat@irisa.fr, fandre@irisa.fr

We address the problem of determining the communication and computation sets induced by the user-supplied distribution of arrays. The work presented in the paper is related to [2, 18], [17] and [6] that use respectively polyhedrons, regular sections and overlaps (rectangular sections) to represent these sets. The problem has also been studied in the framework of the compilation of array statements in [7] and [11]; this time, a finite state machine and triplets permit the characterization of the different sets.

The paper is organized as follows. We first give the principles of the optimized compilation scheme in section 2 and then illustrate the technique in section 3. Notations and definitions are posed in section 4 in order to present code generation in 5. Experimental results for well-known kernels are shown in section 6.

2 Principles of the Optimized Scheme

The optimized compilation scheme separates the generated SPMD code into a communication part and a computation part. The generation of each part relies on a domain analysis that takes advantage of the user-partitioning of the arrays into rectangular blocks in order to achieve symbolic restriction of iteration domains and message aggregation. Furthermore, this domain analysis is symbolic, *i.e.* independent of the number of blocks of each array involved in the parallel loop nest.

Our optimized compilation method applies to parallel loop nests where array references and loop bounds are affine functions of the enclosing indices and where each loop stride is equal to one. As regards data distribution, we assume that an array is either replicated on all processors (the array is owned by each processor) or distributed, that is partitioned into rectangular blocks with constant sizes (known at compile-time), each block being assigned to exactly one processor. Scalar elements are systematically replicated.

Because we assume that the loop bounds and the array access functions are affine, the data access domains can be characterized by polyhedrons and the generated code execution will consist in scanning these polyhedrons. Indeed, a loop nest performing the enumeration of its integer vectors can be associated with any non empty bounded polyhedron. Different algorithms can be used to solve the polyhedron scanning problem [13, 8, 14]; the algorithm implemented in the PANDORE compiler is detailed in [15].

3 Example

For the sake of concreteness, let us consider the following (contrived) parallel nest:

```
for i₁ = 1 , 1000
    for i₂ = i₁ , 2 * i₁ + 1
        S(i₁, i₂) :  X[i₁, i₂ - i₁] := Y[i₂, 2 * i₁ - 2]
```

where arrays X and Y are partitioned into 8 blocks numbered from 0 to 7, as indicated in figure 1.

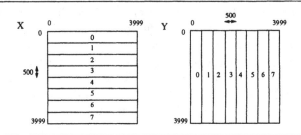

Fig. 1. Partitioning of Arrays

Communication Code Generation.

a - The set of vectors $(j^X \, j^Y \, i_1 \, i_2)$ where j^X (resp. j^Y) $\in 0..7$ is a block of X (resp. Y), $(i_1 \, i_2)$ an iteration vector such that $S(i_1, i_2)$ writes in j^X and reads in j^Y, can be characterized by the polyhedron $\mathcal{P}_1$ defined by the system:

$$\begin{cases} 0 \leq j^X \leq 7 \\ 0 \leq j^Y \leq 7 \\ 1 \leq i_1 \leq 1000 \\ i_1 \leq i_2 \leq 2 * i_1 + 1 \\ 500 * j^X \leq i_1 \leq 500 * j^X + 499 \\ 500 * j^Y \leq 2 * i_1 - 2 \leq 500 * j^Y + 499 \end{cases}$$

b - The enumeration code of polyhedron $\mathcal{P}_1$ can be computed by one of the algorithms [15, 13, 8, 14]; for instance, the algorithm implemented in PANDORE [15] yields the following nested loop:

```
for j^X = 0 , 2
    for j^Y = max(0 , 2*j^X −1) , min(3 , 2*j^X +1)
        for i₁ = max(250*j^Y +1, 500*j^X) ,
                min(250*j^Y +250 , 500*j^X +499)
            for i₂ = i₁ , 2*i₁ +1
```

It is important to notice that the first two loops of this enumeration code do not scan the whole cartesian product $0..7 \times 0..7$, as it can be seen in figure 2. The subset of $0..7 \times 0..7$ described by the (j^X, j^Y)-loop is defined as the convex-hull of the integer projection of polyhedron $\mathcal{P}_1$ along the i_1, i_2 axes.

c - We then insert two masks and a communication instruction in this enumeration code in order to generate the SPMD send code and then a dual SPMD receive code. The send code is generated as follows:

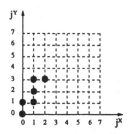

Fig. 2. Restriction of Iteration Domains

```
for j^X = 0 , 2
    if myself ≠ owner of block j^X of X then
        for j^Y = max(0, 2*j^X −1) , min(3, 2*j^X +1)
            if myself = owner of block j^Y of Y then
                for i₁ = max(250*j^Y +1, 500*j^X) ,
                          min(250*j^Y +250, 500*j^X +499)
                    for i₂ = i₁ , 2*i₁ +1
                        pack Y[i₂, 2 * i₁ − 2] in buffer
                send buffer to the owner of block j^X of X
```

The runtime library routine *pack* performs data elements aggregation. Although the previous loop contains masks, the reader should note that these masks are evaluated at the block level and not at the iteration vector level as in the runtime resolution. Furthermore, the (j^X, j^Y)-loop enumerates only a few vectors, as seen in figure 2, and the location of the first mask prevents from enumerating all these vectors.

Computation Code Generation.

a - As before, the set of vectors $(j^X\ i_1\ i_2)$ where $j^X \in 0..7$ is a block of X, $(i_1\ i_2)$ an iteration vector such that $S(i_1, i_2)$ writes in j^X, can be characterized by the polyhedron $\mathcal{P}_2$ defined by the following system:

$$\begin{cases} 0 \le j^X \le 7 \\ 1 \le i_1 \le 1000 \\ i_1 \le i_2 \le 2 * i_1 + 1 \\ 500 * j^X \le i_1 \le 500 * j^X + 499 \end{cases}$$

b - The vectors of $\mathcal{P}_2$ can be enumerated by the nested loop:

```
for j^X = 0 , 2
    for i₁ = max(500*j^X, 1) , min(500*j^X +499, 1000)
        for i₂ = i₁ , 2*i₁ +1
```

which shows that the blocks 3..7 of X are not written during the computation (the j^X-loop scans the convex-hull of the integer projection of polyhedron $\mathcal{P}_2$ along the i_1, i_2 axes).

c - Finally, a mask is inserted to produce the SPMD computation code:

```
for j^X = 0 , 2
    if myself = owner of block j^X of X then
        for i₁ = max(500*j^X, 1) , min(500*j^X +499, 1000)
            for i₂ = i₁ , 2*i₁ +1
                X[i₁, i₂ − i₁] := Y[i₂, 2 * i₁ − 2]
```

4 Notations and Definitions

If x is a row or column vector with n components, x_q $(1 \le q \le n)$ stands for the qth component of x. Given a row or column vector u with n components $u_1, \ldots, u_n$, $X[u]$ denotes the reference $X[u_1, \ldots, u_n]$ to array X. If the access function associated with an array reference is affine, for instance $X[i+3, 2i+j+1]$, the reference may be noted in matrix form as follows:

$$X[\begin{pmatrix} 1 & 0 \\ 2 & 1 \end{pmatrix} \begin{pmatrix} i \\ j \end{pmatrix} + \begin{pmatrix} 3 \\ 1 \end{pmatrix}]$$

Finally, for row vectors u and v with n and p components respectively, $(u\ v)$ stands for the vector with $(n+p)$ components $(u_1 \ldots u_n\ v_1 \ldots v_p)$. This notation can be extended to an arbitrary number of vectors.

Notations related to Distributed Arrays. In order to simplify the notations, we assume that the lower bound is 0 in each dimension of an array. Let X be a m-dimensional distributed array and let h_p^X (resp. s_p^X) be the number of elements (resp. the block size) of array X in the pth dimension $(p \in 1 .. m)$.

We note $Part(X) = \{p \in 1 .. m\ /\ s_p^X < h_p^X\}$ the set of partitioned dimensions of X and $d(X, q)$ the qth partitioned dimension of X if $q \in 1 .. |Part(X)|$. For arrays Y and Z given in figure 3 for instance:

$h_1^Y = 400 \quad h_2^Y = 800$
$s_1^Y = 200 \quad s_2^Y = 250$
$Part(Y) = \{1, 2\}$
$d(Y, 1) = 1 \quad d(Y, 2) = 2$

$h_1^Z = 500 \quad h_2^Z = 700$
$s_1^Z = 500 \quad s_2^Z = 300$
$Part(Z) = \{2\}$
$d(Z, 1) = 2$

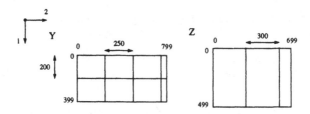

Fig. 3. Partitioning of Arrays

Let n be the number of partitioned dimensions of array X. We term block of X indexed by the vector j, where j is a row vector with n components such that $\forall q \in 1..n$ $\quad 0 \le j_q \le \lceil h^X_{d(X,q)}/s^X_{d(X,q)} \rceil - 1$, and we note $Block(X,j)$, the block $X[lbnd_1..ubnd_1,\ldots,lbnd_m..ubnd_m]$ of array X defined by

$lbnd_{d(X,q)} = j_q s^X_{d(X,q)}$ and $ubnd_{d(X,q)} = min(j_q s^X_{d(X,q)} + s^X_{d(X,q)} - 1, h^X_{d(X,q)} - 1)$ for each partitioned dimension $d(X,q)$ of X ($q \in 1..n$),
$lbnd_p = 0$ and $ubnd_p = h^X_p - 1$ for each dimension p of X which is not partitioned.

Intuitively, the components of j are related to the coordinates of $Block(X,j)$ in the space of the blocks of array X when all the dimensions of X are partitioned. In the general case, j must be related only to the coordinates of $Block(X,j)$ associated with the partitioned dimensions of X. For arrays Y and Z for instance:

$Block(Y,(0\ 1)) = Y[0..199, 250..499]$, $Block(Y,(1\ 3)) = Y[200..399, 750..799]$.
$Block(Z,(0)) = Z[0..499, 0..299]$, $Block(Z,(2)) = Z[0..499, 600..699]$.

and more generally:

$Block(Y,(j_1\ j_2)) = Y[200j_1..200j_1 + 199, 250j_2..min(250j_2 + 249, 799)]$ $\forall j_1 \in 0..1$ $\forall j_2 \in 0..3$,
$Block(Z,(j_1)) = Z[0..499, 300j_1..min(300j_1 + 299, 699)]$ $\forall j_1 \in 0..2$.

Finally, for a vector u with m components and a vector j with n components, we note $Belong(X,u,j)$ the set of inequalities that must be satisfied by vector u so that the reference $X[u]$ belongs to the block $Block(X,j)$ of X:

$j_q s^X_{d(X,q)} \le u_{d(X,q)} \le j_q s^X_{d(X,q)} + s^X_{d(X,q)} - 1$ for each $q \in 1..n$,
$u_p \le \lceil h^X_p/s^X_p \rceil - 1$ for each partitioned dimension p of X such that h^X_p is not a multiple of s^X_p.

Indeed, if p is a partitioned dimension of X, the constraints $u_p \le \lceil h^X_p/s^X_p \rceil - 1$ where h^X_p is a multiple of s^X_p are implicit in this system and thus useless. For instance, for the vector $u = (i_1 + 1\ \ i_1 + 2i_2)$:

$Belong(Y,u,(j_1\ j_2)) = \{200j_1 \le i_1 + 1 \le 200j_1 + 199, \quad 250j_2 \le i_1 + 2i_2 \le 250j_2 + 249, \quad i_1 + 2i_2 \le 799\}$,
$Belong(Z,u,(j_1)) = \{300j_1 \le i_1 + 2i_2 \le 300j_1 + 299, \quad i_1 + 2i_2 \le 699\}$.

Notations related to Nested Loops. In the following, a perfectly nested loop whose (row) iteration vector is i, iteration domain $\mathcal{D}$ and body B will be noted

$\quad$ **for** i **in** $\mathcal{D}$ $\qquad$ or $\qquad$ **for** $i : Ai^T + b \ge 0$
$\quad\quad B$ $\qquad\qquad\qquad\qquad\qquad\quad B$

if the iteration domain of the nested loop is a polyhedron defined by the set of affine constraints $Ai^T + b \ge 0$.

Polyhedrons for Code Generation. Let us consider a parallel loop nest whose iteration vector is i and whose iteration domain is defined by the system of affine constraints $Ai^T + b \ge 0$. The generation of the communication and computation codes for the loop nest lies in the synthesis of polyhedrons called $\mathcal{P}_1$ and $\mathcal{P}_2$ which are functions of the references to distributed arrays appearing in the nest assignment.

Given two references $X[C^X i^T + d^X]$ and $X'[C^{X'} i^T + d^{X'}]$ to distributed arrays in the parallel nest assignment, $\mathcal{P}_1(X[C^X i^T + d^X], X'[C^{X'} i^T + d^{X'}])$ is the set of (row) vectors of the form $((j_p^X)_{p \in 1..|Part(X)|} \quad (j_q^{X'})_{q \in 1..|Part(X')|} \quad i)$ and satisfying the system of inequalities:

$$\forall p \in 1..|Part(X)| \quad 0 \leq j_p^X \leq \lceil h_{d(X,p)}^X / s_{d(X,p)}^X \rceil - 1$$
$$\forall q \in 1..|Part(X')| \quad 0 \leq j_q^{X'} \leq \lceil h_{d(X',q)}^{X'} / s_{d(X',q)}^{X'} \rceil - 1$$
$$A i^T + b \geq 0$$
$$Belong(X, \; C^X i^T + d^X, \; (j_p^X)_{p \in 1..|Part(X)|})$$
$$Belong(X', \; C^{X'} i^T + d^{X'}, \; (j_q^{X'})_{q \in 1..|Part(X')|})$$

One can easily check that this system defines a polyhedron because all its constraints are affine (the references to arrays X and X' are affine). In other terms, $\mathcal{P}_1(X[C^X i^T + d^X], X'[C^{X'} i^T + d^{X'}])$ is the set of vectors $((j_p^X)_{p \in 1..|Part(X)|}$ $(j_q^{X'})_{q \in 1..|Part(X')|} \quad i)$ such that the references $X[C^X i^T + d^X]$ and $X'[C^{X'} i^T + d^{X'}]$ belong to $Block(X, (j_p^X)_{p \in 1..|Part(X)|})$ and $Block(X', (j_q^{X'})_{q \in 1..|Part(X')|})$ respectively.

For the references $Y[i_1 + 1, i_1 + 2i_2]$ and $Z[i_2 - i_1, 3i_1 - 2]$ to the arrays shown in figure 3, located in a parallel nest whose iteration domain is defined by $\{1 \leq i_1 \leq 230, \; i_1 + 1 \leq i_2 \leq 350\}$, the constraints satisfied by the vectors $(j_1^Y \; j_2^Y \; j_1^Z \; i_1 \; i_2)$ of $\mathcal{P}_1(Y[i_1 + 1, i_1 + 2i_2], Z[i_2 - i_1, 3i_1 - 2])$ are the following:

$$0 \leq j_1^Y \leq 1, \quad 0 \leq j_2^Y \leq 3$$
$$0 \leq j_1^Z \leq 2$$
$$1 \leq i_1 \leq 230, \quad i_1 + 1 \leq i_2 \leq 350$$
$$200 j_1^Y \leq i_1 + 1 \leq 200 j_1^Y + 199, \quad 250 j_2^Y \leq i_1 + 2i_2 \leq 250 j_2^Y + 249, \quad i_1 + 2i_2 \leq 799$$
$$300 j_1^Z \leq 3i_1 - 2 \leq 300 j_1^Z + 299, \quad 3i_1 - 2 \leq 699$$

For a reference $X[C i^T + d]$ in the parallel nest, the polyhedron $\mathcal{P}_2(X[C i^T + d])$ denotes the set of (row) vectors of the form $((j_p)_{p \in 1..|Part(X)|} \quad i)$ satisfying the set of affine inequalities:

$$\forall p \in 1..|Part(X)| \quad 0 \leq j_p \leq \lceil h_{d(X,p)}^X / s_{d(X,p)}^X \rceil - 1$$
$$A i^T + b \geq 0$$
$$Belong(X, \; C i^T + d, \; (j_p)_{p \in 1..|Part(X)|})$$

More simply, each vector $((j_p)_{p \in 1..|Part(X)|} \quad i)$ of $\mathcal{P}_2(X[C i^T + d])$ defines an iteration vector i such that the reference $X[C i^T + d]$ belongs to the block $Block(X, (j_p)_{p \in 1..|Part(X)|})$ of X.

With the same iteration domain as previously, $\mathcal{P}_2(Y[i_1 + 1, i_1 + 2i_2])$ is the set of vectors $(j_1 \; j_2 \; i_1 \; i_2)$ satisfying:

$$0 \leq j_1 \leq 1, \quad 0 \leq j_2 \leq 3$$
$$1 \leq i_1 \leq 230, \quad i_1 + 1 \leq i_2 \leq 350$$
$$200 j_1 \leq i_1 + 1 \leq 200 j_1 + 199, \quad 250 j_2 \leq i_1 + 2i_2 \leq 250 j_2 + 249, \quad i_1 + 2i_2 \leq 799$$

and each vector $(j_1 \; i_1 \; i_2)$ of $\mathcal{P}_2(Z[i_2 - i_1, 3i_1 - 2])$ is such that:

$$0 \leq j_1 \leq 2$$
$$1 \leq i_1 \leq 230, \quad i_1 + 1 \leq i_2 \leq 350$$
$$300 j_1 \leq 3i_1 - 2 \leq 300 j_1 + 299, \quad 3i_1 - 2 \leq 699$$

5 Code Generation

Actually, two compilation schemes are defined depending on whether the left hand side (*lhs*) of the assignment refers to a distributed array or a replicated array.

5.1 Compilation Scheme if the lhs refers to a Distributed Array

In this case, the parallel loop nest is of the form

$$\text{for } i : Ai^T + b \geq 0$$
$$X[C^X i^T + d^X] := Exp \, (Dist \uplus Repl)$$

where the array X referenced in the *lhs* is a distributed array, $Dist$ the set of references to distributed arrays in the expression Exp and $Repl$ the set of references to replicated variables (arrays or scalar variables) in Exp.

Communication Code Generation. Let us note $Com = Dist - \{X[C^X i^T + d^X]\}$ the set of references in $Dist$ that *may* generate communications between processors (it is clear indeed that, if $X[C^X i^T + d^X]$ belongs to $Dist$, this reference does not lead to any interprocessor communication). It should be highlighted that the set Com can be reduced still further if some references in $Dist$ are aligned (in a HPF-manner) with $X[C^X i^T + d^X]$. In the following code for instance:

```
!HPF$ ALIGN X(K,L) WITH Y(L+1,K)
   DO I = 0, N-1
      DO J = 0, N-1
         X(2*I,2*J) = X(2*I,2*J) + Y(2*J+1,2*I) * Z(I+J)
      END DO
   END DO
```

the set Com is only composed of the reference $Z(I+J)$. Actually, the communication code generated by the compiler is a sequence of communication codes, one code being produced for each reference $Y[C^Y i^T + d^Y]$ in Com as follows:

a - Compute the code enumerating the vectors $(j^X \, j^Y \, i)$ of polyhedron $\mathcal{P}_1(X[C^X i^T + d^X], Y[C^Y i^T + d^Y])$ by one of the algorithms [15, 13, 8, 14]. This yields the nested loop:

$$\text{for } j^X \text{ in } \mathcal{D}_1$$
$$\text{for } j^Y \text{ in } \mathcal{D}_2(j^X)$$
$$\text{for } i \text{ in } \mathcal{D}_3(j^X, j^Y)$$

where $\mathcal{D}_1$, $\mathcal{D}_2(j^X)$ and $\mathcal{D}_3(j^X, j^Y)$ denote the iterations domains associated with the iteration vectors j^X, j^Y and i respectively.

b - Insert two masks and communication instructions in this nested loop to produce the SPMD send code:

```
for j^X in D_1
    if myself ≠ owner of Block(X, j^X) then
        for j^Y in D_2(j^X)
            if myself = owner of Block(Y, j^Y) then
                for i in D_3(j^X, j^Y)
                    pack Y[C^Y i^T + d^Y] in buffer
                send buffer to the owner of Block(X, j^X)
```

c - Produce the dual SPMD receive code:

```
for j^X in D_1
    if myself = owner of Block(X, j^X) then
        for j^Y in D_2(j^X)
            if myself ≠ owner of Block(Y, j^Y) then
                receive buffer from the owner of Block(Y, j^Y)
                for i in D_3(j^X, j^Y)
                    unpack Y[C^Y i^T + d^Y] from buffer
```

The runtime library routine *unpack* extracts data elements from the buffer and copies them in the local memory of the processor.

Computation Code Generation. The computation code is produced depending only on the *lhs* reference $X[C^X i^T + d^X]$.

a - Compute the enumeration code of polyhedron $\mathcal{P}_2(X[C^X i^T + d^X])$:

```
for j^X in D_4
    for i in D_5(j^X)
```

In this loop, $\mathcal{D}_4$ and $\mathcal{D}_5(j^X)$ stand for the iteration domains associated with j^X and i respectively.

b - Produce the SPMD computation code by inserting an adequate mask:

```
for j^X in D_4
    if myself = owner of Block(X, j^X) then
        for i in D_5(j^X)
            X[C^X i^T + d^X] := Exp (Dist ⊎ Repl)
```

5.2 Compilation Scheme if the lhs refers to a Replicated Variable

The communication code generated by the compiler can be simplified and also optimized, by taking advantage of collective communication routines, when the *lhs* of the parallel loop nest:

```
for i : Ai^T + b ≥ 0
    r := Exp (Dist ⊎ Repl)
```

refers to a variable (array or scalar variable) which is replicated in the local memories.

Communication Code Generation. One communication code is produced for each $Y[C^Y i^T + d^Y]$ in $\mathcal{D}ist$ as follows:

a - Compute the enumeration code of polyhedron $\mathcal{P}_2(Y[C^Y i^T + d^Y])$:

> **for** j^Y **in** $\mathcal{D}_1$
>> **for** i **in** $\mathcal{D}_2(j^Y)$

b - Produce the SPMD send code:

> **for** j^Y **in** $\mathcal{D}_1$
>> **if** $myself =$ owner of $Block(Y, j^Y)$ **then**
>>> **for** i **in** $\mathcal{D}_2(j^Y)$
>>>> **pack** $Y[C^Y i^T + d^Y]$ in $buffer$
>>>
>>> **broadcast** $buffer$

c - Produce the dual SPMD receive code:

> **for** j^Y **in** $\mathcal{D}_1$
>> **if** $myself \neq$ owner of $Block(Y, j^Y)$ **then**
>>> **receive** $buffer$
>>> **for** i **in** $\mathcal{D}_2(j^Y)$
>>>> **unpack** $Y[C^Y i^T + d^Y]$ from $buffer$

Computation Code Generation. According to the owner-computes rule, the parallel loop nest is replicated on all the processors:

> **for** $i : Ai^T + b \geq 0$
>> $r := Exp\,(\mathcal{D}ist \uplus \mathcal{R}epl)$

5.3 Compiling Parameterized Loops

The method previously presented allows the compilation of *parameterized* parallel loop nests, that is to say parallel loop nests depending on variables (not assigned in the loop nest) or surrounding loop counters. Let us note k the vector of parameters associated with the loop nest and $Mk^T + h \geq 0$ the system of constraints, that may be empty, satisfied by k. In this case, the parameterized loop nest is of the form:

> **for** $i : Ai^T + Bk^T + c \geq 0$
>> $lhs\_ref := Exp\,(\mathcal{D}ist \uplus \mathcal{R}epl)$

where $Ai^T + Bk^T + c \geq 0$ defines the iteration domain of the loop parameterized by the vector k. In the following code for instance, the inner i-loop is a parallel loop nest parameterized by the surrounding loop counter k:

> **for** $k = 1$, 100
>
> $\cdots$
>
>> **for** $i = 1$, k
>>> $A[i + k] := B[i] + C[2 * k + i]$
>
> $\cdots$

For these parameterized loops, the SPMD code is generated the same way, the polyhedrons $\mathcal{P}_1$ and $\mathcal{P}_2$ defined in section 4 being now parameterized by k.

Given two references $X[C^X i^T + D^X k^T + e^X]$ and $X'[C^{X'} i^T + D^{X'} + e^{X'}]$ to distributed arrays in the parallel nest assignment, $\mathcal{P}_1(X[C^X i^T + D^X k^T + e^X], X'[C^{X'} i^T + D^{X'} k^T + e^{X'}])$ is the set of vectors $((j_p^X)_{p \in 1..|Part(X)|} (j_q^{X'})_{q \in 1..|Part(X')|} i)$ satisfying the system of inequalities:

$$\forall p \in 1..|Part(X)| \quad 0 \le j_p^X \le \lceil h_{d(X,p)}^X / s_{d(X,p)}^X \rceil - 1$$
$$\forall q \in 1..|Part(X')| \quad 0 \le j_q^{X'} \le \lceil h_{d(X',q)}^{X'} / s_{d(X',q)}^{X'} \rceil - 1$$
$$Ai^T + Bk^T + c \ge 0$$
$$Belong(X, C^X i^T + D^X k^T + e^X, (j_p^X)_{p \in 1..|Part(X)|})$$
$$Belong(X', C^{X'} i^T + D^{X'} k^T + e^{X'}, (j_q^{X'})_{q \in 1..|Part(X')|})$$

For a reference $X[Ci^T + Dk^T + e]$ in the parallel nest, the polyhedron $\mathcal{P}_2(X[Ci^T + Dk^T + e])$ denotes the set of vectors $((j_p)_{p \in 1..|Part(X)|} i)$ satisfying the set of inequalities:

$$\forall p \in 1..|Part(X)| \quad 0 \le j_p \le \lceil h_{d(X,p)}^X / s_{d(X,p)}^X \rceil - 1$$
$$Ai^T + Bk^T + c \ge 0$$
$$Belong(X, Ci^T + Dk^T + e, (j_p)_{p \in 1..|Part(X)|})$$

Again, the algorithms [15, 13, 8, 14] permit the generation of a nested loop scanning these parameterized polyhedrons in the context $Mk^T + h \ge 0$.

6 Experiments

6.1 Runtime Support

The runtime resolution and the optimized scheme rely on the implementation of a paged array management [16] which tries to balance the speed of accesses and the memory requirements. The runtime library routine *pack* used in the optimized scheme performs several communication optimizations. Direct communication is performed whenever possible; what is transferred in this case is a memory zone that is contiguous both on the sender and the receiver, thus eliminating any need of coding/decoding between message buffers and local memories. Message aggregation is also carried out and reduces the effect of latency by grouping small messages into a large message. Furthermore, the routine *pack* eliminates redundant communications that may occur with non injective access functions or when several references to the same distributed array appear in the right hand side.

Because of these optimizations (messages exchanged between processors are generally composed of contiguous memory zones), it should be noted that the compiler does not exactly produce the receive codes given in 5.1 and 5.2; the array elements are not element-wise unpacked from the received buffer.

6.2 Experimental Results

Some results of experiments with the optimized compilation scheme are presented in this section. Performance results are shown in figure 4 for two kernels: Cholesky factorization and Jacobi relaxation; the description of the parallelization of a wave propagation application can be found in [3].

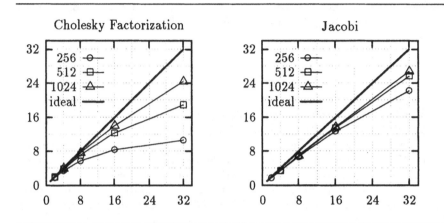

Fig. 4. Speedup

Measurements have been performed on a 32-node iPSC/2. The presented graphs show the speedup against the number processors for several input sizes. Speedup is defined as the parallel time over the time of the original sequential program measured on one node. The obtained efficiencies are satisfactory, ranging from 85% to 95% on 8 processors and reaching around 80% on 32 processors for the largest data size.

7 Conclusion

In this paper, we have presented an optimized compilation technique for parallel loop nests expressed in HPF-like languages. This scheme has been fully implemented in the PANDORE compiler and cohabits with the runtime resolution, thus permitting the compilation of the whole input language. The optimized method performs a symbolic polyhedron-based domain analysis that exploits the partitioning of the arrays involved in the computation in order to achieve restriction of iteration domains and message aggregation. The scope of this scheme can be extended to more general regular loops by integrating parallelization techniques that produce automatically the parallel loops that can be handled by our technique.

The performances obtained on a series of numerical kernels are satisfactory even though enhancements can be made along several axes. First, we plan to improve the compilation technique in order to avoid the multiple enumerations of the same memory location that may occur with non injective access functions or when several references to the same array appear in the right hand side. At the moment, the runtime support prevents from translating these multiple enumerations into multiple sends. This problem can be handled at compile-time by scanning directly the polyhedron affine image, or at least a superset, associated with a right hand side array reference. Moreover, this scanning can be reorganized to exploit the contiguity in the local representation of the distributed arrays in order to maximize *direct communication*, that is the communication of contiguous memory zones.

References

1. R. Allen and K. Kennedy. Automatic Translation of Fortran Programs to Vector Form. *ACM TOPLAS*, 9(4), October 1987.
2. C. Ancourt, F. Coelho, F. Irigoin, and R. Keryell. A Linear Algebra Framework for Static HPF Code Distribution. In *Fourth International Workshop on Compilers for Parallel Computers*, Delft, The Netherlands, December 1993.
3. F. André, M. Le Fur, Y. Mahéo, and J.-L. Pazat. Parallelization of a Wave Propagation Application using a Data Parallel Compiler. In *Nineth International Parallel Processing Symposium*, Santa Barbara, California, April 1995.
4. F. André, M. Le Fur, Y. Mahéo, and J.-L. Pazat. The Pandore Data-Parallel Compiler and its Portable Runtime. In *High-Performance Computing and Networking*, LNCS 919, Springer Verlag, Milan, Italy, May 1995.
5. D. Callahan and K. Kennedy. Compiling Programs for Dis tributed-Memory Multiprocessors. *Journal of Supercomputing*, 2, 1988.
6. B.M. Chapman and H.P. Zima. *Compiling for Distributed-Memory Systems*. Research Report ACPC/TR 92-17, Austrian Center for Parallel Computation, University of Vienna, November 1992.
7. S. Chatterjee, J. R. Gilbert, F. J. E. Long, R. Schreiber, and S.-H Teng. Generating Local Addresses and Communication Sets for Data-Parallel Programs. In *Fourth ACM SIGPLAN Symposium on Principles and Practice of Parallel Programming*, San Diego, California, May 1993.
8. J.-F. Collard, P. Feautrier, and T. Risset. *Construction of DO Loops from Systems of Affine Constraints*. Research Report 93-15, LIP, Lyon, France, May 1993.
9. A. Darte and Y. Robert. Constructive Methods for Scheduling Uniform Loop Nests. *IEEE Transactions on Parallel and Distributed Systems*, 5(8), August 1994.
10. P. Feautrier. Some Efficient Solutions to the Affine Scheduling Problem, Part I, One-Dimensional Time. *International Journal of Parallel Programming*, 21(5), 1992.
11. S. K. S. Gupta, S. D. Kaushik, C.-H. Huang, and P. Sadayappan. *Compiling Array Expressions for Efficient Execution on Distributed-Memory Machines*. Technical Report 19, The Ohio State University, 1994.
12. High Performance Fortran Forum. *High Performance Fortran Language Specification*. Technical Report Version 1.0, Rice University, May 1993.
13. F. Irigoin and C. Ancourt. Scanning Polyhedra with DO Loops. In *Third ACM SIGPLAN Symposium on Principles and Practice of Parallel Programming*, pages 39–50, April 1991.

14. H. Le Verge, V. Van Dongen, and D. K. Wilde. *Loop Nest Synthesis Using the Polyhedral Library*. Research Report 2288, INRIA, France, May 1994.
15. M. Le Fur. Scanning Parameterized Polyhedron using Fourier-Motzkin Elimination. In *High Performance Computing Symposium*, Montréal, Canada, July 1995.
16. Y. Mahéo and J.-L. Pazat. Distributed Array Management for HPF Compilers. In *High Performance Computing Symposium*, Montréal, Canada, July 1995.
17. C.W. Tseng. *An Optimizing Fortran D Compiler for MIMD Distributed-Memory Machines*. PhD thesis, Rice University, January 1993.
18. V. Van Dongen. Compiling Distributed Loops onto SPMD Code. *Parallel Processing Letter*, 4(3), 1994.

Load Balancing
and
Parallel Algorithms II

A Model for Efficient Programming of Dynamic Applications on Distributed Memory Multiprocessors

A. Erzmann, M. Hadeler, C. Müller-Schloer

Institut für Rechnerstrukturen und Betriebssysteme Universität Hannover
Lange Laube 3, D-30159 Hannover, Germany
erzmann@irb.uni-hannover.de

Abstract. We present the TDC programming model which aims to ease the efficient implementation of dynamic applications on distributed memory multiprocessors. This model is based on task descriptors, data objects and capabilities which reside in distinct, globally accessible domains. Dynamic load balancing will be done by the system software and is completely transparent to the user. This often leads to a significant reduction of code complexity. Our prototype of the TDC model on an 128 node nCUBE2 uses a distributed diffusion scheme to balance load dynamically. We have developed a task selection strategy which reduces the load balancing overhead. Measuring and simulation results for a parallel implementation of a block matching algorithm indicate that runtime efficiency close to the optimum can be achieved with the TDC model even for highly parallel systems.

Keywords. Programming Model, Dynamic Load Balancing, Block Matching, Distributed Memory Multiprocessors.

1 Introduction

From the user's point of view two goals are crucial when programming distributed memory multiprocessors: *efficiency* and *ease-of-programming*. Whether both requirements can be met simultaneously depends on the appropriate choice of the *programming model*. The programming model is the description of the virtual parallel architecture as it is seen by the user, i.e. it provides a certain level of abstraction. The better this level fits the application requirements, the easier the programming will be for the user. On the other hand, the implementation of the programming model on a given parallel machine may be the source of substantial efficiency losses if the provided abstraction and the hardware differ too much. A programming model is easy to use if it precisely supports the application needs and on the other hand, may be implemented efficiently if its abstractions closely resemble the underlying hardware. If the problem structure does not naturally map onto the hardware of the parallel machine, then the user has to find a good trade-off between the ease-of-programming and efficiency by carefully choosing the programming model. This choice will be influenced by the application properties and the *target architecture*.

2 The TDC Programming Model

Before the description of the *TDC programming model* (*Tasks, Data Objects and Capabilities*), we define the application class and target multiprocessor architecture:

Application Class

The TDC Programming Model is designed to ease the efficient programming of *dynamic applications*. These applications have at least one *dynamic execution phase* of considerable length with respect to the total execution time. A dynamic execution phase (DP) has the following properties: The work which has to be done during a DP can be split into a certain number of *tasks* which may be created at any time during the DP. All tasks which are existent at a given point of time during the DP can be executed independently and in arbitrary sequence. All information needed to process a task is available as soon as the task is created, i.e. there is no need for direct task interaction. Task dependencies are resolved by delayed creation of the dependent task. The task execution time depends on the input data and cannot be predetermined. Examples for dynamic applications are: ray tracing, volume rendering and block matching algorithms.

Target Architecture

The target architecture is a general purpose distributed memory multiprocessor (MIMD). The nodes of this multiprocessor are linked via an interconnection network. Examples for this class of multiprocessors are: nCUBE 2, Intel iPSC, Intel Paragon.

2.1 Description

The parallelisation of a dynamic application for a distributed memory multiprocessor requires the following steps: (1) The load has to be partitioned into tasks, which can be executed in parallel. (2) The input data has to be partitioned and (3) tasks have to be assigned together with the required parts of input data to the nodes of the parallel machine. Since the task execution times are unpredictable, static assignment of tasks often leads to load imbalance, i.e. low efficiency. To achieve high efficiency it is necessary to balance the load dynamically, which is done by repeated reassignment of tasks and data parts at runtime. Since dynamic load balancing requires complex algorithms especially in highly parallel environments and these algorithms are essentially the same for a wide range of applications, it is desirable to separate dynamic load balancing activities from the application code. The TDC programming model provides the user with the abstractions necessary to program his application easily. Moreover it is designed for efficient implementation on the target architecture.

TDC is based on three separate, globally accessible domains: The *task bag* which contains *task descriptors*, the *data space* which contains *data objects* and the *code space* which contains *capabilities*[1] (Fig. 1).

Worker

The user process, which is written by the programmer, is called the *worker*. It initializes the data objects and inserts task descriptors into the task bag. In order to do work, it removes task descriptors (one after another) from the task bag and executes the task using the specified capability. The task descriptor contains a set of user defined parameters

---

[1] The term capability is not to be confused with an access control mechanism of the same name in the context of data security.

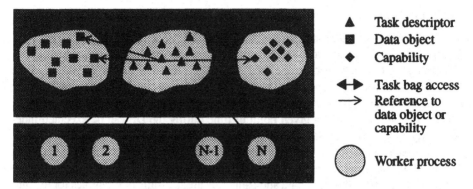

▲	Task descriptor
▣	Data object
◆	Capability
◀▶	Task bag access
⟶	Reference to data object or capability
(○)	Worker process

Fig. 1. The TDC programming model.

which specify details of the task execution process. During the task execution period the worker accesses data objects, which are specified in the task descriptor. Typically there will be a single worker per processing node.

Task Descriptor

A task descriptor is a data structure which contains (1) references to an arbitrary number of data objects and a capability and (2) a set of input parameters, which is used by the capability to distinguish tasks from each other. A task descriptor is created and inserted into the task bag by a certain worker as soon as the corresponding task is executable and will be removed by a potentially different worker in order to execute the specified task.

Data Object

Data objects are contiguous pieces of data associated with an globally unique logical identifier. They are initialized by an arbitrary worker before they are accessed and may be read by any number of workers simultaneously. The size and number of data objects is dependent on the application. Data objects reside in the data space.

Capability

A capability is a piece of code which is used by the worker to process a given task. Capabilities must be loaded into the code space prior to task execution. They can be accessed by an arbitrary number of workers simultaneously.

2.2 Related Programming Models and Tools

In this section two related programming models (Message Passing, Linda) and the tool Dynamo for distributed memory multiprocessors are described and compared to TDC. The suitability of these models for programming dynamic applications is discussed.

Message Passing

In the Message Passing programming model, processes communicate and synchronize by explicit exchange of messages. No globally accessible data structures exist and therefore tasks, data objects and code have to be encapsulated inside the worker processes. Dynamic load balancing can be done (1) by the programmer himself, which is often prohibitive because of the involved implementation complexity, or (2) by an underlying process migration system [1]. The latter however requires that the location of processes is transparent to the programmer. Moreover the number of processes per node must be raised artificially in order to make process migration feasible. Thus the benefit of dynamic load balancing is limited due to the additional overhead and the coarse grain size of the balancing entities, i.e. the processes.

Linda

In Linda [2] workers communicate and synchronize via *tuples*, which reside in the globally accessible *tuple space*. Valid operations on tuples are: insert tuple, remove tuple and read tuple. Since tuples are accessed by contents rather than by address these operation require a costly associative matching process. In Linda tuples do not have a semantic meaning, i.e. the system cannot distinguish between task descriptors and data objects. Load balanced execution of dynamic applications is achieved automatically up to a certain degree since workers remove task tuples from tuple space as needed. This works well for shared memory multiprocessors but is likely to produce overhead on distributed memory machines because the communication latency cannot be hidden (tuples reside anywhere in the system and must be searched for and transferred to the worker which accesses them). The system is not able to support load balancing since task descriptors cannot be identified and load balancing costs cannot be calculated.

Dynamo

Dynamo [3] is a library for dynamic load balancing on distributed memory multicomputers based on the PICL message passing primitives. It provides support for managing local task queues and for writing code which dynamically balances these queues. The main differences to TDC are: (1) The underlying programming model neither supports shared data objects nor capabilities. This limits the range of applications which can be programmed using Dynamo. (2) The dynamo implementation does not use a runtime system, i.e. the programmer must explicitly call the load balancer from its application program (see chapter 3 for the TDC implementation). This synchronizes load balancing and task execution and thus limits the range of balancer algorithms which can be used.

2.3 Comparison of Programming Models

As stated in the introduction our main concern is to provide ease-of-programming and high efficiency. Therefore the question which arises is: How much effort is required by the user to write an efficient implementation of a dynamic application using one of the above-described programming models?

The effort to identify and express parallelism is essentially the same: In all cases a suitable partitioning of load and input data has to be found. Using Message Passing, the partitioning generally is contained inside the code, whereas tasks and data objects have to be created explicitly if Linda, Dynamo or TDC are used. The main difference is the way how dynamic load balancing will be achieved: In Message Passing programs, the programmer has to insert dynamic load balancing operations into the application code, thereby increasing the code complexity substantially, whereas dynamic load balancing will be done by the system software if Linda, Dynamo or TDC are used.

A mechanism which we call *passive load balancing* is inherent to the Linda programming model: Each worker, which becomes idle, requests a new task. This task (a Linda tuple) has to be located in the distributed tuple space and must be moved to the node where the worker resides. The same is true for each data tuple which is accessed during task execution time. The worker remains idle until the requested task and data arrive, i.e. the network latency, which usually dominates the transfer time, cannot be hidden. In TDC the semantics of task descriptors is known to the system. It therefore can perform *active load balancing*, i.e. task descriptors, data objects and capabilities can be moved to underloaded nodes in advance. This enables the system to overlap communication and computation, thereby hiding network latency and minimizing idle times.

3 Implementation

The TDC programming model has been implemented[2] on an 128 node nCUBE 2 as runtime environment on top of the VERTEX® node operating system [4]. Our main implementation goals were:

- *High efficiency.* The local parts of the distributed task bag and data space reside in a portion of memory which is shared by the TDC system and the worker. This avoids unnecessary copying of potentially large data objects and task descriptors. The TDC system itself is implemented in a distributed fashion, i.e. there does not exist any central resource that might become a bottleneck in highly parallel systems.
- *Ease-of-use.* The user accesses the TDC system by a well-defined set of C library functions which are linked to the application code. The TDC system will be configured dynamically and is suitable for future integration into the node operating system.

3.1 Overview

The TDC system consists of two system processes per node (see Fig. 2): The *task server processes* control the task bag and perform dynamic load balancing. The *data server processes* send and receive *data objects*.

3.2 User Interface

The worker process accesses the TDC system by a set of C library functions which are described briefly in this section. These library functions hide the

---

[2] Currently it is assumed that each worker stores the entire set of capabilities. The code space is therefore integrated into the worker processes. This restriction does not affect the general applicability of this implementation but may increase memory requirements.

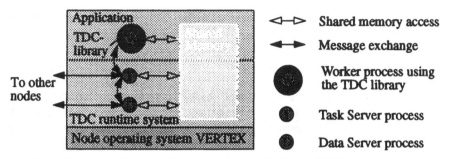

Fig. 2. Overview of TDC implementation on a node of the nCUBE 2 multiprocessor.

tdc_init()   Dynamic configuration of the TDC system. The size and maximum number of task descriptors and data objects are specified as well as the logical identifiers of the locally stored data objects. It synchronizes the workers.

tdc_flush() Delete data objects and capabilities. This may be necessary if multiple dynamic execution phases occur within the same application.

tdc_write() Create and initialize a data object.

tdc_put()   Insert a task descriptor into the task bag.

tdc_get()   Retrieve a task descriptor from the task bag. This function returns end-of-processing if all tasks have been processed, i.e. the task bag is empty.

Example Usage

Fig. 3 shows an worker program written using the TDC programming model. The function `process()` contains the application code which processes the given task.

```
/* Initialize TDC system */
tdc_init(<application specific parameters>);
/* Initialize data objects */
forall(<local data objects>)tdc_write(<data object>);
/* Put tasks into task bag */
create_tasks();
forall(<local tasks>)        tdc_put(<task descriptor>);
/* Process tasks */
while (tdc_get(&task) != EOP) process(task);
```

Fig. 3. Worker program written using the TDC programming model.

4 Implementation of Block Matching Using the TDC Model

In this section we demonstrate how a real application can be parallelized using the TDC programming model and present a modified receiver initiated diffusion algorithm for dynamic load balancing. This algorithm uses a heuristic approach for the task selection strategy which aims to minimize the load balancing overhead thereby maximizing the overall efficiency.

4.1 The Block Matching Algorithm

In a sequence of pictures successive pictures are likely to be quite similar. Therefore the amount of data necessary to store or transmit image sequences can be reduced significantly if only the difference between two pictures is coded rather than coding each picture separately. The picture which has to be coded will be partitioned into square blocks. For each of these blocks the most similar block is searched for in the previous picture. This is done by calculating the *mean absolute error* for each block and choosing the block with the least error value. This technique is called *block matching* and is used by programs with compress image data according to the MPEG standard [5].

In our implementation we choose each image of the sequence to be a *data object* and the matching of one block to be a *task*. Consequently each task requires two data objects (images) to be processed. Tasks which require an identical set of data objects belong to the same *task class*. The maximum number of task classes which can be stored on a node simultaneously is limited by its memory size.

A static assignment of tasks to nodes would lead to load imbalance mainly for two reasons: The task execution time depends on the contents of the images. This is true since the computation of the mean absolute error is stopped as soon as its value becomes greater than the minimum found so far, i.e. finding a good reference block early will lead to shorter execution time. Moreover due to the limited I/O bandwidth the loading of images takes a variable amount of time and therefore prevents nodes from starting with task execution at the same time.

4.2 Dynamic Load Balancing

The load balancing system which is integrated into the task server processes can be divided into four sections:

- Dynamic load balancing strategy
- Task selection strategy
- Local load estimation and load update policy
- Load imbalance detection and balancer activation

Load Balancing Strategy

A variety of dynamic load balancing strategies have been proposed for highly parallel systems ([6],[7],[8],[9]). The load model assumed here has two important differences:

- Task migration may cause data object migration. Thus the task migration overhead cannot be neglected.
- The limited number of distinct task classes per node influences the task selection.

These restrictions imply the use of a task selection strategy which considers the task migration costs and task class limitations. Therefore the receiver (the underloaded node) must control the task selection and migration process. We have chosen the RID strategy (*receiver initiated diffusion*, [8]) for 3 reasons: (1) RID is a completely asynchronous and distributed approach, (2) task migration is controlled by the receiver and (3) this strategy performs comparable or better than the other strategies ([8],[10]).

The *balancing domain* consists of the underloaded node itself (receiver) and its direct neighbors. Each time the algorithm is invoked, it balances load locally. Successive local balancing steps lead to globally balanced load [7]. We describe a local balancing step: Let K be the number of direct neighbors per node, l_0 the receiver's load and l_i the load of its i-th neighbor. The average load l_{avg} in the balancing domain is:

$$l_{avg} = \frac{1}{K+1} \cdot \sum_{i=0}^{K} l_i \qquad \text{(Eq. 1)}$$

The fraction d_i of load which has to be demanded from the i-th neighbor in order to balance load in the local domain is calculated according to the following formulas:

$$h_i = \max(l_i - l_{avg}, 0) \qquad h_{sum} = \sum_{i=1}^{K} h_i \qquad d_i = (l_{avg} - l_0) \cdot \frac{h_i}{h_{sum}} \qquad \text{(Eq. 2)}$$

Task Selection Strategy

The *load balancing strategy* determines how many tasks have to be migrated within one local balancing step, whereas the *task selection strategy* is used to minimize the load balancing overhead by choosing the set of tasks which causes the least cost. We assume that the task migration cost is primarily caused by the involved data object transfers. Thus it is always profitable to select as many tasks of a given class as possible. We use an iterative, heuristic approach with low computational complexity to get a near optimal task selection instead of doing a full search. The receiver executes the following steps:

1. For all neighbors: Calculate the number of tasks d_i, which have to be demanded from neighbor i according to the RID balancing strategy (Eq. 2).

2. For each neighbor i and each task class j in the balancing domain: Let a_{ij} be the number of tasks of this class which are *available* on neighbor i. Calculate the maximum number of tasks r_{ij} of class j which might be requested from neighbor i:

$$r_{ij} = \min(d_i, a_{ij}) \qquad \text{(Eq. 3)}$$

3. For each task class j: Calculate the total number of tasks which could be requested if class j is selected:

$$R_j = \sum_{i=1}^{K} r_{ij} \qquad \text{(Eq. 4)}$$

Determine the cost C_j due to data object migration, which would be caused by the migration of tasks class j. Assign infinite costs to class j if this class cannot be selected due to the limited number of task classes on the receiving node. Calculate the cost per task c_j assuming that R_j tasks will be transferred:

$$c_j = \frac{C_j}{R_j} \qquad \text{(Eq. 5)}$$

4. Determine the task class k with the least cost per task. If no class with finite cost per task can be found then no more tasks can be migrated: Stop here.

5. For each neighbor i: Request r_{ik} tasks of class k and adjust d_i accordingly:

$$d_i \leftarrow d_i - r_{ik} \qquad \text{(Eq. 6)}$$

6. If still tasks remain to demand, i.e. any $d_i \neq 0$, continue with step 2, else stop here.

Local Load Estimation and Load Update Policy

We assume that the average task execution time t_{avg} is constant. This time is estimated locally by averaging the measured task execution times of the tasks which have been processed so far. Since t_{avg} is time invariant, we simply use the number of tasks which still have to be processed as load estimate.

As soon as the local load changes significantly, load update messages will be sent to all neighbors in the balancing domain. These messages contain information about the task classes residing on the node and the number of tasks which are currently available for each of these classes.

Balancer Activation

Performing a load balancing step reduces the probability that nodes become idle and on the other hand causes overhead. Thus the frequency of balancer activation and the degree of load imbalance that can be tolerated must be chosen carefully in order to get the best overall efficiency. We use the number of tasks d_{sum}, which would be demanded if the balancer is activated, as a criterion for load imbalance in the balancing domain:

$$d_{sum} = \sum_{i=1}^{K} d_i = \max(l_{avg} - l_0, 0) \qquad \text{(Eq. 7)}$$

Let $t_{latency}$ be the network latency necessary to load the data objects for a new task class and $l_{latency}$ the number of tasks which can be processed during $t_{latency}$:

$$l_{latency} = \frac{t_{latency}}{t_{avg}} \qquad \text{(Eq. 8)}$$

We distinguish two balancing phases: Phase 1 is active while the local load is greater than $l_{latency}$, phase 2 otherwise. During phase 1 load imbalance will be evaluated whenever the load drops below the threshold l_{bal}, which will be decreased by the constant activation factor f_a after each imbalance evaluation. Load will be balanced if the detected imbalance is greater than $l_{latency}$. During phase 2 load imbalance will be evaluated whenever the node recognizes a load change in the balancing domain. Load will be balanced each time an imbalance of at least one task is detected.

During phase 1 both load imbalance will be determined less frequently and a higher load imbalance will be tolerated compared to phase 2. Thereby unnecessary balancing overhead is avoided unless the local load drops below the critical threshold $l_{latency}$ and on the other hand, the probability that nodes become idle is kept low.

Balancer Activation Algorithm

```
lbal = fa · l
while (not end of balancing)
        if  (lbal > llatency)                           /* Phase 1 */
             if  (l0 ≤ lbal)
                   evaluate dsum
                   if  (dsum > llatency)  balance load
                   lbal = fa · lbal
             endif
        else                                            /* Phase2 */
             if (load in the domain has changed)
                   evaluate dsum
                   if (dsum ≥ 1)  balance load
             endif
        endif
endwhile
```

4.3 Results

In this section the results we have obtained using our TDC implementation on an 128 node nCUBE 2 are presented and compared to simulation results. We have used the block matching algorithm to process the *flowergarden* video sequence as example application. Each picture of this sequence contains 720*576 pixels and is divided into 1620 square blocks. Each node has to compute the motion vectors for one quarter of an image (405 blocks) on average.

Simulation

We have used *event-driven simulation* based on traces of program execution to determine which efficiency could be optimally achieved, if (1) the balancer has global knowledge about the system load, i.e. it can get tasks from any node in the system, (2) dynamic load balancing activities, except the transfer of data objects, do not cause overhead and (3) the network latency is zero. Consequently, only the idle time at the end of the processing phase and the overhead for data object transfer is considered.

In Fig. 4 the efficiency for the block matching algorithm and a constant average load per node is depicted for a varying number of nodes. Additionally the overhead and the

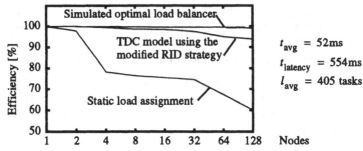

Fig. 4. Measured versus simulated efficiency for the Block Matching Application.

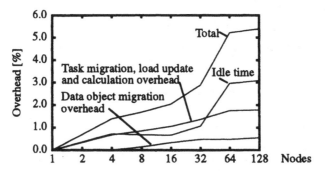

Fig. 5. Idle times and overhead for the RID dynamic load balancer.

idle times which occur if dynamic load balancing is used are shown in Fig. 5. The efficiency decreases as the number of nodes increases primarily for 3 reasons:

- *Statistic properties of the load.* The probability, that at least one node exhibits an execution time close to the maximum increases with the number of nodes. This leads to an increased fraction of idle time, since this node determines the execution time.
- *Number of task classes.* For the considered application the number of task classes is proportional to the number of processing nodes. As the number of task classes becomes higher, task migration becomes more restricted due to the limited number of task classes per node and the overhead caused by data object migration increases.
- *Network diameter.* The higher the network diameter, the more steps might be necessary to migrate tasks from overloaded to underloaded nodes thereby increasing the load balancing overhead and the fraction of idle time.

Fig. 4 shows that the modified RID algorithm is able to keep the efficiency close to the optimum even when the number of processing nodes is high. There is an increasing demand for dynamic load balancing in highly parallel systems since load imbalance tends to increase with the number of nodes for dynamic applications.The overhead for data object migration, which is controlled by the task selection algorithm, is kept consistently low. Our simulations have shown, that although the balancer can only select tasks in the local balancing domain, at most twice the number of data object migrations have been performed compared to the simulated balancer.

4.4 Conclusion

We have introduced the TDC programming model for distributed memory multiprocessors. TDC eases the implementation of dynamic applications since dynamic load balancing is now performed by the system rather than the programmer. The semantics of task descriptors, data objects and capabilities as well as the logical linkage between them is visible to the TDC system. This knowledge is used for active load balancing, i.e. load and the required code and data will be transferred by the system to underloaded nodes in advance thereby hiding network latency and hence reducing idle times.

We have implemented the TDC model on an 128 node nCUBE 2 and used this prototype to write a parallel version of the block matching algorithm. Our measurements and simulation results indicate that the receiver initiated diffusion scheme in conjunction with our task selection strategy leads to a runtime efficiency close to the optimum even for highly parallel systems. Further research is required to proof the suitability of this load balancing system for a broader range of dynamic applications.

References

[1] Ludwig, T.: *Lastverwaltungsverfahren für Mehrprozessorsysteme mit verteiltem Speicher*, Dissertation, Institut für Informatik, TU München, 1993

[2] Gelernter, D.; Ahuja, S.; Carriero, N.: *Linda and Friends*, Computer, Vol. 19, No. 8, Aug. 1986, pp 26-34

[3] Tärnvik, E.: *Dynamo - a portable tool for dynamic load balancing on distributed memory multicomputers*, Concurrency: Pratice and Experience, Vol. 6, No. 8, Dec. 1994

[4] nCUBE Cooperation: *nCUBE 2 Programmer's Guide*, PN 102294, 1992

[5] ISO/IEC 11172-2, *Information technology - Coding of moving pictures and associated audio for digital storage media at up to about 1.5 MBit/s - Part 2: Video*, Annex D.6.2, pp 78-85 Motion estimation and compensation

[6] Lin, F.; Keller, R.: *The Gradient Model Load Balancing Method*, IEEE Transactions on Software Engineering, Vol. SE-13, No. 1, Jan. 1987

[7] Cybenko, G.: *Dynamic Load Balancing for Distributed Memory Multiprocessors*, J. Parallel and Distributed Computing, Vol. 7, pp 279-301, October 1989

[8] Willebeek-LeMair, M.H.; Reeves, A.P.: *Strategies for Dynamic Load Balancing on Highly Parallel Computers*, IEEE Transactions on Parallel and Distributed Systems, Vol. 4, No. 9, Sep. 1993

[9] Gerogiannis, D.; Orphanoudakis, S.C.: *Load Balancing Requirements in Parallel Implementations of Image Feature Extraction Tasks*, IEEE Transactions on Parallel and Distributed Systems, Vol. 4, No. 9, Sep. 1993

[10] Erzmann, A.; Müller-Schloer, C.: *Zur Beurteilung dynamischer Lastausgleichsverfahren*, PARS Mitteilungen, Nr. 13, November 1994

Efficient Solutions for Mapping Parallel Programs*

P. Bouvry[1] and J. Chassin de Kergommeaux[2] and D. Trystram[2]

[1] CWI - Center for Mathematics and Computer Science,
Kruislaan 413, PP.O. Box 94079, 1090 GB Amsterdam - The Netherlands
[2] LMC-IMAG, 46, avenue Félix Viallet, 38031 Grenoble cedex - France

Abstract. This paper describes a mapping toolbox, whose aim is to optimize the execution time of parallel programs described as task graphs on distributed memory parallel systems. The toolbox includes several classical mapping algorithms. It was assessed by computing the mapping of randomly generated task graphs and by mapping and executing on a parallel system synthetic programs representing some classical numerical algorithms. A large number of experiments were used to validate the cost functions used in the toolbox and to compare the algorithms.

Keywords: Parallel environment, Load-balancing, Mapping.

1 Introduction

Efficient use of distributed-memory parallel systems requires the use of specific tools, whose mapping is one of the most important one. The goal of the mapping tools is to minimize the execution time of parallel programs on distributed-memory machines by controlling the use of computation and communication resources. This article describes a toolbox aiming at providing an assignment of the tasks of a parallel program to the available processors to obtain the shortest possible execution time for the entire program. Therefore, mapping algorithms aim at maximizing the (useful) occupation of processors without increasing too much communication costs.

The tasks execution times and inter-tasks communication costs of some regular programs can be entirely determined at compile time. In this case, it is possible to perform static task allocation in advance. This is known as the *mapping* operation whose complexity is exponential in the general case. Thus, it is difficult to obtain an optimal mapping and numerous heuristic solutions have been proposed, representing different tradeoffs between computation cost and quality of mapping [9].

This paper presents a *mapping toolbox*, implementing several "classical" mapping algorithms. This toolbox was used to assess different cost functions by computing the relation between the value of these functions, optimized by the

---

* This work was partially sponsored by the EU's Copernicus programme under contract number CIPA-C193-0251

mapping algorithms, and the actual execution times of parallel programs. The implemented mapping algorithms were also evaluated, by comparing the execution times of a set of representative parallel programs, mapped using the algorithms of the toolbox.

This work is part of the APACHE research project whose aim is the design and development of a general programming environment to balance automatically the load of parallel applications, resulting in reduced development time and increased portability of parallel applications [10].

2 The mapping problem

2.1 Models of machines and programs

A distributed-memory parallel computer is composed of a set of nodes connected via an interconnection network. Each node includes some computation facilities and a local memory. A communication between two processors is much more time consuming than a local memory access. The MIMD model intends to map different executable codes, called tasks, onto processors. Designing a program such that only one task will be allocated on one processor of the target machine would lead to an architecture-dependent and non-scalable code. On the contrary, a too large number of tasks is difficult to manage efficiently. The granularity (size of tasks) is one important parameter for the efficiency of a parallel program.

Most parallel programs can be described using a graph formalism. In most representations, each vertex represents a task and each edge a communication link. We consider that a task can be allocated to a single processor. Any processor can make some communications and computations. We add to this basic model the computation costs of the tasks (execution time) and the amount of information communicated on the links. Often, the user cannot determine the exact values of the program parameters but can only approximate them. The model used in this paper is based, as a large number of related works [9], on tasks graphs without precedence. It is closely related to the programming model used by the transputer based parallel system that was used for experiments, where undirected task graphs are often explicitly described in a separate configuration file.

In the following, we will denote: T, the set of tasks and n their number, P, the set of processors and m their number, $ex(t)$, the computation time of task t, $comm(t, t')$, the total communication time between t and t'.

2.2 Description of the Problem

The parallelization process requires first to distribute data among the different processors. The objective considered here is to minimize the execution time of the whole program. Formally, a mapping is an application (called *alloc*) from T to P which associates to each task t an unique processor $q = alloc(t)$. The number of all possible solutions is n^m.

Mapping tools are part of programming environments. Ideally, the user of a parallel machine would use a parallel compiler which would distribute data among the processors and organize automatically (implicitly) the communications induced by local computations. Practically, parallelization directives can be included in the source code and used to generate a task graph by determining computation and communication costs and analyzing data dependences. This phase is usually followed by a clustering operation, parameterized by the granularity of the target machine. Then, mapping is performed.

2.3 Quality of the solution

Most solutions of the mapping problem are based on the optimization of cost functions, denoted z. There exist in the literature many choices for z. Norman and Thanish propose a classification of the parameters which influence the cost of a mapping [9]. Two opposite criteria have to be taken into account: minimization of inter-processors communications and load-balancing of computations between processors. We chose to minimize the most loaded processor, which is a trade-off between these two criteria:

$$z = \max_{p \in P}(\sum_{t | alloc(t)=p} ex(t) + \sum_{t' | alloc(t') \neq p} comm(t, t'))$$

This basic function does not consider that communications can be overlapped by computations, but it can be adapted by considering the maximum between computation and communication times in place of the second sum. The above cost function does not take into account the length of the exchanged messages nor the topology. Two refinements were introduced to take into account distances between processors.

1. measures on the parallel target system can give the costs to transfer bytes between two processors depending on the number of bytes communicated.
2. communications can be expressed as a linear function of the distance between two processors.

3 Description of the Mapping Toolbox (ALTO)

Many solutions can be found in the literature for solving the mapping problem [4]. Exact algorithms give the optimal solutions but in practical cases they can not be used because of the combinatorial explosion of the number of solutions. The goal of heuristic algorithms is to give good solutions in relatively reasonable time. Two sub-classes of heuristic algorithms were explored: greedy algorithms which construct partially the solution and iterative algorithms whose principle is to improve an existing solution. Obviously, the cost of the mapping algorithm itself must be related to the use of the solution. The more used a given mapping, the greater the time that ought to be invested computing it.

3.1 Basic hypotheses

The mapping toolbox "ALTO" (for ALlocation TOol box) was originally developed to map parallel programs written in a parallel dialect of C, where tasks are source code files, on a transputer based (Supernode architecture) Meganode [7], including 128 T-800 transputers. In parallel C programs, a description of the different tasks and a configuration description must be supplied by the user. The configuration file describes the task interconnection graph, the processor network and the mapping of the different tasks on the processors. To use ALTO, the configuration file must be extended to include cost values (computing and communication costs). In addition, we assume that all processors have the same processing capabilities, that processors may have different memory sizes, and that communication costs between tasks allocated on the same processor are negligible.

3.2 Greedy algorithms

In a greedy algorithm, the mapping is done without backtracking (a choice already done can never be reconsidered). The allocation of the ith task is based on a criterion depending on the mapping of the $(i-1)^{th}$ first tasks. Two kinds of greedy algorithms can be envisaged: either they are based on empirical methods or they come from the relaxation of classical graph theory algorithms which are optimal for some restricted cases. They are easy to implement and have a polynomial complexity. *List algorithms* are the most used greedy algorithms. Tasks are first sorted on a given criterion and then are mapped in this order on the processors. In ALTO, the following greedy algorithms were implemented:

Modulo: the modulo algorithm consists in allocating the ith task onto the ith *modulo m* processor. Theoretically, this algorithm has the same behavior as a random mapping algorithm with a great number of tasks. It was mainly implemented to serve as a reference. The only modification made to the basic algorithm was to skip processors that have not enough memory for a task.

Largest Processing Time First (LPTF): LPTF is a heuristic whose criterion is restricted to load balancing. Tasks are first sorted by decreasing computation cost order, then allocated on the less loaded processor having enough memory.

Largest Global Cost First (LGCF): this greedy algorithm aims at balancing the global load. Tasks are first sorted according to this order, then allocated on the less globally loaded (communication and computation costs taken into account) processor having enough memory.

Struc-quanti: this algorithm uses first a mixed criterion, i.e. qualitative (the number of links of each task) and quantitative (communication and computation costs), to sort tasks. Then, tasks are allocated on the less globally loaded (communication and computation costs taken into account) processor having enough memory.

3.3 Iterative algorithms

All iterative algorithms try to improve an initial solution usually obtained by a greedy algorithm. Most iterative algorithms exchange tasks between processors to improve locally a solution. Most of such algorithms use random perturbations to leave local minima of the cost function and to obtain better solutions. In ALTO two kinds of neighborhood were used: transfering a task from the most loaded processor to another one and exchanging a task from the most loaded processor with another task communicating with it.

Simulated annealing. It is based on an analogy with statistical physics: the annealing technique is used to obtain a metal with the most regular structure possible. It consists of heating the metal and reducing slowly the heat so that it keeps its equilibrium. When the temperature is low enough, the metal is in an equilibrium state corresponding to the minimal energy. At high temperature, there is a lot of thermic agitation which can locally increase the energy of the system. This phenomenon occurs with a given probability decreasing with the temperature. It corresponds mathematically to give the possibility of leaving a local minimum of the function to optimize.

In ALTO a mapping is improved by elementary operations involving task exchanges. The percentage of bad exchanges (leading to a worse solution) is high at the beginning and decreases during the execution of the algorithm. Theoretical studies proved the convergence to the optimal solution of the continuous version if some properties are verified such as a very slow decreasing of the heat, that it is not practical for real problems. It is very hard to tune: finding the starting temperature or the heat decreasing steps have to be done after many experiments. All the parameters were determined according to the literature [2, 6] and a large number of experiments. An estimated value of the average differential value of the cost function between moves denoted δ_f is first computed. Next, using a starting percentage of acceptance of bad solutions of 0.8 (denoted τ) the starting heat is determined ($k = \dfrac{\delta_f}{log\left(\frac{1}{\tau}\right)}$). In this implementation the function $k^{0.98}$ is used for practical heat descent. A bad solution is accepted if $e^{\frac{-\delta_f}{k}}$ is greater than a random number uniformly chosen in $(0, 1)$ (see figure 1).

Tabu search. It is a deterministic meta-heuristic [5]. As for the simulated annealing, a lot of parameters have to be tuned or defined [1]. The tabu search starts from a given solution and improves it by local pair-wise exchanges. Accessible solutions using local moves are called neighbors. At a given step, the best unexplored neighbor is chosen. This implies that the last explored moves must be recorded in a tabu list. Only the last moves can be recorded in order to limit the memory and time costs. Possibilities of cycling are also reduced by this recording. The tabu list length is fixed empirically for each implementation of a tabu search. Aspiration criteria can be used to override a tabu list (e.g. if the proposed move leads to the best ever found value of the cost fonction). If

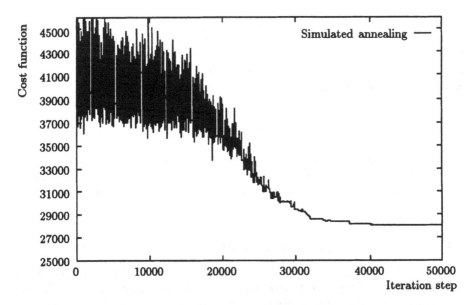

Fig. 1. Typical execution of Simulated annealing

too much time is spent without significative improvements of the solution, diversification factors can be used in order to move to other areas. Intensification factors can be used if some areas seem very promising. Implementation details can be found in [1].

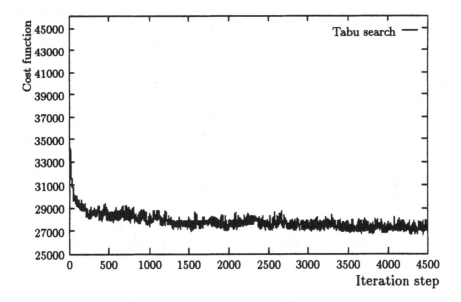

Fig. 2. Typical execution of Tabu search

Figures 1 and 2 examplify the simulated annealing and tabu search methods, for the same example of mapping a randomly generated task graph of 100 tasks on 10 processors. They indicate that the former improves the cost function after a long latence time and is very unstable at the beginning, while on the contrary, the latter is more efficient at the beginning but converges slower. The basic iteration of the tabu is greater than simulated annealing since at each step, it explores all the neighbor configurations to find the best.

4 Validation and experiments

Two kinds of validation were done: first, we generated "artificial" parallel programs using a random task graph generator; then, the mapping algorithms of ALTO were tested on a set of benchmarks, representative of many classical parallel numerical algorithms.

4.1 Task graphs generated randomly

To tune iterative algorithms and to show the behavior of the different mapping algorithms, many task graphs were randomly generated, with the following parameters: number of tasks, maximal computing cost of a task, maximal communication cost, and maximal degree of a task (number of neighbors).

Different task graphs were generated uniformly using these parameters. Figure 3 presents the average improvement (in %) given by the different algorithms versus the behavior of the modulo algorithm. Each value of the table is based on 100 random task graphs. The parameters used in the random task graph generations are: 100 tasks, each task communicating to a maximum of 4 other tasks, 16 processors, a maximal computing cost of 1000 seconds. The cost function used takes into account the sum between communication and computation costs (all the processors being at the same distance). These tests reflect mostly the expectations:

- The most sophisticated mapping algorithms (simulated annealing and tabu) are the most efficient ones.
- LPTF performs well for parallel programs with low communication costs.
- The higher the ratio communication/computation, the more interesting are the iterative algorithms.
- The results of *LGCF* are better than *struct_quanti* which takes into account a qualitative criterion while the quality of results is estimated in terms of quantitative criteria (i.e. the cost function).

The previous results are encouraging but not sufficient since we are not sure that random task graphs are representative of "real" parallel programs.

4.2 Experiments with real programs executed on a real machine

Extensive tests were run on a 128 nodes transputer-based MegaNode, with the VCR software router[3], using the ALPES performance evaluation environment of

---

[3] VCR: Virtual Channel Router, developed by Southampton University.

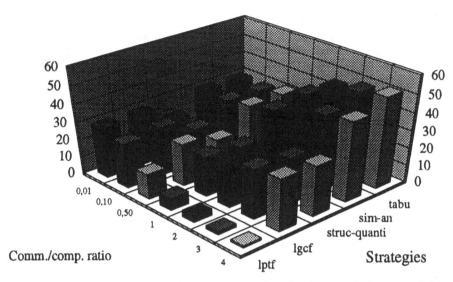

Fig. 3. Percentage of improvements of mapping algorithms relative to modulo

the APACHE project [8]. ALPES provides a modeling language called ANDES, allowing the generation of synthetic programs from the description of an application. Synthetic programs consume resources, as their actual models, although they do not produce any results. Performance measurements were obtained by executing these synthetic programs on an actual parallel computer. Parameters of the synthetic programs (mainly computation/communication ratios) can be easily changed to *emulate* various parallel target architectures. ALPES includes also monitoring tools.

A benchmark for mapping tools was designed using ANDES: it includes the description of classical parallel programs (FFT, matrix-vector multiplication, Gaussian elimination, matrix product using the Strassen algorithm, Divide and conquer, PDE solver, etc.) [3]. Several problem sizes were used for each problem to generate a total of 17 different benchmarks. Each one was run 100 times in order to eliminate the effect of execution indeterminism.

ALTO was coupled with PYRROS which is a complete scheduling platform designed at Rutgers by Gerasoulis and Yang [11]. PYRROS takes as inputs the precedence graphs generated by ANDES to group the tasks. The output of PYRROS, where the orientation of the arcs is not taken into account, is then passed to ALTO.

Adequation of the cost functions. Several mapping experiments were done using various cost functions, in order to determine the best one, whose costs are the closest to the execution times of the benchmarks. The four cost functions defined in section 2.3 were tested on the Meganode, configured as a torus.

Figure 4 presents the cumulated results of the whole set of benchmarks, run on 16 processors for the different cost functions. We observe a linear correlation between all cost functions and execution time. In theory, it is possible to communicate over several transputer links simultaneously and to overlap communications by computations. However, because of the software overhead induced by VCR, this is not the case in practice and the first cost function is not applicable. In addition, since VCR uses packetisation and pipelining mechanisms, the first refinement is not usable. The best cost function is therefore the sum of computation and communication costs (second cost function above), coupled with the second refinement (torus topology, using VCR routing tables).

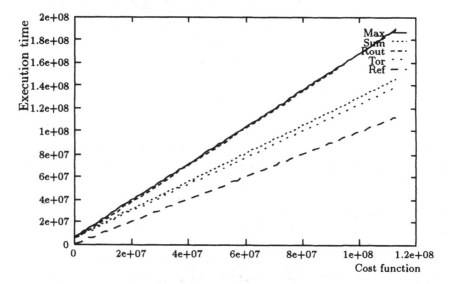

Fig. 4. Regression between cost functions and execution times

In this figure, *Ref* represents the experimental execution time. The best cost function is *Tor*: torus topology with VCR routing tables.

Experimental results. A very large number of experiments were done using synthetic programs. The greedies always delivered their results in less than one second on a workstation, while iterative algorithms could spend up to one hour. To summarize:

- LPTF is better than modulo in most of the tests and may be sufficient when communication costs are low.
- Taking into account communication times is important and LGCF is for this reason the best greedy algorithm.
- Iterative algorithms did not result in important improvements relatively to LGCF. Figure 5 summarizes experimental mapping results by giving the per-

centage of improvement resulting from the use of tabu instead of LGCF, for the cost function which takes into account the torus architecture. The improvement remains low for the majority of the tests (about 15% in the worst case). This may be due to several reasons: the graphs of these benchmarks are well-structured and the ratio communication/computation was not chosen high. Tests using random task graphs demonstrated that iterative algorithms perform better for programs having a high communication/computation ratio.

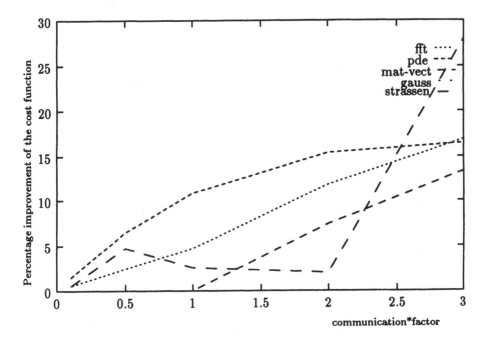

Fig. 5. Comparison between tabu and LGCF

4.3 Use of ALTO

We propose a stepwise process where a first mapping is done with a greedy algorithm. If some parameters are unknown, the greedy uses default parameters. Next, the parallel program is executed using monitoring tools. Monitoring results are used to run an iterative mapping algorithm. If the mapping is not good enough, these steps can be repeated as long as needed and the statistical analysis will try to improve the mapping. Usually, one step is sufficient.

Monitoring is used to determine the mapping parameters, computation and communication costs, and thus improve the quality. Monitoring gives the total execution time of a program, the number of bytes communicated between each pair of tasks, the computing time of each task, the idle time of each task (the time wasted by waiting communications), the total idle time of each processor, and the number of bytes communicated between each pair of processors.

In our benchmarks, the knowledge of communication and computation costs has proved to be very important. To simulate the behavior of an user having only an approximate knowledge of these values and to use the possibility of a feedback mechanism (to use the post-mortem trace analysis), we modified the information given to the tabu for the graph corresponding to the matrix-vector product. In figure 6, the communication costs were multiplied by x for the mapping. The results stress the importance of having a correct estimate of communication times to generate an efficient mapping. They also indicate that it is better to overestimate than to underestimate communication costs.

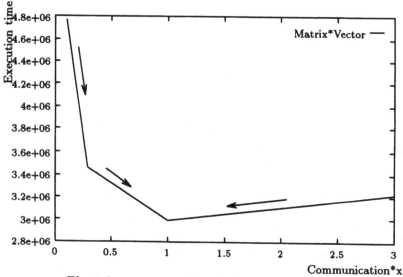

Fig. 6. Improvement of a mapping using feedbacks

5 Conclusion

The ALTO toolbox includes greedy algorithms, *modulo*, *LPTF*, *LGCF* and *struct-quanti* as well as iterative ones, *simulated annealing* and *tabu search*. ALTO was thoroughly assessed to study both the efficiency of the mapping algorithms, that is the time taken to deliver a solution, and the quality of the mapping, that is the value of the cost function optimized by the mapping algorithm.

The first experiments were performed using randomly generated task graphs. A large number of more realistic experiments were performed using synthetic programs modeling the most classical numerical algorithms, executed on a transputer based architecture including 128 processors. These were used to assess the cost functions which can be used in ALTO and which proved to be linearly related to the program execution times. Therefore any of them can be used in the mapping algorithms since decreasing its value will result in improved execution time.

Another experiment studied the sensitivity of the mapping result to the cost estimates done for the programmer for the computation of tasks and inter-tasks communication volumes. It indicated the interest of combining the mapping tools with monitoring tools. The main result of the large number of experiments done with ALTO is that a mapping tool should include several mapping algorithms and a method to use these algorithms.

References

1. J. Błażewicz, P. Bouvry, D. Trystram, and R. Walkowiak. A tabu search algorithm for solving the mapping problem. 1995. European Conference on Combinatorial Optimization, ECCO'95.
2. S. W. Bollinger and S. F. Midkiff. Processor and link assignment in multicomputers using simulated annealing. In *ICPP*, 1988.
3. P. Bouvry, J.-P. Kitajima, B. Plateau, and D. Trystram. Andes: A performance evaluation tool, application to the mapping problem. *submitted for publication*.
4. T.L. Casavant and J.G. Kuhl. A taxonomy of scheduling in general-purpose distributed computing systems. *IEEE Transactions on Software Engineering*, 1988.
5. F. Glover and M. Laguna. *Tabu Search, a chapter in Modern Heuristic Techniques for Combinatorial Problems*. W.H. Freeman, N-Y, 1992.
6. P. Haden and F. Berman. A comparative study of mapping algorithms for an automated parallel programming environment. Technical Report CS-088, UC San Diego, 1988.
7. J.G. Harp, C.R. Jesshope, T. Muntean, and C. Whitby-Stevens. The development and application of a low cost high performance multiprocessor machine. In *ESPRIT'86: results and achievements*, Amsterdam, 1986. North Holland.
8. J. Kitajima. *Modèles Quantitatifs d'Algorithmes parallèles*. PhD thesis, Institut National Polytechnique de Grenoble, Grenoble - France, November 1994. in french.
9. M. Norman and P. Thanish. Models of machines and computation for mapping in multicomputers. *ACM Computing Surveys*, September 1993.
10. B. Plateau. Présentation d'APACHE. Rapport APACHE 1, IMAG, Grenoble, October 1994. Available at *ftp.imag.fr:/imag/APACHE/RAPPORTS*.
11. T. Yang and A. Gerasoulis. PYRROS: static scheduling and code generation for message passing multiprocessors. In *Proceedings of the 6th ACM International Conference on Supercomputing*, pages 428–437. ACM, July 1992.

Optimal Data Distributions for LU Decomposition

THOMAS RAUBER   GUDULA RÜNGER *

Computer Science Dep., Universität des Saarlandes, 66041 Saarbrücken, Germany

Abstract. The paper considers the well–known problem of LU decomposition to study a method to derive data distributions for parallel computers with a distributed memory organization. The importance of the paper lies not so much in the special application but with the principle that the problem of finding an optimal data distribution is formulated as an optimization problem. This is possible by using a parameterized data distribution and a rigorous performance prediction technique that allows us to derive runtime formulas containing the parameters of the data distribution. The parameters are determined in such a way that the total runtime is minimized, thus also minimizing the communication overhead and the load imbalance penalty.

1 Introduction

An important issue in the design of parallel programs for distributed memory machines (DMMs) is the choice of a suitable data distribution. The layout of the data structures of a parallel program among the processors of a parallel machine strongly influences the performance of the program. An inappropriate data distribution may lead to a large communication overhead and a load imbalance which may reduce the speedup considerably. The goal is to find a data distribution that minimizes the overall execution time of a parallel program, thus minimizing the communication overhead and showing a good load balance.

In this paper, we describe a technique to derive a suitable data distribution for any algorithm that uses arrays of arbitrary dimension as data structures. The technique is based on the use of a parallel programming model [RRW95] in which formulas for the global execution time of an algorithm can be derived. These formulas depend on the problem size and on the machine parameters that are used by the programming model. The numerical evidence of the formulas derived in this programming model has already been shown for many numerical applications like Newton iteration, extrapolation methods, and different Runge–Kutta methods, see [RRW95] and the references therein.

This paper extends the performance prediction technique of the programming model by introducing parametrized data distributions. The use of these data distributions leads to runtime formulae that not only depend on the problem size and the machine parameters but also on the parameters of the data distribution.

---

* both authors are supported by DFG

This enables us to apply optimization techniques to determine the parameters of the data distribution such that the global execution time is minimized.

We apply this technique to derive a data distribution for the Gaussian LU decomposition of a matrix. The LU decomposition is chosen as example for two reasons. First, the problem has been extensively studied in the past, see [vdV94] and the references therein. Thus an optimal data distribution for this problem has already been derived by other approaches [FWM94, vdV90] and has been verified by experiments on various parallel machines. This gives us the possibility to verify the results of our analysis. Second, finding an optimal data distribution for LU decomposition is not trivial because both the communication overhead and the load balancing issue have to be taken into consideration. Finally, direct solvers for linear systems are important because they don't impose special requirements on the problem as many iterative solvers do.

The rest of the paper is organized as follows: Section 2 gives an overview of the programming model used. Section 3 introduces a special class of parametrized data distributions which is used in Section 4 for the derivation of formulas for the global execution time of a parallel implementation of the LU decomposition. Section 5 shows how these formulas can be used to determine the parameters of the data distribution such that a minimal global execution time results.

2 Parallel computation model

The important information for the evaluation of a parallel program is the *global execution time*. The global execution time is the time between the start and the termination of a computation of a program and, in case of a parallel program, it consists of the time for computations and the time for communications.

For the theoretical prediction of the execution times, we use the parallel computation model from [RRW95]. The model describes a parallel machine by four parameters: (1) the number p of processors, (2) the time t_{op} to execute an arithmetic operation, (3) the byte transfer time t_c for point-to-point messages, and (4) the startup time τ for point–to–point messages. For a specific machine, the values for t_{op}, t_c, and τ are determined by appropriate benchmark programs.

Parallel programs are specified in an SPMD (*single program multiple data*) programming scheme. The *data exchange* between processors is performed in a synchronous communication phase that is expressed by communication primitives like single–to–single transfer, single accumulation, and single broadcast.

The runtime $t(Prog)$ of a program *Prog* executed by a set G processors is

$$t(Prog) = \max_{q \in G} t_w(q) + \max_{q \in G} t_c(q)$$

where $t_w(q)$ is the computation time for processor q and $t_c(q)$ is the communication time for processor q. The computation times $t_w(q)$ are determined from the arithmetic operations of the program. The communication time depends on the communication primitives used. The costs of one of the communication primitives for a specific parallel machine are expressed by a formula that depends on the number of communicated data, the number of participating processors, and the machine parameters τ and t_c. The transfer time of a message of M bytes between two processors P_1 and P_2 is $t_{s\_s}(M) = \tau(M) + M \cdot t_c(M)$, independent of the special interconnection network of the DMM. The runtime formulae for the other communication primitives depend on the special machine. For a hypercube network, [JH89] addresses the exact runtimes of the primitives. We use the formulae from [RRW95] for our implementations on an Intel iPSC/860:

$$t_{s\_broad}(p, M) = (1 + \log p)(Mt_c + \tau) \tag{1}$$

$$t_{s\_gather}(p, M) = \frac{p-1}{\log p} Mt_c + \left(\frac{p}{\log p} + \log p \right) \tau$$

3 Data Distributions

In order to determine an optimal data distribution that has the minimal global execution time for the LU–decomposition, we consider a theoretical execution time function that contains the information about different data distributions as parameters. For the distribution of an array A, we adopt the parametrized data distribution of [DHR94]: Let A be an array with d dimensions of size $n_0 \times \ldots \times n_{d-1}$. The elements of A are addressed by elements from an index set $I_A \subseteq N^d$. We assume that the indices of dimension i range between 0 and $n_i - 1$. Let $P = \{q_0, \ldots, q_{p-1}\}$ be the processors of the target machine.

Definition 1. (distribution function) A function $\gamma_A : N^d \to P$ is called a *distribution function* for A. A distribution function γ_A partitions the elements of I_A into p index sets $I_0, \ldots, I_{p-1} \subseteq I_A$ with $I_q = \{k \in I_A | \gamma_A(k) = q\}$.

We consider distribution functions that are described by *distribution* vectors of the form $((m_0, b_0), \ldots, (m_{d-1}, b_{d-1}))$ with $p = \prod_{i=0}^{d-1} m_i$ and $1 \le b_i \le n_i$. The value m_i, $0 \le i \le d - 1$, is the number of processors in dimension i. Dimension i is divided up evenly among the m_i processor groups. For simplicity we assume $n_i/m_i \in N$. The value b_i specifies the block size in dimension i. The two–dimensional case is illustrated in Figure 1.

Definition 2. (Parametrized distribution function) We logically arrange the processors in a d–dimensional grid, i.e. processor q is specified by a grid address $G(q) = (j_0, \ldots, j_{d-1})$ with $0 \le j_i < m_i$ for $0 \le i < d$. The distribution function for a distribution vector $((m_0, b_0), \ldots, (m_{d-1}, b_{d-1}))$ is

$$\gamma_A(e_0, \ldots, e_{d-1}) = \left(\left\lfloor \frac{e_0}{b_0} \right\rfloor \bmod m_0, \cdots, \left\lfloor \frac{e_{d-1}}{b_{d-1}} \right\rfloor \bmod m_{d-1} \right) \tag{2}$$

Remark: If $b_i = 1$ for $i = 0, \ldots, d - 1$, the function (2) describes a *cyclic distribution*. If $m_i \cdot b_i = n_i$, the function (2) describes a *block distribution*.

Here, we consider the case $d = 2$ and $n_0 = n_1$, i.e. A is a quadratic matrix, see Figure 1. Each processor owns contiguous blocks of array elements of size $b_0 b_1$. A *superblock* is built by $m_0 m_1$ of these blocks. The number of superblocks in dimension $i = 0, 1$ is $\lceil n/(m_i b_i) \rceil$. For simplicity we assume $n/(m_i b_i) \in N$.

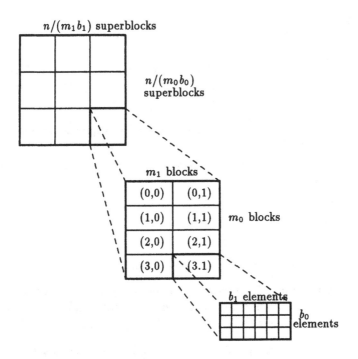

Fig. 1. Distribution of an array with $d = 2$ dimensions among $p = 8$ processors. The figure shows the case $m_0 = 4$, $m_1 = 2$, $b_0 = 3$, and $b_1 = 6$.

Definition 3. (row groups, column groups) For $d = 2$ and a twodimensional grid–numbering of the processors, the set of processors is divided into a partition of m_0 row groups $R_0, \ldots, R_{m_0-1}$ and into a partition of m_1 column groups $C_0, \ldots, C_{m_1-1}$, i.e.

$$\bigcup_{i=0}^{m_0-1} R_i = \bigcup_{i=0}^{m_1-1} C_i = P \quad \text{and} \quad R_i \cap R_j = \emptyset \quad \text{and} \quad C_i \cap C_j = \emptyset \quad \text{for} \quad i \neq j$$

The row and column groups are:

$$R_i = \{q \in P | G(q) = (i, \cdot)\} \qquad C_i = \{q \in P | G(q) = (\cdot, i)\} \tag{3}$$

For $0 \leq i < m_0$ and $0 \leq j < m_1$, it is $|R_i| = m_1$ and $|C_j| = m_0$.

Lemma 4. *For distribution function (2), each row i of A is stored in a single row group R_k with $k \equiv i \pmod{m_0 b_0}$ or $\lfloor i/b_0 \rfloor = \lfloor k/b_0 \rfloor$. Similarly, each column j of A is stored in a single column group C_k with $k \equiv j \pmod{m_1 b_1}$ or $\lfloor j/b_1 \rfloor = \lfloor k/b_1 \rfloor$.*

For a hypercube network, we have $p = 2^x$ and therefore $m_0 = 2^{x_0}$ and $m_1 = 2^{x_1}$ with $x = x_0 + x_1$. We map the two–dimensional processor grid into a hypercube with *reflected Gray Codes* (RGC) [BT88]. The x–bit RGC is a sequence of 2^x distinct binary numbers with x bits each.

Definition 5. (RGC sequence) The 1–bit RGC sequence is $\{0, 1\}$. Let $\{b_0, b_1, \ldots, b_{q-1}\}$ be the $(x - 1)$–bit RGC sequence with $q = 2^{x-1}$. The corresonding x–bit RGC sequence is $\{0b_0, 0b_1, \ldots 0b_{q-1}, 1b_{q-1}, \ldots 1b_0\}$.

We generalize the recursive construction of the RGC sequence: Suppose that $\{a_0, a_1, \ldots a_{m_0-1}\}$ and $\{b_0, b_1, \ldots b_{m_1-1}\}$ are the x_0–bit and x_1–bit RGC sequences. We construct the $m_0 \times m_1$ matrix of x–bit strings $\{a_i b_j | i = 0, \ldots, m_0 - 1; j = 0, \ldots, m_1 - 1\}$

$$\begin{bmatrix} a_0 b_0 & a_0 b_1 & \cdots & a_0 b_{m_1-1} \\ a_1 b_0 & a_1 b_1 & \cdots & a_1 b_{m_1-1} \\ \vdots & \vdots & \ddots & \vdots \\ a_{m_0-1} b_0 & a_{m_0-1} b_1 & \cdots & a_{m_0-1} b_{m_1-1} \end{bmatrix} \tag{4}$$

that represents the mapping of a $m_0 \times m_1$ mesh into a hypercube. The processor p with $G(p) = (i, j)$ is the x–cube node with identity number $a_i b_j$. The rows and columns of matrix (4) represent the row and column groups (3).

Lemma 6. *For a hypercube network, the row (column) groups (3) are hypercubes with m_1 (m_0) processors.*

The fact that row and column groups represent independent substructures makes it possible to assume independent executions on the row and column groups. This is true for every topology in which a grid can be embedded.

4 Parallel Implementation of LU Decomposition

In this section, we describe a general parallel implementation of the LU decomposition that is based on parametrized data distributions as described in the last section and derive formulas for the global execution time that depend on the parameters of the data distribution and the machine model.

4.1 LU Decomposition of a matrix

We consider the LU decomposition of a matrix A without pivoting in order to keep the example comprehensible. The following short description of the LU decomposition introduces the notation that we use for the parallel implementation. The matrix A is factorized into $A = LU$ with a unit diagonal, lower triangular matrix L and an upper triangular matrix U. To compute the n^2 unknown entries of L and U, we proceed row by row (Gauß). The entries of L and U are stored in a single matrix A^{n-1}. We compute A^{n-1} by executing $(n-1)$ elimination steps. Elimination step m consists of subtracting suitable multiples of the mth equation from the remaining equations $m+1, \ldots, n$. The multiples are determined in such a way that the unknown x_m is eliminated from these equations. In general, after the $(m-1)$th elimination step we are left with matrix

$$A^{(m-1)} = \begin{bmatrix} a_{11} & a_{12} & \cdots & a_{1,m-1} & a_{1m} & \cdots & a_{1n} \\ l_{21} & a_{22}^{(1)} & \cdots & a_{2,m-1}^{(1)} & a_{2m}^{(1)} & \cdots & a_{2n}^{(1)} \\ \vdots & \ddots & \ddots & \vdots & \vdots & & \vdots \\ \vdots & & \ddots & a_{m-1,m-1}^{(m-2)} & a_{m-1,m}^{(m-2)} & \cdots & a_{m-1,n}^{(m-2)} \\ \vdots & & & l_{m,m-1} & a_{mm}^{(m-1)} & \cdots & a_{mn}^{(m-1)} \\ \vdots & & & \vdots & \vdots & \ddots & \vdots \\ l_{n1} & \cdots & \cdots & l_{n,m-1} & a_{nm}^{(m-1)} & \cdots & a_{nn}^{(m-1)} \end{bmatrix}$$

In step m, x_m is eliminated from equations $i = m+1, \ldots, n$ by subtraction of $a_{im}^{(m-1)}/a_{mm}^{(m-1)}$ times equation m from each of these equations. This yields the matrix in which the first m rows and $m-1$ columns are the same as those of $A^{(m-1)}$. The remaining elements in column m of $A^{(m)}$ are replaced by $l_{im} = a_{im}^{(m-1)}/a_{mm}^{(m-1)}$ and the other elements are given by $a_{ij}^{(m)} = a_{ij}^{(m-1)} - a_{im}^{(m-1)} a_{mj}^{(m-1)}/a_{mm}^{(m-1)}$ for $i, j = m+1, m+2, \ldots, n$.

4.2 Parallel Implementation

For notational convenience, we use $Ro(k)$ and $Co(k)$ to denote the row group that holds the row with number k and the column group that holds the column with number k. Using distribution function (2), $Ro(k)$ and $Co(k)$ are defined by:

$$Ro(k) = R_i \quad \text{for} \quad k \equiv i \pmod{m_0 b_0}$$
$$Co(k) = C_i \quad \text{for} \quad k \equiv i \pmod{m_0 b_0}$$

We consider the forward elimination step $m \to m+1$ without pivoting. For the array element with index (m, m) there is exactly one processor $r \in P$ with $(m, m) \in I_r$. The following operations are necessary for the elimination step:

1. Broadcast of the pivot row: In order to eliminate the mth column element $a_{im}^{(m)}$ for $i > m$, a suitable multiple of the pivot row $(a_{mm}^{(m-1)}, \ldots, a_{mn}^{(m-1)})$ has to be subtracted from the remaining rows $m+1, \ldots, n$. Therefore, the pivot row has to be sent to the relevant processors. The pivot row is distributed among the processors $q \in Ro(m)$. The element $a_{mj}^{(m-1)}$ of column j has to be sent only to those processors owing some elements of the same column j, i.e. to all $q \in Co(j)$. Thus each processor $q \in Ro(m)$ performs a single broadcast operation to all processors in its column group (group broadcast). The number of elements to be transmitted is $\#\{(m, j) \in I_q | j \geq m\}$.
2. Computation of elimination factors: The processors in the column group of r compute the values l_{im}, i.e. each $q \in Co(m)$ computes l_{im} if $(i, m) \in I_q$. Processor $q \in Co(m)$ computes $\#\{(i, m) \in I_q | i > m\}$ elements.

3. Broadcast of elimination factors: Processor $q \in Co(m)$ broadcasts all computed values l_{im} to all processors owing some elements of row i, i.e. to all $s \in Ro(i)$. The number of elements transmitted is $\#\{(i, m) \in I_q | i > m\}$.

4. Computation of new matrix elements: Each processor q computes $a_{ij}^{(m)} = a_{ij}^{(m-1)} - l_{im} a_{mj}^{(m-1)}$ for all elements $(i, j) \in I_q$. That are $|\{(i, m) \in I_q; i > m\}| \cdot |\{(m, j) \in I_q; j > m\}|$ elements.

The LU decomposition executes $n - 1$ of these steps. There are synchronization points between the broadcast of the pivot row and the computation of the elimination factors l_{im} and between the broadcast of these factors and the computation of the new matrix elements. But there is no need for a synchronization between the computation and the transmission of the values l_{im}. In the two computation phases (2. and 4.) all processors involved in the computation are executing in parallel.

4.3 Runtime Prediction

We assume that the processors are arranged in a topology in which the disjoint row or column groups represent independent substructures. Examples are a hypercube network in which the substructures are also hypercubes and d–dimensional grid structures in which the substructures are $(d - 1)$-dimensional grids. For these topologies, the broadcast operations of the row or column groups can be performed in parallel. Therefore, the maximal communication time needed by the dominating group determines the global communication time. The following lemma summarizes the resulting global execution time of the complete method according to the performance model from Section 2. The global execution time specified represents an upper bound to the exact runtime.

Lemma 7. *The global execution time of the LU–decomposition estimated according to the computational model of Section 2 is:*

$$T_1 = \sum_{m=1}^{n-1} \{ \max_{q \in Ro(m)} t_{s\_broad}(\#Co(q), \#\{(m, j) \in I_q | j \geq m\})$$

$$+ \max_{q \in Co(m)} \#\{(i, m) \in I_q | i > m\} \cdot t_{op}$$

$$+ \max_{q \in Co(m)} t_{s\_broad}(\#Ro(m), \#\{(i, m) \in I_q | i > m\})$$

$$+ \max_{q} (\#\{(i, m) \in I_q | i > m\} \cdot \#\{(m, j) \in I_q | j > m\}) * 2t_{op} \}$$

For the parametrized distribution function (2) the number of elements to be computed or broadcasted are estimated by upper bounds containing the parameters m_0, b_0, m_1, b_1. For the broadcast of the pivot row m, the number of elements to be transmitted by each processor $q \in Ro(m)$ is

$$\#\{(m, j) \in I_q | j \geq m\} \leq \left\lceil \frac{n-m+1}{m_1 b_1} \right\rceil b_1 \leq \left(\frac{n-m+1}{m_1 b_1} + 1 \right) b_1 = \frac{n-m+1}{m_1} + b_1$$

where $\left\lceil \frac{n-m+1}{m_1 b_1} \right\rceil$ is the number of superblocks and b_1 is the number of elements of row m in each superblock. The number of elements l_{im} to be computed or broadcasted by each processor $q \in Co(m)$ is

$$\#\{(i,m) \in I_q | i > m\} \le \left\lceil \frac{n-m}{m_0 b_0} \right\rceil b_0 \le \left(\frac{n-m}{m_0 b_0} + 1 \right) b_0 = \frac{n-m}{m_0} + b_0$$

The parametrized data distribution and the corresponding estimations of the size of the index subsets result in the global execution time that is expressed in the following lemma. Note that the estimation of the number of elements broadcasted or computed is independent of the individual processor. Therefore there is no need to use the maximum function.

Lemma 8. *The parameterized global execution time of the LU–decomposition implemented with the parametrized data distribution $((m_0, b_0), (m_1, b_1))$ is*

$$T_2(m_0, b_0, m_1, b_1) = \sum_{m=1}^{n-1} \left(t_{s\_broad}(m_0, \frac{n-m+1}{m_1} + b_1) \right.$$
$$+ (\frac{n-m}{m_0} + b_0)t_{op} + t_{s\_broad}(m_1, \frac{n-m}{m_0} + b_0)$$
$$\left. + (\frac{n-m}{m_0} + b_0)(\frac{n-m}{m_1} + b_1)2t_{op} \right)$$

where $m_0 m_1 = p$ and $1 \le b_i \le n/m_i$ for $i = 0, 1$.

For a hypercube network, we substitute the time t_{s_broad} for a single broadcast operation by equation (1) and transform the addition over m according to $\sum_{m=1}^{n-1} m = n(n-1)/2$ and $\sum_{m=1}^{n-1} m^2 = n(n-1)(2n-1)/6$. We get for example:

$$\sum_{m=1}^{n-1} t_{s\_broad}(m_0, \frac{n-m+1}{m_1} + b_1)$$
$$= \sum_{m=1}^{n-1} (1 + \log m_0) \left(\left(\frac{n-m+1}{m_1} + b_1 \right) t_c + \tau \right)$$
$$= (1 + \log m_0) \left(\left(\frac{n(n-1)}{2} \frac{1}{m_1} + \frac{n-1}{m_1} + (n-1)b_1 \right) t_c + (n-1)\tau \right)$$

Lemma 9. *The global execution time of the LU–decomposition implemented with the parametrized data distribution $((m_0, b_0), (m_1, b_1))$ on a hypercube network is*

$$T_3(m_0, b_0, m_1, b_1) = (1 + \log m_0) \left(\left(\frac{n(n-1)}{2} \frac{1}{m_1} + \frac{n-1}{m_1} + (n-1)b_1 \right) t_c + (n-1)\tau \right)$$
$$+ \left(\frac{n(n-1)}{2} \frac{1}{m_0} + (n-1)b_0 \right) t_{op}$$
$$+ (1 + \log m_1) \left(\left(\frac{n(n-1)}{2} \frac{1}{m_0} + (n-1)b_0 \right) t_c + (n-1)\tau \right)$$
$$+ \left(\frac{n(n-1)(2n-1)}{6} \frac{1}{p} + \frac{n(n-1)}{2} \left(\frac{b_1}{m_0} + \frac{b_0}{m_1} \right) + (n-1)b_0 b_1 \right) 2t_{op}$$

where $m_0 m_1 = p$ and $1 \le b_i \le n/m_i$ for $i = 0, 1$.

Special cases of the parametrized distributions are the

- row–cyclic distribution with $((m_0, b_0), (m_1, b_1)) = ((p, 1), (1, 1))$
- column–cyclic distribution with $((m_0, b_0), (m_1, b_1)) = ((1, 1), (p, 1))$

The decision which of these distributions is better depends on the number of processors p and the system size n. We consider the difference

$$T_3((p, 1), (1, 1)) - T_3((1, 1), (p, 1)) = (n-1)\left((1+log(p))t_c + \frac{n}{2p}t_{op} - \frac{1}{p}t_c - \frac{n}{2}t_{op}\right)$$

Lemma 10. *The row–cyclic distribution is better than the column–cyclic distribution (i.e. $T_3((p, 1), (1, 1)) - T_3((1, 1), (p, 1)) > 0$) if*

$$n < \frac{t_c}{t_{op}} \frac{2(p(1 + log(p)) - 1)}{p - 1}$$

In some situations, the row– and column–cyclic distributions are suitable for the use of LU decomposition as a module within more complicated problems. An example for this situation can be found in [RR95] which describes the implementation of a diagonal–implicitly iterated Runge–Kutta (DIIRK) method. The DIIRK method executes several Newton iterations where each iteration of the Newton method uses an LU decomposition.

5 Optimal Data Distribution for LU Decomposition

In this section, we derive an *optimal* parametrized data distribution for the LU decomposition, i.e. the data distribution that minimizes the global execution time.

Definition 11. The optimal data distribution for a parallel program *Prog* is the data distribution $((\bar{m}_0, \bar{b}_0), \ldots, (\bar{m}_{d-1}, \bar{b}_{d-1}))$ that minimizes the parametrized global execution time $T_{Prog}((m_0, b_0), \ldots, (m_{d-1}, b_{d-1}))$ of *Prog*, i.e.

$$T_{Prog}((\bar{m}_0, \bar{b}_0), \ldots, (\bar{m}_{d-1}, \bar{b}_{d-1})) = \min_{\substack{(m_i, b_i) \\ i=0,\ldots,d-1}} T_{Prog}((m_0, b_0), \ldots, (m_{d-1}, b_{d-1}))$$

where $\prod_{i=0}^{d-1} m_i = p$ and $1 \le b_i \le n_i/m_i$.

The following lemma states that the block size of an optimal data distribution is 1 in each dimension, if the runtime formula for the execution time of a broadcast operation can be separated into a part that only depends on the number of processors and into a part that only depends on the number of data items transmitted.

Lemma 12. *(Block size of optimal data distribution for LU decomposition) Consider a network in which the time for a single broadcast operation can be represented as $t_{s\_broad}(p, M) = f(p)g(M)$ with g monotonically increasing for $M > 0$. The optimal data distribution minimizing $T_2((m_0, b_0), (m_1, b_1))$ of Lemma 8 fulfills $b_0 = b_1 = 1$.*

Proof. We consider T_2 as a function of b_0 and b_1. The broadcast terms of T_2 are monotonically increasing in b_0 or b_1. The computation term is a positiv quadratic function in b_0 and b_1, i.e. T_2 contains positive terms in b_0, b_1, and $b_0 b_1$. Therefore, T_2 has its minimum at the left hand boundary of the intervall $1 \le b_i \le n/m_i$, $i = 0, 1$, which is independent of m_0 and m_1.

Note that the separation of the variables required by the lemma is possible for most networks like trees, meshes, and hypercubes. For a hypercube network, it is for example according to equation (1): $f(p) = 1 + \log p$ and $g(M) = \tau + M t_c$. Because of Lemma 12 we now have to minimize $T_2((m_0, 1), (m_1, 1))$.

For this minimization, we have to know the dependence of the runtime of the broadcast operation on the number of participating processors i.e. we need a concrete runtime formula. From now on we consider the hypercube network as a specific network and minimize $T_3((m_0, 1), (m_1, 1))$ which we denote by $T_3(m_0, m_1)$. The function T_3 consists of three components: a constant part T_C that is independent of m_0 and m_1, a symmetric part T_S that is a symmetric function in m_0 and m_1, and an asymmetric part T_A.

$$\tilde{T}_3(m_0, m_1) = T_C(m_0, m_1) + T_S(m_0, m_1) + T_A(m_0, m_1)$$

$$T_C(m_0, m_1) = 2(n-1)(t_c + \tau) + 3(n-1)t_{op} +$$
$$(n-1)(t_c + \tau)(\log m_0 + \log m_1) + \frac{n(n-1)(2n-1)}{6} \frac{1}{p} 2 t_{op} \quad (5)$$

$$T_S(m_0, m_1) = \frac{n(n-1)}{2}(t_c + 2 t_{op})\left(\frac{1}{m_0} + \frac{1}{m_1}\right) + \frac{n(n-1)}{2} t_c \left(\frac{\log m_0}{m_1} + \frac{\log m_1}{m_0}\right) \quad (6)$$

$$T_A(m_0, m_1) = (n-1)t_c\left(\frac{1}{m_1} + \frac{1}{m_1}\log m_0\right) + \frac{n(n-1)}{2}\frac{1}{m_0} t_{op} \quad (7)$$

The constant component T_C is independent of m_0 and m_1 (because of $\log m_0 + \log m_1 = \log(m_0 m_1) = \log p$) and does not influence the optimal choice for m_0 and m_1. The symmetric part T_S contains the row broadcast and part of the column broadcast of the pivot row. The asymmetric part T_A contains the communication overhead of broadcasting the pivot element within the column groups and a term that reflects the load imbalance of computing the elimination factors l_{im} only in one column group. For T_S the minimum can be computed analytically, if the arguments are assumed to be real values.

Lemma 13. *(Optimal data distribution for the symmetric part) If T_S is considered as a function of real values, then $T_S(m_0, m_1)$ is minimal for $m_0 = m_1 = \sqrt{p}$.*

Proof. The analytical solution is obtained by differentiating $T_S(m_0, p/m_0)$:

$$\frac{d}{dm_0} T_S(m_0, p/m_0) = \frac{n(n-1)}{2}(t_c + 2t_{op})\left(\frac{1}{p} - \frac{1}{m_0^2}\right)$$

$$+ \frac{n(n-1)}{2} t_c \left(\left(\frac{\log m_0}{p} - \frac{1}{m_0^2}\log\frac{p}{m_0}\right) + \left(\frac{1}{p\ln 2}\left(1 - \frac{p}{m_0^2}\right)\right)\right)$$

It is $\frac{d}{dm_0} T(\sqrt{p}, \sqrt{p}) = 0$ because of $1 - p/m_0^2 = 0$ and $\frac{1}{p}\log m_0 - \frac{1}{m_0^2}(\log p - \log m_0) = 0$ for $m_0 = \sqrt{p}$.

For an integer solution we have to find integer values m_0 and m_1 near $\sqrt{p}$ that fulfill $m_0 m_1 = p$.

The data distribution characterized by $m_0 = m_1 = \sqrt{p}$ is the optimal solution for the symmetric part T_S and also for $T_S + T_C$. The asymmetric part T_A has not been taken into account for the derivation of the solution. This is only justified if the influence of T_A is small. Figure 2 shows for two fixed number of processors that the influence of T_A on the optimal selection of m_0 and m_1 is small. The following lemma shows that T_A is small compared to the global execution time $T_S + T_C + T_A$ for an arbitrary number of processors.

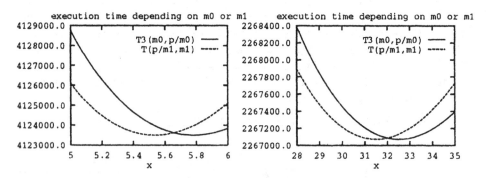

Fig. 2. Global execution time $\tilde{T}_3(m_0, m_1)$ in μs with variable m_0 and setting $m_1 = p/m_0$, and variable m_0 and setting $m_1 = p/m_0$ for $p = 32$ and $p = 1024$ processors. The intersection point of the curves lying at $\sqrt{p}$ is the optimal solution of the symmetric part.

Lemma 14. *Let T_C, T_S, and T_A be the constant, the symmetric, and the asymmetric parts of the global execution time $T_C + T_S + T_A$ according to (5), (6), and (7). The fraction of the asymmetric part T_A on the global execution time is*

$$\frac{T_A}{T_C + T_S + T_A} \leq \frac{1}{X} + \frac{1}{Y}$$

with $X = X(n, p)$ and $Y = Y(n, p)$:

$$X = \frac{n}{2} + \frac{3n}{2p(1 + \log p)} + \frac{n}{\log p} \frac{t_{op}}{t_c} + \frac{(2 + \log p)(t_c + \tau) + 3t_{op}}{(1 + \log p)t_c} + \frac{2n(2n-1)t_{op}}{6p(1 + \log p)t_c}$$

$$Y = 11 + 2n + (n + 1)\frac{t_c}{t_{op}} + \frac{2}{3p}(2n + 1) + \frac{2}{n}(1 + \log p)\frac{t_c + \tau}{t_{op}}$$

Proof. The claim follows by substituting T_C, T_S, and T_A and estimating m_0 and m_1 appropriately.

Note that X and Y do not depend on the special choice of m_0 and m_1 but only on n and p. Figure 3 shows that the value of $1/X + 1/Y$ is smaller than 0.3% for all values of n and p.

fraction of TA on global execution time

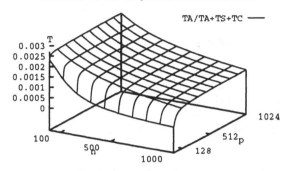

TA/TA+TS+TC ———

Fig. 3. Value of $1/X(n,p)+1/Y(n,p)$ for different system sizes and number of processors.

6 Conclusions

This article shows that the problem of finding a good data distribution for numerical algorithms can be reduced to an optimization problem, if parametrized data distribution functions are used and if the algorithms are formulated within an appropriate computation model. This is illustrated by considering the LU decomposition of a matrix as a representative example. The technique can also be applied to other numerical algorithms that work with arrays of arbitrary dimension. We think that the technique could be a starting point to solve the data distribution problem in parallelizing compilers [DHR94].

References

[BT88]   D.P. Bertsekas and J.N. Tsitsiklis. *Parallel and Distributed Computing.* Prentice Hall, New York, NY, 1988.

[DHR94] A. Dierstein, R. Hayer, and T. Rauber. A Branch–and–Bound Algorithm for Array Distributions. In *2nd Euromicro Workshop on Parallel and Distributed Processing*, pages 528–535, 1994.

[FWM94] G.C. Fox, R.D. Williams, and P.C. Messias. *Parallel Computing Works!* Morgan Kaufmann Publishers, 1994.

[JH89]   S.L. Johnsson and C.T. Ho. Optimum Broadcasting and Personalized Communication in Hypercubes. *IEEE Transactions on Computers*, 38(9):1249–1268, 1989.

[RR95]   T. Rauber and G. Rünger. Performance Predictions for Parallel Diagonal-Implicitly Iterated Runge-Kutta Methods. In *9th Workshop on Parallel and Distributed Simulation*, Lake Placid, USA, 1995.

[RRW95] T. Rauber, G. Rünger, and R. Wilhelm. An Application Specific Parallel Programming Paradigm. In *International Conference on High-Performance Computing and Networking*, 1995.

[vdV90] E.F. van de Velde. Data redistribution and concurrency. *Parallel Computing*, 16:125–138, 1990.

[vdV94] E.F. van de Velde. *Concurrent Scientific Computing.* Springer, 1994.

Detecting Quantified Global Predicates
in Parallel Programs

Mark Minas

IMMD II, Univ. Erlangen–Nürnberg
Martensstr. 3, 91058 Erlangen, Germany
Tel: (+49) 9131 – 857622
Fax: (+49) 9131 – 39388
email: minas@informatik.uni-erlangen.de

Abstract. Global predicates in parallel programs are predicates considering the state of more than one process. They are a useful concept for debugging parallel programs, e.g., for specifying assertions or breakpoints. In this paper ∃-predicates are defined and examined, a restricted class of global predicates. ∃-predicates are defined by two local predicates which have to be simultaneously satisfied by two different processes. Such predicates are frequently needed to express synchronization properties. Efficient centralized and parallel algorithms for detecting satisfaction of ∃-predicates are proposed. Furthermore, it is outlined how ∃-predicates can be used for global breakpoints and where to stop a parallel program reaching such a breakpoint. The underlying machine models is a fixed set of processes communicating by message passing or shared memory.

Keywords: Global predicates; testing; debugging; parallel debugger

1 Introduction

Debugging parallel programs is much harder than debugging sequential programs. Therefore, at least the methodologies proved useful for sequential debugging should be available when debugging a parallel program. One frequently used concept for sequential programs are *predicates*. Either they describe certain program properties (e.g., as *assertions* or *invariants*). Then these predicates are tested when executing the program; each time when a predicate is not satisfied is considered a possible program error. Or they specify *breakpoints*. Then they are used within a debugger. Whenever a predicate is satisfied, the program is stopped in order to examine the current program state. Examples for such predicates are *control breakpoints* specifying certain lines of code or *data breakpoints* being defined by predicates on the program memory state [15]. Predicates have proved to be useful when debugging sequential programs and are needed for parallel programming and debugging, too.

1.1 Predicates in parallel programs

Detecting predicates is more complicated for parallel programs than for sequential programs. In general, parallel systems do not provide for a globally synchronized clock with sufficient resolution. This is obviously true for distributed parallel systems (e.g., a network of workstations), but even some parallel machines (e.g., Thinking Machines CM-5) lack a global clock. But without global clocks a system's *global state* cannot be determined. However, *global predicates*, i.e., predicates related to multiple processes, are defined on global states. Furthermore, a (parallel) program reaching a breakpoint, i.e., satisfying a predicate, must be stopped in the earliest global state possible.

Even if a global clock is available, it makes sense to ignore it when checking predicates. Due to a program's nondeterminism, real simultaneousness of two events is often a matter of pure chance. Not detecting a certain predicate in a particular program run does not mean that this predicate is not satisfied in all other program runs. Therefore, a better suited approach for simultaneousness is necessary for parallel programs.

For several subclasses of global predicates these problems have been efficiently solved. In this paper we examine a further subclass of global predicates allowing efficient predicate detection and program halting. We consider MIMD programs running on parallel machines using message passing or shared memory as well as distributed programs running on an arbitrary distributed system. Programs consist of fixed numbers of processes.

1.2 ∃-predicates

As ∃-*predicates* we consider a restricted class of global predicates: each ∃-predicate, denoted $\exists(P_1, P_2)$, consists of two local predicates (i.e., predicates considering only states of single processes) P_1 and P_2.[1] $\exists(P_1, P_2)$ is satisfied if and only if there are two different processes p_1 and p_2 satisfying P_1 and P_2, resp.:

$$\exists(P_1, P_2) \Leftrightarrow (\exists p_1, p_2 \in \mathcal{P})(p_1 \neq p_2 \wedge P_1(p_1) \wedge P_2(p_2))$$

where $\mathcal{P}$ is the set of all processes. Such predicates are frequently used to describe synchronization properties. As examples consider the following predicates "*No two different processes are ever simultaneously staying within their critical sections.*" and "*One process is in procedure A while another process is in procedure B.*" The predicate of the first example is the negation $\neg\exists(P, P)$ of an ∃-predicate consisting of only one predicate $P \equiv$ "*the process is in one of its critical sections*". The second example's predicate is an ∃-predicate $\exists(P_A, P_B)$ with $P_A \equiv$ "*the process is in procedure A*" and $P_B \equiv$ "*the process is in procedure B*". In the following we present algorithms to detect satisfaction of ∃-predicates. Therefore, the algorithms can detect situations when predicates similar to example 1 (i.e., assertions and invariants represented by negated ∃-predicates) are no longer satisfied. Analogously, the algorithms can detect global states which satisfy predicates like the one in example 2 (i.e., global breakpoints specified by ∃-predicates).

The major contributions of this paper are efficient algorithms that detect as early as possible the satisfaction of ∃-predicates and a proposal when and how to stop a parallel program in a meaningful (global) state as soon as predicate satisfaction has been detected. Related work on global predicates is briefly summarized in Section 2. Vector time necessary for efficient predicate detection is introduced in the following Section 3. Section 4 presents efficient detection algorithms for ∃-predicates. The idea behind the predicate satisfaction algorithm is to check the local predicates of the ∃-predicate in each of

---

[1] There is no real limitation of ∃-predicates to two local predicates, but this restriction makes discussions and algorithms easier.

the parallel processes and to notify an added predicate checker process whenever a local predicate is satisfied. The predicate checker process maintains the information gained from the worker processes and checks for detection of the $\exists$-predicate. In this paper a centralized version providing only one such checker process as well as a parallel version with several checker processes is proposed. Section 5 discusses a means to increase efficiency, and section 6 a method to stop the parallel program as soon as the global predicate is satisfied. We propose to check the program while *replaying* a program run which has previously been recorded [10]. The predicate detection algorithm yields information to reconstruct the earliest global state corresponding with the predicate detection. Finally, we present first experimental results in Section 7.

2 Global Predicates

A *global predicate* is a predicate on the global state of a parallel program. The standard way to define global states in this context uses a system model consisting of a fixed number m of processes running on different nodes [3, 5, 7, 12, 14]. Processes communicate via message passing. This model covers a broad spectrum of distributed and parallel systems: message-passing programs are trivially included, but shared-memory programs are also easily represented.

Processes are considered as sequences of *states*. Transitions from one state to the next one are called *events*. In the following, we will distinguish between *communication events* (sending and receiving a message) and *internal events* (computing steps). When not explicitly stated, events are communication events, and a *local state* is the sequence of internal states between two communication events. Events are considered to happen instantaneously, i.e., to take no time. The *global state* of a parallel program is a set of simultaneous local states, one for each process.

In order to detect such predicates, global states must be determined. Without a global clock, temporal ordering and possible simultaneousness have to be defined in terms of the communication structure [2, 5]: each message in a program run has a send and a receive event. The send event must have happened before the receive event. Furthermore, the events of single processes are temporally ordered. Therefore, there is a partial ordering on the set of all events in a program run called "*happened before*" relation $\prec$ [8]. This relation implies a "*lying before*" relation on local states: A state s lies before state s' ($s < s'$) iff the event e_s^+ immediately after state s happens before or is equal to the event $e_{s'}^-$ immediately before state s' ($e_s^+ \preceq e_{s'}^-$). Two local states s, s' with $s \not\prec s' \wedge s' \not\prec s$ are called $<$-incomparable. Within the program run, s does not lie before s' and vice versa. Therefore, they can be considered simultaneous. This means that s and s' are either actually simultaneous local states, or they can be simultaneous in an equivalent program run, but with a different timing. Therefore, a *distributed global states* is defined as a pairwise $<$-incomparable set of local states, one for each process. Distributed global states comprise actual global states.

In order to check a predicate for a certain program run, every distributed global state must be checked. However, the number of global states grows exponentially with the number of events [3]. Therefore, an efficient algorithm detecting arbitrary global predicates cannot exist. In the literature several restricted classes of global predicates together with algorithms for checking these predicates have been discussed. Quite simple to detect are stable predicates [2], i.e., predicates remaining satisfied when being satisfied once (e.g., "*the entire program has terminated*"). Unstable predicates are more difficult to detect. Most restricted classes of unstable predicates are defined as local predicates connected by boolean operators [5, 7, 12, 14]. $\exists$-predicates are also a member of this class. Furthermore, there are some classes of global predicates going beyond the scope of this abstract.

3 Vector Time

In order to process distributed global states, the "happened before" relation on events must be implemented. The standard way to represent this partial ordering uses time-stamps based on *vector time* [4, 13]: each process i keeps a vector V_i of m counters. $V_i[i]$ is the number of the last event of process i and $V_i[j]$, $j \neq i$, the number of the last event of process j process i is causally dependent on. The timestamp of event e in process i is defined as $V_i(e)$, the value of V_i when e happens. Vectors are updated as follows: be e_i a send event in process i and e_j the corresponding receive event in process j.

$$V_i(e_i)[k] := \begin{cases} V_i(e_i^-)[k]+1, & \text{if } i=k \\ V_i(e_i^-)[k], & \text{else} \end{cases}$$

$$V_j(e_j)[k] := \begin{cases} \max(V_j(e_j^-)[k], V_i(e_i)[k])+1, & \text{if } j=k \\ \max(V_j(e_j^-)[k], V_i(e_i)[k]), & \text{else} \end{cases}$$

where e_i^- and e_j^- are the predecessor events of e_i resp. e_j in the same process. In order to compute $V_j(e_j)$ of the receive event, time stamp $V_i(e_i)$ of the send event must be transmitted piggypacked on the message. It can be shown that $e \prec e'$ iff $V(e)[i] \leq V(e')[i]$ if e happens in process i and $e' \neq e$. Similarly, for two local states s and s' of processes i resp. j, $s < s'$ iff $e_s^+ \preceq e_{s'}^-$ iff $V(e_s^+)[i] \leq V(e_{s'}^-)[i]$ iff $V(e_s^-)[i] < V(e_{s'}^-)[i]$. Thus, the vector time of local states of local states is the vector time of their starting events. In the following, we will call such vector timestamps "*time vectors*", and we will write $V(s) < V(s')$ when actually $V(s)[i] < V(s')[i]$ is meant. Using vector time, testing the "happened before" and the "lying before" relation costs exactly one elementary comparison, and therefore it is easy and efficient to check whether a set of local states is a distributed global state.

4 Detecting $\exists$-Predicates

A straight-forward approach to detect an $\exists$-predicate $\exists(P_1, P_2)$ is quite simple: for each process, we save the timestamps of local states satisfying P_1 resp. P_2. Each time when P_k is satisfied in process i, we compare the corresponding timestamp with saved timestamps of the other processes' local states having satisfied the other local predicate. The $\exists$-predicate is detected if a $<$-incomparable timestamp is found. But the major flaw of this approach is that it is unknown how long such timestamps must be saved before they can no longer serve as partners of a $<$-incomparable timestamp. Heuristically limiting the number of timestamps saved for each process would require that we know upper bounds for message latencies etc. Particularly in distributed systems, upper bounds are unknown or even do not exist.

In this section we propose a centralized and a parallel version of an algorithm detecting $\exists$-predicates in parallel programs consisting of m processes. The algorithm keeps timestamps only as long as absolutely necessary. Heuristics are unnecessary.

4.1 Basics of the Algorithm

In order to detect an $\exists$-predicate $\exists(P_1, P_2)$, we distinguish two classes of processes: user-generated worker processes and checker processes. Worker processes are instrumented such that they inform the checker processes of every local state satisfying a local predicate P_i. The checker processes then determine whether $\exists(P_1, P_2)$ is satisfied. Providing exactly one such checker process yields a centralized version of the algorithm, providing several checker processes on different nodes yields a parallel one. This approach works best if checker processes run on separate processors not being used by worker processes. Then, checker processes do not influence worker processes. However, the approach also works if checker processes have to share processors with worker processes. Especially in this case, checker processes should be highly efficient. The following presents such an efficient solution inspired by Garg and Waldecker's algorithm for detecting conjunctive global predicates [5].

The main idea of checker processes is to consider each of the predicates $P_1(i) \wedge P_2(j)$ for its own. For every pair $(i, j), 0 \leq i, j < m, i \neq j$, the timestamps[2] of i-states[3] satisfying P_1 and those of j-states satisfying P_2 are separately saved. Whenever a new i- or j-state "arrives" indicating that P_1 resp. P_2 has been satisfied in process i resp. j, the predicate $P_1(i) \wedge P_2(j)$ is detected when a $<$-incomparable saved timestamp of process j resp. i is found. The difference to the straight-forward approach is that the arriving timestamp restricts the timestamps that still have to be saved: every timestamp less than the new one cannot contribute to a $<$-incomparable state any longer and may be discarded. Therefore, the algorithm does not save timestamps longer than needed.

We assume that timestamps arrive in ascending order and are processed FIFO by the checker processes. For each pair (i, j), timestamps are best saved in separate queues for i- and j-states. New timestamps are inserted at the end; the heads tell about the eldest timestamps which may be discarded first. Since at least one of the queues is always empty — otherwise there would exist an i- and a j-state being $<$-incomparable such that the $\exists$-predicate is satisfied — one queue for both i- and j-states is sufficient. A flag tells about the process the saved timestamps are coming from.

Figure 1a describes a procedure check_global$(i, j, pred, ts)$ maintaining the queue $q[i, j]$ for a pair (i, j) when process i satisfies P_1 (if $pred = 1$) or when process j satisfies P_2 (if $pred = 2$) in a local state with timestamp ts. Flag $queued[i, j]$ represents the process the timestamps in $q[i, j]$ are coming from.

In order to check the entire $\exists$-predicate, procedure check_global has to be called by the instrumentation code for each local state satisfying P_1 or P_2. Whenever a process i satisfies P_1, check_global must be called for all the pairs (i, j) with $j = 0, 1, \ldots, m - 1, j \neq i$. Analogously, when process i satisfies P_2, check_global must be called for the pairs $(j, i), j = 0, 1, \ldots, m - 1, j \neq i$. The centralized version sequentially executes these invocations, the parallel one executes them in parallel (sections 4.3 and 4.4). The time complexity for the entire algorithm is therefore determined by the time complexity of procedure check_global:

Lemma 1 *The nth invocation of check_global$(i, j, pred, ts)$ with particular values i and j has a mean time complexity, measured as the number of elementary comparisons, of $O(1)$ and a maximal time complexity of $O(n)$.*

---

[2] In this section, timestamps are time vectors of local states. In section 5 pairs of event time vectors will be used as timestamps.

[3] i-state is used as a shorthand for "local state of process i."

procedure check_global($i, j, pred, ts$)
{ **if** *queued*$[i, j]$ = *pred* **then**
   enqueue *ts* in $q[i, j]$
else
{ **while** ¬empty($q[i, j]$) ∧
        ts > head($q[i, j]$) **do**
   dequeue head element of $q[i, j]$;
  if $q[i, j]$ is empty **then**
  { *queued*$[i, j]$:= *pred*;
   enqueue *ts* in $q[i, j]$ }
  else if *ts* ≮ head($q[i, j]$) **then**
  { **case** *pred* **of**
   { 1: ts_1 := *ts*; ts_2 := head($q[i, j]$)
    2: ts_1 := head($q[i, j]$); ts_2 := *ts* }
   global predicate is satisfied:
   $P_1(i)$ at ts_1 and $P_2(j)$ at ts_2 }}}

(a)

procedure clip_queue($i, j, pred, ts$)
{ **if** *queued*$[i, j]$ ≠ *pred* **then**
 { **while** ¬empty($q[i, j]$) ∧
      ts > head($q[i, j]$) **do**
  dequeue head of $q[i,j]$;
  while length($q[i, j]$) > 1 ∧
     ts ≮ second($q[i, j]$) **do**
  dequeue head of $q[i,j]$ }}

(b)

Fig. 1. Core procedure (a) and clipping procedure (b) of the detection algorithm

Proof: We show by induction that the number C_n of time vector comparisons needed for the first n invocations of *check_global* is restrained by $n - q_n \leq C_n \leq 2n - q_n$ where q_n is the number of time vectors in the queue after the nth invocation. This is true for $n = 1$. For $n > 1$, one of three cases can apply. (i) *ts* is inserted into the queue, thus $q_{n+1} = q_n + 1$ and $C_{n+1} = C_n$. (ii) *ts* is less than some time vectors in the queue. Thus, $C_{n+1} = C_n + q_n - q_{n+1} + 2$. (iii) *ts* is greater than all of the time vectors in the queue. Therefore, $C_{n+1} = C_n + q_n$ and $q_{n+1} = 1$. Thus, the mean complexity of each invocation is $C_n/n \leq 2 - q_n/n$. The maximal complexity, $n + 1$, is gained for case (ii) and $q_n = n$, $q_{n+1} = 1$.□

For each pair (i, j), $0 \leq i, j < m$, $i \neq j$, a queue must be maintained. The space required by the algorithm is therefore dominated by the $m(m - 1)$ queues. Each queue always contains the minimal number of elements being necessary to detect the earliest global state satisfying the ∃-predicate. The queue cannot infinitely grow as long as each process occasionally satisfies P_1 as well as P_2. Out-of-date timestamps are then automatically discarded. The space requirement of the algorithm is $O(pm^2)$ where p is the maximum length of each queue. If, however, there is a pair (i, j) of processes such that process i repeatedly satisfies P_k, but process j never satisfies the other local predicate, the queue $q[i, j]$ grows infinitely.

A solution is to periodically notify the checker processes of timestamps of the worker processes when their predicates have not been satisfied for a certain period of time. These "clipping timestamps" can be used to clip the queues: of course, timestamps being <-less than the clipping timestamp can be discarded. But it is also necessary to remove <-incomparable timestamps. Otherwise, the queue $q[i, j]$ of two processes i and j rarely communicating with each other would merely be clipped. Unfortunately, this might result in missing the *earliest* global state satisfying the ∃-predicate since a <-incomparable timestamp has been discarded. But if at least the most recent <-incomparable is left on the queue during clipping, it is guaranteed that a later global state satisfying the ∃-

For each sending of a message from proc i:

   send the array cnt piggypacked
     on the message;

$cnt[i] := cnt[i] + 1;$
$first[1] := \text{true}; first[2] := \text{true};$

For each receiving of a message in proc i;
the message contains the array cnt':

   for $j := 0$ **to** $m - 1$ **do**
     $cnt[j] := \max(cnt[j], cnt'[j]);$
   $cnt[i] := cnt[i] + 1;$
   $first[1] := \text{true}; first[2] := \text{true};$

Whenever a predicate P_k becomes true
in proc i, or when P_k is still true after
an event has happened:

   if $first[k]$ **then**
     $\{ first[k] := \text{false}; clip[k] := \text{false};$
      call local_pred_satisfied$(k, cnt) \};$

Periodically execute:

   if $clip[1] \vee clip[2]$ **then**
     call clip$(cnt);$
   $clip[1] := \text{true}; clip[2] := \text{true};$

Fig. 2. Instrumentation of worker processes

predicate is detected.

    According to these ideas, Fig. 1b shows the procedure clip_queue$(i, j, pred, ts)$ being responsible for clipping the queue $q[i, j]$ when ts is the current timestamp of process i ($pred = 1$) or the one of process j ($pred = 2$). The procedure checks whether the queue contains timestamps of the other process. Every timestamp less than or $<$-incomparable to ts except the most recent one is removed.

4.2 Instrumentation of Worker Processes

Figure 2 shows the instrumentation of worker processes. The first two code sequences describe the instrumentation of code responsible for sending resp. receiving messages. The third code sequence informs the checker process whenever P_1 resp. P_2 is true in the current local state. This sequence must be called either when P_1 resp. P_2 was false and has become true now (i.e., for an internal state not being distinguished within our system model), or when P_1 resp. P_2 has been true all the time and an communication event has happened. The checker process is informed of *every* local state satisfying P_1 resp. P_2 even if P_1 resp. P_2 is satisfied in a period of time covering several local states (e.g., using a predicate "*the process stays in procedure R*"). The checker process(es) are informed by calling local_pred_satisfied(i, cnt) which sends messages to the appropriate checker processes. This procedure depends on the specific predicate checker. It is presented in Fig. 3a and 3b. Flags $first[1]$ and $first[2]$ guarantee that checkers are informed only once when a local state satisfies P_1 resp. P_2. Finally, the fourth code sequence is periodically called (e.g., triggered by a local timer interrupt). It takes care of clipping the queues when P_1 or P_2 has not been satisfied in this process since the last execution of this code sequence.

4.3 Centralized Predicate Checker

The centralized checker in Fig. 3a consists of exactly one checker process. When receiving a notification message on predicate satisfaction or a clipping request from process i, check_global resp. clip_queue is successively called for all the pairs containing i. Due to lemma 1 the mean time complexity of the checker process processing the nth of such

| Within worker processes | Within worker process i |

procedure local_pred_satisfied(k, ts)
{ send $P_k(ts)$ to checker process }

procedure clip(ts)
{ send Clip(ts) to checker process }

| Checker process |

do forever
{ □ on receiving $P_1(ts)$ from worker
　proc. i:
　for $j := 0$ **to** $m-1$ **do if** $i \neq j$ **then**
　call check_global$(i, j, 1, ts)$
□ on receiving $P_2(ts)$ from worker
　proc. i:
　for $j := 0$ **to** $m-1$ **do if** $i \neq j$ **then**
　call check_global$(j, i, 2, ts)$
□ on receiving Clip(ts) from worker
　proc. i:
　for $j := 0$ **to** $m-1$ **do if** $i \neq j$ **then**
　{ call clip_queue$(i, j, 1, ts)$;
　call clip_queue$(j, i, 2, ts)$ }}

procedure local_pred_satisfied(k, ts)
{ **case** k **of**
　{ 1: **for** $j := 0$ **to** $m-1$ **do**
　　if $i \neq j$ **then**
　　send $P_1(i, j, ts)$ to checker
　　proc. on node $(i + j) \bmod m$
　2: **for** $j := 0$ **to** $m-1$ **do**
　　if $i \neq j$ **then**
　　send $P_2(j, i, ts)$ to checker
　　proc. on node $(i + j) \bmod m$
}}

procedure clip(ts)
{ **for** $j := 0$ **to** $m-1$ **do if** $i \neq j$ **then**
　send Clip(i, j, ts) to checker
　proc. on node $(i + j) \bmod m$ }

| Each of the m checker processes |

do forever
{ □ on receiving message $P_k(i, j, ts)$:
　call check_global(i, j, k, ts)
□ on receiving message Clip(i, j, ts):
　call clip_queue$(i, j, 1, ts)$;
　call clip_queue$(j, i, 2, ts)$ }

(a)　　　　　　　　　　　　　　　　(b)

Fig. 3. Centralized (a) and parallel (b) predicate checker

a message for a particular process i is $O(m)$, the maximal space complexity is $O(mq)$ where q is the maximal length of each queue. Number q depends on the frequency of clipping.

4.4　Parallel Predicate Checker

The single checker process is a bottleneck of the centralized version. The iteration loop of the checker process can easily be parallelized and is optimally executed in parallel if each of the updated queues is staying on another node, e.g., when implementing the array q as a distributed array where the queue $q[i, j]$ stays on node $(i + j) \bmod m$. Figure 3b shows the corresponding parallel checker. The queues are distributed over all processors maximizing parallelism. Worker processes satisfying a local predicate or wishing to clip queues have to notify the checker processes on the correct nodes.

The discussion so far assumes that two processes are running on each node: the worker and one checker process. As already described, worker processes must be interrupted when the checker process receives messages. Fortunately, the checker can process the message in constant time on average (lemma 1) and maximal time $O(q)$ where q is determined by the frequency of queue clipping. But in order to maximize efficiency one might run worker processes and checker processes on different nodes. Maximum performance is gained if we have $2m$ processors; worker processes run on processors $0, 1, \ldots, m-1$, and checker processes are executed on processors $m, m+1, \ldots, 2m-1$.

5 State Sequences

As described the checker processes have to be notified of each local state satisfying P_1 or P_2. Local predicates being satisfied for quite a long time (e.g., "*The process is executing procedure R*") may thus cause heavy message traffic to the checkers and high overhead for detecting the global predicate. Obviously, refraining from sending one message for each local state satisfying a local predicate would increase efficiency. The idea is to not notify the checkers of each *single state* within a sequence of local states, each satisfying the same local predicate, but to notify them once of the *entire sequence*. In the following, we propose to use such *state sequences* in order to detect global states satisfying global predicates, in particular ∃-predicates.

A state sequence is a sequence of consecutive local states of one process. Obviously, a state sequence $S = (s_0, s_1, \ldots, s_{n-1})$ lies before another state sequence $S' = (s'_0, s'_1, \ldots, s'_{n'-1})$, denoted $S <^* S'$, iff $s_{n-1} < s'_0$. The following lemma is quite obvious:

Lemma 2 *Given two state sequences* $S = (s_0, s_1, \ldots, s_{n-1})$ *and* $S' = (s'_0, s'_1, \ldots, s'_{n'-1})$, $s_0 \not> s'_0$. *S and S' are $<^*$-incomparable iff there exists s_i within S such that s_i and s'_0 are $<$-incomparable.*

Thus, we do not loose information on local states being $<$-incomparable when using state sequences instead of local states: if we detect that two state sequences are $<^*$-incomparable, each of the sequences contains a local state such that these are $<$-incomparable. The lemma furthermore expresses that one of theses states is the first local state of one of the sequences.

As a consequence we can detect satisfaction of an ∃-predicate[4] by simply searching for $<^*$-incomparable state sequences of two different processes satisfying P_1 resp. P_2. Therefore, the algorithm proposed for local states in section 4 can also be used for state sequences. Even clipping works the same way. The only difference is that the algorithms must deal with state sequences, i.e., compare them. Since state sequences are compared using their first and last state and these are compared using their timestamps, the algorithm has to work with pairs of time vectors: $(ts_1, ts_2) < (ts'_1, ts'_2)$ iff $ts_2 < ts'_1$. This is the only difference for checker processes. The instrumentation of worker processes has furthermore to be modified. It has to detect first and last local states of state sequences satisfying a local predicate and then to send their time vectors to the checker processes.

When local predicates are satisfied for many subsequent local states, using state intervals greatly reduces message traffic to the checker processes and computing efforts to detect the global predicate decrease. As already described, this is in particular essential when worker and checker processes share processors. But using state sequences has also some flaws: the algorithm cannot tell about the exact local states making up the global state satisfying the ∃-predicate (see section 6). And furthermore, the end of a sequence

---

[4] Of course, other global predicate can also be detected by state sequences.

is not known before the first local state not satisfying the previously satisfied local predicate is reached. Therefore, satisfaction of a predicate is delayed until the end of the sequences. This effect can be reduced when long intervals are split into shorter parts and the checker processes are notified on these shorter state sequences.

6 Halting the Program

So far, we have discussed pure detecting $\exists$-predicates only. The algorithms only report satisfaction of the global predicate together with the timestamps of the crucial local states resp. state sequences. This is sufficient when a property of a program run shall be tested. For debugging purposes, e.g., if an $\exists$-predicate is used to specify a global breakpoint, the program has to be stopped at the (earliest) global state found by the checker processes. Since checker processes are running asynchronously to the worker processes, the program cannot be stopped in the right global state when the $\exists$-predicate is detected. The wellknown solution to this problem for other classes of global predicates is stopping the program as soon as the checker detects the global predicate and rolling back the run to a consistent global state satisfying the $\exists$-predicate [5], or replaying [10] the just checked program run and to use the information got in the previous run [12]. Both approaches require that the program run is sufficiently traced in order to correctly roll back or replay the program run. Tracing may be performed during predicate checking (*"online debugging"*). But it also makes sense to trace a program and to check predicates when the original run is replayed (*"post-mortem debugging"*). In the following, we briefly discuss how to use replay to correctly stop the program in a global state satisfying the $\exists$-predicate.

When state sequences are not used, halting in the appropriate global state is easy. The algorithm provides time vectors $ts = (c_0, c_1, \ldots, c_{m-1})$ and $ts' = (c'_0, c'_1, \ldots, c'_{m-1})$ of local states in two processes satisfying the $\exists$-predicate. As shown in section 3, the time vector of a local state contains for each process the number of events being causally dependent on. Therefore, the earliest global state represented by ts and ts' consists in process i of the local state after the event with number $n_i = \max(c_i, c'_i)$. During replay, vector time is not needed any more. Instead, events are simply counted, and process i is stopped after its event with number n_i.

Using state sequences increases efficiency of detecting $\exists$-predicates. But the detection algorithm cannot in general tell the exact local states satisfying the local predicates. The detection algorithm returns two $<^*$-incomparable pairs of time vectors (ts_1, ts_2) and (ts'_1, ts'_2) of state sequences satisfying P_1 resp. P_2 in processes i and j. If ts_1 and ts'_1 are $<$-incomparable, they represent local states where to stop during replay. Therefore, the situation is identical as when detecting $\exists$-predicates without using state sequences. If however $ts_1 < ts'_1$ (the case $ts_1 > tv_2$ is analogous), ts_1 and ts'_1 of process i resp. j do not represent such a global state. But due to lemma 2, $ts'_1 = (c'_0, c'_1, \ldots, c'_{m-1})$ specifies the j-state of the earliest global state satisfying the $\exists$-predicate. Therefore, replay consists of stopping each process k after its event with number c'_k and then to continue each process $k \neq i$ until the next global state with process j satisfying its local predicate is reached. Of course, different from the previous case, vector time is needed here.

7 Experimental Results

We have partially implemented the detection algorithms proposed in Section 4. As a virtual parallel machine we use a cluster of workstations running PVM [6]. The runtime system is made up by a C++ class library providing message passing on top of PVM. Vector time is automatically maintained. Our implementation currently supports only two kinds of predicates: reaching certain lines of code and executing certain procedures. These predicates are easily tested by instrumenting the program. As predicate checker the centralized version supporting state sequences is implemented.

As an sample program we consider a parallel version of Jacobi's relaxation method for partial differential equations which we have used to solve $\frac{\partial^2 u}{\partial x^2} + \frac{\partial^2 u}{\partial y^2} = 4$ for a 34×34-matrix on four workstations (i.e., with four processes). As $\exists$-predicates we have used (1) *"some process exchanges data with its neighbor and some process simultaneously computes its approximation error"*, (2) *"some process distributes its approximation error and some process simultaneously computes its approximation error"*, and (3) *"some process except the first one sends its approximation error before it has received the error of its predecessor"*.

The first two predicates do not mean a program error. Detection rather shows that there is no unnecessary coordination between processes. Both predicates have been detected for several times in each run. Although each of the local predicates is satisfied in each iteration, the maximal queue length was 5.

Satisfaction of the third predicate means that a deadlock has occurred since approximation errors are distributed along the ring of processes. Thus each processor except the first one must not send its error before it has received its predecessor's error. This predicate demonstrates the usefulness of $\exists$-predicates. After deliberately including an error the predicate checker could detect the deadlock.

8 Conclusions

Global predicates are predicates on the global state of the program, where the global state of a program at a particular instance in time consists of local states of all the processes at this time. Detecting such predicates in parallel programs is a problem since global states are in general not observable due to the lack of a global clock. However, the standard concept of the *distributed global state* consisting of one local state of each process and being pairwise causally independent comprises real global states.

In this paper we have discussed the problem of detecting a particular class of global predicates, $\exists$-predicates, in parallel programs during execution. $\exists$-predicates consist of two local predicates, i.e., predicates on local states of single processes. An $\exists$-predicate is satisfied if there is one process satisfying the first local predicate and another process satisfying the other one. Those $\exists$-predicate are most useful for describing synchronization properties.

We considered the usual parallel program model with exactly one process on each node and message passing as a communication means. We proposed a centralized and a parallel efficient algorithm for detecting $\exists$-predicates. Both use special processes running asynchronously to the user processes. The parallel version causes only constant overhead independent of the running time of the program and the number of its processes. Overhead can be reduced and efficiency increased by considering long sequences of local states satisfying a particular local predicate like one single local state. Finally, we showed that ∃-predicates can also be used for specifying global breakpoints. This requires that the entire program is stopped in an appropriate global state as soon as a given ∃-predicate is satisfied. However, stopping in such a global state requires replaying the original program run.

References

[1] R. Chandra, A. Gupta, and J. L. Hennesy. COOL: An object-based language for parallel programming. *Computer*, 27(8):13–26, 1994.

[2] K. M. Chandy and L. Lamport. Distributed snapshots: Determining global states of distributed systems. *ACM Transaction on Computer Systems*, 3(1):63–75, 1985.

[3] R. Cooper and K. Marzullo. Consistent detection of global predicates. *Proc. of the ACM/ONR Workshop on Parallel and Distributed Debugging, published in ACM SIGPLAN Notices*, 26(12):167–174, 1991.

[4] C. J. Fidge. Partial orders for parallel debugging. *Proc. of the ACM SIGPLAN/SIGOPS Workshop on Parallel and Distributed Debugging, published in ACM SIGPLAN Notices*, 24(1):183–194, 1989.

[5] V. K. Garg and B. Waldecker. Detection of weak unstable predicates in distributed programs. *IEEE Trans. on Parallel and Distributed Systems*, 5(3):299–307, 1994.

[6] A. Geist, A. Beguelin, J. Dongarra, W. Jiang, R. Manchek and V. Sunderam *PVM: Parallel Virtual Machine – A Users' Guide and Tutorial for Networked Parallel Computing*. MIT Press, 1994

[7] M. Hurfin, N. Plouzeau, and M. Raynal. Detecting atomic sequences of predicates in distributed computations. In *Proc. of ACM/ONR Workshop on Parallel and Distributed Debugging*, pages 32–42, San Diego, California, 1993.

[8] L. Lamport. Time, clocks, and the ordering of events in a distributed system. *Comm. of the ACM*, 21:558–565, 1978.

[9] L. Lamport. How to make a multiprocessor computer that correctly executes multiprocess programs. *IEEE Trans. on Computers*, C-28(9):690–691, 1979.

[10] T. J. LeBlanc and J. M. Mellor-Crummey. Debugging parallel programs with Instant Replay. *IEEE Trans. on Computers*, C-36(4):471–482, 1987.

[11] Y. Manabe and S. Aoyagi. Debugging dynamic distributed programs using global predicates. In *Proc. 4th IEEE Symp. on Parallel and Distributed Processing*, pages 402–407, Arlington, TX, USA, 1992.

[12] Y. Manabe and M. Imase. Global conditions in debugging distributed programs. *Journal of Parallel and Distributed Computing*, 15:62–69, 1992.

[13] F. Mattern. Virtual time and global states of distributed systems. In M. Cosnard, editor, *Proc. Parallel and Distributed Algorithms*, 1988.

[14] B. P. Miller and J. Choi. Breakpoints and halting in distributed programs. In *Proc. 8th Int. Conf. on Distributed Computing Systems*, pages 316–323, 1988.

[15] R. Wahbe, S. Lucco, and S. L. Graham. Practical data breakpoints: Design and implementation. In *ACM SIGPLAN'93 Symp. on Programming Language Design and Implementation*, Albuquerque, 1993.

Compiling Techniques

Using Knowledge-Based Techniques for Parallelization on Parallelizing Compilers*

Chao-Tung Yang, Shian-Shyong Tseng,
Cheng-Der Chuang, and Wen-Chung Shih

Dept. of Computer and Information Science, National Chiao Tung Univ.
Hsinchu, Taiwan 300, Republic of China
Phone: 886-35-715900, Fax: 886-35-721490
E-mail: ctyang@aho.cis.nctu.edu.tw
E-mail: sstseng@cis.nctu.edu.tw

Abstract. In this paper we propose a knowledge-based approach for solving data dependence testing and loop scheduling problems. A rule-based system, called the K test, is developed by repertory grid and attribute ording table to construct the knowledge base. The K test chooses an appropriate testing algorithm according to some features of the input program by using knowledge-based techniques, and then applies the resulting test to detect data dependences for loop parallelization. Another rule-based system, called the KPLS, is also proposed to be able to choose an appropriate scheduling by inferring some features of loops and assign parallel loops on multiprocessors for achieving high speedup. The experimental results show that the graceful speedup obtained by our compiler is obvious.

1 Introduction

Parallelizing compilers [1, 2, 14, 18, 21] analyze sequential programs to detect hidden parallelism and use this information for automatic restructuring of sequential programs into parallel subtasks on multiprocessors by using loop scheduling algorithms [7, 13, 17]. In particular, loops are such a rich source of parallelism that their parallelization would lead to considerable improvement of efficiency on multiprocessors [14, 21]. Therefore, we investigate the possibility of solving the problem on two fundamental phases, data dependence testing and parallel loop scheduling on loops, in parallelizing compilers.

In brief, the *data dependence testing* problem is that of determining whether two references to the same array within a nest of loops may reference to the same element of that array [5, 12, 10, 15]. Traditionally, this problem has been formulated as *integer programming*, and the best integer programming algorithms are $O(n^{O(n)})$ where n is the number of loop indices. Obviously, these algorithms are too expensive to use. For this reason, a faster, but not necessarily exact, algorithm might be more desirable in some situations. In this paper, we propose

---
* This work was supported in part by National Science Council of Republic of China under Grants No. NSC83-0408-E-009-034 and NSC84-2213-E-009-090.

a new approach by using knowledge-based techniques for data dependence testing [3]. A rule-based system, called the *K test* [16], is developed by repertory grid and attribute ordering table to construct the knowledge base. The K test can choose an appropriate test according to some features of the input program by using knowledge-based techniques [8], and then apply the resulting test to detect data dependences on loops for parallelization. Furthermore, as for system maintenance and extensibility, our approach is obviously superior to others, for example, if a new testing algorithm or testing technique is proposed, then we can integrate it into the K test easily by adding knowledge base and rules.

Another fundamental phase, parallel loop scheduling, is a method that schedules the parallel loops on multiprocessors. In a shared-memory multiprocessors, scheduling decision can be made either statically at compile time or dynamically at runtime. Traditionally, the parallelizing compiler dispatches the loop by using only one scheduling algorithm, maybe static or dynamic. However, a program has the different kind of loops including uniform workload, increasing workload, decreasing workload, and random workload, every scheduling algorithm can achieve good performance on different loop styles and system status [17]. To reduce the overhead and enhance the load balancing, the knowledge-based approach becomes another solution to parallel loop scheduling. In this paper, another rule-based system, named *Knowledge-Based Parallel Loop Scheduling* (KPLS), is also developed by repertory grid analysis, which can choose an appropriate scheduling according to some features of loops and system status, and then apply the resulting algorithm to assign parallel loops on multiprocessors for achieving high speedup. The experimental results show that the graceful speedup obtained by using KPLS in our compiler is obvious.

2 Background

2.1 A Review of Data Dependence Testing

A *data dependence* is said to exist between two statements S_1 and S_2 if there is an execution path from S_1 to S_2, both statements access the same memory location and at least one of the two statements writes the memory location [5]. There are three types of data dependences:

- *True (flow) dependence* (δ) occurs when S_1 writes a memory location that S_2 later reads.
- *Anti-dependence* ($\bar{\delta}$) occurs when S_1 reads a memory location that S_2 later writes.
- *Output dependence* (δ_o) occurs when S_1 writes a memory location that S_2 later writes.

Data dependence testing is the method used to determine whether dependences exist between two subscript references to the same array in a nested loop. The index variables of the nested loop are normalized to increase by 1. Suppose that we want to decide whether or not there exists a dependence from statement S_1 to S_2. Let $\alpha = (\alpha_1, \alpha_2, ..., \alpha_n)$ and $\beta = (\beta_1, \beta_2, ..., \beta_n)$ be the integer vectors of n integer indices within the range of the upper and lower bounds of the n loops. There is a *dependence* form S_1 to S_2 if and only if there exist α and β, such that α is lexicographically less than or equal to β and the dependence equations are satisfied as $f_i(\alpha) = g_i(\beta)$, for $1 \leq i \leq m$. In this case, we say that the system of equations is *integer solvable* with the loop-bounds constraints. Otherwise, the two array reference patterns are said to be *independent*.

The data dependence tests can be classified into three classes: single dimensional tests (e.g., *GCD Test, Banerjee Test* [21], and *I Test* [10]), multiple dimensional tests, (e.g., *Extended-GCD Test* [1], λ *Test* [11], *Power Test* [19], and Ω *Test* [15]), and classification tests [5, 12]. We find these two papers [5, 12] are similar to our approach (*K Test*) in some aspects. Both of them collect a small set of test algorithms, and try to use them to solve the problem both efficient and exact in practical cases. However, our approach is different from theirs in essence.

- *Practical Test* [5]: The test is based on classifying pairs of subscripted variable references. The major difference between the Practical test and our approach is that the Practical test is essentially designed for practical input cases, and its strategy is fixed. However, our approach is not constraint to some kind of input cases.
- *MHL Test* [12]: The major difference between the MHL test and our approach is that the MHL test is a cascaded method; that is, the Extended-GCD test is tried first; if it fails, the next test is applied, and so on. However, our approach uses only the appropriate after the conclusion is drawn.

2.2 A Review of Parallel Loop Scheduling

A loop is called as a DOALL[1] loop if there is no data dependence among all iterations. *Parallel loop scheduling* is used to assign a DOALL loop into each processor as even as possible. There are two kind of parallel loop scheduling strategies which can be made either statically at compile time or dynamically at runtime. *Static scheduling* may be applied when the loop iterations take roughly the same amount of execution time, and the compiler must know how many iterations are run in advance. *Dynamic scheduling* adjusts the schedule during execution, so we use it whenever it is uncertain how many iterations to be run, or each iteration takes different amount of execution time, due to a branch statement inside the loop. Dynamic scheduling is more suitable for load balancing between processors, but the runtime overhead and memory contention must be considered. Up to now there are several loop scheduling algorithms, for example, *SS, GSS* [13], *CSS, Factoring* [7], and *TSS* [17]. We use N and P to denote the number of iterations and the number of processors, respectively. Assume the size of $i_t h$ partition is K_i. The formulas for the calculation of K_i in different algorithms are listed in Table 1, where the CSS/k algorithm partitions the DOALL loop into k equal-sized chunks.

---

[1] Iterations can be executed in any order or even simultaneously

Scheme	Formulas
SS	$K_i = 1$
CSS(k)	$K_i = k$
CSS/k	$K_i = \lceil \frac{N}{k} \rceil$
GSS	$K_i = \lceil \frac{R_i}{P} \rceil,\ R_0 = N,\ R_{i+1} = R_i - K_i$
Factoring	$K_i = (\frac{1}{2})^{\lceil \frac{i}{4} \rceil} \frac{N}{P}$
TSS(f, l)	$K_i = f - i\delta,\ I = \lceil \frac{2N}{f+l} \rceil,\ \delta = \frac{f-l}{I-1}$

Table 1. Various loop scheduling algorithms.

3 Using Knowledge-Based Techniques for Data Dependence Testing

3.1 Knowledge-Based Approach

Knowledge-based systems are systems that depend on a vast base of knowledge to perform difficult tasks. The knowledge is saved in a knowledge base separately from the inference component. This makes it convenient to append new knowledge or update existing knowledge without recompiling the inferring programs. The *rule-based* approach is one of the commonly used form in many knowledge-based systems. The primary difficulty in building a knowledge base is how to acquire the desired knowledge. To ease acquisition of knowledge, one primary technique among them is *Repertory Grid Analysis* (RGA) [9]. RGA is easy to use, but it suffers from the problem of *missing embedded meanings* [8]. For example, when a doctor expresses the features of catching a cold are headache, cough and sneeze, he means if a person catches a cold, he may has those features. However, in RGA, a person is not considered to catch a cold except that he gets all of the features. To overcome the problem, the concept of *Attribute Ordering Table* (AOT) is employed to elicit embedded meanings by recording the importance of each attribute to each object [8].

3.2 The Anatomy of the K Test

The processes of knowledge-based data dependence testing can be described as follows. First, the input, a set of dependence equations, is fed into the inference component. Then, the inference component reasons about knowledge and draw a conclusion, a test. Finally, the resulting test is applied to detect dependence relations for loop parallelization, and generate the answer whether the loop is parallelizable or not. An implementation, called the *K test*, is proposed to demonstrate the effectiveness of the new approach. The K test is a rule-based system. The primary reason we choose a rule-based system is that this type of system is easy to understand; in addition, rule-based inference tools are widely available, which simplify the work of implementation.

The organization of the K test is shown in Figure 1 that the three components are replaced by actual software. We describe them briefly.

- **Knowledge Base:** The knowledge base is constructed as a rule base, i.e., the knowledge is expressed in the form of production rules. These rules can be coded by hand or generated by a translator. In our K test, the latter is adopted. A translator, GRD2CLP, is utilized to translate the repertory grid and attribute ordering table to CLIPS's production rules.
- **Inference Component:** An expert system shell, called CLIPS [4], is used as the inference component. CLIPS, a forward reasoning rule-based tool, is very efficient, and does not increase the execution time of the K test too much.
- **Testing Algorithm Library:** We include four tests in the library. There are GCD test, Banerjee test, I test and Power test for solving the data dependence problem.

It should be noted that the knowledge base and the testing algorithm library shown in Figure 1 are flexible; that is, they are not fixed. You can modify these two components so long as the efficiency and precision of the system are retained. The repertory grid of the K test contains four attributes and four objects which are four existing data dependence tests. The four attributes of the K test are described below:

- Unity_Coef: whether the coefficients of variables are 1, 0, or -1 or not.
- Bound_Known: whether the loop bounds are known or not.
- Multi_Dim: whether the array reference is multi-dimensional or not.
- Few_Var: whether the number of variables in the equation is small or not.

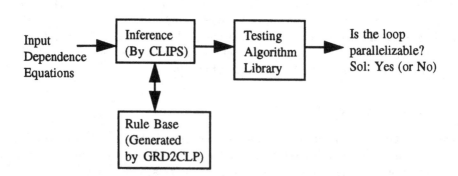

Fig. 1. Components of the K test.

In order to elicit the embedded meanings of RGA of the K test, we construct the AOT. The RGA/AOT of the K test is shown in Table 2. The process is described in dialog form. For example,

Q: If Bound_Known is not equal to 5, is it possible for the Banerjee test to be applied?

	GCD	Banerjee	I	Power
Unity_Coef	1/1	5/2	1/1	1/1
Bound_Known	1/2	5/D	1/1	5/2
Multi_Dim	1/1	1/1	1/2	5/2
Few_Var	5/1	5/1	1/2	1/2

Table 2. The RGA/AOT of the K test.

A: No.

The answer means that Bound_Known dominates the Banerjee test, and hence AOT[Bound_Known, Banerjee]='D'. In AOT, large integer number implies the attribute being more important to the object (e.g. 2¿1).

3.3 The Algorithm of the K Test

We now summarize the discussion of the K test into an algorithm. The algorithm consists of two phases.

Algorithm: K test

Input:

$$(a_0^1, a_1^1, \cdots, a_n^1, M_1^1, N_1^1, \cdots, M_n^1, N_n^1,$$

$$\cdots$$

$$a_0^m, a_1^m, \cdots, a_n^m, M_1^m, N_1^m, \cdots, M_n^m, N_n^m,$$

Unity_Coef, Bound_Known, Multi_Dim, Few_Var)

Output:

True: the input is integer solvable.

or False: the input is not integer solvable.

or Maybe: the input may be integer solvable.

Phase 1: calling CLIPS to draw a conclusion, that is, the most suitable dependence test.

Phase 2: calling the corresponding testing algorithm to check for data dependence.

4 Using Knowledge-Based Techniques for Parallel Loop Scheduling

If the parallelizing compiler can analysis a loop's attributes such as loop style, loop bound, data locality, etc.; then the suitable scheduling algorithms for the particular case should be applied. This leads to select scheduling algorithms by using knowledge-based approach. The processes of knowledge-based loop scheduling method can be described as follows. First, the compiler can get some attributes about a loop by parsing input program. Then, the inference component reasons about knowledge and draw a conclusion, a parallel loop scheduling. Finally, the resulting scheduling is applied for loop partition.

4.1 The Anatomy of KPLS

In this session, we describe our new method, named *Knowledge-Based Parallel Loop Scheduling* (KPLS). We propose this method using *knowledge-based*, because it is easy to understand, implementation, maintenance and extension. This approach has great flexibility as we can add new algorithms to the repertory grid and attribute ordering table, and then use the conversion tool to convert tables to CLIPS rules. We do not need any modification in CLIPS source.

We describe the components of KPLS briefly in the following:

- **Knowledge Base:** The knowledge base is constructed as a rule base, i.e., the knowledge is expressed in the form of production rules. We also use GRD2CLP to translate the repertory grid and attribute ordering table to CLIPS's production rules.
- **Inference Component:** CLIPS is used as the inference component, which is very efficient for inferring, and does not increase the execution time of our KPLS too much.
- **Scheduling Algorithm Library:** There are six scheduling algorithms in the library including static scheduling, SS, CSS, GSS, Factoring, and TSS. It is also the advantage of expert system; whenever, we can easily modify the rules and adding the new scheduling strategy flexibly.

The repertory grid and attribute ordering table of KPLS are shown in Table 3. 'X' means that the attribute has no relation with the object. There are six algorithms and five attributes in both tables. We describe these attributes as follows:

- Loop_Style: means the different styles of loop (1:uniform workload, 2:increasing workload, 3:decreasing workload, or 4:random workload).
- Start_Time: means whether the starting time of each processors is equal or not, influencing the execution time of loop.
- Loop_Bound: means whether the loop bounds are known or not in compile time.
- Overhead: means the different overhead of synchronization primitives on system (0:none, 1:little, 2:fair or 3:high).
- Easy: means whether the implementation of algorithm is easy or not.

4.2 The Algorithm of the KPLS

In this section, we describe our algorithm of KPLS. The algorithm consists of three phases.
Algorithm: KPLS
Input:
The following information can be obtained from input file.

	Static	SS	CSS	GSS	TSS	Factoring
Loop_Style	{1}/D	X/X	{1}/D	{2,4}/D	X/X	X/X
Start_Time	YES/D	X/X	YES/D	X/X	X/X	X/X
Loop_Bound	YES/D	X/X	NO/D	X/X	X/X	X/X
Overhead	X/X	{0}/D	{1,2,3}/D	{1}/2	{2,3}/1	{2,3}/1
Easy	X/X	X/X	X/X	NO/2	X/X	NO/2

Table 3. The RGA/AOT of the KPLS.

1. What kind of loop style? (1-4 styles)
2. Are the start time of processors roughly equal? (Yes/No)
3. Is the loop bound known during compiler time? (Yes/No)
4. What is the synchronization overhead level? (None/Low/Fair/High)
5. Use easy-to-implement methods only? (Yes/No)

A *certainty factor* (CF) [8] value for each question to express the question's importance is given.

Output:

What kind of loop scheduling strategy will be applied. If there are more than one suggestion, the one with maximal CF value will be chosen.

Phase 1: Get the loop attributes from parallelism detector.

Phase 2: Call CLIPS to draw a conclusion by using rules; that is, the most suitable loop scheduling method.

Phase 3: S2m [6] uses the appropriate loop scheduling to partition the DOALL loop on multiprocessors.

5 Experiments

5.1 Integrating K Test and KPLS in PFPC

We integrate K test and KPLS in PFPC to generate the efficient object codes for multiprocessors. The K test is used to treat the data dependence relations and then restructure a sequential FORTRAN source program into a parallel form, i.e., if a loop can be parallelized, then parallelism detector (K test) converts it into DOALL loop. In the previous version of our compiler, Parafrase-2 (p2fpp) is used to treat the data dependence analysis [20, 6]. For improving the capacity of loop partition module in s2m, the KPLS is used, instead of the previous version, to build an intelligent loop scheduling method. Because the restriction of the OS scheduling, the system call for binding any thread onto the appropriate processor is not avaliable and only dynamic scheduling is employed. We can only partition loops and encapsulate with data into threads by s2m and let the OS dynamically choose the threads to run on multiprocessors. The experiments only concerned the performance of KPLS in PFPC.

5.2   Experimental Programs

We show the performance gained by using our parallelizing compiler on the following four examples which are different styles of loops.

- The first example is matrix multiplication, the outer two loops can be parallelized. Since the example is highly load balanced, this kind of loop is called *uniform workload*. The matrix size is 600 × 600.
- The second example is adjoint convolution which exploits significant load imbalance. This kind of loop is called *decreasing workload*. We choose the problem size to be 150 × 150.
- The third example is reverse adjoint convolution which also exploits significant load imbalance. This kind of loop is called *increasing workload*. The problem size is 150 × 150.
- The fourth example is transitive closure. The characteristic of this program is that the workload is dependent on the input data. This kind of loop is called *random workload*. We select the different matrix sizes for testing alone and combining four programs by using 1000 × 1000 and 500 × 500, respectively.

5.3   Experimental Results

There are two parts of the experiments: the first part concerns each execution time and speedup of above four programs, and the other is a combined program, including those four programs. The execution time of four programs is shown in Table 4, and the corresponding speedup in Figure 2 shows that GSS performs poorly when iterations have an decreasing workload like adjoint convolution. CSS/4 is suitable for the uniformly workload like matrix multiplication, and Factoring is suitable for reverse adjoint convolution. Among those scheduling algorithms, none of them is suitable for every case. KPLS can choose an appropriate scheduling and have good results for all programs except transitive closure. In the case of transitive closure, our approach does not choose the fastest one, CSS/4, but chooses TSS, because the imbalance workload in this program is not so obvious, because the control flow is related to the input data, and because the matrix size is 500×500, which is divided exactly by the number of CPUs. On most cases, KPLS makes a better choice than other scheduling even in single loop.

Table 5 shows the experimental execution time and Figure 3 shows the corresponding speedup for the big program integrated from the above four programs. Traditionally, every scheduling algorithm uses only one method through the entire program. But the KPLS can always choose an appropriate scheduling algorithm according to the behaviors of the loop among one program. Like the second part experiment, KPLS chooses different style of loop scheduling for each loop in the combined program. For example, according to the loop behaviors, KPLS selects TSS for the adjoint convolution part of the combined program and CSS/4 for matrix multiplication, instead of only one scheduling method. We concern about the runtime cost of loops. During the execution time, it's important to select a good loop scheduling algorithm by considering about the runtime cost; once compiler specifies the right loop scheduling, program can save the time on execution. Furthermore, for the inference cost of knowledge-based approach, the KPLS only spends a little time. Since no single scheduling algorithm performs well across all applications, our method can now give a good solution to make a compiler more flexible and efficient in loop scheduling.

	Serial	CSS/1	CSS/4	CSS/8	CSS/16	GSS	Factoring	TSS	KPLS
Mat_Mul	854.46	848.18	225.96	230.92	232.73	250.94	259.32	230.74	as CSS/4
Adj_Conv	769.50	776.38	350.80	256.70	239.90	369.54	245.01	237.68	as TSS
Rev_Adj	604.51	632.37	281.01	215.19	171.63	182.01	168.93	177.57	as Factoring
Trans_Col	2310.96	2221.81	695.73	708.83	702.60	730.30	713.62	710.68	as TSS

Table 4. The execution time of four different kind of programs (sec).

	Serial	CSS/1	CSS/4	CSS/8	CSS/16	GSS	Factoring	TSS	KPLS
All	2185.59	2167.99	872.34	683.85	636.38	763.67	651.52	644.43	582.47

Table 5. The execution time of combined program (sec).

6 Conclusions and Further Directions

In this paper we have proposed a new approach by using knowledge-based techniques, which integrates existing data dependence testing algorithms and loop scheduling algorithms to make good use of their advantages for loop parallelization. A rule-based system, called the K test, was developed by RGA and AOT to construct the knowledge base. The K test could choose an appropriate testing algorithm by knowledge-based techniques, and then apply the resulting test to detect data dependences on loops. Another rule-based system, called the KPLS, was also developed by RGA and AOT, which was embedded in our s2m, that could choose an appropriate scheduling and then apply the resulting algorithm for assigning parallel loops on multiprocessors to achieve high speedup. The experiments have shown that the KPLS can apply more suitable loop scheduling strategy. Once we choose the right method for loop scheduling, the program can save more execution time. The experimental results also have shown that the graceful speedup obtained by our compiler is obvious. Furthermore, as for system maintenance and extensibility, our approach is obviously superior to others. In addition, we are going to study whether knowledge-based approaches may be applied to guide the wide variety of loop transformation for parallelization in parallelizing compilers.

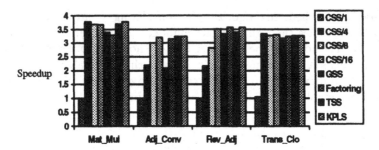

Fig. 2. The speedup for different kind of programs.

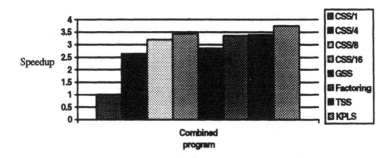

Fig. 3. The speedup for the combined of four program.

Acknowledgments

We would like to thank the anonymous reviewers for suggesting of improvements, and offering of encouragements.

References

1. U. Banerjee, *Dependence Analysis for Supercomputing*, Norwell, Kluwer Academic Publishers, MA, 1988.
2. U. Banerjee, R. Eigenmann, A. Nicolau, and D. A. Padua, "Automatic program parallelization," *Proc. IEEE*, 81(2):211-243, Feb. 1993.
3. B. M. Chapman and H. M. Herbeck, "Knowledge-based parallelization for distributed memory systems," *Parallel Computing, in Proc. of the First International ACPC Conference*, vol. 591, pp. 77-89, Springer-Verlag, Salzburg, Austria, 1991.
4. J. C. Giarratano and G. Riley, *Expert Systems: Principles and Programming*, PWS-Kent Publishing Company, Boston, 1993.

5. G. Goff, K. Kennedy, and C. W. Tseng, "Practical dependence testing," in *Proc. of the ACM SIGPLAN '91 Conf. on Programming Language Design and Implementation*, Toronto, Canada, pp. 15-29, June 1991.

6. M. C. Hsiao, S. S. Tseng, C. T. Yang, and C. S. Chen, "Implementation of a portable parallelizing compiler with loop partition," in *Proc. 1994 ICPADS*, Hsinchu, Taiwan, R.O.C. pp. 333-338, Dec. 1994.

7. S. F. Hummel, E. Schonberg, and L. E. Flynn, "Factoring: A method for scheduling parallel loops," *Commun. ACM*, 35(8):90-101, Aug. 1992.

8. G. J. Hwang and S. S. Tseng, "EMCUD: A knowledge acquisition nethod which captures embedded meanings under uncertainty," *Int. J. Man-Machine Studies.*, vol. 33, pp. 431-451, 1990.

9. G. A. Kelly, *The Psychology of Personal Constructs*, vol. 1, New York, NY: W. W. Norton, 1955.

10. X. Kong, D. Klappholz, and K. Psarris, "The i test: An improved dependence test for automatic parallelization and vectorization," *IEEE Trans. Parallel Distrib. Syst.*, 2(3):342-349, July 1991.

11. Z. Li, P. C. Yew, and C. Q. Zhu, "An efficient data dependence analysis for parallelizing compilers," *IEEE Trans. Parallel Distrib. Syst.*, 1(1):26-34, Jan. 1990.

12. D. E. Maydan, J. L. Hennessy, and M. S. Lam, "Efficient and exact data dependence analysis," in *Proc. of the ACM SIGPLAN '91 Conf. on Programming Language Design and Implementation*, Toronto, Canada, pp. 1-14, June 1991.

13. C. D. Polychronopoulos and D. J. Kuck, "Guided self-scheduling: A practical self-scheduling scheme for parallel supercomputers," *IEEE Trans. Comput.*, 36(12):1425-1439, Dec. 1987.

14. C. D. Polychronopoulos, *Parallel Programming and Compilers*, Kluwer Academic Publishers, MA, 1988.

15. W. Pugh, "A practical algorithm for exact array dependence analysis," *Commun. ACM*, 35(8):102-114, Aug. 1992.

16. W. C. Shih, C. T. Yang, and S. S. Tseng, "Knowelwdge-based data dependence testing on loops," in *Proc. 1994 Int. Computer Symposium*, Hsinchu, Taiwan, R.O.C. pp. 961-966, Dec. 1994.

17. T. H. Tzen and L. M. Ni, "Trapezoid self-scheduling: A practical scheduling scheme for parallel compilers," *IEEE Trans. Parallel Distrib. Syst.*, 4(1):87-98, Jan. 1993.

18. M. Wolfe, *Optimizing Supercompilers for Supercomputers*. Pitman Publishing Co. London, and MIT Press, MA, 1989.

19. M. Wolfe and C. W. Tseng, "The power test for data dependence," *IEEE Trans. Parallel Distrib. Syst.*, 3(5):591-601, Sep. 1992.

20. C. T. Yang, S. S. Tseng, and C. S. Chen, "The anatomy of parafrase-2," *Proceedings of the National Science Council Republic of China (Part A)*, 18(5):450-462, Sep. 1994.

21. H. P. Zima and B. Chapman, *Supercompilers for Parallel and Vector Computers*, Addison-Wesley Publishing, New York, ACM Press, 1990.

Automatic Vectorization of Communications for Data-Parallel Programs

Cécile Germain[1] and Franck Delaplace[2]

[1] LRI-CNRS Université Paris-Sud
[2] Université d'Evry

Abstract. Optimizing communication is a key issue in compiling data-parallel languages for distributed memory architectures. We examine here the cyclic distribution, and we derive symbolic expressions for communication sets under the only assumption that the initial parallel loop is defined by affine expressions of the indices. This technique relys on unimodular changes of basis. Analysis of the properties of communications leads to a tiling of the local memory addresses that provides maximal message vectorization.

1 Introduction

Static analysis of data-parallel programs, for the generation of distributed code, has been proposed by many authors, for instance [5] [6] [8] [10] [15]. Static analysis aims to improve performance over run-time resolution [3] which includes a lot of pure overhead in form of guards and tests. Many static compilation schemes have been considered; they differ in important points such as interleaving computation and communication as in [6], or having identical management of local an non-local data such as in [8]. However, they all use three basic sets: *Compute(s)* is the part of the index set which is local to processor s; *Send(s)* (resp *Received(s)*) is the part of a distributed array that has to be sent (resp received) by processor s when owner computes rule is applied. The central problem of static analysis is to define these sets at compile-time, and in an efficient form.

Two major costs have to be considered for the code generation scheme: the computing cost, and the communication cost. The computing cost is all the overhead required to compute local indices, and, when a communication occurs, to compute the parameters of the communication, the destination processors and the local addresses. As pointed out by [6], naive resolution leads to a symbolic form involving integer divides for each forwarded data, which may be as inefficient as run-time resolution. The communication cost depends on the volume and number of communications. For a data-parallel program, the volume, i.e. the number of data to send to a remote processor, cannot be modified, because it is fixed by the placement function (e.g. ALIGN and DISTRIBUTE directives). At the code generation level, optimization is only directed towards the number of communications, by aggregating all data that are to be sent to the same processor. Although this may seem a very specialized problem, the overwhelming part of startup in message cost makes this optimization a major component of performance, as shown in [15].

To be amenable to static analysis, the references must be affine functions of the parallel loop indices,a reference being an access or alignement function, and the loop bounds must be defined by affine inequalities. These assumptions are the weakest possible. Under these assumptions, deriving efficient closed forms of the previous sets for the most general block-cyclic distribution is an open problem. [8] gives a general compiling scheme under the weakest assumptions, but provides closed forms only when indices are independent: for instance, $T[j, i]$, but not $T[2i + j, i - j]$. [5] uses a finite state machine approach, allowing optimal memory utilization, but restricts references to array sections and uses integer divides. [10] solves the same problem with a virtualization method. Other special cases have been solved, for unit strides in [15], for one-dimensional arrays in [6] and [14].

In this paper, we derive closed forms providing an efficient code generation scheme, under the weakest assumptions, when the parallel arrays are cyclically distributed. Next part formally states the problem and discusses the relationship with the problem of scanning integer polyhedra. Part three analyzes the conditions for message vectorization and proposes an explicit closed form achieving maximal vectorization; part four details the SPMD code and its optimizations, and presents some examples.

2 General Compilation Scheme

2.1 Problem Statement

We consider nested parallel loops, with given alignement and the cyclic distribution, such as described in High Performance Fortran (HPF); we restrict our analysis to the static subset of HPF where arrays are aligned once, at compile-time, and all index functions are affine; moreover, the index set must be described by affine inequations. The generic loop nest is :

```
forall i in C
      X(Bi + b) = f(Y(A₁i + a₁), Z(A₂i + a₂),... )
end forall
```

where B, A_1 and A_2 are integer matrices, and b, a_1 and a_2 are integer vectors.

Some notations must be defined, associated with the cyclic distribution: let $p_1, p_2, \ldots, p_n$ be the extents of the PROCESSOR target of the distribution, p be the vector with coordinates p_i, P the diagonal matrix with coefficients p_i, and $\mathcal{P}$ the processor set, i.e. $\mathcal{P} = \prod_i [0, p_i - 1]$. Template element j is laid on processor s such that $s_i \equiv j_i \bmod p_i$ for all $i = 1 \ldots n$. In the following, the coordinates subscripts are elided, and scalar operations are extended to vector ones by coordinates. Hence, array element j defines a set of spatial coordinates s and a set of memory coordinates t by euclidean division: $j = Pt + s$, with $0 \le s < p$. For any s in $\mathcal{P}$, $\mathbf{Z}_s^n$ is the set of integer vectors congruent with s modulo p.

Distributed code for the previous loop can be generated at compile-time if $Compute(s)$, $Send(s)$ and $Receive(s)$ can be described for each processor s in a convex and generic form. Convex form means that the set can be parametrized by a variable such that the parametrization is one-to-one, and the parameter set is described by an affine inequality, i.e. is a convex polyhedron in $\mathbf{Z}^n$. From a convex polyhedron, generating a loop nest is theoretically possible. The practical issues will be discussed in the following part. As the matrices defining the references (A_1, A_2 and B) will be used to generate such convex sets, we assume that these matrices are constant. Generic means that the distributed program is in SPMD style: code is identical on all processors, possibly parametrized by the processor address.

2.2 An Integer Equation

All our results comme from Lemma 1 which solves equation $Mx = \alpha + Pk$ with x and k as unknowns, where M is an integer matrix and α an integer vector. This lemma is a simple mathematical exercise of unimodular change of basis, but introduces a lot of notations, that will be used throughout this paper.

If D is a diagonal $r \times r$ matrix, let $[D, 0]$ be the $n \times n$ matrix $\begin{bmatrix} D & 0 \\ 0 & 0 \end{bmatrix}$.

Smith normal form theorem [13] states that, given an integer $n \times n$ matrix Q with rank r, there exists a unique $r \times r$ diagonal matrix D such that d_i divides d_{i+1}, all $d_i \neq 0$, and $Q = H[D, 0]K$ with H and K unimodular. Let $\pi = det(P) = \prod p_i$; $\pi P^{-1} M$ is an integer matrix, hence may be decomposed as HDK. From this, the equation to solve may be rewritten:

$$H[D, 0]Kx = \pi P^{-1} \alpha + \pi k \ . \tag{1}$$

Let $\beta = \pi H^{-1} P^{-1} \alpha$ (h is integer because H is unimodular). We can now state our lemma

Lemma 1. *Equation $Mx = \alpha + Pk$ has solutions iff $gcd(d_i, \pi)$ divides β_i. If x_0, k_0 is a solution, the solutions are, for all λ in $\mathbf{Z}^n$*

$$x = x_0 + K^{-1} P' \lambda \ ,$$
$$k = k_0 + H D' \lambda \ .$$

Proof. Let $y = Kx$, $h = H^{-1}k$. From the definitions of y, h and β, (1) becomes

$$[D, 0]y = \beta + \pi h \ . \tag{2}$$

If $d_1, \ldots, d_r$ are the diagonal coefficients of D, and $d_{r+1}, \ldots, d_n$ are defined to be 0, (2) has solutions iff β_i is a multiple of $\delta_i = gcd(d_i, \pi)$. In this case, the gcd algorithm gives a particular solution (y_0, h_0). Let $d_i' = d_i/\delta_i$ and $p_i' = \pi/\delta_i$, and D' and P' the corresponding diagonal matrices; the $n - r$ last components of y_0 are 0, the $n - r$ last diagonal coefficients of D' are 0 and of P' are 1. □

We note *ex-cond(M, P, α)* the condition for existence of solutions; when necessary, subscripts and variables will indicate the dependence on the initial equation of the vectors and matrices involved in Lemma 1.

2.3 Local Sets

Compute Set Generating SPMD code for the compute part of the loop needs to define the local iteration set and the local memory locations that are accessed during each iteration. With Owner Computes Rule, an index i is in $Compute(s)$ if $Bi + b = Pt + s$. Lemma 1 applied to equation $Bi = Pt + (s - b)$ gives:

Proposition 2. *Let $\mathcal{L} = \{\lambda \in \mathbf{Z}^n | CK^{-1}P'\lambda \leq c - Cx_0\}$.*
If ex-cond $(B, P, s\text{-}b)$, $Compute(s) = \{x_0 + K^{-1}P'\lambda | \lambda \in \mathcal{L}\}$
else $Compute(s) = \emptyset$

$Compute(s)$ is parametrized by the λ in $\mathcal{L}$. As K^{-1} is unimodular, and P' has no null coefficient, the enumerating scheme is one-to-one. Finally, $\mathcal{L}$ is a convex polyhedron.

For any index $i = x_0 + K^{-1}P'\lambda$, the local address for array element $Bi + b$ is $t = k_0 + HD'\lambda$, providing the location to write.

The following very simple example is often quoted:
forall $(i = 0{:}n)$ $T(i, i) = 0.0$

Suppose T is cyclically distributed onto a $(4, 8)$ PROCESSOR array. B being the reference matrix (2×2 matrix because T has a 2-D index space), we have:

$$B = \begin{pmatrix} 1 & 0 \\ 1 & 0 \end{pmatrix} \quad \text{and} \quad \pi P^{-1}B = HDK = \begin{pmatrix} 2 & 1 \\ 1 & 0 \end{pmatrix} \begin{pmatrix} 16 & 0 \\ 0 & 0 \end{pmatrix} \begin{pmatrix} 1 & 0 \\ 0 & 1 \end{pmatrix} \ .$$

From this, ex-cond$(B, P, s\text{-}b)$ is 4 divides $s_2 - s_1$. In this case, let $g = (2s_1 - 2s_2)/8$ for short; the compiler has to find a solution of

$$\begin{cases} y_1 = s_2 + 8h_1 \\ 0 = g + h_2 \end{cases}$$

As $1 - 8 * 0 = 1$, the particular solution for y_1 is s_2, for h_1 is 0; $y_2 = 0$ by our algorithm, hence $h_2 = -g$. The compiler can deal with all these symbolic manipulations.

Inequality $0 \leq i \leq n$ is rewritten:

$$\begin{pmatrix} -1 & 0 \\ 1 & 0 \end{pmatrix} \begin{pmatrix} i \\ j \end{pmatrix} \leq \begin{pmatrix} 0 \\ n \end{pmatrix} \ ,$$

If T_s is the local piece of array T, the code is

```
if ((s2 - s1)%4 == 0) then
    g = IntDiv(s1 - s2, 4)
    do l = IntDiv(-s2 + 7, 8), IntDiv(n - s2, 8)
        T_s(-g + 2 * l, l) = 0.0
endif
```

This example points out that the initial solutions (x_0 and k_0) are also symbolic: going back to (2), after simplification, we have to find y_0 and h_0 such that $d'_i y_i = \beta_i + p'_i h_i$, with d'_i and p'_i relatively prime. As we assumed these coefficients to be numerical constants, the gcd algorithm allows to find at compile-time u_i and v_i such that $d'_i u_i = 1 + p'_i v_i$. Hence for run-time β_i, the symbolic form of an initial solution is $(\beta'_i u_i, \beta'_i v_i)$, with $\beta_i = \beta'_i \delta_i$. This must be considered, because β_i are run-time quantities, coming from the processor number and possible variables in the references.

Send and Receive Sets A sending set or a receiving set is related to source and destination references, for instance $A_1 + a_1$ and $B + b$ in our generic example. As sending and receiving sets are symmetrically defined, identical methods can be used to compute both of them, and we present only the method for the sending set. For clarity, subscripts are elided in A_1 and a_1. Formally, we define the sending set on processor s as

$$Send(s) = \{(s', j), s' \in \mathcal{P}, j \in \mathbf{Z}_s^n | \exists i \in \mathcal{C} \exists t' \in \mathbf{Z}^n : Bi + b = Pt' + s'; j = Ai + a\}$$

s' is the remote processor address (processor number) and t' is the remote memory address in processor s'. Let $j = Pt + s$; t is the memory address in processor s. In order to minimize the number of actual communications, this set should be enumerated first along the s' coordinates, and next the t ones. This is the so-called called *message vectorization* [15].

Hence we have to solve in s', t', t, i the system with parameter s:

$$\begin{cases} Ai + a = Pt + s \\ Bi + b = Pt' + s' \end{cases}$$

Valid solution must verify

$$\begin{cases} Ci \le c \\ s' \in \mathcal{P} \end{cases}$$

We defer the solution to the next section, and we first discuss the relationship of code generation with an extensively studied topic, scanning polyhedra [2] [9] [11] [12]. Clearly, the code generation problem may be restated as a polyhedron scanning problem. For instance, *Compute(s)* may be rewritten as the polyhedron in $\mathbf{Z}^n \times \mathbf{Z}^n$:

$$\{(t, i) | Bi = Pt + s; Ci \le c\} \ .$$

In these sets, some variables completely determine other ones (e.g. i defines t in *Compute(s)*). As the final code uses only some variables (t for *Compute(s)*), we need to enumerate the projection of a convex polyhedron, which is not always convex. Many libraries are available for this kind of loop generation (Omega Calculator [12], LIC [11]). However, if these tools scan very efficently the polyhedra created by a block distribution, they generate very poor code or are oveflowed in the cyclic case. For instance, *Compute(s)* of the previous example is defined by

$$\{(t_1, t_2, i) | i = 4t_1 + s_1; i = 8t_2 + s_2; 0 \le i \le n\} \ ,$$

and the best-effort loops generated by the Omega Calculator are:

```
do t1 = IntDiv(-s1 + 3, 4): IntDiv(-s1 + n, 4)
   if ((s1 + 4*t1 - s2) % 8 == 0) then
      t2 = IntDiv(s1 + 4*t1 - s2 + 7, 8)
   endif
```

The test is executed at each loop iteration, while our solution has only one test. The problem is worst for communication, because of the higher dimensionality of the polyhedron. Hence the compiler has to provide some *a priori* tiling of the processors and memory spaces.

3 Vectorization

As vectorization is a major source for communication performance [15], analyzing the conditions where vectorization may occur is the first task. Let the lhs side of the parallel affectation be T[i], i.e. matrix B of the previous part equals Id and $b = 0$. The general problem comes down to this case when B is unimodular; extending our framework to the general case case is straightforward, but leads to clumsy formulas. In this case:

$$Send(s) = \{(s', j), s' \in \mathcal{P}, j \in \mathbf{Z}_s^n | \exists i \in C, \exists t' \in \mathbf{Z}^n : i = Pt' + s', j = Ai + a\} .$$

3.1 Tiling the Index Set

A set of array elements on a processor is candidate to be aggregated in a unique message if all elements have the same destination processor. Such a set will be called *vectorizable* in the following.

Two data i_1 and i_2 have vectorizable images if they are on the same processor, that is $i_1 = Pt'_1 + s'$ and $i_2 = Pt'_2 + s'$, and if their images are on the same processor, that is $Ai_1 \equiv Ai_2 \mod p$. Next definition formalizes this idea:

Definition 3. A subset T of $\mathbf{Z}^n$ is a *remanence set* for A if

$$\forall t_1, t_2 \in T, AP(t_1 - t_2) \equiv 0 \mod p .$$

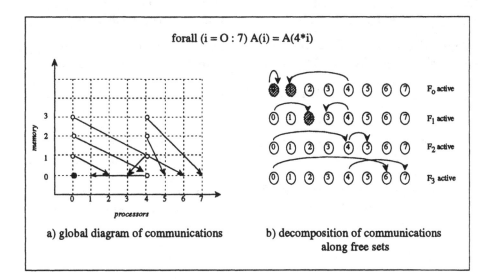

Fig. 1. A remanent but not free communication

Hence data candidate to be aggregated must be defined from a remanent set. This is not a sufficient condition, as exmplified in fig. 1: A and P being

1-dimensional, the remanence property is always true; however, only local addresses congruent modulo 4 can be aggregated inside the same message. This comes from the fact that different data inside the same processor are required by different processors for the same memory slice. Next definition formalizes this idea:

Definition 4. A subset S of P is a *free set* for A if

$$\forall s_1 \neq s_2 \in S, A(s_1 - s_2) \not\equiv 0 \bmod p .$$

Proposition 5 elucidates the relationship between remanence sets, free sets and vectorization.

Proposition 5. *If T is a remanent set and S is a free set, the image by A of $T \times S$ is a vectorizable set on each processor.*

Proof. Let j_1 and j_2 be on processor s, and fulfill the conditions of the previous proposition: $j_1 = A(Pt'_1 + s'_1)$ and $j_2 = A(Pt'_2 + s'_2)$, with t'_1 and t'_2 belonging to a remanence set and s'_1 and s'_2 to a free set. From the fact that j_1 and j_2 are on the same processor, $A[P(t'_1 - t'_2) + s'_1 - s'_2] \equiv 0 \bmod p$. As t'_1 and t'_2 belong to the same remanence set, $A(s'_1 - s'_2) \equiv 0 \bmod p$; thus $s'_1 = s'_2$, because they are in the same free set. $\qquad\square$

From this proposition, tiling the array elements following maximal remanence and free sets creates maximal vectorization. Proposition 6 gives closed form of these sets. Let Smith normal form of the integer matrix $\pi P^{-1}AP$ be $H_1 D_1 K_1$, P'_1 be defined as P'_{AP}, and p'_1 be the vector of the diagonal coefficients of P'_1.

Proposition 6. *Let $T(u) = \{u + K_1^{-1}P'_1 v, v \in \mathbf{Z}^n\}$. The set of $T(u)$, for $0 \leq K_1 u < p'_1$, is a partition of $\mathbf{Z}^n$ is maximal remanent sets. Moreover, for all t in $T(u)$,*

$$APt = APu + PH_1 D'_1 v .$$

Proof. Let t be an integer vector; t belongs to the set $T(u)$ such that $K_1 u$ is the remainder in the integer divison of $K_1 t$ by p'_1. As K_1 is unimodular, and $K_1 u$ is uniquely determined, u exists and is uniquely defined, proving the partition of $\mathbf{Z}^n$ by the $T(u)$. To prove that each $T(u)$ is maximal, let t_1 and t_2 be in $T(u_1)$ and $T(u_2)$; if t_1 and t_2 form a remanent set, the following equality is true:

$$AP(u_1 - u_2 + K_1^{-1}P'_1(v_1 - v_2)) \equiv 0 \bmod p .$$

From lemma 1, this implys

$$u_1 - u_2 + K_1^{-1}P'_1(v_1 - v_2) = K_1^{-1}P'_1 \lambda ,$$

that is $u_1 = u_2 + K_1^{-1}P'_1 \mu$. From unicity of euclidean division, $K_1 u_1 = K_1 u_2$, and from unimodularity $u_1 = u_2$.

If t is in $T(u)$, $t - u = K_1^{-1}P'_1 v$. From lemma 1, this implys $AP(t - u) = PH_1 D'_1 v$. This proves the last part of the proposition. $\qquad\square$

A maximal free set is defined by

$$\mathcal{F}(\lambda) = \{s \in \mathcal{P} | P'\lambda \le Ks < P'(\lambda + 1)\} .$$

However, enumerating all remanence sets and all free sets on each sending processor would create useless iterations. In the example of section 3.3, there are six free sets, but only four need to be enumerated on processor 0. Next section precises our enumeration scheme.

3.2 SPMD Code

The basic idea of our scheme is to enumerate maximal remanence sets, then free sets, to create vectorizable communications. Closed forms are possible because enumeration of the free sets depends on an external index which denotes the remanence set.

The sending set may be expressed as

$$Send(s) = \{(s', Pt + s), s' \in \mathcal{P}, t \in \mathbf{Z}^n |$$
$$\exists t' \in \mathbf{Z}^n : Pt' + s' \in C; A(Pt' + s') + a = Pt + s\} .$$

Let t' be in $\mathcal{T}(u)$; we have to solve in s' and t:

$$A(P(u + K_1^{-1} P_1' v) + s') + a = Pt + s .$$

By proposition 6, this equation becomes

$$A(Pu + s') = P(t - H_1 D_1' v) + s - a . \tag{3}$$

Consider (3) as an instance of $Ax + a \equiv s \bmod p$; solutions exist if $ex\text{-}cond(A, s\text{-}a)$. Note that $ex\text{-}cond$ depends only on s and a. If this condition is satisfied, let $x_0 = x_0(A, P, s - a)$ and $k_0 = k_0(A, P, s - a)$. The solutions of (3) are $s' = x_0 - Pu + K^{-1}P'\lambda$ and $t = k_0 + H_1 D_1' v + HD'\lambda$ with λ in $\mathbf{Z}^n$. A correct SPMD code will be achieved if all constraints on solutions can be expressed in convex form for the parameters (u, λ, v). From the definition of $Send(s)$, and of $\mathcal{T}(u)$, there are three constraints, which define three index sets:

(a) $K_1 u$ is a remainder in division by p_1'. Let $\mathcal{U} = \{u \in \mathbf{Z}^n | 0 \le K_1 u < p_1'\}$.
(b) $s' \in \mathcal{P}$. Let $\mathcal{L}_u = \{\lambda \in \mathbf{Z}^n | -x_0 + Pu \le K^{-1}P'\lambda < -x_0 + P(1 + u)\}$.
(c) $Pt' + s' \in C$. Let $\mathcal{V}_\lambda = \{v \in \mathbf{Z}^n | CPK_1^{-1}P_1' v \le c - C(x_0 + K^{-1}P'\lambda)\}$.

All these sets are convex polyhedra. Finally, the SPMD code for the sending part is:

```
if ex-cond
    compute x_0 and k_0
    do u in U
        do λ in L_u
            do v in V_λ
                send (k_0 + HD'λ + H_1 D_1' v, -Pu + x_0 + K^{-1}P'λ)
```

The first parameter of the *send* it the local address of the data, and the second is the destination processor.

3.3 Example

The current HPF benchmark set is somehow limited. In fact, in all codes that we had, only the block distribution is used. Hence, we have to consider an artificial example.

forall (i= 0:n, j= 0:m) T(i, j) = T(2j, i + j)

on a 4 × 8 PROCESSOR set.

The reference matrix being A, we have

$$A = \begin{pmatrix} 0 & 2 \\ 1 & 1 \end{pmatrix}, \pi P^{-1} A P = \begin{pmatrix} 0 & 1 \\ 1 & 0 \end{pmatrix} \begin{pmatrix} 16 & 0 \\ 0 & 128 \end{pmatrix} \begin{pmatrix} 1 & 2 \\ 0 & 1 \end{pmatrix}, \pi P^{-1} A = \begin{pmatrix} 0 & 1 \\ 1 & 0 \end{pmatrix} \begin{pmatrix} 4 & 0 \\ 0 & 16 \end{pmatrix} \begin{pmatrix} 1 & 1 \\ 0 & 1 \end{pmatrix}.$$

From this, the new index sets are defined by

$$\mathcal{U} = \{(u_1, u_2)|0 \leq u_1 + 2u_2 \leq 1; 0 \leq u_2 \leq 0\} \ ,$$
$$\mathcal{L}_u = \{(\lambda_1, \lambda_2)|0 \leq 8\lambda_1 - 2\lambda_2 - 4u_1 + x_1 \leq 3; 0 \leq 2\lambda_2 - 8u_2 + x_2 \leq 7\} \ ,$$
$$\mathcal{V}_\lambda = \{(v_1, v_2)|0 \leq 8v_1 - 8v_2 + 8\lambda_1 - 2\lambda_2 + x_1 \leq n; 0 \leq 8v_2 + 2\lambda_2 + x_2 \leq m\} \ .$$

The SPMD code is then :

```
if (s1 % 2 == 0)
    x1 = s1; x2 = s1/2 ; k1 = k2 = 0;
    do u1 = 0 : 1
        do l2 = IntDiv(1 - x2, 2) : IntDiv(7 - x2, 2)
            do l1 = IntDiv(7 - x1 + 4*u1 + 2*l2, 8) : IntDiv(3 - x1 + 4*u1 +2*l2, 8)
                do v2 = IntDiv(7 - x2 -2*l2, 8) : IntDiv(m - x2 -2*l2, 8)
                    do v1 = IntDiv(7 - x1 + 2*l2 - 8*l1 + 8*v2, 8) :
                            IntDiv(n - x1 + 2*l2 - 8*l1 + 8*v2, 8)
                        send ( (l2 + 4*v2, l1 + v1), (x1 + 8*l1 - 2*l2 - 4*u1, x2 + 2*l2))
```

The loop bounds were obtained by submitting separately the $\mathcal{U}$, $\mathcal{L}_u$ and $\mathcal{V}_\lambda$ sets to the Linear Inequality Calculator, with constant propagation from each set to the following; here u2 is found equal to 0.

3.4 Analysis

As shown by the form of the general SPMD code, the destination processor does not depend on the innermost loop index v, and all parameters of the *send* primitive are affine functions of the loop indices. For n = m, there are at most 4 messages, proving that good vectorization is possible, even in this complicated case.

Loop bounds are in convex form; only the vector term (c in $Ci \leq c$) depends on an external loop index. Each of the three loops $\mathcal{U}$, $\mathcal{L}_u$ and $\mathcal{V}_\lambda$ is at most as deeply nested as the initial loop; this is a key point: for instance, in the previous (contrivied) example, generating the loop bounds was immediate, but submitting the global system fails. The particular solutions are computed as in the case of *Compute(s)*.

Run-time integer divides appears only in computation of loop bounds; in many cases (see the previous example), there is no actual integer divide, because the divider is always a power of 2.

Another important property that the code is fully symbolic: all matrices are derived from the initial matrix A, the parallel loop bound matrix C, and the processor matrix P, allowing further optimizations of SPMD code based on loop transformations.

4 Optimizations

The most general case is, in fact, quite rare. Most practical programs will present some pecularities that may simplify the compilation process and the output code. Our output code regularly improves with the simplicity of the input code.

4.1 Array Sections

Parallel references using regular spacing are known as *array sections*. A generalization is to allow permutations of the indices, such as $T(i, j) = T(3*j, 3*i)$. In this case, and if the PROCESSOR extents ar all powers of 2, the loop bounds present no integer divides. To prove this, note that in our framework, generalized array sections create a A matrix with only one non-null coefficient on each row (the stride), and a C matrix with only one non-null coefficient on each row, this coefficient being equal to 1. It follows from the form of A that K and $K^{-1} = Id$. On the other hand, all the diagonal coefficients of P' and P'_1 divide π, which is a power of 2. From the form of the sets $\mathcal{U}$, $\mathcal{L}_u$ and $\mathcal{V}_\lambda$, it follows that the divisons will be only by powers of 2.

4.2 Remanent References

If all data required by each processor s' are sent by the same processor (depending on s'), reference A will be called *remanent*. In this case, there is only one maximal remanence set, $\mathbf{Z}^n$ itself; thus loop u would have to disappear, as shown below.

From the definition of remanence sets, A is remanent iff $P^{-1}AP$ is an integer matrix, say B. This condition can be easily checked by the compiler. For instance, A is remanent when it is diagonal, for all one-dimensional arrays, as matrix P reduces to a scalar, and for any PROCESSOR geometry where all p_i are equal.

Let Smith normal form of B be $H_2 D_2 K_2$. From unicity of Smith normal form, $\pi D_2 = D_1$, thus π divides d_i^1; as $p_i'^1 = \pi/gcd(\pi, d_i^1)$, $P'_1 = Id$; finally condition (a) results in $u = 0$, destroying the external loop. With some more manipulation, one can define an index set $\mathcal{W}_\lambda$ such that the final loop becomes:

> *if ex-cond*
>   *do λ in $\mathcal{L}$*
>   *do w in $\mathcal{W}_\lambda$*
>   *send $(k_0 + HD'\lambda + Bw, x_0 + K^{-1}P'\lambda)$*

4.3 Free References

If there is only one free set, reference A will be called free. In this case, a processor always sends its data to the same processor. As the solutions in x of equation $Ax = Pk$ are $x = K^{-1}P'\lambda$, a sufficient condition for A to be free is that $P^{-1}K^{-1}P'$ is an integer matrix, say Q. This condition can be easily checked by the compiler. When A is remanent and free, only one loop remains. This true for shifts, and when matrix A is diagonal with coefficients relatively prime with the p_i. One can choose x_0 such that $[P^{-1}x_0] = 0$, because the only requirement on x_0 is $Ax_0 \equiv s - a \bmod p$, and by the remanence property of A, the solutions in x of this type of equation are defined modulo p. $u = 0$ because A is remanent, $Q\lambda = u$ because A is free and the choice of x_0, ; as $\det Q \neq 0$ (from its definition), $\lambda = 0$. Set $\mathcal{W}$ reduces to $\{w \in \mathbf{Z}^n | CPw \leq c - Cx_0\}$. As A defines a one-to-one mapping of $\mathcal{S}$ onto $\mathcal{S}$, *ex-cond* disappears. The final loop is:

```
do w in W
    send (k₀ + Bw, x₀)
```

On an 8×8 PROCESSOR, the parallel assignment
$$T(i, j) = T(3{*}j, 3{*}i)$$
becomes

```
do w1 = IntDiv(-x1 + 7, 8), IntDiv(n - x1, 8)
    do w2 = IntDiv(-x2 + 7, 8), IntDiv(w1 + x1 - x2, 8)
        send( (k1 + 3*w2, k2 + 3*w1), (x1, x2))
```

This exemplifies the fact that remanent and free communications can be perfectly vectorized.

5 Conclusion

Although many data-parallel languages do propose both block and cyclic distribution, most existing codes only use the block one. The motivation is that blocking provides locality. However, the cyclic distribution may be a key for sparse computations [1], which are a prominent component of numerical codes. The last part of this paper shows that, at least for many frequent cases, the cyclic distribution does not require a larger number of communications than the block one, although it increases the volume of each communication.

In this paper, we focused on the basic sets associated with SPMD code for communications. Another possible application is escaping from Owner Compute Rule, when remote computations are possible. The array elements involved in this local computation may be, once again, determined by our initial lemma. A different communication model is compiled communications, as proposed in [4] and [7]; in this model, the full communication scheme has to be known, to allocate network resources at compile-time. With some adaptation, the scheme presented here meets these requirements.

References

1. R. Asenjo and al. Sparse Block and Cyclick data distribution for matrix computation. In *High Performance Computing, Technology and Applications*, Elsevier, 95.

2. C. Ancourt and F. Irigoin. Scanning polyhedra with DO loops. In *3rd ACM Symp. on Principles and Practice of Parallel Programming*, pages 39–50, 91.

3. D. Callahan and K. Kennedy. Compiling programs for distributed memory architectures. *Jal. Supercomputing*, (2):151–169, Oct. 88.

4. F. Cappello and al. Balanced distributed memory parallel computers. In *22nd Int. Conf. on Parallel Processing*, pages I.72–I.76–, August 93.

5. S. Chatterjee and al. Generating local addresses and communication sets for data-parallel programs. In *Symp on Principles and Practice of Programming Languages 93*. ACM, 93.

6. C.Koelbel. Compile-time generation of regular communication patterns. In *Supercomputing 91*, pages 101–110, 91.

7. A. Feldmann, T.M. Stricker, and T.E. Warfel. Supporting sets of arbitrary connections on iWarp through communication context switches. In ACM, editor, *5th ACM Symp. on Algorithms and Architectures*, pages 203–212, 93.

8. F.Irigoin and al. A linear algebra framework for static HPF code distribution. In *4th Int. Work. on Compilers for Parallel Computers*, pages 117–132, 93.

9. M. Le Fur. Scanning parameterized polyhedron using Fourier-Motzkin elimination. Technical report, IRISA, Sept. 94. PI 858.

10. S.K.S. Gupta and al. On compiling array expressions for efficient execution on distributed–memory machines. In *1993 Int. Conf. on Parallel Processing*, pages II–301–II–305, 93.

11. D.E. Maydan, S.P. Amarasinghe, and M.S. Lam. Data dependence and data-flow analysis of arrays. In *5th Work. on Languages and Compilers for Parallel Computing*, pages 283–292, 92.

12. W. Pugh. The omega test : a fast and practical integer programming algorithm for dependence analysis. *Comm. ACM*, (8):102–114, Aug. 92.

13. A. Schrijver. *Theory of Linear and Integer Programming*. Wiley, 86.

14. J.M. Stichnoth, D. O'Hallaron and T.R. Gross. Generating Communications for Array Statements ; Design, Implementation and Evaluation. *Jal. Parallele and Distributed computing*, (21) 150–159, Apr. 94.

15. C-W. Tseng. *An optimizing Fortran D compiler for MIMD Distributed- memory machines*. PhD thesis, Rice University, 93.

The Program Compaction Revisited: the Functional Framework

Marc Pouzet

VERIMAG, Miniparc-ZIRST, Rue Lavoisier, 38330 Montbonnot St-Martin, France
e-mail Marc.Pouzet@imag.fr.

Abstract. This paper presents a general method to compact the first-order part of functional languages with call-by-value semantics for fine-grain parallel machines like VLIW or super-scalars. This work extends previous works on compaction in two ways. First, it defines a new formal system for the compaction problem usable to design a meta-compiler for these machines. Second, the compaction is directly applied to functional expressions instead of graph based representations (control flow or dependence flow based representations) leading to a very uniform and simple presentation.

1 Introduction

VLIW (Very Long Instruction Word) [14] and super-scalar architectures [11, 5] are fine grain parallel and compiled architectures in the sense that they can execute many instructions per cycle, gathered together by a compiler. VLIW are controlled by a single instruction stream (one program counter) where each processor executes a dedicated field of a long instruction. In a super-scalar machine, the processor executes successive RISC-like instructions belonging to a small window by analyzing at runtime their dependencies.

Fine grain parallelization for these architectures, or *compaction*, statically recognizes and schedules groups of elementary operations that can be executed in parallel. Compaction can be *local* — it is then limited to expressions without branches, or *global* — and it treats conditional expressions. Loops are compiled by *Software Pipelining*.

We propose in this paper a new and formal presentation of compaction, directly applied to functional expressions (terms). It can be used as a first step in the problem of designing meta-compacting compilers but also as a first step toward fast and efficient implementations of functional languages on fine-grain parallel machines.

This paper is organized as follows. The first part motivates the point of view adopted in this paper. We then give some examples. The next part is the formalization: we first define a functional language and its operational semantics. The classical notion of dependence is defined by an equivalence relation named *structural equivalence*, between programs having the *same dependences*. It serves as a guide for the formalization: every program transformations will have to preserve this equivalence. Then we build a transformational system on terms that improves programs for a given machine.

2 Motivations

Compacting compilers and, more generally, parallelizing compilers, can be decomposed into two classes. Compilers in the first class are applied to control flow based representations (basic bloc graphs) where elementary instructions "percolate" in the graph [8, 7, 1, 15, 6]. In this framework, software pipelining is done by iterative methods with a controlled inlining of loops, looking for a repeated behavior [1, 6]. For compilers in the second class, compaction is applied to dependence graph representations of programs, extending scheduling techniques to programs containing control structures [18, 13]. Software pipelining is then applied to graphs with cycles. The tradeoff is between *generality* and *efficiency*. Control based representation is the most general framework since it is the low level representation of every program. Nonetheless, it leads to very poor implementations — operations moves are done in linear time. Dependence graph based representation leads to efficient implementations — operation moves are done in constant time — but only a subset (without tests) of a real language is well treated in this framework. In particular, software pipelining is applied to elementary do loops with no tests or nested loops. When control is added (e.g, Lam's *hierarchical reduction* system [13]), the control is boxed, which forbids the best possible compaction.

This paper investigates a formalization of compaction, thus we have to define an intermediate language and an abstract notion of fine-grain parallel machines. We have to balance this tradeoff: the intermediate language has to be general enough to represent a real subset of classical languages, but it also has to be practical (the representation must lead to efficient implementations). Moreover, this formalization has to be simple enough to allow reasoning about compaction. Then, some program transformations (renaming, duplication, unrolling, etc.) should be possible. Lastly, to be general enough, it has to compact recursive and functional programs: to compact such programs, it makes no sense to translate them into some low level control graph representation and then retrieve their dependences, since in a functional language, dependences are simply read off the syntax. Moreover, in a functional language, sections of programs can be guaranteed to be free of side-effects by the type system [1] and have the Static Single Assignment (SSA) property. As it fails to represent the control of all kind of programs, the dependence graph representation alone is not suited either as an intermediate representation of programs. The solution proposed here is between control flow based representations and dependence flow based representations.

Compaction will be defined by a set of transformations directly applied to functional *terms*, each of them *improving* the term to some extent. The language is an extension of dependence graph representation — a dependence graph is a particular case of a functional expression [2] — but is able to represent the control of program. With the functional representation, the compiler manage at the same

---

[1] Though they manage data-structures (lists,...) represented with pointers.

[2] The let definition in a functional expression defines the sharing, i.e, Directed Acyclic Graphs.

time the dependence and the control information on the program and program transformations are based on the well known substitution principle. In order to define a formal system for the compaction problem, we propose an operational semantics to give a measure to expressions — every compacting transformations will have to improve programs — and a notion of *dependences*. The operational semantics defines the way a fine-grain parallel machine executes a program. The notion of dependences is also important. Indeed, as compaction usually respects this notion in the classical framework, how this notion applies in the functional case, in order to have the same expressiveness? In other words, what are the program transformations a reasonable compiler can do? Here, the notion will be defined by an equivalence relation, named *structural* that will permit classical transformations. Finally, because functional terms can be represented with sharing, it allows better implementations than with the classical control-flow based representation.

3 Examples

Let us try first to compact the simple program P_1 given on the left of the following figure. It executes an addition $(+_1)$ between a variable and a constant. It binds the result to the variable x and then executes the operation $+_2$ and then $-_3$, the test and one of the two branches. Finally, it computes $*_5$ between the value of $(x +_2 4) -_3 x$ and the value of the conditional expression.

$$P_1 = \text{let } x = \overline{y +_1 2}$$
$$\text{in } ((x +_2 4) -_3 x) *_5 \text{ if } \overline{z =_2 0}$$
$$\text{then let } m = \overline{4 +_3 y}$$
$$\text{in } m *_4 n$$
$$\text{else } x *_3 2$$

$$P_2 = \text{let } x = y +_1 2$$
$$\text{in if } z =_2 0$$
$$\text{then } ((x +_2 4) -_3 x) *_5 (\text{let } m = \overline{4 +_3 y})$$
$$\text{in } m *_4 n$$
$$\text{else } ((x +_2 4) -_3 x) *_5 (x *_3 2)$$

$$P_3 = \text{let } x = y +_1 2$$
$$m = 4 +_3 y$$
$$\text{in if } z =_2 0$$
$$\text{then let } x_1 = x +_2 4$$
$$x_2 = m *_4 n$$
$$\text{in let } x_1 = x_1 -_3 x$$
$$\text{in } x_1 *_5 x_2$$
$$\text{else let } x_1 = x +_2 4$$
$$x_2 = x *_3 2$$
$$\text{in let } x_1 = x_1 -_3 x$$
$$\text{in } x_1 *_5 x_2$$

Consider now a machine $\mathcal{M}$ able to execute this program in a left-to-right evaluation order and where three successive and independent instructions can be executed in parallel. The execution time of P_1 on $\mathcal{M}$ is 5. Let us show how a simple transformation *improves* this execution time. Consider the elementary computations that can be executed immediately in parallel. We term these computations *ready sub-terms*. They are overlined here. $+_3$ may be executed speculatively before the test because it is a *safe* computation [3]. We apply a move-up rule to the test, getting P_2. Now, $+_3$ can be moved-up. We then continue the

---

[3] A computation is *safe* when it can be executed speculatively without modifying the semantics.

compaction with the two branches, getting at the end P_3. This program can not be compacted further and its execution time on $\mathcal{M}$ is 4. It is decomposed into groups of independent instructions executed in parallel.

Consider now the case of a simple recursive function F written in a PCF style [10]. It is an iteration on a list where [] stands for the empty list, hd and tl for the head and the tail of the list (x and a are the arguments).

$$F = \text{Fix}_f \left(\begin{array}{l} \lambda\,[x;a].\,\text{if } x = [] \\ \qquad \text{then } a \\ \qquad \text{else } f[\overline{tl(x)}; -(\overline{hd(x)}) + a] \end{array} \right)$$

The global compaction on this program would compact the body of the function, ignoring the possible overlapping between iterations, thus the parallelism. For this reason, we apply an inlining rule: $\text{Fix}_f(a) \rightarrow a[f\backslash\text{Fix}_f(a)]$ meaning that all occurrences of the free variable f are replaced by its definition. We get the following term given on the left. Now the only ready sub-term is the test. We then move the overlined ready sub-terms in the false branch, getting the program on the right.

$$\lambda\,[x;a].\,\text{if } x = []$$
$$\qquad \text{then } a$$
$$\qquad \text{else } F[\overline{tl(x)}; -(\overline{hd(x)}) + a]$$

$$\lambda\,[x;a].\,\text{if } x = []$$
$$\qquad \text{then } a$$
$$\qquad \text{else let } x_1 = tl(x)$$
$$\qquad\qquad x_2 = hd(x)$$
$$\qquad\qquad \text{in } F[x_1; -x_2 + a]$$

The current term to be compacted is $F[x_1; -x_2 + a]$. Because the first argument is computed, the inlining of F will show new ready sub-terms to be executed in parallel with the current ready sub-terms. After the inlining, the following application has to be compacted.

$$(\lambda[x;a].\,\text{if } x = []\text{ then } a\text{ else } F[tl(x); -(hd(x)) + a])([x_1; -x_2 + a])$$

A simple renamming rule is used for simplifying the application. We get the new term:

$$(\lambda a.\,\text{if } \overline{x_1 = []}\text{ then } a\text{ else } F[tl(x_1); -(hd(x_1)) + a])(\overline{-x_2} + a)$$

We can move-up the ready sub-terms. The resulting program is given below, on the left. In this term, the sub-expression $(\lambda a.a)(x_3 + a)$ can be simplified in $x_3 + a$. After the first step of compaction on the false branch, we have the term given on the right.

$$\text{let } x_3 = -x_2$$
$$\text{in if } x_1 = []$$
$$\qquad \text{then } (\lambda a.a)(x_3 + a)$$
$$\qquad \text{else } (\lambda a.F[\overline{tl(x_1)}; -(\overline{hd(x_1)}) + a])(\overline{x_3 + a})$$

$$\text{let } x_3 = -x_2$$
$$\text{in if } x_1 = []$$
$$\qquad \text{then } x_3 + a$$
$$\qquad \text{else let } x_3 = x_3 + a$$
$$\qquad\qquad x_2 = tl(x_1)$$
$$\qquad\qquad x_4 = hd(x_1)$$
$$\qquad\qquad \text{in } (\lambda a.F[x_2; -x_4 + a])x_3$$

The next expression to be compacted is $(\lambda a.F[x_2; -x_4 + a])x_3$. By the renaming rule, this term is simplified in $F[x_2; -x_4+x_3]$. We already saw a very similar term. It is equal, modulo a renaming of its free variables, to the term $F[x1; -x2 + a]$. Compaction does not depend on names so it will produce the same result for this input, hence the process enters in an infinite loop. To stop compaction, we give a name — here ff — to the term and replace it by a call. The final program is the following one.

$$
\begin{aligned}
&\text{let } ff = \text{Fix}_{ff}(\,\lambda[x_1; x_2; a]. \\
&\qquad\qquad \text{let } x_3 = -x_2 \\
&\qquad\qquad \text{in if } x_1 = [\,] \\
&\qquad\qquad\qquad \text{then } x_3 + a \\
&\qquad\qquad\qquad \text{else let } x_3 = x_3 + a \\
&\qquad\qquad\qquad\qquad x_2 = tl(x_1) \\
&\qquad\qquad\qquad\qquad x_4 = hd(x_1) \\
&\qquad\qquad\qquad \text{in } ff[x_2; x_4; x_3]) \\
&\quad \text{in } \lambda[x; a]. \text{ if } x = [\,] \\
&\qquad\qquad \text{then } a \\
&\qquad\qquad \text{else let } x1 = tl(x) \\
&\qquad\qquad\qquad x2 = hd(x) \\
&\qquad\qquad \text{in } ff[x_1; x_2; a]
\end{aligned}
$$

This final program cannot be compacted anymore. It is the *Software Pipelining* version of the initial program, i.e. another inlining followed by the compaction process would produce the same result since we have inlined F as soon as possible.

Note that the recursive call to ff can be implemented here by a direct branch and variable names can be seen as register names. Then, register allocation can be done on the fly with compaction (but it is not necessary). In this case, move instructions between x_1 and x_2, x_2 and x_4, a and x_3 can be eliminated.

This example raises the following questions. In this process, some transformations were done on programs like renaming, moving instructions, reducing *identity* calls. What are the legal transformations a *reasonable* compiler can do? Why would the last program be better than the first one? Does the compaction process always terminate and how can this be formalized? Answers to these questions will be developed in the following sections.

4 Formalization

We present a complete formalization of compaction. The first part deals with the presentation of a first-order recursive language, named $\mathcal{F}$. It is a low level language (an intermediate language). We then present the machine model that will allow discussing about "a program is better than an other one for a given machine". The definition should apply to *sequential* machines as well as *superscalar* or *vliw* machines. The next part deals with the semantical model of fine grain parallelization. It presents the notion of *dependences* in $\mathcal{F}$. We shall see why dependences are defined intentionally by an equivalence relation named *structural equivalence*. The last part is the definition of *software pipelining* and the transformation system to produce it.

4.1 The $\mathcal{F}$ language

The $\mathcal{F}$ language is a recursive language with an ML-like syntax, but with a granularity close to the one of a machine.

Definition 1 The $\mathcal{F}$ language. The definition of the language is the following.

$$a ::= i \mid \text{true} \mid \text{false} \mid x \mid \text{let } x = a \text{ in } a \mid a[a; ...; a] \mid \lambda \vec{x}.a$$
$$\mid op[a; ...; a] \mid \text{Fix}_f(a) \mid \text{if } a \text{ then } a \text{ else } a$$
$$op ::= \text{add\_int} \mid ...$$

Primitives (called op) are those of the architecture. Terms range over a. $\mathcal{F}$ manages scalars (i), variables (x), defines local values (let), n-ary functions $\lambda[x_1; ...; x_n].a$, recursive functions $\text{Fix}_f(a)$, and n-ary primitives (op) and applications $a[a_1; ...; a_n]$. All memory accesses are done by explicit primitives and there are no *side-effects* in the sense that the language has the SSA (Static Single Assignment) property [3]. In the paper, we note $\vec{a}$ instead of $[a_1; ...; a_n]$ and $\vec{a}|_i$ for $[a_1; ...; a_{i-1}; a_{i+1}; ...; a_n]$.

$\mathcal{F}$ is a typed language *à la ML* and we suppose the existence of a typing function — named *type* — returning for each expression of $\mathcal{F}$, its type taken from the type language below for which a classical typing algorithm can be chosen [4].

$$t ::= \tau \mid t \to t \mid [t; ...; t]$$

τ denotes scalar types (int , bool ,...). $t \to t$ is the function type and $[t; ...; t]$ is the product type. Information needed about a type is its complexity, that is, the number of arrows on the left.

Definition 2 Type complexity. We define the function $|.|$, returning the type complexity of its argument.

$$|t_1 \to t_2| = 1 + |t_1| \quad |[t_1; ...; t_n]| = max_i(|t_i|) \quad |\tau| = 0$$

For instance, the type complexity of (int $\to$ int) $\to$ int is 2 whereas the type complexity of int $\to$ (int $\to$ int) is 1. This gives the functionality order. We need a preliminary definition before defining the ready sub-terms of an expression.

Definition 3 Cost. The cost of a term a is defined by the function $||.||$, returning an element from $\mathbb{N} \cup \{\infty\}$.

$$||\text{if } a_1 \text{ then } a_2 \text{ else } a_3|| = \sum_{i=1}^{3}(||a_i||) \quad ||op[a_1; ...; a_n]|| = 1 + \sum_{i=1}^{n}(||a_i||)$$

$$||\lambda \vec{x}.a|| = 1 \quad ||\text{let } x = a_1 \text{ in } a_2|| = ||a_1|| + ||a_2||$$

$$||x|| = ||i|| = 0 \quad ||a([b_1; ...; b_n])|| = \infty \quad ||\text{Fix}_f(a)|| = ||a||$$

The cost is a coarse approximation of the execution time of an expression. All primitives are assumed to be executed in one cycle and the execution time of an expression containing a call is infinite. The cost of an abstraction is 1 as we consider the cost of constructing a closure to be elementary [4]. Now we can define the ready sub-terms of an expression.

Definition 4 Ready sub-terms. Let a be a term of $\mathcal{F}$. $s \prec a$ means that the sub-term s of a is ready in a.

$$\frac{}{s \prec s} \quad \frac{s \prec a_i}{s \prec op(\vec{a})} \quad \frac{s \prec a \quad x_i \not\prec s \quad \|s\| < \infty}{s \prec \lambda \vec{x}.a} \quad \frac{s \prec a_1}{s \prec \text{let } x = a_1 \text{ in } a_2} \quad \frac{s \prec \lambda f.a}{s \prec \text{Fix}_f(a)}$$

$$\frac{s \prec a_1}{s \prec \text{if } a_1 \text{ then } a_2 \text{ else } a_3} \quad \frac{s \prec a_i \quad \|s\| < \infty}{s \prec \text{if } a \text{ then } a_1 \text{ else } a_2} \quad \frac{s \prec a_2 \quad x \not\prec s}{s \prec \text{let } x = a_1 \text{ in } a_2} \quad \frac{s \prec a_i}{s \prec a_0(\vec{a})}$$

A ready sub-term is a sub-term that can be computed immediately. For example, $1 + x \prec \lambda y.(1 + x) * y$. The notion of ready sub-terms is an extension of free variables (hence, a free variable is always ready). For this reason, we will use the classical notation $FV(a)$ containing the set of free variables of a, i.e, $x \in FV(a)$ iff $x \prec a$. Ready sub-terms of special interest are those whose cost is 1, that is elementary computations.

Definition 5 Ready sub-terms substitution. Let t be such that $t \prec a$. The substitution of all occurrences of t in a by b, noted $a[t \backslash b]$, is defined by:

$$
\begin{aligned}
t[t \backslash b] &= b \\
x[t \backslash b] &= x & \text{if } x \neq t \\
(op[a_1; ...; a_n])[t \backslash b] &= op[[a_1[t \backslash b]; ...; a_n[t \backslash b]] \\
(a_0[a_1; ...; a_n])[t \backslash b] &= (a_0[t \backslash b])([a_1[t \backslash b]; ...; a_n[t \backslash b]]) \\
(\lambda x.a)[t \backslash b] &= \lambda x.a & \text{if } x \prec t \\
(\lambda x.a)[t \backslash b] &= \lambda z.(a[x \backslash z][t \backslash b]) & \text{else. } z \not\prec a \wedge z \not\prec b \\
(\text{let } x = a_1 \text{ in } a_2)[t \backslash b] &= \text{let } x = a_1[t \backslash b] \text{ in } a_2 & \text{if } x \prec t \\
(\text{let } x = a_1 \text{ in } a_2)[t \backslash b] &= \text{let } z = a_1[t \backslash b] \text{ in } a_2[z \backslash x][t \backslash b] & \text{else. } z \not\prec a_2 \wedge z \not\prec b \\
\text{Fix}_f(a)[t \backslash b] &= \text{Fix}_f(a) & \text{if } f \prec t \\
\text{Fix}_f(a)[t \backslash b] &= \text{Fix}_g(a[f \backslash g][t \backslash b]) & \text{else. } g \not\prec a \wedge g \not\prec b \\
(\text{if } a_1 \text{ then } a_2 \text{ else } a_3)[t \backslash b] &= \text{if } a_1[t \backslash b] \text{ then } a_2[t \backslash b] \text{ else } a_3[t \backslash b]
\end{aligned}
$$

The substitution of ready sub-terms is very similar to the classical substitution of free variables. For example, $(\lambda x.(1 + y) * x)[1 + y \backslash y] = \lambda x.y * x$. Thus substitution makes it possible to extract computations from a term.

---

[4] A multicycle computation $op(x)$ can be treated, replacing it by $op_1(op_2(...(op_n(x))...))$.

4.2 Operational semantics

The operational semantics has two aims. As usual, it defines the values and the execution order. But, it also express how a fine-grain parallel machine handles a given program. It leads to a measure on programs.

The language has a call-by-value evaluation in a left-to-right order. A machine can be seen as a function, selecting a subset of elementary ready sub-terms and executing them. All sub-terms cannot be selected. A fine grain parallel machine executing some in-line code does not see the entire control structure of the program and is limited by *control-dependences* [12]: an instruction following a function call is *unreachable*. To define machines, we need a preliminary definition to explain what *unreachable* means.

Definition 6 Occurrences and depth. The set of occurrences (access paths), $\mathcal{O}(a)$ of a term a contains words on integers (the empty word is Λ). It is defined as usual by:

$\Lambda \in \mathcal{O}(a)$
For all construction C of the language, $i.o_i \in \mathcal{O}(C(a_1, ..., a_n))$
$$\text{if } o_i \in \mathcal{O}(a_i).$$

We define the Depth of an occurrence in a given term as follows:

$\mathcal{D}_a(\Lambda) = 0$
$\mathcal{D}_{a[a_1;...;a_n]}(1.o) = \sum_{i=1}^{n} \|a_i\| + \mathcal{D}_a(o)$
For all other constructions C, $\mathcal{D}_{C(a_1,...,a_n)}(i.o) = \mathcal{D}_{a_i}(o) + \sum_{j<i} \|a_j\|$.

The *depth* of an occurrence is the number of instructions that are executed before it, in a left-to-right evaluation order. Thus, the depth of $(1+y)$ in $(\lambda x.(1+y) * x)(2 + z)$ is 2 because the argument is executed before the body of the function. The depth of a sub-term on the right of a function call always equals ∞. It means that the computation is unreachable by the machine.

When possible, the occurrence will be omitted and the notation $\mathcal{D}_a(t)$ will be used instead of $\mathcal{D}_a(o)$ if o is the occurrence of the sub-term t in a.

A machine can be seen as a sub-relation of $\prec$. For example, a machine is able to forbid speculative execution. Therefore, instructions under conditionals or abstractions are never ready.

Definition 7 Machine $\mathcal{M}$. A machine $\mathcal{M}$ is a function from terms from $\mathcal{F}$ to set of terms verifying the following constraint: there exists $k_1, k_2 \in \mathbb{N}$ such that for all a with $\mathcal{M}(a) = \{t_1, ..., t_n\}$, we have $n \leq k_1$, $t_i \prec a$ and $\mathcal{D}_a(t_i) \leq k_2$ and there exists at most one t_i such that $\|t_i\| = \infty$.

The number of ready sub-terms (k_1) gives the number of parallel units of the machine and the depth gives the window size (k_2) — the number of instructions that can be fetched every cycle. This window contains at most a function call (an unconditional jump) which is on the right of the others[5]. A *super-scalar* machine also matches this description. A *sequential* machine is the special case where $k_1 = 1$ and $k_2 = 1$. A *vliw* machine is a special case of a machine.

Example 1 VLIW machine. A vliw machine is a maximal machine $\mathcal{M}$ such that: if $t \in \mathcal{M}(a)$ and $\mathcal{D}_a(t) = n$ then $\forall t', \mathcal{D}_a(t') < n \Rightarrow t' \in \mathcal{M}(a)$

Here, the maximal prefix of independent instructions from a window of sequential instructions can be executed in parallel. We call it a VLIW machine, even if it is not a real one — a Multiflow-like machine [14] — because no scheduling is done by the machine.

Pipelined machines enter in this description if the compiler transforms a pipelined instruction $op(x)$ in $\mathsf{nop}(...(\mathsf{nop}(op(x)))...)$.

Example 2 Pipelined machine. A pipelined machine is a machine $\mathcal{M}$ such that: if $t \in \mathcal{M}(a)$ and $t \neq \mathsf{nop}(y)$ then $\mathsf{nop}(x) \prec a \Rightarrow \mathsf{nop}(x) \in \mathcal{M}(a)$.

All nop operations are necessarily executed in parallel with a non-nop operation. A machine will be given by its state automaton that reads only a finite part of the term. Let us see now the definition of the operational semantics of the $\mathcal{F}$ language given in a structural way [16].

The operational semantics is straightforward. Like a classical fine-grain parallel machine, the machine selects a subset of ready sub-terms that can be executed in parallel, executes them and substitutes selected ready sub-terms by their values. Nonetheless, because of the representation of programs, a term of $\mathcal{F}$ contains some *noise*, that is, syntactical constructions that do not generate any computation (in fact, they correspond to no assembly instructions). For example, the let represents *dags* and the expression let $x = 1$ in $x + x$ has the same execution time as $1 + 1$. To reduce this noise, we define an equality.

Definition 8 ϵ-transitions. We define the equality $=_{\mathcal{M}}$. $C(a)$ denotes a term containing the sub-term a.

$$C(\mathsf{let}\ x = x\ \mathsf{in}\ a) =_{\mathcal{M}} C(a)$$
$$C(\mathsf{let}\ x = i\ \mathsf{in}\ a) =_{\mathcal{M}} C(a[x\backslash i])$$
$$C(\mathsf{let}\ x = \lambda y.a_1\ \mathsf{in}\ a_2) =_{\mathcal{M}} C(a_2[x\backslash\lambda y.a_1])$$
$$C(\mathsf{let}\ x = \mathsf{Fix}_f(\lambda y.a_1)\ \mathsf{in}\ a_2) =_{\mathcal{M}} C(a_2[x\backslash\mathsf{Fix}_f(\lambda y.a_1)])$$
$$C(\mathsf{if\ true\ then}\ a_2\ \mathsf{else}\ a_3) =_{\mathcal{M}} C(a_2)$$
$$C(\mathsf{if\ false\ then}\ a_2\ \mathsf{else}\ a_3) =_{\mathcal{M}} C(a_3)$$

$$C((\lambda\vec{x}.a)[b_1;...;x_i;...;b_n]) =_{\mathcal{M}} C((\lambda\vec{x}|_i.a)[b_1;...;;...;b_n])$$
$$\text{if } x_i \in \mathcal{M}((\lambda\vec{x}.a)[b_1;...;x_i;...;b_n])$$
$$\wedge type(x_i)| = 0$$
$$C(\mathsf{Fix}_f(\lambda\vec{x}.a)) =_{\mathcal{M}} C(\lambda\vec{x}.a[f\backslash\mathsf{Fix}_f(\lambda\vec{x}.a)])$$
$$\text{if } \mathsf{Fix}_f(\lambda\vec{x}.a) \in \mathcal{M}(\mathsf{Fix}_f(\lambda\vec{x}.a))$$

---

[5] According to the definition, the depth of a function call is finite if it is not preceeded by any other call.

The constraint on the complexity of the type for the reduction of applications will be explained further. The equality says which constructions are invisible for the machine $\mathcal{M}$. Here, only reachable sub-expressions are reduced: the equality is not applied in all contexts. This is due to the inlining rule for recursions. Indeed, without the use of Mm, the following infinite reduction could occur:

$F[x; y], ..., F[x; op(y)], ..., (\lambda y.F[x; op(y)])(op(y)), ...$

with $F = \text{Fix}_f(\lambda[x; y].f[x; op(y)])$. In our definition, empty computations are erased when necessary.

Definition 9 Operational semantics. The operational semantics of a program on a machine $\mathcal{M}$ is given by the relation $\Downarrow$. $a \Downarrow b$ means that a evaluates to b. Terms are considered modulo $=_{\mathcal{M}}$. The inference rules are:

$$\frac{\mathcal{M}(a) = \{t_1, ..., t_n\} \quad t_i \Downarrow v_i \quad a[t_1 \backslash v_1]...[t_n \backslash v_n] \Downarrow b}{a \Downarrow b}$$

Axioms are of the following form:

$x \Downarrow x$
$\lambda x.a \Downarrow \lambda x.a$
$\text{Fix}_f(\lambda x.a) \Downarrow \text{Fix}_f(\lambda x.a)$
$i_1 + i_2 \Downarrow i_3$ where i_3 is the sum of i_1 and i_2.

The execution time $|a|_{\mathcal{M}}$ of a is the size of the proof of $a \Downarrow v$.

For simplicity, we only give the axiom for integers. With the definition of the execution time, we may compare programs.

4.3 Dependence semantics

We used some program transformations like renaming of inlining in the compaction of the second example. What reasonable transformations should be incorporated in a compacting compiler? In the classical framework, only transformations preserving *dependences* are legal. There is a dependence between two instructions if one instruction modifies a value read by another. These dependences are decomposed into *true-dependences* — or *data-dependences* — when the second instruction reads the value produced by the first, and *false dependences* — *anti-dependences* and *output-dependences* — when the second modifies a value read or written by the first one [2].

Because $\mathcal{F}$ is a functional language, dependences, in the usual sense as *def-use* links are directly given in the text by variables and composition of computations. Thus, x of let $x = a$ in b depends on a — and of all its sub-terms — and every sub-term of b containing x depends on it. The transitive closure of this relation gives the classical notion of dependence graph. It is useless to define another notion of dependences of a term in $\mathcal{F}$ and if it would exist, it would be as complex as the term itself. Our notion of dependences is too rigid here for what we need since no syntactical transformation of the term is allowed.

We prefer to define dependences as an equivalence between "programs having the same dependences". This equivalence will be named *structural equivalence*. How does this equivalence interact with β-reduction[6]? On one hand, two really different programs can be extensionally (beta) equivalent and it is clearly infeasible (in a compiler) to allow all kinds of β-reductions. Moreover, we would have some coherency problems since $1+2$ is not equivalent to 3 but the translation in pure λ-calculus would yield the equivalence. On the other hand, can we limit the equivalence to the syntactic equality? Of course, not. It is reasonable to allow instruction moves, inlining, duplication[7] which are the minimal transformations needed for compaction.

The solution proposed here is to limit β-reductions by the complexity of the type: only β-reductions where the type of the argument is simple (the complexity is 0) are allowed.

Definition 10 Structural equivalence. Let a and b, two terms of $\mathcal{F}$. We say that a and b are structurally equivalent, noted $a \sim b$, when $lim_{n \to \infty} a^n = lim_{n \to \infty} b^n$ where a^n is defined by $a \to a^2 \to \ldots \to a^n$ and by the rewriting relation $\to$ applied to all contexts. $\to$ is defined by:

1. $\mathsf{let}\ x = a_1\ \mathsf{in}\ a_2 \to a_2[x \backslash a_1]$
2. $\mathsf{if}\ a\ \mathsf{then}\ \vec{b}\ \mathsf{else}\ \vec{c} \overrightarrow{\to} \mathsf{if}\ a\ \mathsf{then}\ b\ \mathsf{else}\ c$
3. $\mathsf{if}\ \mathsf{true}\ \mathsf{then}\ a_1\ \mathsf{else}\ a_2 \to a_1$
4. $\mathsf{if}\ \mathsf{false}\ \mathsf{then}\ a_1\ \mathsf{else}\ a_2 \to a_2$
5. $(\lambda\vec{x}.a)\vec{b} \to (\lambda\vec{x}|_i.a[x_i \backslash b_i])\vec{b}|_i$ if $|type(b_i)| = 0$
6. $\mathsf{Fix}_f(a) \to a[f \backslash \mathsf{Fix}_f(a)]$

The first rule allows to duplicate a computation. The second rule is equivalent for the test. The next two rules show that conditions can be simplified. The next rule is a β-reduction when the type of the argument b_i is simple.

4.4 Compaction

We saw in the examples that compaction can be obtained by selecting and moving up ready sub-terms. We first define instruction move by two simple rules and then define how to select a subset of the ready sub-terms.

Definition 11 Move-up. Instruction moves are defined by the relation $a \xrightarrow{t} b$ where t is ready in a, such that:

(MOVE) $a \xrightarrow{t} \mathsf{let}\ x = t\ \mathsf{in}\ a[t \backslash x]$ if $x \not\prec a$

(TEST) $a \xrightarrow{t} \mathsf{if}\ t\ \mathsf{then}\ a[t \backslash \mathsf{true}]\ \mathsf{else}\ a[t \backslash \mathsf{false}]$

if $\mathsf{if}\ t\ \mathsf{then}\ a_1\ \mathsf{else}\ b_1$ is a sub-term of a

---

[6] β-reduction is the following rule $(\lambda x.a_1)a_2 \to_\beta a_1[x \backslash a_2]$.
[7] Duplication is useful when it is cheaper to recompute a value than to communicate it.

Instruction moves are simply inverse β-reductions. Now, to select a subset of the ready sub-terms that can be executed in parallel on the machine, the compaction process needs a *strategy*. For example, the classical *List-scheduling* [9] strategy will select ready sub-terms which are on the longest dependence path.

Definition 12 Strategy. A strategy C is a function C between terms and set of terms such that $C(a) = \{t_1, ..., t_n\}$ and for all t_i, $t_i \prec a$

A strategy is not very different from a machine except that — for the moment — there is no constraint on the position of ready sub-terms in the term. It is the reason why we can deal with $=_C$, replacing $\mathcal{M}$ by C.

Let us see now the compaction system. It is very similar to the operational semantics: at every step, some computations are selected and moved-up in the program. The rest of the program is then compacted.

Definition 13 Compaction. Let ρ be a renaming. Terms are considered modulo $=_C$. The general compaction is defined by the predicates $e \models_{\overline{C}} a \Rightarrow_l b$ given in the figure 1, meaning that in the environment e, the term a is compacted to b, using the strategy C and moving up the selected ready sub-terms in l. An environment is a set $[f_1 \backslash \lambda \vec{v_1}.a_1]...[f_n \backslash \lambda \vec{v_n}.a_n]$ used to record terms.

The (SELECT) rule selects a subset of ready sub-terms from a. It records the current term a in the environment e and compacts a with the selected ready sub-terms. The resulting program may be recursive. Of course, if the compaction of a does not use f, the term $(\text{Fix}_f(\lambda v.b))v$ simplifies to b. The (EQUIV) rule stops compaction when the current term is equivalent modulo a renaming ρ to a recorded term. In this case, the compaction of the current term is a call to the name of the recorded term. The (LAMBDA) rule is compositional rule. The (PRIM), (APP), (CONST) and (VAR) rules are the axioms. The (MOVE) rule moves up a selected ready-sub term and the (TEST) moves up a selected test.

Now, do the resulting program always exists, that is, does the system terminate? What are the conditions under which the compacted program is better than the initial one?

For the termination problem, without constraints on C, the answer is clearly no. Indeed, consider $F = \text{Fix}_f(\lambda[x; y].f[op_1(x); op_2(op_3(y))])$ and $F([x; y])$. Let us see the suite of terms that we shall have to compact. It is,

$$F[x; y], ..., F[x; op_2(y)], ..., F[x; op_2(op_3(y))], ..., F[x; op_2(op_3(op_2(y)))], ...$$

$F[x; y]$ is first inlined and the two ready sub-terms $op_1(x)$ and $op_3(y)$ are substituted. Then, the current term to compact is $F[x; op_2(y)]$, etc. This is a very classical problem of iterative compaction methods [1]: the problem is that ready sub-terms are selected deeper and deeper. In the case of tail recursive functions, i.e. loops, we shall see that compaction is simpler than in the general case and that simple and satisfying conditions over C can be taken. We shall come back on general recursive function at the end of the paper to show the problems.

$$\text{(SELECT)} \quad \frac{\mathcal{C}(a) = l \quad \vec{v} = FV(a) \quad e[f\backslash\lambda\vec{v}a] \models_{\overline{c}} a \Rightarrow_l b}{e \models_{\overline{c}} a \Rightarrow (\text{Fix}_f(\lambda\vec{v}b))\vec{v}}$$

$$\text{(EQUIV)} \quad \frac{b = \rho(a) \quad \vec{v}' = \rho(\vec{v})}{e[f\backslash\lambda\vec{v}a] \models_{\overline{c}} b \Rightarrow f(\vec{v}')} \qquad \text{(LAMBDA)} \quad \frac{e \models_{\overline{c}} a \Rightarrow a'}{e \models_{\overline{c}} \lambda\vec{x}a \Rightarrow \lambda\vec{x}a'}$$

$$\text{(MOVE)} \quad \frac{a \xrightarrow{t} \text{let } x = t \text{ in } a_1 \quad e \models_{\overline{c}} t \Rightarrow t' \quad e \models_{\overline{c}} a_1 \Rightarrow_l b_1}{e \models_{\overline{c}} a \Rightarrow_{\{t\}\cup l} \text{let } x = t' \text{ in } b_1}$$

$$\text{(PRIM)} \; e \models_{\overline{c}} op(\vec{x}) \Rightarrow op(\vec{x}) \qquad \text{(CONST)} \; e \models_{\overline{c}} i \Rightarrow i$$

$$\text{(APP)} \; e \models_{\overline{c}} y(\vec{x}) \Rightarrow y(\vec{x}) \qquad \text{(VAR)} \; e \models_{\overline{c}} x \Rightarrow x$$

$$\text{(TEST)} \quad \frac{a \xrightarrow{t} \text{if } t \text{ then } a_1 \text{ else } a_2 \quad e \models_{\overline{c}} t \Rightarrow t' \quad e \models_{\overline{c}} a_1 \Rightarrow_l b_1 \quad e \models_{\overline{c}} a_2 \Rightarrow_l b_2}{e \models_{\overline{c}} a \Rightarrow_{\{t\}\cup l} \text{if } t' \text{ then } b_1 \text{ else } b_2}$$

Fig. 1. The compaction system

Constraint 1 (Terminal recursions) *A term a is terminal if every sub-term $\text{Fix}_f(b)$ of a is such that f is in a terminal position in b, noted $\mathcal{T}(f, b)$.*

$\mathcal{T}(f, \text{if } a \text{ then } a_1 \text{ else } a_2)$ *if* $f \notin FV(a)$, $\mathcal{T}(f, a_1)$ *and* $\mathcal{T}(f, a_2)$

$\mathcal{T}(f, f(a))$ *if* $f \notin FV(a)$
$\mathcal{T}(f, \text{let } x = a \text{ in } b)$ *if* $f \notin FV(a)$ *and* $\mathcal{T}(f, b)$
$\mathcal{T}(f, \lambda x.a)$ *if* $\mathcal{T}(f, a)$
$\mathcal{T}(f, a(b))$ *if* $\mathcal{T}(f, a)$ *and* $f \notin FV(b)$
$\mathcal{T}(f, a)$ *if* $f \notin FV(a)$ *for the other constructions*

The definition of tail-recursive functions says that recursive calls to f are never followed by a computation. Now, we define a constraint on the strategy that must be bounded to guaranty termination of the compaction system.

Constraint 2 (Bounded strategy) *Let $|a|$ be the number of ready sub-terms of a. A strategy $\mathcal{C}$ bounded by k is a strategy such that if $|a| > k$ then for all t, $t \in \mathcal{C}(a)$ iff $t \in \mathcal{C}(b)$ where $a \rightarrow b$.*

A bounded strategy limits the number of selected ready sub-terms. The implication $t \in \mathcal{C}(a) \Rightarrow t \in \mathcal{C}(b)$ is reasonable: it means, for example, that instructions inside a loop iteration have a priority over the ones belonging to the next iterations. The other constraint is quite unusual: it means that even if a sub-term is ready after an inlining, for example, it cannot be selected if the size of the term is greater than a certain limit. This condition is not so strange: consider a term $F(a)$ where F stands for a recursive function. An argument for termination in iterative methods can be that the recursion is inlined when the size of the argument is bounded (usually, an instruction from an iteration can be moved up when the scheduling time of the previous iteration is less than a certain limit).

How does this constraints act with the classical *List-scheduling* strategy? This strategy selects ready sub-terms which are on the longest path. The constraint means that only bounded paths are considered [8].

Proposition 1 (Termination) *The compaction system $\models_{c}$ terminates with a bounded strategy.*

Proposition 2 (Correction) *The compaction system preserves the structural equivalence.*

We have to prove that this system is useful, that is, it decreases the execution time of programs. This cannot be done for general machines because scheduling is NP-hard [9] and cannot be achieved by a greedy algorithm. Nonetheless, the speed-up can be guaranteed for VLIW machines and a strategy which always select at least the nodes selected by the machine.

Proposition 3 (Speed-up) *Let $\mathcal{M}$ be a vliw machine and C such that $\forall a, \exists c,$ such that $\mathcal{M}(a) \subseteq C(a) \subseteq \mathcal{M}(c)$. Then if $\models_{c} a \Rightarrow b$ then $|a|_{\mathcal{M}} \geq |b|_{\mathcal{M}}$*

The result applies for VLIW machines because the depth of instructions in the program never increase: an instruction that is selected by the machine in the initial program is still selected in the second one (except if it has been executed before).

We can ask now how the resulting program compares with the classical software pipelining principle. Software pipelining for recursive programs can be seen as a finite representation of programs, infinitely inlined and compacted. It is a fixpoint for compaction: the compaction of the inlined version programs yields the same program. Software pipelining is defined from the notion of optimality.

Definition 14 Software pipelining. Let a be a term of $\mathcal{F}$. A program a is optimal for C if $\models_{c} b \Rightarrow a$ where $a \rightarrow b$. A program a' is a *software pipelining* of a by C when $a \sim a'$ and a' is optimal.

Proposition 4 (Optimality) $\models_{c}$ *constructs a software pipelining for tail-recursive functions.*

---

[8] Proofs can be found in [17].

The proposed system is a greedy system and is not well suited to general recursion. Indeed, consider the very simple expression $F = \text{Fix}_f(\lambda \vec{x}.A(\vec{x}, f(op(\vec{x}))))$ where A denotes an $\mathcal{F}$ expression. We have the list of terms to compact:
$F(\vec{x_1}), A(\vec{x_1}, F(\vec{x_2})), A(\vec{x_1}, A(\vec{x_2}, F(\vec{x_3}))), \ldots$
The compaction process only reads the beginning of the term $(op(x_i))$. Here the term grows after the recursive call. Even if compaction is stopped, using conditions over $\mathcal{C}$, we do not have any re-rolling rule for the production of the software pipelining. It is unclear how a greedy algorithm, where software pipelining is obtained using what has been done in previous steps and where terms are inlined *a priori*, can be obtained for non-tail recursive functions.

5 Conclusion and future work

We have presented a method to directly compact the first-order part of functional programs. Compaction is described as a set of program transformations. An operational semantics has been proposed to model the behavior of a fine grain parallel machine that executes a program. A notion of dependences has been given here by the *structural equivalence*: it defines only legal — but minimal — program transformations a parallelizing compiler needs to have. This paper can be seen as a formalization of classical compaction techniques, but also as an extension to the general class of recursive programs. By applying compaction to *terms* instead of control flow based representation, the compiler can take benefit of semantical informations available in the source program (for dependence analysis, for example). Because the representation is more general than dependence based representations — this representation can be obtained with sharing — it can be used to represent dependences of a large class of languages.

Some extensions can be done. First, a better strategy will improve convergence since iteration methods are known to be slow and to produce large resulting code. Secondly, imperative features could be treated with a slight modification of de *ready sub-terms* definition. Thirdly, it could be interesting (and useful) to take into account semantical properties of primitives in order to increase the set of the structurally equivalent terms and, thus, to improve compaction. This could be done by the addition of other simplifying rules (commutative rules,...). It is certainly for this kind of extension that the functional representation of programs is better than the classical control-flow representation. Thirdly, non-tail first-order recursion must be treated and, finally, the compaction of general functional program can be studied.

Acknowledgments

Many thanks to my PhD. advisor Jean-Jacques Lévy and to careful readers Paul Caspi from VERIMAG, Thérèse Hardin and Bernard Serpette from INRIA Rocquencourt. Thanks also to the usefull remarks from the referees.

References

1. Alexander Aiken. *Compaction-based Parallelization*. PhD thesis, Cornell University, 1988.

2. R. Cytron and J. Ferrante. What's in a name ? In *International Conference on Parallel Processing*, pages 19–27, August 1987.

3. R. Cytron, J. Ferrante, B. K. Rosen, M. N. Wegman, and F. K. Zadeck. An efficient method of computing static single assignement form. In *Conference on Principles of Programming Langages*, 1989.

4. L. Damas and R. Milner. Principal type-schemes for functional programs. In *Conference on Principles of Programming Languages*, 1982.

5. Digital. *Alpha Architecture Handbook*. Digital, 1992.

6. Kemal Ebcioglu. A compilation technique for software pipelining of loops with conditional jumps. In *Annual Workshop on Microprogramming*, pages 69–79, December 1987.

7. J. R. Ellis. *Bulldog-A Compiler for VLIW Architectures*. MIT Press, 1985. Ph.D dissertation.

8. J. A. Fisher, J. R. Ellis, J. C. Ruttenberg, and A. Nicolau. Parallel processing: A smart compiler and a dumb machine. In *Symposium on Compiler construction*. SIGPLAN Notices, June 1984. Volume 19, Number 6.

9. M. R. Garey and D. S. Johnson. *Computers and Intractability - A guide to the Theory of NP-completeness*. Freeman, New-York, 1979.

10. Carl A. Gunter. *Semantics of programming languages: structures and techniques*. The MIT press, Cambridge, Mass., London, 1992.

11. IBM. IBM Risc System/6000 technology. Technical Report SA23-2619, IBM, 1990. Copies can be obtained from the local IBM Branch office.

12. M. S. Lam and R. P. Whilson. Limits of control flow on parallelism. *ACM Sigarch. Computer Architecture News*, 20(4), 1992.

13. Monica S. Lam. Software pipelining: An effective scheduling technique for VLIW machines. In *Conference on Programming Language, Design and Implementation*, pages 318–328, Atlanta, Georgia, June 22-24 1988.

14. Multiflow Computer Inc. Trace/300 series. Technical report, Multiflow Computer Inc, Brandford, Connecticut, 1987.

15. Alex Nicolau. Percolation scheduling: A parallel compilation technique. Technical report, Cornell University, 1985.

16. Gordon D. Plotkin. *A structural approach to operational semantics*. Daimi FN-19. University of Aarhus, Computer Science Department Aarhus University Ny Munkegade DK 8000 C Danemark, September 1981.

17. Marc Pouzet. The program compaction revisited: the functional framework. Technical Report Spectre-94-11, Verimag, Grenoble, France, December 1994. Available by anonymous ftp on imag.fr in pub/SPECTRE.

18. R. F. Touzeau. A fortran compiler for the FPS-164 scientific computer. In *Symposium on Compiler Construction*, pages 48–57, June 1984.

Featherweight Threads and ANDF Compilation of Concurrency*

Ben Sloman[1,2] and Tom Lake[2] **

[1] University of Reading, Department of Computer Science, PO Box 225,
Whiteknights, UK, RG6 2AY
[2] GLOSSA, 59 Alexandra Road, Reading, RG1 5PG, UK

Abstract. We present an intermediate representation called ThreadTDF,
a component of the Parallel TDF system for compiling distributed concurrent programs to shared and distributed memory multiprocessors.
ThreadTDF is a parallel extension of the TDF architecture neutral distribution format (ANDF) for sequential programs. ThreadTDF provides
featherweight thread mechanisms for explicitly scheduling dynamic fine-
grain concurrent computations within procedures (and more generally
within static local scopes). Communication between address spaces is
supported by remote service request mechanisms based upon asynchronous
activation of remote threads and synchronous remote procedure calls.
In ThreadTDF variable lifetimes bound the lifetimes of featherweight
threads declared in their scope. We show how a compiler uses thread
lifetime information to integrate resource allocation and communication
with thread scheduling for efficient intraprocedural concurrency. Initial
performance results are given for the SPARC processor.

1 Introduction and Background

Parallel TDF is a system for the architecture neutral representation and compilation of parallel programs. It consists of a family of architecture neutral compiler intermediate representations (IRs), of which ParTDF and ThreadTDF are
currently the most important, and techniques for compiling parallel programs
using these representations. Parallel TDF is based upon TDF[7], an architecture neutral and language neutral distribution format. TDF is a compiler IR
with a standardised external representation. In one scenario, TDF is used to
bridge language-specific compiler front ends (*producers*) and separate target-
specific back ends (*installers*) for distribution of 'shrink-wrapped' software (Fig.
1). TDF cannot create portability[3]: applications must use portable programming
styles and must adhere to standard APIs. Parallel TDF attempts to extend the
functionality of TDF for parallel languages and machines.

TDF is described in detail in [7] and other information is available from the
OSF ANDF web page at *http://riwww.osf.org:8001/andf/index.html* or in [3, 6].

---

* This work was carried out under contract for the UK Defence Research Agency
** The authors can be contacted as {Ben.Sloman,Tom.Lake}@glossa.co.uk.
[3] Though the TDF technology has proved useful for portability *checking* tools.

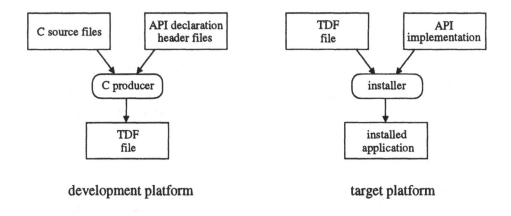

Fig. 1. shrink wrapped distribution using TDF

Parallel TDF provides services for concurrent computation and communication. Its design supports compilation of data parallel and control parallel languages on SIMD and homogeneous shared and distributed memory MIMD machines. Structured parallel languages such as Fortran 90 and occam are compiled into the ParTDF intermediate representation in terms of bags (multisets) of processes. ParTDF allows portability-improving transformations such as distribution of bulk parallelism and conversion of task parallelism for lockstep parallel execution [15]. Other parallel languages are compiled into the ThreadTDF intermediate representation. ThreadTDF provides dynamic manipulation of scoped fine grain threads for efficient concurrency on a narrower range of architectures.

Our contribution is to describe ThreadTDF and show how it can be compiled efficiently to off-the-shelf processor architectures. We show that thread scopes simplify register allocation across threads. We then show how to exploit the register allocation by using cooperative hierarchical scheduling to optimise context switches between threads in the same variable scopes.

2 Introduction to TDF

TDF is a tree-structured language with special features for portability. It preserves more program structure than low level IRs such as the RTL of *gcc*, but has no syntactic sugar and a weaker type system than typical high level languages. The unit of representation in TDF is the *capsule* which contains definitions and declarations of procedures, variables and tokens (see below). A capsule can export these declarations and definitions by binding them to external names. The ANSI C TDF producer converts each separate C file into a compact binary representation of a TDF capsule. A TDF linker allows capsules to be bound together using their external names.

In TDF, any target machine or OS dependences, such as the implementations of C types int and FILE, are deferred using parameterised placeholders, similar to syntax macros, called *tokens*. The TDF linker can be used to bind in token definitions once the target machine is known. The resulting TDF is then converted to object code by an installer and linked using the system linker to produce an executable (see Fig. 1).

TDF producers have been or are being developed for C, Fortran 77, Ada, Dylan and C++ along with installers for SPARC, 80x86, MIPS, Alpha, PowerPC, HP/PA and ARM processors.

2.1 TDF's Tree Structure

The tree structure of TDF is defined as a multi-sorted abstract algebra. Each *sort* can be understood roughly as implementing a particular class of high level language construct. The most important TDF sorts are EXP, which represents executable operations (such as commands and expressions), and SHAPE which describes the types of the static-sized run-time values delivered and manipulated by EXPs. Each sort has a set of *constructors* (operators) each of which takes operands of known sort. Figure 2 specifies some of the EXP constructors. EXPs are annotated with their SHAPEs; there are SHAPEs for integer and floating point numbers, pointers, store offsets, and compounds of these values. The special shapes TOP and BOTTOM are used for constructs that return no usable value or that transfer control respectively.

```
plus (ERROR_TREATMENT,EXP INTEGER(v),EXP INTEGER(v)) -> EXP INTEGER(v)
make_int (v:VARIETY,SIGNED_NAT) -> EXP INTEGER(v)
assign (EXP POINTER(x),EXP(y)) -> EXP TOP
contents (s:SHAPE,EXP POINTER(x)) -> EXP s
integer_test (NTEST,LABEL,EXP INTEGER(v),EXP INTEGER(v)) -> EXP TOP
goto (LABEL) -> EXP BOTTOM
conditional (LABEL,EXP x,EXP z) -> EXP (x ⊔ z)
repeat (LABEL,EXP x,EXP z) -> EXP z
conditional (LABEL,EXP x,EXP z) -> EXP (x ⊔ z)
labelled (LIST(LABEL),EXP x,LIST(EXP)) -> EXP w
sequence (LIST(EXP),EXP x) -> EXP x
variable (OPTION(ACCESS),TAG,EXP x,EXP y) -> EXP y
identify (OPTION(ACCESS),TAG,EXP x,EXP y) -> EXP y
```

Fig. 2. some EXP constructors

The meaning of terms in the TDF algebra is specified in terms of the interleaved 'expression-like' evaluation of EXP constructors. Additional ordering may be imposed by declaration (initialiser before scope), sequence and by explicit jumps to LABELs. Values are delivered from operands to operators or passed via store using assignment and dereference.

The TDF specification [7] defines 53 different SORTS which are combined to produce an EXP for each procedure in a source language program. These EXPs are combined with SORTS describing linking information and global declarations to produce a TDF capsule.

2.2 Declarations and Ordering

Values may be bound to unique numeric identifiers called TAGs. **obtain_tag** delivers the value bound to its operand TAG. **identify** binds the result of evaluating its first EXP operand to a TAG that may then be used during evaluation of its second EXP operand. **variable** is similar but store is allocated to contain the initialising value and the TAG is bound to the address of this store. Declarations are also provided for global TAGs.

A few other EXP constructors also evaluate their EXP operands in order. The simplest is **sequence** which evaluates its operands from left to right and delivers the last operand's result. More general ordering is provided by explicit jumps such as **goto** and **integer_test**; target LABELs are scoped by the declarations **conditional**, **repeat** and **labelled**. **conditional(LB, XA, XB)** evaluates **XA** with LABEL LB available for forward jumps to **XB**. **repeat(LB, XA, XB)** evaluates **XA** then **XB** and LB is available in **XB** for backward jumps to the start of **XB**. Finally, **labelled(XA, LBi, Xi)** declares a list of labels **LBi** and a list of corresponding target EXPs, **Xi**. Evaluation starts with **XA** and any label **LBi** may be used in any EXP operand.

3   ThreadTDF

ThreadTDF extends TDF in a natural way with mechanisms to dynamically create and schedule fine-grain concurrent EXP evaluations that we call *featherweight* threads. These mechanisms are general enough to express a wide range of concurrency: they provide much of the functionality of existing thread libraries, such as POSIX threads, but allow concurrency within as well as between procedure instances. Featherweight threads execute within a shared address space by default, communication between address spaces is added using a notion of remote thread activation.

The execution of multiple featherweight threads within a procedure instance provides new opportunities for integrating resource allocation with scheduling. It often becomes possible to allocate machine resources (stack and registers) statically across threads. An implementation using hierarchical scheduling, described in Sec. 4, groups thread executions by procedure instance to exploit static allocation within the procedure.

Featherweight threads are self-scheduled: there is no notion of a thread handle other than the thread value representing a descheduled thread. We provide lightweight mutual exclusion between threads: other synchronisation operations can be constructed from exclusion and scheduling. More complex services, such as **kill_thread** or priority control, are implemented using self-scheduling. This approach was first proposed in [8] while considering TDF extensions to support compilation of the concurrent object language UC++.

A key aim of ThreadTDF is to allow efficient exploitation of uniprocessors. This is important for many reasons. It allows parallel programs to ride the rapid 'technology curve' of sequential hardware improvements. It supports multiprocessing. It also eases the software development process and encourages portability and scalability.

3.1 Featherweight Thread Operations

A featherweight thread is a concurrent execution of an EXP starting at a label. Thread label declarations have a *Single Entry Single Exit* (SESE) property: a thread is only allowed to complete (fall through) a declaration once all other threads enclosed by the same instance of the declaration have terminated. This means that the lifetime of many threads is bounded by the lifetime of their initial labels. We currently require that threads synchronise explicitly to enforce the SESE property, thereby putting the onus on the ThreadTDF producer. We are also considering adding thread declarations that provide the required thread synchronisations implicitly. Section 4 shows how the SESE property helps code generation.

Figure 3 contains the ThreadTDF constructors. These include a new shape called THREAD for values representing descheduled threads and a new sort called THDLB for thread labels. Modified forms of `conditional` and `labelled`, called `par_conditional` and `par_labelled`, are used to declare thread labels. Procedure return and jumps to external labels are forbidden within these constructs. An instance of a thread label is *replicated* if more than one thread is created or suspended at it or yields to it during its lifetime. Only `par_labelled` labels can be replicated and each of these labels is associated with an optional bound on its degree of replication.

A descheduled thread is created suspended at a THDLB by `create_thread`. An executing thread suspends itself at a THDLB using `suspend_thread`; execution continues in a new thread into which the suspended thread is delivered. Both creation and suspension are parameterised by pointers that address space at which a new thread's internal values can be stored. This space must be allocated explicitly by `variable` or by dynamic store allocation using the size delivered by `thread_size` (parameterised by the amount of store required for user thread-local values). A thread value can be scheduled for eventual execution using `schedule_thread`, and execution is terminated using `stop_thread` or `swap_thread`. Regular use of `yield_thread` is required so that cooperative scheduling can ensure fair independent progress.

A simple extension of thread creation and suspension provides creation and suspension at thread labels declared by previous procedure instances in the current procedure call chain. This can be used to create threads with unlimited lifetimes.

In some cases the new thread created at `suspend_thread` will never block[4] or call or return. In this case `nb_thread` can be used to supply space for the

---

[4] The blocking operations are: `mutex`, `suspend_thread` and `yield_thread`.

```
THREAD -> SHAPE
par_conditional (THDLB,OPT(EXP INTEGER(v)),EXP a,EXP b) -> EXP TOP
par_labelled (
  EXP a,LIST(OPT(EXP INTEGER(v))),LIST(THDLB),LIST(EXP b)) -> EXP TOP
create_thread (EXP POINTER,lb:THDLB) -> EXP THREAD
schedule_thread (EXP THREAD) -> EXP TOP
yield_thread (THDLB) -> EXP TOP
stop_thread -> EXP BOTTOM
suspend_thread (EXP POINTER,THDLB) -> EXP THREAD
thread_size (EXP OFFSET) -> EXP OFFSET
nb_thread -> EXP POINTER
swap_thread (THREAD) -> EXP BOTTOM
nbstop_thread -> EXP BOTTOM
nbswap_thread (THREAD) -> EXP BOTTOM
current_thread (EXP THREAD) ->
access_threadstore (EXP THREAD) -> EXP POINTER
make_null_thread -> EXP THREAD
test_thread (NTEST,LABEL,EXP THREAD,EXP THREAD) -> EXP TOP
KEY -> SHAPE
make_key -> EXP KEY
mutex (EXP POINTER,EXP b) -> EXP TOP
```

Fig. 3. basic thread operators

thread so long as it terminates using **nbstop_thread** or **nbswap_thread**.

Featherweight threads may synchronise using lightweight mutual exclusion. **mutex** takes a pointer to a key and executes its body EXP in mutual exclusion with all other bodies guarded by the same pointer. The body will not contain loops, thread label declarations, procedure calls or returns, or any other construct that may involve a context switch. This means that mutual exclusion comes for free when using cooperative scheduling on a uniprocessor.

ThreadTDF's 'continuation-passing' style of scheduling allows orthogonal combination of scheduling and mutex so, for example, threads can suspend into shared data structures under mutual exclusion. Thread termination within a mutex body or jumps to external labels cause the mutex to be released. Mutexes may be nested but in a correct TDF program the mutex pointer will always be strictly less, in some partial order, than that of any enclosing mutexes to prevent mutex deadlock.

3.2   Distributed Featherweight Thread Operations

We provide three mechanisms for communicating between address spaces. The simplest uses shared global TAGs to communicate static values: the runtime system implements any necessary communication. This mechanism is mainly used to bootstrap other forms of communication during program initialisation.

More complex communication mechanisms use remote values of shape RE-

MOTE. A value is converted to a remote by applying **make_remote**: the resulting value contains the original value, and the identity of the current processor (often an integer). The original value can be extracted from a remote by applying **localise** to it on the processor on which it was originally made.

A remote procedure value is used by **apply_proc_remote** which performs a blocking remote procedure call to the procedure on the processor on which the remote was created.

The *inlet* mechanism allows remote activation of a thread in an existing procedure instance on the target. An inlet is a form of featherweight thread with provision for arguments (similar to TAM inlets [4]). Figure 4 contains the inlet constructors. **make_inlets** declares a group of inlets and delivers their common 'environment'. Each inlet has a THDLB label, a list of formal parameter TAGs and shapes, and a body. **send** and **remote_send** allow asynchronous activation of an inlet using its label and environment. The list of inlet arguments supplied at the send must agree with the formals' declared shapes.

```
INLETENV -> SHAPE
make_inlets (LIST(THDLB),LIST(LIST(TAGSH)),LIST(EXP)) -> EXP INLETENV
send (EXP INLETENV,THDLB,LIST(EXP)) -> EXP TOP
remote_send (EXP REMOTE INLETENV,THDLB,LIST(EXP)) -> EXP TOP
```

Fig. 4. inlet operators

Experiences with active messages [16] and TAM inlets [4] indicate it may be necessary to impose appropriate disciplines on inlet use e.g. to prevent deadlock in the network or to simplify buffer allocation.

4 Implementing ThreadTDF

We now describe implementation techniques for the ThreadTDF operations. We use a form of *hierarchical cooperative scheduling*: preemption could also be used but is more complex. We have used these implementation techniques in a ThreadTDF installer for the SPARC processor built using the existing TDF SPARC installer. The ThreadTDF installer acts as the code generator for a Parallel TDF system for compiling occam and for compiling our own dynamically threaded dialect of C. Section 4.2 gives initial performance results.

Our ThreadTDF installer implements the scheduling of featherweight threads explicitly in terms of operations on a bidirectional ring of bidirectional rings[5]: a global ring of procedure instances and a local ring of thread instances for each procedure instance (shown in Fig. 5). We perform register and store allocation of variables across all threads in a procedure so that we can make context switches

---

[5] The ring structure provides fairness, if fairness were not required a stack would do.

within a procedure (around a local ring) cheap. Context switches between procedures (around the global ring) are usually more expensive. The hierarchy could
be extended to include further subrings for contexts within a procedure.

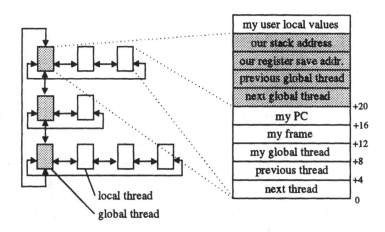

Fig. 5. data structures for hierarchical thread scheduling

A thread is scheduled by inserting it in its local ring but it only actually
executes when this ring becomes current. This 'lazy' scheduling generates more
local concurrency between global context switches and enhances locality[6].

4.1 Implementing Featherweight Threads

The first main task of the ThreadTDF installer is to provide dynamic control
transfer for independent thread progress; the ring-of-rings data structure and
thread data structure we use for this purpose are shown in 5. Below we describe
how register allocation supports scheduling using these structures.

The second main task is to implement procedure local variables. These are
allocated in registers, on a single common stack, and on the heap. The nesting of
variables within thread declarations induces a tree of *frames*, each frame containing nested variables with the same degree of replication and local to the same
threads. Frames are allocated using the most efficient applicable mechanism.
The SESE structure of thread declarations improves this process as it ensures
all lifetimes nest properly and this reduces the connectedness of the variable interference graph. This allows better reuse of registers and store locations which
in turn improves access latency and spatial density and reduces dynamic allocation overhead. The SESE structure also ensures that the degree of replication
nests properly.

---

[6] It is also possible to execute threads eagerly where advantageous e.g. when scheduling
a thread in the current procedure instance that is known to run without blocking.

The third main task is to implement concurrent procedure calls. We wish to reuse the optimised sequential procedure calling convention so each concurrent call potentially requires a new system stack. The installer must also save and restore a procedure's local registers at global context switches and at procedure call. Callee-save registers are a particular issue (see below).

The final task of the installer is to implement as many standard sequential optimisations as possible in the presence of concurrency.

We will not discuss the implementation of inlets in detail here. An inlet is activated using active message mechanisms [16] but the target activation executes in a shared pre-existing procedure instance (see [4] for more detail).

Intraprocedural Concurrency. A THREAD value is simply a pointer to a region of memory containing the thread-local system and user values (shown in Fig. 5, shaded values are present only in global threads). We allocate variables to registers and store in such a way that only the program counter register needs to be saved for a thread. We do this by ensuring that register usage at context switch targets is a subset of the usage at context switch sources. In our implementation all context switches start at yield_thread, stop_thread, or swap_thread (or the non-blocking equivalents) and end at a thread label. The SESE property of thread declarations ensures that only variables in scope or declared in a concurrent operand of an enclosing thread declaration can be live at any point.

Each procedure maintains a pointer to the current local thread, usually in a register. Local context switch can be implemented in three machine operations: (1) load the next local thread's address (2) retrieve its PC (3) jump to it. This seems to work well for our applications because there are usually enough SPARC registers to hold the variables live at context switch targets. When we run out of registers we allocate the remaining variables to store but we could also provide thread-local register allocation if we were prepared to spill these registers at context switches.

Scheduling operations, such as create_thread and schedule_thread are implemented in terms of simple pointer operations on the scheduling data structures. Every thread is created containing the address of its global thread (this may need to be updated in called procedures) so it can always be scheduled by inserting it in the local ring at this thread. Non-blocking threads need no entry in the scheduling data structures so thread operations on non-blocking threads are often particularly simple.

Local Variables. A local variable is *atomic* if its scope contains no thread label declarations. Atomic variables can be allocated to register or stack using sequential techniques because they are never live at any context switch target. Unfortunately non-atomic variables require a more involved treatment.

A procedure's non-atomic local variables are allocated in registers and in a tree of frames spread across the stack and heap. Together these mechanisms provide the logical 'tree-of-frames' structure induced by the nesting of concurrency in variable scopes. The installer analyses the thread declaration structure and local variable declarations to construct the largest possible frames, and to determine the number of replicated instances if possible. Dynamically replicated frames are allocated on the heap, others on the stack. Dynamic allocation is performed on entering a thread declaration and released on exit. create_thread and suspend_thread operations initialise their threads' frame pointers, if required, using the next free frame for the given thread label (the continuation of a suspended thread inherits the suspended thread's frame). If there is no free frame then a new chunk of frames is allocated and added to a free list associated with the label.

Interprocedural Concurrency. Many ThreadTDF procedure calls are purely sequential and can be executed with a normal sequential procedure call. This includes calls outside thread declarations or when the local ring contains only one local thread. External procedures, those that are not generated by the installer, can also be treated as sequential (though not external calls that call back to internal procedures). Run-to-completion calls, using apply_rtc_proc, can also be treated as sequential in many cases. All other procedure calls are concurrent.

Concurrent procedure calls impose a (mainly) small overhead due to the need to manage concurrency. In the worst case a new global thread is allocated and a new stack for the call to execute upon. After this the call uses existing sequential mechanisms. Sometimes it may be possible for an installer to determine the size of stack to allocate at a call, otherwise we resort either to guessing, or to using stack check mechanisms. The stack size problem is particular difficult when calling external procedures, it is probably best to sequentialise these calls on a system stack so that the normal stack checking mechanisms apply. Further overhead may be required to tidy up callee-save registers when a call returns if it has been interrupted for continued execution of a thread in the calling procedure.

Figure 5 shows how a ring of global threads is constructed, one for each procedure instance, to allow independent progress of concurrent calls. A local context switch to the global thread causes, with compiler-controlled frequency, a global context switch to the next procedure instance in the global ring. This switch must save the outgoing thread's registers (and register windows on the SPARC) and restore the registers of the target procedure instance.

We are also experimenting with lazy allocation techniques that reduce concurrency overhead when execution is sequential. For example, procedure calls can execute on their caller's stack so long as the calling procedure is provided with a new stack if it is rescheduled concurrently with the call.

4.2 Measurements

Figure 6 describes the wall-clock durations of individual featherweight thread operations. Times were measured on a SPARCstation 10 model 30 in single user mode. For comparison [11] cites thread creation times in the range 400–1300μs and thread switch times between 21 and 81μs for thread packages (including the

Sun Lightweight Process library) on the SPARCstation 10. Notice that the duration of **thread_create** depends on the degree of replication of any non-atomic variables in the new thread. Dynamically replicated variables are allocated in chunks for many threads at once using **malloc**. Our figures show how the per-thread overhead due to **malloc** increases as chunk size decreases from 1000 thread instances to 1.

Operation	Duration (μs)	
empty call	0.25	empty sequential call
create thread	0.18	no replicated variables
create thread	0.44	statically replicated variables
create thread	0.50–1.90	dynamically replicated variables
schedule thread	0.18	
local yield	0.23	between threads in the same procedure instance
global yield	14.0	between concurrent caller and callee procedures
concurrent call	16.0	set up stack and scheduling structures at call

Fig. 6. thread performance on a Sun SPARCStation 10

Figure 7 compares performance of two simple occam programs compiled using ThreadTDF and using the Southampton Portable Occam Compiler (SPOC)[5]. SPOC compiles occam to C which was then compiled using tcc or gcc (-O2). tcc is the TDF C compiler from which the ThreadTDF installer is derived. *daxpy* is a simple numeric kernel performing a floating point add and multiply per iteration. The inner loop is sequential in the SPOC version and parallel in the ThreadTDF version but the parallelism is eliminated during compilation so the end results are identical. *comstime* passes a value around a ring of channels connecting four occam processes. Here the iteration time measures the cost of four complete channel synchronisations and some internal scheduling overhead.

Platform	Application	Compiler	Iteration Time (μs)
SS10	daxpy	SPOC and GNU gcc	0.30
SS10	daxpy	SPOC and tcc	0.35
SS10	daxpy	ThreadTDF	0.35
25MHz T800	comstime	Inmos occam	12.0
SS10	comstime	SPOC and GNU gcc	12.0
SS10	comstime	SPOC and tcc	23.0
SS10	comstime	ThreadTDF	5.0

Fig. 7. performance of compiled occam

5 Related Work and Conclusion

As far as we know, ThreadTDF is the first language- and machine-independent intermediate representation for compiling concurrency. However many parts of the problem have been considered before.

Much work on compiling parallel languages has considered bulk parallelism and SPMD computation[14, 1, 12]. We believe that ThreadTDF should provide a suitable implementation substrate for these languages, though many optimisations and distribution transformations will be performed outside ThreadTDF, perhaps using ParTDF[15].

Another common approach uses portable libraries, e.g. PVM or POSIX threads, to support the compilation of concurrency. The level of functionality provided by such libraries can impose significant performance costs[10, 13] particularly when the source language allows both communication and concurrency.

Newer libraries, such as MPI and Chant[11], support communication with concurrency. Some, such as Nexus [9], are even designed as compiler targets. Nexus lacks featherweight threads, but otherwise provides services similar to ThreadTDF. It also supports global pointers and heterogeneous machines which ThreadTDF does not, yet. Despite the continued evolution of libraries, we still expect an intermediate representation to offer better performance. Firstly, procedure calls add their own overhead: call and return on a SPARC costs about the same as a *featherweight* context switch. Secondly, procedure calls to libraries prevent sharing in registers. Finally, the structure of an intermediate representation can support many important techniques, such as featherweight threads, that would not otherwise be possible. Technologies based on TDF should be widely portable, though libraries may be more widely available, at least initially.

ThreadTDF is close in spirit to the Threaded Abstract Machine [4]. Inlets and featherweight threads are similar to TAM inlets, but are not bound to execute to completion. Unlike TAM, ThreadTDF preserves sequential control structure and also supports more general thread operations.

In future we hope to improve support for distribution, add further source languages and perhaps add support for restricted scheduling disciplines, such as those considered in [2]. Our implementation techniques could be improved in many areas including register allocation, and dynamic store management. Also outstanding are consideration of remote memory access, memory consistency and of heterogeneous processing.

Finally it is worth noting that the ThreadTDF implementation techniques, if applied widely, may have significant implications for processor design.

References

1. V. Bala and J. Ferrante. Explicit data placement(XDP): A methodology for explicit compile-time representation and optimisation of data movement. *ACM SIG-PLAN notices*, 28(1):28–31, January 1993.
2. Robert D. Blumofe and Charles E. Leiserson. Scheduling multithreaded computations by work stealing. In *Proceedings of the 35th Annual Symposium on Foun-*

dations of Computer Science (FOCS '94), pages 356–368, Santa Fe, New Mexico, November 1994.

3. Frédéric Broustaut, Christian Fabre, François de Ferrière, Éric Ivanov, and Mauro Fiorentini. Verification of ANDF components. In *Proceedings of the 1995 ACM Workshop on Intermediate Representations*, 1995.

4. Daved E. Culler, Seth Copen Goldstein, Klaus Erik Schauser, and Thorsten von Eicken. TAM - a compiler controlled threaded abstract machine. Report, Computer science division, University of California, 1993.

5. Mark Debbage, Mark Hill, Sean Wykes, and Denis Nicole. *Southampton's Portable Occam Compiler (SPOC): User Guide*. University of Southampton, Southampton, UK, March 1994.

6. Stephen L. Diamond and Gianluigi Castelli. Architecture Neutral Distribution Format (ANDF). *IEEE Micro*, 14(6):73–76, December 1994.

7. DRA. *TDF Specification, Issue 3*. Open Software Systems Group, St. Andrews Rd, Malvern, Worcs, WR14 3PS, UK, March 1994. Obtainable via WWW from http://riwww.osf.org:8001/andf/andf.papers/toc.html.

8. P. W. Edwards, D. I. Bruce, D. J. C. Hutchinson, I. F. Currie, and P. D. Hammond. TDF and parallel object oriented languages. Deliverable 2.2 IED3/1/1059, Defense Research Agency, Open Software Systems Group, St. Andrews Rd, Malvern, Worcs, WR14 3PS, UK, 1992. October.

9. Ian Foster, Carl Kesselman, and Steven Tuecke. Nexus: Runtime support for task-parallel programming languages. Technical report, Mathematics and Computer Science Division, Argonne National Laboratory, Argonne, IL, 1994.

10. E. W. Giering, Frank Mueller, and T. P. Baker. Implementing Ada 9X features using POSIX threads: Design issues (draft). Technical report, New York University, Computer Science Department, New York, NY 10003, USA, 1993.

11. Matthew Haines, David Cronk, and Piyush Mehrotra. On the design of Chant: A talking threads package. In *Proceedings of Supercomputing 94*, pages 350–359, November 1994. Washington, DC.

12. S. Hiranandani, K. Kennedy, and C. Tseng. Preliminary experiences with the Fortran D compiler. In *Supercomputing 93*, pages 338–350, November 1993. Portland, Oregon.

13. Wilson C. Hsieh, Kirk L. Johnson, M. Frans Kaashoek, Deborah A. Wallach, and William E. Weihl. Efficient implementation of high-level languages on user-level communication architectures. Technical report, MIT, Massachusetts Institute of Technology, Laboratory for Computer Science, Cambridge, Massachusetts 02139, May 1994.

14. V. B. Muchnick and A. V. Shafarenko. F-code: A portable software platform for data-parallel lanaguages. Technical report, Dept. of Electronic and Electrical Engineering, University of Surrey, April 1992.

15. Ben Sloman and Tom Lake. Extending TDF for concurrency and distribution. Report, GLOSSA, 59 Alexandra Road, Reading, RG1 5PG, UK, January 1995.

16. T. von Eicken, D. E. Culler, S. C. Goldstein, and K. E. Schauser. Active messages: a mechanism for integrated communication and computation. In *Proceedings of the 19th International Symposium on Computer Architecture*, pages 256–266, May 1992. Gold Coast, Australia.

Applications

Parallel N-Body Simulation on a Large-Scale Homogeneous Distributed System *

John W. Romein and Henri E. Bal

Vrije Universiteit, Department of Mathematics and Computer Science,
Amsterdam, The Netherlands, {*john,bal*} @*cs.vu.nl*

Abstract. A processor pool is a homogeneous collection of processors that are used for computationally intensive tasks, such as parallel programs. Processor pools are far less expensive than multicomputers and more convenient to use than collections of idle workstations. This paper gives a case study in parallel programming on a processor pool with 80 SPARCs connected by an Ethernet, running the Amoeba distributed operating system. We use a realistic application (N-body simulation of water molecules) and show that a good performance can be obtained. We measured a speedup of 72 on 80 processors.

1 Introduction

Networks of idle workstations are often used for running parallel applications. Many institutes have a distributed computing system consisting of many powerful workstations, which are idle most of the time. Using this (otherwise wasted) processing power for running coarse-grained parallel applications thus seems attractive.

Unfortunately, this approach to parallel processing also has several disadvantages, which are caused by the heterogeneous nature of such distributed systems. Most institutes have different types of workstations running different operating systems, which were not designed for parallel programming. The workstations usually run dozens of daemon processes that occasionally become active, so the workstations are not really idle. The machines are typically connected by various networks, which are used heavily for file transfers and other applications.

These factors make it difficult to obtain good performance for parallel programs that run on collections of workstations. Load balancing, for example, becomes very difficult on such systems, because processors may run at different speeds or may not have all CPU cycles available for the parallel program. Also, the performance measurements are obscured by many external factors (e.g., congestion of the network due to large file transfers or page swapping) and thus are hard to reproduce.

The problems described above do not occur with multicomputers, since these are usually constructed out of identical processors which all run a single operating system. Also, the interconnection network on modern multicomputers is orders of a magnitude faster than current local area networks, thus allowing more fine-grained parallelism.

---

* This research is supported by a PIONIER grant from the Netherlands Organization for Scientific Research (N.W.O.).

Unfortunately, multicomputers are very expensive, whereas using idle workstations essentially is for free.

An attractive alternative to collections of workstations and multicomputers is the *processor pool model* [8]. A processor pool is a homogeneous collection of processors shared among all users of a distributed system. The processors are used for computationally intensive tasks. At any moment, the pool can run many applications from different users, a parallel application from one user, or a combination of these. The processors are connected by a local area network and do not have any peripheral devices (like displays or disks), thus making them very cheap.

In this paper, we present a case study in parallel processing on a fairly large-scale processor pool. We will show that excellent and reproducible speedups can be obtained for a realistic application. Since processor pools are far less expensive than multicomputers, this case study indicates that they are a feasible platform for parallel processing. Another contribution of this paper is a description of several optimizations that can be applied to such applications, to reduce the communication overhead.

The paper is organized as follows. In Sect. 2, we describe the computing environment we use. The hardware consists of 80 SPARC processors connected by an Ethernet and runs the Amoeba distributed operating system. Next, in Sect. 3, we discuss the application that we have used in our case study. The application is one of the SPLASH [7] applications: the simulation of water molecules. The original N-body simulation program was written for shared memory machines. We have rewritten the program to run on a distributed system. Section 4 describes our distributed water simulation program. Next, in Sect. 5 we study the performance of the program on the Amoeba processor pool and show that high speedups can be obtained. In Sect. 6, we give some conclusions and we look at related work.

2 The Amoeba Processor Pool

This section describes our computing environment. The hardware is described in Sect. 2.1 and the Amoeba operating system is discussed in Sect. 2.2.

2.1 The Processor Pool

The processors in the pool are connected by a 10 Mbit/s Ethernet. To increase the bandwidth of the network, multiple Ethernet segments are used, which are connected by a low-cost switch. There are ten segments of eight processors each. Some special servers (e.g., file servers) are on separate segments.

The segments are connected by a Kalpana switch. The switch forwards Ethernet packets between segments as follows:

- A packet with both the source and the destination on the same segment is not forwarded to other segments.
- A packet with the source and destination on different segments is forwarded with a very small delay (40 μs). The overhead of the switch is negligible compared to the latency of Ethernet packets. The switch uses a crossbar architecture. The advantage

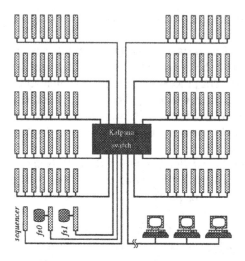

Fig. 1. The Amoeba processor pool.

of using a switch is that multiple pairs of processors can communicate at the same time, provided that the messages do not conflict. Packets sent to the same segment do conflict; in this case the switch can buffer up to 256 packets.
- A multicast packet is forwarded with about the same delay as a unicast packet to all other segments.

The processor boards are SPARCclassic clones made by Tatung. Each board is equipped with one 50 MHz Texas Instruments V8-SPARC processor (a TMS390S10). All processor pool boards have 32 Mb RAM. In addition there is one processor board that has 128 Mb RAM. This board is used by the sequencer [4] of Amoeba's multicast protocol.

The processor pool can be regarded as a low-cost multicomputer. (Its total cost, including 80 SPARCs, 2.5 Gb memory, the network, switch, file servers, sequencer, and packaging is about US$ 350,000). Alternatively, the machine can be regarded as an idealized version of the idle workstations model. It has the same architecture as a homogeneous collection of workstations on a network.

2.2 Amoeba

The operating system we use is Amoeba [8]. Amoeba is designed with the processor pool model in mind. It assumes that the system contains a large number of processors, so all servers (e.g., file server, directory server) run on separate processors, as user processes. User programs are run on the processor pool, using as many processors as the application requires. One of the main advantages of this software organization is that idle processors on Amoeba are truly idle and do not run any daemon processes.

Amoeba is a capability-based microkernel, which basically provides processes, kernel-level threads, synchronization mechanisms, and communication protocols. There are two high-level communication protocols: *Group Communication* [4] and *Remote Procedure Calls* [1].

Reliable communication between two processes is done with the Remote Procedure Call (RPC) primitives `getreq`, `putrep`, and `trans`. A server thread that wants to accept an RPC request calls `getreq` and blocks until a request arrives. Client threads can invoke remote procedures with the `trans` primitive, which blocks until the server thread returns a reply message using `putrep`.

Group communication is supported with multicast messages. A process can send a message to all members of a group using the `grp_send` primitive. The Amoeba kernel buffers the messages until the application does a `grp_receive`. The protocol is reliable and totally-ordered, which means that all machines receive all messages in the same order [4]. The implementation is efficient. A `grp_send` merely costs two low level messages in the normal case, independent of the number of receivers.

3 The 'Water' Program

We have used an N-body simulation program as a case study for programming the Amoeba processor pool. The program, called *Water*, simulates a system in which H_2O molecules move in an imaginary box. The molecules interact with each other by gravitational forces, and the atoms within a molecule also interact with each other.

The computation is repeated over a user-specified number of timesteps. During a timestep (in the order of femto-seconds = 10^{-15} s), the Newtonian equations of motion for the water molecules are set up and solved using Gear's sixth-order predictor-corrector method [3]. The forces between and within the molecules are computed, and the total potential energy of the system is calculated. The box size is large enough to hold all molecules. Physicists use the program to predict a variety of static and dynamic properties of water in liquid state.

The original *Water* program was written in FORTRAN and is included in the Perfect Club [2] set of supercomputing benchmarks. It is completely sequential. The SPLASH [7] version is a rewrite of the sequential FORTRAN code to a parallel C program. This version is designed to run on shared memory multiprocessors.

We have reimplemented the SPLASH version (again in C) to run on a distributed architecture without a shared address space. This program is a complete reimplementation, because many changes were needed to have it run efficiently on a distributed machine. Our implementation uses explicit message passing (RPC and multicast).

A major issue in implementing a program like *Water* on a processor pool is how to reduce the communication overhead. The program potentially sends a very large number of messages over the Ethernet. We have addressed this problem by carefully analyzing the communication behavior of the program and by optimizing the most important cases, as will be discussed in Sect. 4.

Although the three *Water* implementations are quite different from each other, they share the same program structure, as shown in Fig. 2. The statements shown in bold face are only used in our distributed program.

During initialization, the program reads the input data, which contains the number of molecules that should be simulated, their initial positions and velocities, the length of one timestep, how many timesteps the program should simulate, and how often the results

```
int main()
{
        Set up scaling factors and constants;
        Read positions and velocities;
        Estimate accelerations;
        Send updates of accelerations;

        while (compute another timestep)
        {
                Compute predictions;
                Multicast positions;
                Compute forces within a molecule;
                Compute forces between molecules;
                Send updates of forces;
                Correct predictions;
                Put molecules back inside the box if they moved out;
                Compute kinetic energy;

                if (print results of this timestep)
                {
                        Multicast positions;
                        Compute potential energy;
                        Use tree RPC to compute shared sum;
                        Print results;
                }
        }
}
```

Fig. 2. Main loop of the *Water* program.

should be printed. Then it computes the boxsize, some input-dependent and -independent constants, and finally it does some implementation-dependent initializations.

After initialization, the program repeatedly performs the predictions, computes intra- and intermolecular forces, the kinetic energy, places molecules that moved out of the box back inside the box, and corrects the predictions. If the results of that timestep should be printed, the potential energy of the system is computed and displayed.

4   A Distributed 'Water' Program

In this section, we will describe how we developed a distributed *Water* program that runs efficiently on the Amoeba processor pool. In general, porting a program from a shared memory machine to a distributed memory machine requires the following changes:

– The shared data must be partitioned over the available machines, or replicated on several machines. This requires a careful study of the way in which the processes access the shared data.
– Synchronization and access to remote memories must be done by passing messages.
– The parallel algorithm must be adapted such that the number of messages sent across the network is minimal.

We carefully studied the SPLASH implementation, but ultimately decided to rewrite almost all of it (except for some code computing mathematical formulas). The main reason for rewriting the program was to obtain an efficient implementation on a distributed system. We have determined several important optimizations that reduce the communication overhead significantly. In the following subsections, we will discuss the work distribution and data distribution in the program, and we will analyze the complexity of the computations and communication.

4.1 Work Distribution

Both the SPLASH program and the distributed program achieve work distribution by partitioning the molecules over the available processors. Each processor 'owns' a number of molecules and does all computations needed for that molecule. The distribution is done statically. As soon as the input is read (and the number of molecules is known) the molecules are assigned to the processors. No provision is made to dynamically balance the load of each processor. Dynamic load balancing would be very hard to implement efficiently in this application.

4.2 Data Distribution

Apart from some shared sums that are needed for the computation of the potential energy, the most important data structure in the distributed memory program is a large four-dimensional array. This array holds the data for all molecules. Figure 3 shows the declarations of the shared data in simplified form.

```
#define MAX_MOLECULES 4096
#define MAX_ORDER       8 /* POS, VEL, ACC, 3rd .. 6th derivatives, FORCES */
#define NR_ATOMS        3 /* H1, O, H2 */
#define NR_DIRS         3 /* X, Y, Z */

double data [MAX_MOLECULES] [MAX_ORDER] [NR_ATOMS] [NR_DIRS];

#define NR_SHARED_SUMS   6

double potential_energy [NR_SHARED_SUMS];
```

Fig. 3. Shared data declarations.

For each molecule, the *position, velocity, acceleration*, the $3^{rd} \ldots 6^{th}$ *derivatives*, and the *forces* are obtained through the second index value, for *each atom* and in *each direction*.

Each processor allocates storage for the entire array, although this is not strictly necessary, since only a small part of the array is really used. However, even with thousands of molecules only a few megabytes of memory are needed, so this allocation scheme did not turn out to be a problem. Efficient access to the data is more important.

To illustrate how the program distributes the data of the molecules, consider Fig. 4, which shows an example with 12 molecules and 4 processors. Each processor is the

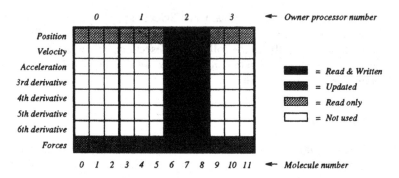

Fig. 4. Example of data distribution on processor 2 if $p = 4$ and $n = 12$.

owner of $\frac{12}{4} = 3$ molecules. Only the home processor of a molecule has all the molecule's data available. The positions and forces are implemented as described below. The remaining pieces of information are private to the owner.

The *positions* of the molecules (or rather the H and O atoms within the molecules) are replicated everywhere. After being computed, the positions are read many times by many processors, so it is evident that they should be replicated to obtain good performance.

The *forces* acting on the molecules are updated (i.e. incremented) very frequently by all processors. As we will describe in Sect. 4.5, updating of the forces can be implemented efficiently by having each processor first compute local sums of partial forces and then communicate the final values of these local sums.

The program tries to overlap communication and computation as much as possible. If a processor knows that other processors will need its data, these data are sent in advance, as soon as they are available. The receiver picks up a message (or waits for it) when it needs the data. This is more efficient than to let the processor that needs the data initiate a request for the data followed by a reply from the supplier. The way it is implemented now, synchronization comes for free: one message is used for both synchronization and shipping data.

In the next three subsections, we discuss three aspects of data distribution in our program: the replication of positions, the implementation of partial sums, and the updating of remote forces. Finally, we will give a complexity analysis of the communication and computation times.

4.3 Replication of Positions Using Multicast Messages

Figure 4 shows that the positions of all molecules are replicated everywhere. As these molecules move in the box, their positions have to be updated sometimes. This happens at two synchronization points (see also Fig. 2):

- after the predictions and before the computation of the inter-molecular forces,
- if the results of the current timestep should be printed, the positions of the molecules are needed for the computation of the potential energy.

To update replicated positions, we use the Amoeba multicast primitives. Each processor marshalls all positions of the atoms in the molecules that it owns into one message and multicasts it to all processors. Next, the processor receives one message from each other processor, containing the positions of the other molecules' atoms. If there are n molecules and p processors, each message contains updates for $\frac{n}{p}$ molecules and for each molecule nine doubles are needed (three atoms, H, O and H, in three directions), so a message contains $72\frac{n}{p}$ bytes of data. In addition, each message has 8 bytes of fixed information, so the total number of bytes transferred over the network is $72n + 8p$. This number excludes the headers prepended by the various network software layers.

4.4 Implementing Shared Sums

A different kind of synchronization is needed for the computation of the potential energy. The total potential energy is the sum of some partial values computed by the individual processors. Processor 0 prints the total potential energy, so only this processor needs to know the total. In fact, six shared sums are computed at the same time.

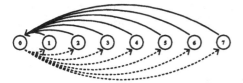

Fig. 5. Naive implementation of computing a shared sum.

Fig. 6. Indirect RPCs in a conceptual tree.

A naive way to implement this is to let each processor send an RPC message to processor 0 containing a partial value, and let processor 0 add those values together (see Fig. 5). The request messages, indicated by a solid line, carry those values. The reply messages, drawn with a dashed line, are empty. This means that processor 0 receives $p - 1$ subsequent RPCs, surely becoming a bottleneck if p is large.

Figure 6 shows a much more efficient implementation, which avoids the bottleneck. Informally, processors receive some RPCs with partial values, add these values together and initiate an RPC to another processor, using a conceptual tree-structure. Processor 0 eventually receives some values and adds these together to obtain the final sum. Most RPCs can be done simultaneously, and no processor receives more than $\lceil \log p \rceil$ messages. We have used this scheme in our program.

4.5 Updating Remote Forces

Computation of the inter-molecular forces is done by computing the pair-wise interactions between molecules. This is an $\mathcal{O}(\frac{n^2}{p})$ problem. If the distance between a pair is *less* than half the boxsize, the force between the molecules is computed by the owner processor of one of them. Otherwise, the force is not computed but neglected. If the other molecule resides on another processor, communication will be necessary.

To compute the force between two molecules one needs the positions of both molecules. Positions are fully replicated, so they are available on the processor that does the computation. Once the force is computed, it has to be added to the total force of both molecules. One of the molecules resides on the processor where the computation is done, so the force can be added immediately. This cannot be done for the other molecule, because it may be on another processor, so we need to do communication here.

The total force acting on a molecule is the sum of partial forces. Each molecule receives updates from approximately half the other molecules, and sends updates to the other half. To reduce communication overhead, we combine updates to several molecules into one RPC. Each processor needs to send an RPC to approximately half the other processors, so the total number of RPCs approximates $p\frac{p}{2} = \mathcal{O}(p^2)$. Each RPC contains updates for $\frac{n}{p}$ molecules, which takes about $72\frac{n}{p}$ bytes. Hence, a total of $36np$ bytes are sent over the network.

4.6 Complexity Analysis of Communication and Computation Time

Before presenting performance measurements, we will first discuss the complexity of the communication and the computations done by the *Water* program. Figure 7 summarizes the total number of messages and the total number of bytes sent during one timestep, as discussed in the last three subsections.

Sync. point	# RPCs	# multicasts	# bytes
Multicast positions	–	p	$72n + 8p$
Update forces	$\frac{p^2}{2}$	–	$36np$
Multicast positions	–	p	$72n + 8p$
Update potential energy	$p - 1$	–	$48(p - 1)$
Total	$\frac{p^2}{2} + p - 1$	$2p$	$36np + 144n + 64p - 48$

Fig. 7. Total number of RPCs, multicasts, and bytes sent per timestep.

With regard to computation time, the most time consuming part of the program is the routine where the inter-molecular forces are computed. For each molecule owned by some processor, the interactions with half the other molecules are computed, thus the complexity for this computation is $\mathcal{O}(\frac{n^2}{p})$.

The amount of time that is needed for the communication is $\mathcal{O}(np)$. If we compare this to the computational complexity, $\mathcal{O}(\frac{n^2}{p})$, we see that the ratio between computation and communication time will be high if n is large. It is important to maintain tens of molecules per processor to obtain reasonable speedups.

5 Performance Measurements

The measurements of the distributed program were done on the Amoeba processor pool described in Sect. 2. All processors ran an Amoeba 5.2 kernel. The application was

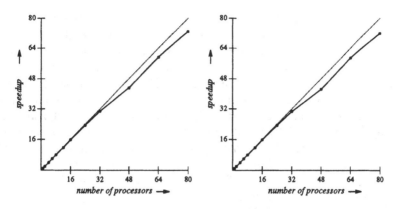

Fig. 8. Speedups obtained on up to 80 processors. The left figure shows speedups without computation of the potential energy, the right figure shows the speedups for the second timestep.

p	# RPCs	# multicasts	# bytes	# RPCs	# multicasts	# bytes
		Theoretical values			*Measured values*	
2	3	4	884816	3	4	884816
80	3279	160	12391376	3317	160	12530136

Fig. 9. Theoretical and measured values for $n = 4096$ molecules.

compiled with gcc 2.5.8 with the -O2 -mv8 options. An input file for 4096 molecules was generated. The molecules were placed in a $16 \times 16 \times 16$ box and initialized with random velocities.

During each run two values are measured. First, the execution time of the second timestep without the computation of the potential energy was measured (as in the SPLASH paper). They did not measure the first timestep, to avoid cold-start cache misses. Second, to get a more realistic impression of the total speedup, the execution time of the entire second timestep was measured. The speedups for the program (relative to the single CPU case) are shown in Fig. 8.

On a single SPARC processor, the entire second timestep takes 7451.9 seconds. On 80 processors, it takes about 103.5 seconds, so a 72 fold speedup is obtained. If the computation of the potential energy is omitted, the speedup is even 73. The efficiency is similar to that obtained by the original SPLASH implementation on a shared-memory multiprocessor, although we use a larger problem size (4096 molecules instead of 288).

The execution times are reproducible. The differences in execution times generally are well below 1%. In one case we measured a difference of 4.1%.

To analyze the performance, we have looked at the RPC and multicast messages generated by the program. Figure 9 shows the theoretical and measured values for the total number of RPCs, multicast messages, and bytes sent on 2 and 80 processors using 4096 molecules. The theoretical values are based on the formulas in Fig. 7. For 80 processors the measured values differ somewhat, because p is not a power of 2 and n is not a multiple of 80, leading to an uneven distribution of the molecules.

It is also interesting to see how large the messages are. With 80 processors, each multicast message and most (97.6%) RPC requests are about 3.6 Kb. All RPC replies are null-messages. Large messages are split into several Ethernet packets.

As an advantage over an architecture with a single Ethernet segment, the Kalpana switch allows simultaneous message delivery in two different ways (see Sect. 2.1). First, the majority of the messages (a little under 90%) are unicast messages that must be forwarded from one segment to another. As long as the destinations are not on the same segment, different messages can be delivered in parallel. Second, about 10% of the messages are unicast messages with the source and destination on the same segment. The switch does not forward these messages, so the other segments are still available for other messages. Finally, 2.4% of the messages are multicast messages that must be forwarded to all other segments. This involves all segments, so different multicast messages cannot be sent simultaneously.

For 80 processors, about 12.5 Mb of data are sent in a little more than 100 seconds. On average, each processor sends about 160 Kb of data. Since the Ethernet has a bandwidth of 10 Mbit/sec, each processor in theory spends only a small amount of time (less than a second) doing communication. However, the communication is very bursty. The network is idle for a long time and then all processors start to send data at the same moment. We have measured that the delays for sending and receiving data at the different synchronization points can be as high as 7 seconds, so the network still is a limiting factor.

Besides the network, another reason why the speedup is less than 80 is the fact that the load is not balanced optimally. With 4096 molecules and 80 processors, some processors are assigned 51 molecules and others get 52 molecules. This leads to a small load imbalance.

We also implemented two alternative schemes for updating the remote forces [6], but measurements showed that the scheme described above yields better speedups and absolute execution times, at least with 80 processors and 4096 molecules.

6 Conclusions and Related Work

We have implemented a parallel N-body simulation program on the Amoeba processor pool. We have used the SPLASH shared-memory program as a starting point, but we rewrote almost all of it. The reason for rewriting it was that several optimizations were necessary to reduce the communication overhead. The result (for a large input problem) is a speedup of 72 on 80 processors. We think this speedup is excellent, given the fact that we use a slow and unreliable network (Ethernet) and fast, modern processors (50 MHz SPARCs).

The experiment thus has shown that good performance can be obtained for a realistic application on the processor pool. The main advantage of the processor pool model over the idle workstations model lies in the possibility to allocate the processors and the network segments exclusively to one (parallel) application. The program will not be slowed down by other activities on the processors or network, such as daemon processes or file transfers. Compared with a multicomputer, the processor pool is far less expensive. As should be clear from the previous sections, however, porting a program like *Water* from a shared memory machine to a distributed system requires a significant effort.

The SPLASH program has also been ported to Jade [5]. Jade is a high-level parallel programming language for managing coarse grained concurrency. The C language is extended to provide the programmer a shared address space and the idea of sequential programming. A Jade programmer provides information about how shared data are accessed. The paper shows several results with their implementation of *Water* running on different parallel architectures. The architecture that looks most like ours consists of 32 SPARC ELCs, connected by a 10 Mbit/s Ethernet. They obtain a speedup of a factor 12 using 24 processors; with more processors the speedup decreases. Using other architectures they obtain considerably better speedups. The reason they get inferior speedups is that they try to automate the communication for fine grained access to distributed shared memory, while we hand-optimized the accesses to global data to minimize the total amount of communication needed.

In conclusion, our case study shows that the processor pool model is a feasible platform for parallel processing. A processor pool is far less expensive than a multicomputer. One disadvantage (shared with the idle workstations model) is the fact that the network interconnecting the processors is slow. We have shown, however, that excellent speedups still can be obtained for a realistic problem. On modern networks with higher bandwidths (such as ATM), one can expect even better performance.

Acknowledgements

Saniya Ben Hassen, Raoul Bhoedjang, Dick Grune, and Koen Langendoen provided useful comments on a draft of this paper.

References

1. A. D. Birrell and B. J. Nelson. Implementing remote procedure calls. *ACM Transactions on Computer Systems*, 2(1):39–59, February 1984.
2. M. Berry et. al. The perfect club benchmarks: Effective performance evaluation of supercomputers. Technical Report CSRD Report No. 827, Center for Supercomputing Research and Development, Urbana, Illinois, May 1989.
3. C.W. Gear. *Numerical Initial Value Problems in Ordinary Differential Equatations*. Prentice-Hall, New Jersey, 1971.
4. M.F. Kaashoek. *Group Communication in Distributed Computer Systems*. PhD thesis, Vrije Universiteit, Amsterdam, December 1992.
5. M.C. Rinard, D.J. Scales, and M.S. Lam. Jade: A high-level, machine-independent language for parallel programming. *IEEE Computer*, 26(6):28–38, June 1993.
6. J.W. Romein. Water — an N-body simulation program on a distributed architecture. Master's thesis, Department of Mathematics and Computer Science, Vrije Universiteit, Amsterdam, August 1994.
7. J.P. Singh, W.-D. Weber, and A. Gupta. SPLASH: Stanford parallel applications for shared-memory. *ACM Computer Architecture News*, 20(1), March 1992.
8. A.S. Tanenbaum, R. van Renesse, H. van Staveren, G.J. Sharp, S.J. Mullender, A.J. Jansen, and G. van Rossum. Experiences with the Amoeba distributed operating system. *Communications of the ACM*, 33(12):46–63, December 1990.

Analysis of Parallel Scan Processing
in Shared Disk Database Systems

Erhard Rahm
Thomas Stöhr

University of Leipzig, Institute of Computer Science
Augustusplatz 10-11, 04109 Leipzig, Germany
E-mail: {rahm | stoehr}@informatik.uni-leipzig.de

Abstract. Shared Disk database systems offer a high flexibility for parallel transaction and query processing. This is because each node can process any transaction, query or subquery because it has access to the entire database. Compared to
Shared Nothing database systems, this is particularly advantageous for scan queries for which the degree of intra-query parallelism as well as the scan processors
themselves can dynamically be chosen. On the other hand, there is the danger of
disk contention between subqueries, in particular for index scans. We present a
detailed simulation study to analyze the effectiveness of parallel scan processing
in Shared Disk database systems. In particular, we investigate the relationship between the degree of declustering and the degree of scan parallelism for relation
scans, clustered index scans, and non-clustered index scans. Furthermore, we
study the usefulness of disk caches and prefetching for limiting disk contention.
Finally, we show that disk contention in multi-user mode can be limited for
Shared Disk database systems by dynamically choosing the degree of scan parallelism.

Keywords: Parallel Database Systems; Shared Disk; Query Processing; Disk
Contention; Dynamic Load Balancing; Performance Analysis

1 Introduction

Parallel database systems are the key to high performance transaction and database processing [DG92, Va93]. They utilize the capacity of multiple locally clustered processing nodes interconnected by a high-speed network. Typically, fast and inexpensive
microprocessors are used as processors to achieve high cost-effectiveness compared to
mainframe-based configurations. Parallel database systems aim at providing both high
throughput for on-line transaction processing (OLTP) as well as short response times
for complex ad-hoc queries. This requires both inter- as well as intra-transaction parallelism. Inter-transaction parallelism (multi-user mode) is required to achieve high
OLTP throughput and sufficient cost-effectiveness. Intra-transaction parallelism is a
prerequisite for reducing the response time of complex and data-intensive transactions
(queries).

There are three major architectures for parallel database systems: "Shared Every-
thing" (SE), "Shared Nothing" (SN) and "Shared Disk" (SD) [DG92, Va93]. Research
has so far focussed on SE and SN, despite the fact that there is a growing number of
commercially available DBMS supporting the SD approach (Oracle, IMS, DB2/MVS,
etc.), although most of them are currently restricted to inter-transaction parallelism.
Presumably, Oracle's "Parallel Server" represents the best-known SD implementation
because it has achieved the highest transaction rates in TPC benchmarks. Furthermore,

it is available for a variety of platforms including a growing number of "cluster" architectures (VaxCluster, SPARCcluster, Sequent, Pyramid, Encore etc.) and massively parallel systems like nCube. Oracle version 7.1 offers initial support for intra-query parallelism. The new DB2-based S/390 Parallel Query Server of IBM also provides intra-query parallelism.

SE refers to the use of shared-memory multiprocessors (symmetric multiprocessing) for database processing. Since it is limited to relatively few processors, SN and SD are generally considered the most important approaches for parallel database systems [Pi90, DG92]. Both architectures consist of multiple loosely coupled processing nodes (distributed memory) connected by a high-speed network. The software architecture is homogeneous in that each node runs an identical copy of the DBMS software. Through cooperation between these DBMS instances, complete distribution transparency (single system image) is achieved for database users and application programs. SN is based on a physical partitioning of the database among nodes, while SD allows each DBMS instance to access all disks and thus the entire database. The latter approach therefore requires a global concurrency control protocol (introducing communication overhead and delays) to achieve serializability. Furthermore, buffer coherency must be maintained since database pages may be replicated in multiple DBMS buffers [Ra86, Yu87, MN91]. On the other hand, SN requires communication for distributed query processing, commit processing and global deadlock detection.

The differences between SN and SD with respect to the database allocation have far-reaching consequences for parallel query processing [Ra93b]. This is particularly the case for scan operations that operate on base relations[1]. Scan is the simplest and most common relational operator. It produces a row-and-column subset of a relation by applying a selection predicate and filtering away attributes not requested by the query. If predicate evaluation cannot be supported by an index, a complete relation scan is necessary where each tuple of the relation must be read and processed. An index scan accesses tuples via an index and restricts processing to a subset of the tuples; in the extreme case, no tuple or only one tuple needs to be accessed (e.g., exact-match query on unique attribute).

In SN systems, a scan operation on relation R typically has to be processed by all nodes to which a partition of R has been assigned[2]. Hence, the degree of scan parallelism and thus the associated communication overhead are already determined by the largely static database allocation. Furthermore, there is no choice of which nodes should process a scan operation. As a result, SN does not support dynamic load balancing for scan and thus for most operations. SD, on the other hand, permits us to dynamically choose the degree of scan parallelism as well as the scan processors since each processor can access the entire relation R. Of course, R must be declustered across multiple disks to support I/O parallelism. In contrast to SN however, SD offers the flexibility to choose a degree of processing parallelism different from the degree of I/O parallelism.

This flexibility of the SD architecture is already significant for parallel query processing in single-user mode. This is because different scan operations on R have their response time minimum for different degrees of parallelism. For instance, a selective index scan accessing only one tuple is best processed on a single processor, while a relation scan accessing all tuples may require 100 processors to provide sufficiently short

---

1. Operations on derived data, e.g. join, can be parallelized similarly in both architectures by dynamically redistributing the operations' input data among processors.
2. Selections on the partitioning attribute, used to define the relation's partitioning, may be restricted to a subset of the data processors.

response times. SN requires to statically choose the degree of declustering and thus the degree of scan parallelism for an average load profile [Gh90]. If both scan queries of our example are processed with equal probability, the relation would thus have to be partitioned among 50 nodes resulting in sub-optimal performance for both query types (enormous communication overhead for the index scan relative to the actual work; sub-optimal degree of parallelism for the relation scan). SD, on the other hand, allows both query types to be processed by the optimal number of nodes (1 for the index scan, 100 for the relation scan), provided the relation is declustered across 100 disks.

The increased flexibility for parallel scan processing of SD is even more valuable in multi-user mode, in particular for mixed OLTP/query workloads [Ra93b]. So, OLTP transactions can always be processed sequentially on a single processing node to minimize the communication overhead and to support high transaction rates. For complex queries, on the other hand, a parallel processing on multiple nodes can be performed to achieve short response times. For these queries, we have the flexibility to base the degree of scan parallelism not only on parameters like relation size or query type, but also on the current system utilization. In particular, it may be advisable to choose a smaller degree of scan parallelism under high load in order to limit the communication overhead and the number of concurrent subqueries. Furthermore, complex queries can be assigned to less loaded nodes to achieve dynamic load balancing. In addition, it may be useful to assign OLTP transactions and complex queries to disjoint sets of nodes in order to minimize CPU and memory contention between these workload types.

However, SD bears the potential problem of disk contention that may outweigh the expected benefits discussed so far. Disk contention can already be introduced in single-user mode if concurrent subqueries of the same query are accessing the same disks. This problem can particularly be pronounced for parallel index scans because it may not be possible to prevent that multiple subqueries access index and data pages on the same disks. Hence, it is unclear to what degree it makes sense employing parallel index scans for SD^3. The disk contention problem is aggravated in multi-user mode when multiple independent queries/transactions are accessing the shared disks. Note however, that disk contention in multi-user mode is not a SD-specific problem but is very difficult to deal with for SN (and SE) as well.

To investigate the performance of parallel scan processing in more detail, we have implemented a detailed simulation system of a parallel SD database system. This model is used to study the relationship between the degree of declustering and the degree of processing parallelism for scan processing. The analysis is made for the three major types of scan queries: relation scan (table scan), clustered index scan, and non-clustered index scan. Furthermore, we study the usefulness of disk caches and prefetching for limiting disk contention. Finally, we show the usefulness to control disk contention in multi-user mode by dynamically choosing the degree of scan parallelism according to the current disk utilization (which is not feasible for SN). While our study focuses on SD, many of our findings equally apply to SE systems because they offer a similar flexibility for dynamic scheduling and load balancing.

Fig. 1 shows the SD architecture assumed in this paper. There are n processing nodes each consisting of m CPUs and local main memory. The processing nodes are loosely coupled, i.e., they communicate by message passing across a network. The nodes are assumed to be locally "clustered", i.e., they reside in one machine room. Furthermore, each node can access all disks as required for Shared Disk systems. All messages including I/O requests and data pages are exchanged across a high-speed and

---

3. Note that Oracle 7.1 only supports parallel relation scans.

scalable interconnection network (e.g., hypercube). The main memory of each disk controller is used as a shared disk cache (DC). Each processing node runs private copies of the SD DBMS, operating system, and application software. Of course, the DBMSs' support the extensions needed for SD, in particular a global concurrency and coherency control protocol. Furthermore, parallel processing of scan queries is supported.

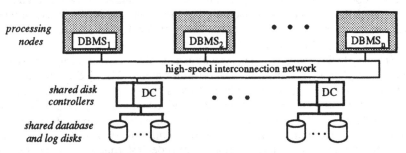

Fig. 1: Shared Disk architecture

The remainder of this paper is organized as follows. The next section briefly discusses different alternatives for data allocation and parallel scan processing for SD. Section 3 provides an overview of the simulation model and the implemented approaches for concurrency/coherency control. In Section 4 we present and analyze simulation experiments for various system and workload configurations to study the impact of disk contention for the different scan query types. In particular, we analyze single-user as well as multi-user experiments with homogeneous and heterogeneous (query/OLTP) workloads. The major findings of this investigation are summarized in Section 5.

2 Parallel Scan Processing

To support parallel query processing, we assume that relations and index structures (B+ trees) can be declustered across several disks according to a physical or logical partitioning strategy. Physical partitioning operates on physical distribution granules like blocks or block sets and can be implemented outside the DBMS, e.g., within a disk array [PGK88]. Such an approach supports I/O parallelism for large read operations, but can cause performance problems in combination with processing parallelism. This is because if the DBMS has no information on the physical data allocation (declustering) it may not be possible to split a query into parallel subqueries so that these subqueries do not access the same disks. Logical partitioning, on the other hand, uses logical database objects like tuples as distribution granules and is typically defined by a partitioning function (e.g., range or hash) on a partitioning attribute (e.g., primary key). DB2 permits a logical range partitioning of relations across several disks, while Oracle supports physical declustering and hash partitioning. Typically, the database allocation in SN systems is also based on a logical range or hash partitioning.

To make *physical declustering* useful for parallel query processing in SD systems we assume that the DBMS at least knows the degree of declustering D and the disks holding partitions for a particular relation. These prerequisites make it easy to support parallel processing of relation scans without disk contention between subqueries. For a degree of declustering D this is possible for different degrees of parallelism P by choosing P such that $$P * k = D,$$ where k is the number of disks to be processed per subquery. For instance, if we have

D=100 we may process a relation scan with P = 1, 2, 4, 5, 10, 20, 25, 50 or 100 sub-queries without disk contention between subqueries. Furthermore, each subquery processes the same number of disks (k) so that data skew can largely be avoided for equally sized partitions. CPU contention between subqueries is also avoided if each subquery is assigned to a different processor which is feasible as long as P does not exceed the number of processors $n*m$. The degree of declustering D should at least be high enough to support sufficiently short response time for a relation scan in single-user mode. As we will see, multi-user mode may require to have higher degrees of declustering, or degrees of scan parallelism P smaller than D.

A physical declustering of index structures is useful to support high I/O rates and thus inter-query/transaction parallelism (multi-user mode) [SL91]. SD can use a declustered index for sequentially processed index scans without problems. Sequential index scans incur minimal communication overhead and are therefore optimal for very selective queries (e.g., exact match queries on unique attribute). However, there may be index scans (e.g., for range queries) that need intra-query parallelism to achieve sufficiently short response times. With a physical declustering, this entails the danger that subqueries may have to access the same disks thereby causing disk contention. Concurrent access to higher-level index pages (root page and second-level pages) is expected to be less problematic since these pages can be cached in main memory or the disk caches. However, disk contention can arise for access to different index leaf pages and data pages stored on the same disk. The impact of disk contention for data pages is also expected to depend on whether a clustered or non-clustered index is being used. Our performance analysis will study these aspects in more detail.

Logical partitioning has the advantage that the DBMS knows the value distribution on disk for the partitioning attribute A. This is useful to restrict scan queries on A to a subset of the disks even without using an index. Furthermore, queries on A can easily be parallelized according to the partitioning function without introducing disk contention. For example, assume that the following range partitioning on A is used for allocating a relation to 100 disks:

A: (1 - 10,000; 10,001 - 20,000; 20,001 - 30,000;...; 990,001 - 1,000,000).

A range query requesting tuples with A values between 70,001 and 220,000 can be processed by 15 (5, 3, 1) parallel subqueries each accessing 1 (3, 5, 15) of the 100 disks. If there is an index for A, the index scan can similarly be parallelized into 1-15 subqueries. To avoid contention for the index, it could also be partitioned into D subindices similarly as in SN systems[4].

Scan queries on different attributes than A cannot take advantage of the logical partitioning. They are similarly processed than with a physical declustering. Hence, parallel index scans for such queries may also suffer from disk contention between subqueries. A general disadvantage of logical partitioning is that it is difficult to define for the database administrator (DBA), in particular for range partitioning. A physical declustering, on the other hand, may only require specification of the degree of declustering D.

---

4. Note however that the increased flexibility of the SD architecture regarding scan parallelism and selection of scan processors is preserved.

3 Simulation Model

For the present study, we have implemented a comprehensive simulation model of a Shared Disk database architecture. The gross structure of this simulation system is depicted in Fig. 2. In the following, we briefly describe the used database and workload models as well as the processing model. Furthermore, we outline the implemented strategy for concurrency/coherency control. The simulation system is highly parameterized. In Section 4.1, we will provide an overview of the major parameters and their settings used in this study.

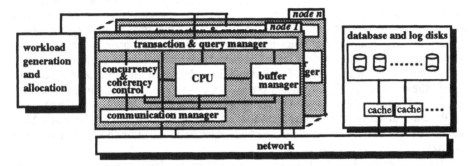

Fig. 2: Structure of the simulation system

Database and Workload Model

The database is modeled as a set of partitions. A partition may be used to represent a relation, a relation fragment or an index structure. It consists of a number of database pages which in turn consist of a specific number of objects (tuples, index entries). The number of objects per page is determined by a blocking factor which can be specified on a per-partition basis. Each relation can have associated clustered or non-clustered B^+-tree indices. Relations and indices can be physically declustered at the page level across an arbitrary number of disks. Declustering of relations is straight-forward. If B is the number of pages per disk (B = relation size in pages / declustering factor D), we simply assign the first B pages to the first disk, pages B+1 to 2B to the second disk and so on. Indices are not partitioned as in SN systems, but have the same structure as in centralized DBMS (only one root page, etc.). Each index level is separately declustered across D disks similarly to relation declustering (the root page is on a single disk, of course).

We support heterogeneous (multi-class) workloads consisting of several query and transaction types. Queries correspond to transactions with a single database operation (e.g., SQL statement). We support the following scan query types: relation scan, clustered index scan and non-clustered index scan. We also support the debit-credit benchmark workload (TPC-B) and the use of real-life database traces. The simulation system is an open queuing model and allows definition of an individual arrival rate for each transaction and query type.

Workload allocation takes place at two levels. First, each incoming transaction or query is assigned to one processing node acting as the coordinator for the transaction/ query. For this placement we support different strategies, in particular random allocation. Furthermore, we can allocate transaction and query types to a subset of the processing nodes allowing us to assign OLTP transactions and complex queries to disjoint sets of nodes. The second form of workload allocation deals with the assignment of sub-operations to processors for parallel query processing. These assignment can be made statically (e.g. random) or dynamically based on the current processor utilization. The number of subqueries (degree of intra-query parallelism) can also be chosen statically or dynamically, e.g., based on the current disk utilization. Details are provided in the next section.

Processing Model

Each processing node of the Shared Disk system is represented by a transaction and query manager, CPU servers, a communication manager, a buffer manager, and a concurrency/coherency control component (Fig. 2). The transaction and query manager controls the execution of transactions and queries. The maximal number of concurrent transactions and (sub)queries (inter-transaction parallelism) per node is controlled by a multiprogramming level. Newly arriving transactions and queries must wait in an input queue until they can be served when this maximal degree of inter-transaction parallelism is already reached. Parallel query processing entails starting all subqueries, executing the individual subqueries and merging their results. Locks may be requested either by the coordinator before starting the subqueries or by the individual subqueries. Similarly, all locks may be released by the coordinator or by the individual subqueries (see below).

The number of CPUs per node and their capacity (in MIPS) are provided as simulation parameters. The average number of instructions per request can be defined separately for every request type. To accurately model the cost of transaction/query processing, CPU service is requested for all major steps, in particular for transaction initialization (BOT), object accesses in main memory, I/O overhead, communication overhead, and commit processing. The communication network models transmission of "long" messages (page transfers) and "short" messages (e.g., global lock request). Query result sets are disassembled into the required number of messages (long or short).

The database buffer in main memory is managed according to a LRU replacement strategy and a no-force update strategy with asynchronous disk writes. Log information is written on separate log disks (1 page per update transaction). The buffer manager closely cooperates with the concurrency control component to implement coherency control (see below).

Database partitions (relations, indices) can be declustered across several disks as discussed above. Disks and disk controllers have explicitly been modelled as servers to capture potential I/O bottlenecks. Furthermore, disk controllers can have a LRU disk cache. The disk controllers also provide a prefetching mechanism to support sequential access patterns. If prefetching is selected, a disk cache miss causes multiple succeeding pages to be read from disk and allocated into the disk cache. Sequentially reading multiple pages is only slightly slower than reading a single page, but avoids the disk accesses for the prefetched pages when they are referenced later on. The number of pages to be read per prefetch I/O is specified by a simulation parameter and can be chosen per query type.

Concurrency and Coherency Control

For concurrency and coherency control, we have implemented a primary copy locking scheme [Ra86] because this approach has performed best in a comprehensive, trace-driven performance study of several concurrency/coherency control schemes [Ra93a]. This approach partitions the global lock authority (GLA) for the database among processing nodes so that each node handles all global lock requests for one database parti- tion. Hence, communication is only required for those lock requests belonging to the partition of a remote node. With this scheme, a large portion of the locks can locally be processed by assigning a transaction to the node holding the GLA for most of the ob- jects to be referenced. For OLTP transactions, such an affinity-based routing can be im- plemented by a table indicating for each transaction type the preferred nodes. Furthermore, the lock overhead can be spread among all nodes in contrast to a central- ized locking scheme.

For page-level locking, coherency control can efficiently be combined with the locking protocol by extending the global lock tables with information (e.g., sequence numbers) to detect invalid page copies. We have implemented such an on-request in- validation approach since it allows us to detect obsolete pages during lock request pro- cessing without extra communication. To propagate updates in the system, we assume that each node acts as the "owner" for the database partition for which it holds the GLA. The owner is responsible of providing other nodes with the most recent version of pages of its partition and for eventually writing updated pages to disk. With this approach, an updated page is transferred to the owner at transaction commit if it has been modified at another node. This page transfer can be combined with the message needed for re- leasing the write lock. Similarly, page transfers from the owner to another node are combined with the message to grant a lock [Ra86, Ra91].

To support query processing, we have implemented a hierarchical version of this protocol with relation- and page-level locking[5]. Relation-level locking is used for rela- tion scans and larger index scans because page-level locking could cause an extreme overhead in these cases. Page-level locking is applied for selective queries accessing only few pages. Relation locks are acquired by the coordinator before the subqueries are started and released after the end of all subqueries. In the lock grant message for a relation lock, the global lock manager indicates all pages of the relation for which an invalidation is feasible at the nodes where the query is to be executed. The respective pages are immediately removed from the buffers and requested from the owner during the execution of the subqueries.

4   Performance Analysis

Our experiments concentrate on the impact of disk contention on the performance of parallel scan processing in SD database systems. For this purpose, we study the rela- tionship between the degree of declustering D and the degree of parallelism P for both single-user and multi-user mode as well as for relation scans, clustered and non-clus- tered index scans. We additionally investigate in how far prefetching is useful for par- allel query processing to improve performance. Furthermore, we show that the SD architecture allows us to control disk contention in multi-user mode by a dynamic query scheduling approach that determines the degree of scan parallelism based on the current system state.

In the next subsection, we provide an overview of the parameter settings used in the experiments. Afterwards, we analyze the performance of parallel relation scans (4.2) and index scans (4.3) for different values of D and P in single- and multi-user mode. Finally, we describe experiments for homogeneous and heterogeneous workloads

---

5. Since the GLA for a relation can be partitioned among several nodes in our implementation, we
   in fact support the additional lock granularity of a relation fragment, consisting of all tuples/pages
   of a relation for which one node holds the GLA. To simplify the description, we assume here that
   the GLA for each relation (and for each index) is assigned to only one node.

showing the need for dynamically determining the degree of parallelism P based on the current disk contention.

4.1 Simulation Parameter Settings

Fig. 3 shows the major database, query and configuration parameters with their settings. Most parameters are self-explanatory, some will be discussed when presenting the simulation results. The scan queries used in our experiments access a 100 MB relation with 125.000 tuples. In the case of index scans, only 1% of the tuples is accessed (scan selectivity). Relation scans also generate a result set of 1250 tuples, but must access the entire relation. The number of processing nodes is varied between 1 and 32.

Parameter	Settings	Parameter	Settings
number of nodes (n)	1 - 32	communication	
#processors per node (m)	1	bandwidth	10 MB/s
CPU speed per processor	30 MIPS		
		relation properties:	(100 MB)
avg. no. of instructions:		#tuples	125.000
BOT	25000	tuple size	800 B
EOT	25000	blocking factor	10 (data), 200 (index)
I/O initialization	3000	index type	clustered / non-cl. B^+-tree
scan object reference	1000	storage allocation	disk
send short message (128 B)	1000	degree of declustering D	varied
receive short message	1000		
send long message (page)	5000		
receive long message	5000	*scan queries:*	
		scan type	relation scan /
buffer manager:			clustered index scan /
page size	8 KB		non-clustered index scan
buffer size per node	500 pages	scan selectivity	1.0 %
		no. of result tuples	1250
disk devices:		size of result tuples	800 B
controller service time	1 ms	arrival rate	single-user, multi-user
# prefetch pages	8 pages		(varied)
avg. disk access time		query placement	random (uniformly over
1 page	11 ms		all nodes)
prefetching 8 pages	18 ms	scan parallelism P	varied
cache size (#pages)	1000		

Fig. 3: System configuration, database and query profile.

The duration of an I/O operation is composed of the controller service time, disk access time and transmission time. For sequential I/Os (e.g. relation scans, clustered index scans), prefetching can be chosen resulting in an average access time of 18 ms for 8 pages rather than 8*11 ms if the pages were read one by one. For message and page transfers we assume a communication bandwidth of 10 MB/s and that no bottlenecks occur in the network. This assumption is justified by the comparatively small bandwidth requirements of our load as well as by the fact that we focus on disk contention in this study.

To capture the behavior of OLTP-style transactions, we provide a workload similar to the debit-credit benchmark. Each OLTP transaction randomly accesses four data pages from the same disks accessed by the scan queries.

4.2 Parallel Processing of Relation Scan

We first study the performance of relation scans in *single-user mode* for the cases without prefetching (Fig. 4a) and with prefetching of pages into the disk cache (Fig. 4b). We vary the number of nodes n from 1 to 32 and use one subquery per node (i.e., P=n) since we assumed a single processor per node. Three cases are considered for declustering the input relation. A degree of declustering D=1 refers to the case where the entire relation is stored on a single disk, while D=n assumes a declustering of the relation across n (=P) disks. D=n/2 assumes two processors per disk for n ≥ 2 (1 disk for n =1). For comparison purposes, we have also shown in Fig. 4b the results where the entire relation fits into the disk cache (or is kept in a solid-state disk).

The results for the cache-resident case show that response times are indeed dominated by disk access times. This is particularly true without prefetching (Fig. 4a) where response times are up to a factor 5 (for D=1) higher than with prefetching. The results show that storing the entire relation on a single disk (D=1) makes parallel scan processing useless since disk utilization is already 85% for sequential scan processing (P =1). Increasing the number of subqueries improves the CPU-related response time portion, but completely overloads the disk preventing any significant response time improvement for P>2. On the other hand, having one disk per subquery (D=n) avoids any disk contention for relation scan in single-user mode allowing optimal response time speedup.

A declustering across n/2 disks is significantly better than D=1, but still suffers from disk contention in particular for smaller degrees of parallelism (P ≤ 8).

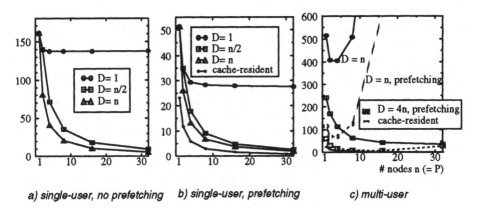

a) single-user, no prefetching   b) single-user, prefetching   c) multi-user

Fig. 4: Performance of relation scan

Prefetching (Fig. 4b) is very effective for both sequential and parallel processing of relation scans. Not only response times are significantly reduced, but also disk utilization (55% for P=1). This lowers disk contention and supports smaller degrees of declustering. Even for D=1, response times can be improved for up to 4 nodes and a speedup of 1.7 is achieved. Response times for D=n/2 are almost as good as for D=n thus permitting the use of fewer disks.

For the *multi-user experiment* (Fig. 4c) we study a homogeneous workload of relation scans on the same relation. The arrival rate is increased proportionally to the number of nodes because we want to support both short response times as well as linear throughput increase. We used an arrival rate of 0.07 queries per second (QPS) per node resulting in a CPU utilization of about 30%. We found that this arrival rate cannot be processed if we have fewer disks than processors (D < n) due to disk over-utilization. The response time results in Fig. 4c refer to the cases of D=n and D=4n and with or without prefetching. For comparison, we again show the results for a cache-resident relation (no disk I/O).

We observe that for D=n, response times are several times higher than in single-user mode (Fig. 4) due to disk waits. Parallel scan processing only allows for very modest response time improvements for 2-4 processors (speedup of 1.25). More nodes lead to significantly aggravated disk contention because we increase both the degree of inter-query (arrival rate) and the degree of intra-query parallelism linearly with n. As a result, the load can no longer be processed for more than 8 nodes and D=n. As Fig. 4c shows the disk bottleneck is largely removed for our arrival rate if we decluster the relation across 4 times as many disks as there are processors (D=4n). While prefetching cannot prevent the disk bottleneck for D=n and more than 8 nodes, it allows for substantially improved response times (factor 5). Furthermore, for up to 4 processors its response times for D=n are better than without prefetching and the four-fold number of disks! For D=4n, prefetching allows us to approach the optimal response times of the cache-resident case. These results demonstrate that multi-user mode requires substantially higher degrees of declustering than single-user mode to keep response times acceptable and to achieve linear throughput increase. Furthermore, prefetching is even more valuable in multi-user mode to keep disk contention low and to limit the number of disks.

4.3   Parallel Processing of Index Scans

We now focus on the performance of parallel index scans in single- and multi-user mode. For our relation (125,000 tuples) we use a 3-level B^+ tree with 625 leaf pages. A range query with scan selectivity of 1% thus requires access to 2 higher-level index pages and 7 leaf pages. The number of additional accesses to data pages for the 1250 result tuples depends on whether a clustered or non-clustered index is used. For the clustered index scan, the tuples are stored in 125 consecutive data pages while up to 1250 different data pages may have to be accessed for the non-clustered index scan. For parallel index scan processing, we assume that the range condition on the index attribute can be decomposed into P smaller range conditions so that each subquery has to access the same number of tuples.

We first analyze the performance of *clustered index scans* (Fig. 5). In this case, we always use prefetching for data pages. The number of nodes n and the degree of parallelism are again varied from 1 to 32. In single-user mode, we study the following degrees of declustering: D=1, D=n/2 and D=n. In multi-user mode, we consider different arrival rates for a homogeneous load of clustered index scans only. Furthermore, the number of disks is up to 8 times higher than the number of processors. The index is always declustered across the same disks than the relation's data pages.

Let's first look at the single-user response times (Fig. 5a). Sequentially processing the clustered index scan achieves an average response time roughly 100-times better as for the relation scan with prefetching (due to the scan selectivity of 1%). However in contrast to the relation scan (Fig. 4b), intra-query parallelism is little useful for the clustered index scan not only for D=1, but also for D=n/2 and even for D=n. This is because in most cases the relevant index and data pages reside also on only one disk due to the clustering according to the index attribute (e.g., for D=32 we have about 390 data pages per disk compared to 125 relevant data pages). The small improvement of D=n/2 over D=1 comes from the fact that the relevant pages for some queries may be on two instead

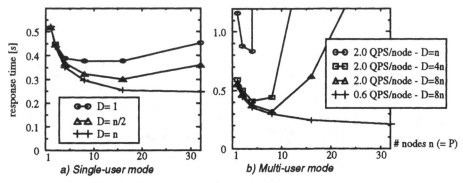

Fig. 5: Performance of clustered index scan

of one disk (the probability of this case increases with D). D = n offers a small improvement for n ≥ 16 since the data of multiple disks needs to be processed in this range. Still, compared to sequential processing only a speedup of 2 is achieved which is clearly not cost-effective.

Multi-user mode (Fig. 5b) leads to increased disk contention so that only modest arrival rates are attained if intra-query parallelism is used. For instance, an arrival rate of 2 QPS per node cannot be sustained for more than a few nodes even if we increase the number of disks proportionally with n (e.g., D=n or D=4n). This shows that selective clustered index scans should be processed sequentially to support high throughput. A small degree of intra-query parallelism may be useful if the data of multiple disks needs to be processed.

For *non-clustered index scans* prefetching is not employed since the result tuples may be spread over many disks. In single user-mode (Fig. 6a), the sequential response time for non-clustered index scan is about a factor 10 better than for the relation scan without prefetching (Fig. 4a) since we have to access about 10% of the data pages. In contrast to clustered index scans, parallel processing of non-clustered index scan is rather effective if the relation is declustered across at least n/2 disks (speedup of 15 for P=32). This is because accesses to the data pages are spread across all disks so that much smaller disk contention arises. However, in contrast to parallel relation scan processing disk contention cannot completely be eliminated even for D=n because of index accesses (not all leaf index pages could be cached). Furthermore, it cannot be excluded that subqueries have to access data pages on the same disks although the probability of this event becomes smaller with higher degrees of declustering. For these reasons, a declustering factor of 4n provides slightly better response times than D=n in single-user mode.

Note however, that a sequentially processed clustered index scan (Fig. 5a) still offers better response times than a 32-way parallel non-clustered index scan. On the other hand, the non-clustered index scan remains always better than a relation scan with prefetching (Fig. 4b) although the differences between the two approaches become smaller for larger degrees of parallelism.

The multi-user results (Fig. 6b) illustrate that the high I/O requirements of non-clustered index scans allow for significantly lower throughput than clustered index scans. While we could support 0.6 QPS for up to 32 nodes and D=8n without problems for clustered index scans (Fig. 5b), this arrival rate causes significant disk contention for non-clustered index scans and cannot be supported for more than 8 nodes. Put differ-

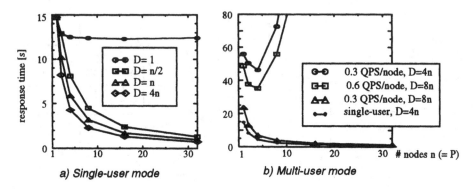

a) Single-user mode   *b) Multi-user mode*

Fig. 6: Performance of non-clustered index scan

ently, non-clustered index scans require a much higher degree of declustering to meet a certain throughput. Similarly as for relation scans (Fig. 4c), in multi-user mode the effectiveness of intra-query parallelism is much smaller than in single-user mode. Increasing the degree of intra-query parallelism while increasing the workload proportionally with n, is only effective for comparatively low disk utilization, i.e., for low arrival rates or few processors.

4.4   The Need for Dynamic Query Scheduling

The experiments discussed so far always used the maximal degree of intra-query parallelism P=n. In combination with inter-query parallelism this caused a high level of disk contention for a larger number of processors even when the number of disks is increased proportionally to n. We now study the impact of the degree of parallelism P for different arrival rates and a fixed number of nodes and disks. This experiment is performed for relation scans using prefetching and a system of 16 nodes and 64 disks.

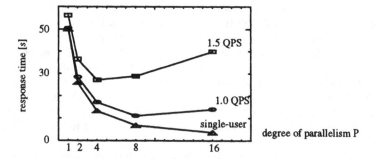

Fig. 7: Degree of parallelism vs. arrival rate (n=16, D=64)

Fig. 7 shows that for sequential processing (P=1) multi-user response times are only slightly higher than in single-user mode, but that the effectiveness of intra-query parallelism decreases with growing arrival rates. In single-user mode response times continuously improve with increasing degrees of parallelism and reach their minimum for P=16. For an arrival rate of 1 QPS and 1.5 QPS, on the other hand, the response time minimum is achieved for P=8 and P=4, respectively. Further increasing the degree of parallelism causes a response time degradation, in particular for the higher arrival rate

1.5 QPS. These results show that the optimal degree of scan parallelism depends on the current system state, in particular the level of disk contention. Under low disk contention (single-user mode or low arrival rates), intra-query parallelism is most effective and achieves good speedup values even for higher degrees of scan parallelism, e.g., P=n. However, the higher the disks are utilized due to inter-query parallelism the lower the optimal degree of intra-query parallelism becomes. Hence, there is a need for dynamically determining the degree of scan parallelism according to the current system and disk utilization. Note that such a dynamic query scheduling approach is feasible for Shared Disk, but not for Shared Nothing. Hence, Shared Disk is better able to limit disk contention in multi-user mode by reducing the degree of intra-query parallelism accordingly. However, we found that disk utilization must be rather high (> 50%) before varying the degree of scan parallelism has a significant impact on performance.

In our final experiment, we studied a heterogeneous workload consisting of relation scans and OLTP transactions. This experiment is based on the same configuration than before (n=16, D=64) but introduces disk contention between OLTP transactions and relation scans. Each OLTP transaction randomly accesses four data pages from the D disks. A fixed OLTP arrival rate was chosen such that it causes an average disk utilization of about 25%. In addition to this base load, we process relation scans with arrival rates of 0.5 QPS and 1 QPS. The resulting response times for different degrees of parallelism for the relation scans are shown in Fig. 8. For the queries (left diagram), we observe a similar response time behavior than for the homogeneous workload. In particular, for higher query arrival rate (disk contention) only a limited degree of scan parallelism proves useful. While P=8 achieved the best response time for 1 QPS and without OLTP load, the optimum is now achieved for P=4. This underlines that the degree of scan parallelism should be chosen according to the current disk utilization, irrespective of whether disk contention is due to concurrent OLTP transactions or other queries.

OLTP response times (right diagram of Fig. 8) are very sensitive to the number of concurrent scan queries as well as the degree of intra-query parallelism. While a query arrival rate of 0.5 QPS did not cause any significant response time degradations for

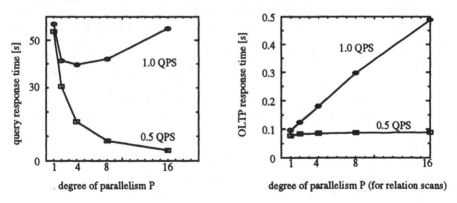

Fig. 8: Response times for mixed query/OLTP workload

OLTP, this was no longer true for 1 QPS. In this case, OLTP response times deteriorate proportionally to the degree of scan parallelism due to increased disk contention. This shows that limiting the degree of intra-query parallelism is not only necessary for obtaining good throughput, but also for limiting the performance penalty for OLTP transactions that have to access the same disks. Furthermore, keeping OLTP response times acceptably small may require a lower degree of scan parallelism than the one minimizing query response time.

5 Conclusions

We have presented a performance analysis of parallel scan processing in Shared Disk (SD) database systems. In contrast to Shared Nothing (SN), SD offers a high flexibility for scan processing because the number of subqueries is not predetermined by the degree of declustering (D) but can be chosen with respect to the query characteristics (relation scan, clustered index scan or non-clustered index scan, selectivity, etc.) as well as the current load situation (disk utilization, CPU utilization, etc.). Furthermore, the scan processors themselves can be selected dynamically to achieve load balancing.

However, even in single-user mode the effectiveness of intra-query parallelism can be reduced by disk contention between subqueries. We found that this problem primarily exists for clustered index scans where the relevant index and data pages typically reside on a single disk. Hence, clustered index scans are best processed sequentially unless the data of multiple disks needs to be accessed. In this case, the number of disks to be accessed determines the maximal degree of parallelism. On the other hand, parallel processing of relation scans permits optimal speedup in single-user mode by assigning the subqueries to disjoint sets of disks. This is easily feasible by choosing the degree of parallelism P such that $P = k*D$. Parallel processing of non-clustered index scans is also quite effective if the relation is declustered across a sufficiently large number of disks (e.g., D=n). Disk contention on the index cannot generally be avoided but is typically less significant for a larger number of data pages to be accessed[6]. A general observation is that physical declustering of relations and indices could effectively be used for parallel query processing indicating that SD database systems can make good use of disk arrays.

Multi-user mode inevitably leads to increased disk contention and therefore requires higher degrees of declustering if an effective intra-query parallelism is to be supported. Prefetching was found to be very effective for relation scans not only to improve response times, but also to reduce disk contention and to support smaller degrees of declustering, in particular in multi-user mode. Even for a high degree of declustering (e.g., D=4n), high arrival rates can lead to significant levels of disk contention and thus high response times for both complex queries and OLTP transactions. In such situations, we found it necessary to choose smaller degrees of intra-query parallelism to limit disk contention and response times degradations. In particular, the degree of scan parallelism should be chosen the smaller the higher the disks are utilized. This flexibility for dynamically controlling disk contention in multi-user mode is not supported by the SN architecture.

While we believe that disks constitute the most significant bottleneck resource for parallel query processing, in future work we will study additional bottleneck resources, in particular CPU, memory and network [RM95]. Furthermore, we want to study parallel processing of other relational operators (e.g., joins) in SD systems. The impact of concurrency and coherency control on parallel query processing also needs further investigation.

---

6. Of course, selective index scans accessing only few data pages should be processed sequentially.

500

6 References

DG92   DeWitt, D.J., Gray, J.: Parallel Database Systems: The Future of High Performance Database Systems. *Comm. ACM* 35 (6), 85-98, 1992

Gh90   Ghandeharizadeh, S.: Physical Database Design in Multiprocessor Database Systems. Ph.D. thesis, Univ. of Wisconsin-Madison, Sep. 1990

MN91   Mohan, C., Narang, I.: Recovery and Coherency-control Protocols for Fast Intersystem Page Transfer and Fine-Granularity Locking in a Shared Disks Transaction Environment. *Proc. 17th VLDB Conf.*, 193-207, 1991

PGK88   Patterson, D.A., Gibson, G., Katz, R.H.: A Case for Redundant Arrays of Inexpensive Disks (RAID). *Proc. ACM SIGMOD Conf.*, 109-116, 1988

Pi90   Pirahesh, H. et al.: Parallelism in Relational Data Base Systems: Architectural Issues and Design Approaches. In *Proc. 2nd Int.Symp. on Databases in Parallel and Distributed Systems*, 1990

Ra86   Rahm, E.: Primary Copy Synchronization for DB-Sharing. *Information Systems* 11 (4), 275-286, 1986

Ra91   Rahm, E.: Concurrency and Coherency Control in Database Sharing Systems, Techn. Report 3/91, Univ. Kaiserslautern, Dept. of Comp. Science, Dec. 1991

Ra93a   Rahm, E.: Empirical Performance Evaluation of Concurrency and Coherency Control for Database Sharing Systems. *ACM Trans. on Database Systems* 18 (2), 333-377, 1993

Ra93b   Rahm, E.: Parallel Query Processing in Shared Disk Database Systems. *Proc. 5th Int. Workshop on High Performance Transaction Systems (HPTS-5)*, Asilomar, Sep. 1993 (Extended Abstract: *ACM SIGMOD Record* 22 (4), Dec. 1993)

RM93   Rahm, E., Marek, R.: Analysis of Dynamic Load Balancing Strategies for Parallel Shared Nothing Database Systems. *Proc 19th VLDB Conf.*, 182-193, 1993

RM95   Rahm, E., Marek, R.: Dynamic Multi-Resource Load Balancing in Parallel Database Systems. *Proc 21st VLDB Conf.*, 1995

Se93   Selinger, P.: Predictions and Challenges for Database Systems in the Year 2000. *Proc 19th VLDB Conf.*, 667-675, 1993

SL91   Seeger, B., Larson, P.: Multi-Disk B-trees. *Proc. ACM SIGMOD Conf.*, 436-445, 1991

Va93   Valduriez, P.: Parallel Database Systems: Open Problems and New Issues. *Distr. and Parallel Databases* 1 (2), 137-165, 1993

Yu87   Yu, P.S. et al.: On Coupling Multi-systems through Data Sharing. *Proceedings of the IEEE* 75 (5), 573-587, 1987

Polynomial Time Scheduling of Low Level Computer Vision Algorithms on Networks of Heterogeneous Machines

Adam R. Nolan , anolan@ece.uc.edu
Bryan Everding, beverdin@ece.uc.edu
Artificial Intelligence and Computer Vision Lab
University of Cincinnati [†]

Abstract

Defining an optimal schedule for arbitrary algorithms on a network of heterogeneous machines is an NP complete problem. This paper focuses on data parallel deterministic neighborhood computer vision algorithms. This focus enables the polynomial time definition of a schedule which minimizes the distributed execution time by overlapping computation and communication cycles on the network. The scheduling model allows for any speed machine to participate in the concurrent computation but makes the assumption of a master/slave control mechanism using a linear communication network. Several vision algorithms are presented and described in terms of the scheduling model parameters. The theoretical speedup of these algorithms is discussed and empirical data is presented and compared to theoretical results.

Keywords: Computer Vision, Heterogeneous Architectures, Scheduling, Distributed Algorithms

1 Introduction

In the past many studies have been performed analyzing the capabilities of various parallel processor – vision algorithm mappings. Thorough surveys can be found in [18][3][2][4][5][17]. Most of these efforts focus on the mapping of a single machine to a single algorithm or mapping a suite of algorithms to a single architecture. [18] Most of the conclusions made in these studies are based on the architectural similarities between the hardware communication configurations and the communication patterns inherent in the vision algorithm (i.e. vision tasks tend to have highly regular communication). Recent research efforts have discussed the mapping of computer vision tasks to networks of workstations with the assumption of homogeneous workstation clusters. [11][7] Additional efforts have focused on scheduling suites of independent programs onto networks of heterogeneous machines. [10] This paper relaxes the assumption of homogeneous workstation clusters and independent program suites. It focuses on the distribution of a single program on a set of architectures connected by the PVM message passing library. [6][13] A framework is presented for the polynomial time scheduling of deterministic local communication algorithms onto a suite of heterogeneous machines using linear communication.

The paper is organized as follows. Section 2 presents the background and motivation. Section 3 develops the analytical description of the scheduling process and introduces a set of conditions necessary for the minimization of the execution time. Section 4 presents the scheduling algorithm. Section 5 presents several low level computer vision tasks and their corresponding scheduling models. Section 6 demonstrates the use of the scheduling method on the computer vision examples, presents theoretical speedups and discusses the elements of nondeterminism inherent in actual run times.

†This work was supported by the NASA – University of Cincinnati Space Engineering Research Center

Section 7 presents several conclusions based on the experimental data, and finally an appendix contains derivations of several conditions presented in the paper.

2 Background

Efforts have been made to develop an Automatic Visual Inspection System (AVIS) for use with various critical aerospace components. These components include high pressure turbine blades (aircraft), injector baffles, oxidation posts, annulus rings(spacecraft). AVIS utilizes several scales of information abstracted from the original image, with each scale requiring a set of low level vision operations. [8][14] The realization of the AVIS paradigm is limited by the tremendous computational burden of these low level vision operations. These algorithms include convolution, difference of Gaussian filtering, morphological filtering, Fourier transform, and Hough transform. In order to increase the speed of AVIS, distributed solutions were investigated. Defining an effective distribution onto the various machines available on the LAN requires models of algorithm decomposition, communication mechanisms, and machine speed for a given algorithm.

Heterogeneous computing is the well orchestrated and coordinated effective use of a suite of diverse high–performance machines to provide superspeed processing. [10] These applications typically contain several types of distinct control and data parallelism. For the purposes of this work data parallelism is of primary interest. Of the available models of parallelism the master/slave paradigm is efficient for most low level computer vision algorithms. The master–slave model utilizes a single controlling machine which issues commands and data to slave machines. In data–parallelism these commands are identical typically operating on different sets of data (the Single Program Multiple Data model–SPMD) or occasionally on identical data sets in the case of distributed search methods. Whereas in control–parallelism the slave machines perform dissimilar tasks on typically dissimilar data sets. Most low level vision tasks exhibit data parallelism with deterministic and localized communication patterns. This characteristic enables the elimination of interslave communication by sending each slave machine the necessary data according to the algorithm neighborhood. As the major computational burden of AVIS corresponds to low level vision algorithms, these are pursued in depth in the upcoming sections.

3 Analytical Development

Before an algorithm can be scheduled a decomposition scheme must be defined for the data. Two popular methods for decomposing image data are row partitioning (or strip mining) and block partitioning. In row partitioning each slave processor receives a number of rows from the original image and the associated neighborhood pixels needed in order to manipulate this row of data. Likewise, in block partitioning each machine receives a given block of data and its associated neighborhood. Typically these blocks must be partitioned onto a square number of homogenous machines, although alternative heuristic schemes have been described for blocking nonsquare numbers of homogeneous machines. [11] Examples of these partitioning schemes can be seen in Fig.1 & Fig.2. Although the total boundary pixels are typically less for block partitioned data than for row partitioned data, $\left(2\sqrt{n} - 2\right)$ vs $(n - 1)$,

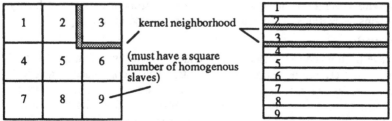

Fig.1 Block partitioning– 9 machines   Fig.2 Row Partitioning – 9 machines

block partitioning introduces many problems in the scheduling of heterogeneous machines. Assuming that an efficient heuristic could be defined that would partition the data onto heterogeneous machines, its inherent nonlinearity would make the analysis and minimization computationally expensive (at least combinatorial in regards to the number of nonlinearities). Hence, row partitioning will be assumed for the upcoming formulations. In order to discuss the analytic model and the conditions necessary for optimal scheduling, terminology involved with the theoretic execution and communication times must be presented. Definitions and terms are presented in Fig.3 .

Definitions:

$\mathcal{S}(n)$ – a scheduling of N homogeneous tasks onto n machines, where

$$N = \sum_{i=1}^{i=n} \eta_i \, , \text{ with each slave machine(i) receiving a task size of } \eta_i \, .$$

γ_i – seconds/operation for each processor(i), where the operation is algorithm dependent .

$T^y_{r(i)}$ – time(secs) spent receiving data from y tasks from processor i .

$T^0_{r(i)}$ – overhead(secs) required for any receive operation .

$T_{r(i)}$ – time(secs) spent receiving data from η_i tasks from processor i .
$$T_{r(i)} = T^0_{r(i)} + T^{\eta_i}_{r(i)}$$

ϕ_r – #bytes needed to receive task size 1 from a slave machine .

$T^y_{s(i)}$ – time(secs) spent sending data associated with y tasks to processor i .

$T^0_{s(i)}$ – overhead(secs) required for any send operation .

$T_{s(i)}$ – time(secs) spent sending data for η_i tasks to processor i .
$$T_{s(i)} = T^0_{s(i)} + T^{\eta_i}_{s(i)}$$

ϕ_s – #bytes needed to send task size 1 to a slave machine .

$T^y_{c(i)}$ – time(secs) required by processor i to compute a task size of y .

$T_{c(i)}$ – time(secs) spent by processor i computing task size η_i , $T_{c(i)} = T^{\eta_i}_{c(i)}$.

ϕ_c – #operations required to compute a task of size 1 .

$T(n)$ – total time to execute $\mathcal{S}(n)$.

$T^{a-b}_{c(i)} = T^a_{c(i)} - T^b_{c(i)}$.

$\lfloor f \rfloor = \max(0, f)$.

Fig.3 Definitions and terminology used in the scheduling model

For the following discussions, a linear single line communication model is assumed. Hence the communication time can be modeled as $T_{communication} = \alpha + \#bytes \times \beta$, where α is the startup overhead for a particular communication process and β is the seconds per byte transmission rate of data to and from a slave processor. This results in a constant aggregate communication time for a given number of processors: $\sum_{i=1}^{n} T_{s(i)} = T_s$, $\sum_{i=1}^{n} T_{r(i)} = T_r$. Similarly, the addition of any new slave machines into the data parallel non interslave communication paradigm results in an additional overhead value: $\sum_{i=1}^{n+1} T_{s(i)} = \sum_{i=1}^{n} T_{s(i)} + T^0_{s(n+1)}$ and similarly: $\sum_{i=1}^{n+1} T_{r(i)} = \sum_{i=1}^{n} T_{r(i)} + T^0_{r(n+1)}$. Some additional assumptions included in the AVIS model are that the slave machines can be organized such that machine(i) is faster than machine(i+1), i.e. $\gamma_i < \gamma_{i+1}$ for the particular type of task set to be scheduled. Also assumed is that the time for communication is not greater than the time for computation, i.e. $T_{c(i)} > T_{s(i)} + T_{r(i)} \; \forall \; i$. These assumptions are necessary for several of the analytic derivations.

As seen in Fig.4 the linear communication model allows for a quick graphical analysis of the optimality of a given schedule. The degree of nonconcurrency in the

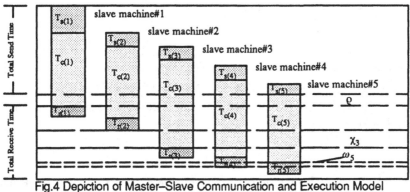

Fig.4 Depiction of Master–Slave Communication and Execution Model

schedule is indicated by the values of ϱ, ω, and χ. The parameter ϱ is a measure of the time spent by the master machine waiting for the first processed data partition to be returned, $\varrho = T_{c(1)} - \sum_{i=2}^{n} T_{s(i)}$. The parameter ω_i is a measure of slave machine wait time caused by contention with the previous slave machine for the linear communication channel, $\omega_i = \lfloor T_{c(i-1)} + T_{r(i-1)} - (T_{s(i)} + T_{c(i)}) \rfloor$. The parameter χ_i is a measure of the master wait time caused by excess computation of machine(i) after machine(i-1) has completed returning its data partition. Although it would appear that $\chi_i = \lfloor T_{s(i)} + T_{c(i)} - T_{c(i-1)} - T_{r(i-1)} \rfloor$, χ_i can be reduced by previous ω_j values, i.e. $\chi_i = \lfloor T_{c(i)} - \sum_{j=i+1}^{n} T_{s(j)} - \sum_{j=1}^{i-1} T_{r(j)} - \varrho \rfloor$. As one would expect, large values of ϱ, ω and χ result in suboptimal schedules. Typically these values cannot be eliminated due to the constraint of integer task size. The total execution time for a given schedule is:

$T(n) = \sum_{i=1}^{n} T_{s(i)} + \sum_{i=1}^{n} T_{r(i)} + \lfloor \varrho \rfloor + \sum_{i=2}^{n} \chi_i$. In order to minimize this execution time, a set of criteria must be established to explicitly define the effects of the values ϱ, ω and χ. The following conditions are used to establish limits on the relative sizes of these parameters.(Derivations can be found in the Appendix.)

Condition 1:

For any given schedule $\mathcal{S}(n)$ in which $\chi_j \geq T^1_{c(j)} + T^1_{c(1)}$, $j > 1$,
there exists an alternative schedule $\tilde{\mathcal{S}}(n)$ with $\tilde{\chi}_j < T^1_{c(j)} + T^1_{c(1)}$ such that
$\tilde{T}(n) < T(n)$. Hence, from this criterion one can conclude that a schedule must
have $\chi_j < T^1_{c(j)} + T^1_{c(1)}$, $j > 1$, otherwise the schedule will be suboptimal .

Condition 2:

Given a schedule $\mathcal{S}(n)$ with $\omega_j \geq T^1_{c(j-1)} + T^1_{r(j-1)} + T^1_{c(j)} + T^1_{s(j)}$ for some j,
there exists an alternative schedule $\tilde{\mathcal{S}}(n)$ with
$\omega_j < T^1_{c(j-1)} + T^1_{r(j-1)} + T^1_{c(j)} + T^1_{s(j)}$ such that $\tilde{T}(n) \leq T(n)$.
From this conclusion, it follows that any minimum time schedule must have
$\omega_j < T^1_{c(j-1)} + T^1_{r(j-1)} + T^1_{c(j)} + T^1_{s(j)}$.

Condition 3:

For any given schedule $\mathcal{S}(n)$ satifying conditions 1&2 with $\varrho > T^0_{s(n+1)} + T^0_{r(n+1)}$,
there exists an alternative schedule $\mathcal{S}(n + 1)$ such that $T(n + 1) < T(n)$.
This presents a condition to indicate when the number of slave machines should be
increased. (Fig.5)

Condition 4:

For any given schedule $\mathcal{S}(n)$ satisfying conditions 1&2 such that
$\varrho < T^0_{r(n)} + T^{\tilde{\eta}_1-\eta_1}_{s(1)} - T^{\tilde{\eta}_1-\eta_1}_{c(1)}$ there exists an alternative schedule $\mathcal{S}(n - 1)$ such that
$T(n - 1) < T(n)$, where $\tilde{\eta}_1$ corresponds to the alternate schedule $\mathcal{S}(n - 1)$ as
defined below in (*) . This presents a condition to indicate when the number of slave
machines should be decreased. (Fig.6)

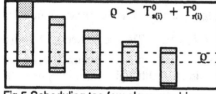

$$\varrho > T^0_{s(i)} + T^0_{r(i)}$$

Fig.5 Scheduling too few slave machines

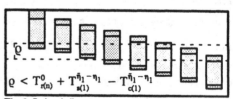

$$\varrho < T^0_{r(n)} + T^{\tilde{\eta}_1-\eta_1}_{s(1)} - T^{\tilde{\eta}_1-\eta_1}_{c(1)}$$

Fig.6 Scheduling too many slave machines

4 Scheduling Algorithm

Relaxing the integral constraint on the scheduled task size, a minimal time schedule (for n machines) can be found in which $\omega_i=0$, $\chi_i=0$. This solution corresponds to
$T_{c(i)} + T_{r(i)} = T_{c(i+1)} + T_{s(i+1)}$. Using this relation in conjunction with the definition

of total task size, $\sum_{i=1}^{i=n} \eta_i = N$, the n values of η_i can be determined explicitly using Gaussian elimination on the n linear equations shown in Fig.7 .

(1) $T_{c\,(1)} + T_{r(1)} = T_{c(2)} + T_{s(2)}$

$\vdots$

(n–1) $T_{c\,(n-1)} + T_{r(n-1)} = T_{c(n)} + T_{s(n)}$

(n) $\sum_{i=1}^{n} \eta_i = N$

Fig.7 Set of linear equations defining schedule with $\chi_i = 0$, $\omega_i = 0$ for all i

Although no closed form solution for n exists, an appropriate number of slave machines can be determined by the evaluation of ϱ as described by conditions 3&4. The computational cost of finding the appropriate number of machines is very low due to the assumption of linear communication. As $\varrho = T_{c(1)} - \sum_{i=2}^{n} T_{s(i)}$, a change in the number of slave machines requires only the recalculation of η_1 in order to evaluate the new ϱ value. Constructing the linear system of equations as:

(1) $\eta_2 = a_2\eta_1 + b_2$

(2) $\eta_3 = a_3\eta_1 + b_3$ where $a_i = \left(\dfrac{\gamma_{i-1}\phi_c + \beta\phi_r}{\gamma_i\phi_c + \beta\phi_s}\right)a_{i-1}$ for $i > 1$,

$\vdots$

(i) $\eta_i = a_i\eta_1 + b_i$ $b_i = \dfrac{T^0_{r(i-1)} - T^0_{s(i)}}{\gamma_i\phi_c + \beta\phi_s} + b_{i-1}$ for $i > 1$,

$\vdots$

(n–1) $\eta_n = a_n\eta_1 + b_n$ $b_1 = 0$, $a_1 = 1$.

We can calculate η_1 directly for any n (after the a_i and b_i values are found) using:

$$\eta_1 = \dfrac{N - \sum_{i=1}^{n} b_i}{\sum_{i=1}^{n} a_i} \quad (*)$$

Hence the algorithm requires 2p steps to construct the a_i and b_i values, a maximum of p steps to define an appropriate number of slave machines, and a maximum of p steps to define the η_i values for the schedule, where p is the total number of slave machines.

   As an actual schedule must stick to integer task sizes, the real valued task sizes must be converted to integral values in a manner which does not violate conditions 1,2,3,4. This integer approximation, $\overline{\eta}_i$, must also satisfy the condition: $\sum_{i=1}^{n} \overline{\eta}_i = N$. A histogram based thresholding technique is used on the non–integral portions of the η_i values. This procedure selects a threshold ζ such that $\sum_{i=1}^{n} \overline{\eta}_i = N$ and requires kn steps where k is the number of bins used in the histogram. As shown in the Appendix, this thresholding method does not violate conditions 1 or 2.

5 Low Level Vision Modeling

The low level computer vision tasks needed for the AVIS computations are: convolution, difference of Gaussian, Fourier transform, Hough transform, and morphological filtering operations. Although explication of these of these algorithms is beyond the scope of this paper, thorough discussions can be found in [1][4][5][12][16][17][18]. For the purpose of this study, the key algorithmic elements are contained in the model parameters: $\gamma_i, \phi_c, \phi_s, \phi_c, T_s^0, T_r^0$. These algorithm specific parameters are presented in Fig.8.

	Convolution	DoG	Morphological	2D FFT	Hough
γ_i	$\dfrac{secs}{mult + add}$	$\dfrac{secs}{mult + add}$	$\dfrac{secs}{2logical\ Ops}$	$\dfrac{secs}{cmplx(mult + add)}$	$\dfrac{secs}{mult + trig\_lookup}$
ϕ_c	$M^2 N$	$\left(M_1^2 + M_2^2\right)N$	BN	$Nlog_2N$	1
ϕ_s	N	N	N	N	0
ϕ_r	N	N	N	N	1
$T_{s(i)}^0$	$\alpha + (M^2 + (M-1)N)\beta$	$\alpha + (M_1^2 + M_2^2 + (M_1 - 1)N)\beta$	$\alpha + (B + (M-1)N)\beta$	α	$\alpha + N^2\beta$
$T_{r(i)}^0$	α	α	α	α	α

Fig.8 Table of scheduling parameters for the low level vision algorithms.(α is the communication channel overhead (sec), β is the sec/byte transfer rate of the communication channel, the image is size NxN, the kernel(i) size is M_ixM_i, and the number of elements in the morphological kernel is B.)

6 Experimental Results

The heterogeneous distributed architecture included several machine types and configurations. The machines included HP 9000 715/33s, a MasPar MP–1(1024 processors), and SUN SPARCstations– IPXs, LXs, IIGXs, 5s, 20s(1&4processor). For a given algorithm, a testing set was generated and run on each architecture. Based on the results of the test suite, a single γ value was assigned to each architecture for that algorithm type. The sample mean values of the experimental gamma distributions were used for this single value. These values were stored and selectively loaded depending on the configuration of the parallel virtual machine being used. Similarly, the sample means of the α and β values were used in the scheduling experiments(8000μs&19μs/pixel for the XDR protocol). The scheduling algorithm is depicted in the graphic user interface (Fig.9).

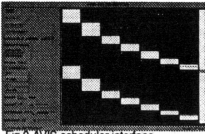

Fig.9 AVIS scheduler interface

Comparison of theoretical and experimental speedups of the modeled schedules are shown in Fig.10&Fig.11 for the convolution and DOG algorithms. As one would expect, the observed speedups were lower than the theoretical. The primary cause for this degradation was the nondeterminism of the communication and execution rates on the various machines. As the current scheduling algorithm uses only sample mean approximations of these nondeterministic values, it is susceptible to variances in these parameters. Efforts were made to run experiments during low usage periods in the day in order to minimize these effects. However, even in an isolated distributed system nondeterminism is evidenced due to memory coherency, operating system overhead, and communication protocols. Discussion of these nondeterministic issues can be found in [15].

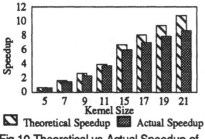

$\blacksquare$ Theoretical Speedup $\boxtimes$ Actual Speedup

Fig.10 Theoretical vs Actual Speedup of
Convolution

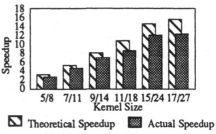

$\blacksquare$ Theoretical Speedup $\boxtimes$ Actual Speedup

Fig.11 Theoretical vs Actual Speedup of
DOG

7 Conclusions

The AVIS GUI Scheduler enables the visualization of the speedup of a given distributed algorithm. The scheduling technique presented enables the generation of a minimum time schedule in polynomial time. The relaxation on machine architecture homogeneity enables efficient solutions to low level vision problems using any set of Unix machines one has at their disposal. This makes for a system which is both cost effective and reconfigurable.

Analyses were presented in terms of machine specific $T^0_{s(i)}$, and $T^0_{r(i)}$ values. These enable a precise description of specific slave communication overheads. Similarly, the definition of machine specific neighborhood functions($\phi_{c(i)}$, $\phi_{s(i)}$, $\phi_{r(i)}$) is a simple extension of the current algorithm and may allow for a more precise description of architectural differences between platforms (i.e. memory configuration, pipeline depth, vectorization) and communication protocols(XDR, NFS, AFS). Although the formulations presented assume a single β value, they also can be extended to machine specific β_i. Defining β_i enables non–local machines to participate in the distributed algorithm more effectively than the current model allows. It is hoped that the inclusion of these parameters will reduce the parameter variance. As the parameter variance is the primarily cause for error in the predicted speedup of the schedule, this should create a more accurate theoretical model.

Acknowledgements

The authors would like to thank the reviewers for their time and helpful suggestions.

References

[1] Computer Vision, Dana H. Ballard, Christopher M. Brown, Prentice–Hall, Englewood Cliffs, New Jersey, 1982.

[2] Parallel Algorithms for Machine Intelligence and Vision(Vipin Kumar Editor) ,"Parallelism in Computer Vision: A Review", Vipin Chaudhary, J. K. Aggarwal, Springer–Verlag, NY 1990.

[3] Parallel Architectures and Parallel Algorithms for Integrated Vision Systems. Alok N. Choudhary, Janak H. Patel, The Kluwer International Series In Engineering and Computer Science, Kluwer Academic Publishers Boston, 1990.

[4] "SIMD Architectures and Algorithms for Image Processing and Computer Vision", Robert Cypher and Jorge L. C Sanz, *IEEE Trans on ASSP*, Vol. 37, No. 12, Dec. 1989.

[5] "Parallel Algorithms for Low Level Vision on the Homogeneous Multiprocessor", R.V Dantu, N.J Dimopoulos, K.R. Li, R.V Patel, A.J. Al–Khalili, *Computers Elect. Eng*, Vol. 20 No. 1, pp51–60, 1994.

[6] Jack Dongarra, PVM3.3 Users Guide, 1994.

[7] "Parallel Programming Systems For Workstation Clusters", Yale University Department of Computer Science Research Report, YALEU/DCS/TR–975, August, 1993.

[8]"Generalization of an Automated Visual Inspection System(AVIS)", Bryan S. Everding, Adam R. Nolan, William G. Wee, SAE Aerospace Atlantic Conference, April 1994.

[9] "Heterogeneous Processing", Richard F. Freund, Howard Jay Siegel,Computer , June 1993, p 13.

[10] "The Challenges of Heterogeneous Computing", Richard F. Freund, Proceedings of the Parallel Systems Fair, Cancun, April 1994.

[11] "Efficient Parallel Image Processing Applications On a Network Of Distributed Workstations", Chi–kin Lee, Mounir Hamdi, *Proceedings of the Parallel Systems Fair*, Cancun, April 1994.

[12] Vision. A Computational Investigation into the Human Representation and Processing of Visual Information, David Marr, W.H Freeman Press, San Francisco, 1982.

[13] "LINDA and PVM: A comparison between two environments for parallel programming", Alfonso Matrone, Pasquale Schiano, Vittorio Puoti, Parallel Computing 19(1993) 949–957.

[14]"Performance Issues of an Automated Visual Inspection System(AVIS)", Bryan S. Everding, Adam R. Nolan, William G. Wee, AIAA Jet Propulsion Conference, June 1994

[15] "Effects of Nondeterminism on the Predicted Speedup of Scheduling Low Level Computer Vision Algorithms on Networks of Heterogeneous Machines", A. R. Nolan, B. Everding, W. G. Wee, 5th International Conference on Parallel Computing, Belgium, September, 1995.

[16] Digital Signal Processing. Oppenheim, A.V., and Schafer, R.W., Englewood Cliffs, NJ, Prentice–Hall,. 1975.

[17] "Mapping Vision Algorithms to Parallel Architectures", Quentin Stout, *Proceeding of the IEEE*, Vol. 76. No. 8. August, 1988.

[18] "DARPA Image Understanding Benchmark for Parallel Computers", Charles Weems, Edward Riseman, Allen Hanson, Azriel Rosenfeld, *Journal of Parallel and Distributed Computing*, Vol. 11 No. 1 Jan. 1991, pp1–24.

Appendix

Condition1: For any given schedule $\mathcal{S}(n)$ in which $\chi_j \geq T^1_{c(j)} + T^1_{c(1)}$, $j > 1$,

there exists an alternative schedule $\tilde{\mathcal{S}}(n)$ with $\tilde{\chi}_j < T^1_{c(j)} + T^1_{c(1)}$ such that $\tilde{T}(n) < T(n)$.

Proof : For a given χ_j , there exists a corresponding task size η_{χ_j} defined as :

$$\eta_{\chi_j} = \text{int}_{\min}\left(\frac{\chi_j}{T^1_{c(j)} + T^1_{c(1)}}\right), \ \tilde{\chi}_j = \chi_j - T^{\eta_{\chi_j}}_{c(1)} - T^{\eta_{\chi_j}}_{c(j)} \text{ which results}$$

in the following bound : $0 \leq \tilde{\chi}_j < T^1_{c(j)} + T^1_{c(1)}$.

Case 1) If $\chi_i = 0 \ \forall \ i < j$ in a given schedule $\mathcal{S}(n)$, the corresponding execution time is :

$$T(n) = \sum_{i=1}^{n}T_{s(i)} + \sum_{i=1}^{n}T_{r(i)} + \lfloor \varrho \rfloor + \chi_j + \sum_{i=j+1}^{n}\chi_i$$

defining a new schedule $\tilde{\mathcal{S}}(n)$ such that $\tilde{\eta}_1 = \eta_1 + \eta_{\chi_j}$, $\tilde{\eta}_j = \eta_j - \eta_{\chi_j}$.

$$\tilde{\chi}_j = \chi_j - T^{\eta_{\chi_j}}_{c(1)} - T^{\eta_{\chi_j}}_{c(j)}$$

The execution time for that schedule is $\hat{T}(n) = \sum_{i=1}^{n} T_{s(i)} + \sum_{i=1}^{n} T_{r(i)} + \tilde{\varrho} + \tilde{\chi}_j + \sum_{i=j+1}^{n} \chi_i$

$$\text{where } \tilde{\varrho} = \varrho + T_{c(1)}^{\eta\chi_j} + T_{s(1)}^{\eta\chi_j}$$

Hence, $\hat{T}(n) = \sum_{i=1}^{n} T_{s(i)} + \sum_{i=1}^{n} T_{r(i)} + \varrho + T_{c(1)}^{\eta\chi_j} + T_{s(1)}^{\eta\chi_j} + \tilde{\chi}_j + \sum_{i=j+1}^{n} \chi_i$

If $\varrho \geq 0$, $T(n) - \hat{T}(n) = \chi_j - T_{c(1)}^{\eta\chi_j} - T_{s(1)}^{\eta\chi_j} - \tilde{\chi}_j = T_{c(j)}^{\eta\chi_j} - T_{s(1)}^{\eta\chi_j} > 0$,

$$\text{by assumption of } T_c > T_r + T_s$$

If $\varrho < 0$, $T(n) - \tilde{T}(n) = \chi_j - \left\lfloor \varrho + T_{c(1)}^{\eta\chi_j} + T_{s(1)}^{\eta\chi_j} \right\rfloor - \tilde{\chi}_j$

$$= T_{c(j)}^{\eta\chi_j} + T_{c(1)}^{\eta\chi_j} - \left\lfloor \varrho + T_{c(1)}^{\eta\chi_j} + T_{s(1)}^{\eta\chi_j} \right\rfloor$$

$\min\left(T(n) - \hat{T}(n)\right) = T_{c(j)}^{\eta\chi_j} - T_{s(1)}^{\eta\chi_j} > 0$, $\max\left(T(n) - \hat{T}(n)\right) = T_{c(j)}^{\eta\chi_j} + T_{c(1)}^{\eta\chi_j} > 0$

Case 2) If $\chi_i > 0$ for some $i < j$ in a given schedule $\mathcal{I}(n)$:

$$\chi_i = \left\lfloor T_{c(i)} - \left(\sum_{k=i+1}^{n} T_{s(k)} + \sum_{k=1}^{i-1} T_{r(k)} + \lfloor\varrho\rfloor \right) \right\rfloor$$

for $i < j$, $\tilde{\chi}_i = \left\lfloor T_{c(i)} - \left(\sum_{k=i+1}^{n} T_{s(k)} - T_{s(j)}^{\eta\chi_j} + \sum_{k=1}^{i-1} T_{r(k)} + T_{r(1)}^{\eta\chi_j} + \lfloor\tilde{\varrho}\rfloor \right) \right\rfloor$

as $\tilde{\varrho} = \varrho + T_{c(1)}^{\eta\chi_j} + T_{s(j)}^{\eta\chi_j}$, $\tilde{\chi}_i = \chi_i - \left\lfloor \varrho - T_{r(1)}^{\eta\chi_j} + T_{c(1)}^{\eta\chi_j} \right\rfloor$, $\tilde{\chi}_i \leq \chi_i$

$T(n) - \hat{T}(n) = \chi_j - T_{c(j)}^{\eta\chi_j} - \tilde{\chi}_j + \chi_i - \lfloor\tilde{\chi}_i\rfloor > 0$

Condition 2 : Given a schedule $\mathcal{I}(n)$ with $\omega_j \geq T_{c(j-1)}^{1} + T_{r(j-1)}^{1} + T_{c(j)}^{1} + T_{s(j)}^{1}$

for some j , there exists an alternative schedule $\tilde{\mathcal{I}}(n)$ with

$$\omega_j < T_{c(j-1)}^{1} + T_{r(j-1)}^{1} + T_{c(j)}^{1} + T_{s(j)}^{1} \text{ such that } \hat{T}(n) < T(n) .$$

Proof : For any given $\omega_j \geq T_{c(j-1)}^{1} + T_{r(j-1)}^{1} + T_{c(j)}^{1} + T_{s(j)}^{1}$ an alternate

mapping can be defined as : $\tilde{\eta}_{j-1} = \eta_{j-1} - \eta_{\omega j}$, $\tilde{\eta}_j = \eta_j + \eta_{\omega j}$

$$\text{where } \eta_{\omega j} = \text{int}_{\min}\left(\frac{\omega_j}{T_{c(j-1)}^{1} + T_{r(j-1)}^{1} + T_{c(j)}^{1} + T_{s(j)}^{1}} \right)$$

Case 1) $j = 2$, $\tilde{\varrho} = \varrho - T_{c(1)}^{\eta\omega j} - T_{s(1)}^{\eta\omega j}$,

If $\varrho \geq T_{c(1)}^{\eta\omega j} - T_{s(1)}^{\eta\omega j}$, $T(n) - \hat{T}(n) = T_{c(1)}^{\eta\omega j} + T_{s(1)}^{\eta\omega j} > 0$.

If $\varrho < T_{c(1)}^{\eta\omega j} - T_{s(1)}^{\eta\omega j}$, $T(n) - \hat{T}(n) = \varrho \geq 0$.

Case 2) $j > 2$, $\tilde{\chi}_{j-1} = \chi_{j-1} - T^{\eta\omega}{}_{j_{c(j-1)}} - T^{\eta\omega}{}_{j_{s(j-1)}}$

$$T(n) = \sum_{i=1}^{n} T_{s(i)} + \sum_{i=1}^{n} T_{r(i)} + \lfloor \varrho \rfloor + \sum_{i=2}^{n} \chi_i$$

$$\tilde{T}(n) = \sum_{i=1}^{n} T_{s(i)} + \sum_{i=1}^{n} T_{r(i)} + \lfloor \varrho \rfloor + \sum_{i=2}^{j-2} \chi_i + \tilde{\chi}_{j-1} + \tilde{\chi}_j + \sum_{i=j+1}^{n} \chi_i,$$

As $\tilde{\chi}_j \leq 0$, If $\tilde{\chi}_{j-1} \geq 0$, $T(n) - \tilde{T}(n) = T^{\eta\omega}{}_{j_{c(j-1)}} + T^{\eta\omega}{}_{j_{s(j)}} > 0$.

If $\tilde{\chi}_{j-1} < 0$, $T(n) - \tilde{T}(n) = \chi_{j-1} \geq 0$.

Condition 3: For any given schedule $\mathcal{S}(n)$ with $\varrho > T^0_{s(n+1)} + T^0_{r(n+1)}$, satifying conditions 1&2 there exists an alternative schedule $\mathcal{S}(n+1)$ such that $T(n+1) < T(n)$.

Proof: Define a new mapping $\mathcal{S}(n+1)$ such that $\tilde{\eta}_1 = \dfrac{N - \sum\limits_{i=1}^{n+1} b_i}{\sum\limits_{i=1}^{n+1} a_i}$ as defined in (*)

The schedule $\mathcal{S}(n+1)$ has an execution time of $T(n+1) = \sum\limits_{i=1}^{i=n+1} T_{s(i)} + \sum\limits_{i=1}^{i=n+1} T_{r(i)} + \lfloor \tilde{\varrho} \rfloor$

$$T(n+1) = \sum_{i=1}^{i=n} T_{s(i)} + T^0_{s(n+1)} + \sum_{i=1}^{i=n} T_{r(i)} + T^0_{r(n+1)} + \lfloor \tilde{\varrho} \rfloor$$

$$\tilde{\varrho} = \left\lfloor T^{\tilde{\eta}_1}_{c(1)} - \sum_{i=2}^{n} T_{s(i)} - T^0_{s(n+1)} - T^{\eta_1 - \tilde{\eta}_1}_{s(1)} \right\rfloor$$

$$T(n) - T(n+1) = \varrho - \lfloor \tilde{\varrho} \rfloor + \sum_{i=1}^{i=n} T_{s(i)} + \sum_{i=1}^{i=n} T_{r(i)} - \sum_{i=1}^{i=n+1} T_{s(i)} - \sum_{i=1}^{i=n+1} T_{r(i)}$$

Case1) $\tilde{\varrho} \geq 0$, $T(n) - T(n+1) = T^{\eta_1 - \tilde{\eta}_1}_{c(1)} + T^{\eta_1 - \tilde{\eta}_1}_{s(1)} - T^0_{r(n+1)} > 0$.

Case2) $\tilde{\varrho} < 0$, $T(n) - T(n+1) = \varrho - T^0_{r(n+1)} - T^0_{s(n+1)} > 0$.

Condition 4: For any given schedule $\mathcal{S}(n)$ with $\varrho < T^0_{r(n)} + T^{\tilde{\eta}_1 - \eta_1}_{s(1)} - T^{\tilde{\eta}_1 - \eta_1}_{c(1)}$ satisfying conditions1&2, there exists an alternative schedule $\mathcal{S}(n-1)$ such that $T(n-1) < T(n)$.

Proof: $\mathcal{S}(n)$ with the above constraints results in $T(n) = \sum\limits_{i=1}^{i=n} T_{s(i)} + \sum\limits_{i=1}^{i=n} T_{r(i)}$

Define a new mapping $\mathcal{S}(n-1)$ such that $\tilde{\eta}_1 = \dfrac{N - \sum\limits_{i=1}^{n-1} b_i}{\sum\limits_{i=1}^{n-1} a_i}$ as defined in (*)

$$T(n-1) = \sum_{i=1}^{i=n} T_{s(i)} - T^0_{s(n)} + \sum_{i=1}^{i=n} T_{r(i)} - T^0_{r(n)} + \lfloor \tilde{\varrho} \rfloor$$

$$\tilde{\varrho} = T^{\tilde{\eta}_1}_{c(1)} - \sum_{i=2}^{n} T_{s(i)} - T^0_{s(n)} - T^{\tilde{\eta}_1-\eta_1}_{s(1)} = \varrho + T^{\tilde{\eta}_1-\eta_1}_{c(1)} + T^0_{s(n)} - T^{\tilde{\eta}_1-\eta_1}_{s(1)}$$

$$\eta_n = \sum_{i=1}^{n-1} \eta_i - \tilde{\eta}_i \; , \; T_{c(n)} < \sum_{i=1}^{n-1} T_{r(i)}$$

$$T(n) - T(n-1) = T^0_{s(n)} + T^0_{r(n)} - \lfloor \tilde{\varrho} \rfloor \; .$$

Case 1) $\tilde{\varrho} \leq 0$, $T(n) - T(n-1) = T^0_{s(n)} + T^0_{r(n)} > 0$

Case 2) $\tilde{\varrho} > 0$, $T(n) - T(n-1) = T^0_{s(n)} + T^0_{r(n)} - \left(\varrho + T^{\tilde{\eta}_1-\eta_1}_{c(1)} + T^0_{s(n)} - T^{\tilde{\eta}_1-\eta_1}_{s(1)} \right)$

$$= T^0_{r(n)} - \left(\varrho + T^{\tilde{\eta}_1-\eta_1}_{c(1)} - T^{\tilde{\eta}_1-\eta_1}_{s(1)} \right) > 0 \text{ if } \varrho < T^0_{r(n)} + T^{\tilde{\eta}_1-\eta_1}_{s(1)} - T^{\tilde{\eta}_1-\eta_1}_{c(1)}$$

Effect of threshold, ς, and associated approximation $\tilde{\eta}_i$ on χ_i :

Define $\tilde{\eta}_i = \text{int}(\eta_i)$, $\tilde{\eta}_i = \overline{\eta}_i$ if $\eta_i - \overline{\eta}_i < \varsigma$, $\tilde{\eta}_i = \overline{\eta}_i + 1$ if $\eta_i - \overline{\eta}_i \geq \varsigma$

$$\chi_i \leq \lfloor \gamma_i \phi_c \tilde{\eta}_{i-1} + \phi_s \tilde{\eta}_{i-1} + T^0_{s(i-1)} - \gamma_i \phi_c \tilde{\eta}_{i-1} - \phi_r \tilde{\eta}_{i-1} - T^0_{r(i-1)} \rfloor$$

$$\max(\chi)_i \leq \gamma_i \phi_c (1 - \varsigma) + \phi_s (1 - \varsigma) - \gamma_i \phi_c \varsigma - \phi_s \varsigma$$

$$\max(\chi)_i \leq T^1_{s(i)} + T^1_{c(i)} - \varsigma \left(T^1_{c(i)} + T^1_{s(i)} + T^1_{c(i-1)} + T^1_{r(i-1)} \right)$$

$$\max(\chi)_i \leq T^1_{s(i)} + T^1_{c(i)} < T^1_{c(j)} + T^1_{c(1)} \; .$$

$\therefore$ thresholding will not violate condition 1 .

Effect of threshold, ς, and associated approximation $\tilde{\eta}_i$ on ω_i :

$$\omega_i = \lfloor T_{c(i-1)} + T_{r(i-1)} - \left(T_{s(i)} + T_{c(i)} \right) \rfloor$$

Define $\tilde{\eta}_i = \text{int}(\eta_i)$, $\tilde{\eta}_i = \overline{\eta}_i$ if $\eta_i - \overline{\eta}_i < \varsigma$, $\tilde{\eta}_i = \overline{\eta}_i + 1$ if $\eta_i - \overline{\eta}_i \geq \varsigma$

$$\omega_i = \lfloor \gamma_i \phi_c \tilde{\eta}_{i-1} + \phi_r \tilde{\eta}_{i-1} + T^0_{r(i-1)} - \gamma_i \phi_c \tilde{\eta}_i - \phi_s \tilde{\eta}_i - T^0_{s(i)} \rfloor$$

$$\max(\omega_i) = \gamma_i \phi_c (1 - \varsigma) + \phi_r (1 - \varsigma) - \gamma_i \phi_c \varsigma - \phi_s \varsigma$$

$$\max(\omega_i) = T^1_{c(i-1)} - \varsigma T^1_{c(i-1)} + T^1_{r(i-1)} - \varsigma T^1_{r(i-1)} - \varsigma T^1_{c(i)} - \varsigma T^1_{s(i)}$$

$$< T^1_{c(j-1)} + T^1_{r(j-1)} + T^1_{c(j)} + T^1_{s(j)} \; .$$

$\therefore$ thresholding will not violate condition 2 .

Mapping Neural Network Back-Propagation onto Parallel Computers with Computation/Communication Overlapping

B. Girau

Laboratoire d'Informatique du Parallélisme - CNRS URA 1398
46 allée d'Italie, 69364 Lyon cedex 07, France
phone: + 33 72 72 85 47   fax: + 33 72 72 80 80   email: bgirau@lip.ens-lyon.fr
URL: http://www.ens-lyon.fr/~bgirau

Abstract. It is shown in [6] that mapping neural networks onto existing parallel computers leads to an unsatisfactory efficiency, except for irregularly connected networks, with several distinguishable highly connected regions. This paper shows how a four step decomposition of the back-propagation algorithm allows to introduce computation/communication overlapping so as to improve any parallel mapping of differentiable feedforward neural networks. This solution can adapt to both irregular and regular feedforward neural structures. Its computational complexity is estimated for multilayered networks. Unlike most network partitioning schemes, it can deal with multilayer networks using non-standard neurons, such as wavelet networks. Unlike a pattern partitioning algorithm, it is able to implement the stochastic gradient learning algorithm. Numerical results show that this solution should be considered as soon as communication overlapping is available.

1   Introduction

Many algorithms have been developed so as to parallelize neural network applications. A satisfactory survey of existing schemes to parallelize back-propagation can be found in [11]. The choice of the best parallelization method strongly depends on both neural network application and employed parallel machine. See [14] for a comparison between some standard methods.

Pattern partitioning schemes are coarse-grained methods. They require large pattern sets, and they are not able to implement a *stochastic gradient learning* algorithm, where the neural network parameters are updated after each pattern presentation. See [13] for a study on a ring, [9] for an improved version, and [7] for a study on several different parallel architectures.

Network partitioning schemes are medium to fine-grained methods. They apply to large neural networks. Their efficiency frequently depends on the density of the neural network connections. Some of them use efficient parallel implementations of the algebraic computations that are performed in a multilayer perceptron (MLP). See for instance [15], or [11, 18] in a less obvious way. Other ones try to *map* the natural parallelism of a neural network onto the parallel computer, by partitioning the neurons among the processors. A general study of this solution has been performed in [6]. It leads to a rather pessimistic conclusion about the efficiency of a neural network *mapping* onto existing machines. Moreover, such a mapping is ill-adapted to regular neural network structures such as MLPs, which are among the most employed neural networks in standard applications. A rather intuitive mapping for MLP is proposed in [16], but its satisfactory results are obtained on a particular parallel computer and it uses beyond measure MLPs.

The aim of this paper is to show how a precise study of the back-propagation algorithm allows an efficient *mapping*. It takes advantage of a general form of the back-propagation so as to introduce computation/communication overlapping. It applies to a general feedforward neural network model, including MLP, wavelet networks, RBF networks, and any irregularly connected feedforward neural network. A processing time model is provided for regular multilayer structures. The main drawback appears in the minimum size of the neural network layers that is required to allow the computation/communication overlapping. Numerical results show that, thanks to the introduced communication overlapping, the general unsatisfactory efficiency of neural network mappings is overcome for the particular case of the back-propagation implementation of large enough neural networks.

Section 2 shortly describes the general neural network model and the associated back-propagation. Section 3 focuses on the new parallelization method. Section 4 deals with the case of regular multilayer neural networks.

2 General feedforward neural networks

2.1 Neural network learning

In a learning phase, a pattern set is given. It contains inputs and the corresponding expected outputs. A learning iteration starts with an error computation. It estimates the difference between the expected outputs and the computed outputs for some selected patterns. Then the network parameters are modified to reduce this error. Several learning iterations are performed, with the same patterns or with different ones.

The error function is assumed to be differentiable. Then a *gradient descent* algorithm can be used for the learning iterations. If $P(t)$ is the parameter vector of the network at time t, and if $\mathcal{G}P(t)$ is the gradient of the error function with respect to the coordinates of $P(t)$, then $P(t+1) = P(t) - \epsilon\,\mathcal{G}P(t)$, where $\epsilon \in \mathbb{R}_+^*$. If the error function is computed for only one pattern, then the *stochastic gradient* algorithm is used (a new pattern is randomly chosen for each learning iteration). If the whole pattern set is considered, then it is called the *total gradient* algorithm. If every learning iteration uses only part of the pattern set, and if the size of this part is constant, then a *block-gradient* algorithm is used. It has often been pointed out that the convergence time of a neural network learning grows with the number of patterns handled by the error computation. Therefore, the fastest learning is the stochastic one.

The back-propagation algorithm is often employed, since many neural network applications use MLPs with a gradient descent learning and a *back-propagated* computation of the gradient.

2.2 Feedforward neural networks

A theoretical study of a general feedforward neural network model is proposed in [4, 5]. It shows that the back-propagation algorithm can adapt to any differentiable feedforward neural network. A MLP is only a particular feedforward neural network.

In this theory, a feedforward neural network is a DAG (directed acyclic graph), in which the predecessor set of each node has been totally ordered. The vertices are differentiable vectorial functions $f_i(x_i, p_i)$, $1 \leq i \leq I$, where x_i is the input vector of vertex i, and p_i is its parameter vector. Layers can be defined so that any f_i in layer l can compute its output as soon as all f_j in layers $0, \ldots, l-1$ have computed their own outputs. If f_i has no predecessor in the graph, then it is an input vertex, and it belongs to the first layer. Else its input is obtained by appending together the outputs of all its predecessors. Then the whole neural network $\mathcal{N}$ is defined as follows: the inputs of the input vertices form the input vector of $\mathcal{N}$, the parameter vector of $\mathcal{N}$ is $P(t) = (p_1, \ldots, p_I)$, and the output of $\mathcal{N}$ is obtained by appending together the outputs computed by the vertices that have no successor in the graph. To simplify, functions f_i may be called *neurons*. This formal definition allows to show that the function computed by a neural network may be considered as a neuron.

2.3 Back-propagation

In any general feedforward neural network, $\mathcal{G}P(t)$ can be computed thanks to a back-propagated algorithm, which is faster than the natural gradient computation that considers $\mathcal{N}$ as a composite function. See [4] for a mathematical description of this general back-propagation, and a full study of its complexity. This algorithm requires *local* operations (it may be described as a sequence of computations performed by each neuron thanks to local data only).

Let $\mathcal{G}P_i$ be the gradient of the error function with respect to p_i. Let $\mathcal{G}X_i$ be the gradient of the error function with respect to x_i. Let $f_1^{(i)}, \ldots, f_{s_i}^{(i)}$ be the successors of f_i in the graph. For each $j \in \{1, \ldots, s_i\}$, let $\mathcal{G}X_j^{(i)}$ be the gradient of the error function with respect to the input of f_j that is received from f_i (i.e., $\mathcal{G}X_j^{(i)}$ is the part of $\mathcal{G}X_j$ that corresponds to the connection from f_i to f_j). Let $\mathcal{J}X_i$ be the matrix of the local differential (jacobian matrix) of f_i with respect to its input and let $\mathcal{J}P_i$ be the local jacobian matrix of f_i with respect to its parameter. Then the back-propagation theorem implies that:

$$\mathcal{G}P_i = \sum_{j=1}^{s_i} \mathcal{G}X_j^{(i)} \mathcal{J}P_i \quad \text{and} \quad \mathcal{G}X_i = \sum_{j=1}^{s_i} \mathcal{G}X_j^{(i)} \mathcal{J}X_i$$

According to this mathematical description, two steps can be defined for the local computation of each neuron:

1. Within the forward step, a neuron waits for its inputs from its predecessors, then it computes its own output and forwards it to its successors.
2. Within the backward step, it waits for the gradients from its successors. Then it applies their sum to its local differentials, and thus obtains the gradient of the error function with respect to its parameters and to its inputs. It sends the latter $(\mathcal{G}X_i)$ backwards to its predecessors.

3 Back-propagation and mapping

3.1 Computation/communication overlapping

Let $\mathcal{N} = \{f_1, \ldots, f_I\}$ be a feedforward neural network. Let $\mathcal{M}$ be a mapping of $\mathcal{N}$ onto a parallel computer: $\mathcal{M}(f_i)$ is the processor on which neuron f_i has been mapped.

Principle

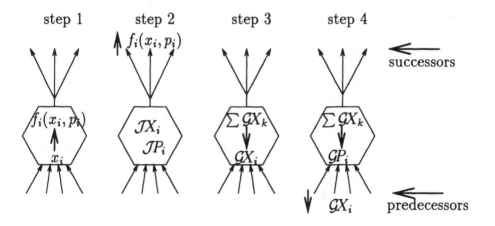

Fig. 1. Four steps of back-propagation

Instead of performing only two steps, forward and backward, each **local** computation can be divided into four steps (see figure 1):

1. Neuron F_i computes its output $(f_i(x_i, p_i))$ thanks to the received inputs (x_i) and then it sends this output to its successors.
2. Neuron F_i computes its local differentials, $\mathcal{J}X_i$ and $\mathcal{J}P_i$, which only depend on the forwarded data (i.e., the already received inputs).

3. Thanks to the backpropagated gradient $(\sum \mathcal{G}X_k)$ that have been sent by its successors, neuron F_i computes the gradient of the error function with respect to its input $(\mathcal{G}X_i)$, and then it sends this gradient to its predecessors.
4. Neuron F_i computes the gradient of the error function with respect to its parameter vector $(\mathcal{G}P_i)$.

This decomposition allows an interesting computation/communication overlapping, if the machine allows asynchronous non-blocking communications:

> Each neuron may send its computed output while it computes its local differentials (the computation of step 2 overlaps the forward communication). In the same way, it may send the gradient of the error function with respect to its inputs while it computes the gradient of the error function with respect to its parameters (the computation of step 4 overlaps the backward communication). Moreover, the neural network can be locally updated within step 4 by means of $p_i(t+1) = p_i(t) - \epsilon \mathcal{G}P_i(t)$.

Algorithm

Each processor p performs the following algorithm for one iteration of the back-propagation. *This algorithm will be called* CCO *algorithm from now on.*

FIRST INITIALIZATION: I_p is the set of input neurons that $\mathcal{M}$ maps on p.
FIRST LOOP:
do: 1. Step 1 performed for each neuron in I_p
    2. Simultaneously:
       – Step 2 performed for each neuron in I_p.
       – Non-blocking one-to-all (worst case) communication to communicate the computed outputs to the other processors. Indeed, this message has to be received only by the processors that contain successors of any neuron in I_p.
    3. I_p updated as follows: it is the set of the neurons mapped by $\mathcal{M}$ on p, for which steps 1 and 2 have not been performed and for which all required inputs have been received from the other processors.
until: Steps 1 and 2 have been performed for every neuron mapped on p.
SECOND INITIALIZATION: I_p is the set of output neurons mapped by $\mathcal{M}$ on p.
SECOND LOOP:
do: 1. Step 3 performed for each neuron in I_p
    2. Simultaneously:
       – Step 4 performed for each neuron in I_p (possibly including the local parameter updating).
       – Non-blocking one-to-all (worst case) personal communication to communicate the computed gradients to every other processor.
    3. I_p updated as follows: it is the set of the neurons mapped by $\mathcal{M}$ on p, for which steps 3 and 4 have not been performed and for which all required back-propagated gradients have been received from the other processors.
until: Steps 3 and 4 have been performed for every neuron mapped on p.

In this algorithm, several patterns may be simultaneously handled. In this case, each communication gathers the data for all patterns.

Implementations of gradient descent algorithms

Any gradient descent algorithm can be implemented with a neural network parallel mapping, and therefore with the CCO algorithm. Each computation step may be processed for a single pattern as well as for the whole pattern set, provided that it does not exceed the per-processor memory. Another way to introduce computation/communication overlapping is to pipeline the patterns, but this solution can not implement the stochastic gradient algorithm.

3.2 Suitable mappings and parallel architectures

The efficiency of the algorithm depends on the neural network and on the chosen mapping $\mathcal{M}$. The choice of $\mathcal{M}$ chiefly depends on the neural network structure, but it depends on the parallel computer architecture too.

Architecture

A good criterion to choose the parallel architecture is the total number of messages implied by both all-to-all communication (multinode broadcast within step 2) and all-to-all personal communication (multinode scattering within step 4). If a non-blocking communication call is modelled as a constant startup time, and if the transfer time is overlapped by computation, then the communication cost of the CCO algorithm is proportional to the number of messages. Table 1 recalls both number of messages and communication times for some standard architectures. The hypercube structure should be chosen if available. Indeed, hypercube-like communications can be simulated on other hardware architectures without loss of performance (e.g. on the Cray T3D).

		ring	grid/torus	hypercube
all-to-all	messages	$\mathcal{O}(p)$	$\mathcal{O}(\sqrt{p})$	$\mathcal{O}(\log(p))$
	total time	$\mathcal{O}(p)$	$\mathcal{O}(p)$	$\mathcal{O}(p)$
personal	messages	$\mathcal{O}(p)$	$\mathcal{O}(\sqrt{p})$	$\mathcal{O}(\log(p))$
all-to-all	total time	$\mathcal{O}(p^2)$	$\mathcal{O}(p\sqrt{p})$	$\mathcal{O}(p\log(p))$

Table 1. Communication costs for several parallel architectures

Since each communication uses several messages, the computation of steps 2 and 4 has to be sliced, so that the parallel implementation performs the computational operations and the non-blocking communication calls by turns. Reliable computation and communication time models are required to obtain a precise overlapping.

Mapping

Any feedforward neural network implies sequential computation (e.g. neurons in layer l have to wait for neurons in layer $l-1$ in the forward step). Therefore, a good mapping probably performs a quite vertical sectioning, i.e., it partitions the neurons of each layer quite regularly among the processors.

For very irregular structures, the study of [6] provides suitable mappings. Another method is to consider any feedforward neural network as a reversible task graph, and then to use any standard scheduling algorithm. See [7] for a study of the Modified Critical Path scheduling with both forward and backward phases.

For regular structures, such as multilayer neural networks, the strict vertical sectioning (see next section) is a satisfactory mapping. In the *checkerboarding* method proposed by [11], each neuron is mapped onto several processors. But this solution limits itself to multilayer perceptrons, since they perform large matrix-vector products (that do not appear in a wavelet network for instance).

4 Multilayer networks

4.1 Notations

Let L be the number of layers. Let n_l be the number of neurons in layer l. Each neuron in layer 1 receives n_0 inputs, which are the network inputs. For each $l \in \{2, \ldots, L\}$, each neuron in layer l receives n_{l-1} inputs, and computes one output in $\mathbb{R}$. These inputs are the outputs of the neurons in layer $l-1$. Therefore, consecutive layers are fully connected. The outputs of the neurons in layer L are the outputs of the network. The standard quadratic error function is used. All neurons are identical (f_i does not depend on i).

It is assumed that the computation time of a neuron is linear with respect to its number of parameters. In the same way, the computation time of its differentials is linear with respect to its number of parameters. It is also assumed that its number of parameters is proportional to its input size. Sigmoid neurons, wavelet neurons and RBF neurons satisfy these conditions.

Therefore, the computation time of step j ($1 \leq j \leq 4$) will be modelled as: $\gamma_j + \delta_j n_{l-1}$ for any neuron in layer l (updating might be taken into account by step 4). For the last layer, the differential of the error function has to be computed: δ_e for one output neuron.

A *vertical sectioning* with p processors is used. Each processor deals with n_l/p neurons in layer l. To simplify, it is assumed that each n_l is a multiple of p. In practice, if a layer contains too few neurons, it may be interesting to map the whole layer onto one processor, and to perform only one-to-all and all-to-one communications for this layer. Indeed, standard applications often have small numbers of output neurons.

In what follows, the diameter of the parallel architecture is called d. It is equal to $\log_2(p)$ for a hypercube, and $2\sqrt{p}$ for a grid. A constant time model, $\beta_{c/c}$ is used for the non-blocking communication calls. With existing machines, this model is simple, but satisfactory. See [7] for a full study with the Intel iPSC 860 (also available in my URL).

4.2 Computational complexity

Let k be the number of simultaneously handled patterns.

STEP 1 FOR LAYER l:	$k(\gamma_1 + \delta_1 n_{l-1})\frac{n_l}{p}$
STEP 2 FOR LAYER l $(l < L)$:	$k(\gamma_2 + \delta_2 n_{l-1})\frac{n_l}{p} + 2d\beta_{c/c}$
	(no transfer time, on account of over-lapping)
STEP 2 FOR LAYER L:	$k(\gamma_2 + \delta_2 n_{L-1})\frac{n_L}{p}$
STEP 3 FOR LAYER L:	$k(\gamma_3 + \delta_3 n_{L-1} + \delta_e)\frac{n_L}{p}$
STEP 3 FOR LAYER l $(1 < l < L)$:	$k(\gamma_3 + \delta_3 n_{l-1})\frac{n_l}{p}$
STEP 3 FOR LAYER 1:	0, since the gradient with respect to the network inputs is useless.
STEP 4 FOR LAYER l $(1 < l)$:	$k(\gamma_4 + \delta_4 n_{l-1})\frac{n_l}{p} + 2d\beta_{c/c}$
STEP 4 FOR LAYER 1:	$k(\gamma_4 + \delta_4 n_0)\frac{n_1}{p}$

The expected speedup is then $\dfrac{pT_{\text{seq}}}{T_{\text{seq}} + 2(L-1)dp\beta_{c/c}}$, with

$$T_{\text{seq}} = k\left[\Gamma(\sum_{l=2}^{L} n_l) + \Delta(\sum_{l=2}^{L} n_{l-1}n_l) + \delta_e n_L + (\Gamma - \gamma_3)n_1 + (\Delta - \delta_3)n_0 n_1\right]$$

where $\Gamma = \sum_{i=1}^{4} \gamma_i$ and $\Delta = \sum_{i=1}^{4} \delta_i$.

4.3 Minimum layer size

The first condition to obtain this speedup is that the communication overlapping is allowed. Therefore, the computation loads have to exceed the message transfer times. If τ is the transfer time for one real, two conditions must be satisfied:

overlapping within step 2: $\forall l \in [1, L-1]$ $2p\tau \leq (\gamma_2 + \delta_2 n_{l-1})$ (1)

overlapping within step 4: $\forall l \in [2, L]$ $2dpn_{l-1}\tau \leq (\gamma_4 + \delta_4 n_{l-1})n_l$ (2)

For the particular case of a MLP, an optimization may be introduced. Step 2 may be enclosed in both step 3 and step 4 without significant loss of time, since these steps are equivalent to scalar multiplication applied to both local input and parameter vectors. Therefore, step 2 only performs an all-to-all communication, whereas step 4 communication is still overlapped by computation. Dealing with a MLP is *the worst case for the* CCO *algorithm*.

4.4   Results

Comparison with network-partitioning schemes

Various works were considered, such as [16] (based on the same vertical partitioning as in section 4, but outperformed by [11]), [14], [15] or [18]. The checkerboarding method of [11] (hereafter called CB algorithm) is finally taken as a reference, with regard to its high efficiency and scalability. Of course, only the case of a MLP is considered, since the CB method only applies to this type of neural network. Therefore, only condition 2 is taken into account to estimate the minimum layer size, since communications are not overlapped in step 2. The minimum values of the number of neurons are reported on figure 2.

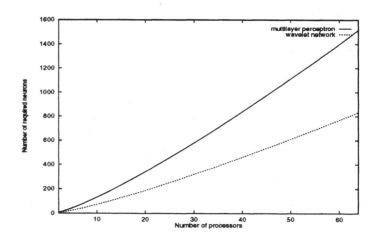

Fig. 2. Minimum number of neurons in each layer for the CCO algorithm

Comparison conditions

Speedups are computed with the same number n of neurons in each layer of the MLP. For this paper, experiments have been performed on an iPSC 860. The theoretical performance models of this paper and of [11] are therefore applied to this particular machine.

Speedups are given for 2-layer perceptrons in tables 2, 3 and 4. The box remains empty when overlapping conditions are not fulfilled. For the experimental results of table 4, the speedups are computed with respect to the theoretical sequential processing time, when the problem size does not allow one processor to handle as large MLPs as the parallel implementation can do. Moreover, the box remains empty when the neural network requires too much per-processor memory even for the parallel implementation.

In many experiments for the CCO algorithm, the per-processor memory limit did not allow to perform the computation for several patterns within a single forward-backward processing (too many data to store for each layer). In this case, the different patterns had to be processed one after each other. Therefore, all the given speedups of both CCO and CB methods are given for $k = 1$. It corresponds to the worst case for the theoretical speedup of both algorithms, but it shows what happens when the stochastic gradient is implemented.

	$p = 4$	$p = 16$	$p = 64$
$n = 30$	1.68	1.51	1.17
$n = 250$	3.78	12.39	28.45
$n = 1500$	3.97	15.51	57.04

Table 2. MLP: theoretical speedups for the checkerboarding parallelization ($k = 1$)

	$p = 4$	$p = 16$	$p = 64$
$n = 30$	2.26		
$n = 250$	3.85	13.1	
$n = 1500$	3.98	15.57	57.13

Table 3. MLP: theoretical speedups with the CCO algorithm ($k = 1$)

	$p = 4$	$p = 16$	$p = 64$
$n = 30$	1.19		
$n = 250$	3.65	13.3	
$n = 1500$		15.51	56.55

Table 4. MLP: experimental speedups with the CCO algorithm ($k = 1$)

	$p = 4$	$p = 16$	$p = 64$
$n = 30$	3.81		
$n = 250$	3.99	15.91	
$n = 1500$	4	16	63.94

Table 5. WN: theoretical speedups with the CCO algorithm ($k = 1$)

	$p = 4$	$p = 16$	$p = 64$
$n = 30$	3.51		
$n = 250$	3.93	15.68	
$n = 1500$		15.94	63.55

Table 6. WN: experimental speedups with the CCO algorithm ($k = 1$)

	$p = 4$	$p = 16$	$p = 64$
$k = p * 1$	0.44	0.39	0.38
$k = p * 10$	2.20	3.21	3.65
$k = p * 100$	3.69	11.45	24.13

Table 7. MLP: theoretical speedups with pattern-partition ($n = 250$)

	$p = 4$	$p = 16$	$p = 64$
$k = p * 1$	1.60	1.93	2.04
$k = p * 10$	3.48	9.25	15.88
$k = p * 100$	3.94	14.91	49.12

Table 8. WN: theoretical speedups with pattern-partition ($n = 250$)

Result comment

Overlapping provides very satisfactory performance, slightly better than the CB algorithm. But the CCO solution is available for a minimum number of neurons which is proportional to $p \log(p)$, whereas CB only requires a number of neurons proportional to $\sqrt{(p)}$.

Some loss of performance appears with experiments, when compared with the theoretical performance model. It can be explained by the fact that there is no autonomous DMA in an iPSC 860. Therefore, non-blocking communications imply a limited loss of performance during overlapping computation.

Comparison with pattern-partitioning schemes

Results for MLP are given for $n = 250$ in table 7 and in the second row of table 3. Results for wavelet networks (WN) are given for $n = 250$ in table 8 and in the second row of table 5. Speedup formulae for pattern-partitioning on hypercube architectures are taken from [7]. Let us recall that with the pattern partition, if each processor deals with b patterns, then the number of handled patterns is $k = p * b$.

Result comment

The performance of pattern-partitioning collapses when small blocks of patterns are handled and when many processors are used. Wavelet networks imply so much computation[1] that the parallel efficiency is usually greater than 99% when the CCO algorithm is used. Communications are easily overlapped by computations for this particular neural network.

When available, the CCO algorithm outperforms the pattern-partitioning method, which should still be used with reduced-sized neural networks and large training sets.

5 Conclusion

This paper introduces computation/communication overlapping in any parallel mapping of the neural network back-propagation algorithm. Overlapping appears thanks to a 4-step decomposition of this algorithm, whereas standard decompositions only use two steps.

It allows some performance improvement for MLP when it is compared to other network-partitioning schemes. But its main drawback is to require a number of neurons proportional to $p \log(p)$, if p is the number of useful processors. Nevertheless, unlike most network-partitioning schemes (particularly unlike the most efficient ones), it can be applied to any feedforward neural network.

The pattern-partitioning scheme also applies to any neural network structure, but its efficiency collapses when a small number of patterns is used. The parallel solution of this paper allows to use such small pattern sets. Moreover, it can implement the stochastic gradient, so that the learning time is reduced.

Some modified versions of this CCO implementation are under development. They reduce the number of required neurons per layer.

---

[1] for neuron i in layer l (see [17] for an introduction to wavelet networks), $\prod_{j=1}^{n_{l-1}} h(d_j^{(i)}(x_j - \theta_j^{(i)}))$, where $h(x) = -x \exp(-x^2/2)$. The $d_j^{(i)}$ and the $\theta_j^{(i)}$ are the parameters.

References

1. L. Bottou and P. Gallinari. A Framework for the Cooperation of Learning Algorithms. In R.P. Lippmann, J.E. Moody, and D.S. Touretzky, editors, *Neural Information Processing Systems*, volume 3, pages 781–788. Morgan Kauffman, 1991.
2. M. Cosnard, J.C. Mignot, and H. Paugam-Moisy. Implementations of multilayer neural networks on parallel architectures. In *Proc. 2nd IEE Int. Spec. Seminar on the Design and Application of Parallel Digital Processors*, pages 43–47, April 1991.
3. C. Gégout, B. Girau, and F. Rossi. NSK, an object-oriented simulator kernel for arbitrary feedforward neural networks. In *ICTAI Int. Conf. on Tools with Artificial Intelligence*, pages 95–104. IEEE Computer Society Press, 1994.
4. C. Gégout, B. Girau, and F. Rossi. A general feedforward neural network model. Technical report NC-TR-95-041, NeuroCOLT, Royal Holloway, University of London, 1995.
5. C. Gégout, B. Girau, and F. Rossi. Generic back-propagation in arbitrary feedforward neural networks. In R.F. Albrecht D.W. Pearson, N.C. Steel, editor, *Artificial Neural Nets and Genetic Algorithms – Proc. of ICANNGA*, pages 168–171. Springer-Verlag, 1995.
6. J. Ghosh and K. Hwang. Mapping neural networks onto message-passing multicomputers. *Journal of parallel and distributed computing*, 6:291–330, May 1989.
7. B. Girau. Algorithmes parallèles et modélisations pour les réseaux d'opérateurs. Master's thesis, LIP-ENSL, 1994.
8. B. Girau. Neural network parallelization on a ring of processors : training set partition and load sharing. Research report 94-35, LIP, 1994.
9. B. Girau and H. Paugam-Moisy. Load sharing in the training set partition algorithm for parallel neural learning. In *Proc. IPPS 9th Int. Parallel Processing Symposium*, pages 586–591. IEEE Computer Society Press, 1995.
10. R. Hecht-Nielsen. Theory of the backpropagation neural network. In *Proc. Int. Joint Conf. Neural Networks*, volume 1, pages 593–605, 1989.
11. V. Kumar, S. Shekhar, and M.B. Amin. A scalable parallel formulation of the back-propagation algorithm for hypercubes and related architectures. *IEEE Transactions on Parallel and Distributed Systems*, 5(10):1073–1090, October 1994.
12. Y. Le Cun. A theoretical framework for back-propagation. In D. Touretzky, G. Hinton, and T. Sejnowsky, editors, *Proc. of the 1988 Connectionist Models Summer School*, pages 21–28. Morgan-Kaufmann, 1988.
13. H. Paugam-Moisy. On a parallel algorithm for back-propagation by partitioning the training set. In *Proc. Neuro-Nîmes*, pages 53–65, 1992.
14. A. Pétrowski. Choosing among several parallel implementations of the backpropagation algorithm. In *Proc. ICNN*, pages 1981–1986, 1994.
15. A. Pétrowski, G. Dreyfus, and C. Girault. Performance analysis of a pipelined back-propagation parallel algorithm. *IEEE Transactions on Neural Networks*, 4(6):970–981, Nov. 1994.
16. H. Yoon and J.H. Nang. Multilayer neural networks on distributed-memory multiprocessors. In *Proc. INNC Paris*, volume 2, pages 669–672, 1990.
17. Q. Zhang and A. Benveniste. Wavelet networks. *IEEE Trans. On Neural Networks*, 3(6):889–898, Nov. 1992.
18. X. Zhang, M. McKenna, J.J. Mesirov, and D.L. Waltz. The backpropagation algorithm on grid and hypercube architectures. *Parallel Computing*, 14:317–327, 1990.

Language Implementation II

Super Monaco: Its Portable and Efficient Parallel Runtime System

J. S. Larson   B. C. Massey   E. Tick

University of Oregon, Eugene OR 97403, USA

Abstract. "Super Monaco" is the successor to Monaco, a shared-memory multiprocessor implementation of a flat concurrent logic programming language. While the system retains, by-and-large, the older Monaco compiler and intermediate abstract machine, the intermediate code translator and the runtime system have been completely replaced, incorporating a number of new features intended to improve robustness, flexibility, maintainability, and performance. There are currently two native-code backends for 80x86-based and MIPS-based multiprocessors. The runtime system, written in C, improves upon its predecessor with better memory utilization and garbage collection, and includes new features such as an efficient termination scheme and a novel variable binding and hooking mechanism. The result of this organization is a portable system[1] which is robust, extensible, and has performance competitive with C-based systems. This paper describes the design choices made in building the system and the interfaces between the components.

KEYWORDS: logic programming, parallelism, native code, runtime systems.

1 Introduction

Monaco is a high-performance parallel implementation of a subset of the KL1, a concurrent logic programming language [15], for shared-memory multiprocessors. "Super Monaco" is a second-generation implementation of this system, consisting of an evolved intermediate instruction set, a new assembler-generator, and a new runtime system. It incorporates the lessons learned in the first design [16], improves upon its predecessor with better memory utilization (via a 2-bit tag scheme and the use of 32-bit words) and garbage collection, and includes a number of new features: 1) Termination detection through conservative goal counting. 2) A new mechanism for hooking suspended goals to variables. 3) A specialized language for implementing intermediate code translators. 4) A clean and efficient calling interface between the runtime system and compiled code.

We have found that our changes to Monaco have increased the robustness, portability, and maintainability of the system, while increasing the performance. The system now has less than 1,000 lines of machine-dependent code, completely

---

[1] Available by anonymous ftp from `ftp.cs.uoregon.edu:pub/sm.tar.gz`.

encapsulated behind generic interfaces. The new assembler-assembler makes native code generation simple and declarative, while supporting the use of standard debugging and profiling tools. A conservative goal-counting algorithm implements distributed termination detection. The intermediate code is evolving toward a more abstract machine model, and thus toward more complex instructions. A new data layout makes for more compact use of memory, in conjunction with a novel hooking scheme which maintains references to suspended goals with a hash table indexed by variable address.

This paper discusses the design choices made in this second-generation system, its implementation and performance. Because of space limitations, we cannot review the compiler and assembler here (see Tick *et al.* [18]).

2 Monaco Intermediate Code

The Monaco instruction set presents an abstract machine which is at an intermediate level between the semantics of a concurrent logic program and the semantics of native machine code. The abstract machine consists of a number of independent processes which execute sequences of procedures and update a shared memory area. Each process has a set of abstract general-purpose registers which are used as operands for Monaco instructions and for passing procedure arguments. Control flow within a procedure is sequential with conditional branching to code labels. See Tick *et al.* [18] for intermediate code samples.

There are two unification operations. Passive unification verifies the equality of ground values (in contrast to systems such as JAM Parlog [4], which also verify the equality of terms in which uninstantiated variables are bound together). An attempt to passively unify a term containing uninstantiated variables will result in suspension of the process until those variables become instantiated. Active unification, on the other hand, will bind variables to other variables or to values in order to ensure equality of terms. As is customary in logic programming implementations, no "occurs check" is performed during unification for efficiency reasons. Variables are bound only through assignment operations or active unification.

The Monaco instruction set consists of about sixty operations. The operations are broadly categorized as: 1) Data constructors for each data type (constant, list, struct, goal record, variable). 2) Data manipulators for accessing the fields of aggregates. 3) Arithmetic operations. 4) Predicates for testing the types of most objects and for arithmetic comparisons. Predicates store the truth value of their result in a register. 5) Conditional branches based on the contents of a register. 6) Interfaces to runtime system operations for assignment, unification, suspension, and scheduling. 7) Instructions for manipulating the suspension stack. The instructions take constants or registers as their arguments and return their results in registers. There is no explicit access to the shared memory except through operations which access the fields of aggregates.

Each data constructor has a variant which serves to batch up allocation requests into a large block, and then initialize smaller sections of the block.

Batching up the frequent allocation requests increased performance on standard benchmarks, as discussed below in Section 5. In addition, aggregates which are fully ground at compile time are statically allocated in the text segment of the assembled code. This decreases execution and compilation times.

The instruction set is modeled after a reduced instruction set architecture, on the theory that such small instructions may be easily and efficiently translated to native RISC instructions with a simple assembler. However as frequent idioms are identified and coalesced, the Monaco instruction set has been evolving toward more complex instructions. There a few reasons for this trend: 1) Higher-level intermediate instructions better hide the runtime system implementation. 2) As the amount of work per instruction gets larger, more machine-specific optimizations can be made in the monaa code templates. (This is in contrast to systems such as [8], a sophisticated multi-level translation scheme producing good code by intelligent generation of simple intermediate instructions.)

3 The Runtime Data Layout

The previous memory layout [16] had three tag bits on each word, and words were laid out on eight-byte boundaries in memory. This prodigious use of memory was not merely a concession to the three tag bits; the unification scheme required each object to be lockable. As a consequence, some of the "extra" 32 bits of each word were used as a lock. While this led to a fine granularity for locking, it doubled the system's memory consumption. All objects are now represented as 32-bit words of memory aligned on four-byte address boundaries. This alignment restriction allows the low-order two bits of pointers to be used as tag bits, without loss of pointer range. The four tagged types are *immediates, list* pointers, *box* pointers, and *reference* pointers. Immediates are further subdivided into *integers, atoms,* and box *headers.* Integers have the distinction of being tagged with zero bits, allowing some optimizations to be made in arithmetic code generation. On most architectures, the pointer types suffer no inefficiencies from tagging, since negative offset addressing may be used to cancel the added tag.

List pointers point to the first of two consecutive words in memory, the head and the tail of the list, respectively. The *nil* list is represented as a list-tagged null pointer. Box pointers point to an array of n consecutive words in memory, the first of which is a box header word which encodes the size of the box and the type of its contents. Boxes are used to implement structs, goal records, and strings, as well as objects specific to the runtime system such as suspension slips.

There is only one mutable object type — the *unbound variable*, represented as a null pointer with a reference pointer tag. When a variable is bound, its value is changed to the binding value. When a variable is bound to another variable, one becomes a reference pointer to the other. Successive bindings of variables create trees of reference pointers which terminate in a root, which is either an unbound variable or some non-variable term. The special Monaco instruction deref must thus be applied to all input arguments of a procedure before they are examined. This operation chases down a chain of references to its root, and returns the root value or a reference to the unbound root variable. Thus, a conservative estimate of whether the variable is bound can be made quickly. In practice, this is a performance, not correctness, issue: the process may try to suspend on a recently instantiated variable, in which case the runtime system will detect its instantiation and resume execution of the process.

In old Monaco, one of the tag types was a *hook pointer*, which was semantically equivalent to an unbound variable, but pointed to the set of goal records suspended on that variable. All of the code which dealt with unbound variables also had to test for hook pointers and handle them separately. However, profiling revealed that suspension is a relatively rare event: most variables are never hooked. Therefore the new data layout keeps the association between unbound variables and suspended goal records "off-line." This new organization seems promising (see Section 4.3); contention for buckets is indeed rare, and we were able to simplify some critical code sections in unification.

4 The Runtime System

The runtime system is responsible for memory management, scheduling, unification, and the multiprocessor synchronization involved in assignment and suspension. It consists of about 2000 lines of machine-independent C code, and about 300 lines of machine-dependent C for a particular platform. It has been ported to the Sequent Symmetry and MIPS-based SGI machines.

Old Monaco used libraries provided by the host operating system [12] to implement parallel lightweight threads and memory management. Here we use a more operating system independent model. We create UNIX processes executing in parallel and communicating through machine-specific synchronization instructions in shared memory, using the **fork** and **mmap** system calls. The machine-dependent runtime system requires only a few synchronization primitives: 1) atomic exchange operation, 2) atomic increment and decrement, 3) simple spin locks, and 4) barrier synchronization. For the Symmetry port, atomic increment, decrement, and exchange are provided by the instruction set, while locks and barriers are synthesized with atomic exchange. The machine-independent code assumes globally reliable writes. The runtime system's interface with the compiled code is small and regular.

The resulting framework is portable since it does not rely on UNIX implementations' libraries for thread and memory management, but there are tradeoffs. UNIX debuggers are too low level. The shared memory must be managed explicitly; consequently, every runtime system data structure which must be visible to all worker processes be a C global, hindering code modularity. The UNIX scheduler infrequently interacts badly with our threads, as in [1].

4.1 Scheduling and Calling Interface

The Monaco abstract machine produces many thousands of processes during a typical computation, too many for implementation via UNIX kernel processes.

We treat UNIX "worker" processes as a set of virtual CPUs, on which we schedule Monaco processes in the runtime system.

A *goal record* records the procedure name and arguments of a Monaco Process. A ready set of goal records is maintained by the runtime system. Each worker process starts in a central work loop inside the runtime system. This loop executes until some global termination flag is set, or until there is no more work to do. The worker takes a goal record out of the ready set, loads its arguments into registers, and calls its entry point. The worker then executes a compiled procedure, including sequences of tail calls, until the compiled code terminates, suspends, or fails. These three operations are implemented by a return to the control work loop in the runtime system with a status code as the return value. In addition, the intermediate code instructions for enqueueing, assignment, and unification are implemented as procedure calls from the compiled code into the runtime system. Such calls return back to the compiled code when done, possibly with a status code as a return value. Control flow during a typical execution is illustrated in Figure 1. The runtime system invokes a Monaco procedure via a goal record (1), which tail-calls another procedure (2). This procedure attempts a passive unification via a call into the runtime system (3), which returns a constant *suspend* as an indication that the caller should suspend (4). The caller then suspends by returning the constant *suspend* to the runtime system (5).

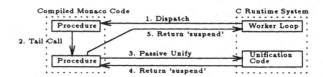

Fig. 1. Sample Control Flow in the Monaco System

The high contention experienced when the ready set is implemented as a shared, locked global object leads to the necessity of some form of distributed ready set implementation. In our scheme, each worker has a fixed-size local ready stack, corresponding to an efficient depth-first search of an execution subtree [14]. If the local stack overflows, local work is moved to a global ready stack. If workers are idle while local work is available, a goal is given to each idle worker, and the remaining local work is moved to the global ready stack. This policy is designed to work well both during normal execution, when many goals are available, and during the initial and final execution phases, when there is little work to do.

4.2 Termination

Execution of a Monaco program begins when goal records for the calls in the query are inserted into the ready set, and ends when there are no more runnable goals. At this point the computation has either terminated successfully, failed, or deadlocked — the difference can be easily determined in a post-mortem phase which looks for a global failure flag and suspended goals. A serious difficulty for a parallel implementation is efficiently deciding when termination should occur.

Many approaches to termination detection are susceptible to race conditions. The previous implementation maintained a monitor process which examined a status word maintained by each worker process, terminating the computation when it recognized that each work had maintained an idle state for some time. A locking scheme was used to avoid races by synchronizing the workers with the monitor, which hurt worker efficiency. Most importantly, the monitor process itself consumed a great deal of CPU time without performing much useful work.

In Super Monaco, we have adopted a different and (to the best of our knowledge) novel approach. We maintain a count of all outstanding goals: those either in the ready set or currently being executed by workers. Termination occurs when this count goes to zero. The count increases when work is placed in the ready set, and decreases when a goal suspends, terminates, or fails. The count is *not* changed by the removal of a goal from the ready set, since the goal makes a transition from the ready state to the executing state. There is a temporary overestimate of the number of goals outstanding during the transition interval between the time the goal suspends, terminates, or fails, and the time the count is decremented. However, this will not cause premature termination, since the overestimate means that the counter must indicate a nonzero number of outstanding goals. Because the count is not incremented until after a parent has decided to spawn a child goal, there is also a temporary underestimation of the goal count during this interval. As long as the count is incremented before the parent exits, this will not cause premature termination either: Since the parent has not yet exited, the count must be nonzero until after the underestimation is corrected. Thus, since mis-estimates of the number of outstanding goals are temporary and will not cause premature termination, our termination technique is both efficient and safe. On the Symmetry, we implemented this goal counting scheme with atomic increment and decrement instructions. We observed no contention on Symmetry, and hypothesize no contention on faster multiprocessors because work within a task overshadows locking.

4.3 Hooking and Suspension

In order to awaken suspended processes when a variable becomes instantiated, there must be some association between them. As noted in Section 3, old Monaco represented this association explicitly: some unbound variables were represented as pointers to sets of hooks. Figures 2a illustrates the old representation.

However, for our benchmark set, the vast majority of variables are never hooked. For a variety of reasons, the most important being the fact that we wanted to adopt two bit tag values to represent five types (immediates, lists, box pointers, variable pointers, and reference pointers), we chose to represent variables using a single word. Super Monaco continues to use suspension slips to implement suspension and resumption, as in systems such as JAM Parlog [4] and PDSS [10], except that the association between variables and hooks is reversed.

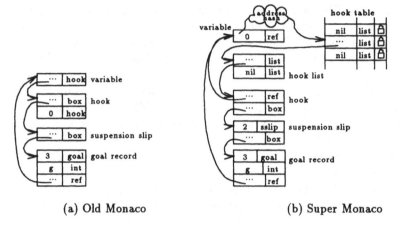

(a) Old Monaco   (b) Super Monaco

Fig. 2. Monaco Hook Structures

Each hook contains a pointer to the variable it is suspended upon. Hooks are grouped into sets according to a hashing function based upon variable addresses. A global hook table contains a lock for each such set.

Since any operation on an uninstantiated variable necessarily involves the manipulation of the hook table, the locks on the buckets of the hook table may serve as the only synchronization points for assignment and unification. This gives a lower space overhead for the representation of variables on the heap. There will be some hash-related contention for locks which would not occur in a one-lock-per-variable scheme, but since we are dealing with shared-memory machines with a moderate number of processors, the rate of such hash collisions can be made arbitrarily low by increasing the size of the hook table.

To instantiate a variable, its bucket is locked, the unbound cell is bound to its new value, all corresponding hooks are removed from the bucket, and the lock is unlocked. All hooks are then examined. To bind a variable to another variable, both buckets are locked (a canonical order is chosen to prevent deadlock) and the set of hooks of on the second variable are extracted and mutated into hooks on the first variable. These hooks are then placed in the first variable's bucket, and the second variable is mutated into a reference to the first. The result is that future dereferencing operations will return a reference to the new root, or its value when instantiated. Figure 2b illustrates the new representation.

To evaluate the performance of our hooking scheme, we replaced it with a more traditional technique. In the latter approach, a list of suspension slips for goals suspended on an unbound variable is maintained in the cell following the variable on the heap. When the variable is bound, the binding process picks up the list directly: the garbage collector will eventually reclaim the extra cell. The traditional implementation requires a locking scheme for variables. We adopt the convention that a locked variable is represented by a reference to itself, i.e., to the location of the locked variable. This representation has an interesting advantage: readers of the variable will spin dereferencing its location until the lock is released, and thus do not have to be modified to be aware of variable locking. The actual lock operation is conveniently implemented with atomic exchange on architectures which have this capability.

Table 1 shows the performance comparison (see Section 5 for benchmark descriptions). In general, there is insignificant performance difference between the two representations (the poor performance of **wave** needs further investigation). In general, most of the differences are due to the longer typical-case path length of the table-based scheme (20 instructions versus 15), which in turn is an unavoidable consequence of the scheme's more complex nature. Although the two-cell representation is slightly faster, future runtime system optimizations may reverse this advantage.

benchmark	hooking performance			inlining performance		
	two-cell	hash table	slowdown	inlined	non-inlined	slowdown
hanoi(14)	2.3	2.4	4%	2.3	2.5	9%
nrev(1000)	11.9	13.1	10%	11.9	16.0	34%
pascal(200)	4.1	4.2	2%	4.1	4.7	14%
primes(5000)	9.3	9.8	5%	9.3	11.3	21%
queen(10)	28.3	30.5	7%	28.3	29.1	3%
cube(6)	38.0	38.9	2%	38.0	38.0	0%
life(20)				20.5	20.9	2%
semigroup	140.7	147.8	5%	140.7	142.8	1%
waltz	26.6	27.0	2%	26.6	27.0	2%
wave(8,8)	7.4	9.2	24%	7.4	7.7	4%

Table 1. Hooking Scheme and Inlining Performance Impacts (Seconds, Symmetry)

4.4 Memory Management

Memory is allocated in a two-tiered manner. First, there is a global allocator which allocates blocks of memory from the shared heap. Access to the global allocator is sequentialized by a global lock. Second, each worker uses the global allocator to acquire a large chunk of memory for its private use. All memory allocation operations attempt to use this private heap, falling back on the global allocator when the private heap is exhausted. When the global heap is exhausted, execution suspends while a single worker performs a stop-and-copy garbage collection of the entire heap. Garbage collection overheads are acceptably low now, but a parallel garbage collector will be implemented in the near future.

The heap holds not only objects created by the compiled code, but also dynamically created runtime system structures. Strings, which are allocated by the parser, are stored as special boxes. Suspension hooks and suspension slips are stored in list cells and small boxes respectively. Sets of objects are either represented as statically-limited tables (such as suspension stacks) or as lists (such as hook lists). All sets were first implemented as lists on the heap, avoiding static limits on set sizes, and also speeding development time through reuse of general-purpose code. However, using statically-allocated resources not only reduces memory-allocation overhead, but also reduces contention by shortening critical sections. If no reasonable limit to set size is known at compile time, such as for the set of ready goals, a hybrid scheme is used where dynamically allocated storage is used to handle the overflow of statically-allocated tables.

4.5 Unification

In early benchmarking, we found that the high frequency of active unification made it a performance bottleneck. We have largely solved this problem through the implementation of "fast paths" through the active unification process. The approach is based on the Monaco compiler's identification of certain active unifications as *assignments* whose left-hand side is likely (but not certain) to be a reference directly to an unbound, unhooked variable, and whose right-hand side is likely to to be a bound value. Assignments comprise the bulk of active unification performed during execution.

The main optimization of assignments is to arrange for inline assembly code to test that the conditions for the assignment are met, and if so, perform the assignment inline. If the assignment is too complex to perform inline, it is passed to a specialized procedure which attempts to optimize some additional common cases. Thus the general active unifier is infrequently executed.

Table 1 shows the performance of the inlined and non-inlined versions (for the two-cell scheme). Differences are substantial in several benchmarks, and in no case do the extra tests degrade performance. For example, nrev(1000) performs about 500,000 assignments (and 1000 general unifications). Of the assignments, all but 12 are handled inline, resulting in 34% overall performance improvement.

5   Performance Evaluation

Super Monaco was evaluated on two sets of benchmarks executed on a Sequent Symmetry S81 with 16MHz Intel 80386 microprocessors. The first set, consisting of small, standard programs, is used for comparisons with other systems: KLIC [3] and Monaco. The second set, containing larger programs, is used for runtime system analysis. Table 2 compares Super Monaco, (original) Monaco [17], and KLIC (uniprocessor version) performance. All times are the best of several runs, using the sum of user- and system-level CPU times. In all cases, Super Monaco improves on the performance of the previous system, despite the fact that it is more robust. Tick and Banerjee [17] compared the old Monaco's performance to that of comparable systems available at the time, such as Strand [5], JAM [4], and Panda [14]. Monaco was found to outperform these systems in a uniprocessor configuration by factors ranging from 1.6 to 4.0, and to maintain such ratios for 1–16 processors (PEs). The new implementation of Monaco maintains this competitive performance. The uniprocessor performance relative to KLIC is respectable for all benchmarks, and especially good for the larger, more realistic benchmarks, where the geometric mean slowdown is only 20%. As for object code size, Super Monaco executables are 20 Kbytes smaller on average than KLIC.

	benchmark	KLIC	Super Monaco	KLIC:SM	original Monaco	Monaco:SM
	hanoi(14)	0.6	2.3	0.261	4.4	1.91
	nrev(1000)	5.9	11.9	0.495	19.2	1.61
small	pascal(200)	1.7	4.1	0.415	9.0	2.19
	primes(5000)	4.4	9.3	0.474	12.8	1.37
	queen(10)	10.4	28.3	0.368	43.4	1.53
	cube(6)	15.5	38.0	0.408		
	life(20)	29.6	20.5	1.45		
large	semigroup	85.9	140.7	0.610		
	waltz	18.8	26.6	0.709		
	wave(8,8)	11.6	7.4	1.56		

Table 2. Comparison of Uniprocessor Performance (Seconds, Symmetry)

Tick *et al.* [18] present the multiprocessor execution times of Super Monaco. Times were measured for the longest running PE from the beginning of the computation until termination. The geometric mean speedups of the small benchmarks (as defined above) on 16 PEs are 10.3, 10.7, and 11.1 for Super Monaco, old Monaco, and JAM Parlog. However, the geometric mean execution times on 16 PEs are 0.76, 1.2, and 3.0 seconds, respectively. For the large benchmarks, Super Monaco achieves a geometric mean of 10.5 speedup on 16 PEs.

The **mona** assembler facilitates profiling our compiled code with standard UNIX tools. We analyzed the performance of compiled code and the runtime system using the UNIX **prof** facilities. Table 3 gives the breakdown of the execution time for differing numbers of PEs, as an arithmetic mean percentage over the larger benchmarks. The top portion of the table is runtime system overheads. The bottom portion is compiled thread execution. Runtime Alloc. and Compiled Alloc. are memory allocation overheads (not including GC). System scalability to larger numbers of PEs is limited by the increasing overhead of scheduling operations and the overhead of shared lock contention. We believe that almost all lock collisions are due to scheduling operations. The system is not yet balanced, with compiled code running below 40% of total execution time; however, these statistics are influenced a great deal by the benchmark suite.

	1 PE	2 PE	4 PE	8 PE	12 PE	16 PE
Unification	30.6	29.2	27.7	26.6	24.4	21.0
Scheduling	16.9	17.0	16.9	16.6	17.6	16.8
Suspension	4.8	5.1	5.0	5.3	4.1	3.6
Runtime Alloc.	5.1	5.6	6.3	6.1	5.7	4.7
Idling	0.2	1.6	3.4	4.3	6.0	9.8
Contention	0.0	0.0	0.1	1.0	3.2	7.8
Compiled Code	41.2	40.2	39.5	39.1	37.9	35.5
Compiled Alloc.	1.3	1.3	1.1	1.1	1.1	0.9

Table 3. Execution Time Breakdown (by Percentage)

6 Related Work

Among the first abstract machine designs for committed-choice languages were an implementation of Flat Concurrent Prolog [15] by Houri [9], the Sequential Parlog machine by Gregory *et al.* [6], and the KL1 machine by Kimura [10] at ICOT. A good summary of work on Parlog appears in Gregory's book [6]. The JAM Parlog system [4] is a commonly-used Parlog implementation which compiles Parlog into code for an abstract machine interpreter. The implementation of JAM Parlog features many innovations which are still in current use by both our system and others, including tail call optimization and goal queues. In spite of a layer of emulation, JAM Parlog is reasonably efficient. An outgrowth of work on Flat Parlog implementation, the Strand Abstract Machine [5] was originally designed for distributed execution environments, but also achieved good performance on shared-memory parallel machines. More recent work includes the ICOT KLIC system [3], which translates KL1 code into portable C code, achieving excellent performance. Uniprocessor and distributed-memory versions [13] have been released. The jc Janus system is a similar uniprocessor-based, high-performance implementation [7]. See Chikayama [3] for an in-depth performance comparison among KLIC, jc, Aquarius Prolog, and SICStus Prolog.

7 Conclusions

Super Monaco has obsoleted its predecessor in robustness, capability, and execution performance, on the shared-memory hosts we are targeting. The novel contribution of this paper is the development of a real-parallel concurrent logic programming language implementation that achieves speeds competitive with the fastest known uniprocessor implementations, while retaining speedups comparable to the best shared-memory implementations. Other contributions include an efficient termination detection algorithm, a new hooking scheme, an assembler-assembler framework that facilitates portability, and support for native profiling, debugging, and linking. Future work includes exploring optimizations, such as lazy resumption and uses of mode analysis, to further reduce overheads.

Acknowledgements

J. Larson was supported by a grant from the Institute of New Generation Computer Technology (ICOT). B. Massey was supported by a University of Oregon Graduate Fellowship. E. Tick was supported by an NSF Presidential Young Investigator award, with matching funds from Sequent Computer Systems Inc. We thank C. Au-Yeung and N. Badovinac for their help with this research.

References

1. T. Anderson *et al.* Scheduler Activations: Effective Kernel Support for the User-Level Management of Parallelism. *ACM Trans. on Comp. Sys.*, 10(1):53–79, 1992.
2. C. Au-Yeung. A RISC Backend for the 2nd Generation Shared-Memory Multiprocessor Monaco System. Bachelor's thesis, University of Oregon, December 1994.
3. T. Chikayama *et al.* A Portable and Efficient Implementation of KL1. In *Int. Symp. on Prog. Lang. Impl. and Logic Prog.*, pp. 25–39, 1994. Springer-Verlag.
4. J. A. Crammond. The Abstract Machine and Implementation of Parallel Parlog. *New Generation Computing*, 10(4):385–422, August 1992.
5. I. Foster and S. Taylor. Strand: A Practical Parallel Programming Language. In *North American Conf. on Logic Prog.*, pages 497–512. MIT Press, October 1989.
6. S. Gregory. *Parallel Logic Programming in PARLOG: The Language and its Implementation*. Addison-Wesley Ltd., Wokingham, England, 1987.
7. D. Gudeman *et al.* jc: An Efficient and Portable Sequential Implementation of Janus. In *Joint Int. Conf. and Symp. on Logic Prog.*. MIT Press, 1992.
8. R. C. Haygood. Native Code Compilation in SICStus Prolog. In *International Conference on Logic Programming*, pages 190–204, Genoa, June 1994. MIT Press.
9. A. Houri *et al.* A Sequential Abstract Machine for Flat Concurrent Prolog. In *Concurrent Prolog: Collected Papers*, vol. 2, pp. 513–574. MIT Press, 1987.
10. Y. Kimura and T. Chikayama. An Abstract KL1 Machine and its Instruction Set. In *Int. Symp. on Logic Prog.*, pp. 468–477. IEEE Computer Society Press, 1987.
11. S. Kliger and E. Y. Shapiro. From Decision Trees to Decision Graphs. In *North American Conf. on Logic Prog.*, pages 97–116. MIT Press, October 1990.
12. A. Osterhaug, editor. *Guide to Parallel Programming on Sequent Computer Systems*. Prentice Hall, Englewood Cliffs, NJ, 2nd edition, 1989.
13. K. Rokusawa *et al.* Distributed Memory Implementation of KLIC. *New Generation Computing*, vol. 14, no. 3, 1995.
14. M. Sato *et al.* Evaluation of the KL1 Parallel System on a Shared Memory Multiprocessor. In *IFIP Work. Conf. on Par. Processing*. North Holland, 1988.
15. E. Y. Shapiro. The Family of Concurrent Logic Programming Languages. *ACM Computing Surveys*, 21(3):413–510, 1989.
16. E. Tick. Monaco: A High-Performance Flat Concurrent Logic Programming System. In *Conf. on Parallel Arch. and Lang. Europe*, LNCS no. 694, pp. 266–278. Springer Verlag, 1993.
17. E. Tick and C. Banerjee. Performance Evaluation of Monaco Compiler and Runtime Kernel. In *Int. Conf. on Logic Prog.*, pages 757–773. MIT Press, June 1993.
18. E. Tick *et al.* Experience with the Super Monaco Optimizing Compiler. University of Oregon, Dept. of Computer Science Technical Report CIS-TR-95-07.

Quiescence Detection in a Distributed KLIC Implementation

Kazuaki Rokusawa* Akihiko Nakase** Takashi Chikayama***
{rokusawa,nakase,chikayama}@icot.or.jp

Institute for New Generation Computer Technology
2-3-3, Shiba, Minato-ku, Tokyo 105, JAPAN

Abstract. Quiescence detection is a fundamental facility for parallel and distributed processing. This paper describes schemes for quiescence detection in a distributed KLIC implementation. KLIC is a portable implementation of concurrent logic programming language KL1. Termination is detected using the *weighted throw counting* (WTC) scheme. Based on the scheme a scheme for global suspension was invented. The postmortem system built-in predicate which provides meta programming facilities was designed, and its distributed implementation is also presented.

Keywords: concurrent logic programming, termination detection, quiescence detection, distributed implementation, weighted reference counting

1 Introduction

This paper describes schemes for quiescence detection (termination and global suspension detection) in a distributed KLIC implementation. KLIC [1] is a portable implementation of concurrent logic programming language KL1 [2] which compiles into C code.

Quiescence detection is fundamental to parallel and distributed processing. It is not easy to detect quiescence for distributed computation because of the difficulty in obtaining a consistent global state. Although some parallel programs can detect termination by itself, for example, using the *short circuit* technique, extra computation is usually needed; the same number of extra unifications which close *switches* as generated processes are required in general. In addition, detection may be incorrect because of bugs. Deadlock or perpetual suspension occurs frequently in developing parallel programs, which is hard to find and fix, especially when processes are distributed among processors. Therefore, parallel programming systems themselves should provide global suspension detection.

Considering the above, we adopted quiescence detection in the distributed KLIC implementation. Termination is detected using the *weighted throw counting*

---

* R & D Group, Oki Electric Industry Co., Ltd., since April 1, 1995.
** R & D Center, Toshiba Corporation, since April 1, 1995.
*** Dept. of Electronic Eng., University of Tokyo, since April 1, 1995.

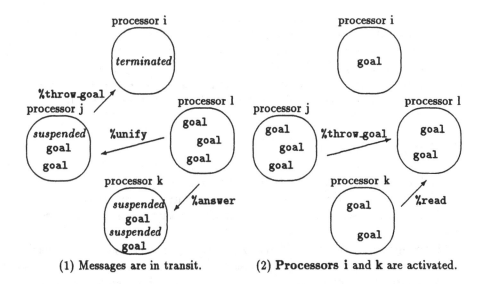

(1) Messages are in transit. (2) **Processors i and k** are activated.

Fig. 1. Execution behavior in distributed environments.

(WTC) scheme [3], which has been employed for several years in previous KL1 implementations on Multi-PSI and PIMs [4, 5]. A scheme for global suspension detection based on the WTC scheme was invented.

We also designed the **postmortem** system built-in predicate, which provides programmers with meta programming facilities. An implementation of the predicate for distributed environments was also invented.

This paper is organized as follows. Section 2 describes execution behavior of KL1 programs and quiescence detection problems in distributed environments. Section 3 presents schemes for termination detection and global suspension. Experimental studies of the WTC scheme for termination detection on a PIM/m machine are given in section 4. Section 5 describes the design and distributed implementation of the **postmortem** predicate.

2 Computation Model

This section gives a sketch of the execution behavior of KL1 programs in distributed environments, and defines the quiescence detection problems.

2.1 The KL1 Language

KL1 is a concurrent logic programming language based on GHC (Guarded Horn Clauses) [6]. Its basic execution mechanism is common with other languages of the family, such as Concurrent Prolog [7], Parlog [8] or Janus [9].

Unlike GHC which is a theoretical language, KL1 is designed as a practical language for writing an operating system and application programs to execute on parallel computers. It also provides primitives for load distribution, which is done by means of *pragma* attached to goals of the form *goal@node(Proc)*. A goal with the pragma is thrown to specified processor. Note that the semantics of programs with pragmas are the same as with the pragmas removed.

2.2 Execution Behavior

In distributed environments, goals are distributed over processors. Each processor executes goal reductions independently. The reduction may succeed, suspend, or fail. In the first case, the goals with pragmas are thrown out to other processors.

Throwing of a goal is done by sending a %throw_goal message [4], which carries some identifier and encoded arguments relating to the goal. A processor may also send a message in order to perform distributed unification, remote value fetch, and distributed garbage collection. Messages carry a unify request (%unify), a read request (%read), and a dereferenced result (%answer), etc [5]. Since messages are delivered with an arbitrary finite delay, there may be messages in transit at a given time. Figure 1 shows the execution behavior in distributed environments.

2.3 Definition of the Problems

A processor is *locally terminated* when all goals in it terminate and no suspended goals reside in it. If some goals are suspended, but no active goals reside, the processor is *locally suspended*. We define the following stable states as *termination* and *global suspension* respectively.

Termination: All processors are locally terminated, and no messages are in transit.

Global suspension: All processors are either locally terminated or suspended, and no messages are in transit. At least one processor is locally suspended. This state includes deadlock and perpetual suspension.

3 Quiescence Detection

This section first describes why quiescence detection is difficult in a distributed KLIC implementation. After that, schemes for termination detection and global suspension detection are presented.

---

[4] In this paper, message names are marked by prefixing them with a percent sign.
[5] Details are described in [10, 11].

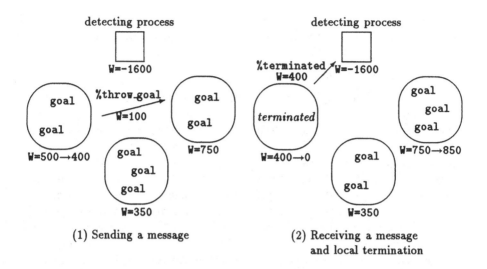

(1) Sending a message

(2) Receiving a message
and local termination

Fig. 2. Snapshots under the WTC scheme.

3.1 Difficulty

Unlike sequential computation, quiescence detection is not trivial for distributed computation because of the difficulty in obtaining a consistent global state.

Since messages may be in transit at a given time, even when each processor is in a stable state, it does not mean that the whole computation has become globally stable. There may be such messages in transit that carry goals, or bring dereferenced results and wake up suspended goals. In figure 1 (1), processor i and k are stable; processor i is locally terminated and processor k is suspended. However, both became active in figure 1 (2) after receiving messages; processor i receives a %throw_goal message from processor j, and processor k resumes suspended goals after receiving an %answer message from processor l.

3.2 Termination Detection

We present here a scheme for termination detection called the *weighted throw counting* (WTC) scheme [3]. The scheme is an application of the *weighted reference counting* (WRC) scheme [12, 13], which is a garbage collection scheme for parallel processing systems[6]. In previous KL1 implementations on Multi-PSI and PIMs, the WTC scheme has been employed to detect termination.

The WTC Scheme

A *detecting process* is placed on one of the processors to actually detect termination. The WTC scheme associates some *weight* to the detecting process, each

---

[6] Derivation of termination detection from the WRC scheme is described in [14].

processor, and each message in transit. The weight of a message in transit and that of a processor are positive integers, while the weight of the detecting process is a negative integer. The WTC scheme maintains the invariant that:

The sum of the weights is *zero*.

This ensures that the weight of the detecting process reaches zero if and only if all processors locally terminate and no messages are in transit[7].

When a processor sends a message, it assigns a weight to the message and subtracts the same amount from its weight. The new weight of the processor and that assigned to the message should both be positive, and the sum of the two weights is equal to the original weight of the processor. When a processor receives a message, it adds the weight of the message to its (positive) weight.

When a processor locally terminates, it sends a %terminated message to the detecting process to return its weight. On receiving a %terminated message, the detecting process adds the weight carried to its (negative) weight. If the weight of the detecting process reaches zero, a global termination is detected. Figure 2 shows snapshots under the WTC scheme.

When the Weight Becomes One

When the weight of a processor becomes one, the processor cannot send a message, because the weight cannot be divided.

In this case, the processor sends a %request message requesting more weight to the detecting process. Message sending is suspended until the weight becomes more than one. On receiving a %request message, the detecting process sends back a %supply message which carries a large amount of weight to the sender processor. When a processor receives a %supply message from the detecting process or some other message with some weight from another processor, it adds the weight to its weight, which enables it to send any suspended messages.

How to Assign a Weight

We discuss here the strategy to assign a weight which decreases the number of requesting weight. In the worst case, a %request message is sent on each message sending, while no %request message is sent in the best case.

- A %throw_goal message should bring some large amount of weight, because it may reach a locally terminated processor which has no weight. The reactivated processor may send messages, which requires some amount of weight.
- Messages carrying a value (%answer and %unify) need not have a large amount of weight. Although a locally suspended processor may receive those messages and it may resume message sending, the weight of the processor is expected to be large enough. When a locally terminated processor receives those messages, no more computation will begin.

---

[7] Essentially the same scheme named the *Credit Distribution and Recovery* algorithm [15] was independently invented after the WTC scheme was. *Credit* corresponds to *weight* in the WTC scheme.

- Only a small amount of weight is enough for a read request message (%read), because it brings no computation to the destination processor.
- A %supply message should carry a very large amount of weight. Although the weight assigned to a message sent by a processor must be less than the weight of the processor, the weight carried by %supply does not have this limitation, because a %supply message is sent by the detecting process.

Considering above, we adopted the following strategy.

- Assign a fixed large amount of weight (say 2^{12}) to a %throw_goal message if the weight of the processor is more than twice of that; otherwise assign half of the weight of the processor.
- Assign a fixed small amount of weight (say 10) to %unify, %read, and %answer messages if the weight of the processor is more than twice of that; otherwise assign half of the weight of the processor.
- Assign a very large amount of weight (say 2^{24}) to a %supply message.

Once a processor receives a %supply message, it can send a message at least 2^{12} times without receiving any weight.

3.3 Global Suspension Detection

In previous implementations on Multi-PSI and PIMs, perpetual suspension within a processor could be detected using MRB [16, 17] and local garbage collection [18]. However, they had no function for distributed environments.

We describe here a basic concept and two schemes for global suspension detection. Both the two schemes are based on the WTC scheme.

Basic Concept

In the state of global suspension, each processor is either locally suspended or locally terminated and no messages are in transit. Since a terminated processor has no weights, the sum of the weights of the detecting process and the suspended processor becomes zero, which can be used to detect global suspension.

Returning Weight Scheme

If a locally suspended processor returns its weight, global suspension can be detected in the same way as termination detection.

When a processor becomes locally suspended, it also returns its weight by sending a %suspended message to the detecting process. When the weight of the detecting process reaches zero, either termination or global suspension is guaranteed. This is because a locally suspended processor can be reactivated and can terminate at any time. If the communication channels are FIFO, when the last message is %suspended, global suspension is guaranteed. However, if the channels are non-FIFO, or, the last message is %terminated, no decision can

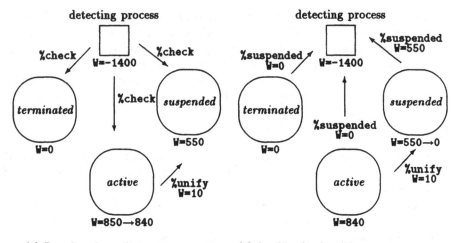

(1) Broadcasting a %check message   (2) Sending back a %suspended message

Fig. 3. Global suspension detection using the *collecting weights* scheme.

be made. To decide between the two states, the detecting process broadcasts a message asking for a report of the state. If the detecting process receives a report of *termination* from all processors, termination is guaranteed. Otherwise, global suspension is detected.

Since this scheme requires no originator, the delay of detection can be min-imaized. However, as the weight of a processor is returned back on each local suspension, the weight of a processor may become one frequently, and frequent %request/%supply messages may degrade the performance. Therefore, this scheme must be effective in a debugging phase where high performance is not required, but frequent global suspension is expected.

Collecting Weights Scheme

We present here a scheme where the detecting process collects the weights of suspended computation, and decides whether global suspension occurs or not.

On start of detection, the detecting process allocates the *ack counter*, and sets the initial value at the number of processors. The detecting process then broadcasts a %check message which asks for a return of the weight of suspended computation (figure 3 (1)).

On receiving a %check message, if the processor is locally suspended, it sends back a %suspended message which carries all its weights. Otherwise, that is, when the processor is active (it has some active goals) or locally terminated, it sends back a %suspended message with no weight (figure 3 (2)).

Table 1. Execution results on PIM/m.

Programs		execution		number of messages				
		time (sec)	reductions	%throw	%unify	%term	%req	%sup
MGTP	32 PEs	1,986	6,916 M	842	549,841	47	36	36
	256 PEs	348	7,432 M	1,280	639,856	306	281	281
Gene	32 PEs	5,457	12,962 M	8,670	9,048	1,056	1,054	1,054
	256 PEs	793	12,962 M	8,670	9,248	8,642	8,670	8,670
Router	64 PEs	104	32 M	701	236,540	449	447	447
LogSim	256 PEs	356	983 M	2,554	8,219,263	257	255	255
DisPool	32 PEs	53	26 M	1,030	32,222	441	339	339
	256 PEs	249	231 M	7,750	1,972,286	2,685	2,583	2,583
Pentomino	32 PEs	665	1,974 M	13,639	20,933	389	387	387
	256 PEs	134	1,974 M	56,872	68,982	4,445	4,443	4,443
COMPILE	21 PEs	282	43 M	151	7,150	354	228	228

On receiving a %suspended message, the detecting process adds the received weight to its (negative) weight, and decrements the *ack counter*.

When both the weight of the detecting process and the *ack counter* reach zero, either termination or global suspension is guaranteed. The decision between the two states can be made by the same operations as those in the *returning weight* scheme. If the value of the *ack counter* only reaches zero, it is guaranteed that some processors are active, or some messages remain in transit.

Unlike the *returning weight* scheme, this scheme requires an originator which demands the detecting process to start detection operations. Although when and how to originate the detection operations depends on each application, the *repeated observation* at regular intervals (for example ten senconds) must be applicable to many cases.

4   Experimental Studies of the WTC Scheme on PIM/m

As mentioned before, the WTC scheme has been employed for several years in KL1 implementations on the Multi-PSI and PIMs. We evaluate here the effectiveness of the WTC scheme for termination detection through the experience on a PIM/m machine, which is one of the five models of PIM.

Execution Results

Table 1 shows execution times, reductions, and the number of messages related to termination detection for several programs[8]. The following are brief explanation of the programs.

[8] Messages for remote value fetch and garbage collection are not concerned.

Table 2. Additional messages of the two schemes.

Programs		Ack	WTC	Ack/WTC
MGTP	32 PEs	550,683	119	4,628
	256 PEs	641,136	868	739
Gene	32 PEs	17,718	3,164	5.6
	256 PEs	17,918	25,982	0.7
Router	64 PEs	237,241	1,343	177
LogSim	256 PEs	8,221,817	767	10,719
DisPool	32 PEs	33,252	1,119	30
	256 PEs	1,980,036	7,851	252
Pentomino	32 PEs	34,572	1,163	30
	256 PEs	125,854	13,331	9.4
COMPILE	21 PEs	7,301	810	9.0

MGTP: A parallel model-generation based theorem prover. It exploits OR-parallelism for non-Horn problems and AND-parallelism for Horn problems [19]. Open problems in finite algebra have been proved using MGTP [20].

Gene: A parallel application program for genetic sequence analysis based on an iterative improvement technique [21].

Router: A LSI routing program based on a concurrent objects model. Each line segment is represented as a object, and routing paths are decided by communication of the objects [22].

LogSim: A parallel logic simulator for VLSI circuits to verify their logical and timing specifications. The program adopts a virtual time algorithm [23].

DisPool: A benchmark program for the *distributed pool* [24] which is a table maintenance utility that provides various forms of tables with arbitrary keys and data. As the distributed pool is used with many application programs, this benchmark program shows characteristic of a real application.

Pentomino: A program to find out all solutions of a 6×10 packing piece puzzle. The *Multi-level dynamic load balancing* scheme [25] is employed.

COMPILE: Distributed compilation of AYA language processor [26] which is written in KL1. The language processor consists of 21 KL1 source program files, each of which is compiled on different processor.

Comparison with Using Acknowledgements

Termination can be detected using acknowledgements. Each processor has a counter which is incremented on sending a message, and is decremented on receiving an *acknowledge* message. When the value of the counter reaches zero, it is guaranteed that no messages are in transit [27].

We compare the number of additional messages of the two schemes. Under the scheme using acknowledgements, an *acknowledge* message is an additional

Table 3. Frequency and cost of additional messages of the WTC scheme.

Programs		exec. time (sec)	additional messages	exec. time/msg (msec)	(K red[a])	extra time (msec)[b]
MGTP	32 PEs	1,986	119	16,689	10,013	6 (0.0%)
	256 PEs	348	868	401	240	43 (0.0%)
Gene	32 PEs	5,457	3,164	1,725	1,035	158 (0.0%)
	256 PEs	793	25,982	31	19	1,299 (0.2%)
Router	64 PEs	104	1,343	77	46	67 (0.0%)
LogSim	256 PEs	356	767	464	278	38 (0.0%)
DisPool	32 PEs	53	1,119	47	28	56 (0.1%)
	256 PEs	249	7,851	32	19	393 (0.2%)
Pentomino	32 PEs	665	1,163	572	343	58 (0.0%)
	256 PEs	134	13,331	10	6.0	667 (0.5%)
COMPILE	21 PEs	282	810	348	209	41 (0.0%)

[a] The performance is 600 KLIPS in append on a PIM/m single processor.
[b] It takes the detecting process about 50μsec to handle each additional message.

one which is sent in response to %throw_goal or %unify messages. Under the WTC scheme, %terminated, %request, and %supply are additional messages.

Table 2 shows the number of the additional messages of the two schemes. As can be seen, except for Gene, the additional messages sent under the WTC scheme are almost negligible compared with the ones of the scheme using acknowledgements.

The detecting process can be a bottleneck ?

Under the WTC scheme, additional messages for termination detection are all sent or received by the detecting process. Therefore, if the additional messages are sent frequently, the detecting process becomes bottleneck.

The frequency and cost of sending or receiving additional messages are shown in table 3; the execution times per one additional message and the extra times consumed for handling additional messages are indicated. The execution times are also represented in *append kiloreductions*. The table demonstrates that the frequency is low enough and the extra time is negligible. Thus it can be concluded that the detecting process never becomes bottleneck.

5 The postmortem predicate

The postmortem predicate provides programmers with meta programming facilities. The form of the predicate is as follows.

```
postmortem(+GOAL,-RESULT)
```

The predicate registers the *postmortem* goal specified by the GOAL, which is executed after detection of quiescence (termination or global suspension). As a postmortem goal has arbitrary arguments, it can access any data objects generated before quiescence detection through those arguments.

When registration is done, RESULT is unified with ⎕. Waiting for the instantiation will prevent further processing from being executed before the completion of the registration. If this predicate is called more than once, the newly specified goal is appended to the old ones.

Distributed Implementation

Implementation of the postmortem predicate in distributed environments consists of the following three phases:

1. Memorizing the postmortem goals.
2. Detection of quiescence.
3. Execution of the memorized goals.

Operations on each phase are as follows.

Memorizing the postmortem goals: The processor where the postmortem predicate is executed memorizes the postmortem goals. If the processor already has postmortem goals memorized, it appends the new goal to the old ones.

Detection of quiescence: The detecting process detects quiescence using the scheme described in section 3.

Execution of the memorized goals: When the detecting process detects quiescence, it broadcasts a %start message demanding execution of the postmortem goals memorized. A %start message, like %supply, also brings a large amount of weight to a destination processor. On receiving a %start message, if postmortem goals reside in it, the processor adds the weight carried to its weight, and starts the execution of the goals. Otherwise, the %start message is treated in the same way as the case of a %supply message.

Note that a processor need not be concerned with quiescence. A processor which starts execution of postmortem goals can send a message at any time. Although the message may reach the other processor earlier than a %start message does, the processor need not be concerned with the order.

6 Summary

Schemes for termination and global suspension detection in a distributed KLIC implementation are described.

Quiescence detection is fundamental to parallel and distributed processing. It is not easy to detect quiescence for distributed computation because of the difficulty in obtaining a consistent global state, especially when there can be messages in transit. We have solved the problems using the *weighted throw counting* technique. Experimental studies on a PIM/m machine have shown that the scheme is superior to the scheme using acknowledgements, and the detecting process never becomes a bottleneck.

The **postmortem** predicate which provide meta programming facilities for programmers was designed, and distributed implementation was done for the first time.

References

1. T. Chikayama, T. Fujise, and D. Sekita, "A Portable and Efficient Implementation of KL1," *Proc. International Symposium on Programming Language Implementation and Logic Programming*, LNCS 844, pp.25–39, 1994.
2. K. Ueda and T. Chikayama, "Design of the Kernel Language for the Parallel Inference Machine," *The Computer Journal*, Vol.33, No.6, pp.494–500, 1990.
3. K. Rokusawa, N. Ichiyoshi, T. Chikayama, and H. Nakashima, "An Efficient Termination Detection and Abortion Algorithm for Distributed Processing Systems," *Proc. International Conference on Parallel Processing*, Vol.I, pp.18-22, 1988.
4. K. Nakajima, Y. Inamura, N. Ichiyoshi, K. Rokusawa, and T. Chikayama, "Distributed Implementation of KL1 on the Multi-PSI/V2," *Proc. International Conference on Logic Programming*, pp.436–451, 1989.
5. K. Hirata, R. Yamamoto, A. Imai, H. Kawai, K. Hirano, T. Takagi, K. Taki, A. Nakase, and K. Rokusawa, "Parallel and Distributed Implementation of Concurrent Logic Programming Language KL1," *Proc. International Conference on Fifth Generation Computer Systems 1992*, pp.436–459, 1992.
6. K. Ueda, "Guarded Horn Clauses: A Parallel Logic Programming Language with the Concept of a Guard," Technical Report TR-208, ICOT, 1986.
7. E. Shapiro, "Systems Programming in Concurrent Prolog," *Logic Programming and its Applications*, M. van Canegham and D.H.D. Warren (eds.), Albex Publishing Co., pp.50–74, 1986.
8. K. Clark and S. Gregory, "PARLOG: Parallel Programming in Logic," *ACM Transactions on Programming Languages and Systems*, Vol.8, No.1, pp.1–49, 1986.
9. V. A. Saraswat, K. Kahn, and J. Levy, "Janus: A Step Towards Distributed Constraint Programming," *Proc. North American Conference on Logic Programming*, pp.431–446, 1990.
10. N. Ichiyoshi, K. Rokusawa, K. Nakajima, and Y. Inamura, "A New External Reference Management and Distributed Unification for KL1," *New Generation Computing*, Ohmsha Ltd., pp.159–177, 1990.
11. K. Rokusawa, A. Nakase, and T. Chikayama, "Distributed Memory Implementation of KLIC," *Proc. Workshop on Parallel Logic Programming and its Programming Environments*, Technical Report CIS-TR-94-04, University of Oregon, pp.151–162, March, 1994. Also *New Generation Computing*, Ohmsha Ltd., to appear.
12. P. Watson and I. Watson, "An Efficient Garbage Collection Scheme for Parallel Computer Architectures," *Proc. Parallel Architectures and Languages Europe*, LNCS 259, Vol.II, pp.432–443, 1987.
13. D. I. Bevan, "Distributed Garbage Collection Using Reference Counting," *Parallel Computing*, Vol.9, No.2, pp.179–192, 1989.
14. G. Tel and F. Mattern, "The Derivation of Distributed Termination Detection Algorithms from Garbage Collection Schemes," *Proc. Parallel Architectures and Languages Europe*, LNCS 505, Vol.I, pp.137–149, 1991.

15. F. Mattern, "Global Quiescence Detection Based on Credit Distribution and Recovery," *Inf. Proc. Lett.*, Vol.30, No.4, pp.195–200, 1989.

16. T. Chikayama and Y. Kimura, "Multiple Reference Management in Flat GHC," *Proc. International Conference on Logic Programming*, pp.276–293, 1987.

17. Y. Inamura, N. Ichiyoshi, K. Rokusawa, and K. Nakajima, "Optimization Techniques Using the MRB and Their Evaluation on the Multi-PSI/V2," *Proc. North American Conference on Logic Programming*, pp.907–921, 1989.

18. Y. Inamura and S. Onishi, "A Detection Algorithm of Perpetual Suspension in KL1," *Proc. International Conference on Logic Programming*, pp.18–30, 1990.

19. R. Hasegawa and M. Koshimura, "An AND Parallelization Method for MGTP and Its Evaluation," *Proc. First International Symposium on Parallel Symbolic Computation*, pp.194–203, 1994.

20. M. Fujita, J. Slaney, and F. Bennett, "Automatic Generation of Some Results in Finite Algebra," *Proc. IJCAI-93*, 1993.

21. M. Ishikawa, T. Toya, and Y. Totoki, "Parallel Application Systems in Genetic Information Processing," *Proc. International Symposium on Fifth Generation Computer Systems 1994*, pp.129–138, 1994.

22. H. Date and K. Taki, "A Parallel Lookahead Line Search Router with Automatic Ripup-and-reroute," *Proc. EDAC-EUROASIC 93*, 1993.

23. Y. Matsumoto and K. Taki, "Parallel Logic Simulator Base on Time Warp and Its Evaluation," *Proc. International Conference on Fifth Generation Computer Systems 1992*, pp.1198–1206, 1992.

24. M. Sato, M. Yamauchi, and T. Chikayama, "Distributed Pool and Its Implementation," *Proc. International Symposium on Fifth Generation Computer Systems 1994*, pp.90–99, 1994.

25. M. Furuichi, N. Ichiyoshi, and K. Taki, "A Multi-Level Load Balancing Scheme for OR-Parallel Exhaustive Search Programs on the Multi-PSI," *Proc. Second ACM SIGPLAN Symposium on Principles and Practice of Parallel Programming*, pp.50–59, 1990.

26. K. Susaki, *et al.*, "Programming in KL1 and AYA," Technical Report TR-831, ICOT, 1993.

27. N. Shavit and N. Francez, "A New Approach to Detection of Locally Indicative Stability," *Proc. International Colloquium on Automata, Languages and Programming*, LNCS 226, pp.344–358, 1986.

Compiler Optimizations in Reform Prolog: Experiments on the KSR-1 Multiprocessor

Thomas Lindgren, Johan Bevemyr and Håkan Millroth

Computing Science Department, Uppsala University
Box 311
751 05 Uppsala, SWEDEN
e-mail: {thomasl,jb,hakanm}@csd.uu.se

Abstract. We describe the compiler analyses of Reform Prolog and evaluate their effectiveness in eliminating suspension and locking on a range of benchmarks. The results of the analysis may also be used to extract non-strict independent and-parallelism.

We find that 90% of the predicate arguments are ground or local, and that 95% of the predicate arguments do not require suspension code. Hence, very few suspension operations need to be generated to maintain sequential semantics. The compiler can also remove unnecessary locking of local data by locking only updates to shared data; however, even though locking writes are reduced to 52% of the unoptimized number for our benchmark set, this has little effect on execution times. We find that the ineffectiveness of locking elimination is due to the relative rarity of locking writes, and the execution model of Reform Prolog, which results in few invalidations of shared cache lines when such writes occur.

The benchmarks are evaluated on a cache-coherent KSR-1 multiprocessor with physically distributed memory, using up to 48 processors. Speedups scale from previous results on smaller, bus-based multiprocessors, and previous low parallelization overheads are retained.

1 Introduction

An important challenge in parallel processing is to keep parallelization overhead low: it does not make sense to use up two or more processors just to break even with sequential code. Another challenge is to make sure that designs scale with the size of the machine. The design of the Reform Prolog system is an attempt to meet these challenges without making programming much harder than in the sequential case.

Reform Prolog has been implemented on a varity of shared address space multiprocessors. The parallel implementation is designed as extension of a sequential Prolog machine [1]. The implementation imposes very little overhead for process management, such as scheduling and load balancing.

We have previously described the compilation scheme [14, 15], execution model [2, 3], and parallel abstract machine [2, 3] of Reform Prolog. In this paper we describe a set of compiler analyses and optimizations for increasing available parallelism and reducing parallelization overheads. We discuss the effectiveness of the optimizations and the runtime space/time efficiency of the compiler. The system is evaluated on a cache-coherent large-scale multiprocessor with physically distributed memory.

2 Reform Prolog

The Reform Prolog system supports a parallel programming model where a single conceptual thread of control is mapped to multiple low-level threads. Each thread runs an instance of the same recursive program in an asynchronous parallel computation. This model is often called SPMD (Single Program Multiple Data). The programming model is realized by a compilation technique that translates a regular form of recursion to a parallelizable form of iteration [14, 15].

Example 1. The following program compares a sequence B with a list of sequences. Each comparison, carried out by match/3, computes a similarity value V that is stored in a sorted tree T for later access. The tree is implemented as an incomplete data structure.

```
:- parallel match_seqs/3.
match_seqs([],_,_).
match_seqs([A|X],B,T) :-
    match(A,B,V),
    put_in_tree(T,V),
    match_seqs(X,B,T).
```

Assume that we invoke this program with a call containing an input list of four sequences. The programmer can then think of the recursive clause as being unfolded four times:

```
match_seqs([A1,A2,A3,A4|X],B,T) :-
    match(A1, B, V1), put_in_tree(T, V1),
    match(A2, B, V2), put_in_tree(T, V2),
    match(A3, B, V3), put_in_tree(T, V3),
    match(A4, B, V4), put_in_tree(T, V4),
    match_seqs(X,B,T).
```

Of course, this is not how Reform Prolog actually compiles the clause. However, the compiled code behaves *as if* the recursion is completely unfolded. When computing the call, four parallel processes are simultaneously spawned (the two calls within each process are executed sequentially):

$$\text{match}(A_1, B, V_1), \text{put\_in\_tree}(T, V_1),$$
$$\text{match}(A_2, B, V_2), \text{put\_in\_tree}(T, V_2),$$
$$\text{match}(A_3, B, V_3), \text{put\_in\_tree}(T, V_3),$$
$$\text{match}(A_4, B, V_4), \text{put\_in\_tree}(T, V_4),$$

The four calls to put_in_tree/2 are sequenced by synchronization on the shared variable T. However, the processes descend through the tree in parallel, temporally suspending when encountering not-yet-created subtrees.

The parallel execution model of Reform Prolog restricts the nondeterministic behaviour of parallel programs so that the following properties hold [2, 3]:

- *Parallel programs obey the sequential semantics of Prolog.* This implies that time-dependent operations (type tests, etc.) on shared, unbound variables are carried out only when leftmost is the sequential computation order.

- *Parallel programs do not conditionally bind shared variables.* This is similar to binding determinism as defined by Naish [16] in that shared variables can only be bound when the process is deterministic. However, in contrast to Naish's binding determinism, nondeterministic bindings to *local* variables are allowed.

In order to ensure these properties, the Reform Prolog compiler performs a global dataflow analysis and generates code that suspends processes and perform atomic updates only when necessary [17]. In particular, the compiler can generate precisely the code for a sequential Prolog machine when data are local.

3 Compiler analyses

The compiler analyses in the Reform Prolog compiler are based on *abstract interpretation* [6]. The abstract interpreter for Reform Prolog shares most of the characteristics of an abstract interpreter for sequential Prolog. This is natural, since each parallel process executes almost as a sequential Prolog machine.

We have modified Debray's dataflow algorithms [7, 8] for analysis of parallel recursive predicates. These algorithms compute call and success patterns for each procedure in the program. Call and success patterns describe the abstract values of the variables in a procedure call at procedure entry and exit, respectively.

The compiler carries out four different analyses using the same basic algorithm. The abstract domains of these analyses are described below.

3.1 Types

The type domain is similar to that of Debray and Warren [9], extended to handle difference lists [17]. For our present concerns it suffices to note that the type analysis can discover ground and nonvariable terms. The analysis precision is similar to that of Aquarius Prolog [20].

3.2 Aliasing and linearity

The analyzer derives possible and certain aliases by maintaining equivalence classes of possibly or certainly aliased variables. This is similar to the techniques used by Chang [4].

A term is *linear* if no variable occurs more than once in it. To improve aliasing information, the analyzer tracks whether terms are linear [13]. Three classes of linearity are distinguished: **linear, nonlinear,** and **indlist**. The latter denotes lists where elements do not share variables. The domain is thus:

$$\text{linear} \sqsubseteq \text{indlist} \sqsubseteq \text{nonlinear}$$

Consider a variable X that is 'split' into several subterms $\{X_1, \ldots, X_n\}$ by unification $X = [X_1, \ldots, X_n]$ or some similar operation. Assuming that there are no other live aliases of X in the rest of the clause, the analyzer uses linearity information as follows in this situation:

- If X is **linear**, then $X_1, \ldots, X_n$ are also **linear** and unaliased.

- If X is **indlist**, then $X_1, \ldots, X_n$ are **nonlinear** and unaliased.

- If X is **nonlinear**, then $X_1, \ldots, X_n$ are **nonlinear** and aliased.

Our domain does not express covering properties, so the compiler cannot exploit linearity information when there are still aliases of X alive in the current clause.

Linearity information is maintained for each equivalence class of aliases.

3.3 Determinism

The analyzer determines where each process may create a choice point. The compiler needs this information since it must keep track of variables that may be bound within the scope of a choice point. The determinism domain is quite simple:

$$\text{det} \sqsubseteq \text{nondet}$$

As long as there is no possibility that a process may have created a choicepoint, it has status **det**. When a choicepoint may have been created, the status is changed to **nondet**. Cuts reset the determinism status to a value saved when the predicate is entered, similarly to what is done in the concrete implementation.

To improve precision, the compiler uses *abstract indexing* to approximate the first-argument indexing that will occur at runtime. This technique selects the possible paths for the inferred types of the first argument, based on standard WAM indexing [21].

3.4 Locality

The analyzer maintains a hierarchy of data locality information:

- shared variables exposed to time-dependent operations by another process (clause indexing, arithmetic, type tests, etc.) are **fragile** and cannot be modified out of the sequential order;

- shared variables not subjected to time-dependent operations are **robust**;

- robust variables become **wbf** (will-be-fragile) when subjected to time-dependent operations—to subsequent processes, **wbf** variables will be seen as **fragile**;

- unshared data are **local**.

The locality domain is thus:

$$\text{local} \sqsubseteq \text{robust} \sqsubseteq \text{wbf} \sqsubseteq \text{fragile}$$

This locality domain can furthermore be used to detect non-strict independent and-parallelism [12]. As long as a process does not contain fragile data, it is independent of the results of other processes. Such independent programs can still construct shared data structures in parallel.

4 Compiler optimizations

The Reform Prolog compiler uses the information obtained by the analyzer for two purposes: verifying parallelizability and reducing parallelization overheads.

Our experience is that the compiler is able to filter out almost all unintended violations of the parallelizability conditions. Moreover, the analyzer can often help the programmer to identify code sections that cause unintended process suspensions.

Suspension and locking overheads can be reduced by optimizations that exploit the results of the compiler analyses.

4.1 Cost of process suspension

Suspension overheads occur in two situations, based on the execution model: (a) to preserve the sequential semantics, fragile variables cannot be bound unless the process is leftmost and (b) to ensure binding determinism, shared variables must not be bound conditionally.

The compiler can eliminate suspension instructions when data is **local** or known to be instantiated, or the process is deterministic and data are non-**fragile**.

4.2 Cost of locking unifications

Locking overheads occur when trying to bind possibly shared variables. Write accesses to shared variables must be locked to avoid data races and premature access to shared structures.

A locking write is required only when the heap cell being assigned is not **local**. In the WAM, writes (get/unify-instructions) are conditional depending on whether the accessed cell is bound or not. The compiler exploits type and locality information to strength-reduce locking instructions into non-locking ones where possible.

On the KSR-1, locking unification is done by simulating an atomic exchange operation. At present, this is done by locking the cache line of the variable to be bound, writing the variable and releasing the lock. A shared variable binding is then done as follows.

```
swap_x = Atomic_Exchange(x,y);
if (swap_x != x) {
    if (!unify(swap_x,y))
      Global_Failure();
}
```

Structures that may be bound to shared variables are constructed privately, and then atomically bound to the variable as described above.

If both suspension and locking overheads can be optimized away, then procedures called from a parallel predicate execute standard WAM code at full sequential speed.

5 Experimental setup

We have evaluated the system using three small (0.5 KB and 20-50 lines of code) and three medium-sized (3-12 KB and 100-425 lines of code) benchmark programs. The small benchmarks are:

map A function is mapped over a list of 5000 elements, producing a new list. The function simply decrements a counter 1000 times.

nrev A list of 1300 elements is reversed using the 'naive reverse' program.

tree 50,000 elements are inserted into a sorted, incomplete, binary tree.

The medium-sized benchmarks are:

tsp The travelling salesman problem of 48 cities is solved by an approximation algorithm that visits the nodes of the minimal spanning tree.

ga A population of 48 individuals is evolved for 5 generations using a genetic algorithm. The application is the travelling salesman problem with 120 cities.

sm A string is compared to 96 other strings using the Smith-Waterman string matching algorithm (a standard dynamic programming algorithm often used for comparing, e.g., DNA sequences). Each string contains 32 characters. Each comparison results in a similarity value, which is stored in a sorted, incomplete, binary tree.

The source code of the benchmark programs is available by ftp from ftp.csd.uu.se in the directory pub/reform/benchmarks.

The runtime statistics of the compiler were obtained on a Sun 630/MP with 4 40-MHz Sparc-2 processors and 64 MB of memory during a normal workday. The compiler was run in native code compiled SICStus Prolog version 2.1.6.

The performance measurements of the compiled parallel programs were obtained on a Kendell Square Research KSR-1 with 64 processors, each with 32 MB of memory. However, we were not able to allocate more than 48 processors due to external constraints.

6   Compiler performance

The time required for analysis and total compilation time were (ms):

	Analysis	Total	Ratio
map	260	620	0.37
nrev	480	840	0.57
tree	850	1360	0.62
tsp	6149	8519	0.72
ga	7670	13870	0.55
sw	3850	5390	0.71

Thus, the analysis requires around 60-70% of the total compilation time; we consider this a reasonable overhead. Furthermore, the absolute compilation times (0.6 to 14 seconds) are quite reasonable, in particular when considering that the SUN 630/MP is not a particulary fast machine by today's standards. Aquarius Prolog seems to have similar absolute analysis times on similar hardware [11].

7   Analysis results

We measured analysis results for arguments in procedures called from parallel predicates.

The following table shows the percentages of ground arguments and the locality information of non-ground arguments. The 'total' percentage is weighted with respect to the total number of predicate arguments in all benchmarks.

	ground	local	robust	wbf	fragile
map	60	40	-	-	-
nrev	25	-	12	12	51
tree	–	60	-	-	40
tsp	38	52	10	-	-
ga	35	59	2	-	4
sm	34	60	-	-	6
total	35	55	4	1	5

All benchmark programs are deterministic in the sense that they do not leave choicepoints when finished. Shallow backtracking does occur. The analyzer was able to verify these facts.

From these results we can see that:

- 90% of the arguments do not refer to data that require locking (i.e. the data are ground or local);

- 95% of the arguments do not refer to data that require suspension (i.e. the data are not fragile).

The 90% of arguments that do not require locking translates to a reduction to 52% of the original number of executed locking instructions.

8 Performance of compiled programs

We measured execution times of sequential code and parallel code using up to 48 processors. The results (in seconds walltime) are:

	seq	1	2	6	12	24	48
map	81.6	81.8	40.9	13.8	6.98	3.60	1.86
nrev	18.7	22.6	12.5	4.11	2.20	1.13	0.82
tree	44.9	50.1	25.7	9.42	6.10	5.20	10.1
tsp	104	107	54.8	17.8	9.06	4.74	2.64
ga	77.0	82.0	40.9	13.9	7.68	4.24	3.40
sm	73.1	75.5	37.8	12.6	6.30	3.46	1.76

The speedups w.r.t. parallel code on one processor are:

	1	2	6	12	24	48
map	1	2.00	5.95	11.7	22.7	44.0
nrev	1	1.81	5.52	10.5	19.9	27.6
tree	1	1.95	5.31	8.20	9.63	4.97
tsp	1	1.95	6.00	11.8	22.6	40.5
ga	1	2.00	5.90	10.7	19.3	24.1
sm	1	2.00	6.00	12.0	21.8	42.9

The speedups w.r.t. sequential code are:

	1	2	6	12	24	48
map	1.00	1.99	5.93	11.7	22.7	43.9
nrev	0.83	1.50	4.55	8.66	16.6	22.8
tree	0.90	1.75	4.77	7.37	8.60	4.50
tsp	0.98	1.91	5.87	11.6	22.1	39.6
ga	0.94	1.88	5.53	10.0	18.2	22.6
sm	0.97	1.93	5.81	11.6	21.1	41.5

We see that the parallelization overhead is very low: 0–17%, with the larger benchmarks in the range of 2–6%.

The absolute speedup is very good on three benchmarks (map,tsp,sm), ordinary on two programs (nrev,ga) and bad on one program (tree). The three programs with ordinary or bad speedup all suffer from lack of exploitable parallelism: the nrev and tree programs are sequentialized by fragile variables, and the ga program invokes a sequential sort routine after the parallel computation (this limits the speedup according to Amdahl's law).

The key characteristics of the programs are:

map	no suspension and no communication
nrev	heavy suspension and communication
tree	almost only suspension and communication
tsp	some communication and little suspension
ga	sequential sort after parallel computation
sm	some suspension and little communication

9 Effectiveness of optimizations

To measure the effectiveness of optimizations (elimination of suspension and locking instructions) we compiled the benchmark programs without exploiting global analysis.

9.1 Elimination of suspension instructions

To evaluate the effectiveness of removing suspension instructions, we rewrote the benchmarks to suspend whenever unbound heap cells were read by time-dependent operations, or written. Since there is no knowledge on what data is shared or fragile, this is required to retain sequential semantics.

The execution times without analysis were the following. We were unable to allocate 48 processors for this experiment and so show execution times for up to 24 processors.

Program	1	2	6	12	24
map	90.9	45.3	15.4	7.90	4.10
nr	30.5	34.4	37.0	42.3	51.3
tree	49.3	30.0	9.90	5.80	5.80
tsp	123.4	126	136	148	197
ga	74.5	37.7	14.1	7.70	6.10
sm	86.9	87.8	93.0	103	131

On 24 processors, there is comparable efficiency in the map, tree and ga benchmarks. For the map benchmark, the parallel computation consists of independent and trivial work that does not allocate heap data. The tree program can only write data when leftmost and so is essentially the same with or without analysis. The ga program performs all computations using scalar or ground data; all unbound variables are found on the stack. Since data on the stack cannot be shared, the engine can determine the outcome of suspension instructions even without analysis. The presence of extra suspension operations still has a cost: on 24 processors, the analyzed version of ga is 44% faster than the unanalyzed one.

Nrev, tsp and sm show net slowdowns when parallelized without global analysis. Tsp and sm perform considerable local work, which the no-analysis version delays until leftmost almost immediately and so sequentializes the program. For nrev without analysis, only the leftmost worker of nrev can write data at any time. With analysis, a 'pipeline' of processes appears and allows quicker completion.

Our conclusion is that there are substantial benefits to detecting computations local to a process (e.g., tsp, sm), and that more complex communication patterns (e.g., the nrev 'pipeline' effect) can be exploited transparently by the compiler.

9.2 Elimination of locking instructions

The elimination of locking instructions is ineffective: there is no measurable difference in execution times when the number of locking unifications are reduced to 52% of the original number. Two factors contribute to this phenomenon:

First, locking instructions are infrequent even in unoptimized code. Locking is spatially infrequent, since assignments to heap variables is a small fraction of the total amount of data written in Prolog implementations [19, 10]. Locking is temporally infrequent, since our Prolog implementation is based on byte-code emulation of WAM [21] instructions. In unoptimized code, 2100–3700 machine instructions were executed for each locking operation on the three larger benchmarks.

Second, single locking instructions are, on average, fast due to cache organization: cache lines owned by a single processor do not need global invalidations. Shared cache lines are infrequently invalidated by our programs since shared variables are written at most once (bindings of shared variables cannot be undone by backtracking). This means that a shared cache line is invalidated at most k times, where k is the number of variables per line ($k = 4$ in our implementation on the KSR-1).

10   Conclusion

We have described compiler analyses that allow us to:

– verify that 95% of the predicate arguments do not refer to data that require suspension instructions;

– verify that 90% of the predicate arguments do not refer to data that require locking instructions.

The elimination of suspension instructions is very effective, since it makes otherwise quite sequential programs highly parallel. However, the elimination of locking instructions is ineffective, in that there is no measurable difference in execution times when locking instructions are removed. The most important contributing factor to this effect is that the single-assigment, non-backtrackable shared variables of Reform Prolog result in few invalidations of shared cache lines.

This cache behaviour is notable, since an increasingly important problem in parallel processing is to hide the latencies of physically distributed and comparatively slow memories. It is reasonable to expect that most future single adress-space architectures will have distributed memories and to expect a continuing increase in processor to memory speed ratio [18].

The performance measurements on the KSR-1 can be summarized as follows.

– Low parallelization overhead (0–17%, with the larger benchmarks in the range of 2–6%).

– Good absolute parallel efficiency on 48 processors (82–91%) provided that there is enough parallelism in the program.

Our data indicate that each process executes in a mostly sequential fashion: suspension and locking is rare. Hence, sequential compiler technology should be largely applicable to our system. We intend to employ such techniques to improve absolute execution speeds further. Future work also includes a detailed quantitative characterization of the memory system behaviour of Reform Prolog programs on different architectures.

Acknowledgements. We thank the University of Manchester for providing access to their KSR-1 computer.

References

1. J. Bevemyr, *A Recursion Parallel Prolog Engine*, Licentiate of Philosophy Thesis, Uppsala Theses in Computer Science 16/93, Uppsala University, 1993.
2. J. Bevemyr, T. Lindgren & H. Millroth, Exploiting recursion-parallelism in Prolog, *Int. Conf. PARLE-93* (eds. A. Bode, M. Reeve & G. Wolf), Springer LNCS 694, Springer-Verlag, 1993.
3. J. Bevemyr, T. Lindgren & H. Millroth, Reform Prolog: The language and its implementation, *Proc. 10th Int. Conf. Logic Programming*, MIT Press, 1993.
4. J.-H. Chang, *High performance execution of Prolog programs based on a static dependency analysis*, Ph.D. Thesis, UCB/CSD 86/263, Univ. Calif. Berkeley, 1986.
5. M. Codish, A. Mulkers, M. Bruynooghe, M. Garcia de la Banda & M. Hermenegildo, Improving abstract interpretations by combining domains, *Proc. 1993 Symp. Partial Evaluation and Program Manipulation*, ACM Press, 1993.

6. P. Cousot & R. Cousot, Abstract interpretation: a unified lattice model for static analysis of programs by construction or approximation of fixpoints, *Proc. 4th ACM Symp. Principles of Programming Languages*, ACM Press, 1977.

7. S.K. Debray, Static inference of modes and data dependencies in logic programs, *ACM Trans. Programming Languages and Systems*, Vol. 11, No. 3, pp. 418–450, July 1989.

8. S.K. Debray, Efficient dataflow analysis of logic programs, *J. ACM*, Vol. 39, No. 4, October 1992.

9. S.K. Debray & D.S. Warren, Automatic mode inference for logic programs, *J. Logic Programming*, Vol. 5, No. 3, 1988.

10. M.A. Friedman, *A characterization of Prolog execution*, Ph.D. Thesis, University of Wisconsin at Madison, 1992.

11. T.W. Gentzinger, *Abstract interpretation for the compile-time optimization of logic programs*, Ph.D. Thesis, University of South California, Report 93/09, 1993.

12. M.V. Hermenegildo & F. Rossi, Non-strict independent and-parallelism, *Proc. 7th Int. Conf. Logic Programming*, MIT Press, 1990.

13. N. Jones & H. Søndergaard, A semantics-based framework for the abstract interpretation of Prolog, report 86/14, University of Copenhagen, 1986.

14. H. Millroth, Reforming compilation of logic programs, *Proc. 1991 Int. Symp. Logic Programming*, MIT Press, 1991.

15. H. Millroth, SLDR-resolution: parallelizing structural recursion in logic programs, *J. Logic Programming*, to appear.

16. L. Naish, Parallelizing NU-Prolog, *Proc. 5th Int. Conf. Symp. Logic Programming*, MIT Press, 1988.

17. T. Lindgren, *The compilation and execution of recursion-parallel Prolog on shared-memory multiprocessors*, Licentiate of Philosophy Thesis, Uppsala Theses in Computer Science 18/93, November 1993.

18. D.A. Patterson & J.L. Hennessy, *Computer Organization & Design: The Hardware/Software Interface*, Morgan Kaufmann Publ., 1993.

19. E. Tick, Memory- and buffer-referencing characteristics of a WAM-based Prolog, *J. Logic Programming*, Vol. 11, pp. 133–162, 1991.

20. P. Van Roy, A. Despain, The benefits of global dataflow analysis for an optimizing Prolog compiler, *Proc. 1990 North Am. Conf. Logic Programming*, MIT Press, 1990.

21. D.H.D. Warren, An Abstract Prolog Instruction Set, SRI Tech. Note 309, SRI International, Menlo Park, Calif., USA, 1983.

Interconnection Networks II

Bidirectional Ring: An Alternative to the Hierarchy of Unidirectional Rings

Muhammad Jaseemuddin and Zvonko G. Vranesic

Department of Electrical & Computer Engineering
University of Toronto, Toronto, Canada, M5S 1A4
Email: (jaseemud, zvonko)@eecg.toronto.edu
Tel: 416-978-5032, Fax: 416-971-2326

Abstract. A hierarchy of unidirectional rings has been used successfully in distributed shared-memory multiprocessors. The fixed cluster size of the hierarchy prevents full exploitation of communication locality. The bidirectional ring is presented as an alternative to the hierarchy. Its relative performance is evaluated for a variety of memory access patterns and network sizes. It gives superior performance for low communication locality and for large networks. Another useful feature of the bidirectional ring is that the network load tends to be balanced over the two constituent unidirectional rings. These features make the bidirectional ring an attractive possibility as a network structure for scalable NUMA multiprocessors.

1 Introduction

A hierarchy of unidirectional bit-parallel rings has been used successfully in distributed shared-memory multiprocessors [2, 8]. In a hierarchical design, clusters of processors are connected in a fashion that enables addition of more clusters as the machine expands. Clustering is an architectural feature that is effective in exploiting communication locality of parallel programs. Unidirectional rings have been used to form clusters of processors, as well as to interconnect clusters in the hierarchy. The cluster size is dependent on the configuration of a particular machine. This may hinder full exploitation of locality when an application does not map well onto the clusters that are naturally available.

This paper proposes a bidirectional ring that exhibits dynamic clustering and exploits communication locality very effectively. In this case, a cluster is formed by spanning any number of consecutive nodes in the ring. This is done simply by allocating the required number of contiguous processors to a process that is conducive to a cluster of a particular size.

The paper gives an assessment of the relative performance of the bidirectional ring in comparison with the hierarchy of unidirectional rings. The problems of static clustering of the hierarchy are discussed in section 2. Section 3 introduces the bidirectional ring and dynamic clustering. The simulation environment is described in section 4, and the results of simulations are presented in section 5. Finally, the main results are summarized in section 6.

2 Hierarchy of Unidirectional Rings

The hierarchy of unidirectional rings that we will use for comparison purposes is similar to the hierarchy used in Hector [8] and KSR1 [2] multiprocessors. Figure 1a shows a simple example of a 2-level hierarchy, in which *local* rings connect a certain number of nodes and these rings are interconnected by a second-level ring. A node consists of a processor, a memory unit (holding a portion of shared address-space), and a communication switch. Larger hierarchies are implemented by increasing the number of levels in the system.

Each local ring in the hierarchy forms a cluster of processors. Thus, the size of a cluster is fixed. The static nature of the cluster causes two problems. First, it favors the assignment of processors to a process to suit the cluster size. Second, the performance of the network becomes very sensitive to the memory access patterns that exhibit variable amount of inter-cluster communication. A process that spawns as many threads as the number of processors in a cluster can naturally fit in one cluster, but the addition of one more thread causes it to span two local rings. This introduces a communication overhead proportional to the size of the second-level ring connecting the two local rings. We call this the *spanning overhead*. If it takes more levels for a packet to cross to reach the destination ring, then each level will add a factor to the overhead proportional to the size of the ring at that level. Furthermore, when a packet ascends or descends the hierarchy it passes through several inter-ring interface buffers, each of which contributes a variable amount of time to the overhead. In this case, depending upon the system load and the amount of inter-cluster communication, the benefits of more parallelism (threads) may diminish.

The hierarchy is particularly effective in exploiting the communication locality that is concentrated within clusters. It is less effective when there exists a low degree of communication locality where each processor communicates frequently with processors that are not necessarily a part of the same cluster.

3 Bidirectional Ring

Bidirectional rings have been considered mainly for the local area network environment [3]. In this paper, the bidirectional ring is viewed as a network structure for a multiprocessor, where due to communication locality the proximity of interacting processors is the main issue to deal with. A key property of the bidirectional ring is dynamic clustering.

In the bidirectional ring data traffic flows in both clockwise and counter clockwise directions. This is realized by having two rings that run in opposite directions, as shown in figure 1b. A node selects the ring to transmit to another node based on the shortest distance between the source and the destination. This keeps the distance between the two nodes to not more than half the ring size. A simple transmission scheme based on a request-response protocol, discussed in section 4.2, can be used to control the flow of traffic on the rings.

The bidirectional ring adapts to the application and forms clusters of processors dynamically. If a process is scheduled to run on a set of adjacent processors,

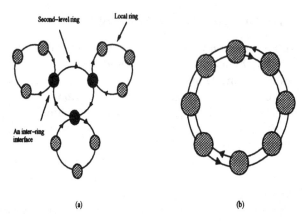

Fig. 1. An example of: (a) the hierarchy of unidirectional rings, and (b) bidirectional ring

then these processors automatically form a cluster where all communication among the processors takes place within a portion of the ring occupied by this cluster. Thus, traffic created by two or more processes tends to be contained within their own clusters. The number of processors forming a cluster is not constrained by the physical structure of the network.

The dynamic clustering in a bidirectional ring offers two advantages over the hierarchy of unidirectional rings. First, the spanning overhead is non-existent, which improves the performance of a process scheduled to run on two or more clusters (local rings) in the hierarchy. However, expanding the cluster increases the communication cost proportional to the additional links. Second, the variable size of the cluster promotes assigning a processor to every thread. This allows the number of threads to match the desired parallelism (the parallelism exhibited by the algorithm) of a large program.

Clusters in a bidirectional ring are not rings in the true sense; rather, they form chain-like structures in both directions. The round trip delay varies depending upon the positions of the source and the destination in the cluster. The maximum round trip delay is of the order of $2P$, where P is the number of nodes in the cluster.

The bidirectional ring is expected to show a smooth performance improvement with increasing locality. This is because, unlike the hierarchy, the bidirectional ring does not show jumps in the communication cost. Instead, it increases proportionally as the distance between the nodes is increased. Therefore, for each node, the cost of communicating with a node of equivalent distance is the same. As the communication locality increases, the neighborhood of a given node decreases; that is, the node communicates mostly with only a few of its nearest neighbors.

4 Experimental Setup

We have simulated the bidirectional ring and the hierarchy of unidirectional rings of different sizes to assess their relative performance using a simple but real communication protocol and synthetic workloads that are tuned by carefully selecting the parameters to reflect the actual workloads. A similar approach is used in evaluating the performance of a hierarchical ring-based system in [5]. The use of synthetic workloads allows us to study the behavior of each network under many possible interesting situations, and it also makes the simulation of large-scale networks manageable. In [1] real applications are used to analyze medium scale systems using a slotted-ring and running different cache coherence protocols. A different approach is used in [7], where first an analytical model of the SCI ring is developed and then a simple synthetic workload is used to analyze and validate the analytical model with the simulation of the actual network. This section explains the environment and parameters of the simulator. Section 4.1 describes the system model. The network protocol is discussed in section 4.2. Section 4.3 explains different workload models used in the simulation.

4.1 System Model

A node consists of a processor, a memory unit and a communication switch. The network is connected to the memory through the switch, and receives only those memory requests which are not satisfied by the local memory. This is modeled by taking a fraction of all requests generated by the processor. The request rate is a parameter which indicates the average number of requests generated by the processor per cycle. It is fixed at 0.05 which corresponds to 20 cycles between two consecutive cache misses. This rate is supported by real workloads [5]. The ring cycle time and the processor clock cycle time are considered to be the same. The ratio of the ring cycle time to the memory access time is 10:1. For instance, a word read takes 10 ring cycles. However, for a cache line read, the first word takes 10 cycles, but each subsequent word is available after every 5 cycles. The ring is a slotted ring [6].

The communication locality can be modeled as groups of *nearby* nodes around a source processor and assigning access probability to each group indicating that the target memory is in that group when the request is not to the local memory. This model is similar to the clusters of communication locality model used in [5]. A group of size s and access probability p consists of all nodes within a distance of $s/2$ from the source. A request generated at the source goes to a node in this group with a probability p given that the request is not to the local memory. The distribution of destination addresses within a group is uniform. For instance, in a system of 1024 processors with a local memory target probability of 0.9, $GS = (512, 768, 1024)$ and $GP = (0.8, 0.95, 1.0)$ defines 3 groups, where GS and GP indicate group sizes and their corresponding access probabilities. The local memory serves on average 90% of all requests. The first group consists of 512 nodes and 80% of the remaining remote requests involve nodes within this group. The second group is formed by adding 256 more nodes to the 512 nodes of the first group. The access probability of this enlarged group is 0.95, meaning that 95% of remote requests go to the nodes of this group. Finally, all 1024 nodes form the third group, and all remote requests are within this group. The communication locality defines the local memory target probability, the number of groups, the size of each group, and the access probability of each group.

The invalidation packets introduced by the cache coherence scheme are not considered in the network traffic. Ignoring the invalidation traffic has no major effect on the overall results. For common applications, average number of shared writes causing invalidations is not more than 2 to 3 percent of total requests, and the average invalidation per shared write involves not more than 2 packets [4]. Assuming one packet per invalidation, the percentage of invalidation packets becomes less than 10% of the total request packets. This value decreases further if it is considered as a fraction of the sum of request and response packets.

4.2 Request-Response Protocol

A Hector-like request-response protocol [8] is used for network transactions. A subset of possible transactions is used which is sufficient to give a good indication of the relative performance that may be expected from the bidirectional ring. The three types of requests modeled are: i) READ a memory word, ii) READ a CACHE LINE (Cache line transfer), and iii) WRITE a memory word. Each processor can have only one outstanding request. A single packet is used to transmit a request. The response can involve multiple packets, such as for a READ CACHE LINE. The data to be written is included in the WRITE packet. For writes, the acknowledgments are issued after queuing the WRITE packets for later storing in the memory. A negative acknowledgement (NACK) is issued when the request cannot be buffered at the receiving node. The sender retransmits the same request after receiving the NACK. Another occasion when a sender retries is after a time-out, which is a mechanism used to recover from a packet loss. When a node cannot gain access to the network, it is said to be *blocked*, and the time it remains blocked is called *blocking time*. During this period the node continues to serve requests from remote processors.

In the hierarchy of unidirectional rings a WRITE packet is turned into an acknowledgement packet by simply changing the request type. In a bidirectional ring this scheme cannot work, otherwise the advantage of shorter distance will be compromised. A separate acknowledgement packet is formed and transmitted on the ring running in the opposite direction. This requires an acknowledgement buffer for each ring at every node to queue the acknowledgement packets for later transmission when the network is busy. We used this simple protocol to highlight the potential problem spots in the network structures. We used a 32-deep receiving and acknowledgement buffer each, and a 64-deep inter-ring interface buffer in the simulated system.

4.3 Workload Models

A number of workloads have been used to model different request traffic patterns. It is shown in [5] that substantial ring contention is observed when more than 10% of memory requests are to remote memory modules. Hence, to examine the network's effect on latency, 80% of requests are targeted to the local memory, and 20% are transmitted through the network to remote memories. The salient features of the workload models are discussed below.

1. **Bursty:** This workload models multiple request packets transmitted in a bunch, such as for cache line writes, multiple outstanding requests, and cache line prefetching. The two parameters that characterize this model are the average number of packets in a burst (burst length), and the average interval between two bursts. The average burst length is set to 5, and the average interval is fixed at 100. All the packets in a burst are directed to the same destination. This is because: i) a cache line write is sent to a single destination, and ii) due to spatial locality consecutive cache misses are served by the same target memory.
2. **Uniform:** This workload model selects the destination node randomly within a group.
3. **Hotspot:** There are periods when requests originating at different processors are destined to the same memory module due to synchronization or false sharing. In such a situation a single node receives a slew of requests from many nodes. Different hotspots are selected randomly each for 10% of total hotspot transactions. Hotspot transactions are 3% of total requests, which is in the range of practical values [5]. The other 97% of packets are generated using the uniform workload model.
4. **Mirror:** The destination address is predetermined for each source and is at the same distance from the other extreme as the source is from one extreme, that is *destination = (number of nodes − source) mod number of nodes*. This model does not exhibit communication locality, thus it serves as the stress test for a network designed to exploit communication locality.

5 Comparing Performance of the Bidirectional Ring and the Hierarchy of Unidirectional Rings

The main performance metric used to compare the performance of different networks is the request latency, which is defined as the number of cycles spent from the time when a processor issues a request to the memory to the time a response is received from the memory. Thus, the request latency is a sum of blocking times at both ends (source and destination), network propagation delays, and cumulative time spent in all the inter-ring interface buffers by the request and the response packets. Different memory requests experience different latencies. The *average latency* for each request type is computed first, and then the weighted averages of the three types of latencies are calculated.

Another important performance measure is *network utilization*, which is defined as the average percentage of busy slots over the total number of slots in the ring at any given time. This average is calculated over the total number of execution cycles. For the results presented in this section, a single application is assumed to be running.

Systems of various sizes, ranging from 16 to 1024 processors, have been simulated using the above workload models. Following are the three different network configurations considered.

1. **Hierarchy:** This is a hierarchy of unidirectional rings where 16 processors are attached to each of the lowest-level rings. Table 1 shows the configuration of different sizes in terms of the branching factor of each level of the hierarchy, from the lowest to the highest level.

Table 1. Configurations of different sizes

No. of Processors	Hierarchy
16	16,1
32	16,2
64	16,4
128	16,2,2,2
256	16,4,2,2
512	16,4,4,2
1024	16,4,4,4

2. **Bi-1:** A bidirectional ring where the channel width of each of the two rings is half the channel width of a unidirectional ring in the hierarchy. This is simulated by doubling the number of packets per cache line transfer on the bidirectional ring in comparison with the hierarchy. A request is assumed to be transmitted in a single packet.
3. **Bi-2:** A bidirectional ring where each ring has the same channel width as the hierarchy.

Two models of communication locality are considered, where the system consisting of N nodes is divided into three groups of communication locality:

1. **CLM1:** Local memory target probability=0.8, $GS = \{N/2, 3N/4, N\}$, and access probability is assumed to be $GP = \{0.8, 0.95, 1.0\}$. This represents an application showing low communication locality.
2. **CLM2:** Local memory target probability=0.8, $GS = \{4, 20, N\}$, and the access probability is assumed to be $GP = \{0.8, 0.95, 1.0\}$. This is representative of applications showing very high communication locality.

5.1 Network Performance

In this section, the simulation results for three workload models—uniform, bursty, and mirror—are presented. Hotspot workload is discussed in the next section. For brevity, the term hierarchy is used for the hierarchy of unidirectional rings, and latency for the average latency.

Uniform Workload. For small networks, the performance of the hierarchy and Bi-1 is not significantly different, as shown in figure 2. Latency in the hierarchy becomes considerably worse for large networks, mainly because of congestion at high level rings. In this situation inter-ring interfaces become points of high activity, even losing some packets, as shown in figure 3. It is interesting to observe the effects of high utilization of the high-level ring in the hierarchy in comparison with the bidirectional ring. In the hierarchy, inter-ring interface buffers are congested resulting in some packet losses. On the other hand, high utilization of the constituent rings in a bidirectional ring shows high contention for the network, but does not result in loss of packets, as indicated by increasing blocking time in figure 3.

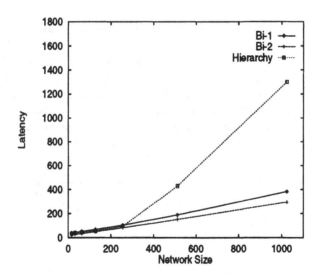

Fig. 2. Latency for uniform traffic and CLM1

The simulation results show a marginal difference between the utilization of the two rings in a bidirectional ring, which is due to the fact that different rings are used for transfer of request and response packets between any two nodes. Hence, the network load tends to be balanced between the two rings.

The causes of packet loss in the two networks are different. In the hierarchy, packets are lost mainly due to the lack of buffer space at the inter-ring interfaces. In a bidirectional ring packets are lost when acknowledgement packets are

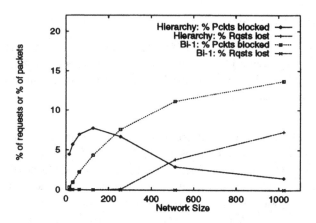

Fig. 3. Blocked Packets and Lost Requests for uniform traffic and CLM1

dropped due to the shortage of acknowledgement buffer space. This occurs very seldom, and appears only in those cases where momentary bursts of requests are received by some nodes. Therefore, packet loss is only observed in the hotspot workload.

Bi-2 results in improved performance for networks of all sizes, as shown in figure 2.

The hierarchy is very sensitive to communication locality. In CLM2, 96% of communication takes place within a distance of 4; that is, most of the communication is confined to the local ring. As shown in figure 4, the hierarchy shows a large reduction in latency for CLM2, as compared to CLM1. The response of a bidirectional ring is also favorable to high communication locality, and its performance is comparable to the performance of the hierarchy.

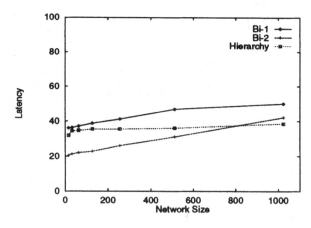

Fig. 4. Latency for uniform traffic and CLM2

Bursty and Mirror Workloads. Results for the bursty workload are shown in figure 5. The latency of the hierarchy for small systems is slightly less than the latency of Bi-1. For large systems the hierarchy shows much worse latency.

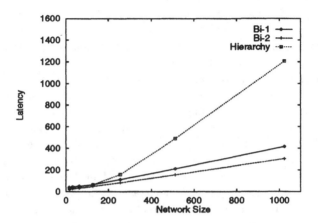

Fig. 5. Latency for bursty traffic and CLM1

Lack of communication locality in the mirror workload increases the latency in both types of networks, as shown in figure 6. The adverse effect is more pronounced in the hierarchy, because a large number of transactions occur between the nodes located in different rings which causes packets to traverse many levels. Every time a packet moves either up or down in the hierarchy, it may spend some time in an inter-ring interface buffer.

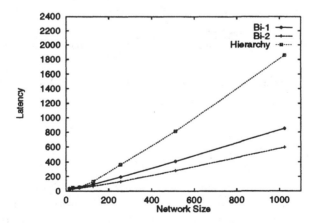

Fig. 6. Latency for mirror traffic and CLM1

5.2 Hotspot Workload

The relative performance of the bidirectional rings and the hierarchy for hotspot workload shows the same trends found for other workload models, as indicated in figure 7. However, the difference between the latencies of the hierarchy and Bi-1 is much less for large networks, as compared to the uniform workload case. The main reason for the smaller difference is the large number of retries that appear on the bidirectional ring. In the hierarchy, a request packet passes through several buffers, one at each inter-ring interface, before reaching the destination node. This spreads out the load at the buffer of the destination node. In contrast, a single buffer in the bidirectional ring receives an equivalent number of requests. This results in many requests being dropped after reaching the destination, which in the hierarchy may find space in one of the inter-ring interface buffers. Another important difference is the contribution of a retry to the latencies on the two networks. In the hierarchy a request may be dropped by an inter-ring interface, which adds less time to the latency than would be the case if the request is dropped by the destination node. In contrast, a request may be dropped only after reaching the destination in the bidirectional ring, and thus every retry adds a round trip delay to the latency.

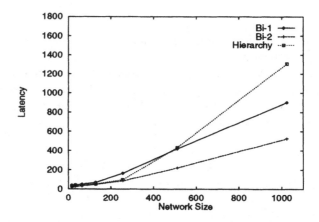

Fig. 7. Latency for hotspot traffic and CLM1

6 Concluding Remarks

The bidirectional ring is presented as an alternative to the hierarchy of unidirectional rings. The relative performance of these networks has been evaluated for different memory access patterns and network sizes, ranging from 16 to 1K processors. The fixed cluster size of the hierarchy makes it very sensitive to the communication locality, especially for large networks. In contrast, the bidirectional ring shows a smooth improvement in performance as the communication locality is increased. The optimal locality for the hierarchy occurs when the communication is confined within clusters. Even for such workloads the performance of the bidirectional ring is comparable to the hierarchy. For low communication locality the bidirectional ring outperforms the hierarchy for all network sizes. In the absence of communication locality, the degradation in the performance of the bidirectional ring is much less pronounced than in the hierarchy.

For hotspot workload, the bidirectional ring outperforms the hierarchy, but not as significantly as in the case of other workload models. In the bidirectional ring, the receiver buffer at the hotspot creates a problem in handling momentary bursts of requests. This is less of a problem in the hierarchy, because the inter-ring interface buffers in the communication path share the load.

Another advantage of the bidirectional ring over the hierarchy is the load balancing in the network. Under certain conditions, such as low communication locality, the hierarchy may experience problems with saturation of high-level rings, whereas the low-level rings remain underutilized at the same time. In contrast, the bidirectional ring shows an effectively uniform load on both rings.

The third advantage of the bidirectional ring is that it has better reliability because a communication protocol may be defined that can tolerate the failure of one link. These factors make the bidirectional ring an attractive choice for scalable NUMA multiprocessors.

References

1. L.A. Barroso, and M. Dubois, *The Performance of Cache-Coherent Ring-based Multiprocessors*, Proc. ISCA, pp. 268-277, May 1993.
2. H. Burkhardt III et al, *Overview of the KSR1 Computer System*, Technical Report KSR-TR 9202001, Kendall Square research, February 1992.
3. I. Cidon, and Yoram Ofek, *MetaRing - A Full-Duplex Ring with Fairness and Spatial Reuse*, IEEE Trans. Communications, Vol. 41, No. 1, pp. 110-120, January 1993.
4. A. Gupta, and W.-D. Weber, *Cache Invalidation Patterns in Shared-Memory Multiprocessors*, IEEE Trans. Computer, Vol. 41, No. 7, pp. 794-810, July 1992.
5. M. Holliday, and M. Stumm, *Performance Evaluation of Hierarchical Ring-Based Shared Memory Multiprocessors*, IEEE Trans. Computer, Vol. 42, No. 1, pp. 52-67, January 1994.
6. A. Hopper, and R. Williamson, *Design and Use of an Integrated Cambridge Ring*, IEEE Journal on Selected Areas in Communications, November 1983.
7. S.L. Scott, J.R. Goodman, and M.K. Vernon, *Performance of the SCI Ring*, Proc. ISCA, pp. 403-412, May 1992.
8. Z.G. Vranesic, M. Stumm, D.M. Lewis, and R. White, *Hector - a Hierarchically Structured Shared-Memory Multiprocessor*, IEEE Computer, Vol. 24, No. 1, pp. 72-79, January 1991.

A Formal Study of the Mcube Interconnection Network

Nitin K. Singhvi and Kanad Ghose

Department of Computer Science
State University of New York at Binghamton, NY 13902–6000.
{nitin, ghose}@cs.binghamton.edu

Abstract

The Mcube network has been proposed in [11] as a highly recursive and symmetrical interconnection network based on twisted links [1]. The Mcube topology has been developed and defined in terms of the structural constraints between components to enforce structural symmetry instead of specifying edges between node pairs. Mcubes have almost half the diameter of a comparable hypercube, a lower average internode distance than most other twisted networks and an uniform spatial node distribution. Unlike most twisted cube–based networks, randomly destined traffic results in uniform traffic flow through every node in the Mcube and links in the Mcube saturate more slowly than hypercubes. The Mcube is recursively partitionable and allows several parallel algorithms to execute as fast as or faster than on a hypercube. We establish the node distribution for the Mcubes to be uniform with the internode distance. Based on the constraints imposed by the construction and the routing algorithm, we derive an expression for the average internode distance for Mcubes. We also introduce an efficient broadcasting algorithm for the Mcube interconnection and show how Mcubes can be reconfigured into hypercubes. Finally, we show how representative parallel algorithms can be directly implemented on the Mcube topology.

Keywords: interconnection Network, hypercube, massively parallel, twisted cube.

1 Introduction

Many variations of the popular hypercube interconnection have been explored over the recent years [2–9, 12–14]. Among these variations, a large class of networks attempt to improve on some of the properties – notably the network diameter and average internode distance – by redirecting edge pairs, i.e., by twisting appropriately chosen pair of links. These improvements to the hypercube due to twisting are bought about without any increase in the number of links, nodes or node degrees. If switches are used to move between the normal and twisted configurations, the usual advantages of hypercube can also be retained, in addition to exploiting the advantages of twisting. Examples of twisted cubic networks include the Twisted Cube [6], the Mobius Cubes [3] and the Crossed Cube [4]. Unfortunately, as shown in [1], twisted links introduce asymmetry in the network, leading to skewed traffic flow and its consequential delays, obscuring the benefits of twisting links. The goal of this paper is to formally study several aspects of a new variation of a twisted hypercube based network, introduced by us in [11], that unlike previous twist based networks, is *structurally symmetric*.

The Mcube interconnection network proposed in [11], is a new class of hypercube based structure using twisted links. The basic properties of the Mcube are as follows:
1) The Mcube interconnection network is designed as a structure that uses the twisting of links to provide the advantages of low diameter like other twist–based structures but

unlike these interconnections, it is structurally symmetrical and possesses a lower average internode distance.

2) The design of the Mcube ensures a uniform distance distribution and under random traffic every node in an Mcube experiences the same traffic load. Thus, undesirable skewed traffic patterns that plague the performance of other twisted structures such as the twisted cube [6] are absent.

3) An Mcube has the same low diameter as the other twist–based interconnections mentioned above. Additionally, it has a lower average internode distance than the other twist–based networks. Consequently, message latencies in an Mcube are significantly low under heavy message traffic and none of its links saturate faster than hypercube links under similar traffic patterns.

4) Mcubes are highly recursive in nature and can be partitioned easily to allow subnetwork allocations in a multiprogrammed system that uses space partitioning.

5) Fully distributed algorithms for optimal routing and broadcasting are possible for an Mcube.

6) Several classes of parallel algorithms can be mapped onto Mcube based systems in a manner that allows them to execute faster than on a comparable hypercube based system.

The Mcube is defined as a composition of smaller Mcubes by specifying the structural constraints that must be satisfied among its component structures. These constraints dictate the placement of 'twisted' links in an Mcube. This construction technique departs from the more conventional approach of specifying interconnections on the basis of links between nodes with specific addresses. The constraints used in the construction of the Mcube are, however, flexible enough to allow a large number of variations in the topology of the resulting networks.

This paper extends the basic concepts of Mcubes, as introduced in [11], by presenting: (i) A fully distributed broadcasting algorithm and an algorithm for constructing routing tables (ii) A formal proof of uniform distance distribution (iii) The computation of the average internode distance (iv) Hypercube emulation techniques (v) Reconfiguration of Mcubes as hypercubes and the computation of the number of switches required and (vi) Mapping of other classes of parallel algorithms.

1.1 Definitions and Notation

A static interconnection network G can be modeled by a graph $G = (V,E)$ where V is the set of processing nodes and E is the set of links in the network. A subnetwork of a network G is a network corresponding to a subgraph of the graph of G. Hereafter, we will use the terms network and graph, and subnetwork and subgraph, interchangeably.

Definition 1: A *1–1 (one–to–one) connection* between two disjoint networks $G_1 = (V_1,E_1)$ and $G_2 = (V_2,E_2)$ where $|V_1| = |V_2|$, is a set of edges $E = \{(v,f(v)) | v \in V_1 \text{ and } f(v) \in V_2$, and $f : V_1 \to V_2$ is a bijection}, i.e. each node in G_1 is connected to a unique node in G_2 and vice versa.

Definition 2 : A *static hypercube network* of dimension n (also called a binary n–cube) contains 2^n nodes which are connected as follows: all nodes are given distinct binary addresses using n bits, and two nodes are connected by a link if and only if their binary addresses differ in exactly one bit position. The link connecting two nodes is numbered j (denoted link#j) if the position of the differing bit in their binary addresses is j. Bit positions are numbered 0 to n–1 from the LSB to the MSB.

We now describe the notations used henceforth in this paper.

Let E be a 1–1 connection between two networks $G_1 = (V_1, E_1)$ and $G_2 = (V_2, E_2)$.

Let G = (V1 | V2, E1 | E2 | E). Then

(1) "G1 c~ G2" denotes the assertion that G1 is 1–1 connected to G2.

(2) The network G is denoted by {G1 :: G2}.

(3) For a node s1 in G1, "s1 ∈ V1" is also written as "s1 ∈ G1".

(4) For an edge (x,y) in G1, "(x,y) ∈ E1" is also written as "(x,y) ∈ G1".

(5) If node p1 ∈ G1 is connected to node p2 ∈ G2, we denote this as c~(p1,G2) = p2.

(6) We denote the set of edges E, by {(G1,G2)}.

(7) A path between two nodes p1 and p2 traversing n links is denoted as $p1 \xrightarrow{n} p2$.

(8) $\omega(x,G)$ denotes the binary address of a node x in G if G is an Mcube.

Definition 3: A network G is *1–1 partitionable* if G = {$G_1 :: G_2$} for some networks G_1 and G_2.

Definition 4: If p_1 and p_2 are two nodes in a network G, then the *distance* $d(p_1,p_2)$, between nodes p_1 and p_2 is the length of the shortest path from p_1 to p_2 under a given routing algorithm R.

Definition 5: For any network G, the *diameter* of G under a routing algorithm R, is given by diameter(G) = max{$d(p_1,p_2)$} for all p_1,p_2 ∈ G, under R.

Definition 6: In a network G, the distance distribution function for a node j, with respect to the nodes in a subnetwork K of G and some routing algorithm R, is denoted as $D_j(i,K)$, whose value is given by $D_j(i,K) = |A|$, where A = {x | x is a node in K and d(j,x) = i}. We call the distance distribution in G uniform iff $D_j(i,G)$ (also written as $D_j(i)$), is the same for all j in G, for each possible given value of i. The Average Path Delay (APD(j)) from a node j in a network G to all other nodes in G is $(1/N)\Sigma_{i=1}^{d} (i * D_j(i))$ where N is the number of nodes in G, and d is the diameter of G. The average internode distance in G is $(1/N)\Sigma APD(j)$, summing over all nodes j in G.

2 Mcube Construction

The construction of an Mcube commences with a pair of 2–dimensional hypercubes. Each hypercube is called a 2–dimensional Mcube (referred to as a 2–Mcube). The two hypercubes are 1–1 connected using the Mcube construction method defined below, to form a 3–Mcube. In general two k–Mcubes are 1–1 connected to construct a (k+1)–Mcube. Therefore a k–Mcube has the same size (number of nodes) and the same number of links as a k–dimensional hypercube.

2.1 Construction Constraints

Before defining the construction of an Mcube we need to provide terms for certain components of Mcubes for simplifying the construction constraints.

Definition 7: If A is an Mcube of 2^r nodes and A is 1–1 partitionable as follows: A = {A_{P0} :: A_{P1}} and A = {A_{L0} :: A_{L1}} such that A_{P0} = {A_{00} :: A_{01}}, A_{P1} = {A_{10} :: A_{11}}, A_{L0} = {A_{00} :: A_{10}}, and A_{L1} = {A_{01} :: A_{11}}, where

$A_{P0}, A_{P1}, A_{L0}, A_{L1}$ are Mcubes of 2^{r-1} nodes and $A_{00}, A_{01}, A_{10}, A_{11}$ are Mcubes of 2^{r-2} nodes

then A_{P0} and A_{P1} are called *principal components* of A, or principals, for short,

A_{L0} and A_{L1} are called *lateral components* of A, or laterals, for short and
A_{00}, A_{01}, A_{10}, A_{11} are called *corner components* of A, or corners, for short.
CS(A) is the set of four corners of A.

Definition 8: An Mcube of dimension k (k–Mcube) is defined for $k \geq 0$, as follows:
(I) For $k \leq 2$, a k–Mcube is a hypercube of dimension k i.e. k–cube.
(II) For $k > 2$, given (k–1)–Mcubes A and B, M = {A :: B} is a k–Mcube if the following
<u>construction requirements</u> are met:
(R1): for each $X \in CS(A)$: $X \, c\sim Y$ where $Y \in CS(B)$
    such that {X :: Y} is a (k–2)–Mcube,
(R2): for $X_1, X_2 \in CS(A)$ and $Y_1, Y_2 \in CS(B)$
    [$(X_1 \, c\sim Y_1)$ and $(X_2 \, c\sim Y_2)$ and $\neg(X_1 \, c\sim X_2)$] $\Rightarrow$ $(Y_1 \, c\sim Y_2)$.
(R3): {A_{L0} :: B_{L0}} and {A_{L1} :: B_{L1}} are (k–1)–Mcubes   (end of construction).

Note that the only two possibilities that satisfy construction requirement (R2) are (a)
$A_{00} \, c\sim B_{00}$, $A_{10} \, c\sim B_{10}$, $A_{01} \, c\sim B_{11}$, $A_{11} \, c\sim B_{01}$ and (b) $A_{00} \, c\sim B_{10}$, $A_{10} \, c\sim B_{00}$, $A_{01} \, c\sim$
B_{01}, $A_{11} \, c\sim B_{11}$. Figure 1 shows principals, laterals and corners of a 2–cube (2–Mcube).
Figure 2 shows a 3–Mcube and its components.

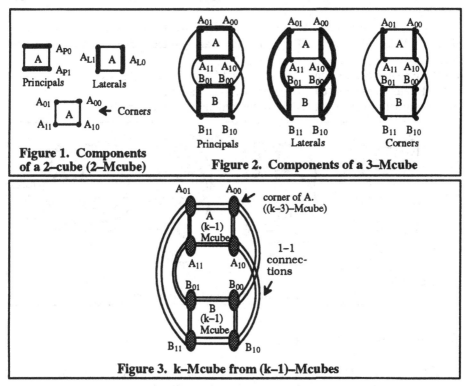

**Figure 1. Components
of a 2–cube (2–Mcube)**

Figure 2. Components of a 3–Mcube

Figure 3. k–Mcube from (k–1)–Mcubes

2.2 Algorithmic construction of an Mcube

Definition 9: In an Mcube M a link l is called a *principal connection link* or a *PCL* of M if l
$\in$ {(M_{P0}, M_{P1})} and a *lateral connection link* or an *LCL* of M if $l \in$ {(M_{L0}, M_{L1})}.
Definition 10: In an Mcube M, a path traversing three links, an LCL, a PCL and an LCL, in
that order, is called a *principal semi–loop* in M.

In Figure 3, a path $p_1 \xrightarrow{1} p_2 \xrightarrow{1} p_3 \xrightarrow{1} p_4$ where $p_1 \in A_{01}, p_2 \in A_{00}, p_3 \in B_{00}$ and $p_4 \in B_{01}$ is a principal semi–loop.

Construction algorithm: A $(k+1)$–Mcube M, $k \geq 2$, is constructed from two k–Mcubes AB and CD where $AB = \{A :: B\}$, $CD = \{C :: D\}$ and A, B, C, D are $(k-1)$–Mcubes (Figure 4) :

Let $(AB)_{L0} = \{A_{L0} :: B_{L0}\}$, $(AB)_{L1} = \{A_{L1} :: B_{L1}\}$, $(CD)_{L0} = \{C_{L0} :: D_{L0}\}$ and $(CD)_{L1} = \{C_{L1} :: D_{L1}\}$.

(a) Add a link (p_1, p_2) where $p_1 \in A_{L1}$ and $p_2 \in D_{L1}$.

(b) Add a link (q_1, q_2) where $q_1 \in B_{L0}$ and $q_2 \in D_{L0}$.

Make a "Dual connection" (defined below) between $(AB)_{L1}$ and $(CD)_{L1}$ *with reference to* (p_1, p_2) and between $(AB)_{L0}$ and $(CD)_{L0}$ *with reference to* (q_1, q_2). The Dual connection copies the structure of AB into $\{(AB)_{Li} :: (CD)_{Li}\}$, $i = 0, 1$.

Dual connection (Figure 4): Let AB and CD be k–Mcubes as explained above. Let (p_1, p_2) be such that $p_1 \in A_{L1}$ and $p_2 \in D_{L1}$, where $(AB)_{L1} = \{A_{L1} :: B_{L1}\}$ and $(CD)_{L1} = \{C_{L1} :: D_{L1}\}$. A Dual connection between $(AB)_{L1}$ and $(CD)_{L1}$ *with reference to* (p_1, p_2), is made as follows:

(I) If $k=2$ **then** add link (p_3, p_4) where $B_{L1} = \{p_3\}$ and $C_{L1} = \{p_4\}$,

(II) else

(a) Make a Dual connection between A_{L1} and D_{L1} with reference to (p_1, p_2),

(b) Add a link (y, z) where $y \in B_{L1}$ and $z \in C_{L1}$, and y is the node reached by a principal semi–loop in AB, from p_1, and $z = c{\sim}(p_2, C)$,

(c) Make a Dual connection between B_{L1} and C_{L1} with reference to (y, z).

A Dual connection between $(AB)_{L0}$ and $(CD)_{L0}$ is similar.

This construction can be proved to conform to the Mcube definition [10].

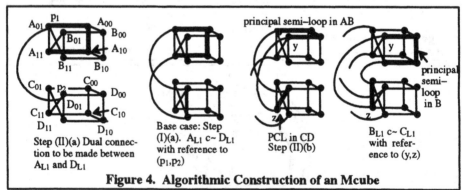

Step (II)(a) Dual connection to be made between A_{L1} and D_{L1}

Base case: Step (I)(a). A_{L1} c$\sim$ D_{L1} with reference to (p_1, p_2)

PCL in CD Step (II)(b)

B_{L1} c$\sim$ C_{L1} with reference to (y, z)

Figure 4. Algorithmic Construction of an Mcube

3 Routing and Diameter in an Mcube

Mroute–k is a distributed routing algorithm for the Mcube that exploits the recursive structure of a k–Mcube. Let M be a k–Mcube $(k > 2)$ where $M = \{A :: B\}$, and A and B are $(k-1)$–Mcubes. Message routing in M, from a source 'S' to a destination 'D', under Mroute–k, falls into three cases: (Figure 5.)

Case(i) S and D are both within the same principal of M (A or B.)

Case(ii) S and D are both within the same lateral of M ($\{A_{L0} :: B_{L0}\}$ or $\{A_{L1} :: B_{L1}\}$.)

Case(iii) Neither Case(i) nor Case(ii) applies. Without loss of generality let us assume that $S \in A_{00}$, $D \in B_{L1}$ and A_{00} c~ B_{00}. Therefore A_{01} c~ B_{11} (see Mcube construction). Since $B_{L1} = \{B_{01} :: B_{11}\}$ it follows that $D \in B_{01}$ or $D \in B_{11}$.

subcase(a) If $D \in B_{01}$ we use $S \xrightarrow{1} c\text{~}(S,B_{00}) \xrightarrow{x} D$ where x steps are taken using Mroute–(k–2) recursively in (k–2)–Mcube B_{P0}.

subcase(b) If $D \in B_{11}$ we use $S \xrightarrow{1} c\text{~}(S,A_{01}) \xrightarrow{x} D$ where x steps are taken using Mroute–(k–2) recursively in (k–2)–Mcube $\{A_{01} :: B_{11}\}$.

On the basis of these cases, Mroute–k can be recursively defined as follows:

If $k \leq 2$ use hypercube e–cube routing.

If $k > 2$ then follow the above three cases:

Case(i): Use Mroute–(k–1) within principal.

Case(ii): Use Mroute–(k–1) within lateral.

Case(iii)(a): Use $S \xrightarrow{1} c\text{~}(S,B_{L0})$, then use Mroute–(k–2) within (k–2)–Mcube B_{P0}.

Case(iii)(b): Use $S \xrightarrow{1} c\text{~}(S,A_{01})$, then Mroute–(k–2) within (k–2)–Mcube $\{A_{01} :: B_{11}\}$.

Using the fact that Mroute–k can be expressed in terms of Mroute(k–2) with one additional routing step and Mroute–(k–1), *the diameter of a k–Mcube (of 2^k nodes) is shown in* [11] *to be* $\lceil (k+1)/2 \rceil$ *under Mroute–k*, about half that of a comparable hypercube.

Node Numbering: The nodes and links in a k–Mcube, for k < 3, are numbered as in a hypercube. Let $M = \{A :: B\}$ be a k–Mcube, k > 2, where A and B are (k–1)–Mcubes. We assign a new address to a node x in M as $\omega(x,M) = 0.\omega(x,A)$ for $x \in A$ and $\omega(x,M) = 1.\omega(x,B)$ for $x \in B$. Once all nodes in an Mcube are numbered, links are numbered as follows (link#(L) denotes the number of a link L): If $L = (v_1,v_2)$, then link#(L) = the position of the most significant differing bit in the binary addresses of v_1 and v_2. Therefore, in a k–Mcube M, with k > 0, if $L \in \{(M_{L0},M_{L1})\}$ then link#(L) = 0. Similarly, if $L \in \{(M_{P0},M_{P1})\}$ then link#(L) = k–1. Note that conventional hypercube e–cube routing can now be used to provide a diameter of k for a k–Mcube.

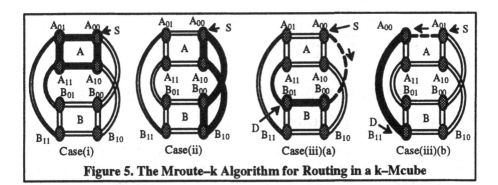

Figure 5. The Mroute–k Algorithm for Routing in a k–Mcube

Routing Tables: The implementation of the Mroute algorithm requires two tables at each node for completely distributed routing [11]. Mroute uses hypercube e–cube routing as the default routing. The tables contain entries for those message destinations that require non–default routing from the source or relaying node. Table RT2 is used if the source and destination are in different laterals of M and Table RT1 is used if they are in the same lateral of M. The tables provide the link number along which the message is to be sent. The table–based routing algorithm is:

if 0th bit in source and destination address differ **then**
    (* source and destination are in different laterals *)
    if destination address is found in RT2 **then** route message along link#0;
    else use default routing;
else   (* source and destination are in the same lateral *)
    if dest address is found in RT1 **then** route message along link number listed in table
    entry;
    else use default routing;

Figure 6 shows the algorithm for determining table entries for both tables. In [11] where the routing table sizes are are shown to be $O(k)$ for RT2 and $O(k^2)$ for RT1 in a k–Mcube and the routing algorithm is shown to be $O(k)$.

```
Calculate_Table(k) {/*for k-Mcube*/

for each node 'p' in an Mcube
{ count := 0;
  for t := 2 to k-1
    /* for table_1 */                    Add_Table(p, t, t1, s, count,
    { s := peer of 'p' in dim 't';                          tableno) {
    for i := t+1 to k-1                   for i := t1-n downto 1
    { s1 := peer of node 's'             { x := peer of node 's'
           in dimension 'i';                    in dimension 'i';
      table1(p)(count).node := s1;        if(tableno = 1){
      table1(p)(count).linkno := t;       table1(p)(count).node := x;
      count := Add_Table(p,t,t,s1,        table1(p)(count).linkno:= t;
               count+1,1);                 }
    }                                     else
  }                                       table2(p)(count) := x;
  table1(p)(count).node := -1;            count := count + 1;
  /* table_2 */                           count := Add_Table(p,t,t1-1,
  s := peer of node 'p'                            x,count,tableno);
         in dimension 0;                  }
  count:=0;                              return(count);
  for t := 2 to k                       }
  { s1 := peer of node 's'
         in dimension 't';
    table2(p)(count):=s1;
    count := count + 1;
    count := Add_Table(p,t,t,
             s1,count,2);
  }
}
}}
```

Figure 6. Algorithm for Determining Routing Table Entries

4 Broadcasting in an Mcube

This section presents a broadcasting algorithm for a k–Mcube $M = \{A :: B\}$ where A and B are (k–1)–Mcubes. Assume, without loss of generality, that p is the source node of the broadcast where $p \in A_{01}$ and $A_{00} c\sim B_{00}, A_{10} c\sim B_{10}, A_{01} c\sim B_{11}$ and $A_{11} c\sim B_{01}$. Let $r = c\sim(p,B_{00})$ and $s = c\sim(p,A_{01})$ (See Figure 7).
If $k \leq 0$ then use conventional hypercube broadcasting.
If $k > 0$, the broadcast can be handled by sending the message as follows:
(i) to p_1 over LCL, where $p_1 = c\sim(p,A_{00})$.
    Then p_1 relays the broadcast to nodes in the (k–2)–Mcube $\{A_{00} :: B_{00}\}$.
(ii) to p_3 over PCL, where $p_3 = c\sim(p,B_{11})$.
    Then p_3 has the responsibility of covering the two, intersecting (k–2)–Mcubes $B_{P1} = \{B_{01} :: B_{11}\}$ and $B_{L1} = \{B_{11} :: B_{01}\}$ avoiding multiple relays to common points.

(iii)   to p_2, where $p_2 = c\sim(p, A_{11})$, over link#x where x = link#(PCL)–1. The node p_2 then has the responsibility of covering the (k–2)–Mcube A_{P1}.

The source node p itself assumes the responsibility of covering A_{01}.

The partitioning of the Mcube into smaller Mcubes here is very similar to that done by Mroute. The algorithm targets four sub–Mcubes of dimension k–2 of the k–Mcube M , viz. A_{P1}, B_{P1}, $\{A_{00} :: B_{00}\}$ and B_{L1}, and one sub–Mcube of dimension k–3, viz. A_{01}. Since the largest sub–Mcube to which the algorithm is now recursively applied is a (k–2)–Mcube it is easy to see that the number of communication steps required for the algorithm to complete a broadcast in a k–Mcube is $\lceil (k+1)/2 \rceil$. When node p_2 receives the broadcast with a header indicating that it has to relay the broadcast in a sub–Mcube of dimension k–2 whose LCL's are #0 links then it is easy for p_2 to identify the required sub–Mcube as A_{P1} and to implement the broadcast in it. p_3 can do the same for B_{P1}. The structure of $\{A_{00} :: B_{00}\}$, when we view A_{00} and B_{00} as its laterals, is the same as that of $\{A_{00} :: A_{01}\}$ i.e. A_{P0}. The only difference is that the LCL's of A_{P0} are the #0 links in M whereas the LCL's in $\{A_{00} :: B_{00}\}$ are the links that 1–1 connect A_{00} to B_{00}, i.e. links numbered k–1 in M. All the other links of $\{A_{00} :: B_{00}\}$ including its PCL's have the same numbering as in A_{P0}. Hence p_1 can recursively implement the broadcast in $\{A_{00} :: B_{00}\}$ by using the link numbered k–1 as the LCL. The case with B_{L1} is similar. In the case of (k–3)–Mcube A_{01} which has links numbered 1 to k–3, the LCL's are the links numbered k–3. Hence, in general the broadcast can be recursively executed within any sub–Mcube if the relaying node knows the dimension of the sub–Mcube and the link number of the LCL link. The link number of the PCL's is always identified as r–1 for a sub–Mcube of dimension r. Note that p_3 must cover two intersecting (r–2)–Mcubes B_{P1} and B_{L0}. However the intersecting portion, B_{01}, is a lateral of each of these Mcubes. Hence it is not too complex a task to avoid sending duplicate messages in these two intersecting broadcasts. The broadcasting algorithm is similar, in the case of p being in any of the other corners of A or B. A broadcast can easily be implemented in a subnetwork by the use of proper parameters in the algorithm. Note that a conventional hypercube broadcasting algorithm can also be used but would require k steps to complete.

The following algorithm is first invoked by the broadcast source with my_dim = k, my_LCL = 0:

Procedure Broadcast(message, my_dim, my_LCL)

if my_dim $\leq$ n **then** use standard broadcast method for a (my_dim)–dimensional hypercube;

else begin

   if my_LCL = 0 **then** Lateral_recipient_LCL = my_dim – 1;

   else Lateral_recipient_LCL = MY_LCL – 2;

   (i) Send(message, my_LCL, my_dim – 2, Lateral_recipient_LCL);

   (ii) Send(message, link#(my_dim – 1), my_dim – 2, my_LCL);

   (iii)DSend(message, link#(my_dim – 1), my_dim – 2, my_LCL

      Lateral_recipient_LCL);(recipient corresponds to c~(p, B_{11}) for source p in A_{01});

   (iv)Broadcast(message, my_dim – 3, Lateral_recipient_LCL – 2);

end;

The call *Send(message, outlink, dim, LCL)* inside the *Broadcast* procedure by source and intermediate sending nodes results in the broadcast message along with the values of the two parameters *dim* and *LCL* on the specified output link, *outlink*. The recipient node of *Send* message invokes the procedure Broadcast(message, my_dim, my_LCL) with *my_dim = dim* and *my_LCL = LCL*. Procedure *DSend(message, outlink, dim1, LCL1, LCL2)* is a modified version of *Send*. *Dsend* requires the recipient node to be responsible for relaying the broadcast within two intersecting sub–Mcubes SM1 and SM2, that it is part of. Both SM1 and SM2 are of dimension d and has links numbered LCL1 and LCL2, respectively, as their LCLs. The intersecting portion of SM1 and SM2 is a lateral of each. Procedure *Broadcast* can be implemented to avoid duplicate messages in the intersecting broadcasts. A broadcast can easily be implemented in a subnetwork by the use of proper parameters in the broadcast procedure by the source. The broadcast takes $\lceil (k+1)/2 \rceil$ steps.

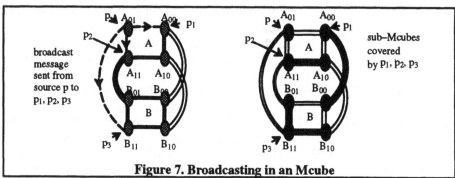

Figure 7. Broadcasting in an Mcube

5 Distance Distribution

We now show that an Mcube has a uniform distance distribution, i.e. the distance distribution function is the same for every node in an Mcube, under Mroute.

5.1 Uniform Distance Distribution

Theorem1: $\exists$ a function $F_k: Z \rightarrow Z \ni$ for any node p in any k–Mcube M, $D_p(i,M) = F_k(i)$ under Mroute(k) (identical distance distribution function for any node in any k–Mcube under Mroute(k)).

Proof: We prove the theorem using induction on k.

Basis: $k \leq 2$. Trivially true since the distance distribution is uniform in a hypercube under the e–cube routing used by Mroute. In this case $F_k(i) = {}^kC_i$.

Induction Step: Let the claim be true for all k–Mcubes for $k < t$.

Consider a t–Mcube $M = \{A :: B\}$, constructed from (t–1)–Mcubes A, B.

Consider any node $p \in M$. Assume, without loss of generality, that $p \in A_{00}$ and $A_{00}\ c\sim B_{00}$, $A_{10}\ c\sim B_{10}$, $A_{01}\ c\sim B_{11}$ and $A_{11}\ c\sim B_{01}$.

Case(i) Distance from p to nodes in A:

By the induction hypothesis $D_p(i,A) = F_{t-1}(i)$ under Mroute(t–1) on A.

Case(ii) Distance from p to nodes in B_{L0}:

$D_p(i,B_{L0}) = D_p(i,M_{L0}) - D_p(i,A_{L0})\ \therefore\ D_p(i,B_{L0}) = F_{t-1}(i) - F_{t-2}(i)$

by the induction hypothesis, using Mroute(t–1) on M_{L0} and Mroute(t–2) on A_{L0}.

Case(iii)(a) Distance from p to nodes in B_{01}:

Let $r = c\sim(p,B_{00})$. Then $D_p(i,B_{01}) = D_r(i-1,B_{01})$ for $i>1$ and $D_p(1,B_{01}) = 0$.

$D_r(i-1,B_{01}) = D_r(i-1,B_{P0}) - D_r(i-1,B_{00})$ (Recall $B_{P0} = \{B_{00} :: B_{01}\}$.)

$\therefore\ \mathbf{D_p(1,B_{01}) = 0}$ and $\mathbf{D_p(i,B_{01}) = F_{t-2}(i-1) - F_{t-3}(i-1)}$ for $i > 1$.

Case(iii)(b) Distance from p to nodes in B_{11}:

Assuming $s = c\sim(p,A_{01})$, using similar reasoning as in Case(iii)(a) we have

$D_s(i-1,A_{01}) = D_s(i-1,\{A_{01} :: B_{11}\}) - D_s(i-1,A_{01})$.

∴ $D_p(1,B_{11}) = 0$ and $D_p(i,B_{11}) = F_{t-2}(i-1) - F_{t-3}(i-1)$ for $i > 1$.

The same reasoning (Cases (i), (ii) and (iii)) applies for p being in any part of M.

∴ $D_p(i,M) = F_t(i)$ for any node p in any Mcube M where

$F_t(1) = F_{t-1}(1) + 1$, $F_t(i) = 2F_{t-1}(i) + 2F_{t-2}(i-1) - F_{t-2}(i) - 2F_{t-3}(i-1)$ for $i > 1$ and $F_s = sC_i$
for $s < 3$.

5.2 Average Internode Distance

Since an Mcube has a uniform distance distribution under Mroute, the average internode distance is the same as the average distance distribution for any node in the network. We can, therefore, calculate the average internode distance in a k–Mcube M = $\{A :: B\}$ as follows: Consider any node $p \in M$. Assume, without loss of generality, that $p \in A_{00}$ and A_{00} c~ B_{00}, A_{10} c~ B_{10}, A_{01} c~ B_{11} and A_{11} c~ B_{01}. Let $r = c\sim(p,B_{00})$ and $s = c\sim(p,A_{01})$. Let us denote the average distance distribution from p to nodes in a sub–Mcube G of M, under Mroute, as $AD_p(G)$. Let N be the number of nodes in M. If M is a hypercube $AD_p(M) = N/2$. Otherwise

$AD_p(B_{L0}) = 2(AD_p(\{A_{L0} :: B_{L0}\})) - AD_p(A_{L0})$.

$AD_p(B_{01}) = 1 + 2(AD_r(B_{P0})) - AD_r(B_{01})$ and $AD_p(B_{11}) = 1 + 2(AD_s(\{A_{01} :: B_{11}\})) - AD_s(B_{11})$.

Then $AD_p(M) = 1/N(\; N/2(AD_p(A)) + N/4(AD_p(B_{L0})) + N/8(AD_p(B_{01})) + N/8(AD_p(B_{11}))$

$= 1/2(AD_p(A)) + 1/4(2AD_p(A_{L0} :: B_{L0})) - AD_p(A_{L0}))$

$\qquad\qquad + 1/8(1 + 2AD_r(B_{P0}) - AD_r(B_{01})) + 1/8(1 + 2AD_s(\{A_{01} :: B_{11}\}) - AD_s(B_{11}))$

Uniform distance distribution ⇒ $AD_x(W) = AD(k)$ for any k–Mcube W and any node x in W.

∴ $AD(k) = 1/2AD(k-1) + 1/4(2AD(k-1) - AD(k-2)) + 1/8(1 + 2AD(k-2) - AD(k-3))$
$\qquad\qquad\qquad\qquad\qquad\qquad\qquad + 1/8(1 + 2AD(k-2) - AD(k-3))$

∴ $AD(k) = AD(k-1) + 1/4(AD(k-2) - AD(k-3) + 1)$

This reduces to $AD(k) = k/3 + 4/9 + (1/18)(-1/2)^k - (1/2)^{k+1} \approx k/3 + 1/2$.

Figure 8 presents a graph comparing average internode distances of Mcubes, Twisted Cubes [6], Crossed Cubes [4] and hypercubes. (Mobius Cubes are excluded from this comparison because their average distances are difficult to calculate exactly [3].)

6 Hypercube Emulation

A special class of Mcubes called Hypercube Emulator Mcubes (or HEM's) can be used to emulate hypercubes of the same size. In an HEM only one extra routing step is required for emulating a hypercube connection over any dimension. HEM's are constructed as follows:

i) A k–HEM is a k–Mcube for $k \leq 2$.

ii) A k–HEM ($k > 2$), is constructed from two identical (k–1)–HEM's as follows:
Let A be an (k–1)–HEM. Let B be identical to A.

(a) Interchange B_{L0} and B_{L1} in B, by complementing the 0th bit in the address of each node in B.

(b) For every node $p_1 \in A_{L0}$, add a link (p_1,p_2) where $p_2 \in B_{L0}$ and $\omega(p_1,A) = \omega(p_2,B)$. (hypercube connection.). This gives A_{00} c~ B_{00} and A_{10} c~ B_{10}.

(c) Add a single link (q_1, q_2) where $q_1 \in A_{01}$ and $q_2 \in B_{11}$. Make a dual connection between A_{L1} and B_{L1}, with reference to (q_1,q_2). (as explained in Section 2.2).

Figure 9 shows an HEM. Note that after interchanging B_{L0} and B_{L1}, B_{L0} is identical to A_{L1}. Therefore $\{A_{L0} :: B_{L0}\}$ is identical to $\{A_{L0} :: A_{L1}\}$. That an HEM conforms to Mcube construction requirements, follows from this and the fact that $\{A_{L1} :: B_{L1}\}$ is formed using the algorithmic construction method. At each step of the construction of an HEM one of the two laterals connects pairs of nodes from the 2 principals, that have the same address within the principals. Therefore the HEM construction ensures that each node has access to a hypercube connection for all levels, either directly, or by using the link#0 as an extra step, i.e, for any pair of nodes p and q in a k–Mcube M such that $|\omega(p,M) \oplus \omega(q,M)| = 1$, the following is true: either (p,q) is a link in M or (p_1,q_1) is a link in M where (p,p_1) and (q,q_1) are LCL's in M. This allows for hypercube emulation in constant time.

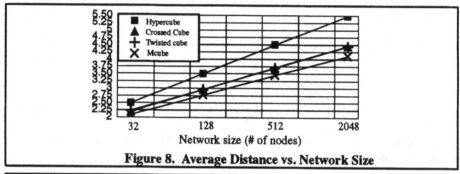

Figure 8. Average Distance vs. Network Size

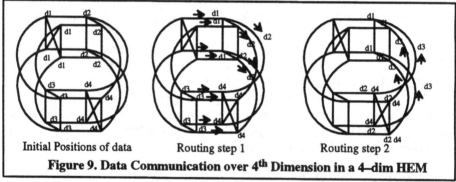

| Initial Positions of data | Routing step 1 | Routing step 2 |

Figure 9. Data Communication over 4th Dimension in a 4–dim HEM

7 Reconfiguration as a Hypercube

Since an Mcube can be viewed as a hypercube with some crossed links we can introduce simple 2x2 switches between those links to statically reconfigure a k–Mcube into a k–dimensional hypercube and vice versa. In this section we calculate the number of such switches required.

Theorem 2: The number of 2x2 switches required to allow the reconfiguration of a k–Mcube (HEM) into a k–dimensional hypercube and vice versa, is at most $(k-2).2^{k-2}$.

Proof: (Induction on k.) Let $M = \{A :: B\}$ be a k–Mcube. Assume A_{00} c~ B_{00}, A_{10} c~ B_{10}, A_{01} c~ B_{11} and A_{11} c~ B_{01}.

Basis: k = 3. In this case we require 1 switch and $1 < (3-2)2^{3-2}$.

Induction Step: k > 3. Let A and B be (k–1)–Mcubes. Assume A and B require at most $(k-3)2^{k-3}$ 2x2 switches each, to switch back and forth between (k–1)–Mcubes and (k–1)–dimensional hypercubes. The connection A_{L1} c~ B_{L1} is a permutation of 2^{k-2} points. Since a permutation on 'n' numbers can be obtained by at most (n–1) exchanges, we need at most $2^{k-2}-1$ switches to reconfigure $M_{L1} = \{A_{L1} :: B_{L1}\}$. Since M is an HEM, "$A_{L0}$ c~ B_{L0}" satisfies hypercube requirements, requiring no additional switches for M_{L0}. The number of switches required is thus at most $2(k-3)2^{k-3} + 2^{k-2} - 1 < (k-2)2^{k-2}$.

8 Algorithm Mapping

In [11] is was shown how the recursive doubling class of parallel algorithms can be implemented to execute faster on an Mcube than on a hypercube. In this section we demonstrate the efficient mapping of some other types of algorithms on Mcubes.

8.1 Algorithms Using Broadcasts

One of the virtues of the Mcube interconnection is its ability to implement broadcasts in about half the steps required by a comparable hypercube. Many broadcast intensive algorithms can potentially benefit from this feature. The execution of the rank sorting algorithm on a Crossed Cube is given as an example in [4]. We show here, its efficient execution on an Mcube.

Rank Sort: In this algorithm n elements are sorted using n^2 processors. The algorithm works by placing the n elements along a row and copying the row n times creating an n x n matrix of elements a_{ij} where $a_{rj} = a_{sj}$ for any r and s. The value of a_{ii} is compared to all elements in row i. A value of '1' is produced in row i column j if $a_{ii} > a_{ij}$ and a '0' is produced if $a_{ii} < a_{ij}$. If $a_{ii} = a_{ij}$ then i < j gives a '0' and i > j gives a '1'. The total number of 1's produced in column j is the rank of a_j, denoting the number of elements larger than a_j. This algorithm can be implemented in a hypercube of dimension 2m to sort 2^m elements. m communication steps are required to make 2^m copies of the row. The broadcasting of a_i in row i takes m communication steps. Lastly the totalling of the 1's in column j takes m communication steps and m addition steps. This gives a total execution time of $3mT_{Comm} + mT_{Add}$. In a 2m–Mcube the same algorithm can be implemented starting with the 2^m elements in any sub–Mcube which is an m–Mcube. It takes m steps to make m copies of the sub–Mcube, in Stage 1 of the algorithm, just as it does in a hypercube. For example we can start with the elements in nodes numbered 0 to 2^m-1. Each node then sends its value along all links numbered higher than m–1 and each node that receives a value along a link with number r sends that value along all links with number x such that m–1 < x < r. In Stage 2, a_{ii} is broadcasted in each m–dimensional sub–Mcube containing the 2^m elements and a 0 or 1 is computed at each node. Finally, the ranks are calculated by each node returning its calculated value along the link from which it received a value in Stage 1. A value is returned along a link numbered m–1+i only in the ith addition step. Stage 2 takes (m+1)/2 communication steps. The other steps have the same complexity as in the hypercube. The total execution time on the Mcube is therefore $^{5m}/_2(T_{Comm}) + mT_{Add}$.

8.2 Hypercube–Based Algorithms and Irregular Algorithms

As shown in Section 7 it is possible to use switches to reconfigure a k–Mcube into a k–dimensional hypercube. The hypercube configuration can be used to execute the large variety of algorithms that map well onto a hypercube. In the alternative HEM's can be used to execute such algorithm with the use of at most one extra routing step per dimension with no change in the complexity of the algorithm – at most the routing steps are doubled.

In general the lower average internode distance, low diameter and low communication delay in Mcubes can benefit applications where the communication pattern is either unpredictable and/or lacks regularity. Many AI applications based on the connectionist model fall into this category as do general classes of branch and bound algorithms. Branch and bound algorithms can usefully take advantage of the lower broadcasting delay for quick broadcasts of current bounds.

9 Conclusions

We presented the k–Mcube, a static interconnection network that connects 2^k nodes for any given $k \geq 0$, with the use of $k2^{k-1}$ links. Any set of 2^k nodes, $k > 2$, can be connected to form a k–Mcube which has a diameter of $\lceil (k+1)/2 \rceil$. This is about half the diameter of a hypercube. In this paper we have formally validated some of the results and techniques presented in [11]. We have also described techniques for fast broadcasting, hypercube emulation, algorithm implementation and reconfiguration between Mcubes and hypercubes. Advantages of Mcubes, as shown in this paper and [11], include a low network diameter, low internode distance, uniform distance distribution, partitionability, low communication delay and efficient execution of parallel algorithms.

References

[1] S. Abraham and K. Padmanabhan, "An Analysis of the twisted Cube Topology," *Proc. 1989 International Conference on Parallel Processing*, Vol. 1, pp.116–120.

[2] N. Bhuyan and D. P. Agrawal, "Generalized Hypercube and Hyperbus structures for a Computer Network," *IEEE Trans. on computers*, vol. C–33, No. 1, April 1984, pp. 323–333.

[3] P. Cull and S. Larson, "The Mobius Cubes," *Proc. 6th Distributed Memory Computing Conference*, April 1991, pp.699–702.

[4] K. Efe, "The Crossed Cube," *IEEE Trans. on parallel and distributed systems*, Vol. 3. No. 5, September 1992, pp. 513–524.

[5] K. Ghose and K. R. Desai, "The Design and Evaluation of the Hierarchical Cubic Network," *Proc. 1990 International Conference on Parallel Processing*, Vol. 1, pp. 355–362.

[6] P. A. J. Hilbers, M. R. J. Koopman and J. L. A. van de Snepscheut. "The Twisted Cube," *Parallel Architectures and Languages Europe*, June 1987, pp. 152–159.

[7] K. Hwang and J. Ghosh, "Hypernet: A Communication Efficient Architecture for Constructing Massively Parallel Computers," *IEEE Trans. on Computers*, Vol. C–36, No. 12, Dec 1987, pp. 1450–1466.

[8] S. Lakshmivarahan and S. K. Dhall, "A New Hierarchy of Hypercube Interconnection Schemes for Parallel Computers," Journal of Supercomputing, Vol. 2, 1988, pp. 81–108.

[9] F. P. Preparata and J. Vuillemin, "The Cube–Connected Cycles: A Versatile Network for Parallel Computation," Comm. ACM, Vol. 24, No. 5, May 1981, pp. 300–309.

[10] N. K. Singhvi and K. Ghose, "A Detailed Study of the Mcube Interconnection Topology," Technical Report No. CS–TR–93–14, Dept. of Computer Science, SUNY Binghamton, 1993.

[11] N. K. Singhvi and K. Ghose, "The Mcube: A Symmetrical Cube Based Network with Twisted Links," Proc. 9th International Parallel Processing Symposium, 1995, pp. 11–16.

[12] N. K. Singhvi, "The Connection Cubes: Symmetric, Low Diameter Networks with Low Node Degree," *Proc. 1993 International Parallel Processing Symposium*, pp. 260–267.

[13] L. D. Wittie, "Communication Structures for Large Networks of Microcomputers," *IEEE Trans on Computers*, Vol. C–30, No. 4, April 81, pp. 264–273.

[14] H. Sullivan and T. R. Bashkow, "A Large Scale, Homogeneous, Fully Distributed, Parallel Machine I," *Proc. Fourth International Symposium on Computer Architecture*, March 1977, pp. 26–38.

Multiwave Interconnection Networks for MCM-based Parallel Processing

Shinichi Shionoya, Takafumi Aoki and Tatsuo Higuchi

Graduate School of Information Sciences, Tohoku University
Aoba-ku, Sendai 980-77, Japan

Abstract. This paper presents *multiwave interconnections* – optical interconnections that employ wavelength components as multiplexable information carriers – for next-generation multiprocessor systems using MCM technology. A hypercube-based multiprocessor network called the *multiwave hypercube* (MWHC) is introduced, where multiwave interconnections provide highly-flexible dynamic communication channels. A performance analysis shows that the use of integrated multiwave optics enables the reduction of network complexity on a MCM substrate, while supporting low-latency message routing.

In this paper, we also present the experimental fabrication of wavelength detectors for the proposed system, and discuss the physical limit on the number of wavelength components at the present state of technology.

Keywords: Multichip module (MCM), optical interconnections, wavelength division multiplexing (WDM), interconnection networks, parallel processing, message-passing multiprocessors.

1 Introduction

Multichip module (MCM) technology is a high-density packaging technology in which unpackaged chips are mounted directly onto a substrate incorporating the interchip interconnection network. It has recently caught the attention of research community as a promising technology for developing cost-effective parallel computers for on-line signal and data processing applications [1],[2]. In reaching for performance with MCM, however, one finds that the current technologies have the definite performance limitation: the high cost of communication in area, power and delay. More profoundly, interchip interconnections restrict the entire architecture of an MCM-based parallel processing system within narrow limits of local communication and minimized input/output.

Motivated by these limitations, this paper is to explore a new interconnection technology for MCM, called *multiwave interconnections*, which employ optical wavelength components as multiplexable information carriers. The wavelength division multiplexing (WDM) technique has already been used with success in telecommunications due to the potential to support extremely higher bandwidth. Recent breakthroughs in new materials and technology offer a possibility of integrating multiwavelength optical systems as well. In this paper, we also present a hypercube-based multiprocessor network called the *multiwave hypercube* (MWHC), and analyze the impact of wavelength multiplexing on various network parameters (concerning performance and complexity).

Recently, several researchers have proposed the use of WDM optical fiber channels for high-performance parallel computers [3]–[5]. However, most of the reported designs are based on assemblies of sophisticated discrete optical components such as star couplers and WDM demultiplexers, that are not suitable for high-density integration on a MCM substrate. In this paper, we assume only three kinds of key components: waveguides, laser diodes with different wavelengths and wavelength-selective photodetectors. As for waveguides, we assume only simple point-to-point optical waveguides having 90°-corner-bend structures. Recent advancement in polyimide waveguide technology makes it possible to fabricate this type of waveguides in micrometer dimensions and to integrate them on a single silicon substrate [6]. We also assume multiwavelength surface emitting lasers [7] as currently available light emitters. As for wavelength-selective photodetectors, on the other hand, most of the reported devices are designed for telecommunications, and hence are not suited for integration. Thus, this paper also presents an experimental fabrication of simple wavelength detecting devices using dielectric multilayer thin-film (DMF) filters [8]. On the basis of the experimental results, we discuss the physical limit on the number of wavelength components available at the present state of technology, and analyze their impact on the proposed network architecture. Our initial results seem to indicate that the use of integrated multiwave optics makes possible both the reduction of network complexity and the reduction of average message distance of the network.

This paper is organized as follows. Section 2 provides functional models of multiwave interconnections,which are classified into two types: static and dynamic. Section 3 describes the structure of the multiwave hypercube (MWHC). Section 4 provides the comparison of topological characteristics (such as the number of links, diameter, average message distance, traffic density and network complexity) of the MWHC and binary hypercube. In Section 5, we discuss implementation issues.

2 Multiwave Interconnections

A conventional MCM has multilayer, thin-film polymer interconnect structure (typically copper/ polyimide) built on a ceramic or silicon substrate. Bare (unpackaged) chips are mounted and electrically connected to the interconnection substrate by wire bonds, tape-automated bonds (TABs), or solder bumps [9]. Eliminating separate chip packages can achieve a 5-to-1 to 10-to-1 reduction in substrate area. However, current MCMs use about $20\mu m$-wide interconnections and there is one-order-of-magnitude gap between VLSI line width and MCM line width. Also, current MCMs have average and maximum chip-to-chip signal path length of about 3 and 9 inches, respectively [2]. These thin and long chip-to-chip interconnections run into severe limitations in high-speed parallel processing applications.

One concern is the increase of interconnection complexity. For the real-time applications in the next generation, parallel processing architectures with very low latency will become essential. One of the central issues in their design relates to the realization of densely connected global interconnections over which many processing modules communicate. Clearly, as the number of modules increases, the characteristics of the global interconnections become critical to overall system performance and cost.

The other concern is the timing error caused by a contribution of signal-propagation delays and circuit rise-time delays. The problem of timing errors has been aggravated by the gap between VLSI and MCM geometries. One way to control timing errors is to keep the distance between chips short, which minimizes propagation delay as well as the resistance and capacitance that contribute to rise-time delay. However, this severely restricts the entire architecture of a multiprocessor system within narrow limits of local communication and minimized input/output, resulting the increase of network latency at the system level.

Consequently, low-latency parallel processing architectures in the next decade require breakthroughs in interconnection technology. The most important technological challenges might concern (i) the reduction of interconnection network complexity while maintaining a specific performance level, and (ii) the reduction of signal propagation delay on global interconnections. Multiwave optical interconnections proposed in this paper present an interesting solution to this problem. They are already used with success in telecommunications known as WDM transmission technology. This paper is the first attempt to explore the potential of integrated multiwave optics for realizing MCM-based multiprocessor systems.

It has long been recognized that integrated optical interconnections promise several advantages over their electrical counterparts such as large bandwidth ($\sim 10^9$ Hz), reduced propagation delay and reduced power (for long interconnections) [10]. In addition to these features, the use of multiple discrete wavelengths offers a means for reducing the complexity of a multiprocessor network without loss of its processing concurrency, and reducing its message delay by wavelength switching.

Fig. 1 depicts the proposed structure of multiwave interconnections for MCMs, which employs two separate substrates: an optical substrate for integrating waveguides, and an electronic substrate for integrating processing elements with light emitters and detectors. In this structure, micron-size optoelectronic devices are key components. Fig. 2 summarizes three critical technologies: integrated waveguides, laser diodes which will emit multiple wavelengths, and wavelength-selective photodetectors which can discriminate multiplexed wavelengths. Here, waveguides are assumed to have simple point-to-point connection structures including only 90° corner bends. This type of waveguides can be fabricated with polyimide in micrometer dimensions [6]: their width is on the same order as the wire width of current MCMs. We also assume multiwavelength surface emitting lasers [7] as currently available technology. As for wavelength-selective photode-

Top
Cross Section
Laser Diode
Core
Clad
Optical Substrate
Si
MCM Substrate
CMOS Circuit
Wavelength
Detector

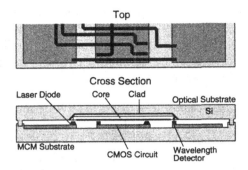

Fig. 1. Multiwave interconnections for MCM technology.

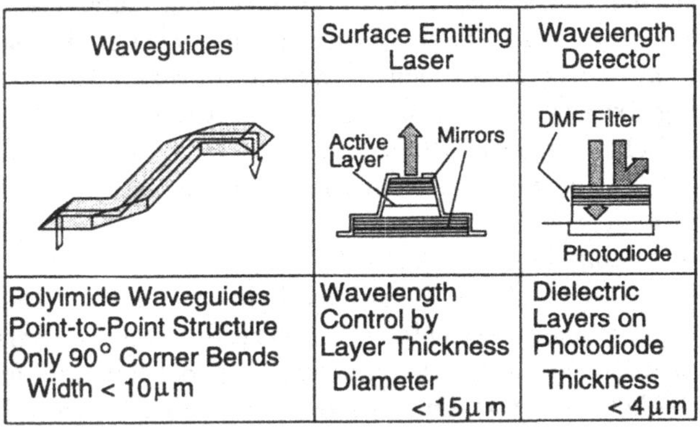

Waveguides
Surface Emitting Laser
Wavelength Detector
Active Layer
Mirrors
DMF Filter
Photodiode
Polyimide Waveguides
Point-to-Point Structure
Only 90° Corner Bends
Width < 10μm
Wavelength
Control by
Layer Thickness
Diameter
< 15μm
Dielectric
Layers on
Photodiode
Thickness
< 4μm

Fig. 2. Opto-electronic devices for multiwave interconnections.

tectors, we assume simple compact devices using dielectric multilayer thin-film (DMF) filters which will be described in detail in Section 5.

On the basis of the above assumptions, we shall develop a functional model of multiwave interconnections. We first classify the multiwave interconnections into two types: static and dynamic, according to rearrangeability of wavelength channels.

Static Multiwave Interconnections Fig. 3(a) and (b) schematically illustrate the physical link and the embedded logical links (wavelength channels) of a static four-wave interconnection. There are two groups of processing nodes: the source nodes $PN_0^S, \cdots, PN_3^S$ which transmit messages, and the destination nodes $PN_0^D, \cdots, PN_3^D$ which receive the massages. We expect that each group will be implemented with a single VLSI chip or with a group of chips. Every processing node has its own light emitter (or detector) whose lasing (or detecting) wavelength is specified in advance. The source nodes $PN_0^S, \cdots, PN_3^S$ transmit messages with wavelengths $\lambda_0, \lambda_1, \lambda_2, \lambda_3$, respectively, which are multiplexed on a waveguide. Then, each destination node, say PN_2^D, receives the specified wavelength λ_1 to establish the logical subchannels shown in Fig. 3(b). In general, when the degree of multiplexing (the number of processing nodes per group) is w, we call it the static w-wave interconnection.

Dynamic Multiwave Interconnections Static multiwave interconnections can support only fixed wavelength channels. Dynamic multiwave interconnections, on the other hand, can support the "wavelength switching" function which dynamically switches a processing node from one channel to another by tuning wavelengths. The methods to realize the wavelength switching function are classified into two types.

1. Source-tuning method (Fig. 3(c));
   The destination nodes $PN_0^D, \cdots, PN_3^D$ have photodetectors of fixed wavelengths $\lambda_0, \cdots, \lambda_3$, respectively. Switching of wavelength channels is performed at the source nodes using wavelength-tunable lasers or more practically using fixed-wavelength lasers with electronic switching circuitry. By tuning the light emitter of the source node PN_j^S to a specific wavelength λ_i ($0 \leq i \leq 3$), the message from the node can be routed to any specific destination node PN_i^D.

2. Destination-tuning method (Fig. 3(d));
   The source nodes $PN_0^S, \cdots, PN_3^S$ have light emitters of fixed wavelengths $\lambda_0, \cdots, \lambda_3$, respectively. Switching of wavelength channels is performed at the destination nodes using wavelength-tunable photodetectors or using fixed-wavelength photodetectors with electronic switching circuitry. By tuning the photodetector of the destination node PN_j^D to a specific wavelength λ_i ($0 \leq i \leq 3$), the destination node can receive the message from any specific source node PN_i^S.

Thus, the dynamic multiwave interconnection realizes dynamically rearrangeable logical links on a single waveguide.

The optical link efficiency might be further increased by introducing time division multiplexing technique that employs extremely large bandwidth of optical signals. However, design decision will depend significantly on practical system specifications. We shall omit such discussions to simplify our model.

3 Multiwave Hypercubes

The main feature in our system is to use two-level hierarchy in its architecture to fully utilize both the high bandwidth of multiwave optics and the high functional density of electronics. Our approach is to group the total N processing nodes in the system into several *processing groups*, each consisting of w nodes, where w is called the *degree of multiplexing*. Thus, assuming $N = w \times 2^s$, there are total 2^s processing groups. We assume the w processing nodes in a group are implemented with a single VLSI chip or with a group of VLSI chips. Multiwave

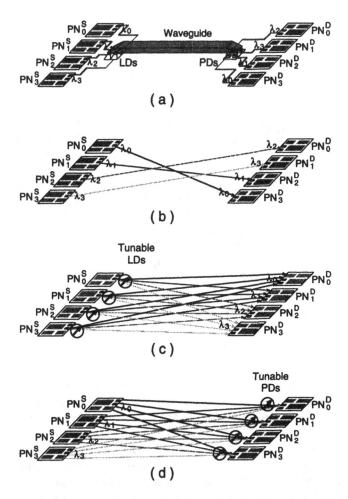

Fig. 3. Model of multiwave interconnections; (a)physical configuration, (b)logical structure of a static multiwave interconnection, (c)logical structure of a dynamic multiwave interconnection with source tuning, (d)logical structure of a dynamic multiwave interconnection with destination tuning.

optical interconnections using w wavelengths provide group-to-group global communication channels in a specific topology. In this section, we formally define the structure of a hypercube-based multiprocessor network, called the *multiwave hypercube* (MWHC), for the inter-group communication. We also evaluate the impact of wavelength multiplexing on various network parameters concerning its complexity and performance.

A (w, s)-MWHC network consists of $w \times 2^s (= N)$ nodes. A *node address* is represented by a pair of an s-bit binary representation $(g_s \cdots g_1)$ and an integer v $(0 \leq v \leq w - 1)$ as $(g_s \cdots g_1)[v]$. The binary representation $(g_s \cdots g_1)$ is called

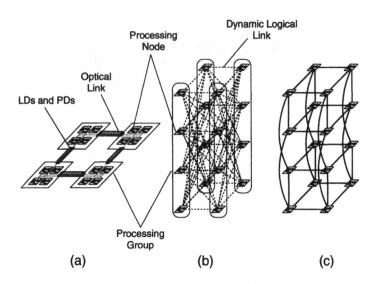

Fig. 4. A (4,2)-MWHC network:(a) physical structure, (b)logical structure. A binary 4-cube network of the same number of nodes is illustrated in (c) for comparison purpose.

the *group address*. A node $(g_s \cdots g_1)[v]$ means the v-th processing node in the group $(g_s \cdots g_1)$. In a (w, s)-MWHC, each processing group $(g_s \cdots g_1)$ will be connected to groups $(g_s \cdots \overline{g_l} \cdots g_1)$ for all $1 \leq l \leq s$, where $\overline{g_l}$ is the complement of g_l. Thus, 2^s groups are connected in the binary s-cube structure with optical links.

The remaining problem is to determine the logical network topology realized with wavelength channels. Given a specific physical network, say binary s-cube, one can embed various distinct logical structures into it. Such logical network can be determined either *statically* or *dynamically*. In the following discussion, we focus on the use of dynamic w-wave interconnections for the above mentioned inter-group network. In this case, a node $(g_s \cdots g_1)[v]$ can be connected to nodes $(g_s \cdots \overline{g_l} \cdots g_1)[u]$ for all $1 \leq l \leq s$ and $0 \leq u \leq w - 1$ with dynamic logical links.

Fig. 4(a) illustrates schematically the physical structure of the (4,2)-MWHC, which is equivalent to the binary 2-cube topology. The network consists of four processing groups; each contains four processing nodes. The four groups are connected by dynamic 4-wave optical interconnections in the form of binary 2-cube structure. (Each optical link is assumed to be bidirectional hereafter.) Fig. 4(b) shows the logical structure of the (4,2)-MWHC. The total number of nodes is 16 which is the same number as that in the binary 4-cube network shown in Fig. 4(c). It is interesting to note that the (4,2)-MWHC does not support direct connections within a common processing group, but supports highly-flexible dynamic logical links between adjacent groups.

As an example of higher-dimensional networks, Fig. 5 shows a binary 6-cube network and a (4,4)-MWHC network embedded in a plane.

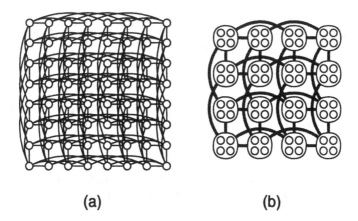

Fig. 5. Comparison of physical structures: (a)binary 6-cube, (b)(4, 4)-MWHC.

In the (w, s)-MWHC network, the number of routing steps required for the communication between two nodes in two distinct groups is equal to the Hamming distance between their group addresses. As for broadcasting in the (w, s)-MWHC, any processing node can send a message to all other processing nodes in just s steps.

4 Analysis of MWHC structures

In this section, the performance of MWHC structures will be compared to that of other structures under the assumptions of constant channel bandwidth and the same number of processing nodes: $N = 2^n$. Here, we shall compare a $(w, n-\lg w)$-MWHC network [1], a binary n-cube network and a fully connected network of N nodes, where the degree of multiplexing w is assumed be a power of two. The links are assume to be bidirectional in the following discussion.

A. Number of Links The total number of *physical links* in the $(w, n - \lg w)$-MWHC is given by

$$L_m = \frac{2^{n-1} \cdot (n - \lg w)}{w}.$$

In these physical links, wL_m *logical links* will be established at a particular time instant. These logical links can be dynamically rearranged through wavelength switching; there exist total $w^2 L_m$ available logical links. As the degree of multiplexing w increases, the number of available logical links $w^2 L_m$ increases, while the number of physical links L_m decreases.

---

[1] Knuth's notation for the base-two logarithm $\lg \triangleq \log_2$ is used throughout this paper.

On the other hand, the total number of links in the binary n-cube network and that of the fully connected network are: $L_b = 2^{n-1}n$ and $L_f = 2^{n-1}(2^n - 1)$, respectively.

B. Diameter The diameter of $(w, n - \lg w)$-MWHC is equal to the diameter of its physical structure: the binary $(n - \lg w)$-cube structure, and thus is given by

$$r_m = n - \lg w.$$

The diameter of the binary n-cube network and that of the fully connected network are given by $r_b = n$ and $r_f = 1$, respectively.

C. Average Message Distance and Traffic Density The average message distance provides a measure of the expected packet delay.

The average message distance of the fully connected network $\overline{d_f}$ is clearly given by $\overline{d_f} = 1$. For the binary n-cube, its average message distance $\overline{d_b}$ is given by

$$\overline{d_b} = \frac{n}{2} \cdot \frac{N}{N-1} \simeq \frac{n}{2} \quad (N \gg 1).$$

For the (w, s)-MWHC, the average message distance $\overline{d_m}$ is given by

$$\overline{d_m} = \frac{\Sigma_1 + \Sigma_2}{N - 1},$$

where Σ_1 is the sum of distances measured from a specific node in a specific group to all the nodes in other groups, and Σ_2 is the sum of distances within the same group. The Σ_1 and Σ_2 are given by

$$\Sigma_1 = w \cdot \sum_{d=1}^{n-\lg w} \binom{n - \lg w}{d} d,$$

$$\Sigma_2 = 2 \cdot (w - 1).$$

Therefore, we have

$$\overline{d_m} = \frac{1}{N-1} \left(\frac{n - \lg w}{2} \cdot N + 2(w - 1) \right) \simeq \frac{n - \lg w}{2} \quad (N \gg 1).$$

Fig. 6 plots the average message distance of the binary n-cube, $(4, n-2)$-MWHC, $(16, n-4)$-MWHC, $(64, n-6)$-MWHC and fully connected network. For large N, as the degree of multiplexing w increases to $4, 16$ and 64, the average message distance of the MWHC is reduced by $1, 2$ and 3, respectively, compared with that of the binary n-cube.

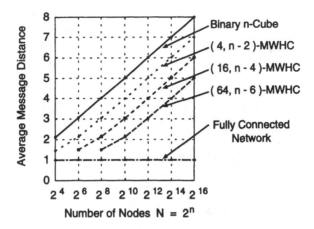

Fig. 6. Average message distance for $N = 2^n$.

Thus, MWHC structures can support small message delay through dynamic wavelength switching. However, the number of logical links established at a particular time instant is much smaller than that of the corresponding binary hypercube structure (see item **A** in this section). This brings up the question: How much message traffic must be supported in each link? The *average traffic density* provides a measure of the potential packet delay by illustrating how much of the total packet traffic each link must support. The average traffic density is defined as the product of the average message distance and the total number of nodes, divided by the total number of communication links. The average traffic density of the $(w, n - \lg w)$-MWHC and that of the binary n-cube are given by

$$\rho_m = \frac{1}{N-1}\left(N + \frac{4(w-1)}{n - \lg w}\right)$$

and

$$\rho_b = \frac{N}{N-1},$$

respectively. Thus, the traffic density in the MWHC and that in the binary hypercube are insensitive to variations in network size, and approach a common value 1 for large networks. From this analysis it is expected that the MWHC network achieves smaller packet delay in comparison with the corresponding binary hypercube under the condition of constant traffic density.

D. Network Complexity MCM systems are wire-limited. The cost of these systems are predominantly that of connecting devices. Thus, to achieve higher performance, the network must make efficient use of the available area. The network must be mapped into a two-dimensional substrate so that it exhibits

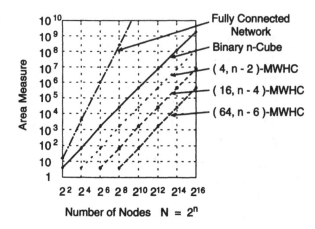

Fig. 7. Area measure for $N = 2^n$.

lower topological complexity and occupies a smaller area. Here, we compare the complexity of networks in terms of *wire density*, the number of wires crossing a cut that divides the network into two pieces.

In general, for a binary n-cube embedded in a plane by a simple mapping rule [12], the maximum wire density occurs at the cut which runs near the center of the network. This maximum wire density is about 2^{n-1} since there are one-to-one connections between two groups of 2^{n-1} nodes at the center cut. To evaluate the area occupied by a network, we introduce an *area measure*, which is defined as the square of the maximum wire density of that network. For a binary n-cube network, the area measure A_b is given by $A_b \simeq 2^{2(n-1)}$.

The physical structure of the $(w, n - \lg w)$-MWHC network is equivalent to the binary $(n - \lg w)$-cube network, and thus its area measure A_m is approximately $2^{2(n-\lg w-1)}$. This gives the area reduction ratio $A_m/A_b \simeq 1/w^2$. Fig. 7 plots the area measure for the binary n-cube, $(4, n - 2)$-MWHC, $(16, n - 4)$-MWHC, $(64, n - 6)$-MWHC and fully connected network. As the degree of multiplexing increases to 4, 16 and 64, the area measure of the MWHC decreases by the factors of 1/16, 1/256 and 1/4096, respectively, compared to that of the binary n-cube. This demonstrates the potential of multiwave interconnections for reducing network complexity, while maintaining low latency in message routing.

5 Implementation Issues

5.1 Optoelectronic Devices for Multiwave Interconnections

The key issue for implementing multiwave interconnection networks is how to realize the functions of guiding, emitting and detecting plural wavelengths. In particular, these functions must be implemented with micron-size compact devices. As for integrated waveguides and light emitters, several devices that are

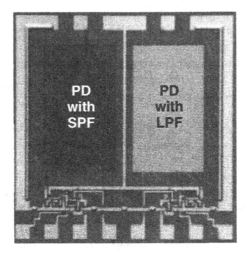

Fig. 8. Experimental chip that integrates photodiodes (PDs) with short-pass (SPF) and long-pass filters (LPF).

suitable for multiwave interconnections have already been reported[6], [7]. These waveguides and lasers can be directly applied to multiwave interconnection systems.

As for wavelength detectors, however, most of conventional devices were designed for fiber communications, and are not compact enough to be used in MCM interconnections. Addressing this problem, we have fabricated a new wavelength detector by combining a dielectric multilayer thin-film (DMF) filter [13] and a photodiode in a single device [8]. The DMF filter is composed of alternate layers of high- and low-index materials, and its spectral characteristics can be controlled by changing the number and thickness of layers. In our experimental fabrication, short-pass and long-pass filters made of SiO_2 and TiO_2 are deposited on pn photodiodes to discriminate red and infrared optical signals. Fig. 8 shows the experimental chip.

5.2 Physical Limit on the Number of Wavelengths

In Section 4, we have observed that the number of wavelengths w directly affects the complexity and the performance of the MWHC network. This gives rise to the question: How many wavelength components are available at the present state of technology? We take up this question in this section, and discuss its physical limitation on the basis of experimental studies of the key components: waveguides, laser diodes and wavelength detectors. It is useful at the outset to list the limiting factors for the three kinds components here:

– Waveguides;
   In the case of a micron-size waveguide, optical diffraction occurs at its edge

and this makes the output light have an angular distribution. The degree of diffraction effect depends on the width of the waveguide Δ and the optical wavelength λ. When a wavelength detector receives the output light, its angular distribution causes the equivalent changes in spectral characteristics of the DMF filter. When the optical wavelength $\lambda = 0.7\mu\text{m}$ and $\Delta \geq 2\mu\text{m}$, however, the diffraction effect is negligible small.

– Laser diodes;

Emitting wavelength of a vertical-cavity laser can be controlled by changing the thickness of layers. However, the total gain bandwidth (the range of lasing wavelength) of laser diodes is limited to a certain width W_{LD}.

– Wavelength detectors;

Selectivity and bandwidth of a DMF filter is limited by its structure. In general, a wavelength detector employs a band-pass filter whose structure is represented as

$$(AL)^p A,$$

where A is the stack of $(HL)^q(2H)(LH)^q$, and L and H are SiO_2 and TiO_2 layers with a quarterwave optical thickness. Larger p and larger q imply sharper cutoff and narrower passband width, respectively. The values for p and q that we can choose are limited by a certain thickness T of the DMF filter.

Also, we must take account of the deviations of spectral characteristics of laser diodes and DMF filters due to the limited controllabilities in fabrication process. We assume the total effect of these deviations corresponds to $\pm\delta$ in wavelength domain.

Taking these factors into consideration, we shall evaluate the number of wavelength components. We assume each DMF bandpass filter is designed to pass more than 50% of the energy of the wavelength to be detected, and to pass less than 10% of the energy of the adjacent wavelengths. In this case, the number of available wavelengths w is estimated as

$$w = \left\lceil \frac{W_{LD}}{W_{10\%}} \right\rceil$$

under the design constraint:

$$W_{50\%} \geq 4\delta,$$

where $W_{10\%}$ and $W_{50\%}$ denote the 10% and 50% passband widths of DMF filters. Fig. 9 plots the number of wavelengths as a function of δ under the conditions: $\Delta \geq 2\mu\text{m}$, $\lambda = 0.7\mu\text{m}$, $W_{LD} = 100\text{nm}$ and $T = 10\mu\text{m}$. When $\delta = 1\text{nm}$, which seems to be realizable in the near term, we can use at least 16 wavelength components. This number offers a potential of reducing the complexity of hypercube-based interconnection networks by the factor of 1/256 in terms of area measure, and reducing the average message distance by 2.

Another important technological challenges in fabrication is how to install opto-electronic devices into MCMs. Future opto-electronic devices are likely to be made of III-V semiconductors, and thus new techniques for hetero epitaxy

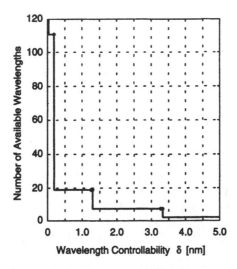

Fig. 9. The number of wavelengths as a function of δ.

of highly mismatched materials, GaAs on Si, will be required. More details concerning fabrication studies have been reported in [10], [14]. At an early stage, however, flip-chip bonding technique seems to provide an economical way of installing relatively small number of opto-electronic devices into an MCM substrate.

6 Conclusions

MCM technology offers a promising way for developing cost-effective multiprocessor systems for on-line signal and data processing applications in the next decade. But, it also raises serious interconnection problems that are inherent in increased network complexity using conventional techniques. We have presented in this paper multiwave interconnection scheme for MCM-based parallel processing and analyze its impact on a new hypercube-based interconnection network, called the multiwave hypercube (MWHC).

An important feature in our system is the two-level hierarchy in its architecture; high-density electronics for localized processing modules and high-bandwidth multiwave optics for global inter-chip interconnections. Our initial results indicate that the use of multiwave optics enables the reduction of network complexity, while maintaining lower latency in message routing. Also, relaxing the interconnect physical distance requirements at a particular data-rate might have significant system cost implications.

The key to success with the proposed approach lies in developing compact multiwave opto-electronic devices suited for integration. Practical implementations require cooperative study in many fields.

Acknowledgments

The authors wish to thank Dr. Shoji Kawahito (Toyohashi University of Technology) and Mr. Yukio Watanabe (Tohoku University) for their aid in experimental study of wavelength detectors.

References

1. P. R. Mukund and J. F. McDonald, "MCM: The high-performance electronic packaging technology," *IEEE Computer*, Vol. 26, No. 4, pp. 10–12, April 1993.
2. R. K. Scannell and J. K. Hagge, "Development of a multichip module DSP," *IEEE Computer*, Vol. 26, No. 4, pp. 13–21, April 1993.
3. P. W. Dowd, "Wavelength division multiple access channel hypercube processor interconnection," *IEEE Trans. Computers*, Vol. 41, No. 10, pp. 1223–1241, October 1992.
4. K. Ghose, R. K. Horsell, and Singhvi N. K., "Hybrid multiprocessing using WDM optical fiber interconnections," *Proc. 1st Int'l Workshop on Massively Parallel Processing using Optical Interconnections*, pp. 182–196, April 1994.
5. T. Takimoto, T. Aoki, and T. Higuchi, "Design of multiplex interconnection networks for massively parallel computing systems," *Proc. 24th IEEE Int'l Symp. Multiple-Valued Logic*, pp. 231–238, May 1994.
6. R. Selvaraj, H. T. Lin, and J. F. McDonald, "Integrated optical waveguides in polyimide for wafer scale integration," *IEEE J. Lightwave Technol.*, Vol. 6, No. 6, pp. 1034–1044, June 1988.
7. C. J. Chang-Hasnain, J. P. Harbison, C. Zah, M. W. Maeda, L. T. Florez, N. G. Stoffel, and T. Lee, "Multiple wavelength tunable surface-emitting laser arrays," *IEEE J. Quantum Electron.*, Vol. 27, No. 6, pp. 1368–1376, June 1991.
8. T. Aoki, Y. Watanabe, T. Higuchi, S. Kawahito, and Y. Tadokoro, "Multiwave computing circuits using integrated opto-electronic devices," *ISSCC Digest of Technical Papers*, pp. 134–135, February 1994.
9. W. Daum, W. E. Burdick Jr, and R. A. Fillion, "Overlay high-density interconnect: A chips-first multichip module technology," *IEEE Computer*, Vol. 26, No. 4, pp. 23–29, April 1993.
10. A. Iwata and I. Hayashi, "Optical interconnections as a new LSI technology," *IEICE Trans. Electron.*, Vol. E76-C, No. 1, pp. 90–99, January 1993.
11. L. N. Bhuyan and D. P. Agrawal, "Generalized hypercube and hyperbus structures for a computer network," *IEEE Trans. Computers*, Vol. 33, No. 4, pp. 323–333, April 1984.
12. W. J. Dally, "Performance analysis of k-ary n-cube interconnection networks," *IEEE Trans.Computers*, Vol. 39, No. 6, pp. 775–785, June 1990.
13. J. Minowa and Y. Fujii, "Dielectric multilayer thin-film filter for WDM transmission systems," *IEEE J. Lightwave Technol.*, Vol. 1, No. 1, pp. 116–121, March 1983.
14. I. Hayashi, "Optoelectronic devices and material technologies for photo-electronic integrated systems," *Jpn. J. Appl. Phys.*, Vol. 32, No. 1B, pp. 266–271, January 1993.

Scheduling

Scheduling Master-Slave Multiprocessor Systems *

Sartaj Sahni

Computer & Information Sciences Department
University of Florida
Gainesville, FL 32611, USA

Abstract. We define the master-slave multiprocessor scheduling model and provide several applications for the model. $O(n \log n)$ algorithms are developed for some of the problems formulated and some others are shown to be NP-hard.

1 Introduction

The problem of scheduling a multiprocessor computer system has received considerable attention [1, 2, 3, 4, 5, 6, 7, 8]. In this paper, we develop a model to schedule a parallel computer system in which the parallel computer operates under control of a host processor. The host processor is referred to as the *master* processor and the processors in the parallel computer are referred to as the *slave* processors. The nCube hypercube is an example of such a parallel computer system. When programming such a system, one typically writes a program that runs on the master computer. This is a sequential program that spawns parallel tasks to be run on the slave processors. When these tasks complete, the sequential thread on the master continues and possibly (later) spawns a new set of parallel tasks on the slaves, and so on. The number of parallel tasks spawned is always less than or equal to the number of slave processors.

If we examine the execution profile of such a computer system, we see that, in general, there are time intervals in which only the master is active, only the slaves are active, both the master and the slaves are active. With each task to be run on a slave processor, we may associate three activities:

1. *Preprocessing.* This is the work the master has to do to collect the data needed by the slave and includes the overhead involved in initiating the transfer of this data as well as the code to be run by the slave.
2. *Slave work.* This includes the work the slave must do to complete the assigned computation task, receive the data and code from the master, and transfer the results back to the master. Into this work, we also include the transmission dalays experienced in receiving the data and code from the time the master initiates transmission to the time the slave receives as well from

---

* This work was supported in part by the National Science Foundation under grant MIP-9103379

the time the slave initiates transmission of the results to the time the master receives the results.

3. *Postprocessing.* This is the work the master must do to receive the results and store them in the desired format. It also includes any checking or data combining work the master may do on the results.

In addition to applications to parallel computer scheduling, the master-slave model can be used to model scheduling problems that arise in industrial settings. The master-slave scheduling model has the following attributes:

1. there is a single master processor
2. thre are as many slave processors as parallel jobs
3. associated with each job, there are three tasks: pre-processing (performed by the master), slave work (performed by the slaves), and post-processing (performed by the master).
4. for each job, the tasks are to be performed in the order: pre-processing, slave work, post-processing.

Let $a_i > 0$, $b_i > 0$, and $c_i > 0$, respectively, denote the time needed to perform the three tasks associated with job i and let n be the number of jobs as well as the number of slaves. In this paper, we shall use the notations a_i, b_i, c_i to represent both the tasks of job i as well as the time needed to complete these tasks.

When we are scheduling a parallel computer system using the above model, we are interested in schedules that minimize the finish time. However, when scheduling industrial systems using the above model we may be interested in minimizing either the schedule finish time or the mean finish time of the jobs.

In this paper, we do the following.

1. In Section 2, we show that obtaining minimium finish time no-wait-in-process (MFTNW) schedules (i.e., schedules in which once the processing of a job begins, it continues without interruption to completion) is NP-hard for each of the following scheduling disciplines:
   (a) Each job's pre-processing must be done before its post-processing. No other constraint is put on the master.
   (b) The pre-processing and post-processing orders are the same.
   In this section, we also develop an $O(n \log n)$ algorithm to obtain MFTNW schedules when the pre-processing order is required to be the reverse of the post-processing order.
2. In Section 3, we develop $O(n \log n)$ algorithms to minimize finish time for each the following scheduling constraints:
   (a) The pre-processing and post-processing orders are the same.
   (b) The pre-processing order is the reverse of the post-processing order.

2 No Wait in Process

Our NP-hard proofs use the subset sum problem which is known to be NP-hard [GARE79]. This problem is defined below:

Input A collection of positive integers x_i, $1 \le i \le n$ and a positive integer M.
Output "Yes" iff there is a subset with sum exactly equal to M.

From any instance of the subset sum problem, we may construct an equivalent instance of MFTNW as below:

$a_i = c_i = x_i/2$, $b_i = \epsilon$, $1 \le i \le n$
$a_{n+1} = c_{n+1} = S - M + 1$, $b_{n+1} = M + n\epsilon$
$a_{n+2} = c_{n+2} = M + 1$, $b_{n+2} = S - M + n\epsilon$

where S is the sum of the x_i's and $0 < \epsilon < 1/n$.

In the no wait case, the master processor cannot preempt any job as such a preemption would violate the no wait constraint. In the preceding section, we remarked that there is no advantage to preemptions on slave processors. So, we may assume non-preemptive schedules. Since $a_{n+1} = c_{n+1} > b_{n+2}$, the pre-processing and/or post-processing tasks of job $n+1$ cannot be done while a slave is working on job $n+2$. Similarly the pre-processing and/or post-processing tasks of job $n + 2$ cannot be overlapped with the slave task of job $n + 1$. Hence, every no wait schedule has a finish time f that is at least the sum of the task times of these two jobs. That is,

$$f \ge a_{n+1} + b_{n+1} + c_{n+1} + a_{n+2} + b_{n+2} + c_{n+2} = 3S + 4 + 2n\epsilon$$

There are exactly two templates for schedules with this length. One has job $n + 1$ processed before job $n + 2$ and the other has $n + 2$ preceding $n + 1$ (see Figure 1).

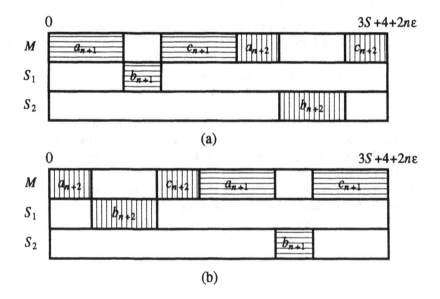

Fig. 1. Templates for NP-hard proof

To complete the schedule using either of the templates and not exceed the finish time of $3S + 4 + 2n\epsilon$, some of the remaining jobs must fully overlap with b_{n+1} and the remainder with b_{n+2}. For this, the sum of the first groups task times cannot exceed $b_{n+1} = M + n\epsilon$ and the sum of second groups task times cannot exceed $b_{n+2} = S - M + n\epsilon$. Since the sum of the task times for the remaining jobs is $S + n\epsilon$ and $\epsilon < 1/n$, the only way to accomplish this is when there is a subset of the x_i's that sums to M. Hence, MFTNW is NP-hard.

We can modify the above proof to show that order preserving MFTNW (OP-MFTNW) is also NP-hard. The task times for the $n + 2$ jobs are:
$$a_i = c_i = x_i, \; b_i = S - x_i + 1, \; 1 \le i \le n$$
$$a_{n+1} = c_{n+1} = S - M + 1, \; b_{n+1} = M$$
$$a_{n+2} = c_{n+2} = M + 1, \; b_{n+2} = S - M$$
The finish time is at least the sum of the master processor task times. So,

$$f \ge \sum a_i + \sum c_i = 4S + 4$$

It is easy to see that there is an order preserving no wait schedule with length $4S+4$ whenever there is a subset of the s_i's that sums to M. We shall show that whenever there is a schedule with this length, there is a subset that sums to M.

As in the previous proof, the tasks of jobs $n+1$ and $n+2$ cannot overlap. So, jobs $n+1$ and $n+2$ are done in sequence. Suppose that job $n+1$ is done before $n+2$ (the case $n+2$ before $n+1$ is similar). Since the sum of the task times for these two jobs is $3S + 4$, the only way to finish processing by time $4S + 4$ is for the master processor to be busy throughout the time the slaves are working on tasks b_{n+1} and b_{n+2} and for task a_{n+1} to begin by time S. The first requirement means that there are only S other time units when the master can work on the remaining S units of pre- and post- processing needed by jobs $1, \cdots, n$. There are three cases to consider:

Case 1: *There is at least one job whose pre-processing is done before a_{n+1} and whose post-processing is done after a_{n+1}.* Let u, $1 \le u \le n$, be the first such job. The post-processing of this job must be done while a slave is working on b_{n+1} as $a_{n+1} + b_{n+1} = S + 1 > b_u = S - x_u + 1$. Hence, we have the situation shown in Figure 2 (a).

The tasks (if any) scheduled between a_{n+1} and c_u, must be pre-processing tasks. To see this, note that to schedule a post-processing task here, the corresponding pre-processing task must have been scheduled either before a_u (in which case u is not the first job with pre-processing before a_{n+1} and post-processing after a_{n+1}), or in between a_u and a_{n+1} (in which case the order requirement is violated as the post-processing of this job precedes that of u), or between a_{n+1} and c_u (which is not possible as the sum of task lengths for each of jobs $1 \cdots n$ exceeds $S + 1$ which in turn is larger than b_{n+1}.

The tasks scheduled between a_u and a_{n+1} are either post-processing tasks of jobs started before a_u or pre-processing tasks of jobs that will finish after c_u (because of the order requirement). Hence, the tasks beginning with a_u and ending just before c_u that are processed by the master correspond to different jobs. The total amount of time from the beginning of a_u to the start of c_u is

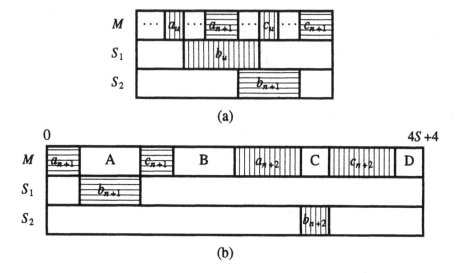

Fig. 2. Templates for order preserving NP-hard proof

$a_u + b_u = S + 1$. Subtracting a_{n+1} from this leaves us with M units of time, all of which must be utilized by the master in order for the schedule to complete by $4S + 4$. This can happen iff there is a subset of the x_i's that sums to M.

Case 2: *There is at least one job whose pre- and post- processing are done before a_{n+1}.* Let u be one such job. Since the sum of the task lengths of u is $S + x_u + 1$, task a_{n+1} cannot begin until $S + x_u + 1$ and so the schedule cannot complete by $4S + 4$. Therefore, this case is not possible.

Case 3: *Task a_{n+1} is the first task scheduled.* Figure 2 (b) shows the scheduling template for this case. For the schedule length to be $4S + 4$, the total time represented by the regions A, B, C, and D must be $2S$. The master processor cannot be idle in any of these regions as the amount of pre- and post- processing not scheduled in Figure 2 (b) is exactly $2S$. Because of the order constraint, in region A, we can schedule only the pre-processing of some subset of the jobs $1, \cdots, n$. Hence, there needs to be a subset of the x_i's that sums to $b_{n+1} = M$.

Hence, OP-MFTNW is NP-hard.

The MFTNW problem is quite easy to solve when the post-processing is to be done in the reverse order of the pre-processing. In this case, there is at most one feasible solution. Hence, if such a solution exists, it has minimum finish time and also minimum mean finish time. Note that when there is no ordering constraint between pre- and post- processing and also when these two orders are required to be the same, there is always at least one feasible solution (i.e., process the jobs in sequence using any permutation). When the post-processing order is required to be the reverse of the pre-processing order and no wait is permitted in process, then the processing of the jobs must be fully nested. That is, the processing of the j'th scheduled job must begin and end while a slave is working on the $j - 1$'th job. As a result, if jobs are pre-processed in the order 1, 2, $\cdots$, n, then the following must be true:

$$b_i \geq a_{i+1} + b_{i+1} + c_{i+1}, \quad 1 \leq i < n \tag{1}$$

Since the a_j's and c_j's are positive, it follows that:

$$b_1 > b_2 > \cdots > b_n \tag{2}$$

The preceding inequality implies a unique ordering of the jobs. The algorithm to determine feasibilty, as well as a feasible schedule that minimizes both the finish and mean finish times is:

1. **(Verify Equation 2)** Sort the jobs into decreasing order of b_j's. If such an ordering does not exist, there is no feasible schedule. In this case, terminate.
2. **(Verify Equation 1)** For $i = 1, \cdots, n-1$, verfify that $b_i \geq a_{i+1} + b_{i+1} + c_{i+1}$. If there is an i for which this is not true, then there is no feasible schedule. In this case, terminate.
3. The minimum finish time and mean finish time schedule is obtained by pre-processing the jobs in the order determined in step 1.

The complexity of the above algorithm is readily seen to be $O(n \log n)$.

3 Same Pre- and Post- Processing Orders

In this section, we develop an $O(n \log n)$ algorithm to construct an order preserving minimum finish time (OPMFT) schedule. Without loss of generality, we place the following restrictions on schedules we consider in this section:

R1: The schedules are non-premptive.

R2: Slave tasks begin as soon as their corresponding pre-processing tasks are complete.

R3: Each post-processing task begins as soon after the completion of its slave task as is consistent with the order preserving constraint.

First, we establish some properties of order preserving schedules that satisfy these assumptions.

Definition 1. A *canonical* order preserving schedule (COPS) is an order preserving schedule in which (a) the master processor completes the pre-processing tasks of all jobs before beginning any of the post-processing tasks, and (b) the pre-processing tasks begin at time zero and complete at time $\sum_{i=1}^{n} a_i$.

Because of restrictions R1 – R3, every COPS is uniquely described by providing the order in which the pre-processing is done.

Lemma 2. *There is a canonical OPMFT schedule.*

Proof: Consider any non-canonical OPMFT schedule. Let c_j be the first post-processing task that the master works on. Since the schedule is non-canonical, there is a pre-processing task that is executed at a later time. Let a_i be the first of these. Slide a_i to the left so that it begins just after the pre-processing task (if any) that immediately precedes c_j (if there is no such task preceding c_j, then slide a_i left so as to start at time 0). Slide the post-processing tasks beginning with c_j and ending at the post-processing task that immediately preceded a_i (before it was moved) rightwards by a_i units. Slide the slave and post-processing tasks left so as to satisfy restrictions R2 and R3. The result is another OPMFT schedule that is closer to canonical form. By repeating this transormation at most $n - 1$ times we can obtain a canonical OPMFT schedule. $\square$

Lemma 3. *If $a_i = c_i$, $1 \leq i \leq n$, then every COPS is an OPMFT schedule.*

Proof: Because of the preceding lemma, it is sufficient to show that all COPS have the same length. Each COPS is uniquely identified by the order in which the pre-processing tasks are executed. We shall show that exchanging two adjacent jobs in this ordering does not increase the schedule length. Since we can go from one permutation to any other via a finite sequence of adjacent exchanges, it follows that no matter what the pre-processing order, canonical schedules have the same finish time when jobs have equal pre- and post- processing times. Hence, all COPS are OMFT schedules.

Consider two jobs j and $j + 1$ that are adjacent in the pre-processing order (Figure 3). Let t_j and t_{j+1}, respectively, be the times at which the master begins tasks c_j and c_{j+1}. Slide job $j + 1$ left by a_j so that all its tasks begin a_j units earlier than before, slide tasks a_j and b_j right by a_{j+1} units so that they begin a_{j+1} units later than before, and move task c_j so that it begins just after c_{j+1} finishes. As a result, task c_{j+1} now begins at $t_{j+1} - a_j = t_{j+1} - c_j \geq t_j$. Hence, the rescheduling of job $j + 1$ does not result in the master working on two or more jobs simultaneously. In addition, the post-processing of job $j + 1$ does not begin until after its slave task is complete. The post-processing of task c_j now begins at $t_{j+1} - a_j + c_{j+1} = t_{j+1} - c_j + a_{j+1} \geq t_j + a_{j+1}$ which is greater than or equal to the time at which the slave finishes b_j. Task c_j finishes at $t_{j+1} + a_{j+1}$. Hence, the schedule for the remaining jobs is unchanged. $\square$

Lemma 4. *Consider the COPS defined by some permutation σ. Assume that job j is pre-processed immediately before job $j + 1$ (i.e., j immediately precedes $j + 1$ in σ). If $c_j \leq a_j$ and $c_{j+1} \geq a_{j+1}$, then the schedule length (i.e., its finish time) is no less than that of the COPS obtained by interchanging j and $j + 1$ in σ.*

Proof: A diagram of the schedule with job j immediately preceding job $j + 1$ is shown in Figure 4 (a). In this figure, t is the time at which the pre-processing of job j starts, A is the elapsed time between the completion of task a_{j+1} and the start of the post-processing of job j (note that $A \geq \sum_{k \text{ follows } j+1} a_k + \sum_{k \text{ precedes } j} c_k$), $\Delta > 0$ is the time between the start of c_j and c_{j+1}, and τ is the time at which c_{j+1} completes.

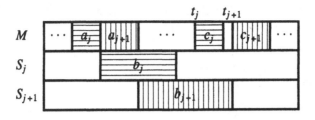

Fig. 3. Figure for Lemma 3

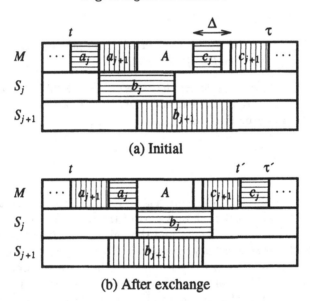

Fig. 4. Figure for Lemma 4

Let σ' be the permutation obtained by interchanging jobs j and $j+1$ in σ. The schedule corresponding to σ' is shown in Figure 4 (b). Let t' and τ', respectively, be the times at which c_{j+1} and c_j finish in this schedule. If $\Delta \geq a_j$, then $t' \leq \tau - a_j$. Also, from Figure 4 (a), we observe that $b_j \leq a_{j+1} + A \leq c_{j+1} + A$. So, b_j finishes by t' in Figure 4 (b). Hence, $\tau' = t' + c_j \leq \tau - a_j + c_j \leq \tau$. As a result, the post-processing tasks of the remaining jobs can be done so as to complete at or before their completion times in σ and the interchanging of j and $j+1$ does not increase the schedule length.

If $\Delta < a_j$, then c_{j+1} starts at time $t + a_{j+1} + a_j + A$ in σ'. So, $t' = t + a_{j+1} + a_j + A + c_{j+1}$. The time at which b_j finishes in σ' is $t + a_{j+1} + a_j + b_j \leq t + 2a_{j+1} + a_j + A \leq t + a_{j+1} + a_j + A + c_{j+1} = t'$. So, c_j finishes at $t' + c_j = t + a_{j+1} + a_j + A + c_{j+1} + c_j \leq \tau$. Consequently, the OPS defined by σ' has a finish time that is $\leq$ that of the OPS defined by σ. $\square$

Theorem 5. *There is an OPMFT schedule which is a COPS in which the pre-processing order satisfies the following:*

1. *jobs with $c_j > a_j$ come first*
2. *those with $c_j = a_j$ come next*
3. *those with $c_j < a_j$ come last*

Proof: Immediate consequence of Lemma 4. □

Lemma 6. *Let σ define an OPMFT COPS that satisfies Theorem 5. Its length is unaffected by the relative order of jobs with $a_j = c_j$.*

Proof: Follows from Lemma 4. □

Lemma 7. *There is an OPMFT COPS in which all jobs with $c_j > a_j$ are at the left end in non-decreasing order of $a_j + b_j$.*

Proof: From Theorem 5, we know that there is an OPMFT COPS in which all jobs with $c_j > a_j$ are at the left end. Let $\sigma = (1, 2, \cdots, n)$ define such an OPMFT COPS. Let j be the least integer such that:

1. $a_j + b_j > a_{j+1} + b_{j+1}$
2. $c_j > a_j$
3. $c_{j+1} > a_{j+1}$

If there is no such j, then the lemma is established. So, assume that such a j exists. Figure 4 (a) shows the relevant part of the schedule. A denotes the time span between the finish of task a_{j+1} and the finish of the task that immediately precedes c_j (in the figure, this happens to coincide with the start of c_j). Figure 4 (b) shows the relevant part of the schedule, σ', that results from interchanging the jobs j and $j + 1$. We shall show that $\tau' \leq \tau$. As a result, the finish time of σ' is no more than that of σ. So, σ' is also an OPMFT schedule. By repeated application of this exchange process, σ is transformed into an OPMFT that satisfies the lemma.

case(a) $b_j \leq a_{j+1} + A$ and $b_{j+1} \leq A + a_j$
Now, $b_j < c_{j+1} + A$ and $b_{j+1} < A + c_j$. So, $\tau = t + a_j + a_{j+1} + A + c_j + c_{j+1} = \tau'$.

case(b) $b_j \leq a_{j+1} + A$ and $b_{j+1} > A + a_j$
The conditions for this case imply that $A + a_j + b_j < A + a_{j+1} + b_{j+1}$ or $a_j + b_j < a_{j+1} + b_{j+1}$ which contradicts the assumption on j. Hence, this case cannot arise.

case(c) $b_j > a_{j+1} + A$ and $b_{j+1} \leq A + a_j$
Since, $c_j > a_j$, $b_{j+1} < A + c_j$, $\tau = t + a_j + b_j + c_j + c_{j+1}$, and $\tau' = t + a_{j+1} + a_j + \max\{A + c_{j+1}, b_j\} + c_j$. For τ' to be $\leq \tau$, we need:

$$b_j + c_{j+1} \geq a_{j+1} + \max\{A + c_{j+1}, b_j\}$$

So, if $b_j \geq A + c_{j+1}$, we need $b_j + c_{j+1} \geq a_{j+1} + b_j$ or $c_{j+1} \geq a_{j+1}$. This is true by choice of j. If $b_j < A + c_{j+1}$, we need $b_j + c_{j+1} \geq a_{j+1} + A + c_{j+1}$ or $b_j \geq a_{j+1} + A$. This is part of the assumption for this case.

case(d) $b_j > a_{j+1} + A$ and $b_{j+1} > A + a_j$

This time, $\tau = t + a_j + \max\{b_j + c_j, a_{j+1} + b_{j+1}\} + c_{j+1} = t + \max\{a_j + b_j + c_j + c_{j+1}, a_j + a_{j+1} + b_{j+1} + c_{j+1}\}$, and $\tau' = t + a_{j+1} + \max\{b_{j+1} + c_{j+1}, a_j + b_j\} + c_j = t + \max\{a_{j+1} + b_{j+1} + c_{j+1} + c_j, a_j + b_j + c_j + a_{j+1}\}$. Since, $a_j + b_j > a_{j+1} + b_{j+1}$, $a_j + b_j + c_j + c_{j+1} > a_{j+1} + b_{j+1} + c_{j+1} + c_j$. Also, since $c_{j+1} > a_{j+1}$, $a_j + b_j + c_j + c_{j+1} > a_j + b_j + c_j + a_{j+1}$. Hence, $\tau > \tau'$. □

Lemma 8. *There is an OPMFT COPS in which all jobs with $c_j < a_j$ are at the right end in non-increasing order of $b_j + c_j$.*

Proof: Similar to that of Lemma 7. □

Theorem 9. *There is an OPMFT COPS in which the pre-processing order satisfies the following:*

1. *jobs with $c_j > a_j$ come first and in non-decreasing order of $a_j + b_j$*
2. *those with $c_j = a_j$ come next in any order*
3. *those with $c_j < a_j$ come last and in non-increasing order of $b_j + c_j$*

Proof: This follows from Theorem 5 and the fact that the proofs of Lemmas 6, 7, 8 are local to the portion of the schedule they are applied to. □

Theorem 9 results in the simple $O(n \log n)$ algorithm given below to find a pre-processing order that defines a COPS which is an OPMFT schedule.

Step 1: Partition the jobs into three sets L, M, and R such that $L = \{j | c_j > a_j\}$, $M = \{j | c_j = a_j\}$, and $R = \{c_j < a_j\}$.
Step 2: Sort the jobs in L such that $a_j + b_j \leq a_{j+1} + b_{j+1}$. Let $\bar{L}$ be the resulting ordered sequence.
Step 3: Sort the jobs in R such that $b_j + c_j \geq b_{j+1} + c_{j+1}$. Let $\bar{R}$ be the resulting ordered sequence.
Step 4: The pre-processing order for the COPS is: $\bar{L}$ followed by the jobs in M in any order followed by $\bar{R}$.

4 Reverse Order Post-processing

While there are no-wait-in-process master-slave instances that are infeasible when the post-processing order is required to be the reverse of the pre-processing order, this is not the case when the no-wait constraint is removed. For any given pre-processing permutation, σ, we can construct a reverse-order schedule as below:

1. the master pre-processes the n jobs in the order σ
2. slave i begins the slave processing of job i as soon as the master completes its pre-processing
3. the master begins the post-processing of the last job (say k) in σ as soon as its slave task is complete

4. the master begins the post-processing of job $j \neq k$ at the later of the two times (a) when it has finished the post-processing of the succesor of j in σ, and (b) when slave j has finished b_j

Schedules constructed in the above manner will be referred to as *canonical reverse order schedules (CROS)*. Given a pre-processing permutation σ, the corresponding CROS is unique. It is easy to establish that every minimum finish-time reverse order (ROMFT) schedule is a CROS. So, we can limit ourselves to finding a minimum finish-time CROS.

Lemma 10. *Let $\sigma = (1, 2, \cdots, n)$ be a pre-processing permutation. Let $j < n$ be such that $b_j < b_{j+1}$. Let σ' be obtained from σ by interchanging jobs j and $j + 1$. Let τ and τ', respectively, be the finish times of the CROSs S and S' corresponding to σ and σ'. $\tau' \leq \tau$.*

Proof: If $j > 1$, then let t be the time at which job $j - 1$ finishes in S and S'. If $j = 1$, let $t = 0$. Let s_j (s_j') be the time at which task b_j finishes in S (S'). s_{j+1} and s_{j+1}' are similarly defined. From the definition of a CROS, we get:

$$s_j = \sum_1^j a_k + b_j \qquad s_{j+1} = \sum_1^{j+1} a_k + b_{j+1} \tag{3}$$

$$s_j' = \sum_1^{j+1} a_k + b_j \qquad s_{j+1}' = \sum_1^{j+1} a_k - a_j + b_{j+1} \tag{4}$$

Let q (q') be the time at which c_j (c_{j+1}) finishes in σ (σ'). It is sufficient to show that $q' \leq q$. We see that:

$$\begin{aligned} q &= \max\{\max\{t, s_{j+1}\} + c_{j+1}, s_j\} + c_j \\ &= \max\{t + c_j + c_{j+1}, s_{j+1} + c_j + c_{j+1}, s_j + c_j\} \end{aligned} \tag{5}$$

and

$$\begin{aligned} q' &= \max\{\max\{t, s_j'\} + c_j, s_{j+1}'\} + c_{j+1} \\ &= \max\{t + c_j + c_{j+1}, s_j' + c_j + c_{j+1}, s_{j+1}' + c_{j+1}\} \end{aligned} \tag{6}$$

From Equations 3, 4, 5, and the inequality $b_j < b_{j+1}$, we obtain:

$$\begin{aligned} s_j' + c_j + c_{j+1} &= s_{j+1} + b_j - b_{j+1} + c_j + c_{j+1} \\ &< s_{j+1} + c_j + c_{j+1} \leq q \end{aligned} \tag{7}$$

and

$$\begin{aligned} s_{j+1}' + c_{j+1} &= s_{j+1} - a_j + c_{j+1} < s_{j+1} + c_{j+1} \\ &< s_{j+1} + c_{j+1} + c_j \leq q \end{aligned} \tag{8}$$

From Equations 7, 8, 5, and 6, it follows that $q' \leq q$. $\square$

Theorem 11. *The CROS defined by the ordering $b_1 \geq b_2 \geq \cdots \geq b_n$ is an ROMFT schedule.*

Proof: Follows from Lemma 10. □

Using Theorem 11, one readily obtains an $O(n \log n)$ algorithm to construct an ROMFT schedule.

5 Conclusion

In this paper, we have introduced and motivated the master-slave scheduling model. We have shown that obtaining minimum finish-time schedules under the no-wait-in-process constraint is NP-hard when the schedule is required to be order preserving as well as when no constraint is imposed between the pre- and post- processing orders. The no-wait-in-process minimum finish time problem is solvable in $O(n \log n)$ time when the post-processing order is required to be the reverse of the pre-processing order.

When the no-wait constraint is eliminated, OPMFT as well as ROMFT schedules can be found in $O(n \log n)$ time.

References

1. G. Chen and T. Lai, Preemptive scheduling of independent jobs on a hypercube, *Information Processing Letters*, 28, 201-206, 1988.
2. G. Chen and T. Lai, Scheduling independent jobs on partitionable hypercubes, *Jr. of Parallel & Distributed Computing*, 12, 74-78, 1991.
3. P. Krueger, T. Lai, and V. Dixit-Radiya, Job scheduling is more important than processor allocation for hypercube computers, *IEEE Trans. on Parallel & Distributed Systems*, 5, 5, 488-497, 1994.
4. S. Leutenegger and M. Vernon, The performance of multiprogrammed multiprocessor scheduling policies, *Proc. 1990 ACM SIGMETRICS Conference on Measurement & Modeling of Computer Systems*, 226-236, 1990.
5. S. Majumdar, D. Eager, and R. Bunt, Scheduling in multiprogrammed parallel systems, *Proc. 1988 ACM SIGMETRICS*, 104-113, 1988.
6. C. McCreary, A. Khan, J. Thompson, and M. McArdle, A comparison of heuristics for scheduling DAGS on multiprocessors, *8th International Parallel Processing Symposium*, 446-451, 1994.
7. S. Sahni, Scheduling multipipeline and multiprocessor computers, *IEEE Trans on Computers*, C-33, 7, 637-645, 1984.
8. Y. Zhu and M. Ahuja, Premptive job scheduling on a hypercube, *Proc. 1990 International Conference on Parallel Processing*, 301-304, 1990.

Time Space Sharing Scheduling: A Simulation Analysis

Atsushi Hori, Yutaka Ishikawa, Jörg Nolte,
Hiroki Konaka, Munenori Maeda, Takashi Tomokiyo

Tsukuba Research Center
Real World Computing Partnership
Tsukuba Mitsui Building 16F, 1-6-1 Takezono
Tsukuba-shi, Ibaraki 305, JAPAN
TEL:+81-298-53-1661, FAX:+81-298-53-1652
E-mail:{hori,ishikawa,jon,konaka,m-maeda,tomokiyo}@trc.rwcp.or.jp

Abstract. We explain a new job scheduling class, called "Time Space Sharing Scheduling" (TSSS) for partitionable parallel machines. TSSS is a combination of time-sharing and space-sharing job scheduling techniques. Our proposed "Distributed Queue Tree" (DQT) is an instance of TSSS. We evaluate and analyze DQT behavior in more detail with a number of simulations. The result shows that DQT performs very well in low-load to high-load situations, almost independent of system size and task size distribution. We also compare our DQT and ScanUp batch scheduling, and we find that our DQT performs as well as ScanUp scheduling in processor utilization, but that both DQT and ScanUp have drawbacks in terms of scheduling fairness. Finally, we find that TSSS can inherently achieve higher processor utilization.

1 Introduction

Work on job scheduling on parallel machines has mostly been on batch scheduling with space-sharing where processors are partitioned and jobs are allocated on these partitions [1, 5, 9]. Some commercially available parallel machines have time-sharing facilities [8]. Few of them, however, tackle both time-sharing and space-sharing [2, 3]. Table 1 shows a categorization of job scheduling systems targeting parallel machines. Time-shared job scheduling on parallel machines can take on a different aspect from that on sequential machines, if the targeting parallel machine supports variable partitions. This is because space-sharing with variable partitions[1] can bring an extra dimension to time-shared job scheduling.

In this paper, we explain a new job scheduling class called **Time Space Sharing Scheduling (TSSS)** to create an interactive programming environ-

---

[1] "Variable partition" means that partitioning can be controlled using software. "Dynamic partition" enables the partition in which a task or a job is running to be dynamically changed on hardware capable of variable partitioning. This definition was proposed by Larry Rudolph at IPPS'95 Workshop on Job Scheduling Strategies for Parallel Processing

Table 1. Categorization of job scheduling for a parallel machine

	Batch	Time Sharing
Fixed partition	Conventional scheme	**CM-5 (CMOST)** [8]
Variable partition	Many works [1, 5, 9] and so on.	**Distibuted Hierarchical Control** [2] **Distributed Queue Tree** [3]

ment for parallel machines. TSSS is a combination of a time-sharing and space-sharing job scheduling techniques for parallel machines with variable partitions. We have already proposed the **Distributed Queue Tree (DQT)** [3], and DQT is an instance of TSSS. In the primary report on DQT [3], we described some of its characteristics and proposed several task allocation policies. We did not, however, reveal enough DQT characteristics. In this report, DQT is evaluated and analyzed with a number of simulations. Here, we focus on: i) the scalability of scheduling performance, ii) the relation to task size (the number of processors required by a task) distribution, and iii) fairness of scheduling.

In the next section, we summarize Scan batch scheduling [5], and then explain TSSS. In Section 3, DQT, as an instance of TSSS, is introduced briefly. Then the simulation results are shown in Section 4. The behavior of DQT is analyzed in Sections 4.2 and 4.4, and compared with some batch scheduling techniques proposed so far in Section 4.3.

2 Job Scheduling for Parallel Machines

2.1 Scan Scheduling

Krueger et al. proposed a space-sharing scheduling technique called Scan [5]. The queuing system consists of multiple queues, and each queue is responsible for a partition size. Scan scheduling is centralized and relatively simple. One of the queues is selected and the tasks in the queue are scheduled. If the queue becomes empty, then the next queue becomes the current queue. If the current queue pointer moves toward a queue of larger size, then the scheduling is called ScanUp; the opposite is called ScanDown. It has been reported that ScanUp always exhibits better performance than ScanDown [5]. Scan scheduling is considered to be the best job scheduling scheme among those proposed so far.

2.2 Time Space Sharing Scheduling

Time Space Sharing Scheduling (TSSS) is a new class of job scheduling techniques which provides an interactive multi-process programming environment. It is a combination of time-sharing and space-sharing job scheduling techniques and is covered in the lower right of Table 1. Figure 1 shows a schematic view of TSSS. TSSS can inherently achieve higher processor utilization, because late-coming tasks can remove fragmentation of the processor space. One major draw-back of TSSS is the heavier scheduling overhead. If TSSS performs better than batch scheduling, then it may be worth implementing TSSS from the viewpoint of resource utilization. To clarify this, we will compare our DQT and ScanUp scheduling with simulation (Sections 4.3 and 4.4).

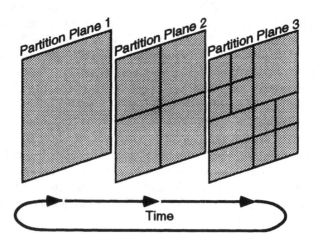

Fig. 1. Example of TSSS

In this paper, a process is defined as an execution entity of a task. With TSSS, a process exclusively occupies a partition in a certain time slot. Each processor could be multiplexed at thread level, not at process level. However, this could result in a larger working set and processor thrashing [2]. A parallel machine is multiplexed in terms of time and processor space with TSSS. A TSSS scheduler should schedule a process to a time slot and map onto a partition. A partition at a certain time slot is a virtualized parallel machine and a processor address space from the user's viewpoint.

We assume that the target parallel machine is homogeneous, and that the user cannot specify the partition to which a process allocated. Only the TSSS scheduler can decide which partition is allocated. The same situation can be seen in the conventional TSS, where the user cannot specify the time slot. The oper-ating system views a partition as a computational resource. The TSSS scheduler is also a virtual parallel machine server of various sizes. Partitions should be allo-cated by a TSSS scheduler according to the status of the entire system, normally, to balance the system load.

To develop a scheduling technique with TSSS, the following items should be taken into account.

- The scheduling process should be distributed and must avoid any bottle-necks. In time-sharing, processes can often change state from running to waiting and vice versa, especially when the processes are waiting for terminal input. If a time-sharing scheduling scheme is implemented with a centralized queue system, as is the case in conventional sequential machines, this can cause a severe bottleneck.
- A TSSS scheduling scheme should be hardware independent, especially for network topology. In most cases, job scheduling is a part of the operating system and operating systems are hard to maintain. If a TSSS scheduling scheme imposes a network topology, then the portability of the operating system would be lost.
- The processor utilization ratio can be a measure of TSSS performance. The strategies of partitioning and partition allocation for a process are very important. A similar problem can be found in memory allocation [6].
- Fairness in scheduling can also be the other measure of TSSS performance. Fairness, however, may be traded off against processor utilization in some situations.
- It is desired that TSSS performance does not saturate with an increase in workload, and exhibits the same characteristics in the system size (number of processors in a system) and pattern of given workload.

3 Distributed Queue Tree

We proposed a **Distributed Queue Tree (DQT)** [3], which we briefly explain in this section. DQT is a distributed tree structure for process scheduling management. Each DQT node has a process run queue. Every process in the queue requires that the number of processors does not exceed the partition size of the node. The DQT tree structure should reflect the nesting of partitioning. Each DQT node should be distributed to the processor in the partition corresponding to that node. When a process is suspended, it should be dequeued from the process run queue. In DQT, this queue operation is needed only in a processor that plays the role of a DQT node.

Figure 2·(a) shows an example of a DQT structure. Each DQT node has a process run queue that is represented by small rectangles on the right side of the node, with the number of rectangles being equal to the length of the queue. The root node, N0, is responsible for the entire processor space (full partition). Each of the nodes N1 and N2 is responsible for a halved partition. Each of the nodes N3, N4, N5, and N6 is responsible for a quartered partition.

Figure 2 (b) shows a DQT scheduling example, corresponding to the DQT in Fig. 2 (a). In this figure, the jth process in the queue Q_i of the ith node is denoted as "$Q_i(j)$". The entire processor space is assigned to $Q_0(0)$ at time slot 0 and $Q_0(1)$ at time slot 1. In time slot 2, halved partitions are assigned and two processes are simultaneously running in adjacent partitions. In time slot 3, the right-hand side halved partition is halved again, while the left-hand side halved

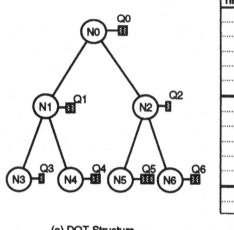

(a) DQT Structure

Time Slot #	PE0	PE1	PE2	PE3
0	$Q_0(0)$			
1	$Q_0(1)$			
2	$Q_1(0)$		$Q_2(0)$	
3	$Q_1(1)$		$Q_5(0)$	$Q_6(0)$
4	$Q_3(0)$	$Q_4(0)$	$Q_5(1)$	$Q_6(1)$
5	$Q_3(0)$	$Q_4(1)$	$Q_5(2)$	$Q_6(0)$
6	$Q_0(0)$			
7	$Q_0(1)$			
8	$Q_1(0)$		$Q_2(0)$	
9	$Q_1(1)$		$Q_5(0)$	$Q_6(1)$
10	$Q_3(0)$	$Q_4(0)$	$Q_5(1)$	$Q_6(0)$
11	$Q_3(0)$	$Q_4(1)$	$Q_5(2)$	$Q_6(1)$
12	$Q_0(0)$			
:	:			

(b) DQT Scheduling

Fig. 2. Example of DQT

partition is left as is since there are two processes in queue Q_1. Every process is scheduled at least once in 6 time slots in this case.

DQT scheduling consists of two major parts. One is a distributed scheduling algorithm and the other is task allocation to balance the DQT load.

3.1 DQT Scheduling

The DQT scheduling process is distributed over the DQT nodes, and the DQT nodes are distributed to the processors in a corresponding partition. Each node communicates and synchronizes with its supernode and subnodes only. Thus the scheduling process is distributed and parallelized.

A DQT node is activated when a process in the queue of a node is scheduled. At a certain time, the line connecting activated DQT nodes in a tree diagram is called a **front**. Figure 3 (a) shows an example of a front movement in a DQT. In this figure, each small rectangle in a DQT node represents a process in a process run queue in that node. If the DQT load is well-balanced, the front is a horizontal line moving repeatedly downward. Lines $t0$, $t1$ and $t2$ in Fig. 3 (a) are examples. The front moves faster on the DQT branch with the lighter load (denoted by $t3$). If a part of the front hits the bottom of the tree (right half of $t3$), then it moves back to the node where the load is unbalanced ($t4$). Consequently smaller tasks may be scheduled more often than larger tasks. This is to keep processors as busy as possible. Predictably, this strategy can cause unfairness. To clarify the effect of this scheduling strategy, we propose an alternative scheduling strategy, called "Fair-DQT." Fig. 3 (b) is an example of Fair-DQT corresponding Fig. 3 (a). Every process is scheduled exactly once in a round. The front never goes

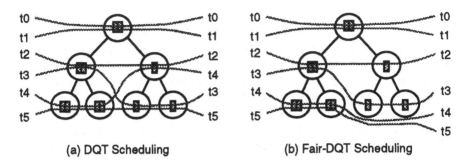

(a) DQT Scheduling   (b) Fair-DQT Scheduling

Fig. 3. Example of front movement

up until every part of front is synchronized at the bottom of the DQT. This strategy can result in fairer scheduling but lower processor utilization. We will show some simulation results to compare these two DQT scheduling strategies (Sections 4.3 and 4.4).

3.2 Task Allocation

The policy used to decide which partition is to be allocated when a process is created is very important to balance the DQT load. A well-balanced DQT exhibits not only good processor utilization, but also a shorter response time and fair scheduling [3]. We proposed various task allocation policies [3].

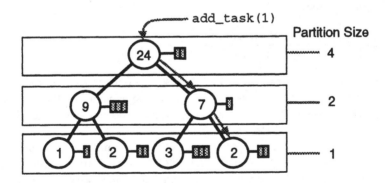

Fig. 4. Example of task allocation

Figure 4 shows an example of one of the proposed policies. The number on each DQT node represents the load on the branch. In this case, it is the number of virtual processors needed to schedule all processes in the sub-DQT at once.

For example, the number on the left node in the second level is 9, because the node itself requires 6 virtual processors (three processes times partition size two) and 3 virtual processors in the subnodes (one for the left subnode and two for the right subnode). The **add_task** message is sent to the root when a partition for a new process is required. This message is forwarded to the subnode whose load is lighter, until it reaches the node that has the required partition size (in this case, the required size is one). This task allocation policy performs very well in various situations [3], and is very simple. In this paper, every simulation of DQT uses this task allocation policy.

4 Simulation

4.1 Simulation Conditions and Measurements

Each task size is rounded up to the nearest partition size, in this case a power of 2. The processor utilization numbers shown in these simulation results were optimistic, since we ignore internal fragmentation and processors which are idle because of communication delays, synchronization and/or waiting for an I/O operation. The task size distributions we simulated are uniform, proportional, and inversely proportional to the rounded size of the task. Tasks that require the full configuration are omitted because they behave in the same way as a single queue system. The distribution of the ideal execution time (task length) is exponential with an average of 1,000 time units. Every task is independent, and can be scheduled and preempted at any time. The simulation time is 10^6 time units, and the time quantum is one time unit. The scheduling overhead is ignored.

The task arrival distribution is geometric, and the mean task arrival time $(\overline{T_{interval}})$ is calculated as

$$\overline{T_{interval}} = \frac{\overline{task\_size} \times \overline{task\_length}}{P \times W_{target}}$$

where $\overline{task\_size}$ is the mean value of the task size (calculated from system size and task size distribution), $\overline{task\_length}$ is the mean value of the task service time, P is the number of processors in the system (system size), and W_{target} is the ratio of workload to system size.

To evaluate scheduling behavior, the system size (number of processors) is varied at 128, 256, 512, 1024, 2048 and 4096. The targeting workload is also varied at 0.2, 0.4, 0.6, 0.8, 0.9, 0.95, 0.97 and 0.99. Since task size, task arrival and task service time are randomized independently, the actual workload may differ from the target workload. So, we define the actual workload (W_{actual}) as

$$W_{actual} = \frac{\sum_{l=0}^{L-1}(task\_size_l \times task\_length_l)}{P \times T}$$

where $task\_size_l$ is the task size of the lth task, $task\_length_l$ is the task length of the lth task, L is the number of tasks arrived, and, T is the simulation time.

The actual workload could exceed 1.0, even though the target workload is less than 1.0. We discard the simulation results in such a situation.

Processor utilization (U_t) at time t is defined as $U_t = P_t^*/P$, and the average processor utilization $(\overline{U})$ from time t_1 to time t_2 is defined as

$$\overline{U} = \frac{\sum_{t=t_1}^{t_2} P_t^*)}{P \times (t_2 - t_1 + 1)}$$

where P_t^* is the number of potentially busy processors (or the sum of the numbers of processors in activated partitions) at the tth time quantum, and P is the number of processors in the entire system.

Here, the **Real Execution Time Ratio (RETR)**[2] of the lth task (R_l^{RET}) is defined as

$$R_l^{RET} = \frac{t_l^{task\_end} - t_l^{task\_entry}}{task\_length_l}$$

where $t_l^{task\_entry}$ is the time of task entry, and $t_l^{task\_end}$ is the time the task ends. This RETR represents how much slower the execution of a task is than the ideal situation.

4.2 DQT Simulation Results

Figure 5 shows the DQT simulation result. The three graphs in the upper row show the processor utilization curves when varying the workload on each system size with the same scale. In those graphs, actual workload values are given on the horizontal axis. To show the difference more clearly, only part of high load situations are drawn. The graphs in the lower row show mean RETR curves in the same scale. In those graphs, in both rows from left to right, the task size distributions are proportional, uniform, and inversely proportional to task size respectively.

Overall, those simulation results show good linearity to the given workload. In all graphs, DQT behaves almost independently of system size. Generally, the saturation of processor utilization means that the number of remaining tasks in the system increases rapidly. These simulation results also show the stability of DQT in high-load situations.

DQT exhibits a somewhat poor performance with uniform task size distribution. With a proportional distribution, the processor utilization can remain high because of larger tasks, while with an inversely proportional distribution, a number of small tasks can be enough to balance the DQT load in high-load situations.

---

[2] **Real Execution Time** is defined as the total duration that a task is in a process run queue. In this sense, RETR is different from elapsed time.

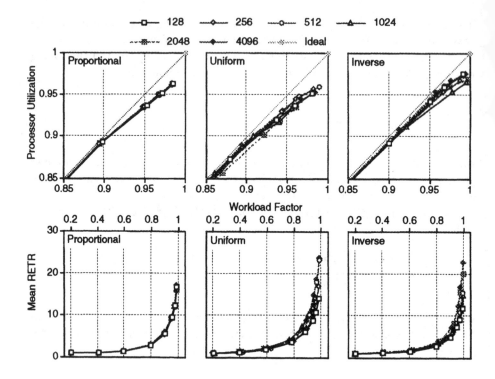

Fig. 5. DQT Simulation Results

4.3 DQT vs. Batch

Figure 6 shows graphs of the simulation results of DQT, Fair-DQT, First-Come-
First-Serve scheduling with Binary Buddy allocation strategy (FCFS-BB), and
ScanUp using exactly the same situation as in Fig. 5, but with the number of
processors fixed at 1024. Overall, ScanUp scheduling also exhibits good processor
utilization for proportional and uniform distribution (the RETR curves of DQT
and ScanUp are almost overlapped in the figure). However, it exhibits relatively
lower processor utilization for inversely proportional distribution.

Interestingly, only a small degradation in processor utilization can be found
in high-load situations with Fair-DQT. The possible explanation of this phenomenon is that the latecoming tasks cancel fragmentation. The linearity of
DQT in processor utilization found in Fig. 5 is also obtained for the same reason. Figure 7 shows RETR curves of Fair-DQT under the same condition as in
Fig. 6. The DQT scheduling strategy always results in shorter mean RETRs. In
these graphs, we show mean RETR values. However, the situation is the same
with the maximum values of RETR. Thus the DQT scheduling strategy is very

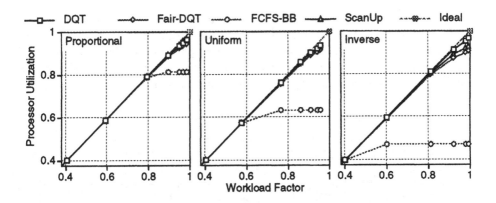

Fig. 6. DQT vs. Batch Scheduling

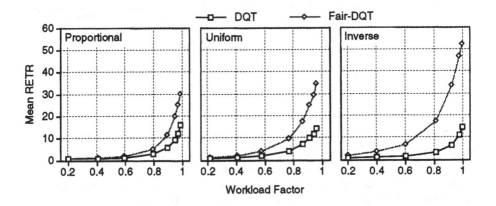

Fig. 7. RETR of Fair-DQT

efficient to reduce RETR values. This means that the strategy can result in a shorter response time.

As expected, FCFS-BB exhibits the worst performance. The processor utilization depends strongly on the task size distribution. This phenomenon comes from external fragmentation. Larger tasks are forced to wait for the space occupied by smaller and longer task(s).

4.4 Scheduling Fairness

In Fig. 8, the correlation coefficient between task size dimension $(log_2(task\_size))$ and RETR obtained at the simulation results in Fig. 6 on DQT, Fair-DQT, and ScanUp scheduling is plotted . In most cases, the correlation coefficients of DQT are positive. This means the larger the task size, the less the opportunity for scheduling. As described in Section 3.1, this phenomenon happens because smaller tasks tend to be scheduled more often to keep processors as busy as possible. As supposed, Fair-DQT exhibits better fairness.

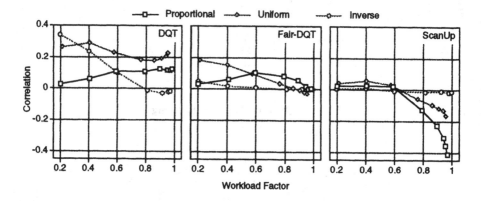

Fig. 8. Task Size Correlation (2^{10} processors)

With uniform and inversely proportional distributions, the correlation coefficient of DQT tends to be higher in lower-load situations. This phenomenon may be because DQT (and Fair-DQT as well) may not have a sufficient number of tasks to fill the load imbalance. A positive correlation coefficient has one advantage; users might hesitate to enter large tasks and this situation could prevent the thoughtless wasting processor utilities.

It was reported that ScanUp scheduling has good scheduling fairness [5]. However, we found that the correlation coefficient between task size and response time depends on the task size distribution and workload. With the inverse distribution, fairness is almost guaranteed. However, when larger tasks are entered more often, the response time for larger tasks becomes shorter for higher workloads.

5 Summary

We have explained a new scheduling class called Time Space Sharing Scheduling combining time-sharing and space-sharing for partitionable parallel machines. On evaluation through simulations, we found that our proposed DQT [3], which is an instance of TSSS, performs as well as ScanUp scheduling which is possibly the best batch scheduling system so far [5]. DQT shows good linearity over given workloads, and good independency from task size distribution and system size.

In terms of fairness, however, both DQT and ScanUp scheduling exhibit some dependency on task size distribution and workload.

Importantly, this paper shows that TSSS can inherently achieve higher processor utilization due to the cancellation of external fragmentation of processor space by late-coming tasks. Thus, the scheduling overhead of TSSS may be acceptable.

DQT scheduling will be implemented on the RWC-1, parallel machine that is under development in our RWC project [7]. RWC-1 will be implemented with some architectural support for TSSS. With TSSS and architectural support [4], an interactive programming environment can be implemented on parallel machines and it is as practical as time-sharing on sequential workstations.

References

1. P.-J. Chuang and N.-F. Tzeng. A Fast Recognition-Complete Processor Allocation Strategy for Hypercube Computers. *IEEE Transactions on Computers*, 41(4):467–479, 1992.
2. D. G. Feitelson and L. Rudolph. Distributed Hierarchical Control for Parallel Processing. *COMPUTER*, pages 65–77, May 1990.
3. A. Hori, Y. Ishikawa, H. Konaka, M. Maeda, and T. Tomokiyo. A Scalable Time-Sharing Scheduling for Partitionable, Distributed Memory Parallel Machines. In *Proceedings of the Twenty-Eighth Annual Hawaii International Conference on System Sciences*, volume II, pages 173–182. IEEE Computer Society Press, January 1995.
4. A. Hori, T. Yokota, Y. Ishikawa, S. Sakai, H. Konaka, M. Maeda, T. Tomokiyo, J. Nolte, H. Matsuoka, K. Okamoto, and H. Hirono. Time Space Sharing Scheduling and Architectural Support. In D. G. Feitelson and L. Rudolph, editors, *Job Scheduling Strategies for Parallel Processing*, volume 949 of *Lecture Notes in Computer Science*. Springer-Verlag, April 1995.
5. P. Krueger, T.-H. Lai, and V. A. Dixit-Radiya. Job Scheduling Is More Important than Processor Allocation for Hypercube Computers. *IEEE Transactions on Parallel and Distributed Systems*, 5(5):488–497, 1994.
6. J. L. Peterson and T. A. Norman. Buddy System. *Communication of the ACM*, 20(6):421–431, June 1977.
7. S. Sakai, K. Okamoto, H. Matsuoka, H. Hirono, Y. Kodama, and M. Sato. Super-threading: Architectural and software mechanisms for optimizing parallel computation. In *Proceedings of 1993 International Conference on Supercomputing*, pages 251–260, 1993.
8. Thinking Machines Corporation. *Connection Machine CM-5 Technical Summary*, November 1992.
9. Y. Zhu. Efficient Processor Allocation Strategies for Mesh-Connected Parallel Computers. *Journal of Parallel and Distributed Computing*, 16:328–337, 1992.

"Agency Scheduling"
A Model for Dynamic Task Scheduling*

Johann Rost [1], Franz-Josef Markus [2] and Li Yan-Hua [3]

[1] J. Rost GmbH
Glockenhofstr. 24, D-90478 Nürnberg, Germany

[2] Medizinische Universität zu Lübeck
Institut für Technische Informatik
Ratzeburger Allee 160, D-23538 Lübeck, Germany
(email: markus@iti.mu-luebeck.de)

[3] Beijing Research Institute of Telemetry
P. O. Box 9212, 100076 Beijing, P. R. China

Abstract: This paper describes a class of algorithms for scheduling parallel programs represented by macro dataflow graphs (task precedence graphs) onto a multiprocessor system such that the total execution time is minimized. The schedule will be computed dynamically during the runtime of the process system. The model allows to represent centralized and fully distributed algorithms as well as intermediate forms. The algorithms are able to schedule static as well as dynamic dataflow graphs. Knowledge of the execution times of the tasks is not necessary. Some variants of the model have been implemented using a multi-transputer system. Practical experiences are included in the paper.

1 Introduction

MIMD multiprocessor systems are increasingly applied in wide areas of computer science. In order to take advantage of the potential increase of computation power, it is first necessary to split the algorithm into parallel processes. In a second step, these processes are to be assigned to the individual processors of the multiprocessor. In existing applications, a specific assignment for a given multiprocessor and for the current problem is often developed by the software engineer. Even though this solution may be slightly more efficient than automatic scheduling, it still has the disadvantages of high development costs, weak portability and a high degree of fault-proneness.

In recent years several variants of the task scheduling problem received increasing scientific attention. Many authors published especially on the following three problems:

(1) Load Balancing Problem

In a multiuser multitasking environment, the processes are started at any point in time. The tasks are to be assigned to the machines of a multiprocessor such that the load of all processors is balanced. Often deadlines and additional resource requests have to be considered. On the other hand, there is usually no communication structure assumed [LüM93] between the tasks. An overview is given in [CaK88].

---

* This work is partially supported by Deutsche Forschungsgemeinschaft DFG under contract number Ma 1412/1-2

(2) Task Scheduling with Task Interaction Graph

For each pair of tasks (t1, t2), the amount of communication between t1 and t2 is given. The data transmission can become necessary at any time during the runtime of the process system. Contrary to (1), all tasks are started at the same time. The problem here is to find a mapping of the tasks to the multiprocessor making the best possible use of the interprocessor network. Solutions of the problem are suggested in e.g. [Lee-88, Lo88]. An introductory overview is given in [CHL80].

(3) Task Scheduling with Task Precedence Graph

For some pairs of tasks (t1, t2), the dataflow graph (sometimes called "task precedence graph") defines that t1 must be finished before t2 can start. A schedule must be found which minimizes the execution time of the process system by minimizing both the communication overhead and the idle time of the processor. The problem can be solved either statically (before the process system is started) or dynamically. While the static solutions usually require good estimations for the execution times of the tasks and a fixed (static) structure of the dataflow graph, the dynamic algorithms consume an increased overhead for communication. Static solutions are given, for example, in [KaN84, MaL86]. A dynamic solution which could be called "Team Scheduling" is suggested in [RoM90].

This paper mainly focuses on dynamic solutions of problem (3). Overviews to the subject are given in [Bok87, ReF87, Hwa93].

2 Problem Description

2.1 Machine Configuration Graph

The multiprocessor (here only distributed memory machines are considered) is modelled as a graph with nodes (PMU, processor memory units) and edges (communication links, connections). The processor nodes are labelled with processing power and memory capacity while the edges carry a link capacity. The machine configuration graph as well as the labels are assumed to be given.

2.2 Dataflow Graph

The dataflow graph (Fig. 1) is a bipartite graph consisting of task nodes (circles), data nodes (squares) and edges. The data nodes describe results produced by one task and required by another one. Usually the execution time of the individual tasks is unknown. Sometimes estimations are available. Note that in some kinds of parallel programs the structure of the dataflow graph is not completely known in advance. The degree of branching or the number of loop iterations may be unknown at design time. If more than one dataflow graph can be executed simultaneously, this is called "space sharing". A model ("D^{2}R", Dynamic Dataflow Representation") which is able to express such features is described in [Ros94].

Fig. 1 shows a dataflow graph which can be used to parallelize some kinds of iterative algorithms for solving partial differential equations ("PDE"). For example, a heatened sheet is divided into two imaginary stripes. This division is made by t0 and will result in data sets d1 and d2. Then an iteration loop (named "loop") is entered. The graphic representation expresses the REPEAT structure of the loop (with at least one iteration). To identify the nodes of different iterations, the loop name is added to the node names within the loop body. During runtime the loop name is substituted by the loop counter value to provide the needed unique identification of the nodes. D^{2}R provides a similar mechanism when dynamic forks are used which are not applied in the example above. Each of the tasks t1.\loop and t2.\loop executes one iteration step in one stripe. After completion of the iteration step, new data will be created (dl1.\loop, dl4.\loop). Moreover, the boundaries of the stripes must be exchanged (dl2.\loop, dl3.\loop). Finally the iteration is converging and the data is passed to "tx".

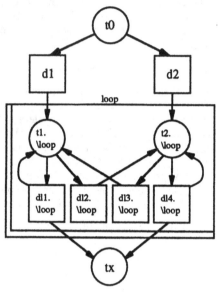

Fig. 1. Dataflow graph

3 Agency Scheduling Model

Up to now only few dynamic algorithms for the task scheduling problem have been suggested. The model suggested permits to easily characterize a wide range of algorithms. According to this model, an algorithm consists of eight rather independent components for which heuristics will be suggested.

3.1 Basic Ideas

There are a number of agencies each of which is responsible for a so-called "employer area". The employer areas constitute a partition of the processors of the multiprocessor, i.e. each processor is assigned to exactly one employer area. In addition, each agency is equipped with an employee area which may either match the employer area or exceed it in size and thus overlap with other employer areas. Jobs generated within the employer area of an agency are reported to the agency, which allocates them within its employee area. In the case of matching areas, the jobs may be allocated via a command protocol. Otherwise a bidding phase is required. If temporarily charged with heavy duty, an agency can delegate jobs to neighbouring areas via a load balancing mechanism. The processor carrying out the function of the agency can be dedicated to this job or can execute user tasks in addition. Moreover, a parameter N is given, defining the number of user processes which are permitted to be executed simultaneously, i.e. multitasking of user processes is allowed. Such agencies are best illustrated by comparing them with human labor offices.

The specification of an algorithm consists of the following eight components:

(1) A set of PMUs (the agencies).

(2) The corresponding employer areas.

(3) The corresponding employee areas.

(4) A boolean variable called "dedicated".

(5) The maximum number of user tasks running simultaneously on one PMU. On each processor, N virtual machines are running, each of which is executing its own protocols for reporting finished tasks and assigning unsolved jobs respectively. The individual user tasks may be running with different priorities.

(6) The protocol for allocating jobs. If each processor is assigned to exactly one agency, an easy command protocol can be applied. Otherwise possible conflicts have to be resolved - for example by using a bidding protocol.

(7) The protocol for reporting finished jobs.

(8) The strategy of balancing the load among the agencies.

Load balancing has been researched intensively. An overview is given in [CaK88].

3.2 "Team Scheduling" A Fully Distributed Variant of the Agency Scheduling Model

In the Team Scheduling algorithm, each processor maintains a *local knowledge* containing the idle and working PMUs, the location of the data sets and the state of the processes. This local knowledge is updated via a *broadcast mechanism* whenever a task is started or finished. After a task t has been finished, the scheduling algorithm will check if t has successors which can be started at that point. In this case, a bidding phase with presumably idle processors is triggered, during the course of which the successors are allocated. For more detail see [RoM90].

Team Scheduling is an extreme example of Agency Scheduling. Each processor is its own (non-dedicated) agency. The employer area is constituted by the processor only. The employee area is established by the entire multiprocessor.

It can be shown [Ros94] that the execution time of the schedule computed by Team Scheduling is at most twice as long as the execution time of the optimum schedule.

$$T_{TeamScheduling} \leq T_{opt} * (2-1/NumberProcessors)$$

4 The Components of the Agency Scheduling Model

4.1 Agencies and Areas

An easy way of defining the areas lies in the manual division of the multiprocessor. Using a regular mesh-like connection network, the whole multiprocessor can be divided into X*Y rectangular areas. The agency function will be assigned to a central processor (geometric center of gravity). An example for applying this strategy is given in Fig. 2. In this example, the multiprocessor is divided into four areas of equal size and matching employer and employee areas. The agency of each area is marked by an "A".

In the example of Fig. 3, the employee areas are overlapping. To avoid confusion, the employer areas are not displayed in the graphics - they are identical with the areas of Fig. 2. Note that in this example the employee areas exceed the employer areas in size. While in the former example an easy command protocol can be used to allocate tasks, in the latter a more complex bidding phase is required which consists of "bid task", "accept task" or "not accept task", and "transfer task". On the other hand, overlapping areas open up a new prospect in load balancing: in this case, it is possible to balance the load without an explicit load balancing function. Instead (implicitly), tasks are assigned to the areas of the neighboring agencies. Applying overlapping areas in heavily loaded systems may cause several (or even many) agencies to send a "bid task" message as soon as an employee gets idle because the idle employee may belong to more than one employee area. To minimize the overhead caused by this message, an additional decision rule can be applied which says that in heavily loaded systems an agency bids a task mainly in its employer area. In other terms, in heavily loaded parts of the systems the overlapping areas are temporarily switched off.

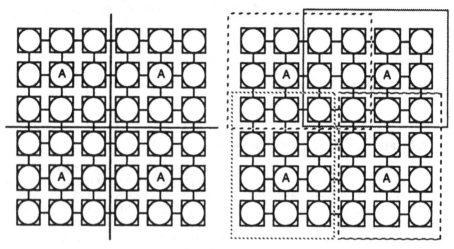

Fig. 2. Disjunct areas   **Fig. 3.** Overlapping areas

To demonstrate the flexibility of the model by means of extreme examples, a central configuration is shown in Fig. 4. Central scheduling algorithms can be implemented more easily and often cause less dynamic overhead than distributed ones. However, the main disadvantages here are that the central agency constitutes a potential bottleneck ("monitor bottleneck") in larger-scale systems and that it is more difficult to solve the problems of fault tolerance. On the other hand, the extreme example demonstrates the wide scope of the model.

Quite the reverse of the central solution is the fully distributed configuration shown in Fig. 5, which is applied in the "Team Scheduling" algorithm. The drawback of the fully distributed configuration is that "Team Scheduling" needs broadcast messages to be distributed among the agencies (i.e. messages from one agency to all others) to maintain the local knowledge. Since in the discussed configuration all processors perform the agency function, the broadcasts among the agencies are, in fact, broadcasts all over the system, which may cause quite a dynamic overhead in large multiprocessor systems. We have already developed a variant of "Team Scheduling" which needs no global broadcast; it is, however, more difficult to implement this variant. For more details see section 4.3.

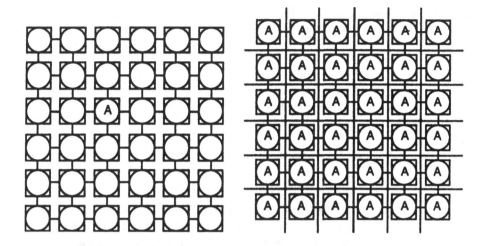

| Fig. 4. Central configuration | Fig. 5. Fully distributed configuration |

4.2 Allocation of tasks

An interesting question arises if a task t depends on the results of more than one task, as for example t1 and t2 (see Fig. 6). In this case there must be an agreement between the agency which has allocated t1 (abbreviated as Agency(t1)) and Agency(t2) as to the question who is responsible for starting t. We tested three rules to achieve this agreement.

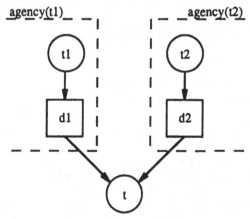

Fig. 6. Task t depending on multiple predecessors

In the following discussion, t_x is an arbitrary successor of t and the value WaitingTime is the time which a broadcast needs to be received all over the system. The function Ord(task) defines the lexicographic order of the name of the tasknode - in the easiest case the node number.

Our first idea was that Agency(t_x) is responsible for task t, if and only if t_x is the predecessor which finished *last*. The advantage is that at this time all required input data is available and t_x can be started immediately. However, if t_1 and t_2 are finishing at almost the same time this rule can cause a conflict. Both Agency(t_1) and Agency(t_2) feel the other one to be responsible for starting t. To avoid this conflict, rule 1 uses a WaitingTime.

Rule 1:

case 1:   if ($\forall$ i ((i ≠ x) => t_i is finished))
           Agency(t_x) is responsible

case 2:   if ($\exists$ i ((i ≠ x) ∧ t_i is not yet started))
           Agency(t_x) is not responsible

case 3:   else:
           -    Agency(t_x) broadcasts "t_x is finished"
           -    Agency(t_x) waits for at least two WaitingTime units
           - 3.1   Agency(t_x) receives a "finish" broadcast from another Agency(t_i)
                The agency with the smaller PMU number is responsible
           - 3.2   else
                Agency(t_x) is not responsible

Rule 1 has some disadvantages:
    - Two broadcasts are required (after start and after finishing of a task).
    - The WaitingTime constitutes a source of dynamic overhead.
    - Case 2 implies the execution times of a task to be at least WaitingTime units.

Rule 2:

Similar to rule 1 but without broadcast at the start of a task.
=>   case 2 cannot arise
      disadvantage: WaitingTime occurs almost always.

Rule 3:

case 1: $\forall$ i ((i ≠ x) => Ord(t_i) < Ord(t_x))
           Agency(t_x) is responsible

case 2: else
           Agency(t_x) is not responsible

Rule 3 is based on the idea that Agency(t_x) is responsible, if and only if t_x has the highest lexicographic order among all predecessors of t. The disadvantage of this rule is the more complex implementation. According to the former rules, all input data of t was already computed when an agency became responsible for a task t. This is usually not applicable to rule 3. Therefore, each agency maintains a list of processes for which it is responsible, but which cannot yet be started. After computation of new data sets, this list is searched for tasks which can be started at that point. Despite its complexer implementation we preferred rule 3 because of the dynamic overhead caused by the WaitingTime in rule 1 and 2.

4.3 Maintaining the local knowledge without broadcast

Among other things the local knowledge contains the information which task has been finished on which processor (the so-called "address component"). Parts of this information are necessary to find out the location of the input data of a task to be started. In the first version of "Team Scheduling", the local knowledge was maintained via a global broadcast mechanism [RoM90]. Since broadcast constitutes a source of dynamic overhead, we have been searching for other solutions.

Note that it is not necessary to inform each agency about every task which is being finished. It is sufficient to send a message to those agencies which are responsible for the predecessors of all successors of the task (perhaps "P"). One difficulty is how to find out the identity of the agencies which are responsible for the predecessors of all successors of P.

Suppose that Agency(P) which has allocated task P wants to send the "finish" message for P to Agency(t) which is responsible for task t. Task t is one of the predecessors of a successor of P. The idea here is to use quite another agency ("A") acting as an intermediary. The trick, however, is that the identity of A = A(P, t) can be computed from the node names of P and t.

One example for function A() is given in the following formula:

(1) Transform the node names of P and t to integer (named "int(P)" and "int(t)"). If the node names are given by ASCII strings, the transformation int() could be the sum of the ASCII values of the individual characters.

(2) Compute A := (int(P) + int(t)) modulo (number of agencies in the system).

If Agency(P) does not know the identity of Agency(t), Agency(P) will act according to the following algorithm:

(1) Agency(P) sends the "finish" message to agency A and requests agency A to transmit the "finish" message to Agency(t).

(2) If agency A knows the identity of Agency(t), it will transmit the message, and the problem is solved; else, A will store the message and steps (3) to (5) are performed.

(3) Later, Agency(t) will be confronted with the similar problem of wanting to tell Agency(P) that t has been finished. If it does not know the identity of Agency(P), it must ask A for help (step (4a)); else, it performs step (4b).

(4a) Due to the message agency A has received in the course of step 1, A knows the identity of Agency(P). So A is able to transmit both of the messages, and the problem is solved.

(4b) Agency(t) sends Agency(P) a message that t has been finished.

(5) Following step (4b), Agency(P) receives the message from Agency(t) *without* the aid of A. Agency(P) sends the message that P has been finished to Agency(t) and tells A that the problem with regard to the identity of Agency(t) is now solved.

5 Test results

5.1 Evaluation of scheduling algorithms

For judging the quality of a schedule, it is necessary to know what to compare the schedule to. The most obvious way, i.e. to compare it with the optimum schedule, fails because the computation of the optimum schedule falls into the class of NP-hard problems. This means that the time needed for computation of the exact solution grows exponentially with the problem size. Therefore, only a few minor problems can be solved to optimum. To cope with this fact, bounds were looked for, the computation of which is easier than that of the exact solution. Two important lower bounds for a given dataflow graph are constituted by the "critical path" and the "efficiency bound". The critical path is the longest path from an input node to an output node of the dataflow graph (the highest sum of execution times). Whatever scheduling algorithm is employed, the execution time of the process system cannot be shorter than the length of the critical path. The efficiency bound says that the speedup cannot be higher than the number of processors. In other words: efficiency ≤ 1. Both bounds are very important and widely applied (see for example [KaN84]). They deliver a rather good estimation in many cases, but unfortunately not in all.

In addition we applied a third bound expressed in the formula given below. Different to the two bounds described above, which provide a bound for a *given dataflow graph*, the third bound measures only the dynamic overhead of a *given schedule* and cannot judge the overall quality of a schedule. The formula computes the fictitious starting times of the processes if the given schedule could be executed on a multiprocessor system with an infinitely fast communication system and with no computation time required for the decision heuristics. In this way the formula reflects an intuitive idea of the "dynamic overhead".

If (t is an input task) $\wedge$ (t is the first task at the processor PMU(t))
StartTime(task t) := 0
else StartTime (task t) := min$_x$ (x fulfils condition (*) as well as condition (**))

$\forall$ p (p is a predecessor of t) =>
$\quad$ x $\geq$ StartTime(p) + ExecutionTime(p) $\qquad$ (*)
AND
$\forall$ p ((PMU(p) = PMU(t)) AND (Order(p) < Order(t))) =>
$\quad$ x $\geq$ StartTime(p) + ExecutionTime(p) $\qquad$ (**)

In this formula according to the given schedule, the expression "PMU(t)" represents the processor which is executing task t and the phrase "Order(p) < Order(t)" means that task p is executed before task t. (*) is a formal description of the critical path rule: a task t cannot be started before all predecessors are finished. (**) states that the user tasks on the same PMU are executed strictly sequentially.

5.2 Measurement of the dynamic overhead

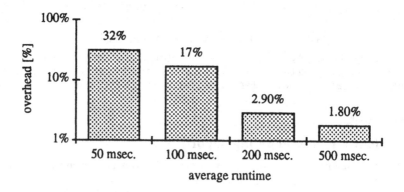

Fig. 7. Variation of execution times

For the measurements we used the multi-transputer system DAMP [BBM91], which is a multi-user system where the users allocate static partitions. More than 2000 measurments were made using up to 28 nodes of our DAMP system configured as tori. The user-applications were modeled by randomly created artificial dataflow graphs with up to 400 task nodes with varying execution times equally distributed in fixed intervalls. The mean execution times and the observed dynamic overhead are given in Fig. 7. Very short execution times of 50 msec cause an overhead of about 32%. Tasks with medium granularity with execution times of 0.5 sec can be scheduled with an overhead of approx. 1.8%.

Multiple user tasks on one PMU

In a second test, the usefulness of multiple simultaneous user tasks executed on each processor has been analysed. The advantage of such a feature could be denied because, on the one hand, the switching of the multiple simultaneous tasks constitutes a source of dynamic overhead. On the other hand, no advantage is expected here as compared with the alternative of executing the tasks strictly sequentially.

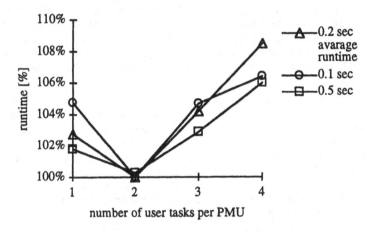

Fig. 8. Variation of the number of user tasks per PMU

In Fig. 8, we measured the execution time for a given example and configuration, and compared it with the best configuration *for this example*. We measured that two user tasks on each processor lead to minimum execution times. Further investigation disclosed the underlying reason as described below.

The allocation of tasks consumes a rather long time (in the test implementation at least some 10 msec) for performing the protocols and transmitting the data. However, most of this time the PMU is waiting idly (sometimes more than approx. 98% to 99%). If the processor has a second task it can use this time in a productive way.

Influence of statistical knowledge on the execution time

In many applications the execution times are not known exactly. One reason might be that the execution times are data-dependent. There arises the question as to the quality of the solutions for static and dynamic task scheduling under such restrictions.

To answer this question, the execution times of the tasks were replaced by estimates (random numbers). The estimates were exponentially distributed. The expectation of the random numbers was identical with the actual value. To these approximately 250 examples, a static optimum algorithm was applied. The computed results were about 4.6% weaker than the mathematical optimum produced by the same algorithm with exactly known execution times. I.e., a static scheduler cannot produce solutions for the examples given which are better than 104.6% of the minimum schedule length. On the other hand, the dynamic scheduler suggested computed solutions of these problems which were only about 3.4% weaker than the optimum. Due to these experiences we assume that the superiority of static task scheduling is limited to special applications. Note that, different to the actual measurements given in the sections above, these numbers are computed with a simulation tool.

6 Conclusion

Agency Scheduling is a model permitting the representation of a wide variety of dynamic task scheduling algorithms including centralized and fully distributed ones as well as intermediate forms. The model consists of eight almost independent components for which examples are given. An extreme case of the model is the fully distributed "Team Scheduling" algorithm. The model has been implemented and tested using the multi-transputer system DAMP [BBM91]. Measurements with artificial loads have shown that Agency Scheduling is suitable for a wide variety of applications. For medium to large grain dataflow graphs with execution times greater than a few hundred milliseconds the measured overhead is less than 5 %.

As described in [BMM94], we have extended our scheduling system by means for fault tolerance. The basic idea is that the input data is always available on two different PMUs: the PMU which executes the task and that one which keeps the so called checkpoints. After a failure of one processor, the corresponding tasks can be easily restarted by the processors which store the checkpoints. If the checkpoints are replicated again after a failure, a subsequent second failure can be tolerated as well and fail-soft behaviour is achieved. The decision which processor gets which checkpoint under the restriction of limited memory capacity leads to a so called "Bin-Packing-Problem", which in itself is anything but trivial [CGJ87]. In our scheduling system we have tackled this problem by using a simple heuristic. Details of the fault-tolerant algorithm are given in [BMM94].

The measurements presented in this paper are based on automatically created artificial loads to cover a wide variety of load characteristics. Further measurements using real applications are currently under way. For the near future we plan to spend more effort in studying and comparing the performance of our scheduling scheme with others. Furthermore we plan to develop a graphical user environment. It will not only be used to aid the user in developing his application but will also supply help for debugging and performance evaluation. Therefor we want to use the monitoring tool DELTA-T [MaO92] also developed at our institute.

Acknowledgement

The authors wish to thank Prof. Dr. E. Maehle for his continuous support of this work.

References

[BBM91] Andreas Bauch, Reinhold Braam, Erik Maehle: DAMP - A Dynamic Reconfigurable Multiprocessor System With a Distributed Switching Network. In A. Bode (Ed.): Distributed Memory Computing. Lecture Notes in Computer Sciences, Vol. 487, Springer-Verlag 1991, pp. 495-504.

[BMM94]   Andreas Bauch, Erik Maehle, Franz-Josef Markus: A Distributed Algorithm for Fault-Tolerant Dynamic Task Scheduling. Proc. 1994 EUROMICRO Workshop on Parallel and Distributed Processing, Malaga, IEEE Computer Society Press 1994, pp. 309 - 316

[Bok87]   Shahid H. Bokhari: Assignment Problems in Parallel and Distributed Computing. Kluwer Academic Publishers 1987.

[CaK88]   Thomas L. Casavant and Jon G. Kuhl: A Taxonomy of Scheduling in General-Purpose Distributed Computing Systems. IEEE Trans. on Software Engineering, Vol. 14, No. 2, February 1988, pp. 141-154.

[CGJ87]   E. G. Coffman, Jr. and M. R. Garey, D. S. Johnson: Bin Packing with Divisible Item Sizes. Journal of Complexity 3, 1987, pp. 406-428

[CHL80]   Wesley W. Chu, Leslie J. Holloway, Min-Tsung Lan, Kemal Efe: Task Allocation in Distributed Data Processing. IEEE Computer, Nov. 80, pp. 57-69.

[Hwa93]   Kai Hwang: Advanced Computer Architecture. Mc Graw Hill, 1993.

[KaN84]   Hironori Kasahara, Seinosuke Narita: Practical Multiprocessor Scheduling Algorithms for Efficient Parallel Processing. IEEE Trans. on Computers, Vol. C-33, No. 11, Nov. 1984, pp. 1023-1029.

[LeA87]   Soo-Young Lee, J. K. Aggarwal: A Mapping Strategy for Parallel Processing. IEEE Trans. on Computers, Vol. C-36, No. 4, April 1987, pp. 433-442.

[Lo88]   Virginia Mary Lo: Heuristic Algorithms for Task Assignment in Distributed Systems. IEEE Trans. on Computers, Vol. C-37, Nov. 1988, pp. 1384-1397.

[LüL93]   Reinhard Lüling, Burkhard Monien: A Dynamic Distributed Load Balancing Algorithm with Provable Good Performance, Proc. of the 5th ACM Symposium on Parallel Algorithms and Architectures (SPAA '93), 1993, pp. 164-173

[MaO92]   Erik Maehle, Wolfgang Obelöer: DELTA-T: A User Transparent Software-Monitoring Tool for Multi-Transputer Systems. Proc. EUROMICRO 92, Microprocessing and Microprogramming, 1992, Vol. 32, pp. 245-252

[MaL86]   Pauline Markenscoff, Weikuo Liaw: Task Allocation Problems in Distributed Computer Systems. Proc. Conf. on Parallel Processing, Aug. 86, pp. 953-960.

[ReF87]   Daniel A. Reed, Richard M. Fujimoto: Multicomputer Networks - Message Based Parallel Processing. The MIT Press, Cambridge MA, 1987.

[RoM90]   Johann Rost, Erik Maehle: A Distributed Algorithm for Dynamic Task Scheduling. In H. Burkhart (Ed.): CONPAR 90 - VAPP IV. Proc. Joint Intl. Conf. on Vector and Parallel Processing, Zürich 1990, Lecture Notes in Computer Science, Vol. 457, Springer-Verlag, 1990, pp. 628-639.

[Ros94]   Johann Rost: Dynamic Distributed Task Scheduling on Multicomputers based on Dataflow Graphs. Ph.D. Thesis, University Paderborn, Germany, June 1994 (in German).

Fault Tolerance and SIMD Arrays

FFTs on a Linear SIMD Array

Mattias Johannesson

Department of EE, Image Processing Laboratory
Linköping University, S-581 83 Linköping
Sweden
E-mail: mattjo@isy.liu.se

Abstract

This paper describes different ways to implement one- and two-dimensional Fast Fourier Transforms, FFTs, on the linear SIMD architecture family VIP. VIP, Video Image Processor, is a bit-serial linear array SIMD architecture developed at the Image Processing Laboratory at Linköping University aiming at real-time low-level image and radar signal processing. Since the processing elements in the linear array only communicate via a shiftregister there is a large communication overhead to PEs far away in the array but we nevertheless obtain very fast FFT implementations. We show for instance that it is possible to build a 512-PE VIP system capable of Fourier transforming 512^2 images at video rate (25 frames per second).

1 The VIP Architecture

The VIP project started in the late eighties aiming at a row-parallel bit-serial SIMD architecture for real-time image processing [1]. The architecture has subsequently been upgraded for more demanding tasks such as radar signal processing, both ground-based, RVIP [2], [3], [5], and airborne, FVIP, [6], wood inspection [4], WVIP, and infra-red image processing, IVIP, [7].

Using an SIMD, Single Instruction Multiple Data, architecture means that all PEs execute the same instruction synchronously, but on different input data. To be able to perform different operations in different PEs we have now implemented a status register in each PE. This can be used to turn off PEs conditionally, thus allowing for a limited form of data dependent operations. The version presented here, called TVIP or Transform-VIP, is, apart from the status register, very similar to the RVIP/FVIP/ WVIP/IVIP architectures. The RVIP chip has been fabricated and tested by Ericsson Microwave Systems (formerly Ericsson Radar Electronics) during spring 1995.

1.1 TVIP Design

The layout of a 128 PE TVIP chip can be seen in Fig. 1. The layout of one Processing Element, PE, can be found in Fig. 2. Data I/O to each PE is performed via a 32x4 bit dual-ported (orthogonal) register. Read/write to/from the chip is performed asynchronous with the PE processing 32 bits in parallel. However, internally each PE can only read/write one bit at the time. Internal neighbor communication is performed on a 16-32 bit wide parallel shift register (parameter W). The internal SRAM memory can be up to 16 Kbits. With the VLSI technology available today we can implement 1-2 Kbit memory in each PE, but within 2-3 years we believe that up to 16 Kbit RAM/PE can be implemented in a reasonably sized VIP chip. An example of a VIP-similar PE array combined with a very large internal RAM can be found in [8].

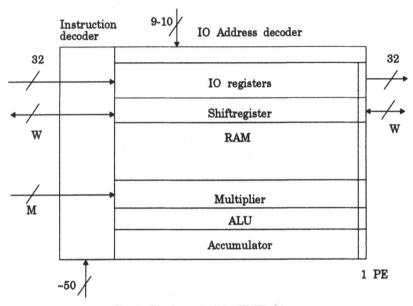

Fig. 1. The layout of the TVIP chip.

The computing unit in each PE consists of three tightly connected units, a serial-parallel multiplier, an ALU, and an accumulator. The serial-parallel multiplier has M parallel bits (16-32), and common coefficients can be loaded to all PEs by an external controller in one clock cycle. The output of the multiplier is connected to the $2M$ bit accumulator via the ALU. This makes it possible to perform a multiply and accumulate, MAC, operation in the same number of clock cycles as a multiplication. The performance for some typical b by b-bit operations are shown in Table 1 (We use the notation that complex data with the precision p has $b = 2p$ bits). The RAM operand can be exchanged for any other register on the PE bus, i.e. the IO register or the shiftregister with the same performance. The possible extension of the shiftregister and the multiplier to 32-bits is to faciliate the use of 32-bit integer precision.

Table 1.

Operation	Op 1	Result	Cycles
Addition,	Acc	Acc	b+1
Addition	RAM	RAM	3b+2
Multiplication/MAC, bxb -> 2b	External	Acc	2b+1
Multiplication/MAC, bxb -> 2b	RAM	Acc	3b
Complex Multiplication	External	RAM	10p+4

Table 1.

Operation	Op 1	Result	Cycles
Complex MAC	RAM	RAM	16p
Butterfly	RAM	RAM	24p
Multiplex	Acc	Acc	p+1
Multiplex	RAM	RAM	3p+1

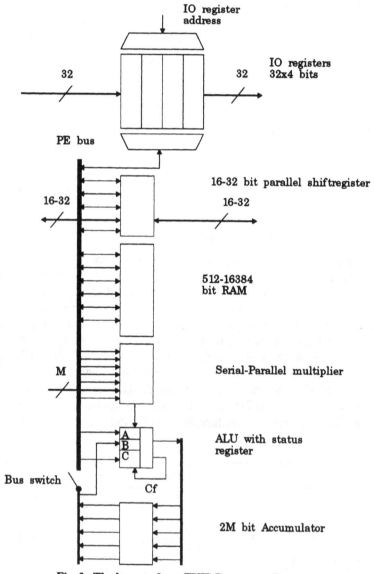

Fig. 2. The layout of one TVIP Processing Element.

1.2 System Design

Each TVIP chip will consist of 128 PEs and four of those chips and one local controller will be mounted inside one Multi Chip Module, MCM, approximately 2"x2" in size [3]. Thus, each module will have 512 PEs and it will run at a clock frequency of 50 MHz. If more than 512 PEs are needed several modules can be connected in series. In an RVIP system for instance, up to 4096 PEs are connected in series [3]. The IO and shift register frequency however, is limited to 25 MHz to avoid clock skew problems between modules. Thus the relative shift clock, R, is two.

2 Fourier Transforms

Fourier transforms are common in signal processing. We studied different ways to implement DFT/FFT algorithms on VIP. A DFT algorithm will have at least $O(N)$ complexity on a linear N-PE array, but with an FFT algorithm we should theoretically be able to obtain $O(logN)$ performance.

2.1 The Discrete Fourier Transform

The discrete Fourier transform, DFT, of a 1D discrete signal sampled from 0 to $N-1$ is defined as

$$F(u) = \frac{1}{N}\sum_{x=0}^{N-1} f(x)e^{\frac{-i2\pi ux}{N}} = \frac{1}{N}\sum_{x=0}^{N-1} f(x)\omega^{ux} \qquad (1)$$

where the phase factor ω^j is called twiddle factor. The twiddle factor for each fourier component $F(u)$ rotates with a different frequency, and any part of the signal $f(x)$ having that same frequency will be collected in that fourier component. Since the computation of each of the N fourier components requires N complex multiplications the complexity of the algorithm is $O(N^2)$. However, the DFT can be computed with $O(NlogN)$ complexity with a technique called Fast Fourier Transform, FFT [10]. The FFT exploits the fact that an N-point DFT can be computed with $O(N)$ operations from two $N/2$ long DFTs on the original data. This subdivision can then be carried out recursively $logN$ steps until only $N/2$ DFTs of the length 2 remains (if N is an even power of 2). This FFT technique is called decimation-in-time radix 2.

A 2-point FFT is computed by a so called butterfly operation

$$A_{i+1} = A_i + B_i\omega(i) \qquad (2)$$

$$B_{i+1} = A_i - B_i\omega(i) \qquad (3)$$

where $\omega(i)$ is the twiddle factor for butterfly i. Thus, each butterfly is composed of one complex multiplication and 2 complex additions and the whole FFT algorithm can be computed with $N/2*logN$ complex multiplications and $NlogN$ complex additions/subtractions. A 2D Fourier transform is computed by taking one 1D transform in each direction.

If the input data is real, the resulting transform is an even function, and if input data is imaginary the resulting transform is an odd function. This can be exploited by computing the transform of two real-valued sequences in one transform, setting one as the real part and one as the imaginary part of the input, and then separating them into the odd and even parts afterwards.

3 1D FFTs in VIP

We have studied three different implementations, one where the number of PEs is equal to N, e.g. VIP is used for row parallel processing and the row-wise FFT is only one part of the total algorithm [6]. One where the number of PEs is equal to $N/2$. The use of only $N/2$ PEs is more effective than N since each layer contains $N/2$ butterflies. Actually, if we have an N PE array and wish to compute two N long FFTs we will show that it is much more effective to compute them in parallel, each using half of the array, than one after the other. Finally we also studied where an FFT is computed within one VIP PE. To compute one FFT within each PE can be desirable if 2D FFTs are computed but it requires extensive internal RAM. Of course it is also possible to use $N/4$, $N/8$.. PEs but that generalization will not be treated here.

4 FFTs in N PEs

First we study the case where each PE is used to compute one Fourier component, i.e. each PE computes "half" of a butterfly operation in each layer. The computation of a butterfly is $A+/-\omega^j$, but in our implementation each PE computes $A+B\omega^j$ and the "other half" of the butterfly is computed in an other PE with the phase ω^j rotated 180°, giving $A-B\omega^j$. If the input data is organized in bit reversed order the result will be in correct order.

The VIP FFT implementation can be broken down into four separate parts: bit-reverse sorting the input data, shifting data to the correct PEs before each butterfly layer, distributing twiddle factors ω^j and computing $A+B\omega^j$, see Fig. 3.

4.1 Bit-reverse Sorting Data

The FFT operates on data which are sorted in bit-reverse order and produces output in correct order (or vice versa). If the VIP array starts with the FFT operation the input can be written into the array bit-reversed since the IO registers can be addressed arbitrary. Otherwise the sorting operation must be done within the VIP array. The bit-reverse operation is performed by shifting data and multiplexing the shifted data with mask patterns. For instance, if $N = 16$ five different shift lengths, 0,2,5,7,9 are needed. The maximum shift lengths must be less than N in each direction. If the number of non-zero shift-lengths are D and the data length b the number of clock cycles needed for the operation is approximately

$$C_{BR} = 2b(D+2) + 2R \cdot N\left\lceil \frac{b}{W} \right\rceil \qquad (4)$$

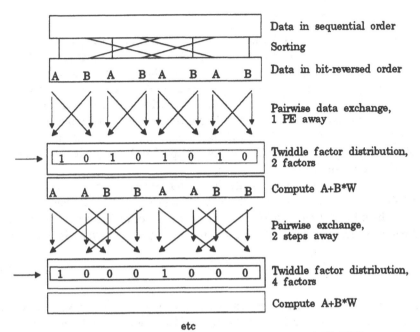

Data in sequential order

Sorting

Data in bit-reversed order

| A | B | A | B | A | B | A | B |

Pairwise data exchange,
1 PE away

Twiddle factor distribution,
2 factors

| 1 | 0 | 1 | 0 | 1 | 0 | 1 | 0 |

Compute A+B*W

| A | A | B | B | A | A | B | B |

Pairwise exchange,
2 steps away

Twiddle factor distribution,
4 factors

| 1 | 0 | 0 | 0 | 1 | 0 | 0 | 0 |

Compute A+B*W

etc

Fig. 3. The FFT algorithm implementation on an N-PE TVIP.

The number of shift lengths, D, can be computed using the formula

$$D = \frac{3^{\left\lfloor \frac{\log N}{2} \right\rfloor} - 1}{2} \qquad (5)$$

and $2D$ mask patterns stored in the internal RAM are required for the multiplexing.

4.2 Shifting Data to the Correct PEs

In a shift operation before each butterfly layer pairs of PEs exchange data. This is done with a double shift and multiplex operation to ensure that each PE has the correct A and B. Each Mux operation requires $3b$ cycles. The shift lengths needed to get the data to the correct PE are 1,2, 4, up to $N/2$ long, which means that a total of less than N shifts in each direction is needed. Thus, the number of cycles needed to complete the data shifting for an N-point FFT is approximately

$$C_S = 6b \log N + 2R \cdot N \left\lceil \frac{b}{W} \right\rceil \qquad (6)$$

One mask pattern is needed for each butterfly layer, which means that $\log N$ patterns are required for an N point FFT.

4.3 Distributing Twiddle Factors

The twiddle factors can be distributed to the PEs in at least two ways, via the IO register or via the parallel load port on the multiplier. The reason that the multiplier is feasible to use comes from the fact that many PEs share the same coefficient. In the first layer only two different twiddle factors occur, in the second there are four and so on. The use of the multiplier port is even more attractive when a large array is used to compute several smaller FFTs in parallel because then the twiddle factors are common for all the parallel Fourier transforms in the array [6]. Another feature is that twiddle factors input when needed do not occupy $b\log N$ bits of RAM which they would if input via the IO register.

Using the parallel register of the multiplier for IO we need approximately $3N$ cycles to distribute one unique word to each PE (a mask bit is input to the status register to control which PE that receives the data). The number of different twiddle factors in each butterfly layer is 2,4 up to N, and thus the total number of cycles is less than

$$ C_{TW} = 2\left(3N\left\lceil \frac{b}{M} \right\rceil + b\log N \right) \tag{7} $$

A mask pattern is needed for each butterfly layer giving $\log N$ masks to determine which PE is receiving the current twiddle factor. The mask in each layer can then easily be moved one step with the shiftregister to obtain the next PE mask in the same layer, see Fig. 3.

4.4 Half Butterfly Computation

The operation in each PE is "half" of a butterfly operation which is a complex MAC operation. The twiddle factors have at the most M bit precision, where M is the size of the parallel part of the multiplier. Thus the complexity for all half butterfly operations is approximately

$$ C_{BF} = 16p\log N = 8b\log N \tag{8} $$

4.5 DFT Computations

As a measurement of the FFT efficiency we compare it with a DFT implementation. In a DFT operation data must be shifted so that each PE access all input data. This can be implemented using the shiftregister. If the shiftregister can be rotating, i.e. the first and last PEs are connected, the communication can be made concurrent with the processing almost without any overhead.

The fastest way to obtain the N twiddle factors is to input the correct phase increment to each PE and store this in the RAM, and then the twiddle factor for the next operation is found as a multiplication of the previous twiddle factor and the phase increment. Thus each PE have a twiddle factor rotating with the correct speed, and this phase increment requires $14p$ cycles for each input data. Storing all twiddle factors in internal RAM instead requires bN bits.

If we compute a DFT we can in each PE use complex MACs requiring $16pN$ cycles to compute the fourier components.

Thus the optimum DFT performance is around $15bN$ clock cycles ($8bN$ if the all twiddle factors are stored internally).

4.6 Total FFT Complexity

The best case FFT complexity for an N PE array, with twiddle factors stored in RAM and bit-reversed input data, is

$$C_{FFT1} = 14b\log N + 2R \cdot N\left\lceil \frac{b}{W} \right\rceil \approx 8N + 450\log N \tag{9}$$

and the worst case FFT complexity with bit-reverse sorting and twiddle factor distribution is

$$C_{FFT2} = 12N + 16b\log N + 4R \cdot N\left\lceil \frac{b}{W} \right\rceil + 2b(D+4) \approx 28N + 510\log N \tag{10}$$

and the minimum DFT complexity is

$$C_{DFT} = 8Nb \approx 250N \tag{11}$$

If we study the approximative figures given above (for $b = 2*16$ and 16 bit shift register) we clearly see that the difference between the FFT and DFT implementations is that the FFT implementations have a small linear complexity and a large logarithmic ditto, whereas the DFT has a large linear complexity. The computational complexity of 1D FFT/DFTs of different lengths are shown in Table 2. For long transforms, when the linear term dominate, the complexity decrease significant with the 32-bit shiftregisters. All figures in the table are theoretical values but an implementation of a 64-point FFT on the RVIP architecture has been made. The result was close to the theoretical value. Thus we feel that our theoretical figures are valid.

Table 2.

Version	128	512	2048	8192
FFT1, W =16	4160	8128	21312	71360
FFT1, W =32	3648	6080	13120	38592
FFT2,W = 16	8128	21632	70848	259456
FFT2, W = 32	6336	14464	42176	144768
DFT, W = 32	81920	327680	1310720	5242880

Note that in the FFT when the computational complexity increase because of the long shift operations the twiddle factor generation complexity also increase. However, the shift operations can be performed concurrently with the twiddle factor distribution, and the total complexity might therefore be smaller than the sums indicated above.

5 FFTs in N/2 PEs

If we only use VIP for FFT computations, and therefore can optimize the array size to fit this problem, it is not optimal to use one PE for each fourier coefficient as above. Instead, since each butterfly layer consists of $N/2$ butterflies, it is more effective to use $N/2$ PEs. Since a butterfly operation requires $24p$ and a complex MAC, used in the N-PE implementation, $16p$ the PEs*cycles product decrease from $16pN\log N$ to $12pN\log N$. Also, since the array length is halved compared with an N-PE implementation the required shift lengths half. Furthermore, since the distribution of both $\omega(i)$ and $\omega^*(i)$ is avoided the twiddle factor distribution complexity is also halved.

The best case FFT complexity, with input data in correct order and twiddle factors in internal RAM (W and p is 16), is then approximately

$$C_{FFT1} = 20b\log N + RN\left\lceil \frac{b}{W} \right\rceil \approx 4N + 640\log N \qquad (12)$$

And the worst case FFT complexity, with twiddle factor distribution and bit-reverse sorting is

$$C_{FFT2} \approx 16N + 700\log N \qquad (13)$$

Actually the complexities are slightly less, the first layer requires no shift and no multiplication since the first twiddle factor is 1. We see that compared with the equations presented for the N PE case the logarithmic complexity is larger but the linear complexity smaller. In Table 3 we see the corresponding figures for the same transforms as above. Note however, that here we use half as many PEs as in the previous table, and to be able to do a fair comparison the numbers in Table 3 should be *divided* by two.

Table 3.

VIP FFT N/2	128	512	2048	8192
FFT1, W = 16	4544	7360	14784	40640
FFT1, W = 32	4288	6336	10688	24256
FFT2, W = 16	7008	15456	43488	146400
FFT 2, W = 32	6112	11872	29152	89056

A comparison of 1D FFT execution time in milliseconds on a 8192 PE VIP array and a 2D 8192 PE MasPar-1 array [9] can be found in Table 4.

Table 4.

FFT size	64	512	8192	16384
MasPar	2.5	4	5.4	6.1
VIP	0.15	0.25	1	1.6

The data precision is 32 bits and the total number of data points used is always 16384. We see that the VIP array perform 4-16 times better (observe however that the VIP clock frequency is four times the MasPar's, but that the MasPar has 4-bit Processing elements. Also, the MP1 has only 16 PEs without internal memory on each chip).

6 FFTs in One PE

Of course it is also possible to compute an FFT within one PE. Then no communication overhead is required. The computations needed are $(N/2)\log N$ butterflies, and since the twiddle factors can be input direct to the multiplier the butterfly complexity is $20p$. Thus, the total complexity is approximately $5bN\log N$. This seems very large, but since we compute in a linear array each PE computes its own transform, and if we have N PEs the complexity for each transform is $5b\log N$. The internal memory requirements are at least bN bits to store input data and intermediate results.

7 2D FFTs in TVIP

7.1 Without External Corner Turning

To compute a 2D FFT within one linear array we first compute a transform along the PEs and then after computing N such and storing the results internally, each PE computes its own transform. If we assume that the input (image) data is real-valued we know that the 2D FFT result is Hermitian (has conjugate symmetry) [10], i.e.

$$F(u, v) = F^*(-u, -v) = F^*(N-u, N-v) \qquad (14)$$

This means that we can use $N/2$ PEs to first compute N N-long x-axis transforms, and then compute $N/2$ N-long y-axis transforms by computing one transform within each PE and still obtain all the information in the 2D FFT. Thus, the total complexity for an $N{x}N$ 2D FFT in an $N/2$ TVIP array is

$$C_{2DFFT} = N\left(20b\log N + RN\left\lceil\frac{b}{W}\right\rceil\right) + N5b\log N \approx 800N\log N + 4N^2 \qquad (15)$$

If we compute 512^2 transforms with 16 bit precision (W = 32) in a 256 PE array each transform requires approximately 80 ms, and if we assume that we have a 512 PE module, 2 512^2 transforms in 80 ms. If we use 2 MCM TVIP modules with a total of 1024 PEs it is thus possible to perform 2-dimensional fourier transforms in video rate (50 Hz frame rate) if the input sequence is divided between the modules. However, the realization of a TVIP chip with 16 Kbit SRAM/PE (which is required for 512^2 transforms) is not feasible with the current VLSI technology.

The MGAP is capable of computing a 32x32 2D FFT in a 32x32 PE array in 2.15 ms [11], a 16 PE TVIP array would require 2 ms for the same task. If we use the same amount of PEs the effective 32x32 FFT time can be as low as 0.03 ms in a TVIP.

7.2 With External Corner Turning

Another way of implementing 2D FFTs in TVIP is to pipeline 2 arrays with a corner turning between them. Thus, the first array can compute the x-axis transforms and the second the y-axis transforms. Then it is easy to exploit real valued input data and conjugate symmetry, and thus halving the work loads for the arrays. The system layout can be seen in Fig. 4. We see that one N-PE array is used for the odd-even transformation and two N/2 PE arrays for the fourier transforms. Now, if we use one N-PE array where the first N/2 PEs compute x-axis transforms and the second y-axis transforms the same array can be used for all the processing. Thus, the processing needed for each image row is approximately $0.5(4N+640logN+200) = 2N+320logN$ since only N/2 transforms need to be computed in each direction. If we compute 512^2 transforms with 16 bit precision (W=32) in a 512 PE array each image row requires 65 μs (video rate is 64 μs) and the image time is 33 ms. Since 512^2 frame rates usually are around 25 Hz this is faster than videorate. Furthermore it is not necessary to implement chip with 16 Kbit internal RAM memory, but on the other hand several external VRAMs are required for the corner turning.

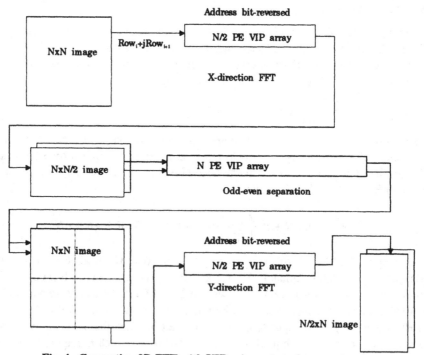

Fig. 4. Computing 2D FFT with VIP using external corner turning.

8 Conclusions and Discussion

We have shown that the VIP architecture is very well suited for 1D and 2D FFT computations, and the performance figures given comparable to or better than other SIMD array implementations [9], [11]. We show that a 512 PE array is capable of transforming 512^2 images at a frame rate of above 30 Hz. A study of the width of the shiftregister showed that a wider register gives very large performance gain for long transforms.

Of course only performing FFTs on data is rather pointless, but the VIP architecture has capacity to also perform many low level signal processing tasks [1]. A pipelined system with three TVIP arrays, one performing forward FFTs, one processing data in the fourier domain and one inverse transforming is one possible system layout. In [6] one dimensional fourier transforms of different lengths are implemented as one step of a complex 2D radar algorithm implemented on a 13000 PE VIP array.

Acknowledgments

The author wish to thank Anders Åström and Per Ingelhag for valuable discussion and suggestions. This work has been supported by NUTEK.

References

[1] Åström A., Danielsson P-E., Chen K., Ingelhag P., Svensson S., *Videorate signal processing with PASIC and VIP*, Proc. Barnaimage '91, Barcelona, Spain, September, 1991.

[2] Ingelhag P., Åström A., Ehlersson T., *Radar Signal Processing Using A 512-Processor Array Chip*, Proc. of the International Conference on Digital Signal Processing, Florens, 1991.

[3] Johannesson M., Åström A., Ingelhag P., *The RVIP Image Processing Array*, Proc. of CAMP '93, New Orleans, 1993.

[4] Hall M., Åström A., *High speed wood inspection using a parallel VLSI architecture*, Proc of 3rd International Workshop on Algorithms and Parallel VLSI Architectures, Leuven, Belgium, August, 1994.

[5] Arvidsson R., *Massively parallel SIMD processor for search radar signal processing*, Proc of RADAR '94, Paris, 1994.

[6] Åström A., Johannesson M., Edman A., Ehlersson T., Näsström U., Lyckegård B., *An Implementation Study of Airborne Medium PRF Doppler Radar Signal Processing on a Massively Parallel SIMD processor architecture*, To appear in RADAR '95, Washington, 1995.

[7] Åström A., Isaksson F., *Real-time Geometric Distorsion Correction and Image Processing on the 1D SIMD architecture IVIP*, Proc of MVA 1994, Kawasaki, 1994.

[8] Yamashita M. et. al., *A 3.84 GIPS Integrated Memory Array Processor with 64 Processing Elements and a 2-Mb SRAM*, IEEE Journal of solid state circuits, Vol 29, No 11, 1994.

[9] Munthe-Kaas H., *Superparallel FFTS*, Siam J. Sci. Comput, Vol 14, No 2, pp. 349-367, March 1993.

[10] Bracewell R.N., *The fourier transform and its applications*, McGraw-Hill, 1986.

[11] Owens R.M. et. al., *Computer Vision on the MGAP*, Proc of CAMP'93, New Orleans, 1993.

Tolerating Faults in Faulty Hypercubes Using Maximal Fault-Free Subcube-Ring

Jang-Ping Sheu and Yuh-Shyan Chen

Department of Computer Science and Information Engineering
National Central University, Chung-Li 32054, TAIWAN
sheujp@mbox.ee.ncu.edu.tw

Abstract. In this paper, we present a reconfiguration approach to identify the maximal fault-free subcube-ring for tolerating faults in faulty hypercubes. The fault-free subcube-ring is connected by a ring of fault-free subcubes with dilation 3. By exploiting the size of fault-free subcubes as large as possible, the maximal fault-free subcube-ring with higher processor utilization is obtained. Using this approach, we can tolerate more than n faults in n-dimensional hypercubes. To demonstrate the fault-tolerant capability of our approach, we implement a fault-tolerant matrix-multiplication algorithms on the nCUBE/2E hypercube machine with 32 processors. The simulation results show that our reconfiguration approach has low performance slowdown and high processor utilization.

1 Introduction

The n-dimensional hypercube (n-cube) is one of the most popular interconnection topologies for parallel computers. As the size of the hypercube system increases, fault tolerance has become an important issue for such a large system to continue operations after failure of one or more processors/links. In this paper, we study how algorithms that are originally designed for fault-free hypercubes can be implemented on hypercubes that contain any number of faults with reasonable slowdown. To measure the efficiency of processor utilization, several researchers use *slowdown* ratio [4] [10], which is the execution time in the faulty n-cube divided by its time requirement in the fault-free hypercube. The lower the *slowdown* ratio is, the higher the processor utilization of system obtains.

Most of the recently proposed fault-tolerant strategies address the issue of *reconfiguration* once the faulty processors are identified. These reconfiguration strategies have been developed [4] [5] [6] [7] [9] without adding any redundancy to the desired architecture. They attempt to mask the effects of faults by using the healthy part of the hypercube architecture. One approach of the reconfiguration strategies is to identify the *largest fault-free subcube* and use the subcube to emulate the entire hypercube [5]. However, this approach results in a tremendous underutilization of resource and high degree of performance slowdown. A different but related approach, which is to identify the *maximal incomplete subcube*, is proposed by Chen and Tzeng [6] by using a *reject-region* concept.

An effective approach, namely the *free dimension*, is presented by Raghavendra, Yang, and Tien [7] to achieve the fault tolerance in a faulty n-cube. Using free dimension approach [10], simulation of any SIMD algorithm on faulty n-cube takes 2 slowdown ratio of computation and 4 slowdown ratio of communication when the number of faulty nodes is no more than $\lceil \frac{n}{2} \rceil$. Sheu, Chen, and Chang [9] proposed a subcube partitioning method for designing a fault-tolerant sorting algorithm that can tolerate at most n - 1 faulty processors on n-dimensional hypercubes. However, all of these algorithms only can tolerate at most n - 1 faulty processors.

Recently, Bruck, Cypher, and Soroker [4] proposed a technique in n-cube using the *subcube-partitioning* approach. In the approach, any regular algorithm can be implemented on an n-cube that has fewer than n faults with slowdown ratios of 2 for computation and 4 for communication. Moreover, this is the first result showing that an n-cube can tolerate more than n arbitrarily placed faults with a constant factor slowdown. Developing an efficient reconfiguration strategy, which can tolerate arbitrarily number of faulty nodes and reduce the performance slowdown for any regular algorithms, is consequently the purpose of our study. Our fault model, similar to [4], is defined as follows. All faults including node/link faults are permanent. We only consider node faults and an edge fault is assumed that one of the nodes incident upon it is faulty. We also assume that faulty nodes can neither perform calculations nor route data.

In this paper, we firstly present a recognition algorithm which can recognize all possible largest fault-free subcubes in faulty hypercubes. Each fault-free subcube with same size is treated as a processing unit. Our reconfiguration approach identifies the *fault-free subcube-ring* which is constructed by a ring of these processing units with dilation 3 at most. Based on these recognized fault-free subcubes, we propose an efficient algorithm to identify the maximal fault-free subcube-ring. For illustrating the fault-tolerant capability of our approach, we implement a fault-tolerant matrix-multiplication algorithm on the nCUBE/2E hypercube machines with 32 processors. If the number of faults is less than n the *slowdown* ratio is smaller than 2. This is due to the reason that the processor utilization of our approach is larger than 50%. The average *slowdown* ratio of our fault-tolerant scheme is smaller than 2.5 as long as number of faults $\leq 2^{n-2}$.

2 Preliminary

Let Q_n be n-cube which consists of 2^n nodes with each node representing a processor and each edge between two nodes in Q_n corresponding to a communication link between two processors. Every node b has address $b_n b_{n-1} \cdots b_1$ with $b_i \in \{0, 1\}$, $1 \leq i \leq n$, where b_i is called the i-th bit (also called dimension i) of the address. Each m-subcube Q_m has a unique address $x_n x_{n-1} \cdots x_1$ with $x_i \in \{0, 1, *\}$, $1 \leq i \leq n$, where exactly m bits take the value $*$, ($*$ is a don't care symbol). For example, $*^{n-1}0$ and $*^{n-1}1$ denote the two $(n-1)$-subcubes separated by dimension 1, where $*^i$ stands for i consecutive $*$'s.

Now we introduce the concept of *prime-subcube* [5]. Let F denote a set of faulty nodes in a faulty n-cube. Given a nonfaulty node P, a prime-subcube with respect to a nonfaulty node P is a fault-free subcube which involves P but is not

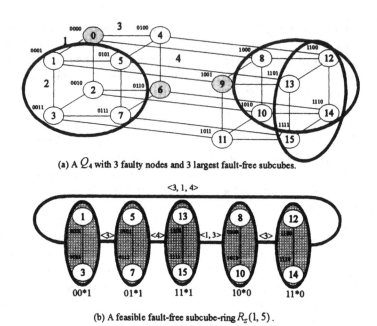

(a) A Q_4 with 3 faulty nodes and 3 largest fault-free subcubes.

(b) A feasible fault-free subcube-ring $R_s(1, 5)$.

Fig. 1. A feasible fault-free subcube-ring $R_s(1,5)$ from a 4-cube with 3 faulty nodes.

contained entirely in any other fault-free subcube involving P, where $P \in Q_n - F$. Note that there may be more than one prime-subcube corresponding to P. For example, given a faulty 4-cube with set $F = \{0000, 0110, 1001\}$ as shown in Fig. 1(a), there exists one prime-subcube 0**1 with respect to node 0001 and 3 prime-subcubes *10*, 1**0, and 11** with respect to node 1100. The work presented here is different from those carried out in [5] in the sense that all maximum fault-free subcubes can be recognized by our algorithm and each healthy node only keeps the status of its neighboring nodes. In our algorithm, we will recognize all prime-subcubes for each healthy node P. Our reconfiguration scheme with more processor utilization can be identified from these recognized prime-subcubes. Assume there exists a sequence of k disjoint fault-free m-subcubes $[Q_m^1, Q_m^2, \cdots, Q_m^k]$. Sequence $[Q_m^1, Q_m^2, \cdots, Q_m^k]$ is selected from set of prime-subcubes which are collected from all prime-subcubes of each healthy node. Each m-subcube is treated as a processing unit and we reconfigure these processing units into a ring with dilation 3 at most, namely *fault-free subcube-ring* $R_s(m, k)$, which is defined as follows.

Definition 1. Let $R_s(m, k)$ be a sequence pair $([Q_m^1, Q_m^2, \cdots, Q_m^k], [j_1, j_2, \cdots, j_{k-1}, j_k])$ to denote a feasible fault-free subcube-ring, where $[Q_m^1, Q_m^2, \cdots, Q_m^k]$ is a sequence of k disjoint fault-free m-subcubes and $[j_1, j_2, \ldots, j_{k-1}, j_k]$ is a sequence of dimension sequences, for each dimension sequence $j_i = <d_1^i, \cdots, d_w^i>$, $d_w^i \in \{1, 2, \cdots, n\}$, $1 \le w \le 3$, and $1 \le i \le k$. The $R_s(m, k)$ is constructed by each node in Q_m^i connects to a node in $Q_m^{(i \bmod k)+1}$ along dimensions $d_1^i, \cdots, d_w^i$. Therefore,

$$Q_m^1 \xleftrightarrow{j_1} Q_m^2 \xleftrightarrow{j_2} Q_m^3 \xleftrightarrow{j_3} \cdots Q_m^{k-1} \xleftrightarrow{j_{k-1}} Q_m^k \xleftrightarrow{j_k} Q_m^1.$$

If the connection $Q_m^k \xleftrightarrow{j_k} Q_m^1$ does not exist, then a fault-free subcube-chain, denoted by $C_s(m, k)$, is constructed. For example, a $R_s(1,5) = 00*1 \xleftrightarrow{<3>} 01*1 \xleftrightarrow{<4>} 11*1 \xleftrightarrow{<1,3>} 10*0 \xleftrightarrow{<3>} 11*0 \xleftrightarrow{<3,1,4>} 00*1$ is constructed in Fig. 1(b).

3 Identifying the Maximal Fault-Free Subcube-Ring

3.1 Recognizing the prime-subcubes

Without loss of generality, we focus on recognizing a set of prime-subcube with respect to a given node P, where $P \in Q_n - F$. Assume that the i-dimensional neighboring node of P is P_i', where $1 \le i \le n$. Before running our recognition algorithm, nonfaulty node P keeps a variable $\gamma = (\gamma_n, \gamma_{n-1} \cdots, \gamma_1)$ to record the status of its i-dimensional neighboring node P_i'; if P_i' is nonfaulty then set bit $\gamma_i = 1$; else set bit $\gamma_i = 0$, for all $1 \le i \le n$. Assume that the address of node P is $x_n x_{n-1} \cdots x_{i+1} x_i \cdots x_1$ and address of node P_i' is $x_n x_{n-1} \cdots x_{i+1} \overline{x}_i \cdots x_1$, where $x_i \in \{0,1\}$ and $1 \le i \le n$. Let H_i^P represent an i-subcube whose address is $x_n x_{n-1} \cdots x_{i+1} *^i$. We denote $\mho_{H_i^P}$ as a set of prime-subcube with respect to node P and subcube H_i^P such that each subcube in set $\mho_{H_i^P}$ involving P is not contained entirely in part of any other fault-free subcube of H_i^P. Similarly, $\mho_{H_i^{P'}}$ is the set of prime-subcube with respect to node P_i' and subcube $H_i^{P'}$, where $1 \le i \le n$. As a consequence, $\mho_{H_n^P}$ is the set of prime-subcube with respect to node P and Q_n. As an example, consider a faulty hypercube Q_3 with $F = \{000\}$ as shown in Fig. 2. For a given node P is 011 and its 2-dimensional neighboring node P_2' is 001. Subcube H_2^{011} is $0**$ and sets $\mho_{H_2^{011}}$ and $\mho_{H_2^{001}}$ are $\{01*, 0*1\}$ and $\{0*1\}$, respectively.

Our recognizing prime-subcube (RPS) algorithm is an ASCEND algorithm to recursively concatenate smaller healthy subcubes into larger healthy subcube. Initially, sets of $\mho_{H_0^P}$ and $\mho_{H_0^{P'}}$ are the respective addresses of node P and P_i'. The set $\mho_{H_i^P}$ is derived by the $SC(\mho_{H_{i-1}^P}, \mho_{H_{i-1}^{P'}})$ (subcube-concatenation or SC) operation. The $SC(\mho_{H_{i-1}^P}, \mho_{H_{i-1}^{P'}})$ operation is defined here to repeatedly recognize $\mho_{H_i^P}$, where i is ranging from 1 to n. The SC operation is divided into two phases as described in what follows.

In phase I, if node P_i' is fault-free, then node P sends its set $\mho_{H_{i-1}^P}$ to node P_i' and receives a set $\mho_{H_{i-1}^{P'}}$ from node P_i'. After this phase, node P contains sets $\mho_{H_{i-1}^P}$ and $\mho_{H_{i-1}^{P'}}$ and then continue to perform phase II of SC operation. If node P_i' is a faulty node, then set $\mho_{H_i^P}$ to be $\mho_{H_{i-1}^P}$ and skip the phase II of SC operation.

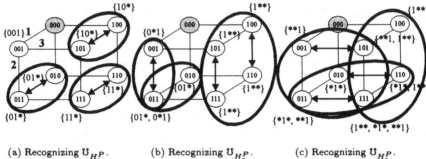

(a) Recognizing $\mho_{H_1^P}$.   (b) Recognizing $\mho_{H_2^P}$.   (c) Recognizing $\mho_{H_3^P}$.

Fig. 2. Recognizing prime-subcubes on a 3-cube with faulty node 000.

In phase II, each node P performs the *bit-concatenation* (BC) operation $\alpha = \oplus(x, y)$ for each element $x = b_n b_{n-1} \cdots b_1 \in \mho_{H_{i-1}^P}$, $y = b'_n b'_{n-1} \cdots b'_1 \in \mho_{H_{i-1}^{P'}}$ to recognize a new set $\mho_{H_i^P}$ with $\alpha = z_n z_{n-1} \cdots z_1$. The $\oplus$ is a bitwise operator on each pair of b_k and b'_k, i.e., $z_k = b_k \oplus b'_k$ for $1 \leq k \leq n$. The bit operation $\oplus$ is divided into three cases and defined as follows. In case 1, it yields 0, 1, and $*$ if the bits b_k and b'_k have the same value "0", "1", "$*$". In case 2, if one of bits is "0" and another one is 1, then it yields $*$. In case 3, if one of bits is "$*$" and another one is "0" (or "1") then it restores to 0 (or 1). Let subcubes x and y are neighboring subcubes, symbol $x + y$ denotes the union of subcubes x and y and all links connecting x and y.

Proposition 2. *If subcubes $x \in \mho_{H_{i-1}^P}$ and $y \in \mho_{H_{i-1}^{P'}}$ are two disjoint neighboring subcubes then subcube $\oplus(x, y)$ is the prime-subcube containing node P and belongs to $x + y$.*

Proposition 3. *If subcubes a and b are not disjoint then subcube $\oplus(a, b)$ is the intersection subcube of subcubes a and b.*

If a is a subcube of b then equation $a = \oplus(a, b)$ holds. For each $x \in \mho_{H_{i-1}^P}$ and $y \in \mho_{H_{i-1}^{P'}}$, subcubes x and y are two disjoint neighboring subcubes and let $\alpha = \oplus(x, y)$, then set $\mho_{H_i^P}$ is recognized as follows.

$$\mho_{H_i^P} = \begin{cases} \mho_{H_i^P} \cup \alpha & \text{if } x = \oplus(x, \alpha) \text{ and } \alpha \notin \mho_{H_i^P} \\ \mho_{H_i^P} \cup x \cup \alpha & \text{if } x \neq \oplus(x, \alpha) \text{ and } x \notin \mho_{H_i^P} \text{ and } \alpha \notin \mho_{H_i^P} \end{cases}$$

After applying the two phases of $SC(\mho_{H_{i-1}^P}, \mho_{H_{i-1}^{P'}})$ operation for n times, in final, $\mho_{H_n^P}$ is a set of prime-subcube for node P. Recall above example, for a given pair of neighboring nodes P (011) and P'_3 (111), the set $\mho_{H_2^{011}}$ is {01*, 0*1} and $\mho_{H_2^{111}}$ is {1**}. To obtain $\mho_{H_3^{011}}$, the SC operation is performed on sets $\mho_{H_2^{011}} = \{01^*, 0^*1\}$ and $\mho_{H_2^{111}} = \{1^{**}\}$. Equations $\oplus(01^*, 1^{**}) = {}^*1^*$ and $\oplus(0^*1, 1^{**}) = {}^{**}1$ hold. Thus, $\mho_{H_3^{011}} = \{^*1^*, {}^{**}1\}$ is obtained. The total time cost of T_{RPS} is

$$T_{RPS} = O(2n \cdot \sum_{i=1}^{n} (C_{\lceil i/2 \rceil}^{i})^2) = O(n^2 \cdot N), \text{ where } N = 2^n.$$

Note that if $|F| \leq n$, the size of $\mho_{H_{i-1}^P}$ is $1 \leq |\mho_{H_{i-1}^P}| \leq i$. The total time cost of T_{RPS} becomes $O(2n \cdot \sum_{i=1}^{n} i^2) = O(n \frac{n(n+1)(2n+2)}{6}) = O(n^4)$.

3.2 Identifying the maximal fault-free subcube-ring $R_s(m, k)$

In this subsection, we show how to effectively identify the $R_s(m, k)$ from the prime-subcubes. The algorithm of identifying maximal fault-free subcube-ring $R_s(m, k)$ (IMSR) is divided into four steps. In the first three steps, each node will determine its fault-free subcube-ring individually.

In step 1, each nonfaulty node sends its own prime-subcubes to host node. It is assumed that the hypercube has one host which has a direct connection to each cube node, like the nCUBE/2E [1]. Then the host collects the prime-subcubes in set $\mho$ and broadcasts the set $\mho$ to each nonfaulty node.

In step 2, let's recall the description of maximal fault-free subcube-ring $R_s(m, k) = ([Q_m^1, Q_m^2, \cdots, Q_m^k, Q_m^1], [j_1, j_2, \ldots, j_{k-1}, j_k])$. For each subcube of $Q_m^1, Q_m^2, \cdots,$ and Q_m^k, we observe the fact that all '*' occur on the same positions of each subcube's address. In the following, we explain how to obtain these subcubes from set $\mho$. We firstly define the *subcube-sequence*. For given a subcube $x = b_n b_{n-1} \cdots b_i \cdots b_1$, $b_i = \{0, 1, *\}$ and $1 \leq i \leq n$, let *subcube-sequence* $S(x)$ be $<s_j, s_{j-1}, \ldots, s_1>$ such that $b_{s_k} = \{*\}$ and $b_h = \{0, 1\}$, where $1 \leq k \leq j$, $1 \leq h \leq n$, and $h \notin s_j, s_{j-1}, \ldots, s_1$. For given a subcube x, the *subcube-sequence* $S(x)$ is used to eliminate useless subcubes existed in set $\mho$. The useless subcube is one existed in set $\mho$ has different *subcube-sequence* $S(x)$.

Before describing how to select subcubes from set $\mho$, we must exploit a subcube and then use this subcube to eliminate useless subcubes in set $\mho$. Such subcube is called as the *bridge-subcube* throughout this work. We devoted to the basic aspects of finding the *bridge-subcube* in the following. For each nonfaulty node P, considering each pair of nodes P with $\mho_{H_n^P}$ and P_i' with $\mho_{H_n^{P'}}$, for $1 \leq i \leq n$, all pair of $x \in \mho_{H_n^P}$ and $y \in \mho_{H_n^{P'}}$ are selected to find the *bridge-subcube*. The *bridge-subcube* or $BS(x, y)$ is defined as follows. First, if x and y are not disjoint, then *bridge-subcube* is the intersection subcube of x and y; that is, $BS(x, y) = \oplus(x, y)$ by proposition 3. Second, if x and y are two disjoint neighboring subcubes, then $BS(x, y)$ is the intersection subcube of x and $\oplus(x, y)$; that is, $BS(x, y) = \oplus(x, \oplus(x, y))$, where $\oplus(x, y)$ is the prime-subcube containing node P and belong to $x + y$ by proposition 2. The criterion to determine $R_s(m, k)$ is the maximum value of m will be exploited and then to identify $R_s(m, k)$ with largest value of k. Thus, we select the maximum *bridge-subcube* which is denoted as MBS and satisfy the following max function.

$$MBS = \max_{x \in \mho_{H_n^P}, y \in \mho_{H_n^{P'}}} BS(x, y)$$

Since each subcube Q_m^i of $R_s(m, k)$ has the same *subcube-sequence* $S(Q_m^i)$, for $1 \leq i \leq k$, therefore, we only keep subcubes from set $\mho$ with same *subcube-sequence* $S(MBS)$. This work can be achieved as follows. All subcubes $x \in \mho$ with

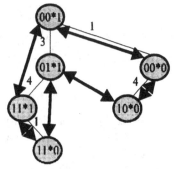

(a) Identifying a largest fault-free subcube-ring from a *subcube-tree T*.

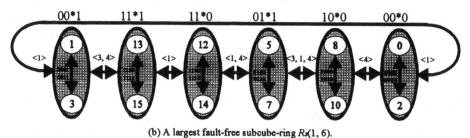

(b) A largest fault-free subcube-ring $R_s(1, 6)$.

Fig. 3. Identification of a largest fault-free subcube-ring $R_s(1, 6)$ from the *subcube-tree T*.

the same *subcube-sequence* $\mathcal{S}(MBS)$ are collected into set Ψ. If $|x| > m$, then subcube x is partitioned into m-subcubes with same *subcube-sequence* $\mathcal{S}(MBS)$ and collected into set Ψ.

In step 3, each node P constructs a *subcube-tree T* based on set Ψ and MBS. Fully using the whole *subcube-tree T*, a feasible fault-free subcube-ring with dilation 3 is identified. The *subcube-tree T* is constructed as follows. Each node of *subcube-tree T* is a subcube of set Ψ. The total nodes of *subcube-tree T* is at most 2^{n-m} and all subcubes in set Ψ construct T. The *subcube-tree T* is a Breadth-First-Searching spanning tree. Root of tree T is the selected MBS and branches of tree T represent the possible neighboring subcubes. Each node v of *subcube-tree T* probes each of the $n - m - 1$ neighboring m-subcubes. If the neighboring m-subcubes exist in set Ψ but not exist in *subcube-tree T*, node v connects to the m-subcube. Repeatedly performing above operations until no neighboring m-subcube can be further found, the *subcube-tree T* is constructed.

Continually, the whole *subcube-tree T* is used to identify the $R_s(m, k)$ for the purpose of maximizing the processor utilization. It is known that an N-node ring can be one-to-one embedded with dilation 3 in any connected N-node network [2]. A *subcube-tree T* is a connected network, as a consequence, a largest fault-free subcube-ring with dilation 3 can be identified. Consider a faulty hypercube Q_4 with $F = \{6, 9\}$. The *subcube-tree T* is constructed as shown in Fig. 3(a).

Fig. 3(a) also displays how to identify a largest fault-free subcube-ring $R_s(1,6)$ from the *subcube-tree* T. A $R_s(1,6)$ is constructed as shown in Fig. 3(b).

Finally, in step 4, the maximal fault-free subcube-ring $R_s(m,k)$ is determined among these largest fault-free subcube-ring. Each nonfaulty node $P \in Q_n - F$ has constructed its largest fault-free subcube-ring. Then each node P sends its largest fault-free subcube-ring to host node by the direct links. The host node determines the maximal fault-free subcube-ring $R_s(m,k)$ from the view of the processor utilization. If there exist more than one of largest fault-free subcube-ring with same processor utilization, host node randomly selects one from them. Finally, host node broadcasts the final $R_s(m,k)$ to each nonfaulty node P.

We now analyze the total time cost T_{IMSR} of algorithm IMSR. The maximum number of prime-subcubes with respect to a given nonfaulty node P is $C^n_{\lceil n/2 \rceil}$ [6], where $P \in Q_n - F$. From Stirling's approximation, $C^n_{\lceil n/2 \rceil} \approx \frac{2^n}{\sqrt{n}}$ for a large n [6]. In step 1, time $O(\frac{2^n}{\sqrt{n}} \times nN)$ is needed for each nonfaulty node sending its prime-subcubes to host node. In step 2, we take time $O(n^2 \times (\frac{2^n}{\sqrt{n}})^2)$ to determine the MBS. We takes time $O(\frac{2^n}{\sqrt{n}} \times nN)$ to keep elements in set $\mho$ with the same *subcube-sequence* $S(MBS)$. The total number of nodes in the *subcube-tree* T does not exceed 2^n and each probing step takes $O(n)$ to probe whether its children exist or not. The time cost of step 3 is $O(nN)$. In step 4, time cost $O(N)$, where $N = 2^n$, is needed. Thus, the total time cost of T_{IMSR} can be measured by the following equation.

$$T_{IMSR} = O(\frac{2^n}{\sqrt{n}} \times nN) + O(n^2 \times (\frac{2^n}{\sqrt{n}})^2) + O(\frac{2^n}{\sqrt{n}} \times nN) + O(nN) + O(N)$$
$$= O(n \times N^2)$$

The total time cost T of T_{RPS} and T_{IMSR} is $O(n^2 \times N) + O(n \times N^2) = O(n \times N^2)$.

4 Fault-Tolerant Matrix-Multiplication Algorithm

J. Berntsen [3] proposes a communication efficient matrix multiplication algorithm on n-cube. The n-cube includes a two-dimensional mesh interconnect with wrap around which is mapped by a binary Gray code. The matrix multiplication $C = A * B$ is performed where C, A, and B are full $N \times N$ matrices. Since there are $P = 2^n$ identical processors, the matrices are distributed on a $\sqrt{P} \times \sqrt{P}$ mesh of processors. In order to compute C, the neighbour to neighbour communication and computation for each processor are needed to perform [3]. Based on J. Berntsen's algorithm, we simulate each fault-free subcube of $R_s(m,k)$ as a processing unit. Our major concentration then is to arrange the jobs between each pair of neighboring processing units of the maximal fault-free subcube-ring $R_s(m,k)$. Our algorithm is divided into two phases. The first phase is to redistribute the matrices C, A, and B onto a $R_s(m,k)$. Consider a $R_s(m,k)$, there are k m-subcubes each containing 2^m nodes. Each m-subcube of $R_s(m,k)$ includes a ring which is mapped by a binary Gray code. A two-dimensional mesh interconnect with wrap around containing $k \times 2^m$ processors is formed. The matrices C, A, and B are distributed into a $k \times 2^m$ mesh of processors as follows. Let

LCM(x, y) denote the least common multiple of x and y. First, we split the full $N \times N$ matrices into $\mu \times \mu$ submatrices, where $\mu = \text{LCM}(2^m, k)$. The matrix C is divided in square submatrices C_{ab} holding the elements c_{ik}, with $Na/\mu \le i < N(a+1)/\mu$, $Nb/\mu \le k < N(b+1)/\mu$ and $0 \le a, b < \mu$. Similarly, matrices A and B are split up in the same way. Second, we evenly partition the $\mu \times \mu$ submatrices onto $k \times 2^m$ processors of $R_s(m, k)$. As a result, each processor contains $(\mu/2^m) \times (\mu/k)$ submatrices of C, A, and B.

The second phase is to rearrange the jobs of the neighbour to neighbour communications and computations of each processor of $R_s(m, k)$. Since each processor contains $(\mu/2^m) \times (\mu/k)$ submatrices of C, A, and B, it can be viewed as a matrix with $(\mu/2^m)$ rows and (μ/k) columns. The communication and computation are modified as follows. First, each processor must multiply the respectively submatrices of A and B and sum the product to the respective part of C. Then, we let all submatrices of A shifts left one row. The shift left operation of boundary column is achieved by sending leftmost column with $(\mu/2^m)$ submatrices of A to the west and receiving a column with $(\mu/2^m)$ submatrices of A from the east. Third, we let all submatrices of A shifts up one row. The shift up operation of boundary row is achieved by sending the top row with (μ/k) submatrices of B to the north and receiving a row with (μ/k) submatrices of B from the south. After executing above communication and computation steps μ times, matrix C is thus obtained.

The derivation of time cost T_{FM} of the fault-tolerant matrix-multiplication algorithm is described as follows. Assume that τ is the time to do a floating multiplication or addition, t_{comm} is the time to communicate a single real word and t_{start} is the startup time. The total time cost T_{FM} is

$$T_{FM} = \mu \left(2 \times \frac{\mu}{2^m} \times \frac{\mu}{k} \times (\frac{N}{\mu})^3 \tau + 2t_{start} + (3 \times (\frac{\mu}{2^m} + \frac{\mu}{k}) \times (\frac{N}{\mu})^2) t_{comm} \right)$$
$$= 2\frac{N^3}{P}\tau + 2\mu t_{start} + \frac{3 \times (k+2^m)N^2}{P} t_{comm}, \text{ where } P = 2^m \times k.$$

5 Experiment Results

It is obviously that the processor utilization and diameter of $R_s(m, k)$ are $2^m \times k$ and $3 \times \lceil k/2 \rceil + m$, respectively. The larger value m and k are, the higher percentage of processor utilization and the higher diameter will be. There is a tradeoff to determine the suitable value of m and k such that both the high percentage of processor utilization and the low diameter are achieved. In our scheme, we consider to possibly select the largest subcube to avoid the high diameter problem. Let there exist two suitable fault-free subcube-rings $R_s(3,3)$ and $R_s(2,7)$ in a faulty Q_5 with only one faulty node. The percentage of processor utilization of $R_s(3,3)$ and $R_s(2,7)$ are respective 75% and 87.5%, and the diameter of $R_s(3,3)$ and $R_s(2,7)$ are respective 9 and 15. Here we select the $R_s(3,3)$ as our result.

Our simulation is executed on an nCUBE/2E hypercube machines with 32 processors each contains 4 Mega bytes of local memory. In our simulation, two cases of number of faulty processors are assumed. The addresses of faulty processors are randomly generated on each of 10000 simulations for fixed n and

Table 1. Distributed percentage of processor utilization of the maximal fault-free subcube-ring $R_s(m, k)$ in faulty 5-cube with $|F| = 1, 2, \cdots$, and 8.

Percentage of processor utilization	$R_s(m, k)$	$|F| = 1$	$|F| = 2$	$|F| = 3$	$|F| = 4$
10% ~ 20%	(1, 2), (1, 3)	0	0	0	0
20% ~ 30%	(1, 4)	0	0	0	0
30% ~ 40%	(2, 3)	0	0	0	0
40% ~ 50%	(1, 7)	0	0	0	0
50% ~ 60%	(2, 4)	0	4.74	5.64	7.65
60% ~ 70%	(2, 5)	0	4.6	26.54	38.53
70% ~ 80%	(2, 6), (3, 3)	100	84.6	65.45	50.67
80% ~ 90%	(2, 7)	0	6.25	4.37	3.15

Percentage of processor utilization	$R_s(m, k)$	$|F| = 5$	$|F| = 6$	$|F| = 7$	$|F| = 8$
10% ~ 20%	(1, 2), (1, 3)	0	0	0	0.02
20% ~ 30%	(1, 4)	0	0.05	0.11	0.53
30% ~ 40%	(2, 3)	0.51	1.26	3.01	5.51
40% ~ 50%	(1, 7)	2.82	9.28	17.65	27.20
50% ~ 60%	(2, 4)	2.70	8.84	16.10	20.85
60% ~ 70%	(2, 5)	60.28	64.06	55.98	42.74
70% ~ 80%	(2, 6), (3, 3)	31.35	15.99	7.05	3.12
80% ~ 90%	(2, 7)	2.34	0.52	0.10	0.03

$|F|$. In the case of $|F| < n$, the requirement of processor utilization is demand to at least larger than 50% for improving the slowdown factor. If percentage of processor utilization of $R_s(m, k)$ is larger than 50%, the slowdown factor of computation will reduce to be smaller than 2. The percentage of processor utilization of any recognized $R_s(m, k)$ is larger than 50% when the number of faulty nodes is smaller than n. This is because that there at least existed a $R_s(0, 2^{n-1})$ on a faulty n-ncube with $n - 1$ faulty nodes [11]. All possible $R_s(m, k)$, processor utilization, and distributed percentage of processor utilization under fixed n and $|F|$, where $n = 5$, $1 \leq |F| \leq 4$ are shown in Table 1. As shown in Table 1, 100%, 84.6%, 65.45%, and 50.67% cases to exploit the 75% processor utilization in a faulty Q_5 when $|F|$ is 1, 2, 3, and 4 respectively. This indicates that the percentage of processor utilization of maximal fault-free subcube-ring $R_s(m, k)$ is always larger than 50% if $|F| < n$. Furthermore, if the number of F is larger than n, we exploit the maximal fault-free subcube-ring $R_s(m, k)$ such that the processor utilization of $R_s(m, k)$ is as high as possible. Two factors, the value of $|F|$ and the locations of faulty nodes, mainly effect the processor utilization. The percentages of processor utilization under the fixed n and $|F|$, where $n = 5$ and $5 \leq |F| \leq 8$, are also shown in Table 1. For instance, there are 96.67%, 89.41%, 79.23%, and 66.74% cases to exploit the processor utilization higher than 50% in a faulty Q_5, where $|F|$ is 5, 6, 7, and 8, respectively. The smaller the value of $|F|$

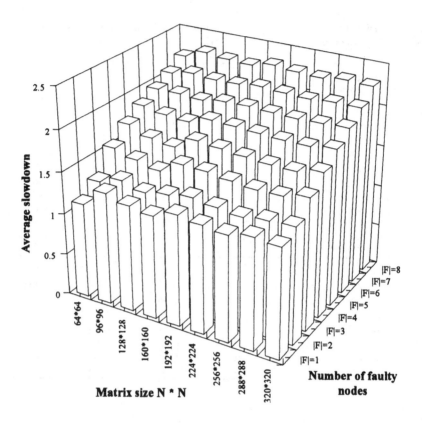

Fig. 4. The average slowdown of the fault-tolerant matrix multiplication algorithm running on 5-cube with set $|F|$ whose value is ranging from 1 to 8.

is, the maximal fault-free subcube-ring with high processor utilization generally be determined.

We simulate our fault-tolerant matrix-multiplication algorithms on a Q_5. Simulation here compares the execution time of our fault-tolerant algorithm with subcube-partitioning scheme [4] in a faulty hypercube. Using the subcube-partitioning scheme, J. Berntsen's matrix-multiplication algorithm at least has 2 performance slowdown if $|F| < n$. The simulation result of our fault-tolerant matrix-multiplication algorithm on $R_s(m, k)$ is depicted in Fig. 4. The number of data elements of matrices C, A, and B are ranged from 64×64 to 320×320. As illustrated in Table 1, if Q_5 with $|F| < 4$, $R_s(2, 7)$, $R_s(3, 3)$, $R_s(2, 6)$, $R_s(2, 5)$, $R_s(2, 4)$ are identified. The slowdown ratio of our algorithm in $R_s(2, 7)$, $R_s(3, 3)$, $R_s(2, 6)$, $R_s(2, 5)$, $R_s(2, 4)$ is less than 2 since processor utilization is larger or equal than 50%. As depicted in Fig. 4, when $|F| < 5$, average slowdown ratio of our fault-tolerant matrix-multiplication algorithm running on $R_s(m, k)$ is smaller than 2. For illustrating algorithms running on our reconfiguration scheme with reasonable slowdown even when $|F| > n$, we also simulate above fault-tolerant matrix-multiplication on faulty 5-cube with different value of set $|F|$, where $5 \leq |F| \leq 8$. As illustrated in Fig. 4, the more the data element is, the low the slowdown ratio obtains. The average slowdown of all cases of running the matrix-multiplication algorithm are smaller than 2.5.

6 Conclusion

In this paper, a new reconfiguration approach, identifying the maximal fault-free subcube-ring $R_s(m, k)$, is presented for tolerating more than n arbitrarily placed faults in hypercubes. We can reconfigure a faulty hypercube into the maximal fault-free subcube-ring $R_s(m, k)$ with dilation 3 so as lower potential performance degradation is obtained. To demonstrate the fault-tolerant capability of our approach, we implement the fault-tolerant matrix-multiplication algorithm on the nCUBE/2E hypercube machines. Using the approach, if the number of faults is less than n, the *slowdown* ratio of running the application algorithms on $R_s(m, k)$ is smaller than 2. Moreover, if number of faults is not larger than 2^{n-2}, the average *slowdown* ratio of running the application algorithms on $R_s(m, k)$ is smaller than 2.5 by our simulation results.

References

1. NCUBE corporation: nCUBE/2 processor manual. NCUBE corporation. (1990).
2. F. T. Leighton: Introduction to parallel algorithms and architecture: array · tree · hypercube. Morgan Kaufmann Publishers. (1992).
3. J. Berntsen: Communication efficient matrix multiplication on hypercubes. Parallel Comput. **12** (1989) 335-342.
4. J. Bruck, R. Cypher, and D. Soroker: Tolerating faults in hypercubes using subcube partitioning. IEEE Trans. Comput. **41**, 5 (1992) 599-605.
5. H. L. Chen and N. F. Tzeng: Quick determination of subcubes in a faulty hypercube. Proc. of 21th Int. Conf. Parallel Processing. **3** (1992) 338-345.
6. H. L. Chen and N. F. Tzeng: Distributed identification of all maximal incomplete subcubes in a faulty hypercube. Proc. of the 8th Int. Parallel Processing Symp. (1994) 723-728.
7. C. S. Raghavendra, P. J. Yang, and S. B. Tien: Free dimension - an effective approach to achieving fault tolerance in hypercubes. Proc. of Int. Symp. Fault-Tolerant Comput. (1992) 170-177.
8. J. P. Sheu: Fault-tolerant parallel k selection algorithm in n-cube networks, Information Processing Letters. **39**, 2, (1992) 93-97.
9. J. P. Sheu, Y. S. Chen, and C. Y. Chang: Fault-tolerant sorting algorithm on hypercube multicomputers. J. Parallel and Distributed Comput. **16**, 2 (1992) 185-197.
10. S. B. Tien, and C. S. Raghavendra: Simulation of SIMD algorithms on faulty hypercubes. Proc. of 20th Int. Conf. Parallel Processing. **1** (1991) 716-717.
11. Y. C. Tseng and T. H. Lai: Ring embedding in an injured hypercube. Proc. of 22th Int. Conf. Parallel Processing. **3** (1993) 149-152.

Communication in Multicomputers with Nonconvex Faults*

Suresh Chalasani[1] and Rajendra V. Boppana[2]

[1] Dept. of ECE, University of Wisconsin-Madison,
Madison, WI 53706-1691, USA
[2] Computer Science Division, The University of Texas at San Antonio,
San Antonio, TX 78249-0664, USA

Abstract. A technique to enhance multicomputer routers for fault-tolerant routing with modest increase in routing complexity and resource requirements is described. This method handles solid faults in meshes, which includes all convex faults and many practical nonconvex faults, for example, faults in the shape of L or T. As examples of the proposed method, adaptive and nonadaptive fault-tolerant routing algorithms using four virtual channels per physical channel are described.

1 Introduction

Many recent experimental and commercial multicomputers and multiprocessors use direct-connected networks with mesh topology [1, 13, 12, 6, 14]. These computers use the well-known dimension-order or e-cube routing algorithm in conjunction with *wormhole* (WH) switching [8] to provide interprocessor communication. In the WH technique, a packet is divided into a sequence of fixed-size units of data, called *flits* and transmitted from source to destination in asynchronous pipelined manner. The first flit of the message makes the path and the tail flit releases the path as the message progresses toward its destination.

The e-cube routing algorithm is simple and provides high throughput for uniform traffic. The e-cube achieves its simplicity by using, always, a fixed path for each source-destination pair, though the underlying network may provide many additional paths of the same length (in hops). Therefore, the e-cube cannot handle even simple node or link faults, because even one fault disrupts many "e-cube communication" paths.

Adaptive and fault-tolerant routing for multicomputer networks has been the subject of extensive research in recent years [5, 9, 7, 11, 2, 10, 3]. Most of the current techniques to handle faults in torus and mesh networks require one or more of the following: (a) new routing algorithms with adaptivity [5, 7, 10, 11], (b) global knowledge of faults, (c) restriction on the shapes, locations, and number of faults [5, 7, 11, 3] and (d) relaxing the constraints of guaranteed delivery, deadlock- or livelock-free routing.

---

* Chalasani's research has been partially supported by NSF grant CCR-9308966 and Boppana's research by NSF Grant CCR-9208784.

In this paper, we present fault-tolerant routing methods that can be used to augment the existing fault-intolerant routing algorithms with simple changes to routing logic and with modest increase in resources. These techniques rely on local knowledge of faults—each fault-free node needs to know the status of only its links and its neighbors' links, and can be applied as soon as the faults are detected (provided the faults are of specific shapes). Messages are still delivered correctly without livelocks and deadlocks.

The fault model is a generalized convex fault model, called solid fault model. In the convex fault model, each connected set of faults has a convex shape (for example, rectangular in 2D meshes) [3, 5]. In the solid fault model, a connected fault set is such that any cross-section of the fault region has contiguous faulty components. Fault regions with a variety of shapes, for example, convex, +, L, and T in a 2D mesh, are examples of solid faults.

Our approach in this paper is to demonstrate techniques to enhance known fault intolerant routing algorithms to provide communication even under faults. To illustrate this, we apply our techniques to the non-adaptive e-cube and a class of fully-adaptive algorithms [9] for meshes with solid faults. Our results in this paper expand on our earlier results for convex faults [3, 4].

The rest of the paper is organized as follows. Section 2 describes the solid fault model and the concept of fault-rings. Section 3 describes our fault-tolerance techniques for the nonadaptive e-cube algorithm. Section 4 applies these techniques for fully-adaptive algorithms. Section 5 concludes the paper.

2 Preliminaries

We consider n-dimensional mesh networks with faults. A (k, n)-mesh has n dimensions, denoted $\text{DIM}_0, \ldots, \text{DIM}_{n-1}$, and $N = k^n$ nodes. Each node is uniquely indexed by an n-tuple in radix k. Each node is connected via bidirectional links to two other nodes in each dimension. Given a node $x = (x_{n-1}, \ldots, x_0)$, its neighbors in DIM_i, $0 \leq i < n$, are $(x_{n-1}, \ldots, x_{i+1}, x_i \pm 1, x_{i-1}, \ldots, x_0)$; if the ith digit of a neighbor's index is -1 or k, then that neighbor does not exist for x. We denote the link between adjacent nodes x and y by $x \leftrightarrow y$.

We assume that a message that reaches its destination is consumed in finite time. If a message has not reached its destination and is blocked due to busy channels, then it will continue to hold the channels it has already acquired and not yet released. Therefore, deadlocks can occur because of cyclic dependencies on channels. To avoid deadlocks, multiple logical or virtual channels are simulated on each physical channel and allocated to messages systematically [8]. When faults occur, the dependencies are even more common, and more virtual channels may need to be used or the use of channels may have to be restricted further. Using extra logic and buffers, multiple virtual channels can be simulated on a physical channel in a demand time-multiplexed manner. We specify the number of virtual channels on per physical channel basis and denote the ith virtual channel on a physical channel with c_i.

In the remainder of this section, we describe the fault model and the concept of fault-rings for 2D meshes. Our results can be extended to multidimensional meshes and torus networks with suitable modifications. We label the sides of a 2D mesh as North, South, East and West.

2.1 The fault model

We consider both node and link faults. For fault detection, processors test themselves periodically using a suitable self-test algorithm. In addition, each processor sends and receives status signals from each of its neighbors. A link fault is detected by the processors on which it is incident by examining these status signals. A processor that fails its self-test, stops transmitting signals on all of its links, which appears as link faults to its neighbors. A fault-free processor ignores the incoming signals on its links determined to be faulty. So, faulty nodes do not generate messages.

We model multiple simultaneous faults, which could be connected or disjoint. We assume that the mean time to repair faults is quite large, a few hours to many days, and that the existing fault-free processors are still connected and should be used for computations in the mean time. We develop fault-tolerant algorithms that can work with only local fault information—each node knows only the status of links incident on it and on its neighbors reachable via its fault-free links.

A node fault is equivalent to making the links incident on that node faulty. Therefore, given a set F with one or more node faults and some link faults, we can represent the fault information by a set F_l which contains all the links incident on the nodes in F and all the links in F. Two faulty links $a = x \leftrightarrow y$ and $b = u \leftrightarrow v$ in F_l are *adjacent* if one of the following conditions hold:

1. a and b have different dimensions and are incident on a common node, or
2. node x is adjacent to node u and y is adjacent to v, or
3. node x is adjacent to node v and y is adjacent to u.

A pair of links adjacent by the above definition are said to be connected. Two nonadjacent links $a_1, a_p \in F_l$ are connected if there exist links $a_2, \ldots, a_{p-1} \in F_l$ such that a_i and a_{i+1}, for $1 \leq i < p$, are adjacent. A faulty node and a faulty link a are connected if there is at least one link incident on the faulty node to which link a is connected. A set with a single faulty link represents a trivially connected fault set. A set of faulty links F_l with two or more components is connected if every pair of links in F_l is connected. A set F of faulty nodes and links is connected, if the corresponding set F_l of faulty links is connected. The fault sets $F_1 = \{(1,0) \leftrightarrow (1,1), (0,1) \leftrightarrow (1,1)\}$, $F_2 = \{(0,4) \leftrightarrow (0,5), (1,4) \leftrightarrow (1,5)\}$, $F_3 = \{(2,2) \leftrightarrow (2,3), (3,2), (4,1)\}$, and $F_4 = \{(4,4)\}$ in Figure 1 are examples of connected fault sets. F_2 is an example of the connected fault based on the last two adjacency rules given above.

Before defining solid faults, we need to define cross sections of networks and faults. Each connected fault set describes a subnetwork of the original mesh. Given a subnetwork or network, all of its nodes that match with one another in all but one component of their n-tuple representations and the links among them form its 1-D cross section. For example, in a 2D mesh, each row and each column is an 1-D cross section of the network. The column cross sections of F_3 in Figure 1 are $\{(4,1),(3,1)\leftrightarrow(4,1),(4,1)\leftrightarrow(5,1)\}$ and $\{(3,2),(2,2)\leftrightarrow(3,2),(3,2)\leftrightarrow(4,2)\}$, and its row cross sections are $\{(2,2)\leftrightarrow(2,3)\}$, $\{(3,2),(3,1)\leftrightarrow(3,2),(3,2)\leftrightarrow(3,3)\}$, and $\{(4,1),(4,0)\leftrightarrow(4,1),(4,1)\leftrightarrow(4,2)\}$. Each faulty link not incident on a faulty node of a connected fault set is an 1-D cross section of the connected fault.

A connected fault-set F, with all of its links given by the set F_l, indicates a *solid* fault region, or *f-region*, if the following condition is satisfied.

If two links $a, b \in F_l$ are in the same 1-D cross section, then all the nodes between a and b are also faulty.

A set of faults is valid if each connected fault in the set is a solid fault. All the faults in Figure 1 are examples solid faults. The faults F_2 and F_4 are also examples of convex (rectangular block-shaped) faults. The faults F_1 and F_3 are not convex faults.

2.2 Fault rings

For each connected fault region of the network, it is feasible to connect the fault-free components around the fault to form a ring or chain. This is the fault ring, f-ring, for that fault and consists of the fault-free nodes and channels that are adjacent (row-wise, column-wise, or diagonally) to one or more components of the fault region. For example, the f-rings for the various solid faults in Figure 1 are shown with thick lines. It is noteworthy that a fault-free node is in the f-ring only if it is at most two hops away from a faulty node. There can be several fault rings, one for each f-region, in a network with multiple faults. Fault rings provide alternate paths to messages blocked by faults.

A set of fault rings are said to overlap if they share one or more links. For example, the f-rings of F_3 and F_4 in Figure 1 overlap with each other on link $(3,3)\leftrightarrow(4,3)$. Forming a fault-ring around an f-region is not possible when the f-region touches one or more boundaries of the network (e.g., F_2 in Figure 1). In this case, a *fault chain*, f-chain, rather than an f-ring is formed around the f-region. In this paper, we do not consider solid faults that form f-chains or overlapping f-rings.

2.3 Formation of fault rings

Fault-rings can be constructed for every connected fault set. To see this, consider a single fault region in a 2D mesh. The formation of a f-ring around this f-region is a two-step process. Each node with at least one faulty link incident on it sends a message to each of its nonfaulty neighbors. The rules using which each node determines its neighbors on the f-ring are given in Figure 2. The first six cases apply when at least one faulty link is incident on x, the node trying to determine its f-ring neighbors. The other cases apply when x has no faulty links.

Even with nonoverlapping f-rings, a node may appear in up to n f-rings in a (k, n)-mesh with solid faults. For example, nodes $(2,1)$ and $(1,2)$ appear in the f-rings of F_1 and F_3. There can be at most two faulty links incident on a fault-free node even with multiple f-regions. If multiple faults occur simultaneously,

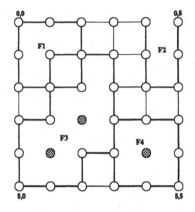

Faulty Links	Neighbors
East & South links of x	N_x, W_x
East & North links of x	S_x, W_x
West & South links of x	N_x, E_x
West & North links of x	S_x, E_x
East or West link of x	N_x, S_x
North or South link of x	E_x, W_x
North link of E_x or East link of N_x	N_x, E_x
South link of E_x or East link of S_x	S_x, E_x
North link of W_x or West link of N_x	N_x, W_x
South link of W_x or West link of S_x	S_x, W_x

Fig. 1. Examples of solid faults in a mesh. Faulty nodes are shown as filled circles, and faulty links are not shown. Thick lines indicate the corresponding fault rings.

Fig. 2. Determining the neighbors of a node on an f-ring. Let x be the node whose neighbors are to be determined. N_x, E_x, S_x, W_x denote the nodes adjacent to x in the North, East, South, and West directions, respectively.

a node may send or receive messages about multiple f-regions. Using the faulty link direction and dimension provided in each fault status message, it is feasible to separate the messages on faults for different f-regions. For multidimensional meshes, each solid fault creates multiple fault rings, one for each 2D cross section of the fault. In summary, f-rings are formed for any connected fault set using only near-neighbor communication among fault-free processors.

The definition of solid faults can be used to check if a fault can be characterized as a solid fault. In a 2D mesh, the boundary of a solid fault crosses each row and each column exactly zero times or twice. A special type of message, called shape finding worm, can be circulated around an f-ring and the number of times the worm crosses each row and column can be counted. If any row or column is visited more than twice, then the corresponding fault is not a solid fault. Otherwise, the fault is a solid fault, and the routing techniques described in the remainder of the paper can be used to route messages without any further network reconfiguration. If a fault is not a solid fault, then disabling selected nodes and links so that the result is a solid fault is still an open problem. For the remainder of the paper, we assume that only solid faults can occur in networks.

3 Fault-Tolerant Nonadaptive Routing

We first show how to enhance the well-known e-cube routing algorithm to handle solid faults in 2D meshes. The e-cube routes a message in a row until the message reaches a node that is in the same column as its destination, and then routes it in the column. For fault-free meshes, the e-cube provides deadlock-free shortest-path routing without requiring multiple virtual channels to be simulated. At each point during the routing of a message, the e-cube specifies the next hop, called e-cube hop, to be taken by the message. The message is said to

---

Procedure Set-Message-Type(M)
/* Comment: The current host of M is (a_1, a_0) and destination is (b_1, b_0). When a message is generated, it is labeled as EW if $a_0 \geq b_0$ and as WE otherwise. */
If M is an EW or WE message and $a_0 = b_0$,
    change its type to NS if $a_1 < b_1$ or SN if $a_1 > b_1$.

Procedure Set-Message-Status(M)
/* Comment: Determine if the message M is normal or misrouted.
The current host of M is (a_1, a_0) and destination is (b_1, b_0). */

1 If M is a row — EW or WE — message and its e-cube hop is not blocked, then set the status of M to **normal** and return.
2 If M is a column — NS or SN — message and $a_0 = b_0$, and its next e-cube hop is not on a faulty link, then set the status of M to **normal** and return.
3 Set the status of M to **misrouted**,
    determine using Table 1 the f-ring orientation to be used by M for its misrouting.

Fig. 3. Procedures to set the status and type of a message.

be blocked by a fault, if its e-cube hop is on a faulty link. The proposed modification uses four virtual channels, c_0, c_1, c_2 and c_3, on each physical channel and tolerates multiple solid faults with nonoverlapping f-rings.

To route messages around f-rings, messages are classified into one of the following types using Procedure Set-Message-Type (Figure 3): EW (East-to-West), WE (West-to-East), NS (North-to-South), or SN (South-to-North). A message is labeled as either an EW or WE message when it is generated, depending on its direction of travel along the row. Once a message completes its row hops, it becomes a NS or a SN message depending on its direction of travel along the column. Thus, EW and WE messages can become NS or SN messages; however, NS and SN messages cannot change their types. These rules are summarized in procedure Set-Message-Type. EW and WE messages are collectively known as *row* messages and NS and SN as *column* messages.

In addition to its type, each message also provides its current status information: normal or misrouted. A row message is termed **normal**, if its e-cube hop is not blocked by a fault. A column message whose head flit is in the same column as its destination is **normal** if its e-cube hop is not blocked by a fault. All other messages are termed **misrouted**. Procedure Set-Message-Status in Figure 3 gives these rules.

3.1 Modifications to the routing logic

Normal messages are routed using the base e-cube algorithm. A normal message blocked by a fault is treated as a misrouted message and routed on the corresponding f-ring using the logic given in Figure 6 *until it becomes normal again*. Sometimes a message may travel on f-ring before being blocked by the fault con-

Table 1. Directions to be used for misrouting messages on f-rings.

Message Type	Traversed on the f-ring	Position of Destination	F-Ring Orientation
WE	No	In a row above its row of travel	Clockwise
WE	No	In a row below its row of travel	Counter Clockwise
EW	No	In a row above its row of travel	Counter Clockwise
EW	No	In a row below its row of travel	Clockwise
NS or SN	No	(don't care)	Either one orientation
Any message	Yes	Don't care	Choose the orientation that is being used by the message

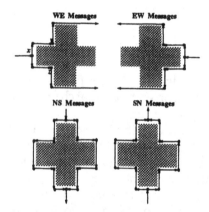

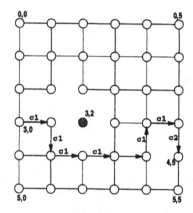

Fig. 4. Routing of misrouted messages around fault rings.

Fig. 5. Example of nonadaptive fault tolerant routing.

tained by the f-ring. In such cases, the message is forced to use the f-ring orientation compatible with its travel on the f-ring up to that point. For example, a WE message may be blocked at node y in Figure 4 after traversing a hop on the f-ring. In that case, the message should traverse the f-ring in the clockwise orientation to get around the fault.

In other cases, a message is blocked the first time it arrives at a node on an f-ring (for example, node x for a WE message in Figure 4). In such cases, a message may use clockwise or counter clockwise orientation depending on other conditions. The orientations and conditions are given in Table 1.

If a message takes a normal hop on a link that is not on an f-ring, then the virtual channel to be used is given by the base e-cube algorithm. Under the e-cube, a message may use any virtual channel in its normal hop without deadlocks. (In fact, with e-cube routing, there can be only one type of messages using each

---

Procedure Fault-Tolerant-Route(Message M) /* Specifies the next hop of M */
1. Set-Message-Type(M).
2. Set-Message-Status(M).
3. If M is **normal**, select the hop specified by the base algorithm.
4. If M is **misrouted**, select the hop along its f-ring orientation.
5. If the selected hop is on an f-ring link, route the message using virtual channel c_0 if M's type is EW, c_1 if WE, c_2 if NS, or c_3 if SN.
6. If the selected hop is not on an f-ring link, route the message using the virtual channel specified by the base algorithm.

Fig. 6. Fault-tolerant routing algorithm.

physical channel that is neither faulty nor part of an f-ring.) Sometimes a message may travel on an f-ring using the base e-cube algorithm because its normal hop is on the f-ring. In addition, a message may travel on an f-ring because it is blocked by the corresponding fault. In both cases, messages traveling on f-rings can use only the following virtual channels: EW messages use c_0 for all hops on f-rings, WE messages use c_1, NS messages use c_2 and SN messages use c_3.

Consider a message M from (3,0) to (4,5) in the mesh with two solid faults in Figure 5. M begins as a WE message and is routed to (3,1), where its e-cube hop is blocked by the faulty node (3,2). It is misrouted in the counter-clockwise orientation to (4,1) to be compatible with its previous hop, which is on the f-ring. After routed by the base e-cube from (4,1) to (4,4), it is blocked by the faulty link $(4, 4) \leftrightarrow (4, 5)$, and is misrouted in the (randomly chosen) clockwise orientation. M is routed as an NS message for its final hop. The use of virtual channels per the enhanced routing logic is as indicated. The hop from (4,3) to (4,4) is by the e-cube on a link not on any f-ring; so, any of the four classes of virtual channels may be used for this hop as per the e-cube.

If a message is destined to a faulty node, then it can be detected and removed from the network using our misrouting logic. A message, say, M, destined to a faulty node will eventually become a column message, say, an NS message, with our misrouting logic. Upon further routing, M will reach a point where it has just completed misrouting by reaching a south row of the f-ring, but its destination is directly above its current host node and its e-cube hop is on the faulty North link of its current host node. Upon detecting this anomaly, the message M can be removed from the network.

3.2 Proof of deadlock and livelock freedom

Lemma 1. *The algorithm* Fault-Tolerant-Route *routes messages in 2D meshes with solid faults and nonoverlapping f-rings free of deadlocks and livelocks.*

Proof. Each type of messages (EW, WE, SN, and NS) uses a distinct class of virtual channels. This can be easily seen for the virtual channels simulated on physical channels forming f-rings. For each physical channel not on any f-ring, there can be only one type of message using that physical channel because of e-cube routing. Therefore, in all cases, each message type has an exclusive set of virtual channels for its hops. Furthermore, row messages (EW and WE) can become column messages, but not vice-versa. Thus, deadlocks among two different types of messages cannot occur, since NS and SN messages do not depend on any other message type. Hence, to prove deadlock-freedom, it is sufficient to show that there are no deadlocks among messages of a specific type.

Deadlocks among NS messages. Deadlocks can be among NS messages waiting for virtual channels at nodes on a single f-ring only or at nodes on multiple f-rings. (The NS messages waiting for virtual channels at other nodes will be routed by the deadlock-free e-cube and cannot be part of deadlocks.) Furthermore, a NS message may use counter clockwise or clockwise orientation to travel on an f-ring. The set of physical channels used for each orientation are disjoint. Misrouted NS messages with clockwise orientation never use the channels on the west-most column of an f-ring. (For example, the link $(2,0) \leftrightarrow (3,0)$ constitutes the west-most column of the f-ring for F_1 in Figure 5.) Similarly, NS messages misrouted counter clockwise on an f-ring never use the east-most column of the f-ring (for example, the two links between nodes $(2,3)$ and $(4,3)$ for the f-ring of F_1 in Figure 5). Therefore, the paths used by NS messages on an f-ring are acyclic. So, a single f-ring does not cause deadlocks among NS messages.

The f-rings can be given a partial-order by their topmost row numbers, and NS messages traverse them satisfying this partial order. Therefore, multiple f-rings do not cause deadlocks among NS messages.

Livelock freedom and correct delivery. A message is misrouted only by a finite number of hops on each f-ring, and it never visits an f-ring more than twice (at most once as a row message and once as a column message). So, the extent of misrouting is limited. This together with the fact that each normal hop takes a message closer to the destination proves that messages are correctly delivered and livelocks do not occur.

□

3.3 Extension to multidimensional meshes

We now consider solid faults with nonoverlapping f-rings in a (k, n)-mesh and show how to enhance the e-cube to provide communication. The e-cube orders the dimensions of the network and routes a message in dimension 0, until the current host node and destination match in dimension 0 component of their n-tuples, and then in dimension 1, and so on, until the message reaches its destination. From the definition of solid faults in Section 2.1, it is easy to verify that each 2D cross section (consists of all nodes that match in all but two components of their n-tuples and the links among them) of a solid fault in a (k, n)-mesh is a valid solid fault in a 2D mesh. Therefore, fault-tolerant routing in a (k, n)-mesh is achieved by using our results for 2D meshes and the planar-adaptive routing technique [5].

The routing algorithm to handle nonoverlapping f-rings still needs only four virtual channels per physical channel. Let A_i, where $0 \leq i < n$, to denote the set of all 2D planes (2D cross sections of the (k, n)-mesh) formed using dimensions i and $i + 1 \pmod n$.

A normal message that needs to travel in DIM_i, $0 \leq i < n$, as per the e-cube is a DIM_i message. A DIM_i message that completed its hops in dimension DIM_i becomes a DIM_j message, where $j > i$ is the next dimension of travel as per the e-cube algorithm. A message blocked by a fault uses the f-ring of the 2D cross section of the fault in the 2D plane formed by dimensions $i, i + 1 \pmod n$ and has the current host node to get around the fault. A DIM_i message, $0 \leq i \leq n - 2$, uses a 2D plane of type A_i for routing and virtual channels of class $c_{2(i \bmod 2)}$ or $c_{2(i \bmod 2)+1}$ depending on its direction of travel in DIM_i. A DIM_{n-1} message will use an A_{n-1} plane; it will use virtual channels of classes c_2 or c_3 if n is even, or c_0 or c_1 in DIM_{n-1} and c_2 or c_3 in DIM_0, otherwise. There is a partial-order on the planes used and the sets of virtual channels used for these planes are pairwise disjoint. So, the proof of deadlock free routing is straight forward and is omitted.

4 Fault-Tolerant Adaptive Routing

The adaptive fault-tolerant routing algorithm described in this section uses the technique developed in the previous section. The fault intolerant version of the algorithm is based on the general theory developed by Duato [9]. The particular one we use here can provide adaptive routing with as few as two virtual channels: one for deadlock free e-cube routing and another for adaptive routing. Since we need four virtual channels for deadlock free routing under faults, we describe the base adaptive algorithm, A, for fault-free networks using four channels (Figure 7). At any point of routing, a message has two types of hops: the e-cube hop and adaptive hops. The e-cube hop is the same as before: the hop specified by the e-cube algorithm. The adaptive hops are all other hops that take the message closer to its destination. Algorithm A first tries to route a message M using an *adaptive channel*—c_1, c_2, or c_3—along any of the dimensions that take M closer to the destination (Step 2). If this fails, A tries to route M using the non-adaptive channel c_0 on its e-cube hop (Step 3). If this step also fails, the same sequence of events is tried after a delay of one cycle.

To enhance this algorithm for fault-tolerant routing, we classify messages into normal and misrouted categories, as before. While normal messages may have adaptivity, misrouted messages do not. The top level description of our fault-tolerant adaptive routing is the same as that for the nonadaptive case in Figure 6, with the algorithm in Figure 7 as the base routing algorithm. An important amendment to the routing logic is for normal messages: (a) if a message's e-cube hop is on an f-ring, then adaptive hops cannot be used; or (b) if message's e-cube hop is not on an f-ring, but one or more of its adaptive hops are on f-rings, then those adaptive hops cannot be used. A message with its e-cube hop on a link that is faulty or part of an f-ring is routed exactly the same as in the e-cube case, because e-cube routing is the basis for deadlock freedom in the adaptive routing. The adaptivity is used only when the message does not have to travel on f-rings.

```
Procedure Adaptive-Algorithm(M, x, d)
/* Current host is x and destination d, d ≠ x. */
1 Determine all the neighbors of x that are along
  a shortest path from x to d. Let S be the set of
  such neighbors.
2 If a virtual channel in the set {c₁, c₂, c₃} is avail-
  able from x to a neighbor y ∈ S, route M from
  x to y using that virtual channel; return.
3 If virtual channel c₀ is available from x to a
  neighbor z along the e-cube hop of M, route
  M from x to z using c₀; return.
4 Return and try this procedure one cycle later.
```

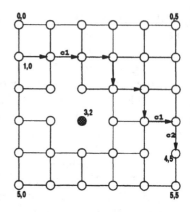

Fig. 7. Pseudocode of the adaptive algorithm enhanced for fault-tolerance.

Fig. 8. Example of fault-tolerant adaptive routing.

Once again the virtual channel allocation is crucial for deadlock avoidance. In the fault-tolerant adaptive routing, channels c_0 to c_3 are used for messages around f-rings. Virtual channels on links that are not on f-rings are used for normal routing by **Adaptive-Algorithm**. The four virtual channels on physical channels not on f-rings are partitioned into nonadaptive and adaptive subsets. The channels in the nonadaptive category are c_0 channels, which are used to ensure deadlock free routing. Furthermore, only one type of messages may use the nonadaptive channel on a physical channel not an f-ring. Thus, no virtual channel can be used for normal routing by one message and for misrouting or adaptive routing by another message. Therefore, each message type has an exclusive set of virtual channels for deadlock free routing. Given this argument, the proof of deadlock-freedom is similar to that of the nonadaptive case. Figure 8 gives an example of our method. The message uses specific channels for its hops on the f-ring links $(1, 0) \leftrightarrow (1, 1)$, $(3, 4) \leftrightarrow (3, 5)$, and $(3, 5) \leftrightarrow (4, 5)$. For its other hops, the message uses virtual channels as per the original adaptive algorithm.

5 Concluding Remarks

We have presented a technique to enhance the nonadaptive and adaptive algorithms for fault-tolerant wormhole routing in mesh networks. This technique works with local knowledge of faults, handle multiple faults, and guarantees livelock- and deadlock-free routing of all messages. We have used the solid fault model, which generalizes the convex fault model used in previous studies. In the convex fault model, any 2D cross-section of the fault has the shape of a rectangle. In the solid fault model, additional fault shapes such as +, T, L, and ◇ can be handled. The concept of fault-rings is used to route around the fault-regions.

The main costs of the proposed fault-tolerant routing technique are (a) a special bit in message header to indicate the misrouted status, (b) additional routing logic, which is used by the nodes on f-rings, and (c) additional virtual channels to avoid deadlocks around f-rings. Also, some processing overhead is incurred in forming f-rings.

Our technique extends to related networks such as tori. The number of virtual channels required for tori is doubled, however, because of the wraparound connections. Currently, we are evaluating the performance of the proposed technique and extending the results to more complex fault shapes and for more general network topologies.

References

1. A. Agarwal et al., "The MIT Alewife machine: A large-scale distributed multiprocessor," in *Proc. of Workshop on Scalable Shared Memory Multiprocessors*, Kluwer Academic Publishers, 1991.
2. K. Bolding and L. Snyder, "Overview of fault handling for the chaos router," in *Proceedings of the 1991 IEEE International Workshop on Defect and Fault Tolerance in VLSI Systems*, pp. 124–127, 1991.
3. R. V. Boppana and S. Chalasani, "Fault-tolerant wormhole routing algorithms for mesh networks," *IEEE Trans. on Computers*. To appear. Preliminary results presented at Supercomputing '94.
4. S. Chalasani and R. V. Boppana, "Adaptive fault-tolerant wormhole routing algorithms with low virtual channel requirements," in *Int'l Symp. on Parallel Architectures, Algorithms and Networks*, Dec. 1994.
5. A. A. Chien and J. H. Kim, "Planar-adaptive routing: Low-cost adaptive networks for multiprocessors," in *Proc. 19th Ann. Int. Symp. on Comput. Arch.*, pp. 268–277, 1992.
6. Cray Research Inc., *Cray T3D Architectural Summary*, Oct. 1993.
7. W. J. Dally and H. Aoki, "Deadlock-free adaptive routing in multicomputer networks using virtual channels," *IEEE Trans. on Parallel and Distributed Systems*, vol. 4, pp. 466–475, April 1993.
8. W. J. Dally and C. L. Seitz, "Deadlock-free message routing in multiprocessor interconnection networks," *IEEE Trans. on Computers*, vol. C-36, no. 5, pp. 547–553, 1987.
9. J. Duato, "A new theory of deadlock-free adaptive routing in wormhole networks," *IEEE Trans. on Parallel and Distributed Systems*, vol. 4, pp. 1320–1331, Dec. 1993.
10. P. T. Gaughan and S. Yalamanchili, "A family of fault-tolerant routing protocols for direct multiprocessor networks," *IEEE Trans. on Parallel and Distributed Systems*, vol. 6, pp. 482–497, May 1995.
11. C. J. Glass and L. M. Ni, "Fault-tolerant wormhole routing in meshes," in *Twenty-Third Annual Int. Symp. on Fault-Tolerant Computing*, pp. 240–249, 1993.
12. Intel Corporation, *Paragon XP/S Product Overview*, 1991.
13. M. D. Noakes et al., "The J-machine multicomputer: An architectural evaluation," in *Proc. 20th Ann. Int. Symp. on Comput. Arch.*, pp. 224–235, May 1993.
14. C. L. Seitz, "Concurrent architectures," in *VLSI and Parallel Computation* (R. Suaya and G. Birtwistle, eds.), ch. 1, pp. 1–84, San Mateo, California: Morgan-Kaufman Publishers, Inc., 1990.

Posters: Extended Abstracts

Parallelising Programs with Algebraic Programming Tools

Anatoly E. Doroshenko and Alexander B. Godlevsky

Glushkov Institute of Cybernetics
National Academy of Sciences of Ukraine
Glushkov prosp., 40, Kiev 252650, Ukraine
E-mail: dor@d105.icyb.kiev.ua

Abstract. A rewriting based approach to dynamical parallelization of a general class of sequential imperative programs by means of the algebraic programming system APS is proposed. It gives advantages of rapid prototyping and evolutionary development of efficient parallelizers. The paper shows major features of a dynamical parallelizer implemented in the APS as well as techniques for designing efficient parallelizers.

1   Introduction

The dominant trend in automating programming for parallel computers is connected with compiler technology and remarkable achievements have been made in last decade in this area. (e.g. [3]). Nevertheless to develop a compiler for parallel computer system is still a difficult and expensive task that imposes a lot of restrictions and language simplifications for compiler to be practical and efficient. Therefore prototyping is an important tool to save efforts and time especially in its declarative form [1]. We follow an integrated compiler/interpreter approach to parallel software design having in mind that writing interpreter is much easier task than developing compiler but interpreters are commonly known to be inefficient. The emphasize is maden on program transformations and dynamical issues of parallelization that can be solved in compile-time and run-time respectively at low cost. Such approach that we call *dynamical parallelization* has been proved to be acceptable in large-grained computations for macroconveyer parallel multicomputers [6]. Recently likely approach was undertaken for run-time parallelization of functional languages [4].

   In this paper we report on exploiting the approach of dynamical parallelization of programs on a new platform of the algebraic programming system APS [5] based on rewriting rules programming techniques. Early experience of application of the APS system for this purposes is described in [2]. It was not our goal to propose a new method of data dependence analysis and in this part we follow well known decisions adopted in parallelizing compilers. What is significant and new is to provide declarative treatment of programs analysis and transformations by means of rewriting techniques in the system of algebraic programming. It gives a great deal of flexibility of parallelizers and allows extracting parallelism independently on multiprocessor architecture and number of processors available in parallel system. Besides of rapid prototyping the advantages consist in controlability and verifiablity of the whole process of evolutionary program development.

2 The APS Main Features

The APS is an integrated rewriting rule based programming system. A methodology of the system application consists in flexible integration of four main paradigms of programming: procedural, functional, algebraic and logical that is achieved by adjusted use of corresponding computational mechanisms. The main objects in the system are terms of the algebra that is considered as absolutely free algebra of infinite (but finitely represented) trees. As a values of names these trees may have common parts and may be used to represent arbitrary labelled graphs. There are three types of system objects: *algebraic programs* (ap-modules), *algebraic modules* (a-modules) and *interpreters*.

Algebraic programs are texts in APLAN language syntax [5]. Each program contains the description of some signature of underlying algebra with syntax for constructing algebraic expressions (terms). It defines also the set of names and atoms. These objects together with numbers and strings constitutes the set of *primary objects*. The sets of names and atoms together with the signature of an ap-module define the *type* of this ap-module.

Algebraic modules contain internal representation of the data structures defined in ap-modules. They are being created by system commands that refer to ap-modules as a new object generators. The notion of a-module is dynamical one. It has a state which may changes in time. The change of the state of a-module takes place as a result of executing procedures located in it by means of interpreters. System interpreters are programs destined for the interpretation of the procedures written in APLAN. They are developing in C language on the base of libraries of functions and data structures to work with internal representation of system data structures. Each interpreter is connected with a distinct type which defines the restriction to algebraic modules which can be executed by the given interpreter. Each interpreter specifies the operational semantics of APLAN for the given class of a-modules and provides efficient implementation of the procedures, functions and strategies of rewriting for the systems located in the given module.

3 Rewriting Techniques for Dynamical Parallelization

To give a flavor of the APS and to demonstrate the rewriting style programming for parallelization we consider a short fragment of ap-modules that realises a piece of data dependency analysis implemented in our dynamical parallelizer — evaluation of the fact that two sets of array variables are disjoint.

If we designate the property of intersection nonemptyness of two sets of array variables V and W with predicate $Int(V, W)$ and a function evaluating the number of dimensions of array variable x with $art(x)$ then we can write following recurrence relations:

$$Int(V, W) \iff (\exists x, i, j)(x(i) \in V, x(j) \in W)$$

$$\& \ (n = art(x) \ \& \ Indx(i, j, n)$$

$$Indx(i, j, n) \iff (i = (i_1, \ldots, i_n),$$

$$j = (j_1, \ldots, j_n)) \ \&$$

$$(\forall l : 1 \le l \le n)(Noncomp(i_l, j_l) = 0)$$

$$Noncomp(k, m) \iff (k \ne m) \ \& \ (k, m \ are \ integers)$$

Informally, these relations mean that intersection is nonempty iff both sets V and W comprise two elements of the same array that in every component of index sets have expressions or coinsided integers.

The following fragment of APLAN code realises these relations using rewriting rules (abbreviated rs) in functional style to which standard interpreter is applied.

```
Int:=rs(x,x1,i,y,y1,j)(
    (nil,x) = 1, (x,nil) = 1,
    Indx(x(i) || x1,x(j)) ->
        ( (x(i) || x1,x(j) || y1) =
          Int(x(i) || x1 ,y1)),
        (x(i) || x1,x(j) || y1) = 0,
    compare(x,y) ->
        (( x(i) || x1,y(j) || y1)=
          Int(x1,y(j) || y1)),
        ( x(i) || x1,y(j) || y1 ) =
          Int(x(i) || x1,y1)
);
```

Its formal parameters x, i and j meaningly stand for just the same variables that in relation system of Int, others are additional. Fragment contains logical connection -> (implication), logical constants 0 and 1 and use ordered list representation of variable sets with nil standing for empty list and || for concatenation of list elements. These rewriting rules essentially consist of two parts. The second part prefixed with predicate $compare(x, y)$ is to seive two array variable sets and deleting from them all the variables whose names are different. The first part is to test index expressions of array variables with the same name for compatibility in the sense of Int.

4 Techniques for Parallelizers Development

To enhance dynamical parallelizers based on data dependency analysis some additional computational mechanisms aimed to breaking data dependences and transforming source programs to improve locality of computational activities for parallelization are developed. They are not new and are commonly used in compilers but we try to treat them as rewriting rules. Below are enumerated some of such techniques being intensively used in our parallelizer.

Concretization of variables. This rewriting technique consists in substituing values in algebraic expression instead of variables to reduce data dependences. Special but very important case of this technique is achieved when variables to be concretisized are indeed variables that body and/or condition of a loop are dependent on.

Localization of variables. This technique belongs to preliminary program transformations. The meaning of a localization constructs $loc(x)$ consists in generating a new copy of variable x whose scope is delimited syntactically by $loc(x)$ itself and the nearest construct *endloc*. This gives a possibility to delete data dependence of constructs embraced on variable x with purely syntactic tools.

Coarse-grained computations. Defining some piece of computations as a *basic* operator we thereby represent it as a single operator (perhaps depending on parameters) in program dynamic parallelization. This technique of computations consolidation may be preferable due to at least two reasons. Firstly, it is tightly connected with coarse-grained parallelism in distributed memory multiprocessor systems and networks. Secondly, it is extremely agreed with dynamical mode of parallelization because it provides reducing parallelizer's workload, assists in transfering purely computational activity from parallelizer to processors of parallel system.

References

1. M. Chen, J. Cowie, Prototyping Fortran 90 Compilers for Massively Parallel Machines, *ACM SIGPLAN'92 Conf. on Programming Language Design and Implementation*, ACM Press, pp. 94-105, 1992.
2. A. B. Godlevsky, A. E. Doroshenko, Parallelizing Programs with APS, *ISSAC'93: Proc. ACM SIGSAM Int. Symp. on Symbolic and Algebraic Computation*, ACM Press, 1993, pp. 55-62.
3. S. Hiranandani, K. Kennedy, C.-W. Tseng, Compiling Fortran D for MIMD Distributed-Memory Machines, *Commun. ACM*, vol. 35(8), pp. 66-80, 1992.
4. L. Huelsbergen, J. Larus, Dynamic program parallelization, *Proc. 1992 ACM Conf. Lisp and Functional Programming*, ACM Press, pp. 311-323, 1992.
5. A.A.Letichevsky, J.V.Kapitonova, S.V.Konozenko, Computations in APS, *Theoretical Computer Science* 119, 1993, pp.145-171.
6. V.S.Mikhalevich, Ju.V.Kapitonova, A.A.Letichevsky, On models of macroconveyer computations, in: *Information Processing 86* (IFIP, Amsterdam, 1986) 975-980.

Parallel Prolog with Uncertainty Handling

Katalin Molnár

IQSOFT Intelligent Software Ltd.,
Teleki Blanka u 15-17, H-1142 Budapest, Hungary
molnar_k@iqsoft.hu

CUBIQ is a toolset that is built on top of Aurora [Carl 92], an OR-parallel implementation of Prolog for shared memory multiprocessors that provides support for the full Prolog language. CUBIQ introduces frames, blackboard handling, functional notation and uncertainty handling incrementally and independently of each other. As part of the CUBIQ project we investigated how parallelism can be exploited in deduction in uncertain knowledge bases.

Several models of uncertainty are suitable for parallel execution [Pear 88], [Ram 90], [Roj 93]. Logic programming languages have been extended to deal with support logic [Bal 87b], certainty functions [Nara 86] and fuzzy sets [Geig 94]. Meta-interpreters to handle uncertain information in Prolog have been designed by [Ster 86], [Yalç 90].

We used a compiled version of Yalçinalp and Sterling's layered interpreter [Yalç 90] in the CUBIQ toolset. The uncertainty is modelled after support logic programming as described in [Bal 87b] that represents Dempster-Shafer-style uncertainty and incorporates representation methods for fuzzy information and probabilistic rules.

1   Uncertain knowledge representation

Support logic programming assigns necessary support and possible support as a pair of values *[Sn,Sp]* to every clause. The rules of the knowledge base are represented by Prolog clauses that are extended with support pairs.

(Head:- Body) : [Sn,Sp].

Uncertainty can be assigned not only to whole clauses, but to individual arguments as well (so called fuzzy arguments). Following [Bal 87b] we use semantic unification instead of the Prolog unification for fuzzy arguments. The first use of a fuzzy argument has to be preceded by a CUBIQ declaration of the form:

:- fuzzy(Name,[(Value:Membership_grade),...])

There is a smooth transition between logic and uncertain knowledge inside the same knowledge base. One can invoke logical rules from uncertain ones and vice versa through CUBIQ built-in predicates:

unc(:Call_to_uncertain_knowledge, -Unc)
logic(:Call_to_logic_knowledge, +Unc)

Prolog built-in predicates are handled as having either [1,1] or [0,0] outcome (true or false). Meta-predicates (findall, if-then-else, call, etc) and cut and commit operators are not yet supported.

2 Parallel aspects of uncertainty handling

In this project, we focused on those aspects of uncertain knowledge bases in which the scope for exploiting OR-parallelism was most significant.

When evaluating logic knowledge it may be interesting to find either *one* or more solutions. One solution generally means the first evaluation path that leads to a solution. In an uncertain knowledge base, we have to explore *all* paths leading to the same solution in order to get the combined uncertainty that is calculated from the uncertainties of the different paths leading to that solution. The main problem is to decide which of the different solutions is considered the answer. In the best case there is one solution that has a significantly higher degree of certainty (less uncertainty) than all the other solutions. Searching for one solution in a logic knowledge base thus becomes searching for all solutions in an uncertain knowledge base. Searching for all solutions is obviously more effective when done in parallel than sequentially. Note that negated goals (negation by failure in Aurora) are evaluated through full search both in logic and in uncertain knowledge—thus in the case of negated goals, parallel execution in logic knowledge is exploited as much as in uncertain knowledge.

3 Implementation

Each predicate with uncertainty is extended with an additional argument, in which its uncertainty is returned. During the execution of the body of a goal the constituent subgoals are evaluated and their uncertainty is combined according to the support logic rules for the AND (Prolog ','), OR (Prolog ';') and NOT (Prolog '\+') operators [Bal 87a]. We have to preserve the uncertainty calculated for one evaluation path until all the other paths leading to the same solution are evaluated. Following the layered interpreter approach [Yalç 90] we use the Prolog dynamic database for asserting the solutions of a goal. Every solution is stored together with a unique identifier and its uncertainty measure. After all solutions of a goal have been found, the uncertainties of unifiable solutions are combined to give the general uncertainty of the solution.

As a first step we implemented a straightforward, unsophisticated Prolog interpreter without considering parallelism. We interpreted a knowledge base using multiple workers and found that the parallel evaluation takes more time than the sequential evaluation. The reason for this slowdown was that a worker performing a dynamic database update will suspend its branch, unless it is leftmost in the OR-tree (to preserve Prolog semantics). As the order of the solutions is not important, we could use the asynchronous database predicates of Aurora, and so avoid unnecessary suspensions.

Another source of the parallelization bottleneck was the improper use of cuts. In many cases the asynchronous database handling predicates had been suspended because they were in the scope of a cut [Haus 90]. This was due to bad programming style of placing cuts at the end of clauses. We restructured the CUBIQ interpreter by placing cuts as early as possible in the alternatives. This helped to get rid of most suspensions.

Finally, we substituted the interpreter with a compiler. The compiled code runs about three times faster than the interpreted code.

We used the ship knowledge base described in [Bal 87a] to evaluate the performance of an uncertain knowledge base. This is a classification problem about recognising warships and ordinary ships on the base of visual, acoustic and radar information. The knowledge base contains 112 clauses.

The table below shows performance results for the ship program in various stages of our implementation. We present execution times in milliseconds for 1, 3 and 4 workers on a SEQUENT/DYNIX system with 4 of 50Mhz Intel486 processors.

	1 worker	3 workers(speedup)	4 workers(speedup)
simple interpreter	1526	2020 (0.75)	2178 (0.71)
interpreter	1591	638 (2.49)	515 (3.12)
compiler	593	241 (2.46)	193 (3.07)

4 Future work

The main problem is the representation of the uncertain knowledge in the Prolog language in such a way that all the language structures of Prolog are allowed. The current model of uncertainty in CUBIQ does not fulfill this requirement. The uncertainty of built-in procedures and especially meta-predicates (findall, if-then-else, etc.) should still be investigated.

We devoted some effort to exploring possible interpretations for the cut operator in uncertain knowledge bases. In Prolog we use cut operators when we want to prune the evaluation of other alternatives after some subgoals in an alternative have been found true. We plan to introduce an uncertain cut operator with the following meaning: the cut operator is executed when the preceding subgoals are evaluated with high support (near to true) and ignored when the support for the preceding subgoals is low (near to false). The applicability of the cut operator may also depend on the general support of the containing clause.

A further area to explore is the uncertainty in frames with multiple inheritance [Itz 94]. In this model the ancestor relationship is extended to allow uncertain parent(s). In the CUBIQ tool-set the knowledge engineer is allowed to provide his/her own definition of ancestorship. One may consider using this mechanism for experimenting with such extended forms of inheritance.This may also lead to a search mechanism that is highly parallel.

5 Conclusion

Aurora Prolog has been extended with uncertainty handling and experiments show a reasonable speedup on multiple workers. We have found that there is a bigger scope for exploiting parallelism in an uncertain knowledge base than in an ordinary logic knowledge base because of the nature of calculating uncertainty.

Our experiments contributed to expanding our knowledge on applicability of parallel Prolog. We have found the asynchronous database handling predicates of Aurora useful for implementing efficient information transfer between the parallel branches of the search tree. We have found that in a parallel environment one has to pay attention to careful use of the non-logical features of Prolog (such as the cut operator), as improper use may lead to serious performance degradation.

6   Acknowledgement

This work has been supported by the European Union in the framework of Co-operation in Science and Technology with Central and Eastern European Countries (CUBIQ — PECO Project 10979).

The author is much indebted to Péter Szeredi for his valuable comments and encouragement.

References

[Bal 87a]   Baldwin, J. F., Martin, T. P., Pilsworth, B. W.: FRIL Programming Language Reference Manual.

[Bal 87b]   Baldwin, J. F.: Evidential Support Logic Programming in Fuzzy Sets and Systems **24**, (1987) 1–26

[Carl 92]   Carlsson, M., et al.: Aurora Prolog User's Manual.

[Geig 94]   Geiger, C., Lehrenfeld, G.: The Application of Concurrent Fuzzy Prolog in the Field of Modelling Flexible Manufacturing Systems, in Proc. of 2nd Int. Conf. on the Practical Applications of Prolog, London, (1994) 233–251

[Haus 90]   Hausman, B.: Pruning and Speculative Work in OR-Parallel Prolog, Dissertation, Stockholm, Sweden, (1990)

[Itz 94]   I. Itzkovich, I., Hawkes, L. W.: Fuzzy extension of inheritance hierarchies, in Fuzzy Sets and Systems **62**, (1994) 143–153

[Nara 86]   Narain, S.: MYCIN: The Expert System and Its Implementation in LogLisp, in van Caneghem, M., Warren D. H.: Logic Programming and its Applications in Ablex Series in AI, (1986) 161–174

[Pear 88]   Pearl, J.: Probabilistic Reasoning in Intelligent Systems: Networks of Plausible Inference. USA, (1988)

[Ram 90]   Ramsey, C. L., Booker, L. B.: A Parallel Implementation of a Belief Maintenance System, in Proc. The Fifth Ann. AI Systems in Gov. Conf., (1990) 180–186

[Roj 93]   Rojas-Guzman, C., Kramer, M. A.: Comparison of Belief Networks and Rule-Based Expert Systems for Fault Diagnosis of Chemical Processes, in Engineering Appl. of AI, Vol. 6, Iss 3, (1993) 191–202

[Ster 86]   Sterling, L., Shapiro, E. H.: The Art of Prolog. MIT Press, (1988)

[Yalç 90]   Yalçinalp, L. Ü., Sterling, L.: Building Embedded Languages and Expert System Shells in Prolog, in Proc. of 2nd Int. IEEE Conf. on Tools for AI, (1990) 56–62

A Special-purpose Coprocessor for Qualitative Simulation*

Gerald Friedl, Marco Platzner, Bernhard Rinner
E-mail: marco@iti.tu-graz.ac.at

Institute for Technical Informatics
Graz University of Technology

keywords: specialized coprocessor, FPGA, qualitative simulator QSIM

1 Introduction

Qualitative simulation is applied more and more in design, monitoring and fault-diagnosis. However, poor performance of current qualitative simulators complicates or even prevents its application in technical environments.

In our research project [3] a special-purpose computer architecture for the widely-used qualitative simulator QSIM [2] is developed. The design of this special-purpose computer architecture is mainly based on an extensive analysis [4] of current QSIM implementations. Figure 1 presents an overview of the runtime ratios of QSIM kernel functions and their hierarchical structure. An improved performance is achieved by mapping QSIM functions onto a multiprocessor system and executing runtime intensive functions on specialized coprocessors. In this paper, we present the current state of a part of this research project — i.e. the design and implementation of a specialized coprocessor for the *constraint check functions (CCFs)* of QSIM [1]. The constraint check functions are primitive kernel functions, but due to their frequent execution they dominate the overall kernel execution time. For most models, the CCFs require more than 50 % of the kernel runtime.

2 CCF Coprocessor

Current QSIM implementations include many types of CCFs (D/DT, ADD, MULT etc.). This section presents the design, implementation, and first experimental results of a coprocessor for the most complex CCF, the MULT-CCF.

2.1 Analysis of the MULT-CCF

Figure 2 shows the data dependency diagram for the MULT-CCF. This function is partitioned into 4 subfunctions SF1 to SF4. SF3 consists of n iterations. All

---

* This project is partially supported by the Austrian National Science Foundation *Fonds zur Förderung der wissenschaftlichen Forschung* under grant number P10411-MAT.

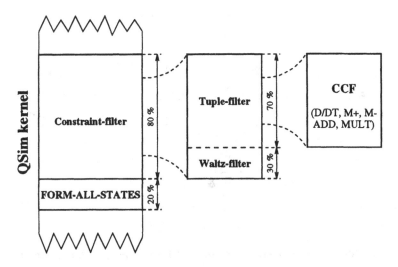

Fig. 1. Runtime analysis of the QSim kernel. Kernel functions are hierarchically structured and their runtimes are informally presented with regard to the runtime of the calling function. The presented runtime ratios are extracted from various runtime measurements of a QSim system implemented on a TI Explorer LISP workstation.

subfunctions produce a boolean result. Two facts can be taken from the data dependency diagram. First, the subfunctions SF1, SF2, and all iterations of SF3 are dataflow–independent. Therefore, they can be executed in parallel. Second, subfunction SF4 performs a logical AND-operation on the results of SF1 to SF3. QSim uses *short circuit evaluation* for this logical AND-operation.

2.2 Design of the MULT-CCF Coprocessor

The MULT-CCF coprocessor was designed at the gate- and register level to obtain maximum execution speed. Main features of the design are:

- data structures are optimized for the application QSim
- operations use maximum parallelism
- customized memory architectures allow parallel access

The block diagram of the MULT-CCF coprocessor is shown in Fig. 3. The blocks SF1, SF2, and SF3 correspond directly to the subfunctions in Fig. 2. Primitive operations of these subfunctions are comparisons and evaluation of boolean functions. These operations are supported by optimized comparators and lookup-tables. The input and output controller establish communication to the host processor (digital signal processor TMS320C40) via two separate communication channels. The operands and the instruction code are packed into a 32 bit word for communication from host to coprocessor. The function controller decodes the instruction, handles the data transfer to the functional blocks, and controls the execution of the instruction. The function controller also

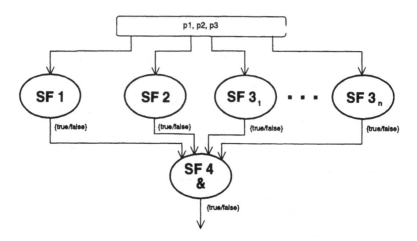

Fig. 2. Data dependency diagram for the MULT-CCF. p_1, p_2, and p_3 are input variables.

handles the short circuit evaluation mechanism. SF3 iterations are sequentially executed in the current design.

2.3 Experimental Results, Further Work

In order to compare the coprocessor to a SW reference system we consider two execution paths of the MULT-CCF. In the first case the SW implementation stops after the first executed subfunction due to short circuit evaluation. In the second case, all subfunctions have to be executed, including 4 iterations of SF3. The first execution path represents the worst case for the coprocessor.

The MULT-CCF coprocessor was implemented in an FPGA of type Xilinx XC4013 running at a clock frequency of 15 MHz. We compared experimentally the coprocessor to a SW reference running on a TMS320C40 at 32 MHz. For the first execution path the runtime improvement is given by a factor of 6, for the second execution path the gain is 20.7.

Further work includes:

- performance improvement due to routing optimization
- exploration of design alternatives (pipelining of SF3 iterations vs. simultaneous execution of SF3 iterations on several SF3 function blocks)

References

1. G. Friedl. Entwurf und FPGA-Implementierung eines Coprozessors für qualitative Simulation. Master's thesis, Graz University of Technology, 1995.
2. B. Kuipers. *Qualitative Reasoning: Modeling and Simulation with Incomplete Knowledge*. Artificial Intelligence. MIT Press, 1994.

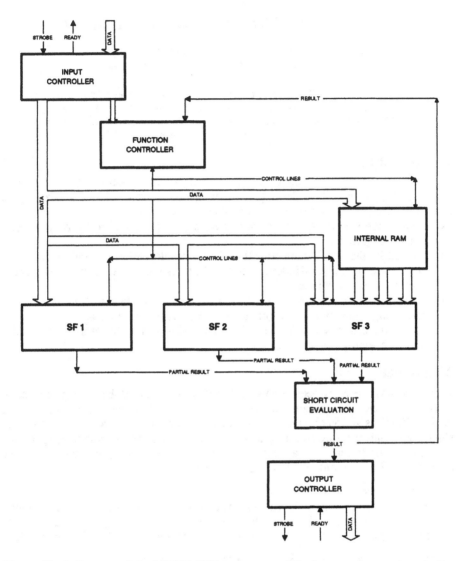

Fig. 3. Block diagram of the MULT-CCF coprocessor. The input and output controller connect the coprocessor to the host processor via an 8 bit data bus and two handshake lines (STROBE, READY). For simplification control lines between input/output controller and function controller are not shown.

3. M. Platzner, B. Rinner, and R. Weiss. A Distributed Computer Architecture for Qualitative Simulation Based on a Multi-DSP and FPGAs. In *3rd Euromicro Workshop on Parallel and Distributed Processing*, pages 311–318, San Remo, January 1995. IEEE Computer Society Press.
4. B. Rinner. Konzepte zur Parallelisierung des qualitativen Simulators QSIM. Master's thesis, Graz University of Technology, October 1993.

Portable Software Tools for Parallel Architectures

Catherine Barnes
Programme Manager, EPSRC[1]

Chris Wadsworth
Technical Coordinator, RAL[2]

Abstract. Portable Software Tools for Parallel Architectures (PSTPA) is a five-year programme of collaborative research funded by the UK Engineering and Physical Sciences Research Council. This paper summarises the scope and aims of the programme and the set of 15 projects recently started.

1 Scope and Aims

The scope of the PSTPA programme covers the spectrum from research in parallel programming methods to development of generic tools including application generators. The programme seeks in particular:

- to widen the application programmer base and to improve productivity by an order of magnitude,
- to maximise the exploitation potential of tools developed in the programme,
- to maximise architectural independence of the tools and to maximise the leverage of open systems standards,
- to focus on easy-to-use tools which can provide particular benefit to the engineering, industrial, and information processing user sectors, and
- to prove the effectiveness of the tools and the value of the standards to potential users with appropriate demonstrations.

2 Projects

15 projects have recently been announced. Both projects to aid the porting of existing software and ones that research methods and tools to reduce the effort in developing new applications software have been selected. Each project is academically-led with significant planned commitment from one or more industrial (or commercial) partners. The rest of this paper gives a brief description of each project, grouped under five headings. For brevity only the lead partner is listed here.[3]

2.1 Application Generators

Application generators are tools with which applications can be built by specifying their parameters, usually in a domain-specific input language, analogous to the "fourth generation" approach adopted, for instance, in commercial areas for scalar machines.

An Application Generator for Spatial Interaction Modelling on a Scalable Computing Platform   (Prof Peter Dew, University of Leeds)

An application generator will be developed for non-linear optimisation problems with embedded spatial interaction models, targeted at the WPRAM computational model. As well as generating parallel code for the final application, code will also be generated for calibrating and bootstrapping the model. Practical techniques including randomised hashing and software asynchronous combining will be implemented to support a shared address space and scalable concurrent data access.

---

1. Engineering and Physical Sciences Research Council, Polaris House, North Star Avenue, Swindon SN2 1ET, UK. (Tel: +44 1793 444428, Fax: +44 1793 444006, Email: scbn0@ib.rl.ac.uk)
2. Rutherford Appleton Laboratory, Chilton, Didcot, Oxon OX11 0QX, UK. (Tel: +44 1235 445101, Fax: +44 1235 445945, Email: cpw@inf.rl.ac.uk)
3. For full summaries of the projects including contact details, please contact the first author.

A Distributed Application Generator in the Search/Optimisation Domain
(Dr Hugh Glaser, University of Southampton)

The distinctive nature of computational problems that require management in a sophisticated, heuristic fashion will be studied and a generator built for implementations on networks of workstations and related architectures. Research is also included on experimentation with distribution strategies and the design and specification of novel input languages attuned to the application domain. A prototype will be built and evaluated for optimisation problems in decision support.

A Framework for Distributed Application (Prof Phil Treleaven, UCL)

The project will develop standard distributed communications and object manipulation protocols, comprising a Framework, and a Generic Application Generator (GAG) tool. The Framework will comply to industry standards, such as CORBA, OLE and DDE, to allow network transparent development and execution across a heterogeneous network of machines including PCs and workstations. The GAG tool, built using the Framework, will facilitate rapid, seamless integration and execution of tools by allowing developers to visually build and configure applications. The tools will be demonstrated on a direct marketing utility in the advertising sector and on financial application in the retail banking sector.

2.2 User Environments

This area covers run-time utilities, design and development tools, tools for managing parallel systems, and integrated environments.

Portable Software Tools for the Parallelisation of Computational Mechanics (CM) Software (Prof Mark Cross, University of Greenwich)

Analysis and restructuring techniques for the parallel implementation of CM codes will be studied, building on earlier research in the CAPTools and JOSTLE projects. In the first phase the earlier partitioning tool for structured mesh (SM) codes will be extended to unstructured mesh (UM) and multi-block structured (MBS) codes. Extension of the analysis and optimisation techniques to handle recursion, pointers, etc in F90/HPF and C will then be addressed in the second phase.

Parallel Software Tools for Embedded Signal Processing Applications
(Dr Andy Downton, University of Essex)

The objective is to build an integrated visual programming toolkit for embedded applications characterised by requiring a real-time response to streams of input data. A stylised, generic design methodology will be developed, building from existing studies using pipelines of processor farms, and exercised on a range of applications selected from fields such as image processing, computer vision, speech processing, and real-time control. A particular aim is to capitalise on the stylised nature to improve the accuracy of performance prediction and to assist in the consideration of tradeoffs at design time.

An Integrated Environment for Modelling High-Performance Parallel Database Systems (Prof Tony Hey, University of Southampton)

The issues of performance optimisation and capacity planning for parallel database systems will be studied. The project will build on novel ideas in analytical modelling supported by calibration and interpolation, and by automated acquisition of performance characteristics for parallel database systems, to provide high accuracy and predictive capability. The involvement of four industrial partners will ensure wide applicability.

A BSP Programming Environment (Dr Bill McColl, University of Oxford)

The Bulk Synchronous Parallel (BSP) model provides a unified framework for the design and programming of scalable parallel systems. The Oxford BSP Library is already being for the design and implementation of parallel software which is efficient, scalable, and fully portable. This project is a major effort to extend the practical methodology, with: training materials, tutorials and case studies; design, analysis and implementation tools (performance analysis and prediction, benchmarking, debugging); and higher level "synthetic" elements (collective communications, superstep structuring and transformation).

Application Sizing, Capacity Planning and Data Placement for Parallel Database Systems (Prof Howard Williams, Heriot-Watt University)

A set of tools to assist the migration of database applications to parallel computing platforms will be investigated and developed. Techniques will be developed to determine: how best to distribute the user's data (data placement); the best configuration to meet the user's needs (application sizing); and how to adjust the data placement, possibly dynamically, to improve performance once the system is running (capacity planning). Trend analysis, simulation, and benchmarking are among the methods that will be assessed. The tools will be validated on two different parallel platforms and two different database management systems using standard benchmarks (TCP-B, TCP-C, AS3AP).

An Environment for the Design and Performance Evaluation of Portable Parallel Software (Dr Steve Winter, University of Westminster)

An integrated environment will be developed to support a rapid, effective, and flexible approach to the engineering of portable parallel software using standard programming tools, such as compilers. The environment will be formed from three principal tools: a simulation tool for generating behaviour and performance data, based on an abstract machine execution model for skeleton parallel programs, supported by library modules to realise specific implementations; a visualisation tool for extracting and presenting the relevant characteristics and data generated by the simulator; and a graphical configuration tool for rapidly (re-)configuring programs.

2.3 Portable Software Platforms

Portable software platforms define interfaces below which machine-dependent optimisations can be performed, and above which portable programs may be constructed. They are the lowest level at which portability is considered in this programme. They also provide appropriate targets for application generators and for compilers. (Only one project is specifically listed, but see also the projects led by Dew, by McColl, and by Jesshope based on WPRAM, BSP, and f-code, respectively.)

A Portable Coprocessor Model for Parallel Image Processing
(Prof Danny Crookes, QUB & Dr Philip Morrow, University of Ulster)

A portable software platform, EPIC (Extensible Parallel Image Coprocessor), initially targeted at the image processing domain will be defined and developed. Associated tools will include a rule-based transformation which allows the set of programming abstractions to be extended and automatically optimised. The extensible nature of the coprocessor is key to obtaining optimised execution for portable abstractions. Generalisation(s) from this domain-specific model, which provides efficiency and portability from the outset, toward a general-purpose model will also be investigated.

2.4 Tools for Building and Using Libraries

Tools for creating libraries and modules, interface standards, and for building applications from library components and modules are included.

Portable Software Components
(Dr Peter Dzwig, Queen Mary & Westfield College)

PSC aims to develop a set of tools to assist non-expert users by provision of a "literate programming", modular database of generic library components and graphical tools for parallel and distributed systems. An object-oriented coordination model will be used, built in UC++ (EUROPA parallel C++). The toolkit will enable the user to visualise system configurations and to generate these transparently. Target applications in the commercial (banking) sector will be demonstrated.

Automatic Generation of Parallel Visualisation Modules
(Mr Andrew Grant, University of Manchester)

A comprehensive environment for the development of parallel visualisation modules will be developed, including: an automatic parallel module generator, a dataflow network editor for building parallel visualisation modules, and a development environment for (remote) computational steering. The environment will be portable between networks of workstations and MPP systems and will be made available for both virtual shared memory and distributed memory parallel machines.

2.5 Languages and Compilers

This area covers language developments that have the potential to fit in with likely future hardware developments, and parallelising compiler techniques such as analysis, restructuring, and mapping techniques. (See also the project led by Cross.)

The Inference of Data Mapping and Scheduling Strategies from Fortran 90 Programs on the Cray T3D (Prof Chris Jesshope, University of Surrey)

A novel access subtyping system will be studied and developed for the inference of mapping and scheduling strategies for data parallel languages on distributed memory architectures. The techniques will be demonstrated and evaluated by the compilation of (non-annotated) Fortran 90 programs for a Cray T3D. Portability will be ensured by the use of an underlying portable software platform (f-code).

Automatic Checking of Message-Passing Programs
(Dr Denis Nicole, University of Southampton)

Symbolic model checking will be investigated as a technique for assuring the correctness of the communications components of message passing programs, in order to catch possible deadlock, livelock, and other problems during the program design cycle. A model checking environment for MPI Fortran is the principal target, but a preliminary study will be made for occam as it serves as a bridging language between application programming, protocol design, and hardware specification.

occam for All (Prof Peter Welch, University of Kent)

A set of architecture-neutral tools, based on occam, will be developed that support the design, implementation, optimisation, and maintenance of high-performance applications. Systems constructed with these tools will be portable across a wide range of (MIMD) parallel computing platforms, on which they will operate with high levels of efficiency. Based initially on occam2, research will also be pursued to extend the tools efficiently and portably for the new high-level features in occam2.5 and occam3.

Boosting the performance of workstations through WARPmemory

Christoph Siegelin*, Ulrich Finger and Ciaran O'Donnell

Ecole Nationale Supérieure des Télécommunications
Département Informatique
46 rue Barrault, 75634 Paris Cedex 13, France
E-mail {siegelin, finger, ciaran}@inf.enst.fr

1 Introduction

Networks of workstations have become widely available. The consoles are mostly occupied, whilst the aggregate computational power remains idle. This problem has been addressed by several software packages that allow the remote management of processes and the communication between them. These solutions work reasonably well for message-passing programming and applications with a very coarse grain parallelism. The shared memory programming model is preferable, but its implementation on top of message-passing is cumbersome. Applications with a finer grain of parallelism yield unacceptable performance.

At ENST, we are currently designing a device called WARPmemory that makes shared memory physically available to a number of workstations. Each workstation has a direct access link (high bandwidth, low latency) making data sharing and synchronisation very fast. Message-passing can be optimised also. It is important to our approach that an existing programming interface is used, thereby preserving existing investment in parallel software. WARPmemory is a transparent accelerator for parallel programming on a network of workstations.

2 Background

The most widely used parallel programming package is currently PVM [2]. To transform a network of workstations into a *Parallel Virtual Machine*, daemon processes are initiated that communicate with each other and with the user tasks via UDP and TCP sockets respectively. A user library provides routines for the control of remote processes and communication and synchronisation between them. This design is advantageous when portability and use in heterogeneous configurations are the primary design goals, but it is penalising for performance. Frequent system calls (socket-level communications management), data copying and network accesses lead to communication latencies of the order of the millisecond, consequently reducing the performance. Results for a typical application using message-passing are reported [4] in which communication latencies

---

* Supported by a Graduate Fellowship (HSPII) of the German Academic Exchange Service.

amount to 40 % of the total execution time. When implementing (distributed) shared memory on top of PVM message-passing [3], the overhead increases since shared memory programming tends to exploit a finer grain of parallelism.

3 Hardware

The architecture of WARPmemory is derived from our research in the SAXO-SMM architecture [1]. It is composed of a plug-in card for a workstation, fiber optic links and a multiported memory module. Each workstation addresses the multiported memory as a part of its own memory space. Cache coherence is ensured using a directory-based write-invalidate protocol [5].

The plug-in card (Fig. 1) interfaces to the processor-memory bus (e.g., Sun's Mbus) and to the fiber optic link. The controller is designed to translate the transactions on the bus (snooping coherence) to the link protocol (directory-based coherence) and vice-versa. Note that it is also possible to interface to an I/O bus such as PCI, but cache coherence must then be assisted in software.

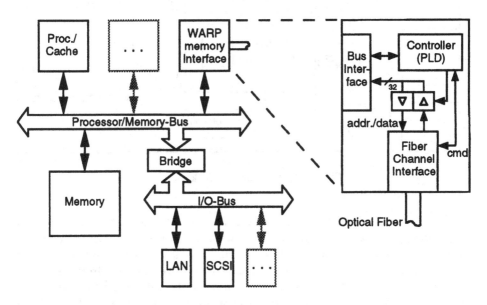

Fig. 1. Workstation block diagram

The links are built of standard parts implementing the Fiber Channel Standard (1 Gbaud/s). The chip sets (Siemens [6]) have a parallel interface hiding the complexity of data coding, multiplexing and clock extraction completely.

The design of the memory module (Fig. 2) is original in that a fast RISC microprocessor (DEC Alpha [7]) is used as an intelligent switch. Its high-bandwidth system bus is directly connected to two banks of SRAM (simplifying the design) and to the links. Memory accesses have a cache-line granularity, their latency is hidden through the use of *prefetch* accesses. Links are accessed in 32 bit quantities. The processor moves data (assembling and disassembling memory blocks) and manages the directory-based protocol. Importantly, its superscalar architecture allows to execute data accesses and protocol operations (i.e. integer instructions) in parallel. The protocol code fits into the instruction cache, the data cache stores recently used directory information. The complexity of the implementation is lower (compared with a conventional implementation using shift registers etc.), thus design efforts can be concentrated on the bus interface. The link protocol is implemented in firmware, allowing for flexibility (critical word first, e.g.), subsequent extensions (partial access, e.g.) and easy correction of bugs. No dedicated memory for the directory is needed.

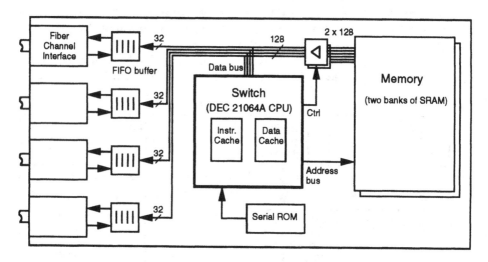

Fig. 2. WARPmemory block diagram

The performance of WARPmemory is mainly determined by the latency of data serialization on the link, and by data moving and execution of protocol code on the switch. For a 32 byte cache line, the link latency amounts to 300 ns approximately. A 200 MHz DEC Alpha can move 32 bytes from or to the links within 160 ns, these accesses are consequently hidden. Further assuming 20 cycles for directory lookup, data moving within the processor etc. leads to a software overhead of 100 ns. We therefore expect the overhead of a cache-fill operation from WARPmemory (compared with a fill from the workstation's memory) to be in the order of 400 ns. The switch has a projected bandwidth of 190 MByte/s, thus significant contention is not expected.

4 Software

The system described so far provides coherent shared memory, atomic read/write transactions and a reliable message-passing mechanism (also for interrupts). Custom low-level software must be written for memory allocation *(shared malloc)* and synchronisation *(test-and-set)*.

For process creation and communication, existing software running on top of the local network is used in a first phase. We chose PVM [2] for its availability on various platforms and its wide user base. The resulting system will augment the functionality of the basic PVM configuration with powerful and efficient shared memory primitives.

At this point, performance will again suffer from the latencies of PVM operations, including barriers. The system has therefore to be incrementally optimised in a second phase by replacing PVM functions (using the local network and TCP/IP) with much faster native (WARPmemory) implementations. This will include an optimised message-passing mechanism. To by-pass the time-consuming operating system barrier (context switches), these functions will be entirely implemented in user space.

5 Conclusions

In this paper, we have described a device to accelerate the execution of parallel programs on a network of workstations. It provides physically shared memory, avoiding the drawbacks of distributed shared memory (DSM) machines. The design of the serially multiported memory is conceptually simple, yet powerful. We provide a standard programming interface. Finally, the prototype exploits the existing functionality of PVM on a local network, allowing the quick realisation of a running system. Subsequent replacement of PVM functionality with native implementations leads to optimisation of performances.

References

1. Siegelin, C., Finger, U., O'Donnell, C.: SAXO-SMM: a distributed multiprocessor and a balanced architecture. Proceedings of the 2nd International Workshop on Massive Parallelism, Capri, Italy, October 1994.
2. Manchek, R.: Design and implementation of PVM version 3. MSc thesis, University of Tennesse, Knoxville, USA, May 1994.
3. Demeure, I., Cabrera, R., Meunier, P.: Phosporus: adding shared memory to PVM. Proceedings of the 1st European PVM Users' Group Meeting, Rome, Italy, October 1994.
4. Femminella, A., Omodeo, A.: PVM-based parallel computing: a case study on power plant simulation. Short note at the Euromicro'94 conference, Liverpool, England, September 1994.
5. Censier, L., Feautrier, P.: A new solution to coherence problems in multicache systems. IEEE Transactions on Computers, December 1978.
6. 1 GBaud Transceiver. Product Brief, Siemens.
7. DECchip 21064 and DECchip 21064A Alpha AXP Microprocessors. Hardware Reference Manual, Digital Equipment Corporation, 1994.

A Monitoring System for Software-Heterogeneous Distributed Environments*

Aleksander Laurentowski, Jakub Szymaszek, Andrzej Uszok,
Krzysztof Zieliński

Institute of Computer Science
University of Mining and Metallurgy (AGH)
Al. Mickiewicza 30, Cracow, Poland
e-mails: {pinio,jasz,uszok,kz}@ics.agh.edu.pl

1 Introduction

Emerging trends in high performance computing tend to exploit massively parallel systems (like SPP 1000) and distributed memory architectures (e.g. SP1, SP2), as well as workstation clusters. The most appropriate computational model for this kind of systems is built of a set of autonomous objects, communicating via message-passing mechanism. Advanced applications within this model may be engineered of components implemented in various programming languages. Hence, particular parts of such applications can be executed in those programming environments which inherently express the nature of computation. This allows mixing various programming and execution paradigms (e.g. imperative, functional, object-oriented or logic programming) in one software-heterogeneous system. Taking advantage of software components reuse and easier implementation process, this technique can speed-up the development of new, modern applications – unfortunately, much increasing their complexity at the same time.

Tools for monitoring, debugging and maintaining such applications could substantially help in that case. Our Managed Object-based Distributed Monitoring System (MODIMOS) aims at monitoring of large distributed software-heterogeneous applications, organized according to an object wrapping technique. The area of its application covers visualization of the systems' structure and activity, management of their logical configuration, thus enabling appropriate tuning. This influenced characteristic features of MODIMOS, like e.g. configurability of its modules, information management and filtering mechanisms, expandability of monitored environments set.

2 MODIMOS Architecture

The functionality of MODIMOS is determined by an abstraction we call the Uniform Model of Computation, pertinent to the object-based environments used

* This work was sponsored by the Polish State Committee of Scientific Research (KBN) under grant no.: 8 S503 015 06.

for wrapping of programming modules. Well-known distributed systems used for wrapping technology show some similarity of their computational models. We have analyzed a set of them and decided that the abstract model should be a superset (union) of their models of computation. Hence, in our Uniform Model the following levels of abstraction have been recognized: environment, application, container, object, interface and method. The detailed mapping of them into a couple of popular programming environments, e.g. ANSA[1], SR[2], and a CORBA-compliant[3] (Orbix) is shown in the table below.

Unit of abstraction	Environment		
	ANSA	SR	Orbix
application	—	makefile	—
container	capsule	virtual machine	process
object	object	resource, global	object
interface	interface	resource spec.	interface
method	operation	operation	operation

A set of relevant events is associated with each abstraction unit. These events are reported to the monitoring subsystem. Events concern the aspects of the items' behavior, such as initiation, creation, destroy, change of state, operation call/reply, etc.

MODIMOS has a multi-layer architecture shown below. Functionality of these layers may be described as follows. The Environments Layer consists of an

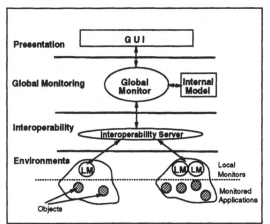

expandable set of popular distributed programming environments. Any new object-wrapping environment can join the Environments Layer, provided it fits at least partially the Uniform Model and supports basic mechanisms of communication with the outside world. The Environments Layer consists of Monitored Applications sublayer and Local Monitoring sublayer.

The Monitored Application Sublayer represents original application code, instrumented by special preprocessors with addition of notification functions. The events reported by notification functions are collected in the Local Monitors sublayer. Each local monitor is a managed object written in a language provided by the given environment. It has three interfaces: Monitored Events, Management and Reported Events. Management Interface is used for monitoring policy setting, that determines which events received via Monitored Events Interface are forwarded through Reported Events Interface. Information sent via Reported Events Interface is structured according to the Uniform Model. Therefore, above the first layer only the abstract semantics is recognized.

The second layer deals with interoperability aspects. The aim of the Interoperability Layer is to ensure a universal and general platform for operations dispatching between local monitors and Global Monitoring Layer. The dispatching mechanisms used for this purpose are transparent to the local monitors. This layer dispatches invocations concerning reported events notification to the Global Monitoring module and, respectively, the management decisions from the global monitor (i.e. the user) down to local monitors.

Global Monitoring Layer collects reported events in a database called Internal Model (reflecting the architecture, configuration and current state of the monitored environment), cooperates with Graphical User Interface in the process of information visualization, implements the selective monitoring policy, and ensures consistency of collected data.

3   Basic Features of the System

As MODIMOS is itself a software heterogeneous application, the general interoperability mechanisms proposed and employed during its construction can be used in further multi-paradigm systems. We have analyzed and compared several variants of those mechanisms during design and construction of Interoperability Layer. The first choice is its base platform: a primitive communication interface (such as sockets) or an integrating *glue* environment, which offers more abstract notion of communication providing localization, binding, dispatching, name service, etc. We have chosen the latter solution and implemented Interoperability Layer in Orbix CORBA-compliant system. Messages are sent by invocations of functions from remote servers' interfaces, what frees the programmer from buffers construction. This also ensures well structuring and encapsulation of IL functionality into environments' objects. The *glue* environment must be somehow integrated with the monitored environments. The perfect solution would be construction of an object being a full member of the *glue* and a given monitored environment at the same time. It means that this object should be able to call and receive invocations from both these environments, so it may act as a *gateway* between them. However, there is a lot of environments which do not fulfill this assumption. A solution for this problem is an idea of a *plug* [7]. It is a regular *glue* environment object, which, however, represents the given monitored environment in the *glue* system. It receives remote operations' invocations from the given environment's local monitors, translates them into *glue* system's remote operation calls format, and invokes them on behalf of the local monitors. Invocations from all *plugs* are in an ordinary *glue* system form. The *glue* environment serves as a communication framework for *plugs*, it localizes the global monitor, binds *plugs* to its interface and dispatches their invocations to it.

Applications running in the environments to be visualized consist of items composing a hierarchical structure (a tree), described in terms of the computational model specific for the particular environment, and in terms of the Uniform Model. In order to visualize the items' hierarchy, we have implemented methods of "box-like", two-dimensional trees visualization, in which "child" level figures are placed into the figures representing "parent" levels of the hierarchy.

High performance computing imposes substantial requirements on monitoring tools, e.g. ability to cope with large amount of data, high speed and intensity of interactions. In contrast to systems like IPS-2 [4], Paragraph [5] or Falcon [6], MODIMOS is not intended to present the whole program execution history. Introduction of filtering and selection mechanisms enables the user to significantly limit the amount of collected data and focus on the the most interesting and "hot" areas of the monitored system's activity. Filtering can take place at Environments Layer, where selection rules can be set up at preprocessing time and through the management interfaces of local monitors, as well as at the Global Monitoring level. Moreover, selection options at GUI enable the user to eliminate a group of objects or levels in the Uniform Model hierarchy during a particular visualization process. We employ two kinds of the visualized tree nodes' selection: *horizontal* (eliminating items from one logical level, e.g. all containers) and *vertical* (eliminating particular tree nodes with its subtrees).

To assure high flexibility of the system, we employed advanced software engineering techniques during MODIMOS's design and construction. As an object-oriented framework [8], the system consists of a set of cooperating software components, thus enabling easy extensions (new monitored environments, multiple monitors, GUI's, etc.). We use design patterns [9] to describe architecture, functionality and interfaces of those software-heterogeneous components.

The system is currently under development. Having implemented the Environments, Interoperability and prototype Global Monitoring layers, we are currently investigating methods of ensuring consistent global state of the monitoring trace. We are also designing the management mechanisms for global and local monitors.

References

1. *ANSAware 4.0 — Application Programmer's Manual*, APM Ltd. Cambridge, 1992.
2. G.R. Andrews, R.A. Olsson, *The SR Programming Language: Concurrency in Practice*, Benjamin/Cummings Publishing Company, 1992.
3. *Draft Common Object Request Broker Architecture Revision 1.1*, OMG Report 91-12-1, OMG Inc., 1991.
4. B. P. Miller, M. Clark, J. Hollingsworth, S. Kierstead, S. Lim and T. Torzewski, "IPS-2: The Second Generation of a Parallel Program Measurment System", *IEEE Trans. on Parallel and Distributed Systems*, 1,2, April 1990.
5. M. T. Heath and J. A. Etheridge, "Visualizing Performance of Parallel Programs", *IEEE Software*, 8(5), September 1991.
6. W. Gu, G. Eisenhauer, E. Kraemer, K. Schwan, J. Stasko, J. Vetter, N. Mallavarupu, Falcon: On-line Monitoring and Steering of Large-Scale Parallel Programs, Georgia Institute of Technology, Technical Report No. GIT-CC-94-21, April 1994.
7. A. Uszok, G. Czajkowski, K. Zieliński, Interoperability Gateway Construction for Object-Oriented Distributed Systems, *Proceedings of the 6th Nordic Workshop on Programming Environment Research*, Lund, Sweden, June 1994.
8. R. Campbell, N. Islam, A Technique for Documenting the Framework of an Object-Oriented System, *Proc. IWOOS'92*, IEEE Computer Society Press, Sep. 1992.
9. E. Gamma, R. Helm, R. Johnson, J. Vlissides, *Design Patterns: Elements of Object-Oriented Software Architecture*, Addison-Wesley, 1994.

A metacircular
data-parallel functional language [1]

Gaétan Hains [2] and John Mullins [3]

Abstract

We describe and relate two data-parallel semantics for the simply-typed
λ-calculus and obtain a semantic function expressible in its object language. The explicitly distributed semantics allow the formal specification
of the interpreter's effect on data partitioning and communications.

1 Introduction

The CMU Scandal project's VCODE [2] demonstrates the usefulness of a parallel
intermediate language abstract enough to be portable yet explicit about parallel
data. DPML and its latest implementation Caml FLight [5], were designed with
these goals in mind. Caml Flight extends the sequential language Caml Light
in a deterministic and portable way but looses its *metacircularity*, a symptom
of a loss of expressive power. A language which can express its own interpreter
is called metacircular [1]. This paper describes the semantics of a metacircular
DPML-like language.

Data-parallel functional programming is often formalised through *data fields*
or *parallel data as functions* [9]. We use instead (generalised) concrete data
structures [4, 6] whose data elements called *states* are built more elementary
pieces called *events*. We label *events*, not states with *indices*, i.e. explicit locations, and obtain a space of concrete states we call *arrays* [7] supporting a
dual *macroscopic/microscopic* view of data, characteristic of data-parallelism
[3]. Equivalence of the centralised-macroscopic and the distributed-microscopic
semantics leads to metacircularity. We first define the category of domains of
arrays, then our two denotational semantics and conclude.

2 Concrete- and Array Data Structures

A *concrete data structure* or CDS [6] is a tuple $(C, V, E, \vdash)$ where C is a countable
set of *cells*, V is a countable set of *values*, $E \subseteq C \times V$ is the set of possible *events*
(c, v) or cv. The *enabling* relation $\vdash$ is between finite sets of events and cells. It
induces a *precedence* relation on cells: $c \ll c'$ iff $\exists y, v. \, y \cup \{cv\} \vdash c'$. Precedence
must be well-founded. A cell c is called *initial* if $\emptyset \vdash c$. If $y \vdash c$, then y is

---

[1] Work supported by Fujitsu Labs and NSERC
[2] ISIS, Fujitsu Labs, 1-9-3 Nakase, Mihama-ku, Chiba 261, Japan
[3] Dept. Computer Science, University of Ottawa, Ottawa K1N 6N5, Canada

an *enabling* of c. Let M, M', N denote CDSs from now on. A *state* of M is a set of events $x \subseteq E_M$ which is functional (at most one value per cell) and safe (contains an enabling for every cell it fills). Define $(\mathcal{D}(M), \subseteq)$ to be the poset of states of M. For example let $\text{Bool} = (\{B\}, \{T, F\}, \{BT, BF\}, \vdash)$ where $\vdash B$. Then $\mathcal{D}(\text{Bool})$ is $\{\emptyset, \{BT\}, \{BF\}\}$, the flat domain of booleans. $\text{Nat} = (\{N\}, \mathbf{N}, \{Nn \mid n \in \mathbf{N}\}, \vdash)$ where $\vdash N$ has states $\{\emptyset, \{N0\}, \{N1\}, \ldots\}$, the flat domain of naturals. Posets $(\mathcal{D}(M), \subseteq)$, called *concrete domains* are consistently complete Scott domains with set union and intersection as operations.

Bookes and Geva's *generalised* concrete data structure or gCDS [4] are CDSs with a partial order $\leq$ on cells. We may safely think of a gCDS as a CDS. The *generalised* concrete domains are also consistently complete. Their category **gCDScont** has continuous functions as arrows. The product $M_1 \times M_2$ simply superposes events without interaction. The exponential $M \to M'$ is a gCDS of cells $C = \mathcal{D}_{\mathbf{fin}}(M) \times C_{M'}$, where $\mathcal{D}_{\mathbf{fin}}(M)$ is the finite states of M ordered by $\subseteq$. The values are $V = V_{M'}$, cell ordering, events and enablings are defined appropriately. An event $xc'v'$ of $M \to M'$ associates an event $c'v'$ of M' to a finite state x of M. The exponential preserves gCDSs through the isomorphisms $a \mapsto \lambda z \in \mathcal{D}(M). \{c'v' \mid \exists x \subseteq z. \ xc'v' \in a\}$ and $f \mapsto \{xc'v' \in E \mid c'v' \in f(x)\}$. Continuous functions and states of the exponential structure are interchangeable. **gCDScont** is a CCC.

We define now *array structures* [7]. Cells, values and events are labelled by network locations called *indices*. Communication is represented by the enabling relation in analogy to the way S communicates to B, N in **Bool+Nat**. Array indices thus represent addresses in a static multiprocessor network underlying all data, including functions. Assume the existence of a fixed countable directed graph (I, L) between indices $\vec{\imath} \in I$. Let $M = (C_0, \leq_0, V_0, E_0, \vdash_0)$ be a given gCDS. The array data structure, (ADS) or *array structure* over M, $M^{\square}$ is a gCDS $(C, \leq, V, E, \vdash)$ where: $C = I \times C_0$, $\leq$ is local to every $\imath$, $V = V_0$ and $E = I \times E_0$. Enablings follow links: $\{\vec{\imath}'c_1v_1, \ldots, \vec{\imath}'c_kv_k\} \vdash \vec{\imath}c$ when $(\vec{\imath}', \vec{\imath}) \in L$ and $\{c_1v_1, \ldots, c_kv_k\} \vdash_0 c$. The elements t of poset $\mathcal{D}(M^{\square})$ are called *arrays* over M. Because a cell can be enabled either locally or remotely, enablings in $M^{\square}$ are not unique even when they were so in M: cells of $t \in \mathcal{D}(M^{\square})$ can be enabled remotely, the set $t\vec{\imath} = t \cap (\{\vec{\imath}\} \times C_0 \times V_0)$ is not, in general, a state of $\mathcal{D}(M)$. This is how our arrays generalise data fields.

Define now the category **ADScont** on array structures with continuous transformations between their domains as morphisms. Its product is a special case of the product of CDSs. Its exponential operator is also a special case because $(M^{\square} \to N^{\square}) \cong (M^{\square} \to N)^{\square}$, through the isomorphisms $a \in \mathcal{D}(M^{\square} \to N^{\square}) \mapsto \{\vec{\imath}xe \mid x\vec{\imath}e \in a\}$ and $t \in \mathcal{D}((M^{\square} \to N)^{\square}) \mapsto \{x\vec{\imath}e \mid \vec{\imath}xe \in t\}$. **ADScont** is thus a CCC. In fact the following more general isomorphism holds:

Proposition 1 *For any gCDSs* M, N $\qquad (M \to N^{\square}) \cong (M \to N)^{\square}$

3 Sum structures, types and two semantics

The structure $\mathbf{Bool} + \mathbf{Nat}$ has cells $\{SEL, B, N\}$ values $\{L, R\} \cup V_{\mathbf{Bool}} \cup V_{\mathbf{Nat}}$, events $\{SELL, SELR\} \cup E_{\mathbf{Bool}} \cup E_{\mathbf{Nat}}$ and enablings $\vdash S$, $SELL \vdash B$, and $SELR \vdash N$. Its domain is isomorphic to the lifted sum of $\mathbf{Bool}$ and $\mathbf{Nat}$. It is straightforward to generalise this construction to a countable family of gCDS $\{M_j\}_{j \in J}$ whose sum $\sum_{j \in J} M_j$ has one central selector cell SEL and where $SELj$ enables the initial cells of M_j. The states of $\sum_j M_j$ are $\emptyset$ and $\bigcup_j \{\{SELj\} \cup x \mid x \in \mathcal{D}(M_j)\}$. For every j there is a monomorphism $\mathrm{inj}_j : M_j \to \sum_i M_i$ which adds $\{SELj\}$ to a state. Its left-inverse is the continuous $\pi_j : x \mapsto x \cap E_{M_j}$.

Let K be a countable set of base types and construct the set of types as terms $T = T_{\times, \to}(K)$. We give each type two interpretations for every $\tau \in K$, M_τ is a given gCDS so $M_\tau^\square$ is an ADS. This is extended to every type by interpreting $\times$ and $\to$ in the appropriate category, $\mathbf{gCDScont}$ or $\mathbf{ADScont}$. Define $M_{\sigma \to \tau}^\square = M_\sigma^\square \to M_\tau^\square$ which is not isomorphic to $(M_\sigma \to M_\tau)^\square$.

Consider now a state x of $\sum_\tau M_\tau^\square$. Either $x = \emptyset$ or $x = \{SEL\tau'\} \cup x'$ where x' is a state of $M_{\tau'}^\square$. By construction x' is almost a state of $(\sum_\sigma M_\sigma)^\square$, so define the correspondence $\mathrm{inc} : \sum_\tau M_\tau^\square \to (\sum_\sigma M_\sigma)^\square$ such that $\mathrm{inc}\, x = x' \cup \bigcup_{\iota \in I} \{\iota SEL\tau'\}$ if $x \neq \emptyset$ and $\mathrm{inc}\, \emptyset = \emptyset$. This is a continuous injection. Its partial inverse π is discontinuous. The sum $\sum_{\sigma \in T} M_\sigma^\square$ is a gCDS but not an array structure. Its states are suitable data for a macroscopic semantics (sums of arrays): they realise a kind of centralised control. Meanwhile, the "arrays of sums" structure $(\sum_{\sigma \in T} M_\sigma)^\square$ is suitable for a microscopic semantics because the selection of its type is distributed. But it introduces a form of non-determinism. In general its states are not I-indexed families of scalar states: different scalar types may overlap at any given index ι.

Let now $\mathbf{Var}_\perp$ be a flat CDS whose values are typed variables $x_\tau \in \mathbf{Var}$. Define a macroscopic environment to be a strict continuous $\hat{\rho} : \mathbf{Var}_\perp \to \sum_\tau M_\tau^\square$ such that $\hat{\rho} x_\tau \in \mathrm{inj}_\tau(M_\tau^\square)$. A microscopic environment $\check{\rho}$ has codomain $(\sum_\tau M_\tau)^\square$ and equals $\mathrm{inc} \circ \hat{\rho}$ where $\hat{\rho}$ is a macroscopic environment. Remark that $\check{\rho} x_\tau$ is then a state of $M_\tau^\square$ plus selector events at each ι. Let $\mathbf{Term}$ be the set of typed λ-terms built from typed constants c_τ and variables x_τ.

For $t \in \mathbf{Term}$, the macroscopic semantics $[\![t]\!] \hat{\rho} : \sum_\tau M_\tau^\square$ is defined through transformation functions inj, π from the standard semantics in $\mathbf{gCDScont}$. The application rule for $s_1 : \sigma \to \tau, s_2 : \sigma$ is $[\![s_1 s_2]\!] \hat{\rho} = \mathrm{inj}_{M_\tau^\square}((\pi_{M_\sigma^\square \to M_\tau^\square}([\![s_1]\!] \hat{\rho})) \cdot (\pi_{M_\sigma^\square}([\![s_2]\!] \hat{\rho})))$ (using $\mathbf{gCDScont}$'s application $\cdot$). The abstraction rule for $s : \tau$ is $[\![\lambda x_\rho . s]\!] \hat{\rho} = \mathrm{inj}_{M_\sigma^\square \to M_\tau^\square}(\lambda t \in D(M_\sigma^\square). \pi_{M_\tau^\square}([\![s]\!](\hat{\rho}[x \leftarrow \mathrm{inj}_{M_\sigma^\square} t])))$. It follows that $[\![\,]\!]$ is well typed and that $[\![s]\!] \hat{\rho} \in \mathrm{inj}_{M_\sigma^\square}(M_\sigma^\square)$ for $s : \sigma$.

A microscopic semantics can be defined without transformations, directly in $\mathbf{ADScont}$: $[\![t]\!]\check{\rho} \in (\sum_\tau M_\tau)^\square$. Again $[\![\,]\!]$ is well typed and for $s : \sigma$, $[\![s]\!]\check{\rho} \in \mathrm{inc} \circ \mathrm{inj}_{M_\sigma^\square}(M_\sigma^\square)$. We can verify the equivalence $[\![s]\!]\check{\rho} = \mathrm{inc}([\![s]\!]\hat{\rho})$. This is interesting because the microscopic semantics is itself an array, expressible by a λ-term. Indeed, by repeated application of proposition 1, we obtain $[\![\,]\!] \in (\mathbf{Term} \to (\mathbf{Var}_\perp \to \sum_\tau M_\tau)^\square \to \sum_\tau M_\tau)^\square$. Metacircularity can be proven immediately as follows: encode the λ-terms in the CDS LAMBDA [6] whose enablings correspond to syntactic occurrence paths. Then conclude by the above remarks that **Term** is a gCDS and **[]** an arrow of **ADScont**. Then express it as a λ-term itself, using fixpoint and conditional constants.

While this work is preliminary, it mathematically solves a first goal of the CMU Scandal project (*Scandal project overview*, under http://www.cs.cmu.edu) namely support for higher-order functions, and prepares formal methods for a second goal: the optimisation of data layout on parallel computers. Future work will involve the denotational design of distributed algorithms [8] for **[]** and a data-parallel interpreter in Caml-Flight.

References

[1] H. Abelson and G. J. Sussman, *Structure and Interpretation of Computer Programs*, MIT Press, 1985.

[2] G. Blelloch and S. Chatterjee, *VCODE: a data-parallel intermediate language*, in 3rd IEEE Symp. Frontiers of Massively Parallel Comp., 1990.

[3] L. Bougé, *On the semantics of languages for massively parallel SIMD architectures*, in PARLE-91, E. H. L. Aarts and J. van Leeuwen, eds., no. 505 and 506 in L.N.C.S., Eindhoven, June 1991, Springer.

[4] S. Brookes and S. Geva, *Continuous functions and parallel algorithms on concrete data structures*, in MFPS'91, L.N.C.S., Springer, 1991.

[5] E. Chailloux and C. Foisy, *Caml-Flight alpha: Implantation et applications*, in Journées Franco. Lang. Applicatifs, C. Queinnec, V. V. Donzeau-Gouge, and P. Weis, eds., no. 13 in Collection Didactique, INRIA, Janvier 1995.

[6] P.-L. Curien, *Categorical Combinators, Sequential Algorithms and Functional Programming*, Birkhäuser, Boston, second ed., 1993.

[7] G. Hains and J. Mullins, *A categorical model of array domains*, Rapport de Recherche RR94-43, LIP, ENS-Lyon, December 1994.

[8] ———, *Array structures and data-parallel algorithms*, Research Note RR-95-1E, ISIS, Fujitsu Labs, Makuhari, Japan, 1995.

[9] P. Hammarlund and B. Lisper, *Data parallel programming: A survey and proposal for a new model*, Tech. Rep. TRITA-IT-9308, Swedish Royal Institute of Technology, Stockholm, 1993.

Efficient run-time program allocation on a parallel coprocessor

Jurij Šilc and Borut Robič

Jožef Stefan Institute, Computer Systems Department
Jamova 39, 61111 Ljubljana, Slovenia
E-mail: jurij.silc@ijs.si

Abstract. One way to obtain higher computational performance of a computer H is to use a parallel coprocessor unit C which is attached to H and can efficiently solve computationally demanding applications. If such a unit C can be used for concurrent execution of several independent executable programs, the problem of efficient run-time (i.e. dynamic) allocation of programs to C arises. Our aim is to find an allocation strategy that maximizes throughput of the overall system H-C.

We present two dynamic allocation approaches for C with mesh-connected architecture. In both cases we reduce the allocation problem to the weighted bipartite matching problem which must be solved during the run-time each time a set of waiting executable programs is to be allocated space in C. The two approaches differ in the way they search for free space in C.

1 Introduction

One way to obtain higher computational performance of a computer system is to use special parallel coprocessor units (e.g. processor meshes) which are attached to the host and can efficiently solve computationally demanding applications. We are particularly interested in coprocessor units where each node is capable of executing I/O operations such as 2D or 3D data-driven hex meshes [6, 8]. Having high I/O bandwidth, these meshes are particularly suitable for computationally intensive applications. In addition, they simplify the mapping process and can serve as general-purpose coprocessor units. The qualification of these meshes for computationally intensive applications is complemented by advances in VLSI/WSI technology which offer a higher rate of on-chip communication, a higher number of processor nodes per chip, and complex node architecture.

Clearly, given such a coprocessor unit we should strive to improve the computing performance of the overall system. To do this, we might use the coprocessor unit for concurrent execution of several independent executable programs. Allocation of programs can either be static (during the compile-time) [1] or dynamic (during their execution). In what follows we will discuss the dynamic allocation of executable programs to the processor array with mesh-connected architecture aiming to improve the systems overall performance.

2 Mapping optimization

The first step towards performance optimization is to improve program mappings during the compile-time so that during their run-time they occupy as small number of nodes as possible. This also reduces communication time between remote nodes and consequently the program execution time. Several approaches to such a *mapping compression* were described in [3, 4]. Due to yield problems, however, some of the nodes are going to be faulty [7]. Methods for mapping compression in presence of faulty nodes were discussed in [5]. Using mapping compression larger programs can be mapped on the coprocessor unit. Alternatively, several executable programs can be placed on the unit concurrently. This results in the problem of *dynamic allocation* of executable programs.

3 Dynamic allocation

Let H denote the host and C the coprocessor unit attached to H. Suppose that at some moment there is a set $\mathcal{P}_R$ of *running* programs in C, and a set $\mathcal{P}_W$ of compressed executable programs *waiting* in H to be allocated space (i.e. nodes) in C. The aim is to find an allocation strategy that would maximize throughput of the H-C system. Each node of C is either *idle*, *faulty*, or *busy* (running part of a program from $\mathcal{P}_R$). Accordingly, we write $C = C_i \cup C_f \cup C_b$, where C_i, C_f, and C_b are sets of idle, free, and busy nodes, respectively. A local optimization approach decides which programs from $\mathcal{P}_W$ will be allocated to C_i and how this will be done. In order to decide on this, each program in $\mathcal{P}_W$ is associated with information describing its size. The size is determined after the program compression during the compile-time. We also monitor the shape of C_i and update it as soon as either a program in $\mathcal{P}_R$ has completed its execution and set free some of the nodes, or a program in $\mathcal{P}_W$ has been selected for execution and allocated nodes in C_i. A similar problem has been discussed in [2] where it was reduced to the three dimensional packing problem. In our case, however, this approach is not useful since the execution times of programs in $\mathcal{P}_W$ are not known in advance.

Fixed polygons: Let $P_1, P_2, \ldots$ be a sequence of convex polygons of m sides such that P_i is the *largest* such polygon for which we have $P_i \subseteq C - C_f - \bigcup_{j=1}^{i-1} P_j$. We will take into consideration only a finite subsequence $\Pi(m, \alpha) = P_1, P_2, \ldots P_k$ such that $area(P_k) \geq \alpha > area(P_{k+1})$, where α denotes the smallest area allowed. Informally, the faultless part of the coprocessor is partitioned into k largest pairwise disjoint polygons. Efficient algorithms for the construction of the largest P_i for $m = 4$ (rectangle) and $m = \infty$ (circle) exist. That is, largest empty rectangle or circle can be constructed in time $\mathcal{O}(n \log n)$, where $n = |C_f|$. $\Pi(m, \alpha)$ is described by the *allocation table* (AT) located at H. The i-th row of AT describes the $status(P_i)$, $size(P_i)$, and $position(P_i)$ of P_i in C. The status is either free or occupied. Sizes of circles or rectangles are given by their radii or side lengths, respectively. Also at H is located the *program table* (PT) which describes the size of each $p_j \in \mathcal{P}_W$, i.e., the size of the *smallest bounding poly-gon* B_j of p_j. Now, let $\mathcal{B}$ be the set of all such bounding polygons of programs in $\mathcal{P}_W$, and let $\Pi^{\text{free}}(m, \alpha)$ be the subsequence of those $P_i \in \Pi(m, \alpha)$ having $status(P_i) = $ free. Define the cost of placing $p_j \in \mathcal{P}_W$ into $P_i \in \Pi^{\text{free}}(m, \alpha)$ to be

$$Cost(j, i) = \begin{cases} size(P_i) - size(B_j), & \text{if } size(P_i) \geq size(B_j) \\ \infty, & \text{otherwise.} \end{cases}$$

The problem of optimal allocation of waiting programs to C can now be described in terms of the *weighted bipartite matching problem* between $\mathcal{B}$ and $\Pi^{\text{free}}(m, \alpha)$ with the cost function as defined above. The time complexity of this problem is known to be polylogarithmic, i.e., $\mathcal{O}(\frac{ne \log n}{\max(1, \log \frac{e}{n})})$, where n is the number of vertices in $\mathcal{B}$ and $\Pi^{\text{free}}(m, \alpha)$, and e is the number of edges between the two sets. Allocation of a program p_j to some P_i moves p_j from $\mathcal{P}_W$ to $\mathcal{P}_R$, deleting B_j from PT, and setting $status(P_i) = $ occupied in AT. This status is set back to free after the p_j has finished its execution and freed the space in C.

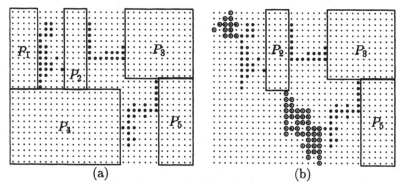

(a)   (b)

Fig. 1. We are given C with 27×33 nodes (depicted by ·) of which 68 are faulty (depicted by •). Fixed polygon method for $m = 4$ and $\alpha = 45$ results in $\Pi(4, 45) = P_1, \ldots, P_5$ (Fig.1a). Fig.1b shows the situation after the allocation of programs p_1 ($size(B_1) = 9 \times 3$) and p_2 ($size(B_2) = 13 \times 7$), allocation of p_3 ($size(B_3) = 5 \times 3$), and deallocation of p_2 (busy nodes are depicted by ⊙). This results in $\Pi^{\text{free}}(4, 45) = P_2, P_3, P_5$ which is 32.5% of C.

Variable polygons: In spite of the application of the weighted matching algorithm a situation may develop where waiting p_j is placed into P_i although B_j is much smaller than P_i, i.e., $size(P_i) - size(B_j) \geq \alpha$. In such cases it is much more space-efficient to allocate only a part of P_i to p_j and either returning the rest of P_i (appropriately partitioned into smaller empty polygons) to the set of free polygons, or recomputing the whole set of free polygons from the idle part of the C. According to this, AT has to be either updated or reconstructed each time a program is allocated/deallocated space in C.

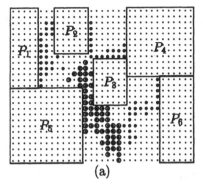

		fixed polygons		variable polygons	
	action	k	A (%)	k	A (%)
1.	initialization	5	69.6	5	69.6
2.	p_1 and p_2 allocated	3	34.1	5	59.3
3.	p_3 allocated	2	26.3	5	58.5
4.	p_2 deallocated	3	32.5	6	74.1

(a)   (b)

Fig. 2. If variable polygon method is applied, the same sequence of allocations/deallocations as in Fig.1 results in the situation depicted in Fig.2a. Notice, that now 74.1% of C can be used for allocation (Fig.2b).

4 Conclusions

Two dynamic allocation approaches have been presented. Both improve the performance of a H-C system, where H is a host and C is a parallel coprocessor with mesh-connected architecture. Both approaches reduce the allocation problem to the weighted bipartite matching problem which must be solved during the run-time each time a set of waiting executable programs is to be allocated space in C. The incurred overhead is not severe, however, since the latter problem can be solved in polylog time. The two approaches differ in the time they spend in optimizing the utilization of C, i.e., in the way they search for free space in C.

References

1. Kvas, A., Ojsteršek M., Žumer V.: Evaluation of static program allocation schemes for macro data-flow computers. Proc. EUROMICRO 94 (1994) 573–580
2. Li, K., Cheng, K.H.: Job scheduling in partitionable mesh connected systems. ICPP 89 (1989) II.65–72
3. Mendelson, B., Koren, I.: Using simulated annealing for mapping algorithms onto data driven arrays. Proc. ICPP 91 (1991) I.123–127
4. Robič, B., Kolbezen, P., Šilc, J.: Area optimization of dataflow-graph mappings. Parallel Comput. **18** (1992) 297–311
5. Robič, B., Šilc, J.: Fault-tolerant mapping onto VLSI/WSI processor arrays. Proc. EUROMICRO 94 (1994) 697–703
6. Sérot, J., Quénot, G., Zavidovique, B.: A functional data-flow architecture dedicated to real-time image processing. IFIP Trans. **A-23** (1993) 129–140
7. Trobec, R., Jerebic, I.: Optimization of diagnostic examination. Lect. Notes Coput. Sc. **854** (1994) 761–772
8. Weiss, S., Spillinger, I.Y., Silberman, G.M.: Architectural improvements for a data-driven VLSI processing array. J. Parallel Dist. Com. **19** (1993) 308–322

A program manipulation system for fine-grained architectures *

Vladimir A. Evstigneev, Victor N. Kasyanov

A.P.Ershov Institute of Informatics Systems
Siberian Division of Russian Academy of Science
630090, Novosibirsk-90, Russia

E-mail:{eva,kvn}@iis.nsk.su
Fax: (07-383-2) 32-34-94

Abstract. The PROGRESS system being implemented at the Institute of Informatics Systems in Novosibirsk is discussed. The system is intended to support rapid prototyping of compilers for high level languages (e.g. Fortran-77, Modula-2, SISAL) and for a family of architectures exploited fine-grained parallelism. The next goal of the project is to develop an environment for investigation of optimizing and restructuring transformations of programs to be parallelized.

Key words: parallel processing, fine-grain architectures, transformational approach, program restructuring, multifunctional cooperation

1   Introduction

One of the problems of parallel processing is that of a rapid development of a compiler prototype for a new computer. Having such compiler prototype one can begin to exploit the computer, to reveal its merits and demerits, and to evaluate its performance. To achieve this goal, we have begun the project PROGRESS aimed at rapid prototyping of compilers for a family of high-level languages and for a family of architectures exploiting fine-grained parallelism [1].

The next goal that we should like to achieve is to develop an environment for investigation of optimizing and restructuring transformations of the programs to be parallelized. From this point of view, the system under development is also intended to study currently available transformations and to create new ones (in particular, composite transformations involving existing ones) for programs written in high-level languages which are extended by facilities to annotate programs.

We are also planning to use the PROGRESS system as an integrated collection of tools to support the following opportunities:

— to convert a sequential program into a parallel one written in a parallel dialect of the input language,

— to optimize programs at the input language level using various criteria of quality,

— to compare versions of the programs with respect to complexity,

* Partially supported by the Russian Foundation for Fundamental Research under Grant 95-01-01334a

— to include most of the capabilities of modern symbolic algebra systems,

— to tune the compilation process upon a given architecture.

2 The PROGRESS system

The PROGRESS system includes the following subsystems:

— the translating subsystem (TRSS) which supports conversion of a source program into the basic intermediate form (abstract syntax tree);

— the intermediate representation subsystem (IRSS) which supports conversion of the basic program representation into other intermediate forms (program dependence graph, hierarchical task graph, ideograph and so on);

— the transformation subsystem (TSS) which supports program transformations and extraction of program properties needed;

— the retranslating subsystem (RTSS) which supports conversion of an intermediate program into high-level language program to be pretty printed or visualized;

— the evaluation subsystem (EVSS) which supports static program analysis and · program run simulation to evaluate program quality and performance;

— the code generator subsystem (CGSS) which supports a code generation for a given target computer;

— the specialization subsystem (SSS) which supports a design of compiler prototype for a given input language and a given target computer by means of concretizing transformations;

— the information subsystem (INSS) and others.

Each subsystem is designed as an abstract data type — through the set of operations supported by this subsystem. Interaction between the subsystems is accomplished by a special interface subsystem.

We assume a compiler prototype being constructed to have several components, P_1, ..., P_k, where compilation process consists in applying P_1 to source program and, in general, in applying P_j to the result of applying P_{j-1}. Of course, some modifications of input languages, of program transformations implemented in the system or of target architectures may require corresponding modification of one or several subsystems. So, each subsystem should be open to include new features. However, we suppose that many components of compiler prototypes may be constructed from corresponding subsystems of the PROGRESS system on the base of concretizing transformations [2].

3 Input languages and target architectures

We are planning to have both the imperative languages (Fortran 77, Fortran-90, C, Pascal, Modula-2) and the applicative language SISAL [3,4] as input ones.

It is assumed that source programming languages are extended by the so-called annotations which are formalized comments in the source programs and intended for permitting advices and partially relaxing the limits on the source language. That is, the program manipulation system accepts not only the source program, but also some annotations being directions (guidances) on how to do the transformation. However, annotations are not just pragmas or hints for a manipulation system (e.g., how to better parallelize a sequential program). They can be used to modify the semantics of the source program, but only in a very moderate manner [5].

Our current interests are connected with fine-grained architectures which include VLIW, superscalar, superpipelined and others. The importance of these architectures is connected with the existence of a tendency to offer both kinds of parallelism: coarse-grained and fine-grained ones.

4   Current state and related works

Today many programming tools and environments are being constructed to coordinate the disjoint activities of editing, debugging, and tuning complex applications designed to run on parallel architectures. The DELTA system, Faust, PTOPP, ParaScope and others can be mentioned among them.

Like DELTA [6], our system is a program manipulation one to study optimizing and restructuring algorithms, to design new transformations, to find out transformation application order mostly suited for the given classes of programs and computers. Unlike DELTA and other similar systems, the PROGRESS system uses a number of intermediate representations (such as the abstract syntax tree, the control flow graph, the program dependence graph, etc.) for programs being transformed, manipulates with annotated programs and can be used for the rapid prototyping of parallelizing compilers for different input languages and different target computers.

The initial version of the system manipulates with programs written in the Fortran-77 and Modula-2 languages extended with program annotation facilities and supports data flow analysis and optimizations. For program transformed, it uses such intermediate presentations as an abstract syntax tree, a control flow graph and SSA-form [7].

Multifunctional integration method aimed at solving the compaction problems for fine-grained computers and based on multiple-function multiple-data procedures has been developed. A computer-aided integrator for Fortran programs and a library of multifunctional procedures for the ES-2706 computer with the VLIW architecture have been implemented [8], [9].

Now the next version of the system is under development in which the translating subsystem will include the Fortran-90, C and SISAL languages, the intermediate representation subsystem will be extended on the program dependence graph and IF1, the program transformation subsystem will support restructuring transformations. Moreover, the system will be enriched by an evaluation subsystem.

References

[1] Evstigneev, V., Kasyanov, V.: The PROGRESS program manipulation system; In: Proc. of the International Conf. Parallel Computing Technologies (PaCT'93), Vol.3, Obninsk, 1993, 651 – 656.

[2] Kasyanov, V.N.: Transformational approach to program concretization; Theoretical Computer Science 90,1 (1991), 37 – 46.

[3] Feo, L.T.: SISAL; LLNL, Preprint UCRL-JC-110915, July 1992.

[4] Cann, D.: Retire Fortran? A debate rekindled; Comm. ACM 35, 8 (1992), 81-89.

[5] Kasyanov, V.N.: Tools and techniques of annotated programming; Lecture Notes in Computer Science 477 (1991), 117 – 131.

[6] Padua, D.: The DELTA program manipulation system. Preliminary design; University of Illinois at Urbana-Champaign, CSRD Rep. 880, June 1989.

[7] Software intellectualization and quality / Ed. by V.N.Kasyanov, Novosibirsk, 1994, (in Russian).

[8] Evstigneev, V.: Some peculiarities of the software for the computers with large instruction word; Programmirovanije, 2 (1991), 69 – 80. (In Russian).

[9] Bulysheva, L.: Methods and tools for optimization of computation for processors with VLIW-architectures; Computing Center of Sib. Div. of the RAS, Preprint 975, Novosibirsk, 1993. (In Russian).

Real-Time Image Compression Using Data-Parallelism

P. MORAVIE[1], H. ESSAFI[1], C. LAMBERT-NEBOUT[2], J-L. BASILLE[3]

[1] LETI (CEA – Technologies Avancées), DEIN – CE/S, F91191 Gif sur Yvette.
[2] Centre Spatial de Toulouse, 18 Av. Belin BP 1421, F31055 Toulouse Cedex.
[3] ENSEEIHT, 2 rue camichel, 31071 Toulouse Cedex.

Abstract

The purpose of this paper is to present this new parallel image compression algorithm. We present implementation results on several parallel computers. We also examine load balancing and data mapping problems. We end by presenting a well-suited architecture for Real-Time image compression.

Keywords : Data-Parallelism, Image Compression, Wavelet Transform, Vector Quantization, Huffman Coding.

1 Introduction

Today, in the digitized satellite image domain, the needs for high dimension images increase considerably. To transmit or to stock such images (6000 by 6000 pixels), we need to reduce their data volume and so we have to use image compression technics. In most cases, these operations have to be processed in Real–Time. But the large amount of computations required prohibits the use of common sequential processors. To solve this problem, CEA in collaboration with CNES developed and evaluated a new parallel image compression algorithm for general purpose parallel computers using data-parallelism. This paper introduces this new parallel image compression algorithm. Thus, in a first section, we briefly describe the image compression technics on which our algorithm is based. In section two, we develop our algorithm. We also present implementation results on several parallel computers and we examine load balancing and data mapping problems. As a conclusion, we present a well-suited architecture for Real-Time image compression.

2 Sequential Image Compression Algorithms

Image compression is classically achieved in three steps. The image is first transformed in a set of decorrelated coefficients. Then, the transformed coefficients are quantized. Finally, the quantized values are entropy coded.

During the past few years several design algorithms have been developed for each step. It has been shown that compression algorithms based on Wavelet Transform[1], Vector Quantization[3] and Huffman Coding[4] provide one of the best trade-off between compression rates and quality. Therefore, we based our algorithm on all these technics.

2.1 Wavelet Transform (W.T)

The Wavelet Transform is a powerful tool for signal, image processing. For image compression, using wavelet transform offers two essential advantages. First, the produced coefficients are well decorrelated due to the good localization of the wavelet function in both space and frequency. And the multi-resolution of wavelet transform is suitable with quantization: each sub-image produced by W.T can be quantized using an adapted quantizer.

In order to reduce the computation time, we used one of the fastest wavelet transform algorithm (designed by Mallat[2]). It is based on a subband coding scheme, i.e it uses linear filter convolutions and image shrinking.

2.2 Vector Quantization (V.Q)

Quantization is the most essential part of common image compression algorithms. In fact, it is the part which provides the major bits rate reduction. Indeed, this technic reduce the number of grey levels used to code the image and so reduce the number of bits required to represent each pixels. According to Shannon's rate distortion theory, better results are always obtained when vectors rather than scalars are encoded. Therefore, our algorithm is based on vector quantization.

This technic is achieved in three steps. First, the pixels are organized into k-dimensional vectors. Then, each vector is approximated by a vector (named centroid) belonging to a predefined catalogue (named codebook). And finally, each vector to be coded is replaced by the reference of its centroid.

2.3 Huffman Coding (H.C)

Huffman coding[4] is the most popular lossless compression technique. It is a statistical data compression technique which gives a reduction in the average code length used to represent the symbols of a alphabet. In fact, it assigns codes to input symbols in such a way that each code length in bits is approximatively $\log_2(symbol\ probability)$.

Usually, a Huffman code is built as follow. First, we rank all symbols in order of probability of occurrence. Next, we successively combine the two symbols of the lowest probability to form a new composite symbol. And finally, we trace a path to each leaf, noticing the direction at each node. The code assign to each symbol is the path.

3 Our Parallel Image Compression Algorithm

3.1 Parallelization mode

After studying implementations of all the technics described above, on MIMD, SIMD and message passing architecture, we concluded that using data-parallelism and pipeline technics are the best way to parallelize this type of algorithm. This is due to the regularity of the processing involved. Indeed, each block of pixels is processed in the same way and all these have to be chained in good order. As our aim is to define a parallel algorithm for general purpose machine, we developed our parallel image compression algorithm solely using data-parallelism.

3.2 Data Organization

From implementations of these technics on several parallel machines (such as Connection–Machine CM5, Maspar, Symphonie, Sympati2) we noted that for each network and memory organizations, there are few data organizations which allow a real speed–up. This is due to the large amount of regular communications required by all these technics. In fact, these data organizations respect two essential conditions.

- Each processor must have the same amount of data in order to ensure correct load–balancing
- The amount of communications required by the processes must be minimum. It means:
  - *(V.Q)* Each vector must be stocked in one processor memory.
  - *(W.T)* Each processor only gets adjacent pixels in its memory.

An interesting point we underlined is that if a data organization is optimal for Wavelet Transform, then it is also optimal for the quantization. As the wavelet transform do not change data organization, we recommend to optimize the data organization according to wavelet transform and to architecture.

3.3 The Parallel Image Compression Algorithm

The parallel algorithm can be described as follow :
  - Get an new image and map the pixels into the processors memories.
  - Apply a double Wavelet Transform Decomposition on the image.
  - Quantify each sub-image (vector) with the adequate codebook.
  - Encode each result using a Huffman encoder.
Vector quantization and Huffman encoding consist in replacing a group of pixels (vector or reference) by a code. By using an appropriate codebook it is possible to mix this 2 process and so to speed-up the computations.

3.4 Implementing results

Each part of this algorithm has been evaluated on several parallel machine with several parameters. In table 1, we give few results for a 8:1 compression ratio and a quality of 36 DB (PSNR).

	SYMPATI-2 (32 proc.)	SYMPHONIE (32 proc.)	CM5 (32 proc.)	Cm200 (4096 proc.)
W.T (Float. point)	1502	200	250	1855
W.T (16 bits)	115	7	-	1870
V.Q + H.C (16 bits)	190	22	-	-

Table 1. *Computation time in Milliseconds (256x256 image).*

We note that when the computations is process using floating or fix point precision operations, the best results are obtained by Symphonie. This is due to its well suited architecture. In fact, Symphonie do not have floating point processors but its architecture has been designed for Real-Time Image Processing.

4 Real-Time image compression architecture

To process the satellite image compression in real–time, we need to execute our algorithm in less than 4 milliseconds. Using fix point precision, Symphonie fitted out with 32 PE processes our algorithm in 29 milliseconds. But, using floating point precision, it processes in 420 millisecond. As quality test shows that in most of cases using 16 bits fix precision to do all the calculations, we can estimate that Symphonie architecture (fitted out with 1024 PE) is well suited for process real–time image compression.

From studying all the implementations we have made, we pointed out the main characteristics of Symphonie (*in italic*) which are interesting for satellite image compression :

- Symphonie is a *Multi-SIMD* architecture where each node is a linear array of superscalar processors. Each PE consists mainly of *32 bits processor, a co-processor dedicated to memory address computation, a floating point accelerator* and a communication module. Symphonie is also fitting out with two communications networks (one asynchronous and one synchronous).

5 Conclusion

We presented here a new parallel image compression algorithm which likely to be implemented on SIMD and MIMD architecture. We evaluated this algorithm on several machines. We showed that when the computation is done using fix point precision, it allows us to process the image compression in real time.

References

1. M. Antonini, M. Barlaud, P. Mathieu, I. Daubechies. Image coding Using Wavelets Transform. *IEEE Trans. on Image processing* 1(4):205–220, 1992.
2. S. G. Mallat. A theory for multiresolution signal decomposition: The wavelet representation. *IEEE Trans. on Pattern Analysis and Machine Inte lligence*, 11(7):674–693, 1989.
3. A. Gersho, R.M. Gray Vector Quantization and Signal Compression. Kluwer Academic Publisher, Boston, 1992.
4. M. Nelson. The Data Compression book. Prentice Hall, Redwood Cityes, 1991.
5. M. J. Quinn. *Designing Efficient Algorithms for Parallel Computers.* McGraw-Hill, New York, NY, 1987.
6. R. W. Hockney and C. R. Jesshope. *Parallel Computers: 2 Architecture, Programming, and Algorithms, 2nd Ed.* IOP Publishing Ltd., Pennsylvania, 1988.

Congestion control in wormhole networks: First results

Abdel-Halim Smai

Department of Teleinformatics, Royal Institute of Technology
Electrum 204, S-164 40 Kista, Sweden

Abstract. We present the first results of a congestion control scheme for computer wormhole networks. The basic idea of this scheme is to require pre-selected nodes to restrict their packet injection in order to reduce and possibly eliminate congestion in the whole network. The scheme employs randomization to select nodes. Our preliminary performance measurements indicate clearly that the proposed scheme improves network performance. Some of the remaining studies are implementation cost, such as the impact of the scheme on the input/output queues in the nodes. Another further study would be to compare such flow control schemes with other trends such as that of adaptive routing algorithms.

1 Introduction

Wormhole routing has been introduced to reduce network latency in message-passing multicomputers. Apart from deadlock, one of the main issues in wormhole networks is channel and network congestion. While previous research on multicomputer networks focused mostly on designing and comparing various adaptive routing algorithms and network topologies, little work has been devoted to flow control. Furthermore, most of the studies have ignored the problem of congestion. Channel congestion occurs when two or more packets simultaneously require the same channel. Only one packet acquires the channel while the other packets are blocked. Several channel congestions create network congestion. Since in wormhole routing a packet is not removed from the network when it is blocked, it can rapidly lead to more blocked packets and therefore to more congestion, especially with large packet lengths and network sizes.

We present the first results of a congestion control scheme for computer wormhole networks. The basic idea of this scheme is to request pre-selected nodes to restrict their packet injection in order to reduce and possibly eliminate congestion in the whole network. This approach can be used in combination with other flow control schemes based on virtual channels [1,3]. In Section 2, we give an insightful illustration of the problem and discuss our approach. In Section 3, we report some performance measurements based on a simulation study. Concluding remarks are given in Section 4.

2 The congestion control scheme

We first give an example to grasp the problem. Figure 1 illustrates the effect of congestion on packet delays. Packets m1, m2, m3, and m4 are all l flits long and their destinations are d1, d2, d3, and d4, respectively. To make the illustration simple and to emphasize the effect of congestion on packet delay, it is assumed that the routes taken by m1, m2, m3, and m4 are (...,n4, n1, n2, d1), (..., n1, n2, n3, d2), (..., n2, n3, n4, d4, d3), and (..., n3, n4, d4), respectively. Packet m4 is not blocked and can immediately advance towards its destination. However, packet m3 waits for m4, packet m2 waits for m3 and m4, packet m1 waits for m2, m3, and m4. Assuming it takes one clock cycle to transmit a flit, the blocking times for m1, m2, m3, and m4 are $3*l$, $2*l$, l, and 0 respectively. The average blocking time is $1.5*l$ clock cycles, but we should keep in mind that the maximum is $3*l$. For example, the average blocking time is 24 clock cycles for $l=16$, but the blocking time for m1 is 48 which is in average about two and half times the time it takes to forward the head flit to its destination in a congestion-free network, assuming a 2D mesh network of size 32x32. Notice that, the longer the message packets are the longer the blocking time is.

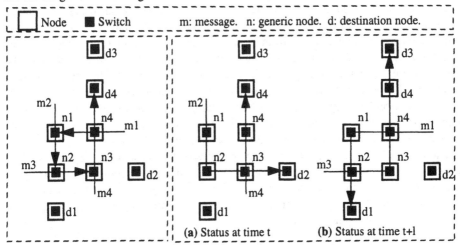

Fig. 1. Illustration of congestion in wormhole   **Fig. 2.** Congestion avoidance

This example is a very simple case because only four packets are involved. In networks with thousands or more nodes, much more packets are involved and the blocking time cumulates very easily and can be very considerable. As an example, if a short packet, say of length 4, has to wait for 10 long packets, say of length 64, then the blocking time would be 640 clock cycles, while it takes only 20 cycles, in average, for the head flit to reach the packet destination. The delay has been increased by a factor of 32. Again this is a rather simplified situation, since in reality thousands or more packets, possibly of different lengths, can simultaneously exist in the network.

Now let us compare the situations depicted in figure 1 and figure 2, respectively. In figure 2a, m1 and m3 have not been injected yet, they are still stored in their respective source node. In such a case, m2 and m4 do not interact at all, and can advance freely to their respective destinations. Some clock cycles later, when m2 and m4 have reached their destination, m1 and m3 acquire their respective resources as shown in figure 2b. This time also packets do not block each other; m1 and m3 advance towards their destination without having to wait. The blocking time in the network is zero in figure 2, compared to $1.5*l$ in figure 1. Thus, the improvement of the average packet delay can be drastic. If we do not restrict packet injection, the network can reach a saturated state rapidly, resulting in prohibitive network delay. The cost is to delay packet injection in the selected nodes.

The proposed scheme performs as follows: 1) Select randomly a node where packet injection must be restricted. 2) Require the selected node to suspend injecting possible packets into the network for a certain period of time.

The node selection can be done at regular time intervals (congestion avoidance) or on-demand (congestion detection and recovery). Hence, we distinguish two approaches for the node selection: 1) Continuous randomized selection and 2) On-demand randomized selection. Randomization is introduced because it can provide fairness. In the continuous randomized selection, nodes are continuously selected to suspend packet injection, irrespective of the network load and status. Note that the selection being continuous means that it is performed at regular and uniform time intervals. This approach has the advantage that it does not require any status information. Its disadvantage is that it is applied when no congestion occurs. In the on-demand randomized selection, congestion control is applied whenever a node discovers that congestion is building up or has reached a pre-defined level. Such a node will randomly choose a remote node to which it sends a message to order a packet injection suspension. The scheme is fair because it allows all the nodes to suspend their packet injection with equal probability. It has the property of being universal because it is independent of the characteristics of the interconnection network. Also, it does not require global network information. Flow control based on priority can easily be combined with these congestion control schemes. For instance, it would probably be interesting if no restrictions at all are put on short packets.

3 First results

Our first experiment consists in testing the basic idea, i.e.putting restriction on packet injection. Instead of applying randomized selection, we consider four testbeds, each including a particular subset of nodes where congestion control is applied. These subsets are defined in table 1.

Testbed #1	All the nodes are concerned
Testbed #2	All nodes (i,j) such that i mod. 4 = 0 and j mod. 4 = 0
Testbed #3	All nodes (i,j) such that 8<= i,j & i,j <=24 and i mod. 2 = 0 & j mod. 2 = 0
Testbed #4	All nodes (i,j) such that 8<= i,j & i,j <=24 and i mod. 4 = 0 & j mod. 4 = 0

Table 1: Four testbeds

We assume a 2D mesh network with 1K nodes. The packet generation rate is set to 0.2, which brings the network to saturation after few clock cycles, when no congestion control is applied. The traffic pattern is uniform and the packet length is set to 16 flits. The number of virtual channels is fixed to 4. The packet injection suspension time is fixed to the mean time between the generation of two successive packets.

Figure 3 shows the delay without congestion control, and with congestion control for the different testbeds. Improvements in the delay is obtained in all cases. For testbeds number 4 and 2, the delay is reduced by 64% and 26%, respectively, whereas for testbed number 1, a reduction of only 9% is obtained. Figure 4 shows the throughputs corresponding to the delays measured in figure 3. The throughput is improved in two cases, with testbeds number 2 and 3, by 13.5% and 7%, respectively. However, the worst case in throughput degradation is obtained with testbed number 4, which is 32%. But recall that for this same testbed the delay was improved by 64%. In almost all the cases we studied, the delay has been decreased, whereas in few cases the throughput was improved. Surprisingly, we obtain both improved delay and throughput for some testbeds, e.g. testbeds 2 and 3. For instance, with testbed number 2 we improve simultaneously both the delay (26%) and the throughput (13.5%), which is difficult to achieve.

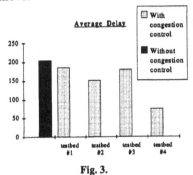

Fig. 3.
Delay with and without congestion control

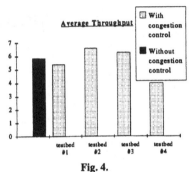

Fig. 4.
Throughput with and without congestion control

4 Conclusion

We presented a scheme to control congestion in wormhole networks. Preliminary experiments were carried out with various testbeds. The results showed that both network delay and throughput can be improved. The scheme is simple, and does not require any global information such as the concept of global clock or information about the load at remote nodes. No modifications are needed to the router design.

Although the evaluation showed clearly that the congestion control scheme can yield improved performance, the problem of fairness amongst nodes in the entire multiprocessor system needs more careful consideration. Assuming one type of traffic, the congestion control should not favour some particular nodes, as this can lead to starvation or unnecessary synchronization delays for example. A further study would be to compare such flow control schemes with other trends such as that of adaptive routing algorithms. Some other remaining studies are related to implementation issues, such as the impact of the scheme on the input/output queues in the nodes.

References

1. W. J. Dally. Virtual channel flow control. IEEE Transactions on Parallel and Distributed Systems, 3(2) pp. 194-205. March 1992.

2. A-H. Smai, Flow control in wormhole multicomputer networks. Technical report TRITA-IT R94:32, Royal Institute of Technology, December 1994.

3. A-H. Smai and L.-E. Thorelli, Dynamic allocation of communication bandwidth in multicomputers. In Proc. PARLE'94, Springer-Verlag LNCS 817, 1994.

Author Index

Author Index

Lecture Notes in Computer Science

For information about Vols. 1–903

please contact your bookseller or Springer-Verlag